European Government

McGRAW-HILL SERIES IN POLITICAL SCIENCE

Adrian / State and Local Governments

Adrian and Press / Governing Urban America

Bone / American Politics and the Party System

Christenson and McWilliams / Voice of the People: Reading in Public
  Opinion and Propaganda

Gerberding / United States Foreign Policy

Harmon / Political Thought: From Plato to the Present

McClosky and Turner / The Soviet Dictatorship

Millett / Government and Public Administration

Millett / Management in the Public Service

Neumann / European Government

Pierson and Gil / Governments of Latin America

Powell and Parker / Major Aspects of American Government

Pritchett / The American Constitution

Pritchett / American Constitutional Issues

Turner / Politics in the United States: Readings in Political Parties and
  Pressure Groups

Vandenbosch and Hogan / Toward World Order

Wilson / Police Administration

fourth edition

EUROPEAN GOVERNMENT

Robert G. Neumann

Professor of Political Science
University of California, Los Angeles

Formerly published under the title of **EUROPEAN AND COMPARATIVE GOVERNMENT**

McGRAW-HILL BOOK COMPANY

New York   St. Louis   San Francisco   Toronto   London   Sydney

EUROPEAN GOVERNMENT

Library of Congress Catalog Card Number 67–25357

46310

1 2 3 4 5 6 7 8 9 0   MAMM   7 5 4 3 2 1 0 6 9 8

Preface

This is the fourth edition of a book which presents itself to the reader under a new title and with a somewhat revised form. The first three editions, published in 1951, 1955, and 1960, respectively, appeared under the title *European and Comparative Government*. This edition's title, *European Government*, reflects two thoughts in my mind:

1. There are now available a great number of books dealing with political institutions and political phenomena on a comparative basis, utilizing a variety of methods and approaches. These were not available in the early 1950s. It seems to me, therefore, that the comparative approach for students of comparative government can now be accomplished more adequately through such separate works than through a necessarily brief section of a book on European governments. By using

v

many sources, the teacher and the reader can utilize and be exposed to an entire gamut of methodological approaches. Therefore the earlier pattern of this book, which included a fifth part entitled "Government in Comparison," has been abandoned in this revision.

2. The new fifth part, entitled "Toward a More United Europe and Atlantic Partnership: The Emergence of Community," represents a novel and experimental endeavor. It is an attempt to place a totally new phenomenon, namely, the rise of the European Communities, in a setting of comparative government rather than of international relations. The introduction to Part 5 deals more fully with this idea. Here I want only to summarize by saying that a number of important European states have decided to undertake continuous, common, and collective action on a number of important matters of common concern and that they have done so through common organs which are responsible to the respective Communities and not to their individual member governments. This is a very different approach from that of the traditional international organizations such as the United Nations. These new Communities, through their common organs, establish policies, set rates, settle disputes, and negotiate important matters for their Community as a whole. So interwoven have these affairs become that, for instance, it is now impossible for the United States or for other countries to negotiate tariff reductions with individual countries if the latter are also members of the most important of these Communities, the European Economic Community, better known as the Common Market. Instead, the common organ thereof, the European Commission, negotiates for its six member countries collectively in a complex procedure, an example of which was the Kennedy Round.

Nobody would claim that these Communities constitute superstates or that they are likely to become such in the foreseeable future. But they are equally and substantially different from the traditional form of international organizations. They are phenomena *sui generis* which (in the area in which they have been able to function) have developed constitutions, organs, and a politics of their own. Some critics have argued that these institutions are in decline or that they have not fulfilled the hopes which accompanied their birth. There is something to the latter assertion. Certainly those who had expected that there would be a quick and perhaps easy road from economic to political integration were disappointed, and now the road, if feasible at all, seems very much longer indeed. The distinction between economic and political integration, however, strikes me as somewhat artificial. The largest part of the business of any sovereign government concerns economic matters. The setting of rates, of taxes, of tariffs, licensing regulations, agricultural policies, etc., has been traditionally considered part of the sovereign functions of government. When these functions or important parts thereof are transferred to supranational organisms to such an extent that national action and national legislation in those fields becomes difficult and even impossible, then something closely akin to a partial transfer of sovereignty has taken place, and the Communities have by the same token gradually begun to have more in common with states than with traditional international organizations.

Other critics have pointed to the mounting opposition to supranationalism, especially the opposition of the French government of General Charles de Gaulle. That opposition policies and actions have placed the European Communities in grave peril cannot be denied; their progress has very probably been retarded. It is highly significant, however, that these crises have been successfully overcome and that the Communities continue to exist and to prosper without any important structural changes — the very changes that the French government wished to impose. In other words, the fact that the Communities have overcome and survived the assault of their strongest member and Europe's strongest political leader gives evidence of the extraordinary vitality of the Community idea.

Today the survival of these Communities is no longer debatable: it is a fact. Development in the legislative sphere has been frustrated; but the Community institutions in the executive and judicial spheres have grown. The Communities continue to regulate economic activities in most important sectors. The validity of national executive action is constantly tested and sometimes overruled by supranational authorities. Batteries of lawyers argue cases before national and European Community courts, based on Community law. So great is the magnetic attraction of the success and accomplishment of these Communities that other European countries are constantly endeavoring to become full or associate members, and the future membership of Great Britain has become one of that country's most important political issues. In other parts of the world, attempts have been made to copy the success of this experiment, notably in Central America and in Africa.

The continued existence of a less advanced type of Atlantic community, the North Atlantic Treaty Organization (NATO), is not quite so certain. Here the assault has had more serious impact. Future editions of this book will testify whether the inclusion of a section on NATO remains justified or not. It is included here largely because of the strong direct ties between European integration and Atlantic partnership. Partnership is difficult when there is great inequality of power, and the growth of European integration has a direct bearing on the probability or the improbability of a true Atlantic partnership. Moreover, the attack against that partnership, although ostensibly made in the name of Europe, is in fact also directed against Europe. In substance, the attacks on the Atlantic community are of a nationalistic nature, and if they succeed in destroying the Atlantic partnership, national egotisms are not likely then to be submerged within a greater European unification. If nationalism prevails over Atlantic partnership, it can result only in the recrudescence of French, German, Italian, etc., nationalism, not in the rise of a "European nationalism"—which is a contradiction in terms.

As far as the choice of countries to be included in this book is concerned, I have stated in the preface to previous editions that "the leading and rival forms of government which put their mark on the rest of the world are to be found primarily in Europe and in the United States." Despite a considerable passage of time since those lines were first written, I see little reason to change my mind on this point. It is of course true that since the first edition of this book was published, a great number of countries have achieved their independence and have endeavored to find political and constitutional frameworks suitable to their needs. In this search they have found American and European models, including that of the Soviet Union, to be of varying validity, but thus far none of them has succeeded, in my view, in establishing clearly recognizable systems of their own or in establishing patterns which other states might fruitfully emulate. In time, no doubt, they will succeed. I do not make here any arrogant assumption that there is nothing, or can be nothing, new under the sun of government and politics; but I continue to claim that the accumulated experience in the art of government and politics embodied in the political and institutional history of the Atlantic world and of the Soviet Union still forms the indispensable bedrock of knowledge without which one attempting to venture into new fields cannot fruitfully proceed. To be fully effective, however, study of the cumulative experience of the political systems mentioned above should not be limited to their separate, national incarnations, but must be supplemented, as is the endeavor here, by examining their new and exciting forays into the process of Community building.

Since the first edition of this book, the field of political science has seen a methodological revolution, though without unity in the approaches. Many of these new methods stem from the desire to avoid overconcentration on formal institutions, which has been characteristic of traditional political science. Others reflect the ever-present desire to stress the scientific element in political science and to infuse an element of greater certainty into political analysis. The hope is to increase greatly those elements of the political system which can be made subject to precise measurement.

There is nothing wrong with any of this. Where I do sometimes feel quarrelsome is toward a degree of simplification and oversimplification which occasionally crops up in the pursuit of these methods. Also, because of the desire to increase probability through measurement, there exists a tendency to restrict analysis of politics to those criteria which are easily subject to measurement. The danger there is not that of simplification in itself — all analysis and pattern formation require simplification — but that (1) oversimplification may tend to suit methods which are still in their infancy, and (2) some extreme exponents of these methods may simplify to the point of losing touch with reality. It should be recognized, however, that these dangers are not intrinsically a result of the new methodologies as such.

Whichever method is followed, one way of protecting the student and reader reasonably well from landing on cloud nine rather than on earth is to give him a thorough grounding in the realities of the political systems and the institutions of which the life of governments and Communities is made. The student of government should then be in a position to judge which theories and methods he might follow for more advanced work and which generalizations remain valid within the scope of the facts which he has learned. To that end, I hope this book will make a useful contribution.

At the same time, no author can reasonably present all the facts and only the facts. There are far too many facts available on any system of government for them all to be used in one work. Selection is therefore necessary, and this in turn necessitates interpretation, weighting, and ordering of facts in order to analyze the meaning of institutions and events, the possible impact of certain personalities on events, and the likely progress of certain trends. Obviously, machinelike impartiality and objectivity are not going to be possible in this process. The only possible course, therefore, is for an author to make an honest attempt to consider all available factors and to interpret them in the fashion he deems most likely to be correct. Absolute certainty is not possible in the study of human institutions. Not only the rational, but also the irrational, characterizes human behavior; and the irrational has an important impact on political developments, as this text will note from time to time.

In the preparation of this manuscript, I have had more help and advice than I can easily acknowledge here. The new fifth part has been reviewed by Ambassador J. Robert Schaetzel, for several years Deputy Assistant Secretary of State for Atlantic Affairs and more recently American Ambassador to the European Communities in Brussels and Luxembourg. The section on the Soviet Union was brought up to date with the help of Dr. John DeLuca, former White House Fellow, a member of the Stanford Research Institute. In the sections on France and Germany in particular, the author relied to a large extent on his own numerous contacts and frequent visits to those countries. In all sections, the research assistance of Mrs. Anne Bodenheimer has been invaluable, and the secretarial work of Mrs. Christa Eichhorn and Mrs. Trudy Woods is gratefully acknowledged.

In the preface to the first edition in 1950, I somewhat facetiously thanked my "son Ronald for not playing cowboy in his father's study." In the preparation of this fourth edition the same Ronald Eldredge Neumann, recently a graduate fellow in political science at the University of California at Riverside, has rendered invaluable service and assistance in the editing and the rethinking of much of this book. His fresh and intelligent approach has been of enormous help, and his labors have gone far beyond the most extreme interpretations of filial duty.

An expression of deep gratitude also goes last, but certainly not least, to the author's wife who, despite numerous and important civic responsibilities, has given unstintingly of her time and wisdom, both intellectually and by physical labor. Her contributions too went far beyond the call of duty.

This edition also represents a milestone in my personal work and application. Having recently been appointed United States Ambassador to Afghanistan, I am taking temporary leave of a long preoccupation with European and Atlantic affairs in order to return, for the time being, to an earlier love affair with Moslem culture. The clear separation between the subject matters treated in this book and my new responsibilities should make it absolutely clear that this book represents the work of a private person and academician, written entirely before I had or knew of my present appointment, and it should in no way be interpreted as a statement of United States government policy in any form, shape, or manner. I alone am responsible for what has been said between these covers and, of course, for all errors and omissions.

ROBERT G. NEUMANN

Contents

preface   v

Part 1   GREAT BRITAIN

    Introduction   1

1.   The Origins of the Constitution   5
2.   The Idea of the Constitution   20
3.   Parties and Politics   27
4.   The Crown   68
5.   Parliament   107
6.   Law and Justice   139
7.   Local Government   150
8.   The Commonwealth   165
9.   The Outlook   176

xii   Contents

Part 2 FRANCE

Introduction   179
1. Early Constitutional and Political Development   185
2. The Rebirth of France   200
3. France at Low Tide: The Fourth Republic   209
4. The Political System and the Parties   222
5. Constitutional Government in France   288
6. De Gaulle's Foreign Policy   356

Part 3 GERMANY

Introduction   365
1. Historical Introduction: From the Holy Roman Empire to the Second Reich   369
2. From Strong Empire to Weak Republic   375
3. The Rise and Fall of National Socialism   385
4. From Military Occupation to the New Republic   394
5. Political Life in Germany   408
6. Constitutional Government   446
7. Government in Eastern Germany   490
8. Germany and the World   499

Part 4 THE UNION OF SOVIET SOCIALIST REPUBLICS

Introduction   505
1. Historical Antecedents   511
2. Revolution and Consolidation   514
3. From Lenin to Stalin   523
4. The U.S.S.R. after Stalin   535
5. Marxism-Leninism: The Theoretical Foundations of the State   545
6. The Communist Party   553
7. Soviet Federalism   595
8. The Soviets   604
9. The Administration   614
10. Law and Justice   625
11. The Position of the Individual   633
12. The Soviet Union and the World   640
13. Conclusions   652

Part 5 TOWARD A MORE UNITED EUROPE AND ATLANTIC PARTNERSHIP: THE EMERGENCE OF COMMUNITY

Introduction   657
1. The Evolution of an Idea: Concepts of European Unity, Old and New   661
2. The Council of Europe   674
3. The Dawn of Community: The European Coal and Steel Community—Schuman Plan   681

4. The European Economic Community—The Common Market   692

5. The European Atomic Energy Community   720

6. A Partial Atlantic Community? The North Atlantic Treaty Organization   727

APPENDIXES

A. The Constitution of France Adopted by the Referendum of
    September 28, 1958   743

B. Basic Law for the Federal Republic of Germany, 1949, as Amended   758

C. The Constitution of the U.S.S.R., 1936, as Amended   789

selected bibliography   805

index   855

European Government

part 1

Great Britain

England is not governed by logic; she is governed by Parliament.
Benjamin Disraeli, Lord Beaconsfield

A famous wit once described Great Britain[1] and the United States as "two countries separated by the same language." This remark bears the obvious stamp of Shavian exaggeration, but it tends to remind us that the many close ties existing between the two countries are not solely, or even primarily, based on the use of a more or less common language. Above and beyond that linguistic kinship there is a vast common heritage in the origin and the practice of many institutions and ideas which are characteristic of free government.

The twentieth century has witnessed the development of increasingly strong British-American relations in the field of international affairs. Actually, it is the whole of Europe, not only the British Isles, which is the cornerstone of our military and diplomatic strategy in Europe, but the special relationship between the two countries is nevertheless a reality. Such increasing interdependence does not always make for the smoothest of relations, but the fact that our two countries are firmly welded together by innumerable ties is incontestable.

A thorough understanding of British affairs, the nature of her government, and the atmosphere in which it operates ought therefore to be of great concern to an informed American public. Yet, such understanding is made difficult by a certain vagueness of institutions and frequent absence of definitions, which a distinguished Englishman has epitomized in these words:[2]

> It is a commonplace that the characteristic virtue of Englishmen is their power of sustained practical activity, and their characteristic vice a reluctance to test the quality of that activity by reference to principles. They are incurious to theory, take fundamentals for granted, and are more interested in the state of the roads than in their place on the map.

The apex of this approach is the British "constitution," a generic term covering a multitude of statutes, decisions, customs, and conventions dealing with the institutions of state and government and the rights of the citizens. Its principal parts are the customs and conventions, which relate to both form and the actuality of practice. Since the rate of change of form is often much slower than that of practice, there is a tendency to overlook the actual changes in practice which constantly occur in British life.[3] These changes have brought about transformations, from feudalism to democracy, from being the greatest empire in the world to being a slightly junior member of the Atlantic Alliance, which have been enormous and, more remarkably, for the most part free of bloodshed.

These transformations have frequently bewildered foreigners, because they are often hidden behind ancient ritual and immutable facades. The Britisher, who, no

[1] The term "Great Britain" as used throughout this book is meant to stand for the United Kingdom, which includes England, Wales, Scotland, and Northern Ireland.
[2] R. H. Tawney, *The Acquisitive Society,* New York, 1920, p. 1.
[3] Ramsey Muir, *How Britain Is Governed,* Boston, 1935, 3d ed., p. 2.

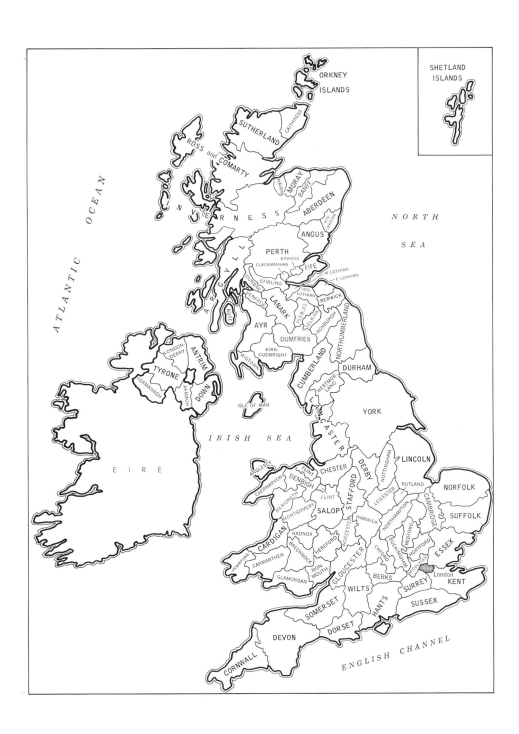

matter how radical, is always to some extent a disciple of Burke, values the stability and security which come from accepted and affectionately regarded institutions. But he is also a realist and quite willing to try out some new course of action; consequently, an increasing discrepancy develops between the form of institutions, which remains the same, and the substance, which changes. The British understand that perfectly well. They are not greatly troubled by questions involving the purity of a theory or the consistency of an approach; they are primarily interested in successful performance. Therefore they are quite prepared to accept the discrepancy between the form and the substance of institutions and to defend both with equal conviction.

Still more difficult for the foreign observer to understand has been the unusual restraint of British politics, a restraint based, not upon law, but on an undefinable sense of what is, and is not, proper. Walter Bagehot, in his classic work on the English constitution,[4] declared that such a system of government was possible in England only because there existed certain prerequisites: mutual confidence among electors, a calm national mind, and the gift of rationality. These qualities all add up to an adult and practical nation.

The brilliant days of Palmerston, Disraeli, and Gladstone are gone. London is no longer the hub of the universe. But a healthy Europe and a strong free world are unthinkable without Britain playing a major role, and in her civic discipline as well as in the free association of her Commonwealth, the world may find much to admire and emulate.

It must always be remembered that modern Great Britain is a state *sui generis*, and not really a part of Europe, except by an accident of geography. Her ties and interests have long emphasized the Empire and Commonwealth, rather than Continental relations. Bagehot, when seeking comparison or contrast, looked to the United States, not to France or Germany. Britain has been hesitant about getting too closely embroiled in the affairs of Europe for fear of losing her place as the center of the Commonwealth. Common economic, political, and military dangers have driven Britain reluctantly to closer cooperation with the Continent, but membership in European agencies has often been reluctant, and such mighty steps toward European unity as the Coal and Steel Community (Schuman Plan) and the European Economic Community (Common Market) met British opposition. It is only in the sixties that this policy has changed, despite the setback which Britain received in 1963 when General de Gaulle slammed shut the door to the Common Market. The student of British government will therefore do well not to fix his eyes on the European character of Britain, but to treat Britain as a world in itself—a world which has by no means been oblivious to its environment, but which has nevertheless retained its own characteristics.

[4] Walter Bagehot, *The English Constitution*, first published in 1867.

1

The origins of the constitution

Neither the 461 years of Roman occupation nor the rule of the Angles, Saxons, and Danes who succeeded the Romans left any appreciable mark on the central government of England. Only in the field of local government did the Anglo-Saxon period leave a lasting impression. The townships and especially the shires—later renamed counties—remained, as did the boroughs, especially London. From these remains, such enduring symbols of government as the sheriff (*shire-reeve*) developed.

The Norman-Angevin[1] period

The constitutional history of England begins, then, with the Norman conquest of 1066. The Normans themselves were of Scandinavian origin, and their own institutions were hardly more sophisticated than those of the Saxons. But the Nor-

[1] Derived from the Anjou dynasty (from Anjou province, France; capital, Angers) which came to power in England with Henry II (1154) and called itself Plantagenet.

mans had settled in France in the tenth century and had come in contact with the vastly superior organization of the declining Carolingian monarchy, the Frankish empire. From it they accepted two principal ideas: royal absolutism and feudalism, the two centers of English constitutional developments.

William the Conquerer transplanted these ideas to England—chiefly because he knew them to be the most effective ways of ruling a country. Moreover, so many parallels could be found between Anglo-Saxon and Norman customs[2] that the transition was fairly smooth, especially as the wise Norman rulers ostensibly granted their Anglo-Saxon subjects continuance of some of their ancient laws, but modified —if not to say falsified—sufficiently to make them acceptable to the demands of Norman rule.[3]

As was customary in those days, William declared all English land forfeited to him, which gave him an opportunity to dispossess the native lords and invest his own followers with their holdings. This was the feudal system which was thus transplanted to England. In other countries, especially Germany, it led to the dissolution of the empire because it created mighty lords who challenged the King's power. But in England most of the Norman-Angevin kings retained a high degree of control and thus established a regime which was not only feudal and absolute, but also centralist.

Local customs prevailed in the feudal courts, but the King sent his own royal judges on circuit. These judges—an institution derived from Charlemagne and the Frankish empire—inquired into local customs and law and in their jurisdiction fused them more and more into a unified body of rules. But these judges were usually ecclesiastics who had studied the Church (canon) law, which in turn had taken most of its precepts from the Roman law. Thus, Roman-law ideas and expressions entered into English law. On the whole, the royal law which was established by these itinerant judges was superior to and more equitable than the local, feudal rules which it gradually replaced. This was the origin of one of the proudest possessions of the English-speaking nations, the common law, the law which was common to the entire realm, in contrast to local, feudal law.

At the same time, the jury made its first appearance. Under the Anglo-Saxon rule, the free warriors (*thanes*) had participated in the rendering of the verdict. Now they were called upon to give evidence as to the facts in the case, a combination of witness and jury. This, and the separation of royal from ecclesiastic courts, further strengthened the system of royal justice.

In his role as a ruler, the King was assisted by two bodies, the Grand Council

[2] George B. Adams, *The Origin of the English Constitution,* New Haven, Conn., 1920, 2d ed., pp. 17–18.
[3] The cultural development and civilization of the Normans were incomparably higher than those of the Anglo-Saxons. This is attested by the fact that most expressions of the English language which pertain to the professions, arts, and science or otherwise concern a higher type of life are of French origin. The Norman predilection for written records and orderly procedure alone made them superior administrators.

(*Magnum Concilium*) and the King's Court (*Curia Regis*). Both bodies were feudal assemblies to which the nobles were summoned as part of their duties of vassalage to the King. Of the two, the *Curia Regis* was the smaller but more important. Theoretically the two councils were one; every nobleman had a right to sit in the Curia, and the smaller group had all the rights of the larger one. In actuality, however, no vassal appeared at the Curia who was not specifically summoned. Moreover, the assembly of all the vassals, the *Magnum Concilium,* met only three times a year, when the King was in England, and that was not enough to conduct all the business of the state. Hence the growing importance of the *Curia Regis.*

The Norman dynasty declined after the death of the conqueror, but it was succeeded in 1154 by the energetic Henry II of Anjou (Plantagenet). By that time, certain important events had taken place. The royal courts had ceased to be merely temporary makeshifts, and had become permanent features. The common law which they established was recognized, and it was generally assumed that the King was subordinate to the law. Such obligations upon the otherwise absolute King were by no means illogical, since the entire feudal system and the lord-tenant relationship were based on a contract imposing mutual obligations.

Most of the courts of that time were assembly courts, i.e., assemblies like the *Curia Regis* which also discharged judicial functions.[4] But the trend toward more professional courts was already clear in the twelfth century. The *Curia Regis,* which was sometimes difficult to distinguish from the *Magnum Concilium,* had become a permanent, almost professional body. Later it was to be called the Permanent Council. But certain sections of the Curia acquired more and more independent functions until they became separate bodies.[5] This is the origin of the Exchequer (as a court for the settlement of fiscal disputes), of the Court of Common Pleas (for pleas under common law for which the presence of the King was not required),[6] and later of the Court of King's Bench, the Chancery, and the Privy Council. At the same time, criminal justice was improved by the imposition of a permanent jury system whose functions were more like those of our modern grand jury than of the trial jury.

Magna Carta

The institutions just described were not "democratic" as the term was later understood; they were part of the feudal system. But they had become so generally accepted that a lawless king who attempted to do with them as he pleased ran into

[4] See Charles H. McIlwain, *The High Court of Parliament and Its Supremacy,* New Haven, Conn., 1910.
[5] D. Pasquet, *An Essay on the Origins of the House of Commons* (trans. by R. D. G. Laffan), Cambridge, England, 1925, pp. 6–8.
[6] According to Adams, *op. cit.,* pp. 136–143, the Court of Common Pleas did not originate in the *Curia Regis* but had a distinct and separate origin.

serious difficulties. This happened to King John, who was forced to accept in 1215 that famous document known as Magna Carta.[7] The Great Charter was not a contract between the King and the nation—there was hardly a nation—nor was it a charter of civil liberties. It was a purely feudal document, in which the King guaranteed to the nobles the rights which, in their opinion and probably correctly, they already possessed. It was not called the "great charter of liberty" (*magna carta libertatis*), but the "great charter of liberties" (*magna carta libertatum*), namely, the liberties of the barons. When the Charter speaks of "free man" (*homo liber*), it refers to the nobles, as it does when referring to the jury trial as "judgment by his peers."[8]

Thus the Charter confirmed primarily the feudal rights of the barons, guaranteeing them their possessions against unlawful interference by the King, and the right to be punished or fined only by the judgment of their peers. It also stopped the arbitrary removal of a case from a baronial court to a royal court and prevented the King from interfering too drastically with the right of inheritance.

However, the Charter's most notable contribution was the provision contained in Section 61, which established a machinery for keeping the King under control. The barons realized that a mere promise, extracted from the King when his fortunes were low, could not be relied upon to protect them once he had regained his power. Therefore the Charter established a committee of twenty-five barons to be freely elected by their peers. Any complaint of a violation of the Charter was to be brought to the attention of four of the twenty-five, who would demand that the King or one of his officers redress the wrong. If that were not done within forty days, the four barons were to refer the matter to the rest of the twenty-five, who would review the case. If they agreed that a violation had occurred, they had the right under the Charter to rise in arms, together with the rest of the barons, to seize the King's possessions or to injure him in any way until redress had been made.

Thus was established for the first time in history the principle of a limited monarchy—the first step toward constitutional government. It was contained in two great ideas: that the King was bound by the law, and that his subjects had a right to set up machinery to enforce this obligation, if necessary by civil war. Such an arrangement was quite clumsy, but "considering that the men of 1215 had no precedent to go upon, no model of any such machinery to follow, no literary expression of such ideas, no theorizing about such procedure, they did very well."[9]

The long-range significance of the Charter made its appearance only gradually. However, with every subsequent dispute, the Charter became an increasingly strong weapon for free, constitutional government, which would be quoted by the oppo-

---

[7] The definitive work on the Great Charter is still M. S. McKechnie's *Magna Carta: A Commentary on the Great Charter of King John*, Glasgow, 1905. See also F. Thompson, *The First Century of Magna Carta: Why It Persisted as a Document*, Minneapolis, 1925.

[8] This term is preserved in the title of "peer," the official designation of a member of the present House of Lords.

[9] Adams, *op. cit.*, pp. 179f.

nents of arbitrary power as an argument for their cause.[10] This was possible because the Charter bore in the two above-mentioned principles the germ of all future constitutional developments. In this sense one might accept the famous dictum of Bishop Stubbs that the whole of English constitutional history is merely one long commentary on Magna Carta.[11]

Up to the thirteenth century the Great Council and the Curia retained their purely feudal character. It is now generally agreed that in 1254 representatives of the counties were summoned to the Council, for which the term "Parliament" became current.[12] There is no evidence that much was achieved at that time, as the reason for the summons was the chronic need of the King (Henry III) for money, and the nobles were reluctant to grant the requests without the consent of those to whom a part of the burden would be passed on. At any rate, the act of calling lesser men than the peers of the realm to Parliament was far more significant than the meeting itself, which produced few results.

In subsequent years, the custom of summoning the representatives of the counties grew, especially as the need for financial support increased. Simon of Montfort, after his victory over Henry III, again summoned the knights of the counties in 1264 to meet with the Council the subsequent year. At that time, representatives from the cities appeared as well. However, the reputation of Simon of being the father of the House of Commons appears to be ill founded. There was no House of Commons in 1265 nor for many years thereafter. Everybody met in one assembly, and there is no evidence to show that later meetings were greatly influenced by the gathering of 1265.

The rise of Parliament

The Parliament which King Edward I summoned in 1295 has been termed the "model Parliament." This laudatory expression is acceptable only with considerable caution. Apart from the nobles and the clergy, there were summoned two knights from each county, two citizens from each city, and two burghers from each borough. All this was not new. Each of these groups had been summoned to Parliament before. But the innovation consisted in their being called all to one and the same gathering, and this remained the model for later sessions, though by no means all of them followed it.

There is evidence that the groups deliberated separately at times, but in order to make a decision, they had to meet in one body, which was the rule. There was then as yet no House of Commons, but only one Parliament.

Some doting historians have chosen to present the story of the rise of Parlia-

---

[10] Frederic A. Ogg, *English Government and Politics,* New York, 1936, 2d ed., p. 16.
[11] W. Stubbs, *The Constitutional History of England,* Oxford, 1880, Vol. II, pp. 2*ff.*
[12] First used in the reign of Henry II. See A. F. Pollard, *The Evolution of Parliament,* London, 1920, p. 32. Used more definitely by Matthew Paris, *Historia Anglorum* (1237). Pasquet, *op. cit.,* p. 3.

ment as an example of the steady growth of popular demands for self-government. Others have interpreted Edward's statement to the clergy, to the effect that "what touches everyone should be approved by everyone," to mean that the King decided to share the rule of the realm freely with his subjects. Both theories are without foundation. The subjects and nobles were most reluctant to make use of these institutions. The King had to bring great pressure on those whom he summoned in order to make them appear at the session of Parliament. To travel to Oxford, or London, must have taken weeks or longer for some of the delegates. Sometimes the King prorogued Parliament quickly, and summoned it again later, causing great inconvenience. There can therefore be no question of a popular "demand" for parliamentary representation. Nor could so strong-willed a King as Edward I be suspected of wishing to share his power with anyone. The fact was simply that the King desired to strengthen his hand by obtaining the support of the cities and counties, and by imposing a more reliable tax basis on them than was possible if he dealt with the nobles alone. Parliament was therefore largely an institution which the King forced on more or less unwilling subjects for purposes of his own.

The Parliament which was convoked in 1295 was, like its predecessors, above all a court, and many writers refer to it as the "High Court of Parliament." There was no idea of legislation. In the Middle Ages, laws were generally not passed but "found" in the customs and conventions of the realm. Deliberations in Parliament had the character of court proceedings, and few acts of Parliament are recorded from those days which would qualify as "legislation" by modern standards. But there were a great many petitions to redress wrongs, and in that manner the King learned a great deal about the state of the realm. With the consent of the urban groups he could also collect taxes more easily.

We cannot fix an exact date when the House of Commons originated. It is certain that it did not exist under Edward I, who reigned from 1272 to 1307, and it is equally certain that it did exist under Edward III, who reigned from 1327 to 1377. We may, however, surmise that the representatives of the communes, or *communitates*—from whom the name of the house is derived—appeared before the "bar" of Parliament, of which they were not full-fledged members; that they withdrew, or were urged to withdraw, to deliberate among themselves; and that they appointed a "speaker," who alone had the right to speak in Parliament. Thus they submitted their petitions for the redress of grievances, which were enrolled as statutes. These common pleas required common deliberation and common action on the part of county and city representatives. This habit became an institution, and eventually a house. It grew slowly and imperceptibly, and therein lies its strength.

In the fourteenth century, the clergy generally withdrew from Parliament into their own assemblies. Therefore there remained essentially two bodies, and it is of the utmost significance that, for reasons which are not entirely explored, the lesser nobility joined forces with the "commons," thus giving them both strength and new blood. But it was not until the sixteenth century that the division became official, and we hear officially used the term "House of Lords." Until then, the Commons, although they deliberated separately, were essentially a committee of Parliament. Their power grew immeasurably when the lesser nobility joined and lent their wealth and experience. Gradually, under the guise of "petition" and extreme humility, the Commons established their power, especially in financial matters. By 1407, it was accepted doctrine that financial legislation had to originate in the Commons, and that the two groups, the Lords and the Commons, should confer among themselves and then report to the King upon their full agreement.

The power inherent in Parliament was not quickly realized. The reluctance of members to serve persisted for some time. There was certainly no thought that Parliament was sovereign, for sovereignty as understood by Bodin or Hobbes belongs to a later period. The royal power before the Tudors was of a feudal nature. It emanated from the King as the tenant-in-chief to the magnates of the realm, and from them to their tenants, and so forth down. In this framework, neither Parliament nor any other body of men could claim "sovereignty" for themselves. There was no national ambition for self-government, partly because there was as yet no nation. Moreover, as long as the power of the great lords was overabundant, no national consciousness could arise, for each was lord in his own domain, and his country was Norfolk or Essex or Cornwall, not England. It was only when the cities and counties began to be more interested in sending delegates to Parliament that this situation began to change. What caused the change is impossible to say. Perhaps it was, as one writer put it, "that general stirring of national impulse in English bones of which Wycliffe, Langland, and Chaucer were some of the exponents." Perhaps the close confines of an insular existence emphasized the common weal. The progress of education, which produced some of England's most famous colleges, may have had something to do with it, and the Peasants' Revolt of 1381 would seem to indicate some political consciousness on the part of the lower classes. Whatever the reasons, we notice that after the middle of the fifteenth century more interest was shown in Parliamentary representation. Attendance at meetings picked up, and the representation of a borough or county in Parliament was at last considered an asset rather than a liability. In 1533 a borough member was elected Speaker of the House of Commons for the first time, and only a few years later it is reported that the Speaker had asked for access to the King on behalf of himself and his colleagues. At the same time, even elder sons of peers sought election to the House of Commons.

This increased interest in the House of Commons produced a more careful organization and the keeping of a Journal. Being a member of the House of Commons now brought prestige and public recognition, and men were praised for being great parliamentarians.

The Tudor period was the last great preparatory period which Parliament, especially the House of Commons, had to undergo before facing its crucial test under the Stuarts. A number of writers have dismissed the Tudor period as one in which Parliament was merely a rubber stamp. There is some truth in this, but it misses the point. Henry VIII (1509–1547) was the first king who might truly be called a "sovereign." He held the total power of the realm, which was brought to bear upon all subjects, high and low alike. No longer was there a process of delegating power, as was the case under feudalism. But on the other hand, the King sought to dignify his administration by having many of his acts enrolled as acts of Parliament. The King therefore caused Parliament to be in session much more often than before. A common experience and procedure were created, and the House of Commons began to maintain control over its own members. The House did support Henry VIII and Elizabeth in their major actions, but its members were jealous of their right to speak freely, and individual members spoke out in a clear voice against royal acts of which they disapproved.

Although the Tudors generally gained the support of the House of Commons, they were nevertheless aware of its sensibilities. But their successors, the Stuarts, attempted to make an absolute political theory of their supremacy and to relegate the Commons to the lower depths. The House of Commons, which, as we have seen, had gained much in stature and especially in solidarity, was not likely to look kindly upon such endeavors.

The viewpoint of the King was explained in a tract written by himself (James I, 1603–1625) entitled *The Trew Law of Free Monarchies,* published in 1598. Its thesis was simple to grasp. The King's power derived from God, and it was therefore blasphemy to call him to account. "The state of monarchy is the supremest thing upon earth: for kings are not only God's lieutenants upon earth and sit upon God's throne, but even by God himself they are called Gods." Consequently "kings were the authors and makers of the laws, and not the laws of the kings," and therefore "that which concerns the mystery of the king's power is not lawful to be disputed."

The opposing viewpoint was well stated by the great exponent of the common law, the Chief Justice Sir Edward Coke: ". . . the king cannot change any part of the common law, nor create any offense by his proclamation which was not an offense before, without Parliament. . . ."[13] Now this was an extreme statement, and hardly in accordance with the facts.[14] But while the Commons and Coke might have been short on theory, they were long in the clarity of their political conception. What the King demanded was not a return to the Middle Ages or even to the Tudors, but the establishment of royal absolutism and the abdication of Parliament. Had the Commons elected to surrender, England would have followed the path of France. True, royal absolutism might have been shed later, as in France, but that could have been done only by revolutionary means, which would have deprived

[13] The Question of Royal Proclamations (1610), Coke, *Reports,* XII, pp. 74*f.*
[14] Coke's extreme views also sought to restrain Parliament when it interfered with the common law. See Dr. Bonham's case, *ibid.,* XII, p. 75. "It appears in our books, that in many cases, the common law will controul [*sic*] acts of Parliament, and sometimes adjudge them to be utterly void."

English institutions of that steady growth which is their principal strength. Fortunately the Commons chose to fight.

The outcome of this struggle is well known. Charles I (1625–1649) lost his head. But the triumphant House of Commons was hardly less arbitrary than the King. Political opponents were eliminated, the House of Lords was abolished, and a Commonwealth (republic) was proclaimed. Oliver Cromwell became the actual ruler, as Lord Protector, but he and the army were scarcely less difficult to bear than the Stuarts. The Commonwealth never became rooted in popular sentiment and did not long survive the death of Cromwell. The rebelling Commons had not really meant to abolish the monarchy when they began their uprising,[15] and the Commonwealth had been the product of the victorious moment, rather than of a carefully conceived plan. The depressing effect of Puritan rule and the excesses of the army quickly made the monarchy popular again, and when General Monk contrived to bring Charles II, the son of Charles I, back to England in 1660, there was general relief. Charles II (1660–1685), a quite inconsequential and frivolous person, managed to ride the tide, but James II (1685–1688) burned with the fire of the divine-right-of-kings theory. To make matters worse, he was a Catholic, and Catholics were not popular in England at that time.[16] When the King proceeded to grant far-reaching rights to Catholics and Nonconformists, and to restore the arbitrary Elizabethan Court of High Commission, the House of Commons decided to get rid of him. They called upon Prince William of Orange, governor (*stadtholder*) of the United Netherlands and husband of James's daughter Mary, to assume the English throne. James fled the country, and it is perhaps typical that this bloodless shift of power is referred to as the Glorious Revolution (1688–1690).

The triumphant Commons were in no mood to entrust their liberties to any monarch unprotected. This time their rights were to be put down in black and white. But certain legal difficulties developed.[17] In order to be effective, the new king had to accept certain conditions before his coronation. Yet, without a king, no legal Parliament could be convoked. This dilemma was resolved in the following way: A number of members of Parliament and certain other officers assembled at Westminster, declared the throne vacant on account of James II's flight, and called upon Prince William and Princess Mary to rule the country. Therefore William and Mary, by the advice of the lords spiritual and temporal and "diverse principal persons of the commons," caused a new Parliament to be elected. This Parliament has been called the "Convention Parliament" because it met on January 22, 1689, without being legally convoked. This "Parliament" then drew up a declaration of its rights[18] which was accepted on February 13. Thereupon William and Mary were proclaimed King and Queen. On February 22, the "Convention Parliament" was

[15] See the Grand Remonstrance of 1641.
[16] It should be pointed out, however, that the divine-right-of-kings theory is a Protestant, not a Catholic, concept.
[17] Frederic W. Maitland, *The Constitutional History of England,* London, 1908, pp. 281–288.
[18] Containing a list of grievances against James II, a method which was later adopted in the American Declaration of Independence.

legalized by royal action, and finally on December 16, the now legal Parliament reenacted its previous declaration with certain additions which became known as the Bill of Rights.[19]

The Bill of Rights of 1689 is one of the fundamental documents of the constitution.[20] It creates no innovations, but it crystallizes the growth and achievements of parliamentarism in England. It provided that Parliament "ought to be free" and held frequently; that Parliament should make laws and that there should be granted no dispensation from them except by act of Parliament; that all ancient rights and liberties be confirmed; and that no Catholic should ever ascend to the throne. These provisions were further broadened in the Toleration Act (1689), which increased the rights of Nonconformists; the Triennial Act (1694), which provided that Parliament should meet at least once every three years; the Trial for Treason Act (1696), which modified criminal procedure; the Act of Settlement (1701), which established the line of succession to the throne and thereby established the important principle that monarchs ascended to the throne by virtue of an act of Parliament; and finally, under Queen Anne, the Act of Union with Scotland (1707). To these important statutes must be added an earlier one which constitutes one of the proudest possessions of the English-speaking world, the Habeas Corpus Act (1679).

With these acts, but especially in view of its demonstrated strength, the victory of Parliament was achieved. Parliament, however, meant now and henceforth the House of Commons. The House of Lords continued to exist, but the tail now wagged the dog.

What did this mean? The King was still, as a medieval writer has stated, "in his court, in his council, in his parliament."[21] The King's powers had greatly declined, while Parliament had become exalted. But while the King had become nearly powerless, the Crown, the symbol of government, had gained immeasurably by the newly found unity of the nation. Yet Parliamentary government, as it emerged in the seventeenth century, had two major flaws: it was not representative and was too unwieldy as a government. A large number of seats in Parliament were filled by members who represented no electorate other than a handful of landowners who made and unmade members at will. Those were from the "rotten boroughs," as they came to be called. On the other hand, there were large cities without representation. Much corruption prevailed, and the House of Commons, in sovereign arrogance, declared men elected who had not obtained the necessary number of

---

[19] For text see Stephenson and Marcham, *Sources of English Constitutional History,* New York, 1937, pp. 599–605.

[20] Some distinguished authorities have opined that the Bill of Rights is the nearest thing in English history to a written constitution. G. B. Adams, *Constitutional History of England,* New York, 1934, 2d ed., p. 358. This seems to be debatable, as Cromwell's Instrument of Government (1653) is far more like a constitution and is probably the oldest written constitution.

[21] Fleta, II, c. 2, quoted by F. Pollock and F. W. Maitland in *History of English Law to the Times of Edward I,* London, 1911, 2d ed., Vol. I, p. 179.

votes, while duly elected members were not seated. Favors and offices were bought and sold, and political opponents were sometimes persecuted. At the same time, this proud and unrepresentative body could not actually govern the country because it was too large and diversified. Consequently the actual powers of government were often wielded by various cliques of politically ambitious men and women who were essentially responsible to nobody.

The growth of the cabinet system

In other countries, such conditions frequently lead to revolution and counter-revolution. In England, this was happily not the case. The fortunate tradition of institutions which grew out of experience and fortuitous accident produced the cabinet system which the leading authority on the subject has described as the "core of the British constitutional system."[22] Parliamentary supremacy had been established in 1689. Nobody could doubt that. But at the same time the King considered himself to be the real executive, and this idea was shared by Parliament, which attempted to check his power by reaffirming its own power of impeachment.[23] The King soon found that he was most likely to get on with Parliament if he selected those men for his advisers who had the confidence of the majority of Parliament. This development really came into its own when the Hanoverian dynasty ascended to the throne in 1714. George I (1714–1727) was a German prince who knew no English and cared little for England. He withdrew from cabinet council meetings, leaving the conduct of business to its chairman, who began to be called Prime Minister.[24] There was little change under George II (1727–1760). George III (1760–1820) made an attempt to recover the prerogatives of royal power, but Parliament was far too strongly entrenched, and alert to its danger, to permit him to turn the clock back. The loss of the American colonies, the resignation of the Lord North cabinet, and finally the insanity of the King put an end to such endeavors. The prestige of the Crown sank further under the regency and George IV (1820–1830). But William IV (1830–1837) and Victoria (1837–1901) restored its reputation, which increased thereafter. The First and Second World Wars brought new heights of popularity to the monarchs, who shared in the privations of their subjects. But there was no question of giving the King any real power. Queen Victoria had tried to have a hand in the selection of her Prime Ministers and repeatedly attempted to keep the seals of office from the Liberal party leader, William Gladstone. But she was completely unsuccessful, and no subsequent king has dared to make a similar attempt.

It is the English cabinet system which has permitted Britain to become a crown republic, because it vests the real executive power, not in an untouchable

---

[22] W. Ivor Jennings, *Cabinet Government,* Cambridge, England, 1951, 2d ed., p. 1.
[23] See the Act of Settlement of 1701, 12 & 13 William III, c. 2. Since "the King could do no wrong," the executive power could be curbed only by impeaching the King's ministers.
[24] The first person so called was Sir Robert Walpole.

king, but in a responsible cabinet—responsible, that is, to the real sovereign, Parliament, and ultimately to the people.

The cabinet system is one of Britain's outstanding gifts to the science and practice of government. Yet this institution, like so many others, was never "created." It grew imperceptibly, with the result that when it was firmly established, it was already so generally accepted that no serious protests against it were forthcoming. This is generally the advantage of gradually developed institutions over created ones. How unaware even sophisticated contemporaries were of this tremendous innovation is demonstrated by the fact that the wise and well-educated founders of the American Constitution gave little attention to the cabinet problem and none to the concept of a responsible ministry. Likewise, when in 1791 the Pitt government in England framed a government for Canada which was to be based on the English model, no responsible cabinet was created or even proposed.

An essential part of the system of cabinet government is the responsibility of the cabinet to the legislature. This too was a feature which emerged gradually. William Pitt still resisted ouster by a hostile majority in the House of Commons, but when Sir Robert Walpole lost his majority in the House in 1742, he resigned as a matter of course. When it was firmly established that a Prime Minister must resign as soon as he has lost the confidence of Parliament, the older remedies of ouster, impeachment, and act of attainder fell into disuse.[25] For a while governments believed it necessary to have the confidence of the Crown as well as of the House of Lords in addition to that of the Commons. As late as 1839 Sir Robert Peel refused office because he felt that he did not possess the confidence of the Crown, and in 1850 a British cabinet (Russell) found it necessary to ask for a special vote of confidence from the House of Commons because it had received a vote of nonconfidence from the House of Lords. But soon thereafter the cabinet's sole responsibility to the House of Commons was fully recognized, and in 1868 Prime Minister Disraeli resigned upon the defeat of his party at the polls, without waiting to meet Parliament as had hitherto been the custom.

Thus it was recognized that the people, in voting ostensibly for members of the House of Commons, actually elect a new government. That has been standing practice ever since. It would be inconceivable for the King to call anyone but the leader of the victorious party to Buckingham Palace to entrust him with the seals of office; nor will the displeasure of the House of Lords ever again endanger the stability of a cabinet. Lord Salisbury was the last Prime Minister (1895–1902) to sit in the House of Lords, rather than the House of Commons. So much importance was attributed to the Prime Minister's ability to represent the government in the House of Commons that, when Prime Minister Bonar Law resigned in 1923 because of ill health, Stanley Baldwin became his successor and not the favored Lord Curzon.

---

[25] The last case of impeachment was that of Lord Melville in 1805.

Broader representation

The close relationship between the cabinet and the House of Commons would not have been possible had the House not become much more broadly representative than it had been in the eighteenth century. We have seen how unrepresentative the House of Commons was before 1832.[26] Large municipal areas were unrepresented, while ruined hamlets "sent" members to Parliament. Worse, rich landowners, who themselves may have been members of the House of Lords, the House of Commons, or the cabinet, "appointed" members to seats which they controlled and sometimes sold in the most open and shameless manner. More than half the seats in the House of Commons came from such "rotten" or "pocket" boroughs, a situation which John Locke described in the following terms:[27]

> To what gross absurdities the following custom, when reason has left it, may lead, we may be satisfied when we see the bare name of a town of which there remains not so much as the ruins, where scarce so much housing as a sheepcote, or more inhabitants than a shepherd is to be found, send as many representatives to the grand assembly of lawmakers as a whole county numerous in people and powerful in riches.

And one of England's most notable statesmen, himself once the "representative" of a "rotten" borough, William Pitt the younger, declared on the floor of the House of Commons, "This House is not the representative of the people of Great Britain; it is the representative of nominal boroughs, of ruined and exterminated towns, of noble families, of wealthy individuals, of foreign potentates."[28]

After a considerable struggle,[29] the great Reform Bill finally became law in 1832. It did not solve all outstanding problems by any means, but it was a mighty step in the right direction. It abolished the "rotten boroughs" and created new constituencies in hitherto unrepresented or underrepresented areas. Moreover it ended the chaos of conflicting voting qualifications by substituting a single system of property qualifications[30] and by establishing a registration system. The Reform Bill of 1832 did not yet turn England[31] into a fully democratic country in the modern

---

[26] E. Porritt, *The Unreformed House of Commons: Parliamentary Representation before 1832,* Cambridge, England, 1909, 2d ed., 2 vols., is the most authoritative work.
[27] John Locke, *Two Treatises of Government,* ed. by W. S. Carpenter, London and New York, 1924, p. 197.
[28] Ogg, *op. cit.,* p. 261.
[29] The bitter opposition of the House of Lords was overcome only after a general election, a second passage of the bill in the House of Commons (after it had once been rejected by the Lords), and the clear understanding that King William IV would, if necessary, create enough Liberal peers to upset the Tory majority in the House of Lords.
[30] Different standards were established for owners and tenants. English tenants, unlike those in some other countries, are on the whole substantial farmers whose tenancy has been handed on in the same family, often for many generations. They cannot be compared with the sharecroppers of the southern United States.
[31] Similar acts were passed for Scotland and Ireland.

sense. Only 1 million new voters were added to the lists. But it opened up the era of electoral reform which eventually resulted in a fully representative House of Commons. Subsequent acts introduced new classes of people to the polls. The Representation of the People Acts of 1867 and 1884 enfranchised the urban classes, who had not been included in the bill of 1832, and together with the Redistribution of Seats Act of 1885 created a more equitable system of constituencies and created uniform regulations for town and country. At the same time illegal and corrupt election practices were outlawed by a series of statutes, beginning in 1854.

However, inequalities remained, and in fact became more pronounced in certain areas as a result of the passage of time and social change. The First World War set a temporary halt to reforms, but it also gave an opportunity for sober reflection. A commission of outstanding persons was called together to consider remedies. The results produced by this "Speaker's Conference on Electoral Reform"[32] culminated in the far-reaching Representation of the People Act of 1918, which wiped out nearly all unreasonable voting qualifications, especially property qualifications in national elections, reorganized the entire electoral procedure, and granted the suffrage to women thirty years of age or older. The Equal Franchise Act of 1928, known to contemporaries as the "Flapper Bill," finally gave full rights to women by reducing their minimum voting age to twenty-one, the same as for men. The last vestiges of inequality among voters were removed in 1948 when the university constituencies and the business-premises votes, which gave certain groups of people a double vote, were eliminated.

The Reform Bill of 1832 had not only remodeled the House of Commons but had also affected the House of Lords in two ways. By abolishing the "rotten boroughs," it deprived the Lords of much control over the lower house. Secondly, the willingness of the monarch to create enough peers to upset the Tory control of the House of Lords served unmistakable notice that the House of Commons would not be deterred in its course by the opposition of the noble Lords.

However, the problem was kept boiling until 1909 when a predominantly Conservative House of Lords rejected the budget of the Liberal Asquith government, as presented by Lloyd George, the Chancellor of the Exchequer. Although by no means an illegal or unconstitutional action, the behavior of the Lords caused a tremendous upheaval. The government, after receiving a new mandate from the people, was determined to break the power of the House of Lords once and for all, and in 1911 forced the enactment of the Parliament Act. It removed the Lords' influence in financial matters almost entirely by providing that all money bills must receive the consent of the upper house within one month or receive the Royal Assent[33] without it. In all other matters, the Lords could, however, apply a sus-

---

[32] *Letter from Mr. Speaker to the Prime Minister,* Cmd. 8463, London, 1917. Sir W. H. Dickinson, *The Reform Act of 1918,* London, 1918. E. M. Sait and D. P. Barrows, *British Politics in Transition,* Yonkers, N.Y., 1925, pp. 82–93.

[33] The Royal Assent, a pure formality which cannot be withheld, is the final act which gives a statute the force of law.

pensive veto which could delay enactment for two years. Ever since that time, the House of Lords has played in a strictly minor key, but reform movements have nevertheless been active. The Labor party especially, when in power, facing a hostile majority in the upper chamber and fearing undue delays in its nationalization program, has been critical of the House of Lords. Although the Lords, mindful of their political weakness and their historical anachronism, cannot be said to have given the Labor government too much trouble, their power has been further curbed by the Parliament Act of 1949, which limits the operation of their suspensive veto to one year. However, this further reduction of the Lords' power and the creation, in 1958, of life peers (who may be women) have largely silenced criticism of the institution.

2

The idea of the constitution

Few topics are as easy and at the same time as difficult to explain to a non-British reader as the nature and content of the British constitution.[1] The American or Continental European reader must first of all free himself from nearly all the concepts which he may have derived from the American, French, or German constitutions. Our American Constitution is a single, written document, which is declared to be the "supreme law of the land." Laws or other acts which are in contradiction thereto are declared null and void as soon as a court has an opportunity to review them. To be sure, that is not the whole story; even the most perfunctory student of American government knows that our Constitution grows by means other than formal amendments—by court decisions, by legislative and executive acts, by custom and convention. Yet there is always the written document, which cannot be trifled with, and departure from a practice hitherto considered constitutional must be laboriously justified in the courts.

[1] This part is concerned mainly with the English constitution. Major differences in Scotland or Northern Ireland will be pointed out.

Quite different is the situation in Great Britain. The foreign visitor who enters the British Museum and demands to see the "constitution" cannot be accommodated; if a guide, made wise by past experience with foreigners, wanted to give him a measure of satisfaction, the best he could do would be to hand him two books: a history of England and a treatise on the character of the English people.

The answer is simply that there is no single document which may properly be called "the British constitution." There are many written documents scattered throughout the constitution, but for the most part the constitution is unwritten, i.e., is based on custom and convention. This raises some extraordinary problems. The written sections are occasionally quite misleading, because they sometimes convey powers which could almost certainly not be exercised. Certain powers granted the Home Secretary and the Minister of Labor lie nearly dormant. Other powers may have been exercised once but have since fallen into disuse. Yet they are rarely actually removed from the statute books, and who can say that they will not, one day, be revived?

A certain amount of light can be brought into this apparent confusion if one remembers first of all that when we speak, quite properly, of the British "constitution" we mean the sum total of "rules which directly or indirectly affect the distribution or the exercise of the sovereign power in the state."[2] This would include the rules which constitute the organs of government, their branches and divisions, the relationship between these organs, and the relationship between them and the people, as well as the manner in which the functions of government shall be exercised. Understood in that fashion, the British constitution is not quite so unusual, because all other constitutions, too, have their written and unwritten laws, their statutory and conventional rules. What makes the British constitution unique is the uncommonly large number of its rules which are based solely on convention, and the fact that no act has a higher degree of authority than a simple act of Parliament.

Written and unwritten constitution

Lecturers on the subject of the constitution sometimes make a point of distinguishing between the "written" and the "unwritten" rules. Now, it is quite true that large sections of the constitution are written and larger ones unwritten. However, as a great master of the subject has pointed out, this distinction misses the point.[3] Certain rules may be unwritten but have nevertheless the effect of law. Very often such rules are eventually written into the law. For instance, the fact that a minister, by countersigning a measure or affixing his seal thereto, becomes responsible for it is certainly constitutional law but is not written law. On the other hand, written law may have long fallen into disuse, like the process of impeachment, or it may not mean what it says, like the legal right of the King or (reigning) Queen

[2] A. V. Dicey, *Introduction to the Study of the Law of the Constitution,* London, 1889, 3d ed., pp. 22f.
[3] *Ibid.,* p. 28.

to appoint all officers. Everyone knows, of course, that he or she has ordinarily no choice in the matter.

Law and convention

The important distinction is not between "written" and "unwritten" laws, but between "laws" and "conventions."

Law may take the form either of common law, i.e., the law based on the body of precedents established by judicial decisions, or of statute law, i.e., acts of Parliament. Among all categories of constitutional rules, the latter is the highest ranking and most final type of law, as has been expressed in the famous statement by Bagehot that "Parliament can do anything except make a man a woman, or a woman a man." This means simply in practical terms that Parliament does not submit to any higher law. There is no higher authority than its own acts. Not even past acts of Parliament can preclude contrary later action.[4] Moreover, Britain does not have a doctrine of expressed and enumerated powers. Any field may be invaded by the legislative action of Parliament, and the courts will abide by such laws, although they will try to interpret them wisely and, if possible, in conformity with precedent and international law.[5] It is certainly a fact that Parliament may invade the field of executive discretion (royal prerogative) and impose such limitations as it may see fit.

Nevertheless there are vast and important areas in which statute law does not greatly interfere. For instance, in the important field of civil liberties the English Bill of Rights is not nearly so explicit and comprehensive as its American counterpart. In actuality, the important civil liberties, such as freedom of speech, press, assembly, and religion, are primarily safeguarded by the common law, the great body of court decisions and precedents.[6]

This apparent predominance of statute law and its author, Parliament, must be viewed against the background of British and not of American constitutional life. In the United States the executive and legislative branches of government are largely independent of each other and are presumed to check and balance each other jealously. The British constitution is built on an entirely different principle. The real executive, the cabinet, is a committee and indeed the leader of the legislature. A need for "checks and balances" between the two is inconceivable, since the whole system is based on harmony between the two branches. Without such harmony the cabinet would fall. The supremacy of statute law is therefore merely an expression of the supremacy of the "Crown in Parliament," that is, of cabinet and Parliament working in concert.

[4] Ellen Street Estates Ltd. v. Minister of Health, 1 K.B. 590 (1934); A. B. Keith, *The Constitution of England from Queen Victoria to George VI,* London, 1940, Vol. I, p. 10.
[5] But if Parliament alters international law, the courts must give it effect no matter what other consequences may arise therefrom. See The Zamora, 2 A.C. 77 (1916).
[6] Hiram M. Stout, *British Government,* New York, 1953, p. 21.

Statute law is not necessarily of a higher order than conventional rules, even though statute may overrule convention. But statute law is usually expressed in more precise terms, and it has the added dignity of extracting unquestioning obedience from everybody. With due deference to Justice Holmes's famous dictum that "the quest for certainty is an illusion,"[7] we may state that the existence of a particular law is at least reasonably certain, and a well-trained constitutional lawyer ought to be able to say approximately what the laws of the constitution are at a given moment, although he may differ with his colleagues and the courts as to the interpretation thereof. When it comes to the conventions of the constitution, we are less fortunate. For one thing, we cannot say with absolute certainty just when a convention is in effect and when it is not. We may surmise that conventions are based on usage and acquiescence. Their binding force is derived from the willingness of the country—meaning government and Parliament—to be so bound. They are based on the assumption, agreed to by virtually all, that there are things which are or are not done by gentlemen.

So far the difficulty may not seem to be so great, but it increases when a challenge arises. This is especially likely to happen because politicians in England and nearer home are prone to shout "unconstitutional" when in effect they mean to say: "I don't like this." And what one person may call constitutional practice, another might regard as merely an accident of history. Prime Minister Lord Salisbury once wrote to Queen Victoria, "Our constitutional law is based on precedents. If the House of Lords reverses its course, under threats, because a majority of the House of Commons object to their policy, it will, by that very act, become constitutional law that the House of Lords is bound to submit to the House of Commons."[8] This view is doubtless exaggerated. It takes more than one precedent to create a constitutional rule. But it is quite impossible to state categorically how many precedents it takes to make a rule. Here again demonstrable acceptance and usage are the key; yet, a government or Parliament may by a single act set aside constitutional conventions. Such an act, if sustained in Parliament, would not necessarily create a new rule, but it would certainly abrogate the old one, or at the very least place it under serious doubt. For instance, it is a constitutional rule that the members of the cabinet bear collective responsibility as well as individual responsibility. But in 1932 the coalition ("National") government was composed of such divergent elements that they "agreed to differ," i.e., permitted ministers of one group to speak against the policy of another group. This has not become a constitutional rule, and at the present time, a minister who felt that he could not go along with the majority of his colleagues would undoubtedly be expected to resign from his post before voicing any criticism.

Despite this flexibility, the conventions of the constitution carry grave weight. Their weight is not derived from any idea that they are the supreme law of the

[7] O. W. Holmes, *The Common Law,* Boston, 1881, p. 1.
[8] *Letters of Queen Victoria,* 2d Series, Vol. III, pp. 559*f.,* quoted from W. Ivor Jennings, *Cabinet Government,* Cambridge, England, 1951, 2d ed., p. 6.

land, but rather from the fact that they are related to the idea of constitutional government and democracy with which nearly all Britishers find themselves in agreement. This island race simply prefers to retain proven procedures when there is no particularly strong reason to adopt innovations, and has thereby produced a system of time-honored customs and conventions which are observed because they are based not only on precedent but also on reason. One example will suffice. Governmental measures needing royal action are submitted to the King or (reigning) Queen in the form of "advice." It is a constitutional convention that the monarch must abide by the advice of his ministers, especially the Prime Minister. There is no law to compel him to do so, but let us consider the consequences of the King's refusal to accept the advice of his Prime Minister. The government would of course have to resign, as it could not be responsible for acts or omissions which are not of its making. The King would have to call on the leader of the Opposition to form a government. If the latter accepted—which is more than doubtful— Parliament would have to be dissolved, since the government formed by the opposition party would not have a majority in the House of Commons and would be defeated on its first appearance. General elections would be held, which would center very much on the constitutional question raised by the King's attitude. If the new government found itself and the King's action sustained by the people, it might get away with it. But if it were defeated, it would constitute a defeat for the King, and his fate as well as that of the monarchial institution itself would be seriously endangered. Win or lose, if the King became a partisan, his role would be materially changed, and the whole-hearted acclaim of the nation, which alone permits a monarchy to endure, would be lost. Consequently the King would seriously endanger and probably destroy his own foundation were he to refuse to take his Prime Minister's advice. It is thus in political reality that the conventions of the constitution are founded.

The conventions of the constitution cover an enormous range. The rules of procedure in both houses of Parliament rest entirely on convention.[9] So does the procedure concerning the dismissal and appointment of governments. In fact the whole cabinet system, the core of the British system of government, is convention.[10]

It has been stated before that acts of Parliament are supreme and must be obeyed by the courts. Acts of Parliament can therefore abrogate convention. Yet such action will not be undertaken lightly unless the convention is clearly outdated or inapplicable. Similarly, a government which possesses a comfortable majority in the House of Commons can set aside convention, but in so doing it may arouse the country and give such strong ammunition to the Opposition that it may face a difficult test at the next elections. Such emotions would be aroused, however, only

[9] The authoritative reference work on Parliamentary procedure is Sir Thomas Erskine May, *A Treatise on the Law, Privileges, Proceedings and Usage of Parliament*, rev. by Sir G. Campion, London, 1950, 15th ed.
[10] The Ministers of the Crown Act of 1937 does recognize the existence of the cabinet, but only in so far as certain pay raises are concerned.

if the convention is still strongly entrenched and is clearly relevant to existing problems. In the last analysis, therefore, the validity of constitutional conventions will be determined by political realities.

All this would seem to add up to a somewhat uncertain state of affairs. We have seen that the constitution consists of laws and conventions. Of the two categories, law is more dependable than convention, but it is also far from reliable, for an enormous gulf often exists between legal rights and the actual use or nonuse of those rights. This fact has been clearly expressed by the Judicial Committee of the Privy Council when it interpreted the Statute of Westminster of 1931: "The Imperial Parliament could, as a matter of abstract law, repeal or disregard Section 4 of the Statute. But that is theory and has no relation to realities."[11]

Even greater uncertainty exists in the field of the conventions. Not only can they be set aside, as we have seen, but their exact status and scope are never certain. A former Prime Minister, Stanley Baldwin, has described the situation in the following terms:[12]

> The historian can tell you probably perfectly clearly what the constitutional practice was at any given period in the past, but it would be very difficult for a living writer to tell you at any given period in his lifetime what the constitution of the country is in all respects, and for this reason . . . there may be one practice called "constitutional" which is falling into desuetude, and there may be another practice which is creeping into use but is not yet constitutional.

The guiding principles of the constitution

Dicey has stated that the British constitution is governed by two basic principles: the rule of law and Parliamentary supremacy.[13] Both are fundamental but must be understood in their broadest form. The "rule of law" means essentially that no one is above the law and that no one can be punished or otherwise be made to suffer except as provided by law. But law comes down not only in the form of a statute but also in that of judicial decision; hence the rule of law does not mean immutable text so much as orderly procedure. The essential emphasis of this principle is freedom from arbitrariness.

The principle of Parliamentary supremacy must also be understood in its proper frame of reference. It does not mean that Parliament is supreme over other branches of government. As the British cabinet forms part of Parliament, in fact its leading part, it is difficult to speak of Parliamentary supremacy in executive-legislative relationships. Moreover, as has already been stated and will be elaborated later, Britain is the country of cabinet government, not of parliamentary govern-

[11] British Coal Corporation v. Rex A.C. 500 (1935); Keith, *op. cit.,* p. 10. Section 4 of the Statute of Westminster stipulates that no law enacted by the United Kingdom Parliament shall extend to the Dominions without the consent of the latter.
[12] Quoted by Jennings, *op. cit.,* p. 12.
[13] Dicey, *op. cit.,* 1939, 9th ed., pp. 188–195.

ment (in the narrower sense of that term). In the United States the term "presidential government," or, as Woodrow Wilson put it, " Congressional government," would denote the supremacy of one branch over the other. But as employed by Dicey and others,[14] it means the principle of the unity of powers (as distinguished from the separation of powers as interpreted in the United States) and the concept that acts of Parliament are not subject to a ruling document and are therefore immune from review of their constitutionality by a court (judicial review).

These two principles are not only essential, they also hold each other in balance. The unitary principle of Parliamentary supremacy makes for speed and efficiency in government—especially when understood as an aspect of cabinet government; the rule of law ensures orderly procedure and reasonable safeguards against arbitrariness. These principles remain fixed. Their actual meaning in concrete application depends a good deal on the changing forms of the political struggle and the shape of the times. These principles of the constitution are, therefore, more permanent than the actual content of the constitution; and in this manner they ensure both its perpetuation and its flexibility.

[14] Sidney D. Bailey, *British Parliamentary Democracy,* New York, 1958, p. 6.

3

Parties and politics

Through the political parties and their network of organizations the public pulse is constantly being felt, and changes and adjustments are constantly being initiated as a result of the sentiments which reach the surface in such a process. To be sure, each candidate for Parliament is an individual with his own record to defend, but that record is far less important to the voter than the program and the record of the candidate's party. Now it might be argued that these programs are not established by broad masses of people but by small committees, although they may be approved by larger gatherings. This is of course true to a certain extent. No program on earth can ever be written by more than a handful of people. But it is not true to imply that such programs are created in a vacuum. Every political party wants to get its candidates elected. Every political party wants to be in office or be returned to office. This is possible only if it receives a large number of votes; every party is therefore sensitive and receptive to wishes and demands expressed by significant elements among the electorate.

Moderation

This constant process of new intellectual growth from the "grass roots" would, however, have only limited scope if the British parties were strictly class parties. In that case, ideas could come only from a relatively narrow section of the population and they would not necessarily have to be heeded, as the members of a specific class would have little choice but to support their class party. Fortunately this is not the case, despite the common belief abroad that British parties are class parties. The Labor party is largely supported by the trade unions and hence by the workers, and the Conservative party has many of the business and financial interests behind it, but two important factors greatly mitigate this picture. First, not all workers vote Labor, and not all businessmen support the Conservatives. Consequently the Conservatives have to be mindful of the workingman, and Labor cannot completely disregard business. In the second place, there is a vast mass of people between the laboring classes and the moneyed interests. No generic term can cover it; it is the middle class, the white-collar workers, the clerks, the lower to middle civil servants.

In recent years their votes have tended to become more consistently "left" rather than "right," and studies undertaken under the auspices of Nuffield College, Oxford,[1] have suggested that this floating vote may in fact be a Liberal vote lacking Liberal candidates to support. But this only adds to its floating character, and it can influence closely contested elections.

This has important consequences. Party lines are easily and frequently crossed, especially by the middle classes. A party in power may expect to be in opposition a few years hence, while the existing minority party may look forward with some confidence to the day when it will be in office. This has an extremely sobering effect on both. The majority party must remain mindful of the rights of those who occupy the Opposition benches for sooner or later it will be sitting there. The minority party must guard against extreme, purely propagandistic, slogans without practical value, for some day they would come back to haunt it at an inopportune moment.

Another important result of this situation is that since both major parties must appeal to substantially the same, decisive electorate, their differences of views cannot be too wide. This does not mean that there have not been most bitter contests. The repeal of the corn laws and the issue of Irish home rule divided the country deeply. But the division was not solely between the parties but also within them, and it was not permanent. The landowners who wanted to keep the oppressive corn laws supported the Tories, but it was a Tory leader, Sir Robert Peel, who effected the repeal of the laws. William Gladstone, the great Liberal leader, suffered several defeats over his advocacy of Irish home rule, but the Parliament which gave home rule to Ireland had a Conservative majority.

---

[1] Michael Steed, "The Results Analysed," in *The British General Election of 1964,* ed. by D. E. Butler and Anthony King, London, 1965, pp. 337–359.

Both parties have long been steeped in this tradition. Although precise definitions may not be found in party literature, there is no question but that both political parties and of course the remnants of the nearly defunct Liberal party understand thoroughly the respective roles of government and Opposition. There must be a government or chaos would reign. Therefore the Opposition will make a spirited attack upon the government program, and the government will expect and meet it. The government will not try to shut off debate, for that would imply conceding the Opposition's point. A genuine parliamentary life depends, therefore, on the existence of a vigorous Opposition.

On the other hand, the Opposition recognizes that the country must have a government which will be able to govern. The Opposition will therefore oppose, but it will not ordinarily obstruct. After the debate has had its course and the minority has spent its maximum effort to influence the course of policy, the division (vote) on the measure finally settles the issue. Obstruction, filibusters, and similar devices by which a minority may try to frustrate the will of the majority are extremely rare in the United Kingdom. They may be attempted, at most unusual and rare instances, when the Opposition feels that the government is taking an unfair advantage of its position. But ordinarily there is quite a sense of fairness and a mutual and profound understanding of proper democratic procedure.

A good example is the story of the bill for the nationalization of the iron and steel industry, which preceded the election campaign of 1950. The Opposition had fought previous nationalization bills but had not seriously attempted to stop the government. However, the nationalization of a complicated, vast, and on the whole successful industry was another matter. The Conservative party felt that the nationalization of steel would affect the entire economy, and to a far greater degree than had been the case with previous nationalization bills. It felt that the government's mandate, received in 1945, did not extend to such actions. It promised a bitter fight, which could have lasted for some time, with the help of the predominantly Conservative House of Lords. The Labor leaders conceded the point in effect, though other reasons entered too. They made an agreement with the Conservative party by which the steel bill was passed but its execution postponed until after the general election. Thus, the nationalization of the steel industry became an election issue of the first magnitude.

Most of these rules are based on experience and tradition. If all the rules of the Parliamentary game were to be put down in black and white and with the utmost precision, huge loopholes would appear and frightful confusion would ensue. However, the British distrust logic and precision and trust experience, and the system works.

Two-party system

The existence of a two-party system in Britain is an historical accident which the plurality system of elections and the single-member constituency (district) have helped to preserve.[2] Under the British (and American) electoral system, third-party candidates are not easily elected, because a plurality is sufficient to send a candidate to the House of Commons. The British tend to be pragmatic thinkers rather than doctrinaires, do not generally care to waste anything, and consequently look upon elections as a contest between two possible governments, the incumbents and the hopeful Opposition. The third party, not being a possible government, is thus increasingly ignored. Third-party candidates may accumulate a sizable national vote, but they rarely carry many constituencies, and consequently a vote for them—unless cast strictly as an act of protest—is largely wasted. Third parties have an opportunity to arrive in front only if they come upon the scene at a time when one of the major parties begins to disintegrate. This favored the Labor party, which was able to replace the Liberal party as the second party and thereby return the country to the two-party system.

It must also be remembered that general Parliamentary elections are the sole opportunity by which the mass of the British people may determine policy. There is no popular initiative and referendum, there is no recall, there is nothing like an American presidential election. All issues must be determined in the Parliamentary elections. Consequently, popular attention is focused on a few key issues: whether there should be a return to limited socialism; whether there should be more or less economic planning; whether the standard of living and general economic security would eventually increase through more austerity and planning, or whether there ought to be some relaxation and confidence in a freer play of economic forces; whether Harold Wilson or Edward Heath, leaders of the Labor and Conservative parties, respectively, shall be in charge of the country for some crucial four or five years to come. Between these pairs of fairly clear alternatives, a third party, advocating what seem to many to be half measures, is likely to be ground into pulp.

The years since World War II have shown the two-party trend with considerable clarity. The House of Commons in 1945 contained scattered Liberals of different factions, two Communists, two Irish Nationalists, and sixteen Independents.[3] By 1959 there remained only one Independent and six Liberals. In 1966 only the Liberals remained in addition to the two main parties. The Liberals have come up to twelve seats, and they still have a voter base of something over 2 million, but their supporters are much too scattered for the Liberal party to gain many more seats.

These events naturally have intensified the desire among Liberals to bring about a change in the electoral system which works so obviously to their disadvantage. A system of proportional representation—that of the single transferable vote

---

[2] For a different view, see Leslie Lipson, "The Two-Party System in British Politics," *American Political Science Review*, Vol. XLVII (1953), pp. 337–358.

[3] For the 1951 period, see Ivor Bulmer-Thomas, *The Party System in Great Britain*, London, 1953, pp. 83–91.

Table 1. *Distribution of votes and seats in the House of Commons among major parties*[a]

Year		Conservative	Labor	Liberal	Total
1945	Votes	8,693,858 (35%)	11,985,733 (48%)	2,253,197 (9%)	25,018,393
	Seats	189 (29.5%)	396 (61.8%)[b]	25 (3.9%)[c]	640
1950	Votes	11,518,360 (41.7%)	13,295,736 (46.4%)	2,621,489 (9.1%)[d]	28,769,477
	Seats	298 (47.7%)	315 (50.4%)	9 (1.4%)	625
1951	Votes	13,718,069 (48.05%)	13,949,105 (48.72%)	730,552 (2.53%)	28,596,695
	Seats	320 (51.2%)	296 (47.4%)	6 (1.97%)	625
1955	Votes	13,266,526 (49.8%)[e]	12,405,246 (46.3%)	722,395 (2.7%)	34,855,907
	Seats	345 (54.8%)	277 (44%)	6 (0.95%)	630[f]
1959	Votes	13,750,935 (49.4%)	12,216,166 (43.8%)	1,640,761 (5.9%)	27,862,708
	Seats	365 (57.9%)	258 (40.95%)	6 (0.95%)	630[g]
1964	Votes	12,002,407 (43.4%)	12,205,576 (44.1%)	3,093,316 (11.2%)	27,650,213
	Seats	303 (48%)	317 (50.3%)	9 (1.7%)	630
1966	Votes	11,406,255 (41.9%)	13,049,455 (47.9%)	2,320,021 (8.5%)	27,228,421
	Seats	253 (40.1%)	363 (57.6%)	12 (1.9%)	630[h]

[a] All election reports list the Speaker as nonparty. Despite the fact that elections would seem to be cut and dried affairs, there is actually a certain difference of opinion as to exactly how many votes were cast in a given election and even how many seats were held by a given party at a given time. This last view is the result of differing opinions as to where certain small parties should be counted. Thus, the figures given here will not be in complete agreement with those found either in A. D. Allen, *The English Voter*, London, 1964, or in D. E. Butler, *The Electoral System in Britain*, Oxford, 1963. Lest this unduly disturb the reader, it should be added that these books do not agree with each other.
[b] Including 3 Independent Labor party seats.
[c] 13 Liberal National and 12 Liberal.
[d] A total of 983,630 votes was cast for five different categories of National Liberals. None obtained a seat.
[e] Including associates.
[f] Including 2 Irish Sinn Fein who do not take their seats in the House of Commons.
[g] Including one Independent.
[h] Including 1 Irish Independent Liberal.

—and a majority system with an alternative vote[4] have been favored. But while such changes would render fairer results in the distribution of seats in Parliament, it would make the small Liberal party the decisive element in the government because of the even balance of the two major parties. Such an outcome would certainly not be a just reflection of the will of the British voter. The British, with their preference for proven experience rather than abstract justice, are highly unlikely to change the present electoral system.

The disappearance of splinter groups and Independents and the absorption of their voters by the major parties has furthered the development of a situation in which the two major parties are not only nearly even in national voting strength and in Parliament but in which a large number of electoral contests are won by small margins. This has greatly intensified the energy with which the parties undertake their campaigns.

The development of the contemporary party system

It is hardly possible to speak of a modern party system prior to the Reform Bill of 1832, although its origin lies further back. Jennings suggests that the beginnings of political parties may be seen in the Reformation and the eventual emergence of the Tories as the "Church party." A more common date is the restoration of the Stuarts in 1660. The Tories were the partisans of the King, while the Whigs were the spokesmen of Parliament. But since one party was in Parliament and the other outside, the situation was quite different from the present one. The final victory of Parliament in 1689 made this division obsolete.

The French Revolution profoundly affected English public opinion and divided Parliament into those who took a serious view of the French "danger"—men like William Pitt and Edmund Burke—against those who were less concerned, like Charles James Fox. In this may be seen the beginning of a new party division between a more conservative and a more liberal party, the former imperialistic, the latter disinclined toward foreign ventures and stressing reforms at home. However, until 1832 both parties were essentially aristocratic and dominated by a few great families.

The Industrial Revolution brought about both social and political changes.

---

[4] A system by which the voter designates an alternative if the candidate favored by him in first place does not win. Alternate votes are added until a candidate has a majority. The Proportional Representation Society, quoted by Bulmer-Thomas, *ibid.,* p. 103, figured out that under that system the Conservatives would have received 302, Labor 303, Liberals 15, others 4, while the actual results were 320, 296, 6, and 2. Under proportional representation the Liberals would have been the arbiters of the situation. Such conclusions are however, inaccurate because a change in the electoral system would also change some voting habits, and the Liberal vote would be likely to increase further. In effect, the Liberals did become the new arbiters in 1964 because the Labor majority was small, but they lost that role again in 1966.

A common front developed between the manufacturers, who were inadequately represented in Parliament and who wanted free trade, and the workers, who wanted free trade and the repeal of the corn laws.

The Reform Bill of 1832 was carried through by the Whigs and a dissident Tory group, but the outstanding spokesmen were outsiders like Richard Cobden and John Bright, powerfully supported by the theories of Adam Smith.

The debate over the Reform Bill was the first true Parliamentary controversy between two rival Parliamentary parties. The King remained neutral and followed the advice of his Prime Minister. Also significant was the fact that the Act of 1832 required the registration of voters, which gave rise to political registration societies. These had the purpose of "getting out the vote" for the parties of their choice and thus were the origins of local party organizations, although the nomination of candidates remained left to chance, the desires of public-spirited men, and the endeavors of men of influence.[5]

Benjamin Disraeli, later Lord Beaconsfield, succeeded in winning the Tory party away from extreme reaction. In that spirit he was responsible for a number of health and welfare measures as well as trade-union and factory acts. It was he who carried to victory the Reform Bill of 1867, which enfranchised a far greater number of people, especially among the working population, than the Act of 1832 had done. The increase in the electorate, as well as the lessons learned by Disraeli from the defeat of his party in 1852, pointed the way toward tighter central party organization. However, it was the Birmingham Liberal Association which, under the leadership of Joseph Chamberlain and his assistant Francis Schnadhorst, became the prototype of an organized political party. It had dues-paying members and ward committees, and it elected delegates to an executive committee which chose the official party candidate for Parliament.

The bitter controversy over the Irish Home Rule Bill caused a certain realignment of political forces. Part of the Liberal party, especially the great Whig families, seceded and joined the Conservatives as "Unionists."[6] Thus class lines were more sharply drawn between the two great parties, Liberal and Conservative.

The ambitious social reform program of the Liberal governments of William Gladstone and Lord Rosebery ran into difficulties as a result of the slim majorities those governments maintained. This revealed the need for strengthening party leadership, and an executive committee was set up in 1896 charged with preparing the agenda for the meetings of the representative council (National Convention) and the general committee of the party. To preserve the committee's independence, Members of Parliament were excluded from it. This actually resulted in weakening the committee and strengthening the Parliamentary party leadership, a situation which has been typical of British parties ever since.

[5] G. M. Trevelyan, *The Two-party System in English Political History*, Oxford, 1926.
[6] As a result, the Conservative party officially bore the name Unionist for many decades. It never became popular and was officially abandoned on Winston Churchill's suggestion.

The great Liberal victory of 1906 brought a great many social and political reforms which changed the country substantially and which are associated with the names of Sir Henry Campbell-Bannerman and Herbert Asquith, but especially with that of David Lloyd George. The reform of the House of Lords, the Trade Disputes Act, and a vast array of social legislation marked this era.

The First World War put a halt to domestic reforms, and in 1915 an all-party coalition government took over.

The great coalition proved successful in war but disintegrated in peace and broke the back of the Liberal party. Some dissident Liberals, calling themselves Independent Liberals, split off and together with the new Labor party returned to the Opposition benches. The Conservatives and regular Liberals remained united, but in the 1918 election the Conservatives obtained a majority of seats within the coalition as well as in the House of Commons. When the next elections came in 1922 the Conservatives, naturally enough, decided to free themselves from the coalition shackles and by their victory returned the country to the familiar system of responsible party government. The Liberal party never recovered and in 1924 decided to support a minority Labor government, thereby demonstrating that Conservatives and Labor, not Conservatives and Liberals, were the real alternatives before the voters. Labor thus became officially the second party, while the remnants of the once great Liberal party moved steadily toward the outer darkness.

The present Labor party is of much more recent origin. When small segments of the working class rose to political consciousness in the first half of the nineteenth century, they naturally allied themselves with the rising Liberal party. As early as 1868 an attempt was made to elect Labor members to Parliament, but failure resulted. The lessons of this were drawn by the Trades-Union Congress, which had already created a Parliamentary committee for general lobbying purposes. Also individual unions had occasionally been able to elect some of their leaders to Parliament—usually with the help of the friendly neutrality of the Liberal party. One of them received its baptism of fire in the 1874 election, in which it ran thirteen candidates but elected only two. By 1892 fifteen Labor leaders were elected; the number was reduced to twelve in 1895.

While the trade unions prepared the mass basis of the future Labor party, the intellectual direction and programmatic crystallization came from other sources. They were the Social Democratic Federation,[7] the Fabian Society, and the Independent Labor party. The Social Democratic Federation, led by Henry M. Hyndman, practiced a somewhat unscientific Marxism. It became a victim of factionalism, and a major part of it became the British Socialist party, the nucleus of the later British Commonwealth party.[8] The influence of the Social Democratic Federation was negligible among the masses, but it stressed the need for action as a

[7] Founded as the Democratic Federation in 1881, it took the name Social Democratic in 1884, emulating the Socialist parties of other countries, especially Germany.
[8] Hyndman and his close followers rejoined the Labor party.

socialist technique when that approach was not generally understood. Moreover many men who later rose to roles of prominence once belonged to the Federation.[9]

⤲   Of far greater significance was the so-called Fabian Society.[10] It originated within an ethical and utopian organization called the Fellowship of the New Life. A small group of members broke off and founded the Fabian Society in 1883. In the next few years they were joined by that group of outstanding people who gave the Society its direction, George Bernard Shaw, Sidney Webb, H. G. Wells, Graham Wallas, Annie Besant, and others. The Society first attracted attention through the publication of the Fabian Essays[11] in 1889, which were followed by a large number of tracts designed for popular consumption.

✕   The Fabian Society set the course which was later followed by the Labor party. It established the dominant ideology of the party and thereby set it markedly aside from other Socialist parties on the Continent. The core of Fabianism was the theory of Sidney Webb that the progress from capitalism to socialism was part of a gradual development which had begun during the period of capitalist domination. With this theory it set itself in sharp contrast to the Marxist doctrine—then propagated by the Social Democratic Federation—according to which the increasing misery of the working class and the inability of capitalism to solve its inner contradictions were bound to lead to violent revolution and the radical transformation of society. In contrast to Marx's theory of increased misery, Webb pointed out that the position of the workers had actually improved and was continuing to do so by means of the numerous works of social-reform legislation which marked the end of the nineteenth and the beginning of the twentieth century. After social reform, he envisaged the next step toward socialism through a more equitable distribution of income, brought about by progressive taxation and eventual public ownership of industries. He repudiated the idea of revolution by showing that the rise of capitalism had also led to increasing governmental action on behalf of the worker.[12] Fabianism therefore denied the Marxist concept of the class struggle and relied on persuasion.

✕   It was largely the merit of Beatrice Potter, later Mrs. Sidney Webb,[13] that the Society's attention was directed to the need for effective workers' organization. Her

[9] M. Beer, *A History of British Socialism*, London, 1948; J. Clayton, *The Rise and Decline of Socialism in Great Britain, 1889–1924*, London, 1926; G. D. H. Cole, *A Short History of the British Working Class Movement, 1789–1927*, London, 1932; and T. Rothstein, *From Chartism to Labourism*, London, 1929.

[10] Named after a Roman general, Quintus Fabius Maximus, called Cunctator (the hesitant), who defeated Hannibal's Carthaginian forces by delaying tactics. His name was adopted as a symbol for gradualism.

[11] Newly edited by G. B. Shaw, London, 1931. See also E. R. Pease, *History of the Fabian Society*, London, 1925, 2d ed.; G. B. Shaw, *The Fabian Society: Its Early History*, Fabian Tract No. 41, London, 1892; for a Marxist criticism, see L. D. Trotsky, *Whither England?* New York, 1925.

[12] The Society also rejected Marx's theory of value—now considered untenable by many Marxists—and followed the marginal utility school of W. S. Jevons, A. Marshall, and others. This fitted well into the generally neo-utilitarian philosophy of the Fabians.

[13] Margaret Cole, *Beatrice Webb*, London, 1949.

work and that of her husband led them to a reassessment of the importance of political action.[14] Due to their influence, the Fabian Society gave the future Labor party a political ideology and a sense of direction.

It never became a mass movement; that was the contribution of the Independent Labor party, which was founded by Keir Hardie, a Scottish labor leader, a fiery speaker, and an effective journalist although not a profound thinker. In 1893 he was instrumental in founding the Independent Labor party, whose task it was to convince the trade unions of the necessity for a Socialist program and for separate representation in Parliament.

Increasing dissatisfaction of trade-union leaders with the Liberal party made them receptive to his ideas. The Trades-Union Congress of 1899 adopted a resolution calling for a special congress of cooperative societies, socialist groups, and other labor organizations, in order to devise ways and means for securing the return of an increased number of Labor members to the next Parliament. The congress met in 1900 and founded the Labor Representation Committee, whose sole task it was to secure the election of Labor representatives to Parliament.[15]

The Committee met with only indifferent success; the cooperative movement and the mineworkers remained outside; and the Social Democratic Federation withdrew. But a decision of the House of Lords holding trade unions liable for action of their officers in carrying out a strike[16] created great bitterness among labor and caused the trade unions to redouble their efforts for greater political action. As a result, in 1906, the Labor Representation Committee was renamed Labor party, and that designation has remained.

The new party succeeded in electing twenty-nine of its members to Parliament that same year. It worked in close alliance with the Liberal party and benefited from the wave of reform legislation which the Liberal majority put through the House. Its strength increased steadily despite severe financial difficulties.[17]

The First World War created a crisis in the Labor party between the integral pacifists, led by Ramsay MacDonald and Philip Snowden, and those who, like the trade-union leaders and Arthur Henderson, supported the war effort. But this split was not as serious as in other countries. The Henderson wing of the party retired from the government in 1917, and the electoral campaign of 1918 saw Labor reunited. It obtained only fifty-seven seats, and most of its prominent leaders were defeated. But accident would have it that this small party became nevertheless the official opposition in the House of Commons, and this situation remained true after

---

[14] Sidney and Beatrice Webb, *The History of Trade Unionism,* London, 1894, and *Industrial Democracy,* London, 1897, 2 vols.

[15] For the text of the resolution, see D. E. McHenry, *His Majesty's Opposition,* Berkeley, 1940, p. 7.

[16] The Taff-Vale case, A.C. 426 (1901). See also Quinn v. Leathem, A.C. 495 (1901).

[17] The trade unions had supported the party and paid modest salaries to their members in Parliament, who then received no compensation from the government. The House of Lords declared that practice illegal, Osborne v. Amalgamated Society of Railway Servants, A.C. 87 (1910). A partial remedy brought the Trades Union Act of 1913.

the elections of 1923 had broken up the once mighty Liberal party. The Conservatives had a decided plurality in the House with 258 seats against Labor's 191 and the Liberals' 158. But the Conservative government had called the election and had failed to receive a majority; by British standards, it had been repudiated by the country, and it resigned. Ramsay MacDonald, leader of the Labor party and leader of the Opposition, was called to the palace "to kiss hands,"[18] and thus began the unhappy nine months of the first Labor government of Great Britain.

The fall of this minority government in 1924 came as a relief to all, because it marked the return to normal majority and party government. Both Labor and the Liberals lost heavily in the 1924 election,[19] the former dropping to 152, the Liberals dropping from 158 to 42. Stanley Baldwin, supported by 415 Conservatives in the House of Commons, returned to 10 Downing Street.[20]

The following years saw increasing economic difficulties. On May 4, 1926, the Trades-Union Congress called a general strike as a countermeasure against conditions in the mining industry. But government and public reacted strongly, which was natural in a country with a tradition which prescribes that political changes should be sought only through the ballot box. The general strike was a complete failure, and after it was broken Parliament enacted the Trade Disputes and Trades Union Act to prevent the recurrence of such a situation. Numerous restrictions were placed on the unions, especially on their right to call sympathy strikes and to use funds for political purposes. This act and adverse public reaction caused the loss of a million union members to the Labor party.

These events were soon overshadowed by the deepening world depression, and Labor gained again. In 1929 another Labor minority government appeared when the Labor party won 288 seats against the Conservatives' 260. The 59 Liberals were again able to decide the issue.

The second MacDonald government began under auspicious circumstances but suffered under Ramsay MacDonald's inability to work with his colleagues, especially with his Foreign Secretary, Arthur Henderson. Worst of all, the government proved itself utterly incapable of coping with the depression and the fearfully mounting toll of unemployed. The abandonment of the gold standard seemed indicated but was fiercely resisted by the Chancellor of the Exchequer, Philip Snowden, and by MacDonald, who was incapable of understanding fiscal policies and relied completely on Snowden.

The government came under increasing attacks from within and without. The party's left wing held the crisis to be insoluble within the capitalist order and demanded large-scale socialistic measures. The Liberals, whose support was essential, rejected these ideas and favored a policy of economy.

[18] It is a custom that the Prime Minister-designate kiss the hand of the sovereign.
[19] In this election an important role was played by a letter purporting to have been written by G. Zinoviev, Secretary-General of the Communist International.
[20] The official residence of the Prime Minister, located just off Whitehall, the government center.

The Conservative and Liberal pressure for deflationary policies was well received by MacDonald and Snowden, who were conservative at heart. An investigating committee with heavy Conservative predominance, headed by Sir George May, chairman of the Prudential Insurance Company, proposed a policy of heavy retrenchment, including drastic cuts in unemployment benefits.

In the face of this report the government showed an extraordinary incapacity to act, and it was clear that the acceptance of the May report would split the Labor party wide open. Already the Independent Labor party had reaffirmed its independent position at its Birmingham conference in 1930 and several ministers had left to form the "New Party" under the leadership of Sir Oswald Mosley.[21]

On August 23, 1931, MacDonald announced in cabinet meeting that he would present the resignation of the entire cabinet to the King. He left everybody with the impression, although it was not clearly stated, that he would be succeeded by Stanley Baldwin heading a Conservative minority government or by a Conservative-Liberal coalition.[22] But he returned from the palace with the surprising announcement that he had been entrusted with the formation of a "national," i.e., coalition, government. It is generally believed that the King induced MacDonald to take this step, though it is certain that he must have found a very willing listener. MacDonald split the Labor party by this move, and only very few followed him and Snowden into the "national" government.

The cabinet of the "national" government had an equal number of Conservative and "national" Labor members (four each), with the Liberals holding two posts. But there was no question as to the men who held the upper hand and determined policy. After the "national" Labor leaders had accomplished the task assigned to them, namely, to destroy their former party, they dropped out in bewilderment or bitterness, depending on character. In the general election of 1931 the Conservatives were pleased to leave the brunt of the battle to MacDonald, Snowden, and their friends, being satisfied with reaping the rewards, which were considerable. The Labor party, disorganized, unable to put up a proper campaign because its leaders had already endorsed most of the policies which were now put into effect by the "national" government, and pursued by the most venomous attacks of its former leaders, made a poor showing and lost 2 million votes. Its Parliamentary defeat was even more catastrophic. It dropped from 289 seats to 46, plus 5 ILP members and 1 Independent who went along with Labor. The Liberals lost even more votes, but through fortuitous circumstances were able to increase their representation from 59 to 72. "National" Labor managed to send 13 members into the House of Commons but only because they sailed under the coalition label; they had no following of their own and soon passed into oblivion. Despite the crisis, the Communists did not obtain a single seat.

[21] Aneurin Bevan, John Strachey, and George Strauss followed Mosley, but later returned to the Labor fold.
[22] For an eyewitness report, see Sidney Webb, *What Happened in 1931: A Record,* Fabian Tract No. 237, London, 1932, p. 8.

Nor was this all. Most of Labor's leaders were defeated at the polls. Among them were Henderson, Clynes, Greenwood, and many others. Of former cabinet members only old George Lansbury returned to take the leadership of a small, demoralized, and inexperienced group of men. His principal aides were Clement Attlee and Sir Stafford Cripps.

We have dwelt on this disaster to such an extent because it helps to explain the subsequent development of Labor and especially of the Labor government which came to power in 1945 and was returned in 1950 and 1964. The Labor party learned from bitter experience that it could hope to achieve little by nibbling reforms. It returned to the doctrine of its left wing, that a future Labor government could hope to accomplish its aims only by bringing about a fundamental change in the social and economic picture of Britain. The Labor party did not then and does not now advocate complete nationalization or integral planning on the Soviet model. Nor has its devotion to democratic measures been affected. But the party realizes that it must be able to influence strongly the entire economy, even the private sector, in order to solve those problems which it believes to be inherent within the capitalistic system. The policies of the Labor government after 1945 reflect these convictions.

Only the Conservative party benefited from the events of 1931. The sorry remnants of "national" Labor evaporated. In the 1935 elections, its representation in the House declined to eight, and Ramsay MacDonald was overwhelmingly defeated in his own constituency of Seaham. He was handed the safe Tory seat of the Scottish universities through the intercession of Stanley Baldwin, but died in 1937. He had been obliged to hand the premiership to Baldwin in 1935.

The Liberals also suffered from the splitting disease. At first they had all joined the "national" government, with the exception of a small group around Lloyd George. But soon one section led by Sir Herbert Samuel (later Lord Samuel) went into the Opposition,[23] while another group under Sir John Simon (later Lord Simon) remained in the government and became practically indistinguishable from the Tories.

For the Labor party, troubles were not yet over. The Independent Labor party had long strained at the reins and did not want to submit to party discipline in the form of the standing orders which controlled voting in Parliament. After prolonged and fruitless discussions, the final break eventually came in 1932 when the ILP decided at the Bradford conference to secede from the Labor party. This was accomplished, not without a split in the ILP. A few seats remained under the control of this party, but it lost them all in 1950 and is now a factor of little importance.

For a while the Labor party vegetated under the Parliamentary leadership of George Lansbury, who was seventy-three years old when he became leader of

---

[23] When the government became frankly protectionist, Snowden, by then a viscount and Lord Privy Seal, resigned too.

the Opposition in 1932. He was beloved by all, a man of the highest moral stature. But he was a convinced pacifist—a creed which was of little help in the years of Hitler's rise to power and Mussolini's increasing aggressiveness. Labor, like its brethren in other countries, had to consider what policy it should adopt in the face of this menace. The Communist agitation for joint action was vigorously opposed by the Labor party, which found little choice between Communism and Fascism. Whatever stand was taken by Socialist parties elsewhere, the British Labor party— in its overwhelming majority—always stood foursquare against communism in all its forms.[24] In 1935 Lansbury, who insisted on his pacifism on grounds of Christian principles, was overruled by the party conference and resigned. He was succeeded by his chief lieutenant, Clement Attlee.

The elections of 1935 produced a Parliament which was to remain in office ten long years, but that could hardly have been foreseen then. The Labor party recovered partially from the 1931 shock and won 154 seats. But the Conservatives still predominated with 387, to which must be added 33 National Liberals who supported the government.

Stanley Baldwin resigned in 1937, at the height of his career, before the consequences of his vacillating foreign and military policy became obvious. His successor was Neville Chamberlain.

A serious split in the Labor party occurred over the possibility of a united front. In January, 1937, the Communist party, the ILP, and the Socialist League had reached an agreement for united action. The Socialist League was part of the Labor party. Its spokesman was Sir Stafford Cripps. The Labor party Executive condemned any and all common action with the Communists and the ILP and expelled the Socialist League from the Labor party. Then at the party conference at Bournemouth in 1937 Cripps and his group were overwhelmingly defeated. However the "united-front" or "popular-front" agitation continued, and when Sir Stafford Cripps circulated widely a memorandum which had been turned down by the Executive, of which he was a member, he was expelled from the Labor party.[25] Also expelled were Aneurin Bevan, Sir Charles Trevelyan, and G. R. Strauss.

The outbreak of the war laid this controversy to rest. The Labor party and the Trade Union Council supported the war wholeheartedly, although they were still distrustful of the Chamberlain government and refused to enter it. The Soviet-German Nonaggression Pact of August, 1939, and the Soviet Union's subsequent attack on Finland ended, probably for good, all talk of a "united" or "popular" front. Aneurin Bevan and G. R. Strauss returned to the Labor party; Sir Stafford Cripps remained outside for a longer time, as he did not wish to accept the con-

---

[24] The Labor party issued a manifesto, *Democracy versus Dictatorship* (London, 1933), which placed Nazism and Communism ("reaction of the left") on the same level and condemned them both.

[25] At that time, however, Cripps concentrated more on collaboration with the Liberals than with the Communists. The "popular front," different from the earlier "united front," was to include all parties opposed to the Conservative government with the exception, of course, of the fascists.

ditions of the party executive. However he cooperated with the party and rejoined it later.

Under the impact of military disaster, the Chamberlain government was overthrown by a rebellion within the Conservative party to which Labor lent active support.[26] On May 12, 1940, Winston Churchill became Prime Minister of a coalition government in which Labor participated.

The coalition government presented a picture of odd bedfellows. Churchill was an imperialist, in many respects a Victorian. In some fields he was quite progressive, but his progressivism was that of Disraeli. To the Labor party, Churchill was the man who had crushed the general strike in 1926, and had sought to destroy them through the Trades Union and Trade Disputes Act. But both sides realized that they needed each other. Since the Conservatives had a majority in the House, the premiership would have been theirs in any case. What was needed in the year of disaster 1940 was a fighting man with indomitable will. That fitted Winston Churchill to a T. And modern warfare necessitated the greatest effort of workingmen, which could be assured only by the Labor party and the trade unions. Moreover, national unity was imperative in the face of the imminent danger of invasion.

Churchill as Prime Minister also took on the duties of Minister for National Defense, which gave him an opportunity to control the war effort effectively. The supreme direction of affairs was taken from the cabinet as a whole and vested in the War Cabinet, which combined supreme military and civil authority. Besides Churchill, it contained the leading members of the Labor and Liberal parties. These men worked together as a team. Churchill gave high praise to the leader of the Labor Opposition who thus became his colleague:[27]

> In Clement Attlee I had a colleague of war experience long versed in the House of Commons. Our only differences in outlook were about Socialism, but these were swamped by a war soon to involve the almost complete subordination of the individual to the State. We worked together with perfect ease and confidence during the whole period of the Government. . . . Never did a British Prime Minister receive from Cabinet colleagues the loyal and true aid which I enjoyed during the next five years from these men of all Parties in the State.

The coalition held together until the end of the European war, and the electoral truce was observed. However, when the German armies surrendered unconditionally and victory over Japan was clearly only a matter of time, the Labor party decided to leave the coalition. Churchill had hoped to preserve the coalition for another five years, during reconstruction, or failing that, at least until Japan was

---

[26] Chamberlain was not overthrown by a vote of nonconfidence. On the day of his resignation, May 10, 1940, he still commanded a majority of eighty-one in the House. But he realized that his personality and record were too controversial to provide the kind of leadership that Britain needed. His resignation proved him to be a patriot and earned him more respect than his ineffective and uncomprehending leadership.

[27] Winston S. Churchill, *Their Finest Hour,* Boston, 1949, pp. 13, 26.

conquered. However, the Labor leaders, under increasing pressure from their restive followers, were eager for a contest. That they desired this, after the danger to the nation had passed, is quite understandable. There had been no general election since 1935, and 1935 had not been a good year for Labor. Moreover, the Labor party felt that it had a concrete program for reconstruction on which the electorate was entitled to pass judgment.

The postwar political picture

The election of July, 1945, did not turn out as was generally expected. The Conservatives entered the race expecting to retain the leadership of Parliament, although with a diminished majority. Their campaign centered around the dynamic personality of Churchill, who had led the country in its darkest days. This approach failed for several reasons. Most Britishers had a tremendous admiration for Churchill as a man, but they distinguished clearly between the man and the party. And the party was the one which had stumbled its way into the war and fumbled, or appeared to fumble, the ball in regard to social welfare. Further, Churchill diminished his own stature by his highly partisan attacks on Attlee and the Labor party in which he denounced them as totally irresponsible. After the share Attlee had played in the war government, this simply was not credible.

In addition to these weaknesses, the Conservatives had allowed their party machinery to run down during the war. Labor, on the other hand, had kept its organization in fighting trim. Entering the campaign with somewhat moderate hopes, the Labor party sealed the breaks in its ranks that had formed during the war and went to the country with a strong program of social improvement. It emphasized that nationalization would be gradual and for the time being confined to about 20 percent of the industrial sector, with fair compensation for all.

The Conservatives also spoke for increased welfare,[28] but in such general terms and with so many qualifications that they appeared to be primarily making promises for the election only. They could not shake off their image as the party of an often dreary past. When the results of the election came in, it was clear that Britain had opted for the future.

The outcome of the election was a surprise to everyone, including the Labor leaders. In the House of Commons it took on the proportions of a landslide, returning Labor with 394 seats against 202 Conservatives. The Liberals obtained only 25 seats, divided between Independent Liberal (12) and National Liberal (13). ILP and Commonwealth received 5 seats, while the Communists won 2.

[28] Full employment in free enterprise, housing through private enterprise but local subsidy, stable market and adequate prices for agriculture, insurance plan of 1944, comprehensive health service, improvement of primary schools, encouragement of overseas trade, stimulation of scientific research, hearings of complaints against monopolies, removal of controls, encouragement of small business, central authority for more efficient fuel and power, better transport, and continued high taxation. "Mr. Churchill's Fourteen Points," *The Manchester Guardian Weekly,* June 15, 1945.

However these figures give a distorted picture of the popular vote. The Labor party polled nearly 12,000,000 votes, the Conservatives nearly 10,000,000, the Liberals 2,500,000, and all others 750,000. The Labor party was thus in a minority of about 1,000,000 as against all other parties, but it is the peculiarity of the British electoral system that it usually overemphasizes the strength of the leading party and thus provides a working majority in Parliament.

The election showed something else. Labor had become a more truly national party. Many of the rural areas, the cathedral towns, the Midlands—all traditionally Conservative strongholds—returned Labor candidates.[29] The class structure of previous elections was broken. To be sure, most workingmen voted Labor, and the remaining wealthy voted Conservative, but Labor had made large inroads into the middle class. This was the class which Labor would have to retain in future elections if it wanted to be returned to office. Labor, therefore, would have to concentrate on national, rather than class, policies. This had been the trend for some time, but the elections of 1945 made that point quite clear and all subsequent elections proved it convincingly.

When Clement Atlee rose to the premiership it became fashionable in many quarters to disparage him. Churchill's unkind quip, "an empty car drove up and out stepped Mr. Attlee," made a quick trip all over the world. Of course, no greater contrast can be imagined than that between Clement Attlee and Winston Churchill. Yet, after his two full terms in office, there is no doubt that Clement Attlee was a far stronger man than was generally believed. The wisdom of his policies will forever be a matter of debate, but there can be no doubt that he went about his task with a clear mind and great determination. There is also no doubt that he and no one else was the Prime Minister of the Labor government. Other, reputedly stronger, men cracked under the strain of their office, but Attlee did not.

The life of the two Labor governments (1945–1950, 1950–1951) of Prime Minister Clement Attlee was overshadowed by the extremely difficult economic crisis in which Great Britain found herself as the result of her almost superhuman war effort, the long neglect of her industrial machinery, and the disappearance of some of her markets. Thus, while these governments vigorously went about instituting some of the reforms long urged by them, the emphasis had to be placed on increasing production, which naturally bewildered many of the Labor party's faithful followers. Moreover, because general employment and wages were high, many workers were better off than before the war, despite the continued policy of austerity, and were often unable to comprehend fully the seriousness of the situation which the government tried to get across in the slogan, "We are up against it: we work or we want."

Many of the austerity measures taken by the Labor government were thus the result of the national crisis and not caused by the socialistic program of the administration. In substance, that was conceded by the Opposition. But where the dif-

[29] See R. B. McCallum and A. Readman, *The British General Election of 1945,* Oxford, 1947.

ference of opinion entered was the question as to the most effective means of increasing production and export and thus weathering the crisis. The Conservatives
believed that a return to a modified free-enterprise system would provide the necessary incentive, and they pointed to Belgium as a shining example. The Labor party,
on the other hand, believed that only careful planning would be successful and that
the nationalization of key industries was essential, partly in order to improve their
efficiency, partly in order to control the entire economy more effectively. Whatever
one might think about this argument, the accusation that Labor placed socialism
before the national interest was not justified. To the Labor party, limited socialism
and planning were the answers to the crisis.

The economic plan of the first Attlee government may conveniently be divided into four parts:[30]

1. Creation of a central planning organization for the purpose of making an
inventory of the national income, manpower, and raw material, and of recommending the most suitable use and distribution thereof.

2. A long-range plan involving the nationalization of basic industries and the
direct control of such other industrials as serviced the entire national production mechanism, or were in dire need of reorganization, or had reached such
an advanced state of monopoly that private ownership could be considered
"socially dangerous." Consequently, coal, the Bank of England, gas, electricity,
rail transportation, and long-distance trucking were nationalized, with steel,
cement, sugar, and others to follow later. The nationalized industry was to
comprise 20 to 25 percent of all industry.

3. Development plans for industry left under private ownership, in order that
it might operate in conformity with the national economic plan.

4. A long-term development of agriculture in order to make the nation less
dependent on the import of food.

If nationalization and economic planning constitute the long-range aspects of
Labor policy, social services represent immediately realizable goals. The combination of both aspects has long been the essence of the Labor party program, but its
own ardent supporters admit that Labor cannot claim full credit for its social-
service program.[31] That belongs, to a large extent, to Lord Beveridge, a Liberal,
whose famous report on *Social Insurance and Allied Services* was published in
1942 and formed the basis of the Labor government's legislative program in that
field. Other important reports on employment policy, national health service, and
workmen's compensation were all adopted under the Churchill coalition govern-

---

[30] Francis Williams, *Socialist Britain,* New York, 1949, pp. 86*f.*
[31] Barbara Wootton, "Record of the Labour Government in Social Services," *Political Quarterly,* Vol. XX (1949), p. 101; Margaret Cole, "Social Services and Personal Life," in *Socialism: The British Way,* ed. by Donald Munro, London, 1948, pp. 89–91.

ment. Labor claims, of course, that the Conservatives gave only lukewarm support —a claim which is denied by their opponents. It is true that two major legislative projects, the National Insurance Act and the Industrial Injuries Act, were passed by the wartime Parliament without dissent, but on the other hand the National Health Service Act was the subject of considerable controversy.

At any rate, the Labor government carried out these ideas with great vigor and added to them. In substance, these are the achievements of the Labor government in the field of social services:

1. The entire population is now covered to a certain extent against the loss of earning power, and a uniform practice has been established.

2. The National Health Service Act, which came into operation in July, 1948, provides free medical care, including hospital and dental services, for all. Each citizen contributes a small weekly sum to this program, and all services are free except for a small fee for prescriptions. Other small fees were later added. The contributions have been found completely inadequate, and the government discovered that it had to spend much more than it had expected. The opponents of the measure claim that this was caused by a run on medical facilities by people who had no real need for them, while the defenders of the policy, notably former Minister of Health Aneurin Bevan, replied that the miscalculation merely proves that the health of the British people was in even worse shape than had been estimated.

3. Housing has been a serious problem for many years and no quick or easy solution is feasible. The tightness of the island, the large industrialization, and inadequate progress in the building industry and trades have produced slum conditions. Added to that was the considerable destruction of dwellings by bombing and the V weapons, as well as the deterioration of houses which could not be repaired during the war because of shortages of supplies. A good deal of progress has been achieved, and war damage had been largely repaired by 1947. A number of temporary housing units were produced, and measures were taken to make unused houses available for rent. Long-range solutions were approached through the Town and Country Planning Act and the New Towns Act. However, in that sector progress was not considerable.

4. Educational reforms were already begun under the Churchill coalition government, which caused Parliament to pass the Education Act of 1944. It raised the school-leaving age, prescribed universal secondary education up to the sixteenth year of age, abolished fees in (public) secondary schools, and provided for closer inspection of private schools. Further measures for post-school education were planned. Much remains to be done in this sector, although no substantial disagreement exists between the major parties, and no insurmountable difficulties have arisen.[32]

[32] The quality of British schools, however, is excellent.

Conservative growth

The Conservative party, still led by the redoubtable Winston Churchill, reorganized its shattered forces after 1945. Under the keen, efficient direction of Lord Woolton and R. A. Butler, it rebuilt its organization from the bottom up, paid much attention to the younger element in the party, and girded for the next bout. It accepted and endorsed virtually the entire social-service program of the Labor government, and even pledged itself to broaden it somewhat. It emphasized the fact that it had already endorsed most of those measures during the war, and thereby attempted to demonstrate that their acceptance did not constitute a recent change of heart. Labor opponents, however, pointed to the record of prewar Conservative governments, and Prime Minister Attlee inquired in an election speech why previous Tory governments had not carried out such reforms if the Conservative party was so much in favor of them.

Although the Conservatives had resisted much of this nationalization, they pledged themselves in 1950 and 1951 to maintain what had been achieved, but in 1951 promised to denationalize only the iron and steel industry and road haulage. They pledged themselves to relax austerity by abolishing rationing just as soon as possible and by encouraging production through private enterprise. They promised to cut taxes radically and to effect sizable savings in the bureaucratic machinery of the government. They envisaged more incentive for the investment of risk capital, foreign and domestic.[33]

The Conservatives charged that nationalization had retarded production because of the inevitable confusion accompanying reorganization on such a vast scale. They maintained that the only reason why the evil effect had not become obvious to all had been the lavish American aid which alone kept Britain above water.

They attacked with special fervor the topic of regimentation and the alleged danger to freedom. While Labor went into the 1950 campaign endorsing a mixed economy[34] of nationalized and private industry, the Conservatives maintained that Labor was inevitably committed to eventual total nationalization. The Labor government's plans to control such things as sugar, fruit, and vegetable marketing and to nationalize the wholesale meat business, and the government departments' practice of buying what they liked in order to sell it to retailers gave, in the opinion of the Conservatives, some credence to this assumption.

The 1950 election and its consequences

With these records and achievements, the two major parties went into the election of February 23, 1950. The Labor party was in a highly confident mood. It published a self-congratulatory manifesto, called *Let Us Win Through Together,*

---

[33] See the Conservative party declaration, *The Right Road for Britain,* London, 1949; R. A. Butler, "Conservative Policy," *Political Quarterly,* Vol. XX (1949), pp. 317–325; Quintin Hogg, *The Left Was Never Right,* London, 1945.
[34] *Labour Believes in Britain,* London, 1949, issued by the National Executive Committee of the Labor Party, pp. 10–13.

which suddenly attempted to create an atmosphere of optimism, although Sir Stafford Cripps had declared only a few weeks before that Britain was teetering on the brink of economic disaster. The manifesto also managed to give all credit for maintaining the standard of living to the Labor government without mentioning Marshall Plan aid in a single word. These were only natural manifestations of politics in an election year, such as might be expected from any government party, but they did reflect strong confidence that socialist planning would be permitted to have another five years of operation.

The outcome of the election was a shock to such confidence. The Labor party lost 81 seats in the House of Commons, maintaining only 315, two more than a majority. The Conservatives breathed hard on their opponent's neck, obtaining 298 seats. The Liberal party, which had hoped to wax stronger by the votes of those who would turn their backs on Labor but who would not want to endorse the Tories, obtained only 9 seats in the House. The small Communist party lost both its seats in Parliament. The popular vote of 13,295,736 for Labor and 11,518,360 for the Conservatives reflected the same picture as the distribution of seats. The Liberals maintained their vote at 2,621,489 but found it scattered to such an extent as to approximate extinction in the House of Commons.

The Labor party hoped that the election would give it a mandate for the continuation of its program. Such a mandate was obviously not received. On the other hand, no mandate was given to the Conservative party to lead the country according to its lights. Inasmuch as the election was fought largely for or against socialism, it might be said that there was a socialist defeat. But in a positive sense the elections were inconclusive.

The swing back toward the Conservatives was the product of a variety of factors. As has been noted, the party had completely reorganized its machinery and was able to work much more effectively at the grass-roots level. In addition it had tapped new funds and was able to bring into the field large numbers of bright new candidates. Then too, the glamor of Labor had faded, and socialism was seen as much less of a panacea for the ills of Britain. Perhaps the most important factor was the switch of the crucial middle-class vote. The workers had greatly improved their position and the upper classes had in many cases also done well, but the middle class had not found its incomes rising enough to keep pace with the rise in prices. For a variety of reasons the middle class was feeling pinched from both sides of the social scale, and it made known its discontent with a turn back to the Conservatives.

The Conservatives return to power

The election of 1951 was really a continuation of the 1950 contest.[35] Nationalization of industries became less of an issue because the second Attlee govern-

---

[35] H. G. Nicholas, "The British General Election of 1951," *American Political Science Review,* Vol. XLVI (1952), p. 398. For a more complete study see D. E. Butler, *The British General Election of 1951,* London, 1952.

ment had too feeble a majority to undertake much beyond forcing through the iron and steel nationalization. Both parties emphasized the continuation of the welfare state and promised a better housing program. But greater prominence was given to foreign affairs. This was not so much the result of any deep disagreement between Attlee and Churchill but was rather due to events and tendencies within the ranks of the Labor party. In April, 1951, Aneurin Bevan, Minister of Health, and Harold Wilson, President of the Board of Trade, resigned from the Attlee government, ostensibly over the size of the government's military effort, but actually over a more and more fundamental disagreement on foreign policy. Bevan became the recognized spokesman of the Labor party's left wing, which is certainly not Communist but which regards the United States with almost as much suspicion.

Although Bevan and his friends certainly did not prevail, their weight helped to focus the campaign on a "peace versus war" issue which tried to pin the "warmonger" label on Churchill. The electorate seemed unimpressed by this artificial issue. Both parties displayed their best organizational efforts. Television was used for the first time, though on a much more limited scale than in the United States.

The outcome was a Conservative success, though far from a landslide. The Conservatives won almost everywhere, but with margins only slightly over their 1950 results. But the Liberals dared to run candidates in many fewer constituencies than in 1950, and the majority of their former supporters seemed to have turned to the Conservatives. Practically all the important leaders of the Liberals were defeated. Of their remaining six members in the House of Commons, five were elected without Conservative opposition and with Conservative help.

Although the Conservatives won a majority in the House of Commons with 321 seats against Labor's 296, their total popular vote of 13,717,538 was smaller than that of the Labor party, 13,948,605. Taking into consideration the fact that four of the Conservative seats from Northern Ireland were unopposed and therefore produced a light vote, it might be said that the two parties were just about even.

The period of the last Churchill government was beset by a severe economic crisis as well as by other controversies. A special chapter was that of foreign affairs, in which the moderate leaders of the Labor party, especially Attlee and Morrison, tried hard to keep a semblance of a bipartisan approach, while the party's rebels, led by Aneurin Bevan, were most vigorous in their opposition. In fact, on one dramatic issue, that of German rearmament within the framework of a European Defense Community, the rebels came within eight votes of carrying the day in a private vote of the Parliamentary party.[36] Further cleavages developed over the Paris agreements for Western European Union, the successor to the defunct European Defense Community, and over the establishment of the Southeast Asia Treaty Organization (SEATO). Bevan resigned from the Labor "shadow cabinet" in protest, and together with sixty other members of Parliament, he abstained from supporting an official Opposition amendment to the government's defense policy.

[36] The persistence of anti-German sentiment in Britain was again revealed as late as 1958 during the state visit of German Federal President Theodor Heuss.

Thereupon the "whip was withdrawn" from them (i.e., they were expelled from the Parliamentary party) amidst a clamor of protest from Labor's rank-and-file constituency organizations.

This was the situation when the great political career of Sir Winston Churchill[37] came to a close. He had turned eighty in November, 1954, his health had become increasingly frail, and on April 5, 1955, he resigned his office.[38] His successor was Sir Anthony Eden, long Churchill's understudy and faithful lieutenant. Soon thereafter, Parliament was dissolved and new elections proclaimed for May 26.

There were few outstanding issues. The Labor leaders hinted at a reduction in the length of military service and assailed the high cost of living. But the economic situation had been improved and this issue did not make a very profound impression, especially as the government had brought about a welcome cut in the exceedingly high taxes. The Labor party also pushed for nationalization of the extremely powerful and efficient chemical industry on grounds of power concentration and monopoly. But additional nationalization apparently no longer is a vote-getting device in Great Britain. Moreover the Labor party's chances were marred by a series of strikes which broke out around election time.

The result was a major Conservative victory. For the first time since the end of the Second World War, the Conservatives could claim a majority of both popular votes and seats in Parliament. In the House of Commons, the Conservatives now had a majority of sixty-eight over their Labor opponents or of sixty seats over the combined opposition. Their record had been vindicated; the premiership of Sir Anthony Eden, for which he had waited so long and so patiently, began under the best possible auspices. But his was to be one of the briefest and most luckless premierships in modern British history.

The abrupt refusal of the United States to help build the Aswan Dam in Egypt had been countered by the equally peremptory decision of Egypt's President Gamal Abdel Nasser to nationalize the Universal Suez Canal Company in June, 1956. Although this step actually had nothing to do with the question of freedom of navigation through the canal,[39] the Western powers, especially Great Britain and France, were deeply disturbed about the possibility of a hostile power gaining a stranglehold on what they regarded as one of their principal life lines. The unclear attitude of the United States further complicated the picture. Military operations began in October, 1956. Israel was first to strike against Egypt, and its action in the Sinai Peninsula was soon followed by British and French bombardments and landing operations in the area of the Suez Canal. Militarily the action presented few

---

[37] He was knighted in 1954.

[38] But he continued as a member of the House of Commons until 1964. He died on January 24, 1965, at the age of ninety.

[39] Freedom of navigation in the Suez Canal was guaranteed by the Constantinople Convention of 1888 in which the company was not even mentioned. The company never did have any control over freedom of navigation. That was always in the hands of the power controlling the canal zone: Great Britain until the withdrawal of its forces in 1954, and Egypt thereafter. Incidentally, the company's concession was to expire in 1968.

problems, and the outcome was never seriously in doubt. But especially for the British government the action proved a political disaster of the first magnitude. World public opinion was immediately extremely hostile. America, caught by total surprise in the midst of a presidential election campaign, was indignant; the Commonwealth countries were skeptical or, like Canada, hostile; British opinion was deeply divided, with the Labor party solidly opposed and the Conservatives far from united. At the same time, the Soviet Union issued threats of intervention and "volunteers."

Had the British and French struck as swiftly as the Israelis, political disaster might have been avoided and the world would have been another *fait accompli* richer.[40] But the operation was badly bungled; enough time elapsed between the first Anglo-French bombing raids and the actual landing of troops to mobilize formidable diplomatic and political pressure. Thus, although the British and French paratroopers reached their objectives, their fight was lost before it started, and under increasing pressure and the impact of condemnation by the United Nations, the expeditionary forces retired.

The impact of this blow shattered the British government. Under a hailstorm of bitter criticism and deeply undermined in his health, Sir Anthony Eden resigned on January 6, 1957, and was succeeded by Harold Macmillan.

It was thought that the Conservative government was finished. And indeed it faced many difficulties. It did poorly in by-elections and suffered severe reverses in the municipal elections of 1958. But toward the end of 1958 the tide had turned. The great skill of Macmillan ("Super-Mac," as he was often called) bore fruit; the Conservatives began doing vastly better in by-elections. At the same time Hugh Gaitskell, who had succeeded Clement Attlee (now Lord Attlee) in the leadership of the Labor party in 1955, ran into much criticism from his own party. Observers of the 1958 Labor party conference have criticized the seeming absence of new ideas. The position of Aneurin Bevan within the party became extremely strong, and his post as "foreign secretary" in the shadow cabinet became very firm, but he dumbfounded some of his radical followers by taking a more moderate line on the question of atomic armament, contradicting his own position of long standing.

By the end of 1958 the Conservatives and the Labor party seemed again to have pulled even, with the former having a tenuous edge. Macmillan had sucessfully resisted pressure to dissolve the House of Commons. As the country prepared for the general election of October 8, 1959, the Conservatives met the challenge with much confidence. The economic situation was fair. In the field of foreign affairs, British prestige had almost completely recovered from the disaster of the Suez affair. The partnership with America was restored. The series of top-level East-West meetings, which began in 1959 and which much of the British public ardently desired, was quite rightly ascribed in part to Prime Minister Macmillan's persistent advocacy of such meetings. Moreover, in "Super-Mac" the British found that father

[40] But Arab nationalism would hardly have been contained by a victory over Nasser, for Nasser is not the father of this nationalism but merely its child.

image which voters of all countries cherish. Certainly, few would deny that the Conservative party's comeback was largely the work of this gifted political leader. The contrast between him and the very intelligent but deadly dull Labor leader Gaitskell was distinctly to the advantage of the former. It was therefore scarcely surprising that the British electorate gave Macmillan and his Conservatives another and much larger majority which prolonged the Conservative government's life beyond the ten years which had hitherto been the outer limit for the rule of any British party in time of peace.

After the 1959 elections, the sure touch of "Super-Mac" seemed to wane. The Conservative government was up against a number of difficult problems. Many foreign, especially American, observers had long felt that Great Britain's drive toward a national nuclear force, although closely coordinated with the American power, would prove to be a costly and relatively unproductive venture. These predictions seemed to come true in 1962 when the American government decided to discontinue further development of an air-launched missile, the so-called "Skybolt," on whose development British plans had depended. The hastily convoked Nassau conference in December, 1962, produced certain alternative proposals centered around the Polaris submarine, which failed, however, to soften the political storm which broke in Britain. The abrupt refusal by General de Gaulle to permit Britain's entry into the European Common Market[41] also weakened the government.

During the same period the government was shaken by a number of espionage cases and scandals, which set off what Macaulay once called the ridiculous spectacle of the British public in one of its periodic fits of morality. The first case was that of a clerk in the Admiralty, John Vassall, who was convicted of having spied for the Soviet Union. A junior minister, Thomas Galbraith, was for a time under suspicion, and although he was completely cleared, disturbing flaws in the security arrangements of Britain were discovered. Fuel was added to the flames by the flight to Moscow of Harold Philby, a former British diplomat and later newspaper correspondent who was believed to have been connected with an earlier espionage affair involving two other former foreign service officers.

The culminating affair was that of the Minister of the Army, John Profumo, who was found to have been conducting an affair with a woman who had also had relations with a Soviet naval attaché. The most dramatic aspect of the affair was not the presumed espionage, which was not proved, but the fact that Profumo lied to the House and denied his involvement only to confess the truth some two months later in a letter to the Prime Minister. Macmillan acted quickly by bringing in a resolution condemning Profumo for an act of contempt to the House of Commons and by appointing an investigation commission. The harm was done, however, and more than 50 percent of a Gallup sample reported being "shocked" by these events, while an even larger sample of the public felt that the government was not taking adequate security precautions.[42]

[41] Press conference of Jan. 14, 1963.
[42] D. E. Butler and Anthony King, *The British Elections of 1964,* London, 1965.

These events were not designed to improve public confidence in the Macmillan government. In October, 1963, the Prime Minister, whose health had been failing, announced his resignation. He had already seen to it that Lord Home, later Sir Alec Douglas-Home, would be his successor. This choice did not receive unanimous applause within the Conservative party, and the man whom many had considered a better choice, Richard Austin Butler, retired from political life the following year.

The return of Labor

In the same period important developments also occurred in the Labor party. It had been rent by deep internal divisions. A vocal minority advocating unilateral disarmament and profound changes in Britain's alliance with the United States had gained strength in the Labor party and in the trade-union movement. One of the top labor leaders, Harold Wilson, had been considered close to this minority but had never formally given it his adherence. What had happened was that in Wilson's rivalry with the leader of the party, Hugh Gaitskell, Wilson had received and accepted the support of the left and pacifist wing. However, in 1962 the party leadership was able to win a number of important contests with the left wing, both in the party congress itself and in the congress of the trade-union movement. This victory was further emphasized by the expulsion of Arthur Horner, an open Communist party member, who had been for many years general secretary of the powerful trade union of electrical workers. Also, under Gaitskell's influence, the Labor party moved closer to a favorable attitude toward Britain's eventual joining of the Common Market.

Early in 1963 Gaitskell suddenly and unexpectedly died, and the contest for his succession became spirited if not bitter. Chief contenders for the leadership were Harold Wilson, who was initially considered to be the candidate of the left, and George Brown, the candidate of the right. On February 14, 1963, Wilson won the election of the Parliamentary Labor party (the party's caucus in Parliament) with a vote of 144, against 103 for Brown and 2 abstentions. On the first ballot, Wilson had received 115 votes, Brown, 88, and James Callahan, who later retired from the race, 41. However, this had not been a straight left-versus-right contest. Wilson, although not entirely trusted by many in the party, was finally considered to be the ablest man to lead the party in the next election and quite possibly in the government. That Wilson's choice was certainly not to be labeled a "victory of the left" immediately became clear when he formed his shadow cabinet in which the right wing dominated, with members Patrick Gordon Walker, Denis Healey, and Charles Pannell, who had been considered the late Hugh Gaitskell's closest collaborators. Only one member of the shadow cabinet, Richard Crossman, could be clearly identified as a representative of the left wing. Wilson also clearly succeeded in gaining the wholehearted cooperation of his unsuccessful rival George Brown, and the two arrived at complete agreement about the policy to be followed.

At the annual conference at Scarborough, the Labor party exuded confidence and unity. Wilson displayed a moderate attitude, stressing that the strength, economic health, and influence of Great Britain depended, not on sentimental illusions and nuclear ambitions, but on the speed with which the country adjusted itself to a changing world. The party conference, beating down all left-wing resolutions, adopted a program stressing economic growth, the steady rise of the standard of living, and the easing of hardships caused by industrial automation through severance pay and pensions, but it rejected a proposal for the nationalization of the construction industry and also rejected a proposal for the nationalization of land. The conference adopted far-reaching measures for the reform of the British educational system. It also adopted a resolution favoring a reduction to sixty of the minimum age for the receipt of social security payments, although this was opposed by the party's executive. In the field of foreign affairs, the conference favored extensive action within the United Nations and the creation of a permanent international police, and emphasized disarmament. It also favored the admission of Communist China's representatives to the United Nations.[43] Although such resolutions do not formally bind a future government, the conference ended on a high note of confidence and unity.

The elections of October 15, 1964, brought the Labor party back to power, but it would be difficult to speak of a Labor victory. Compared with 1959, the Labor party increased its vote by only 0.3 percent, from 43.8 percent to 44.1 percent. The Conservatives, on the other hand, declined from 49.4 percent to 43.4 percent of the vote, the difference being made up by the Liberals, who increased their holdings from 5.9 percent to 11.2 percent but who gained only 9 seats as compared to their 6 in 1959. The meager gains of the Labor party and the increase in the Liberal vote spelled out clearly the meaning of the election, namely, that more people had lost confidence in the Conservative government than had gained confidence in a Labor administration. This was also revealed in the parliamentary situation, in which the Labor party held only the slim majority of five over the combined total of the Conservative and Liberal parties. This later declined to three and for a while to two, as a result of subsequent by-elections.

Altogether the Conservatives had not done too badly. But many Conservative leaders felt that the colorless personality of Sir Alec Douglas-Home had been a detriment despite his ability. Moreover, his aristocratic lineage had possibly helped to deepen the image of the Conservative party as a "party of privilege." The sensitive Sir Alec gave in to these criticisms and declared his resignation as leader of the Opposition. On July 28, 1965, the Parliamentary group of the Conservative party, acting for the first time under the new rules for the election of a leader which were instituted in 1964, elected as its new leader Edward Heath.

It was the first time that a man of humble origins had risen to that position

---

[43] Great Britain had been the first major power to recognize the government of Peiping and to maintain diplomatic relations with it.

in the Conservative party. Edward Heath had been the principal spokesman for Britain's entry into the Common Market and had been the Macmillan government's representative in the complicated negotiations on the Common Market which came to an abrupt end as the result of General de Gaulle's ban. Heath's closest rival had been Reginald Maudling who had been Chancellor of the Exchequer in the Conservative government and who became Heath's deputy in the shadow cabinet. Heath's and Maudling's rise to leadership emphasized a partial shift to younger men in the Conservative party. Other new leaders were Christopher Soames, Churchill's able son-in-law; Ian Macleod, who had reorganized the Conservative party; and the strong-willed and independent Enoch Powell. However, Sir Alec Douglas-Home remained in the shadow cabinet, and a former foreign secretary, Selwyn Lloyd, also joined it in an unusual comeback.

The new Labor government had considerable difficulties at first, and a brief life span was generally predicted for it. With such a slim majority, highly controversial measures like the renationalization of the iron and steel industry were, of course, out of the question and were shelved for the time being. But a drastic 15 percent import levy imposed by the new Wilson government came in for harsh criticism, especially as the measure was in clear violation of international agreements. Many difficulties in the British economy added to the Wilson government's initial woes, and a number of unpopular measures had to be taken in view of Britain's continuing lag in economic growth. These measures were particularly resented because life seemed good, there was full employment, and there was a considerable degree of affluence. The coming problems and Britain's unfavorable competitive position were not clearly visible to the man in the street.

In the field of foreign affairs, any suspicion of Wilson's "left" leanings were quickly dispelled. The Anglo-American alliance remained as solid as it had been under Macmillan and Home. Despite opposition of the now much weakened left wing of the party, Wilson gave vigorous support to America's foreign policy, especially to America's action in Vietnam.

During the first month of the new Labor government's life, several events produced a number of reverses which diminished its already very small majority in the House of Commons. Particularly painful was the double defeat of Patrick Gordon Walker, one of its most senior and most highly respected leaders, who lost his seat in his former constituency of Smethwick in the general election and lost again on January 21, 1965, in the theoretically "safe" constituency of Leyton. The latter defeat was particularly painful because both there and in Smethwick there had been racial overtones.[44] Gordon Walker resigned from the cabinet and was replaced as Foreign Secretary by Michael Stewart, who had been Minister of Education.

A deep, searching review of general defense, with results published in Febru-

---

[44] The immigration of Jamaicans and other people from the Commonwealth had, for the first time, brought a color problem to Britain.

ary, 1966, also revealed Britain's difficult adjustment to her reduced power in the world. It was an attempt to bring her farflung responsibilities into line with her diminished economic and financial capabilities while still retaining an important role "east of Suez," a role which Britain could obviously play only in the closest cooperation with the United States. In this respect, too, the continuity in the foreign and defense policies of the Conservative and Labor governments was complete.

The defense review dealt a heavy blow to the prestigious Royal Navy by refusing its demands for aircraft carriers and drastically diminishing its role. Instead, the Navy was to receive four United States Polaris submarines. But much of the Navy's role would be taken over by the Royal Air Force, to which 50 American F-111A's were to be added. This produced the strong opposition of one of the Labor ministers, Christopher Mayhew, who resigned in protest as First Lord of the Admiralty (Navy Minister), as did Sir David Luce, First Sea Lord.[45] However, despite this disturbance in naval circles, the drastic measure caused fewer political ripples than had been anticipated.

In spite of these numerous difficulties, the Wilson government achieved a number of solid advances. The government had acted with balance and a high degree of responsibility. It had skillfully avoided a number of major difficulties, including major strikes. The ability of some of its new, partly untried leaders in government had been impressive. Particularly outstanding were Denis Healey, Michael Stewart, and Roy Jenkins. Towering above them all was the Prime Minister himself, Harold Wilson, whose aplomb and skill as well as tireless energy were dazzling. He had silenced the most vociferous leaders of the left opposition, either by taking them into the government (but in relatively minor positions, e.g., Frank Cousins, Richard H. S. Crossman, and Barbara Castle) or by isolating them outside. The government and its leaders had clearly gained greatly in both national and international respect. The Labor party had proved itself thoroughly capable of governing the country in an efficient and responsible manner.

Thus, by the beginning of 1966 the public opinion polls showed that the Labor government was starting to profit from its performance. The Labor party was now ahead of its Conservative and Liberal opponents, and the margin seemed to be increasing.

At the same time there was trouble in the Conservative party. The initial enthusiasm about Edward Heath's election as leader of the opposition had given way to a more critical spirit. Although a more experienced parliamentarian than Sir Alec Douglas-Home, he nevertheless found it difficult to counter the rapierlike parliamentary thrusts of Harold Wilson. To many intra-party critics, he seemed not too eager to engage the government in real battle. This criticism increased as the party did not oppose the government vigorously enough, at least in the opinion of some Conservatives, on the sensitive issue of how to bring the rebellious Rhodesia to terms.

---

[45] Similar to the American position of Chief of Naval Operations.

Angus Maude, who held the Colonial portfolio in the shadow cabinet, broke out into open opposition and resigned. But more powerful opposition to Heath's policies came from the stern Enoch Powell, who was in charge of defense matters in the shadow cabinet. And finally, at the end of February, 1966, the Labor party won a stunning victory in the important constituency of Hull.

It seemed therefore to Prime Minister Harold Wilson that this was the time to call for new elections in the hope of increasing the Labor party's delegation in the House of Commons to a more workable majority. Hence Parliament was dissolved, and elections were scheduled for March 31, 1966.

British election campaigns are always spirited and often rough—a far cry from the gentlemanly picture the world has of most British undertakings. Heckling is rude, and insults fly. But even with these precedents, the 1966 election campaign was one of the roughest in British memory. Perhaps the fact that there were so few differences between the policies and programs of the two major parties served to increase the desire in both camps to make up in passion what was lacking in programs. The election rallies of both parties were broken up or seriously disturbed, and the Prime Minister was hurt in the eye, though only temporarily, by a stink bomb.

But the Conservatives proved to be no match for Wilson's Laborites. No doubt many voters felt that the small majority which the Labor party had received in 1964 had not really given it a chance and that it ought to be given an opportunity to show what it could do. No doubt also, many skeptics had found the brief record of the Wilson government good and the quality of its ministers good-to-impressive. Certainly no one could really see wild radicalism in the generally prudent and middle-of-the-road policies of the government.

At the same time the Conservatives really never hit their stride. Being in the opposition, they should have been on the attack, but Wilson adroitly managed to pin on them the shortcomings of all previous Conservative governments, and forced them into the defensive. This was all the more remarkable in a matter on which the Conservatives and their leader, Edward Heath, should have had the better of the debate, namely, Britain's entry into the Common Market.

The Macmillan government had originally been opposed to the European Economic Community (Common Market) and especially to Britain's entry therein. Economic realities forced it into a different path. When Britain and the Common Market countries began negotiations for the former's entry, Heath had been the government's principal spokesman and negotiator. The country had come to accept this position, and the Labor party had remained generally out of step until shortly before General de Gaulle in the press conference of January, 1963, put an end to the whole affair. The Conservatives had the better record on this issue, and Heath was in good shape, since he had been the government's principal representative in the talks with the Common Market negotiators.

Thus, when in March, 1966, General de Gaulle hinted, though undoubtedly for tactical reasons only, that Britain might after all be admitted, he created an election issue which should have benefited Heath—particularly since Wilson, in an election speech, placed conditions on Britain's entry which were clearly unacceptable to the members of the Common Market. Heath misjudged the hurt which his countrymen had felt over General de Gaulle's previous brusque rejection and showed perhaps too much eagerness to pick up the new hint.

Labor gained a resounding victory. With 47.9 percent of the votes and 363 seats in the House of Commons, against 41.9 percent and 253 seats for the Conservatives, Wilson at last had the majority he desired. The Liberals, who had gained 12 seats but only 0.02 percent over their 1964 vote, were no longer needed to support the government in a tight squeeze, and their chances for survival appear increasingly hopeless.

Without the slightest doubt, the star of the election was Harold Wilson. It was he who carried the brunt of the attack, it was his personality, his leadership which was the real and principal issue of the campaign. Hence, the outcome must be interpreted as a resounding vote of confidence for the Prime Minister. This was bound greatly to strengthen his hand. On the Conservative side there was disappointment, disarray, and doubt about Heath's leadership. However, in all fairness it must be said that Labor, and especially Wilson, was in "high form" in March, 1966, and even Macmillan—"Super-Mac"—in his prime would have had a difficult time to stand up to the Wilson performance.

No doubt Wilson had much need of his increased power and prestige. Britain's nagging economic problems, her increasingly unfavorable competitive condition, had not been solved and would not go away. The defense review had given an indication of some very hard decisions ahead. Rhodesia remained a sore point. Though the intra-party opposition of the left wing in the Labor party could no longer bring the Wilson government down, that very fact gave the left greater freedom to oppose the party leadership. Having that built-in attitude of moral rectitude which characterizes radicals of left and right in all countries, they felt no need to be impressed by Wilson's massive victory. However, he had stood up to them unflinchingly before and during the elections; he could be counted upon to give a good account of himself in the interparty and intra-party battles which lay ahead.

Party organization in Parliament

One of the conditions of an orderly and responsible party system in Parliament is party discipline. This is a difficult and touchy subject. Too much party discipline makes Members of Parliament into mere rubber stamps to "be voted" by their leaders as they see fit. Too little discipline produces unstable governments and irresponsible legislatures. In the British Parliament a good measure of discipline prevails, although dissent is possible and common.

It is said that a Member of Parliament becomes officially a member of a Parliamentary group by accepting its "whip,"[46] which means that he accepts the discipline of the party and its parliamentary leadership. Each party has a chief whip and several assistant whips; the chief whip of the government party being the Parliamentary Secretary of the Treasury, with the Junior Lords of the Treasury as his assistants. The chief whip of the Opposition and his assistants have no such salaried positions, but their authority is also great. The whips of the opposing parties confer frequently with one another and together help to prepare the work of the House.

While it is the general duty of the whips to keep in touch with the members of their parties and to keep them informed of what is expected of them, their most important task comes at "division" (vote) time, when they see to it that everyone is present and doing his duty by his party. While this task has always been important, it has been of special significance since 1950, with the two major parties being separated by such a small margin of votes. In addition the power of the whips has undoubtedly been increased by the facts that Independents have fared very badly in recent elections and that the expulsion of a member from his party would almost certainly terminate his political career as soon as the next election is held. The "whip may be withdrawn" from a member—meaning that he is expelled from the Parliamentary group by decision of the leader of the Conservative party or by decision of the Parliamentary party for Labor members.

Of pivotal importance in the operation of the Parliamentary group is the personality of the leader, who is automatically leader of his party in Parliament and in the country, and who is normally designated Prime Minister when his party wins and leader of the Opposition when it loses. Since 1964 both the Conservative and the Labor leaders have been chosen by the members of the House of Commons from their respective parties. In both parties leadership has usually been uncontested, but there have been exceptions. In the Conservative party, contests were rare as long as the leaders were chosen either by their predecessors or in a highly informal process by a narrow "in-group" of leaders. The fact that Lord Curzon was passed over for the leadership in 1923 was doubtless due not only to his peerage but also to certain personality traits. By contrast, Winston Churchill's rise in 1940 was forced on the party by an aroused country which demanded strong war leadership, to which urging the Conservative leaders had to accommodate themselves.[47] Anthony Eden (Lord Avon), Macmillan, and Home had each been the choice of his predecessors, but as we have seen, Edward Heath's selection was carried out under the new (1964) rules of election by the Parliamentary group. Actually, Heath won a majority on the first ballot, with 150 votes against 133 for Maudling and 15 for Powell. However, the rules required that the winner should obtain at least 15 percent more of the votes than his nearest rival. Hence a second

[46] Bulmer-Thomas, *op. cit.,* p. 109, reminds us that the expression is derived from "whipper-in," a huntsman's assistant who kept the hounds in line.

[47] Many old-line Conservative leaders regarded Churchill, who had twice "crossed the floor" (changed parties), as unreliable and a radical.

ballot was necessary, where the 15 percent clause would no longer apply. Both Maudling and Powell withdrew their candidacies and Heath was declared elected.

In the Labor party, lively contests were more frequent. As long as Ramsay MacDonald remained in the fold, there was no question about who was leader. After his defection, the Labor party went down to defeat in the elections, as we have seen, and all its first-rank leaders failed to gain reelection. In this situation George Lansbury was elected leader and Clement Attlee his deputy. When Lansbury resigned in 1935, Attlee was elected in his stead. This was the only occasion on which there was a real contest, for both Herbert Morrison and Arthur Greenwood were candidates. Nevertheless Attlee was later reelected by a large majority. As a result of a previous agreement among the principal leaders of the Labor party, the election of Hugh Gaitskell as successor to Attlee in 1955 was not seriously contested, but as we have seen, Wilson had real opposition in 1963.

These party leaders are not absolute lords and masters—party leadership is a matter of teamwork—but their position is extraordinarily strong. Nevertheless, the sentiments expressed in party meetings will of course influence the leadership, although the leadership determines how great that influence will be.

In the Labor party, the leaders take an exceptionally active part in the meetings of the Parliamentary Labor party.[48] There is a much more formal organization than the Conservatives have, and there is even a kind of executive committee which is called the Parliamentary committee. When the Labor party is in the government, this committee has a heavy backbencher note.

The meetings of the Parliamentary Labor party are much more important than those of the Conservatives because the Labor party meeting makes policy decisions which are binding on its members, while the Conservative meeting has no such right. However, since the 1964 reforms, the power and influence of the Conservative meeting has risen. Experience will tell, several years hence, whether this is likely to diminish the once almost limitless power of the Conservative leader.

The standing orders of the Parliamentary party commit the members to strict obedience to the decisions of the meetings except in certain cases of deeply felt personal opinions and matters of conscience. In practice the members are held to those rules only within limits, and some opposition has been tolerated, but persistent violators have been expelled. It is one of the attributes of party leadership to know when force or leniency is to be applied.

National party organization: Conservative

Outside Parliament, the Conservative party is organized on the constituency (electoral district) level. Sometimes these constituencies are subdivided. The Conservative constituency association is a rather loosely organized unit of individual members, most of whom reside in the area, although members may merely have

[48] Ordinarily the Labor members of both the House of Commons and the House of Lords meet together.

their business interests therein. Each constituency organization makes its own rules, usually guided by central headquarters. Such guidance, however, is given only when desired. Sometimes men and women are in the same association; sometimes there is a separate women's branch. There is always a young Conservative organization. Branches are organized around each ward (similar to precincts). Each association elects its own officers. One of its principal functions is the approval of parliamentary candidates whose names are proposed by the executive committee of the association, but no candidate will be endorsed who has not been approved by a (national) advisory committee on candidates. For part of its work the party relies on a string of auxiliary organizations. Especially well known are the Primrose League, the Imperial League (with a junior branch), and the Conservative Workingmen's Clubs.

Each constituency endeavors to have a professional agent, preferably of the full-time variety, who is the professional campaign manager of the party's candidate. These agents belong to a respected profession, and the Conservatives, naturally more affluent than their Labor opponents, have nearly succeeded in having a professional agent in every constituency.

For better organization the Conservatives have established regional groupings whose principal function is the coordination of the work of the various associations. At the national level there is the loosely organized National Union of Conservative and Unionist Associations. It is the purpose of this National Union to promote Conservative party activity all over the country and to work in close cooperation with all affiliated associations, including the Scottish Unionist Association and the Ulster Unionist Council.

The National Union has a central executive committee, a central council, and an annual conference. Its executive committee is reconstituted every year and is composed of the leader of the party, other party officials, the chairmen of the various central advisory committees, five representatives appointed by each provincial area, one representative of Conservative Lords, four representatives of the Conservative Members of Parliament, and various other representatives of Conservative associations.

The central council of the National Union consists of representatives of various groups such as constituency associations, provincial areas, and Conservative peers. It is a larger body than the executive committee but not as large as the annual conference.

Every year a Conservative conference is held. All members of the central councils have the right to attend, and each constituency association and various other groups are entitled to delegates. Approximately ten delegates attend from each constituency as well as representatives of the central council and leadership. Thus between 5,000 and 6,000 persons have a right to attend, and there are as many as 1,000 visitors. Actual attendance has varied between 2,500 and 4,000.

The Conservative conference is a general policy meeting at which the main issues before the party are discussed, but at which party policy is not determined.

That is the prerogative of the leader, who does not take part in the work of the conference itself but addresses it when invited (which is usually the case).

The nerve center of the party's organizational effort is the central office (the headquarters of the national party organization). Its officers and staff are salaried and are more or less permanent. The central officers are behind every concentrated publicity campaign and work directly with the constituency election agent. They also conduct a training program, give examinations, and grant certificates. They supply publicity material, bolster the courage of sagging local organizations, and do whatever else may be necessary to keep the organization in full swing (especially at election time). It is generally agreed among Conservatives that the 1945 election was lost largely because of overconfidence and neglect of the party organization. Under the leadership of Lord Woolton and later of Ian Macleod, the central office was reorganized and has now reached a very high degree of efficiency.[49]

National party organization: Labor

In contrast to the Conservatives, the Labor party is much more tightly and centrally organized. It is also based on a different organizational principle because it has two types of members, namely, affiliated organizations and individual members. The great majority of members are in the affiliated organizations, especially the trade unions, which means that people join an organization which in turn is a collective member of the Labor party. This somewhat unusual principle is the result of the history of the Labor party, which started out as a roof organization over trade unions, the Fabian Society, the Independent Labor party, etc.—for the purpose of electing representatives to Parliament.

The Labor party has constituency organizations like the Conservatives, but they must adopt rules which are laid down by the annual (national) party conference. These constituency Labor parties are subdivided into ward organizations to which the individual members are primarily attached. In each ward[50] there is a ward committee consisting of individual members, a women's section, and usually a section of the Labor League of Youth. The ward committees of a constituency together with the affiliated organizations (mostly local branches of trade unions) form the constituency Labor party. Delegates from the various ward committees form the general committee, which holds an annual meeting at which officers are elected.

The constituent Labor parties do not have as many paid agents as the Conservatives, although their number is increasing. In many places they have part-time agents.

Like the Conservatives, the Labor party has regional councils and federations,

[49] Samuel H. Beer, "The Conservative Party of Great Britain," *Journal of Politics,* Vol. XIV (1952), pp. 41–71.
[50] The equivalent to the American precinct is called "ward" in a borough and "polling district" in a county.

but its principal organ is the annual Labor conference. This consists of delegates from the various affiliated organizations.[51] Generally one delegate is appointed for each 5,000 members. Voting is by number of members of affiliated organizations, which means that the trade unions have the overwhelming power at the annual conference. For instance, the Transport and General Workers' Union casts votes for over 800,000 members.

The annual conference hears reports on various aspects of policy, elects the members of the National Executive Committee, and adopts resolutions. Since the Labor conference establishes at least theoretically the policy to be followed by the party in Parliament, debates are exceedingly keen and sometimes heated. When the party is in opposition it has generally been more inclined to follow the guidance of the annual conference than when it bears the burden of office. A casual listener at these conferences may often have a wrong impression about the prevailing sentiment because the representatives of the party's left wing are usually very much in evidence, make fiery speeches, and are hotly applauded, while the more middle-of-the-road element appears less prominent. But when the discussion has ended, and the votes are tabulated, the radicals are usually snowed under by the millions of votes represented by the trade unions and cast under the direction of their more conservative leadership.

While the delegates normally vote in a body, election of the members of the National Exectuive Committee is done by sections (divisions). Twelve members of the "Executive," as the National Executive Committee is commonly called, are nominated by the trade unions and elected by their delegates. One member each is nominated by Socialist, cooperative, and professional organizations and elected by their delegates. Seven members are nominated by constituency Labor parties and their federations and elected by their delegates. Five women members may be nominated by any affiliated organization and are elected by the entire conference. The leader of the party and the Treasurer are ex-officio members, bringing the entire membership to twenty-seven. While the Treasurer is elected by the annual conference, the leader of the party is not; the party simply accepts the choice of its Parliamentary group.

The election of the constituency members of the Executive is usually the most heated because it is there that the left wing of the party makes its greatest effort. For a number of years the late Aneurin Bevan and his friends dominated this side of the picture, but since the trade unions are assured of twelve members of the Executive, and by their preponderant number can elect the five women members if they so desire, the left wing had little chance of dominating the party. In recent years, however, trade-union resistance to the left wing has become weaker and less united because of splits in the trade-union ranks and the role of Frank Cousins as a defender of unilateral disarmament. However, after Labor came to power in 1964 and while Cousins was silenced by a ministerial post, trade-union unity was largely restored. This, however, did not guarantee that the Labor government would

[51] Technically the constituency Labor parties are as much affiliated organizations as the trade unions, Fabian Society, etc.

always have its way with the workers, as was painfully demonstrated by the ruinous seamen's strike of 1966.

Like the Conservatives, the Labor party has a central headquarters, which is commonly known as "Transport House."[52] Its chief full-time official is the General Secretary of the Labor party, and there is a considerable paid staff. Transport House is in close contact with the constituency agents, and the constituency and regional organizations of the party. Like its Conservative counterpart, it provides leadership in the publicity endeavors of the party and supplies the bulk of the publicity material. In contrast to the Conservative party, the national Labor party leadership keeps close tab over the choice of prospective candidates for Parliament and allows the constituency organization much less leeway. Nobody may run for Parliament as a Labor candidate who does not have the approval of the National Executive. Such endorsement will be given only if the candidate promises to abide by the standing orders of the Parliamentary Labor party, if elected. Very frequently candidates are urged upon local organizations for reasons of national policy.

Party program and policy: Conservative

As the name of their party implies, the Conservatives stand for the essential preservation of the main features of British economic and social life. Traditionally they have advocated free enterprise and as little government control as possible. In their election publicity they have strongly denounced socialism and planning.[53] But in actual practice they have had to recognize three salient facts: (1) that Great Britain, as a result of the war and of an overaged, neglected industrial machinery, was confronted by such a serious economic situation that it seemed improbable that private industry would recover unaided and without considerable government direction; (2) that many of the social reforms and services instituted by the Labor government were obviously popular and well liked and that any party which advocated their wholesale abolition would commit political suicide; (3) that it was obviously futile to try to denationalize the nationalized coal industry. What was once scrambled could not again be unscrambled.[54] It might also be added that Britain did not have quite the American type of free-enterprise ideology, because for many years much of her economy had been planned and directed by private cartels, not by the government. What the Conservatives object to is not so much planning in itself as the growth of bureaucratic control inherent in state planning. Attacks against an overgrown and unwieldy bureaucracy are usually popular and politically profitable.

---

[52] The Labor party shares offices in that building with the Transport and General Workers' Union and the Trades-Union Congress; hence the name.

[53] *United for Peace and Progress,* London, 1955, the Conservative election manifesto. John Boyd-Carpenter, *The Conservative Case: Choice for Britain,* London, 1950; Quintin Hogg, *The Case for Conservatism,* London, 1948; and Bernard Braine, *Tory Democracy,* London, 1948.

[54] The denationalization of the iron and steel industry and of road haulage seemed easier because the companies had remained intact. Even so, denationalization proved a major headache for the Conservative government.

The Conservatives have gone to great lengths to prove that they are not opposed to the social reforms and services undertaken by the Labor government. They point out, not without justification, that the major planning and spadework for these reforms and services was undertaken under the wartime coalition government headed by Winston Churchill. This is certainly true with regard to such measures as the National Health Service, the Town and Country Planning Act, the Education Act, and many others. However, one is permitted to suspect that the Conservatives' enthusiasm for these measures was not quite so great as that of their Labor opponents, who had been concerned with these ideas for a long time. At any rate the Conservatives promised to keep these services and reforms but to administer them better.

In foreign and Commonwealth affairs the Conservatives have always been traditionally nationalist and imperialist.[55] For that reason the Labor party tried to pin the "warmonger" label on them in the 1951 elections. This, however, proved unsuccessful, in view of Sir Winston Churchill's persistent advocacy of a "big-four" conference to undertake the settlement of the East-West conflict. Actually there is little difference between Labor and Conservative foreign policy when the parties hold office, though whichever party is the Opposition tries to make an issue of it. Thus, when Churchill was in the Opposition, he strongly advocated a united Europe and berated the Labor government for its negative attitude. But when he became Prime Minister again, he kept Britain out of such a union just as Attlee had. The 1955 election manifesto, *United for Peace and Progress,* contained a section on "Western Unity," but it was kept in very general terms.

Very little of the Empire remains, and the questions associated with it have tended to cut across party lines as well as between parties. On the delicate issue of Rhodesia the Conservatives, in spite of opposition within the party, supported the Wilson government for a time, but later split from Labor's hard line and demanded that Rhodesian independence be recognized. Where this will lead and whether this issue will inject new vitality into the Conservative party are, for the present, open questions.

Party program and policy: Labor

The British Labor party is a party of democratic socialism, and it is proud of that designation. But at the same time it is not Marxist or revolutionary in a violent sense. Nor does it believe that all features of life should be socialized. It has advocated the public ownership of all basic industries as well as those which are natural monopolies, like public utilities, believing that these industries can be better run that way and be more dedicated to the public good—plus the fact that they would be means by which the rest of the national economy could be controlled. In 1964 the renationalization of the iron and steel industry was again proposed but then not carried out because of Labor's small majority in the elections

---

[55] "Imperialist" in the British use of this term means the preservation of the British Empire and Commonwealth rather than its expansion.

of that year. It was finally reinstituted in 1967, but remains a latent issue of which neither side can quite rid itself and the country.

If Labor leaders have frequently stated, especially at the beginning of the Attlee Labor administration, that they intend to nationalize only 20 percent of the industry, this should not be interpreted as a hard and fast rule. It is rather another instance of British gradualism and a reluctance to plan every step ahead. Presumably after about 20 percent of the industry, including all basic industry, had been nationalized, a second look would be cast and the situation reviewed. Thus while the general economy would be brought into line with the over-all economic plan of the government, no attempt would be made to regulate every facet of individual economic behavior. The Labor party is as democratic as its Conservative opponents, and there is no thought of interfering with the freedom of parties, of elections, or of personal liberties.[56]

Therefore the Labor party has been consistently vigorous in its opposition to Communism and its program of dictatorship. Whatever the difference may be between some Americans and some British Laborites with regard to the place of Communists in the public service, the Labor party has been vigorous and successful in keeping its own ranks free from Communist infiltration.

It goes without saying that the Labor party considers it the responsibility of the government to ensure an ever-increasing standard of living and personal development to the citizens. Because it is primarily a *labor* party, it has concentrated on increasing the income and purchasing power as well as the general welfare of the working population in order to create greater equality, although the complete equalization of wages is not a Labor policy. Taxation has been used to reduce the status of the remaining upper classes, but generally heavy taxation has been inevitable in Britain since the beginning of the war because of the general economic situation of the country. It is thus difficult to say what part of taxation is social policy and what is economic policy.

The health and education programs of the Labor party have been largely fulfilled and have been discussed elsewhere.

The Labor party's foreign policy is not an easy thing to discuss because of the notable discrepancy between the party's policy when in power and when in opposition. Traditionally the party is pacifist, but its coming to power after the war and during the rapid worsening of East-West relations has certainly imprinted the realities of the situation on the party's leadership. Thus the party has had to endorse the continuation of conscription and the heavy military establishments at home and abroad. If Labor felt at times that America was too extreme in its opposition to the Soviet Union, such sentiments could also be found among Conservatives, and both the Labor and the Conservative governments have on occasion

---

[56] Herbert Tracey, *The British Labour Party,* London, 1948, 3 vols.; Donald Munro (ed.), *Socialism: The British Way,* London, 1948; Francis Williams, *Socialist Britain,* New York, 1949, and "The Program of the British Labour Party: A Historical Survey," *Journal of Politics,* Vol. XII (1950), pp. 189–210; and Bertrand de Jouvenel, *Problèmes de l'Angleterre Socialiste,* Paris, 1947.

believed it to be their task as America's principal ally to try to slow down a bit their "impetuous cousins" across the water.

There is, however, a segment of the Labor party which differs more profoundly with the Conservatives, with America, and with its own leadership. This group, largely but not entirely composed of intellectuals, looks upon America with as much suspicion as the Communists do, though it is certainly not communist. To these men, America is the symbol of capitalism—an economic and social order which they dislike and for which they see no future. While they do not find Russia or China blameless for the existence of world tension, they suspect that America is largely motivated by a desire to destroy the socialist-communist experiment. They therefore advocate that Britain should free herself from all vestiges of American leadership and should endeavor as the leader of a "third force" to negotiate with the communist world. Their statements and resolutions are therefore often strongly critical of American policies and personalities.

After Prime Minister Harold Wilson made clear his strong support of America's policy in Vietnam, the now much-diminished left opposition concentrated its fire on that, without however significantly denting the Labor party's strength or unity.

Certainly in the field of foreign affairs, little difference can be found between the Conservative and Labor parties—a normal situation in modern countries. Like the Conservative party, but a little more slowly, the Labor party has come around to favoring Britain's entry into the European Common Market when negotiations once more become possible, probably after General de Gaulle leaves the scene. Anglo-American relations have been as close as under the Conservative government, and the defense review undertaken by Defense Minister Denis Healey left no doubt that Anglo-American cooperation is still in the center, taking precedence over all other considerations, although British participation has been much weakened by the projected withdrawal "East of Suez." In line with its tradition and free election promises, the Labor government has pressed for arms control and in particular for a treaty outlawing the proliferation of nuclear weapons, but has predictably had little more success than its predecessors, since the decisive elements lie outside British control.

Pressure groups and social conditions

Pressure groups fall into the familiar categories of those promoting certain economic interests of their members and those embracing general political, moral, or other causes. The Federation of British Industries (FBI) and the National Union of British Manufacturers (NUBM) have both industries and individuals among their members, but the FBI tends more toward the larger industries and is by far the more important of the two. There are also the local Chambers of Commerce organized on a national basis in the Association of British Chambers of Commerce. These organizations are naturally politically active. There is also an unusual organization called The Institute of Directors, in which the great majority of Britain's top managerial personnel can be found. The British Employer's Confederation is concerned primarily with the relationship between its members or with generalized problems and professes not to be involved in political questions. There is also the important National Farmers' Union, comprising nearly all the farmers in England and Wales.

Then there are important professional associations such as the British Medical Association (BMA), the National Union of Teachers, and the National and Local Government Officers' Association. A powerful organization for a long time has been the Cooperative Union, the most important of the vast and wealthy cooperative movements in Britain. The trade-union movement is almost entirely within the Labor party, of which the various individual trade unions are collective members.

All these organizations keep close contact with the respective government departments and try to further their interests. In the Conservative party there are also a number of important company directors who are also Members of Parliament. However, government or Opposition policy is influenced far more through attempts to persuade the government or government departments of the desirability of a certain course of action than attempts to put pressure on individual members, who, being subject to a certain amount of discipline, especially as far as Labor is concerned, have only limited influence. For the same reason, economic pressure groups do not ordinarily expend much activity on the constituency level in support of or opposition to specific candidates. This does not mean that financial aid is not given to campaigns, but it does mean that certain pressure groups will habitually support Conservatives and others habitually support Labor candidates, rather than shift support from the one side to the other in order to attain specific advantages.

Britain also has a long tradition of general political, noneconomic pressure groups. They are too numerous to mention, and their causes usually last only for a limited period. Particularly notable were the suffragettes before World War I, ladies of highly diverse social and political backgrounds who banded together to achieve the women's vote. In more recent years, the Committee on Nuclear Disarmament and its later offshoots have staged large demonstrations, often directed against American Polaris bases although the movement does not necessarily have a specifically anti-American tendency. Although this group has at times been able to bring considerable crowds into the streets, its effectiveness has diminished during the Wilson Labor government because most of its followers were favorable to Labor, and now that the Labor party is the government, its opportunity for putting pressure on the government has been reduced.

By and large, the influence of pressure groups has not been small in Great Britain, but it has been more orderly and less corrupting to the general political process than in many other countries. Possibly the fact that the economic pressure groups of both capital and labor have operated rather openly on and within the two major political parties has added to this situation.

4

The crown

A. THE MONARCH

Walter Bagehot in his memorable and pioneering work on the English constitution distinguished between its *dignified* and *efficient* parts. The first is to appeal to the imagination of the people, while the second does the work. This does not mean that the *dignified* sections of the constitution are pure propaganda. They have their most definite place, and many could not be dislodged without very serious disturbances. An outstanding example of this category is the place which royalty holds in the governance of Britain.

The British monarchy is an institution which is more widely known than understood. It is often fancied that the throne is merely the relic of past greatness, having preserved a fraction of its former popularity. Americans, especially, who are by tradition republicans (but suspiciously fond of aristocracy), often feel that the preservation of the monarchy is just another proof of an alleged British "backwardness" and "quaintness," which must of course eventually give way to a more "modern" concept. A closer examination of history will give little comfort to such misconceptions.

The monarchy was by no means always popular, even if one disregards the fate of Charles I and James II, and under such rulers as George IV it descended to a level of contempt. In fact it might be said that the monarchy, as a popular institution, steadily declined under the Hanoverians in the eighteenth and nineteenth centuries, until Queen Victoria restored and ameliorated its reputation. Genuine popularity came only under her successors. Edward VII, a far more democratic and jovial monarch than his formidable mother, made many friends, but even he was not so close to the people as were George V and especially George VI, as well as the present monarch Elizabeth II.[1] Undoubtedly the two world wars enhanced the reputations of these two kings because of the way in which they shared dangers and privations. George VI, who together with his family remained in London during the entire German blitz bombings and the later attacks by V-1 and V-2 weapons, added enormously to the people's morale. It is probably not exaggerated to state that the personal popularity of the monarch and the sincere interest of the people in her and her family's doings have never been greater than they are today. It is a well-known fact among journalists that a front-page story about the royal family will immediately boost the sales figures of newspapers.

The reputation and the resulting significance of the monarch rest almost entirely on psychological factors, although the belief that monarchy is a form of "father fixation," as has been suggested, might be challenged. But it is certain that the monarch lends flesh and blood to the idea of government, and while to many people the idea of a constitution may be incomprehensible, the existence of a living king is always easily understood.

In a world of many and frightening changes, in which the quest for security becomes ever more desperate, the British monarchy breathes stability and continuity. The Englishman, bewildered and upset over so many difficulties, confronted by the far-reaching changes which the Empire has undergone, finds a contemplation of the ancient pageantry of monarchy most reassuring. Despite the changes which he has had to endure there is then, after all, one seemingly permanent institution which, despite, or perhaps because of, the loss of many prerogatives, has stood the test of time. To most Britishers, the monarchy is a symbol of the enduring qualities of their race and living proof that, whatever the future may bring, it will not break too radically with the tried and proven concepts of the past. The tremendous interest in Queen Elizabeth's coronation in 1953 gave most telling proof of this sentiment, and royal and parliamentary pageantry mixed most impressively and harmoniously in Sir Winston Churchill's grandiose funeral in 1965. By this greatest of all commoners being given a funeral worthy of a great king, the unity of the monarchy and the country was once more symbolically asserted.

[1] The designation Elizabeth II is controversial among Scottish nationalists, who claim that Mary, Queen of Scots, was their rightful monarch and not Elizabeth I. They maintain therefore that the present Queen is the first Elizabeth to reign over England and Scotland.

The monarch's position rests on his deportment; it is necessary for him to be close to the people and yet remain on the pedestal of his august position. That is why the abdication crisis of Edward VIII, now the Duke of Windsor, cut so deep. It is idle to speculate now whether the King's conduct and his proposed marriage scandalized the majority of his subjects or not. It certainly divided the country on an issue concerning the royal person, and that is the very opposite of what a monarch ought to do. But the issue was broader than merely the relationship between the King and Mrs. Simpson and their marriage plans. The government stood four-square against the whole idea, and the Prime Minister, Stanley Baldwin, made it quite clear to the King that even though Mrs. Simpson could never be Queen, neither the British Parliament nor the Dominion Parliaments would sanction a morganatic marriage.

Here was a test case to show whether the King must abide by the advice of his Prime Minister even in matters affecting his private life, and it was largely because of this constitutional issue that the leadership of the Labor party, which was then in opposition, rallied to the government. Winston Churchill, perhaps more passionate than prudent at the time, toyed for a moment with the idea of leading a "king's party"; fortunately, nothing came of so wild a plan, which would certainly have done the monarchy irreparable damage, and the will of the government prevailed. Edward extricated himself from his difficulties by resigning the throne—an act which has been condemned as dereliction of duty, but which gave Britain a monarch whose conduct was above reproach. Baldwin's action was naturally condemned by those of all ages and sexes who considered romance more important than constitutional government. If there has ever been any doubt in recent years as to the authority of the Prime Minister's advice over the King, there is no doubt now.

The position of a reigning Queen is exactly the same as that of a King, but while a King's spouse is called Queen, the husband of a reigning Queen is never called King. Queen Victoria's husband, Prince Albert, received the title Prince Consort during the later years of his life. But the husband of Queen Elizabeth II has not received this title and is not likely to, because to history-conscious Englishmen this designation is forever tied to the memories of Victoria and Albert. At present Prince Philip, the Queen's husband, is usually addressed by his title as Duke of Edinburgh, but his growing influence is indicated by his appointment as one of the Councillors of State who would appoint a regent in the case of the death or incapacity of the Queen, during the minority of the Heir Apparent (Prince Charles), who has now officially been designated as the Prince of Wales.

Power and influence

In abstract theory the powers of the monarch are truly formidable. The Queen, wrote Bagehot in 1872, "could disband the army, she could dismiss all the officers from the General Commanding-in-Chief downward; . . . she could sell off all our ships of war and all our naval stores; she could make a peace by the sacrifice of Cornwall, and begin a war for the conquest of Brittany. . . ." But of course that is pure theory and has no relation whatsoever to fact. In theory all acts of government are acts of the monarch to which he must give his consent, either personally or by proxy. But since the monarch is not responsible to Parliament, the rules of responsible government demand that these acts be countersigned by a minister of the crown, who is responsible. Thus all acts become in effect governmental acts, to which the King or Queen has no choice but to give his or her consent. This does not mean that they are without influence. We know now from the correspondence of Queen Victoria that her influence was considerable and that she attempted many times to have her own way outside constitutional practices. Her desperate attempts to keep Gladstone—whom she loathed and distrusted—from becoming Prime Minister are a matter of history. She even attempted to indulge in intra-party feuds in order to accomplish her aim. We also know that Edward VII's influence was not negligible, although not as great as some historians believed. About more recent events we have only scant information, although there is some evidence that King George V and King George VI at times took a hand in politics. It would appear that Queen Elizabeth II has made her influence felt less strongly than did her father and grandfather. However, the relationship between a monarch and her Prime Ministers is of a highly confidential character, and frequently details become known only long after the individuals have passed away. On the other hand, there are numerous indications that the influence of the Duke of Edinburgh has steadily grown, although the consort of a reigning Queen can never equal her formal position and potential influence.

The most important function of the monarch is undoubtedly the selection of the Prime Minister, but usually he has virtually no choice in the matter. Ordinarily each party has its clearly designated leader who, as long as the two-party system exists, will be either Prime Minister or leader of the Opposition. If the government party wins again, there is no question that the Prime Minister will remain in office if he chooses; but if the government loses, he resigns, and the leader of the Opposition is called to Buckingham Palace to receive a commission to form a government. No other course is open to the monarch, and the people in voting for a particular party know very well that they are thereby voting for a particular Prime Minister. Englishmen had no doubt that when the Conservative government of Winston Churchill was defeated in 1945, Clement Attlee would be the next Prime Minister, or that in the election of 1964 the choice would lie between Sir Alec Douglas-Home and Harold Wilson.

Queen Victoria attempted to preserve the royal prerogative—already obsolete —of appointing her own candidate, but she was unsuccessful, and it is not likely that any present or future monarch will try to repeat her performance. A certain amount of choice exists when, because of death, illness, or resignation, a vacancy occurs which may not have been foreseen. However, even under such circumstances, the Queen's choice is circumscribed by the fact that whoever is appointed must have a majority in the House of Commons. The choice must therefore be made in close contact with the leadership of the majority party. As an example, the succession of Lord Home (Sir Alec Douglas-Home after his renunciation of the peerage) to the position of Prime Minister in 1963 was unquestionably the sole, personal choice of his predecessor, Harold Macmillan.

We have already seen that the monarch cannot fail to abide by the "advice" of his Prime Minister. This is the very cornerstone of the constitution, and the abdication crisis of 1936 revealed that it applies even to the most private and personal acts of the King. If the King were to refuse his assent, the resignation of the cabinet would become inevitable, and this would be followed by a general election in which the entire prestige and foundation of the monarchy would be at stake. For the same reason the monarch could not dissolve Parliament against the advice of his government. But there are two cases on record in which the government reluctantly agreed to a dissolution and general elections on the urging of the King, who believed that the government ought to receive a new mandate from the people before proceeding to certain far-reaching decisions. Both cases occurred in 1910, when Edward VII urged dissolution over the question of Lloyd George's budget[2] and George V pressed for the same action before the powers of the House of Lords were to be curbed.

It is quite difficult to see how the monarch could refuse dissolution,[3] since any cabinet crisis would be bound to bring about general elections. There is of course absolutely no question about the Royal Assent to acts of Parliament; it cannot be refused.

But there is considerable doubt whether the monarch must "pack" the House of Lords with government supporters if the Lords persist in their frustration of the government's program. The fact that at least two kings, William IV and George V, were reluctantly ready to do so cannot be considered conclusive. However, the King's discretion must be viewed against the probability that a majority of the House of Commons which had been continuously frustrated by the Lords would eventually proceed to drastic reforms, if not abolition, of the upper house. In view of the greatly reduced power of the House of Lords, this is of little practical importance today.

In order to appraise the position of the British monarch, it is necessary to distinguish between his power and his influence. Theoretically he has great powers; he resides resplendently in his castles, he receives a handsome allowance known as the Civil List,[4] and all acts of government are accomplished in his name. Actu-

---

[2] Lloyd George was Chancellor of the Exchequer in the Asquith government.
[3] But the King's representative in Canada, Governor-General Lord Byng, did once refuse to grant the Prime Minister, Mackenzie King, a second dissolution, and the Governor-General of South Africa refused a first dissolution to Prime Minister Hertzog.
[4] The Civil List of the present monarch, Queen Elizabeth II, is £475,000, while the Duke of Edinburgh receives £40,000. This includes the salaries and pensions of the household, maintenance, and various services, and the privy purse of the Queen. The Crown lands, which are managed by the government, usually yield more than the amount of the Civil List.

ally, as we have seen, he has virtually no power at all. But he has a surprising amount of influence. Bagehot was the first to point out that the King has three rights: the right to be consulted, the right to encourage, and the right to warn. To this he adds, "And a king of great sense and sagacity would want no others." The august position held by the King and the long experience which he is bound to accumulate through the years of his reign give his advice great weight. He is informed about all decisions taken by the cabinet. He is informed about all problems of importance. He is in constant contact with his Prime Minister. An intimate atmosphere of mutual understanding and respect usually develops. It is true that the King can never have his way against a determined Prime Minister who opposes him. But while we do not have too much knowledge of the private conversations between the nominal and the real heads of the country, there is considerable evidence to show that the advice or the warning of the King is not lightly dismissed. The influence of the King will therefore grow in direct proportion to his wisdom and his discretion.

A wise monarch must be well informed but never partisan. This is sometimes rendered somewhat difficult because of the fact that the King's or Queen's most intimate connection is with the government in power, while more than formal relations with the Opposition would be considered improper and evidence of bias. He is therefore largely dependent on the help and advice which he receives from his staff. It is perhaps not an exaggeration to say that the monarch's staff, especially his secretary, is the keeper of his conscience; and that the wisdom and sagacity the monarch displays—in addition to his native intelligence and experience—is in large part a contribution of his staff. It has therefore been suggested that staff posts be made regular civil service appointments. This is not the case at present, but recent appointments have been made with great care and success.

Thus the monarch appears as a symbol of government and state, as a counselor and adviser, and as a reassurance of the application and validity of the British tradition of government. Moreover he is a great convenience. As the official and symbolic link between the mother country and the dominions and colonies, he makes possible an extraordinary flexibility which the best draftsman could not write into any other constitutional form or document. George VI and Elizabeth II have emphasized this point through their extensive travels. How widely accepted this notion is may be gleaned from a passage written by an eminent socialist couple, Sidney and Beatrice Webb:[5]

> If we pass from the constitutional theory of the text-books to the facts as we see them to-day, what we have to note is that the particular function of the British monarch . . . is not the exercise of governmental powers in any of its aspects, but something quite different, namely, the performance of a whole series of rites and ceremonies which lend the charm of historic continuity to the political institutions

[5] Sidney Webb and Beatrice Webb, *A Constitution for a Socialist Commonwealth of Great Britain,* London, 1920, p. 61.

of the British race, and which go far, under present conditions, to maintain the bond of union between the races and creeds of the Commonwealth. . . .

B. THE CABINET

The real executive is not the King but the cabinet, though the cabinet is much more than that. Walter Bagehot, who first pointed to the significance—indeed, the existence—of the cabinet, also demonstrated its peculiar role. The theory expounded by Montesquieu and repeated by others that the genius of English government consists in the separation of powers is completely false. The outstanding characteristic of the English government is the almost complete fusion of legislative and executive functions; and it is the cabinet which effects this fusion and makes it work.

This all-important body of men which we call the cabinet is an oddly informal group. Until 1937 it was unknown to the law of the land, although it had been a living reality for two centuries. Its head, the Prime Minister, still receives his salary as the First Lord of the Treasury, although he leaves the administration of the Treasury to his Chancellor of the Exchequer.[6] Cabinet proceedings have been regularly recorded only since 1917 when the cabinet secretariat was established by Lloyd George, and cabinet decisions take the form either of orders of the Privy Council (Orders in Council) or of advice to the King.

Historically the cabinet emerged as a committee of the Privy Council, and it still retains this fiction as a matter of convenience. Since the Privy Council is composed of every individual who has once held cabinet rank, as well as other persons of note, it is far too big to carry on any governmental business, and meets with its entire membership usually only once in each king's reign and only for ceremonial functions. But the cabinet or even two or three members thereof usually act for the whole Council.

The Prime Minister

By far the most significant man in any cabinet is its leader, the Prime Minister. If he is strong like Sir Winston Churchill, Harold Macmillan, or Harold Wilson, he will imprint his stamp on the cabinet. If he is endowed with fewer leadership capacities, like Lord Rosebery or Lord Salisbury, the entire course of his cabinet will be lacking in decisiveness. Other ministers may temporarily overshadow their chief. Sir Stafford Cripps and Ernest Bevin were more prominent than Attlee. But they can never hope to prevail against the Prime Minister, as Lord Palmerston found out to his peril.

We have already seen that under ordinary circumstances the choice of the Prime Minister is determined by the electorate. The chosen leaders of both major

---

[6] Who in turn leaves the administration of the Exchequer proper to the Auditor and Comptroller General.

parties are well known to the people, and those who voted in the general election of 1964 had no doubt that if they voted Conservative they voted for a Home government, while those who voted Labor obviously favored a Wilson cabinet. Thus it may be stated that the people of Britain elect their Prime Ministers no less than the American people elect their presidents. This is of course based on the assumption that the two-party system will continue to function, but the entire cabinet system is in fact based on that very same assumption, as we shall see.

Ordinarily, therefore, the Prime Minister is the chosen leader of the party winning a majority at the polls, and if the fortunes of political warfare are reversed, the King or Queen sends for the leader of the Opposition as a matter of course in order to entrust him with the seals of office. There have been some partial exceptions to this rule, as has been noted in the section on the monarch, but in general the rule holds fast.

It is important to remember that the Prime Minister and his colleagues in the government are party leaders of long standing and experience. Even in the rare cases where a party does not have a declared leader, the man who will eventually lead the party's destinies will be chosen from among a small group who have stood in the forefront of the political battle—a battle which is carried out in the House of Commons. It follows therefore that no party leader—and consequently no Prime Minister—is ever a "dark horse" in the American sense. To become a party leader he must have proved his mettle in countless Parliamentary skirmishes, and must have won the acclaim and confidence of his followers. To gain distinction in the House of Commons is not an easy thing, for some very keen minds are always to be found there. Undoubtedly not all members are outstanding, but a good many are, since membership in the House of Commons, once called "the world's most exclusive club," is considered a great distinction, which is eagerly sought by many bright young men. If a man is able to maintain himself in such company, and through the years eventually climbs to the pinnacle of leadership, he has certainly proved that he is a man of considerable ability. Laski was therefore right in saying that "no simple man can ever be Prime Minister of England."

Until 1965 the leader of the Conservative party, who would become Prime Minister in case his party obtained a majority in the House of Commons, was chosen through a highly informal and confidential process by the most significant Conservative leaders; no outsider could state with any certainty who these "electors" were. By contrast, the leader of the Labor party was chosen by the Parliamentary Labor party (i.e., the Labor party caucus, in American nomenclature). In 1964, however, the Conservative party adopted the Labor party method. Edward Heath was the first Conservative leader to be chosen in that fashion in 1965.

The position of the Prime Minister is a formidable one. He determines the outlines of policy, and all important decisions of the other ministers are cleared with him first. Sir Robert Peel was known to take a detailed interest in the administration of every department, in effect reducing his ministers to virtual undersecretaries. That feat was never repeated thereafter and would be quite impossible now in view of the greatly augmented business of government. Sometimes Prime Ministers have retained control over certain government departments: Lord Salisbury was Prime Minister and Foreign Secretary at the same time; MacDonald performed the same dual function in the first Labor cabinet of 1924. However, the combination of the premiership with the direct administration of a department has always worked to the disadvantage of both offices concerned.

There have also been Prime Ministers who had such a strong hand in the formulation of policy in a particular department that they reduced the status of the responsible minister and undermined cabinet morale. This was the case with Neville Chamberlain, who conducted foreign policy frequently without bothering to consult his Foreign Secretary, Sir Anthony Eden. Sir Winston Churchill's primary interest in foreign affairs also tended to overshadow Foreign Secretary Eden and the Foreign Office. On the other hand, Prime Minister Harold Macmillan overshadowed Foreign Secretary Selwyn Lloyd largely as the result of his greater ability and skill, rather than because he wanted to invade the Foreign Secretary's domain. Harold Wilson also easily overshadows his cabinet colleagues.

The relationship between the Prime Minister and his colleagues depends very largely on the personalities involved. The Prime Minister selects the ministers of the crown. This is an exercise of great power, but it is by no means unrestricted. In every party there are men who must obviously be included in any government if the unity and support of the party in the House of Commons is not to be endangered. There are also other members whom the Prime Minister must include in payment of political debts. Conservative governments have found it necessary to divert minor posts to men who had given the party prominent financial or other support, while Labor governments have contained deserving former trade-union officials whose loyal support demanded reward. Also, if the contest for leadership has been a lively one, the winner is likely to make his principal competitor his chief aide in order to assure unity in the party ranks. Thus, Edward Heath chose Reginald Maudling, and Harold Wilson chose George Brown.

The distribution of portfolios is very largely in the hands of the Prime Minister, but here again he cannot completely disregard the wishes of prominent party leaders. It is well known, for instance, that MacDonald did not wish to put Henderson in charge of the Foreign Office, but Henderson would not take any other post, and since he could not very well be excluded, the Prime Minister gave in.

Every party which comes to power has a number of leaders who are so obviously important that, as we have seen, they cannot be excluded from the government and the cabinet without causing such rifts and animosities that the effectiveness of that party's hold on the government would be seriously impaired. This also means that, despite the Prime Minister's preeminent position, government policy is generally the result of constant consultations. Even Sir Winston Churchill, who liked to run things alone, was not exempt from this rule, although his immense prestige allowed him great liberty of action. The Labor government of Harold Wilson has come the closest to being dominated by the Prime Minister, who makes decisions in virtually all fields, so that one is inclined to call this almost a "presidential" regime.

Apart from the appointment of important party leaders, other considerations must also play a role in the nomination of ministers of the crown. Both major political parties of Great Britain contain elements who find themselves in some opposition to their party's leadership. Often a Prime Minister finds it useful to appoint one or two of his opponents to cabinet positions, partly in the hope that the burden of responsibilities will have a sobering effect on the appointee, partly because cabinet secrecy and cabinet solidarity will make it more difficult for the men concerned to voice their objections. There is little doubt that Attlee's choice of Aneurin Bevan for the post of Minister of Health did not stem from any high regard for that gentleman. That such action is effective was perhaps clearly enough demonstrated when Aneurin Bevan and the like-minded Harold Wilson resigned from the Attlee cabinet in 1951 in order to regain their freedom of action.[7] Similarly, Harold Wilson muted the opposition of Frank Cousins (who had favored unilateral disarmament) and of R. H. S. Crossman, an often oppositional left-wing intellectual, by taking them into his first government.

The geographic distribution of cabinet posts is far less important than is the case in the United States. Nevertheless, the Secretary of State for Scotland always comes from that part of the country, and it is generally considered wise not to leave other Scotsmen and perhaps a Welshman entirely out of the government.

The inclusion of some gifted younger men is very important. Failure to do so would not only cause intense dissatisfaction among many Members of Parliament but would also fail to assure the continued supply of leadership material to the party. It is also necessary to appoint several Lords to the cabinet in order to assure the government's leadership in the House of Lords. The Lord Chancellor is of course always a member of the House of Lords, but there must be at least one other member to represent the government, for the Lord Chancellor presides over the upper house and cannot effectively represent the government.

The Prime Minister, in appointing ministers and heads of departments, also designates who shall be members of the supreme policymaking body, the cabinet, for not all ministers are cabinet ministers. The selection of cabinet posts has varied from cabinet to cabinet. There are certain departments which are always represented: the Treasury, the Foreign Office, the Ministry of National Defence,[8] the Home Office, the Commonwealth Relations Office, the Colonial Office, the Scottish Office, and the Lord Chancellor. The Lord Privy Seal and the Lord President of the (Privy) Council also rate seats in the cabinet on grounds of rank alone, but these "sinecure" posts are frequently filled by very important leaders who are thus freed from departmental responsibilities in order to devote themselves to tasks of

---

[7] The immediate cause was a disagreement over budgetary policies.

[8] In 1946 the three defense departments, the War Office, the Admiralty, and the Air Ministry, were unified under a Ministry of National Defence which became a cabinet office. The three original departments were dropped from cabinet rank.

special importance.[9] The Ministers of Health and Labor are rarely excluded, and the Minister of Agriculture and Fisheries also rates a cabinet seat as a general rule but was excluded from the Churchill (1951), Macmillan, and Wilson governments. The Minister of Housing and Local Government is also often included. The Board of Trade had been excluded from several cabinets in the past, but that has proved impractical in view of the increasing importance of economics and trade in the making of high policy, and it may be assumed that the Board of Trade is now ordinarily found in the cabinet. In addition to the incumbents of these offices, the Prime Minister may also include other ministers of his choice. Ordinarily a cabinet will be composed of fifteen to twenty people, but some cabinets have been above that number and some below.

Over this body of men, the Prime Minister presides. It is a distinguished group of political leaders, most of whom have held public office before. Some of them may be more brilliant than the Prime Minister; yet he holds their destinies in his hands, and the degree to which he wishes to impose his will upon his colleagues is largely determined by his tact and his capacity for self-restraint. Generally a good Prime Minister is one who gives leadership but does not try to be the whole show. Harold Wilson's premiership has been unusually strong in this regard. This is partly a result of the fact that he was the only member of the cabinet (after the departure of Patrick Gordon Walker) with previous major cabinet experience. Also, the exceptional difficulties confronting this government, together with its razor-thin majority of three in the 1964–1965 House of Commons, made necessary an unusual amount of deft maneuvering of which Wilson held only himself capable— probably correctly. There are always, however, certain fields in which the Prime Minister takes a special interest. He is chairman of the Committee of Imperial Defence, and therefore bears direct responsibility in the field of military preparedness and strategy. In times of crisis he will keep very close to those departments which handle the most crucial issues of the day. At present and undoubtedly for some time to come, these are economic and foreign affairs.

These vast responsibilities of the Prime Minister do not rest on statutory grounds. They rest almost entirely on political considerations. He is the leader of the majority party in the House of Commons. His party has entered the electoral fight under his leadership, and the people who voted for it have thereby unmistakably voted for his premiership. Having achieved a clear majority, the leader of the party and his cabinet are secure against removal by the opposition party unless the margin of seats is very small; ordinarily a leader can be removed only when he loses the support of his own party. That does not occur often. A party which overthrows its leadership in effect confesses failure, and it is only too likely that the electorate will confirm that judgment. Such confirmation is bound to be swift, for

[9] Past examples are Clement Attlee in the Churchill coalition government and Herbert Morrison in the Attlee government.

if the government falls, general elections are the logical consequence. To be sure, there are exceptions. Strong internal pressure removed Herbert Asquith in 1916, Neville Chamberlain in 1940, and Anthony Eden in 1957. Macmillan's resignation in 1963 was his own choice, due to illness, but it was doubtlessly influenced by increasing opposition to his leadership and by the growing possibility of defeat at the polls. Finally, the Conservative leadership was so obviously unhappy with Sir Alec Douglas-Home's image in the 1964 elections that he retired voluntarily after only one electoral defeat—a narrow one at that. As a rule, however, the majority party remains intact and rallies to the support of the government. Even if they do not like their leader, they usually like the leader of the Opposition even less, and it is he who may expect to be the beneficiary of a cabinet crisis. It must also be remembered that party discipline is greater in Britain than in the United States, and the government whips usually succeed in corralling the necessary majority of Members of Parliament.

In the exercise of his vast powers, the Prime Minister is therefore reasonably assured of a full term in office between general elections. He may expect to remain in office as long as he is able to win elections. He has therefore an indefinite term of office, which tends to strengthen his leadership. If he loses an election, he becomes leader of the Opposition, with good prospects of becoming Prime Minister again when the fortunes of political war are again reversed. But if he loses two or three elections in a row, intra-party pressure is likely to compel his retirement.

For a fuller understanding of the Prime Minister's position it must always be remembered that cabinet and Parliament—or more precisely the House of Commons—are one. The struggle between the legislative and executive branches, so typical in American government, is totally missing in England. The cabinet leads the House, and a serious conflict between the two would lead only to the dissolution of both. As long as the government is in office, it expects to have its legislative program passed by the House of Commons without serious changes or amendments. Yet it is certainly an exaggeration to speak of "cabinet dictatorship." In a democratic state, such as Great Britain, leadership is never a one-sided affair, but can exist only when there is a measure of confidence between the leader and the led. The cabinet does indeed lead Parliament, but it can do so successfully only as long as it remains mindful of the basic need for unity on which the entire cabinet system is based. The cabinet cannot ride roughshod over Parliamentary opposition, but must seek agreement. Naturally such agreement will rarely be unanimous, especially on the Opposition benches. But the government, knowing that close cooperation with the House of Commons is of the essence, always seeks agreement whenever possible, even when it is assured of the necessary votes for victory. So it is receptive to the views of Parliament, and even Opposition views may find their way into legislation. Parliament is not a machinery for checking and balancing the cabinet, but rather a forum for a broad and open discussion of policy—a forum which the ministers can ill afford to ignore.

Power of dissolution

Some writers, especially French ones, have seen a special significance in the power of the Prime Minister to bring about (by "advice" to the King) the dissolution of the House of Commons. They apparently believe that this is a power which ensures government control in the House. We have seen, however, that government control is based on quite different factors, and that the "threat" of dissolution is a threat to the government in precisely the same proportion as it is a threat to the House of Commons. It is quite true that the Prime Minister uses the power of dissolution; hardly any Parliament remains in session to the very last day of its legal existence. But the power of dissolution serves primarily a tactical purpose; it enables the government to select the moment which it deems most auspicious for a general election. Thus, Prime Minister Attlee resisted strong pressure both within his party and among the Opposition for a general election in the fall of 1949, and postponed it to February, 1950, in the hope that a mild winter and the effects of currency devaluation would produce a more favorable situation for the Labor party. Although naturally criticized, the Prime Minister's decision was entirely in agreement with custom and precedent.

There is also another occasion at which dissolution may take place. When a question of great and far-reaching importance has to be decided, or when a major change in policy or the reversal of a very controversial policy is concerned, the cabinet may wish to assure itself of the people's support by calling for a general election. This is the nearest approach to a plebiscite known to the British system of government, and it has worked very effectively. Most notable have been the two dissolutions of 1910 in which the (Asquith) government was upheld.

When there is no clear majority in the House, the power of dissolution says in fact to the possibly unruly Commons: "Either make government possible, or surrender your seats and entrust yourselves to the vote of the people." The House can thus, by its attitude, decide which it shall be. But in any case a fairly firm government will be the result, usually after a new House has been elected.

It is said that in matters of dissolution the Prime Minister alone determines the issue. This is true only in so far as the Prime Minister bears responsibility for it and the final decision must therefore be his. But it cannot be assumed that he will stake the cabinet's life on an election without consulting his colleagues.[10]

The cabinet system

The British cabinet system has many advantages. Perhaps its most outstanding virtue is the fact that it usually creates clear lines of responsibility. The government

[10] The former Prime Minister Asquith wrote: "Such a question as the dissolution of Parliament is always submitted to the Cabinet for ultimate decision." Oxford and Asquith, *Fifty Years of the British Parliament,* Boston, 1926, Vol. II, p. 195; W. Ivor Jennings, *Cabinet Government,* Cambridge, England, 1951, 2d ed. p. 387. This is possibly a stronger statement than is justified.

has an opportunity to carry out the program on which it has been elected and cannot pass on the blame for its failures and omissions to the legislature or to any other authority. It remains responsible before the people, who thus have a clear choice and will give a clear answer in endorsing or rejecting the government.

The responsibility borne by cabinet members is individual as well as collective. The difference between these two categories depends largely on political circumstances. When a minister is taken to account because of a personal mistake or worse, the responsibility will, as a rule, be confined to him, and the stability of the rest of the cabinet may not be affected. When Chancellor of the Exchequer Hugh Dalton imprudently revealed to a favored journalist certain facts about the forthcoming budget message—a gross breach of custom and possibly of law[11]—he resigned in the ensuing storm without shaking in any way the solid foundation of the Attlee government.

A quite different case was the resignation in 1935 of the then Foreign Secretary, Sir Samuel Hoare, over the Hoare-Laval Agreement concerning Abyssinia. At that time, the agreement evoked such a scandal in England that the Prime Minister, Baldwin, had to sacrifice his Foreign Secretary. Yet it is difficult to believe that so important a step as the Hoare-Laval Agreement could have been concluded without the knowledge of the Prime Minister and at least some of the cabinet members. But in this case Sir Samuel was permitted to take sole blame for the act, and the life of the cabinet was spared. We might conclude, then, that in case a cabinet member is blamed for a political, rather than a personal, mistake, the consequences will depend on the depth to which the Prime Minister and the rest of the cabinet are involved or wish to be involved, and on the extent to which the commotion dies down after the sacrifice of a minister. Of course if the Prime Minister himself is involved in a debacle, as Anthony Eden was in the unhappy Suez venture, the government has to resign. His successor may then pick up as many pieces (ministers) as the situation might indicate.

Collective responsibility is feasible only if there is a high degree of cabinet solidarity. Uniformity of opinion cannot be expected, as the cabinet is composed of men of great experience and judgment. Decisions are therefore frequently based on compromise, which can be effected successfully only when ministers may debate their views freely without having to fear political and personal repercussions if they change their minds or concede a point. Cabinet secrecy is therefore vital to a successful conduct of business. This secrecy is technically assured by the Official Secrets Act, the Privy Councillor's oath, and the fact that all cabinet decisions take the form of "advice" to the King, which ought not to be disclosed without his permission. In actuality, however, it is political necessity rather than legal prohibition which protects the confidence of ministers. The violation of confidence would make a useful cooperation of ministers impossible, and the culprit would find it difficult to gain admittance to any future government. Of course, sometimes a min-

[11] The Official Secrets Act.

ister finds the cabinet position so incompatible with his convictions that he resigns, and in the ensuing debate in the Commons some cabinet facts will invariably be disclosed. But on the whole, official secrecy is preserved, and it is left to later historians and of course to the inevitable memoirs of prominent men to lift an edge of the curtain.

Collective responsibility means, in the words of Lord Salisbury, that "each member [of the cabinet] who does not resign is absolutely and irretrievably responsible, and has no right afterwards to say that he agreed in one case to a compromise, while in another he was persuaded by his colleagues."[12] This has always been a standing rule, except for the strange "agreement to differ" in 1931, which was found quite unworkable because it tended to destroy the idea of party responsibility on which the British system of government is founded.

It must be clear from the foregoing that a government cannot tolerate a minister who opposes government policy but does not resign. This extends not only to cabinet members, but to all ministers, under-secretaries, parliamentary secretaries, junior lords, and other political appointees. How far this can go was demonstrated by Prime Minister Attlee when he caused the dismissal of five private parliamentary secretaries who had voted against the government in connection with a bill regulating Britain's relationship to Eire (Republic of Ireland). This is strong proof of the correctness of Gladstone's saying that a person who enters a government gives up a certain amount of freedom of expression because whatever he says is bound to commit his colleagues. It is obvious, however, that this principle works best when the government is composed of members of one party only. Holding coalition governments together has generally been an unhappy and unsuccessful experience except in times of war.

Until 1917 the secrecy surrounding cabinet meetings was carried so far that there were not even cabinet minutes. The only documentary evidence was the summary of the Prime Minister, which he might have made in support of his own memory or for the purpose of reporting to the sovereign. This "informal" procedure broke down under the weight of decisions which had to be taken in the course of the First World War, and Prime Minister Lloyd George—never a venerator of tradition—established the cabinet secretariat, headed by an uncommonly able man, Colonel (later Sir Maurice) Hankey.[13] This brought order and permanent records into cabinet meetings, and the institution was retained despite some initial opposition.[14]

---

[12] Lady Gwendolyn Cecil, *Life of Robert, Marquis of Salisbury,* London, 1921, Vol. II, pp. 219–220. See also Jennings, *op. cit.,* p. 217, and Harold J. Laski, *Parliamentary Government in England,* New York, 1938, pp. 212f.

[13] This was originally the secretariat to the Committee of Imperial Defence, of which the Prime Minister is chairman. The secretariat of the Committee became the secretariat of the War Cabinet, and in 1917 the cabinet secretariat.

[14] The Haldane Committee (Ministry of Reconstruction, *Report of the Machinery of Government Committee,* London, 1918, p. 6) recommended the retention of the secretariat. Prime Minister Bonar Law opposed it, but it survived and has become an indispensable fixture.

During the Second World War two further cabinet offices were added: the Economic Section and the Central Statistical Office.

The Haldane Committee of 1918 described the main functions of the cabinet as follows:

1. The final determination of the policy to be submitted to the Parliament.

2. The supreme control of the national executive in accordance with the policy prescribed by Parliament.

3. The continuous coordination and delimitation of the activities of the several departments of state.

Among these broad functions, the first is easily the most important. A cabinet may get away with poor administration and would probably be protected from its worst mistakes by the diligent efforts of ubiquitous civil servants, but it can never afford to neglect Parliament. It is no exaggeration to say that the most important function —or at any rate one of the most important functions—of the British executive is primarily legislative in nature. The presentation of policy in Parliament, the answering of questions, and the securing of passage of needed legislation take much of the ministers' time.

It is of course true, as we have seen, that a government may usually expect to have its measures passed in Parliament by a comfortable majority, but no matter how conclusive the majority, the government must still subject itself to the scrutiny of the legislature. It has often been stated that the chief function of Parliament is to criticize—a function which makes the Opposition the most important part of Parliament. Now it might perhaps be expected that a government which enjoys a safe and well-disciplined majority need not pay much heed to criticism. Such an attitude, however, would be extremely dangerous for any government to adopt. Members of Parliament are very conscious of the dignity and sovereignty of their House, and a high-handed attitude on the part of the government would be greatly resented. Moreover, it sometimes happens that some issue which is brought up in the House of Commons captures the imagination of the people to such an extent that even a "safe" government finds it prudent to beat a hasty retreat. The Hoare-Laval Agreement and its repercussion present an example of this.

The government finds Parliament a convenient medium through which it can expound its ideas to the country. Attention is always focused on the debates in the House of Commons, and the government has thus a ready-made sounding board of which it makes frequent use. No press conference, no "fireside chat" over the radio can quite equal the picture of high policy at work which a debate in the House of Commons presents.

All this is true of governments with a comfortable majority in the House. It is even more true of governments with slender leads and of minority governments. That the latter, like the Labor governments of 1923–1964, are able to function at all is primarily due to the high sense of responsibility prevailing in the House of

Commons, which makes most Members of Parliament realize that there ought to be a government. A minority cabinet or one with a small majority may therefore count on a fair degree of tolerance in the House. But naturally its scope of action may be seriously restricted. The Wilson government of 1964 managed quite well with a majority of only three, largely because the Conservatives were neither anxious to take office in the face of exceptionally difficult problems, nor certain that a new election would not favor the Labor party.

The preoccupation of ministers with their role in the House of Commons naturally cuts down the time which they can spend on administrative work. Consequently, they must depend on the work of their civil service staff, a phenomenon common to all modern governments. Some critics have been very unhappy about this and have complained that "the Cabinet has arrogated to itself, half blindly, a series of colossal responsibilities which it cannot meet, which it will not allow Parliament to tackle, and which are not met at all except in so far as they are assumed by the bureaucracy behind the cloak of Cabinet omnipotence."[15] This is indeed a strong indictment, if true. Now it is correct that no mortal man can hope to have expert knowledge of everything that pertains to a government department, but such expert knowledge is neither necessary nor desirable. It is an axiom of democratic government that "the expert should be kept on tap but not on top," because he is too likely to be insensitive to popular sentiment and is apt to have an exaggerated conception of the significance of his special field. That is why policy-making officials ought to be politicians: (1) in order to tell the civil servant, in the famous words of Sir William Harcourt, "what the public won't stand," and (2) in order to coordinate the departmental with the over-all policy for which the government is responsible before Parliament and the electorate.

We have observed that cabinet ministers are not born but are made through experience. Their background ought to enable them to read the one-page memoranda of their permanent staffs, listen to their arguments, and then apply that princely gift of the successful top man, judgment. The amount of judgment which a minister possesses is the measure of his success and of his future. It is this quality which has generally made civilian leadership in war more effective than military leadership. It cannot be pretended that every British minister has been the epitome of wisdom. But the majority of ministers have usually had enough experience and good sense to treat advice from their permanent staff with intelligent detachment. It is not the minister's job to check the technical accuracy of the reports which are placed before him. He must have confidence in his staff, for if there are chronic mistakes and notorious misinformation in their work, that fact will become known soon enough. Generally such confidence will not be misplaced. But where the minister comes in is in his ability to see the broader ramifications of a project and to gauge its effect on government policy. Once he has made up his mind, he always has his way. No civil servant can ever prevail against a minister

[15] Ramsey Muir, *How Britain Is Governed*, Boston, 1935, 3d ed., p. 105.

who has made up his mind on an issue. Moreover, terms of office usually last several years, and the minister has a good chance to learn a great deal about his department. The picture, therefore, of a puppet minister directed by the hands of an anonymous civil servant is a gross exaggeration.

The War Cabinet

The cabinet originally emerged from the informal meetings of certain members of the Privy Council when the latter had become too big and cumbersome. During the First World War, even the cabinet seemed to be too large for the big and far-reaching decisions which had to be taken. The result was the creation of a "War Cabinet" in 1916 by Prime Minister Lloyd George. It was composed of five members,[16] only one of whom had any departmental responsibility (Treasury). This group was almost constantly in session and in effect conducted the war and handled the questions arising from it. After the fighting was over, difficulties arose because of the exclusion of the heads of departments whose problems now moved to the forefront of the day. The Machinery of Government (Haldane) Committee recommended a new type of "inner" cabinet, modeled on the War Cabinet, but composed of heads of departments. However, the idea was abandoned; only the Committee on Imperial Defence remained. Its head was the Prime Minister, and its principal task was the coordination of the fighting services.

In the Second World War, Prime Minister Churchill resurrected the idea of the War Cabinet. Again five men were selected, only one of whom bore departmental responsibility (Foreign Office). This War Cabinet was not merely a committee of the cabinet; it was *the* cabinet for the purpose of conducting the war, to which all other matters were subordinate. Churchill describes the situation as follows:[17]

> All the responsibility was laid upon the five War Cabinet Ministers. They were the only ones who had the right to have their heads cut off on Tower Hill if we did not win. The rest could suffer for departmental shortcomings, but not on account of the policy of the State. Apart from the War Cabinet no one could say "I cannot take the responsibility for this or that." The burden of policy was borne at a higher level.

The "inner" cabinet

Despite the dissolution of the War Cabinet in 1945, the idea of a central nucleus within the cabinet structure has remained. The Labor governments of 1945 and 1950 certainly contained a core of principal leaders with whom the Prime Minister conferred more than with others. Thus something like a hierarchy within

---

[16] In 1918 General Smuts was added.
[17] Winston Churchill, *Their Finest Hour*, Boston, 1949, p. 13.

the cabinet developed. However, this so-called "inner" cabinet was quite different from the War Cabinet. The latter was, as Churchill reminds us, the official policy-making committee which consequently bore full and exclusive responsibility for the conduct of affairs. The informal "inner" cabinet was only a group of men who were closer to the Prime Minister and more important than other cabinet members and who helped him to draft policy. But as a group they bore no formal responsibility. Responsibility remains with the cabinet as a whole, and if ministers are expected to bear responsibility, they also expect to have a decisive voice. An informal "inner" cabinet is therefore at best a kind of "general staff"; it can never be a "high command" like the War Cabinet.

Committees of the cabinet

Despite the abandonment of the War Cabinet idea for peacetime purposes, the cabinet works quite efficiently, chiefly because of the frequent use of committees. Some are permanent; others are created for special purposes. Their organization and operation differ widely from cabinet to cabinet depending on the personalities and working methods of the cabinet members and especially of the Prime Minister.

The merit of committees studying specific issues for recommendation to the larger body of the cabinet is obvious. Committees may also keep certain important problems under continuous observation and thus guarantee that the cabinet is kept well informed. Cabinet committees may also call upon noncabinet members to participate in their work.

Among the Standing Committees, the best known is the Defence Committee, of which the Prime Minister is chairman. Under Churchill's premiership this committee became especially significant. Another but less well-known committee is the Legislation Committee, which is engaged in reviewing all proposed bills of ministers and recommending the lines of parliamentary procedure to be followed. Other committees deal with economic and many other problems. Their number and structure are subject to periodic changes as circumstances demand.

One of the principal advantages of the cabinet committees is the fact that they provide an opportunity for controversial measures to be thrashed out in an informal exchange of opinion of which no record is kept and to which no publicity is given. Thus, when such measures reach the full cabinet it is likely that a large measure of agreement has already been reached.

The composition of the cabinet

The composition of the British cabinet is, as we have noted, decided to a large extent by the Prime Minister. This discretion extends not only to the persons who are to fill the principal offices of government, whether in the cabinet or other ministries (some sixty altogether), but also to the arrangement of the government departments themselves. The Attlee government made an unusual number of changes. The three armed services were unified in 1946, and a Ministry of Defence with cabinet rank was created. The three service departments, the War Office, the Admiralty, and the Air Ministry, were dropped to subordinate status and are no longer in the cabinet. A Ministry of Economics was created, but in the Churchill government the preeminent position of the Treasury was restored, and there was left only a Minister of State for Economic Affairs, who was not of cabinet rank. By contrast, Prime Minister Harold Wilson elevated the Ministry for Economic Affairs to top rank and made the Minister his permanent deputy as well as First Secretary of State. The latter title had been used for the first time in the Macmillan cabinet and given to Richard Butler.

A number of new ministries have been created, while others have been transformed or dropped. In 1947, the Attlee government transformed what had been the Dominion Office into the Office for Commonwealth Relations. The India Office was abolished for obvious reasons. Ministries for Fuel and Power, Supply, Food, National Insurance, Civil Aviation, and Town and Country Planning were added at one time or another, all outside cabinet rank. In 1951 Churchill appointed a Secretary of State for Transport, Fuel, and Power with a seat in the cabinet. This office absorbed the former Ministry of Civil Aviation. In the same year the former Ministry of Town and Country Planning absorbed most of the local government functions of the Ministry of Health and was renamed the Ministry of Housing and Local Government. Prime Minister Wilson added a Secretary of State for Wales, as well as Ministers of Technology and Overseas Development. Power and Transport were again separated.

At the present time the cabinet is composed of the following officers: the Prime Minister (who is also First Lord of the Treasury and Chairman of the Committee on Imperial Defence), the Foreign Secretary, the Chancellor of the Exchequer, the Lord President of the Council, the Lord Privy Seal, the President of the Board of Trade, the Minister of Defence, the Lord Chancellor, the Home Secretary, the Secretary for Commonwealth Relations, the Colonial Secretary, the Secretary for Transport, Fuel, and Power, the Secretary for Scotland, the Secretary for Wales, the Minister of Labor and National Service, the Minister of Housing and Local Government, the Minister of Education and Science, the Minister of Transport, the Minister of Agriculture, Fisheries, and Food, the Minister of Power, the Chancellor of the Duchy of Lancaster, the Minister of Technology, the Minister for Overseas Development, the Parliamentary Secretary of the Chancellor of the Exchequer and Chief Whip.

Outside the cabinet, but included in that body of heads of government departments often called the "ministry," are the following: the First Lord of the Admiralty, the Secretary of the Army, the Minister for Air, the Minister for Pensions and National Insurance, the Minister of Health, the Minister of Works, the Minister of State for Foreign Affairs and Permanent Representative at the United Nations (subminister under the Foreign Secretary), the Attorney General, the Solicitor

General, the Lord Advocate, and the Solicitor General for Scotland. Outside the cabinet are also the Ministers of State for Economic Affairs and for Scotland, who are essentially subministers.

For practical purposes it is possible to distinguish between four distinct ranks in the Ministry, leaving out such junior officials as Parliamentary Secretaries, Under-secretaries, Junior Lords of the Treasury, etc. At the bottom of the scale are the Minister of Pensions, the Postmaster General, and at times (but not now) the Chancellor of the Duchy of Lancaster. The next higher group is composed of all other ministers not of cabinet rank. In the cabinet itself there are two groups, the top one being composed of that core of chief advisors to the Prime Minister who are sometimes called the "inner cabinet," while the second highest group is formed of the other cabinet ministers.

The appearance of a "hierarchy within a hierarchy" has been noted with some misgivings. In some instances it has led to jockeying for the support of certain key figures, and it endangers equality of discussion in the cabinet. It may diminish departmental responsibility, it may promote factionalism, and it may narrow down the possible range of choice for future party leadership because of inbreeding. But this, it would seem, is the inevitable result of the growth of governmental functions and the growing complexity of their nature. It is also furthered by the trend toward increasing specialization, which was particularly pronounced under the Labor government. The times when Sir Robert Peel could personally control every department of government now lie in the past. To some it seems that now even the cabinet is too cumbersome, and they advocate the adoption of the recommendation of the Haldane Committee that a cabinet of not more than ten members be created. This ideal is far from realized today, and the British government finds itself as vexed by the increase of its responsibilities as every other government in the world.

It has attempted, with a measure of success, to streamline its business by the above-mentioned use of cabinet committees. In addition, recent years have produced the institution of the coordinating ministers, called "overlords."[18] Under the Churchill government the already mentioned Secretary of State for Transport, Fuel, and Power coordinated the Ministries of Transport and Civil Aviation and the Ministry of Fuel and Power. The Lord President of the Council took on general direction of the British food supply. In the Wilson government, Minister of Economics George Brown was placed in general charge of planning and revitalizing the country's economy.

The Treasury

After the Prime Minister's office, the most important department is usually the Treasury. During periods when a tense international situation prevails, the Foreign Office may be more in the forefront of public attention, but for purposes of administration and much of the top-level policy, the Treasury is a key post, and its

[18] Herbert Morrison, *Government and Parliament,* London, 1954.

chief, the Chancellor of the Exchequer, is not infrequently considered the logical successor to the Prime Minister, should the latter step down. Both Stanley Baldwin and Neville Chamberlain were Chancellors of the Exchequer before they became Prime Ministers upon the withdrawal of their former chiefs.

The importance of the Treasury is emphasized by the fact that the Prime Minister is its nominal head as First Lord of the Treasury. This is a relic from the days when the government maintained itself in office to a large extent by the judicious use of what Americans call the "spoils system," i.e., patronage administered by the Treasury, the office concerned with the payment of salaries. When civil service reform set in and the Civil Service Commission was created in 1855, it was placed under the Treasury and under the direction of the Prime Minister. As a result, the highest civil service positions are not necessarily filled from the staff of the department concerned, but transfers are frequent, thereby avoiding narrow compartmentalization on the top level and creating a sense of unity of which the Treasury is the logical hub. Treasury control of the civil service also means the power of general regulation over the entire civil service, which presumes good relations and cooperation between the Treasury and other departments. It has made for a unified service, but it has also created some friction between departments and the Treasury, which is fortunately becoming less frequent.

Treasury control goes far beyond the civil service. Its most important power is its control over fiscal matters in general. The Treasury controls the collection of taxes and other revenues, prepares the budget, supervises the disbursement of funds, exercises considerable borrowing power, and prescribes and supervises the manner in which the public accounts shall be kept. But it is essentially a staff, not an operating, agency. The actual operations are performed by such departments as the Board of Inland Revenue and the Board of Customs (which are under Treasury supervision) while the control over the legality of expenditures and the auditing function rests with the Exchequer and Audit Departments headed by the Comptroller and Auditor General.

Many of the Treasury's functions entail a certain amount of regulatory power over other departments, which is increased by the manner in which Parliament appropriates money in large sums, dedicated for certain general purposes, leaving the actual disbursement to the Treasury, which cannot exceed the appropriations but can diminish them. In practice the sanctions at the disposal of the Treasury are sparingly used. What actually happens is that administrative officers of diverse departments, when they seek departure from previous practice—especially when such departure entails increase in expenditures—seek informal contact with their "opposite number" in the Treasury and iron out difficulties in an informal manner before the issue comes to a head.[19]

It must of course be remembered that the Chancellor of the Exchequer is not

---

[19] T. L. Heath, *The Treasury*, London, 1927. This authoritative work is one of the Whitehall Series, which deals with the principal government departments.

an isolated official rendering dictatorial decisions, but a member of the cabinet which settles policy. Treasury control in other than purely technical questions is therefore subject at all times to cabinet control.

Both the "spoils" origin and the key role of the Treasury are reflected in its organization. It is headed, as stated, by the Chancellor of the Exchequer; he is assisted by a Financial Secretary of the Treasury, who is the most important of all junior ministers, is usually a Member of Parliament, and often represents the Treasury there. There is also an Economic Secretary, whose chief function is economic planning. At times there has also been a Minister of Economics, who has always been subordinate to the Chancellor of the Exchequer.

There is also a Parliamentary Secretary of the Treasury. In other government departments, the Parliamentary Secretary is the chief assistant to the minister and fills the role which in the Treasury is played by the Financial Secretary. However, the Parliamentary Secretary of the Treasury has practically nothing to do with the Treasury. He is the government's chief whip in the House of Commons and is at the present time a member of the cabinet. He is assisted by several Junior Lords (Lords Commissioners) of the Treasury, who likewise have little to do with the Treasury (and are not Lords) but are assistant whips. There are also four assistant whips.

Apart from the various boards, offices, and commissions under the Treasury which carry out its operating functions, there are certain ministries which are subordinate to it. Among them are the Paymaster General's Office (which is often headed by a minister) and the office of the Postmaster General (who is always a minister). The latter has a more independent department, whose financial operations are under Treasury control. Also under Treasury control but with a separate budget are a large number of offices and commissions too numerous to mention here.[20]

Some other departments

The other departments of government present a picture which looks more confusing than it is. Some are called "Offices," like the Foreign Office, and are headed by Secretaries of State; others are called "Ministries," like the Ministry of Health, and are headed by a minister; still others are called "Boards" and are headed by a President, as in the case of the Board of Trade, or by a First Lord, as in the case of the Admiralty. Most of them are, however, organized in a similar manner.[21]

As to their responsibilities, that of the Foreign Office is clearly the handling

[20] Among them are such offices as the Civil Service Commission, the Mint, the Public Record Office, the Historical Manuscript Commission, etc. Their budgets, while separate, appear in the national budget under the Treasury vote. For a list see Jennings, *op. cit.,* p. 526.
[21] The departments also have deputy ministers called "parliamentary secretaries" (when under ministers) or "under-secretaries" (when under secretaries of state). The political deputy to the Chancellor of the Exchequer is the Financial Secretary; the Parliamentary Secretary is chief government whip.

of international problems. The Home Office is concerned with questions of domestic security. It is in charge of the metropolitan police of Greater London and supervises the provincial police systems. During World War II, it exercised tremendous power over aliens and Englishmen alike; under Defence Regulation 18B the Home Secretary could intern virtually anybody who was suspected of endangering the security of the state. The Home Office is in charge of the naturalization of aliens—largely a discretionary power—and exercises the power of pardon[22] and reprieve. It operates the Extradition Act[23] and wields some influence over local government, although it is not the principal government department in that field. The Home Office has various other miscellaneous functions, such as liquor control, and it provides a channel for all government business for which no other authority is prescribed. As in many other countries, the Home Office is a "catchall" department, to which was added the vast responsibility for civilian defense which it discharged so splendidly during the days of the great blitz and the V-weapon attacks on England during the Second World War.

For Scotland and Wales, the Scottish Office and the Welsh Office respectively exercise many of the functions which in England are carried out by the Home Office,[24] the Ministry of Health, the Ministry of Housing and Local Government, and the Ministry of Agriculture and Fisheries.

The Ministry of Labor and National Service has become one of the most important government departments. Its general preoccupation is with conditions of labor, unemployment compensation and insurance, and conciliation. During the war it had vast powers over the labor supply, which were used extensively in order to utilize manpower to best advantage for the prosecution of the war. Thus all men and women found themselves directed into either military or civilian occupations which were connected with the war effort. One of the most spectacular incidents of that period was the drafting of men for work in the mines, an action which, while obviously necessary, caused much resentment.

Although until 1950 the Ministry of Labor and National Service had vast powers of compulsion over labor under the National Service Act and the Control of Engagement Order, it used them in only 600 cases, preferring to operate by persuasion.

The Ministry of Health was formerly a more important department than the name would imply. It had considerable power over two seemingly unconnected fields: health and local government. As with much of the facade of British government, solid historical reasons lay behind this combination. However, since 1951 the control over local government has passed to the Ministry of Town and Country Planning which in turn has been renamed the Ministry of Housing and Local Government.

---

[22] The prerogative of mercy is exercised in the form of advice to the King. In actuality the Home Secretary is in charge.

[23] However, the decisive element is usually a court.

[24] Except pardon, alien affairs, naturalization, extradition, drug control, workmen's compensations, etc. Control over Northern Ireland reverted to the Home Office in 1920.

The Ministry of Health administers the old-age, widows', and orphans' in-surance schemes and, since the National Health Act of 1946, is in charge of the vast machinery of the socialized medical services. In recent years, Ministers of Health have not been members of the cabinet.

The Board of Trade is theoretically a committee, but it never meets. For all practical purposes it is a ministry like others, with the President of the Board of Trade as the minister. While comparable to the United States Department of Commerce, it is a good deal more important than its American counterpart. Its signifi-cance has been greatly increased in view of the directed economy of Britain even under a Conservative government, and the tight control over exports and imports.

A peculiar department in every way is that of the Lord Chancellor. This dignitary, whose office is very ancient and who according to protocol outranks the Prime Minister, is the final refutation of the theory of the separation of powers. He is a cabinet minister, the presiding officer of the House of Lords, and a judge. In addition he performs important functions in the administration of the estab-lished Church, for which reason he ought to be a member of the Church of En-gland. He is usually an eminent jurist,[25] as well as a distinguished politician. As a member of the cabinet and its principal legal adviser, he takes part in all its deci-sions and is sometimes entrusted with special missions. As presiding officer of the upper house, the Lord Chancellor exercises the same functions as the Speaker does in the House of Commons, but he possesses less authority. Technically, he need not be a peer, but he invariably is one, or is created a peer shortly after his appointment.

He is one of the judges in the House of Lords, and he presides over the Judicial Committee of the Privy Council—the two highest judicial offices in the country. He is a member of the High Court of Justice and of the Court of Appeals. He is a member of the rules committee of the Supreme Court of Judicature, which determines the rules of procedure, and he confirms the decisions of the county courts rules committee. He has many administrative duties, especially in connection with appointment of certain judges, and he has certain powers regarding some of the administrative tribunals. He also wields authority over the Land Registry and the Public Trustee's Office.

Other law officers of the Crown are the Attorney General and the Solicitor General. They are both ministers, and some Attorney Generals have been in the cabinet. Their principal duty is to represent the Crown and the departments in court. In some important cases they may prosecute for the Crown, but most prose-cutions are still conducted by private barristers. The duties of the two ministers have been lightened by the appointment of a Director of Public Prosecution.

In Scotland these duties are carried out by the Lord Advocate and the Solici-tor General for Scotland. The law officers, including the Lord Advocate, are almost always Members of Parliament, where they are expected to support the government.

[25] Lord Sankey and Lord Maugham were exceptions.

The "sinecure" offices

A peculiarity of the British administrative system is the existence of certain so-called "sinecure" offices. Those are offices without many official duties which, nevertheless, because of their historical significance, give the incumbent high rank. There is above all the Lord Privy Seal, who has no departmental duties, and the Chancellor of the Duchy of Lancaster, who has few. The Lord President of the (Privy) Council, although not strictly a sinecure minister, is in a similar category.

The chief advantage of this institution is that it provides an opportunity to appoint a distinguished public servant to a high-ranking office in which he is free to devote himself to such duties as the Prime Minister may assign to him. In the Attlee government Herbert Morrison, one of the principal leaders of the Labor party, became Lord President and leader of the House of Commons. For some time he was also chief planner for the government. Similarly the Lord Privy Seal is usually a very distinguished leader in the government. In 1929 J. H. Thomas was appointed to this office with the special task of finding an answer to the unemployment problem. In 1932 Anthony Eden received this office and was placed in charge of Britain's relationship with the League of Nations. The Chancellorship of the Duchy of Lancaster has also been used for important assignments and has sometimes found a place in the cabinet. More often, however, the Chancellor of the Duchy of Lancaster has operated under the direction of the Foreign Office. For a while, Chancellor Lord Peckenham was in charge of the occupied areas in Germany and Austria.

C. THE PUBLIC SERVICE

In the preceding section we have seen that cabinet ministers lead very busy lives. They have party duties to perform, they have to spend much time in Parliament and in cabinet meetings, and they cannot easily escape many social functions. Consequently the time which they can devote to the administration of their respective departments is limited. At the close of the nineteenth century Lord Salisbury could boast that he had written all the important dispatches of the Foreign Office himself, but that is hardly practical today. Now the enormously increased burden which rests on each and every government department demands a much greater amount of time and effort as well as expert knowledge, none of which the minister will ordinarily possess. He must therefore rely on having much of his work done or prepared for him in such a way that all pertinent information is carefully digested so that he may familiarize himself speedily with the subject and render a final decision. Even then he will ask for recommendations, although he need not necessarily follow them.

It is clear, therefore, that in order to function properly, the minister must be able to rely on the honesty, efficiency, impartiality, and complete loyalty of the civil service. A civil service which is corrupt, intriguing, or disloyal, which is composed of "empire builders" or of people determined to oppose the minister, would wreck the entire structure of the administration. If the cabinet is the apex of the English system of government, the civil service makes that system possible.

There are people who have many valid objections to all kinds of civil services, but there are few who would deny that the British civil service is one of the best, quite possibly the best, in the world. Before 1853, the government services were inefficient and corrupt. The turn to the better began with the Northcote-Trevelyan report of 1853, which has rightly been called an epoch-making document. John Stuart Mill thought that the proposed reforms would constitute the greatest single improvement in the machinery of government. Graham Wallas described it as the greatest British contribution to the practice of politics in a century.[26] Whether this estimate is exaggerated or not, the Northcote-Trevelyan report, the establishment of the Civil Service Commission in 1855, the Superannuation (Retirement) Act of 1859, the Order in Council of 1870 providing for open competition and division into classes, and the Order in Council of 1920 creating the Whitley Council are milestones in the development of the civil service.

The high quality of the service is possible because it attracts excellent men and, to an ever-increasing extent, women. The pay is, on the whole, quite good and, in the higher brackets, fairly comfortable. At any rate, it compares not unfavorably with salary rates in equivalent private employment. In addition, there are paid holidays, sick leave, and a noncontributory pension which may amount to two-thirds of one's highest pay. If a civil servant shows great ability, he can go to the top of his class, and although promotions from one class into a higher one are not too plentiful, they are possible. At least one civil servant, Sir Horace Wilson, reached the top position of Permanent Secretary of the Treasury. The knowledge that it is possible to get to the very top inspires men of high ability to enter the service. It must also be remembered that civil servants are highly respected and hold a lofty social rank without necessarily having become like the old-style German *Beamter* who was puffed up with his own importance and considered himself a little tin god because he represented the all-powerful "state." It might also be that the qualities which one expects from a civil servant—quiet efficiency, loyalty, a sense of fairness, and a passion for anonymity—are also qualities which one expects to be prominently displayed among Englishmen.

Because the civil servant is permanent and therefore works for governments of changing political texture, it is necessary for him not only to be impartial, but also to refrain from such action and association as might reflect unfavorably on his impartiality. This means that a higher civil servant may not run for public office[27] and that he may not propagate his political views too vigorously. Since the repeal in 1946 of the Trades Disputes Act of 1927, civil servants may again join

---

[26] H. R. G. Greaves, *The Civil Service in the Changing State,* London, 1947, p. 19. See also W. J. M. Mackenzie and J. W. Grove, *Central Administration in Britain,* London, 1957.
[27] Exceptions are made for certain civil servants in local offices. A civil servant who is elected to Parliament is presumed to have resigned.

trade unions, although strikes are strongly disfavored; but since the civil service has a very effective system for redressing grievances by means of the Whitley Councils, this has not become a question of first-rate importance. Nor do British civil servants high-pressure their government in the manner frequently found in France.

An additional check on improper activities may be seen in the fact that civil servants serve "during the King's pleasure," which means that their tenure rests on custom, rather than on law. This is also true of their retirement benefits, which may be withheld under certain circumstances. These disciplinary measures may be used when the interest of the service requires it. Thus a Permanent Secretary of the Air Ministry was removed because he used his official knowledge for private gain, and an official of the Ministry of Health was once dismissed because he criticized the foreign policy of the government in an anonymous article. Since 1948 membership in the Communist party may lead to transfer or suspension from the service. However, there are some safeguards to guarantee due process.[28]

Treasury control

The control of the entire civil service reposes in the Treasury. An Order in Council[29] describes it as follows: "The Treasury may make regulations for controlling the conduct of His Majesty's civil Establishments, and providing for the classification, remuneration, and other conditions of service of all persons employed therein, whether permanently or temporarily." Chief of the civil service is the Permanent Secretary of the Treasury. Under him is the Establishments department, which is in direct contact with the establishment and organization officer in each department of government. The origin of this system is, of course, the financial responsibility of the Treasury. This has the advantage of uniformity and enables civil servants to move around from department to department, thereby preserving wider vision and acquiring much broad knowledge. On the other hand, Treasury control tends to be restrictive and is sometimes lacking in imagination. According to Gladstone, it is the business of the Treasury to say "No, no, no," but while great care in spending money is the mark of good government, a leading observer points out that "the Treasury should always ask itself whether it is chastity it is defending or an obsession about its chastity."[30]

In order to exercise its extraordinary power, the Treasury must have an intimate knowledge of the working of all departments. Only through such understanding—and, it might be added, sympathy—can the friction between Treasury and the departments, of which the Haldane Committee spoke, be mitigated.

Treasury control has enormous potentialities. It may work as a harmonizer

---

[28] Especially tribunal procedure.

[29] Order in Council No. 1976 (1920), quoted in H. Finer, *The British Civil Service*, London, 1937, p. 52.

[30] *Ibid.*, p. 61.

and streamliner. It has unparalleled opportunities for smoothing out differences and for effecting needed coordination. But there is an inherent danger in such over-all control exercised by a fiscal agency. It is inclined to view expenditures from a standpoint of prudent economy rather than of service, and it is understandably suspicious of experimentation. In an age in which the demand for government services is on the increase, such an attitude is in danger of losing touch with political realities.[31]

The Treasury controls the service itself; entry into the service is controlled by the Civil Service Commission. It is made up of three members appointed by the Crown, i.e., the cabinet. They are completely nonpartisan and independent. Because entry into the civil service is accomplished through competitive examinations, a large number of examiners are employed by the Commission. Most of them are academic personnel, and some are taken from the civil service itself, usually retired persons.

Examinations

As in the United States, the use of competitive examinations has marked the transition from patronage to the merit system. But especially in the higher brackets of examinations, the British approach is unlike the one used in America or on the Continent. In America, civil service examinations contain a fixed set of questions on subjects which presumably have some relationship to the candidate's future work. This is not the case with the British higher civil service examinations, which are geared to the educational system of the country. A candidate for the top Administrative class, for instance, may choose to be examined in any field or combination of fields. He may choose political science or Sanskrit, ancient history or organic chemistry. This field examination counts for a major portion of the entire test, 700 possible points out of a total of 1,400. The other 700 points may be obtained from five additional tests which are prescribed. There is an essay test (100 points), a paper on the use of English (100), a paper entitled "Present Day," which is a broad current-affairs test (100), a foreign-language test (100), and an oral examination (300). This method, now often referred to as Method I, has been implemented by a simplified Method II open to honors students of the universities. Only 25 percent of the vacancies in the Administrative class are filled by Method II.[32]

This system might seem rather incredible to foreign observers, but there is some very sound reasoning behind it. First of all, Method I is required only of the highest, numerically smallest, but most important group of civil servants, the Ad-

[31] This problem was studied by a Royal Commission headed by Lord Tomlin and therefore usually referred to as the Tomlin Commission. It reported in Cmd. 3909, 1931.

[32] For a discussion as seen especially from the universities, see Ernest Barker, "The Home Civil Service," *The British Civil Servant,* ed. by W. A. Robson, London, 1937, pp. 29–45. See also Finer, *op. cit.,* pp. 66–108; A. H. M. Hillis, "The British Civil Servant of To-Morrow," *Public Administration Review,* Vol. XI (1951), pp. 173–179.

ministrative class. It is the British contention that the best preparation for such a career is a broad, sound, and penetrating liberal education. It is felt that, whatever specialized knowledge is needed, the candidate will get it from in-service training and experience, while any vocational training at the university level will invariably encroach on the liberal-arts subjects. This system is designed to favor the broadly educated, highly cultured man over the narrow specialist. This may be important because in the course of his lifetime career the civil servant tends to become too narrowly specialized anyway. It is therefore particularly important that he have a broad background before he enters the service. The system minimizes, although it does not eliminate, cramming for the examination, thereby testing the real and permanent knowledge of the candidate. It does not force the educational institutions to make too many concessions in the direction of vocationalism, but allows them to proceed with their proper task.

But there are some disadvantages. This system is geared to the curriculum of the universities, especially to the great institutions of Oxford and Cambridge. It finds its justification in the tutorial system, where the student learns how to appraise and tackle a problem—a knowledge which will be of incalculable value to him in his higher civil service career. But—and this is a big but—only a small proportion of British youth have an opportunity to study at the universities, and still fewer enroll at Oxford or Cambridge. Despite the increase in the number of scholarships, the group from which higher civil servants are chosen will be found to be a small and select one, which cannot be called representative of the nation and which is also likely to hold social and economic views that may tend to be on the conservative side.[33]

Much criticism has been directed against the oral examination, which counts for a great deal. It does not test specific things but rather general attitude, alertness, etc. Tests have shown great variation in appraising the same candidate, and undue attention may have been paid to nice manners over ability in the raw.

Classes

The British civil service is divided into classes. At the top of the pyramid stands the already mentioned Administrative class. It is the smallest in number, having around 4,000 members. Most of them are recruited by competitive examination, as we have seen, or are taken directly from the honor students of the universities. A smaller number enters by promotion from the lower civil service classes. Below the Administrative class is the Executive class. It fills its ranks by promotion and examination, but promotion is preferred when suitable candidates are available. This class does the higher work in the more specialized branches of the departments, and some of its members become the heads of large units of government engaged in routine operations.

[33] Harvey Walker, *Training Public Employees in Great Britain,* New York, 1935.

On the lower level there is the Clerical class, divided into a Higher Clerical class and a Clerical class. The nature of this group's duties is indicated in its name. Most of its members are appointed after examinations, but some are obtained by promotion from the still lower class of Clerical Assistants. There is furthermore a group of Typists, Assessors, Collectors, etc. In addition to these regular classes, there are specialists such as lawyers or physicists, as well as inspectors of various kinds, and others.

All this applies primarily to the national civil service. There are also different services within *the* civil service, such as the Colonial or the Foreign Service. What we have said above applies primarily to the home civil service. The Foreign Service test is now quite similar to the test for the Administrative class, but the grading system differs.

The Whitley Councils

To ensure harmonious relationships between the government and its civil servants, the so-called Whitley Councils[34] were established in 1919.[35] They are more than grievance committees or conciliation boards. In effect, they cover much of the field of public personnel policy. There are a National Whitley Council, 70 departmental councils, and a number of district and office committees. The latter groups function in the governmental industries. All councils are composed of employers' and employees' representatives in equal measure.

The councils consider practically all questions of public personnel policy, such as recruitment, promotion, salary, discipline, etc. They are also supposed to improve the service by devising means by which knowledge and training may be better utilized, and by suggesting better training. The decisions of the councils, especially the National Whitley Council, enjoy great prestige and have been at the bottom of many recent reforms. It is of course true that the Whitley Councils cannot definitely commit the minister, whose decision is final; in practice, however, decisions of this kind are made on the basis of understanding between both sides so that a publicly announced decision of the council in effect constitutes an already reached agreement.

Wage disputes, however, are submitted to compulsory arbitration, for which the Civil Service Arbitration Tribunal is the proper forum.[36]

The higher civil service

It will easily be seen that the key to the entire British civil service system is the Administrative class. Its duties have been well defined by Sir Horace Wilson,

[34] Named after J. H. Whitley, chairman of the committee which worked out this plan.
[35] *Report of the National Provisional Joint Committee*, Cmd. 198, 1919. See L. D. White, *Whitley Councils in the British Civil Service*, Chicago, 1933.
[36] In the government industries, industrial courts perform the same task.

then Permanent Secretary of the Ministry of Labor, in his remarks to the Tomlin Commission:

> Broadly speaking, the main quality that is required seems to me to be a capacity to take the facts about a particular subject, to put them into shape, to suggest the deductions that might be drawn from them, to propose the lines of policy that might be adopted in relation to them, and generally to apply a constructive analytical mind to what I would call the policy of the Ministry.

During the past decades criticisms of the service have been numerous. One line of criticism is that it is not possible to diagnose such qualities with certainty in a person under twenty-six and that in any case the whole system of an Administrative class creates a group which is cut off from the world which its decisions affect, yet which tends to regard administration as something which only the initiated can understand. Remedies have been suggested, notably the recruitment of older men, experienced in various social services, into the Administrative class and an intensive in-service training including sound academic work in the theory of public administration.

Other critics complain that higher civil servants, being the product of the universities, especially of Oxford and Cambridge, are likely to originate from the upper strata of society; that this system may have been of use in the olden days when higher civil servants and their ministers came from the same social class and could confer with one another in an atmosphere of social equality, but that it is quite possibly out of step with the present day; and that, since a very broad system of scholarships does not exist, this present method of recruitment for the civil service excludes a vast reservoir of manpower, among whom great but unknown talents may be slumbering.

These criticisms may well be exaggerated, but that they are not entirely without foundation may be gleaned from the fact that over half the men appointed to head departments[37] in recent years have not entered the Administrative class through the regular avenue of competitive examinations. Since it was necessary to go outside the regular group to seek out men competent enough for great responsibility, it is safe to assume that not all is well among the lower strata of the Administrative class.[38]

The objections which have been stated so far are somewhat mitigated by the fact that they can be overcome by a better personnel policy, by the infusion of new blood into the machinery, and by devising means through which civil servants may gain knowledge and experience in the broader, "outside" fields which are affected by their actions. If past experience is any guide, it may be assumed that these weaknesses will be remedied as far as possible, and some progress has already been achieved.

[37] Permanent secretaries.
[38] Greaves, *op. cit.,* p. 60.

While the higher civil servants are still recruited from the universities, the graduates of these institutions of learning no longer belong exclusively or even predominantly to the social upper classes. The impoverishment of the upper strata of society on the one hand and the increasing use of scholarships for gifted students from impecunious families on the other hand have considerably modified the social composition of university student bodies. Also promotions from one civil service class to a higher one are now much easier. For instance, 20 percent of the vacancies arising in the Administrative class are to be filled by candidates from the Executive class who compete successfully in examinations especially administered for them. There is also a better system of in-service training now.

There is, however, a further objection which may be directed to all civil services, but which has particular validity in Great Britain in view of the many services which the government has taken over since 1945. It is said that the civil service, as it exists today, was devised for a type of government whose principal administrative duties were control functions. To exercise efficient control, the necessary virtues are impartiality, discretion, caution, and keeping a jaundiced eye turned toward radical innovations. But under the leadership of the Labor party, Britain has been transformed more and more into a so-called "welfare state" or "service state," which the Conservatives can hardly undo, with the result that the rendering of services, rather than the exercise of control, is becoming more important. The very characteristics which were virtues in a control administration tend to become vices in a service administration. Instead of being impartial, the service-administering official is supposed to believe passionately in what he is doing, thus increasing the efficiency and the scope of the service he is rendering. Instead of being cautious, he is supposed to be a bold innovator and to embark on experiments which, in the last analysis, can alone determine the wisdom or failure of a particular course of action. Instead of saying "No, no, no," to new expenditures, as Gladstone suggested, he is supposed to consider the social aspects of a prospective service, rather than the financial effects on the Treasury. Civil servants are frequently accused, and not entirely without reason, of lacking imagination, of paying excessive devotion to precedent and self-developed rules, and of a plodding and disinterested slowness in the execution of business "through channels." It is certainly no disparagement of the quite excellent British civil service to wonder whether it is really geared to the demands of the new "service state."

The administration of nationalized industry and other public corporations

Because of these considerations, the British government has sought new ways in the administration of its nationalized industries. Experimentation with alternative forms antedates the Labor government by many years, and outstanding examples of earlier public corporations are the British Broadcasting Corporation, the Central Electricity Board, and the London Passenger Transport Board. The forms of organization established for those corporations were perhaps more accident than design, but their semiautonomous character was conceived in order to combine two divergent principles: that of sound business administration, which demands independence from a national bureaucracy, and that of responsibility, to which all sections of governmental activities must ultimately be subjected. Naturally, where there is government responsibility there must be government control.

The nationalized industries use a form of organization which was inaugurated in 1947 by the National Coal Board[39] and has spread, with some differences, to the Transport Commission (Railroads) and the British Electricity Authority. The Iron and Steel Corporation, however, had an entirely different setup. The principles by which the nationalized industries are governed can be best shown by the example of the coal industry, the oldest of the nationalized industries, which is concerned with the most basic enterprise in Britain. Under private ownership,[40] there had been some larger and some smaller companies, but none of them was excessively large. Only in a few was there any considerable hierarchy.[41] Now there is a formidable machinery. At its top is the National Coal Board itself, a kind of coal "cabinet." Below, are eight divisional boards which are smaller in number of members (six) but largely duplicate the functional division of the National Board. Under the divisional boards there are no fewer than forty-eight areas, each under an area general manager, under whom are the heads of departments. Finally there are the many colliery managers. The difficulties of such an arrangement are clear. The lower levels are faced by many confusing lines of authority, and there is a tendency—well known in the civil service—to escape responsibility by passing "the buck" higher up.

The other nationalized industries have not had quite the same problem as the coal industry. The British Electricity Authority, which took over on April 1, 1948, found an already efficiently working system of distribution which had been administered by the Central Electricity Board. A similar arrangement was made for nationalization of gas, which took effect on May 1, 1949. There are twelve area boards and an advisory Central Gas Council. The British Transport Commission took over the railroads on January 1, 1948. It learned much from the experiences of the London Passenger Transport Board, which was created in 1933. The Transport Commission found the railroads already largely consolidated since 1921, when four major companies had been created out of a multitude of others. These railways were now placed under a Railway Executive, under which there are now six "regions," each headed by a chief regional officer and by various functional executives. Just what advantages there are in the "consolidation" of four companies into six regions is not quite clear. A more flexible form of administration was set up

---

[39] The National Coal Board took over on Jan. 1, 1947. Cf. National Coal Board, *Annual Report and Statement of Account,* 1947; William W. Haynes, *Nationalization in Practice: The British Coal Industry,* Boston, 1953.

[40] One could hardly speak of private *enterprise.* The price cartel agreements of 1930 eliminated all competition, and in 1937 the government acquired all mineral rights.

[41] Charles L. Mowat, "The Anatomy of British Nationalization," *Antioch Review,* 1949, pp. 274ff. See also A. A. Ragow, *The Labour Government and British Industry, 1945–1951,* Ithaca, N.Y., 1955.

for the Road Haulage Executive, which was in charge of long-distance trucking. Quite different forms of administration have been applied to such special public corporations as the British Broadcasting Corporation, the British Overseas Airways Corporation, the British European Airways, and the Bank of England. The latter is particularly significant because its control over credit touches the lives of all citizens.

The scheme for the Iron and Steel Corporation, which was designed to control the nationalized steel industry, departed from the above system. The various firms remained intact, even under their former names, in order to retain the large amount of good will and reputation attached to certain internationally famous firms. They also remained largely under their former managerial personnel. However, the Churchill government denationalized both the iron and steel industry and the trucking industry. This measure ran into considerable difficulty, as private interests were rather reluctant to repurchase the stocks of these companies for fear that a possible future Labor government might renationalize them, as the Labor leaders have threatened to do.

These public corporations are subordinate to an appropriate minister who in turn is answerable for their activities in Parliament. However, the exact line between ministerial responsibility and control on the one side, and the corporations' autonomy on the other, has never been entirely determined, and ministers have refused to answer questions in Parliament on matters which they felt lay within the autonomous powers of the corporations. As the ordinary machinery of Parliamentary control was not easily adjustable to the nationalized industries (although the industries' accounts are scrutinized by the Public Accounts Committee), a special Select Committee of the House of Commons was established in 1955 in order to gain better information and report to the House. However, it is generally conceded that the Select Committee has found its work difficult and has not been very effective.

Another avenue to public control has been sought by means of consultative councils attached to most public corporations, but they have been generally unsatisfactory and have been accused, rightly or wrongly, of reflecting merely the position of management.

From an administrative standpoint, the nationalized industries have raised many problems. Their cumbersome structure, especially in the coal industry, will have to be streamlined. The National Coal Board admitted at one time an increase of 4,799 persons in the administrative and nonindustrial staff as compared to the personnel before nationalization. While some additions were undoubtedly necessary, the situation, as well as other difficulties, would seem to indicate that the administration of a large industry from a central command post is not an easy thing and is certainly not learned overnight.

There are also other problems. There is not as yet a merit system in the nationalized industries comparable to the civil service. Standards are difficult to develop on account of the great diversification of the industries. Moreover, in order to retain the managerial skill of former executives, it has been necessary to pay salaries which are comparable to the top positions in private industry and are substantially higher than comparable civil service salaries. This has caused considerable criticism and opposition.

There have also appeared new problems of labor relations. Strikes have occurred, but have generally been discouraged by the unions, especially while a Labor government was in office. On the other hand, unions not affiliated with the Trades Union Congress have been squeezed out in some places. In contrast with France, there are no workers' representatives as such on the boards or executives.

It is true some trade-union leaders became members of these boards in their personal capacity, and the close tie between the former Labor government and the unions has forced the latter to urge more production and to discourage certain wage demands—an attitude which runs counter to the fighting tradition of a union. On the other hand, there is no conclusive evidence that nationalization has appreciably affected the workers' morale, and they may perhaps be excused if they find that the new bosses look—and sometimes behave—suspiciously like the old ones. It cannot be assumed that the oft-proven British skill for adaptation will be found wanting; the shortcomings of the nationalized industries are openly discussed and studied, and improvements are undertaken vigorously. But just as the development of the British civil service had to go through many stages, so the administration of the nationalized industries is in its infancy, and its definitive analysis must be left to an endeavor which still lies in the distant future.

Nationalization and large-scale governmental planning have apparently raised more questions than they have solved. This is not in itself an argument against the measures undertaken by the Labor government, because a situation of this kind must be expected in any period of transition. However, there are many people who wonder whether the time-honored methods of control still operate today, or whether checks and balances need to be developed in order to keep the enormously growing scope of executive power within the confines of democratic government. In the past, checks and balances have not characterized the British system.

The relatively short time during which nationalized industries have operated in Great Britain does not permit any final conclusions. One thing is certain, however, and that is that nationalization has not fulfilled the expectations of either its protagonists or its opponents. It has not raised production beyond the level achieved in comparable branches of private industry. In some cases the level has remained lower. Nor has greater economy or efficiency prevailed; labor relations have not markedly improved, and the working man is no happier working for a public corporation than for a private one. In fact, at the annual meeting of the Trades-Union Congress in 1953, several delegates voiced the opinion that it was easier to deal with the old bosses than with the new ones. Certainly in the mining industry, the most ailing before nationalization, higher wages[42] have diminished neither absenteeism nor the ever-growing difficulty of recruiting new labor.

On the other hand, nationalization has certainly not ruined the British econ-

[42] Miners' wages are among the highest of Britain's industrial workers.

omy as was widely predicted, and it is unlikely that private management would have done any better either in labor relations or production. In fact, considering the austere days after the war, industrial unrest would probably have been greater under private management, especially in the coal fields, when labor would not have been restrained by its unions.

It is difficult to deny that nationalization has not fulfilled the high expectations of its Labor-party advocates. While some may take satisfaction in the fact that certain private interests have been shorn of their great power, Britain's major economic problem, the increase and greater efficiency of her production, has not been appreciably enhanced by nationalization beyond what has been achieved in the private sector of the economy. As a result, enthusiasm for nationalization has cooled in Labor-party circles. The Conservative government denationalized only the iron and steel industry and the trucking business. In the election campaign of 1964, the Labor party demanded the renationalization of the steel industry, but the small majority with which Labor won that election made realization of this goal impractical until 1967. In any case, while iron and steel remain controversial, further nationalization in other parts of the economy has now become fairly unlikely. It is interesting to note, however, that in making a case for renationalization the Labor party has lately emphasized the supposedly greater efficiency of such an enterprise and resulting gains for Britain's competitive ability, rather than earlier political and ideological arguments. In other words, socialist measures are defended in nonsocialist terms.

Problems of big government

As the government has extended its power and influence into many fields, there are pessimistic voices complaining that these powers tend to become arbitrary and unduly free from restraint. Parliament, being overburdened by an ever-increasing legislative load, is increasingly inclined to pass "skeleton" legislation, leaving "details"—often very extensive—to the decision of executive departments, which thus exercise what is sometimes termed "delegated legislation."[43] But then the executive often goes one step further and also establishes ministerial and departmental tribunals or quasi-tribunals which decide disputes arising under these orders and regulations. As long as the decision is within the scope of this broad grant of power given by Parliament, it is legal, and the justice or wisdom of the ministerial decision itself cannot be reviewed by a regular court of law.[44] This means that when the law says "the decision of the Minister is final," some anonymous civil servant is in a position to make a nonreviewable final decision which may affect the livelihood and property of individuals very deeply. Moreover, the "minister," or rather

---

[43] The executive orders given as a result of such delegation have many names. They may be called "orders," "rules," "regulations," "warrants," "minutes," "schemes," "bylaws," etc.

[44] In the United States, review by the courts is made possible in such cases by the use of the "due process of law" clause of the United States Constitution. There is no equivalent in Great Britain.

the civil servant, is not governed by the rules of judicial procedures which are incumbent upon the courts and may therefore make decisions without a hearing and without giving the affected party an opportunity to submit evidence.[45]

It is a fact that on the whole the British administration leans over backward to be fair and to enable all parties to make their points. Even when the ministers have extraordinary powers, they prefer to rule by persuasion rather than by compulsion. Nor is there any appreciable degree of dishonesty in the wielding of the extraordinary powers and discretions which the civil service frequently possesses. The speed, publicity, and severity with which the Attlee government dealt with a corrupt Parliamentary Secretary of the Board of Trade[46] shows that the government is fully aware of those dangers and is intent upon maintaining the integrity of the administrative machinery. But it is nevertheless true that the increasing number of regulations which economic austerity, planning, and nationalization have brought to England cause many decisions to be made by anonymous civil servants and behind closed doors. This has also the further disadvantage that the civil servant, unlike the judge, is not necessarily bound by precedent, with the result that the citizen remains somewhat uncertain as to the outcome of his case.[47]

On the other hand, the defenders of the present system reply in the following manner to the critics of this form of "delegated legislation" and administrative justice: there is no reason to assume, they say, that a judge is necessarily wiser than a civil servant, although he is of course more independent. Moreover, ministerial decisions frequently involve questions of policy, rather than of abstract justice, and the minister is responsible for that policy before Parliament, and ultimately before the nation. Decisions implementing policy might therefore be said to be quite properly before the minister or his agent, rather than before an independent judge who bears no responsibility for the policy of the government and may even be hostile to it.

The Committee on Ministers' Powers[48] suggested certain remedies such as greater publicity in the performance of quasi-judicial functions. When Parliament is of the opinion that the ordinary courts are not suitable for the determination of certain issues arising out of the administrative work of a department, the disputes should be referred to an independent tribunal and not to the discretionary power of the minister. This would have meant the establishment of an administrative court system on the French model.

[45] The principal critic was the Lord Chief Justice Lord Hewart of Bury, *The New Despotism*, New York, 1929. See also C. K. Allen, *Law and Orders: Delegated Legislation and Executive Powers in England*, London, 1945; M. A. Sieghart, *Government by Decree*, London, 1950; and W. A. Robson, *Justice and Administrative Law: A Study of the English Constitution*, London, 1947, 2d ed.

[46] This was the Belcher case. Cf. Rebecca West, "The Tribunal That Stirred England," *Harper's Magazine*, Vol. 198 (June, 1949), Part I, pp. 21–33; *ibid.* (July, 1949), Part II, pp. 37–50.

[47] In practice, however, the civil servant is not much less impressed by his own precedents than the judge is, and sometimes more so, even though there is no official rule of *stare decisis* in the civil service.

[48] *Report of the Committee on the Ministers' Powers*, Cmd. 4060, 1932.

Most of these recommendations have not as yet been carried out, although isolated instances of tribunals of the kind envisioned above do exist. While all these dangers and difficulties exist of necessity in an age which demands unprecedented services from its government, and while they ought to be remedied, there is no factual reason as yet to speak of "despotism" or "dictatorship." It is important to remember that the British civil service is not a "state within the state," as the German civil service used to be, but is part of a democratic and responsible form of government in which large-scale abuse of power would lead to a quick and drastic public reaction which would cause some "heads to roll." On top of the civil servant there is still the responsible minister, whose function it is "to tell the civil service what the public won't stand."

5

Parliament

A. THE HOUSE OF COMMONS

Wherever there is a parliamentary form of government in the world, England is the model, and all comparisons eventually center around the magnificent building on the river Thames which is called the House of Parliament. Indeed this "mother of Parliaments" is a remarkable establishment, but like so many other British institutions it is somewhat different in scope and methods from what the casual observer might expect.

On one thing all are agreed: when we speak of Parliament, we mean the House of Commons. To be sure, there is still the House of Lords, and a later section will show that it is by no means a negligible quantity despite its progressive loss of substantive power. But the sovereignty of Parliament resides in the House of Commons, for it alone is representative of the nation as a whole, and in its chamber are heard the great political debates of the country.

A preceding chapter has demonstrated that the British cabinet and legislature are not separate entities, but one, and that their relationships are based on political realities rather than on any constitutional "checks and balances." Parliament does not rule; no body of more than 600 persons could do that. It actually interferes far less with the administration of government departments than does the United States Congress. Nor does policy emanate from Parliament; that is the business of the cabinet. Yet Parliament stands at the very center of the political stage—is, in fact, the political stage—and if the cabinet is the head of the body politic, then Parliament is its heart.

The election of members

The House of Commons is a large body. At present it is composed of 630 members. They are now all elected from single-member districts. Before the House of Commons (Redistribution of Seats) Act of 1944 and the Representation of the People Act of 1948, there were several two-member districts in London. There was also the so-called business-premises vote, which permitted a person who occupied an office or land having a rental value of at least £10 to vote in the constituency in which his business premise was located, as well as in the constituency[1] of his residence. Moreover, holders of university degrees could also vote (by mail) in special university constituencies in addition to their regular voting residence. However, after 1918 and before 1948 no person was allowed to cast more than two ballots in any one election. This system of plural voting was of course a residue from an older age when even so enlightened a man as Bagehot could speak of the "rich and wise" on the one hand and the "poor and stupid" on the other. This system benefited the Conservative party, whose members were more likely to hold business premises or country estates, and who also predominated among the university voters.[2] At any rate, few Liberals had been elected from university constituencies, and no regular Labor man. There was little justification in the business-premises vote, but the university constituencies were hotly defended. It was contended that they permitted the election of men who had attained public distinction, but were not prepared to submit to the rough-and-tumble of an electoral campaign. Such exceptional men were indeed selected at times, though certainly not always, but the same was also true of the former "rotten boroughs" of the days before 1832. At any rate, no really satisfactory answer was found to the Labor party argument "one man, one vote," and plural voting is now a matter of the past. Distinguished men who desire a place in the high council of the nation but do not wish to stand[3] for a seat in the House of Commons can now be accommodated only in the House of Lords.

[1] The English call both the electorate of a district and the electoral district itself "constituency."
[2] In 1945 it was estimated that 20,000 people were qualified to cast a business-premises vote, and 175,000 a university vote. H. Finer, *The Theory and Practice of Modern Government*, New York, 1949, rev. ed., p. 231*n*.
[3] The different attitude of the two major English-speaking countries is reflected in the use of terms. An American "runs" for Congress, but an Englishman "stands" for Parliament.

The Parliamentary constituencies are now more or less evenly distributed all over the country, i.e., England and Wales, Scotland, and Northern Ireland.[4] But the United Kingdom has never known the method of periodic redistribution of seats which the United States Constitution provides after each decennial census. By 1944 large movements of population had taken place, which were not reflected in the distribution of constituencies. In 1942 a departmental committee on electoral machinery[5] recommended a permanent boundary commission. This recommendation was endorsed by the Speaker's Conference on Electoral Reforms and Redistribution of Seats in 1944. The Act of 1944 established four separate boundary commissions[6] with the Speaker as chairman of each, but all other members of the House of Commons and of the Parliament of Northern Ireland excluded from membership therein. The commissions effected a considerable redistricting of constituencies. Their principal departure from past practice is that changes in boundaries of constituencies will now be recommended by the commissions and carried out by order in council, rather than by an act of Parliament, although Parliament has an opportunity to intervene.

The elections themselves are fairly simple, though spirited, affairs. When the Prime Minister has decided on the date of the general election, a royal proclamation dissolves Parliament. Writs of election are then dispatched to the election officials all over the country. Eight days after the proclamation (Sundays and holidays not counting), all candidates must have been nominated. This is known as "election day." The formal requirements for candidates are exceedingly simple. All they have to do is to fill out forms giving name, address, and profession as well as the names of voters of the constituency who nominate and second each candidate, and the names of eight more voters who "assent." They must also deposit the sum of £150, which is forfeited unless they manage to poll at least one-eighth of the total vote cast in the constituency. This is a measure designed to discourage hopeless and insincere candidates.

Each candidate must have an election agent (manager) who is required by law to handle and account for all campaign expenses (except the candidate's personal expenses). If an agent is guilty of corrupt practices under the law, the election may be declared invalid. It should be noted that there are no residence requirements: in other words, a candidate need not be a resident of his constituency. This is very advantageous, because it enables any number of able men to run for office. It also enables political parties to shift their candidates around so that a strong leader may capture a constituency which a less prominent man might have lost. This was demonstrated in 1945 when Herbert Morrison changed constituencies in order to capture a doubtful seat for the Labor party.

Certain persons are, however, ineligible even if they possess other qualifications. Election officials are disqualified, and so are civil servants (who may run but

---

[4] Northern Ireland also has a legislature of its own.
[5] Cmd. 6408, December, 1942.
[6] England, Wales, Scotland, and Northern Ireland.

would be deemed to have resigned from the service upon election). United Kingdom peers and Scottish peers are ineligible, but Irish peers who have not been
elected representative peers may be candidates. Peeresses in their own right (that
is, those who have inherited the title in the absence of a male heir) are eligible,
since they are not permitted to sit in the House of Lords. But life peeresses may
now sit in the House of Lords and are therefore not eligible. Likewise, wives of
peers may sit in the House of Commons. American-born Lady Astor was a well-
known example. Persons convicted of certain crimes, including corrupt practices,
may be declared ineligible, and so are lunatics. A residue from the days when
religious tests were demanded is the provision that clergymen of the established
churches of England and Scotland and priests of the Roman Catholic Church are
also ineligible.[7]

Simple as candidacies may be under those rules, it is quite a bit more difficult
to be a successful candidate, which now means usually to be officially endorsed by
a major political party. Ordinarily the local party organization, or rather its leadership, picks the "official" candidate. Sometimes advice may be asked from national
headquarters. In the Labor party, central control is generally stronger than among
Conservatives, as it requires close consultation with headquarters and endorsement
of candidates by the national leadership.

The two-party system successfully accomplishes its mission by often, though
not always, presenting a clear majority and therefore a fully responsible government. But as in the United States, the distribution of votes and that of seats in the
House of Commons do not always coincide.

Usually, as has been shown, the winning party will have a larger percentage
of the seats than it has of the votes. It is obvious that this system greatly discrimi-
nates against small parties. In 1951 and 1955 the Liberal party received 2.53 percent and 2.7 percent of the vote but only 0.95 percent and 0.97 percent of the
seats. In 1959 the Liberals more than doubled their vote to 5.9 percent but still
received only 0.95 percent of the seats. In 1964 they doubled their vote once more
and reached 11.2 percent. But their seats remained a bare 1.7 percent of all the
seats. Or, put in a different way, in 1964 the Labor party obtained five times as
many votes as the Liberals but received more than thirty-five times as many seats.
In 1966, the Labor party polled nearly six times as many votes as the Liberals and
won thirty times as many seats.

Election campaigns are short, especially when compared to the American
practice. We have seen how candidates must file on "election day," eight days after
the proclamation dissolving Parliament. Nine days later, on "polling day," the
votes are cast. Of course, it is usually known that an election is impending, and the
parties warm up, hold their conferences, and issue their programs, but the actual
electoral campaign is over after seventeen to nineteen days. There are no long

---

[7] However, since the Church of England was disestablished in Wales in 1914, ministers of that
church from Wales may be elected.

ballots. Only Members of Parliament are elected on "polling day." Local and other officials are elected at quite different times, and of course there are no referendum questions to answer. The election is therefore simple and straightforward. The British voter merely casts his ballot for one single person.

Party programs, usually adopted on a long-range basis, not merely for electoral purposes, have assumed increasing importance in recent years. The victory of the Labor party in 1945 can certainly be credited in no small degree to the fact that it had a definite program for the solution of the country's problems. But usually the electorate has a few very distinct alternatives before it, and the votes are mostly cast on that basis. The radio and television are not used as extensively as in the United States, but political meetings are more significant. One peculiarity of campaigns is the habit of "heckling," which tests both the stamina and the sense of humor of the candidate. While this habit may seem startling and rude to foreign observers, it forces the candidate to "think on his feet," a habit which will stand him in good stead when he takes his seat in the House of Commons.

Campaign expenses

Expenditures play a less significant role in Britain than in the United States; the fabulous sums expended in America are not equaled anywhere else in the world. The shortness of the British campaign helps to make it inexpensive; the small size of the constituencies makes it possible for the candidate to travel about in a small car, and Britishers do not expect big shows or barbecues from their candidates. Nevertheless there are some expenses, and they are regulated, chiefly because the eighteenth- and early nineteenth-century history of England fairly reeked with political corruption. The Corrupt and Illegal Practices Prevention Act of 1883 and subsequent legislation, including substantial sections of the Representation of the People Act of 1948, regulate the legal scope of electoral campaigns. A significant distinction is made between corrupt practices, involving moral turpitude, and illegal practices, which are merely unfair and therefore outlawed. In the first group are such offenses as bribery, fraud in counting or reporting the results, intimidation, and the publication of false statements concerning a person's character. In the second group are such practices as illegally paying for certain services which may be permitted only when rendered voluntarily, and voting in more than one place.

In addition to the establishment of this "moral code" of elections, these laws also limit the candidate's expenses. The allowable sums used to be very small, but the Act of 1948 now permits each candidate a basic expenditure of £450, plus 2d for each registered voter in a rural constituency (county) and 1½d for each voter in an urban area (borough). In effect even these modest amounts (about $3,000 to $4,000 on the average per candidate) are rarely fully spent—an extraordinary contrast to American practices. Each candidate must have a single agent, who is obliged to submit a sworn statement of all receipts and expenditures to the election officials. All money spent for the campaign must be paid through this agent. Should a newly elected member sit before his agent has submitted his sworn statement, he may forfeit £100 ($280) per day to any person who sues for it. The expenses of the election itself (polling booths, clerks, etc.) are covered by the government.[8] There is some uneasiness in Britain as to the scope of the 1948 act. Indications are that not only the expenditures made during the brief election period are included, but also all others. A former Attorney General, Sir Hartley Shawcross, once threatened to include the campaign of certain firms, notably the sugar industry, against nationalization, but nothing of the sort happened.

Every British subject, male or female, who is of age and not incapacitated mentally or through conviction for a criminal offense, is entitled to vote, provided he is registered as a voter. The registration of voters is undertaken by public authority, not by the voter himself as in the United States. The voter merely reassures himself, if he wishes, that his name is properly listed, and may make representations if he finds that this is not the case. Since the Act of 1948, two registration lists are prepared annually.

Elections may be contested by anyone who has reason to believe that there has been an error in tabulating the vote or in the eligibility of candidates, or that any corrupt or illegal practices have taken place. Judgment is rendered by two judges of the High Court of Justice, or of the Court of Session for cases affecting Scotland. Only the question of legal eligibility is still left to the House of Commons.

Technically, a member of either house may not resign his office. Until 1963 this rule was fatal for a peer, as he had absolutely no opportunity to refuse the "writ of summons" which installed him in the upper house, provided he had inherited the title. Brilliant political lights had thus been dimmed by the inheritance of a title, because a top-flight career is possible only in the House of Commons. This peculiar state of affairs was changed by legislation in 1963, when peers who had received their titles by inheritance were permitted to renounce them for their lifetime (which means that their sons would nevertheless inherit them). A number of political leaders have made use of this, the best known case being that of Lord Home, who became Sir Alec Douglas-Home in 1964 and ran successfully for a seat in the House of Commons.

Resignation from the House of Commons, however, is possible through the use of a fiction. It is customary for a member who wishes to resign to ask for appointment to the sinecure office of the Stewardship of the Chiltern Hundreds, since an appointment under the Crown is incompatible with a seat in the House of Commons. This appointment, which has been in use since 1740, results in the automatic vacating of the seat in the House, whereupon the nominal and unpaid office of the stewardship is promptly resigned. Upon the resignation or death of a member of the House of Commons, or his elevation to the peerage, a special election known as a "by-election" is held to fill his seat. Apart from replenishing the membership in Parliament, by-elections afford valuable indications of public opinion between

[8] See James K. Pollock, *Money and Politics Abroad,* New York, 1932, chaps. 2–10.

general elections. The rules for by-elections are the same as those for general elections. They also often enable an important party leader who has been defeated in a general election to return to the House.

Influence on public opinion

The expression and guidance of public opinion is a function of the House, and in the exercise thereof, the House informs the public how it is being governed. England is a small country. No place is farther than 40 miles from the sea, and every Member of Parliament may visit his constituents easily over the week end—without the use of a plane. Moreover, constituencies are generally not large. Consequently the sentiment back home is usually quite easily discernible, and the members of the House are bound to reflect the views of their constituents when they return to Westminster. Issues which interest the public will quickly find their way to the floor of the House, and the government will be questioned closely. No matter how formidable the majority which the government may control in the House, it can neglect such expressions of sentiment only at its peril. Public opinion must therefore be placated wherever possible, and the government knows very well that the attitude which it takes toward the expression of widely felt grievances will determine the degree to which it may hope to be returned at the next election.

While Parliament thus brings issues and public sentiments to the attention of the government, the government in turn brings its views to the attention of the people. A successful government must lead as well as listen. Weak governments never have found favor with either public or Parliament. The electorate looks upon its representatives and its government as agents who are supposed to use their judgment within the framework of their electoral mandates. The British do not regard Members of Parliament as servants whose actions are constantly dictated by demands from their constituents.

In telling the public about its policies, the government affects and often changes public opinion. This is what Bagehot called the "teaching function." "A great and open council of considerable men cannot be placed in the middle of a society without altering that society." In the House of Commons, the government finds its best forum. Radio, and now television, may carry the Prime Minister's voice and face into millions of homes, but nothing can equal the atmosphere of the House of Commons. Here are to be found all the symbols of majesty, in the use of which the British have no equal. There is the crowded, but intimate, chamber in which the members and ministers speak quite informally, almost conversationally. There is the formidable figure of the Speaker on his throne with his wig, and there is the mace on the table of the House, the symbol of sovereignty. But at the same time the frontbench speakers may lean on that table and may sometimes even stretch their weary feet on it. Members, whether ministers or private members, speak from their places—a custom which is as practical as it is discouraging to unnecessary oratory; they do not march to a rostrum as they do in France or Ger-

1. The Speaker
2. The Prime Minister
3. Leader of the Opposition
4. Clerks of the House
5. The table
6. The mace
7. Government front bench, occupied by Ministers
8. Opposition front bench
9. Back benches
10. Minor Opposition parties
11. Press gallery
12. Members gallery
13. Commonwealth gallery
14. Peers and distinguished strangers gallery
15. Strangers gallery

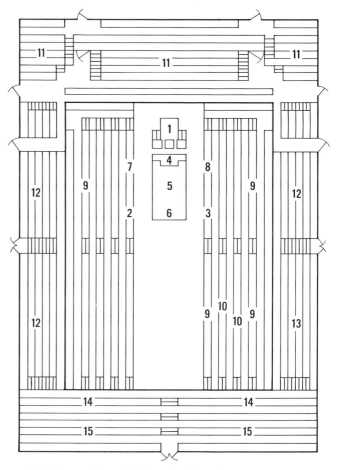

many. The House is not semicircular and amphitheatric, like the French National Assembly, the Weimar and Bonn legislatures, and the United States Congress, but oblong, with the table dividing the government and Opposition benches—a visual manifestation of the two-party system. The Prime Minister therefore speaks directly to the leader of the Opposition, who sits opposite him and who then rises and attempts to blast his speech.

When there is an important speech or debate, the chamber is crowded. Many members are unable to find seats, and their crowding of the chamber increases the emphasis on the importance of the occasion. That happens only on important occasions, but at such times the attention of the country is focused on the House. The public at large knows that it is witnessing government in action to a far greater degree than could be the case in the United States, where only one branch of the government can usually be observed at a time. When the chamber of the House of Commons was rebuilt after the destruction of the Second World War, it was again constructed with fewer seats than members.

Debate

The extent to which the actual content of Parliamentary debates shapes public opinion is an open question. The substance of these debates is carried on radio and television. The television is nationally owned and both by law and by tradition does its best to be fair to both sides. However voters' opinions are formed, whether by the news media, by the content of debates, or by reaction to the content of proposals, the implications of their opinions are soon felt by Parliament. In this way, Parliament may be said to be the focus of interaction between government and governed, in which each molds the other.

The effectiveness of Parliament is possible because it rests on certain assumptions which all or most members hold in common. It is agreed that there must be a government and that it must be able to govern. It is also agreed that there must be an Opposition which must be given adequate opportunities to oppose. Thus the Opposition fights the government tooth and nail, and when such redoubtable orators as Winston Churchill, in his prime, or Harold Macmillan, Aneurin Bevan, or Harold Wilson step into the arena, strong words fly. But when all is over and done and the majority has had its way, there is rarely an attempt at sabotage. The Opposition is mindful of its political opportunities in creating campaign issues, but it nevertheless often supports the government when, in its opinion, the good of the country requires it. At any rate, when the government carries its program to the floor of the House and the Opposition fights against it, it is understood that both are thereby fulfilling their constitutional functions, and that democratic government would be impossible unless both sides enjoyed considerable freedom. The Prime Minister who debates the leader of the Opposition knows that he is debating his probable successor. The members of the victorious majority party know that it is very rare for a party to enjoy a majority in the House for more than ten years and that consequently they will, one day, sit on the Opposition benches. It is therefore necessary for both sides that the rules of the game be observed.

The epitome of this system may be found in the Speaker, who presides over this contest. Once elected by the House, he divests himself of all party connections and rules with absolute impartiality. As a result, he retains his position as long as he chooses and is ordinarily reelected to Parliament. The Speaker used to be re-elected, unopposed. But in recent elections there has been ineffective opposition. No Speaker has ever failed to gain reelection although he never campaigns, as that would make him a partisan. In 1945 the Labor party received an overwhelming majority of seats in the House of Commons, but the Speaker, Colonel Clifton

The spirit of the House of Commons shines in the debates. A leading observer describes it as follows:[9]

> . . . you must remember that here are phlegmatic Englishmen and dour Scots. The "Celtic fringe" is too small to change the atmosphere, especially since the Irish went to enliven their own assembly in Dublin. Scenes are rare. There is no banging of desks; there are no desks to bang; and they would not be banged if there were. The moments of excitement are so rare that they go down in the political annals. . . . The task of the Speaker is easy. A calm word, a humorous comment, usually restores order. He has no bell, no hammer. The Speaker rises, the members sit, and the House is quiet. . . .

Debates may be spirited, but courtesy will usually be observed. New members and new cabinet ministers are customarily congratulated by the Opposition for their first speeches—after which they may be vigorously attacked. Many members remain in the House for many years, and have to learn to get along with each other. In America, there are many roads to political leadership, but in Great Britain there is only one—the House of Commons. Thus, this assembly of the great, the nearly great, and the merely dull has acquired an atmosphere of its own which emphasizes the British belief that the most desirable type of humanity is the gentleman.

School for leadership

In order to become a national figure in the public life of the country, a man has first to make a name for himself in Parliament. He will be listened to if he has something to say, but not otherwise. He will have some pretty sharp debating to do, and the manner in which he conducts himself will make a name for him—or not. A party may get a good many men elected, but it cannot make them leaders. Only after some years in the House do the talents begin to crystallize and the future leadership to emerge. The House is courteous, but not necessarily patient. It does not care much for insincerity or empty oratory. The halting speaker who has something to say is more likely to succeed than the dispenser of glittering generalities. A man who gains a reputation in the House of Commons is one who has faced sharp opposition almost daily and has stood his ground. It is after all no small thing to speak, knowing that sharp-witted opponents will put every word under a magnifying glass.

What is the result of all this? It is that leadership grows gradually as a man proves his worth in the daily Parliamentary struggle. "Dark horses," as we have noted, have no place in England. Leaders are almost always men who have served fairly long terms in Parliament, who have learned the art of give-and-take, and who have learned to get along with one another. By the time they become "frontbenchers," they have become steeped in Parliamentary tradition and House of Commons lore. "I am a child of the House of Commons," said Winston Churchill, with his gift for accurately descriptive prose.

---

[9] W. I. Jennings, *Parliament,* London, 1939, p. 20.

This is a most democratic way of attaining leadership. It is not democratic in the sense of ancient Greece, where citizens were held equally capable of holding office to such a degree that they were simply selected by lot, but it is democratic in the modern sense of the idea, which requires that all men should have an equal chance for leadership but that leadership itself be attained by talent and ability. The Conservative party may send the dull sons of famous houses to Parliament, the Labor party may send deserving but equally dull retired trade-union secretaries to the House, but from there on they are on their own. Winston Churchill was once distrusted by the leaders of the Conservative party because he had "crossed the floor"[10] before and was not considered safe. Sir Stafford Cripps had once been expelled from the Labor party. He too was not considered safe by the party leadership. Yet later their place was undisputed, even if they continued, like all strong men, to have their opponents on both sides of the House.

Grievances

Another function of the House is the airing of grievances. When a public official has made an unjust or arbitrary ruling, when negligence or gross inefficiency has been reported to exist in a branch of the public service, when an order or law has been applied unfairly, or when there are other real or imaginary grievances against the government or its agents, a Member of Parliament is bound to hear about it from a constituent. In that case he may bring the matter up in the House. He will question the responsible minister, ask for information on the matter, and demand to know what the minister intends to do about it. Now a minister may have a very comfortable margin of support in the House, but his reputation and leadership are bound to suffer if very many complaints are lodged against the manner in which he administers his department. The minister will therefore usually investigate the case unless the complaint is clearly unfounded, and if it is justified, some redress will usually follow.

This function works well in execution but it works even better by its mere existence. A minister may take pride in improving conditions which have been criticized in Parliament, but he much prefers not to be criticized. Consequently he keeps his eyes open for acts of maladministration, and is likely to press for improvements before the matter has a chance to reach the House. If the shortcomings are of major proportion, the government may appoint an impartial investigating board, sometimes even a Royal Commission whose recommendations usually carry great weight and also prevent the Opposition from making excessive political capital out of the defects found in the government's armor.

This method is not only effective in itself, it is also an excellent and convincing proof of democratic government. Any Member of Parliament, and through him the electorate at large, may put a mighty minister, even the Prime Minister himself, on the stand and demand an explanation. As long as that is possible, all talk of "dictatorship" in England will remain greatly exaggerated.

[10] I.e., changed political parties.

It must be clear from what has been said that Parliament accomplishes its task primarily by means of debate. Deprecators of democracy have been pleased to speak of it as a "talking shop" or a "debating society." Actually, the House of Commons may take pride in these designations. Debate is the essence of democracy; in the debate, different points of view may come into the open freely and without fear. Only where there is government by debate can decisions be made which are afterward obeyed without recourse to police sticks, concentration camps, or forced labor.

Debate is essential, but it can exist only when there is challenge. The members of the government party are somewhat subdued by considerations of party discipline and the desire not to show up their own leaders. But the Opposition is under no such restraint. The more vigorous its challenge, the better. The importance of the Opposition is now officially recognized, as the leader of the Opposition receives a salary which is charged to the Consolidated Fund and is thus not subject to annual appropriations. In return for this salary, he has no other obligation than to oppose the government. This fulfills two vital tasks: it keeps the government on its toes, and it provides a capable alternative government, should the cabinet in power fail.

Why the system works

This remarkable system operates on the basis of certain basic assumptions and conditions. In the first place it presupposes a two-party system. Its physical organization, its procedure, the assumption of the basic stability of governments, and the opportunity to carry out a clear electoral mandate are products of the prevailing two-party system. The fact that all previous experiences with coalition governments have been unsatisfactory, except in times of war, further underscores the validity of these stipulations.

Secondly, the British Parliamentary system presupposes a close relationship between the Members of Parliament and their constituents. This is necessary because, as we have seen, one of the functions of Parliament is to articulate prevailing public opinion on major issues and to voice grievances encountered by constituents. The fulfillment of this function is all the more vital because, short of elections, there are few other ways in which public opinion may press forcefully upon the government. There is no referendum, and public petitions are little used.[11] This close relationship between legislator and constituents is made possible by the single-member districts which are customary in the English-speaking world. This is true even though, as we have already seen, members do not have to reside in the constituency from which they are elected.

A third factor which ought not to be underestimated is the high reputation of

[11] The so-called "Peace Ballot" of 1935 was organized by the British League of Nations Union and had the nature of a petition. However, it attained such wide coverage that it is possible to speak of a quasi-referendum in this one isolated case.

Parliament, which causes able men to be attracted by a political career. In Britain the term "politician" does not have to contend with the same disparagement which it suffers in America, and a seat in the House of Commons is considered an outstanding achievement by many businesses and professions. The House of Commons may not be "the world's best club" because, as one writer stated, "there are too many bores in it," but it is still the meeting place of such great or near great as the current generation possesses.

Perhaps the most important condition of all is that in order to succeed, in order to provide for that common acceptance of the traditions and procedures of Parliament, it is necessary that Parliament be composed of "moderate men," who, in the words of Cardinal Newman, "are hard to be worked up to the dogmatic level." It might be easy to dismiss this by simply referring to an innate quality in the British which makes them moderate, but to be moderate in all cases and under every circumstance might border dangerously on an absence of conviction. Such an accusation cannot legitimately be made against the British people, and it has become quite absurd since their performance in the Second World War, especially when they stood alone. Bagehot and Laski intimated that this moderation springs from a common belief and a common philosophy, which in their view are caused by a common economic basis and similar economic interests. Others feel that this view is somewhat exaggerated and that all which is needed is that there should be no fundamental disagreement over the issue of constitutionalism.[12] Laski wonders whether such "moderation," which he recognizes to be the foundation of British parliamentarism as we know it, could endure if a socialist government were to take over the reins of government.

There is no doubt that this is an important point. Only moderate men can compromise, and freedom in a world of divergent views is hardly possible without compromise. Have the drastic economic changes which have taken place in England shaken the parliamentary system to its foundations? Obviously not. The victory of the Labor party in 1945 and its aftermath left the parliamentary system intact. Perhaps this is a manifestation of an increasing realization that the basic cleavage in the world of today is not between rival economic systems, but between rival political systems, between free government and dictatorship. On that issue, most of the British are of one mind, and apparently they can therefore still "safely afford to bicker."

The Speaker

The presiding officer of the House of Commons, and at the same time its official representative before the Lords and the Crown, is the Speaker. He has a number of formal duties, such as reading messages from the monarch, referring to the proper authorities the bills that are passed, and watching over amendments by

---

[12] Carl J. Friedrich, *Constitutional Government and Democracy,* Boston, 1946, p. 161.

the House of Lords to House of Commons bills, lest they infringe upon the financial privileges of the lower house.

His principal function, however, is that of presiding officer, in which capacity he controls the debate. He determines who shall speak, being guided by the consideration that ample time be provided for the presentation of both sides in an issue. Thus if a cabinet minister has made a statement, the Speaker will then call on the principal member of the Opposition who wishes to speak, and start the ball going back and forth. Beyond that, the Speaker wields considerable power in recognizing members. Sometimes such members may ask their whips to let the Speaker know of their desire to address the House, but it has been charged that the Speaker is more likely to recognize a member whose forensic abilities and sense of humor will hold the interest of the House than one who is deadly dull. Happily also, for the House, the Speaker does not allow speeches to be read.

The Speaker rules on points of order, and his powers are extensive. He may refuse a motion for closure or a motion whose purpose is, in his judgment, to cause delay. He may refuse motions which are irregular or improper. For instance, he will refuse a motion creating a tax or fee which has not been recommended by the Crown, or a motion which anticipates matters which have been reserved for later consideration. He may also rule out a bill if it is introduced as a private bill but ought to have been a public one, or if the proper committee stage has not been observed. More often, however, he will call the attention of the House to motions or bills which are out of order and will attempt to secure their voluntary withdrawal.

The Speaker has considerable disciplinary powers to prevent disorder. The most frequently employed device is the custom that no member may stand and speak while the Speaker stands. Thus when the Speaker rises, the member who is on his feet must sit down, and the Speaker must be heard in silence. This is usually sufficient. When it is not, the Speaker may "name" a member for the purpose of disciplinary action by the House, leading to that member's suspension. He may cause the suspension of a member or his withdrawal, by placing a nondebatable motion to that effect before the House. He may also reprimand members and call them to order. None of his rulings on points of order can be challenged when they are issued. To do so would entail disobedience and might result in disciplinary punishment. Challenge is permissible only later and after notice has been given.

The Speaker is also in charge of the administrative department and of officials who perform the "housekeeping" functions. The Clerk of the House is under him, although appointed independently. The Speaker receives a salary of £5,000 ($14,000) per year and his apartment in the Palace of Westminster. On his retirement, he is offered a viscountcy and a pension.

Since 1855, the Chairman of Ways and Means has been Deputy Speaker. If he is absent, a Deputy Chairman (of Ways and Means) takes over the chair.

The party whips also play an important role in the maintenance of orderly procedure in the House, because they exercise primary control over their party members and maintain liaison between their Parliamentary party and the chair.

Privileges of members

Members of Parliament enjoy the customary privileges and immunities of legislators in all democratic countries. It should be noted, however, that their freedom from arrest extends only to civil cases and is therefore virtually extinct, because arrest for civil offenses is no longer in use. Technically the House may itself sentence a member to imprisonment for contempt, but this right is not in use. Members may be arrested and tried for ordinary criminal offenses, and the House will not interfere. In fact, during the Second World War, a Member of Parliament, Captain Ramsay, a member of the British Union of Fascists and associate of the notorious Sir Oswald Mosley, was interned without trial for the duration of the war under orders of the Home Secretary (Herbert Morrison) in conformity with Section 18B of the Defence of the Realm Regulation. In most other countries, members of parliament are immune from arrest for criminal offenses in order to protect them from political persecution. The British, however, appear to be unworried about such a contingency, which seems remote in view of their attitude and training. It goes without saying, however, that a Member of Parliament is not answerable for criminal words uttered in the House. As to other crimes committed in the House, opinion is divided, especially as it would be difficult to show that such a crime was part of the proceedings of the House.

Members of Parliament (Commons) receive a stipend of £1,750 ($4,900) per year plus £2 per day when the House is in session (except Fridays). The leader of the Opposition receives £2,000. They receive no office space and no assistance for secretarial help.

Procedure

Freedom of debate is assured in the Parliament, but the public may be excluded at any time. It is a privilege of ancient origin that if a member takes notice that "there are strangers in the House,"[13] the Speaker is obliged to clear the galleries. This privilege is rarely used, because it is difficult to keep secret a matter which has been revealed to over 600 people. More often the government will simply refuse to discuss a question which bears on the national security. However, during the darkest days of World War II, when the Prime Minister wished to fortify national unity by taking the House into his confidence, secret sessions were held very successfully.

Closely connected with the right to exclude strangers is Parliament's control over the publication of its debates and proceedings. They have been published for

---

[13] This is merely a formula, as there are always strangers in the House.

a long time, and although they have been reported officially ever since 1910, they are still colloquially referred to as "Hansard," after the printer who was first authorized to publish Parliamentary debates in 1809.[14] However, both Houses have retained the privilege to forbid publication of a particular debate.

Most of the rights and privileges of Parliament, which can be found in the formidable volume of Sir Thomas Erskine May (usually quoted by its abbreviated title, *Parliamentary Practice*),[15] are based on convention. So also is the pageantry which surrounds Parliament. The wigged Speaker on his throne is a formidable-looking figure. An air of formality prevailing in the House, even though the tone may be conversational, is revealed in the requirement that all members be "honorable," if they are not "Right Honorable,"[16] that all lawyers be "learned" and all officers "gallant."[17] At "division" time, when a vote is to be cast, the members file into the two "division lobbies," and are counted upon their return into the House, whereby a generally reliable and unexcited result is achieved.

The opening of a new session of Parliament provides an exceptional opportunity for pageantry. The government declaration, comparable to the American President's "state of the Union" message to Congress, is presented in the form of the "speech from the throne," read by the monarch or by the Lord Chancellor in the House of Lords and by the Speaker in the House of Commons.[18] The speech itself is of course drawn up by the government, and the Queen's private views do not remotely enter into it.

Once a new House has been elected, it is convoked within a few weeks. There is no "lame-duck" session. The House may adjourn at any time, regardless of what the House of Lords does. But only the government (Crown) may prorogue, and both houses must be prorogued together. Adjournment merely interrupts the session; prorogation terminates all business, which cannot be taken up again except *de novo*, i.e., beginning all over. Thus a bill which has passed its second reading before adjournment may pass on to its ultimate passage, but the same bill whose course has been interrupted by prorogation must be taken up all over again just as if it were an entirely new bill.

The dissolution of Parliament is the prerogative of the Crown, i.e., the government, as we have seen. Usually this takes the form of a prorogation followed by a proclamation of dissolution. If the House is not dissolved or if it has its life prolonged by act of Parliament, it expires automatically after five years according to the Parliament Act of 1911. However, this is never actually allowed to happen,

---

[14] There are Parliamentary records considerably antedating Hansard's, but the consistent, complete, and continuous record begins in 1809.
[15] Sir Thomas Erskine May, *A Treatise on the Law, Privileges, Proceedings and Usages of Parliament*, 15th ed. by Sir Gilbert Campion, London, 1950. See also Sir Gilbert Campion, *An Introduction to the Procedure of the House of Commons*, New York, 1950, 2d ed.
[16] The title Right Honorable is given to all Privy Councillors.
[17] Jennings, *op. cit.*, p. 19.
[18] To reaffirm their independence, both houses give a sham bill a first reading before proceeding with the debate on the speech. Nothing further is done about this bill.

and the government always makes use of its privilege of determining the date of a general election which appears most auspicious for its reelection. But at times of exceptional crisis, especially during war, Parliament has prolonged its life far beyond its ordinary limits. The Parliament of 1910 lasted until 1918; the Parliament of 1935 until 1945.

Until 1867, Parliament was automatically dissolved by the monarch's death, called "demise of the Crown." Now this is no longer the case, but it is customary that Parliament meet immediately and take the oath once more. This was also the case in 1936 when the abdication of Edward VIII was declared to be a demise of the Crown.

The leadership of the government manifests itself very clearly in the order of business. The House meets at 2:45 P.M. on Monday through Thursday and at 11 A.M. on Friday. Precedence is normally given to government business. Before Easter, Wednesdays are allowed for motions by private members[19] and Fridays for their bills (second reading). After Easter these are allowed only on certain Fridays and not at all on Wednesdays, but even that modest amount of time may be curtailed.

The period from 3 to 3:45 P.M. is set aside for questions. This, as we have seen, is an opportunity to bring up grievances. It is also an opportunity to elicit information on facts and intentions of the government. Sometimes the questions provide an opportunity for harassing the government, and the number and intensity of questions will increase when there are strong feelings on a subject. Due notice of a question is given in writing so that the minister may prepare himself, but under certain conditions of urgency, verbal notice may be acceptable. However, there ought to be no surprises in the question period, and the questioner is not allowed the elaborate speeches which are associated with interpellations in the French parliament. All elaboration must be left to the time set aside for debate.

Not all questions call for an oral reply, and the minister is not legally bound to answer any question, but of course the House will draw its own conclusion if he does not.

In the question period the British government does not risk its life in the same manner as the French government does when there is an interpellation. Nevertheless, the skill with which this period is handled by the respective ministers will have a strong bearing on their political futures and the regard which the people have for them. The question period is not only a tool in the hands of the Opposition or of private members in order to cause the government embarrassment; it can also become an effective means for the government to make important declarations, defeat whispering campaigns, and generally assert its leadership. On the other hand, the question period serves to remind the government of its ties to the House of Commons and of the limits beyond which it cannot go. Every democratic government needs an occasional reminder of this kind.

---

[19] A Member of Parliament who is not a member of the government.

As the time of the House of Commons is carefully rationed in order to provide an orderly continuity of business, it becomes clear that some measure for an enforced closure of debate is necessary. Ordinarily an agreement is made "behind the Speaker's chair" between the government and the Opposition with regard to the amount of time allowed for debate, and the Speaker will see to it that the agreement is carried out. If that fails, however, there are several ways in which closure can be brought about. Methods for closure became necessary in 1881 when the Irish Nationalists obstructed the government to such an extent that there was danger of the ordinary procedures of Parliament being destroyed. The result was the adoption of the so-called "simple closure" by which a member moves "that the question be now put."[20] The Speaker is free to allow or disallow the motion, having due deference to the rights of the minority and the demands of a fair and orderly procedure. But if the Speaker does entertain the motion, it must be supported by a majority of members present, or at any rate by not less than 100 members. If adopted, this motion brings the debate to an end.

A more drastic closure method, adopted in 1887, is known as the "guillotine." It presupposes that a motion will be made, seconded, and passed by the House whereby the debate will cease at a certain, specified time, and all issues bearing on the measure or bill in question will be brought to a vote. By this measure, a precise timetable may be established for every phase of a pending bill.

A rather unique form of closure is the so-called "kangaroo," first used in 1909. In contrast to the "guillotine," this does not specify a time for ending debate, but the Speaker or Deputy Speaker is empowered to select those clauses and amendments of a bill which he thinks most appropriate for discussion and to exclude all others. This invests the presiding officer with grave responsibility, but there is virtually no evidence of real abuse. If well administered, this method allows a maximum of useful debate within a minimum of time.

These rules for shortening debate have been indispensable, in view of the volume of business. But they also have the disadvantage of sometimes preventing a member from properly informing himself of an issue before the House.

Legislation

The process of legislation, which takes up a large portion of Parliament's time, is a reasonably simple one. Any member, be he a backbencher or a proud inhabitant of the Treasury bench,[21] has the right to introduce a bill. If he is not a member of the government, his bill will be termed a "private member's bill." It is deposited on the Speaker's table after due notice, but without special permission. The title of the bill is then read, and that action constitutes "first reading," although

---

[20] Not to be confused with the motion "that the previous question now be put," which puts the principal issue up for vote immediately.
[21] The front bench on the majority side of the House on the Speaker's right, on which cabinet members sit, is called the Treasury bench.

the bill as first deposited is likely to be merely a dummy. There is no debate at such occasions, but under the "ten-minute ride," the member introducing a bill may make a brief introductory speech in order to dispel possible misconceptions, and an equally short rebuttal statement will follow. Most bills may be introduced either in the House of Commons or in the House of Lords. Financial bills must originate in the House of Commons, while judiciary bills are first presented to the House of Lords.

The second reading of the bill is its real hurdle. It is fully debated on a specific date. If there is organized opposition to it, its enemies will propose motions designed to destroy it. Such a motion either may be a direct negative, which pigeonholes the bill for the day, or it may be a motion that the bill be read six months later—at which time the House is probably not meeting—thus killing the bill for the session, or it may be a resolution which affects the character of the bill and thus kills it too. Only the general scope and idea of the bill are discussed on second reading, and the Speaker prevents the debate from becoming too technical.

Government bills are likely to pass because of the safe majority which is usually at the disposal of the government, unless the latter takes the whips off and leaves the matter to the individual conscience of the members. Private bills may have tougher sledding, and the casualty rate is considerable.

Committees

After the second reading has been passed successfully, the bill goes to committee. The committee stage is familiar to all bona fide legislatures, but the British approach is in marked contrast to its American, French, and German counterparts. Parliament knows four types of committees: Committees of the Whole House, Select and Sessional Committees, Standing Committees, and Joint Committees.

Much business is transacted in the Committee of the Whole House, which is merely the entire membership of the House deliberating under an informal procedure and under the presidency of the Chairman of Committees, also called Chairman of Ways and Means. When dealing with taxation the Committee of the Whole House is called the Committee of Ways and Means or the House in Ways and Means; when dealing with appropriations it is termed Committee of Supply or the House in Supply.

Ordinarily a bill will go to a Standing Committee unless it is a money bill. The nature of the Standing Committee is derived from its history. Originally all bills were considered by the Committee of the Whole House. In 1882 two committees were created, whose number was raised to four in 1907. In 1919 the number was increased to six, but later diminished, and at present there are just five Standing Committees. One of them is the Scottish Committee, which considers all bills concerned with Scotland. The others are simply called Committees A, B, C, and D. Select Committees are appointed for examining a specific problem, and report to the House on their findings. A special form of Select Committees are the Sessional

Committees, which function during an entire session of the House of Commons, particularly the Committee of Selection (which in America would be called a committee on committees), the Committee on Standing Orders (the American term would be rules committee), and the Committee on Public Accounts.

When a bill solely affecting Wales and Monmouthshire is under consideration, all the members from that area must be put on the committee. The members of the committees are chosen by the Committee of Selection, which is appointed at the beginning of each session and is composed according to the proportional strength of parties in the House.

If the bill is a money bill, it will go to the Committee of the Whole (House), but the House may always rule by motion that any other bill shall also go to that Committee. Private bills go to the Private Bill Committee or to the Committee on Unopposed Bills. Bills to confirm a provisional order are treated like private bills. Certain bills may also go to Select Committees, but they can only report, and the bills must then still be considered in the Committee of the Whole.

The committee system was established to relieve the congestion of business in the House, caused partly by the obstructive tactics of the Irish Nationalists as mentioned above, and consequently the committees are *not* small expert bodies undertaking special studies of the merits of bills, but rather miniature editions of the House, headed by a chairman whose powers and functions are very much like those of the Speaker, including the closure rules.[22] Each committee has a regular membership of twenty, but the Committee of Selection may add as many as thirty for special bills. There are rarely fewer than thirty all told.

The Standing Committees do not have special subjects, as is customary in other democracies, but the Speaker assigns bills to them more or less at will. The purpose of the committees is to put the bill into final shape for adoption after its general character has already been approved at second reading and before it has to be reported out. Public hearings are not conducted by Standing Committees. Where such hearings seem desirable they are usually held by an extraparliamentary body appointed by the government, such as a Royal Commission, but that is done before the bill is introduced.

The British committee system has worked quite well within its frame of reference, i.e., in doing work which would otherwise have to be accomplished by the entire House with resulting loss of time. But it usually brings no expert scrutiny to bear upon a bill. The House adopts bills on second reading primarily on their general merits, and the Standing Committees are neither capable of screening the technical details nor staffed for the purpose of doing so. There is therefore the danger that Parliament may be abdicating its role and becoming a rubber stamp, since at no time in the procedure does a member find out—except possibly from government sources—just what a technical bill is all about. Small wonder therefore that there has been some agitation for more expert committees. But an expert committee is likely to contradict the government and to burden bills with amendments

---

[22] However, the "guillotine" is not in use.

which were neither proposed nor desired by the government, so all governments to date have preferred the greater docility of the present system.

Eventually the bill is reported out and subjected to a third reading. At this stage debate may again break out, although all viewpoints are likely to have been aired, and the fate of the bill is probably quite certain. Substantial amendments are not accepted at this stage unless the bill is to be referred back to committee. The "division" (vote) is taken, and that is the end as far as the House of Commons is concerned.

The treatment given ordinary bills is not unlike the procedure applied to private bills and the confirmation of provisional orders. The demarcation line between public and private bills is not absolutely fixed, because the House may declare any bill a public bill. But ordinarily a private bill is one which deals with a special local situation. Before a private bill can be introduced, a petition must be filed with the "examiner of private bills," an officer appointed in each House. It is also demanded that certain preliminary steps be taken in order that all persons affected by the bill may be duly notified. After the second reading, the bill is assigned to a Select Committee of four persons (five in the House of Lords) which conducts such hearings as seem appropriate. If there is no opposition, the bill is assigned to the committee on unopposed bills. From there on it follows the same course as do ordinary bills.

This method of dealing with private bills saves the House a great deal of work, but since hearings are held, witnesses heard, and evidence collected, it takes an inordinate amount of time from the members who are assigned to sit on such committees. Nor are political laurels to be gathered in such hearings, because the treatment of private bills is distinguished by a nonpartisan character.

In order to diminish the number of private bills, government departments have statutory authority to issue orders, which generally need subsequent sanction by Parliamentary act. These orders are usually assembled in groups which may be passed in one act. Such Confirmations of Provisional Orders are handled like private bills. To an ever-increasing extent Parliament vests direct, statutory authority in government departments to issue orders without subsequent confirmation by Parliament. Such "delegated legislation" naturally increases the power of the administrative machinery and has already been touched upon.

Quite different from private bills are "private members' bills." These are simply bills proposed by an ordinary member of the House of Commons, usually a backbencher, and not by the government or on behalf of the government. Such bills may be introduced during brief periods on two days of the week, and few members avail themselves of this opportunity, because their chances of success are virtually nil. The time alloted for the critical second reading is also very brief, and often government business is allowed to cut into it. Moreover, not every private member's bill actually receives a second reading, and if there are more such bills than time allows, lots are drawn in order to determine which one shall receive a second reading. If the government opposes a private member's bill, it has no chance to come to life. If the government acquiesces, it may eventually be enacted. But the government does not care for this invasion of its legislative leadership. Moreover, the passage of a bill requires so many little details which are ordinarily performed by a number of experienced people, but which, in the case of a private member's bill, he must perform himself, that most members find such an effort not very rewarding.

There is one more type of legislation, apart from money bills, which will be dealt with separately. There is an established church in England, which has the right to submit certain measures to Parliament for enactment. Usually this submission is a formality, but not always, as was indicated in 1927 and 1928 when the House of Commons refused to accept certain changes in the Book of Common Prayer. When such a step is proposed to Parliament by the National Assembly of the Church of England, Parliament can only accept or reject; it cannot amend.

If a bill has originated in the House of Commons, it goes to the House of Lords after having passed its third reading. There it undergoes very much the same treatment as it received in the House of Commons. There are no regular Standing Committees in the House of Lords,[23] but Select Committees are frequently resorted to, and ample use is made of the Committee of the Whole. If the Lords agree, the bill is submitted to the Royal Assent, which makes it final. If the Lords do not agree, attempts are made to compromise the difficulties. Such conference committees, however, deal only in written messages nowadays; a "free" conference, i.e., a really negotiating (oral) committee, is no longer used. More often, informal discussions between party leaders will bring results.

If the Lords refuse to compromise or give in, and if the House remains equally stubborn, the bill (but not a financial bill) becomes law even without the consent of the Lords after one year's delay, as stipulated under the Parliament Act of 1911 as amended in 1949. Private bills and confirmations of provisional orders are not under the protection of the Parliament Act as amended, and the Lords can therefore kill such measures outright. However, such an attitude on the part of the Lords is neither practical—as will be seen later—nor expected.

The final step is the Royal Assent. This is a pure formality, since it must be given and cannot be refused. The refusal formula, *le roy s'avisera* (the King will consider it), has not been employed since 1707. Using the ancient legal formulas in archaic French, the Royal Assent is given in the words *la reine le veult* (the Queen desires it) for ordinary bills, *soit fait comme il est desiré* (be that as it is desired) for private bills, and *la reine remercie ses bons sujets, accepte leur bénévolence, et ainsi le veult* (the Queen thanks her good subjects, accepts their benevolence, and thus desires it) for money bills.

Money bills

The enactment of money bills is somewhat different from that of others. In the first place they must originate in the House of Commons and in the Committee

---

[23] The so-called "standing" committee for textual revision is formed at the beginning of each session.

of the Whole. No appropriation for the public service nor any other drain on the public revenue will be considered by the House unless it has been proposed by the government (Crown). Nor will any taxation measure be taken up unless recommended by the Crown. The government thus has undivided power of initiative in financial matters.[24]

The burden, responsibility, and power of proposing appropriations, especially the budget (estimates), rests with the Treasury and its chief, the Chancellor of the Exchequer. But in so far as the budget is an expression of cabinet policy, the entire cabinet shares in this responsibility.

Parliament prepares for the budget by appointing the Committee of Supply and the Committee of Ways and Means at the beginning of each session. But this is a formality since both committees are merely the Whole House deliberating under an informal procedure. The budget message itself is invariably presented by the Chancellor of the Exchequer in person, and strict secrecy is preserved until the budget is announced in the House of Commons.[25] The budget bill then goes to committee. The duration of the debate on each item and on the total is strictly regulated and limited; if the allotted time is exceeded, the "guillotine" rule is applied. Revenues and expenditures are discussed during the same period and follow the same procedure. All proposals are handled in groups and passed in the same manner.

All resolutions are then assembled in two statutes, the Appropriation Act and the Finance Act. Earlier in the session, Parliament has passed a Consolidated Fund Bill, in order to make up any deficiency and hold funds on account for the current year. The Appropriation Act now authorizes all necessary expenditures to be made from the general fund (Consolidated Fund)[26] while the Finance Act approves all necessary revenues.

Having passed the House of Commons, the money bills now go to the House of Lords. Since the Parliament Act of 1911, the upper house has lost all control over finance bills. If a bill, duly certified by the Speaker to be a money bill,[27] has been received by the House of Lords at least one month before the end of its session, it receives the Royal Assent and becomes law either upon the approval of the Lords or a month after it has been submitted to them, whether they have passed or even considered it or not. But even if the House of Lords considers a money bill, it may not amend it under any circumstances.

Opinion is divided on the advantages or demerits of the British system of financial legislation. From the government's standpoint, the British system is nearly ideal. It permits the government to prepare a consolidated budgetary plan with the virtual assurance that it will not be seriously changed. The kind of treatment which

---

[24] A private member may move that the government ought to spend more or less on certain subjects.

[25] An ill-advised remark on the budget by Chancellor Hugh Dalton led to his resignation on Nov. 13, 1947.

[26] Not all expenditures come from the Consolidated Fund.

[27] The Speaker decides what is a money bill and what is not. His decision cannot be challenged.

the budget usually gets from ax-wielding Congressmen in the United States is unknown in Great Britain. The government is therefore in no position to blame any shortcomings on the failure of Parliament to appropriate the necessary funds. Its responsibility before the public is clear and unequivocal.

On the other hand, it is obvious that the so-called power of the purse which Parliament is alleged to possess is not a reality, even though its theoretical existence might conceivably have a sobering effect on the government. At no time is the budget really scrutinized or seriously debated in either house. "Budget Day," when the Chancellor of the Exchequer makes his great budget speech and presents the document to the House of Commons, is indeed one of the greatest days, if not *the* greatest day, of a Parliamentary session. The speech is long and detailed, invariably lasting several hours, and the ensuing debate is extremely fierce. But the debate may deal only with the general character of the budget, not its details; in effect it is the entire government policy which is at stake, and the Opposition brings out every objection and grievance it can think of. The vote on the budget is then a test of confidence in the government which, in a House where the government has a clear majority, can never be in serious doubt.

Nor can the members of the House and its committees be expected to discharge their alleged responsibilities as "holders of the purse strings." We have seen that all initiative must come from the government as far as financial legislation is concerned, that bills which involve expenditures are not accepted from private members, only from the Crown (government). Parliament may not even increase the appropriations over what the government asks. Theoretically it may decrease them, but that is theoretical to the point of nonexistence. A vote to decrease expenditures below the government figure would be tantamount to a vote of nonconfidence, at the very least in the government department for which the outlay is being asked; at the most it would be a vote of nonconfidence in the government as a whole. That is unthinkable as long as the government has a majority in the House, which is ordinarily the case.

There is not even enough time for an itemized scrutiny of the budget, or enough expert knowledge in the House to evaluate the intricate relationship between the figures in the budget and the inner working of the departments and activities for which they are designed. If there were a great deal of time to study the estimates, some remedy might be found, but the whole bulky document must be whipped through in a mere twenty-six days. Thus an evaluation of the budget would be impossible even if it were contained in a clear and precise statement. But that is by no means the case. In fact, by failing to give an understandable picture of the country's financial situation, the budget hides more than it reveals.

A further handicap is the unwieldy character of the Committee of Ways and Means—which is none other than the Committee of the Whole. A detailed examination of a large technical document would be quite impossible in a body of that size.

This all adds up to one inevitable conclusion: the so-called "power over the purse strings" of Parliament is largely a fiction. It does not exist. Power over the purse rests in the cabinet, especially in the Treasury. This situation is mitigated by the already discussed need for harmony between government and Parliament, and the resultant desire on the part of the government to compromise—preferably before the situation comes to a head—issues on which strong feelings exist in the House. And if a government were ever to be imprudent enough to try to maintain itself without the basic confidence of the House of Commons, the dormant financial powers of the House could be put to good advantage. As far as the control of the legality and propriety of government spending is concerned, it is adequately exercised by an independent official, the Comptroller and Auditor-General.[28]

Criticism of this situation has naturally been protracted. The Ninth Report of the Select Committee on National Expenditure of 1918 gave the following reasons for a needed reform:

1. Control in Committee of Supply is not in fact a control over the Estimates.
2. Treasury control, invaluable as it is up to a point, is not a substitute for Parliamentary control.
3. Control by ministers is not enough—such a doctrine would convert the responsibility of ministers into irresponsibility.

The result has been the establishment of a Select Committee on Estimates which has functioned with some interruptions since 1920. However, the impact made by that committee has been disappointing. As the estimates still go their customary route, the Committee on Estimates has looked into only a few of the items. It has made some suggestions for possible improvements, which have been quite valuable, but they have in no way restored financial control to Parliament. The Committee on Public Accounts has made even less of an impact, although its chairman is always a member of the Opposition.

Criticism of Parliament has often centered on the fact that the House is overworked and is therefore unable to give adequate attention to bills. Various schemes for the devolution of powers have been suggested as possible relief measures. One group of proposals favored regional assemblies, composed of members of the House of Commons for the area concerned, plus a Council of Peers. But these schemes have not proved practical or acceptable. Too much of the business of legislation is national in character, and Parliament derives its great reputation and influence from its role as the single national assembly of political leaders.

The other group of suggestions has attempted to propel the House of Com-

---

[28] The Exchequer and Audit Departments Act of 1866 (29 & 30 Vict., c. 39), as amended in 1921 and 1939, established the office of the Comptroller and Auditor-General, who reports directly to the House of Commons, who may be removed only upon Joint Address of Parliament, and who has tenure like a judge of the High Court. He controls the issue of all public money, audits the accounts of all departments, and reports on them to the House of Commons. It is his job to see to it that all pertinent rules are observed, but he has no power over the rules themselves.

mons in the direction of the American Congressional committee system. Naturally such a possibility is not regarded with favor in government circles, who fear that their well-laid plans might be carved up and rendered unrecognizable by an all-too-independent committee. Opposition members have viewed such proposals usually with somewhat more favor than the government. But since opposition parties become government parties sooner or later, nothing has come of such ideas, nor is any far-reaching reform likely to occur in the foreseeable future, especially as many British and other observers prefer the British system by which bills are drafted into final shape by the respective government departments under cabinet control, rather than by legislative committees and their staffs as is the practice in the United States.

A novel institution was adopted in 1966 with the creation of a Parliamentary Commissioner. This was modeled after the Scandinavian *ombudsman,* whose function it is to ferret out grievances and shortcomings and to instigate remedial action. He may be called a procurator of the public interest or a one-man review board. In view of the complexity of modern government, this institution has been discussed in many countries and was introduced outside Scandinavia in Australia and New Zealand.[29] There is also a certain similarity to the German Defense Commissioner (*Wehrbeauftragter*) whose functions, however, extend only to matters related to the military services.

B. THE HOUSE OF LORDS

Among the many quaint and ancient institutions which exist in the United Kingdom, the House of Lords is one of the most archaic. Its nature, role, and composition are unique in comparison with the second chambers of other countries. The Parliament Acts of 1911 and 1949 have shorn the "other house," as the House of Lords is sometimes called, of much of its former power, but it still leads a vigorous life, and its reform is still a much debated question. Its role is by no means nominal.

Composition

Countries which desire a second chamber have been exercised over the problem of how to make the "upper house" representative, but at the same time have it composed in such a way as to prevent it from becoming an exact replica of the "lower house." No such problem confronts the British: the House of Lords is completely unrepresentative, and it is never a replica of the House of Commons.

Its members are the princes of the blood (who take no part in the consideration of controversial issues) and the hereditary peers, who are either the descendents of peers (the majority) or newly created lords. In addition there are the so-

[29] Vincent Powell Smith, "An Ombudsman for Britain?", *Law Journal,* Vol. 115 (1955), p. 657. In Sweden there are actually two such procurators, one in charge of civil affairs (*justitieombudsman*), and the other for military affairs (*militieombudsman*). Cf. Nils Andrén, *Modern Swedish Government,* Stockholm, 1961.

called "representative peers" of Scotland and Ireland. These peers are selected by and from the peers of their respective groups to sit in the House of Lords. There are a few Irish lords left,[30] and their Scottish brothers number only sixteen. A fifth group is the Lords Spiritual who represent only the English branch of the Church of England.

The sixth group are the Lords of Appeal in Ordinary, often called "Law Lords." Since the House of Lords is the highest court for the United Kingdom, the inclusion of jurists is desirable. Nine Lords of Appeal in Ordinary are created for that purpose. They hold tenure for life, and receive a salary for their judicial work. They retain their membership in the House of Lords even after resigning their offices as Lords of Appeal, but their seats are vacated upon their death and do not descend to their heirs.

A seventh group, the life peers, was created in 1958. This is the only group which has women members entitled to sit in the House of Lords.

While appointment to the peerage may be declined, until 1963 there was no way of escaping hereditary peerage. Since a peer may not sit in the House of Commons this effectively stifled some promising careers. As has been noted, this rule was changed in 1963 to allow peers to resign their peerage for life and thus sit in the House of Commons. The 1963 change also allowed Scottish and Irish peers to sit in the Commons.

The formidable array of titles and the ancient pageantry which indicates the derivation of the House of Lords from the Grand Council (*Magnum Concilium*) of the Norman and Angevin kings give the impression that the upper house is an aristocratic body. This is not true unless "aristocracy" is to be understood as a purely formalistic and meaningless term. Not "aristocracy" but "plutocracy" is the word for the House of Lords. The ancient titled families of England form but a very small minority in the House; few titles date back further than the eighteenth century, and half of them were created in the twentieth century. The wealth of the country represented in the House of Lords was originally based primarily on landed property, but the Industrial Revolution shifted the emphasis toward the upper middle classes, the new capitalists.[31] Of course not all men in the House of Lords are wealthy; peerages are also created for "political and public services." In fact, an ever-increasing number of newly created peers are former politicians who, after spending their prime in the House of Commons, are permitted to achieve semi-retirement in the House of Lords. Thus an opportunity is created to retain certain men in public life when they are no longer willing to submit to the rough-and-tumble of periodic election campaigns. Much of the actual work of the upper house

---

[30] The summoning of the Irish lords for the purpose of electing representative peers was accomplished by writ issued by the Lord Chancellor of Ireland. After the demise of that office in 1920, the responsibility passed on to the Lord Lieutenant, but that office has also ceased to be, and there appears to be no legal way in which representative peers may be elected from Ireland.

[31] There is hardly any large corporation which does not have one or several of its directors in the House of Lords.

is done by them, and their ranks swell especially when a Liberal or Labor government is in office, attempting to increase its slender representation in the House of Lords.

Finally, appointment to a peerage and a seat in the House of Lords is an excellent opportunity to confer a much-coveted honor on a man who has gained great distinction in the sciences, arts, or other fields.

Because the overwhelming majority of the noble Lords represent wealth or are descendants of wealth, the political composition of the House is overwhelmingly Conservative. About 600 members of the House of Lords are Conservative, less than 100 profess allegiance to the Liberal party, whereas a few more than 20 belong to the Labor party. Of course there are never that many peers at any one session, but the Conservative majority is still formidable. Also permanent officials and legislators have a well-known tendency to become more conservative, with the result that the majority of the upper house is not only Conservative in party affiliation and sympathy, but actually is even more conservative than the leadership and majority of their party in the House of Commons. They are Conservative not so much out of party loyalty as because they are convinced that the country would go to ruin unless governed by Conservative principles.

Party affiliation is a matter of preference, not of necessity, for peers. Their positions are secure, they need not be concerned about the good graces of a party leadership, and they need not appeal to the country for a vote of confidence. They need not follow the party whip, and they may defy the government with impunity. In summation, they are responsible to no one—but then no one is responsible to them. The life of the government depends in no way on the wishes of the House of Lords. Were it otherwise, only Conservative governments could exist.

Procedure and organization

The atmosphere in the House of Lords is quite different from that of the House of Commons. The debate is more leisurely than in the House of Commons, but the daily sessions are not nearly as long. There is a tradition that noble Lords ought to be allowed their dinners at home, and members raising questions dangerously near the dinner hour are regarded with disfavor. There is no pressure on members by their constituents—for they have none. Few of the members hold office in the cabinet. Freedom of speech is virtually unrestricted, because the presiding officer, the Lord Chancellor, has far more limited powers over the debate than are enjoyed by the Speaker in the House of Commons. Moreover the Lords will not hesitate to overrule the Lord Chancellor, who, after all, is a partisan and therefore cannot be regarded as an impartial officer of the type presented by the Speaker.

A visitor to the House of Lords will often find the level of the debate high, and on certain occasions higher than in the House of Commons. This does not mean that there is more talent in the House of Lords—as a matter of fact, a large majority of the Lords are exceedingly and sometimes painfully dull. But most of that type do not attend meetings. It simply means that approximately one-fourth of the Lords are former members of the House of Commons, and a good many are retired statesmen, administrators, professors, etc., all of whom are more likely to attend, especially when an interesting topic is scheduled for debate. It may also be said that since most Lords belong to the same party, they do not have to debate party politics; their discussion may therefore center on the technical problems of the bill or motion under consideration. Many motions will be made and amendments proposed, but most of them are usually withdrawn if the government refuses to accept them.

The organization of the House of Lords closely parallels that of the House of Commons. The presiding officer is, as we have seen, the Lord Chancellor, a member of the cabinet. He presides while sitting on the traditional "wool-sack," which is technically outside the confines of the House of Lords in order that a man who is not a peer may nevertheless be Lord Chancellor. But the point is not important, since Lord Chancellors are invariably peers or are created peers immediately after their appointment.

There is also the Lord Chairman of committees, who corresponds to the Chairman of Ways and Means in the lower house and presides over the Committee of the Whole. There is the clerk, called Clerk of the Parliament, and the equivalent to the sergeant at arms, who bears the more colorful title of "gentleman usher of the black rod." The "Leader of the House of Lords," i.e., the representative of the government, is usually the Lord President (of the Privy Council).

Powers

Originally the House of Lords was coequal to the House of Commons. The Lords could not dismiss a government, but they could stop legislation dead in its tracks. This situation came to a head in 1909 when the Lords defeated the budget of the Liberal Asquith government which was presented by Lloyd George, the Chancellor of the Exchequer. By that time the reform of the House of Lords had already been under serious consideration, and the speech from the throne in 1907 had alluded thereto. It was therefore with a singularly bad sense of timing that the Lords decided to defeat the budget which suggested a number of social reforms. The argument of the Lords was that a measure of such far-reaching nature should not be passed without a new mandate from the people, although the Liberal party had been put into power in 1906 with the largest majority any party had ever received up to that time. The Lords' action was especially objectionable because it ran counter to the longstanding tradition giving the House of Commons predominance in financial matters.

The election of 1910 sustained the Liberal government, and the House of Lords passed the bill, but the government was determined to prevent a recurrence. Various proposals for reform were made, one even emanating from the House of

Lords itself. But while the Liberal government wished to reform the House of Lords and make its membership more representative, it considered a curb on the Lords' powers a more urgent issue. A bill to that effect was carried by the House of Commons, but the outcome in the House of Lords was doubtful, although a second election in the same year (1910), which was fought specifically on that issue, again sustained the government. The decisive factor was the King, George V, who let it be known that he would, on recommendation of the government, create enough Liberal lords to give the government a majority in the House of Lords, if that became necessary. The opposition thereupon collapsed, and the result was the Parliament Act of 1911.

This Act[32] distinguished between money bills and other public bills. If a money bill is passed by the House of Commons, as discussed in a previous section, and sent to the House of Lords at least one month before the end of the session, it may be submitted to the Royal Assent and become law after one month whether passed by the House of Lords or not. A public bill, according to the Parliament Act of 1911, could be passed over the Lords' veto[33] only after it had been passed by the House of Commons in three successive sessions, and after it had been submitted to the House of Lords at least one month before the end of each session and been rejected by the Lords in each case. Upon being passed by the House of Commons a third time, it could be submitted to the Royal Assent and become a law. In the latter case, two years at least had to elapse between the first and third sessions.[34] The Parliament Act of 1949 has reduced this period to one year and has reduced the sessions from three to two.

These two Acts appeared to many people as the end of the House of Lords. But this was by no means the case. It had been clear ever since 1832, when King William IV promised the government then in power to appoint enough Whig lords to pass the Reform Bill, that in a real showdown the Commons would always prevail. It had been the pride of the Duke of Wellington that he preserved the House of Lords by prevailing upon it to yield. Bagehot therefore was able to write in 1867:

> Since the Reform Act the House of Lords has become a revising and suspending House. It can alter Bills; it can reject Bills on which the House of Commons is not yet thoroughly in earnest—upon which the nation is not yet determined. Their veto is a sort of hypothetical veto. They say, We reject your bill for this once, or these twice, or even these thrice; but if you keep on sending it up, at last we won't reject it. The House has ceased to be one of latent directors, and has become one of temporary rejectors and palpable alterers.

Does the House of Lords, then, perform a useful function? Or should it be

[32] It also fixed the five-year term of Parliament.
[33] Inaction on the part of the Lords is deemed to be rejection.
[34] Technically between the second reading in the first session and final passage in the third session.

condemned in Winston Churchill's biting words spoken in more radical days—
"the House of Lords—unrepresentative, irresponsible, absentee!" To the believers
in legislative supremacy, the House of Lords will not be any more acceptable than
the entire system of British government. To those who believe that the majority
must always have its way without restriction, the House of Lords with its accidental
membership and unrepresentative character must seem repugnant. Those who insist that a legislative body must, above all, be representative of the electorate will
also reject the House of Lords.

Even if one believes in the desirability of a second chamber to curb the possible exuberance of the House of Commons, it is difficult to be entirely pleased with
the House of Lords. It is so obviously, even outrageously, unrepresentative and
nonresponsible that it cannot dare to stand in the way of the representative part of
Parliament, the House of Commons, when the latter is really determined to have
its own way; and if it tried to do so, it would be swept away.

Believers in second chambers therefore frequently feel that the House of
Lords does not do its job as a true second chamber should and that, even when it
tries to act as a curb on the lower house, it does so only when a Liberal or Labor
government is in power. A Conservative cabinet need not fear great difficulties
from the House of Lords. This does not mean that the peers submit to Conservative party discipline under all circumstances. But on the whole, a Conservative
government will find the House of Lords willing to go along, while a Labor government is in a less fortunate position.

With all its serious faults, the House of Lords performs some useful tasks.
Its treatment and examination of private bills is recognized as being far superior to
that of the busier House of Commons. When the Lords feel that a major measure
proposed by the government does not possess the clear support of the country and
was not included in the mandate which the electorate gave the government at the
last election, they can be very obstreperous and turn down government measures
as long as the revised Parliament Act will permit. This is a form of obstruction
which is not always designed to defeat measures but rather to force the government
to ask the people for a new mandate. Of course the Lords usually believe that the
people will sustain them—a belief which has often been erroneous. But again, history records such action on the part of the upper house only when Liberal or Labor
governments were in power.

It is not surprising, therefore, that a reform of the House of Lords has frequently been debated in England. Even the Conservatives have realized that some
change is necessary, and they gave their support to the far-reaching suggestions of
the committee headed by Lord Rosebery in 1911.

Nothing came of it, and numerous other plans followed, all without results.
The Conservatives were not eager to lose their stronghold but were willing to agree
to a reform of the membership of the House of Lords if it would receive the powers
which it possessed before 1911. In the meantime they were in no great hurry to
effect a change. The Labor party, on the other hand, was naturally hostile to the

upper house, which it could not hope to control. At its annual conference of 1934, the National Executive Committee submitted a report which was adopted by the conference and which read in part as follows: "A Labour Government meeting with sabotage from the House of Lords would take immediate steps to overcome it; and it will, in any event, take steps during its term of office to pass legislation abolishing the House of Lords as a legislative Chamber."[35] A similar provision was put into the election platform of the party in 1935. Earlier, in 1920, the famous work of Sidney and Beatrice Webb on the future socialist Britain declared, "There is, of course, in the Socialist Commonwealth, no place for the House of Lords, which will simply cease to exist as part of the Legislature."

After the Labor party came to power in 1945, it proceeded to bring into operation its vast nationalization and planning program. The Lords, somewhat overwhelmed by the tremendous size of Labor's majority in the House of Commons, made no frontal attack against the first part of the government program. However, they proposed amendments—some good, some less so—which the government frequently accepted rather than face costly delay by having to override the Lords' veto.

There has been some rumbling about drastic reforms of the upper chamber if Labor were to regain a majority,[36] but there is a tendency to go slow. Under the present system, the House of Lords is fairly tame. Occasionally it can still wage a tremendous fight, as evidenced by the debate over the nationalization of the steel industry. But its teeth have been drawn with the imposition of the one-year rule in the Parliament Act of 1949. The government may well prefer the known disadvantages of the present system to the unknown faults of a new scheme. One thing is certain; no British government wants a second chamber which has any remote similarity to the United States Senate or to the Senate of the Third French Republic. Thus the matter stands.

[35] *Report of the Thirty-fourth Annual Conference of the Labour Party,* 1934, p. 263.
[36] None of these reform plans touch the judicial functions of the House of Lords, which are virtually separate. See Chap. 6.

6

Law and justice

Many are the achievements of which Englishmen may justly boast. In preceding chapters, Parliament and cabinet government were presented as outstanding English contributions to the political process. Now we may add another pearl to the crown: the English common law, and the idea of the "rule of law."

There are many legal systems in the world, but none has had and still has a more profound effect than the systems of the Roman (civil) law and the English common law. Some writers who affected a kind of "historical nationalism," like Freeman, Froude, and Stubbs, have maintained that the common law is wholly English and Anglo-Saxon in origin. This theory has been definitely exploded: we know that it is of Norman and feudal, rather than of Anglo-Saxon, origin, and we are discovering more and more about significant traces of Roman influence. And yet, while the English law is no more "pure" in its historical development than Englishmen are in racial origin, it is nevertheless very decidedly a specialty of the English-speaking world.

Common law

In a preceding chapter we have seen how the Norman kings adopted a method instituted by Charlemagne by which itinerant judges (*missi dominici*) traveled about the country rendering justice in the King's name, and how this kind of justice was preferred over the cruder baronial courts of the feudal period.

The strong hand of Henry II increased the scope of the royal judges, who in turn sought to discover common elements in their decisions, and who found it convenient to follow their own and each others' precedents in ever-increasing measure. Thus an amorphous and at times ill-defined, but very real, body of law was formed which later became known as the common law. The basis of the law was the rule *stare decisis* (*et quieta non movere*)—let the decision stand. Under this rule a court decision establishes a precedent which later cases ought to follow when the situation is analogous. This was the law which rose to such proportions that Bracton could write in the thirteenth century that "the king was under God and the [common] law."

These decisions were collected and to some extent systemized by a succession of great legal scholars, beginning with Glanville in the twelfth century, continued by Bracton, Littleton, Fitzherbert, and Coke, and finally culminating in Blackstone's *Commentaries on the Laws of England* in the eighteenth century. From the days of Edward II to Henry VIII, cases were also reported by skilled lawyers in the so-called Year Books.

In the meantime, other developments took place which affected the common law. The jury system which we have already encountered shortly after the arrival of William the Conqueror became more generally adopted, chiefly as a defense against the peculiar system of "witnesses," or rather oath-helpers, through which any rich and noble scoundrel could get exonerated by producing twice as many oath-helpers in court as his opponent.[1] The jury was not an ideal system because the jurors would give their verdict on the basis of what they already knew of the case or had learned about it out of court, and not on the basis of the evidence presented in court. However, it was a great improvement over the method of oath-helpers, which continued to be used for some time.

The prevalence of the jury system profoundly affected the rules of evidence which were developed over the centuries. They were made strict in order not to influence unduly a jury of laymen. They are much laxer in countries in which juries are less frequently employed, because there it is presumed that the learned judge will be able to discern fact from fiction.

Equity

At the same time the common law developed a formalism of great strictness which was quite in evidence by the thirteenth century and was considered oppres-

---

[1] The oath-helper (witness) would merely swear to the credibility of the party concerned. He was an early form of "character witness," who knew nothing about the case itself and whose testimony, often given out of fear or for love of money, was notoriously unreliable.

sive. A man might have paid his debt and there might even have been witnesses to his payment, but if he failed to apply certain formalities, such as exchanging certain sealed documents, he could and would be compelled under common law to pay anew. Here a historical process repeated itself. Just as royal justice had once been brought in to mitigate the arbitrariness and lack of uniformity of the feudal, baronial courts, so now a new type of royal justice was instituted. The King, as the fountain-head of justice, was always entitled to set aside judgments of the common-law courts, and this he did through his principal officer, the Lord High Chancellor. This type of justice was therefore dispensed in chancery—the Lord Chancellor's department—and became known later as "equity." Often it turned out to be a superior type of justice, partly perhaps because the earlier Chancellors were church-men who knew their Roman law, which often suggested a remedy when the English law did not.[2] Equity is therefore much more influenced by Roman law than is common law.

The Chancellor, who was later replaced by deputies called "masters in chancery," was reasonably free in the rendering of his judgments because he was considered to be the "keeper of the King's conscience." When the common law was manifestly unfair, he could render a contrary decision. As the bulk of equity rules increased and also acquired a certain formalism, the judges who rendered judgments in equity became separated from the Lord Chancellor's office and had their own court, the Court of Chancery. Today there is not a separate court but a division, the Chancery Division in the High Court of Justice, which still applies equity when there is no remedy at common or statute law, or when there is danger of irreparable damage. Actually the application of equity is more or less confined to certain fields of law, and in certain instances is a matter of choice for the parties in a suit.[3]

The legal profession

Both common law and equity are forms of law based on precedents. Such precedents can be discovered only after a study of relevant cases; common law and equity are therefore forms of case law. The student of such law must study a great many cases, and it has been the English tradition that he does not study them at law school or at the university, but at the place where the living law daily unrolls itself. These places are called the Inns of Court. Their origin is obscure and very old. Undoubtedly there were law students before there were any Inns of Court. But in the reign of Edward II (1307–1327) a group of students took up quarters in the confiscated former home of the Knights Templars, and as their number grew,

[2] However, due to the nonexistence of printing and the rarity of manuscripts, Roman law often entered not in its original version but in the way in which the Chancellor remembered it from his ecclesiastical studies.

[3] Equity applies only in civil cases. There is no criminal equity. The sorry distinction of having established a crude system of criminal quasi-equity belongs to the Nazis and certain other dictatorships.

they divided into an Innter Temple and a Middle Temple. Another group took over Lincoln's Inn. Others again took up residence in the former home of Lord Grey de Wilton, which was henceforth called Gray's Inn. Students of chancery law took over a number of smaller inns, called Chancery Inns.

Fortescue, one of the greatest legal luminaries, explained in the fifteenth century that law could not be studied at the university, but that far more suitable places were available, near enough to the King's court at Westminster so that the law might be observed in its daily operation.

Full-fledged members of the bar, called "barristers," would instruct and supervise the legal training of the students. To be an instructor (reader) was considered a great honor, and the position was avidly sought.

The Courts of Chancery influenced this development in many ways. It was there that a new type of lawyer emerged, the solicitor, whose learning and knowledge were frequently broader than those of the barristers. Moreover, the chancery lawyer, having fewer precedents to go on than his common-law colleague, developed a broader basis of judicial wisdom and philosophy. Yet the connection between common and chancery lawyers was close, and there was much intellectual cross-fertilization.[4]

The administration of justice in contemporary England is profoundly influenced by the experiences of the past. The students still congregate in the Inns of Court. Lawyers still divide into barristers, who alone are permitted to plead in the regular courts, and solicitors, who hire them, prepare the case, and take care of general legal business. Thus, a practical division of labor is accomplished. This is all the more important because the judges are appointed from among the barristers, who have "taken silk" (who have been made "Queen's Counsel") at least seven years before becoming judges, or in the case of the High Court, ten years. The English judge, like his American colleague, is therefore a man who has seen the practical side of law and has had opportunity to witness and experience the economic, political, and social effects of judgments. This distinguishes English and American judges from their French or German brethren, who ascend to the bench directly from their theoretical law studies and remain in their career for life, carefully preserved—unless they possess great personal wisdom—from the raw winds of social and economic realities.[5]

---

[4] Gradually the chancery bar and the common-law bar merged, and both types of lawyers became students at the Inns.

[5] The most extensive and phenomenal study on the history of English law is W. S. Holdsworth, *History of English Law,* London, 1922–1938, 2d ed., 12 vols. A brilliant and standard treatise on the earlier period is F. Pollack and F. W. Maitland, *History of English Law to the Times of Edward I,* Cambridge, 1898, 2 vols. An excellent summary is E. Jenks, *The Book of English Law: As at the End of 1938,* London, 1938, 5th ed. See also W. M. Geldart, *Elements of the English Law,* London, 1912; H. Potter, *A Historical Introduction to English Law and Its Institutions,* London, 1949, 3d ed. On the common law specifically, see O. W. Holmes, *The Common Law,* Boston, 1881; F. Pollock, *The Expansion of the Common Law,* London, 1904, and *The Genius of the Common Law,* New York, 1912; R. Pound, *The Spirit of the Common Law,* Boston, 1921.

Statute law

Today, common law and equity exist side by side with statute law, i.e., the acts of Parliament. Acts of Parliament used to confine themselves, more or less, to the field of public law, but an ever-increasing invasion into private law has taken place. Wherever there is statutory law, it is supreme over common law. There is no judicial review in the United Kingdom because there is no written constitutional document like the Constitution of the United States. Acts of Parliament are therefore supreme and must be enforced by the courts. The latter may not declare a statute void because of "unconstitutionality," nor may the clear wording of a law be set aside because it is alleged to be contrary to public policy. However, when the statute is not all-inclusive, the courts exercise wide powers of interpretation, especially in questions involving public policy, and the charge has been made by a brilliant partisan commentator[6] that the judges have exercised their powers in order to restrain certain trade-union and other activities very much along the course of action which the Supreme Court of the United States pursued prior to the Jones and Laughlin case.

For the purpose of evaluating the English legal and judicial system, it is perhaps of little importance to determine the exact line of demarcation which separates statute from common law—if such a thing were possible. What is important, however, is to note that the entire legal fabric, be it statute or common law, is permeated by the common-law system, whose principal genius, in England as in the United States, lies in the rule of precedent, trial by jury, and the doctrine of the rule of law. The significant element of the use of precedent as a source of judicial interpretation is the application of reason to judicial experience. Thus, the judge relies on past decisions in concrete situations, rather than on abstract textual interpretation as is so often done on the Continent. But since no past case is likely to be exactly identical with a later one, there is always some leeway which permits the judge to exercise that infinite quality called wisdom. Therefore Oliver Wendell Holmes could write in his well-known book on the common law: "The life of the law has not been logic, it has been experience."

The bench

In order to exercise their functions properly, it is necessary that the courts be independent of the executive branch of the government. We have seen above that the courts cannot set aside legislative action on the part of Parliament because of unconstitutionality. But they can invalidate executive action on grounds of illegality. Here the courts enter a twilight zone, because the American doctrine of expressed and enumerated powers in the hands of the national government does

---

[6] Laski, *Parliamentary Government in England,* New York, 1938, pp. 303–326. Numerous cases cited there. See also the Taff-Vale case, A.C. 426 (1901), and Osborne v. Amalgamated Society of Railway Servants, A.C. 87 (1910).

not apply to England. There, executive power (prerogative) extends to all fields not specifically limited by statute or by the conventions of the constitution. But the courts have sometimes placed restrictive interpretations on existing prerogative power, which has tended to limit the expansion of executive influence.[7] However, as in all other states, there is increasing evidence of "delegated legislation," i.e., rule-making power given by Parliament to government departments who also review grievances and complaints thereunder. In such cases the courts are severely limited because they can only examine whether a department acts *ultra vires,* i.e., beyond its legal powers. Very often, however, delegated legislation is drafted by Parliament in very general terms, with the result that no act *ultra vires* can be found, and when that is the case the courts are powerless to examine the departmental, quasi-judicial decision on its merits.

The personal independence and tenure of judges dates from the Act of Settlement of 1701. Judges are now appointed for good behavior and may be removed only on grounds of misconduct or upon joint address of Parliament. However, the caliber of English judges is such that removal of a judge is virtually unknown. Judges of the county courts are appointed by the government (Crown) upon the recommendation of the Lord Chancellor, and justices of the peace are nominated by local authorities and committees and appointed by the Lord Chancellor. All other judges are appointed by the Prime Minister.

The independence of judges is furthered by very high salaries, which are much greater than in France or Germany. Moreover there is virtually no promotion, so that a judge need not ingratiate himself with authorities as is the case in some Continental countries where the government wields such power through the Minister of Justice. Proper performance of functions is guaranteed by the rule of publicity, which requires all hearings, except for rare exceptions, to be held in open court. The judge is immune, civilly and criminally, for any action performed in court. He is further protected by the rules for contempt of court which shield him from undue attacks, but the right to reasonable and constructive criticism of judicial action has been repeatedly upheld.

We have said before that the jury is one of the essential features of the English system of justice, but today the jury is markedly in decline, and in criminal cases the grand jury has been abolished except for a few unimportant instances.[8]

In civil cases the jury has suffered a similar decline. Since 1933 a party to a lawsuit no longer normally has the right to a jury, although he may make application for jury trial in certain types of cases.[9] Even then the judge may refuse the request if the trial involves prolonged local investigation or documentary or scien-

---

[7] The Zamora, 2 A.C. 77 (1916); Attorney-General v. De Keyser's Royal Hotel, A.C. 508 (1920).

[8] 23 & 24 Geo. V, c. 36 (1933). Treason committed overseas, certain offenses against governors, and violations of the Official Secrets Act.

[9] Libel, slander, malicious prosecution, false imprisonment, seduction, breach of promise, and other cases in which a charge of fraud is made against a party and he demands a jury.

tific evidence. The judge's discretion is virtually unrestricted in this case. Generally, jury verdicts have met with greater favor of public opinion than judgments rendered by a single judge, but on the other hand the use of a jury in a civil case greatly increases the cost of litigation to the parties.

The court system

The United Kingdom has no unified court system. There is one system for England and Wales, there is another for Scotland, and there is still another for Northern Ireland. The Dominions of course have their own. The system with the greatest significance is that of England, and we shall be primarily concerned with it.

There was no judicial unification in England before 1873. Three great common-law courts existed: the Court of King's (Queen's) Bench, the Court of Common Pleas, and the Exchequer. Next to the common-law courts, there were others: the Court of Chancery, which decided equity cases; the Court of Admiralty, which goes back to an act of Richard II; a special Divorce Court; and a Court for the Relief of Insolvent Debtors (Bankruptcy Court). Appeals were a difficult and intricate business, and there was no appeal system from criminal judgments at all, although there were ways in which an error could be brought up to the House of Lords.

The obvious need for reform produced the appointment of a Royal Commission, which reported in 1869; as a result the great Judicature Act was finally passed in 1873. This act and subsequent amendments constitute the major portions of the English judiciary system. It created the so-called "Supreme Court of Judicature" which is a somewhat misleading term, because it is neither supreme nor a court. In fact the "Supreme Court of Judicature" is a covering name for a court system which never meets as one court but is composed of parts which are entirely separate. One part is a High Court of Justice which divides into three separate divisions: the Queen's (King's) Bench; Chancery; and Probate, Divorce, and Admiralty. Another is a Court of Appeals which divides into the Court of Appeals proper and the Court of Criminal Appeals.

On the lower level, below the "Supreme Court," there are now the county courts. Criminal cases of grave nature are tried in the "assize" courts, which are traveling circuit courts, except the one in London, which is called the Central Criminal Court, better known to readers of detective fiction as "Old Bailey." Above the "Supreme Court," there is the House of Lords, whose judicial decisions are rendered by the Lords specifically appointed for that purpose and known as the "Lords of Appeal in Ordinary." The Lord Chancellor presides over them.

There is another "Supreme" court, the Judicial Committee of the Privy Council, which handles appeals from the ecclesiastic courts, from colonial tribunals, and from the courts of those Dominions which still permit such appeals.

Civil cases—i.e., litigations between private individuals or corporations—are tried before county courts if the sum under dispute is less than £200 ($560).

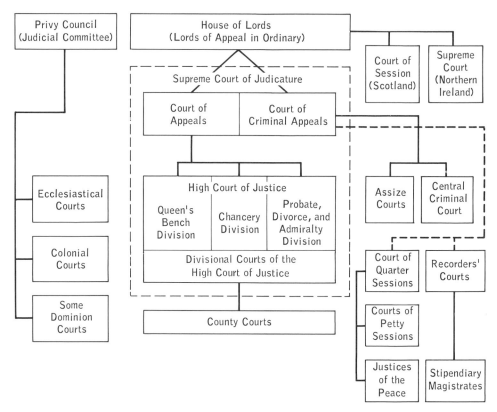

The name "county court" is misleading, because the area covered by each court has no relationship to the county. There are 500 county courts in England and Wales, which are grouped into sixty circuits. To each circuit, the Lord Chancellor assigns one judge, who must hold court at least once every month in each of the county courts assigned to him. This volume of work might seem insurmountable, but because of the small sums and issues involved in a majority of cases, the permanent staff assigned to each court, the registrar and his aides, are usually able to settle a great many matters before they reach a hearing in open court.

In the county court the litigants may demand a jury if the sum at issue exceeds £5, but that is quite unusual and would be extremely uneconomical. An appeal may be made to a divisional court of the High Court of Justice, composed of two or more judges taken from the Queen's Bench Division. There the matter ordinarily rests, but the Court of Appeals may allow one more step and take the case unto itself.

If the sum under litigation exceeds £200, or when a party wishes it, the case goes before the High Court of Justice; that is to say, before one of its three divisions, the Queen's Bench Division if it is a trial at common or statutory law in general, the Chancery Division for decisions at equity, and the Probate, Divorce, and Admiralty Division in appropriate cases. The Queen's Bench Division is composed of a Lord Chief Justice—who is not the highest judge in the land—and twenty puisne (associate) judges. The Chancery Division consists of the Lord Chancellor—whose position is nominal—and five judges. The Probate, Divorce, and Admiralty Division has a President and four judges. Trials are handled either by single judges or by small panels of judges.

An appeal from the High Court of Justice goes to the Court of Appeals, which is composed of the "Master of the Rolls" (president) and eight Lord Justices of Appeal. From there a final appeal may be carried to the House of Lords in session composed of the Lord Chancellor and nine Lords of Appeal in Ordinary. In addition the Lord Chief Justice, any former Lord Chancellor, and other peers with high judicial experience may sit. Ordinarily three lords to each case are sufficient, although five is the more frequent number. Technically the "law lords" sit as the House of Lords as a whole; their proceedings are legislative rather than judicial in form and are entered on the Journal of the House. In actuality, however, the House of Lords as a judicial body is entirely separate from the House as a legislature, and the separation could easily be made final and practical without harm to anyone. However, with their love for antiquity and time-honored institutions, the people of England prefer to leave well enough alone.

Appeal to the House of Lords can be made in civil cases only upon permission of the Court of Appeals. It is an exceedingly expensive affair and therefore not very frequent. Moreover since 1948 lords are no longer tried "by their peers" as the Magna Carta decreed. A further factor which diminishes the judicial work of the Lords is the extreme rigidity of their reliance on their own previous decisions. But on the other hand, the House of Lords is the only true United Kingdom court, because it accepts appeals from the highest courts of Scotland and Northern Ireland as well as from England and Wales.

Quite outside the regular court hierarchy is the Judicial Committee of the Privy Council. Just as the House of Lords is technically a legislative body but is actually also a judicial one, so the Judiciary Committee of the Privy Council is theoretically an administrative body but is in reality also a court. It is composed of the Lords of Appeal in Ordinary (law lords) with the addition of several judges from the Commonwealth.

Criminal cases are handled differently. Usually no indictments are rendered by a grand jury, but charges are filed by local officials. There is also a national officer, the Director of Public Prosecutions, who performs this task in cases of exceptional difficulty. The prosecution in court itself may be conducted by a public prosecutor or by a barrister who has been appointed for this purpose by the Crown and given the title of Queen's (King's) Counsel (Q.C. or K.C.). But whether the prosecution is conducted by a public official or a private person retained for this purpose, it is always in the name of and at the expense of the Crown.

A person who is charged with a criminal offense is taken before a justice of the peace or in large cities before a full-time "stipendiary magistrate" (in London called metropolitan magistrate). Justices of the peace are unpaid officials who perform their duties because of the honor and the prestige involved. Most of them belonged to the class of country squires, but in recent years members of other professions have found access to appointment. Justices of the peace are the only members of the judicial branch who are not learned in the law; they are appointed by the Lord Chancellor upon recommendations by local organizations. They are very numerous[10] and easily accessible. They have jurisdiction only in minor cases of misdemeanors, such as traffic violations, and they may not impose fines of more than £5 ($14) or imprisonment for more than two weeks. Two justices of the peace sitting together form a Court of Petty Sessions, which may try a wider range of misdemeanors for which maximum punishment does not exceed six months unless the defendant consents. Single justices and petty sessions may concern themselves with cases which are too grave for their jurisdiction, but in those instances the justices of the peace merely exercise the function discharged by the grand jury in the United States or the *juge d'instruction* and *Untersuchungsrichter* in France and Germany respectively. They investigate whether there exists enough prima-facie evidence to commit the accused to trial, and they decide what court shall hear the case, depending on the severity of the transgression. In the cities, stipendiary magistrates exercise the same functions.

Appeals from single justices of the peace of petty sessions may be heard in the assembly of all justices of the peace in each county or important part thereof, known as the Court of Quarter Sessions,[11] which hears all cases *de novo*. In some areas this Court is presided over by a barrister appointed by the Home Secretary and called "the Recorder." Courts of Quarter Sessions may also try more serious crimes but not those for which the death penalty or life imprisonment can be asked. Here the jury is used, and an attempt has been made to make the presiding officer a learned jurist lest he be too much under the thumb of the clerk. Under certain circumstances appeals may be directed to the Court of Criminal Appeals, while in rating and licensing matters the High Court of Justice may be asked to intervene on certiorari. In larger cities, a learned jurist, the Recorder, has similar functions.

Grave crimes are brought before the Assizes or, if in London, before the Central Criminal Court. One or two judges of the Queen's Bench[12] are out on circuit and hold court in the more important places. Here, the jury is always used.

The accused has a right to appeal to a higher court, the Court of Criminal Appeals, which is composed of three judges from the Queen's Bench. This appeal may be undertaken on questions of law in any case, but on questions of fact only with the permission of the trial judge or of the Court of Criminal Appeals. Once a case is appealed, however, the Court of Criminal Appeals has great freedom; it

[10] Nearly 20,000, less than half of whom exercise juridical functions.
[11] Meeting four times each year. For appeal purpose they act through committees.
[12] The "Queen's Bench Division" is not only a court division but also a pool of judges who may be used for various judicial purposes.

may reduce or increase the sentence, or it may quash the entire case, but the possibility of increase keeps the number of appeals down to a minimum.

Ordinarily the Court of Criminal Appeals is the highest court in criminal cases. An appeal to the House of Lords is possible at infrequent instances, provided the Attorney General consents to it, but such an appeal may never come from the prosecution.

One particular characteristic is the English method of creating rules of procedures. In most other countries, these are laid down in the form of legislative acts and codes. These acts may be well organized, or they may be quite confusing, but they are always formidable barriers to simple and speedy trial and are the joy of the lawyer who can save his client only by riding procedural tricks. In England a rules committee does the job. It is composed of the Lord Chancellor, the Master of the Rolls, the Lord Chief Justice, four other judges, two barristers, and two solicitors. This truly "expert" committee, composed of eminently experienced men, has the task of establishing and constantly adjusting the rules of procedure. They have performed exceedingly well, and have produced satisfactory and speedy trials.[13]

No administrative courts

The court system described above is the only one existing in England.[14] There are no administrative courts as in France or Germany, and many English judges and lawyers treat the very idea with absolute horror, congratulating themselves on having avoided this "monster" in England. But, as we have seen above, there is an increasing tendency toward "delegated legislation" and the power of government departments to make rules, and disputes break out which must be decided in the interests of justice and in order to permit the orderly carrying on of business. Since the courts can, as we have mentioned, examine only the question whether the administrative procedure was *ultra vires* or not, a great number of disputes would remain unresolved unless the government departments themselves took it upon their shoulders to give a fair hearing to people who believe that they have a grievance. Thus, quasi-judicial tribunals, departmental boards, etc., are to be found everywhere, which may be considered "administrative courts" of sorts.

Another question, intimately connected with the problem of administrative justice, is the liability of the government for acts of its agents. If a person incurs damages as a result of the action of a government agent, he has to sue that man, and not the "state" as in France. However, the government stands behind its agents to an increasing degree, and since 1947 it is possible to sue the government for damages incurred as a result of action by an agent which was not necessarily illegal but which caused damages, even though possibly committed in good faith.

[13] R. M. Jackson, *The Machinery of Justice in England,* 2d ed., Cambridge, England, 1953; H. G. Hanbury, *English Courts of Law,* London, 1944; C. P. Patterson, *The Machinery of Justice in Great Britain,* Austin, Tex., 1936. See also S. Amos, *British Justice: An Outline of the Administration of Criminal Justice in England and Wales,* London, 1940.
[14] Ecclesiastic courts and prize courts are not being considered here.

7

Local government

It is a matter of historical experience that national government changes more frequently and more violently than local government. New masters often rewrite the constitution of a country, but leave the structure of local government fairly well alone. England[1] is somewhat of an exception in this development because local and national governments show a remarkable degree of parallelism; both are deeply rooted in the past, both have institutions of most ancient origin, both have undergone very fundamental changes a little over a century ago, and both have had to make adjustments to fit into the postwar period.

Local government is of great importance and is an interesting and significant indicator of the general relationship between the English people and their government. The many services which the citizen needs for the normal comfort of his daily life are, to a very large extent, provided by local authorities. There are the

[1] We are discussing English local government. Insignificant differences exist in Scotland and Northern Ireland.

police for the protection of life, liberty, and property—and the English police are second to none in the world. There are the schools, certain health and welfare functions, the building and maintenance of roads and bridges, and the use of open spaces; Town and Country Planning introduce an even closer relationship, though in a new garb.

Local government is also a school for democracy and the beginning of a political career. While local government is not as independent in England as it is in the United States, it is infinitely more self-reliant than is customary on the European continent. There is a closer tie-in to the national government than in America, but there is no all-powerful Minister of the Interior, as in France, whose hand weighs heavily on the shoulders of local authorities. Under such circumstances, free men may assemble in their councils, pretty much as of yore, and impress the mark of their personalities on their environment. Many leading statesmen began their careers in the councils of local government; most notable among them were Joseph and Neville Chamberlain, both of whom were Lord Mayors of Birmingham before entering the national scene, while one of the outstanding Labor leaders, Herbert Morrison, first became prominent as President of the London County Council.

Development

Modern English local government began in the nineteenth century, but significant elements are discernible much earlier.[2] From the Anglo-Saxon period there remains little that is of great significance except place names. But the feudal society which the Normans brought to England was a different matter. In those days, the basic unit of local government with which the citizen came into contact was the parish. A straight line of authority reached from the King down to the people in the parishes—a system based on the ownership and tenancy of land which was characteristic of feudalism. Above the parishes were the counties. If the parishes were the most important units of local government for the citizens concerned—because they saw to the keeping of the peace—the counties were the most important units from the King's standpoint. It was through the county administration that the King kept the barons in line. This was done through the sheriffs, who were royal proconsuls, through the royal judges, and also with the help of the clergy who were learned in the canon law. True, the local lords were permitted to maintain their own baronial courts, but royal justice was so much better that it gained the upper hand, as we have seen in a preceding chapter.

[2] The most famous and all-inclusive treatise on the history of local government is the formidable work of Sidney and Beatrice Webb, *English Local Government from the Revolution to the Municipal Corporations Act,* London, 1906–1927, 9 vols. A briefer treatment may be found in W. A. Robson, *The Development of Local Government,* London, 1948, 2d ed., and a detailed historical introduction is contained in J. J. Clarke, *The Local Government of the United Kingdom,* London, 1945, 13th ed. A very useful book has been published in the new Town and County Hall Series by K. B. Smellie, *A History of Local Government,* London, 1947.

In the thirteenth century an important addition was made to local administration in the form of the justices of the peace. Soon social and economic changes caused their functions to increase steadily. But they found it difficult to discharge them through the existing parish organization, which had a tradition of self-government, while the justices of the peace were appointed by and responsible to the King. Thus a habit of compromise between the two principles, local autonomy and central direction, was established, which marks local government today even though the instrumentalities have greatly changed. At the same time, the King gave special autonomy to certain cities—mostly for political reasons—and exempted them from much of the regular county organization; this was the origin of the later county boroughs.

The Tudor period saw the first integral attempt at a thorough organization of the country along modern lines. The justices of the peace were placed under the close scrutiny of the King's council and the Star Chamber, while a large number of laws regulated many of the functions of local government. The parishes in turn were brought under the justices of the peace, and the overseers of the parishes were put in charge of the administration of the Poor Laws.

The great social and economic changes which accompanied the Industrial Revolution were not at first reflected in the organization of local government. A straight channel of command still led from the King, via the Lord Lieutenant and the Sheriff, to the justice of the peace. In actuality, unwritten changes took place, but no uniformity or system was maintained. In 1832 there existed 15,000 parishes, each a distinct organization which operated a good deal as it pleased. Area, methods of administration, and methods of appointment varied from place to place. Many offices were held by unpaid officials who allowed them to decline. Since the parish vestry was the only assembly (other than Parliament) entitled to impose taxes, there was usually a small group of influential and wealthy people who ran things as they saw fit. Abuse was frequent and corruption abounded.

With the growth of the population and the establishment of many new towns in the North and the Midlands, the local government officials were grossly overworked, and many a prosperous and well-bred citizen exempted himself from a rotating parish office by paying his way out, while those who were unable to do so were determined to make their office pay off. The new towns tended to submerge the parish organization, and additional work was placed on the shoulders of the justice of the peace. In 1765 Blackstone wrote: "Such an infinite variety of business has been heaped upon them, that few care to undertake and fewer understand the office."

In line with the increasingly difficult times, the office of the justice of the peace—once the pride of the country squire—came increasingly under the control of doubtful and rough characters; moreover, politics set in between Whigs and Tories, and between Church of England men and Dissenters, with the result that the whole system was being torn to shreds. The village constable was unable to control the increasing criminality of the industrial age. Nor could the parish and county organization establish effective control over the new industries and the people they brought in. It became increasingly clear that local, piecemeal reform was inadequate, that only comprehensive action from the top down could furnish remedies.

The need for reform was great everywhere, but nowhere was it greater than in the overcrowded industrial cities. There it was inextricably interwoven with the problem of poor relief. Those were the days of the oppressive corn laws and the movement for their repeal.[3] The results were two statutes: the Poor Law Act of 1834 and the Municipal Corporations Act of 1835. Of the two, the Poor Law Act was the more basic.

A Poor Law Commission had been set up in 1832 under the chairmanship of Lord Brougham. It employed a large number of investigators and thus began the system of inspectors. The principal recommendation of the Commission was the establishment of a central board to control the administration of the Poor Law. This board was to be empowered to combine as many parishes and establish as many workhouses as it saw fit. It was to establish standards for the appointment of administrative officers who applied the Poor Laws. This was done in 1834, and thus was established one of the principal tenets of English local government, that of central control. The three Commissioners and the Secretary who were appointed to administer the Poor Law eventually became the Ministry of Health.

The Municipal Corporations Act of 1835 laid down the broad outlines which all local government eventually followed. It established the municipal corporation as a legal person which expressed itself through an elected council. The rights of the corporation were strictly circumscribed and were not extensive at first. Moreover, although the Poor Law Act went deeply into the question of central control, the Municipal Corporations Act merely touched on it. The permission of the Treasury was required for local government loans as well as alienation of property, and the Privy Council could veto local government bylaws.

Gradually more and more functions were taken on, especially in the fields of public health, parks, libraries, sanitation, fire departments, and police. In 1867 Manchester obtained legislation which in effect gave it the first legal basis for slum clearance. Also, a number of commissions were set up for the purpose of controlling public utilities. Eventually, all these functions and more were brought together in the Municipal Corporations Consolidation Act of 1882 and extended to twenty-five more boroughs.[4]

In the meantime the Poor Law Commissioners had not been idle. From pure administrators, they developed into something like social reformers. They began to look into the reasons for poverty and they found terrible health conditions. The

[3] They were laws taxing the import of corn and thus keeping the price high. Repeal became a great political question and was finally successful in 1841. It marked the alliance of worker and manufacturer and became the source of what is sometimes called "Manchester liberalism." See D. G. Barnes, *A History of the English Corn Laws from 1660 to 1846,* London, 1930.
[4] Except for the City of London (the center part of the metropolitan area, in which few people live), the word "city" is not used legally. "Borough" is the official term.

secretary to the Poor Law Commission, Edwin Chadwick, was able to show conclusively that Poor Law expenditures could be reduced only if a drastic improvement of public health were brought about. Epidemics showed the national character of the health menace, and in 1848 a new central authority, the General Board of Health, was established with powers of a large and varied nature. The Board met so much opposition that it was abolished in 1858, but the idea had taken root. Ten years later, a Royal Sanitary Commission was appointed, and its report led to the Public Health Act of 1875, establishing the Local Government Board, which inherited the poor relief from the Poor Law Board, the public health functions which the Board of Health had exercised and which had later gone to the Privy Council, and the local government work of the Home Office.

It is not exactly surprising that so much effort was spent on borough (urban) government and so little on county (rural) government. By 1875, approximately two-thirds of all Englishmen lived in towns. Nevertheless, the Municipal Corporations Act of 1835 and subsequent legislation had set the pattern for county government too. When piecemeal reform and the giddy piling up of unrelated boards had made county government nearly unmanageable, the Local Government Act of 1888 and that of 1894 brought relief and carried the counties alongside the boroughs.

The Local Government Act introduced an entirely new system of local units, the so-called "administrative county," which sometimes is identical with the old historical county and sometimes is not. The Act also established councils which followed the pattern established in the boroughs. It transferred nearly all the vast powers of the justices of the peace to the new County Councils. Only petty justice and a certain influence over the police remained in the hands of the justices of the peace. This democratization of local government was carried further down in 1894, when parish councils were established and urban district councils set up in the former Local (Sanitary) Board Districts. On the other hand, many more towns claimed exemption and "county borough" status than had originally been anticipated.

One other innovation might be mentioned: women entered local government before they were admitted to Westminster or Whitehall. In 1894 they became eligible for parish and district councils, and in 1907 they became eligible to the borough and county councils and could become aldermen.[5]

After rural government had caught up with the hitherto more advanced municipal (borough) area, it was time to undertake the final step in the direction of a better integration at the top. We have seen how a great deal of improvement was achieved by the establishment of the Local Government Board in 1875. But the overlapping and duplication of efforts was still great, especially as Parliament

---

[5] Women's activities in such political associations as the Primrose League (Cons.) and the Women's Liberal Congress helped to obtain these concessions.

created new commissions for all kinds of purposes; one might wonder for instance why the august Privy Council had to approve the rules of the Central Midwives Board, while the protection of infant life was placed under the Home Office.

The Haldane Commission, which we had occasion to mention before, gained another claim to fame by proposing the creation of a Ministry of Health with very wide powers. This was accomplished a year later, in 1919, and a Parliamentary Secretary was appointed under the Minister, to be in charge of the work of the former Local Government Board and the Insurance Commissions.[6] Subsequent legislation abolished further independent boards and simplified the administration, but the Ministry of Health has remained the major feature in the whole realm of local government.

This relationship, the like of which cannot be found elsewhere, is also unique from another viewpoint. It is a subtle relationship, like many others in the framework of British government. There is central control, but, as we have seen, there is no Minister of the Interior or prefect as in France who may directly interfere with, and indeed run, local government. Local officials are elected locally and have no duty of obedience to the national government, although most of their powers are regulated by national law. Moreover, local government has its own income resulting from an age-honored system of property taxes called "rates," but it is not independent financially for it must rely heavily on grants-in-aid of the central government.

The counties

Today the system is as follows: there are two types of counties, the historical and the administrative counties. The fifty-two historical counties are relics of former times and are shorn of all important functions. They have no elected council and have only three principal officials, the Lord Lieutenant, the Sheriff, and the justice of the peace. The first two, especially the Sheriff, are election officials for Parliamentary elections. The functions of the justices have been discussed above. All three are appointed by the government.

There are now sixty-two administrative counties superimposed over the historical counties. The governing authority of each is an elected council whose chief functions are administrative rather than legislative, especially since most basic local government legislation is accomplished in Parliament. Councilors are elected in single-member districts, very much like Members of Parliament. Before the Second World War the suffrage was restricted by property qualifications, but this was abolished thereafter, and the right to vote in local elections is now exactly like that in national elections.

The county councils are responsible for the policy and the administration of

---

[6] However, control over local elections was shifted to the Home Office in 1921.

the county and supervise the work of subordinate bodies, such as the district councils. They establish the rates[7] and appropriate money. With the consent of the central government, they may also borrow. Otherwise they maintain the ordinary local services, buildings, and asylums. They also administer the licensing laws except for liquor,[8] and they appoint the regular administrative personnel of the county, most of whom are, however, part of a local civil service system.

New and very considerable powers and duties were imposed on the councils as a result of two important national statutes: the Education Act of 1944 and the Town and Country Planning Acts of 1944 and 1947. The Education Act made the county and county borough councils responsible for all primary, secondary, and related education.[9] It also broadened considerably the scope of public education;[10] before 1944 the elementary schools had continued until the student was fourteen, but secondary education had begun at eleven. In fact, 90 percent of otherwise eligible children were excluded from secondary education, most of which was private. Now, under Section 7 of the Act, a definite system of education in three progressive steps—primary, secondary, and further education—has been instituted. The Act also ordered the establishment of kindergartens, special schools for the handicapped, and, for the first time in history, an examination of the desirability of boarding schools, hitherto reserved to the well-to-do. Private schools are not thereby outlawed. The act distinguishes between three types of voluntary (private) schools: controlled, aided, and special-agreement schools. But the increasingly heavy financial burden on schools groaning under the ever-increasing demands for higher education is forcing them more and more in the direction of controlled schools. Even the parochial (Roman Catholic) schools are negotiating to enter into a special-agreement category by which the state would pay many of their expenses, but the conditions offered by the Church have been found unacceptable by the Minister of Education.

Town and country planning

The Town and Country Planning Acts grew out of the conditions created by war. Devastated areas were to be reconstructed in line with a general plan, rather

---

[7] The rates are property taxes based on an Elizabethan system by which the needs of the local government are determined and then are distributed among property owners, to be paid according to assessed evaluation. This is now the function of the Treasury's Board of Inland Revenue, but collection is done by local government. However, more and more money is being received from the central government as block grants-in-aid, especially since land and real property used for agricultural, manufacturing, or transport services either have been exempted altogether (agriculture) or have had their rates drastically reduced.

[8] Liquor licenses are still issued by the justices of the peace.

[9] Under the control of the Minister of Education.

[10] Meaning public education as understood in the United States as well as in Britain. This has nothing whatever to do with the so-called "public schools" (especially Eton, Harrow, Winchester, Westminster, Rugby, Shrewsbury, Charterhouse, St. Paul's, and Merchant Taylor's), which are very exclusive preparatory schools from which the public is excluded.

than haphazardly. Moreover, poorly or wrongly developed areas were to be directed toward more useful exploits. General as well as very detailed direction was vested in a new government department, the Ministry of Housing and Local Government. Under it, local authorities are entitled to acquire land which in overcrowded county boroughs may actually be slightly outside the corporation limits. Development on such land remains thus under local and central government control,[11] and even the owner of certain types of property must await the consent of the authorities for certain improvements he might desire to make.

The operation of the Town and Country Planning Acts is a good example of the extent to which local government has absorbed new functions which it exercises under central direction. It is also an example of the attitude of the British government, which desires to have a maximum of consultation before embarking on planning activities and which in this case finds local government a suitable medium for carrying out this design. The acts charge local bodies (county and county borough councils) with the drafting of plans for their respective areas. Considerable power of delegation and extensive opportunities for hearing affected interests exist. All such plans have to be approved by the Minister of Town and Country Planning, and local recommendations are sometimes overlooked or forgotten at that stage. New land can be acquired either directly through the local authorities or through the Central Land Board, an agency of the Ministry which only manages land and sets certain rates and charges.[12]

An even more ambitious scheme has been the planning of new towns,[13] partly in order to relieve congestion, partly to attract new industries into undeveloped areas, and partly to further the new urban type of "satellite cities."

Outstanding results were not achieved, but the scope of the act was nevertheless enormous. Two types of new towns were planned. One was intended to take population and industry away from overcrowded towns; the other envisaged the satisfaction of immediate industrial needs through expansion and new industries in hitherto undeveloped areas. So far, fourteen new towns have been designated. But this was to be merely a beginning. Eventually 3,000,000 people were to be accommodated in these new communities, which would mean that fifty or sixty of them would have to be built.[14]

The New Towns Act constituted a bold step on the part of the government in the direction of meeting some of Britain's worst needs. But on the other hand a

[11] Under the 1944 act, a distinction was made between war-damaged, "blitzed," areas and "blighted" areas, i.e., underdeveloped or wrongly developed regions.

[12] It also pockets increments in value accrued by private owners because of government improvements. This is to take speculation out of the business.

[13] The New Towns Act of 1946, 9 & 10 Geo. VI, c. 68. Preparatory to this entire system of town and country planning were two reports, that of the Departmental Committee on the Utilization of Land in Rural Areas (Scott Report), London, 1942, and the *Final Report of the Expert Committee on Compensation and Betterment* (Uthwatt Report) of the same year. New Towns Committee (Reith), *Final Report*, Cmd. 6376, 1946.

[14] A. E. Telling, "New Towns, Progress and Prospects," *Town and Country Planning*, Vol. X (1948), p. 80.

number of critics are disturbed about the manner in which the act has been administered. Since the recommendation of the Reith Commission—that new towns be built where no urban centers existed—was largely ignored by the then Minister of Town and Country Planning, difficulties with property owners and other interested parties arose. These issues illustrate some principal objections raised by opponents of the act. Under the law, which was upheld by the House of Lords,[15] the Minister of Town and Country Planning did not need to "sell" his case to the local citizenry but needed merely to hear objections. Thus a former Minister (Silkin), who was thoroughly committed to the plan, was the one to decide disputes raised by local objections. This made him a judge in his own case, with the result that local opinion found it difficult to make much of an impression.

The counties and county boroughs are also local education authorities and are charged with maintaining institutions of primary and secondary education, and frequently various training schools as well. Yet the system is controlled and standardized by the Minister of Education. Similar examples of the interweaving of local and national government functions may be found in almost every other field of local government endeavor.

County councils and aldermen

Numerous duties are performed by elected councils in the counties and the county boroughs. Many of them are required by statute. The latter are cities (boroughs) with the quasi-status of a county; we may think of them as urban counties.

Since counties vary greatly in size, membership in the county councils varies accordingly. The council elects a number of aldermen, who may be councilors (in which case there is a by-election) or may be chosen from the outside. Their number is one-third of the regular councilors except in the London County Council, where they amount to only one-sixth. Aldermen are elected for a term of six years, half of them being reelected when a new council convenes.

The system of aldermen is unique, for although they are selected on a different basis than the councilors, they sit with them as one body. However, aldermen are chosen for their wisdom and experience and generally enjoy greater prestige than ordinary councilors.

The county councils are too large to work effectively as administrative bodies. Most of their work is therefore done in committee and in cooperation with their staffs. The organization of the councils, the number of their principal committees, and their general procedure are fixed by the Local Government Act of 1929. But other committees may be established on the council's own initiative. There are also committees in which both the council and other authorities are represented.

The county councils also have limited legislative power to issue by-laws, which need, however, the approval of the appropriate ministry.

[15] Franklin and Others v. Minister of Town and Country Planning, A.C. 87 (1948).

The staff

Because of the steady increase in administrative work, a major portion of the load is actually performed by a staff of permanent officials, among whom the county clerk (in county boroughs, town clerk) is the most important and has the most ancient office. He serves as coordinator and supervisor over the other heads of departments, such as finance officer, surveyor, chief constable, education officer, and health officer. Under each one in turn is a staff the size of which depends of course on the size and character of the county or county borough. The high standards of British local government depend in no small degree on these officials, who are not under a formal civil service statute but who actually have tenure and look upon their work as a career. Moreover, it is the practice that these officials meet regularly with the appropriate committees of the council, thus helping to blend into an efficient combination the democratic principle of elected officials with the need for expert advice.

Districts

The rural and urban districts which form the subdivisions of the county are organized very much like their parent bodies, with their own councils, rates, and permanent staffs. At times an urban district may become a borough, but that is not done in a systematic manner. The parishes, however, have deteriorated. In urban centers they merely have ecclesiastic functions, while in the rural parishes very minor administrative duties have been retained.[16]

The boroughs

A unit of local government of a special kind is the borough, which is simply a town with a charter. There are two different types of boroughs: the county borough, which, as we have seen, is a county unto itself and exempt from any other county jurisdiction, and the ordinary borough, which forms part of the county in which it is located. County boroughs are usually the more important cities, with inhabitants of 100,000 or more, but no general rule can be applied to the entire system because it is impossible to apply any rational yardstick to determine which town ought to be a borough and which ought to be content with being an urban district.

In order to become a borough, a district must "petition Her Majesty in Council" for a charter. No minimum population or ratable value is required in the law, but in practice a minimum population of 20,000 is expected. This applies only to

[16] The parish meeting is the only British institution comparable to the New England town meetings. In English (not Scottish or Northern Irish) parishes, there is also a Parish Council if the parish has more than 300 inhabitants or if it has between 200 and 300 and has made application for the establishment of a council.

new boroughs; among older ones there is a great discrepancy in size and importance. The Privy Council appoints a committee to report on the matter while an
inspector of the Ministry of Health conducts local hearings. If the inspector's report
is unfavorable, the petition is dead but may be revived at a future, more opportune
date. If the inspector's report is favorable, the charter may be granted either by
order in council or by act of Parliament.

The borough is governed by a borough council, constituted similarly to a
county and district council. Its presiding officer is the mayor or, in more important
towns, the Lord Mayor. The term of office for councilors is three years, as in the
case of county councilors, with one-third being elected each year. Aldermen are
elected as in the county councils. The borough status gives a town a much greater
degree of dignity and civic pride; it also means somewhat larger expenses for pomp
and circumstance. Much ceremonial attention is paid to the mayor or Lord Mayor,
although he actually wields much less power than most American mayors. He
heads no special department; apart from being presiding officer of the council, he
is merely one of the councilors, who casts his vote like other members. In most
cases there is no salary, while the duties and expenses may be quite heavy. Often
the Lord Mayors must be wealthy men in order to stand the strain, although this
tendency is somewhat less emphasized now.

The council is the chief legislature and administration of the borough. In a
county borough it also absorbs the functions ordinarily held by the county council.
It manages the corporate estate and the borough fund. It establishes the borough
rates. It has its own budget and appropriates money. Subject to approval by the
central government, it may borrow money. It also administers the municipal services, which are often quite extensive.

Just like the county council, the borough council operates chiefly through
committees; however, because of the vast extent of municipal and social services
required from a city, the regular staff on quasi-civil service looms especially large.
Since these officials have tenure, the establishment of a city "machine," which still
plagues some American cities, is unlikely in England. However, lack of uniformity
in selection and inadequate standards are causing some difficulties which may possibly lead to a more far-reaching reform at some future date.

Central government control

In describing the powers and responsibilities of local government, it has been
necessary at various instances to point to the existence of central control. The pivot
of this system was the Ministry of Health and is now the Ministry of Housing and
Local Government, but other departments, chiefly the Treasury, the Home Office,
the Ministry of Transport and Civil Aviation, the Ministry of Education, the Ministry of Agriculture and Fisheries, and the Ministry of National Insurance, are also
concerned.

Like all other institutions, local government is of course subject to the supreme authority of Parliament and such laws as it may enact. Beyond that, the various government departments concerned supervise the work of local government and see to it that statutory authority is not exceeded.[17] The Home Office inspects and to a certain extent supervises the police forces, except in the Metropolitan District of London, where the police are directly administered under the Home Office. The latter, logically enough, is also in charge of local civil defense work, especially the Home Guard. The Treasury must give its consent to borrowing by local government. Of principal interest are the grants-in-aid which enable local government to render its many services, and considerable central control is maintained there. There are two types of grants: allocated grants, which are directed toward certain services, and block grants, which are without specified instructions. The first category has been criticized because it leads to ill-conceived expansion purely for the purpose of earning grants, while block grants, which are gaining in favor, do not show the same tendency. About half of local government expenditures are covered by grants.

Generally speaking, the appropriate central departments supervise the work of local authorities, keep them in line, and establish rules with regard to procedure, organization, qualifications of officials, equipment, and general objectives.

Central departments may invalidate local ordinances which go beyond powers granted to the local authorities, and they may compel obedience by recourse to the courts. They, especially the Ministry of Housing and Local Government, audit local government accounts and give appropriate advice. They watch over the efficiency of the local services; for instance, one-half the net expenditures for the police services is refunded if the local force has been found efficient. But under the Local Government Act of 1948, grants given to local governments depend on the extent to which each is above or below a national average of financial strength. This is a process of equalization. National ministries also approve certain appointments and bylaws and, since 1948, participate even in the assessment of property for local tax purposes. Recently the great expansion into the fields of public housing and socialized medicine has broken new ground for central government control, and the end is not yet in sight. Nevertheless, the over-all record of English local government is splendid. The preoccupation of the councils and their committees with administrative matters guarantees that democratic procedures are maintained on all levels and tends to prevent the rise of an all-powerful officialdom. At the same time, the intimate collaboration of councilmen and career officials creates a high level of administrative efficiency and a minimum of friction between elected and appointed officials.

Much can also be said for the exercise of national control over local government, which has generally tended to improve and increase local services without

---

[17] In the constitutional theory of the United States, the federal government has only expressed, enumerated, implied, and inherent (see the Curtiss-Wright case) powers, while state powers are inherent and reserved. The opposite is true in England. The powers of local government are not reserved or inherent but solely statutory.

being arbitrary or leading to the unimaginative uniformity of the French system. In particular, national control appears not to have stultified the great vitality of local government or prevented many a pioneering venture.

Despite the generally satisfactory nature of local government and of central-local relationship, there is some uneasiness among certain observers concerning the future of local government.[18] There is a steady invasion of former local government preserves by the national government. The establishment of the National Health Service has relieved local authorities of some responsibilities while creating others, but generally under a greater measure of national control. The nationalization of electricity and gas has deeply affected many local government administrations which used to own and operate their own public utilities—sometimes at lower rates. Local poor relief was made a national matter by the National Assistance Act of 1948.

Another matter for long-standing concern has been the great disparity in size between different counties and county boroughs, which makes local administration unwieldy and encourages central direction. Therefore a great deal of thought has been given to the reform of local government, and the Local Government Boundary Commission has proposed a series of radical changes.[19] Private agencies and local government associations have also shown deep concern.[20] But so far these proposals have remained on paper, and until Parliament acts nothing can be done.

Despite these difficulties, local government still constitutes a major part of the British fabric of government and an outstanding school for future statesmen.

Politics and local government

Until fairly recently, elections to the numerous local government councils were nonpartisan. But this is now a matter of the past. Spearheaded by the Labor party, local elections are now contested on party lines and often on the basis of national rather than local issues. In the same manner, many leading national politicians have formerly been active in local government. This has been more frequently the case with Labor-party leaders than with Conservatives, because the former often saw in local government an opportunity to carry out some of their ideas in the field of social reform.

As a result, local elections have often been regarded as a barometer of national trends. Such an evaluation, however, must be treated with considerable caution. The voting participation is much smaller in local elections than in national ones. There are a number of candidates who run as independents or as candidates of major parties and groups. Moreover local issues do sometimes count in certain

[18] Especially since government departments (central and local) are not required to apply court procedures and may therefore decide a dispute against a person without granting him a hearing. Local Government Board v. Arlidge, A.C. 120 (1915).
[19] *Report of the Local Government Boundary Commission for 1947*, London, 1948.
[20] "Local Government Reorganization," *Public Administration*, Vol. XXXI (1953), pp. 176–188, 285–295.

localities. Consequently voting trends in national and local elections have frequently been quite dissimilar.

The government of London

Many countries have special forms of government in their capital cities. The large size of some has sometimes been the cause. Some governments, especially conservative ones, have wanted to keep a potentially "radical" population of the capital city under control and prevent undue local pressure from trying to influence the central authorities. In many countries, therefore, capital cities possess less self-government than other towns, while only a few have more extensive powers. Examples of the first category are Washington, D.C., and Paris; of the second, Vienna.

But London, like many other British institutions, is in a category by itself. In the first place there are several Londons. There is the so-called "City of London" which comprises only the inner heart of the city, primarily the business and financial center, in which over a million people are active during the day but in which few people live at night. Then there is the administrative county of London under the London County Council, which consists of twenty-eight metropolitan boroughs. Finally there is the Greater London area, chiefly the Metropolitan Police District, which comprises the territory of the administrative county of London plus sections of a number of surrounding counties.[21]

A closer integration of these systems has been advocated for over a century, but has always been defeated, ever since the "City" was able to marshal enough strength to achieve the exclusion of London from the provisions of the Municipal Corporations Act of 1835.

The City of London, properly speaking, is an area of about one square mile, located in the heart of London and divided into twenty-six wards. Its constitution, archaic in every way, is a residue of the guild-dominated city system of the Middle Ages. The City is under the control of three "courts," the Court of Aldermen, the Court of Common Council, and the Court of Common Hall.

The City of London relies on the county for its municipal services, although it has a small police force and courts. It administers a number of services and extensive trusts. It also controls certain areas outside the city limits. The City of London is the scene of magnificent ceremonies, especially on the annual "Lord Mayor's Day," but it is an anachronism which serves little purpose and only helps to deprive the boroughs of some very lucrative tax property.

The major government of London is carried out by the London County Council. Its structure and that of the twenty-eight metropolitan boroughs are now consolidated in the London Government Act of 1939, which does for London what the Local Government Act of 1929 has done for the counties, but it is peculiar that the largest metropolitan area in the world is governed like a rural county. The

[21] Parts of Kent, Surrey, Middlesex, Herts, and Essex.

functions of the London County Council however, differ in many ways from those of ordinary counties. This is also true of the twenty-eight metropolitan boroughs, whose powers are much more extensive than is ordinarily the case in other boroughs. A special feature is the Metropolitan Boroughs Standing Joint Committee, which is composed of representatives of the borough and county councils. It is a coordinating body; its chief functions are the maintenance of London's over-all interest, and consultation with the county council and ministries concerned with municipal problems.

The administrative county of London is the only county which does not control its own police. The Metropolitan Police is directly administered by the Home Secretary, who appoints commissioners in order to carry out the actual operations. The Metropolitan Police District is larger than the area of the London County Council, and includes also the county boroughs (Croydon, East Ham, West Ham) and the parts of counties which are located outside the control of the London County. The Metropolitan Police District and similar administrative areas, such as the Metropolitan Water District, the Port of London Authority, and the London Passenger Transport Board, also extend beyond the boundaries of the London County.[22]

[22] In addition to the already mentioned works by the Webbs, Robson, and Clarke, see J. Warren, *The English Local Government System,* London, 1946; E. L. Hasluck, *Local Government in England,* London, 1948, 2d ed.; G. D. H. Cole, *Local and Regional Government,* London, 1947; H. Finer, *English Local Government,* London, 1950, 4th ed.; S. E. Finer, *A Primer of Public Administration,* London, 1950; V. D. Lipman, *Local Government Areas, 1834–1945,* Oxford, 1948; C. R. Attlee, *Borough Councils,* London, 1946, 2d ed. (a brochure); W. J. Jennings, *Principles of Local Government Law,* London, 1947, 3d ed.; J. A. Hawgood, *The Citizen and Government,* London, 1947; and others. See also E. W. Weidner, "Trends in English Local Government," *American Political Science Review,* Vol. XXXIX (1945), p. 337; W. W. Crouch, "Trends in British Local Government," *Public Administration Review,* Vol. VII (1947), p. 254; W. A. Robson, "Reform of Local Government," *Political Quarterly,* Vol. XIX (1948), p. 254; V. Usill, "Democracy in British Local Government," *National Municipal Review,* Vol. XXXV (1946), p. 620; W. A. Robson, *The Development of Local Government,* London, 1948, 2d ed., and *The Government and Misgovernment of London,* London, 1948, 2d ed.; also E. W. Cohen, *Autonomy and Delegation in County Government,* London, 1953. Among older works, see especially H. J. Laski et al. (eds.), *A Century of Municipal Progress,* London, 1935.

8

The commonwealth

The special genius of the British nation has long been expressed in its adaptability to regional differences and change. While French and German administration stress uniformity and logic, British administration suggests diversity and experience. As a result, the British Empire and Commonwealth was and is an extraordinarily complex organization, which is more easily described than defined. Its expansion is immense; it comprises approximately one-fourth of the land surface of the earth and nearly a quarter of the earth's population. Its parts may be found on every continent and in every ocean. There are few important maps on which a section is not printed red, the traditional color of the British Empire.

This Commonwealth includes areas which are directly governed by colonial administrations, but it also includes completely independent states over which London exercises no control whatsoever and over which its influence is most tenuous.

The most varied manners of acquisition were used in placing these territories under the British flag. Rudyard Kipling, the bard of imperial glory, summed it up in these words:

> Some we got by purchase,
> And some we got by trade,
> And some we got by courtesy
> Of pike and carronade.

Some lands were acquired by ostensibly private companies, such as the famous East India Company, but were later taken over by the Crown when the abuses and the maladministration of the companies became obvious. Other lands were taken in the name of the Crown when they were either uninhabited or seemed otherwise desirable. Some were acquired from other powers through treaties of cession— often as a result of war. Many were appropriated because of economic or strategic reasons. In some parts of the empire the original inhabitants have become nearly extinct, while in others they constitute the overwhelming majority. Hundreds of different languages and dialects are spoken, all important races of mankind are included, and every possible type of climate is represented, in both the Northern and Southern Hemispheres. Every stage of cultural development may be found, from the virtual stone-age civilization of the Australian aborigines to the sophisticated culture of the great metropolitan centers of Melbourne, Montreal, or Capetown. Nearly every form of government may be found, from the Governorship of Gibraltar to the self-governing Dominion of Canada or the Republic of India.

The present status and nature of the Commonwealth are the result of evolution, rather than design. A characteristic of British constitutional development has been that men groped more or less blindly for the institutions and legal forms which they considered right, making and formulating their demands, which found fulfillment sooner or later. Of course this development was not always peaceful, as exemplified by the secession of the thirteen American colonies and the uprising in Canada in 1837. More recently, the disturbances which heralded India's independence and the separate status of Pakistan, as well as the bloody incidents in Palestine preceding the expiration of the mandate, the Mau-Mau trouble in Kenya, the Communist guerrillas in Malaya, and the fighting in Cyprus have been examples of the same sort. Nevertheless, although the British record is certainly not spotless, no other country has found it possible to give complete independence to so many of its former possessions and yet keep them within a broader Commonwealth.

It would be quite impossible to evaluate the British colonial administration within the framework of this book. The infinite variety of the Empire and Commonwealth alone would make that impossible. Perhaps it might also be said that successful colonial administration is a contradiction in terms; if the motherland helps its dependent people to obtain a higher standard of living and better education, it also arouses automatically desire for self-government and independence. It is therefore not exaggerated to say that a successful colonial rule rules itself out. But while colonial rule may be on the road to extinction, it has made many contributions to the development of many races and continues to do so. The British, at any rate, do not consider the idea of empire to contain any nefarious connotation but regard it rather as a source of justified pride.

The desire for self-government stirred early in the most advanced colonies. In America, demand for home rule and independence was negligible until 1764–1765, when a new system of taxation was imposed. The lesson of the American War of Independence was drawn rather slowly. Three-quarters of a century later, the Canadian colonies raised similar demands. Canada did not leave the Empire, but its progress toward self-government was fairly rapid. In 1867 it received a constitution—ostensibly in the form of an Act of (the Imperial) Parliament, the British North America Act—and assumed the generic title of "Dominion."[1] Other areas followed, notably Australia in 1900 and South Africa in 1909.

The development toward self-government in these most advanced imperial territories was especially marked in the field of foreign relations. The dominions participated in technical conferences and expected to be consulted with regard to commercial treaties and other questions affecting them. A significant step forward was made during and after the First World War. The dominions had made tremendous contributions to Britain's victory. The fame of the Anzac (Australian and New Zealand Army Corps) troops resounded throughout the Middle East, while the Canadians shed their blood freely at Vimy Ridge, and Indian troops were in evidence in most theaters of war. Imperial leaders, notably General (later Field Marshal) Smuts of South Africa, were consulted on the conduct of the war, and Smuts joined the War Cabinet. The Imperial Conference of 1917 decided to hold a special conference in order to deal with the future constitutional position of the component parts of the Empire. This conference was to recognize the dominions as "autonomous nations of an Imperial Commonwealth," while India was to become "an important portion of the same." India and all dominions except Newfoundland participated in the peace conference of 1919, and certain dominion representatives acted on behalf of the entire Empire in other councils and conferences. The peace treaties were signed and ratified by each dominion and India, which thereby became original members of the League of Nations. Thus the dominions, and to a lesser degree India, had gained equality with each other and with the mother country as well as with foreign states.

In 1920 the British government consented to the establishment of a Canadian legation in Washington, and the principles of equality and self-government were specifically recognized in the Constitution of the Irish Free State of 1922 as enacted by Parliament. In 1923, it was agreed that the dominions were entitled to conclude treaties with foreign states without any participation by United Kingdom representatives.[2]

[1] Although the term "dominion" was used in the British North America Act of 1867, it came into general use only after the Imperial Conference of 1907.
[2] A. J. Toynbee, *Conduct of British Empire Foreign Relations since the Peace Settlement,* London, 1928, pp. 100–104.

The Statute of Westminster

A milestone of the utmost significance was the Imperial Conference of 1926. A number of questions were in doubt and needed settlement; particularly the role of the King's representative in the dominions, the Governor-General, and the right of secession as propounded by the nationalist Prime Minister of the Union of South Africa, General Hertzog.

The Imperial Conference of 1926 defined the position and mutual relations of the United Kingdom and the dominions as follows:

> They are autonomous Communities within the British Empire, equal in status, in no way subordinate one to another in any aspect of their domestic or external affairs, though united by a common allegiance to the Crown, and freely associated as members of the British Commonwealth of Nations. . . . Every self-governing member of the Empire is now master of its destiny. In fact, if not always in form, it is subject to no compulsion whatever. . . . But the principles of equality and similarity, appropriate to *status,* do not universally extend to function.

This definition was undoubtedly premature and, at that time, incorrect. But it clearly foreshadowed changes which were soon enacted.

The legal crystallization of these principles took place in the Statute of Westminster of 1931.[3] It established the Crown as the common symbol of the members of the Commonwealth as well as their common allegiance.[4] Most important of all, however, is the provision that no act of the London Parliament shall extend to any dominion unless that dominion has expressly requested it and it is so stated in the act. The dominion parliaments, in turn, are unlimited in their legislative power except in so far as their own constitutions impose limitations. The dominions may also abolish the power of the Governors-General to "reserve," i.e., veto, bills.

The Commonwealth today

The true nature of the Commonwealth can hardly be discerned from the Statute of Westminster. The Statute itself is vague enough. It points out some of the things which the members of the Commonwealth may or may not do. But with a full application of the British genius for accepting realities and avoiding definitions, it does not tell us what the Commonwealth is. At the enactment of the Statute of Westminster the "British Commonwealth" consisted of the following dominions: the Dominion of Canada, the Commonwealth of Australia, the Dominion of New Zealand, the Union of South Africa, the Irish Free State, and Newfoundland. A somewhat hybrid status existed in Southern Rhodesia and India.

---

[3] 22 Geo. V, c. 4. Australia and New Zealand accepted but did not ratify the Statute.
[4] Therefore the dominions had to be consulted in questions concerning the succession to the throne and similar questions. This point was brought out by Prime Minister Baldwin in the abdication crisis of 1936.

Since that time the situation has become vastly more complicated. New-foundland relinquished its independence in 1933, because of financial difficulties, and was administered by a United Kingdom-Newfoundland Commission until 1948, when it elected (by an unimpressive majority and on second try) to join the Do-minion of Canada and thus became its tenth province on April 1, 1949.

Ireland, never happy in any form of association with England, rapidly shook off all vestiges of its former bondage. It had become a Free State in 1922. In 1937 it proclaimed a new constitution in which the state, then called Eire, was declared to be "sovereign," "independent," and "democratic." The Governor-General was replaced by a President (*Uachtaran nah Eireann*) who is elected by direct vote of the people and who in turn appoints the Prime Minister (*Taoiseach*). The Com-monwealth was not mentioned at all in the 1937 constitution, but Art. 29 em-powered the government to join any group or league of states for certain purposes.

In the Second World War, Ireland chose to remain neutral and thus deprived itself of much sympathy among Allied nations, especially since its neutrality was very helpful to the Germans and tended to render Britain's convoy losses much more serious than they probably would have been had Irish naval and air bases been available. Finally in 1949, exactly thirty-three years after the outbreak of the famous "Easter Rebellion," the last remnants of dominion status were shed, and Eire became officially the Republic of Ireland.

Burma, a former colony, chose to become independent on October 17, 1947 (effective January 6, 1948) and is not a member of the Commonwealth. Another colony, Ceylon, became a dominion in 1948.

But a new status was assumed by the former Indian empire. India had first come under British control as a result of the activities of a group of powerful traders organized in the famous East India Company. By stages the Crown assumed greater control, and after the bloody mutiny of 1857 the Crown took full control, and in 1858 Queen Victoria became Empress of India.

Indian nationalism grew slowly, but by the time of the First World War it was becoming a force to be reckoned with. This pressure resulted in the Govern-ment of India Act of 1919, which granted India some measure of self-government on the local level and for the first time declared the goal of British government to be responsible government for India. Indian self-government continued to expand during the years before World War II, as the result of both official acts and un-official changes made by various Viceroys.

During World War II Indian pressure for independence became fierce. The British were caught between their willingness to let India go eventually and their need for India's resources and strategic location during the war. All attempts to find a solution failed, largely as a result of the split between the Indian nationalists who wanted a unified India and the Moslem nationalists who for a variety of rea-sons were determined to form the separate Islamic state of Pakistan.[5]

---

[5] Meaning "land of the pure," but its letters stand for the names of the various provinces.

The defeat of the Conservative government in 1945 had far-reaching consequences for India. L. S. Amery, the Conservative Secretary of State for India, who
had been thoroughly detested by the Indian leaders, left office and was replaced
by Lord Pethick-Lawrence, of the Labor party. The Viceroy, Lord Wavell, was
directed to renew negotiations.

On February 20, 1947, the British government announced its intention to
grant India its freedom, and on June 3 of the same year revealed its decision to
partition India into two separate entities, with August 15 to be the new independence day. The Indians had already set up a constituent assembly, and despite
enormous difficulties, they and the Moslem League finally accepted the British
proposals.

The appropriate bill passed Parliament on July 18, 1947. Everything in India
was divided between India and Pakistan, from troops right down to typewriters and
paper clips. This process was not smooth, and was followed by bloody riots, termed
"communal," because they involved fighting between religious and racial communities.[6] Over 8 million terrified people crossed the border in each direction. Even
an age like ours, which had become accustomed to cruelty, found the Indian spectacle a chilling experience. Rioting eventually died down under the shock of
Gandhi's assassination in 1948, although later flare-ups occurred, especially in
Bengal.

Most princely states declared their accession either to India or to Pakistan
and were merged with adjacent provinces or formed various types of combinations,
such as the six big "unions" of the larger states. A few of the largest continue to
exist as component parts of the Indian Union. Hyderabad was brought into India
by force in 1949, while Kashmir remains in dispute between India and Pakistan—
a dispute which the United Nations has been trying to solve without success.

India was committed to the adoption of a republican form of government. It
may be surmised that Jawaharlal Nehru, India's Prime Minister and principal
leader of the times, was quite prepared to accept dominion status, but nationalist
pressure and the wording of the new Indian Constitution demanded the proclamation of a republic, which took place in January 26, 1950. Therefore a new formula
had to be found if India wished to remain in the Commonwealth. A Commonwealth
Conference—the new title for the former Imperial Conferences—was held in London in April, 1949, and adopted the following declaration:

> The Governments of the United Kingdom, Canada, Australia, New Zealand,
> South Africa, India, Pakistan and Ceylon, whose countries are united as members
> of the British Commonwealth of Nations and owe a common allegiance to the
> Crown, which is also the symbol of their free association, have considered the
> impending constitutional changes in India.
>
> The Government of India have informed the other governments of the
> Commonwealth of the intention of the Indian people that, under the new Consti-

[6] The biggest difference is neither religious, nor racial, but cultural.

tution which is about to be adopted, India shall become a sovereign independent republic. The Government of India have, however, declared and affirmed India's desire to continue her full membership of the Commonwealth of Nations and her acceptance of the King as the symbol of the free association of its independent member nations and, as such, the head of the Commonwealth.

The governments of the other countries of the Commonwealth, the basis of whose membership of the Commonwealth is not hereby changed, accept and recognize India's continuing membership in accordance with the terms of this declaration.

Accordingly, the United Kingdom, Canada, Australia, New Zealand, South Africa, India, Pakistan and Ceylon hereby declare that they remain united as free and equal members of the Commonwealth of Nations, freely cooperating in the pursuit of peace, liberty and progress. . . .

It will be noted that this significant declaration introduces a number of innovations. The section dealing with the past speaks of a "common allegiance to the Crown" and of a "British Commonwealth of Nations." The section dealing with the present, after India has become a republic, speaks only of the "acceptance of the King as the symbol of the free association of its [the Commonwealth's] independent nations." The King (or Queen) is however the "head of the Commonwealth." The word "Dominion" is carefully excluded, and the new association is referred to as the "Commonwealth of Nations," the word "British" having been dropped.

The road taken by India, Pakistan, and Ceylon has been followed by others, with more to come. Malaya was next. Singapore then united with Malaya in the Federation of Malaysia, but was forced out of the Federation in 1965 much against its will. However, both Malaysia and Singapore have remained in the Commonwealth. In Africa, Ghana, formerly known as the Gold Coast, became self-governing in 1950.[7] Seven years later, Ghana became an independent republic and member of the Commonwealth. In 1960 Nigeria, Britain's largest and richest African possession, acquired the same status, as did South Africa. But in 1961 the Republic of South Africa (formerly called Union of South Africa) left the Commonwealth over the increasingly bitterly fought issue of its racial policies (*apartheid*).

Gradually most of Britain's possessions have become independent republics but have chosen to remain members of the Commonwealth on the model of India. Some, like Aden and the South Arabian sheikhdoms, are scheduled to attain that status later. Some others, like Bermuda or Gibraltar, have remained Crown Colonies.

Britain had tried to form a Federation of Rhodesia and Nyasaland but this endeavor failed. Northern Rhodesia became Zambia and Nyasaland became Malawi. Both remained in the Commonwealth. However, the ruling white minority in (Southern) Rhodesia, headed by Prime Minister Ian Smith, refused to heed British demands for free elections and for the enfranchisement of the African majority and

[7] John R. E. Carr-Gregg, *Self-rule in Africa: Recent Advances in the Gold Coast,* International Conciliation Pamphlet 473, New York, 1951.

in 1965 declared its independence. The British government declared Rhodesia to be in a state of rebellion, but to date British and United Nations sanctions have failed to bring the Smith government to terms.

The Commonwealth has thus become a smaller United Nations. In the field of legislation, the members of the Commonwealth enact their own laws exclusively. The Parliament in London may not legislate with binding effect in the territories of the Commonwealth overseas unless the particular country in question specifically requests it. Even then the member of the Commonwealth may repeal such a law with regard to its own land at any time.

Although most of the constitutions of the dominions were originally enacted formally as acts of the British Parliament, like the British North America Act, the dominions have generally enacted legislation, ratified as a matter of form by the British Parliament, according to which the amendment of those constitutions is solely a matter for the dominion concerned. In Canada this right extends only to federal matters, and constitutional amendments concerning the provinces and a few other matters would still have to be ratified by the British Parliament. This is a matter of form only. There is no intention on the part of the British Parliament to take sides in a dominion's constitutional issues. Comparable situations also exist in Australia and New Zealand, but all these residues of past imperial realities have little practical effect today.

Those members of the Commonwealth which have retained dominion status and thus continue to recognize the monarch as their common sovereign continue to have the monarch's representative, the Governor-General, in their capitals. In years past, Governors-General have exercised prerogatives which would never be permitted to the Queen in the United Kingdom. In particular, they have, on occasion, vetoed or "reserved" bills. Now this right is in disuse. The Governor-General still gives the assent to all bills, but it is quite impossible for him to refuse. In India, of course, there is no governor-general, since India is a republic. There, the head of state is an elected president.

Governors-General are appointed by the Crown, but in all cases they are nominated by the Commonwealth government concerned. Some Governors-General hail from the United Kingdom, while others are natives of the dominion in which they serve.

In their executive functions, the dominions are as free as in their legislative powers. The fiction of "royal" action is preserved via the Governor-General, but such action takes place only on the advice of responsible ministers, just as in the United Kingdom—but of course these are dominion, not United Kingdom, ministers. The monarch therefore may on occasion act technically in contradiction to himself. For instance, during the period of 1939 to 1945 the King was at peace in Eire, then still a dominion of sorts, but he was at war in all the rest of the Commonwealth and Empire.

Being fully sovereign and independent, all members of the Commonwealth are in full command of their own foreign relations. They receive and send diplomatic representatives, and they are all members of the United Nations, several of them having served or serving as members of the Security Council. A special relationship exists between them and the United Kingdom. Although such relations are "foreign relations" for all practical purposes, they are not handled through the usual channels of the Foreign Office and diplomatic representatives, but are in the hands of the Secretary of State for Commonwealth Relations in London and of the various Commonwealth ministers for External Affairs.[8] Instead of diplomatic agents, High Commissioners act as chief representatives on both sides.

A few tenuous strings between the United Kingdom and the Commonwealth nations are preserved in the field of judicial appeal. The Judicial Committee of the Privy Council is the highest court of appeal for the Empire. However among the Dominions, only New Zealand still permits appeal to the Privy Council.[9]

One cannot truly speak of a common policy of the Commonwealth, either in foreign or in domestic affairs. Not only is there no common authority to impose uniformity of action, but the interests of the Commonwealth countries concerned have sometimes been at cross purposes. The sharp antagonism between India and Pakistan over the Kashmir question broke into open warfare in 1965. India and the Republic of South Africa were also constantly at loggerheads over the treatment of Indians in South Africa, until South Africa left the Commonwealth in 1961.

To iron out some of these and lesser problems, occasional Commonwealth Conferences (formerly called Imperial Conferences) are called, usually at the initiative of the British government. But these conferences constitute neither a common executive nor a common legislature. They are merely diplomatic meetings between the representatives of sovereign states. Yet the relationship between these countries is different from ordinary diplomatic relationships. There is no constitution, no law, no rule to bind them together, but there are often a common history, a similarity of procedures, an unspoken affinity which defies definition. Somehow these countries feel a bond, and this sentiment is stronger than any treaty. But this bond is much stronger in those Commonwealth countries which have retained effective democratic and parliamentary government than in those which have not. In fact, in the deep crises which have beset some Commonwealth countries, the Commonwealth has been unable to assert itself. Thus the bitter, bloody 1965 war between India and Pakistan was settled by the Soviet Union and the United States. Neither was it possible in 1965 and 1966 to prevent the bloody disorder and the steady deterioration of the situation in once-promising Nigeria. Nor has it been possible to keep Rhodesia from defecting.

[8] However, on January 1, 1965, the staffs of the Foreign Ministry and of the Commonwealth Relations Office were amalgamated.
[9] In 1940 the Supreme Court of Canada held that the Parliament of Canada had power to abolish the right of appeal to the Privy Council. This was upheld by the Privy Council [A.C. 127 (1947)]. In 1949 the Canadian Parliament enacted the Supreme Court Act (*The New York Times,* Dec. 23, 1949) making the Supreme Court of Canada the final Court of Appeals. Although Australia has not formally abolished appeals to the Privy Council, no such appeals have been made since 1950 and this form of appeal may in effect be considered defunct.

Other parts of the Empire

While the members of the Commonwealth of Nations are without doubt the most important parts of the former British Empire, they are not the only ones. There are a great many Crown Colonies which are administered in various fashions by officials of the Colonial Office, all of which have certain but varying measures of self-government. In some regions this degree of self-government is very high. There are also "condominia," areas held in common with other countries.

Some areas are termed "protectorates" because they are technically not British possessions but are subject to British control, under limitations determined by treaty. Such British control always extends over military matters and foreign affairs, but it also penetrates to varying degrees into the domestic affairs of the protectorate. In actuality, there is little substantitve difference between protectorates and Crown Colonies.

A new type of overseas possession was introduced after the First World War in the form of mandates, which later, under the United Nations and with significant changes, became the network of trusteeships. Trust territories are former enemy possessions whose relationship to the trustee is determined by treaty between the United Nations and the trustee. However, the conditions imposed by the United Nations Charter and the above-mentioned treaties are not too stringent. Different from the mandate system of the League of Nations, the trusteeship system of the United Nations permits arming of trust territories for purposes of self-defense and related objectives, and a trust territory may be designated a "strategic area," in which case military and naval use is virtually unlimited.

Britain is responsible to the United Nations, especially to the Trusteeship Council, for its stewardship in the trust territories.[10] Unfortunately, however, the Trusteeship Council, together with all other organs of the United Nations, has been made a battleground for East-West controversy, and has accommodated the taste of excolonial states for baiting their former masters. The British feel that much of the criticism which Britain has had to endure has been caused by political maneuvering, unrelated to the facts. They have therefore taken a cool attitude toward the Trusteeship Council and have curtailed the right of the United Nations to send inspectors to trust territories. Since none of Britain's trust territories appears to be capable of immediate independence, it is probably safe to assume that they will soon be indistinguishable from ordinary Crown Colonies.

It is extremely difficult to classify the governmental system of British overseas possessions because of their large variety and the constant change in their status. There is always a governor, whose powers may be very large or more limited, depending on the advancement of the colony concerned. There is also usually an ex-

---

[10] That the obligations under the trusteeship system are not empty words may be gathered from the strenuous attempts of the Republic of South Africa to incorporate her trust territory, the former German South-West Africa, into her territory—an endeavor which has been strongly opposed by the natives.

ecutive council with advisory function, on which natives may or may not be represented. More advanced colonies have legislative assemblies with varying powers. Local government is usually left to local chieftains with varying degrees of British supervision. There are also colonial courts whose verdicts may be appealed to the Judicial Committee of the Privy Council in London.

The general tenor is constant advancement toward ever greater degrees of self-government. Another trend in British colonial administration has been toward favoring regionalism, although most of such attempts, like the Central African Federation, have failed. Still another approach has been the creation of a Commissioner-General for Southeast Asia who does not supersede the existing colonial administrations but helps to coordinate their particularly difficult problems. Closely related is an ambitious regional development scheme known as the Colombo Plan,[11] which envisages a long-range program of rehabilitation, economic improvement, and technical assistance in Southeast Asia through Commonwealth cooperation and American participation.

The trend toward independence is seemingly irreversible. As the British defense review of 1966 graphically illustrated, Britain is unwilling and unable to carry for long the burden of colonialism and the enormous financial outlays which it requires. Some instances of common administration or at any rate of common defense have appeared, especially with the United States and Australia. But direct British control outside the British Isles is certain to shrink further, and fusion of the Colonial and the Commonwealth Relations Offices is now a fact.

[11] John R. E. Carr-Gregg, *The Colombo Plan: A Commonwealth Program for Southeast Asia,* International Conciliation Pamphlet 467, New York, 1951.

9

The outlook

The choices Britain faces in the late 1960s are not easy. Despite a traditional suspicion of Continental governments and a deep attachment to the Commonwealth, the state of Britain's economy is steadily pushing her closer to Europe and the Common Market. This economic necessity is not coupled with any great enthusiasm for European integration and thus contrasts with the widespread desire for greater European unity which exists both on the Continent and in the United States.

Simultaneously, the growing split between Britain's responsibilities and her power, between her resources and her need for military security, as well as her long enjoyment of a special relationship with the United States, are pulling her toward this country. Internal and external, physical and spiritual problems all face the British as they move toward the fourth quarter of the twentieth century.

Britain also feels that her security requirements are best met by close collaboration with the United States. For this reason Britain has retained a military presence "east of Suez," although economic necessities have made the British Army of the Rhine an increasingly skeletal force in NATO. That these forces, as well as those east of Suez will be further reduced was clearly heralded by the defense review of 1966. After 1970 the British presence east of Suez is scheduled to cease.

At such a time Great Britain is particularly blessed to have a stable form of government. The British political party system continues to show such vitality that its future and its development can hardly be in doubt. Nor can there be much doubt about the fact that although the Liberal party has shown a certain talent for survival and was able to increase its vote considerably in both the 1959 and 1964 elections, its ability to turn that often thinly spread vote into a much larger representation in Parliament was proven unavailing once again in 1966. The basic fact that Britain has in the main a two-party system is therefore not likely to change in the future.

Another highly significant factor has been that neither political party is strictly a class party and that both appeal to a wide stratum of occupation and education. Both parties vie for the adherence of the middle class, although that class is hard to define, since objective ratings are faulty and subjective ratings (people's own estimates of their class adherence) are even faultier.[1] Further, the degree to which one or the other party appeals to the more educated voter has had less bearing than might have been expected because, despite the vastly extended educational facilities in Britain, higher education is still reserved to a relatively small percentage of the population. The great majority of the voters, that is, the group which is so large that both parties must derive their major support from it, have had similar, not very extensive, educational experience.[2] No doubt a more equal and less stratified population is emerging in Britain, but it is emerging in both political parties and is therefore a unifying and not a divisive element.

All these factors have had a deeply moderating influence on both major parties. The Conservatives are fully aware of the fact that the many far-reaching changes which Britain has undergone since the end of World War II now form a solid part of the country's national life. For the Labor party, on the other hand, nationalization and planning, although still favored, have proved somewhat less than the cure-all that an earlier doctrine envisioned. And the trade unions have come to realize that it is no easier to deal with the state as employer than to deal with private owners; if anything, the private owner, being less powerful, is more easily overcome.

This hugging of the middle of the road by each party is essentially a way of showing that both are in effect national parties following national policies. It has, naturally, not been pleasing to the more extreme wing of either party. The overlapping of the policies of the two parties does interfere with neat distinctions and abstract classification. But it is also the mark of a basically mature and increasingly balanced society.

[1] John Bonham, *The Middle Class Vote*, London, 1954; Mark Denney et al., *How People Vote*, London, 1956; R. S. Milne and H. C. Mackenzie, *Straight Fight*, London, 1955.
[2] Richard Hoggart, *The Use of Literacy*, London, 1961; Mark Abrams, "New Routes of Working Class Conservatives," *Encounter*, May, 1961, pp. 57–59.

part **2**

France

All my life, I have had a certain conception of France, which emotion as well as reason have inspired in me. The emotional side of me tends to imagine France as the princess in the fairy tales, or the Madonna in the frescoes, as dedicated to an exalted and exceptional destiny. Instinctively I have the impression that Providence has created her either for complete success or for exemplary misfortunes.

Charles de Gaulle, Mémoires de guerre: L'Appel, 1940–1942

Many are the ties of friendship and common cause which exist between the United States and France. Great are the contributions of France to civilization and the arts of government. Yet few Americans have been able to suppress feelings of impatience, frustration, and exasperation when contemplating the French political and economic scene in the past or in the present. How difficult it is to understand a country which does much brilliantly but so often to excess!

Here is a country which nature has endowed with abundant blessings. Well-supplied with natural resources and a fertile soil, France has an ideal balance between rural and urban population. Hers is a people of diligence and many skills. Her educational system is of a high order, producing a well-informed, intelligent, and politically sophisticated population, although overcrowded facilities present difficult problems.

Of most outstanding interest for the student of political science is France's lasting and continuing contribution to the realm of political ideas and institutions. Few events, if any, in the entire history of mankind have ever electrified the human race as did the French Revolution of 1789. All Continental European ideas of liberty, of popular sovereignty, and of the republican form of government either are directly derived therefrom or owe France a heavy debt.

The student who considers the nature of parliamentary democracy is inclined to think first of England. But the Third and Fourth Republics of France have given the world a different approach to that same subject—the system of assembly government—which has found many, though often involuntary, followers. And the Fifth Republic has contributed a unique type of presidential leadership and a special system combining features of presidential and parliamentary government.

Less spectacular, but just as significant, is France's leadership in the highly important field of administrative justice, which we in the United States have only recently discovered and about which we can learn much from the genius of France's Council of State.

But for a long time France experienced great difficulties in finding herself. Her disunity, her relatively slow rate of recovery, the weakness of her fiscal system, her difficulty in creating a positive foreign policy weakened the resonance of her voice in the council of states until the return to power of General de Gaulle in 1958. And afterwards, when there was stability and firmness in all domains, many observers began to feel that stability and firmness were turning into obstinacy and a determination to unravel the precious threads of an increasingly united Europe and of the North Atlantic Alliance.

At the root of the problem stands a fact stated time after time by a galaxy of writers, namely, that Frenchmen are individualists of an extreme kind. French individualism differs substantially from the English and American variety. In the English-speaking world, individualism expresses itself in a reluctance to accept too readily the ministrations of a paternalistic government. At the same time, the members of the Anglo-American family have been by no means adverse to voluntary group action, a habit fostered especially by the growth of Protestantism and an-

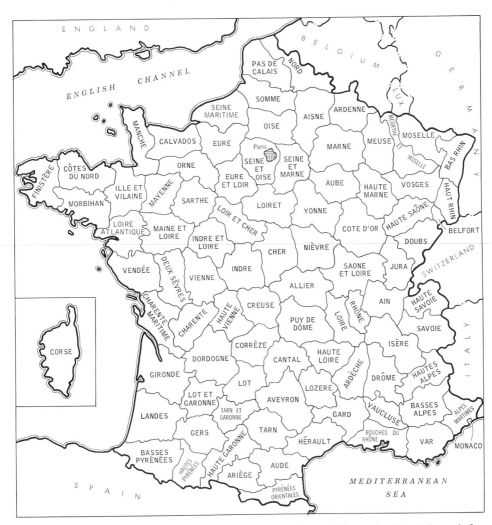

chored in the modalities of the new industrial society.[1] Thus, the English and the Americans, as well as such other nations as the Swiss and the Scandinavians, have that rare gift which makes democratic government a living reality, namely, voluntary discipline. To the Anglo-American peoples, individualism is a modern idea, well suited to the industrial age and its demand for collective action as long as it is the result of a free exchange of ideas and is carried out after a full hearing and under due process of law.

[1] On the relations between religion, capitalism, and democracy, see especially Max Weber, *Protestant Ethic and the Spirit of Capitalism,* London, 1930, and R. H. Tawney, *Religion and the Rise of Capitalism,* London, 1926.

French individualism is essentially a quest for personal independence. "At the end of his day's work the English miner goes to play football; the French miner, who has remained a peasant, goes into his garden."[2] To preserve this precious independence, a Frenchman will toil from dawn till dusk, he will live a most frugal existence, and he will always try to make ends meet. Once he has saved enough, he is likely to retire to live on the interest of his investments, as a *rentier,* though economic developments have now made that quite difficult. He thus becomes the prototype of the French "solid citizen," the *bourgeois.* One of the keenest observers, himself a Frenchman and a patriot, has characterized him thus: "To acquire a little property, a little house, a little business, a little pension is the dream of millions of Frenchmen. It is a precise, limited aim without romanticism: he who pursues it is a realist and may even be called wise, but he borders on the mediocre."[3]

While a part of French business remains as described above,[4] a huge process of modernization has taken place. In 1964 France's gross national product rose from NF 395.6 billion to NF 431.9 billion. When the European Economic Community (Common Market) was first created in 1957, French business and industry had been apprehensive about their ability to cope with competition, especially Germany's. But the results were excellent, and French industry has truly come into its own. Much credit for this has been given to France's planning organization, *Commissariat Général du Plan;* experts from all over the world, including the United States, have flocked to Paris to study the operation. But even greater praise is probably due to a new, chiefly young class of managers, sometimes called "technocrats," who are essentially apolitical and who are imbued with a passion for making things work.

The political stability created by the Fifth Republic, the abandonment of the drain of the Algerian conflict, and the opportunities created by the Common Market set the stage for French economic rebirth.

However, none of this has killed French individualism, which embodies the idea of life in isolation, economically, socially, and intellectually. The gregarious, frivolous, risqué Frenchman so often portrayed in drama and novels is not typical of his country but represents only a small group which impresses foreigners far more than it impresses Frenchmen. Unfortunately, the French ideal of individualism belongs to a day long gone by when life in isolation was possible. Modern society poses quite different problems: not of individual versus group action, but of voluntary versus enforced group action.

His individualism causes the Frenchman to be suspicious of his government and to take a cynical attitude toward it. Yet his intellectual clarity of mind—the mark of an old civilization and of mature reflection—coupled with a Latin tem-

---

[2] Paul Morand, *Paris-Tombouctou,* Paris, 1929, p. 84, quoted by André Siegfried in *Tableau des partis en France,* Paris, 1930, p. 14.
[3] Siegfried, *op. cit.,* pp. 28–29.
[4] David S. Landes, "French Business and the Businessman: A Social and Cultural Analysis," in *Modern France,* ed. by E. M. Earle, Princeton, 1951, pp. 334–353.

perament, causes him to embrace idealistic schemes which are totally unconnected with his personal interests. He is ready to die for his country, but not to pay its taxes. Even if he is a *bourgeois,* he may fervently embrace the spirit of the French Revolution and cast his vote for a radical candidate—as long as his privacy and his property are not interfered with. "The French carry their heart on the Left and their pocketbook on the Right" is a much-quoted saying.

It is difficult to induce such people to unite except in a dire emergency, and, short of war, it is not easy to convince them that such an emergency exists. To stress the need for unified action has been the earnest endeavor of every succeeding French government since the liberation. "It was imperative then and . . . it is essential now that the French people reacquire the desire and taste for authority, an authority freely accepted. We felt that our main task was to persuade Frenchmen gradually to resume the necessary practice of civic discipline," declared a leading French statesman who was several times Premier.[5] General de Gaulle had a different approach:[6]

> Only great undertakings are capable of holding in balance the ferments and scattering which its (France's) people carry in themselves. And our country, such as it is, among the others, such as they are, must, under pain of mortal danger, aim high and hold itself straight. In a word, as I see it, France cannot be France without greatness [*grandeur*].

And indeed, General de Gaulle did unite France, at least for a while, in "great undertakings." France's road to recovery and her entry into the European Communities, especially the Common Market, were begun before De Gaulle took office, particularly under Jean Monnet and the late, great Robert Schuman. But probably no other man than De Gaulle could have freed France so radically and so completely from her terrible mortgage in Algeria. It is quite probable that only a man of his great historical stature and incredible tenacity could have raised France to an importance in world affairs which neither friend nor foe can always appreciate and which has given France a weight that exceeds considerably her resources in manpower, territory, or wealth. Whatever one might think of it, it was without doubt a dazzling example of statecraft of the utmost virtuosity.

For this there was a price to pay. The Constitution of the Fifth Republic is a democratic one. Although there have been excesses, the press and speech are free. Political parties of all descriptions exist and pursue their activities. And yet, for most of the duration of the Fifth Republic, France has been governed by one-man rule. Certainly not one-man rule of the Hitler or Mussolini type, nor even like that of a Latin American *caudillo,* but one-man rule nevertheless, in the sense that only one man counted and only one man made all important decisions. The government

[5] From a speech by Robert Schuman, then Premier of France, delivered at Poitiers, Apr. 18, 1948. *Le Monde,* Apr. 20, 1948.
[6] General de Gaulle, *Mémoires de guerre,* Paris, 1955, Vol. I, *L'Appel, 1940–1942,* p. 1.

ministers became a group of executors, practically of secretaries carrying out the President's wishes. The parliament, although its free debate was in no way curtailed, was cowed by its own sense of impotence, and the traditional political parties were pursued by a sense of failure and frustration.

Strangest spectacle of all, France, that country of the never-ending political debates, the passionate intellectual hair-splitting, that "political country" par excellence, suddenly seemed to have become "depoliticized." Frenchmen continued to criticize this or that aspect of De Gaulle's policy but then proceeded to shrug their shoulders, either because they thought that he after all knew best, or because nothing really could be done and things were not running so badly. Even a few months before General de Gaulle's return to power, no observer had foreseen such a transformation. And as the presidential elections of December 5 and 19, 1965, approached, practically all observers foresaw a shoo-in for General de Gaulle and a continuation of his regime as before.

But this was not to be. True, General de Gaulle was reelected by a comfortable majority on the second ballot. But the election, the first popular election of a French president in over 100 years, and the appearance of opposing candidates on television revived that which many observers had thought to be dead, namely a political debate. Perhaps the most significant result of that remarkable election was not the fact that General de Gaulle was refused the "massive and open support of the citizens" which he demanded,[7] but that the apathy and somnolence of the Fifth Republic were over. And this popular verdict was confirmed by the parliamentary elections of 1966, which gave General de Gaulle only a razor-thin and uncertain majority.

Where all this will lead is difficult to say as these lines are written. But one thing is certain: only a nation of great vitality could have moved so swiftly from the chronic disease of the Fourth Republic to the stability and power, excessive in the views of some, of the Fifth. And only that same brilliant and creative spirit could again have engendered the reaction of December, 1965. Those who have written France off as passé were proven wrong at least twice. And there is further proof: all the great and creative ideas of the post-World War II period, whether they were carried out, like the Schuman Plan and the Common Market, or failed, like the European Defense Community, had Frenchmen among their spiritual fathers—while other Frenchmen rose as their most determined opponents.

This then is France: a country of contrast and diversity, an old land with many new ideas, a country with almost an oversupply of talents, some of which neutralize each other, a country whose determination can be glorious and whose obstinacy can be exasperating, a fascinating subject for study, an object of marvel and despair to friend and foe alike.

---

[7] Radio and television address by General Charles de Gaulle, Nov. 4, 1965.

1

Early constitutional and political development

In a very real sense France's modern political and constitutional history begins in 1789, the year of the great Revolution. True, earlier developments left their trace, but the Revolution was a break with the past, and there are few modern concepts and problems which cannot be traced back to that epoch.

The *ancien régime*

The prerevolutionary era, known as the *ancien régime,* was characterized by a combination of absolutism and centralism, devised to keep the various feudal lords under control. It reached into every region and was exercised by a well-organized bureaucracy under the leadership of the King's council.

The *ancien régime* did not permit a legislature in which the legitimate complaints of the people could be debated openly. A general assembly, the Estates

General, had been known for centuries but had no legislative functions and was usually convoked only in times of great crisis.

Accordingly, public indignation over the severe social inequalities found no outlet until it erupted into violent revolution. The intellectual fathers of the Revolution had no actually existing state of affairs in mind when they described their ideas, with the exception of the American example and a misconception of the British form of government. The idea of the Revolution was therefore conceived in the abstract. But this idea had many origins. There was the influence of Rousseau's theories as expressed in the new nationalism of the Revolution. There was the political individualism of the natural-law school and the economic individualism of the physiocrats. The nationalism which the French Revolution engendered led everywhere to a serious intensification of political struggles. Wars which had hitherto been dynastic, almost private affairs, now became the struggle of great masses rising to the new nationalist battle cries. But this nationalism, so disastrous to the stability of the world, also carried with it the new ideas of individual rights, of representative institutions, and of liberalism.

The Declaration of the Rights of Man

The outstanding expression of the natural-law concept and the resulting belief in individual rights is the "Declaration of the Rights of Man and of the Citizen" of 1789. Several authorities have offered impressive evidence that it was in fact modeled on its American counterpart.[1]

The Declaration asserted the principles of personal freedom and equality, the rights of man to liberty, property, security, and resistance to oppression. It recognized the right of the citizen to participate either directly or through representatives in the legislative process. It recognized the freedom of thought and religion, of speech, press, and assembly. It forbade arrest and indictment except as prescribed by law, and prohibited the taking of private property without just compensation.

The Declaration formed the preamble of the Constitution of 1791 and was repeated or expressly recognized in subsequent documents, including the present Constitution of the French Republic.

The intellectual influence of the Declaration on European thought and practice was enormous. Everywhere men were inspired to think in terms of individual

---

[1] Georg Jellinek, *Die Erklärung der Menschen und Bürgerrechte,* Munich, 1927, 4th ed., pp. 7ff.; H. E. Bourne, "American Constitutional Precedents in the French National Assembly," *American Historical Review,* Vol. VIII (1903), pp. 466–486; J. H. Robinson, "The French Declaration of the Rights of Man," *Political Science Quarterly,* Vol. VI (1899), pp. 653–662; Crane Brinton, "Declaration of the Rights of Man," *Encyclopaedia of the Social Sciences,* Vol. III, pp. 49–51. Brinton cites a French pamphlet published in 1791 showing connections between the American documents and the French Declaration.

rights. Its specific constitutional significance in France, however, has always remained questionable because it has never been a true constitutional document in the Anglo-American sense; it was rather a syllabus of aims and purposes or, in the words of a distinguished writer, a part of the "social" constitution as distinguished from the political. It was, and it has remained a philosophical call for action which was sometimes heeded and sometimes not. It has never constituted the specific limitations on government which were instituted by the comparable provisions of the United States Constitution.

The Revolution

The government of France which the Revolution established was as powerful as that which it had overthrown. In contrast to certain British and especially American ideas which emphasize the limitations of governmental power, the French were more concerned with the control of that power than with its extent. According to the concepts of popular sovereignty this control, hitherto in the hands of an all-powerful king, would now be wielded by the sovereign nation itself. But in a modern, large state, popular sovereignty is always rather theoretical, because the people as a whole cannot rule. From a political and institutional point of view this meant that sovereignty was actually exercised by the legislature, the *convention.* From a sociological standpoint, control was now in the hands of the *bourgeoisie,* the victor of the Revolution. While the Revolution was not able to establish direct rule by the citizens themselves, it made the rise of a strong executive most difficult. Hence, legislative supremacy, also called assembly government or *gouvernement conventionnel,* became identified with the spirit of the Revolution and with those political groups which consider themselves the true custodians of the nation's revolutionary heritage.

The Revolution is tied to the republican tradition of France. An affirmative attitude toward the Republic is supposed to entail an acceptance of the ideas of the Revolution. It is therefore not unusual for otherwise very conservative citizens to give their vote to parties which profess to be revolutionary and hence acting in the true spirit of France.

The Revolution went a long way toward creating a nation. But it also created profound cleavages which are not overcome even today. This is most sharply defined in the now wholly historical struggle over the relationship between state and church in which the parties which consider themselves as belonging to the traditional "left" regard the Catholic Church as antirevolutionary and therefore as an enemy, despite the fact that these terms have lost all meaning today. But in France historical struggles are carried on regardless of the pertinence of the question to contemporary issues. In a way, the entire question about the direction in which "progress" lies has divided and continues to divide the French nation and often prevents it from busying itself with less fundamental, but more practical and urgent tasks. Such fundamental cleavages also make for intransigence which renders most difficult the daily compromises on which all government is based.

The first constitutions

The National Assembly which drafted the first Constitution of France, that of September 3, 1791, was actually nothing but the so-called Third Estate of the Estates General (*états généraux*), a quasi-legislature of medieval origin. After a history during which the Estates General were sometimes influential, especially when the king needed money, and sometimes not, popular pressure and dire financial strain caused Louis XVI to revive the institution and even to double the representation of the burghers, the Third Estate (*tiers état*).

The Constitution of 1791 was a curious mixture of monarchical and republican principles. It established in most solemn manner the fundamental rights of the citizen. Its references to popular sovereignty were, however, difficult to implement. A number of fruitless attempts were made in a series of constitutions which followed one another rapidly: the already mentioned one of 1791, that of 1793, and that of 5 Fructidor, Year III (August 22, 1795).[2] But the Constitution of 22 Frimaire, Year VIII (December 13, 1800), finally abandoned the attempt by proclaiming that "the government is entrusted to three Consuls who are appointed for six years and are reeligible."

These constitutions were influenced by Jean Jacques Rousseau's doctrine of popular sovereignty, but they failed to respond to his demand that this sovereignty be exercised directly and not through deputies. In actual application, therefore, the legislative branch which, according to prevailing beliefs, most closely represented the will of the people became sovereign rather than the people themselves. Rousseau's demand for direct government was fulfilled only in the form of elections and plebiscites. The latter, however, were frequently abused and do not have a good reputation in France despite their continued existence.

The principle of popular sovereignty was also anchored in the maxim that the people alone could change the Constitution and that they could change it at will. It is true that the manner in which such constitutional changes could be brought about was prescribed in the Constitution, but ever since the Revolution it has been a time-honored tenet that the people cannot be restrained by mere form in the exercise of their sovereign will. Consequently constitutional changes have more often than not been the result of revolutions and of *coups d'état*.[3] For the same reason, judicial review of legislation or any other form of constitutional restraint on legislatures has been generally in disfavor, although the Constitution of the Year VIII did take some wholly theoretical steps in that direction.

[2] The First French Republic attempted to reorganize the calendar. The years were counted from the beginning of the Revolution; the months were renamed and completely rearranged. Fructidor, for instance, lasted from August 18 to September 16.

[3] Jean Brissaud, *A History of French Public Law* (trans. by J. W. Garner), Boston, 1915, p. 545.

Napoleon

Despite the Revolution's professed belief in popular sovereignty, there were many instances of short-lived strong executive leadership. Most notable was the revolutionary Committee of Public Safety, which developed into a dictatorship as absolute as any royal government had ever been. The Constitution of the Year III marked a reaction against the broad basis of its predecessors. Voting qualifications were reinstituted, a second chamber, the Council of Elders, was established, and the executive power was vested in the Directory of five members.

The Constitution of the Year III was the last democratic organic act of the revolutionary period. Its successor, the Constitution of the Year VIII, was strictly authoritarian, and its machinery was placed under the exacting control of the First Consul, Napoleon Bonaparte. Its principal legislative body, the "conservative Senate," was appointed for life and was self-perpetuating. It had power to annul unconstitutional acts, but by decree (*sénatus-consulte*) it amended the Constitution by establishing the Consulate for life in 1802 and the Empire in 1804.

Schoolbooks generally emphasize the belligerent exploits of Napoleon, but far more lasting and significant were his administrative reforms. The judicial system, already streamlined by the Revolution, was made more uniform by Napoleon. Judges, who in the earlier revolutionary period had been elected, were again appointed. In order to satisfy the French concept of the separation of powers, the Council of State (*Conseil d'État*) and prefectural councils were established for the purpose of rendering administrative justice.

Formidable was the work of codification which created the great series of legal codes: the Code of Civil Law (1804), the Code of Civil Procedure (1807), the Code of Criminal Law (1808, supplemented in 1810), and the Code of Commercial Law (1807).

French local government also took its final form under Napoleon. The old territorial divisions of the *ancien régime* had been irregular, inconsistent, and full of enclaves. They were the results of dynastic considerations, acquisition by marriage and conquest, and historical accident. The royal regime used these divisions effectively by imposing on them royal agents designed to keep in check the centrifugal tendencies of the nobles. The Revolution swept all that away and created a unified system of local government composed of departments, districts, cantons, and communes. Some forms of local councils were established, but because of the complete absence of experience with local government, these resulted in chaotic conditions. In order to alleviate them, the central government reverted to the methods of the *ancien régime* by sending delegates at large with considerable power to the various regions. Through them, local government quickly became the creature of the central authorities.

Under Napoleon this system was regularized and the government established permanent strict control over local government, even in the most minute detail, through the departmental prefect.

The restored Bourbons

Upon his first return from long exile, the restored Bourbon monarch Louis XVIII enacted the Constitutional Charter of June 4, 1814, which was full of allusions to divine providence and the other customary formulas of legitimism, but satisfied neither the reactionaries, for whom it did not go far enough, nor the liberals, to whom it smelled of the *ancien régime*. After the death of Louis XVIII in 1824, his brother, Charles X, immediately proceeded to go the *ancien régime* one better; but the cup finally flowed over, and the Revolution of 1830 chased the King out of the country.

Constitutional monarchy

The rebellious burghers called to the throne Duke Louis Philippe of Orléans, the son of the man who, under the name of Philippe-Égalité, had been a member of the Revolutionary Convention, had voted for the death sentence against his cousin, Louis XVI, and had finally gone to the guillotine himself as a member of the Girondist party.

The regime of Louis Philippe was that of a constitutional monarchy with reasonably liberal content. Its Constitutional Charter of August 14, 1830, avoided the provocative preamble of the Charter of 1814. But the imagination of the regime was exhausted with these initial reforms. It resisted all further change, which was fatal at a time which knew great advances in human thinking. It gradually lost all support and, at the first show of force against it, it collapsed. On February 24, 1848, Louis Philippe left the country, never to return.

The Second Republic

If the constitutional monarchy had been lacking in imagination, the Second Republic possessed this fault to an even greater extent. Its sole contribution was the institution of universal suffrage. But the government proved itself incapable of coping with a serious economic condition and met with the bitter resistance of the workers who, under the influence of socialist ideas, rose in arms in June, 1848. After a bloody battle, the workers were defeated, and their movement stepped into the background of the political stage, from which it returned only many years later.

The Constitution of November 4, 1848, was modeled on the American example and created a presidency of the Republic in which was vested all executive power. Then, on December 2, the French people went to the polls and by overwhelming majority elected to this all-important post none other than Louis Napoleon Bonaparte, a nephew of the great emperor. The new President attempted from the outset to discredit the legislature, a majority of whom were both antirepublican and anti-Bonapartist. Since the Constitution had made the president ineligible to succeed himself, Louis Napoleon accomplished his aim by a *coup d'état* on December 1–2, 1851. Having seized power and abrogated the offensive presidential election laws, Louis Napoleon demanded that a plebiscite give him power to write a new constitution. The response was overwhelming: 7,439,216 voted "yes," while only 640,757 voted "no," and 36,820 ballots were invalid.

The Second Empire

The Constitution thus sanctioned in advance was promptly promulgated on January 14, 1852, very much in the image of the Constitution of the Year VIII. Like that earlier document, it was merely a stepping stone to the restoration of the Empire. It was established in late 1852, by a Senate vote which pronounced Louis Napoleon Bonaparte Emperor of the French under the name of Napoleon III. The Senate resolution was submitted to a plebiscite, which gave its consent to the reestablishment of the Empire by the stupendous majority of 7,824,189 votes against a mere 153,145. Once again it was demonstrated that universal suffrage and free elections are no guarantee against the rise of autocracy.

In the beginning the Second Empire was strictly authoritarian, but after 1860 somewhat more popular government was instituted and greater emphasis was placed on parliamentary government. The Constitution of May 21, 1870, was even more liberal and constituted a real concession to the mounting disaffection among the people.

A new and promising era seemed to dawn over France. But on July 19, 1870, Napoleon III plunged his country into a hasty and ill-considered war against Prussia, and on September 1 the dream of the Second Empire vanished in the disastrous battle of Sedan together with the tarnished crown of the Emperor. When this dreadful news reached Paris, the legislature reinstituted the Republic and set up an emergency government.

A renowned historian and philosopher once remarked that outstanding historical facts and personalities frequently appear twice in the course of history. Another observer commented that he might have added, "once as a tragedy, and once as a farce." "If Napoleon I was the tragedy, Napoleon III was the farce."

The Third Republic

The period 1870 to 1875 not only gave rise to the Third Republic, but also created the foundations of the Fourth, its nearly identical successor, and set the stage on which the Fifth Republic eventually appeared.

The end of the Second Empire brought about various propositions concerning the future course to be followed. For a while they were all brushed aside by the people of Paris, who set up spontaneously a provisional Government of National Defense whose guiding spirit was the fiery Italian-born Léon Gambetta. But despite Gambetta's ardor in raising new armies in the provinces, and despite the diplomatic efforts of such respected men as Thiers and Ferry, the Germans ruled the field, occupied much of France, and besieged Paris, which capitulated on January 28, 1871.

The electoral campaign of 1871 centered on the issue of peace or war. And the victory of the conservative forces who favored peace with Germany was decisive. The majority favored a constitutional monarchy, but this came to naught because they were divided between the "legitimists," adherents of the Bourbon monarchy, whose candidate was the pretender, the Count of Chambord, a grandson of Charles X, and Orléanists, whose candidate was the Count of Paris, a grandson of ex-King Louis Philippe. There was also a small group of Bonapartists who remained faithful to Napoleon III and, after his death in 1873, to his son, the Prince Imperial.

Thiers

By a resolution of February 17, 1871, Adolphe Thiers was elected "Chief Executive" rather than President, thus avoiding the creation of a strictly republican institution. He was a man of great prestige, experience, and dignity and got along well with Bismarck, which was important. Although he was to exercise his power under the control of the National Assembly, he dominated it by his enormous prestige and eloquence. But after he had suppressed the uprising of the Paris Commune by force, the National Assembly no longer considered him indispensable.

Undoubtedly he would have been succeeded by a monarch had the monarchist cause not been defeated by the incredible blindness of the principal pretender, the Count of Chambord. He was surrounded by a coterie of faithful followers who were as much out of contact with France as he was, and insisted that the French nation must expiate its sins before it could return to the law and order which he proposed to give it. The symbol of his own limited mind was his stubborn insistence that the tricolor flag of France, originally of revolutionary origin, but now accepted by almost all, had to be abandoned and replaced by the white-lily banner, the symbol of the *ancien régime*.

The attitude of the pretender dealt a mortal blow to the monarchist cause. The results of the July, 1871, elections held in forty-six departments showed a decisive shift of public opinion toward republicanism.

As a result, the Rivet law of August 31, 1871, moved a little closer to republicanism. But two years later the growing conflict between President and Assembly resulted in a curtailment of presidential powers and Thiers's downfall.

His successor was Marshal MacMahon, Duke of Magenta, hero of the Crimean and Franco-Austrian Wars, who had been badly defeated and captured at Sedan during the Franco-Prussian War.

The Constitution of the Third Republic

Under MacMahon the character of the presidency changed radically and took on the form which it kept through the Fourth Republic. The shift resulted from a difference in personality rather than from the passage of new laws. Thiers had been an extraordinary politician and statesman, a splendid orator, and a renowned historian. MacMahon was brave and dull, personally an honest man, but a convinced monarchist and reactionary. About politics he knew little and cared less. He was quite content to play the role of a formal head of state and leave the actual government of the country to his ministers. Among them the Vice President became Premier in everything but name.

The National Assembly took due notice of this change and on November 20, 1873, adopted a law removing the President from responsibility to the Assembly and giving him a fixed term of seven years, the so-called *septennat* which is still in effect today.

In subsequent constitutional debates, a number of proposals were submitted, especially by deputies Casimir Périer and Laboulaye, which would have established a clear-cut republican form of government, but which were rejected by the predominantly monarchist Assembly which was prevented from following its natural inclinations only by the intransigent attitude of the pretender.

Finally, amidst general confusion, deputy Wallon proposed an amendment which read as follows: "The President of the Republic is elected by an absolute majority of the Senate and the Chamber of Deputies joined together in the National Assembly." This amendment was designed to separate the Republic from the person of the Marshal and thus make the Republic permanent. The crucial vote on the Wallon amendment was taken in breathless excitement. The result was adoption by 353 against 352. Thus by indirection and amidst confusion, the Third Republic was created by a majority of one in a predominantly antirepublican Assembly which had no intention of creating anything lasting. Few people in that year of 1875 believed that the Republic was to remain for long. Yet it existed for 65 years and, after the four years of the Vichy régime, found its resurrection in the Fourth and Fifth Republics. Never was more justice done to the French saying that nothing lasts as long as the provisional.

After the narrow adoption of the Wallon amendment, the militant opposition against the Republic subsided. Soon a number of constitutional laws followed, "on the organization of the Senate," "on the organization of the public power," and "on the interrelationship of the public power." "The organic law concerning the election of Senators" and "the organic law concerning the election of deputies" completed the constitutional framework of the Third Republic. "Do not search for the principles which guided us," said some of the members of the Assembly, "everything was done without method, without design, blindly, through the imperceptible balance of indecisive minorities; chance was our master."[4]

Subsequent amendments transferred the seat of parliament from Versailles to Paris and "deconstitutionalized" the articles of the Law of 1875 which dealt with the elections to the Senate, thus opening the way for a new electoral law to the Senate to be passed by ordinary legislation.

The government created in 1875 and later was that of a parliamentary de-

---

[4] Joseph-Barthélemy and Paul Duez, *Traité élémentaire de droit constitutionnel,* Paris, 1926, p. 33.

mocracy. Headed nominally by a President of the Republic, its chief executive was actually the Premier, whose official title was President of the Council of Ministers.

The legislature was bicameral, consisting of a Chamber of Deputies and a Senate. The Chamber was elected in single-member districts by majority vote and run off election. The Senate was elected indirectly, each department forming an electoral college similar to the present method of electing members of the Council of the Republic. A minimum age of forty and a term of nine years prescribed for Senators made the Senate a very aged and very independent body which, for practical purposes, was coequal to the Chamber of Deputies. While the Senate did not overthrow cabinets outright, it was known to make their lives so impossible as to force them to resign. This whip was used against both right-wing governments (Tardieu, Laval) and those of the left (Blum). But the general character of the Senate was conservative, whatever the party label, and it was therefore particularly the Socialists and Communists who urged its abolition.

A strange feature in this picture was the fact that in the land of "liberty, equality, and fraternity," women did not possess the suffrage despite the fact that they had always played an important and significant role in the public life of France. Only after the Second World War were women given full political rights.

The Constitution of the Third Republic was characterized by the predominance of parliament. Yet in times of extreme crisis, cabinets were frequently invested with practically unchecked power to rule by decree. Of this regime, the leading French historian of that period has written as follows:[5]

> It is not one of those beautiful, straightforward constructions in whose establishment the theoreticians of the last century took pride, comparable to the famous constitutions of 1791, 1793 and 1848, with their majestic pillars of a Declaration of the Rights of Man, the wise order of uniform style and with the ingenious symmetry of three separate and balanced powers. No, this is an incoherent monument whose architect one cannot even find, for the whole world has had its hand in it; master-builder and brick-layer alike. A monument? Not even that. At the most it is a piece of masonry, a clump of separate cabins without apparent intercommunication. Less than that, it is a scaffold of chance, a work without name. Not even the word constitution is written on its gable while on its roof sits the menacing amending clause, the permanent stamp of the provisional.

Emerging political parties

At the inception of the Third Republic the principal political division was between monarchists and republicans. This was not merely over the head of state. The monarchists were also, by and large, the economically and socially more conservative element, while the republicans tended to be more progressive and liberal. But this division must be accepted with considerable reservation as all shades of opinions existed in either camp.

[5] Gabriel Hanotaux, *Histoire de la France contemporaine,* Paris, 1903, Vol. III, p. 423.

The situation was also further complicated by the injection of the so-called "religious question." France is a Catholic country, which does not mean that the majority of the French people are practising Catholics but rather that the Catholic religion is by far the strongest among the religions of France and that a predominantly Catholic cultural pattern permeates the country, even among those who have little to do with the Catholic Church. Church questions are therefore sensitive ones.

In the minds of republicans the Catholic Church is identified with antirepublican thought and action. Graduates of Catholic schools are suspected of being automatically antirepublican. Time and again, during the Third Republic, attendance at mass or even the attendance of his wife would retard or even break the career of a soldier or civil servant. Nor was much of the Catholic element less uncompromising, and when Pope Leo XIII[6] and Cardinal Lavigerie recommended acceptance of the Republic, their action was deeply resented by some die-hard groups as practically treasonable.

The religious issue complicated the political picture enormously because a politician who was arch-conservative in economic matters could be regarded as "left" if he opposed the church, whereas a Catholic who approached the socialist position might be labeled as "right."

The Socialists

The nineteenth century, which produced the great wave of industrialization in most countries, also brought forth the proletariat and the workers' movement which found its home in the ranks of socialism. It was essentially a movement of protest against intolerable social conditions and the vast cleavage which existed between the workers and other classes. In a way the passing of feudalism had not abolished the feudal system but had only changed the ruling groups and made their methods more subtle. The French worker, in contrast to his American colleague, still has no hope or expectation of individual success. Only as a class can he hope for the improvement of his lot.

French workers' class consciousness antedates Marxism. But in contrast to German socialism, which quickly adopted the Marxist formula and which was forged into a powerful party by the German love for organization and discipline, French socialism was, at first, more individualistic than collectivistic. Neither the theories of Proudhon[7] nor the political action of August Blanqui[8] created a real movement. Eventually Jules Guesde, representing Marxist integralism, and Jean Jaurès, representing the emphasis on humanitarian motives, forged the Socialist party into one (1905).

[6] In the encyclical, *Inter Multiplices Sollicitudines.*
[7] Pierre Joseph Proudhon's principal work, *Système des contradictions économiques, ou philosophie de la misère,* Paris, 1846, 2 vols., was subjected to acid criticism by Marx in his *Misère de la philosophie,* Brussels, 1847.
[8] Blanqui was an old revolutionary who was genuinely popular, but he died in 1881. See Alexandre Zevaès, *Histoire du socialisme et du communisme en France,* Paris, 1947.

Because the party professed to be revolutionary, it never was accused of being an "enemy of the state" as was its German counterpart, since the revolutionary tradition is part of the life of France. But because it was French, it never rose to great organizational accomplishment. Jaurès remained the most popular and brilliant of Socialist leaders until his death by assassination on the eve of the First World War.

It was Jaurès's influence over the Socialist party which made it more humanitarian than Marxist, more gradualist and reformist than revolutionary. But this course was not followed unanimously, and to this day French socialism is divided on the issue of radicalism versus reformism; this inner cleavage contributes to the weakness of the party.

The Communists

The world-wide split within the international socialist movement which followed the First World War also took place in France. At the party convention of Tours (1920) the split between Socialists and Communists became permanent. The majority of the leaders fought the Communist strength vigorously, but the majority of the party was not with them. Had Jaurès still been alive, it might have been different. With the majority going Communist, the control over the party's assets, especially its chief newspaper, *L'Humanité,* became Communist. The Socialist remnants established themselves under great difficulties as the French section of the Second (Socialist) International (SFIO).[9]

Until the Second World War the Communists were not successful in taking over the trade-union movement. The General Confederation of Labor (CGT) remained outside their fold and largely Socialist-controlled. The Communists tried to infiltrate various locals and eventually founded a rival movement which they called "Unified" General Confederation of Labor. But this split merely helped the Christian Federation of Labor (CFTC) and sometimes the employers.

The interwar period

The First World War left the French nation united and victorious but, by the standards of those days, physically almost destroyed, for France had been the principal battleground, and the loss of life had been fearful. Over 1,600,000 were dead—out of a population of 40,000,000—with, at that time, a dangerously declining birth rate. From then on, fear, revulsion against war, any war, long remained a dominant element in French political thinking.

The governments between the two wars were usually coalitions either of the left or of the right, but in actuality the difference between them was not so great. While the governments of the right were truly right, those of the left, usually domi-

---

[9] *Section française de l'internationale ouvrière.*

nated by the Radical Socialist party, which was neither radical nor socialist but actually quite conservative, were little different. On the whole, French politics of the Third Republic were dominated by personalities such as Raymond Poincaré, André Tardieu, Pierre Laval, Édouard Herriot, and Édouard Daladier far more than by rigid party lines.

But France did not remain immune from fascism. A number of groups appeared, among which the Patriotic Youth (*Jeunesses Patriotes*), the *Action Française,* the "hooded men" (*Cagoulards*), and the Fiery Cross (*Croix de Feu*) were best known. On February 6, 1934, the pent-up emotions resulted in widespread demonstrations which produced some shooting and swept away the Daladier government.[10] This was the first time that a left government had been overthrown by pressure from the "street," and the lesson was not lost. The parties of the left pulled closer together, establishing the so-called "Popular Front." It was composed of the Communists, Socialists, and Radical Socialists. Although such an organization may have seemed logical at the time, it had some serious consequences. Most important of all, it produced a great strengthening of the Communists, and their association with the other parties made them "respectable" and permitted them to infiltrate many organizations, especially the trade-union movement. The common-action program of the Popular Front was announced in 1936, a year of general elections, which also brought to the Communists considerable success. Not that their vote had so greatly increased, but the Popular Front gave them allies and coalition partners for the first time and thus made it possible for many Communist candidates to win runoff elections with Socialist and Radical support.

The Popular Front government, headed by Socialist leader Léon Blum, found itself confronted on the one hand by the profound suspicion of the right and on the other hand constantly pushed into more precipitate action by the Communists. In order to appease the workers, the government had to accept hasty reforms which certainly did much good but also increased the cost of production and weakened output. In order to appease the flight of capital, the government had to adopt half-hearted fiscal measures which satisfied no one. On top of this, the Popular Front governments were confronted by the Spanish Civil War, which produced complex problems of foreign policy, while the Senate constantly sniped at the governments, and made their lives miserable. All this brought confusion to France at a time when Hitler was already in power in Germany and the German rearmament effort was going forward full blast. Léon Blum, now keenly aware of the danger which confronted France, attempted to create a government on a broad national basis but was only partly successful. Faced by Senate refusal to grant him the requested plenary powers, Blum resigned, and on April 13, 1938, he was succeeded by

---

[10] See Alexander Werth, *The Twilight of France,* New York, 1942. Generally the best work on the political parties of the Third Republic days is by François Goguel, *La Politique des partis sous la IIIème République,* Paris, 1946, 2 vols.

Édouard Daladier, who was supposed to be a strong man but hardly deserved this reputation. The Popular Front experiment had come to an end.

Defeat and Vichy

France entered the Second World War without enthusiasm and as a deeply divided nation. Many Frenchmen hated one another more profoundly than they hated the enemy. Marcel Déat, once of the left, wrote his famous article, "Why Die for Danzig?" and scored a smashing hit. The rapid defeat of France was breathtaking and awe-inspiring. When the dazed Frenchmen compared the machine-like efficiency of their conquerors with the spectacle of their own disorganized army retreating in confusion, a feeling of hopelessness and fatalism often overcame them. In this situation, the appearance of Marshal Philippe Pétain was especially significant. He was one of two surviving marshals of France, the hero of Verdun, the symbol of past French glory. Pétain's decision to establish an authoritarian government in order to cope with the extraordinary problems of defeat and reconstruction met with less resistance than might otherwise have been expected, because the supposed superiority of authoritarian regimes had been so tellingly demonstrated by the overwhelming victory of the German juggernaut. Had Pétain's predecessors, especially Daladier and Reynaud, possessed the fortitude to hold out against the Armistice and perhaps transfer the seat of the French government to North Africa, a considerable element of public opinion would undoubtedly have rallied around them. But France's collapse was not only military, it was moral as well, and to many Frenchmen further resistance seemed useless.

The transition from the defunct Third Republic to the Vichy regime[11] was effected smoothly and with that strict obedience to legal forms with which authoritarian regimes like to cloak their violation of the legal spirit. An act to call a national assembly for the purpose of amending the Constitution was passed in the Senate by a majority of 225 to 1 and in the Chamber by 385 to 3. The Communists were barred. The National Assembly, which was convened on July 10, 1940, gave full powers to Marshal Pétain by an act passed by a majority of 569 to 80. No one party voted against the act as a solid bloc. The Socialists were the largest group among them, but a majority of Socialist deputies and Senators voted for the act. All the more glory, therefore, to the 80 who showed such conspicuous courage, which led most of them to imprisonment and some of them to death.

The debate over Pétain's real motives did not die down with the aged Marshal's imprisonment and death. Some see in him a traitor, others a misguided patriot who tried to do the best for France in trying days. But whatever Pétain's motives, he was surrounded by men who had gone over to the Germans, lock, stock, and barrel, partly out of convictions and partly out of belief in Hitler's ulti-

---

[11] Paris, being occupied by the Germans, had been abandoned, and a temporary capital of unoccupied France was established at the city of Vichy (Allier), a well-known spa.

mate victory. Many of the atrocities committed against patriots in those days were the work of French militiamen who showed that they had learned well the lessons of their German masters.

Fortunately, far more Frenchmen were in the Resistance than supported these shameful acts. The Resistance movement was indeed of such broad nature and covered itself with so much glory that no one has a right to speak of French decadence. The majority of the people, however, merely tried to get by, being neither in the Resistance nor among the fascists. Many of them might have repeated the words of that famous aristocrat who, when asked what he did during the great Revolution, replied simply, "I survived."

2

The rebirth of France

General Charles de Gaulle

While France lay prostrate before her conqueror, and some of her self-appointed leaders tried to ape their goose-stepping masters, the tricolor flag was again unfurled across the Channel. General Charles de Gaulle had not been prominent before the war. He was a professional soldier and a tank specialist whose works were read with far greater attention in Germany than in France. Daladier propelled him into the under-secretaryship of war, and as a field commander he fought one of the few moderately successful engagements with the Germans which French arms could record in 1940.

General de Gaulle became identified with the idea of utmost resistance to Germany and was advised to leave France when all resistance crumbled. He did so on June 17, 1940, and both he and Winston Churchill have given us graphic descriptions of those memorable events. The same evening De Gaulle addressed the French nation over the network of the British Broadcasting Corporation. "France has lost a battle," he declared, "but she has not lost the war." With these ringing phrases, "Fighting France" was reborn.

The significance of De Gaulle's move was not immediately realized. France was in utter confusion. Her army was, on the whole, loyal to Marshal Pétain, and with its peculiar military logic regarded De Gaulle as a traitor. No political group survived intact, for all of them had some collaborationists in their midst. Moreover the Communists gave more than passive support to the Germans as long as the Soviet-German Pact of August, 1939, governed their actions in France as it did all over the world. Their leader, Maurice Thorez, deserted from his regiment early in the war and took up his residence in Moscow. This situation lasted until the invasion of the Soviet Union impelled the Communists to take so active and gallant a part in the Resistance movement that they could claim for themselves, not without reason, the somber title of *"parti des fusillés"* (Party of Executed Men).

The Resistance

The Resistance movements and underground groups which sprang up had little coherence at first, and their effectiveness was small. Moreover Frenchmen had been without dictatorship for so long that conspiratorial habits had not been developed, and Gallic love of intrigue was not enough to counter the Gestapo. In this situation, General de Gaulle fulfilled an extremely useful function by providing both a headquarters beyond German reach and the symbol which French patriots needed. Slowly, gradually, and not without some ugly scenes, the many independent resistance and underground groups coalesced into the Resistance and the French Forces of the Interior. In the meantime, De Gaulle had been able to hold on to a portion of France's overseas empire, and good and reliable communications were established with the French mainland.[1]

The Resistance did more than fight the Germans and give effective aid to Allied forces and agents. It gave much thought and attention to the future of France. Criticism of the Third Republic was abundant and sharp; few Resistance fighters wished to return to the system of 1875. Many found the American presidential system attractive and hoped that a reasonable adaptation thereof might solve the chronic and permanent crises of France.[2] This thinking and planning received further momentum from the creation of a kind of underground government, the National Council of Resistance, which was founded by Jean Moulin in 1943, and whose work was later carried on by Georges Bidault.

[1] Among the many books on the French underground, see especially Rémy (Gilbert Renault-Roulier), *Memoirs of a Secret Agent of Free France* (trans. by L. C. Sheppard), New York, 1948. Charles de Gaulle, *Mémoires de guerre*, Paris, 1955, Vol. I, *l'appel, 1940–1942*, and Paris, 1956, Vol. II, *L'Unité, 1942–1944*.

[2] For an excellent and penetrating account, see Gordon Wright, *The Reshaping of French Democracy*, New York, 1948, pp. 30–40.

At that time very few people had much good to say for the Third Republic, which was saddled with blame for much of the disaster that had befallen France. Only the remnant of the once-mighty Radical Socialist party defended the Third Republic. But its voice was weak, partly because it shared so much of the blame, partly because so many of its leaders had become collaborationists.

Many adherents of right-wing parties joined the Resistance, and many former left-wingers became collaborationists. But on the whole, the overwhelming majority of the Resistance belonged to the left—to the Communists, the Socialists, and a group of Christian Democrats.

There was much talk and writing in the Resistance about the "new France," which would be so different from the old, and about the "dead" political parties of the past. Actually this kind of talk was never too realistic. The Communists, who had stayed out as a body until the invasion of the U.S.S.R., joined as a body and entered the fight with their customary discipline and devotion. Thus, other political groups, especially the Socialists, were forced to look to their own political fences. General de Gaulle himself favored the abandonment of the traditional political party system and supported the idea of a broad national front. But in 1943 he suddenly sent instructions to encourage the old-line parties and offer them representation on the National Council, by which act he actually recreated artificially certain groups which would otherwise have possessed no right to existence. It is not known for certain just what caused the General to change his mind, but the desire to rid himself of the reputation of fascist tendencies may have been of influence. It may also have been his fear that a single, unified Resistance movement might come under the spell of the Communists. But whatever his motives, it is worthy of note that it was General Charles de Gaulle himself who restored the galaxy of parties of which he complained so much later on.

The liberation of French North Africa brought new vigor to the Gaullist movement, even if its relations with its allies were not always smooth. Now there was again a French government on French soil. Naturally enough, thoughts were directed toward the long-range future, and a study committee (*Comité Général d'Études*) was formed, which pronounced itself in favor of a strong executive form of government. This, as a matter of fact, was a very current trend of mind within the Resistance movement; even Léon Blum,[3] the socialist doctrinaire of yesteryear, expressed sympathy for that idea. Perhaps it was not so clear then as it became later that, at least in the period immediately following the liberation of France proper, only one strong executive was feasible, and that was Charles de Gaulle. But the Communists did understand this, and in 1944 they vigorously denounced the idea of a strong executive. They also condemned any attempt to return to France with a ready-made constitution; only the people of France had the right to

---

[3] Blum was imprisoned, first by Pétain, later by the Germans. While in prison he wrote down his thoughts in a book entitled *A l'échelle humaine* (For All Mankind), New York, 1946.

determine their future form of government. This Communist action stopped effectively the incipient trend away from the traditional French course of government by assembly. Moreover, made bold by their success, the Communists developed their ideas further by proposing a system through which legislators could be recalled by the electorate before their term of office was up. On this and other points, unanimity of opinion could not be reached in the Resistance movement or in Algiers, and thus there already was foreshadowed the later constitutional debate.

Liberation

With the liberation of France there began a very strange period of French history. General Charles de Gaulle returned to France with unparalleled power and prestige. He had no political party of his own, but a government not headed by him was unthinkable. He was the man of the hour who had restored France's honor, and he alone was enshrined in the hearts of his people. There was no constitution—the Vichy Constitution was, of course, unacceptable—and few people wanted to pick up the remnants of the Third Republic where they had dropped them in 1940. Therefore De Gaulle ruled without any real restraint. A "dictatorship by consent," one writer called it.[4] Yet De Gaulle did not attempt to hold on to power and defy the politicians, nor did he try a *coup d'état* like Louis Bonaparte, nor was a coup constantly in the air as it was during the Boulanger episode.[5]

This strange attitude of De Gaulle's has remained a mystery to many observers. But it is also a key to the man's character. His background is primarily military. Like many general officers and products of military academies, he is used to giving high-level orders with the calm expectation that they will be carried out to the letter by the lower echelon. For this rigidity De Gaulle paid in failure. But he learned the lesson well, as the events of 1958 were to prove.

The Communists

De Gaulle's policy was that of a broad coalition which was to be representative of France. But in actuality that meant a coalition of the political left. The Communists had established themselves very firmly. Their Resistance record greatly outweighed their inglorious attitude of 1939–1940. Moreover they had been able to achieve virtually absolute domination of the now unified General Confederation of Labor (*Confédération Générale de Travail,* CGT), and although the old Socialist Léon Jouhaux was still nominal leader, Benoît Frachon, a militant Communist, became general secretary and hence real boss. Thus the workers were more likely to

---

[4] Wright, *op. cit.,* p. 51.
[5] General Georges Boulanger was a man of high ambition who played with the idea of a *coup d'état* for a long time without ever carrying it out.

obtain their demands from the Communists than from the Socialists, and the subsequent electoral figures bore that out.

The Socialists

The Socialists, now reduced or about to be reduced in strength, were badly
split between a left wing, headed by Guy Mollet, and a majority of the leadership,
dominated by the much-mellowed Léon Blum who, despite advanced age and delicate health, had gained greatly in prestige as a result of his courageous stand before
the Vichy-conducted trials of Riom.

The MRP

Perhaps the greatest phenomenon was the newly created Popular Republican
Movement (*Mouvement Républicain Populaire,* MRP), a genuine child of the
Resistance, although a nucleus had existed under the Third Republic. The MRP
was one of the several Christian (Catholic) democratic movements which gained
prominence after the Second World War. Its principal spokesman was Georges
Bidault, diminutive professor at the Lycée Louis-le-Grand and, since 1943, president of the clandestine National Council of Resistance. The movement followed the
trend of progressive Catholicism that began with the encyclical *Rerum Novarum*
of Leo XIII. On the philosophic and literary side the movement was influenced by
such figures as Jacques Maritain, François Mauriac, and Georges Bernanos. Much
of its early strength came from the common belief, carefully nurtured by the party
itself, that it was the party of De Gaulle. But it also received strength from the
record of its leaders, especially Bidault and Maurice Schumann,[6] the youthful editor
of the party paper, *L'Aube,* whose voice had become familiar to millions of Frenchmen as the voice of Free France from London. While more conservative than the
Communists and Socialists, the party nevertheless was definitely of the left, believing in large-scale social reforms, and quite determined not to be forced to the right.

Other groups

In the early days of liberated France, these three groups represented France.
The Radical Socialist party, the giant of the Third Republic, was tainted with the
failure of the regime that had come to such an ignominious end in 1940. The
parties of the right were deeply implicated in collaborationism, notwithstanding
certain outstanding republican figures such as Louis Marin. Courts of honor were
set up in order to eliminate those politicians who had voted in favor of plenary
powers for Marshal Pétain in 1940. Only a good Resistance record could reinstate

[6] Not to be confused with Robert Schuman, another leader of the MRP and several times
Premier and Foreign Minister.

such a man to a place on the ballot or in public office.[7] In that way, many of the political leaders of the Third Republic were excluded, and many of those who remained, like Édouard Herriot, who had never compromised with Vichy, were very old and past their prime.

Had De Gaulle identified himself with one of those parties, especially the MRP, its victory would have been assured, and while his political basis would have been smaller, it would have been much firmer. But De Gaulle preferred to be a symbol rather than a political leader.

Ever since April 21, 1944, it had been established that a future national assembly would decide the form of government.[8] The same ordinance issued by the government (Committee of National Liberation) proclaimed the suffrage of all adult men *and women,* thus ending once and for all the exclusion of women from the polls. But it was not until October 21, 1945, that the return of most French prisoners of war made an election to the National Assembly possible. The political picture was confused. The old parties had not completed their reorganization and were caught off guard. The great Resistance movement was falling to pieces as a political force. For a while De Gaulle had toyed with the idea of placing himself at the head of a Resistance bloc, but the disintegration of the movement was inevitable, because, like all movements with limited objectives, it lost its reason for existence when its objective, the defeat of the Germans, was attained. Perhaps De Gaulle was also motivated by fear of the prominent role of Communists in the Resistance. At any rate he placed himself at the head of the tripartite coalition. Apart from the MRP, the Resistance had produced only two political groups: the French Unified Movement of Reconstruction (*Mouvement Unifié de la Renaissance Française,* MURF), which was for all practical purposes an appendix to the Communist party, and the Union of Democratic and Socialist Resistance (*Union Démocratique et Socialiste de la Résistance,* UDSR), which was at first in the Socialist camp. Both these groups were of rapidly diminishing significance.

The three principal parties, Communists, Socialists, and MRP, all agreed on the necessity of a new constitution, not merely a revision of the regime of 1875, which the remnants of the Radical Socialists would have preferred. But the MRP disliked the kind of concentration of power in the hands of a unicameral legislature which the Socialists and especially the Communists demanded. They favored the establishment of a second chamber with a suspensive veto. Few people wanted to restore the Senate of the Third Republic with its great powers.

[7] One of those reinstated was Robert Schuman, whose Resistance record and imprisonment by the Germans saved him from political extinction. The purge was by no means confined to the right. Over one-half the Socialist deputies voted for Pétain and were purged later for the most part; among them was the party secretary, Paul Faure. Only the Communists, who were not allowed to attend the 1940 session of the legislature, were spared the opportunity to compromise themselves, and their leadership corps therefore remained largely intact, thanks to the "anti-Communism" of the Vichy regime.

[8] *Journal Officiel,* 1944, p. 325. For a good account of the drafting of the Constitution, see *A Constitution for the Fourth Republic,* Washington, D.C., Foundation for Foreign Affairs, 1947.

The Constitution of the Fourth Republic

Largely under left-wing pressure, France elected the members of the Constituent Assembly under the unfortunate system of proportional representation. This system, which had been tried in France before and found wanting, and which had been utilized in Weimar Germany with such devastating results, helped establish party discipline and stifled all political independence. Thus, all constitutional issues were settled on strictly a party basis and determined by the nearly sovereign party leaders. One could imagine what kind of instrument, if any, would have been produced in Philadelphia in 1787 had the founding fathers labored under a similar system.

The elections confirmed the preeminence of the three coalition parties. The Communists and affiliates (MURF) received 5,004,121 votes (25.1 percent), the Socialists and affiliates (UDSR, etc.) 4,491,152 votes (23.4 percent), and the MRP 4,580,222 (23.9 percent). The *Rassemblement des Gauches Républicains,* composed mainly of the Radical Socialists, received only 2,018,665 votes (10.6 percent). The sensation of the election was the great strength of the MRP and the decline of the Radical Socialists. However, it had to be assumed that much of the electoral strength of the MRP was derived from right-wing voters who wanted to vote against Communism but did not otherwise share the liberal aspirations of the MRP. Another significant event was the considerable representation of overseas France, which proved very influential in the Assembly and foreshadowed possible future consequences of great importance.

Drafting the Constitution

The Communists were determined to establish a government by assembly. They and the Socialists were agreed that the future legislature should be unicameral, that the future Premier should be elected by the Assembly, and that the role of the President of the Republic should be essentially ornamental. The MRP, on the other hand, fought for a bicameral legislature and for a somewhat stronger executive. It also favored the right of the Premier, under certain circumstances, to dissolve the Assembly.

But before the draft was completed, a steadily widening split between the left wing and De Gaulle came into the open. Its immediate cause was his opposition to a deep cut in the military appropriations, but the actual sources of the conflict lay deeper: De Gaulle did not deny the right of the Assembly to overthrow his government, but while he was in office he wanted a fairly free hand. The Socialists and Communists, however, insisted on a constant guidance of the government by the Assembly, in other words, that assembly government which De Gaulle and the MRP detested.

Embittered by these problems, General de Gaulle suddenly resigned on January 20, 1946. At that time he was still immensely popular, and had he chosen to carry his case to the people, the leftist parties would have been swept away. But he decided to remain silent and thus created an enigma which has not been solved to this very day.

De Gaulle's resignation made the Communists and Socialists bolder and deepened the differences between them and the MRP. The break finally occurred on the question of a second chamber, which the MRP demanded and the other two groups rejected. When the Communist-Socialist majority finally refused to accept measures designed to test the constitutionality of laws, the MRP *rapporteur,* François de Menthon, resigned, and the MRP declared that it would reject the entire draft.

The draft constitution was submitted to a referendum. The Socialists and Communists were confident of victory, as the MRP alone bore the main burden of agitating against acceptance. General de Gaulle cloaked himself in dignified silence. Moreover the majority coalition had polled nearly a majority of votes, and the rest, so it was expected, would be made up by the voters, who in the entire history of France had never defeated a proposition submitted to them by referendum.

But the unexpected happened. On June 2, 1946, the draft constitution was rejected by 10,584,000 (52.9 percent) votes against 9,454,000 (47.1 percent).

Election to the Second Constituent Assembly brought the Communists some gains; the Socialists suffered severe losses. The MRP, on the other hand, obtained 28.22 percent of the electorate and became, for the time being, the largest party of France. The Second Constituent Assembly produced a final draft within four months. Relatively few changes were made, and a number of controversial points were avoided. A second chamber was proposed, as this was clearly the will of the electorate, but the National Assembly remained formidable, and thus this draft too provided for essentially a government by assembly.[9]

Deputy Paul Coste-Floret (MRP), general *rapporteur,* was correct when he spoke of a modified unicameralism and politely termed the second chamber, the Council of the Republic, a "chamber of reflection." By and large, the second draft constitution created a somewhat faded, somewhat weakened, carbon copy of the Third Republic.

As the work of the Second Constituent Assembly neared its end, General Charles de Gaulle suddenly emerged from his seclusion. In no uncertain terms he condemned the work of the Assembly. He scored the absence of a strong executive in the proposed constitution. But the remedies he suggested were vague. Even then, however, it was clear that he favored that peculiar combination of the presidential and parliamentary systems which later became the core of the Fifth Republic. That was not to be in 1946. Still, his attacks had their effect. On October 13, 1946, the

[9] Robert K. Gooch, "Recent Constitution-making in France," *American Political Science Review,* Vol. XLI (1947), p. 438.

tired French voters went to the polls again. They cast 9,257,432 votes for the Constitution and 8,125,295 votes against it. Eight million people abstained, an unusually high figure for France.

The Constitution was formally adopted. But the plebiscite was nevertheless an unexpected triumph for De Gaulle. Although all three major parties supported the Constitution, the General, who had no party organization, could claim with considerable justification that a decided majority of the French people had withheld their consent from the document. Under these doubtful auspices did the Constitution of the Fourth Republic come into force. Those who were alarmed by the unfavorable auspices with which the Fourth Republic saw the light of day cheered themselves with the thought that the Third Republic had been accepted with even less enthusiasm and yet had endured for seventy years.

But such qualified optimism was ill founded. The Fourth Republic came to an unlamented end after less than twelve years.

3

France at low tide:
the Fourth Republic

The twelve years of the Fourth Republic (1946–1958) constitute a period about which historians are likely to have little good to say. In that they will perhaps not be entirely just. France did settle down under reasonably orderly government after the turbulent war years, and although the rate of her political and economic recovery may have been slower than that of other European countries, especially Germany and Belgium, it compared more than favorably with major sections of the earth.

One of France's greatest deeds during this period was her leadership of the movement toward a more united Europe. Under the inspired leadership of Robert Schuman, the treaty setting up the Coal and Steel Community (better known as the Schuman Plan) was signed on April 18, 1951; it was the first step, not only toward greater collaboration among European nations, but also toward a degree of Franco-German reconciliation which had long been considered an utter impossibility. It was followed in 1957 by the signing in Rome of both the Treaty Establishing the European Economic Community (Common Market) and the Treaty Establishing the European Atomic Energy Community (EURATOM). Both had great Frenchmen among their most important founders. All people striving for a more united and integrated Europe would acknowledge Jean Monnet as one of their most important "spiritual fathers."

At the same time, the French economy, despite chronic fiscal weakness and currency instability, took mighty strides forward. There was full employment in France after the liberation of 1944. Farmers produced ever-increasing yields per acre; productivity per man-hour increased greatly in every branch of industry, and France finally even overtook mighty Germany in the rate of growth of her production, though not in her total output. French enterprise and engineering skill produced records and "firsts" in every sector. Even in the crisis year of 1958, visitors familiar with France could not help but notice that the well-being of the French people steadily increased. In fact, among the countries of the North Atlantic Treaty Organization (NATO), France had the highest per capita income after the United States, though some of this advantage was canceled by high prices.

The Constitution of the Fourth Republic was scarcely much worse than that of the Third,[1] which it closely resembled. Nor was the party system so decisively different. It will long be debated whether institutions or men were primarily at fault. The most probable answer is that neither measured up to the exceptional problems which confronted the Fourth Republic.

The domination of parliament

Parliament, under the Fourth Republic, was as predominant as it had been under the Third, although the second chamber (the Senate, as it had been called under the Third Republic), the Council of the Republic, as it was now called, was less in evidence. Governments could be overthrown with equal ease, although the cumbersome investiture procedure of the Fourth Republic made the establishment of a government more difficult, at any rate until the constitutional reforms of 1954. But the political structure had changed sufficiently to make solid majorities almost impossible.

The Communists, who regularly polled between 26 and 28 percent of the popular vote, were assured a large representation in the National Assembly, thanks to the working of the proportional representation system; even the peculiar list-coupling arrangement of 1951 (*apparentement*) did not much curb their power. The right was never strong enough to govern alone and at times was weakened by uncooperative and intransigent groups like the Rally of the French People (RPF), the first postwar Gaullist movement, or the Poujadists, who were strong for a short time between 1956 and 1958.

---

[1] For a comparison between the Constitutions of the Fourth and Fifth Republics, see the next two chapters.

The political left, which traditionally had the slight edge on the French vote, was permanently disunited and disabled by the strength of the Communist party. Hence the only government which could hope to command a majority in the National Assembly was a coalition between left and right groups, a government which had to rely on the support of parties ranging from the Socialists to the far right. Obviously, such a coalition could agree on very little and would break up at the slightest provocation.

Thus French cabinets found themselves continuously confronted by impossible situations. The serious problems which they had to face, especially in the fields of economics and foreign affairs, and later in the corrosive Indochinese and Algerian crises, demanded long-range, often radical, solutions. No such solutions were possible because the parties composing the coalitions were fundamentally at odds. In this hopeless struggle, cabinets quickly exhausted their energy and collapsed in frustration.

Léon Blum, a former Premier of the Third and Fourth Republics, said:[2]

> Cabinets do not fall or fall only rarely over questions of general policy. The votes which end their existence have very seldom produced anything which resembles a regroupment of political forces. They [the cabinets] fall because their active strength is exhausted, because they have gasped their last breath, because they have come to the end.

Yet these odd coalitions, so riddled by inner tensions which caused them to break up at increasingly frequent intervals, were the only ones mathematically conceivable in the divided parliament. Hence, after each crisis, the same groups, very often the same persons, had to try to form a government again. This accounted for the peculiar fact that, although French cabinets were extremely unstable, the ministers who manned them frequently succeeded themselves. Especially in such offices as foreign affairs, there were often fewer changes than occurred in Great Britain or the United States during the same period of years.[3]

It has often been said, quite correctly, that the seriousness of French cabinet crises was exaggerated. When one government fell and another came in, very little actually changed. Few new appointments were made, and most policies were fairly stable. Scarcely ever did France experience the considerable personnel and policy changes which often follow presidential elections in the United States. In fact, the weakness of France was not the rapid changes of governments, but rather the inability of any French government whatever to undertake those policy changes which the serious problems of the times demanded. One might well say that not instability but an excessive degree of the wrong kind of stability was the chief curse of the Fourth Republic.

Naturally many French thinkers considered reforms which might remedy this

---

[2] Léon Blum, *La Réforme gouvernmentale,* Paris, 1936.
[3] Maurice Duverger, "Public Opinion and Political Parties in France," *American Political Science Review,* Vol. XLVI (1952), pp. 1069–1078; Roy C. Macridis, "Cabinet Instability in the Fourth Republic (1946–1951)," *The Journal of Politics,* Vol. XIV (1952), pp. 643–658.

situation. Since it was fairly obvious that the political party system was immune to decreed changes, most of their suggestions bore on the institutions of the country. Some believed, for instance, that if the government were given the power to dissolve parliament, it would force that recalcitrant assembly into longer and more reliable periods of cooperation. Others thought that a change in the electoral system would produce a more manageable party system and hence more solid and long-lasting governments.

Perhaps the most far-reaching conclusion was drawn by a study committee headed by Georges Vedel.[4] This committee concluded that a partial reform of the French Constitution was hopeless. Vedel suggested that the difficulty lay in the absence of stable majorities; French majorities were formed and re-formed on each question, thus producing frequent upsets. He concluded that a surprisingly similar condition existed in the United States, where there was also an absence of stable majorities in Congress, but where the stability of the government was guaranteed by the presidential system which was impervious to changing majorities in Congress. He proposed, therefore, that France adopt the presidential system.

But all these suggestions came to naught. In the minds of many French people, presidentialism was infected with "Caesarism," particularly with the fate of the Second French Republic, which had a presidential constitution and then threw itself into the arms of Prince Louis Napoleon, later Napoleon III. The left in particular strongly resisted all such suggestions. A change in the electoral system was also frustrated by the coalition of Communists and MRP who, despite profound differences on other questions, thought that they would lose much through a return to the direct electoral system and the single-member district. And although many deputies gave lip service to the principle of the government's right to dissolve parliament, they were reluctant to take concrete steps in that direction and to entrust themselves too frequently to the good will of the electorate.

In all of this, the Third and the Fourth Republics were quite similar. However, the cabinet crises, which were frequent enough under the Third Republic, became more frequent under the Fourth. Worse, as governments' lives shortened, the period needed to establish new cabinets lengthened, thus illuminating the gravity of the dissension. The French public became increasingly cynical as the crises seemed obviously pointless. For instance, the cabinet of Socialist Premier Guy Mollet, established in 1956, was the first to take strong measures in Algeria and thus obtained the backing of the right. But when Mollet asked parliament to give him the necessary financial means to carry out the measures, that same right defeated him.

Yet when a very similar cabinet was formed under Maurice Bourgès-Maunoury and was forced to ask for the same appropriation, it received it from the same parliament, without serious difficulties. Later on, however, that government attempted to effect certain reforms in Algeria which were encompassed in the

---

[4] Georges Vedel, *L'Instabilité gouvernementale,* Paris, Comité d'Etudes pour la République, 1956.

enabling act (*loi cadre*) of 1957. Thereupon the right turned on the government furiously and brought it down. But its almost identical successor, headed by Felix Gaillard, obtained consent to a virtually identical act without too great difficulties. And finally, the Gaillard government fell on the issue of accepting the recommendations of a British-American good-offices mission (Murphy-Beeley mission), after the bombing of Sakhiet Sidi-Youssef, a Tunisian village on the Algerian border, in the spring of 1958, whereas General de Gaulle carried out those recommendations without any serious difficulties.

As government crises became deeper and more frequent, it seemed at times almost as though they were a kind of a game.[5] Those familiar with the corridors of the National Assembly will remember the atmosphere of excitement, the mounting tension which produced the growing conviction that a particular cabinet had to come down. Eventually the increasingly confused situation would produce the "assassins," the men who by various maneuvers would carry out the execution. And yet it all seemed without purpose, without results.

Perhaps because Frenchmen have often tended toward cynicism, the parliament paid little attention to the growing disgust which overcame the French people. Had its members been more sensitive, they would not have tried to curb public discussion of public problems, like the parliament which protested against a radio and television program which presented a kind of panel discussion of various public matters, such as is very familiar to American listeners. The argument against it was that such a program violated the primacy of parliament as the principal arena for discussion of public questions.

In spite of this cynicism, despite worsening government crises, few observers believed in the early demise of the Fourth Republic. Most believed that these situations were deeply embedded in the French system and perhaps the French character and that little could be done about them. Had times been fairly normal, these observers would almost certainly have been correct, and French governments would simply have muddled on from crisis to crisis, no better and no worse than many others before them.

But the fact of the situation was that France was confronted by an exceptional problem which profoundly divided the nation and imperatively demanded solution. It was obvious to even the most faithful defender of the Fourth Republic that the weak and divided governments were incapable of producing a solution or even substantial progress. This problem was the Algerian crisis, which finally in its fifth bloody year destroyed the Fourth Republic.

The agony and death of the Republic

The Algerian crisis, which revealed the basic sickness and heralded the end of the Fourth Republic, was much more than a colonial crisis. There had been

[5] Nathan Leites, *Du malaise politique en France,* Paris, 1958 (translated as *On the Game of Politics in France,* Stanford, Calif., 1959).

other colonial wars ending in France's withdrawal from the territory concerned, especially the bloody war in Indochina (1946–1954), and they had produced violent political debates and the disruption of governments without shaking to the core the form of government or the political system.

But Algeria was different in many ways. About four times the size of France, Algeria lies close by. The distance between Marseilles and Algiers is shorter than that between Los Angeles and San Francisco. When the end came, Algeria had been French as long as California had been American. Although the European population of Algeria constituted only a little over one-tenth of the total population, that was a relatively large proportion compared with other colonial areas, and was comparable only to the situation in the Union of South Africa. Furthermore, the majority of the Europeans in Algeria were either non-French (Italian, Spanish, Maltese, etc.) or considered Algeria, rather than France, their home, although they all were consciously proud French citizens.

Despite the official doctrine and administrative organization, Algeria had never really become "just another part of France" even though French investment, enterprise, and education had raised the living standards of Algeria far beyond those of other countries in the Arab world. As a result Algeria had become quite different from the rest of North Africa and the Middle East.

When the struggle for independence finally did break out, it started relatively late, compared with other countries in the area, and its aims were at first obscure. In fact, the earlier leaders of the uprising fought for the rights of full French citizenship before they began to fight for an independent Algeria.

As the struggle dragged on, year after year, it caused profound divisions inside France. These divisions were by no means clear-cut between left and right for both sides were divided internally on this question. The government which had first sent out as Governor-General Jacques Soustelle, later one of the most intransigent defenders of a "French Algeria," was the leftist government of Pierre Mendès-France. The government which sent the first sizeable military reinforcements to Algeria was the government headed by Socialist Guy Mollet. One of the most controversial French Governors-General in Algeria was another Socialist, Robert Lacoste.

Agony and deadlock continued for years. France's military domination of Algeria was never in doubt for a minute, but final settlement eluded her, partly because weak and irresolute French governments could never make up their minds what to do. To effect a true integration would have required a deployment of military forces of which France was almost certainly not capable and certainly not in favor. All other methods were always too little or too late. The Europeans of Algeria, who had powerful allies in Paris, persisted in deluding the French government and the French public—and possibly themselves—about the true state of affairs. Added to all this was the attitude of the French Army.

When the Fourth Republic came to an end in 1958, France's professional officers and soldiers had fought in wars without interruption for twenty years, first in World War II, then in Indochina, then in Algeria. They were a highly skilled professional group and theirs was the bitter conviction that they had always fought effectively and well, only to be betrayed by the politicians. The retreats which had been forced upon them in the Levant, in Indochina, and in Egypt rankled deeply. Now they feared that the same would happen in Algeria, which they considered the sacred soil of France. Talk of rebellion against the politicians, against the allegedly "abandonist" governments in Paris, was heard with increasing frequency in 1957 and 1958.

The last "regular" government of the Fourth Republic, that of Félix Gaillard, gave up the ghost on April 15, 1958. At first, it seemed a crisis like others, and even General de Gaulle thought it was that, as he remarked to this author at the time. Several candidates tried and failed to form a new government. The rumbling from Algeria increased rapidly. It was now clear that serious repercussions might be expected if a prime minister came to power in Paris whose name had been associated, rightly or wrongly, with the idea of abandoning Algeria. Mendès-France was generally considered to be such a person, but this was not the reputation nor the reality of the man who was finally designated Premier, Pierre Pflimlin (MRP).

Meanwhile matters came to a head in Algiers. On May 13, 1958, a huge crowd moved towards the Forum in front of the palace of the Minister-Resident (Governor-General) for Algeria. The crowd was composed mainly of Europeans, with a large sprinkling of students and paratroopers, some in civilian clothes and some in uniform but ostensibly off duty. The demonstrations were not spontaneous, for there had been plenty of wire-pullers. There was Alain de Serigny, the influential publisher of *L'Écho d'Alger,* the organ of European intransigence. There was Léon Delbecque, a student leader from Algiers, later an official in the French Ministry of War, who had mysteriously disappeared from his Paris office in time to show up in Algiers, while at the same time, the Minister-Resident, Robert Lacoste, was equally mysteriously absent from his Algiers office, ostensibly in order to cast his vote in the French National Assembly.

It is nevertheless uncertain that anyone planned to have events take the turn that they did. The crowd became increasingly violent and uncontrollable, broke through the gate of the Minister's palace, and stormed the palace itself. In this general confusion, Brigadier General Jacques Massu, the popular commander of the tough parachutists, appeared on the balcony of the palace, addressed the frenetic crowd, and announced the take-over of power. In a subsequent interview, General Massu declared that he had decided to do this on the spur of the moment, in order to prevent the crowd from getting completely out of hand and after he thought he had read at least tacit assent in the eyes of General Raoul Salan, commander in chief in Algiers.

Thereafter, the take-over was swift and smooth throughout the country. "Committees of public safety" were formed in many places without resistance. Only in Oran did the Socialist superprefect refuse to hand his office over peacefully. He was bodily ejected.

These events stunned France, especially as the Pflimlin government was obviously completely unable to command the obedience of the Army in Algeria. There was also uncertainty about the role of General Salan, who seemed to favor the rebels while at the same time accepting the government's commission as its general delegate for Algeria, an action through which the government hoped to regain control.

There followed now a short period of impasse. The French government was unable to restore order in Algeria or even to assert itself there. But the army leaders in Algeria were equally unable to impose their will on France. A few abortive attempts to establish committees of public safety in a few French towns fizzled.

The impasse was finally broken by the rebellion's jumping over to Corsica, where it established a temporary regime under the command of Colonel Thomazo, one of the brains of the May 13 Movement. Jules Moch, Minister of the Interior, sent detachments of security forces to Corsica to restore order, but either they arrived too late or they were unable to land.

This affair, too, has remained very obscure. But it convinced the Pflimlin government that reliance on the support of the police and the security forces was impossible. The government's authority was further undermined by the flight of the firebrand, Jacques Soustelle, who broke house arrest and managed to slip away into Algiers. The Communists called for support of the Republic and were joined by some Socialists and the followers of Pierre Mendès-France, but the government was embarrassed by such one-sided support, and moreover these demonstrations were not particularly impressive. Everybody knew that the situation could not last. Now the deputies of the National Assembly were repaid for their many sins of omission and for their game of assassinating government after government by the massive indifference of the French people when the regime was in dire peril. One thing was certain: the French people had no desire to defend the parliamentary regime which had served them so poorly.

It was considered likely that, if some solution did not appear soon, tough paratroopers from Algeria might drop on Paris at any moment, with incalculable consequences.

In that desperate hour when France seemed prostrate and on the eve of civil war, the eyes of an increasing number of French people turned toward the man who once before in a desperate hour had been a symbol of union and rebirth, General Charles de Gaulle. General de Gaulle's ties to the events of May 13 also remain obscure, and only future historians may be able to throw some light into that interesting corner. It is virtually certain that the General was not a wire-puller of the rebellion and did not directly influence its course. In fact, there is much evidence that some of his followers who were involved desperately desired a word or a sign from him but were disappointed. It is almost certain that he was kept informed of events, but there is no trace of evidence that he had either warned or encouraged. He was still in self-imposed exile at his country home at Colombey-les-deux-Eglises. In preceding months, he had begun to sense the deterioration of the general situation and had begun to come to Paris once a week to keep his fingers on the French pulse. Yet he had said nothing and he was not saying anything now.

Now it became increasingly clear that no other man had the national stature and prestige to put France together again. It was De Gaulle or the abyss. And still De Gaulle said nothing. Even those who shouted for his return did so for very different, sometimes opposite reasons. The conservatives called for him in the hope that he would overthrow the regime in Algeria; the liberals wanted him in the hope that he would preserve it. General de Gaulle held a press conference in which he declared his readiness to serve France again in "republican legality." But he was enigmatic about his program and vague about the manner in which the transfer of power might be effected. He maintained no open contact with the army's rebellion in Algeria, but he said that he "understood it," an expression which was to become famous later. At the same time, he also said that he "understood" why the non-Europeans had taken up arms against France.

The political left and center were uneasy about General de Gaulle's intentions; many people were apprehensive because of his austere figure and his military background. The ice was finally broken by an exchange of communications between the Socialist leader, Guy Mollet, and General de Gaulle, and by a visit to Colombey of former president Vincent Auriol, also a Socialist. At the same time Premier Pflimlin opened his contacts with the General. Evidently they all were reassured by De Gaulle, and although there were some obscure last-minute maneuverings, the coast was now clear for De Gaulle to form a government.

There were some last-minute efforts to prevent this, but there clearly was no other alternative. President René Coty took the unusual step of sending a special message to the National Assembly in which he threatened to resign if General de Gaulle were not invested as Premier. Clearly, if there were no government and no president, only chaos could be the result.

Thus General de Gaulle was named Premier-designate and amid breathless excitement entered the Palais Bourbon, the seat of the National Assembly, which had not seen him in more than twelve years. His brief declaration made it clear that he had spent his years in exile profitably and had learned much. Where he had once been unfailingly rigid and standoffish, he now showed that he could, if necessity required, be urbane and suave. So great was his success that one committee's deputy was heard to remark, "First Operation Subversion, and now Operation Seduction." On June 1, 1958, General de Gaulle and his cabinet were formally invested by the National Assembly by a vote of 329 to 224.

In form this was still a government—in fact, the last official government—of the Fourth Republic. But the transition was quickly undertaken. Almost immediately, on June 3, three laws were passed—one of which was a constitutional law amending Article 90 of the Constitution of 1946, giving the government the right to draw up an entirely new constitution with the advice (but not the consent) of a special consultative committee. That constitution was then to be submitted to a popular referendum. It was not to be submitted to parliament.

The law outlined a few very general principles which were to be honored by the new constitution, such as universal suffrage, separation of powers, and responsibility of the government to parliament, as well as the independence of the judiciary and some form of association between metropolitan France and the overseas territory. Another law was passed which gave the government the power to rule by decree for a period of six months. Another law granted special emergency powers in Algeria, a right which had been given as a matter of routine to practically every new government.

The new De Gaulle government was a shrewdly balanced group. Besides the General, who was Premier and Minister of National Defense as well as Minister of Algeria, there were four Ministers of State, one of whom was De Gaulle's predecessor, Pierre Pflimlin, and one the Socialist leader, Guy Mollet, who had rallied the majority of his party to De Gaulle; another was Louis Jacquinot, a right-wing independent of great energy, and the fourth was Félix Houphouet-Boigny, a leader of the African Democratic Rally (RDA) and one of Africa's most outstanding Negro leaders, who later became President of the independent Ivory Coast. There were representatives of both left and right in the cabinet, but the General had assured his control by placing nonpolitical civil servants in the key ministries of Foreign Affairs (Maurice Couve de Murville), Interior (Emile Pelletier), Armed Forces (Pierre Guillaumat), and in the post of Minister of Justice, with the responsibility of drafting the new constitution, one of his most faithful lieutenants, Michel Debré.

A rapid series of other measures was taken to restore order and bring about resumption of normal production and other activities. Meanwhile, a major part of the government's concern remained concentrated on the drafting of the new constitution. This document will be analyzed in subsequent chapters. It contained the principal ideas to which the General had been devoted since Resistance days and which he had first formally announced on June 16, 1946, in a speech in the city of Bayeux. It provided for a strong executive, the President of the Republic, and was to be a combination of presidential and parliamentary forms of government; in reality it turned out to be much more presidential than parliamentary though in many respects quite different from the American system.

This proposed constitution was submitted to a referendum to be held in late September, 1958. In order to assure it massive support, the General himself led the campaign in its favor. He traveled over the length and breadth of France and visited even the far corners of France's overseas territories, especially those in Africa. There on August 27, 1958, at Dakar, he made the extraordinary statement which no other government before his would have dared to make, that the people of the overseas territories were free to vote against the constitution if they chose and that by doing so they would automatically obtain their independence. Those who voted for the constitution would still have an opportunity to choose various forms of association and could even obtain their independence later on.

De Gaulle's success was phenomenal. Altogether, 31,123,483 people (82.5 percent of the vote) voted "yes"; 6,556,073 (17.5 percent of the vote) voted "no."

Blank ballots were cast by 418,298. Of the overseas territories, only Guinea voted "no," and it immediately received its independence. Most significant was the result in metropolitan France. With 84.9 percent of the electorate voting, 17,668,790 (79.2 percent of the vote) voted "yes"; 4,624,511 (20.8 percent of the vote) voted "no."

There were additional features of interest. The Communist party had organized a strong campaign in favor of a "no" vote. A section of the Radicals led by Pierre Mendès-France also opposed a new constitution. So did minority groups of the Socialists and others. Yet the "no" vote remained a million votes below the 1956 vote for the Communists alone. As Marcel Servan, a member of the Communist Politburo, openly admitted at a meeting of the Communist Central Committee,[6] the Communists had actually lost more than a million votes because others than Communists voted "no." Thus for the first time since the liberation of France, the Communists, who hitherto had always polled approximately one-quarter of the total vote with seemingly uncheckable discipline, had suffered a resounding defeat. Nor was this blow merely a passing incident, as was demonstrated in subsequent elections, even though the Communists made some partial recoveries later.

General de Gaulle's return to power was followed by an extraordinary display of leadership bordering on political wizardry. In a series of trips to Algeria, he liquidated the army's rebellion and its European allies, step by step, though not without creating many bitter enemies who rose and threatened him later on. In France itself, order was quickly restored, confidence returned, and France proceeded resolutely on a course toward economic prosperity which had already begun under the Fourth Republic.

It was sheer wizardry indeed, for in effect nothing had really changed. The Algerian War, which had consumed and destroyed the Fourth Republic, was by no means brought to an end in 1958 when General de Gaulle returned to power. It dragged on until 1962; in other words, it lasted as long under De Gaulle as it had under the preceding regime. It was finally brought to an end, not by any ingenious scheme, but by total abandonment, but so great was the strength of this remarkable man and the confidence which he exuded that he was able to bring about this surgical operation which no government of the Fourth Republic would have survived. True, he obtained an enormous majority in the referendum on the new constitution, but he had no majority in the last parliament of the Fourth Republic, and even the much diminished parliament of the Fifth Republic could have given him a lot of trouble had it wished, since he did not have an assured majority until the elections of 1962.

What made De Gaulle irresistible was both the enormous impact of his personality and the knowledge of failure on the part of the old-style politicians. It was this combination of factors which made all resistance crumble before him for seven long years. The extraordinary thing was that General de Gaulle never relied on any

[6] *Le Monde,* Oct. 7, 1958.

army, political party, or other organization, but only on himself. The army was always against him or at best neutral,[7] and even the political party which was hastily formed in 1958 to support him, the Union for the New Republic (UNR), drew strength from him rather than contributing strength to him. It played little part in his decisions.

This is one of the rare cases where a single man's personality, a single man's will, has made an enormous difference—not only in France, but throughout the world, and if such a development puzzles some, it is perhaps partly because there is a curious reluctance in our age to admit the possibility of individual greatness. A study of social phenomena and environmental circumstances will not suffice to explain the phenomenon of Charles de Gaulle. When, in the dark days of June, 1940, he decided to go to England and unfurl the banner of Free France, he was just one of many obscure Brigadier Generals, a man totally without following, commission, or recognition. He did what he did solely out of an inner sense of mission, out of an inner compulsion and conviction that he was destined to embody the immortal soul of France. Even then he held on to that role, not because of his army, which was small and scattered, nor because of any brilliant ideas that he contributed to the Allied cause, but solely because he personified and stubbornly upheld a moral principle. He is a master at the use of power, but even his enemies would not claim that he is seduced by its glitter and paraphernalia or that he seeks power for his own sake.

He is a brilliant strategist and an even more brilliant tactician in politics and diplomacy, using the element of surprise, striking hard, granting no quarter, and expecting none. He has many aides and counsellors, but his decisions are shared by no one. To say that anybody has real influence over him is to claim an absurdity. Many are the times when his most important cabinet ministers literally do not know what policy is until he announces it to them, at times even in a public ceremony mislabeled a "press conference." His concept of leadership has always been constructed around the idea of loneliness and remoteness as qualities indispensable in a leader of men. These ideas have long grown in him and can be found in his earliest writings.[8]

General de Gaulle spoke the literal truth, although it must have seemed strange and flamboyant to many, when he said in his first press conference after his return and emergence from long retirement, *"Je suis un homme seul. Je n'appartiens à personne. Et j'appartiens à tout le monde."* (I am a man who stands alone. I belong to nobody, and I belong to everybody.) The verdicts of his contemporaries and of history about his stewardship are and will remain divided. In one

---

[7] Paul-Marie de la Gorce, *The French Army: A Military-Political History* (trans. by Kenneth Douglas), New York, 1963. See also Raoul Girarded (ed.), *La crise militaire française 1945–1962*, Paris, 1964.

[8] Charles de Gaulle, *Le fil de l'épée*, Paris, 1932; *La France et son armée*, Paris, 1938; *Mémoires de guerre*, Paris, 1954, Vol. I, *L'Appel, 1940–1942*.

sense, his appearance has been enormously reassuring[9] to those who were seeking evidence that man was not just the helpless product or victim of his material environment. This extraordinary type of leadership has established a very personal regime somewhat in the Bonapartist mold. Despite the efforts of the UNR, there is in a very real sense neither a Gaullist movement nor a Gaullist idea. There is only Charles de Gaulle, who in the memories of friend and foe alike will remain a giant.

[9] Romain Gary, "The Man Who Stayed Lonely To Save France," *Life,* Dec. 8, 1958, pp. 144*ff.*

4

The political system and the parties

Far above and beyond the political parties, there now exists the massive political factor of General Charles de Gaulle. He is not a party leader, although there is a political party, the Union of the New Republic (UNR), which is dedicated to unconditional support of his policies. He is not the leader of the UNR, he is not even a member of it; he stands quite apart and acts separately and independently from it. The UNR relates to De Gaulle; De Gaulle does not relate to the UNR except for short-term, purely tactical reasons of passing significance.

It is a unique situation for which there is no parallel anywhere in the world. There are and have been other strong leaders, like Winston Churchill, Konrad Adenauer, or the two Roosevelts and Lyndon B. Johnson. But they have all worked with and through large political parties and groups which they led and dominated. Or there were strong dictatorial figures like Joseph Stalin and Adolf Hitler, who ruled their countries in total exclusiveness and in complete control of

222

every facet of public and private life. But the single, solitary figure of General de Gaulle, who dominates much of but not all the public scene, who operates in uneasy coexistence with, and almost separate from, the political party system, constitutes a unique phenomenon. A slightly flippant but not inaccurate characterization might state that the French political system consists of the political parties and General de Gaulle. It is possible that the order of sequence ought even to be reversed. Nevertheless, an understanding of French political parties is vital to an understanding of French political life.

To a Frenchman the political party system of France seems entirely clear and simple, whereas the American equivalent appears confused and incomprehensible. Americans, on the other hand, have exactly the opposite impression. Is this merely a case of mutual misinformation? No, the difference lies rather in divergent concepts and definitions of political parties. Americans are inclined to look upon political parties from the standpoint of their purpose, namely, the struggle for control. Frenchmen look primarily for the political philosophy which the parties embrace. Thus Benjamin Constant defined a political party simply as "an assembly of men who profess the same political doctrine."[1]

To a Frenchman, therefore, the galaxy of French parties is utterly clear because each one stands, or at least professes to stand, for a particular philosophy, whereas he is utterly confused by the two big parties of America which he sometimes cannot distinguish from each other. When he learns that some "right" Democrats are farther to the "right" than some "left" Republicans, his confusion is complete. An American, however, cannot understand why the French parties remain separate and thus condemn themselves to a relatively small-scale existence, nor can he easily comprehend what the constant formation and destruction of coalitions is all about.

In order to arrive at a better understanding of the French party system, we will do well to keep both the American and the French concepts in mind, for both doctrinal differences, which Frenchmen take very seriously, and the struggle for power, which everybody takes very seriously, are much in evidence. Unfortunately, these things are not so neatly arranged in practice as they might be in theory, for in politics words are frequently used to obscure meaning rather than to illuminate it. Thus a passionate appeal to an idea may hide a determined quest for power, while an opportunistic action may have been engaged in to further the victory of an idea.

The French attention to political ideas makes for stirring debates and beautiful writing. But it also has an atomizing effect, making cooperation difficult for political factions. Compromise over practical issues is obviously easier than over philosophical differences.

These centrifugal tendencies in the French political tradition have undoubtedly

---

[1] Benjamin Constant de Rebecque, *De la doctrine politique qui peut réunir les partis en France,* Paris, 1822.

received much fuel from the electoral systems. Both the majority-single-member-district system with runoff elections and proportional representation with or without *apparentement* greatly encourage the existence of a multiplicity of parties.

We have already seen that such political fractionalization made for weak government under the Third and Fourth Republics. But this was not a uniquely French situation. What was unique was the fact that these parties regrouped themselves in different blocs or loose coalitions according to several distinct dividing factors. In most countries the most important factor is the attitude toward social and economic questions; thus groups of parties align themselves on opposite fronts according to their degree of liberal or conservative convictions.[2] In France, however, a most important dividing line is still the religious question, although this is a purely historical problem which has very little basis in reality; unfortunately French memories are extremely long.[3]

The picture which emerges is approximately this: over "religious" questions (such as the important issue of state support to private schools), the Communists, Socialists, and the otherwise very conservative Radicals make common cause against the otherwise leftist MRP, the right-wing Independents, and parts of the Gaullist UNR. In the broad area of social and economic questions the Communists, the Socialists, and the Catholic MRP face the Radicals, Independents, and many UNR members. On the question of East-West orientation, the Communists and a handful of "progressives" often fight it out against all the rest. On problems of European integration the UNR may have to fight it out alone against the rest although the Communists have occasionally relaxed their opposition to European integration for tactical reasons. And on problems of NATO and the Atlantic partnership, the Communists and the UNR are likely to hold more similar views than all the rest. The importance of the religious question is shown by the fact that the Socialists have long been far more ready to make an electoral coalition with the conservative but anti-Church Radicals and with the Communists than with the moderately left-wing but Catholic MRP.

Party shifts since the liberation

Since liberation, France has seen quite considerable political shifts. At first the political horizon was dominated by the three big parties of the left: Communists, Socialists, and MRP. The Radicals and the right were powerless, discredited partly by collaboration with the Vichy and occupation regimes, partly by too close iden-

---

[2] Words are tricky. The terms "liberal" and "conservative" may take many meanings, but they are used here as commonly and colloquially understood in America. Let it be noted, however, that in Continental Europe the word "liberal" stands for opposition to government regulation and planning and for something approaching *laissez faire*. Hence the European use of the term "liberal" corresponds closely to the American concept of "conservative." French newspapers would refer to men like Antoine Pinay, Joseph Laniel, or Paul Reynaud as "liberals," while American papers would call them "conservatives."

[3] Maurice Duverger, "Public Opinion and Political Parties in France," *American Political Science Review*, Vol. XLVI (1952), pp. 1069–1078.

tification with the then disparaged Third Republic. The increasing East-West tension and the primary loyalty of the Communists to every twist of the Russian political line gradually drove a wedge into the left and separated the Communists from their erstwhile allies. Meanwhile, beginning in 1947, conservative tendencies became strengthened, producing the first Gaullist movement, Rally of the French People (RPF), which achieved great, but not dominant, strength for a time. At its head General Charles de Gaulle appeared for a while within inches of recapturing the reins of power which he had so abruptly cast aside in 1945. But beginning in 1951 Gaullism began to fade, and a part of its remnants joined the traditional right.

At the same time, the Communists preserved their position, but the electoral law of 1951 operated against both them and the Gaullist RPF, with the result that the middle-of-the-road parties were able to hold on to an unstable majority. Shortly thereafter General de Gaulle abandoned the RPF, and its remnants ceased to be a threat to the government parties.

By the election of 1956, political fortunes had not changed a great deal, except for the decline of the Social Republicans (as the former RPF was then known), but the center parties were split, largely over the Algerian problem and over the bitter controversy which Pierre Mendès-France unleashed in his quest for the leadership of the left bloc. As a result, as Table 2 shows, the electoral law and its list-coupling arrangements did not play a very large role. Without gaining in percentage of the vote, the Communists were able to increase the size of their group in parliament greatly.

This was the last election of the Fourth Republic. By November, 1958, the political situation had changed radically. The great majority of the French people quite obviously wanted no return to the sterile parliamentary game of the past. De Gaulle was their champion, and they turned vigorously against all parties which opposed him. Chief victim of this development was the Communist party, which suffered its first sizable reverse since liberation. Most other opponents of De Gaulle were obliterated. The second chief sufferer was the Radical party, which had exhausted itself in internal struggles between the Mendècists and their adversaries, but both wings were considered symbolic of the Fourth Republic and went down to defeat. Another extremist group, the Poujadists, who had risen steeply to an overall vote of 12 percent in 1956, disappeared almost without a trace. The Socialists a majority of whom had supported De Gaulle in his return to power in 1958, increased their vote slightly; whereas the MRP suffered a temporary split. The right-wing Independents, who gave De Gaulle considerable support, increased their strength. The great victor of 1958, however, was the newly formed Gaullist party, the Union for the New Republic (*Union pour la Nouvelle République,* UNR), which had been organized almost at the last minute, just before the elections. Nobody knew much about its aims and aspirations, and few people cared. The French wanted to vote for De Gaulle, and they therefore gave their vote in large measure to the UNR, the party which they identified, rightly or wrongly, with De Gaulle. There might have been some doubt in November, 1958, about what

Table 2. *Distribution of votes and seats in the General Assembly*

Parties	In 1946 Percent of vote	In 1946 Seats	In 1951 Percent of vote	In 1951 Seats	In 1956 Percent of vote	In 1956 Seats	In 1958 Percent of vote on first ballot	In 1958 Seats	In 1962 Vote on first ballot	In 1962 Percent of vote after first ballot	In 1962 Seats after second ballot	In 1967 Vote on first ballot	In 1967 Percent of vote after first ballot	In 1967 Seats after second ballot*
Communists, PCF	28.6	166	26.4	106	25.5	150	18.9	10	3,992,431	21.8	41	5,029,808	22.46	73
PSU and Left Socialists							1.8		449,743	2.5	5	506,592	2.26	5
Socialists, SFIO†	17.9	90	14.4	104	14.8	95	15.5	66	2,319,662	12.6	67	4,207,168	18.79	116
Radicals and RGR†	12.4	55	11.0	93	13.6	91	11.5	16	1,384,998	7.6	44			
MRP‡	26.3	158	12.4	85	10.9	83	11.6	57	1,635,452	8.9	38	2,864,272	12.79	27
Right and Independents†	14.5	75	12.3	110	14.2	95	19.9	136	2,458,998	13.4	50	1,136,191	5.08	15
RPF, Social Republicans, UNR-UDT§			21.6	119	4.2	22	17.6	189	5,847,403	31.9	234	8,453,512	37.75	244
Poujadists and extreme right					12.0	52	3.3	1	159,682	0.9	1	194,776	0.87	

* Not listed here are 5 independent Left deputies as well as 2 from French Somaliland and French Polynesia who were elected later.
† In 1967 Socialists and Radicals ran as a single group under the name of Federation of the Left.
‡ In 1967 the MRP together with other center elements ran under the name of Democratic Center.
§ In 1967 this included 43 Independent Republican deputies pledged to Giscard d'Estaing.

the French people voted for; but there could be no doubt about what they voted against. They voted against the parliamentarism of the Fourth Republic and proved that point in a startling fashion. Out of 437 deputies from metropolitan France in the old Assembly of the Fourth Republic, only 128 were returned to the first parliament of the Fifth. A more crushing denunciation could hardly be imagined.

Only 17.6 percent of the electorate made a clear-cut "Gaullist" decision and voted for the UNR, although a good many of the 19.9 percent who voted for rightists and Independents probably also wanted to express themselves in De Gaulle's favor. This was equally true of some of the 11.6 percent who voted for the Popular Republican Movement and the Christian Democratic splinter group. The vote, therefore, was not clear-cut.

But the parliamentary picture was quite different. The disarray and disorganization among the old-line parties and the rush of enthusiasm throughout the country to express support for General de Gaulle made it possible for UNR candidates to arrange for many advantageous coalitions in the runoff election on November 25, 1958. Thus, the UNR became by far the largest group in the National Assembly, with 189 seats, although on the first ballot it had obtained only 17.6 percent of the vote.

Just how this proportionate voting system worked can be seen in the fact that the Socialists, with 15.5 percent on the first ballot, obtained 66 seats while the Communists, who with 18.9 percent on the first ballot actually polled more than the UNR, obtained only 10 seats. However unfair the distribution was, the National Assembly did represent in some peculiar manner the sentiment of France, because in 1958 even the opposition parties were temporarily more or less "Gaullist" and not all those voting Socialist or MRP intended to vote against De Gaulle.

What followed then were seven years of absolute Gaullist domination. It was not so much that the other parties were wiped out or even that their vote declined so radically, although some of that happened in 1962. It was rather that the parties which had ruled the Fourth Republic felt the sting of public disapproval and even disdain. For the first time in their long history, they realized that they were in a vacuum and that they had seemingly lost the ability to influence events. In addition, the new Constitution greatly curtailed the power of parliament, the traditional stamping ground of the parties.

The parties were not even able to make full use of the not inconsiderable powers which remained in the National Assembly, because they knew that the General could crush them at any time by appealing to the will of the people. This he demonstrated in four referenda, September 28, 1958, January 8, 1961, April 8, 1962, and October 28, 1962, when 79.3, 75.5, 90.7, and 6.7 percent of the votes cast endorsed the propositions which he had submitted to the electorate. It is true that the referendum propositions were carefully chosen and even more carefully worded by De Gaulle.

The referendum of September 28, 1958 endorsed the new Constitution and was thus part of his triumphant return to power.

Table 3. *Votes on referenda on De Gaulle's program*

Plebiscites	Votes yes		Votes no		Abstentions, %
	Number	%	Number	%	
Sept. 28, 1958	17,668,790	79.3	4,624,790	20.7	15.1
Jan. 8, 1961	15,200,547	75.5	4,999,479	24.7	23.5
Apr. 8, 1962	17,508,607	90.7	1,795,060	9.3	24.4
Oct. 28, 1962	12,808,196	61.7	7,932,453	38.3	22.8

The two propositions of January 8, 1961, and April 8, 1962, dealt with the future status of Algeria. The first one was designed to strengthen De Gaulle's hand against the increasingly bitter opposition of the army, the right-wing elements, and the European settlers in Algeria to his Algeria policy, and thus was supported by many voters on the left whose orientation was not normally pro-Gaullist. The abortive rebellion of the army in Algeria and of the European element of April 22 to 26, 1961, showed how very serious the situation had become, a fact which was underlined by several assassination plots against De Gaulle from which he narrowly escaped. The second referendum, of April 8, 1962, ratified the independence of Algeria that had been agreed upon in the Evian Conference of March 7 to 18, 1962, and here the left voted solidly in favor, as did many elements of the center and the right. In fact, only 9.3 percent of the vote cast was "no," although there was an all-time high abstention rate of 24.41 percent.

By contrast, the referendum of October 28, 1962, dealt with a constitutional change providing for the direct popular election of the President of the Republic. Here the opposition, especially on the left, was rather strong. The declared ground for opposition lay in doctrine, in general aversion to what looked like an approach to the American presidential system, and also in the memory of the one preceding popular election in French history, by which in 1848 Prince Louis Napoleon had come to power—only to become an autocratic emperor four years later. More concretely, many saw in this referendum an issue on which the opposition to De Gaulle could unite. In fact, the "no" vote on this referendum reached an all-time high of 38.25 percent, while the "yes" vote was the lowest of them all, 61.75 percent. Some argued that if the entire registered vote were counted, De Gaulle's proposition would have been supported only by a minority of 46.44 percent. This, however, was a dubious argument, as the abstention rate of 22.75 percent was lower than that of the preceding two referenda.

Nevertheless, the opposition felt encouraged by these results and viewed De Gaulle's powers as being in decline. In contrast to 1958, when the parties had been dispirited and afraid, the campaign leading to the elections of November 18 and 25, 1962, was spirited, and the mood of the parties moderately optimistic. The buoyancy of the parties was also encouraged by the fact that the elections had been called as a result of the first vote on censure against the government which had succeeded in the National Assembly. Article 89 of the Constitution clearly stated that the Constitution was to be amended on the basis of a proposal passed by both houses of parliament and then submitted either to a referendum or to a special parliamentary convention composed of both houses sitting jointly. De Gaulle, however, proposed to circumvent his own Constitution by bypassing parliament and submitting the text of the amendment directly to a referendum. Thereupon, parliament rose in wrath and on October 5, 1962, enacted its first (and thus far its last) successful motion of censure of the government. The resignation of the cabinet, the dissolution of parliament, and new elections were the results. It is not unlikely that De Gaulle deliberately chose this method in order to provoke a direct confrontation and to strike down the parties of the opposition.

The results of the referendum did not fulfill all the expectations of the opposition parties. Altogether the deputies who voted against the government on October 5 represented three-quarters of the electorate according to the 1958 elections, yet De Gaulle obtained 61 percent of the "yes" vote. Nevertheless, many politicians consoled themselves with the fact that the Cuban crisis had broken out only one week before the referendum took place and that, since De Gaulle had hinted his intention to retire if the referendum vote were not massively in his favor, many voters had undoubtely hesitated to place the strong government of France in peril at a moment of world crisis.

However, by the time of the National Assembly election, the Cuban crisis was well over. Moreover, the politicians hoped that in a legislative election where General de Gaulle was not directly a candidate, his great influence and charisma would play a lesser role. Besides, the opposition of the traditional parties to De Gaulle and the UNR had now become quasi-unanimous, since the resignation of the MRP ministers from the cabinet.

Alas, the electoral campaign so hopefully undertaken by the parties of the opposition ended in an unmitigated disaster. A triumphant UNR jumped from 17.6 percent in 1958 to 31.9 percent on the first ballot in 1962, ending with 40.5 percent of all votes on the second ballot. The Communists gained votes also, moving from 18.9 percent in 1958 to 21.78 percent in 1962, but they were still considerably short of the 25 to 28 percent which they had regularly polled under the Fourth Republic. The Socialists descended from 15.5 to 12.65 percent. The MRP, the Radicals, and the right all took heavy losses, and the extreme right was crushed.

Even ghastlier for the opposition was the new distribution of seats in the National Assembly. Together with the small UDT (*Union Démocratique du Travail* —Democratic Union of Labor) with which it fused after the election, the UNR obtained 234 seats, the largest representation ever attained by a French party. The UNR-UDT, together with thirty-two Independent Republicans organized in support of the government by Finance Minister Valéry Giscard d'Estaing, now gave the government a virtually unshakeable majority. For the first time in history all the deputies elected from Paris belonged to one and the same party—the UNR-UDT. Of the 280 deputies who had supported the vote of censure against the government, only 113 won reelection. For the time being, the parties of the opposition were effectively excluded from any influence on the course of events.

In some respects one could argue that the reasons for the opposition's setback were even worse than the results. Certainly General de Gaulle's still-great prestige played a large role, especially as he had now successfully terminated the war in Algeria. But the parties of the opposition had greatly helped to dig their own graves. They had attempted to make a show of unity without much reality behind it. Thus they underlined De Gaulle's contention that the opposition was incapable of providing a valid alternative capable of governing. Also much to blame, undoubtedly, was the Socialist chief Guy Mollet's decision to conclude an electoral pact with the Communists.

On October 8, 1962, Mollet had proposed a general electoral agreement to all "politicians choosing to accept major responsibility for the defense of the Republic."[4] This seemed to open all possible coalitions. But on November 12, Mollet had advised his followers to vote for a Communist in the runoff election wherever the choice might lie between a Communist and a member of the UNR. It proved a doubly massive miscalculation. While Mollet had defended his decision, saying that no more than ten to twelve seats would be at stake under such conditions and that a few more Communists in the National Assembly would not matter, it turned out that there were in effect no fewer than 103 such direct UNR-Communist party duels, and 90 of them ended with a UNR victory. By contrast, there were only 58 duels of direct contests between UNR and Socialists, of which the UNR won 35. The Socialists won 23, indicating that the Communist voters had maintained greater discipline in shifting their votes to Socialist candidates on the second ballot than did the Socialists—many of whom apparently failed to support Communists despite their leader's advice. More important, many voters had been repelled by what they regarded as a new Popular Front. Some of the most important leaders of the opposition had gained reelection only because of Communist support. Among them were Guy Mollet himself (Arras), Jules Moch (Sète), François Mitterand (Chateau-Chinon), and even the veteran Catholic priest and longtime mayor of Dijon, Canon Kir. In fact, Mollet and Moch, who had once been in the forefront of the fight against Communism, chose to hold common electoral meetings with important Communist leaders. Their long anti-Communist records prevented this from doing them permanent harm, but it made a poor impression on many of the middle-of-the-road opponents of General de Gaulle.

As a result of the 1962 elections the public political scene suddenly seemed less interesting. The country which had been perhaps the most vibrantly political of all, where political discussion was the order of the day, now seemed, oddly, to take on the character of a country whose public cared little about politics. Many articles were written on the theme of the "depolitization" of France. True, vivid political debates continued in the newspapers, but they no longer reflected the country as a

[4] Jean Paul Charnay, *Les scrutins politiques en France de 1815 à 1962*, Paris, 1964, p. 229.

whole. Most people seemed content, even when they disagreed, to leave matters in the experienced hands of General de Gaulle. The vivacious and constantly quarreling intellectuals had lost much of their influence with the Fourth Republic, and the rest of the people seemed to settle into the strange and unaccustomed role of turning their backs on politics. And so it was, until the picture changed dramatically within two or three short weeks before the presidential elections of December 5, 1965.

Although the outward manifestation of this change emerged in the extremely short period of a few weeks, many factors had been working to produce it. France's economy had recovered well and was forging ahead in a remarkable fashion, but the policy of stabilization with which Finance Minister Valéry Giscard d'Estaing was identified was hard, especially on the lower-income groups. Added to this was chronic dissatisfaction among the farmers, and growing apprehension about the future of the Common Market. Despite continued high quality of instruction the situation in the schools, especially in higher education, had become very bad. Nowhere else were classrooms so overcrowded and laboratories so inadequate to accommodate masses of students. In all fairness, one would have to admit that these conditions in the schools and universities were largely the fault of previous regimes which had failed to take the necessary steps to anticipate the increase in enrollment, but the trouble hit the universities during the Gaullist regime, and under such circumstances, the existing government is always blamed.

There was great restiveness in the army, many of whose officers felt bitter, betrayed first by De Gaulle's Algerian policy and then by the harsh sentences against those like Generals Raoul Salan and Maurice Challe who had openly risen in armed rebellion against the government of France. It was even more difficult to understand the arrest of General Paul Vanuxem who was kept in prison for two years, and then tried—and acquitted. A great many highly decorated officers retired from the armed forces with bitterness in their hearts. The uneasiness within the army remained one of the problems of the regime for some time.[5]

There was also growing apprehension among those who believed in a united and more integrated Europe about General de Gaulle's increasingly sharp rejection of this idea. First his attitude caused the resignation of the MRP ministers; then he bluntly rejected Great Britain's entry into the Common Market, announcing this at a "press conference" on January 14, 1963; and finally he addressed a series of ultimata to France's partners in the Common Market which led to the virtual breakdown of France's relations with the European Communities and to a near paralysis of the Common Market on June 30, 1965. Only after the presidential elections was the Common Market to be refloated by an "agreement to differ" reached at a conference in Luxembourg on January 29, 1966.

But to return to December, 1965. Besides these reasons for dissatisfaction at

[5] Paul-Marie de la Gorce, *The French Army: A Military-Political History* (trans. by Kenneth Douglas), New York, 1963.

the end of De Gaulle's first term, there was also the effect of normal wear and tear on the conduct and the record of a government which had been in power seven long and difficult years. However, perhaps the greatest amount of irritation stemmed from that which is sometimes called the "style" of the general, but which is a great deal more than that.

I have said before that France is not a dictatorship and that General de Gaulle is not a dictator. The French press resounds with critical voices and views, political meetings protesting any aspect of government policy can be and are held constantly, and no restrictions are placed on a French citizen who wishes to leave his country temporarily or permanently and go anywhere in the world. Nevertheless, General de Gaulle does simply as he pleases. If he can have his way within the existing constitutional framework, he will follow that path. But if he finds this inconvenient, he is not averse to setting himself above law and Constitution and acting as though they did not exist.

Moreover, as time went on, General de Gaulle's cabinet became increasingly one of technicians rather than politicians, and this was clearly the type of cabinet that he preferred. Men like Maurice Couve de Murville, Foreign Minister and career diplomat; Louis Joxe, career civil servant and trouble-shooter extraordinary of the cabinet; and above all Georges Pompidou, Prime Minister, former teacher, editor of an anthology of poetry, and managing director of the Bank of Rothschild, who never before had run for elective office, were the types of men with whom De Gaulle preferred increasingly to work. They and their colleagues had several qualities in common, among them total loyalty to De Gaulle.

Nevertheless, in spite of all these factors, nobody dreamed that General de Gaulle would have the slightest difficulty in being reelected to the presidency of France if he chose to run. In view of his age (he was 75 in 1965), there were some observers who thought that he might decide not to run. There was also the known desire on the part of Madame de Gaulle to retire with her general to Colombey-les-deux-Eglises, their country house. There were also those who thought that he could assure his succession more certainly if he were to nominate a successor and put his own considerable prestige behind his election.

But whether General de Gaulle had actually considered these alternatives or not, in October, 1965, he announced his decision to run for his second term. He had intended to do almost no campaigning. He addressed the nation by radio and television on November 4, 1965, for the first time as a candidate, and said:[6]

> Should the massive and open support of the citizens pledge me to remain in office, the future of the new Republic will be decidedly assured. If not, no one can doubt that it will collapse immediately, and that France will have to suffer—but this time with no possible recourse—confusion in the State even more disastrous than that it experienced in the past.

[6] Press and Information Service, French Embassy, New York.

It was an incredible declaration, not only for its Olympian, almost disdainful tone, but even more for its assertion that General de Gaulle was the only person who could lead France and that without him France would collapse—a terrible indictment, if it were to be taken seriously, not only of the opposition but of De Gaulle's own collaborators as well.

Despite this, every observer, commentator, and public opinion institute and all the foreign embassies in Paris predicted a decisive victory for De Gaulle on the first ballot. The only question was the size of the majority he would get. Even opponents of the regime or of important parts of General de Gaulle's policy saw no hope in the opposition. They felt that De Gaulle was confronted, not by an opposition, but by a void. And they did not want to vote for a void.

The start of the opposition had certainly not seemed particularly promising. Encouraged by a campaign of the left-wing newspaper *L'Express,* the Socialist leader and mayor of Marseilles, Gaston Defferre, had attempted to put together a large movement of the left and center and had failed, torpedoed by the leader of his own party, Guy Mollet. Now the principal candidates against de Gaulle were François Mitterand, a former leader of a small left-wing movement who had gained the support of Communists and Socialists; Jean-Louis Tixier-Vignancour on the extreme right, who had undertaken an exceptionally long campaign which at times created a certain circuslike atmosphere; two other right-wing candidates of little consequence, Pierre Marcilhacy and Marcel Barbu; and fairly late in the campaign, the new and important candidate, Jean Lecanuet, president of the MRP.

Perhaps the greatest influence on the outcome was wielded by (1) television, and (2) Jean Lecanuet. (1) Until the presidential election, radio and television had been virtually closed to the opposition parties. The press continued to be free, and was open to all political figures of significance. However, not only were radio and television owned and controlled by the government, but the government had deliberately used its control to prevent even the mention of opposition candidates whenever possible. Their faces rarely appeared, even in newsreels. However, as election day approached, the law which provides for a certain amount of time to be given to all candidates came into effect, and the French public suddenly awakened to the facts that there was an opposition to General de Gaulle, that its candidates were able and attractive men, and that they presented a reasonable point of view. Moreover, although the old General spoke in terms of the future, there was a startling visual contrast between the 75-year-old statesman and his young and attractive-looking opponents, especially Lecanuet and Mitterand. Television and radio also made it possible for these candidates to direct the spotlight of attention onto the shortcomings of the regime, its diplomatic isolation, the danger to the Common Market, etc.

(2) Jean Lecanuet's candidacy in itself was very significant. This highly photogenic, able, and sincere candidate clearly intended to appeal to that middle-of-the-road vote which was dissatisfied with De Gaulle but might nevertheless have voted for De Gaulle in order not to support a candidate (Mitterand) who was sus-

tained by the Communists. Lecanuet, by his candidacy, gave this important group a candidate.

The results of the first ballot for the presidential election of December 5, 1965, came as a startling surprise. For the first time, the electorate, which had gone to the polls with the largest number of voters ever (85 percent), failed to give De Gaulle that "massive support" for which he had asked. De Gaulle received 43.71 percent of the vote cast in metropolitan France (i.e., only 36.78 percent of eligible voters) or 44.64 percent including the overseas vote. François Mitterand obtained 32.23 percent in metropolitan France or 31.72 percent including the overseas vote. Lecanuet obtained 15.85 percent or 15.57 percent, while Tixier-Vignancour obtained only 5.19 percent. The other candidates obtained only 1.7 percent and 1.1 percent of the vote respectively.

For the first time since coming to power in 1958, General de Gaulle found that he had to pay attention, not only to "France," with which he had totally identified himself, but also to Frenchmen who did not agree with him. Of course, on the runoff ballot on December 19, he won a second term with 54.49 percent of the votes in metropolitan France and 55.18 percent counting the overseas vote as well. In this runoff in which, according to the law, only the two top-ranking candidates could compete, about half of those who had supported Jean Lecanuet on the first ballot had with obvious reluctance shifted their votes to De Gaulle rather than support a candidate who was sustained by the Communists. But nobody could overlook the fact that, in an election which the General himself had turned into a plebiscite that was to give or withhold from him "massive support," the majority of the voters had turned against him.

One thing was already clear as the year 1965 came to a close: from now on, the simple assumption that De Gaulle would always win, would always have his

Table 4.

Candidates	Votes cast	Percent of vote cast	Percent of eligible voters
Presidential election			
First ballot, Dec. 5, 1965			
Charles de Gaulle	10,828,521	44.64	39.45
Francois Mitterand	7,694,005	31.72	26.60
Jean Lecanuet	3,777,120	15.57	13.06
J.-L. Tixier Vignancour	1,260,208	5.19	4.35
Pierre Marcilhacy	415,017	1.71	1.43
Marcel Barbu	279,685	1.15	0.96
Second ballot, Dec. 19, 1965			
Charles de Gaulle	13,083,697	55.19	45.26
Francois Mitterand	10,619,735	44.21	36.75

way, was no longer valid. France had become "repoliticized" and the debate was on. Moreover, as Jacques Fauvet, one of France's leading political commentators, said, "General de Gaulle was the victim of an even older error which pertains viscerally to his fundamental concept of politics. For him, the parties are nothing but factions which break up the unity of France."[7]

The General Assembly elections of 1967 were rightly regarded as the "third ballot" of the presidential elections of 1965. They were expected to herald either the definitive survival of the Fifth Republic or its demise. But history does not often favor us with such clear-cut decisions, and in many respects this third ballot remained inconclusive. Nevertheless a significant number of conclusions can be drawn from the 1967 elections.

1. The forces of Gaullism had remained basically stable from 1962 to 1967. Although the percentage had increased from 31.9 in 1962 to 37.75 in 1967, the latter figure contains the votes cast for the 43 deputies who were pledged to Giscard d'Estaing and who in 1962 had run under the separate label of Independent Republicans.

2. What had changed was the far greater discipline and confidence of the left. Encouraged by the results of the presidential elections, François Mitterand had finally succeeded in the task in which Gaston Defferre had failed, and had created a seemingly viable Federation of the Left (*Fédération des Gauches*), the core of which were the Socialist and Radical parties but which had also drawn other leftist votes. The Federation's total vote was not much different from the combined total of the Socialist and Radical parties in 1962, but the Federation's representation in parliament was somewhat larger and its self-confidence infinitely superior to that of the distraught opposition parties after the 1962 bout. The Communists, on the other hand, who had gained only 0.6 percent over 1962, profited greatly from electoral coalition with the Federation of the Left, and their number rose from 41 to 73 seats.

3. The earlier promise of Jean Lecanuet was not fulfilled in 1967. Although his Democratic Center obtained 12.79 percent of the vote against the MRP's 8.9 percent in 1962, his representation in parliament has actually declined because of the isolated position of the center. Hence, his hope of becoming the decisive balancing factor between Gaullists and anti-Gaullists was not fulfilled.

4. Lecanuet's biggest rival for the "decisive middle" position, Giscard d'Estaing, had certainly gained in stature and position. Although he still supported De Gaulle, his "yes, but" position had been assailed by the Gaullists and by De Gaulle himself. Nevertheless he had held well and had strengthened his position as well as his independence.

The 1967 elections have been called the "first election of the post-Gaullist

[7] *Le Monde,* Dec. 7, 1965.

period." Afterwards Gaullists and anti-Gaullists settled down to an uneasy and frequently negative stability. When given a sufficient number of alternatives, a considerable majority of Frenchmen opposed De Gaulle, as clearly shown in the first ballots of the 1965 and 1967 elections. Yet it was most unlikely that the French people had opted for a return to the Fourth Republic. As long as the opposition parties acted with determination and responsible unity, the opposing forces were likely to remain in balance. But if they were to return to their bickering and the irresponsible conduct of the past, De Gaulle would certainly seize the opportunity to dissolve parliament to get a new popular verdict which might well sustain him.

The 1967 elections had given De Gaulle merely a razor-thin majority in the National Assembly, which could be upset at any time by even minor defections or by the tactical judgment of Giscard d'Estaing and his followers. But this power to upset was more apparent than real. If the opposition were to return to irresponsible "assassinations" of government, if it were to show that it had learned nothing, then De Gaulle might well find the French people on his side. The power of the opposition to upset the government therefore continued to be severely limited for these practical, political considerations, and De Gaulle continued to do as he pleased. But with every self-willed act, with every action which found widespread opposition, the chances of Gaullism surviving De Gaulle diminished. This was particularly illustrated by the Middle East crisis of 1967 when De Gaulle's opposition to Israel was clearly rejected by his country, of which it was said that "the left is pro-Israel and the right anti-Arab."

Thus De Gaulle, who undoubtedly has done much for the power and prestige of his country, may leave the political scene with almost as big a question mark as he entered it. His UNR has shown considerable staying power but only because of his own immense prestige. That it will survive him is likely, but that it will remain as strong or outwardly united as it has been is extremely unlikely. Possibly Valéry Giscard d'Estaing may some day build a majority out of remnants of the UNR and some of its opponents. Whatever develops, the elections of 1965 and 1967 made clear the fact that the party system, although weakened, had survived De Gaulle's onslaught with new strength.

The Communist party

The French Communist party (*Parti Communiste Français,* PCF) is a phenomenon worthy of study.[8] Second only to the Italian Communist party, it is far stronger than any other Communist party outside the iron curtain. In fact, the others are all numerically insignificant in comparison to their French and Italian counterparts.

---

[8] There are a number of excellent studies on the Communist party of France. A. Rossi, *Psychologie du Parti Communiste Français,* Paris, 1948, with an abbreviated English translation; *A Communist Party in Action,* New Haven, Conn., 1949; M. Einaudi et al., *Communism in Western Europe,* Ithaca, N.Y., 1951; Jules Monnerot, *Sociologie du Communisme,* Paris, 1949; David Caute, *Communism and the French Intellectuals 1914–1960,* New York, 1964; and A. Micaud, *Communism and the French Left,* New York, 1963.

The French Communist party not only is large, but until 1958 it had a remarkable voter discipline. Between the liberation and 1958, the party polled approximately the same vote, roughly between 26 and 28 percent of the total vote cast, at every election. This was a considerable achievement equaled by no other party; it was even more remarkable when one considers the tremendous political changes which occurred in that period—from the left domination and De Gaulle's first presidency to the resignation of De Gaulle, the breakup of the left coalition, the ouster of the Communists from the government, the intensification of the East-West struggle, the Marshall Plan, and the Korean conflict. Amid all these changes the Communist party held on to its voters. Moreover, it is still the most national party of France in terms of geographic distribution. In no *département* have the Communists polled less than 6 percent of the total vote in a national election. No other party can make that claim. This voting distribution is also reflected, though not identically, in the party organization; there is no *département* of France in which the Communist party does not have a sizable organization.

The fact of a constant and strong, though isolated and not dominant, Communist party is seemingly permanent in the political life of France. Yet the picture becomes confusing when one remembers that although the Communist vote has long remained constant, Communist party membership has steadily declined and so have, even more so, the readers of the Communist press. Even more important, the Communist leadership has been consistently unable to move the bulk of its voters or even the majority of its members to overt political action other than voting for the party. This has been particularly in evidence since 1947. The Communist-led demonstrations against Generals Dwight D. Eisenhower and Matthew Ridgway, when they became NATO commanders, were miserable failures, and the party has been unable to produce really massive demonstrations since. Only in 1960 and 1961 when the Army and the Europeans rebelled in Algeria was it able to send sizable masses into the street—and they were not all Communists. Political strikes, when not joined by non-Communist organizations, fizzled, and in many other instances the Communist suggestions for action were ignored by the rank and file of the party. The conclusion is therefore inescapable that the majority of people voting the Communist ticket are not believers in Communism but give the party their support for reasons which have nothing to do with Marxism, Communism, or Russia. What are these reasons?

One source of Communist strength is the revolutionary tradition of France which interprets revolutionary ideology as an eminently "French" matter. Communists have convinced many people, among them many intellectuals, that they are the most revolutionary and left, hence the most "French," party.

Another root lies in the Communist Resistance record. It is true that the Communist leadership collaborated actively with the Germans until the invasion of Russia by the Germans.[9] But after that the Communists threw themselves whole-

---

[9] Documentary proof is presented in A. Rossi, *Les Communistes français pendant la drôle de guerre*, Paris, 1951.

heartedly into the struggle and contributed a majority of the Resistance martyrs. This is understandable because of the customary discipline of the Communist militants and also because the Communists are always largely an underground organization even when their existence is perfectly legal. Thus they were well prepared for the secret war against Vichy and the Germans.

Perhaps most important of all is the Communist hold over the workers. It is of course not complete. A good many workers are not Communists, nor are all Communists workers. But the Communists have found it possible to identify themselves successfully with the workers' numerous and quite justified grievances: their low wages compared to the high cost of living, the unequal tax burden, the lack of social conscience of a good part of management, inadequate housing, etc. If the workers were to look for other champions, where would they go? Neither the Socialists nor the MRP are workers' parties, although both have workers in their midst. Both, in successive governments, did little for the workers. Some workers tried De Gaulle's RPF, but to most workers it was a party of the right, and a French worker does not vote for the right, which he is wont to consider the "class enemy." Some tried the UNR in 1958 and after but it is doubtful that they intended a permanent shift. Thus the apparent paradox: millions of workers have refused to go into the streets and demonstrate when the Communist leadership demanded it; over 2 million workers have left the Communist-led CGT, in disgust over political misuse of the union movement; yet a majority of these same workers continue to vote Communist in election after election because, rightly or wrongly, they believe they have no alternative.

Communism has also made many converts among the rural people, and some purely rural *départements,* like Corrèze, are among the most Communized in the country. However, among the rural population Communism is clearly in decline and is more and more confined to the traditionally left (though not traditionally Communist) regions.[10]

Communism also has much appeal for youth and for intellectuals, to whom it offers a "solution" for all problems. Perhaps more important, it offers them a chance for total dedication. The party, says Rossi, is a church, and its militants seem to participate in a retreat. They form a society of their own, with its own principles, hierarchy, and mores. The party is for the militant Communist the picture of the society to come, a society which he is ready, with missionary zeal, to impose on all others.[11] This is the spirit which gives the party its shock troops on whom it can count in any emergency.

These aforementioned factors add to the strength of the Communist party of France. On the reverse side of the medal there is the complete and slavish following of every twist and turn of Russian foreign and domestic policy. There was the familiar joke about Maurice Thorez, the Communist leader: "When Stalin sneezes,

[10] Gordon Wright, *Rural Revolution in France,* Stanford, Calif., 1964, pp. 172–175.
[11] Rossi, *op. cit.,* pp. 302–303.

Thorez catches a cold." And the same Thorez declared in 1949, ". . . in case of conflict between France and the Soviet Union the French people ought to collaborate with the troops of the Soviet Union."[12] This has caused occasional contortions and disaffections in the party. The thoroughly Moscow-oriented Communist leadership ruthlessly purged every element that did not depend solely on Russia for each word of revelation. Even so popular a figure as Charles Tillon, a member of the Politburo and wartime commander of the Communist Resistance group *Franc-Tireurs et Partisans* (FTP), and the equally popular Resistance leader of the *Massif Central,* Georges Guingouin, were purged and expelled. Ousted also was one of the oldest top leaders, André Marty, when he failed to toe the line. These expulsions caused arguments, even grumblings; some of the Communist Resistance veterans were reluctant to pour mud on their former idols. But all that blew over, and the basic unity of the Communist party was not broken. Even the bloody suppression of the Hungarian Revolution did not shake the basic loyalty of the rank and file.

The crisis of the Fourth Republic in 1958 caught the Communist party unprepared. The government of the Republic which they had so long reviled was now tottering. But the attack came from the colonels in Algeria, from the right, from the groups which the Communists had long called fascist, and whose ranks they could now hardly join. Thus there was no alternative left to the Communists but to take the course of pronouncing themselves the champions of the Republic, in an attempt to take over the leadership of the left and all those opposed to De Gaulle. That action fizzled miserably. The majority of the French people saw the death of the Fourth Republic with scorn and monumental indifference. The Communists, whose late conversion to republican loyalty was hardly believable, failed to arouse the masses. The few demonstrations which they called were quite large, but fell far short of what they could have been had they been supported by the major part of those who had voted Communist. A return of De Gaulle could obviously not be stopped in that fashion. The Communists quickly gave up trying. In fact, when De Gaulle did become Premier, one could hardly speak of more than token resistance on their part.

The Communists had expected De Gaulle to come to power as the prisoner of the extreme right, of the men who had unleashed the Algerian events of May 13, 1958. In that case, they expected the republican element to turn its back on De Gaulle and return to the struggle against him under Communist leadership. Then their turn would come. But De Gaulle's total independence from the right and his extraordinary ability threw them into confusion. He even obtained a measure of grudging admiration from them.

Moreover the leadership of the Communist party faltered in its usually sure sense of the tactical situation when the Soviet Union took a cautious wait-and-see attitude toward the Gaullist regime and when *Pravda* and *Izvestia* at first expressed themselves cautiously and noncommittally about him.

[12] *The New York Times,* Feb. 25, 1949.

The results of these blows were soon apparent. In the referendum of September, 1958, the total "no" vote was one million below the vote obtained by the Communists alone in 1956. Hence, since other groups had also supported the negative vote, the Communist loss was even greater, as their leadership openly admitted.[13]

This defeat was repeated and deepened in the general elections of November, 1958, when the Communists lost nearly 1,800,000 votes, as compared to 1956, and declined from 25.5 percent to 18.9 percent of the total vote. Even worse was the slaughter in parliament. Because of its total isolation, the Communist group in the National Assembly dropped from 150 in 1956 to 10 in 1958. In 1962 and 1967 the Communist vote increased again to 21.78 and 22.96 percent on the first ballot, which was an increase over 1958 but which kept them well below the levels to which they had been accustomed under the Fourth Republic. The distribution of the vote showed that the Gaullists had broken into some Communist strongholds among workers as well as into more middle-class workers' strongholds.

The presidential election of 1965 confronted the Communists with a dilemma. The 1958 and 1962 elections and the various referenda had shown that in a direct confrontation with De Gaulle around one million Communist votes deserted the party and went over to the "enemy." It would, therefore, have been a serious tactical error for the Communists to run their own candidate and thereby reveal their possible weakness. So their aim was to conclude as broad an agreement as possible along Popular Front lines, or failing that, with the Socialists alone. What they were advocating was a common movement, if possible, and a detailed electoral agreement, if necessary.

They were therefore quite cool to the attempt by Gaston Defferre to form a political movement from the Socialists to the center, because Defferre clearly intended to leave the Communists outside and confront them with the choice of giving their votes to him anyway or revealing their weakness by running their own candidate. In the end Defferre's endeavor foundered on the rock of his own party leadership. And when François Mitterand came forward as a new candidate of the left, the Communists leaped at the opportunity to support him. It is impossible to say precisely what percentage of the Mitterand vote was Communist, but the total 1962 vote of the parties pledged to his support was about 10 percent larger than the vote he actually gained in 1965. Since it is not possible to assume that all the losses were taken by the non-Communist parties, it seems highly likely that Communist prudence in not advancing a candidacy of their own was highly justified.

When Mitterand formed the Federation of the Left preparatory to the 1967 elections, the Communists were confronted by a tactical dilemma. They, who had always called for the unity of the left, however spuriously, could not easily oppose such a movement, especially as Mitterand avoided any appearance of overt anti-Communism. They tried to dominate Mitterand; they failed. Finally, they entered

[13] Report of Marcel Servin before the Central Committee of the French Communist Party. *Le Monde,* Oct. 7, 1958.

into an election agreement with his Federation in the time-honored French tradition by which support is given, in the run-off election, to the strongest candidate of the left. This benefitted the Communists more often than the Federation. However, the end result was that the Communists now find a stronger and more determined non-Communist left than they have for many years.

They are further handicapped by the increasingly close relations between De Gaulle and the Soviet Union. Communist opposition to Gaullist foreign policy has therefore often been muted and tortured, and thus has often ceded leadership of the opposition to the Federation of the Left.

Communist party organization begins at the local level, and its smallest and most direct part is called the cell. These cells may be organized in shops and factories, they may cover a few blocks of houses in towns and villages, or they may cover a certain area in rural regions. It is at the cell level that membership is acquired and every member takes part. Even top leaders of the Communist party must not neglect their responsibilities to their local cells.

These cells are grouped together in sections. A section may cover a town or in larger centers part of the town. In these sections too the members take an active and personal part. The sections of a *département* form a Federation, but if there are very many sections, there may be an organization of regions between the sections and the Federation. On the Federation level it is the delegates of the sections rather than the members as a whole who are active.

The delegates of the Federations meet in a national congress which elects a central committee. This in turn elects two other, smaller committees in which the actual leadership of the party is vested: a secretariat, now headed by Waldeck-Rochet as secretary-general, and a political bureau which contains the members of the secretariat and a number of other members. The political bureau meets at least once a week and at every meeting lays down the precise political and propaganda lines to be followed by all segments of the party. In this, it is assisted by a central political control committee, a central cadre committee, and a committee for ideological supervision. Besides the formal party organizations, there are a tremendous number of associations, clubs, and groups, many of them of the camouflaged "front" type.

The tactical line of the Communist party is of course primarily directed toward a fulfillment of the party's major political objectives: defeat of every government, weakening and destruction of the North Atlantic Alliance, prevention of German rearmament, pressure for appeasement of Russia, and the fomenting of every conceivable disaffection in France. To this end the party latches on to every controversy in order to split the other parties. It has been particularly expert and successful in raising the religious and school issue in order to separate the Socialists from the MRP. In the growing Sino-Soviet conflict, the French Communist party has taken the side of Russia. Having once been one of the most "Stalinist" of communist parties, it has not found adjustment to polycentrism too easy. Its leadership has therefore seemed less strong and determined in recent years.

After a long and acrimonious debate between the French and Italian Communist parties, the French one moved closer to the Italian line and took a more positive attitude toward the Common Market. This move, however, like the Italian move, is purely tactical and connotes no conversion whatsoever.

Despite the fact that the Communist party is the second largest and best-organized party of France, it is nevertheless fairly ineffective and unable to make much progress toward its objectives. This is due to its isolation, which condemns it to be consistently outvoted and overruled. However, it would be more than daring to write off French Communism. Despite its reverses, the Communist party is still strong; despite the large number of voters who have abandoned it, its organizational cadres remain intact; and it has shown more than once in its history that it can rise again when conditions favor it.

The Socialist party

The Socialist party of France is important, although less so than its British counterpart. The French Socialist party is beset by profound inner contradictions which handicap it in decisive moments and prevent its success. When it was unified in 1905 it was torn between the doctrinaire Marxist viewpoint of Jules Guesde and the humanitarian, reformist attitude of Jean Jaurès. It never solved this conflict, but absorbed it. It has retained the Marxist phraseology of Guesde, but it has conducted the reformist policy of Jaurès. The latter makes a mockery of the party program's radical words—and so the party loses the workers who were exasperated by the vacillations and the "immobilism" of the regime and wanted a radical policy. But the radical phraseology frequently prevents the party from carrying through its responsible, reformist policies—and so the party loses among the more moderate elements. In fact it declined steadily in voting strength in all national elections from 1945 to 1956. Between the elections to the first and second Constituent Assemblies in 1945 and 1946 respectively, the Socialists lost nearly 400,000 votes. Between the elections to the second Constituent Assembly in 1946 and the elections to the first National Assembly of the same year, they lost over 700,000 votes; a loss of over 1,100,000 in one year. This is often called the "hemorrhage" of the Socialist party. And then between the National Assembly elections of 1946 and 1951, the party dropped another 700,000 votes.[14] It has probably reached its more permanent level by now and is likely to remain an important political group, but no election figures give the Socialists cause for cheering.

The Socialist party was handicapped by its association with the declining years of the Third Republic and its inadequate preparation for national defense. But on

[14] Charles A. Micaud in his interesting work, *Communism and the French Left,* New York, 1963, points to the fact that the losses in Socialist party membership (from 300,000 to 100,000 after 1947) were no greater than those suffered by the Communist party and that party discipline and loyalty were maintained. This is true, but the losses were mostly in the working-class sector, and they changed the character and the inner strength of the Socialist party profoundly.

the other hand its record after the defeat of France did much to restore its reputation. The great majority of Socialist deputies and senators had voted *for* the Pétain enabling act. But thirty-seven of them, the largest group in any party (the Communists had not been "invited" by Pétain), were among the eighty who dared to vote against capitulation to totalitarianism. One year later, André Philip and Henri Ribière tried to reconstitute the Socialist party underground, but its principal leader, Léon Blum, was arrested, and together with several other leading figures, was tried before the court of Riom. Blum easily outshone his codefendants and the prosecution, and gained much prestige for his party. The party organ, *Le Populaire,* reappeared clandestinely from 1942 onward. Socialist leaders were members of the National Council of Resistance, while André Philip escaped to London and played an important role under General Charles de Gaulle. In North Africa, and later after the liberation of France, several Socialists were members of General de Gaulle's government. It was a Socialist, Félix Gouin, who succeeded De Gaulle as provisional President in January, 1946, and it was another Socialist, Paul Ramadier, who in 1947 as Premier ejected the Communists from the government, to which they were never to return. Yet another veteran Socialist leader, Vincent Auriol, became the first and much respected President of the (Fourth) Republic. A Socialist, Jules Moch, was Minister of the Interior in the critical days of 1947 and stood steadfast in the way of Communist tactics of violence and obstruction. He has earned major credit for having turned Communist violence from a danger to a nuisance.

Nevertheless, the Socialists have suffered from a dearth of leadership. Léon Blum developed from the doctrinaire, even arrogant, leader of Popular Front days into a major statesman without personal ambition, a man of profound humanitarian sentiments, conciliatory, and a realist. But he returned from German internment broken in health, too late to lead the party in the critical days after liberation and never again able to pull his full weight. His death in 1948 constituted an irreparable loss for the party. Other experienced leaders were eliminated by other causes: Vincent Auriol by becoming President of the Republic, Félix Gouin because of a financial affair, Paul Ramadier because he was twice beaten for reelection to the National Assembly. Their place was taken by less distinguished men, among whom the general secretary of the party, Guy Mollet, ranks first.

"The Socialist party," writes Fauvet,[15] "is the only and the last one which, at least in its title, calls itself international.[16] It is, however, one of the most French of them all. In any case it has most of the good qualities but still more certainly all the faults which one generally attributes to the French." It shares the French national

---

[15] Jacques Fauvet, *Les Forces politiques en France,* Paris, 1951, p. 65. Also by the same author, *La IVè République,* Paris, 1959.
[16] The official name of the party is still *Parti Socialiste, Section Française de l'Internationale Ouvrière* (SFIO)—Socialist Party, French Section of the Workers' International. This refers to the Second International of the Socialist parties of the world, which has recently been reestablished.

spirit of emphasizing reason and ideas. But it shares the French predilection for failing to check ideas against realities. The Declaration of Principles adopted by the party in 1946 and reprinted as a kind of preamble to the party statute proclaims, "The Socialist Party is an essentially revolutionary party," and later in the same document, ". . . the Socialist Party has always been and continues to be a party of the class struggle based upon the organization of the working people."

Nothing could be further from the truth. The Socialists are mild and earnest men and women who would not dream of mounting a barricade. As Fauvet rightly stated, "The posters (of the SFIO) do not call for revolution, but for comfort." Moreover the Socialist party, quite different from its British and German prototypes, is not a workers' party. There are some workers in it, and in a very few regions like the departments of Nord and Pas-de-Calais they are represented in fair numbers. But elsewhere and in an over-all analysis, the overwhelming majority of Socialist voters come from small, rural communities, and while often impecunious are not of the working class. As for the active party members, they are mostly recruited among schoolteachers, civil servants, and other whitecollar people. It is true that a section of the labor movement, called General Confederation of Labor, Workers' Force (CGT, *Force Ouvrière*), is frequently described as a Socialist union movement. This is, however, a considerable exaggeration. Socialist party and *Force Ouvrière* very frequently do not see eye to eye with one another and actually have little regard for each other. *Force Ouvrière* may come closest to the Socialist party as compared to other parties, but it is consciously independent and does not respond to party directives.

The Socialist party (SFIO) thus presents the phenomenon of a party sincerely trying to represent the workers but actually divorced from the main currents of the workers' movement. It is, and is bound to remain, an important party, but it has made practically no dent upon the far stronger Communist party. Since Socialists and Communists compete for the same groups of the electorate in most European countries, a strong Socialist party always means a weak Communist one, or vice versa, as in France.

This situation became much aggravated after the election of 1951 when it became clear that the parties of the middle had to cooperate in order to support a government. This forced the Socialists, out of a sense of responsibility toward the preservation of the Republic, to collaborate with the government. But since the left was split by the Communists, these governments were essentiallly governments of the right, which gradually deepened their conservative tendencies. In such company the position of the Socialists was far from enviable. Their chance of recapturing the workers' vote was hardly improved by their collaboration with forces which the workers regard as their enemies. On the other hand, if the Socialists went into sharp opposition to the government, they risked making democratic government impossible and ensuring a radical change in the French form of government.

The Socialists had another possibility. They could strengthen the left-wing tendencies by adroit and intimate collaboration with the Popular Republican Movement (MRP), whose social and economic ideas are quite close to those of the Socialists. But such an alliance was made virtually impossible by another, peculiarly French, factor. The Socialists still live mentally in the world of their revolutionary phraseology. They regard themselves as the heirs of the men who made the French Revolution. In France this attitude entails a stand of hostility and suspicion toward the Catholic Church. To be left means traditionally to be hostile to or at the very least extremely suspicious of the Church. And the MRP, while not a "church party" in the narrow sense, is without doubt a primarily Catholic party. The Socialist hostility toward the Church is further heightened by the fact that public school-teachers are the backbone of the Socialist organizations, and these schoolteachers, who are sustained by powerful organizations, regard the Catholic schools as competition, a menace, and the embodiment of an "anti-Republican" conspiracy. This goes back to the not-so-distant days when "Catholic" and "right wing" were regarded as synonymous, and the product of a Catholic school was automatically regarded as a man of the right. The Socialists, who like most Frenchmen are deeply tied to the past, appear to be unable to free themselves and especially their teacher cadres from these deeply ingrained notions. This explains the curious fact that in all recent elections, national and local, the Socialists have collaborated much more with the very conservative Radical party—which, however, shares with them a now fairly mild version of anti-Catholicism, or with the Communist party—which shares with them a vocabulary, than with the MRP. In every party congress of the Socialists one can hear several orators intone the now well-known phrase: "Better the worst Radical than the best Popular Republican" or, "No enemy on the left!"

This conflict between Socialists and MRP was heightened by the Barangé Act of 1951,[17] which provides for a small subsidy for education in public and private schools. To throw this law into the fray was actually a Communist maneuver designed to split the Socialists and MRP and thus weaken the government coalition. It succeeded brilliantly. The Socialists fought the law bitterly; the MRP, whose deputies had been elected mostly from the Catholic regions, had to fight just as hard for the law or be finished politically.

The coolness between the Socialists and the MRP has prevented both parties from making a more effective fight for their social and economic aspirations. In countries like America or Great Britain, where practical considerations play a major role in politics, such a condition would not be allowed to last long. But in France, where dedication to ideas is almost total, even to ideas that have few roots in social reality, this is quite another matter.

The Algerian war, which has been tragic for France, was peculiarly damaging to the Socialist party, for in the years when some relatively mild reforms might have averted the later explosion, some Socialists saw the handwriting on the wall

---

[17] The Barangé Act provided for the extension of a modest scholarship of 1,000 francs ($3) per student and quarter, whether the student attends public or private schools. Thus four-fifths of these funds actually benefit public schools. However, the fight took on a symbolic significance.

more clearly than others. But this was soon forgotten. The curtain rose on this tragedy in 1954 and 1955 when the government of Pierre Mendès-France negotiated the independence of Morocco and Tunisia, which became a fact under his successor, Edgar Faure. This aggravated the situation in Algeria, which did not change in status. When the Socialists returned after the elections of 1956 as relatively the strongest party among the moderates and participated prominently in the formation of a government under their leader, Guy Mollet, Algeria was in flames. Mollet went to Algeria to see for himself and was received by a hail of eggs and rotten tomatoes from the enraged European extremists who feared that he and the Socialists were soft on Algeria. Under this onslaught, which had been well rehearsed in advance, the man who had been one of France's most courageous underground leaders during the German occupation and who had braved a thousand dangers, retreated in disorder. The man whom he had designated as Governor-General of Algeria, General Georges Catroux, resigned without having set foot in Algiers.

In his stead Mollet appointed Robert Lacoste, a trade-union leader from the Dordogne and a Resistance hero; a man of courage, to be sure, but a man only modestly endowed with the gifts of intellect. Under Mollet and Lacoste the slogan for Algeria became "pacification first, negotiations later!" And pacification meant military action. From the French point of view it was Mollet's merit to have been the first of France's chiefs of government to recognize that the disturbance in Algeria was not a police action but a war and to send large contingents of troops there, eventually numbering half a million men. In these energetic measures Robert Lacoste played an important role, but he never understood that the war could not be won by military means alone and that to win it he had to win over the non-European middle classes. For that task his intellect and his sensitivity were inadequate. When this author met him in the spring of 1958, he presented the pathetic picture of an undoubtedly sincere and devoted patriot unable to understand why he could not succeed.

The Mollet-Lacoste policy in Algeria caused profound uneasiness in the Socialist ranks. The liberation of dependent territories had once been a maxim of Socialism, and its memories still lingered. Moreover, the Socialist parties of other countries made no attempt to hide their strong disapproval of the Mollet-Lacoste policies.

Under these circumstances, considerable opposition arose within the Socialist party against Mollet's leadership. But it was disorganized and ineffective. One small group of oppositionists was led by André Philip, who published a bitter criticism of Mollet's leadership[18] and was expelled from the party. More important was the more moderate but nevertheless quite effective opposition of Gaston Defferre, Minister of Defense in the Mollet cabinet, and mayor of Marseille. But Mollet mastered all these crises, even when he announced at the party's Toulouse congress of

[18] André Philip, *Le Socialisme trahi,* Paris, 1957.

1957 the surprising revelation that "it had never been a doctrine of socialism to support national independence." He won, largely because of the fundamental discipline of the Socialist party and because most of the delegates were party officials and party bureaucrats who were used to following the strong Mollet leadership.

But the struggle increasingly weakened and undermined the party. After Mollet's government fell, in June, 1957, other men, non-Socialists, like Bourgès-Maunoury and Felix Gaillard, headed the governments but Mollet remained the real master of the situation without whose support they could not survive. Thus the rebellion of the colonels and the Europeans in Algiers on May 13, 1958, was also directed against Mollet who had become one of the chief symbols of the Fourth Republic. Although he had been determined to remain outside the government, his sense of responsibility did not allow him to refuse the call of the short-term interim Premier, Pierre Pflimlin (MRP), for support. But Mollet soon realized, as did everybody else, that Pflimlin could not last, and the profound question of conscience became that of supporting or opposing the evidently inevitable coming of General Charles de Gaulle.

Mollet had never shared the fear of De Gaulle which imbued some other Socialists. In a conversation with the author four months before De Gaulle returned to power, Guy Mollet categorically rejected the idea that De Gaulle might want to be a dictator. At a crucial moment in May, 1958, he wrote a frank letter to General de Gaulle, who was still in retirement then at Colombey-les-deux-Eglises, and received reassuring answers. Together with Vincent Auriol, who had been first President of the Fourth Republic, he called upon the General and received further assurances. Thereupon he resolutely and without reservations threw his entire support to General de Gaulle's return to power. It was not an easy decision, and it required much courage in the face of some bitter opposition in his own ranks. But it probably saved France from the horrors of a civil war, for without the support of the powerful Socialist party it is doubtful that General de Gaulle could or would have come to power peacefully.

Thus, when General de Gaulle formed his first cabinet on June 1, 1958, Guy Mollet became Minister of State and, in effect, though not in title, deputy premier. In the referendum campaign he strongly supported an affirmative vote. It was scarcely a secret that the two worked well together and that the General hoped that the elections of November, 1958, would return a strong Socialist party, which would then help him to balance the right, with whose policies he disagreed in many respects. This hope was not realized. The Socialist party suffered a strange, bizarre kind of defeat. As far as the vote was concerned, it was no defeat at all. The party obtained very nearly the same vote in 1958 that it had received in 1956 and increased its percentage slightly from 14.8 percent to 15.5 percent. But because of the operation of the electoral law, its representation in parliament declined sharply from 95 in 1956 to 66 in 1958. Thus the hopes of Guy Mollet had come to naught. But his opponents within the Socialist party had fared much worse. All those who had opposed the Constitution and De Gaulle went down to crushing defeat. Even those who had voted for the Constitution but had opposed Mollet, like Defferre, lost their seats in parliament. Thus, despite Mollet's reverses, his position within the party actually grew stronger than before because it was clear that had his opponents prevailed, the party would have been utterly crushed.

After the elections, Mollet withdrew his Socialist party from the government, despite General de Gaulle's attempts to dissuade him from that step, and went into opposition. It was his announced intention to form a loyal opposition in order to prevent that essential role from falling to the Communists. As the Fifth Republic developed, the Socialist party and its leadership became increasingly critical of General de Gaulle and his regime. They resented the fact that his drive was not against this or that party but against the party system as such. They criticized the regime's tendency toward one-man rule, under which parliament had little to say and even cabinet ministers were figureheads or handymen of the President. They objected to the manner in which legal and constitutional forms were often brushed aside in order that the General could have his way. And, although they had little sympathy for the Army generals who had plotted against De Gaulle or for the assassins who sought his life, they found the punishment meted out to be unnecessarily severe, especially when implication was not clearly proven.

In contrast to their German brethren, the French Socialists had been strongly "European" from the beginning. They grew more and more concerned over De Gaulle's increasing hostility toward integration. As a Socialist party, they found that the economic policies of the government were essentially conservative and deflationist, and while they admitted the high degree of stability reached, they thought that the common man had to bear a disproportionate share in the form of high prices and scarce lodging.

Thus, the Socialist party, headed by Guy Mollet, went from support of De Gaulle to partial opposition and finally to complete systematic opposition, i.e., opposition in principle to all measures proposed by the government. In his position as one of the principal leaders of the opposition, Mollet had a choice between at least two courses of action. It was clear that General de Gaulle and his regime constituted a danger to all political parties and that these parties should form as unified a front against his as possible. Therefore the Socialists had the choice of seeking unity toward the center or toward the left. Many moderate elements in the party, like Gaston Defferre and the deputy secretary-general Georges Brutelle, advocated a large federation of the left and center. Others preferred various combinations with the Communists, ranging from occasional collaboration to the renascence of a Popular Front. Between these tendencies Mollet vacillated, and only shortly before the 1962 Assembly elections opted for limited collaboration with the Communists. The result was the setback which has already been discussed, in which the Socialists lost 3 percent of their vote.

Despite this experience, Mollet could not be persuaded that he had made a fundamental error and that a better solution lay in a center-left union. The young leader of the Radical party, Maurice Faure, advocated such a solution. So did the

young and able leaders of the Popular Republican Movement (MRP), Jean Lecanuet and Joseph Fontanet. Still Mollet would not budge.

As 1965 and the presidential election approached, a campaign got under way
destined to create just such a movement around the personality of a future candidate. The independent left-wing periodical *L'Express,* which once had been close
to the Radical leader Pierre Mendès-France, carried article after article designed
to build up an as yet unknown single opposition candidate whom it called "Monsieur X." By and by it emerged that that candidate was none other than Gaston
Defferre, Socialist mayor of Marseille. Indeed he seemed well chosen in many ways,
for although not an arousing speaker, he was sound and respectable. He had given
an excellent administration to the large city of Marseille, where he had consistently
beaten both the Communists and the Gaullists. As Minister of War in the Mollet
government, he had done his share to prosecute the Algerian War and was thus
acceptable to the nationalists, but he had warned against the excesses of the European extremists and was thus acceptable to the liberals. Moreover, on the delicate
religious question, he occupied a unique place: although a Socialist, he was religious
and a regular churchgoer—but he was a Protestant and hence not considered a
menace to the doctrinaire left.

Defferre's movement gathered considerable steam. It met a great deal of
support and he campaigned hard in 1964 and early 1965—well ahead of the presidential campaign—in order to become well known in a country where the best
media for that purpose, radio and television, were closed to him by the government.
The then Secretary of State for Information, Alain Pierrefitte, spokesman for the
government, declared somewhat cynically that since most of the newspapers were
against the government, it was only right that the government balance the picture
by not letting the opposition in on the government-controlled radio and television.

At first Defferre had the grudging support of his own Socialist party and of
Mollet. But Defferre did not want to have a program for his broad federation which
would seem sacrilege to the doctrinaire left; he wanted merely a general declaration
of principles, and nothing whatsoever to do with the Communists. Defferre realized
that the opposition to De Gaulle would not amount to a great deal without the
Communist votes, but he was certain that the Communists, fearing to reveal their
weakness, would not present a candidate of their own and would in the end be
forced to support him as the single or at least the most important anti-Gaullist
candidate.

Mollet and the majority of the Socialist party leadership did not agree with
this diagnosis. They manifested increasing hostility toward Defferre's design, until
finally Mollet pulled the rug from under Defferre. Defferre resigned from his candidacy, and the movement for the creation of a broad center-left federation came
to an abrupt end. Later, Mollet found the candidacy of Mitterand far more acceptable, because he did not attempt a center-left coalition but depended primarily on
Socialist-Communist collaboration.

Why did Mollet choose this course of action? The idea that he is pro-Communist must be discarded at the outset; he has fought the Communists too hard, and has always insisted on his basic antipathy to them. The reason is probably to be found in two factors, one his analysis of the situation and the other his personal ambition. Mollet has always considered that the De Gaulle regime, although it cuts across the board and has support in all sectors of the country and of the population, is essentially a regime of the right and that consequently the logical opposition to it must be a coalition of the left. However, in Mollet's irretrievably Fourth Republic mind, the left is that old left derived from the tradition of the French Revolution and hence it cannot collaborate with the Catholic MRP. Mollet has always been unable and unwilling to understand the nature of the MRP. He has always declared it to be "the party which ought not to exist," and he has never described any other party in that manner. It is not that he hates the MRP; he merely finds no place for it in the neat left-right model of France which he sees.

The second reason for Mollet's opposition cannot be proven, but in my opinion it lies in his personal ambition. It is almost certain that Mollet believes the De Gaulle regime to be merely an interlude, after whose departure from the scene France will again settle into something like the pattern of the Fourth Republic. This is a dubious conclusion. In this expected situation, it is my belief, Mollet hopes to come to power, perhaps as President of the Republic, and since the Communists cannot hope to elect their own candidate, he may well believe that they will be more willing to support him than anybody else. Yet he is sufficiently anti-Communist to expect support from other parties also. This at any rate seems a plausible explanation for Mollet's subborn refusal to consider any other alternative than one based primarily on Socialist-Communist collaboration.

In the presidential elections of December 5 and 19, 1965, it was Mollet who was the real architect of the Mitterand candidacy and who received credit for that candidate's relative success. Mitterand, the leader of a very small political group, seemed to be no threat to Mollet's continued leadership of the Socialist party, and was thus very different from Defferre who, had he succeeded, would almost certainly have taken the leadership of the party away from Mollet. However, the price of this tactic was further deterioration and disunity in Socialist ranks. In January, 1966, a number of important Socialist leaders resigned from the executive committee of the party, among them Gaston Defferre, Georges Brutelle, and Marc Jacquet. They did not leave the party but they demanded a special meeting of the party congress in order to consider their grievances. Mollet, although he almost certainly had the majority of the party members and of the Federation secretaries behind him, refused that demand.

As long as Mollet holds the Socialist party in his grip—and there are no indications of his loss of power—this situation is not likely to change. He envisages the future party constellations of France as falling eventually into four groups, a Socialist-Communist electoral combine, a center group, the Gaullists, and the right. He continues to be deaf to all entreaties to consider the alternative of a broad "labor party" which would include the Socialists, the MRP, the Radicals, and other center elements.

The lowest echelon of the Socialist party organization is the section which the party strives to establish in every town and village (*commune*). Larger cities are divided into several sections. Executive power in the section is wielded by an elected secretary and a treasurer. But frequently the sections are so weak that they cannot produce a secretary, and in that case the central leadership attempts to persuade someone in the locality to take on the job. Frequently schoolteachers are selected for this often thankless job, which increases their importance in the organization.

A *département* with at least five sections totaling a minimum of 100 dues-paying members is entitled to organize a Federation. The representative organ of the Federation is a federal administrative congress which is composed of the delegates of the sections. The number of delegates which each section is entitled to send to the congress varies according to the number of members in the sections. The Federation has its officers, secretary, treasurer, etc. It in turn elects delegates, proportional to its membership, to a national congress which meets annually. The national congress in turn elects an executive committee (*Comité Directeur*) composed of thirty-one members, no more than ten of whom may be members of parliament. The executive committee elects a general secretary and assistant general secretaries, as well as a treasurer and his assistants. The general secretary is the most important party leader, while the assistant general secretaries do the actual administrative work. The present general secretary is Guy Mollet.

Since the national congress meets only once a year, another body, the national council, has been created to keep the party leaders in touch with the rank and file. It is composed of one delegate from each Federation and meets every three months or more frequently.

The effective direction of the party is supposed to lie in the hands of the executive committee. However, more than once the Socialist members of parliament or at any rate their leaders, who are actually in charge of the day-by-day political decisions, have paid little attention to the will of the national congress or the executive committee.

Apart from the regular party organization, the Socialists have organized factory groups which are to serve as centers of persuasion for other workers. There are also other Socialist organizations like the Socialist Youth Movement, vacation clubs, etc. After the liberation, radical elements, many of the Trotskyite variety, found their way into the Socialist Youth Movement, and in 1947 the executive committee found it necessary to dissolve the leadership of the Youth Movement. And although the movement was reorganized, it never recovered from this blow and is leading a meager existence.

While the party has some strong sections, its organization on the whole is weak. But, as has been pointed out previously, there seems to be little connection between its organizational strength and its vote. There are many areas with a small organization and a big vote, others with good organizations and a small vote. This merely emphasizes the reluctance of most Frenchmen to become members of any party. Although the party has relatively few men of great national stature, it is solidly entrenched on the local level. Being old, it has many well-liked and respected men in the smaller towns of France who have become mayors, general councilors, etc., and who give a more solid foundation than the weak organization can provide. This is one of the factors which make the Socialist party (SFIO) a permanent force in the political kaleidoscope of France.

The Left Federation

Although the idea of a broad anti-Gaullist front had died with the failure of Defferre, a different kind of united front made its appearance after the presidential elections of 1965. One of its roots was certainly the desire of François Mitterand and his friends to make use of the popularity and vote-drawing power which he had achieved as the principal opposition candidate in 1965. This was particularly important for Mitterand because his political origins lay in the small Socialist and Democratic Union of the Resistance (UDSR), and in order to play a role of major significance, he had to find a broader vehicle.

To Socialist leader Mollet, Mitterand's "visibility" as the top opposition candidate in the presidential elections was an asset to be used by the entire left opposition; also, Mollet, after having torpedoed Defferre's venture, was probably in need of proving, in some manner, that he was not systematically opposed to all ventures of association with kindred groups. So he initially welcomed Mitterand's role as the leader of a broader federation.

Another important consideration was the hope of the non-Communist left that the Communists could not easily oppose an essentially left federation without running counter to their own slogan of "left unity." Finally, such a left federation might make it possible to pick up such splinter groups as the Unified Socialist party (PSU) of former Premier Pierre Mendès-France, which was weak in voting power but often strong in impressive intellectual membership.

Thus was born in 1966 the Federation of the Left (*Fédération des Gauches*), of which François Mitterand became president and spokesman, but in which the largest single group by far was the Socialists (SFIO). Guy Mollet had every expectation of actually controlling this venture.

The reality of the Federation proved to be somewhat different. What Mitterand had in mind was far more complex than had been anticipated, far more than simply an electoral coalition. He wanted: (1) to create the image of a genuine left group which would gain such wide acceptance that the Communists could not oppose it for fear of becoming splitters of left unity; (2) to assemble men of talent and experience who would elaborate a practical, not overly ideological program that would serve to give the country a genuine alternative to Gaullism, not only in ideas, but also in hardheaded managerial talent; and (3) to knit the Federation so closely together that his, Mitterand's, own role of leadership would not be questioned even though men like Mollet might control larger parties and organizations.

Mitterand reasoned that the left tradition of France had remained a living reality despite the inroads of Gaullism. He believed in the potential existence of a left majority, although he believed that it could not exist in outright opposition to the Communists. Hence his Federation of the Left was to be neither anti-Communist nor pro-Communist. It would never attack the Communists head-on and would even accommodate them when possible, but its composition and program were to be strictly non-Communist and independent. Mitterand reasoned that the Communists would be reluctant to appear as wreckers of left unity and thus would be reluctant to attack as long as the Federation did not give them an opportunity to denounce it as anti-Communist. Moreover, he reasoned, Gaullism and De Gaulle himself had made inroads into the Communist vote, especially by the attacks on NATO and on virtually every aspect of American foreign policy, and the Communists would be reluctant to go into the elections "naked," i.e., without some associations and vote mergers which would disguise significant losses of votes.

Mitterand felt that as the result of such a Left Federation's existence, once it had proven its strength many leftist voters who had voted the Communist ticket in the past would shift their votes to the Federation candidates. Such voters had perhaps never really been Communists but had nevertheless voted for Communist candidates because other parties, especially the Socialists, appeared tainted by collaboration with more or less conservative governments. Now, however, the Federation would give those voters a spiritual home and thus lay a foundation for the emergence of a large, non-Communist party of the left, something like the Labor party in Great Britain.

Thus what Mitterand desired was not only a victory, or more realistically, a relative success against De Gaulle in the parliamentary elections of 1967, but perhaps even more a shift of the vote within the opposition away from the Communists. And this was to be achieved by the Federation never becoming anti-Communist. An ingenious scheme indeed.

The plan described above would also entrench Mitterand in his own right and would make him invulnerable to Mollet's pulling the rug from under him as had been done to Defferre.

Mitterand surrounded himself with an impressive advisory council, which the press somewhat incorrectly dubbed "shadow cabinet" (*contre gouvernement*) but which did produce, in the Program of July 14 (1966), a list of proposals and schemes many of which showed considerable practicability and a high degree of talent. Especially noteworthy were the contributions of the noted economist Pierre Uri. Mollet was a member of the group but found it impossible to dominate it. The Program of July 14 was intended not only to make practical and concrete proposals for the solution of France's problems and thereby to appeal to the young, reputedly pragmatic, generation, but also to show the French people that an impressive number of knowledgable and experienced individuals existed on the opposition side, able to carry on the business of government with efficiency and dispatch.

Naturally, these endeavors remained a secret neither from the Communists nor from Mollet. The Communists countered Mitterand by pressing hard for a joined program, criticizing considerably the Federation's Program of July 14, but in a relatively restrained way. The Communist game was clear; either Mitterand was to receive the kiss of death and become a Communist front, or he was to be maneuvered into a clear rejection of the Communists, in which case he would be denounced as the real wrecker of left unity. Mitterand managed by a series of deft maneuvers, to escape both of these traps although not without making concessions to Communist views which some thought regrettable. In a sense the relationship between Mitterand and the Communists presented the familiar picture of two groups of people extolling unity and cooperation while seeking to cut each other's throats.

Guy Mollet was not particularly pleased over Mitterand's strength and independence with the Left Federation, but continued to cooperate—although reluctant and obviously disgruntled. Only the tiny PSU, in doctrinaire purity, led by the increasingly self-isolated Mendès-France, persisted in going its separate and solitary way while mouthing the gospel of unity.

Mitterand's calculations succeeded up to a point. He outmaneuvered Mollet sufficiently to avoid the fate of Defferre. He gave the Communists no loophole and thus prepared the ground for an electoral coalition with them without losing his independence. And he led the non-Communist left in the 1967 elections under the Federation label. But his hope of taking votes away from the Communists did not materialize, and the vote of 18.79 percent polled by the Federation lies below the combined Socialist-Radical vote of 1962. Still, he had achieved two important things: (1) the non-Communist left emerged stronger, more united, and more confident than it had in many years; and (2) he had established himself as a serious alternative to Mollet as a leader of that non-Communist left.

The MRP

The Popular Republican Movement (*Mouvement Républicain Populaire*), generally referred to by its initials, MRP, is a unique phenomenon on the French political stage. It is essentially a Catholic party although some Protestants, Jews, and even nonbelievers belong to it. But its Catholicism would not make it unique. There are Catholic parties in Belgium, Holland, Italy, and Austria, and Germany's Christian Democratic Union is largely Catholic. What distinguishes the MRP is that it is or tries to be a party of the left in France, where "Catholic" and "right" have been considered synonyms for years.

The MRP is primarily a product of the underground struggle of the Resistance. However, it has its antecedents in earlier periods in men like the philosopher Lamennais, the Dominican preacher Lacordaire, the Count of Montalembert, and the Count Albert de Mun. Their aim was that the Church should inspire social legislation, but like their more conservative coreligionists, they were distrustful of the Republic. They were, as Goguel has pointed out,[19] social Christians rather than

---

[19] Mario Einaudi and François Goguel, *Christian Democracy in Italy and France,* Notre Dame, Ind., 1952, p. 110.

Christian Democrats. To set political forces in motion was left to Marc Sangnier and the movement *Le Sillon* (the furrow), which he founded in 1897. The aim of *Le Sillon* was a social democracy based on Christian principles. But the conservative tendencies which permeated the Vatican after the death of Pope Leo XIII caused Pius X to condemn *Le Sillon*. Marc Sangnier obeyed and dissolved his movement, an act which made it possible for the spirit which he had raised to succeed eventually within French Catholicism rather than outside or against it. Sangnier lived long enough to see the fruits of his endeavor.

In 1911, one year after the condemnation of *Le Sillon,* he and his friends founded a political movement, *La Jeune République* (The Young Republic), which advocated social reforms and fought against nationalism and militarism. Particularly significant was their belief in the collective action of the workers, including strikes.

This movement remained small. Only in 1919 was Sangnier elected to parliament together with a handful of others. In 1936 *La Jeune République* became part of the Popular Front movement.

Politically more significant were the thirteen deputies who, after the elections of 1924, formed a "group of democrats" and later that year were instrumental in founding the Popular Democratic party *(Parti Démocrate Populaire).* The PDP shared the ideas of the *Jeune République* but was perhaps a little more cautious. Although definitely a party of the left, its deputies were elected in the Catholic, traditionally conservative provinces of the West and in Alsace and Lorraine.[20] The party's efforts were aided by the Catholic publisher Francisque Gay who founded the newspaper *L'Aube* (dawn), among whose editorialists was the later MRP leader, Georges Bidault.

Without the defeat of France and German occupation, Christian Democratic thought would probably still be represented by these two small groups. However, the Resistance period caused a complete change. Most of the Popular Democratic deputies, and all those of the *Jeune République,* voted against emergency powers for Marshal Pétain, percentagewise the best record of any political party represented in parliament in those fateful days. Immediately afterward practically every Christian Democrat participated in the Resistance movement, and their importance was recognized when one of their foremost leaders, Georges Bidault, became president of the clandestine National Council of the Resistance.

Bidault, François de Menthon, Pierre-Henri Teitgen, and other Christian Democratic Resistance leaders thought in terms of a Christian alliance, but it was a young university student of Lyons, Gilbert Dru, who gave the movement its form and its direction. It was he who converted Georges Bidault and André Colin (later general secretary of the MRP) to his idea of a large movement which was to fuse the spirit of the Resistance with that of Christianity, democracy, and social progress. In that way Gilbert Dru became the father of the MRP. However, it was not given to him to see the crowning of his work. After returning to his studies and his

[20] Except for the party president, Champetier de Ribes, who was elected in the Pyrenees.

Resistance work in Lyons, he was arrested by the Germans and executed in 1944 in reprisal for an attack on the Gestapo.[21]

The party which emerged from these endeavors first called itself the Republican Movement of Liberation, but soon changed to Popular Republican Movement (*Mouvement Républicain Populaire,* MRP).

Being a new party, the MRP has placed particular emphasis on its political philosophy,[22] which it considers as of greater importance than its more concrete program.[23] It is primarily concerned with man's nature, which it conceives in traditional Christian terms as dual, spiritual and temporal, with the spiritual side being eternal and hence more important. In this dual existence man is a rational being and hence capable of being responsible for his actions. This responsibility he can fully discharge only if he is free in his full physical, moral, and mental development. The essence of the MRP philosophy is thus based on an exceedingly strong concept of liberty.

The emphasis on personal liberty is circumscribed and placed in focus by the realization, not shared by other Catholic groups, that man in modern society is incapable of living alone. He lives in a hierarchical system of groups such as family, profession, labor union, and nation. These groups, however, exist for the individual and not the individual for them. Consequently while they are essential to the full development of the individual, they cannot demand that he surrender his essential rights to them. These considerations lead the MRP to a position which is in sharp opposition to both capitalism and socialism. It reproaches capitalism of the French version for preventing the full development of the individual by turning political democracy into a smoke screen behind which a few powerful individuals are actually in control, leaving the workers the illusion without the reality of free choice. It recognizes that in self-defense and exasperation the workers have frequently embraced Marxism, but that Marxism offers no solution and on the contrary aggravates the objectionable features of capitalism. Under the Marxist doctrine, the power of the few is even more marked in a socialist state than in a capitalist one because the various competitive groups and factors of capitalism no longer exist, and the men who rule the state hold in their hands the totality of economic and political power. The MRP demands of the state that it be social, that is, mindful of the needs of social improvement, but not that it be socialist because, as Gilson put it, "Personal rights belong to persons, and to take them away from persons under the pretext of making them more secure would be a policy

---

[21] Jean-Marie Domenach, editor of *Esprit,* has given him a deeply moving monument in his book *Gilbert Dru, celui qui croyait au ciel* (Gilbert Dru, He Who Believed in Heaven), Paris, 1947.

[22] Basic documents are Etienne Gilson, *Notre démocratie,* Paris, 1948, and Albert Gortais, *Démocratie et libération,* Paris, 1947; see also Einaudi and Goguel, *op. cit.,* pp. 123–132.

[23] This is not unusual in Europe but is totally alien to the American concept of political parties. The difference between philosophy and program may be summarized in that philosophy asks, In what do you believe? What is your concept of the world and mankind? while the program asks, What do you want to achieve? Where do we go from here?

contrary to the very nature of things." The MRP is thus hostile to any form of statism and envisages that such aid as the state must give to the individual for his social improvements should be given through the aforementioned natural groups.

This doctrine places the MRP in opposition to the thinking of both traditional right and left. It contrasts with the right because of its frank condemnation of unbridled capitalism and the attitude which much of French management takes toward the workers. In the eyes of the right, the MRP is simply socialistic. But it is in equal conflict with the left because it opposes the left's belief that social progress can be achieved only by endowing the state with greater power and functions. In addition, the MRP is a Catholic party and in the eyes of the left, therefore, automatically classed with the right.

Because the emphasis of the MRP doctrine is on liberty, the MRP is unreservedly democratic and republican. It wishes to see democracy extended into the economic and social field by giving the workers a share in management and the profits of labor. Management should be in the hands of an elite, but an elite to which all social groups and classes have equal access according to talent and ability. This, the MRP contends, would do away with the class struggle and would free man as an individual, in the full enjoyment of his dignity. This is somewhat further spelled out in a plan submitted in the form of a bill by Paul Bacon in 1946. It proposes the creation of a new type of corporation called the Society of Work and Savings, which would be administered by a board of directors composed of representatives of the stockholders, of the workers, and of permanent consultants. Profit sharing would be applied with at least 50 percent earmarked for the workers.

It should be emphasized that the important thing about this philosophy and program is not so much the concrete proposals, which are vague enough, but rather the endeavor to restore the dignity of the human being by giving him a fuller place in society and by making it possible for him to use his individual talents to the best advantage of himself and of society. It is this attitude rather than any concrete proposals which is the essential part of the Popular Republican point of view.

The MRP has never been in sole charge of the government nor has it even been its dominant force. Concrete actions to give substantive implementation to its ideas have therefore not been too plentiful. There are, however, areas in which the MRP viewpoint has made a strong impact upon the country. The Popular Republicans have been the spokesmen and spearhead of the complicated system of family allocations, which have imposed a tremendous burden on the treasury but without which a very large number of families would not have reached the existence minimum. The MRP has also been active in the support of all measures to increase and broaden social security while at the same time opposing the absorption of the independent social-security agencies into the state. Together with the Socialists, the MRP has never hesitated to press for higher wages and better working conditions and has wholeheartedly supported the principles of labor unions and of strikes.

In conformity with this attitude is also the MRP stand on the tricky school question. Unlike the traditional right, the MRP is not hostile to public education, but it emphasizes the need for private schools in order to provide a real choice between alternatives. Since the financial situation of private schools is desperate, the MRP has advocated vigorously that the state's aid to schools and schoolchildren should be distributed among both public and private schools alike. To the parties of the traditional left, this is absolutely unacceptable as a matter of principle and constitutes the chief barrier to collaboration between the Socialists and the MRP, despite a high degree of agreement between these two parties on other issues of practical policy.

The tactical situation of the MRP is a difficult one in many ways. It was propelled into national significance almost overnight. In October, 1945, it received 24.8 percent of the national vote; in June, 1946, it emerged as the strongest party with 28.1 percent; and in November, 1946, was still formidable with 25.9 percent. But these results were artificial, and the MRP leadership had few illusions on that score. In 1945 and 1946 the traditional right and even the Radicals led only a shadow existence under the onus of collaborationism or too close association with the failure of the Third Republic. Many voters of the traditional right then voted MRP because that party was relatively the most anti-Communist among the "big three" of the day: Communists, Socialists, and MRP. But as soon as the right began to emerge from the debris of its past, and especially after General Charles de Gaulle organized the Rally of the French People (RPF) in 1947, many of those voters returned in droves to their more natural political habitat. The municipal elections of 1947 were catastrophic for the MRP. In cities of over 9,000 inhabitants the MRP declined from 23.8 percent to 10.2 percent. In Paris the party was nearly wiped out. It obtained 12.4 percent of the national vote in 1951, 10.9 percent in 1956, 11.6 percent in 1958, and in 1962 it dipped again, to 8.92 percent.[24]

Although the MRP had lost half of its previous electorate, its organization and cadres remained intact. There was some criticism of the leadership but there were no real opposition factions. In fact the party was remarkable for the close relationship between its leaders and the loyalty of its cadres. All this might lead to the conclusion that those voters who have remained with the MRP were strong believers in its philosophy. Their geographical distribution,[25] however, throws some doubt on this assumption. The MRP obtained its largest vote in traditionally Catholic areas. One might therefore suspect that part of the electorate is more conservative than the party itself. But this point should not be carried to extremes, for there are several Catholic groups competing for the vote of the Catholic regions and hence those who voted MRP must have been less conservative than some of their fellows. Moreover the relatively good showing of the MRP in industrial regions would indicate that it did well in areas where people are aware of social problems. Therefore it undoubtedly had a greater degree of voter homogeneity after 1946 than it had before, but there were enough who voted for the MRP because of

[24] Counting MRP and Christian Democratic votes together.
[25] Einaudi and Goguel, *op. cit.*, p. 186. See also François Goguel, *Géographie des élections françaises*, Paris, 1951, pp. 112–113.

its Catholic character rather than its social program to force it not to be found wanting in the struggle for the Catholic schools, or face the loss of an important segment of its electorate. This is precisely the reason why the collaboration between the otherwise logical partners, Socialists and MRP, was so difficult. The MRP had not sought the fight over the school issue, but once joined, it could not withdraw.

The crisis of the Fourth Republic was also the crisis of the MRP, although to to a lesser extent than it was for the Socialists and the Radicals. Because the MRP was sincerely democratic and republican, it could not refuse to participate in the government if, without that participation, majorities could have been found only by including extremists. But when the Socialists went temporarily into the opposition, the MRP was the only left party in an overwhelmingly right government. In this situation, it was easily outmaneuvered and had little opportunity to realize any part of its program. It tried to get into closer relationship with the Socialists, but found itself rebuffed because of the deep-seated Socialist suspicion of a clerical party.

But if the MRP was rebuffed and frustrated in that respect, it rose to great significance in another. The MRP made itself the principal spokesman for the idea of European unity which had electrified many minds. It was especially Robert Schuman, several times Premier and Foreign Minister, who persistently pursued this idea and who succeeded in producing the first concrete step towards that unity, the European Coal and Steel Authority, better and rightly known as the Schuman Plan.[26]

The European orientation of the MRP brought it both loyal friends and bitter opponents. It is not yet possible to speak of a clear victory or defeat in this struggle over greater European unity, but there is little doubt that the MRP viewpoint had greater success than that of its opponents. In particular this policy, and especially Robert Schuman personally, must receive major credit for having helped to bury the age-old Franco-German animosity, which had so long been regarded as a fixed and unchanging feature of contemporary Europe.

But the Algerian crisis was even harder on the MRP. The social and liberation tendencies in the MRP's ideology found it increasingly difficult to get along with the policy which Mollet and Lacoste were pursuing in Algeria. The fact that many Algerian non-European workers were organized in the Christian trade-union movement (CFTC) also had a bearing on the party's attitude. But in contrast to the Socialists, who were deeply divided by the Algerian problem, the MRP remained solid and increasingly critical of governmental policies, although continuing in the government coalition.

Only Georges Bidault, once the undisputed leader of the party and later its honorary president, spoke increasingly the language of the Algerian ultras (European extremists), and he alienated himself more and more from his party.

---

[26] The basic idea for the Coal and Steel Authority came from Jean Monnet but it was Schuman's merit to grasp its significance immediately and to carry it through the debates in the French government and Assembly as well as in the negotiations with other European powers. The treaty itself was signed in 1951.

The revolt of the colonels and the white settlers in Algeria on May 13, 1958, was directed against a government headed by the MRP leader Pierre Pflimlin and hence found the MRP virtually united, except for the lone dissent of Georges Bidault. But the MRP did not, at any moment, take the extreme position of Mendès-France, and when General de Gaulle assumed the premiership on June 1, 1958, Pierre Pflimlin and several other MRP leaders were in his cabinet. With a few very minor exceptions, the party urged a "yes" vote on the constitutional referendum and continued to participate in the government after De Gaulle ascended to the presidency.

In one of the erratic moods for which he is famous, Georges Bidault attempted to destroy the party which he had once helped to found, by creating a rival Christian Democratic movement, which was to take the place of the MRP and embrace other groups as well. Just what he expected to achieve by this maneuver is difficult to say, except that it helped him to vent his personal displeasure on the MRP, which had refused to allow him to dominate it. The only visible difference between the Christian Democratic movement and the MRP was the attitude on Algeria, in which Bidault embraced the views of the Algerian ultras. But the attempt to replace the MRP failed.

In the elections of 1958, the MRP and Christian Democrats moved separately. Although many people supported the latter, they did so largely because of strong personal ties, dating back to the Resistance period, rather than because of sharing Bidault's views or ambitions. Although he was reelected by a wide margin in his own sixth district of the Loire department, he carried only twelve other Christian Democrats with him, while the MRP elected forty-four.

Bidault went into embittered retirement. He became an ever more violent apostle of the ultras in Algeria, made common cause with the army rebels, and went into voluntary though doubtless well-advised exile in South America and later in Belgium.

It was quite important for France that the MRP had joined the first De Gaulle government as an act of national union, and that Pierre Pflimlin, the last Premier of the Fourth Republic, had entered De Gaulle's cabinet. Yet Robert Schuman watched developments from the sidelines, being well aware of General de Gaulle's hostility to European integration. And it was this hostility which on March 16, 1962, caused the resignation of all five MRP ministers in protest over the General's sharp and haughty rejection of European integration.

In opposition, the MRP concentrated primarily on two goals: one was the continued and vigorous advocacy of European unification, the other was the creation of a broad center-left movement. The party had already considerably rejuvenated itself by placing Jean Lecanuet in its presidency and electing Joseph Fontanet as general secretary, both comparatively young men. At the same time the MRP leaders refused to accept the systematic anti-Gaullism of the Socialists and declared that they would vote for or against government propositions on their merits. This balanced attitude was rendered increasingly difficult by the crescendo of General de Gaulle's fight against European integration, and the brusque manner in which he publicly rejected Great Britain's entry into the European Common Market in January, 1963.

Thus, as the 1965 presidential elections approached, the MRP had generally moved from selective opposition to total opposition with the exception of a few veteran Gaullists like Maurice Schumann. It quietly supported the endeavor of Gaston Defferre for a broad center-left federation. After the failure of that experiment, the MRP leaders kept their own counsel and it was only quite late in the campaign that their president, Jean Lecanuet, presented his candidacy.[27]

The Lecanuet candidacy had an electrifying effect, as discussed earlier. Although he had been a deputy in the Senate as well as a minor cabinet official, he was virtually unknown in France. Now he not only achieved great prominence but also presented a highly photogenic, extremely attractive personality to France's millions of television viewers. He helped to make the French voters aware of the fact that while De Gaulle spoke of himself as a man of the present and the future and of his opponents as men of the past, it was they who were young and he who was old. Lecanuet was also the principal defender of European integration, a goal dear to many Frenchmen and especially to the younger generation, and he challenged De Gaulle effectively and responsibly.

What infuriated the Gaullists particularly was that Lecanuet had deprived De Gaulle of being elected on the first ballot, because Lecanuet admirably fulfilled the function of presenting an alternative to those voters who were opposed to De Gaulle but unwilling to support a candidate sustained by the Communists or reluctant to support the extreme right candidate Tixier-Vignancour, who was the only other practical alternative. The 15.57 percent who voted for Lecanuet (almost twice as much as the whole MRP vote in 1962) thus gave him a very considerable success, even though he did not enter the second ballot, and never had a real chance to do so.

After the first ballot, Lecanuet gave his followers a free choice since he did not want to support openly a Communist-backed candidate. Had he openly espoused the candidacy of Mitterand, the outcome would probably not have been different except that Lecanuet's own postelection plans would have been disturbed. At any rate, on the second ballot, where only De Gaulle and Mitterand could be candidates, the fact that De Gaulle's percentage increased from 44.64 percent to 55.19 percent[28] shows what difference the Lecanuet candidacy had made on the first ballot.

The morning after the second ballot, Jean Lecanuet declared:[29]

If the non-Communist left had made a union with the center instead of accepting

[27] In order to emphasize his appeal to a segment of the population broader than just MRP voters, Lecanuet resigned as president of the MRP.
[28] Including the overseas departments.
[29] *Le Monde,* Dec. 21, 1965.

a common candidate with the Communists, France would today have a republican and democratic president favoring social progress and European unity. The alliance of the candidate [Mitterand] and of the opposition with Communism has helped to reject those voters who have finally rallied to the candidacy of General de Gaulle.

Thus Lecanuet seemingly accepted as the lesson of the first ballot that 56 percent of the voters were opposed to General de Gaulle, and as the lesson of the second ballot that 55 percent were even more opposed to a policy purely of the left, based on Socialist-Communist collaboration. One might question whether total unity of the opposition would really have defeated De Gaulle. But the balloting did illustrate the point that there was evidently room for a strong center movement.

In order to make greater use of the visibility and popularity which he had gained in the 1965 presidential elections, Lecanuet formed, early in 1966, the Democratic Center (*Centre Démocratique*). In this he was encouraged by 40,000 letters demanding the formation of just such a center movement—an unprecedented outpouring in France. This move was applauded by his young and enthusiastic followers and indeed his meetings in the country drew unprecedented crowds long after the presidential elections. His young and attractive personality, his wit, his considerable knowledge of public affairs had undoubtedly made an impression. But, whether all this could be translated into votes and seats in the National Assembly was a question. As far as other parties were concerned, Lecanuet gained little adherence. Maurice Faure, leader of the Radicals,[30] joined his cause but was unable to win over his own party. Bertrand Motte[31] and other "progressive conservatives" cooled off. Even in his own MRP, Lecanuet did not remain unopposed. The respected elder statesman of the party, former Prime Minister Pierre Pflimlin, declared in the summer of 1966 that he would "sit this one out" and not run for national election in 1967. No doubt Pflimlin's precarious position in Gaullist Strasbourg had something to do with his decision but there is little doubt that Pflimlin intended to rebuke Lecanuet's firm anti-Gaullism.

Lecanuet had of course little hope of gaining anything like a majority. But if he were to win 20 percent of the seats or even 15 percent, he and his group would be the decisive element in an Assembly which might produce no clear majority for either Gaullists or anti-Gaullists. In that case Lecanuet would not under all circumstances ally himself with the anti-Gaullists. He would insist, above everything else, on the revision of De Gaulle's anti-European integration policy.

Thus despite his strong and undoubtedly honest convictions, Lecanuet could be classed as the "least unconditionally *anti-Gaullist*" political leader. In a similar way, as we shall see, former Finance Minister Valéry Giscard d'Estaing,[32] has emerged as the "least unconditionally *Gaullist*" political leader on the other side.

[30] See p. 268.
[31] See p. 270.
[32] See p. 271.

It is therefore not surprising that a keen rivalry has developed between these two gifted men who compete, to a considerable extent, for the same electorate.

The outcome of the 1967 elections was inconclusive and disappointing to Lecanuet and the Democratic Center, but the figures alone do not give the full picture. They show the Democratic Center as receiving a higher percentage of the vote than the MRP had ever received since its heyday in 1946, but this success was more apparent than real because the MRP-Democratic Center's inability to enter into electoral coalitions had reduced its parliamentary representation from 38 (in 1947) to 27 (in 1967). When one adds the greater consolidation of the left and the continued strength of the UNR, one sees that Lecanuet failed to gain his hoped-for role of becoming the decisive element in the balance of left and right. That role shifted, at least potentially, to Giscard d'Estaing and his Independent Republicans.

Compared with the MRP, the Democratic Center was now lacking in both cohesiveness and parliamentary effectiveness: first, because it now had several deputies who actually belonged to the classic conservatives and had little sympathy for the social ideas which had characterized the MRP and second, because Lecanuet's decision not to run for a seat in the National Assembly had deprived it of his leadership there.

In September 1967 the step which Lecanuet had advocated earlier was finally taken: the MRP was formally dissolved and left the field to the Democratic Center. Yet the latter's uninspiring parliamentary performance raised uncertainty about whether it would be able to continue the special role formerly played by the MRP, or whether it would turn out to be merely another one of France's many transitory, electoral coalitions. Certainly the hope that it would become the vigorous rallying point of those who wanted neither the left nor the Gaullists had clearly remained unrealized.

The Radicals

The party whose official name is Radical and Radical Socialist party (*Parti Radical et Radical Socialiste*) is in no way "radical" in the American sense. It is rather a conservative party and eminently respectable. Some overenthusiastic historians[33] find its origin in the French Revolution, in the society of Jacobites and the "Mountain" (*La Montagne*) of the Revolutionary convention. Nearer our own time they consider Condorcet and especially Ledru-Rollin, the leader of the Second Republic, as their precursors. However, the Second Empire put an end to this development. Only before the demise of Napoleon the Third's regime did modern radicalism begin to take shape. The declaration of Jules Simon of 1868 and especially the Belleville program of Léon Gambetta in 1869[34] embodied the basic ideas of "radicalism": universal manhood suffrage, democratic administration, strict sepa-

---

[33] Jammy Schmidt, *Les Grands thèses radicals,* Paris, 1931.
[34] Albert Milhaud, *Histoire du radicalisme,* Paris, 1951, pp. 57–58.

ration of state and church, and especially the fighting words "mandatory public, primary education, free of charge" (*instruction primaire laïque, gratuite, et obligatoire*).

The Radical party made its debut in 1885 under the propulsion of Georges Clemenceau, but it was only in 1901 that the party, now officially called Radical and Radical Socialist party, organized itself in permanent form. Since then it has held an annual congress (with the exception of the two wars) every year, and it constitutes the oldest among the presently existing organized parties of France.

The Radical party is a French phenomenon which foreigners find hard to classify. First of all it is a party of personalities; it does not have and it does not wish to have a mass basis. It is built around a considerable number of men of high talent and long reputation in both local and national affairs. What these men have in common is not a program nor truly a doctrine but rather an attitude. This attitude may be described as republican and democratic, with no sharp distaste for anyone. Traditionally the Radicals are opposed to the Catholic Church, but this opposition is now quite mild and its more militant phases have been taken over by the Socialists. In the social and economic sphere the party officially endorses the principle of reform and progress but denounces revolution. In actuality the Radicals do not believe that their acceptance of the idea of progress obliges them to endorse any particular measure or commits them to any rate of speed. Therefore in the daily parliamentary game they have usually been on the conservative side, and even such a measure as the sliding wage scale, which in the United States was instituted by the General Motors Corporation, met with the violent denunciation of the majority of Radical deputies and senators.

Because the criterion of "radicalism" is a personal attitude and not a definite commitment on program, the party has most heterogeneous elements in its midst, ranging from men who are very close to the Socialists (only a few) to outright reactionaries (of whom there are several). In fact, there is no occasion on record on which all deputies of the Radical party have ever voted on the same side.

This used to put the party in a most admirable position. By its philosophy, if that term be applicable, it is a party of the left: rationalistic, humanitarian, antireligious. Consequently during elections in which general principles were primarily at stake, the Radical party formed its most effective coalitions with the left, especially the Socialists. But in its social and economic policy the party in its great majority belongs clearly to the conservative side, and in the daily alignments of the parliamentary struggle as well as in the operation of government, it worked most closely with the right. There are few other countries in which such a situation could long endure. Nothing illustrates better the utter separation between political ideas and political action in the Third and Fourth Republics than the success with which the Radical party worked both sides of the street. Auguste Maurice Barrès, famed French politician and writer, once said, "France is Radical," by which he meant that the Radical party embodies much of the spirit of France, and indeed he who can understand the Radical party already understands a great deal about France.

The unique position occupied by this party made it an indispensable partner of any French government. If it associated itself with a government of the left, it gave it respectability by its presence. If it associated itself with a government of the right, it gave it the stamp of progressivism. To some extent it still plays this role. But for the time being, at least, the Radicals have weakened themselves by an unusual degree of disunity, in particular by the disastrous consequences of the leadership of Pierre Mendès-France.

The Radical party has traditionally been an extremely tolerant party—so tolerant of divergent points of view that it was difficult sometimes to speak of it as a party in the usual European sense.[35] Therefore, there was nothing unusual in the position of the deputy from the Eure department, Pierre Mendès-France, whose views differed from those of the party leadership in many important features.

Mendès-France is an economist and much of his political thinking is influenced by economic considerations. After fighting in the Free French forces during the war (as a navigator), he became Minister of National Economy in the first De Gaulle government after the liberation of France. He advocated a bold program of price and wage stabilization, heavy taxation, and firm reestablishment of the shaky currency, all measures which sooner or later were taken in most other European countries during that same period. In this, Mendès-France was undoubtedly right and his opponents wrong, but his views did not prevail. He resigned from the government in disgust and remained on the outer edge of politics until 1955. In that period he was known primarily as a Cassandra, a voice of doom and gloom which often warned, usually with good reason, of the deterioration of France's affairs. In contrast to many of his countrymen, he was willing to face certain harsh realities; in particular, he became convinced that the murderous war in Indochina could not be won and that it drained France's resources. To restore France's prosperity and financial structure, her losses had to be cut.

However, Mendès-France remained an outsider until the war in Indochina turned very much to the worse and the French suffered the psychologically spectacular defeat of Dien Bien Phu in 1954. Then, like Winston Churchill in Britain in 1940, Mendès-France suddenly became the man whom everybody wanted to have end *la sale guerre* (the dirty war). Although it was the government headed by Joseph Laniel, whose Foreign Minister was Georges Bidault, which inaugurated the peace talks with Ho Chi Minh and the Communist revolutionaries of the Vietminh, it was a government headed by Pierre Mendès-France which brought those negotiations to a conclusion.

For this, he had to pay a heavy political price. Rumors were current that some of his closest associates had contacts with the Vietminh and had persuaded the latter to remain intransigent until the Laniel-Bidault government had fallen. These rumors were never entirely proved or disproved. But profound bitterness remained

---

[35] American parties are of course accustomed to accommodating vastly different points of view in their midst.

between the members of the Laniel-Bidault government and Mendès-France, a bitterness which was greatly aggravated by the latter's habitual arrogance and cutting tongue. In contrast to French parliamentary customs, he continued to flay his predecessors even after they were down and out.

The Mendès-France government which lasted from June 21, 1954, to February 22, 1955, was an unusual spectacle for France. It was very much a one-man show. Mendès-France, who copied some of the techniques of Franklin D. Roosevelt, hardly let a Sunday go by without unveiling some monument or opening some bridge, with the attendant occasion for a speech. Then there were "fireside chats" on the radio practically every weekend. In his speeches, in his dashing around the country, he tried to give the impression of a man of action, and indeed it is undeniable that he enjoyed considerable popularity. In foreign affairs, at least, he was a man of action. It was he again who began the negotiations with Morocco and Tunisia which eventually culminated in the independence of both countries. But in his own field of economics, he accomplished surprisingly little, preferring to concentrate on spectacular schemes such as the fight against alcoholism and the furthering of milk consumption rather than on more solid plans.

The customary coalition of his numerous enemies brought him down early in 1955 but from that defeat he drew a heavy and highly debatable conclusion. He decided that France's ills, primarily her economic ones, were such that only long-range plans and actions could cure them. But no short-lived government could tackle them. Hence a solid, long-lasting government had to be found. Up to this point there can be little quarrel with his reasoning. But this is not the case with what followed. He went on to argue that since the political right did not have a majority in France and was too disunited and helpless in the face of troubles in the overseas territories, only a government of the left could succeed. He advocated the creation of a broad republican front, a bloc of the left, which he hoped would gain enough votes to produce a majority and a solid government. This meant primarily an alliance between Radicals and Socialists. But into this traditional concept of leftism the MRP did not fit, because of its Catholicism.

Guided by these considerations, and also influenced by his intense hatred of Bidault and the entire MRP, Mendès-France proceeded to organize this combination, using his own Radical party as the nucleus. But how could such a disorganized, divergent party be the nucleus of a disciplined republican bloc? The answer was that the Radical party would have to be streamlined and dissenters purged. And so Mendès-France took it upon himself to capture the leadership of the Radical party, an endeavor in which he was supported by Edouard Herriot, the party's grand old man, during the last few months of Herriot's life.

It is difficult to believe that Pierre Mendès-France could have succeeded under any circumstances. A disciplined Radical party is virtually a contradiction in terms. But his failure became inevitable when his hand was forced by the election of 1956. By extremely dexterous maneuvers, Mendès-France's successor, Edgar Faure, also of the Radical Socialist party, had remained in power for a year. Eventually the government's survival became impossible and Faure used a newly revised section of the Constitution to force the dissolution of parliament and new elections on January 2, 1956. This was a heavy blow to Mendès-France because his hold over his party was not yet completely consolidated; and besides, the elections took place under an election law which the Radicals considered unfavorable to them. Nevertheless, the Republican Front became a reality, and Radicals and Socialists fought the electoral campaign together.

The outcome did not fulfill Mendès-France's expectations. The parties of the Republican Front did gain some votes, but because of the split among the center parties, the Communists increased their seats in the National Assembly from the 106 they had had in 1951 to 150. On the extreme right, the Poujadists, a new group, captured 52 seats and 12 percent of the vote. Further, among the partners of the Republican Front, the Socialists had fared better than the Radicals. Hence it was Guy Mollet, the Socialist leader, rather than Pierre Mendès-France, whom President Coty called to the premiership. Mendès-France became deputy premier. But if he had thought that his superior intelligence would dominate the cabinet, he was vastly mistaken. Mollet may not have the intellectual brilliance of Mendès-France but he is a stubborn man and far more experienced in the French internal power struggle. Thus Mendès-France lost more and more ground in the cabinet and found himself in increasingly bitter opposition to the Algerian policy of Mollet and Lacoste. This led to the final break between the two men and the departure of Mendès-France from the cabinet.

Again he turned to the reorganization of the Radical party. He pushed the party from purge to purge. All his adversaries, Edgar Faure, Henri Queille, André Marie, either were expelled or left more or less voluntarily. Finally he seemed to have succeeded. But what remained of the party was a skeleton, a hollow shell of its former self. Although Mendès had the support of a brilliant and successful weekly newspaper, *L'Express,* edited by his friend and admirer Jean Jacques Servan-Schreiber, his political fortunes declined. His speeches became less frequent and more bitter. To the conservatives in parliament and in his own party he became the symbol of an "abandonist" policy in Algeria. Finally enough of his opponents united to bring him down and oust him from the party leadership in 1957. In the two last Radical-led cabinets of the Fourth Republic, he had no position and no influence.

When the Fourth Republic came tumbling down and General de Gaulle's huge shadow was cast over France, Pierre Mendès-France, bitterly resentful of his personal defeat and failure, was unable to see that De Gaulle's ideas were much closer to his own than were those of De Gaulle's opponents. Mendès-France unfurled the banner of the "defense of the Republic" and led the demonstration against De Gaulle, oblivious to the fact that he and his supporters were only a handful among a huge crowd of Communists. After De Gaulle had formed his government, Mendès-France's wounded pride would still not be appeased and he became one of the chief opponents of the new Constitution. For this the French people rewarded him by bringing him and virtually all his supporters down to crushing defeat. He even suffered the indignity of being beaten on the first ballot, when his adversary, a totally unknown young man (Rémy Montagne) won a decisive majority. He has continued to play an active role in French politics, but he has become increasingly isolated.

Although Pierre Mendès-France was no longer the leader of the Radical party when the elections of November, 1958, came, the party nevertheless went down to defeat with him. Completely split into several separate factions, the Radicals were condemned to ineffectualness. Wedged between the highly successful conservative Independents and the MRP, which held its own, the Radicals were able to elect only sixteen members to the National Assembly and almost all their leaders, except Félix Gaillard, Maurice Faure, and André Marie, went down to defeat. Although the combined total vote of all candidates of Radical tendencies amounted to a respectable 11.5 percent, its opposing parts canceled each other out and reduced them to a greater degree of impotency than they had at the moment of France's liberation.

After the smoke of disaster had cleared away, the Radical party tried to reunite under its new president, Félix Gaillard, an able but not very significant man who had been France's youngest Premier, during the last months of the Fourth Republic. Reunification was continued more successfully by an even younger man, Maurice Faure (born 1922), who had been Under-Secretary for Foreign Affairs and Chairman of the National Assembly's Foreign Relations Committee, but who had remained far less identified with the Fourth Republic than Félix Gaillard.

Maurice Faure is a convinced European integrationist and hence an opponent of General de Gaulle's policy. He personally favors the idea of a center-left movement such as had been advocated first by Defferre and later by Lecanuet. Working with the MRP posed no particular problems for him. But it did pose a problem to the party, many of whose leaders feared that such collaboration would deprive the Radicals of the left tradition. Finally the Radical leaders defeated Maurice Faure because of his continued collaboration with Lecanuet and the Democratic Center.

The Radical party is split in many other ways. There is the bitterly anti-Gaullist President of the Senate, Gaston Monnerville, who is convinced that the Fifth Republic will be succeeded by the Fourth or even the Third and who wishes to preserve the full identity of the Radical party and its maneuverability as of yore. There are Radicals and members of associated groups like François Mitterand (UDSR, Union of Democratic and Socialist Resistance) who organized the Federation of the Left.

On quite another side is former Premier Edgar Faure (no relative of Maurice Faure), a man of dazzling ability who has sailed his ship on many divergent courses. After first having been strongly opposed by the Gaullists, he was later given several important missions by General de Gaulle, acquitted himself brilliantly, and finally, in 1966, entered the Gaullist government of Prime Minister Georges Pompidou as Minister of Agriculture, which made his expulsion from the Radical party virtually mandatory.

In the 1962 elections the Radicals, who lost less than 1 percent of their vote, held their own largely because of the absence of the divisive spirit of Mendès-France. In 1967 they ran with the Socialists in the Federation of the Left.

The Radical party has always been known as a *parti des notables* (a party of distinguished men) rather than of formal organization. Unlike the Communists, Socialists, and the MRP, it has no local sections but merely a few local committees. More important are the Federations, the department organizations which enjoy a great deal of independence. These Federations have few members but often great influence. Candidacies for public office and political combinations on the department level are their exclusive domain, and their relationship to central party headquarters is more administrative than political. The annual congress of the party, which is composed of delegates from the Federations, elects the president and certain members of the executive committee and the executive commission. The party's presidency is a position of great importance.

"Moderates" and Independents

It is indicative of the leftist and revolutionary phraseology of France's political life that no party or political group would dare to call itself "conservative." Thus the motley group of right-wing groups and independents are called *les modérés*—the Moderates.

No group is harder to classify. It has no organization, no unified point of view, no recognized leader or leadership committee. Its vote is always split and its members adhere to no discipline. From time to time an abortive attempt is made to bring some organization into this chaos, but soon anarchy reigns again. Yet this was long a highly important group.

The Moderates are by no means a new phenomenon; they have existed for over half a century. In the Third Republic they possessed a certain amount of parliamentary organization, but certainly not much. There was the Democratic Alliance, perhaps the most significant group, which never could get over the personal and political quarrel between its two most outstanding leaders, Pierre-Étienne Flandin and Paul Reynaud. There was the Republican Federation of Louis Marin. And there was the French Social party, the only one with a definite organization, which emerged from the dissolved Fiery Cross (*Croix de Feu*) but was more moderate than that near-fascist organization.

The war discredited the Moderates. Not all were collaborationists. Reynaud was imprisoned by Vichy and later by the Germans, Louis Marin escaped to London and joined De Gaulle, Joseph Laniel was a member of the clandestine National Council of Resistance. But the majority collaborated—or at least did not resist. Consequently in the elections of 1945 and 1946 the right had a hard time to find eligible and untainted candidates and did poorly. Many conservatives gave their temporary allegiance to the MRP.

In order to remedy the situation, a number of deputies and other rightist leaders founded in 1945 the Republican Party of Liberty (*Parti Républicain de la*

Liberté, PRL), which flattered itself as being the "fourth big" (next to Communists, Socialists, and MRP). The PRL defined its aims in terms which were more middle-of-the-road than conservative, but that was in 1945–1946, when it was not the thing to be of the right. "Neither reactionary nor fascist, but strongly attached to the parliamentary regime" were the words of the party's principal spokesman, Joseph Laniel, who as a former member of the National Council of Resistance helped to make the party respectable.

Another group of the Moderates was the Peasant party. What was perhaps most remarkable about it was that it was not prominently composed of or led by peasants. Actually it was a sectional party based mostly on the Massif Central, where there is a tradition of separate political agrarian action, although it did spread somewhat into adjacent areas. Its leader and animator was Paul Antier, but the party split and lost much effectiveness even before the 1951 elections.

Because the electoral law of 1951 favored "national" parties, these moderate groups and independents found it useful to run under common labels, among which the term Union of Independents, Peasants, and National Republicans was the most frequent.

The voting mass of Independents had not become any more coherent by the time the Fourth Republic disappeared. An attempt to unify this group or at least to give it some semblance of direction was made by the ambitious Roger Duchet when he established an Independent Center, which was conceived as a documentation center but which tried to act like a party headquarters. Duchet was no more successful in getting the other Independents to follow his leadership than had been others who tried before him. Thus, although Independents had great success in the 1958 election, obtaining 19.9 percent of the vote and entering the National Assembly with 136 deputies, Duchet has if anything lost some of his influence because he did not have the inside track to De Gaulle and the Debré government.

In 1958 most of the Independents had run as strong supporters of De Gaulle's return to power. In subsequent years that support turned sour for many of them. The General's policy in Algeria as well as his opposition to European integration were the main reasons for their disillusion. One of their most important leaders, Antoine Pinay, broke with General de Gaulle and left the government where he had been Minister of Finance. A majority of the Independents opposed the Pompidou government, and as the style of General de Gaulle's one-man rule became more obvious their opposition became deeper.

But this was costly to the Independents in 1962 when their vote was halved and they went down from nearly 20 percent to 13 percent of the vote. They received even less in 1967, a mere 5.8 percent of the vote, and have disappeared visually from the scene. But they are still there. And since they always act as individuals, their strength is probably just as great as before. It may not matter for the strength of conservatism under what party label they are identified.

Conservatism remains a strong and lasting current in French politics. Most of its adherents are found at present in the Gaullist UNR. But that is almost certainly a temporary affiliation. Once the dominating personality of De Gaulle has left the scene, the conservatives will undoubtedly reconsider their position. That is when the hour of Giscard d'Estaing may strike.

Valéry Giscard d'Estaing is a young politician and a brilliant, though somewhat cold, personality. As Minister of Finance under De Gaulle and Prime Minister Pompidou, he proved an able administrator. He kept his Independent Republicans consciously separate from the rest of the Gaullists, but as long as he was in the government his and their support to De Gaulle was unwavering. However, rightly or wrongly, his fiscal policies were believed to have detracted from the vote for De Gaulle in 1965. He was offered a lesser cabinet post, refused it, and left the Pompidou cabinet in 1966.

Since then, Giscard has become increasingly independent. He and his followers ran on a common ticket with the Gaullist UNR in 1967, but he made clear that his position regarding De Gaulle was not a simple "yes," but a "yes, but." This position was denounced by the integral Gaullists and even by the General himself, but it has remained unshaken. Giscard generally votes the same way as the Gaullists, but always he lets it be known that he has misgivings, that he does not entirely agree, that he is more European, less systematically anti-American, less certain of De Gaulle's unerring wisdom than the UNR.

Because Giscard and his followers nevertheless toe the Gaullist line in their parliamentary votes, his policy may seem hesitant and vacillating to the casual observer. This, however, is quite incorrect. Giscard's policies are neither Gaullist, nor anti-Gaullist, but *post-Gaullist*. As long as the mighty General is in the saddle, Giscard will avoid a confrontation, will try to maneuver close enough to the Gaullists to prevent their turning against him, yet will continue to foster the impression that he is really dubious about the General's policies. This, in essence, is the "yes, but" position. And because he plays this difficult game with uncommon brilliance and because the Gaullists need his vote, he is quite likely to continue it for some time. In particular he wants to avoid a vote against the Gaullist government which might lead to its downfall and force him off his "yes, but" fence.

The purpose of these complicated tactics is for Giscard to become the "available man" after De Gaulle leaves the scene, the man who alone could hammer together a new majority composed of leaderless Gaullists and anti-Gaullists. This would presumably be a majority of the right. In view of Lecanuet's failure to construct a powerful center force and of the absence of any UNR leader capable of inheriting De Gaulle's mantle, Giscard d'Estaing has a very good chance to succeed.

The UNR

The idea of a great national revival, a great rally, had already begun to take shape in General de Gaulle's mind during the war. It became more real after his abrupt resignation from his position as provisional President on January 20, 1946. In his disappointment over the turn being taken by the new Fourth Republic, he launched his ideas of a supraparty national rally, first on March 30, 1947, in a speech at Bruneval and a few days later in more detail in a speech at Strasbourg.[36]

Thus the Rally of the French People (*Rassemblement du Peuple Français*, RPF) was born. Its program was expressed in very vague and general terms; indeed it disclaimed the existence of a program and insisted that it merely had objectives. It was originally intended that people joining the RPF could maintain their previous party affiliations, but this concept was never very realistic, partly because of the resistance of other parties, and partly because of the rigid discipline of the RPF itself.

The RPF's ideas about the "association of capital and labor" were extremely vague and highly idealistic. These ideas had originated within the Resistance movement. But the RPF had somewhat more concrete concepts about the desirable reform of the French constitution, ideas later realized in the Constitution of the Fifth Republic.

The RPF got off to an excellent start. In the municipal elections of 1947, when it was only six months old, it obtained 28.1 percent of the vote in cities over 9,000; and coalition lists which it endorsed won 10.6 percent more. It won majorities or pluralities in all the larger towns of France, including those of industrial regions like Marseille and St. Étienne. A comfortable majority was won in Paris. The cantonal elections of 1949 confirmed and broadened this victory.

But these were Pyrrhic victories. They alarmed the government parties and started them on a way to a revision of the electoral law, designed to make impossible an RPF or Communist victory. Also the RPF's rapid growth rendered impossible the integration of its new cadres and deputies, and rifts soon began to show. Thus, when the 1951 elections came, the RPF was no longer at the height of its success. True, it obtained over 4 million votes (21.5 percent), and entered the National Assembly with the largest bloc of deputies (119). But it had failed to gain enough seats to prevent formation of a government without its participation. Consequently its leadership had to work to prove that no government could exist in France without it by letting no opportunity pass to oppose and obstruct the government.

This proved the undoing, not of the government, but of the RPF. A number of RPF deputies disliked this policy of opposition at any cost and felt a certain affinity for governments under conservative leadership. The first breach occurred on March 6, 1952, when twenty-seven RPF deputies voted for the investiture of conservative Premier Antoine Pinay, contrary to the instructions of their party leadership. The dissident group grew larger in subsequent votes. All attempts of the RPF leaders in parliament to reassert party discipline failed. Further splits occurred, and the party's decline could no longer be denied. The municipal elections of April, 1953, saw the RPF go down to defeat in a veritable tailspin.

[36] Robert G. Neumann, "Formation and Transformation of Gaullism in France," *Western Political Quarterly*, Vol. VI (1953), pp. 250–274.

By that time, General de Gaulle had evidently concluded that his adventure into party politics had been a mistake and had stultified the very idea of a national rally, and he abandoned the RPF. As the party was fighting its losing campaign of 1953, the General undertook a pilgrimage to the hallowed grounds of Fighting France in Africa, and then withdrew to his country seat at Colombey-les-deux-Églises.

What was left of the RPF reorganized itself under the name of Social Republicans, and in the 1956 national elections, only twenty-two of them survived. These lean years for the Gaullist faithful were known as "the march through the desert."

When General de Gaulle returned to power on June 1, 1958, no Gaullist movement existed. The principal leader of the Social Republicans was Jacques Soustelle, former secretary-general of the RPF; although once De Gaulle's right-hand man, Soustelle and the General had long since reached a parting of the ways. Despite newspaper reports which persisted in calling Soustelle De Gaulle's faithful aide, there was great coolness between the two. They had not seen each other for several months, and De Gaulle clearly disapproved of Soustelle's role in whipping up the ultras in Algeria. He admitted Soustelle to only a minor role in his government, and that only after prolonged hesitation.

When the dates for the elections of 1958 (November 28 and 30) were announced, the whole political party structure of France was in utter confusion. No party had any clear concept of how to meet the new situation and how to accommodate itself to De Gaulle's position. Moreover, it was clear that many who had resisted De Gaulle would suffer under the disapproval of the electorate. Quite evidently, a political vacuum existed. It could be filled only by those who should proclaim themselves the loyal followers of De Gaulle, not just for the referendum and the election, but always. The nucleus of such a group was evidently the remainder of the RPF-Social Republicans, among whom there were three general policies: that of Jacques Soustelle which supported activism and an intransigent policy in Algeria; that of Michel Debré whose program consisted primarily of unquestioned loyalty to De Gaulle and the remaking of France's institutions in the image that De Gaulle had proclaimed at Bruneval in 1946; and that of the able mayor of Bordeaux, many times minister, Jacques Chaban-Delmas, whose views were somewhat more moderate and opportunist than those of the others.

Because of resistance to Soustelle's leadership, the efforts to create a united Gaullist movement almost collapsed; only at the very last minute, when the date for filing candidacies had almost passed, was a new, very loosely conceived electoral bloc finally organized. It called itself Union for the New Republic (*Union pour la Nouvelle République,* UNR).

There had been no time to establish a program or an organization for it. Nobody knew what the new UNR stood for, and for that matter few people cared. What mattered was that the UNR was a symbol of persistent loyalty to De Gaulle, because its principal leaders and the nucleus of the movement had been with him in the RPF. This is what the UNR's General Secretary, Roger Frey, wrote a few days before the election;[37]

> More than anyone else we may proclaim the beautiful title that others have betrayed: the party of fidelity. Yes! of fidelity to great and beautiful memories, for the liberator, for fidelity to ourselves, and this fidelity has been logical and necessary because we belong to one spiritual family—Gaullism, which has never despaired of France and whose vocation it is to believe in her and whose duty it is to sacrifice everything for her.

This was enough for the voters, who wanted to give General de Gaulle resounding support and heap confusion on his enemies. Thus the UNR obtained an impressive 3,603,958 votes or 17.6 percent of the electorate and marched into the National Assembly as the largest group, with 189 deputies. Its victory became even more emphatic in 1962 when, together with a smaller movement of Gaullists of the left, UDT (*Union Démocratique du Travail*—Democratic Labor Union), it came close to a majority in the National Assembly. After the 1962 election, the UNR and the UDT merged into the UNR-UDT. As we have seen, it was able to maintain its position in 1967.

The success of the UNR has not solved its problems but has accentuated them. It is still a party without program or clear political tendency. Loyalty to De Gaulle is no program, and some UNR deputies find that duty of loyalty heavily strained as they discover that their views and his diverge. For in the UNR one finds almost everything: extreme reactionaries, as well as people who are virtually Marxists, republicans as well as fascists, and people with wide variations in their views about the integration of Europe.

Nor is there a man who clearly leads the party. Soustelle was the founder, the animator. But many resented and suspected his driving ambition, which eventually led to his expulsion from his party. He became bitterly anti-Gaullist, became involved in several plots, and finally exiled himself from France.

The fortunes of Michel Debré and the UNR became inextricably interwoven after Soustelle's defection. Debré is without doubt the most important and the most difficult leader of the UNR. He was active in the Resistance and joined the first administration of De Gaulle at the end of World War II. As Minister of Justice in the first De Gaulle cabinet, he drafted the 1958 Constitution. Always loyal to De Gaulle, he became one of the leaders of the RPF and remained throughout the "march through the desert." In those years he was an extremist if not to say a fanatic. His speeches were phillipics, harsh and disdainful. He was the most feared heaper of coals on whatever heads the Fourth Republic produced. He agitated constantly against every aspect of its policies, and the bitterness of his effusions poured into a number of books.[38] The slightest shadow on France's sovereignty

[37] *Le Monde,* Nov. 21, 1958.
[38] Cf. particularly Michel Debré, *Ces princes que nous gouvernent,* Paris, 1957.

brought him into the battle, and he opposed vigorously and virulently not only the European Defense Community but also the Schuman Plan, the Common Market, and Euratom, which he called "a plot against France."

As Prime Minister he was not easier to deal with. He was constantly harassed and impatient, and his colleagues—even in the Cabinet—feared the sting of his tongue or of his notes and marginal comments. Such notes often began, "My dear . . ." and ended in such words as these, "I would ask you therefore to act in accordance with this. Failing this, I shall see myself obliged within a week to request the appointment in your place of a responsible person who is less incompetent, blundering and incapable."[39]

At the same time, nobody would dispute his brilliant intelligence and knowledge of the subject with which he dealt. He was almost certainly opposed to De Gaulle's Algerian policy, but when his remonstrances had no visible effect, he submitted and continued to serve loyally. But shortly after peace was restored in Algeria he felt worn out and resigned from the government or, more probably, was asked to resign by De Gaulle. No doubt a less controversial man would serve better for the period of consolidation. He was replaced by Georges Pompidou.

Although the 1962 election gave the UNR a resounding victory, Michel Debré was defeated for reelection. He refused to take another government post, feeling personally repudiated, and it was only after persuasion by another UNR leader, Jacques Chaban-Delmas, that both General de Gaulle and Debré agreed that Debré should run for a seat from an overseas territory, the island of Réunion in the Indian Ocean.

After his return in 1963, Debré took in hand the leadership of the UNR group in parliament. Later, in January, 1966, he was called back to the government as a "Super-minister of Finance," and in general charge of economic affairs. In effect, though not in name, Debré became deputy Prime Minister, and it was clearly his task to bring economic development more in line with political necessities. He performed brilliantly and that placed him in line again for bigger things, perhaps even some day the succession to De Gaulle. But about that, many other people would have something to say, including probably the General himself.

While Debré came from the inner core of the Gaullist movement, Georges Pompidou did not. That is not to say that he was not a Gaullist, for he was. A former professor, he participated with courage and determination in the Resistance movement, and after the war he joined the staff of the office of the provisional President De Gaulle. Later he became interested in both government and business administration and emerged as the managing director of the Rothschild Bank, at the same time undertaking discreet missions for General de Gaulle. In 1958 he returned to government service as chief of the presidential cabinet, dropped out again, was recalled in 1962 as Prime Minister. In between he seemed to find time for other things such as beautiful art objects, the cultivation of roses, and the writ-

[39] Pierre Viansson-Ponté, *Les Gaullistes,* Paris, 1963.

ing of an interesting anthology of poetry. It is an unlikely combination, but Georges Pompidou is not a man like others. Yet he is not of the inner circle. He is not a "companion," and while the other Gaullist leaders accept him as one chosen by the General, they would not have chosen him had they had their way.

Pompidou never ran for office in his life until he became Prime Minister, which is a contrast to Debré, who had many years of parliamentary experience before coming to power. Nevertheless, Pompidou probably has a more natural political talent than Debré and he quickly acquired the outer and inner manifestations of the art. In contrast to the constantly nervous and usually humorless Debré, Pompidou is a man who exudes charm and who is very much at home on the speaker's platform or in the in-fighting of the smoke-filled room. After De Gaulle called him to the premiership, nobody could fail to take seriously his claim to first place in the event of the General's departure.

The third man in influence probably is Jacques Chaban-Delmas, a Gaullist from the first hour and a man of very considerable talent. He must have excellent nerves also. How else could this exceedingly good-looking man, after having accomplished a number of very dangerous missions for the Resistance, then, in March, 1943, take and pass one of the most difficult examinations in the French Civil Service, that of the Inspector of Finance, only to be admitted a few months later into the military delegation of Free France in London? Moreover, a few months later he was promoted to Brigadier General, then became Inspector-General of the Army, and in between had organized the Resistance for the whole of southwestern France.

In contrast to other Gaullist leaders, he has cultivated power not only at the center in Paris but also in the province where he lives. He was among the first to join the RPF and during its heyday became mayor of Bordeaux while remaining for awhile in the RGR (Rally of the Republican Left). When Herriott banned this double membership, "bigamy" as he called it, Chaban-Delmas split the Radicals and took the majority with him into the RPF. While other Gaullists lost their seats in the subsequent debacle of the RPF and its successors, Chaban-Delmas held on to his position and even bettered it. He became minister in several of the cabinets of the Fourth Republic but remained mayor of Bordeaux and did much for his city.

When De Gaulle returned to power, Chaban-Delmas became president of the National Assembly. Many observers wondered why he remained content with this decorative and high-ranking but relatively unimportant office. There is little doubt that he could have had important cabinet appointments had he so desired, but Chaban-Delmas is a man who loves the good and gracious life, and this largely ceremonial office with its residence in a charming villa adjacent to the parliament building may give him that opportunity. Perhaps the fact that Chaban does not openly participate in the race for top positions makes it possible for him to be the confidant of all and to exercise great influence behind the scenes. That may be the proper role for this discreet, loyal, and courageous man.

Among the organizers of the UNR there are Roger Frey, Minister of the Interior, and Senator Jacques Baumel, but there is a good deal more talent available. This is not surprising, because the UNR is not so much a party as an order of knights. It is a group of men with views of great variance, some like André Malraux coming originally from the extreme left, some like Gaston Palewski more from the right. What they have in common is absolute and unquestioned loyalty to General Charles de Gaulle and an unconquerable belief in his destiny.

As long as the General lives, that is perhaps enough. But what then? The UNR has never been able to develop a program, an astonishing omission for a French political party. The nearest to it is a book commissioned by the UNR and written by Michel Debré, called *In The Service of The Nation*.[40] It does not say a great deal. Now there is also a series of political actions by the General which in fact have created a program with which the future post-Gaullist UNR will have to live: extreme nationalism in foreign affairs, pressure for a "Europe of nations" and against an integrated Europe, efforts against American and British influence in Europe, and in domestic affairs an essentially conservative program. Perhaps the main difficulty of the UNR is not so much that it has no real program of its own but that De Gaulle's policies are tailored to his own heroic proportions and cannot easily be made credible in the hands of more ordinary even though gifted men.

The UNR leaders know better than anyone else that the decision will probably be made by the young generation of France. The UNR leaders have correctly assessed the temper of that generation, finding them to be essentially practical and pragmatic rather than doctrinaire as their fathers were. The UNR has therefore centered its appeal on competent and practical administration, on getting things done. In this respect, the objective performance of the UNR and the Gaullist government is quite respectable, yet in the long run, they seem to have failed. According to all observers, the youth of France is by and large not Gaullist, perhaps because they were born too late to witness the magic of June 18, 1940, and of the liberation period. A survey conducted by the French Institute of Public Opinion Research[41] showed that the UNR had a higher proportion of those over sixty-five and a lower proportion of those under twenty-five than any other party. Nevertheless, while indications are that the youth is not Gaullist, there are no clear indications of what the youth is, and hence the UNR retains a chance, even a great one as long as De Gaulle remains active. But in order to use its opportunities after the eventual departure of General de Gaulle, the UNR will be forced more and more to act like other parties. From this one might draw the conclusion that the principal aim of General de Gaulle, to destroy the party system, has failed. It is by no means certain that the old parties will survive as such, but the party system already has.

Splinter parties

There are so many smallish political parties—consider the Radical groups—that the distinction between a regular political party and a splinter group is hard

---

[40] Michel Debré, *Au service de la nation*, Paris, 1963.
[41] *Le Monde*, Nov. 21–22, 1965.

to draw. Some of these groups appear, achieve a certain prominence, and disappear. A good example of such an ephemeral phenomenon is the Poujadist Movement, a rather vulgar extreme rightist group of general protest which rose, fell, and disappeared within a few years.[42]

More typical and representative is a small but not insignificant group of the far left, the Unified Socialist Party (*Parti Socialiste Unifié,* PSU). The title is not an accident: in France, parties growing out of a split have often given themselves the title "Unified." It is a group which arose primarily out of the opposition to the too far right-wing leadership of the Socialist party, in protest against the continuation of the war in Algeria. The word "unified" is justified only in the sense that the PSU regards itself as having a mission to bring the Socialists and the Communists closer together. The PSU has a certain intellectual significance, and has fulfilled the function of engendering a constant debate. Numerically, however, it is likely to remain very small. It won two seats in the 1962 election and four in 1967. It has a vigorous weekly paper *Le Nouvel Observateur* which, while nominally independent, is close to the party. However the PSU has suffered from the old malady of the intellectual left, the tendency toward further splintering, as demonstrated by the long-standing feud between two former editors of the above-mentioned paper, Claude Bourdet and Giles Martinet. Its most significant leader is former Premier Pierre Mendès-France.

Of some significance, in addition to the regular parties, is the so-called club movement, a number of independent clubs dedicated to the discussion of important public problems. Most important and best known among them is the Club Jean Moulin, which also publishes a number of books. The clubs have only a few hundred members each, as membership is not easily acquired, but contain a kind of intellectual elite, and their discussions are always interesting.

For a while it was thought that the club movement might cause the rejuvenation of France's political life. However, it is now fairly certain that this task is beyond their capability. They retain their significance in the intellectual discussion of public affairs, but for a deep impact on the party system one would have to look elsewhere.

Electoral campaigns

French elections are lively but relatively brief affairs. They are generally much cheaper to conduct than those in the United States, as the business of advertising is less developed in France, and fewer monetary resources are available to parties and candidates.

Laws and decrees regulate many phases of the campaigns. The period during which candidacies may be filed is usually brief and fairly close to the date of election. For instance, for the elections of November 23, 1958, candidates could file

[42] Stanley Hoffmann, *Le Movement Poujade,* Paris, 1956.

between October 22 and November 3, and thus November 3 was the official opening day of the campaign, which accordingly lasted less than three weeks. Political parties which present candidates for at least seventy-five seats in parliament are reimbursed for their campaign expenditures and are allotted equal but modest periods of radio and television time on the state-owned broadcasting system. They cannot buy more time for themselves.

An executive order determines the number and size of posters which candidates may display, as well as the number and sizes of circulars and ballots which they may have printed.

One factor which helps to distinguish European from American campaigns is that Europeans, although more heavily motorized than they were, still have fewer cars than Americans do and consequently walk more. Thus many election posters are smaller than ours and contain a good deal of material which can easily be absorbed by a passing pedestrian who stops to read the dozens of posters which may be affixed to a single board but which could not be read from a passing car.

Apart from posters and occasional advertisements, the principal instrument of the electoral campaign is the candidate's campaign meeting. It is usually rather well attended, since most candidates cannot be seen elsewhere because television time is allotted so sparingly. Just how well the candidates' meetings are attended depends on the degree of public concern or apathy at any given campaign. By and large, attendance is decreasing, as many voters seem to make up their minds in the early stages of the campaigns. Yet, when these meetings are addressed by controversial personalities like Pierre Mendès-France, they may turn into lively and even unpleasant affairs, as opponents send flying squads into them with the intention of breaking them up. Less violent but also quite effervescent is the French habit of the *contradictoire,* the right of opponents not just to ask questions but to make speeches of their own. Thus, under certain circumstances, the meeting of a less experienced candidate may actually become that of his opponent. Despite the frequent flare-ups of Gallic temperament, few people are seriously hurt, and elections are usually remarkably honest.

Political impact of the trade unions

The tradition of political trade unionism in Europe is old, and many strikes have had political, rather than economic, motives. In the period between the First and Second World Wars, there existed three major trade-union federations. The largest was the Socialist-dominated General Confederation of Labor (*Confédération Générale du Travail,* CGT), the other two being the Communist-dominated Unified General Confederation of Labor (*Confédération Générale du Travail Unitaire,* CGTU) and the French Confederation of Christian Workers (*Confédération Française des Travailleurs Chrétiens,* CFTC), which was progressive-Catholic and not tied to any particular party.

The Vichy government dissolved the unions, but they were restored after liberation. The split between the CGT and CGTU had been healed before the outbreak of war. In 1943 the CGT and the CFTC united while they were both working in the underground.

But postwar developments quickly destroyed this unity. The CGT had come under the leadership of the Communists during the period of the underground struggle. Nominally the reemerging CGT was nonpartisan and operated under the joint secretaryship of old Léon Jouhaux (Socialist) and Benoît Frachon (Communist), but Frachon and his Communist friends held all the strings in their hands. This was also apparent in the Communist-sponsored and dominated World Federation of Trade Unions.

It was not so much the fact of Communist domination itself which broke up the unity of the French labor movement as the use which the Communist leaders made of the unions. This became quite apparent after the Soviet Union denounced the Marshall Plan, and Communists all over the world began to sabotage it wherever possible. Hand in hand with this development also came the realization on the part of both Socialists and Catholics that cooperation with the Communists was possible only at the price of surrender. The Christian trade unions had never been completely integrated into the CGT and their separation was easily effected. The Socialists, however, had to build anew, with great difficulties. In 1943 Léon Jouhaux reluctantly led his followers out of the CGT and formed a new organization called General Federation of Labor—Worker's Force (*Confédération Générale du Travail —Force Ouvrière*). It is, however, not correct to consider the Workers' Force simply as a Socialist labor union. The Workers' Force is quite independent from the Socialist party and has frequently gone separate ways from it, especially when the Socialists were in the government.

In addition there are a number of independent unions[43] whose membership is larger than one might suppose.

The numerical strength of these unions is subject to considerable speculation, as the figures published by the unions themselves are undoubtedly exaggerated. It was, however, generally conceded that a large majority of workers stand in the ranks of the Communist-dominated CGT, that the Workers' Force unions were weak,[44] and that the Christian unions had rallied after some setbacks.

Since its heyday of 1945–1946, when the Communist-dominated CGT claimed 6 million members (probably exaggerated), it has lost over half its members. But except for those who participated in the original exodus of the CFTC and the Workers' Force, the other 2 million workers have simply dropped out of the union movement. And yet the majority of those who have left the CGT because of its Communist-inspired policy continued to vote Communist because they believed that

[43] The *Confédération du Travail Indépendante* (CTI), formerly the *Comité Général du Syndicalisme Indépendant* (CGSI), *Fédération des Syndicats Autonomes* (FSA), *Confédération Nationale du Travail* (CNT), and various isolated unions.
[44] For a while they were jokingly referred to as the *Faiblesse Ouvrière*, Workers' Weakness.

the Communists were the only party which raises its voice for the workers. Reference to the actual conditions in Communist countries was to no avail. The workers felt too bitter over the inaction of the governments of the Fourth Republic, the unequally distributed tax burden, low wages, and the extremely high cost of living to be concerned with conditions in Poland, Czechoslovakia, or the Soviet Union.

Under the Fourth Republic, there could be little doubt that the huge majority of the working people of France were aligned against the government. This did not mean that all members of the CGT voted Communist or that all those who voted Communist believed in communism. But the prevailing sentiment among the workers was that they were the disinherited of the regime and that they could expect nothing from the government except broken promises.

The fall of the Fourth Republic and the coming of De Gaulle did not intrinsically change the picture so far as the labor unions were concerned. But at least as far as the elections were concerned, it became plain that many workers thought there was some hope in the new regime. In the referenda and in the general elections of 1958 and 1962 a great many workers voted for candidates favorable to De Gaulle. This attitude benefited the new UNR in particular, but it also brought some additional votes to the Socialists. By breaking into the workers' vote, the UNR thus repeated the success of its predecessor, the RPF, in 1951.

Despite their size and discipline, the French labor unions have played only a limited role in the political life of the Fifth Republic. In part they suffered from the general depoliticization which characterized the Gaullist regime for some time, although the first outward manifestations of resistance did come from the trade-union movement. These were sporadic and were not followed up, perhaps because some of the initial propulsion came from the Worker's Force and the Christian trade unions rather than the CGT.

With the CGT, the strong political direction of the Communists has somewhat diminished in the sense that a certain amount of open discussion has now become possible. Although the Communist leaders are no less in control than they were in the past, they have to take greater care not to impose their political will too sharply lest there be an outbreak of dissension. Gradually, the CGT has become less an instrument of the class struggle, though still far from the American type of a "business union."

The Worker's Force (CGT-FO) has done little more than hold its own. It remains solidly implanted among civil servants and some white-collar unions. A left opposition has made itself heard within recent years, but with little effect. There is much talk about unity but little action.

More significant has been the transformation of the Christian trade-union movement, the aforementioned CFTC. It has vigorously marked its independence and even distance from the Catholic Church, though not from the Catholic faith. There have been a number of divisions on political and union tactics which have been barely overcome in the unions of teachers, metal workers, building workers, and chemical workers. As a result, the CFTC has moved somewhat toward the left and has often been more militant than the *Force Ouvrière* or even the CGT. The relative radicalization of the CFTC, which first came to the surface with the election of Eugène Descamps as secretary-general, found its culmination in the change of the union's name from CFTC to CFDT (*Confédération Française Démocratique du Travail*), a symbolic turning away from both the church and the MRP. Nonetheless, the CFDT is a movement deeply animated by Christian principles.

The press, television, and radio

The prewar French press was famous for its brilliance but also for its venality. If most papers were not for sale, they most certainly were for rent. However it is not entirely correct to say, as in a famous *bon mot,* that France's prewar press was "in the pay of every government except that of France," because the French government also participated in bribing the press through the famous "secret funds" at the disposal of the ministers.

This merry state of affairs came to an abrupt end upon liberation, when all papers which had continued to appear during the occupation were suppressed. The left attempted to turn the confiscated papers[45] into a state-owned press trust which would lease its facilities at cost to any group wishing to publish. This extreme suggestion was not carried out, but the confiscated papers were placed under the administration of a National Association of Press Enterprises (*Société Nationale des Entreprises de Presse*) which was to sell them, with preference and loans to be given to groups and parties having a Resistance record. This system, which was instituted by the Law on the Press Property of 1946 and liquidated in 1953, was intended to further the party press over the so-called "press of information"— which comprises both the great nonpartisan journals and the sensational press. It was also expected that the leftist papers would benefit particuarly. The independent newspapers complained that they were required to be self-supporting under difficult economic circumstances while the party papers were heavily subsidized by the treasuries of their respective parties.

Actually the situation developed in a radically different manner from these fears and hopes. The party press, despite the law's favoritism, began to lose steadily from the very beginning. This was particularly marked in Paris, which dominates the country intellectually and politically. The Socialist organ *Le Populaire* dropped from 250,000 subscribers to below 40,000 by 1950. Intermittently it had to be published as a single sheet of two pages and was saved from complete extinction only by repeatedly passing the hat among the Socialist parties of other European countries, notably the British Labor party. The chief organ of the MRP, *L'Aube,* also dropped to about 40,000 by 1950, but having nowhere to go to pass a hat, it

---

[45] Only workers who had not collaborated with Vichy or the Germans were compensated, but they too had to give up their property if their papers had appeared during the occupation.

had to give up the ghost in 1951. There never was a real party press on the right in Paris, and even the RPF could not maintain a daily paper. The UNR has *La Nation,* which however cannot rival the great dailies.

The Communists, because of their greater party discipline, fared somewhat better. Even so the chief Communist newspaper, *L'Humanité,* lost over half its readers, and the Communist evening daily, *Ce Soir,* had to suspend publication in 1952. Even the very popular and well-edited Communist agricultural journal, *La Terre,* lost heavily. This picture is not entirely repeated in the provinces, where the party press has done much better. The Communists have lost several papers there but otherwise have held their own; two Socialist provincial papers, *Nord-Matin* and *Le Provençal,* have circulations of over 200,000, and several others have over 100,000. The Radicals have no proper party press in Paris, but the large daily *L'Aurore* is close to them. They dominate a number of provincial journals, among which the famous *Dépêche de Toulouse* has been resurrected under the name of *Dépêche de Midi.*

The public-opinion field is clearly dominated by the independent press, the "press of information." Although sensation-seeking papers, like *Paris-Presse,* have the largest circulation, the most respected papers are *Le Figaro* and *Le Monde.*

The reason for the victory of the "press of information" over the party press is undoubtedly the fact that the independent press publishes by far the better papers and attracts the better editorialists and writers, most of whom prefer to write without the ideological strait-jackets of the party press. On the other hand, these papers seem to have no more influence on political adherence and the casting of the vote than is the case elsewhere. The diminishing fortunes of the party press have not resulted in a corresponding diminution of the party vote. This is most clearly shown in the case of the Communists, who polled nearly the same percentage of votes at every election between 1946 and 1956 despite the steady decline of their party press.

It is customary throughout Europe that radio and television should be state owned.[46] However, the extent to which the government of General de Gaulle has made use of radio and television is unique. The news is editorialized to an astonishing degree and is constantly designed to fit the domestic and foreign policies of the government. Until the presidential elections of 1965 approached, the opposition was given little opportunity to be heard, either on preceding elections or on the four referenda on which the French people voted. One might surmise that if the law had not specifically required a certain amount of time to be given to opposition candidates in the 1965 election, they would not have been heard then, either. How-

---

[46] Exceptions are the German radio and television channels, which are not owned by the German federal government, but are under the legal authority of the federal states (*Länder*) and are administered by autonomous councils. The British Broadcasting Corporation (BBC) is also an autonomous, public enterprise. There is also a private radio and television enterprise in Luxembourg, which enjoys great popularity and is known as Europe No. 1.

ever, once the opposition candidates appeared, their impact was immediately visible. While the government may in future try to clamp down again, the awareness of the opposition's existence will not go away. What effect this will have on the actual conduct of radio and television programs cannot as yet be assessed, but there is little doubt that television in particular has a greater influence on voters' behavior than any other medium.

Pressure groups

Pressure groups in France have, of course, been active and important politically for a long time. However, in contrast to the United States, their existence and activities have been studied and analyzed only recently.[47]

There are the customary professional organizations of farmers, of small and medium-sized enterprises, veterans' organizations, labor unions, etc. There are some particularly specialized organizations, such as those of the sugar-beet growers, long a powerful group. There are organizations for specific industries. There are Catholic groups which seek to marshal support for state aid to private schools, and there are strong teachers' organizations determined to resist such attempts to the very last. There are also special interests concerned with special measures or bills which they want passed or suppressed.

In this there is nothing unusual. However, the centralized nature of most political parties in France, especially in the years immediately following liberation, made it unprofitable for pressure groups to operate on individual deputies. They therefore shifted their main emphasis to the party leadership which was notoriously in need of money. Later, most parties, except the Communist, reverted to a looser form of organization, and pressure was more easily placed on deputies. However, as long as the proportional-representation system of election existed, the position of a deputy could not be assured just by his private contacts. Hence pressure groups had to operate constantly among the party leadership.

In one respect, pressure groups had exceptional opportunities under the weak governments of the Fourth Republic. They were able not only to infiltrate parliament but at times to see one or another of their close associates enter the cabinet. For instance, a certain Minister of Health was known to be personally interested in, and also associated with, certain industries in the field of pharmaceutical products. Thus the sophisticated observer knew approximately what to expect of him.

Although these phenomena are by no means confined to France, French pressure groups did profit particularly from two aspects of political life under the Fourth

[47] Henry W. Ehrmann (ed.), *Interest Groups on Four Continents*, Pittsburgh, Pa., 1958, and "Pressure Groups in France," *Annals of the American Academy of Political and Social Science*, September, 1958, pp. 141–148. Jean Meynaud, *Nouvelles études sur les groupes de pression en France*, Paris, 1962; and Bernard E. Brown, "Pressure Politics in the Fifth Republic," *Journal of Politics*, August, 1963.

Republic. Political parties and groups were disunited and therefore often no match for the united and strongly directed pressure groups which permeated their structure. The French public was disgusted by the never-ending succession of short-lived coalition governments, the never-completed programs, and the cynicism with which parliament dismissed one cabinet after another; hence the experienced citizen sought his salvation in making his own contacts with the proper quarters. Thus a situation which might otherwise have been intolerable became endurable for many because of the special and private deals which they made in one way or another. Almost everybody knew somebody through whom he could get this or that special favor. This lack of civic spirit, for which the Fourth Republic was noted, made life possible under the uncertain governmental conditions but perpetuated the very system from which it sought relief. It was a vicious circle. It is pointless to discuss whether the government corrupted the people or the people the government.

Under the Fifth Republic, lobbying and the work of interest groups have not decreased but have changed somewhat in tactics. The ministers of the Fifth Republic have been able to remain in office much longer than those of the Fourth and Third but at the same time have been under far greater control from above. Also it is well known that General de Gaulle is not tolerant of scandals; hence the spokesmen and representatives of special interests have had to work farther down in the ministries. Moreover, the very wide field of special legislation for special interests, to which the parliaments of the Third and Fourth Republics were so open, has been materially reduced. But on the other hand, the increasing activity of government in the economic sphere has widened the possibilities for action by special-interest groups.

Under these circumstances, the more open political activities of the major special-interest organizations have increasing significance. One of the most important is the National Council of French Employers (*Conseil National du Patronat Français,* CNPF) which is organized both nationally, along branch lines such as textile, steel, etc., and on an across-the-board basis in the units of local government, the departments. The coverage of this organization is therefore exceedingly wide and so is the effectiveness of its political antennae.

There is a special organization for small and medium businesses, the CNPME (*Conseil National de Petits et Moyens Entreprises*), which is important because of the very large number of small and medium-sized businesses in France. Of great political weight is also the National Federation of Farm Syndicates (*Fédération Nationale des Syndicats des Exploitants Agricoles*).

One of the most potent lobbies is the National Teachers Federation (*Fédération de l'Education Nationale,* FEN) which has a virtual monopoly over public school teachers and plays an important role, not only in professional but also in political questions, even when they are far removed from specifically educational questions. The students in the UNEF (National Union of French Students—*Union Nationale des Etudiants de France*) are also strongly organized. Their union has been in the forefront of many political demonstrations but is also working actively to improve the often deplorable conditions in French universities and the difficult economic situation of many French students.[48]

The future of the French party system

The French political system could be described as consisting of the political parties *and* General de Gaulle. Before December 5, 1965, it might have appeared to many that General de Gaulle totally dominated the political scene, while the political parties were ineffectually and seemingly aimlessly thrashing about. After December, 1965, at least this much is certain: the traditional political parties, although diminished, have maintained significant positions in the political life of France and are quite likely to survive De Gaulle. His fond dream of destroying the party system, not by force, but by his own mastery on the one hand and by their own ineffectualness on the other, may have come close to realization, but not all the way. The parties' survival will mean that even the General's own faithful UNR will, in the post-Gaullist phase, be obliged to act more and more like a political party. Hence, the eventual victory of the party system over the Gaullist concept of society appears assured. But that does not mean that the nature of that future party system is absolutely certain.

Guy Mollet and traditionalist politicians like him seem to expect that after De Gaulle France will simply go back to its previous political habits, or in other words, that the Fifth Republic will be succeeded by the Fourth—while possibly maintaining some of the constitutional forms of the Fifth.

This is a rather daring assumption. The content and the modalities of the French party system in the post-Gaullist period are in truth very uncertain. A new generation is growing up in France. Already half of the electorates are first- or second-time voters. Theirs is a generation for whom the traditional historical struggles and quarrels of France have a great deal less meaning than for their fathers. To be "left" or "right" is no longer a matter of passionate dedication. Here Gaullism has undoubtedly had an impact, for it has straddled this traditional fence. Nor is this generation likely to find quite so important the state-church dispute, which has poisoned France's political life for well over a century. This would indeed be progress, for an issue with less relevance to practical political requirements in modern France could hardly be imagined.

And yet, this generation has largely remained outside the interplay of political forces. We have already seen that the Gaullist UNR has not succeeded in attracting the youth of France; there is no evidence that other parties have been much more successful. Really vital youth movements hardly exist in any of the parties. France does have a rather young political generation among the leading politicians,

---

[48] Meynaud, *op. cit.;* Brown, *op. cit.*

but an uncommonly large number of men and women in their thirties and twenties are standing apart from political life. The most gifted among them are often found in business or similar enterprises where their great talent and excellent educational foundation have found suitable application and have produced excellent results. In a way, this is a generation of managers, of pragmatists who want to see things work properly but who are unconcerned with political and ideological problems. But business and industry, science and technology, cannot operate in a vacuum. They are more dependent on the modern state with its multiple activities than they used to be in the past. Hence, if the government does not function properly, if it channels its resources into undesirable undertakings, these enterprises will suffer, and this new generation of "managers" will be forced, *faute de mieux,* to engage in politics, even if for no other reason than to "make things work."

How they will do this, what forms of action they will choose, what parties they will favor, or whether they will form new organizations cannot as yet be known. But in the light of all these possibilities and uncertainties, the simple assumption that "the Fifth Republic will be succeeded by the Fourth" is quite unlikely.

5

Constitutional government in France

A. THE NATURE OF DE GAULLE'S CONSTITUTION OF 1958

In a preceding chapter we have seen how the Fourth Republic came to an end. What defects in it did the Constitution of the Fifth Republic expect to remedy? First was the constant change of government. True, a change of cabinets did not change a great deal in France and could not be remotely compared with the change from a Democratic to a Republican administration, or vice versa, in the United States. The same men frequently returned to the cabinet after the immediate crisis was over. Thus, the Fourth Republic had no more individuals in the post of Foreign Minister than the United States had Secretaries of State during the same period.

However, the brief life of every cabinet, the uncertainty of its support in parliament, the necessity to compromise constantly between widely different points of view allowed for little continuity of policy and indeed for little policy at all. More-

288

over, the deputies of the National Assembly in the Fourth Republic evidently became much too fond of the parliamentary game, of the plots and counterplots in the halls of the Palais Bourbon, and of the thrill of assassinating yet another cabinet.[1]

Perhaps in ordinary, or at least less disturbed, times these inconveniences would not have been sufficient to bring down the regime. After all, the Third Republic was not that different from the Fourth, yet the former lasted for nearly seventy years. But times were not ordinary, and in the bitter quarrel and dissension over the Algerian war, the Fourth Republic went down as we have seen, accompanied by the disdain of the huge majority of the French people whom the regime had alienated and driven into frustration and apathy.

Was this catastrophe the fault of France's institutions? the fault of France's leaders? or the fault of the French people? Certainly similar institutions worked quite well in other countries. But it became increasingly clear that they were ill adapted to the particularly difficult problems of France. But then, almost every major governmental system works well in some countries and very badly in others.

Since France is a country in which lawyers are very important, it was not surprising that many minds churned out plans for the reform of the 1946 Constitution.[2] Some thought that an automatic dissolution of the National Assembly in case of a vote of confidence being refused to the government would create discipline and more solid majorities. Others thought that one more juggling of the electoral system might produce that elusive stable parliamentary majority. Numerous other suggestions were heard. Few of them, however, contemplated a fundamental reform of the constitution or a basic change in the regime. In fact, many proposals, long and seriously debated in parliament as they were, seemed to many observers like another intellectual exercise rather than practical solutions.

One diagnosis, which enjoyed only short-lived attention, went a little deeper into the problem. A report by Georges Vedel[3] concluded that France's parliamentary system was on the wrong track. The prototype of a successful parliamentary regime was Great Britain, whose system functioned well because of the existence of the two-party system, which gave rise to a stable majority and a loyal minority to which power could shift from time to time. In France, however, the report demonstrated, such a stable majority was impossible; in view of the existing party system, it was not likely to be created. Therefore, it was futile to try to emulate the British system; the solution must be sought in a country which also had no stable majority but which nevertheless had a stable government.

---

[1] For a lurid case study see Nathan Leites, *Du malaise politique en France,* Paris, 1958 (translated as *On the Game of Politics in France,* Stanford, Calif., 1959). For a better criticism see Michel Debré, *Les princes qui nous gouvernent,* Paris, 1958.

[2] Roy Pierce, "Constitutional Revision in France," *Journal of Politics,* Vol. 17 (1959), pp. 221–247; and "France Reopens the Constitutional Debate" *American Political Science Review,* Vol. 46 (1952), pp. 422–437.

[3] Georges Vedel, *L'Instabilité gouvernementale,* Comité d'Etudes pour la République, Paris, 1956.

Surprisingly, perhaps, Vedel found such a country in the United States, where majorities constantly formed and re-formed in Congress according to the different issues at hand, without leading to unstable government. The presidential system accounted for this, he felt, but the report opposed its adoption in France.

However, the Vedel report roused only passing interest, mainly among intellectuals and political scientists, and had no lasting effect. Nevertheless apparently General de Gaulle agreed with at least some of its conclusions, though it would be wrong to ascribe any similarities in the 1958 Constitution to the impact of the Vedel report, since De Gaulle's fundamental ideas about the future of France were of a much earlier origin. In his speech at Bayeux, on June 16, 1946, General de Gaulle had indicated the fundamental ideas and concepts which have been incorporated into the Constitution of 1958.

What are those ideas? The first and foremost constitutes a direct reversal of the constitutional tradition of the Third and Fourth Republics. Ever since the presidency of Marshal MacMahon (1873–1879), the Presidents of the French Republic had been largely figureheads and ceremonial chiefs who, because of their personal qualities and experience, had at times influence but never power. Now, under the Constitution of 1958, the greatly increased executive power centers on the President of the Republic, who, being elected for seven years, is capable of giving France unusual governmental stability. But at the same time, this is not a purely presidential regime for, alongside the President of the Republic, there are also a Prime Minister and a cabinet who are responsible to the National Assembly, which can overthrow the government although not the President of the Republic.

This peculiar regime is not easily characterized. It cannot be called presidential because the government is responsible to parliament, in contrast to the rigid separation of powers between the executive and legislative branches which characterizes the classical presidential regimes. Yet the powerful and independent position of the President makes it difficult to call this a parliamentary regime, even if one were to take the German Weimar Republic (1918–1933) with its strong presidency as an example. Nor is it quite satisfactory to speak simply of a compromise between the two systems, because the De Gaulle constitution has many unique features.

Perhaps the Constitution of 1958 is so difficult to characterize because it is essentially a monarchical constitution, though a monarchical constitution in a republican disguise. Such a constitution existed in France during the reign of the Orléanist king, Louis Philippe (1830–1848). Under such a system, the monarch guarantees the stability and continuity of the government of the country; he rules rather than governs and leaves the day-by-day administration of the government to a cabinet. But in a crisis, he steps in and decides with finality.

The position of the President of the Republic under the 1958 Constitution is very much the same, except that it is far more effective, at least in part because of De Gaulle's far greater ability as compared with that of King Louis Philippe. As under the monarchy, the President guarantees the stability and continuity of the state, while the cabinet administers the daily affairs of government. But it is the

President who, in many ways, has the most decisive voice and who may step into a crisis and settle the issue. As Article 5 of the new Constitution puts it, "He [the President] shall ensure, by his arbitration, the regular functioning of government, as well as the continuity of the state."

It should be added here that the French word *arbitrage* denotes far greater power on the part of the arbiter than is conveyed by the English word "arbitration."

The superior position of the President over the cabinet is also indicated by the title for the head of the cabinet who, under the Third and Fourth Republics, was called President of the Council of Ministers, but is now called Prime Minister or First Minister (*premier ministre*). Undoubtedly British usage has influenced the selection of this term, but when used in the French language, it may tempt Frenchmen strongly to speak of *le premier ministre du roi* (the king's first minister).

Presidential power is greatly enhanced in the 1958 Constitution, and parliament's is considerably reduced.

B. THE EXECUTIVE

The Constitution of 1958 greatly strengthens the executive and diminishes the role of parliament. Another change, as compared to the constitutions of the Third and Fourth Republics, is the shift within the executive, where major emphasis is now placed on the President of the Republic.

1. The President of the Republic

The Presidents of the Third and Fourth Republics were elected by joint session of both houses of parliament for a term of seven years. They presided over the formal sessions of the cabinet, a function which was infrequently exercised under the Third Republic but became more common under the Fourth. In neither case did this position convey any real power, although it did tend to make the President a well-informed man who, because of his knowledge, wisdom, and experience, could sometimes exercise a not inconsiderable measure of influence. He had no veto, and most of his functions were formal and ceremonial. When a government fell, his skill in finding a new cabinet was of considerable significance, and if the political situation allowed any choice at all between candidates, his preference enjoyed some leeway. Both Presidents of the Fourth Republic, Vincent Auriol and René Coty, enjoyed considerable respect and discharged their functions with wisdom and determination. But they had little chance to influence decisively the course of events.

That situation is radically different under the Fifth Republic. In 1958 the President of the Republic was elected for his traditional term of seven years (the *septennat*) by an enlarged electoral college. This comprised all the members of parliament, the members of the general councils of the departments of France (county-like local units of government), and the assemblies of the overseas territories. In addition, it included representatives from the elected municipal councils. This system was changed in 1962 by a law amending the Constitution, adopted by referendum. It provides for direct, popular election of a President of the French Republic, the first since 1848. Any candidate who wins over 50 percent of the total vote cast is declared elected. If no candidate achieves this majority, a runoff election takes place two weeks later, in which only the two candidates with the highest votes can run. No substitutions are allowed. If one of the two top-ranking candidates were to retire or die before the second ballot, the candidate with the next highest number of votes would run. The result of the runoff election is final.

Another innovation is the provision which guarantees all official candidates a fixed amount of radio and television time. As we have seen, this was effectively used by the opposition candidates in 1965.

In the event of the death or resignation of the President, his place shall be taken by the presiding officer of the Senate, who shall have all presidential powers listed in the Constitution, except those of calling for a referendum and dissolving the National Assembly. He also takes over if the President is prevented from exercising his functions. In each case, it is the Constitutional Council which, upon request of the government, rules by a majority of its members on the official existence of a vacancy or an incapacity in the presidency. In the case of vacancy, or where the Constitutional Council declares the presidential incapacity to be definitive, a new President shall be elected within not less than twenty and not more than fifty days after the beginning of the vacancy or the declaration of the definitive character of the incapacity. The Constitution allows an exception when the Constitutional Council declares the existence of *force majeure* (catastrophic intervention beyond human power to prevent, act of God).

The President of the Republic appoints the Prime Minister and terminates his functions when the latter presents the resignation of the government. On the proposal of the Prime Minister, the President appoints the other members of the government and terminates their functions. He also presides over the meetings of the cabinet. Under the Third and Fourth Republics, a distinction was made between the formal meetings of the Council of Ministers and the informal meetings of the cabinet council. The President of the Republic presided over the former, and the Premier (President of the Council of Ministers) over the second. Under the Third Republic, all important decisions were taken in the informal cabinet council and merely ratified in the formal Council of Ministers.

Under the Fourth Republic, the distinction between the two became less important, and the President of the Republic participated in most cabinet meetings. Under the Fifth Republic, all important decisions are taken while he is in the chair.

The President of the Republic has no veto and must promulgate the laws within fifteen days after their formal adoption. He does, however, have a suspensive veto in the sense that he may ask parliament for reconsideration of entire laws or parts thereof, a request which cannot be refused (Art. 10). Under the Constitution of the Fourth Republic, the President had the same right,[4] but custom opposed his exercise of it, and the powerful National Assembly would have made his life

---

[4] Constitution of 1946, Art. 36.

miserable if not impossible had he used it often. These power relationships are now very much reversed in the Fifth Republic, and there is no reason to doubt that the request for reconsideration now constitutes a reality. Although the President must make this request within fifteen days from the transmission of the bill, he has then an opportunity, during the reconsideration, to bring very considerable political pressure to bear on parliament.

On the proposal of the government (but only during parliamentary sessions) or on a joint motion of parliament, he may submit a bill to a popular referendum (Art. 11). The Constitution specifies that such bills must deal with the organization of the powers of government, with the approval of an agreement concerning the French Community, or with ratification of a treaty, but no such bill may be contrary to the Constitution. Probably few bills could not be placed under one of those categories. However, the referendum of October 28, 1962, providing for the popular election of the President, was of doubtful legality as it amended the Constitution without following the amendment procedure outlined in Article 89. The executive may thus carry the fight directly to the people over the heads of recalcitrant deputies. Under a strong President like General de Gaulle, this power can be very great and tends to keep the National Assembly under control.

A new and potentially very important power of the President is that of dissolution (Art. 12). The Third Republic gave the President no such power, although many reformers felt that it was necessary. The Fourth Republic's Constitution did give the Council of Ministers the right of dissolution but under conditions which made it impracticable until the constitutional reform of 1954, and difficult thereafter.[5] Only one French Premier, Edgar Faure, dared to use this provision and bring about general elections on January 2, 1956, but the manner in which the National Assembly and even his own party put him in the political doghouse thereafter was hardly encouraging to a second attempt.

The Constitution of 1958 (Art. 12) leaves the President of the Republic free to dissolve the National Assembly as he sees fit, except that he may not do so again within a year following the election after a dissolution. The Constitution provides that he must consult with the Prime Minister and the presiding officers of the two houses of parliament, but he is quite free to disregard their advice.

Under the Third and Fourth Republics, the value of the power of dissolution was highly problematical, even if the exact provisions of the Constitution could have been approved. A weak government could have threatened the parliament with dissolution, but the threat would also have turned against the government itself. Moreover the electoral system of the Fourth Republic made it unlikely that a new parliament would be a material improvement over its predecessor. In Great Britain the Prime Minister does not use the power of dissolution to force Parliament's hand but, as we have seen, for quite different reasons. The only pertinent experience, therefore, might be that of the German Weimar Republic (1918–1933), which is hardly encouraging.

---

[5] Constitution of 1946, Arts. 51 and 52 as amended.

Under a strong and irremovable president, however, the power of dissolution can take on entirely new significance. It was used in 1962 when the government fell on a vote of censure. As we have seen, the result was a triumph for De Gaulle and the UNR.

The President has the customary powers of appointment of high military and civilian officials, and he is commander in chief of the armed forces. Under the Third and Fourth Republics, these powers were nominal; the actual decisions were taken either by the cabinet or by the ministers in charge of particular subjects. They are, however, exceedingly real under General de Gaulle's presidency. In fact, General de Gaulle has been rather close-mouthed about appointments, and some of the usual juggling for positions has been less in evidence because these maneuvers could not reach the President.

The President also has the right to communicate with the two houses of parliament by means of messages which shall not be immediately debated, and he may call parliament into special session for that purpose (Art. 18). He may also exercise the right of pardon (Art. 17).

An exceptional and much debated power is the emergency provision of Article 16 for which there is no equivalent in the Constitutions of the Third and Fourth Republics but which is reminiscent of Article 48 of the German Weimar Constitution. This article provides that when the institutions of the Republic and the independence of the nation or the integrity of its territory or the fulfillment of its international obligations are threatened in a grave and imminent manner, *and* when the regular functioning of the constitutional authorities is interrupted, "the President of the Republic shall take those measures which the circumstances demand" after official consultation with the Prime Minister and the presiding officers of the two houses of parliament as well as the Constitutional Council.

Several points about this article are noteworthy. Although the exceptional circumstances under which Article 16 may be carried into effect are fairly well defined, the President alone decides whether or not they have actually arisen. No other authority can override him. His consultations with the Prime Minister and the other state officers are mandatory, but the results are in no way binding upon him. The Constitution further demands that these measures which the President might take must be prompted by the desire to place the constitutional authorities in a position to exercise their regular functions again in the shortest possible time; it repeats the requirement that the Constitutional Council be consulted. But there is still no review of the President's actions, which, it must be underlined, can be virtually without limitation. Article 16 further provides that if these exceptional powers are invoked, the parliament shall meet as a matter of right; and the President would presumably have no right to prevent it from so doing, nor could he exercise his right of dissolution (under Art. 12) during the exercise of these emergency powers.[6]

---

[6] Jean Chatelain, *La Nouvelle Constitution et le régime politique de la France,* Paris, 1959, p. 99.

Article 16 has been sharply criticized by a number of French jurists, and the painful history of the abuse of Article 48 of the German Weimar Constitution has been cited. Evidently this article was included in the Constitution to guard against a situation like the one which emerged from the rebellion of the Europeans in Algeria on May 13, 1958, to guard against a possible Communist uprising, or to give the President necessary emergency powers in case of war. It was used effectively from April to October, 1961. The fact that the President cannot prevent the parliament from meeting during the exercise of his emergency powers does constitute a considerable safeguard. Although parliament cannot actually force the President to terminate the emergency, a strong parliamentary protest against his exercise of those powers would make clear that he was in effect engaged in a *coup d'état*.

Although the Constitution (Art. 19) provides that the acts of the President of the Republic shall be countersigned by the Prime Minister and, if circumstances indicate, by an appropriate departmental minister, it exempts the most important and far-reaching presidential powers from that condition. This involves particularly the rights of referendum (Art. 11) and of dissolution (Art. 12), as well as the emergency powers discussed above (Art. 16). In ordinary parliamentary regimes, the necessity for having the President's acts countersigned by the minister concerned actually makes the minister responsible with the President, and the presidential signature is largely a matter of form. Not so in the Fifth Republic where the all-powerful President makes the actual decision, and the signature of the minister is a mere formality—inevitable unless he were to desire the termination of his ministerial status. Thus, the presidential position is formidable. Other aspects of these powers will emerge from our discussion of other branches of the government and their relationship to one another and to the President.

2. The Prime Minister and the Cabinet

The Constitution of 1958 makes a peculiar distinction between the President of the Republic, who is the "supreme arbiter of the state," and the government, which "shall determine and direct the policy of the nation" (Art. 20). The government's operation is directed by the Prime Minister (Art. 21). Under the Third and Fourth Republics, the Premier's nomination was a complicated process which had to be repeated often because of the frequent government crises. The Premier-designate, who was found by the President of the Republic after much diligent search and often several wrong starts, had to submit himself to the uncertainty of the investiture procedure.

Under the Constitution of the Fourth Republic, up to the reform of December 7, 1954, he had to make his plea to parliament alone, and only after having been "invested" by an absolute majority was he able to form his cabinet. The 1954 reform streamlined this procedure by allowing him to form his cabinet first and present himself and the cabinet together. The 1958 Constitution abolishes the investiture procedure altogether. As we have seen, the President of the Republic appoints the Prime Minister and, upon the latter's proposal, the other members of the cabinet, and that is all. No further confirmation by parliament is required. However, the government is responsible to parliament (Art. 20) and can be overthrown by a vote of censure or a vote of nonconfidence. This works in the following fashion: the Prime Minister, after deliberation by the cabinet, but on his own individual responsibility, may demand a vote of confidence from the National Assembly with regard to the program of the government or with regard to a declaration of general policy, as the case may be (Art. 49). If the National Assembly rejects such a motion, the government is forced to resign.

The National Assembly may also take the initiative in bringing down the government by means of a motion of censure. This, however, is a much more complicated affair. At least one-tenth of the members of the National Assembly must sign a motion to that effect, and a vote can take place only after forty-eight hours have elapsed. A motion of censure is considered passed only if an absolute majority of all members of the Assembly vote for it; if the motion of censure is rejected, its signatories may not introduce another motion in the course of the same session. Other signatories may propose such a motion, however. It should be noted in this connection that a simple majority of deputies present and voting is sufficient to bring down the government on a vote of confidence proposed by the government, but that an absolute majority of all members of the Assembly, present or not, is necessary to carry a motion of censure. This makes its adoption difficult. Even under the less stringent provisions of the Constitution of the Fourth Republic, no motion of censure was ever successfully adopted. However, remember that in October, 1962, such a motion did succeed, and it brought down the Pompidou government.

A new element is also added in those cases where the government wishes to tie a vote of confidence to the adoption of a particular bill. Under the Constitution of the Fourth Republic, such a link could be made by a declaration of the government to that effect, but this provision could produce peculiar results. Under the 1946 Constitution, the government was *refused* a vote of confidence if it was *rejected* by an absolute majority of all deputies having a seat in the house, present or not. Thus, the government could tie a vote of confidence to a given bill, the bill would then be rejected but not by the required majority to force the government to resign.

In actual practice, however, a government which had in effect declared that it could not go on without a certain bill would usually resign in such a case anyway. Under the 1958 Constitution, the situation is radically different. The Prime Minister may, after deliberation by the cabinet, pledge the government's responsibility in conjunction with a specific bill. But the text of that bill shall be considered adopted, unless a motion of censure, filed in the succeeding twenty-four hours, is voted under the conditions laid down in the previous paragraph.

In other words, after the Prime Minister has tied the question of confidence to a given bill, that bill, and with it the government, can be defeated only if, within twenty-four hours, one-tenth of the members of the National Assembly sign a motion of censure and then find an absolute majority of all deputies, present or not, to vote for it. It should be emphasized that no vote need be taken on such a bill in order to declare it adopted. It can be defeated, together with the government, only by the procedure just outlined, a procedure which, under those circumstances and within the very brief period of twenty-four hours, is almost impossible to carry through. This provision (Art. 49, Sec. 3) gives the government a strong potential capacity to ram legislation through without a vote. It may be presumed that if this method is used too often, the National Assembly may become so obstreperous that even that measure may no longer be entirely safe. Nevertheless this is a formidable weapon.

Under the Third and Fourth Republics, the government frequently resorted to the so-called "pseudo vote of confidence."[7] Under that practice, the government, without pronouncing the sacramental words "vote of confidence," *let it be known* that it would resign if the required measure were defeated. This was to put pressure on the National Assembly by placing its responsibilities before it. It is difficult to see why the governments of the Fifth Republic should follow that course, as they can proceed more effectively by an official tie between the survival of the government and a given bill.

Another informal fashion of bringing down the government, under the Third and Fourth Republics, lay in the so-called "interpellation." Under that practice, a deputy would "interpellate," i.e., question the government on a certain point and then develop the question, i.e., argue it at length. The government would defend itself, and eventually a motion would be made to pass on to the next point on the agenda (*passer à l'ordre du jour*). This motion was crucial. If it was rejected, the government saw that as an unofficial censure and would resign. As these lines are written, it seems unlikely that this method of bringing down governments will be revived in the Fifth Republic.

Under the Third and Fourth Republics governments did not seek a formal vote of confidence from the second chamber of parliament. However, the powerful Senate of the Third Republic was known to bring down governments of both the right and the left, by making their lives so miserable that they felt they could not go on. This was the main reason why the power of the second chamber (called the Council of the Republic under the Fourth Republic) was drastically reduced. Gradually, however, the power and influence of the Council of the Republic increased, and although there never was a question of seeking a vote of confidence in that body, French governments nevertheless sought upper-house support, though the latter never approached the importance of the National Assembly.

The Constitution of 1958 still does not give the Senate the right to bring down the government. However, Article 49, last section, provides that the Prime

---

[7] Claude-Albert Colliard, "La Pratique de la question de confidence sous la IVè République," *Revue du droit public et de la science politique*, Vol. LXIV (1948), pp. 220–237.

Minister shall have the right to demand a vote of approval of the government's declaration of its general policy. The Constitution does not require the government to step down should such a motion be refused (in contrast to the procedure before the National Assembly), but it is clear that if the government goes so far as to demand such an expression of the Senate's confidence and is refused, it would have lost so much political prestige that its survival might be in serious doubt.

In countries governed by the parliamentary system, it is customary for various cabinet ministers to direct their respective departments with a far greater degree of authority than is allowed a member of the President's Cabinet in the United States. In Great Britain, this independence is somewhat counteracted by the fact that the Prime Minister is the leader of the majority party in the House of Commons. In the French Third and Fourth Republics, this was never the case since there never could be a majority party. Consequently, the Premier had the difficult and unenviable task of leading a team of divergent and exceedingly independent men, each representing parties and groups on whose support the life of his cabinet depended. Each minister directed his department with considerable discretion and not too infrequently in opposition to other ministries occupied by political rivals. Under those circumstances the Premier bore an immense burden. All interpellations, attacks, and questions were primarily directed at him. Although all policies of the governments in those periods were essentially the result of compromise, his was the main responsibility of having to defend and explain them. In a way it could be said that his responsibilities were considerably greater than his powers.

Apparently under the Fifth Republic, certainly under the presidency of General de Gaulle, this situation no longer prevails. True, men of different political parties still make up the government. But the President of the Republic, who cannot be removed during his seven-year term of office, is now their real leader, and the powers of the executive are generally much increased. It is certainly interesting to note that nonpolitical professionals were assigned the ministries which used to be considered the choicest and most important[8] and that the first Prime Minister, Michel Debré, was not the principal leader of his victorious party at that time but a man whose unquestioned obedience to General de Gaulle was never in doubt. This was even more the case in 1962 when Georges Pompidou succeeded Debré. Pompidou cannot in any way be called a leader of the UNR.

In the exercise of their functions, both the President of the Republic and the Prime Minister have considerable staffs at their disposal. The presidential staff includes specialists in all fields (foreign affairs, interior, justice, finance, etc.) who keep the President informed and assure liaison with the ministries concerned. Under the Presidents of the Third and Fourth Republics, the Elysée Palace, in which the President of the Republic has his official residence, was fairly quiet; in the Fifth Republic, the Palace is humming with activity and is likely to prove too small for some of the offices which have now been established in it.

---

[8] Especially those of Foreign Affairs and National Defense.

The Prime Minister and the cabinet are served by a General Secretariat (*Sécrétariat Général du Gouvernement*)[9] modeled on the British cabinet secretariat. Its members assist in drafting all government bills and executive orders, follow up the fate of these bills in the National Assembly, and report to the government on action taken on them and on other bills emanating from parliament. They also help to plan parliament's legislative agenda. In general, they keep the Prime Minister and the cabinet constantly informed about the legislative picture.

Apart from its legislative work, the Secretariat prepares reports on such topics as may be assigned to it, keeps the minutes of cabinet meetings, and is generally at the disposal of the Prime Minister. The Secretariat may also help to iron out differences between the actions of several ministries covering the same subject.

Technically the General Secretariat consists of two services: the Legislative service, and the Administrative and Financial service. The latter is mainly occupied with housekeeping functions for the Secretariat as a whole; the Legislative service carries on the real functions of the Secretariat. The General Secretary heads both services.

Attached to the Secretariat are the Civil Service Office, which will be discussed later; the Document Center; the official journal of the French Republic; and the National School of Administration, as well as technical services such as the French Broadcasting System and the postal, telephone, and telegraph services. However, policy with regard to these particular services has been directed by the ministers who deal with information and the operation of the mails, the telegraph, and telephone.

Also very important is the work of the Council of State, whose principal role as an administrative court will be discussed later.[10] Under the executive order of July 31, 1945, and Article 39 of the Constitution of 1958, the Council of State must be consulted with regard to all legislation originated by the government and is frequently to be consulted in other matters as well. The Council of State may also take other actions within the administration, such as an investigation on behalf of the government, and it may call attention to any need for administrative reform. Moreover, it serves as an inspector over all authorities which exercise functions of administrative justice in metropolitan France and overseas. The great usefulness of the Council of State, especially in drafting government-sponsored legislation, lies primarily in the high degree of *expertise* and experience of its members, and in the extraordinary respect which they enjoy.

Under the Third and Fourth Republics, much juggling preceded the formation of each government. The key ministries of Foreign Affairs, Interior, Finance, and War had to be so distributed that no one party could control too many of them. This rivalry, as well as the widely diverse views which had to be accommodated in order to make a coalition government possible, made it impossible to carry out any

[9] Roy C. Macridis, "The Cabinet Secretariat in France," *The Journal of Politics*, Vol. XIII (1951), pp. 589–603.
[10] See "The Administrative Courts" later in this chapter.

long-range program. Yet the weakness of this system lay not so much in the institutions of parliamentary government, nor even in the multiparty system as such, but rather in the peculiar nature of the French party system.

Ever since 1849, the division between the parties of the left and of the right has shown an amazing degree of constancy, with the votes for the left usually a little larger than those for the right. But the left could not form a coalition government of its own, because the Communists formed the largest part of the left, and no other party could collaborate with them. The right was not strong enough to form a purely rightist government either, because it was not sufficiently numerous, and too many of its members had too many petty differences ever to be able to pull together. Consequently, whatever the outcome of any election, the only possible government in France was a coalition supported by elements of both the left and the right—in other words, a coalition whose members had nothing in common except that they alone could find a mathematical majority in the National Assembly.[11]

As we have seen, in some cabinet offices like Foreign Affairs, there were no more changes in the French scene than in the United States during the same period. Of course, it must be admitted that French governments, especially those of the Fourth Republic, found themselves confronted by an impossible situation. The serious problems which they had to face, especially in the field of economic and foreign affairs, demanded long-range, often radical solutions. No such solutions were possible because the coalition parties and the other groups which supported them in parliament were fundamentally at odds. In this hopeless struggle, as a former Premier, Léon Blum, put it, cabinets died of sheer exhaustion rather than because of policy conflicts.[12]

It was of course quite true that the fall of the government under the Third or Fourth Republics entailed no fundamental change in the country. As the same men often returned or, at any rate, the same political groups had to support the next government, there was rather a remarkable continuity of policy or, more often, the continuity of the policy of having as little policy as possible. At the same time, the efficient civil service carried on and saw to it that there was no interruption in the functioning of government. Yet with continuous change of government there could be no long-range policy. No matter how able their members, governments were unable to provide the radical, long-range solutions France needed.

Moreover, because of the constant threat to the life of a government, every cabinet minister had to spend a major part of his time in parliamentary maneuvers and even then he could expect to stay in office only a brief time.

Because of the mere flicker of life granted to many cabinet ministers and because of their necessary preoccupation with party politics and elementary maneuvers, French ministers, under the two previous Republics, were almost incapable of exercising much actual control over their departments. The permanent civil

---

[11] Maurice Duverger, "Public Opinion and Political Parties in France," *American Political Science Review,* Vol. XLVI (1953), pp. 1069–1078.
[12] Léon Blum, *La Réforme gouvernementale,* Paris, 1936.

servant often was the real administrator and policy maker; usually the best the minister could do was to exercise a certain check and restraint. This dependence on the civil service was unfortunate; civil servants often could sabotage a policy they did not like simply by outlasting the minister. No wonder that a former Premier and long-time Foreign Minister, Robert Schuman, complained bitterly that many of the policies for which the minister received the blame were actually the policies of some civil servant against whom the minister found himself quite powerless.[13]

This has, of course, greatly changed under the Fifth Republic. Governments have been exceedingly stable, and ministers have been administrators much more than policy makers, attaining or even surpassing the stability and longevity of their British and German counterparts, though with far less political significance. As a result they have been able to devote much more time to the management of their ministries, to acquire considerable expertise therein, and to assert their authority. The opportunity for recalcitrant civil servants to sabotage policy or to "outwait" a minister until his inevitable fall, as was so normal under the Fourth Republic, is no longer possible. Moreover the government has not been tolerant toward civil servants who do not fall into line, and those whose views were known to be unfriendly sometimes found themselves shunted off to less important or less desirable posts.

There is also another new factor. According to Article 23 of the new Constitution, membership in the cabinet shall be incompatible with a seat in parliament, as well as with any function of professional representation on a national level, or any public employment, or any other professional activity.[14]

What this far-reaching paragraph means is the following: in the first place, a member of parliament who enters the government must give up his seat in either house. This was designed to lower the appetite of deputies for overthrowing one government in order to have a better chance for a ministerial position in the next. The electoral law of 1958[15] provides that every candidate for the National Assembly shall designate a substitute who will take his place within one month if he enters the government. After leaving the government, the former minister may not resume his seat in parliament until new elections take place.

Hence, the threat of losing a parliamentary position as a price for membership in the government is quite real. If the government lasts for an appreciable length of time, the minister loses his parliamentary contact and it may be difficult for him to resume a position of leadership in his house.

In some respects more serious, however, is the incompatibility of ministerial positions with "functions of professional representation on a national level." Sec-

[13] Robert Schuman, "Nécessité d'une politique," in *Maroc et Tunisie, La Nef,* March, 1953.
[14] An exact rendering of this article into English is extremely difficult. The French text reads: *"Les fonctions de membre du Gouvernement sont incompatibles avec l'exercice de tout mandat parlementaire, de toute fonction de représentation professionnelle à caractère national et de tout emploi public ou de toute activité professionnelle."*
[15] Executive Order of Oct. 13, 1958.

retaries of labor unions, of employers' federations, of agricultural associations, of chambers of commerce, etc., cannot become ministers or must resign those positions before becoming ministers. This is particularly painful for party leaders who in giving up key positions in their party's hierarchy may well endanger their future leadership. It was therefore understandable that Roger Frey, general secretary of the victorious UNR (Union for the New Republic), gave up that position reluctantly when he became Minister of Information. Had Guy Mollet, the Socialist leader, not decided to leave the government after the elections of 1958, he would have been forced to give up his position of secretary-general of the Socialist party, from which his numerous opponents in his own party would have liked to oust him.

Under the circumstances just set forth, cabinet ministers in governments of considerable longevity will probably find their ties to their parties or political associations, as well as to parliament, loosened. They are, therefore, likely to be reluctant to abandon their ministerial positions in a fit of temper over some minor disagreement. Yet this reluctance makes them more dependent on the powerful President of the Republic.

Because of these special circumstances of the De Gaulle presidency, it will be a number of years before one can state with any certainty how much of the presidency's strength is due to its constitutional position and how much to the personal and political power of General de Gaulle. After all, the Constitution does make it possible for governments to be forced out, and in the post-Gaullist period governments may not have quite such an easy time with parliament. Nevertheless, the constitutional system does promise a much greater longevity of governments than was possible under the Fourth Republic. It would seem likely, therefore, that greater stability of the administration and greater responsiveness to governmental direction have become features of the new regime of the Fifth Republic.

3. The ministries

The French Constitution of 1958 does not establish or limit the number of chief government departments (ministries) nor did any of its predecessors. A number of principal government functions, such as foreign affairs, interior, finance, defense, are naturally always represented by ministries. However, President de Gaulle has given a literal interpretation to Article 15, according to which he is commander in chief of the armed forces and chairman of the higher committees and councils of national defense. He has thus diminished the normally more important position of the Minister for the Armed Forces. This is understandable in view of General de Gaulle's military background but may not be a permanent feature of this Constitution.

Beyond that, it may be presumed that the practice of the Third and Fourth Republics, which created new ministries from time to time, partly because of the importance of their functions and partly for political reasons, will be continued. It is also quite customary to appoint ministers without portfolio. They are called

Ministers of State and are usually highly important political personages who have no specific assignment but may be given certain special tasks. A temporary innovation of the De Gaulle period was the position of "Minister Delegate of the Prime Minister," a rather obscure position created largely for the political purpose of giving an important and sensitive person a high-sounding title without much concrete to do. This designation was dropped in the reformed Pompidou government of 1966.

In addition to the ministers, there are usually a number of secretaries of state, who are in effect junior ministers and whose positions are not clearly defined. Normally they may sign executive orders only together with a full minister. Their authorities are derived from whatever the Prime Minister or the minister delegates to them. Yet within that framework, their functions may be quite substantial. Very often, secretaries of state are gifted younger men who are being tried out for eventual top positions. Under-secretaries of state fall into the same category but are definitely of subministerial status, and their position is more uncertain. However, in ministries which have no secretary of state, under-secretaries may be virtual secretaries without the title. Otherwise their position is closer to that of the top civil servants in the ministries concerned.

Ministers and secretaries of state are normally politicians, or, if they are chosen from the diplomatic or civil services (as General de Gaulle has done in certain cases), they are presumed to have left their respective services. Under-secretaries, on the other hand, may be politicians or may be drawn from the top civil service strata. Under the Fourth Republic, practice varied greatly from government to government. On occasion, high commissioners or government commissioners have been appointed, but they rank below under-secretaries and have the character of special assistants to ministers.

As we have seen, the Constitution specifies certain actions which must be taken by the cabinet. Beyond that, the cabinet, theoretically, deals with all questions of high policy and receives all government bills either for information or in order to discuss and approve them. If a poll is taken in the cabinet, the minority is supposed to support the decisions of the majority or to resign. There can be no "cabinet opposition," at least not in a declared form. In 1947 the Communist ministers attempted to chart a novel course by acceding to the decisions of the cabinet majority, while Communist deputies in the National Assembly voted against the government. However the then Premier, Paul Ramadier (Socialist), declared that a party could not be in the government and oppose it at the same time, and as the Communist ministers refused to resign, they were removed from office. There have been no Communists in subsequent cabinets, and the incident is not likely to be repeated, especially under De Gaulle's presidency.

As cabinet meetings tend to be cumbersome, the practice of holding meetings of smaller groups has become rather prevalent. One of these is the Interministerial Council, which is composed of several ministers who have certain common problems to discuss. Such councils may become semipermanent cabinet subcommittees.

Another group is colloquially called the "super-council." It is composed of certain ministers of special eminence whose function it is to evolve government policy on specific questions. This institution comes closer to being an inner cabinet, but the device is infrequently used and only on matters of the gravest importance.[16]

Inner structure of ministries. Functions of most French ministries are divided in the same manner as those of the chief government departments of other countries. In many respects, the Ministry of the Interior is perhaps one of the most important posts, because it is in charge of internal security, controls the police, and administers elections. Through the prefects it maintains tight control on all levels of local government.[17]

Economic affairs have sometimes been divided between different ministries, but General de Gaulle has taken the opposite course and has concentrated most economic power in the hands of the Minister of Finance. In 1966, the Ministries of Economics and Finance were combined. This is logical, because the chief economic problem of France is fiscal: lack of adequate revenues and emptiness of the treasury, both because the country has long lived above its means and because of costly wars, first in Indochina and then in Algeria. A contributory cause of the difficulty is also the poor tax structure, which places principal emphasis on indirect taxation.

In addition to the Ministry of Finance, which even when not combined with the Ministry of Economics might be considered a super-ministry over all economic affairs, there are Ministries of Industry and Commerce, of Agriculture, of Public Works—now called the Ministry of Equipment, and of Industry. Housing is among the problems which have been confided to special secretaries of state. This emphasizes the government's particular concern with a sector of the French economy which a leading Paris newspaper has called the "shame of France."

French ministries are organized on a nearly uniform pattern. One of their peculiar features is a "cabinet" within each ministry. It is headed by a chief (*chef de cabinet*) and is composed of an assistant chief, a secretary, and several attachés. Its members are not part of the civil service but are strictly political, or more accurately, personal appointees of the minister. Relatives of a minister have frequently been chosen. These cabinets were supposed to act as a counterbalance to the overly powerful civil service and thus prevent the minister's isolation in his own department. It was, of course, understandable that the minister, whose parliamentary duties and especially whose short tenure gave him little time to become an expert on technical questions, was somewhat overwhelmed by the permanent officials who had far greater knowledge of the subject matter than he and perhaps different views from his own. In this situation, a cabinet of loyal, devoted friends was a great help. But its value diminished because frequently many of its members were novices with little knowledge of the art of administration in a strongly centralized govern-

[16] Claude-Albert Colliard, *Le Travail gouvernemental et ses méthodes,* Paris, 1948.
[17] See "Local Government" later in this chapter.

ment. At times the result was confusion and demoralization among members of the regular service who regarded the cabinets as personal espionage services of the ministers.

In the Third Republic the situation was particularly bad because some ministers tried to secure high civil service positions for the members of their cabinets, even by special legislation. Under the Fourth Republic, this practice became far less frequent, partly as a result of a civil service reform, partly because the constant return to office of a relatively small number of people improved employment opportunities for members of the cabinets. The author has met several ministers, temporarily out of office, who introduced their *chefs de cabinets* by this title although they had no cabinet at that time. These gentlemen simply stood by and waited until "their" ministers should return to office, which they usually did in short order.

Toward the end of the Fourth Republic, members of the cabinets were chosen increasingly from experts; this seems also to be the trend in the Fifth Republic, which has continued the practice of the cabinet within each ministry although its members are to a very large extent civil servants on detached service or specialists of distinction or promise.

Advisory agencies.   After the First World War, a number of economic advisory agencies and councils were set up, among them an Economic Council which was established by law in 1925 and received enlarged power in 1936, but their achievements have been insignificant.

Article 25 of the French Constitution of 1946 provided for an Economic Council. Articles 69–71 of the Constitution of 1958 established an Economic and Social Council. The Economic Council of the Fourth Republic was composed of representatives of the various professional organizations, labor unions, agricultural federations, etc., and the French government appointed ten people as representatives of French literature and creative thought. The same pattern has been maintained in the Economic and Social Council of 1958.

The Economic Council, as well as its 1958 successor, was designed to satisfy a number of diverse ideas and aspirations. It was to appeal to those who wanted some sort of "interest representation," to those who wanted to see the power of the National Assembly checked by other councils, to those who believed in the need for giving experts a high place in the councils of government, to those who resented the predominance of politics over the economic problems of the country, and to those who had some vague ideas about economic democracy.

The Economic Council of the Fourth Republic fulfilled few of those aspirations, however, and there is little reason to believe that its successor will be much more successful.

The Constitution of the Fourth Republic provided for the *mandatory* consultation of the Economic Council in any question concerning the establishment of an over-all national economic plan. This was also true in regard to any executive order or administrative directive which implemented a law previously submitted to the Council for advice. The Constitution of the Fifth Republic is much more vague on this point. Article 70 states that any plan or bill dealing with a plan of an economic or social character should be submitted to the Economic and Social Council for the latter's advice. It is not quite clear how general a bill has to be in order to qualify as a plan of an economic or social character. Beyond that, the Council is to give its opinion on any bill, executive order, or decree which the government may submit to it. In that case, the Council may emphasize the significance of its reply by designating one of its members to present its opinion to the houses of parliament.

On its face there is no reason to suppose that the Economic and Social Council of the Fifth Republic should have any more significance than its predecessor. Certainly its prerogatives are no greater and its status, if possible, is even less well defined. However, one of the ideas of the Resistance movement, which has permanently influenced Gaullist thought, was the contention that some way should be found toward a certain amount of "interest representation." Thus the Economic and Social Council may be chosen both as an avenue toward that goal and as a high assembly on economic and social questions to help check the National Assembly if that were considered desirable. Under the Fifth Republic, the Economic and Social Council has earnestly dedicated itself to its task. However, it is at best advisory, as the real power is clearly located elsewhere.

4.   The nationalized industries

Nationalization is not a novelty in France. A number of railroads, utilities, and other enterprises have been nationalized for many years. Moreover, the government maintained certain monopolies, i.e., industries which it owned and operated and to which it allowed no competition. In 1936 the Popular Front government had introduced further nationalization, notably of the Bank of France and of the munitions and aircraft industries, and had brought all railroads under its control.

During the struggle for liberation, nationalization was a popular topic of discussion among members of the Resistance. In part this was due to the prevalence of leftist elements, but a powerful argument was found in the large degree of collaboration which existed between some of France's largest industries and the hated German enemy.

Consequently nationalization became an item on the agenda of all postliberation governments. A variety of reasons tended to demand nationalization. Paramount were the political reasons which favored the argument that only nationalization of key industries could free France from the rule of the "trusts." It was felt in certain circles that big, powerful corporations had been able to wield a disproportionate influence through their command of a good part of the press and that they had thus been able to paralyze orderly and constitutional government. It was also known, and revealed from time to time, that certain public officials were not above accepting favors from such sources. Moreover, it was contended that certain corporations, like the steel trust (*comité de forges*), had been notorious for their ties with foreign (German) interests, and it was also remembered that certain financial circles had held the whip hand over the national currency by their constant threat to evacuate their capital from France.

On the economic side of the argument, it was held that only by the direct ownership and administration of key industries could the government hope to control the national economy and direct it into certain well-planned channels. This argument gained many adherents partly because other means of control, such as price and allocation controls, had proven ineffective, partly because of poor administration, partly because of a lack of discipline among the people and their great skill in circumventing the law—a talent developed to a fine art under the German occupation.

Another argument advanced stated that in times of national emergency, during the difficult days of recovery, vital industries should not be in a position to enrich themselves by huge profits. Perhaps it was also hoped that improved morale among the workers would result from nationalization and would produce a higher degree of efficiency.

As a result of these considerations, the most important coal mines, the public utilities corporations (gas and electricity), and certain aviation and automobile manufacturers[18] were nationalized. More important perhaps than these, the same fate reached the most important banks and a majority of insurance companies. This was an important stroke because it enabled the government to control virtually the entire production process, either directly through the nationalized factories or indirectly through the nationalized banks and insurance companies.

The organizational patterns of the nationalized industries have much in common, even though they differ in certain respects according to their needs. The coal industry, for instance, was organized into nine semiautonomous *bassins,* each with a full-fledged administrative staff and a board of directors composed of representatives of the government, the consumers, and the workers.[19] These *bassins* are subordinate to the National Coal Authority (*Carbonnages de France*), which exercises supervisory powers over the administration but controls functions in all financial matters. The other nationalized industries follow this pattern with some variations. The banking and credit institutions have a National Credit Council, which is headed by the Minister of Finance and is composed of representatives of other ministries, financial institutions, labor, industry, agriculture, commerce, etc. Labor has a large representation on this Council as well as on the board of each of the nationalized banks. Actually, however, the Minister of Finance and the officers designated by him dominate the picture.

The situation in the insurance business is very similar, where a National Insurance Council exists, very much like the National Credit Council but with a more

[18] The Renault motor works and the Gnôme et Rhône aircraft corporation were nationalized because of the collaborationist activities of their former managers.
[19] The workers' share of seats is proportionally higher than the others'.

limited representative basis (representing government, policyholders, and employees). The Renault auto works, on the other hand, being a single enterprise, has an appointed president and an advisory board of directors with the usual interest representation. However, the government is clearly dominant. The Renault factory is administered in a very businesslike way and has been a considerable financial success, largely because of excellent management.

All is not plain sailing. On July 24, 1948, André Marie, Premier-designate, declared before the National Assembly: "We want the nationalized industries to become a source of pride for France and to stop being a source of anxiety." Part of the state of affairs to which Marie alluded was caused by the economic difficulties of the postwar period and had no particular connection with the fact of nationalization. But there were and are other factors as well. The tripartite control authority (government, consumers, employees) is composed of elements with very divergent interests. It is sometimes difficult to establish a purposeful business policy. For this reason, a superimposed body, a Special Accounting Office (*Chambre de Comptes*), whose members are all government-appointed, has wielded much control, thereby rendering somewhat theoretical the principle of decentralization which the law tried to establish.

Later it was replaced by a body with similar functions, the Commission for the Verification of Accounts in Public Enterprise (*Commission de Vérification des Comptes des Entreprises Publiques*), whose members were selected from the staffs of the Ministry of Finance and the General Accounting Office (*Cour des Comptes*). Like its predecessor, the Commission may remove boards of directors for demonstrated inefficiency. The appointments to the top administrative positions are controlled by the various ministers in charge (commerce and industry, finance, economics, etc.) and are therefore open to political influence. These positions are of key importance because the tripartite board of directors is often unable to agree, and consequently the appointed officials in effect often determine policy and have veto power in fact.

The situation is complicated by the fact that the excessively large representation of the employees on the boards of directors and councils is composed of people appointed by their respective unions, for the workers vote which union shall represent them and not which individuals. This vests control in outsiders, most of whom belong to the completely Communist-controlled General Workers Federation (*Confédération Générale du Travail*). As a result, political rather than economic reasons have often motivated the actions of the workers' representatives, especially when the Communists made an all-out attempt to wreck the Marshall Plan and subsequent American aid programs.

The nationalization of French industry was the result of special circumstances at the end of the war, rather than of over-all planning. It is now an established fact of French life, and there are few attempts to denationalize, though some talk is occasionally heard. On the other hand few Frenchmen would want any more nationalization. Although it was the political left which once made itself the spokesman of nationalization, it was a coalition regime which brought it about, and no single party can claim credit or accept sole blame for it. Consequently as a political issue nationalization plays no role, and as an economic and administrative factor it is confined to the sector of the economy which it now occupies.[20]

5. The Civil Service

French government is characterized by a strongly centralist regime in which most important decisions are made in Paris and executed by a vast bureaucracy. Even minute problems of local government must frequently be decided on a central level, and the central government embraces many functions which in other countries are partly exercised by other levels of government, partly left to private agencies. Thus the centralized machinery not only administers most of local government and the entire educational system but also manages much of the legitimate stage and opera and many other things.

The pay of the French civil servant is not high, but he is better off than many other parts of the population, for the civil service unions have much power and many political friends and have been able to obtain many concessions. Nor have they refrained from strikes when recourse to this remedy seemed indicated. True, the Council of State has handed down rulings designed to limit certain types of strikes, but this has had little effect. Although civil service strikes have not been frequent, they did occur under the Fourth Republic either outright, as in the summer of 1953, or indirectly by slowdowns, exaggerated enforcements of minute regulations, or nonenforcement of regulations.

Let us not be too harsh on the French civil servant. While strikes and comparable actions on his part seem obnoxious and improper to the American or Briton, they are merely a reflection of French individualistic society in which the special interest of the person or the group is so often allowed to override the interests of the community. In this respect the civil servants do not differ from other people in France, from parliament, industry, trade, agriculture, labor unions, and the public in general. In this environment, the French civil servant actually exhibits a high order of devotion to duty and principle.

Apart from his salary and his family allocations,[21] which are tied to the cost of living, the French civil servant is protected from lawsuits arising from his official functions, for the government is responsible for his acts, except those committed in a strictly personal capacity. At the same time, he may seek redress in the administrative courts (councils) against any superior officer seeking to impair his rights under the civil service laws.

[20] For a balanced account, see Mario Einaudi et al., *Nationalization in France and Italy,* Ithaca, N.Y., 1955.
[21] Under the system of family allocations, the French government pays a subsidy to families, which increases with the number of children and constitutes a substantial supplement to the regular salary earned. These family allocations are of course paid to all qualified persons in both public and private employment.

Before 1945 all matters of personnel management, recruitment, promotion, disciplinary action, etc., were in the hands of the personnel boards of the various ministries. These boards were under the fiscal control of the Board of the Budget and under the legal control of the Council of State. This system worked rather badly, lacked uniformity and central control, and often favored the employees of the Ministry of Finance, who were closer to the Board of the Budget.

This was changed in 1945 and formally enacted in the Civil Service Act of October 19, 1946. Without replacing the Board of the Budget, the Act set up a central office directly under the Premier; it is called the Civil Service Office (*Direction de la Fonction Publique*)[22] and is headed by a director who is assisted by a rather small staff. This office prepares the texts of all laws and executive orders (decrees) concerning the status of civil servants but must consult the Board of the Budget in financial matters. The office is in charge of classifying civil service positions—which is for the first time being done in a fairly uniform manner, supervises and approves regulations for recruitment and promotion, and advises on methods to improve the service.

The Civil Service Office is strictly a staff agency; that is, it is solely concerned with planning and advising. The actual operation of the civil service rests with the personnel boards in the various ministries.

The supervision of the Civil Service is delegated to a Minister or Secretary of State. This has tied the Director of the Civil Service rather closely to the government, but French governments do not ordinarily interfere with the operation of the service and there is little political influence from the top. There is certainly no spoils system.

The 1946 law established a system of consultative councils, each composed half of supervisors and half of staff employees. There are administrative committees representing one class in a ministry, and there are technical committees representing members of the same service regardless of class. The Minister must consult with the appropriate committee on any decision affecting the status of a civil servant. The same is true in disciplinary cases. The Minister is not bound to follow the committee's advice. There is also a Supreme Civil Service Council of twenty-four members headed by the Minister (or Secretary of State) of the Civil Service. It is a high consulting body on general questions affecting several ministries and a board of appeals in individual cases. The Minister is not obliged to carry out its advice but almost invariably does.

The main civil service classes follow the British system very closely. The top group is, as in Britain, the Administrative class (*administrateurs civils*). Second in rank and largest in number is the Executive class (*secrétaires d'administration*), which is followed by the Clerical class (*adjoints administratifs*) and the Subordinate Personnel (typists, messengers, etc.).

---

[22] For an excellent discussion on which much of this presentation is based, see Jean Trouvé, "The French Civil Service Office," *Public Administration Review,* Vol. XL (1951), pp. 180–186.

One may enter the Executive class and the classes below by competitive examinations. These test the desired educational level of the candidate rather than his special preparation for the job. In this respect they follow the British example and are geared to the various levels of (public) education. In contrast to the American practice, a French civil servant who passes his examination successfully enters a so-called "corps of civil servants" of which there are about 1,000. A corps of civil servants comprises a variety of civil service positions to which one is eligible after passing one particular examination. It also comprises a number of given ranks to which one may be advanced according to regulations and without taking additional examinations.

The most important corps are those of the Inspectors of Finance, the Diplomatic Corps, the Court of Accounts, and the Council of State. They form the so-called "Great Corps of State" (*les Grands Corps d'État*). The Inspectors of Finance are generally considered to be the cream of the crop and many of France's most distinguished diplomats or civil servants started out as Inspectors of Finance, such as Foreign Minister Maurice Couve de Murville.

Recruitment to the highest group, the Administrative class, is handled in a different manner. It is open only to graduates of the National School of Administration (*École Nationale d'Administration*). The creation of this school had long been a dream in French administrative circles, and the former Premier Léon Blum was among its special advocates. It was realized only in 1945 under the leadership of Michel Debré, who later became the first Prime Minister of the Fifth Republic.

Admission to the National School of Administration is possible only through one of two sets of exceedingly difficult examinations. One set is given to young civil servants with a minimum of five years' experience. The other is open to graduates of the various Institutes of Political Science (*Instituts d'Éudes Politiques*) attached to the principal universities—Paris, Bordeaux, Strasbourg, Grenoble, etc.[23]

Successful candidates become temporary civil servants and receive a salary while going to school. The course lasts three years and features periodic internships, i.e., work in different branches of the administrative services. The training is divided into four categories among which the student may choose: general administration, economic and financial administration, social administration, and foreign affairs. The rank of each student in each category is determined by examinations which form the basis for later appointment. Rarely do more than 100 students graduate each year.

Special in-service training for high officials is available in three-month courses at the School of Advanced Studies. Both the National School of Administration and the School of Advanced Studies have greatly democratized the civil service and have opened access to the highest positions to all men and women who possess the necessary training and ability.

---

[23] The principal Institute, the one in Paris, is the *Institut d'Études Politiques*. The second type of entrance examination to the National School of Administration is open also to students of other university departments, especially law. But the Institutes prepare specially for it.

C. THE LEGISLATURE

The Constitution of 1958 establishes a fundamentally different system from that of the Third and Fourth Republics. The Senate of the Third Republic was extremely powerful. Under the Fourth Republic it was at first emasculated but later gained weight. Under this new Constitution, the National Assembly and the Senate are more nearly coequal than they were in the Fourth Republic, although both are diminished in stature compared with the power of the executive. Deputy Paul Coste-Floret characterized the system of the Fourth Republic as incomplete bicameralism or modified unicameralism. By the same line of reasoning, the system of the Fifth Republic may be considered as a strongly modified parliamentarism.

Parliament, the entire legislative body of France, is composed of the National Assembly (*Assemblée Nationale*) and the Senate (*Senat*). The National Assembly of the Fourth Republic had 627 deputies,[24] of whom 544 represented metropolitan France. The Council of the Republic had 320 senators. The National Assembly of the Fifth Republic has cut its membership radically to 475 deputies, 465 of whom are from metropolitan France. The number of senators is now 268.

The electoral process

Although Gallic temperament may lead to occasional fisticuffs and the tearing down or defacing of enemy billboards, French elections are usually calm, orderly, and honest. The latter quality is assured by the electoral commissions which control the proceedings and the counting of the ballots. These commissions are composed of regular judges, a member of the department general council, a division chief of the local prefecture, and optional observers from all the political parties.

All French men and women twenty-one years of age or older have the right to vote unless they are specifically disqualified for such reasons as mental incapacity, preventive arrest, or a court order accompanying a verdict in a criminal trial. Unlike American practice, the voters' lists are prepared by the authorities, and no special registration is necessary on the part of the voter.[25] The lists are open to inspection for a certain period, and a qualified voter whose name has inadvertently been omitted can protest and have his name added. The situation is a little different for a naturalized French citizen; he may vote only after he has been a citizen for five years.

Under the Third and Fourth Republics, various elaborate schemes were en-

---

[24] After the elections of 1956, there were only 597 deputies (including the presiding officer), as the 30 deputies from Algeria could not be elected because of the disturbed conditions in that country. For an analysis of that election, the last under the Fourth Republic, see M. Duverger, et al. (eds.), *Les Élections du 2 janvier, 1956*, Paris, 1957.

[25] This system is common in Europe. It is made possible by the fact that every person staying in France must notify the police of his whereabouts. Travelers sign a police registration form at their hotels. French citizens and resident aliens must do the same and must also carry identity cards issued by the Ministry of the Interior.

acted to give some, but not complete, representation to France's overseas possessions. Those efforts were continued under the Fifth Republic. However, practically all these territories, including Algeria, have gained their independence, and the only overseas territories left under French rule are those pre-Revolution territories like the island of Réunion, French Guiana, or St. Pierre and Miquelon[26] which have long been administered like departments of France and where the electoral rules are the same as in the mother country. As far as the National Assembly is concerned, there are three representatives from Martinique, three from Guadeloupe, three from Réunion, and one from French Guiana.

The minimum age for eligibility to the National Assembly is twenty-three, and to the Senate, twenty-five. A candidate must be a French citizen or, if naturalized, must have been a French citizen for at least ten years. He must be a qualified voter who has satisfied the law dealing with military service; i.e., he must have either served or been definitely exempted.

French law further decrees certain cases of ineligibility. Among them are members of the former royal families which have ruled France in the past. Also ineligible are those who have been condemned by a court to "national indignity"[27] but who have had their right to vote restored.

Certain officials—whose number is held to a minimum—suffer a temporary and relative ineligibility because their positions might make it possible for them to influence the outcome of an election. Thus judges of lower courts, certain administrative officials of the prefecture and comparable services, and military commanders of territories may not be candidates. This relative ineligibility ends between six months and two years after the official has ceased to exercise the particular function or office.

Finally, deputies or senators who have been unseated by their respective chambers for corrupt practices are ineligible for two years.

The executive order of October 13, 1958, which regulated the electoral system of the Fifth Republic, further provided that certain positions in private or public life are incompatible with membership in the National Assembly. Directors of national or private enterprises which hold government contracts or enjoy special advantages or privileges from the government, as well as directors of banks, loan companies, or similar companies organized for exclusively financial purposes and publicly engaged in investment or banking, must resign from such positions before occupying their seats in the National Assembly. It will also be remembered that Article 23 of the 1958 Constitution requires a deputy appointed to a cabinet position to resign his parliamentary seat. With this possibility in mind, the executive order of October 13 rules that candidates for the National Assembly nominate substitutes of the same political tendency, who automatically take their seats within 30 days should they be advanced to cabinet rank.

---

[26] See pages 316, 346–347.
[27] Minor collaborationists during the Second World War.

Under the Third, Fourth, and Fifth Republics the method of electing senators has remained fairly constant. But the same cannot be said for the Chamber of Deputies and its successor, the National Assembly. The Third Republic used three systems: the single-member district, the multimember district-list system, and a modified form of proportional representation. Among them the most durable and also the simplest was the single-member district system, a majority system with runoff elections (*scrutin d'arrondissement à deux tours*). This, with some modifications, has been reinstituted for the Fifth Republic.

Although the electoral systems of the Third and Fifth Republics are quite simple, that of the Fourth Republic was incredibly complicated. It provided for multimember districts, basically on the level of the department, and election on the basis of proportional representation, under which the proportion of seats assigned to each party in the National Assembly corresponded roughly to the percentage of votes cast for it. This system may have served the cause of accurate representation of the electorate, but it had other, very serious defects.

It removed the electoral process very far from the voter, who could choose only between lists of candidates set by the various parties. He could not favor one person over another but had to vote for a given bloc of names. Although preferential voting was later added to this system, it proved to be without practical significance, and the voter still had no deputy whom he could regard as "his" representative and to whom he could write his grievances, for his district was represented by several people of divergent political views. In choosing the party for which he cast his ballot, the voter had to decide between abstract party programs (none of which could ever be realized as long as coalition governments were the order of the day). Most serious of all, the system established and strengthened the rule of party bureaucracies which actually decided what candidate should be on what list and in what place,[28] with the result that the candidates were beholden to their party leaders rather than to the voters. At the same time, proportional representation encouraged a multiplicity of parties and splinter groups whose presence in the National Assembly made stable government impossible.

By 1951 the political situation in France had deteriorated to such a degree that the possibility of "a negative majority," i.e., of Communists and Gaullists (RPF) equally opposed to the government, became very real. This would have meant that government itself would have become impossible, for the two antigovernment groups, although able to bring a government down, could not have joined to establish a government of their own. In this situation, the parliament adopted a new electoral law which preserved the essential features of proportional representation but added a possibility of coupled lists (*apparentement*) under which several parties could couple their lists and corner all the seats in a given department if the

---

[28] Those elected were taken from the top of the respective parties' lists. Hence, an unfavorable position on the list precluded election. Sometimes party leaders placed people, especially women, on the list to attract voters but without giving those candidates a real chance.

total number of votes cast for their combined lists constituted a majority.[29] Even where they did not achieve a majority, the coupled lists won certain advantages. Of course, this system did away with the alleged justice of the proportional system, but in 1951 the coupled-list plan achieved at least its purpose of preventing a negative majority from coming into existence. In 1956, however, the middle-of-the-road parties quarreled and list-coupling arrangements were effective in only a minor number of cases.

The electoral system of the Fourth Republic was never popular and was generally considered incomprehensible and purely artificial. The Fifth Republic, under the executive order of October 13, 1958, returned basically to the much simpler and certainly popular district system of the Third Republic, but with certain modifications. When applied under the Third Republic, it was based, in principle, on the small administrative subdistrict known as the *arrondissement*. The regulation of 1958, however, desired a smaller number of deputies from metropolitan France and was therefore forced to create new electoral districts, larger than the *arrondissement* but smaller than the *département,* which correspond to no other district organization in France. Otherwise the system is quite simple. Each electoral district elects one deputy to the National Assembly, and no person may be a candidate in more than one district. Each candidate must deposit the sum of 1,000 francs (roughly $200), which is forfeit unless he obtains at least 5 percent of the votes in the district. Elections are held in two stages: on the first run, a candidate is declared elected if he obtains a majority (50 percent plus one) of all the votes cast. This, however, is not often the case in a country which has so many political parties. Hence a runoff election is held a week later, in which no one may be a candidate who has not already won at least 5 percent of the votes on the first ballot. On the second ballot, a plurality elects. However, between the first and the second ballots, it is customary for candidates with little chance of victory to "desist" and recommend that their supporters vote for other candidates still in the race whose political views may be relatively close to their own. As a result, the candidates who win a plurality on the second ballot are usually the beneficiaries of formal or informal coalitions which may have been formed before or after the first ballot was taken.

One might ask why the French have again adopted a two-ballot system and not the single-ballot Anglo-American system. The answer is that in a country of many political parties, the single ballot would render highly unrepresentative results, as pluralities of 15 to 25 percent of the vote would frequently be sufficient to elect a deputy. Moreover, the Communists, who are the largest single party in France, might well elect a majority of the deputies. Of course, it might be argued that the Anglo-American system discourages a multitude of parties and that its institution in France might have tended to simplify the political picture there. However, such

---

[29] Robert G. Neumann, "The Struggle for Electoral Reform in France," *American Political Science Review,* Vol. 55 (1951), pp. 741–755.

a result is by no means a foregone conclusion, and the risk of instituting it was much too great. The advantage of the present French system is that it is relatively simple and close to the voter. It does not tend to simplify the panorama of political parties, since even small groups often have a good chance for a seat or for the exercise of political power in the juggling of electoral coalitions between the first and second ballot. But the results obtained can be extremely bizarre. For instance, if we take the figures of the second ballot in the 1962 elections,[30] we find the Communists with 21.3 percent of the vote winning 41 seats, while the UNR with a little less than twice as many votes (40.5 percent) obtained over five times as many seats, namely 229. The Socialists, with 15.2 percent, won more than the Communists also, 65 seats.

Article 24 of the 1958 Constitution provides that the Senate shall be elected indirectly and that it shall ensure the representation of the territorial units of the Republic as well as of Frenchmen living abroad. This is spelled out in the following manner: there are now altogether 268 senators, of whom 255 come from metropolitan France, 7 from the pre-Revolutionary overseas possessions of Guadeloupe, Guiana, Martinique, and Réunion, and 6 represent French citizens abroad. In France and in the so-called "old" possessions, each *département* forms an electoral college which is composed of the following persons: (1) all the deputies of the National Assembly elected from that *département,* (2) all the members of the *département's* general council, (3) the delegates of the municipal councils and their alternates. In townships (*communes*) of less than 9,000 inhabitants, electors are chosen by the municipal councils according to a certain ratio to the number of municipal councilors who in turn follow, in their number, a fixed ratio to the town's population. Thus municipal councils of between 9 and 11 members elect 1 elector; of 13 members, 2, going up to 15 electors for towns of 23 councilors. In townships numbering 9,000 to 30,000 inhabitants all municipal councilors are automatically electors; in towns of more than 30,000 inhabitants, 1 delegate in addition to the members of the municipal councils is elected for every 1,000 inhabitants in excess of 30,000.

Départements of 154,000 inhabitants or less are entitled to one senator; all others have one for every 250,000 additional inhabitants. In *départements* entitled to five or more senators, the electoral college elects them under proportional representation. In *départements* of lesser size, a majority is required for election; if no candidate achieves a majority, there is a runoff election. French citizens abroad vote by mail ballot and according to proportional representation.

The organization of the French parliament

Most bicameral legislatures of the world meet in two chambers of the same large building. Not so in France. The National Assembly meets in the sprawling Bourbon Palace, which is situated on the Quai d'Orsay, next door to the Ministry

---

[30] Metropolitan France only.

of Foreign Affairs and overlooking the Seine and the magnificent Place de la Concorde. The Senate is located approximately 1½ miles away in the smaller but lovelier and far more elegant Luxembourg Palace.

The immunities of French legislators go beyond those accorded to their American and British counterparts. They may not be prosecuted or held in any way responsible or answerable for the opinions they express or the votes they cast in the exercise of their duties (Art. 26). Beyond that, they may not be arrested or held for even minor offenses without the authorization of the house to which they belong or, if that house is not in session, without the permission of its officers (*Bureau*). If the house to which the legislator belongs is in session, he may be arrested only *flagrante delicto* (in the very act of committing the crime); if the house is not in session, he may be arrested either *in flagranie* or if his arrest or prosecution had previously been authorized.

In all cases, the detention or prosecution of a member of parliament must be suspended on demand of the chamber of which he is a member.

There is, however, a difference between the first-mentioned immunity (*irresponsabilité*), not being answerable for acts committed in line of duty, and the second category (*inviolabilité*), freedom from criminal pursuit. The former is substantive, and the deputy or senator can never be prosecuted for those acts; the second is procedural, which means that he may be prosecuted after his legislative term expires or if the house to which he belongs lifts his immunity.

It is clear that immunities of this kind are necessary for the proper exercise of legislative functions. However, they have sometimes been abused in France, especially by members of parliament who are newspapermen and who contrive to escape the consequences of a violation of the press law or the law of criminal libel because of their parliamentary status. On the whole, parliament has been disinclined to allow criminal prosecution of its members.[31]

In the life span of the National Assembly, three periods may be distinguished. The legislative term (*legislature*) lasts from the first meeting of a duly elected assembly until its dissolution; this term is five years unless parliament is dissolved earlier by the President of the Republic under the provision of Article 12. Then there are the sessions (*sessions*), which denote the period during a given year (not calendar year) when the Assembly is conducting its business, and the actual meeting (*séance*), which refers to a period of hours during which the Assembly is actually, physically, meeting.

Under the Third and Fourth Republics, sessions often lasted quite a long time, although in 1954 the Premier was given the power, with the consent of the Council of Ministers, to declare closed a session which had lasted at least seven months.

Under the Constitution of 1958, the duration of parliamentary sessions is drastically curtailed. Now there are only two regular sessions per year. The first

[31] This is true even when a member wished to be tried in order to clear himself of charges against him.

begins on the first Tuesday of October and must end on the third Friday of December. The second session opens on the last Tuesday of April and may not last longer than three months. Thus parliament may not be in ordinary session for more than a bit above five months in any parliamentary year (Art. 28). However, parliament may be convened in special session at the request of the Prime Minister or of the absolute majority of all the members of the National Assembly. Such a special session of parliament will then consider an agenda which has been determined in advance and on the basis of which the special session has been called. When this takes place at the request of the Prime Minister, other items may presumably be discussed as well. If the session was called at the request of the National Assembly majority, it must close when the predetermined agenda is exhausted, but in any case no more than twelve days from the date of its first meeting.[32] After this special session is closed, only the Prime Minister may ask for another to meet any earlier than one month thereafter.

In each house, the management of the sessions, as well as the housekeeping duties, is carried on by a group of elected officials, called the *Bureau*. Each *Bureau* is composed of a president (speaker) and several vice presidents, secretaries, and certain other administrators known as questors (*questeurs*). The presidents of both houses are elected by majority vote, and the other officers are elected upon an informal agreement reached by the different parties. If no agreement is possible, plurality prevails.

In contrast to the short life span of French governments under the Third and Fourth Republics, the presidencies of the two houses of parliament have generally been long-term offices. Edouard Herriot, the grand old man of French politics under both Republics, was president of the National Assembly from 1946 to 1954. After his resignation the National Assembly reverted to its old habit of electing a presiding officer for each session; his personality and viewpoint were somewhat representative of the prevailing political tendencies in the house. For the remainder of the Fourth Republic, the National Assembly was presided over by André le Troquer (Socialist), with the exception of one session when Pierre Schneiter (MRP) was in the chair. The election of Jacques Chaban-Delmas (UNR) as president of the first and second parliaments of the Fifth Republic started a new trend, as presiding officers are now elected for the entire legislative period.

In the Senate, consistency was even greater. Since the death of the first president of the Senate (at that time called the Council of the Republic), Champetier de Ribes, in 1947, Gaston Monnerville, a senator from French Guiana, presided over the Senate under both the Fourth and Fifth Republics.

There are six vice presidents, fourteen secretaries, and three questors, but either house may change the number of its officers.[33]

---

[32] Special sessions which have been called at the request of the Prime Minister may presumably be kept in session continuously until a regular session starts.
[33] Normally these officers have been distributed proportionately to the respective parties' strength, except for the Communist party which often received less. In the first National Assembly of the Fifth Republic, the Communists were too weak to elect officers.

The *Bureau* of each chamber is elected for one session. Consequently, when a new session opens, technically it has no presiding officer of its own, since the preceding officers' terms have expired. A session is therefore opened by the so-called "bureau of age" (*Bureau d'Age*), which means that the oldest deputy or senator (in age, not length of service) presides and the youngest serves as secretary. The "age" president has only two functions to perform: he makes a speech and he presides over the election of the permanent *Bureau*.

According to protocol, the president of the National Assembly ranks as the second man in the country, second only to the President of the Republic. The president of the Senate ranks third. Each president presides over the meetings of his house unless he asks one of the vice presidents to replace him temporarily. He watches over the observation of rules and has some disciplinary power, which goes as far as the temporary exclusion of a deputy or senator, but the presidents of the National Assembly and of the Council of the Republic of the Fourth Republic had neither the strong control of the Speaker of the British House of Commons nor the political influence of the Speaker of the United States House of Representatives. There are few indications that this situation is basically changing.

Parliamentary committees (*Commissions*)

The French parliaments of the Third and Fourth Republics functioned with an elaborate committee structure through which passed all legislation. In that they resembled the Congress of the United States and the parliament of Germany rather than the British Parliament. This committee system became firmly established in the Third Republic, and the Constitution of 1946 actually provided that legislation had to be discussed in the committees of the National Assembly before being enacted. Committees were organized, as in the United States, according to the subject matter with which they dealt. They were divided into permanent general committees (*Commissions générales*)[34] and special committees (*Commissions spéciales*). At the end of the Fourth Republic there were nineteen permanent (standing) committees in each house of parliament. In the National Assembly each committee had forty-four members, elected according to proportional representation of party groups.

To streamline parliament's work and probably further to curb its powers, or at least make it harder for parliament to obstruct and delay, the Constitution of 1958 reduced the number of permanent (standing) committees to six in each house. It is, however, highly questionable whether this reduction will serve any useful purpose. The new committees have now become unmanageable giants of between 64 and 120 members each so that, in effect, they must meet as subcommittees, and this in a way restores the previous situation.

The members of committees are still elected according to the proportional representation of party groups, but in effect leaders of the various parties them-

[34] But they were still referred to under the name by which they were known in the Third Republic, *grandes commissions permanentes*.

selves agree upon the number of seats to be allocated to each one and submit to the presiding officer a combined list of nominations. This is then put into effect unless at least fifty deputies object; in that case, a vote is taken. If a single vacancy occurs on a committee, the party to which the former incumbent belonged simply nominates his successor, who is then duly appointed.

Permanent committees are appointed at the beginning of each legislative term for the following two years and are reappointed each succeeding year. Each committee has a *bureau* composed of the president, two vice presidents, and two secretaries. The finance committee of the National Assembly also has a general reporter (*rapporteur général*). Moreover, for each question or bill before a committee, a special reporter (*rapporteur*) is appointed by the committee. All committee officers are members of the committee concerned. Committee meetings are not generally open to the public, but a cabinet minister may attend any of them, and he must be heard. Similarly, but less frequently, other interested persons may be given an opportunity to appear, although hearings of the American type are not customary.

Theoretically it is the purpose of the committees to discuss legislation and to prepare bills for final submission to the full house. However, the permanent (standing) committees also keep a close watch over the government departments which correspond to their field of specialization. Under the Third and Fourth Republics, these committees had great power because of the instability of governments and their small margin of parliamentary majority. Government bills quite often were badly mauled in committee and sometimes were so altered that the government found itself constrained to oppose the bill when it reached the floor.

Since failure to pass an important bill in the National Assembly was sometimes regarded by a cabinet as a vote of nonconfidence, a hostile committee could thus be instrumental in producing a cabinet crisis. The key role in this and other committee affairs was often played by the reporter who was in charge of guiding the bill through the committee, reporting it out to the full National Assembly, and shepherding it through its adoption or rejection on the floor. In the ensuing debate, the reporter constituted a focal point, and his ability, good will, or malevolence had a decisive bearing on the bill's fate. Frequently the personality of the reporter selected for a particularly crucial bill gave a hint about its eventual fate.

The committees of the parliament under the Fifth Republic share the general decline of parliamentary power. Because of this decline it is likely that the main struggle of parliament for such control over governmental action as it may be able to preserve will shift from the floor of parliament to the committee rooms. As we have seen, frontal assault on a government's existence is now much more difficult. The committees, however, retain considerable opportunity for delay and frustration of governmental action. In this connection, it must be considered a minor parliamentary victory to have forced upon the government the rule under which parliamentary committees may meet even though the house in question is not in session. Although this, like other rules, is temporary, an old and much-tested French proverb says that "nothing lasts as long as temporary solutions."

All committees, whether permanent or special, may conduct investigations. If part of an investigation is to take place outside the premises of the National Assembly, a special authorization from the Assembly is needed (*pouvoir d'enquête*). If a committee wishes to subpoena witnesses, it must obtain even more extensive authorization from the Assembly. But in that case it can not only subpoena witnesses, it can also cause them to be punished for refusing to answer, for refusing to take the oath, for perjury, or for bribing a witness.[35] Although parliamentary investigations have occurred in France, especially in cases of scandals and suspected corruption, they have never been undertaken on the scale common in the United States. This is natural because, in a parliamentary regime like that of France, even under the Fifth Republic, a deputy can force a minister to divulge facts by using the implied threat of overthrowing the government. Moreover, the United States is the only country where successful criminal prosecution or investigation is traditionally a steppingstone to political success.

Legislation

The Constitution of the Fifth Republic groups subjects for legislation into three basic categories. The first comprises those subjects where parliament has the right of full and detailed legislation. It is outlined in Article 34 and includes civil rights and the obligations of national defense; nationality; legal capacity of persons; marriage contracts, inheritance, and gifts; criminal law and criminal procedure; as well as the establishment of the judicial system and the status of judges, taxation and currency, electoral system of parliament and local assemblies, the establishment of public institutions, the fundamental rights of civil and military persons, and nationalization and eminent domain.

A second category includes subjects on which parliament shall not legislate in detail but merely determine the fundamental principles. This group comprises the general organization of national defense, local administration, education, property rights and civil law, labor legislation, and social security. Parliament alone may declare war. Martial law may be decreed by the government but it may be prolonged beyond twelve days only upon an authorization by parliament (Art. 36).

Thirdly, some subjects not listed above may be dealt with by executive order (Art. 37). Should parliament invade these residual powers of the government, such legislation may be altered by executive order of the government, but only after consultation with the Council of State, and only after the Constitutional Council has ruled that the legislation concerned is of a kind which the constitution has reserved to executive regulation. In other words, if parliament goes beyond its specific and enumerated powers, especially as listed in Article 34, the government may modify or set aside such legislation after a ruling by the Constitutional Council.

In addition, the government may ask parliament for authority to rule by de-

---

[35] These rules were first established in 1914. Norman L. Stamps, "A Comparative Study of Legislative Investigations: England, France, and Weimar Germany," *Journal of Politics,* Vol. XIV (1952), pp. 592–615.

cree power for a limited period. If that is granted, decrees may establish rules for subject matter otherwise reserved to legislation. After the decree-making power is granted, decrees resulting therefrom shall be enacted in a meeting of the cabinet and after consultation with the Council of State but without need for its consent. After a certain period, which must be established in the enabling act granting the decree-making power of the government, such decree laws must be submitted to parliamentary ratification and become null and void if they are not. However, after the expiration of the period for which the decree power has been granted, parliament may change or amend the laws passed under that power only in so far as they fall into the normal legislative power of parliament.

This peculiar provision of Article 38 highlights the controversial nature of the right to rule by decree, i.e., delegated legislation. The history of the Third Republic, especially after the First World War, is replete with instances in which the government did by decree what would ordinarily have been done by law. The manner in which parliament authorized or tolerated these decree laws differed; the practice was regarded with suspicion, but it existed and flourished. In fact, any government which found itself confronted by a crisis—and few French governments did not— usually asked for some sort of decree powers and often resigned when they were refused. The parties which were in control of the Constituent Assembly in 1945 and 1946 felt that in some mystical way these decree powers held a measure of responsibility for the defeat of France, although other observers might have opined that not the strength but rather the weakness of French governments was to blame. At any rate, the Constitution of 1946 stipulated in Article 13 that the National Assembly could not delegate its right to enact legislation.

However, subsequent developments made it quite clear that delegated legislation and decree laws were not dead in France. French judicial doctrine has always distinguished between legislative power, which belongs to parliament, and regulatory power, which belongs to the executive. The latter could be called derivative, i.e., derived from law. This derivation could be direct, as when the law requires or permits the executive to do certain things; or it might be indirect or implied in the executive's general obligation to see that the laws are faithfully executed and that they attain their objectives.

Through this regulatory power the back door (or was it the front door?) was opened to new decree laws. In two well-known cases, in 1948 and 1951, the government received extensive power by means of that delegated legislation which was presumably forbidden by the Constitution of 1946. Hence, Article 38 of the Constitution of 1958 revives what has never been actually dead.

The right to initiate legislation belongs to the members of the cabinet and to all members of both houses of parliament. Government bills must first be discussed in the cabinet, and the Council of State must be consulted. Finance bills must first be submitted to the National Assembly. However, like the Constitution of 1946, that of 1958 stipulates (Art. 40) that bills and amendments introduced by members of parliament shall not be considered when their adoption would result in either a diminution of public financial resources or the creation or increase of public expenditures.

Bills introduced by a member of the cabinet are called law projects (*projets de loi*); bills introduced by a private member of either house are called law proposals (*propositions de loi*). As in all modern states, however, the great bulk of legislation is introduced by the government, directly or indirectly.

A bill is first sent to the *Bureau* of the house in which it is introduced; sometimes it is also submitted in the course of a regular meeting. In either case, it is immediately referred to the appropriate committee in printed form, and consists of a brief explanation of what it is supposed to achieve (*exposé des motives*) as well as the proposed text itself. Under the Constitution of 1958 (Art. 43), the government may demand that the bill be sent to a special committee, to be established for that special purpose, rather than to one of the permanent (standing) committees. This request must be honored (Art. 43).

The committee then studies and debates the bill in the manner stated above. It must report to the house to which it belongs within three months of the time that the original bill was distributed, and in some instances, within a shorter period. In appropriate cases, bills are referred by the committee to the Economic and Social Council or to the Senate of the Community[36] for an advisory opinion.

Shortly after the bill is reported out of committee, it is submitted to general discussion on the floor. The bill may be killed at this stage, either by moving the previous question or, if the committee has reported negatively, by accepting that report. Bills may also be referred back to committee for further study. Members of parliament and of the government have the right to propose amendments. However, after the debate has opened, the government may oppose the examination of any amendment which has not previously been submitted to committee (Art. 44). On the other hand, the government has an advantage in pushing its own amendments. It may demand that the house vote on the entire bill or a part thereof in one motion, leaving aside only the amendment proposed or accepted by the government. Government may then presumably concentrate its entire energies on getting those amendments accepted.

After the general discussion, the National Assembly or the Senate discusses the bill article by article. At this stage, articles may be removed or amended, subject to the reservations of Article 44 mentioned above. Even an entirely new bill may be proposed as an amendment, although this would seem to be difficult under the new Constitution. After this phase, there may be reference back to committee for consolidation and a second deliberation on the floor. Before the bill finally leaves the floor, a vote is taken on it.

This entire procedure is termed "first reading." After having passed one house on first reading, the bill is sent to the other house with a view toward an identical text being adopted. If that succeeds, the bill is then sent to the government and is

[36] See further discussion in this chapter.

promulgated by the President of the Republic within fifteen days except, of course, where he makes use of his suspensive veto or where parliament has gone beyond its enumerated powers or where the constitutionality of the law is being examined by the Constitutional Council.[37]

When the two houses disagree, the bill is returned to both for a "second reading," unless the government has declared the matter officially urgent. If the second reading produces no agreement, or after the first reading in urgent cases, the Prime Minister has the right to demand the meeting of a conference committee composed of an equal number from both houses. The text which that committee reports out may then be submitted by the government for the approval of both houses. No amendment is permitted to the conference committee's version of the bill, except by agreement with the government.

If the conference committee fails to agree on a text, or if a text is reported out but is not approved by the two houses, the government may ask for yet another reading by both houses; if there is still no agreement, it may ask the National Assembly to rule with finality. In this case, the National Assembly may reconsider either the text prepared by the conference committee or a later text adopted by the National Assembly, or it may consider any of the amendments adopted by the Senate.

A comparison between the Constitutions of 1946 and 1958 reveals a number of significant differences. The original version of the 1946 Constitution had relegated the Council of the Republic to a role without significance, what the French call a *quantité negligeable*. The reform of 1954 did enhance the stature of the second house, but it was still a very secondary chamber. The Constitution of 1958 grants the two houses virtual equality. No longer is the Senate obliged to confine its voting of laws to a narrow time limit or to be considered as having given its consent just by nonaction. It is true, as we have seen, that Article 45 gives the National Assembly the possibility of breaking a deadlock and ruling with finality. But the National Assembly can do so only upon demand of the government and not upon its own initiative. If, for instance, the government opposes a bill and wins the support of the Senate, the bill is effectively blocked. We have already seen that the method of electing the President of the Republic is quite similar to that of electing the Senate. Political agreement between the majority of the Senate and the President is therefore somewhat more likely than between the President and the majority of the National Assembly. This fact, too, enhances the power of the already powerful Senate.

In various sections, the Constitution provides that certain types of legislation must be adopted as "organic laws." This procedure is only slightly different from that used for ordinary legislation. An "organic bill" may be deliberated and voted on only after a period of fifteen days following its introduction. Otherwise, the legislative procedure described above will be followed. But if there is no agreement

---

[37] See under "The Constitutional Council," later in this chapter.

between the houses, and the National Assembly rules with finality as described above, it must do so by an absolute majority of its members, whether present or not. When an organic law deals with the functions of the Senate, it must be passed by both houses in an identical manner. That means that if one house were to pass it with an absolute majority, the other house would have to do the same. All organic laws are automatically submitted to the Constitutional Council for an examination of their constitutionality.

Finance Bills. Proposals concerning revenues and expenditures may be initiated by any deputy. For the most part, such proposals originate with the government and find their most important expression in the annual budget. This budget is prepared and submitted to the National Assembly by the Minister of Finance. In past years, a separate Minister of the Budget has at times taken principal responsibility, but the innovation seems to have been discontinued. Under the Fourth Republic, one of the system's inconveniences lay in the fact that, due to the short life expectancy of a government, the minister who prepared the budget was hardly ever the same one who had to carry it out. In fact, it came to be almost a rule that the minister who prepared the budget was no longer in office when it was to be presented to the National Assembly. It is to be hoped that the greater longevity of governments expected of the Fifth Republic will eliminate that condition.

After the budget has been submitted to the National Assembly, it is referred to the finance committee for consideration. This elevates the finance committee over all other committees. The others are usually concerned with the affairs of a single government department or a group of functions, but the finance committee is concerned with appropriations for, and therefore the management of, all ministries whose representatives are heard as their respective items come up for consideration. The president and general reporter of the finance committee are therefore exceptionally powerful persons who in time have often become Ministers of Finance and Prime Ministers themselves.

The budget is reported out by the general reporter of the finance committee who, in his initial speech on the floor of the Assembly, deals primarily with the financial situation rather than with specific items. These details are presented later by several special reporters appointed by the finance committee.

General discussion of a bill begins right after the presentation by the general reporter. Then the budget is discussed, ministry by ministry, and chapter by chapter. Each chapter is voted on separately. The debate is somewhat curtailed; no deputy may speak more than twice on any one chapter unless replying to a minister. Deputies may propose amendments in the form of separate bills, but as we have seen, the Constitution forbids the moving of amendments to the finance bill itself when such amendments would create new expenditures or curtail revenues. In practice, under the Constitutions of both the Fourth and Fifth Republics, such amendments are proposed, but the government and the finance committee retain the right to separate such amendments from the budget, a demand which must be met. In that case, the amendment becomes a separate bill which goes to the finance committee and the floor in the usual manner. This is to prevent the urgency of passing the budget from being used for the hasty adoption of ill-considered amendments. Yet a deputy who wishes to make an amendment and have it considered together with the budget may transmit it to the finance committee before the finance bill is reported out. In that case, it will be discussed by the committee in connection with the budget. There is no limit to a deputy's right to propose an increase of revenues, except the general limitation on amendments which was discussed above.

If the National Assembly fails to reach a decision on a finance bill on first reading and within a time limit of forty days after the bill has been submitted, the government shall refer it to the Senate, which must rule within a time limit of fifteen days. Otherwise the procedure for ordinary legislation as set out in Article 45 shall be followed. If parliament (both houses) fails to reach a decision within seventy days, the bill's provisions may be put into effect by an executive order. In that case, the government need not simply enact by executive decree the entire finance bill but may enforce certain provisions provided they were contained in the original bill.

If a finance bill which establishes the revenues and expenditures for a given fiscal year has been submitted to the National Assembly too late to be promulgated before the beginning of that fiscal year, the government shall urgently request parliament for an authorization to collect the taxes and shall make available, by executive order, the funds necessary to meet government commitments already voted.

The time limits mentioned above do not prevail when parliament is not in session.

This article (Art. 47) again puts parliament under pressure, not only because of the time limit but because a government can, with the support of the Senate, prevent the National Assembly from demolishing its fiscal policies.

Relationship between parliament and government

Parliament, especially the National Assembly, exercises both direct and indirect control over the Prime Minister and his cabinet. It does not exercise any control over the powerful President of the Republic, except to the extent of being able to refuse its support to certain measures. As we have seen, even that is not always possible. Otherwise it is conceivable that parliament could prove itself so obstreperous as to make a President's life impossible and force him to resign. This has happened with weak Presidents of the Third and Fourth Republics, like Jules Grévy and Alexandre Millerand.

We have seen that the investiture procedure of the Prime Minister and his colleagues, which the Fourth Republic found so burdensome, has been abolished by the Constitution of 1958. However, old parliamentary habits do not die easily. The first Prime Minister of the Fifth Republic, Michel Debré, did ask for a vote of confidence from the National Assembly after he had explained the program of his government. It is of course a fact that a government could not last long against a hostile majority in the National Assembly, but a request for a specific vote of confidence is a throwback to the ingrained habits of the Fourth Republic.

In addition to the interpellations, a potent weapon already discussed, the Constitution of the Fourth Republic knew both "written" and "oral" questions, terms which were misleading, for even the "oral" questions were written. Each of the so-called "written" questions was printed immediately after presentation, and the minister to whom it was directed had a month's time to reply. He might ask for an extension or he might refuse to answer, but only by claiming that an answer might prejudice the public interest. The question, together with the answer, was published again in the verbatim report of the National Assembly. Written questions were and are used a good deal, but it is sometimes difficult to obtain an answer. Moreover, most of them deal with matters of special interest to the deputy or to his particular constituents.

The "oral" question was more important. It was presented to the presiding officer in writing, but the minister answered orally (hence the name), in principle within a week. Under the procedure of the parliament of the Fourth Republic, only five minutes each were allowed to the minister and his questioner, and no other deputy was allowed to speak. Only one day a month was reserved for oral questions, and that procedure did not allow for the lively exchange of views associated with the question period in the British Parliament. Hence the oral question was not used extensively under the Fourth Republic.

The rules for the parliament of the Fifth Republic abolish the right of interpellation. But there is a chance that it may have reentered the Palais Bourbon by the back door, for the oral question has now become more elaborate. And, like the prior interpellation but unlike the prior oral question, it can now provoke a general debate. Here, however, the similarity stops. If a deputy wishes to attach a motion of censure to the oral question, he must do so in the difficult manner of Article 49 which has already been discussed.[38] But could the condition of the Fourth Republic be recreated, under which a motion for ending the debate on the interpellation became a quasi-vote of confidence? If the governments of the Fifth Republic remain determined to prevent it, probably not. The governments of the Fourth Republic were constantly dependent on the Assembly, and collapsed easily at the first indication of parliamentary displeasure. If the Constitution of the Fifth Republic is carried out in spirit and in letter, its governments ought to be less sensitive and hence more solid. The answer cannot yet be given. It will depend on the political development of the Fifth Republic rather than on the legal interpretation of its constitutional text.

We have already seen[39] that the Constitution of 1958 makes it difficult to

[38] See "The Prime Minister and the Cabinet," earlier in this chapter.
[39] *Ibid.*

bring the government down by either a motion of censure or a vote of no confidence. Together with other powers of the executive which we have already mentioned, such as the power of dissolution, the power of referendum, the extensive possibilities of ruling by executive decree, the opportunity to stymie the work of the National Assembly with aid from the Senate, that hampering of censure gives the executive branch of the government the preponderance of power in the Fifth French Republic. Nevertheless, the National Assembly is not exactly taking all this lying down. The government draft for parliamentary rules, which the UNR worked out for presentation in January, 1958, faced a tough debate. A number of modifications had to be accepted. The size of the committees and their ability to meet even when the assemblies are not in session, the use of the oral question, the quasi-investiture to which Prime Minister Debré submitted himself, all indicate that there is still a good deal of fight in the parliament.

In many respects the political situation produced by the elections of 1958 and 1962 created an unusual situation. Normally, on the basis of tradition and inclination, one would have expected the greatly decimated left to be the champion of parliamentary power whereas the right might have been expected to be more inclined to sustain the equality of the executive. But an odd situation developed early in the first term of the first parliament of the Fifth Republic. No one who had really studied General de Gaulle's pronouncements and record should have been surprised that on the Algerian question he moved more and more in a direction which the moderate left approved but which alarmed rightist elements. The left felt less inclined to assault the executive supremacy which the 1958 Constitution established, but a number of emphatic, but newly discovered champions of parliamentarism rose among the disgruntled right. This situation split the right, which had a majority in the National Assembly. Hence a combination of leftists and dissatisfied rightists again was in a position to cause the government trouble and succeeded in doing so in 1962. But it was kept in check by the expression of overwhelming popular approval in favor of President de Gaulle. In that situation, executive supremacy, although not unchallenged, had nevertheless an excellent chance to prevail and to become the pattern for the government of the Fifth Republic.

The presidential elections of 1965 and the parliamentary elections of 1967 have cast some doubt on this situation. Nevertheless, the experience with the 1958 Constitution has been, on the whole, a positive one, and even if the opposition parties become able to win their way back to the center of the stage, stronger executive power than was known under the Fourth Republic is likely to prevail, whoever may eventually reside in the Elysée Palace.

Under De Gaulle, and certainly until 1967, parliament has led a relatively subdued life and has often failed to use properly all the constitutional means at its disposal to assert itself. But there is reason to believe that this will not always remain so. The party system, although battered and bruised, has almost certainly survived. Nor is it at all likely that such overwhelming domination as has been at the disposal of De Gaulle will be available to his successors. Under these circumstances, parliament is likely, once again, to become the arena in which the post-Gaullist regime will undergo its inevitable transformations.

D. THE JUDICIARY

The administration of justice in Continental Europe is dominated by the tradition and the system of the Roman law. This is especially true of France, a country which for the most part was once under Roman domination. Gaul was more quickly Romanized than many other provinces. A number of its inhabitants received Roman citizenship early, and the rest were elevated to that state of distinction by the edict of Caracalla in A.D. 212. The old Gallic legal institutions were quickly dropped, and virtually no trace of them remains except in the research work of legal historians.

In the Middle Ages, feudal customs and conventions took their place beside the tradition of the Roman law, sometimes even submerging the latter. Still, Roman law was known and avidly studied, and large parts of it were retained in the canon law, the law of the Roman Catholic Church. As the great divergence of local and customary law created increasing difficulties for the administration of justice, attempts were made to record customary law in codified forms which received royal sanction and were eventually undertaken by royal command. But this did not mean legal unification, as the codified rules of law showed significant variations from region to region.

On top of these various layers of law came an increasing number of royal decrees which were registered by the various regional courts, known as *parlements*. Some bold *parlements,* especially that of Paris, even refused to register certain ordinances.[40] However, as a rule, royal decrees were registered as a matter of course.[41]

The Revolution put an end to this confused and overlapping system. In 1791 and 1795 the first Penal Code and Code of Criminal Procedure were enacted. But it was only under the rule of Napoleon and under his active furtherance that the crowning edifice, the Civil Code, was finally published in 1804, followed in 1807 by a Code of Civil Procedure. Other codes were enacted subsequently. In all of them, the predominant influence of Roman law is evident. These codes have of course been revised and amended, yet in their principal structure they still stand today, not only as the living law of France, but also as that of numerous other countries which have since adopted them.[42] The spirit of the great Corsican with whom they are

---

[40] Sometimes the king forced the *parlement* to register the edict. In that case the *parlement* indicated this fact by adding to the formula the words *de expresso mandato regis, pluries facto.*
[41] But the habit of consulting *parlement* grew over the years and occasionally had a restraining influence on royal absolutism (Jean Brissaud, *A History of French Public Law* [trans. by J. W. Garner], Boston, 1915, p. 447). Needless to say, the French *parlements* never approximated the significance of the English Parliament.
[42] Some countries, like Egypt, simply translated the codes for their own use.

forever identified as the Code Napoléon has found more endurance there than in most of his more glittering military conquests.

The impact of Roman law

The imprint of Roman law is firmly stamped on the whole edifice of French law and justice. Its watchwords are symmetry, unity, and authority. The French codes are well-balanced pieces of jurisprudential art, utterly systematic and conveniently accessible. In each field, the particular code germane to that subject, the amendments thereof, and the commentaries thereto, are the last and reasonably complete word on the subject. The student need not dig his way through tome after tome of cases and decisions. The law, as embodied in the codes, is clear and easily available. Moreover, only one system of law prevails from one corner of the country to the other. But the law so conceived is not the result of gradual social growth. It is the expression of the will of the state, which lays down in final and authoritative manner what the relationships shall be between citizens and between them and the state. This type of paternalism naturally leaves little room for the judge, who becomes merely the expositor of code and statute. It is true that precedent, while officially nonbinding, actually exists, for a judge who is habitually overruled by an appellate authority will find his path to promotion a rocky one. But precedent has a very much smaller scope in the French system than in its English and American counterparts. Moreover, the judge is not regarded as an independent arbiter between the parties to the suit or between the state and the individual; he is a part of the machinery of the state, though protected from direct political interference by the customary privileges and immunities.

Because the knowledge and the administration of the law are not contingent on a long and arduous study of the case material, as is the case in the English-speaking world, judges are not selected from the bar but choose their career from the very beginning of their law studies. This system, which is current in Continental Europe, produces judges who are well trained in the mechanical rules of law and procedure and who can discharge their duties competently and with reasonable dispatch. But the specialist-judge who grows up in this rarefied professional atmosphere is not likely to become a statesman of the bench of the caliber of John Marshall or Lord Coke. He sticks rather narrowly to the interpretation of statutory provisions and never assumes the social significance and the majesty of the Anglo-American judge. For these reasons, social and economic changes are not readily reflected in judicial opinions. Such changes must come from the legislature, not from the bench. Consequently the French system is generally a good deal more rigid than the common-law approach. But this is not true of the procedure in court.

In order to broaden the background and experiences of judges, a decree of January 8, 1959, created a National Center of Judicial Studies (*Centre national d'Études judiciares*) through which all future members of the bench would have to pass. It was designed to do for the judges what the National School of Administration did for civil servants. The students of this Center, who are known as "attachés of justice" (*attachés de la justice*), are chosen by competitive examinations from among the advanced students at the law schools and those members of the civil service who have had legal training. The attachés receive a salary (like the students at the National School of Administration) and their studies are designed to broaden their understanding of social and cultural factors which may affect their future judicial decisions.

It will of course be many years before the impact of the Center of Judicial Studies on the judiciary will be fully felt, but judging from the experience of the National School of Administration, it is likely to have excellent results.

Appointment of judges

During the Third Republic, judges were in actual practice appointed by the Minister of Justice. This interfered with the independence of judges, because unpopular or obstreperous judges could be denied promotion and could, in some cases, be left in some undesirable provincial or overseas spot until they went to seed. The Constitution of 1946 attempted to remedy this by creating the Superior Council of the Judiciary. This Council was composed of the President of the Republic as chairman; the Minister of Justice (called "Keeper of the Seal"); six persons elected by the National Assembly but not from among its members; six alternates elected in the same manner; four judges and four alternates representing all categories of the judiciary, who were elected by their colleagues; and two members of the legal profession who were neither judges nor legislators and who were appointed by the President of the Republic together with two alternates.

The competence of the Superior Council extended to three groups of problems: the appointment of judges, the supervision of the judiciary with regard to administrative discipline and independence, and the exercise of the right of pardon.

This system has been largely preserved by the Constitution of 1958. The Superior Council of the Judiciary is again presided over by the President of the Republic, and the Minister of Justice is vice president. Its membership has now been reduced to nine, plus the two persons mentioned above. This Council makes nominations for the judges of the highest court, the Court of Cassation, as well as for the First Presidents of the Courts of Appeal. Other judges are nominated by the Minister of Justice, but the Council may express itself thereon. Of course in all these cases, the President of the Republic makes the final choice, but this right is more theoretical than real. The normal way to enter the judiciary is by competitive examination, and the Council accepts the results thereof. For the promotion of judges there is an administrative procedure within the judicial machine which is also normally followed, and the Council merely nominates those proposed by this process. This means that much less has changed in the appointment and promotion of judges than might be indicated by the Council's creation. It is undeniable that the Minister of Justice remains in a key position. However, the existence and the prerogatives of the Council tend to prevent abuses and the appointments so far made have been of a high order.

Control over disciplinary infractions among the judiciary and over alleged infringements of judicial independence is exercised directly by the Superior Council. It is not bound by any nominations or proposals emanating from other sources. But when it sits as a disciplinary court, judging the actions of a judge, the president of the Court of Cassation presides.

The President of the Republic exercises the right of pardon but the Superior Council of the Judiciary assists him. This means that the Council is consulted but that the President alone exercises this right.

A presidential pardon releases a prisoner from all or part of his punishment but does not wipe out the crime. An amnesty, on the other hand, removes the criminal character of certain acts. The Constitution (Art. 34) stipulates that an amnesty must be enacted by law according to the usual legislative procedure.

The establishment of the Superior Council of the Judiciary constitutes a compromise between those who wanted to see all judges elected (Communists) and those who wanted to return to the old system of presidential appointment, which was in effect appointment by the Minister of Justice. So far the new system seems to be quite satisfactory.

It has been pointed out that French judges are not appointed from the bar but directly from a brief apprenticeship and after the conclusion of their academic law studies, to which has now been added a period of three years at the National Center of Judicial Studies. Newly appointed judges are therefore quite inexperienced, but that is not too serious because the French principle is still *"juge unique, juge inique"* (single judge, unfair judge), and most courts have a panel of judges rather than a single judge. These panels are presided over by an older, more experienced judge. Moreover the ordinary French judges do not have the leeway in interpreting the law which their American and British colleagues enjoy: they stick close to the detailed text of the codes, the laws, and the commentaries. It is frequently argued that a French judge is not burdened by the English common-law rule of *stare decisis* and therefore decides only a single case without setting a precedent for future decisions, but that argument must be regarded with caution. In actual fact the appeals courts see to it that the law is applied with considerable uniformity, and judges whose decisions are erratic will find themselves frequently overruled—which will not help their promotion. In actual practice, therefore, judicial decisions tend to create precedents in fact, if not in theory, though not as much as in the French administrative courts and in the American and British courts. One might perhaps say that the courts of Continental Europe follow precedents more than the Anglo-American lawyers think, while the Anglo-American courts follow precedent somewhat less than the European lawyers believe.

One of the peculiarities of the French judiciary is the fact that it consists of two separate, yet interwoven, groups: the actual judges of the bench, known as the "sitting judiciary" (*magistrature assise*), and the State's Attorney's department, known as the "standing judiciary" (*magistrature debout*). The "sitting" judges have been described. The "standing" ones are more like regular civil servants and form a section of the Ministry of Justice known as the *ministère publique*. They staff the State's Attorney's office, known as the *parquet,* attached to each court. They are not independent but are subject to strict orders of the Ministry of Justice and the advocates-general of their respective (appeals court) districts. They represent the interests of the state in all court actions, but primarily they are prosecutors, filling the functions which in the United States are carried out by district attorneys and equivalent officials. In addition they staff the indictment section (*chambre d'accusation*), which may be compared in function, though not in composition, to the American grand jury.

Although the functions of the "sitting" and "standing" judiciary are widely different by Anglo-American standards, French judges are constantly shifted from one to the other. In many cases this means a promotion. A judge may be transferred to a higher place on the *parquet* and later return to the bench in a superior position. But since members of the *parquet* are not independent but subject to strict instructions from the Ministry of Justice, this system somewhat negates the principle of judicial independence. On the other hand these transfers give members of both sections of the judiciary a varied experience which they would otherwise not have.

This system naturally produces an enormous judiciary, but it is not easy to remedy the situation because the adoption of a single-judge court system would heap responsibilities on the members of the bench for which neither their training nor the legal system has prepared them. On the other hand French courts do fulfill their promise of being easily available and inexpensive. On the whole they function satisfactorily and the judges enjoy a high social prestige which makes up somewhat for their notoriously low pay, especially in the lower brackets. The judiciary was streamlined and reduced in size by a series of sweeping measures which took effect on March 1, 1959.

The ordinary court system

France is covered with a network of numerous courts in order that justice may be easily accessible to all. In view of the uniformity of the legal system, this is altogether to the good, making it possible for a Frenchman to get justice at far lower cost than his British or American counterpart. The organization of the courts is simple enough. However, the proliferation of courts slowed down the process of justice. Hence the reforms of 1958–1959. The lowest-ranking judicial authority was the justice of the peace (*juge de paix*) who, in contrast to his British counterpart, was a salaried official with some judicial experience, though not ordinarily a law degree. Justices of the peace had jurisdiction over civil suits involving very small sums. In certain cases where the amounts under litigation were minimal, their judgment was final. Otherwise an appeal to the next higher court, the Court of First

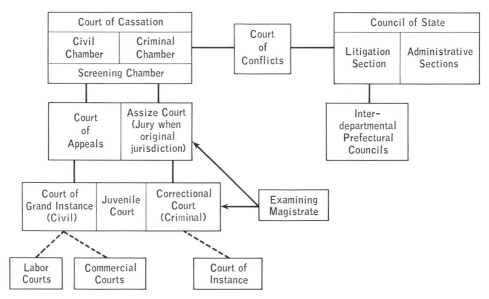

Instance, was permissible. Justices of the peace also had jurisdiction over small infractions (*contraventions*) and minor misdemeanors (*délits*). The principal reason for the institution of the justice of the peace was originally the intention to make him a conciliator who would spare the regular courts some work. However, this institution had become more and more a formality and had retained its original purpose only in those areas where the judge was able to act as a moderator because of his personal knowledge of the litigants—a condition which is possible only in rural districts. The broad reforms of December, 1958 (effective March 1, 1959), swept out 2,918 justices of the peace. Their functions are now exercised by 454 "Courts of Instance" (*Tribunaux d'Instance*) of somewhat enlarged prerogatives.

On the same level in the hierarchical order stand two special courts, the Labor Courts (*Conseils de Prud'hommes*) and the Commercial Courts (*Tribunaux de Commerce*). Both deal with special subjects (labor disputes and disputes under the Commercial Code), and both have as a specially distinguishing feature a panel of judges, composed of employers and employees in the case of the Labor Courts, or of businessmen in the case of the Commercial Tribunals. In more serious cases, appeal from these courts to the Court of First Instance is possible.

The lowest court of the regular judicial hierarchy was the Court of First Instance (*Tribunal de Première Instance*), whose criminal section was known as the Correctional Court (*Tribunal Correctionnel*).[43] In 1959 it was renamed Court of Grand Instance (*Tribunal de Grande Instance*). Courts of first instance could be

---

[43] Although the sections are sufficiently separated to rank almost as separate courts, the judges rotate among them.

found at almost every county (*arrondissement*) seat, but the new Courts of Grand Instance cover large areas, as 351 Courts of First Instance were reorganized into 172 Courts of Grand Instance. In civil cases, these courts have unlimited original jurisdiction as well as appellate jurisdiction from the Courts of Instance, the Labor Courts, and the Commercial Courts. In criminal cases they deal with misdemeanors and the lesser types of felonies. Each case is heard by a panel of three judges. Considering the number of trial sections of courts involved, this makes for an astoundingly large number of judges, probably more than are really necessary. At the seat of each Court of Grand Instance, there is also established a Juvenile Court (*Tribunal pour Enfants*) with one or several judges.

Appeals in civil cases from the Courts of Grand Instance are brought before the Courts of Appeal (*Cours d'Appel*), of which there are twenty-seven. These courts engage in an entire rehearing of the case (*de novo*), and their judgments on the facts and the law involved are final as far as the facts are concerned. In civil cases these proceedings may seem rather dull to us as they consist chiefly of filing and counterfiling written statements.

The courts of appeal for criminal cases are the Assize Courts (*Cours d'Assises*), one of which may be found in session in each of the ninety departments at least once every three months but more frequently in the large centers. Besides being appeal courts, the Assizes also have original jurisdiction over grave crimes, such as homicide. In the latter case, when the court is sitting as a court of original jurisdiction, it employs a jury. Five or more judges hear each case before the Court of Appeals, and three judges in the Assize Courts. In the latter case, the presiding judge is taken from the Court of Appeals while the other two are taken from the local Court of Grand Instance or also from the Court of Appeals if the Assizes meet where a Court of Appeals is located.

The apex of the regular judiciary is the Court of Cassation (*Cour de Cassation*). It is composed of one Chief Justice (First President), four presidents (of sections) and sixty other judges (counselors, *conseillers*); attached to it is the Chief Prosecutor (*Procureur Général*) and his staff. Its first section, the screening chamber (*Chambre des Requêtes*), conducts a preliminary examination and rejects outright those appeals which have no substantial merit. If it is decided to hear the case, it is then referred to either the civil or criminal section of the court.

As the name implies, the court does not technically decide a case, but only quashes (*casser*) it, remanding it to a lower court for retrial. This lower court will be of the same rank as the court from which the appeal was received, but will not be the same court. Should this second lower court again rule contrary to the views of the Court of Cassation, the supreme court may hold a hearing before a panel of not less than thirty-three of its judges, and then remand the case to a third lower court. This court then must execute the will of the Court of Cassation.

The prestige of the Court of Cassation is very high, and while it may not actually decide a case, the reasons for a *cassation* may be tantamount to the same thing. An appeal to the Court of Cassation is relatively easily accomplished in meritorious cases and is fairly inexpensive. However, this fact, together with the litigious nature of the French, burdens the court with a great deal of business and delays its decisions, sometimes for many years.[44]

Criminal prosecution

French judicial procedure is distinguished by a number of characteristics. In criminal cases an accused person is first taken before an examining magistrate, called *juge d'instruction*. He examines the case thoroughly, scrutinizes all the evidence, and then decides whether the case shall go to trial, and if so, whether a Correctional Court or an Assize Court should hear the case. Under the Third Republic the *juge d'instruction* could keep the accused in custody while the often lengthy investigation proceeded. This is no longer supposed to be the case, but in practice the old methods are hard to eradicate.

The institution of the examining magistrate, which is by no means confined to France, has been severely criticized for being a secret pretrial at which the accused is at a disadvantage. There is a certain amount of justification to this, although the accusation of "star-chamber proceedings" is greatly exaggerated. However this pretrial procedure has given rise to the oft-heard but totally false idea that in a French court the accused is considered guilty until he proves himself innocent. Actually no civilized country has such a rule in its criminal procedure. However, the fact that a case does not reach the trial court until a *juge d'instruction* has sifted the evidence and found it compelling may well prejudice the court against the defendant from the outset.

British and American observers have been critical of the lax rules of evidence in French courts, the acceptability of hearsay, the inability of witnesses to excuse themselves on grounds of self-incrimination. However, it must be remembered that the Anglo-American rules of evidence have been specifically designed for the jury trial, chiefly to prevent undue bias on the part of the jury. But jury trials are the exception, not the rule, in France, and it is presumed that the learned judges will treat the evidence presented to them with appropriate caution and erudition. This is also borne out by the fact that the judges take an active role in the proceedings and endeavor to get at the facts themselves.

Actually judges often question the accused in a manner which one might associate with the prosecution rather than with a supposedly impartial judge. In these

[44] Cf. Jean Brissaud, *A History of French Private Law* (trans. by R. Howell), Boston, 1912; Francis Deak and Max Rheinstein, "The Development of French and German Law," *Georgetown Law Journal*, March, 1936; James W. Garner, "The French Judiciary," *Yale Law Journal*, March, 1917; Robert C. K. Enser, *Courts and Judges in France, Germany and England*, Oxford, 1933; A. Grandin, *Bibliographie générale des sciences juridiques, politiques, économiques, et sociales de 1800 à 1926*, Paris, 1926, and annual supplements; A. Esmein, *Histoire de la procédure criminelle en France*, Paris, 1881; A. C. Wright, "French Criminal Procedure," *Law Quarterly Review*, Vol. XLIV (1928), pp. 324–341; Vol. XLV (1929), pp. 92–107.

interrogations French judges frequently make comments about such things as the credibility of the accused or of a witness, or about the hideous nature of the crime, which if made in an American or British court would constitute a mistrial. In France both judge and prosecutor are government officials who are interested in their promotion, and sometimes they seek distinction or notoriety by conducting "sharp" trials. In such instances it is often the prosecutor rather than the judge who sees to it that the accused gets a fair trial.

These tendencies on the part of the judge, which must seem rather shocking to an American or British lawyer, are particularly in evidence in trials of a political nature. The judge's eagerness for ferreting out all the facts may involve him in a controversy with the accused in which the judge does not always emerge as the winner. This was particularly in evidence in the trial of Pierre Laval in which the extremely clever and experienced accused proved himself so much the superior of the court that his conviction almost gave the impression of having been decided in advance. Most observers agreed that although Laval may have been justly put to death, the cause of justice was not well served by the trial.

There is also a question of whether the special procedure established to prosecute those implicated in the several coups in 1960 and 1961 has always served justice well. Nobody would deny that justice had to be meted out, but the severity of treatment was often excessive, and many men were long held in captivity without adequate proof of their guilt.

The High Court of Justice

A High Court of Justice was created by a decree of November 18, 1944, and was organized as a purge court to deal with the higher officials of the Vichy regime. Its trials, especially the earlier ones, were highly emotional affairs, which sometimes reflected little credit on the French administration of justice. Foreign observers were often shocked at the irregularities of procedure, the lax application of the rules of evidence, the way in which everything seemed to be stacked against the defendant. However, one had to remember that in all countries which had been under German occupation, the need to purge collaborationists caused considerable emotional upheaval over which impartial justice did not easily triumph. If one considers that in fifty-two trials of major collaborationists, the court exacted the death penalty in only three cases, one must deem its total record one of admirable restraint.

Belgium, with only one-fifth of France's population, convicted an equal number of collaborationists.

Because of the experience of the purge court, the Constitutions of both 1946 and 1958 sought to install a regular court of impeachment. This court is called the High Court of Justice and is composed of members of parliament, elected in equal number by the National Assembly and the Senate. The Court is elected anew after each new election to the National Assembly and after each partial election to the Senate.

The President of the Republic cannot be held accountable for actions performed in the exercise of his office, except in the case of high treason. In that case, he must be indicted by both houses of parliament and by an absolute majority of the members of both assemblies or by a higher majority if one of the two houses casts its vote in that fashion. Other members of the government shall be criminally liable for actions performed in the exercise of their office, provided these actions are classified as major infractions or crimes. In that case, they may be tried by the High Court of Justice, following the same procedure which it applies to the impeachment of the President, and the High Court is bound by the rules of criminal law.

The High Court of Justice has not yet been called upon to try a President or a minister. And it is not likely to be confronted by this possibility. At one time, a minister of the Fourth Republic, Jules Moch, was almost indicted, but this was the result of a political cabal against a personally very unpopular figure, rather than an expression of a genuine will for impeachment. Generally speaking, impeachment procedures have little significance in a parliamentary regime in which the parliament may cause the minister's downfall. The possibility of the President of the Republic committing treason is highly remote. Although the parliamentary character of the Fifth Republic is modified, a recourse to impeachment nevertheless remains quite unlikely.

No judicial review

None of the aforementioned courts possesses or exercises the right of judicial review as that is known in the United States. The question was raised and laid to rest in 1833, in the case of the newspaper *Le National,* when the Court of Cassation ruled that a law which had been "deliberated and promulgated according to constitutional forms" could not be attacked as unconstitutional. French jurists, who prefer to analyze questions of this kind on grounds of judicial doctrine rather than of workability, frequently declare that judicial review violates the principle of the separation of powers because it allows the judiciary to interfere with the legislative power of parliament. They also argue that it runs counter to the doctrine that law is the expression of the sovereign will.[45] This attitude naturally tends to make the Constitution more of a declaration of principles than a legally binding instrument. It also greatly reduces the status of the judge.

Eminent voices have been heard repeatedly suggesting the introduction of judicial review, but so far to no avail. The majority of the Constituent Assembly found judicial review utterly incompatible with the doctrine of a sovereign legis-

[45] For a refutation of this view see Edward M. Sait, *Government and Politics of France,* Yonkers, N.Y., 1920, p. 23. The administrative courts do (since 1907) examine the constitutionality of executive acts.

lature. Pierre Cot, the *rapporteur* of the first draft, repeatedly referred to President Franklin D. Roosevelt's difficulties with the Supreme Court as a warning example of a situation which should be avoided in France, and his view carried much weight.

The Constitutional Council

Ostensibly as a concession to the promoters of judicial review, the Constitution of 1946 created a Constitutional Committee, which was somewhat strengthened by the Constitution of 1958 and given the title of Constitutional Council. It is composed of nine members who are appointed for nine years and who cannot be re-appointed. One-third of the membership is renewed every three years. Three members are appointed by the President of the Republic, three by the president of the National Assembly, and three by the president of the Senate. In addition, former Presidents of the Republic are ex-officio members for life of the Constitutional Council. The president of the Council is appointed by the President of the Republic from among Council members and has the power to cast the deciding vote in case of a tie.

Membership on the Constitutional Council is incompatible with a cabinet position or membership in parliament or with certain other positions.

Compared with the Constitutional Committee of the Fourth Republic, the Constitutional Council of the Fifth has certain enlarged functions. It assures the regularity of the election of the President of the Republic and decides disputes over contested votes. It also decides in case of contested elections to the National Assembly or the Senate, a right which the Fourth Republic had reserved to the houses concerned. The Constitutional Council also watches over the regularity of referenda and announces their results.

As already stated, organic laws must be submitted to the Constitutional Council before their promulgation, and the Council will rule on their constitutionality. Ordinary laws may also be submitted to it before their promulgation by the President of the Republic, the Prime Minister, or the president of one or the other house. Upon such submission, the Constitutional Council normally has one month to rule on the constitutionality of the measure. However, in case the government declares a measure "urgent," that period shall be reduced to eight days. In any case, referral of a bill to the Constitutional Council suspends the ordinary time limit for promulgation. Once a bill is declared unconstitutional, it may not be promulgated or implemented. No appeal is possible from the decisions of the Council.

Several differences between the Constitutional Committee of the Fourth Republic and the Constitutional Council of the Fifth should be noted. The Council's right to supervise the regularity of elections and referenda is new. Also the text of Articles 61 and 62 speaks bodly of constitutionality and unconstitutionality and avoids the coy wording of Articles 91–93 of the Constitution of 1946. The review function of the Constitutional Committee of the Fourth Republic was tucked away among the articles dealing with amendments; the equivalent provisions in the 1958 Constitution form a separate and distinct section.

Nevertheless, even if one recognizes the greater significance of the Constitutional Council, it is still highly doubtful that one could speak of anything even remotely comparable to judicial review in France. Challenge to the constitutionality of a law is possible only on the basis of the general principles of the law and not on that of its concrete application in a particular case; it cannot be challenged by private individuals but only by the high officials mentioned before. Thus, judging from the experience of other countries which have judicial review, the principal source of challenge has been eliminated at the very outset.

Secondly, the period during which the Constitutional Council must make up its mind is so short that one might think that the framers of this section did not expect it to be applied very frequently. The real role which its 1946 framers wished to confide to its predecessor was that of a conciliator, when a bill passed both houses in different versions. But it played that role only rarely, and there would seem to be little room for it under the Fifth Republic, which has created the institution of the conference committee. Certainly, under the Fourth Republic, there was no real difference between constitutional and ordinary law, and for all practical purposes the French parliament could enact any law it saw fit, whether constitutional or not. In fact, it is no exaggeration to say that in actual practice such unconstitutional but duly enacted and promulgated laws constituted informal amendments of the constitution of the Fourth Republic.

Under the Fifth Republic the Constitutional Council has been more active than its predecessor was but it has not been more significant. This is because its relatively few actions have been directed effectively only against unconstitutional parliamentary procedures. Where its findings were inconvenient for the executive, as was the case in a question regarding the 1962 plebiscite, the General simply ignored the Council and proceeded to have his way.

The administrative courts

The ordinary court system which has been discussed above is only one side of the judicial picture, and not even necessarily the most important part at that. Side by side with it there exists another organization: the system of administrative justice. It must be remembered that the French administrative system is characterized by an enormous degree of concentration and centralization, vesting great power in individual officials. At the same time, not all features have really been brought under one roof, and a complicated system has been established which, according to one observer, becomes comprehensible only when one remembers that it was designed to control the overly powerful administrative staff.[46] The French adminis-

---

[46] Carl J. Friedrich, *Constitutional Government and Democracy,* Boston, 1946, pp. 368*ff.*

trative court system, which sees to it that administrative power is not misused, is therefore a necessary part of this approach.

Parallel to this development runs the French doctrine of the separation of powers, which has declared ever since 1789 that the judiciary has no right to interfere with the acts of the legislature or the executive.[47] Thus, while it became necessary to have a system by which abuse of power could be checked, such a check could not come from the regular judiciary; it had to come from within the executive machinery itself. The organs of administrative justice form therefore a part of the administration itself. To many an observer such a system appeared to be a mockery. The spectacle of the administration ostensibly judging itself while being exempt from ordinary justice seemed preposterous and a far cry from the "rule of law."[48] In actuality, however, time and custom have given the Council of State, the supreme and principal dispenser of administrative justice, a degree of independence and prestige which is rarely equaled by the ordinary courts. At any rate, the fear expressed by these critics has been found groundless for the most part.

Administrative law is an extremely important field. It covers no less than the whole realm of relationships between the public authorities and the individual.[49] And strangely enough, in France, the country of codified law, administrative law is to a very large extent based on precedent, on judicial decision, with which the legislature does not ordinarily interfere and which the administrative courts themselves alter only gradually. Thus, something like *stare decisis* can be found even in France.[50]

The lowest administrative courts are the Interdepartmental Prefectural Councils (*Conseils de Préfecture Interdépartementaux*). Originally they existed in every department and constituted the "consultative" part of the administration, serving the chief official of the department, the prefect. However a decree of July, 1934, reduced the number of councils to twenty-two as an economy measure. Hence the

[47] Law of Dec. 22, 1789: ". . . Judicial power should not trouble local administrative agencies in the exercise of their functions." Law of Aug. 16 to 24, 1790: "The judicial functions are and will remain forever separate from the administrative functions. The judges will not be allowed, under penalty of forfeiture, to disturb in any manner whatsoever, the activities of the administrative corps, nor to summon before them the administrators concerning their functions." Stephen Riesenfeld, "The French System of Administrative Justice: A Model for American Law?" *Boston University Law Review*, Vol. XVIII (1938), pp. 48–82. William Rohkam and Orville C. Pratt, *Studies in French Administrative Law*, Urbana, Ill., 1947, p. 14.

[48] A. V. Dicey, *Law of the Constitution*, London, 1926, 8th ed., chap. XII.

[49] Marcel Waline, *Traité élémentaire de droit administratif*, Paris, 1951, 6th ed. Gaston Jeze, *Les Principes généraux du droit administratif*, Paris, 1925, p. 283. James W. Garner, "French Administrative Law," *Yale Law Review*, Vol. XXXIII (1924), p. 599. F. M. Marx, "Comparative Administrative Law," *University of Pennsylvania Law Review* (1942), p. 118.

[50] This is a relatively recent development; see the case of Casanova, Canazzi, et al., Council of State, Mar. 29, 1901, Dalloz, *Recueil hebdomadaire de jurisprudence*, Vol. III (1902), p. 34. See also C. S. Lobinger, "Administrative Law and *Droit Administratif*," *University of Pennsylvania Law Review* (1942), p. 34; C. L. Hamson, "Le Conseil d'État statuant aux contentieux," *Law Quarterly Review*, Vol. LXVIII (1952), pp. 60–87.

designation "interdepartmental" rather than "departmental." Each council is composed of two or three members (councilors), one of whom acts as president. The others may at any time be delegated to department seats in order to settle minor litigations. The Interdepartmental Prefectural Councils have limited jurisdiction, usually in minor cases, especially concerning taxation. On the same level is the Prefectural Council of the Seine with jurisdiction over the department of the Seine, in which Paris is located.

In the same category are also certain other authorities with special jurisdiction, such as the Council of Public Instruction (*Conseil de l'Instruction Publique*), the Draft Review Boards (*Conseils Militaires de Révision*), and the Departmental Council, a pension-adjustment court. The General Accounting Office (*Cour des Comptes*) is organized like a court and has certain quasi-judicial functions which also fall in the category of administrative justice. Recently, another court was added, the Court of Budgetary Discipline (*Cour de Discipline Budgétaire*), which punishes the incurring of unauthorized expenditures.

The apex and by far the most important court in this system is the Council of State (*Conseil d'État*). The Council of State is not merely a court but has other functions as well; technically, only one section of the Council, the Litigation Section (*section du contentieux*), is an administrative court.

The personnel of the Council of State presents a curious blend of administrative and judicial experiences which adds to the excellence of this body. The Minister of Justice is President of the Council of State, but that position is purely nominal. The actual chairman is a vice president. Under him serve five presidents of sections, forty-six councilors of the regular civil service who have been promoted from the lower echelons of the Council, twelve councilors who are appointed from the outside, forty-nine masters of petition (*maîtres des requêtes*), and forty-eight junior members (*auditeurs*) of the first and second class. All members of the Council, except the twelve outside councilors and the Minister of Justice, are appointed on the basis of highly technical, competitive examinations and are then promoted within the hierarchy of the Council. Thus, a preponderance of great experience is assured. The Council of State contains without doubt the cream of the juridical and administrative elite of France.

In order to transact its business, the Litigation Section of the Council of State is divided into nine subsections, each composed of three councilors and several masters of petitions and junior members. Some less important business can be conducted by some of these sections alone (*contentieux spécial*), but for the rest, two sections must deliberate together (*contentieux général*). There are also larger meetings: that of the Litigation Section, which for this purpose is composed of the president of the section, the presidents of the subsections, two councilors from the subsection directly affected, and the *rapporteur;* and then the plenary meeting (*assemblée plenière*), which has the same members as the above meeting of the Section but in addition has the vice president, the actual head of the Council of State, and instead of the two councilors from one subsection has four councilors from the "administrative" sections (other than the Litigation Section) of the Council.

These enlarged meetings are not appeals sections; rather certain persons (not the parties) have the right to refer certain cases to them. These special people are the vice president of the Council, the presidents of the Litigation Section and its subsections, and the government commissioner (*commissaire du gouvernement*).

The government commissioners are rather unusual people. There are twelve of them and they are usually recruited from the masters of petitions. Contrary to their title they are *not* the attorneys for the government. If the government wishes to have its viewpoint presented by counsel, it must hire one just like any private party. The commissioners represent the public interest; they are not subject to instruction (like the members of the *parquet*) and not dependent on one another. They are men of great knowledge and talent; eventually they are almost certain to be appointed councilors, and the various presidents and vice presidents are often former commissioners.

The Council of State has original, appellate, and final jurisdiction, but these categories are only vaguely defined by law and, rather, emerge as the result of past decisions by the Council of State. It is a court of appeals for judgments rendered by the inferior councils and administrative courts. But ordinarily, cases involving the extent of power and discretion of officials are handled by the Council of State in original jurisdiction.

The jurisdiction of the Council is a good deal broader than might be indicated by the above categories. It is the principal purpose of the Council of State to guarantee the "legality and legitimacy" of the administration. It has therefore been called the "guarantor of administrative morality,"[51] a role which the Council can exercise all the better because a person who is interested in seeing the law applied properly may take his complaint to the administrative courts without the necessity of violating the decree or regulation whose legality he wishes to attack. Originally, the basis of administrative justice was the plea that a certain administrative act was illegal (*exception d'illégalité*). But soon the Council developed more refined doctrines which permitted a closer examination of administrative acts. The next step was that the Council permitted pleas of *ultra vires* (*recours pour excès de pouvoir*), i.e., the complaint that an official had acted beyond the confines of his legal powers. In the interpretation of this category of pleas, the Council distinguishes between personal liability (*faute personnelle*), for which the guilty official must take personal responsibility, and public liability (*faute de service*), in which case the government will redress the wrong if the judgment goes against it.[52] In addition to these two concepts, illegality and *ultra vires,* the Council of State has added another one, that of abuse of power (*détournement de pouvoir*). It is this category which permits the

[51] W. R. Sharp, *The Government of the French Republic,* New York, 1938, p. 317.
[52] *Fautes de service* fall into three categories according to gravity.

Council to look beyond the question of legality and penetrate the motives of the act. Under the definition of abuse of power, the Council may annul actions and assess damages if an official exercises his authority for purposes for which it was not granted, even though the act itself may be neither illegal nor *ultra vires*.

Among those categories the Council of State has been inclined to restrict the extent of personal liability more and more, while expanding the concept of the public liability. It has even gone so far as to grant damages for accidents or inefficiency.

However, not all *fautes de service* make the government liable for damages. This is generally true only for acts in which the government plays the role of the business manager of the administration (*actes de gestion*).[53] But the government will ordinarily not accept liability concerning acts of authority (*actes d'autorité;* also, *actes de puissance publique*) unless they were either illegal or constituted an abuse of power. Acts of authority concern primarily international relations, but also executive-legislative relationship, national defense, and the "state of siege,"[54] as well as certain colonial matters. However, the Council of State has tended to restrict the fields of *actes d'autorité* more and more, except in the field of international relations. A third category, acts of state (*actes de gouvernement*), may not even be the subject of litigation. Such acts concern high-level policy, state security, etc. Their distinction from *actes d'autorité* is not always clear, but the number of cases which may be placed under that category is not large.

Administrative law is the result of practice and precedent. Consequently it is unsystematic and contradictory, and its perimeter is flexible. It is not surprising, therefore, that jurisdictional disputes may arise between the realms of ordinary and administrative justice, but it is surprising that such disputes are few. To decide them, another court has been created, the Court of Conflicts (*Tribunal des Conflits*), which is composed of the Minister of Justice as chairman (who rarely presides), three councilors of the Council of State, three judges of the *Cour de Cassation,* and two others nominated by them.

The French system of administrative justice affords an easy and generally inexpensive way of keeping the administrative machine in line. In a highly centralized country in which the bureaucracy is only inadequately checked by rapidly changing political heads, an institution like the Council of State is an absolute necessity, although Anglo-American jurists will contend that there is no reason why the ordinary courts cannot discharge this function just as well.[55] However, the system of administrative justice would never have worked as well as it did if the executive appointment of members of the bench had not gradually given way to

[53] Many *actes de gestion* come from the administrative staff itself, especially complaints against illegal or unfair treatment of civil servants. The drafting of a Civil Service Code, which was largely undertaken by the Council of State itself, has improved this situation.

[54] An act by which civil government is suspended in a certain area, which is thus placed under military control and martial law.

[55] As a matter of fact, regular courts actually deal with a number of administrative questions.

protection of tenure and judicial independence. The practice of the Council of State has disproved the arguments of those critics who feared that the existence of the Council of State within the French administration would produce collusion because the administration would "judge itself." On the contrary, a distinguished observer reports that the system of administrative justice "has been criticized by some Frenchmen for showing an excess of bias against the government and in favor of private individuals; that it has given more consideration to equity and less to law . . . ,"[56] and another famous jurist has even gone so far as to state that "in France the discretionary act no longer exists,"[57] which is perhaps exaggerated.

One major drawback of this system is to be found in the fact that the Council of State is overrun with litigation and is constantly in arrears. Since 1944 more cases have been received every year than have been decided, and in the first five postwar years the arrears amounted to the staggering number of 10,753 cases, which, as professor Hamson so admirably states, amounts to a denial of justice.[58] This has of course its repercussions in the administrative services. One highly respected and conscientious prefect of a *département* once explained to the author how he had requisitioned housing for his staff knowing full well that his action was of doubtful legality and that the Council of State would overrule him. But he figured that this would take at least two to three years and in the meantime he would find other quarters. And so it was.

A number of proposals have been made for the remedy of this serious shortcoming; the most promising have been those tending to increase the jurisdiction of the interdepartmental prefectural councils, but that is not so easy because the prefectural councils do not possess the high standing and the reputation of the Council of State, and it is this reputation which makes it so effective.

In sum total the Council of State is one of the most admirable institutions of France or any country. Far from being an instance in which "the administration judges itself," it is on the contrary a highly effective device of "forbidding the administration to judge its own acts."[59] At a time when the problem of how to control the now tremendous administrative machinery is a serious question in every country, the French Council of State has made an important contribution, or at least one partial answer, thereto.

In conclusion, attention ought to be drawn to the fact that in many respects administrative justice is an aspect of constitutional jurisprudence, the French answer to judicial review (though not its equivalent). It is true that acts of the legislature cannot be challenged. But French legislation frequently leaves much detail and procedure for the administrator to fill in by the use of his regulatory power, and there the Council of State comes into its own. In a way the Court of Conflicts

56 Garner, "French Administrative Law," p. 626.
57 Léon Duguit, *Law in the Modern State* (trans. by Frieda Laski and Harold Laski), New York, 1919, p. 185.
58 Hamson, *op. cit.,* p. 84.
59 Waline, *op. cit.,* Tit. II, chap. 2, sec. 1, § 1.

is, according to a leading French authority,[60] a constitutional court par excellence, because it deals with the fundamental question of French constitutional doctrine, the separation of powers.

E. THE COMMUNITY

France's overseas empire was exceeded only by that of Great Britain. Almost all of it lay in Africa, especially after Indochina was lost in 1954. But outside Africa and Indochina there were still New Caledonia and other islands in the Australian area and Oceania, and in the Western Hemisphere there were the islands of St. Pierre and Miquelon just off the coast of Newfoundland, Guadeloupe and Martinique in the Antilles, and French Guiana in South America. The French population was not very numerous in those territories. Even while Indochina was French, there were only 42,000 Frenchmen among 25 million Indochinese. In French Equatorial Africa there were only about 5,000 French among more than 5 million native inhabitants. Only in North Africa, especially in Algeria, was there a larger European contingent.

But all this is a matter of the past. The "old" (pre-Revolutionary) colonies of Martinique, Guadeloupe, Réunion, and Guiana have become departments of France and are administered more or less like domestic territories. As far as the vast territories in Africa are concerned, there was hope of holding them in a status of domestic autonomy within a "French Community." Article 76 of the Constitution of 1958 provided that overseas territories had a choice between becoming overseas departments of the Republic, i.e., remaining integral parts of France, or becoming states of the French Community, either singly or in groups. This was a choice which they would have to make within six months after the Constitution came into effect (Article 91).

But even after a state had decided upon its status within the French Community, it could still change its mind. Under Article 86, the legislative assembly of that state could, on the basis of a local referendum, demand a change of its status, or even its independence, and thereby cease to be a member of the Community. Article 77 provided that the states of the Community were to enjoy autonomy and were to administer themselves, and it also proclaimed a single citizenship within the entire Community.

Article 78, on the other hand, provided that the jurisdiction of the Community, that is, of the Community as a whole and not each individual state, was to comprise foreign policy, defense, currency, and common economic and financial policy, as well as policies affecting strategic raw materials. It was also to supervise the tribunals, the institutions of higher education, and the general organization of transport and telecommunications within the Community.

To carry into effect these vast rights and duties, the Constitution provided for

---

[60] M. Hauriou, *Précis de droit administratif et de droit public*, Paris, 1927, 11th ed., p. 948.

three organs of the Community: an Executive Council, a Senate, and a Court of Arbitration. But the President of the (French) Republic was to preside over and represent the Community and was to be represented in each state thereof.

All this has remained a dead letter. The wave of independence which flooded Africa did not stop before the French-speaking territories. Even such areas as Senegal and the Ivory Coast, which were headed by men who were greatly attached to France and had been high in France's councils (Léopold-Sedar Senghor and Félix Houphouet-Boigny), declared their independence. Algeria followed the same road in 1962. It is true that important sentimental, cultural, and economic ties have remained between "Francophone" (speaking French as a second language) Africa and France, but the hoped-for stability of those new countries has been no greater than became evident in other parts of Africa.

In view of this course of events, the "French Community" never had an opportunity to exist. The pertinent articles and paragraphs are still in the text of the Constitution but they have no reality in fact.

F. LOCAL GOVERNMENT

It is a well-known fact that systems of local government usually outlive systems of national administration. Wars, revolutions, and *coups d'état* put their marks far more on the national than on the local level. France is no exception to that rule. Yet gradual changes have occurred to which the Fourth Republic made a small contribution.

Under the *ancien régime* a royal official, the intendant, ruled the principal unit of local administration, the so-called *généralité*. The Revolution of 1789 quickly did away with this institution and replaced it by a totally new system of departments, *arrondissements,* and communes. Departments and communes now elected their councils, which in turn elected their officers.[61] This enlightened system lasted only until 1800, when Napoleon placed local government under rigid central control and created the pivotal position of the prefect. With some modifications, this has remained the system to this day, justifying the famous statement by a former President that "we have the Republic on top and the Empire underneath."[62] This situation has often been termed paradoxical by foreign observers, but the very paradoxicality of the system has created, over the years, a curious blend of authoritarian and democratic threads which is not always apparent to those who confine themselves to a study of the channels of command.

The Third Republic achieved some gradual reforms by a certain amount of democratization and by an increasing tendency to delegate additional functions to units of local government. The Vichy regime, aping its German master, abolished much of this and attempted to reintroduce some features of regionalism. Region-

[61] See V. D. Lipman, "Recent Trends in French Local Administration," *Public Administration*, Vol. XXV (1947), p. 29.
[62] Paul Deschanel, *La Décentralisation*, Paris, 1895, p. 6.

alism has been a frequent discussion topic in France,[63] but its use by the Vichy regime largely discredited it, and the Constituent Assembly of 1946 was not inclined to retain it. The Constitution of the Fifth Republic makes no change in this respect.

Territorial organization

The territorial subdivisions of France are called departments, *arrondissements,* cantons, and communes. There are 90 departments (not counting the seven North African and overseas departments), 281 *arrondissements,* 3,028 cantons, and 38,014 communes. Among them only the departments and the communes are of importance.

While the communes are the product of natural growth, many of them going back to most ancient times, the departments are the artificial creation of the French Revolution. Originally the departments were founded as new areas of self-government. Within a few years of their creation, the departments lost that character completely and became the principal instrument through which the central authorities in Paris controlled the provinces. With some modifications, the Third Republic maintained this institution. Under it, the prefect, who was appointed and controlled by the Minister of the Interior, was both the representative of the central government and the chief executive officer of the department. After 1833, there existed elected general councils in the departments (with some interruptions), although they were still dependent on the prefect for the execution of their orders. Moreover, the prefect had strong control, called "administrative guardianship" (*tutelle administrative*), over the council and the local administration, through which he could see to it that the councilors acted "wisely."

The "founding fathers" of the Fourth Republic unanimously voted for a change of the prefectural system. They were prompted in this by the lessons of the war, which reminded them how easily the Vichy regime had gained control over the prefects and hence over the country. Yet the well-known statement that those in power always like the prefectural system, because it is so convenient for the effective maintenance of control, tended to neutralize the desire to place local government on a completely democratic and "home-rule" basis. The result, which the Fifth Republic has retained, was a compromise which attempted to separate the two principal functions of the prefect. He was to retain his role as the representative of the national government but was to yield his place as chief executive of the department to the department's own elected officials. Thus, the president of each department's general council became theoretically the chief executive for the departments, very much in the same manner as the mayors had been chief executives of the communes.

However, the innovation is more apparent than real. Only a few relatively

---

[63] Charles Brun, *Le Regionalisme,* Paris, 1911; R. K. Gooch, *Regionalism in France,* New York, 1931.

unimportant functions are carried out by the general council: the upkeep of public buildings, the maintenance of certain secondary roads, and similar housekeeping duties. And many of those functions are circumscribed by national law. In effect the constitutional provision dividing power between the prefect and the general council has remained a dead letter because the National Assembly never passed the necessary implementing legislation and, according to one Minister of the Interior, never will do so.

The mayors and municipal councils have somewhat larger functions, chiefly because of their administration of public welfare and communally owned public utilities. All these functions are hamstrung by the very limited right of taxation possessed by all units of local government. Their main income is derived from a small percentage of certain national taxes which are placed at their disposal, income from communal industries, and grants-in-aid. But even these limited budgets are not within the sole province of local government. Over three-fourths of all communal outlays are the result of mandatory national legislation which gives the commune no choice. Problems of education, police, fire, health, etc., are largely removed from the competence of mayor and council, and even in the few areas where they retain functions, as in public welfare, many duties are prescribed for them. This system does not permit or encourage local initiative to any large extent. Postwar disorganization and physical destruction have inspired many mayors and city councils to accomplish heroic acts of reconstruction, proving thereby that the lethargy for which French local government is renowned is not caused by lack of ability on the part of the French people. A remedy is, however, not in sight as long as "unity," or rather uniformity, of administration is considered a virtue[64] and as long as the idea prevails that "France cannot be abandoned to the whims of ninety general councils and 38,000 communes."[65]

The prefects

The prefects are appointed by the President of the Republic in the Council of Ministers, but they are for all practical purposes the appointees of the Minister of the Interior, who is their immediate chief.

Prefects are a curious blend of political and civil service officers. They are usually appointed from among the civil service, yet they are not required to meet any special standards of professional competence. An outstanding expert[66] has described them as being "essentially political agents whose business it is to support and spread the opinions and wishes of the government throughout the whole administration." This implies that while prefects are not necessarily partisans, they

[64] With the exception of Paris and the department (Seine) in which it is located, all French communes and departments have identical organization.
[65] Joseph-Barthélemy, *The Government of France* (trans. by J. B. Morris), New York, 1924, p. 153. (Figures have been adjusted.)
[66] *Ibid.*, p. 134.

are nevertheless chosen for their obedience to the government. Prefects are rarely dismissed; more frequent is the so-called "movement of prefects," i.e., they are shifted around as a new administration takes office. Obedient prefects will be shifted to more important posts, while less pliable ones may be sent to "exile" in the provinces or even to overseas departments. In some cases, prefects are promoted or "kicked upstairs" to the General Accounting Office or even the Council of State.

Within his department the prefect represents the total power of the national government. As such he not only supervises and controls the local administration, but he carries out directly a number of functions and appoints a considerable number of officers.[67] Especially in the fields of education, public works, road construction, and police, his powers are extensive. He plays a particularly important role in the field of public safety, which is strongly centralized in France. The Minister of the Interior controls all the police forces of France—a method which is common on the European continent, with the result that ministries of the interior are of outstanding importance in the political picture—especially in troubled times. The Ministry of the Interior has the *Sûreté Nationale,* a plain-clothes force which operates in secret, under its immediate control. A force of uniformed police, known as the *gendarmerie,*[68] is stationed in each department and is under the control of the Minister of Defense. However, both national and local security agencies may call on them for help.

The local police forces are directly administered by the municipal governments, subject to the control of the prefect. In certain key cities, however, the police are under direct national control. In the department of the Seine, in which Paris is located, there are two prefects, and one, the prefect of police, is in direct charge of that important security force.

The original concept of the prefect as created by Napoleon was that of the nearly omnipotent arm of the central authorities. With the improvement of communications and the growth of a democratic spirit, the power of the prefect deteriorated as the central authorities issued more and more detailed directives and increased the scope of their direct intervention. However, there are enough important functions which remain under his jurisdiction as the "delegate of the government."

This conflict between the traditional tendency toward strictest centralism and the modern trend toward decentralization may in time revive the idea of regionalism, which has been the subject of much argument in the past. The Vichy regime created regional administrations, and the French Committee of National Liberation decided to maintain them. As a result, eighteen administrative regions were created. But after consolidation, the government decided to return to the purely prefectural regime. However, the danger of public disorder caused by the repercussions of the

---

[67] Technically the prefect may even act as an examining magistrate (*juge d'instruction*) (Art. 10, *code d'instruction criminelle*), but such cases are now virtually nonexistent.

[68] It is an American tendency to regard all French policemen as gendarmes. This is quite incorrect. Most French policemen are municipal officers. Gendarmes are vaguely comparable to American state policemen.

East-West controversy prompted the government to impose a tighter security control in 1948 by creating eight superprefectures.[69] The superprefects have largely a coordinating function, primarily in cases of widespread emergency. In such cases they act like regional ministers of the interior. However, the superprefects are permitted to exercise only the functions which are specifically delegated to them— functions which are ordinarily reserved to the Minister of the Interior and not to the prefect. Consequently the superprefect does not diminish the role of the prefect. Prefects of important departments are appointed superprefects in addition to their prefectural duties. Superprefects, even when stationed in the provinces, attend regular monthly conferences at the Ministry of the Interior, where they have an opportunity to brief the government on important over-all developments in the country.

Great as the power of the prefect may be, it is nevertheless circumscribed very considerably by a number of important factors. The rapid extension of the civil service system has curtailed his power of appointment. At the same time his politically ambiguous role has remained. On the one hand he is supposed to lay down the law to the department over which he "rules"; on the other hand he must maintain good relations with the members of parliament from his department, who can make trouble for him in the National Assembly, especially when they belong to a party whose support is important to the Minister of the Interior. The deputy in turn has an attentive ear cocked toward the demands of his constituents, with the result that complaints or requests which ought to be directed to the prefect are actually presented to the deputy from the area concerned, who then intercedes with his considerable influence. To walk the straight and narrow path between pressure from below and possible displeasure from above, the prefect must indeed be a man of remarkable qualities and political talents. He must also be a man of discretion for, in so far as civil service and other regualtions permit, he has a certain amount of patronage to dispense, and there are also certain funds at his disposal which may be used prudently in order to strengthen the position of his minister. People imbued with the Anglo-American concept of local government will be unable to see anything good in the prefect, but in a country which believes in centralization he constitutes an essential element of coordination.

The departmental General Council

While the prefect represents the national government in the department, the local functions are carried out by a General Council (*Conseil Général*), whose chairman is called president. The general councils are important bodies because of their composition, not because of their functions. In order to maintain or build up local strength, virtually all leading politicians are active members of general and often of municipal councils in which they are joined by men of local and often

[69] The official title is *Inspecteurs Généraux de l'Administration en Mission Extraordinaire;* R. S. Abbott and R. Sicard, "A Postwar Development in French Regional Government: The 'Super Préfet,' " *American Political Science Review,* Vol. XLIV (1950), pp. 426–431.

national distinction. General councils have very few functions except for discussion, as the prefect is the real kingpin of the *département*. However they watch the prefect, and the political role of the council's members makes this an important performance. The General Council has a standing committee which often carries on the functions of the entire council. Where it has an auditing function, it is primarily concerned with the supervision of financial affairs.

The *arrondissement* and its subdivisions

The department's subdivisions, called *arrondissements,* are of little significance. It is primarily an administrative subsection of the department, is headed by a subprefect, and is without an independent life of its own. Under the Third Republic it derived a certain amount of importance from the fact that it was an electoral district. The electoral system of the Fifth Republic, however, is based on a different electoral district. The *arrondissement* could easily be abolished, but civic and local pride have been able to prolong its existence.

This has also been said of a further territorial subdivision, the canton, which has no civic life of its own. Yet, it fulfills an unofficial mission by giving a center and cohesion to communities which would otherwise lack them. The canton is grouped around the most important town in the area, which is the seat of a number of necessary officials, especially notaries and court clerks (*huissiers*). Small communities are thereby able to effect a certain amount of consolidation which is otherwise prevented by a senseless uniformity which imposes precisely the same type of municipal government on all towns other than Paris, regardless of size or significance.

Municipal government

Each city elects a city council, which in turn elects a mayor, who presides over it. In communities of 500 inhabitants or less, eleven councilors are elected. In bigger cities their number is proportionately larger, but the maximum number of councilmen, thirty-seven, is reached by cities of 60,000 inhabitants. All larger cities, except Paris, have the same number.

The rules of order, the jurisdiction, and the organization of the city councils are strictly determined by law. The councilors themselves are elected on the basis of a proportional-list system combined with preferential voting, which permits the voter to indicate preferences among the candidates of his party. However, he may not split his vote between different party lists. Municipal elections usually have a partisan character and are often dominated by national, rather than local, issues.

The mayor and his principal assistants (*adjoints*) head the executive departments of the city, which may be simple or complex depending on the size of the community. He prepares and executes the budget, is responsible for public safety and order, administers local licensing and inspection regulations, and maintains housekeeping functions. While the mayor's importance increases with the size of his city, it is nevertheless a fact that he finds himself under stricter control by the prefect when the city is large. Thus, in cities of more than 5,000 inhabitants, the chief of police is appointed by the Minister of the Interior, not the mayor, and in certain larger cities the police force is even more strongly controlled by Paris. In addition, the prefect, in exercising his power of *tutelle administrative,* may dissolve city councils or set aside mayors' ordinances if they are deemed illegal. He may also suspend or dismiss mayors for "improper activities." Although it is the prefect who takes such drastic actions, they are almost invariably ordered by the Minister of the Interior. Political considerations as well as fear of being overruled by the Council of State have greatly limited extreme measures of this kind. However, dismissals of mayors have happened repeatedly in recent years in cases of Communist mayors who fused their public and party functions too closely.

Mayors hold a double position. On the one hand, they are the chief executives of their communities; on the other hand, they are agents of the prefect with regard to functions under national law, such as the maintenance of voting lists. Many mayors occupy a special place because of their national, rather than local, importance. What has been true of the departmental general council, namely, that nationally prominent politicians seek membership there, is even more so in the case of the mayors of France. Many, if not most, leading statesmen of France have sought to be mayors of their home city and have maintained that office concurrently with their national posts. The dean of France's statesmen-mayors was of course Édouard Herriot, many times Premier and cabinet member and in the forties and fifties president of the National Assembly, who was mayor of Lyons for over fifty years. Only the Vichy interlude caused a short interruption of this extraordinary record.

The fact that mayors of important towns can afford to be absent for long parliamentary sessions or for terms in cabinet office is made possible by the first *adjoint,* who does the work in the mayor's absence. On the other hand, the national importance of a mayor-deputy or even cabinet minister can do much for a city.[70]

Paris

A separate case is presented by the city of Paris. In many countries a special status is given the capital city; the nonvoting inhabitants of Washington, D.C., are well aware of that fact. But in other respects Paris cannot be compared to Washington. As a city, Paris is by all odds the most important place of France. The "city of lights" is the political, intellectual, and economic leader of the country. "Who holds Paris, holds France," is a well-known expression. Moreover, all revolutions, of which France has had more than her share, commenced and were decided

---

[70] The permanent town clerk (*secrétaire de la ville;* in larger cities, *secrétaire général de la mairie*) is in charge of the entire staff. In very small communes the schoolmaster may act as clerk.

in Paris. In order to make sure that local issues will not prevail over national ones, Paris has been organized in a special way, as determined by the law of July 24, 1867.

Paris has no mayor but is governed by two prefects for the department of the Seine, one of whom is the regular departmental prefect, while the other is the prefect of police. Paris is divided into twenty *arrondissements,* each headed by a so-called "mayor." But as this official is appointed by the Council of Ministers, upon recommendation of the Minister of the Interior, he is in fact nothing but a sub-prefect. If any one official comes close to being the mayor of Paris, it is the president of the city council, but the prefect of the Seine department actually carries most of the functions which are now ordinarily associated with the position of mayor. For the purpose of planning and coordinating, an Inspector General (Super Prefect) has been appointed for the entire Paris region.

Paris has a city council composed of ninety members, who are elected by the *arrondissements,* or rather their subdivisions, known as "quarters" (*quartiers*). All city councilors are automatically general councilors of the department of the Seine as well. Fifty additional members are elected by the nonincorporated suburbs. The members of the Paris city council receive a salary, which is unusual in France, but in return they find that theirs is nearly a full-time job because of the almost constant sessions of the council.

In its functions, the Paris city council is even more restricted than French city councils ordinarily are. The authority of the prefects and the need for ministerial approval for some of its most important acts transform the Paris city council into something that is largely decorative. Nevertheless, elections to the council are carried out with much of the gusto which characterizes parliamentary contests.

Debatable merit

A wide difference of opinion exists between American and French experts on the relative merits of their respective systems. The belief that home rule is the best road to democracy and representative government makes the absence of real local self-government, as the term is understood in the Anglo-American countries, surprising to us. Movements for home rule exist in France, but they have produced no powerful ground swell and the government has been able to ignore them with impunity.

This divergence in concepts illustrates the vast difference of approach between the English- and French-speaking worlds. The Anglo-American approach to problems has traditionally been inductive and pragmatic. The French approach is deductive and systematic. America especially has generally been content to let local units of government find their own way and has benefited from their experience. Progress in local and municipal government has often been the result of successful experiments by individual states, counties, and municipalities. From those experiences more general rules have been derived. In France, such an approach would be condemned as unsystematic and wasteful—if not worse. The merit of an innovation must first be proved on the basis of theoretical logic and in conformity with accepted doctrines. If such proof is successful, then the innovation must logically be adopted everywhere; a partial adoption would make no sense. Such general adoption, however, can be accomplished only by the national government. Progress, as understood in France, is therefore tied to centralism and uniformity. Home rule is suspected of being capable of becoming the stronghold of reaction; it is feared to be the road to disorder and anarchy, and it is certain to be wasteful.

As this system appears to be acceptable to most Frenchmen, the foreign observer may well remain at ease. It is a system specially adapted to the enforcement of national policy on all levels.[71] In disturbed times such as these, the French system has certain definite advantages.

[71] For a recent comprehensive treatment see Brian Chapman, *Introduction to French Local Government,* London, 1953.

6

De Gaulle's foreign policy

The title of this chapter was not chosen lightly. Although De Gaulle's policy as President is, of course, in every sense, formally and substantively the foreign policy of France, it is nevertheless in a very real sense the policy of one man, having been conceived and implemented solely by Charles de Gaulle.

Domestic policy and foreign policy are greatly interwoven in all countries, but nowhere is this more the case than in France, where General de Gaulle has utilized in daily policies his fundamental analysis of France's need to exist as a nation. I have already quoted the statement from his memoirs to the effect that the rich and imaginative spirit of France pulls that country in many directions, and it can be pulled together only through great enterprises.[1]

De Gaulle's first task was to rid himself and France of the mortgage of Algeria, which he had come to regard as a menace both to France's resources and to

[1] Charles de Gaulle, *Mémoires de guerre,* Paris, 1954, Vol. I, *L'Appel, 1940–1942,* p. 1.

its continued fabric as a state. He succeeded in this, but at the price of embittering a great part of the French army.[2] This uneasiness, if not to say hostility, of the army, he attempted in turn to assuage by diverting the army's attention to modern technology and especially to nuclear weapons. These were essentially tactical aims designed to make all his other aspirations possible—the great design to make France again a great power. General de Gaulle is not unmindful of the limited resources and manpower of France, but he believes that power is a combination of physical capability and will, and that a nation determined to assert its will to the utmost could counterbalance to a considerable extent the possibly greater resources of other countries which might be accompanied by a less determined will.

Within the limitations of these pages, let us examine General de Gaulle's policy for three important areas: the unification of Europe, the defense of the Atlantic area (NATO), and the United Nations.

When General de Gaulle came into power, he found the European Coal and Steel Community already well installed, and the Common Market and EURATOM in the process of implementation. He was quite critical of all these institutions from the very beginning. Those of his followers who were members of the National Assembly or the Senate had already criticized them vigorously and had consistently voted against them. However, they had become obligations of France and De Gaulle went along with their implementation. The initial fear that French industry would find it too difficult to compete with German competition proved unfounded, but still De Gaulle did not want to see the process of integration go too far. In particular he resisted political integration.

Charles de Gaulle has said much in extremely broad and sometimes mellifluous tones about "European unity." But to those who have actually been in the forefront of the struggle for greater European unification, to men like Jean Monnet and the late Robert Schuman, the unification of Europe always meant the creation of durable institutions through which this unity could be practically applied and implemented. General de Gaulle is clearly an adversary of such institutions. Many observers will find it difficult to see how he can, at one and the same time, be for European unity and against any institutions of such unification. One explanation for his attitude is that when he speaks of "Europe" he means a unity of the will among sovereign states, that unified will to be provided by a strong nation and a strong leader, i.e., France. This might seem acceptable logic to those Europeans who see only an inevitable return to nationalism, but many sincere believers in European unity see in it only a thinly disguised wish for French hegemony and say that while the General speaks of "Europe" he means "France."

General de Gaulle's 1963 rejection of Great Britain's application to become a member of the Common Market was quite consistent with his views, although many newspapers considered his dictum to be primarily a reaction to the nuclear

[2] Paul-Marie de la Gorce, *The French Army: A Military-Political History* (trans. by Kenneth Douglas), New York, 1963; Raoul Girardet (ed.), *La crise militaire française 1945–1962,* Paris, 1964; Jean Planchais, *La malaise de l'armée,* Paris, 1958.

"deal" made by the United States and Great Britain at the Nassau Conference of 1962. Their interpretation does little justice to De Gaulle's vast concepts. It is true that the British government itself was not enthusiastic about political integration, but Great Britain would definitely have been a rival to France's claim for leadership of Europe.

By June, 1965, the agricultural problems of the Common Market were increasingly troublesome, and the Commission of the European Economic Community (Common Market) submitted to the Council of Ministers of the member states an ambitious plan which went well beyond the settlement of these agricultural problems. General de Gaulle, on June 30, 1965, used this as an occasion, if not to say a pretext, to bring to a halt all negotiations between France and the Common Market and also within the Common Market. Subsequently, French Foreign Minister Maurice Couve de Murville made it very clear in a speech in the French National Assembly that what was at stake was not merely the proposal of the Commission, nor the form of the agricultural settlement, but much deeper questions of a political nature. Plainly, General de Gaulle was determined to reverse the process of integration by diminishing the power and status of the Commission and by refusing to accept the majority voting formula which was to come into effect within the Common Market on January 1, 1966.

The presidential elections of December 5th and 19th jolted De Gaulle's standing and prestige, especially as it was clear that his hostility toward European unification had been one of the causes of his disappointment. However, this did not lead to any modification of his demands; quite the contrary. On January 17, 1966, when the Foreign Ministers of the six member countries of the Common Market met in Luxembourg, they were confronted by ten French demands, called "proposals," which would in effect have given De Gaulle everything he wanted. The Commission was to be reduced to a definitely subordinate group of civil servants. The unification of the three Communities (Coal and Steel, EURATOM, Common Market) was to lay the groundwork for the removal of all independent-minded Commissioners, especially the Commission's President Walter Hallstein and the Dutch Commissioner Sicco Mansholt. In particular De Gaulle insisted either on a revision of the Treaty of Rome abolishing the majority voting formula or, at the least, a solemn written statement that such would in fact be the case. At this point, the meeting of Foreign Ministers broke up in total disagreement with De Gaulle.

A second meeting took place on January 31, 1966, in which a compromise was reached, but which left many questions unsettled. The diminution of the Commission did not take place, and the other five nations made only a few peripheral concessions which were more in form than in substance. The election of the new Commissioners of the unified Commission was left open, but there was strong resistance to De Gaulle's desire to remove Hallstein and Mansholt. In 1967 Hallstein removed himself from the controversy, but his successor, Jean Rey, is no less a "European" and by no means a Gaullist puppet.

As far as the majority vote was concerned, the ministers "agreed to disagree." They agreed that "in the event of decisions that can be adopted by a majority on the proposal of the Commission, when very important interests of one or several partners are at stake, the members of the Council will attempt within a reasonable period of time to arrive at solutions that could be adopted by all members of the Council. . . ." But there was nothing new in that, because this procedure had already been agreed upon long before. However, the French delegation thought that in such a case, "discussion must be continued until unanimous agreement has been reached," while the other delegations "acknowledged that a difference of opinion remains on what should be done in the event that conciliation cannot be fully attained." In other words, if repeated attempts to bring about unanimity were not successful, the "five" might be prepared to go ahead and adopt the measure concerned by majority vote, in implementation of Article 2 of the Treaty of Rome—and in that case, presumably, another first-rate crisis in the Common Market would erupt.

Two conclusions from these events are permitted: (1) General de Gaulle will continue to resist any further European integration and will veto any new steps; (2) as long as the other members of the Common Market remain firm, he will not be able to disrupt it. And since the presidential elections of 1965, he knows that France's withdrawal from the Common Market might have serious domestic political consequences.

The above-discussed crisis in the EEC is closely tied to the crisis within the North Atlantic Treaty Organization (NATO). General de Gaulle has taken many opportunities to denounce alleged "American hegemony" in NATO. In this he has met some sympathy in other European countries. And even in America there was a good deal of understanding for his point of view, since people recognized that the conditions which had existed in 1949, when the North Atlantic Treaty was drafted and signed, were not the same in the 1960s. However, a basic change was rendered difficult by the facts of the nuclear age, which required, in the opinion of most European countries as well as of the United States, that the deterrent power of America's enormous nuclear arsenal should continue to shield Europe. Most other European countries therefore favored a greater European share in nuclear decision-making along with the continuation of an integrated Atlantic defense system. At the same time, the relative relaxation of East-West tensions (*détente*) made the problem less urgent in the opinion of several governments.

General de Gaulle, while accepting the reality of the *détente,* had a basically different view. Militarily he appeared to accept the thesis promulgated by General Gallois[3] that nuclear weapons had such devastating results that even relatively small nuclear powers, like France, could deter major ones, like the U.S.S.R. Politically, however, the "fallout" was more important. In developing a French national nuclear

---

[3] For a brilliant discussion of this controversy, see Raymond Aron, *The Great Debate: Theories of Nuclear Strategy* (trans. by E. Powell), New York, 1965.

force (*force de frappe, force de dissuasion*) De Gaulle made clear that Germany was not to be given a part in any kind of nuclear decision, and it seemed likely that he envisaged a European defense system centered around France's small nuclear force, which then might enter into a bilateral relationship with the United States. In all this there was to be no integrated command but only strictly national forces united by bilateral agreements and alliances of the type common in the eighteenth and ninteenth centuries.[4]

The situation became further aggravated when General de Gaulle declared that France would leave NATO "in 1969 at the latest," when, under the treaty, member states can withdraw. Suddenly, on March 8, 1966, De Gaulle struck another of his sudden and peremptory blows. Without any attempt at negotiation or conciliation,[5] he declared that all foreign military installations in France had to come under French command or leave French soil. He also announced unilaterally that all French forces still within NATO's structure would be withdrawn.

This referred particularly to two understrength divisions and some air force units stationed in Germany. This declaration was elaborated by individual notes to all NATO governments. In these notes there was a curious statement, contrasting with previous, especially private, statements by the General, that France would not after all make use of Article 13 of the NATO Treaty permitting member states to withdraw officially from NATO in 1969 and thereafter. In view of the cessation of all forms of practical cooperation, this latter point could not be viewed by other NATO partners as having any practical value other than permitting the French government to make further trouble.

De Gaulle also attempted to disrupt NATO procedurally by proposing bilateral discussions to regulate the phasing out of France's position in NATO. This was clearly in conflict with the obligations of any unilateral organization to deal with all fellow members together and not on a selective, bilateral basis. De Gaulle's move was therefore quickly rejected by President Johnson on the very same day.

France's action raised many problems: the moving of NATO installations out of France, the future status of French forces in Germany, the operation of the NATO pipeline, and the use of French airspace. Heartening to the other NATO members, however, was the unanimity with which the need for a continued NATO was asserted by all the other fourteen member states, and with which De Gaulle's move was condemned and rejected. It was obviously the determination of the others

---

[4] An analysis of where Gaullist thinking would logically lead was developed by an important study group of the Study Center on Foreign Policy in Paris and published under the designation XXX, "Faut-il reformer l'Alliance Atlantique?," in *Politique Étrangère* (1965), No. 3, p. 230–244. It is known that General de Gaulle was shown this article before its publication and voiced no objection.

[5] General de Gaulle had suggested, in 1958, a French-British-United States directorate to coordinate allied policy, not just in NATO but world-wide, and this had been rejected by President Eisenhower, who gave his reasons in two lengthy communications. But after 1958 no official French plan for NATO reform was ever submitted.

to carry on without him and to wait for some future government of France to take a more positive attitude toward Western cooperation.

Perhaps the most dazzling example of General de Gaulle's undoubted skill in international affairs has been his policy of seeking "dissolution of the blocs." There are various considerations operating in this sphere. In the first place, De Gaulle has always refused to accept the validity, even the existence, of ideologies in international affairs. To him there is no such thing as communism being an international menace or even a problem; to him there is only a problem of Russian or Chinese national power and interests asserting themselves and using ideology as an excuse and a disguise for their national designs. To him, therefore, there is no essential difference between Communist drives for domination and American-led moves designed to stop such drives. Both are, in his view, national actions undertaken to further purely national interests. Moreover, he objects that such "pseudo-ideological" conflicts are a bipolar struggle between the two superpowers, the United States and the Soviet Union, which tend to override or ignore Europe's interests.

In a bipolar world the voice of a medium-sized power like France would not be heard loudly unless it became fused with the voice of an integrated Europe, but that remedy was, as we have seen, anathema to him. Hence he turned his endeavor, in 1965 and 1966, toward dissolution of the blocs. This he could achieve most easily within the bloc of which France was a member at that time, namely, NATO, but he was also encouraged by strains within the Soviet bloc, notably those caused by Romania among the countries of the Warsaw Pact. His epic journey to the Soviet Union in 1966 was designed to further this "dissolution of the blocs" and undoubtedly had considerable "atmospheric" repercussions. His grand and masterful gestures plus the manner in which he was received in the Soviet Union certainly impressed the many Europeans who had become weary of the cold war and who sought a diminution of the two-bloc situation. To Frenchmen in particular, this journey appeared to be France's grand reentry into the world politics of the great powers. They frequently likened his journey to the visit of President Raymond Poincaré to Tsar Nicolas II in July, 1914.

In his sharp opposition to American policy in Vietnam, General de Gaulle further sought to make himself available as a world arbiter. It seemed to many observers as though the General felt that he could assert himself and France only by opposing the United States at every opportunity, whether on Vietnam, NATO, fiscal policies, or virtually any other subject. Certainly under his rule the relations between the United States and France sank to an all-time low, despite periodic and ritualistic mutual protestations of traditional friendship and the invocation of Lafayette's memory.

In the same direction went General de Gaulle's policy toward the United Nations. For a long time his attitude toward it varied between disdain and contempt. He often referred to the UN as *"le machin,"* which might be liberally translated as "that thing" and was not intended as an expression of endearment. In particular he considered the voting formula in the UN's General Assembly to be totally un-realistic. He bitterly resented various UN attempts to interfere in France's overseas concerns, especially during the Algerian war. He joined the Soviet government in resisting any UN efforts which might be even remotely considered as interfering with national sovereignty. For the same reasons he has opposed UN peacekeeping operations and, together with the Soviet Union, has refused to help pay for them.

This attitude is completely consistent with his view that there must be no limitation whatsoever on France's freedom in the conduct of foreign affairs. This, however, does not mean that De Gaulle, superior tactician that he is, will not use the UN when it fits his purpose. Thus, in the growing controversy between the United States and France over the war in Vietnam and over China's role in the UN, France has made itself felt increasingly in the UN—without changing any of its previous positions and without contributing one franc to the world organization's peacekeeping activities.

The consummate mastery with which General de Gaulle has pursued his course has brought him much admiration inside and outside France, and many people undoubtedly wish that their national leaders had similar skill and statesman-like qualities. Yet to many critics it seems as though many of his successes were mainly visual, almost like dazzling play with mirrors, devoid of much substance. He has succeeded in weakening NATO, possibly even fatally, but he has failed com-pletely to erect another structure or combination in its stead. In particular he has failed to attract other European states to his ideas, with regard either to European integration or the lack thereof, or to his ideas of European defense. Germany in particular has found that De Gaulle's France is in no position to secure German or European security requirements without the strong participation, and in fact leadership, of the United States.

Even in his popular policy toward the dissolution of the blocs, there is a question whether he has achieved anything of a concrete nature, because there are obvious limitations both East and West to this idea, and it has become increasingly clear that if any substantial change is to be made in the world's bipolarity and in the cold war, that can best be achieved by direct negotiations between the United States and the Soviet Union without intermediaries. As the cautious hope rekindles that such negotiations will indeed be possible, the relative significance of France's action is likely to recede again.

There can be little doubt that De Gaulle's policy may be characterized as nationalistic. But it would certainly be incorrect to imply that he is the only nation-alist in France. France is a nation proud of its strong and glorious military tradi-tion. This became evident in 1954 when the long-fought-over project of a European Defense Community (EDC) was defeated in the National Assembly. Although much of the argument then was directed against the alleged militarism of Germany and toward the French dislike of seeing Germans in uniform again, it was only a few months later that the same National Assembly which had killed that European Defense Community voted with a comfortable majority for the West European

Union (WEU) which permitted Germany to establish a national army. Hence, not apprehension over Germany, but opposition to the welding of a strictly national French army into a general "European" one, was the explanation.

No previous regime, no other party in France, has gone as far in its nationalistic design as General de Gaulle. Even a part of his own UNR party does not quite follow him there. The lonely role which De Gaulle has assigned to France is perhaps plausible when it is in the hands of such a master and such an extraordinary personality as his. It will become much less so when France is led, as one day she must be, by a more ordinary mortal.

While this trend continues, the other members of the European Communities and those in the Atlantic partnership can perhaps do little more than hold their own. Where necessary, they can go ahead without France until there is again a government in France which might be more willing and more interested in continuing the trends toward European integration and Atlantic partnership.

To many observers, among them sincere though perhaps erstwhile admirers of Charles de Gaulle, this is a pity, because (1) France has been instrumental in one of the most hopeful developments of post-World War II Europe, namely, the trend toward greater unification, and (2) the extraordinarily high quality of French diplomats and civil servants has often won for France or for Frenchmen positions of leadership within these Communities.

It is not saying too much to say that France as the leader, rather than the opponent, of European integration would have been far more likely to achieve the role of preeminence which its government craves than the France of the anti-integrationist policies pursued by General de Gaulle.

De Gaulle has played a diplomatic game of unsurpassed virtuosity, supported by one of the most highly skilled diplomatic services in the world. The resulting increase of French influence and prestige in the world is unmistakable. And yet, observers may well wonder what the long-range consequences of De Gaulle's policies will be. He has spearheaded the rebirth of European nationalism against both European integration and Atlantic partnership, or "American hegemony" as he prefers to describe it. But while this opposition is often claimed to be in behalf of "Europe," it seems highly unlikely that this reawakened nationalism will easily allow itself to be submerged into some "European" conception. It is far more likely that once on the march, this nationalism will push on and back to the traditional types of French, German, and other nationalism.[6] Moreover, France can play the role of leader only by keeping Great Britain out and Germany down—policies which may well succeed but which make neither for European unity nor for European strength. In other words, the diplomacy which attacks Atlantic partnership also directs itself against European unity, no matter how often it talks in the name of Europe.

That there has been an accretion of power to France can hardly be doubted.

---

[6] George W. Ball, "How Frail Are U.S.-European Ties?" *Washington Post,* Dec. 11, 1966.

But the same has not been true for "Europe" as a whole, and France alone, despite the genius of its leadership and the skill of its diplomacy, is no equal to the superpowers, especially the United States and the U.S.S.R.

As a result, the great issues of the world are increasingly settled or acted upon without the participation, or without the fullest possible participation, of Europe. The fact that this has happened despite Europe's great economic strength and accumulated political, economic, and technical wisdom is a charge against the policies of General de Gaulle which future historians will have to consider.

part 3

Germany

It is characteristic of the Germans that one is rarely completely wrong about them. The German soul has corridors and cross-corridors; there are caves, hiding places, and dungeons; its disorder has much of the charm of the mysterious.

Friedrich Nietzsche

The unconditional surrender of Germany in May, 1945, brought about her temporary demise as a state. The four principal Allies took over all power. Only on the lowest levels of administration did they permit any kind of German government, and that only under rigorous control.

Many believed that Germany could be written off as a powerful nation and a principal factor in international politics. But today, only twenty years later, Western Germany, the German Federal Republic, is the largest state of Continental Europe, in terms of inhabitants, outside the Soviet Union and is the third largest producer in the world. Her industrial potential, know-how, and organization are unequaled anywhere outside the United States. With her regained strength and her diligent, disciplined—perhaps too disciplined—people, Germany is a powerhouse of the first magnitude for whose favor East and West vie alike.

Everything that happens in Germany has profound repercussions in the world at large, because in the contest between the Soviet world and the Western states, the position of Germany is today one of the principal issues. Under the impact of war and catastrophe the idea of a united Europe has found a great many new adherents, but it is clear to anyone that no such unity is feasible unless Germany, at least Western Germany, plays a decisive role therein.

The twentieth century has seen Germany go through a series of the most violent changes imaginable, from a great empire to an unstable republic, to one of the most brutal and murderous dictatorships ever recorded in history, to an utterly crushing defeat, and then to a surprisingly stable, healthy, and respected power. In this process, Germany has become a laboratory of political ideas, plans, and institutions. Here is a country in which a veritable social revolution has been attempted from the outside and by decree. Here is a state in which radically new institutions struggle hard with the customs and prejudices of the past, and here one may study intricate political and constitutional schemes from the blueprint stage up to actual operation and may note the imponderables and problems which emerge in that process. Germany's constitutional fabric, the nature of her parties, and the maturity of her people are problems of world importance.

Much of the recent development of Germany is highly encouraging. Her government has proved the most stable in Europe. Her currency is one of Europe's most reliable. Her economic recovery has been stupendous, and even the tremendous stream of refugees and expellees has been largely absorbed by hard work and sacrifice shared by the entire population. Perhaps most encouraging to the foreign observer is the fact that extremist groups, both Communist and neo-Nazi, have remained so small as to be insignificant. Under the leadership of Chancellor Konrad Adenauer and his successors, Ludwig Erhard and Kurt Georg Kiesinger, Germany resolutely took her place on the side of the West, while the numerous uprisings and revolts in Eastern Germany, especially in 1953, unmistakably demonstrated where those people would stand if they were only given an opportunity to express themselves.

NORTH SEA

BALTIC SEA

SCHLESWIG-
HOLSTEIN

Hamburg

(MECKLENBURG
VORPOMMERN)

Bremerhaven

Bremen

LOWER SAXONY

GERMAN

GERMAN

(BRANDENBURG)

Berlin

DEMOCRATIC

NORTH RHINE-
WESTPHALIA

(SAXONY-ANHALT.)

FEDERAL

REPUBLIC

HESSE

(SAXONY)

(THURINGIA)

RHINELAND-
PALATINATE

REPUBLIC

SAAR

BAVARIA

BADEN-
WÜRTTEMBERG

NETHERLANDS

BELGIUM

LUX.

FRANCE

SWITZERLAND

AUSTRIA

CZECHOSLOVAKIA

POLISH ADMINISTRATION

The late Joseph Stalin is reported to have said: "Without Germany we cannot win, and with Germany we cannot lose." The essential correctness of this analysis remains uncontested.

More than most other nations, the Germans are not only the product, but also the prisoners of their past. The acts and omissions of the Middle Ages, the rise of Prussia, the late unification of the country, to name only a few factors, have profoundly marked Germany. Also the consequences of Hitler's evil reign will long continue to place a heavy mortgage on the shoulders of even the best Germans. This is why considerable attention has been paid to historical material in the pages ahead.

1

Historical introduction: from the Holy Roman Empire to the Second Reich

In the ever-changing maelstrom of human history, mankind has never again seen as long, as glorious, and as relatively stable a period as the 700-odd years of the great Roman Empire. Even after it had passed into history, its memory as the lost "golden age" haunted mankind. It inspired philosophers and theologians, princes and rulers. And when on Christmas Day, A.D. 800, Charlemagne was crowned emperor by Pope Leo III, it seemed to many contemporaries that the great Roman Empire had been revived with even greater glory. That proved to be an illusion.

The "Holy Roman Empire," as this concoction was to be miscalled,[1] had little

---

[1] It was German rather than Roman, and an aristocratic republic rather than an empire. Its "holiness" may also be doubted.

in common with its great predecessor, despite periods of undoubted greatness. More than that, the results of the thousand years of this Holy Roman Empire proved generally unfortunate for Germany, for the process of national consolidation which must precede the establishment of constitutional government[2] was delayed for centuries.

While less powerful rulers were obliged to consolidate their dominions and bring reluctant nobles under the control of the state in order to survive, the German emperors held power sufficient to allow pursuit of the elusive dream of the *Reich*.[3] Even the greatest of the emperors seems to have preferred campaigning in Italy to tending his own back yard. Thus power tended to be split among the larger barons, and German law tended toward territorial law (*Landrecht*).[4]

This trend was further developed under the pressures of the ruinous Thirty Years War, when Germany became the battleground for all of Europe. The bloodletting, devastation, and disintegration brought on by this war, comparable in European history only to the Second World War, left the Holy Roman Empire a mass of petty, feuding, and ineffectual principalities. After 1648 (the Treaty of Westphalia), unity for Germany was farther removed than ever. The Holy Roman Empire continued to exist in name only, and under the hammer blows of Napoleon it collapsed with little more than a whimper.

The rise of Prussia

What was significant in the period between 1648 and 1806 was the final decline of Austria, the holder of the imperial crown, and the ascendance of that country which is usually regarded as the embodiment of all that is undesirable in the German character—Prussia.

Prussia was a relative newcomer to German history. Long after the establishment of the Holy Roman Empire, the central and eastern portion of the territory which later became Prussia was inhabited by lawless, pagan tribes of predominantly Slavic origin, called "Pruzzen."[5] They lived mainly from pillage and were a scourge upon their neighbors, especially the far more civilized Poles. Attempts to Christian-

---

[2] Carl J. Friedrich, *Constitutional Government and Democracy,* Boston, 1946, p. 8.

[3] The term *Reich* has always confounded the interpreter. Derived from the Latin word *regnum,* it means more than "empire," "commonwealth," or "state." In it is embodied the dream of Germany as the hub and heart of occidental civilization, of a commonwealth which is both of the realm of reality and of the realm of idea. It is a term which embodies essentially an historical myth rather than a constitutional or territorial entity. It is significant that the father of the German Constitution of 1919, the then Minister of the Interior, Hugo Preuss, rejected the suggested term "German Federation" and insisted on the retention of the word *Reich* because of the traditional and emotional value attached to that term in the minds of the German people. The original term *Reich* will therefore be used in this discussion, and no further attempt at translation will be made.

[4] The most prominent exposition of both *Landrecht* and the law of feudal relationships (*Lehnrecht*) is *Saxon's Mirror* (*Sachsenspiegel*), written by Eike von Repgow between 1198 and 1235.

[5] Even the name of the capital city, Berlin, is of Slavic (Wendish) origin, meaning "dam."

ize them failed. Then the Polish Duke Conrad of Masovia appealed for help to Hermann of Salza, Grand Master of the Order of Teutonic Knights, whose well-trained "elite guard" defeated the aborigines in a series of battles (1226 to 1283) and absorbed their territory. To consolidate it further, they inaugurated a period of forceful "Christianization," and used the pagan character of most of the inhabitants as a convenient excuse for separating them from their possessions.

The Order of Teutonic Knights was in its turn defeated by an alliance of its neighbors with the Prussian nobles (1410) and was saved from total annihilation only by great diplomatic skill. After a new revolt of the Prussian nobles, who obtained help from Poland, the Order ceded West Prussia and Ermeland to Poland and retained only East Prussia as a Polish fief. Thus was created the "corridor" problem which later plagued German-Polish relations.

Last *Hochmeister,* or chief, of the Order was Albert of Ansbach, a member of the Hohenzollern family, who renounced his Catholic faith in 1525, became a Protestant, and was created first Duke of Prussia by his uncle, the King of Poland. In 1618 the duchy of Prussia and the margravate[6] of Brandenburg were united to form the nucleus of the later Prussian power. Other territory was gained in 1648 as a result of the Westphalian Peace, and in 1660, Frederick William, the "Great Elector,"[7] forced Poland to renounce its nominal overlordship over Prussia. He also obtained other territory, especially in the Ruhr. His son, Frederick, was the first to become King of Prussia (1701).

Quickly, Prussia shed the remaining vestiges of feudalism. The nobility (*Junkers*)[8] was deprived of its remaining independence but compensated by superior positions in the newly formed professional army. Frederick William I (the "Soldier King") forged the Prussian army, which became an instrument of terrible efficiency when led by Frederick II, called by all Germans "the Great." It was this Frederick who began the long power struggle with Austria which eventually ended in Austria's defeat. Casting aside all inconvenient treaties, agreements, or promises, Frederick embarked upon a course of naked power politics which succeeded mainly in eliminating whatever unity had remained in Germany. Prussia itself gained little from the struggle. There is a strange parallel between the Prussia of Frederick II and the Germany of both the Kaiser and Hitler. In order to dominate the scene, Frederick entered into various alliances, especially with France, until both friend and foe suspected his motives with good reason and ganged up on him. As he thus

---

[6] *Mark* was the old Germanic word for frontier. Later it prefixed the names of special frontier counties, especially *Mark Brandenburg;* the rulers thereof were known as *margrave (Markgraf);* in the latinized form they were called *comes marchae* or *marchisus,* from which the word "marquis" is derived.

[7] In the Holy Roman Empire the emperors were elected by the principal barons of the realm, who were therefore called "electors" (German *Kurfürsten*). After 1257 there were seven of them: the Archbishops of Mainz, Trier, and Cologne; the King of Bohemia; the Duke of Saxony; the Margrave of Brandenburg; and the Palatine of the Rhine.

[8] From the Middle High German *junc-herre* (young master). Originally used for the sons of princes and rulers, the name *Junker* (pronounced "yoonker") later covered the Prussian nobility, especially of the agrarian and military type.

faced an "encirclement" of his own making, Frederick, luckier than his later imitators, was miraculously saved by the death of an enemy (the Empress Elizabeth Petrovna of Russia) and the coming to power of an admirer (Tsar Peter III) at the very moment when his position seemed practically hopeless.[9]

Frederick II was an absolute ruler, a king-dictator. His ministers and generals were merely his secretaries and lieutenants. But it is significant to note that his absolutism was not usually arbitrary. He continued and expanded a most efficient and incorruptible civil service, which, together with the army, was the mainstay of his rule. He alone made the laws, but once made, they were observed by all, including the king. To a more modern generation, the distinction between arbitrariness and law-abiding absolutism may seem exceedingly fine. But in those days, the knowledge of where one stood, and what one's rights were, was a distinct advantage.

The people of Prussia took to this idea of "law and order" which gave the subject few rights but allowed him to sleep peacefully in his bed if he had obeyed all laws and commands. Thus the Prussian state was able to unify into a solid phalanx its army, its civil service, and its people and to create for them the idea of the state as an authority (*Obrigkeitsstaat*) which takes care of all matters and supplies all the answers. In this manner, Prussia was able to preserve its state and crown despite revolution and violent upheaval elsewhere. It protected its citizens from the bloodshed and horror of the French Revolution, but it also prevented them from absorbing any "radical" ideas about popular sovereignty, self-government, and the rights of man. When Napoleon's armies occupied large parts of Germany, the fresh air of French progressivism could not be entirely excluded. But such ideas were confined to intellectuals and some dissident members of the middle and upper classes. The large masses of the people were not affected. Thus the frequently heroic struggle which culminated in the unsuccessful revolution of 1848 was in fact stillborn, and left hardly a dent on the body politic. After making some initial concessions to the revolutionaries, the King had no difficulty in breaking his word and returning to the old ways with a vengeance. Had the revolution been a true popular movement, he could not have afforded to do so, but he gauged the temper of the Prussians more correctly than did the well-meaning intellectuals who gathered at St. Paul's Church in Frankfurt.[10]

Once Prussia had successfully survived numerous defeats at the hand of Napoleon and had overcome the revolutionary wave which swept over Europe, it

[9] The ideas and the deeds of Frederick II have always had a powerful influence on German psychology. Few other historical figures embody the spirit of the German state more than this man, who always wrote, and mostly spoke, French and who had a profound contempt for German culture. The last trace of the "Frederick psychosis" occurred in April, 1945, in the final days of the Nazi regime, when Hitler and Goebbels hoped that the death of President Roosevelt might have the same results for them as the death of the Empress Elizabeth had for Frederick II. See H. R. Trevor-Roper, *The Last Days of Hitler*, New York, 1947, p. 100.
[10] The meeting place of the so-called "German National Assembly" on May 18, 1848. It was in commemoration of this spirit of German liberalism that President John F. Kennedy's principal address during his German visit was made at this church on June 25, 1963.

could undertake its final task—the conquest of hegemony in Germany. This meant first eliminating its archrival, Austria.

The German Confederation

Austrian influence in the affairs of the small German states commenced with the ending of the Thirty Years War. This influence was in a sense recognized by the Congress of Vienna which, paying lip service to the idea of German unity, created the German Confederation (1815) under the perpetual chairmanship of Austria. The Confederation was equipped with a parliament but found it impossible to govern effectively, saddled as it was with a unanimity rule and with the necessity for relying upon the individual states to carry out its decisions.

Austria, old, easygoing, and cosmopolitan, with its conglomeration of discordant lands, languages, and cultures, was in no condition to lead itself, let alone Germany. At the same time, its pressure and the structure of the Confederation stood in the way of any gradual unification of Germany. It was these forces which Prussia had to overcome if it was to head a new, united Germany.

Bismarck

The liberal developments of 1848 had not left even Prussia, the fortress of reaction, entirely untouched. Constitutional reforms were grudgingly granted. But when the parliamentary majority refused to sanction the government's military reform, the Prime Minister, Otto von Bismarck, decided to reverse the process of constitutional government by ignoring the will of the legislature and forcing through his entire program. Supported by the crown, the army, and the civil service, Bismarck's course could have been changed only by full-fledged revolution. But the Germans had little gumption for that, and thus a weak-kneed, halfhearted liberalism was brought to bay for the second time. Whatever opposition remained was virtually obliterated by Bismarck's victorious wars of aggression against Denmark (1864) and Austria (1866), which apparently proved him right. The removal of Austria from leadership in Germany opened the way to the final goal of Prussian hegemony.

The North German Federation

After Austria's elimination, a new organization was created under Prussian leadership—the North German Federation. Its constitution came into effect on July 1, 1867. In contrast to the impotent German Confederation, the North German Federation had all the earmarks of a true state. It provided for a Federal Council (*Bundesrat*) composed of delegates from the various state governments and bound by their instructions, as well as a Diet (*Reichstag*) elected by universal manhood suffrage. Bismarck remained the master, being responsible only to the

King of Prussia (the executive head of the new Federation) for his actions and policies. The garb of federalism in no way diminished the authoritative character of Prussian rule.

The pursuit of a secure and unified Germany led next to war with France. By clever maneuvering, Bismarck managed to unify Germans in and out of the Federation over the war question. France's disastrous defeat led to the culmination of Bismarck's policy—the crowning of King William as German Emperor on January 18, 1871, in the magnificent hall of mirrors at Versailles before the princes and military leaders of Germany.

The German Empire

Thus was created the second *Reich*. It was an achievement of Bismarck and his aides, of the nobles, and of the military and civil service. It was not an achievement of the people acting as an independent force. Henceforth the greatness and glory of Germany was forever associated with the throne and the reactionary political and military leaders. The courageous men who fought the forces of absolutism, in order to bring Germany into line with democratic and constitutional developments in other parts of Europe and America, were constantly forced to defend themselves against the accusation of being traitors to the reborn idea of the *Reich*.

2

*From strong empire
to weak republic*

The dominance of Prussia

The imperial constitution of April 16, 1871, declared that it established a permanent federation which was to be called the German *Reich;* the King of Prussia was to be its presiding officer, and indeed Prussia dominated the entire realm. Since Prussia comprised two-thirds of Germany, that situation is not surprising.

Nevertheless the imperial regime does not easily fall into any of the current classifications of government. Despite the existence of a freely elected parliament under universal manhood suffrage, it was certainly not democratic. But neither was it a dictatorship, as even so imperious a figure as Bismarck was not unchecked. Nor was it an autocracy, in the same sense as tsarist Russia was. Nor was it centralist, for true federalism existed.

Imperial Germany was an oligarchic regime ruled by a combination of the

Emperor and his court, the high civil service, the nobility, the military, and to a much smaller extent, certain economic interests. It operated on a basis of complicated interrelationships which worked fairly well as long as the hands of a virtuoso, Bismarck, guided them, but which broke down increasingly in the fumbling hands of his inferior successors.

Parliamentary impotency

Imperial Germany had a freely elected parliament. Debates there were free, and the government was sometimes asked embarrassing questions. But in many respects it was an expensive piece of make-believe. The government was in no way responsible to parliament but only to the Emperor. If the government answered questions posed by deputies, it did so condescendingly, as a matter of privilege not of right. Even in its proper field of legislation, the *Reichstag* found itself sidetracked by the upper house, the Federal Council (*Bundesrat*) in which the government introduced all its legislative proposals. The *Bundesrat* was not an elected body but a chamber of ambassadors from the various federal states (*Länder*) of Germany in which Prussia dominated.

Deprived of any active role, the *Reichstag* could act only in a negative fashion: it could say "No." But even that was difficult because the multiplicity of parties hindered collective action. On the right was the essentially Prussian Conservative party which was authoritarian, anti-Catholic, and antidemocratic. There were a number of liberal parties;[1] a Center party, which was a Catholic group containing both conservative and liberal elements but favoring a democratic and parliamentary regime; and on the far left the Social Democrats, profoundly influenced by Marx but favoring the democratic road to socialism. None of the parties enjoyed what could be called strong popular support. Nor was the situation helped by the fact that at different times the Bismarck government attempted to wipe out the Center party and the Social Democrats. Thus the *Reichstag* could engage in petty politics and endless debate but the real decisions were taken elsewhere. This gave it that terrible cognomen of "gossip club" (*Schwatzbude*) which accompanied it throughout its history and made it difficult for Germans to understand parliamentary government later.

The result was that the German people looked to the government and not to parliament for results and action. And as the German Empire coincided with the period of Germany's greatest expansion and prosperity, the German government's authority was not unwillingly accepted. For, undemocratic as the imperial regime was, it was not arbitrary. The laws were known and were scrupulously observed. The courts and administration were completely free from corruption. No unknown

---

[1] "Liberal" in the European sense historically means opposed to government intervention, in other words, to what might now be termed the welfare state.

dangers lurked in the dark, and the loyal subject who had obeyed all the laws to the letter could rest peacefully in his home secure in the knowledge that nothing would disturb him. Those were the days before the Gestapo and the MVD, and the Germans looked upon the Russian *Ochrana* as a sign of Asiatic barbarity from which Germany was mercifully preserved through the wisdom of her rulers and the loftiness of her *Kultur.* In return for those blessings, Germans were willing to leave the power of government in the hands of competent authority who, after all, knew much better what was good for them.

This concept of the *Obrigkeitsstaat,* the state as a commanding authority, and the "spirit of the subject" (*Untertanengeist*) was beautifully captured by Heinrich Heine, Germany's greatest lyric poet, a man who combined a deep love for Germany with a profound understanding of her weakness, in the following lines:[2]

> Honor your mayor; it is he
> Who guards the state and zealously
> Decides what's best for old and young.
> So listen well—and hold your tongue.

The First World War and army control

In the West the Allies fought the war under civilian control, which was never seriously challenged. This enabled them to achieve a remarkable measure of national unity and confirm French Premier Georges Clemenceau's famous expression, "war is too serious a business to be left to the generals." But in Germany a totally different course was taken. The *Reichstag* virtually abdicated, and by 1916 the Army High Command was in complete charge of the country, exercising an authority which even the Emperor could not challenge.

The German soldiers fought with their customary gallantry and discipline, but the military leadership showed little appreciation of the economic requirements of modern war or of the problems of civil government. As German soldiers stood far on enemy soil everywhere, the possibility of defeat did not occur to them. As late as September, 1917, General Erich Ludendorff, Quartermaster General of the Army and its real leader, demanded that large parts of Belgium and France as well as Kurland and Lithuania should be incorporated into Germany, that Belgium should be divided, and that Germany should acquire a larger colonial empire and naval bases around the globe.[3]

The armistice with Russia at Brest-Litovsk and the subsequent peace treaty of

---

[2] From Heinrich Heine's *"Erinnerung aus Kraehwinkels Schreckenstagen,"* freely translated by Louis Untermeyer. (L. Untermeyer, *Heinrich Heine, Paradox and Poet,* New York, 1937, pp. 317*ff.*)

[3] Memorandum of General Ludendorff concerning war aims, dated Sept. 14, 1917, quoted in Bernhard Schwertfeger, *Die politischen und militärischen Verantwortlichkeiten im Verlaufe der Offensive von 1918,* Berlin, 1927, pp. 102–106.

Bucharest demonstrated that these concepts were not just idle dreams.[4] But on August 8, 1918, the "black day" of the German army,[5] British tank forces penetrated the German lines and revealed weaknesses which could no longer be hidden. This, as well as the collapse of the Balkan front and of the corroded Austrian-Hungarian empire, made defeat inevitable. Ludendorff himself admitted this situation in the following words: "The situation on the western front was extraordinarily tense, especially with regard to the 17th, 2nd, 18th, and 4th armies. The reserves had been diminished, the troops were exhausted. *The war could no longer be won.*"[6]

The new Chancellor, Prince Max of Baden, was thereupon forced by the High Command to negotiate an armistice with the Allies, but after it was accomplished, the army chiefs denied all responsibility for it. To the German people the sudden turn of events came as a terrible psychological shock. The tightly controlled press and the ever-optimistic army communiqués had hidden from them the true state of affairs. Suddenly, within the period of a few days, they tumbled from the conviction of victory to the discovery of defeat.

The "stab in the back" legend and the Republic

The generals who had lost the war stood aside, and the long-neglected members of parliament took over. On them now fell the burden of the impoverished country and the onus of the armistice and the peace treaties. Emperor William II fled the country, after first refusing to abdicate, and the republic was hastily proclaimed. But in the people's minds, the generals remained associated with victory and the politicians became associated with a defeat in which they had no part. A myth of the most insidious kind was born in those days: the "stab in the back" legend. The defeated generals proclaimed to the world that they had not failed, but that a conspiracy of socialists, democrats, Jews, etc., had undermined the nation's will to fight and thus betrayed Germany. "Like Siegfried stricken down by the treacherous spear of Hagen, our weary front collapsed," proclaimed Field Marshal von Hindenburg.[7]

Completely false as the story was, it was nevertheless eagerly believed. For four years Germany had ostensibly marched from victory to victory. Suddenly she was laid low. What easier explanation could there be than "foul play"? In this way, the disappointment, the hatred, and the quest for responsibility were successfully diverted from the responsible militarists and heaped upon the leaders of the new republic who were perhaps not always brilliant but who were certainly innocent as far as the military defeat was concerned.

[4] For an excellent account, see John W. Wheeler-Bennett, *The Forgotten Peace,* New York, 1939.
[5] Erich Ludendorff, *Meine Kriegserinnerungen, 1914–1918,* Berlin, 1919, p. 547.
[6] Quoted by Schwertfeger, *op. cit.,* pp. 362*ff.* (The italics are the author's.)
[7] Paul von Hindenburg, *Out of My Life* (trans. by F. A. Holt), New York, 1921, Vol. II, p. 275.

For the politically inexperienced Germans, the "stab in the back" legend became a potent and fateful drug. And thus the German republic, known to history as the Weimar Republic, came into being against the bitter resentment of many Germans who saw in it a symbol of their misery and defeat.

The Weimar Republic

In form, the new German state which originated on November 9, 1918, was a soviet republic. Revolutionary, self-constituted bodies, the Councils of Workers and Soldiers, had sprung up everywhere. Meeting in Berlin in plenary session on that day, they declared themselves the "holders of political power" and Germany a "socialist republic," and elected an executive committee which in turn designated a cabinet that was called "Council of People's Commissars" (*Rat der Volksbeauftragten*), after the Russian model.

But among the Social Democrats, who had emerged as the strongest party, less revolutionary tendencies prevailed. The political conditions at the end of the war raised the possibility of a German soviet government, but by the election of January 19, 1919, the moderate element emerged victorious. The revolutionary period came to an end. The National Assembly met at the city of Weimar in order to avoid revolutionary pressure, which still abounded in Berlin. Moreover, it was hoped that Weimar, which was associated with Germany's great cultural past, would serve as a reminder that national greatness did not necessarily depend on feats of arms alone.

The Weimar Constitution was democratic and federal, but it gave considerable power to the executive, and made it possible at times to rule by decree. Moreover, by decree of the *Reich* President, the central power could impose itself upon recalcitrant *Länder,* and the *Reich* President had the right, under the notorious Article 48 of the Constitution, to suspend civil liberties in periods of emergency. The *Reichstag,* the lower house of parliament, emerged in full importance.

The first President of the Weimar Republic, Friedrich Ebert, remained scrupulously within his constitutional powers. The second President, Paul von Hindenburg, former commander of the imperial High Command, maintained the practices of his predecessor at first. But after 1930, when the German *Reichstag* was torn apart between warring factions and immobilized by extremists, Germany was ruled virtually without parliament, by means of the decree-making power of the President. Even rents were regulated, and licensing laws for automobiles as well as agricultural marketing regulations were enacted in this fashion. Finally this Article 48 was used to oust the legally constituted government of Prussia.

Thus the German republican regime was in effect liquidated before the Nazis took over, although the Nazis contributed to the paralysis of German parliamentarianism which had brought about the resort to this method of government by decree.

The deterioration of political life

The political picture of the Weimar Republic was forever cursed by the presence of a large number of parties.[8] Their numbers varied considerably as new groups emerged and old ones decayed. At one time as many as thirty parties vied for the favor of the electorate. True, many of these were not of national significance, but their existence made a profoundly unfavorable impression on the German people, an impression which was frequently carried over into contempt for the democratic system which made such conditions possible.

Before the rise of Nazism the German Nationalist People's party (*Deutschnationale Volkspartei*) occupied the extreme right of the stage.

The party of big business and finance was the German People's party (*Deutsche Volkspartei*), the successor to the old National Liberals. It was a conservative but constitutional party. It is chiefly remembered for having given the Weimar Republic its only statesman of real magnitude, Gustav Stresemann.

The middle of the stage was occupied by the Center party (*Zentrum*). Neither reactionary nor liberal, the party stood on strictly republican and constitutional grounds.

An offshoot of the Center was the Bavarian People's party (*Bayerische Volkspartei*), which in 1920 constituted itself as a separate party.

The German Democratic party (*Deutsche demokratische Partei*) was formed in 1918 and attempted to become a focal point for the progressive but anti-Socialist middle classes. In 1930 it vividly illustrated the sorry plight of the Weimar Republic by renaming itself State party (*Staatspartei*),[9] indicating that even the name "democratic" was fraught with disadvantages.

Until 1932 the strongest party in Germany was the Social Democratic party (*Sozialdemokratische Partei Deutschlands*). It was sincerely republican and democratic, but it never rose to the task which history had imposed upon it. Its leaders were party bureaucrats who had gained their places of eminence by long, faithful service rather than by special brilliance or imagination. Although the party polled 40 percent of the vote on the average until 1932, it permitted itself to be constantly outmaneuvered and eliminated from active governmental participation for long stretches of time. After 1930 it had virtually no influence on the course of events.

While the Social Democratic party failed the test of leadership, it nevertheless left a strong mark upon Germany. It gave an unequaled amount of political educa-

---

[8] The disastrous effect of proportional representation on the fate of Germany has been explored definitively by F. A. Hermens, *Democracy or Anarchy,* Notre Dame, Ind., 1941. Only four or five of the fifteen-odd parties represented in the *Reichstag* could have maintained themselves under an Anglo-American type of electoral system, and among them a coalition of Social Democrats and Centrists, perhaps with some of the liberal element, could have commanded a two-thirds majority in the *Reichstag.* Such a government would have been in a strong position to deal with the rising Nazi menace. See Carl J. Friedrich, *Constitutional Government and Democracy,* Boston, 1946, p. 288; and F. A. Hermens, *P.R., Democracy and Good Government,* Notre Dame, Ind., 1943, pp. 21*ff.*

[9] After fusion with a small party of that name.

tion to its members and followers, especially among the workers, which even the iron fist of the Gestapo and the concentration camps could not entirely break. As late as March, 1933, two months after Hitler had come to power, and under conditions of utmost terror and ruthlessness unleashed by the Nazis, over 7,000,000 Germans dared to vote for the Social Democratic ticket. This discipline and tradition enabled the party to revive almost immediately after the collapse of the Hitler regime.

The Communist Party (*Kommunistische Partei Deutschlands*) took from its inception a position of uncompromising hostility toward the Republic. Since it had absolutely no chance of coming to power in Germany, its propaganda carried both nationalistic and socialistic tendencies without being bothered by contradictions. It used every conceivable maneuver to gain advantages, including common actions with the Nazis, especially when directed against the hated Social Democratic government of Prussia. Aided by the mounting depression, the Communist vote steadily increased, but its highest point, over 6,000,000 in 1932, was far from a majority.

Inflation

Perhaps the greatest single blow to the stability of the young Republic, however, was the outbreak of the most fantastic inflation the world had ever known to that day. The German government headed by Wilhelm Cuno wanted to improve German economic conditions before paying reparations. But the Germanophobe French government of Raymond Poincaré proved adamant and occupied the Ruhr Valley in order to force the German government to pay. Since open resistance was out of the question, passive resistance was proclaimed. It was eventually given up, and the Ruhr issue was subsequently solved because of the more conciliatory policy of Poincaré's successor, Édouard Herriot. But in the meantime incalculable harm had been done. In anticipation of possible trouble, the German government accepted short-term enlistments of volunteers who turned out to be the worst type of cutthroats. This was the notorious "Black Reichswehr."

In order to finance passive resistance, the German government resorted to the printing press, and unchecked inflation set in. When it came to an end, in November, 1924, a new currency, the rentenmark, was established at the incredible ratio of 1 rentenmark to 1 trillion old marks. Speculators and profiteers had a field day, but the working population was hard hit and the middle classes were financially wiped out. Henceforth embittered members of the middle class became increasingly attracted to right-wing radicalism, which promised them a rise to their former positions of preeminence once the hated "system" had been overthrown. To those radical groups they brought a reservoir of talent and training which stood them in good stead later on.

The national election of May, 1924, pointed to the catastrophe which had occurred. The Nationalists, determined opponents of the Republic, gained heavily, and so did the Communists, who rose to fourth place. The young Nazi party polled nearly 2 million votes only half a year after its unsuccessful Munich *Putsch*. Chief losers were the Social Democrats and the other parties of the Weimar coalition. The extremists of right and left could of course never hope to form a government coalition together. But together they could obstruct the government most effectively. Cabinet followed cabinet, election followed election,[10] but always with inconclusive results. In 1928, when economic conditions were at their best, the middle-of-the-road parties did achieve success and formed a "great coalition." The extremists all lost heavily; the Nazis went down to 800,000 votes. But the "great coalition" broke up over a relatively minor matter in 1930 and was replaced by a cabinet under Centrist Chancellor Heinrich Brüning.

Brüning was a man of energy and dedication, but faced by the mounting obstructionism of the extremists he lent a willing ear to President Hindenburg's suggestion to keep the government somewhat aloof from parliament. As Brüning's coalition became narrower and as he faced increasing opposition, he resolved to use the presidential emergency powers in order to enact by decree what he could not enact by law. When the *Reichstag* demanded the revocation of the decrees, Brüning prevailed upon Hindenburg to dissolve parliament and call for general elections.

These elections were held at the worst possible moment, on September 14, 1930, when the depression had its sharpest impact and after the government had made itself unpopular by taking strictly deflationary measures by decree. The outcome was a mortal blow to the Republic. The Center party held its own, but all the other moderate parties lost heavily. The beneficiaries were the extremists. The Communists increased their vote by 40 percent, polling over 4½ million votes. The Nazis made the most spectacular gains. From an 800,000 low in 1928 they soared to 6,400,000.

Now parliamentary work became impossible. The extremists shouted and heckled; the Nazi deputies marched in and out in brown-shirt party uniform and showed their contempt for parliamentary procedure in every way. Brüning weathered the storm for a while, but government by decree became more and more frequent until March 26, 1931, when the *Reichstag* adjourned and government was carried on entirely by decree.

Hindenburg's reelection and the fall of Brüning

Presidential elections were held in March, 1932. Chief candidates were Hindenburg, now candidate of the moderate parties, and Hitler. Communists and Nationalists ran candidates of their own. Hindenburg piled up an impressive total of 18,661,736 votes compared with Hitler's 11,338,571, but he failed by less than 1 percent to carry an absolute majority. A runoff election was held on April 10, boosting Hindenburg to well over 19,000,000 and Hitler to over 13,000,000. Hindenburg was elected, but the Nazi total was impressive.

[10] In 1924 and in 1932 elections were held twice in the same year.

For Brüning, who had worked hard for Hindenburg's reelection, this was a Pyrrhic victory. He fell victim to the intrigues of the cliques around the ailing and senile president, which turned Hindenburg's mind against the Chancellor. Having relied on presidential power rather than on parliament, Brüning, who was never defeated in parliament on a vote of confidence, had to give up his post at the express request of Hindenburg.

He was succeeded by a renegade Centrist, Franz von Papen, who misused the emergency powers in order to remove the constitutional government of Prussia. If this sacrificial offering at the Nazi altar was to save Papen's political life, it failed to accomplish its purpose. The Nazis became the strongest party, and the Communists too gained considerably at the expense of the Social Democrats, who paid heavily for having taken Papen's lawless act lying down.

However, internal dissension within the Nazi party gave the party a temporary setback, and between the two elections in 1932 the Nazis lost 2 million votes. But fate was not kind to Papen either. The real power in the clique around Hindenburg was an ambitious general, Kurt von Schleicher. Papen had been his protégé, but now he had become too independent and the general turned against him. Schleicher replaced Papen on December 3, 1932, and it seemed for a little while as if he were to meet with success. Dissension was rife within the Nazi party, and Schleicher was negotiating with one of the dissident leaders, Gregor Strasser. But at this moment of lowest Nazi morale, Hitler threw himself and his resources into a relatively minor election in Lippe and by succeeding therein was able to overcome the dead point of the party's momentum.

Schleicher's position deteriorated thereafter, and Papen threw his entire influence with Hindenburg against him. When Schleicher tried to bluff his way through by obtaining a presidential decree to dissolve parliament, he met with refusal and had to resign.

Hitler becomes Chancellor

Upon taking his leave Schleicher recommended to Hindenburg that he appoint Hitler as his successor—whether out of spite against Papen is not known. Hindenburg's "kitchen cabinet" also supported this suggestion, and Hitler took office on January 30, 1933. The Weimar Republic had come to an end.

Under the empire, the German citizen had been excluded from the realm of government. This was the prerogative of certain privileged classes. But in return for this, he had been furnished with an ideal: the ideal of a dazzlingly glorious and brilliant Germany forging ahead under a determined leadership.

In 1918, this idea suddenly evaporated. The war was lost, the Emperor in ignominious flight, the traditional exponents of power in confusion. The German people were not prepared to rule themselves alone, for they lacked both experience in government and that innate sense of moderation and freely accepted self-discipline that is the essence of democratic government, and has been the genius of the

English-speaking peoples. The unimaginative, uninspiring party bureaucrats took over. But they took over without giving the people another ideal. Thus, to most Germans, the Weimar Republic was form but not substance. For the latter, they dreamed either of the past or of the future, but in any case despised the present. Hitler's genius contrived to combine these dreams for his own purpose and to furnish the German people with what they desired. In that sense Hitler was really what he claimed to be—the embodiment of the German soul—not because he was a typical German, for that he was not, but because he shouted from the rooftops what many Germans had secretly dreamed.

Thus the Weimar Republic was in a real sense the age of transition from Bismarck to Hitler—not because of overt acts (of which there were some, but not many), but because of its omissions, its lack of substance, and its inability to imbue the German people with a new ideal.

From this must be learned an obvious lesson. New democratic forms, seemingly democratic party governments, civil liberties, are the forms, not the substance of democracy. Only when all energies are concentrated on the education of the individual as such, not merely as part of a glorious machine, is there hope of developing personal dignity, the sense of balanced moderation, that innate understanding of generally accepted and therefore unspoken values, which are the mark of a free people.

3

The rise and fall of National Socialism

Hitler

Adolf Hitler was born in Braunau on the Inn on April 20, 1889. The accident of birth made him an Austrian, and he never bothered to acquire German citizenship until just before he became German Chancellor. But he always considered himself a German and during the First World War chose a German, rather than an Austrian, regiment.

After a youth of flotsam and military service he joined a tiny group called the "German Labor Party," an event which he later termed "the most decisive decision of my life."[1]

Munich was the hub of all kinds of antidemocratic activities at that time, and

[1] Adolf Hitler, *Mein Kampf,* Munich, 1938 (German ed.), p. 244.

Hitler found many ready adherents. In this atmosphere he staged his famous "beer-hall *Putsch*" of 1923, which ended in dismal failure. Hitler received a short term of imprisonment during which he wrote that famous conglomeration of platitudes, half-baked philosophy, and propagandistic fulmination which, under the name of *Mein Kampf* (My Struggle), became the Bible of the Third *Reich*.

The failure of the *Putsch* taught Hitler the valuable lesson that it was unwise to challenge the authority of the state directly. Henceforth he was determined to come to power by "legal" means, which did not exclude violence, but by which accusations of illegality might be avoided.

The Nazi party

From 1919 on, Hitler called his party the "National Socialist German Workers party" (*Nationalsozialistische Deutsche Arbeiterpartei,* NSDAP). The only concrete point in its program was anti-Semitism. Otherwise its platform was composed of an assortment of vague, semi-mystical phrases.[2] The speeches and the propaganda were harangues of little meaning, designed to appeal solely to the emotions.

What accounts for the rise to power of a group of men most of whom, if measured by ordinary standards, would have been considered uncouth and commonplace? One thing is certain: Hitler was never the tool of so-called "special interests," "capitalists," etc., but it was rather the other way around. Some of these people might have had illusions of controlling Hitler, but if so they were quickly brought back to reality. As a matter of fact the Nazis had no real political theory,[3] very much like their Italian fascist cousins. The realistic Italians accepted that situation calmly, but the Germans were in greater need of philosophy, of *Weltanschauung*. Hence the paraphernalia of would-be philosophy and "racial" concept of history.[4]

Nazism directed its most powerful attraction toward the disgruntled and impoverished middle classes. It even attracted some brilliant intellectuals, who may not have believed every word but who were ready enough to serve. Patriotism in its most extreme form was another weapon in the Nazi arsenal. Hitler showed his qualities of leadership by identifying himself more and more with the "spirit of the nation," and his command thus became the command of patriotism. To resist it became a moral wrong, an act of treason against the nation. Patriotism is something which in the opinion of many Germans excuses almost anything, and some Germans are still not quite sure they understand why other nations find certain German actions so reprehensible. Also useful was the "stab in the back" legend which

[2] The principal program of the Nazis was to be found, apart from *Mein Kampf,* in Gottfried Feder's "Twenty-five Points," written in 1920.

[3] Franz Neumann, *Behemoth, the Structure and Practice of National Socialism,* New York, 1942, pp. 459–462.

[4] The official exponent of Nazi "philosophy" was Alfred Rosenberg, in *Der Mythus des 20. Jahrhunderts,* Munich, 1930.

blamed German defeat in the First World War on certain groups which were identified with the Weimar Republic. It was easy to believe in this legend, contrary to the facts though it was, because it made possible the continuation of the belief in German superiority. Moreover the clearly militaristic undertones of all Nazi activities tended to convey the impression that only the Nazis were doing anything to help Germany regain a "place in the sun."

The strongest single aid to the Nazi cause was undoubtedly the depression, which created desperation in millions of men and women. Without the depression the Nazis would hardly have come to power. Nor would the depression alone have accomplished that without the Nazi leaders' shrewd appraisal of the German character. The vague Nazi creed, its symbolism, its song of hate, gave every German something to believe in and something to fight against. This does not mean that every German was a Nazi, but Hitler cast a spell over them from which few could keep themselves entirely free.

The first Hitler government

The cabinet which Hitler formed upon his assumption of the Chancellery was composed of surprisingly few Nazis; besides Hitler, only two others, Wilhelm Frick (Interior) and Hermann Göring (Air and Prussian Prime Minister). Quite likely, some of the Nationalists thought that Hitler had reached his zenith and that they would control him. But then came the fantastic burning of the *Reichstag,* according to all available evidence engineered by Göring but blamed on the Communists. This "plot" was used as an excuse for Hindenburg to sign emergency decrees suspending all civil liberties and establishing strict central control. Draconic punishments were imposed for all kinds of old and new crimes, and the death penalty was restored. The decrees also furnished the basis for so-called "protective custody," the name given to imprisonment in the notorious concentration camps.[5] Under these decrees the opponents of the Nazis were hunted down and imprisoned or killed.

Under these conditions of terror the German people went to the polls on March 5, 1933, and it must be considered remarkable that the Nazis obtained only 43.9 percent of the total vote. Only together with the Nationalists did they poll a bare majority of 51.9 percent. It was the last German election in which there was anything like a contest until the collapse of the Nazi regime.

The capstone of this development was the Enabling Act of March 24, 1933, which was rushed through the newly elected *Reichstag* and passed quickly against only the votes of those Social Democrats who were still at liberty to come to the session. The Communists had "received no invitation," and most of them were in jail anyhow.

With the Enabling Act the legislative power was transferred from the *Reichstag* to the government, and it was quite justified to call this law the "Law of Leader-

[5] Ernst R. Huber, *Verfassungsrecht des grossdeutschen Reichs,* Hamburg, 1937–1939, p. 38.

ship" (*Reichsführungsgesetz*). After all power of executive and legislative leadership was thus united in Hitler's hands, the judiciary was quickly brought in line; and after the blood purge of June 30, 1934, Hitler declared himself the "supreme Lord Justice" (*oberster Gerichtsherr*) of the German people.

After legal unification came political unification, and on July 14, 1933, all political parties were declared dissolved. The Nazi party, being presumably a "movement," was excluded from that provision. Finally, the dissident elements within the Nazi party were wiped out in a gigantic purge which killed well over a thousand people. While the killing was going on, accounts with such old enemies as General von Schleicher and Gustav von Kahr (who turned against Hitler in the beer-hall *Putsch*) were also settled in the approved Nazi manner, by assassination. Hitler's power could no longer be challenged. And when old President Paul von Hindenburg died on August 1, 1934, a "testament" almost certainly forged, was conveniently found, suggesting that Hitler be made the old Marshal's successor. Hitler was only too glad to oblige and combined the two offices in his hand. He was to be called "*Führer* (leader) and *Reich* President." Later, with pseudo-simplicity, he caused himself to be "simply" called *Der Führer*.

The *Führer* in power

No man ever wielded more personal power in modern times than Hitler. He was responsible to no one and consulted, if at all, with whom he wished. He did not even have a Politburo like Stalin. Neither the party leadership nor the cabinet filled that role. In the past, several writers have held that certain personalities like Heinrich Himmler, Hermann Göring, and Joseph Goebbels were the actual "powers behind the throne." Today we know that Hitler and Hitler alone counted. Even when the regime was crumbling around him he had no trouble in disposing of these pillars of National Socialism.[6]

Hitler was "the chosen one," a modern incarnation of the divine-right-of-kings concept; and all kinds of fanciful legal, social, and political theories were woven around this concept by servile intellectuals.

The members of the *Reich* cabinet were administrators, underlings who did Hitler's bidding and usually had little share in policy making. Only the degree to which Hitler chose to consult them gave them influence, if any. Under them, however, a fairly well-functioning bureaucracy continued to operate with fair efficiency.

Centralism

Totalitarianism cannot tolerate decentralized power. Hence, Nazism quickly abolished all vestiges of federalism. The *Länder* were "coordinated" by the use of *Reich* governors (*Reichsstatthalter*); and the *Land* governments which remained

---

[6] A graphic account of those events can be found in H. R. Trevor-Roper, *The Last Days of Hitler*, New York, 1947.

retained mainly the function of rewarding party leaders with well-paid offices. Prussia, the largest *Land* by far, was for all practical purposes, abolished as a *Land*. The only thing that remained was the title of Prussian Prime Minister, now devoid of meaning, which Göring, who collected such things, retained for himself.

Centralization was also extended to lower levels. The German Municipal Code of 1935 established a uniform system of local administration. New territories incorporated into Greater Germany, such as Austria and the Sudetenland, were organized into new types of administrative units, *Reichsgaue,* with the regional party leader (*Gauleiter*) as governor in personal union. The *Reichsgaue* were obviously the pattern to be imposed eventually on all of Germany had the Hitler regime lasted longer.

Party organization

The National Socialist German Workers party (NSDAP) was a most elaborate structure. At the top stood the *Führer* and a central executive committee (*Reichsleiter*) who ranked with cabinet members, which some of them were. Below the national organization was that of the regions (*Gaue*), districts (*Kreise*), and towns and villages (*Ortsgruppen*). Each was headed by an appropriate "chief" (*Leiter*). On the precinct level were subordinate block leaders and cell leaders.

Associated organizations comprised the brown-shirted militia (storm troopers, SA), the black-uniformed elite guard (SS), the motorized corps (NSKK), and the youth organizations for boys (Hitler Youth) and for girls (BDM). Other affiliations existed for most professions and interests.

It was not always easy for citizens to keep away from some form of party affiliation. The pressure to join was heavy; certainly promotion and sometimes continuation of business or job depended on it. On the other hand, some convinced Nazis never joined up formally for one reason or another. Membership in the Nazi party or its affiliates was therefore not always an adequate gauge of sentiment, although it might have been a clue.

Above all the party functioned as a superb control mechanism which hovered over every public and private activity of the citizen. Its network was quickly able to spot dangerous tendencies and to take steps toward their neutralization. On the other hand, as the chief "educator," in control of every medium of information, it molded thought and action. Fortunately, in their heavy-handed way, the Nazis overdid it a little and especially with the younger generations were not always as effective as they might have been. But control was complete: No really effective underground could exist, and only external force finally overcame their regime.

Death and destruction

The regime left behind a path of death and destruction that had few equals in the history of the world. Its racial myth was responsible for the mass murder of over 6 million Jews and many more millions of members of other races and nationalities, supposedly "inferior" to the German. The terror of the Secret State Police (Gestapo) is still recalled in many parts of Europe, especially in Germany itself. Despite the many horrors still abounding in the world today, and in spite of many Nazi methods faithfully copied or improved upon by other dictators, the names of the death camps of Dachau, Buchenwald, Ravensbrueck, Bergen-Belsen, Maidanek, Oświecim (Auschwitz), and many others will long be remembered as a horrible proof of the depth of depravity to which a supposedly civilized country may descend.

The Second World War

The outbreak of the Second World War found the Nazis in firm control of Germany. There was little evidence of dissatisfaction. Germany was prosperous, the vast rearmament program had obliterated unemployment, and the country's voice was heard loudly if not lovingly in the concert of nations. No anti-Nazi group, and there were a number, could ever dare to go outside its own small circle; otherwise a police agent would manage to slip in, and before long the names of the conspirators would be read on the well-known orange posters which announced the death penalty against the enemies of the regime. In France, Norway, and Poland, anti-Nazi forces could rely on most of their countrymen to be on their side. But in Germany one never knew who was friend and who was foe.

The first great victories of the German armies silenced whatever opposition there was. But after the blitz on England had failed, and after the battles of Stalingrad and El Alamein, certain members of the high officers' class felt an increasing uneasiness because they knew that the war was not going well. In those circles, Hitler's prestige suffered particularly after Stalingrad, where a large German army was forced to surrender because Hitler's stubbornness had not allowed it to withdraw in time.

This dissatisfaction led to the plot of July 20, 1944. It was not of a grass-roots character—that would have been impossible. It was a conspiracy of certain high military, civilian, and diplomatic leaders.[7]

The plot failed because of a number of accidents and miscalculations. The bomb, placed under Hitler's table by one of the conspirators, Colonel Claus Werner von Stauffenberg, exploded as planned; but in the wooden shed to which Hitler had inexplicably transferred a staff meeting, the walls were blown out, and Hitler was only slightly hurt. Stauffenberg, hearing the explosion and believing the deed accomplished, set into motion the prearranged machinery. The rebels did take over

[7] Ernst Bernd Gisevius, *Bis zum bitteren Ende*, Zurich, 1946, 2 vols. (translated as *To the Bitter End*, Boston, 1947); Allen W. Dulles, *Germany's Underground*, New York, 1947; Fabian von Schlabrendorff, *They Almost Killed Hitler*, ed. by Gerov S. Gaevernitz, New York, 1947; Hans Rothfels, *The German Opposition to Hitler*, Hinsdale, Ill., 1948.

the offices of the home army in Berlin, and their success was even greater in Vienna and Paris, where the Gestapo was temporarily placed under arrest.

But the conspirators, the generals who had moved vast armies with clocklike precision, went about their business in a most dilettante fashion. They failed to secure the lines of communication. Being the products of Prussian militarism, they did not consider the possibility that their orders might be questioned. But a young Nazi officer, a Major Rehmer, became suspicious, contacted Dr. Goebbels, and heard the truth that Hitler was alive. With that, the jig was up. Without decisive leadership, the plot collapsed. The one man who might have led it to success, who was in the plotters' confidence, the popular Field Marshal Erwin Rommel, had been severely wounded by an Allied flier and was out of the fight.[8]

Subsequent investigations showed traces of the plot in practically every major town of Germany. Now the conspirators were hunted down, tried under conditions which constituted a mockery of justice, and executed under frightful torture.

The failure of the plot of July 20, 1944, was a tragedy for Germany; most of the physical destruction of that country occurred after that date. And since all opposition was now crushed, there was no longer anything to stop Hitler from exacting the last drop of blood from the German people. Hitler's famous boast that if he were forced to depart from the scene, he would "shut the door with a bang," was carried out to the letter.

The end of the Nazi regime

The fall of the Hitler regime was entirely due to the armed might of the Allied armies. Hitler himself held the reins of government until his own physical destruction. His last act was that of naming the liquidators. Since his faith in Göring— once his designated successor—was gone, and since he also regarded Himmler as a traitor because of the latter's peace feelers, he designated as his successor Grand Admiral Karl Doenitz, who had set up his headquarters in Flensburg, near the Danish frontier. It fell upon Doenitz to bring the war to a close as far as Germany was concerned.

Occupation

The shape of Germany's future was determined by Allied policy, not by German volition. The outlines of Allied policy toward Germany resulted from several basic considerations. It was believed that the fact of Germany's military defeat had to be brought home to the German people lest another "stab in the back" legend

---

[8] He died in a hospital and was buried with great honors, Hitler himself being present. But it is certain now that he was forced to commit suicide by Gestapo agents; Hans Speidel (Rommel's chief of staff), *Invasion 1944*, Tübingen, 1950; Albert Lidell-Hart (ed.), *The Rommel Papers* (trans. by Paul Findlay), New York, 1953.

were to develop. Therefore unconditional surrender was demanded. It was felt that because of the deep penetration of National Socialism into every aspect of life, existing institutions and available officials could not be trusted. Therefore, not only military occupation but also military government of Germany was called for. Finally it was clear that the occupation of Germany would be a task devolving upon the principal Allied powers acting in concert.

It became clear at an early date that the military occupation and military government of Germany would have to be accomplished primarily on the basis of separate zones of occupation. This was necessary for two reasons: first, because the integration of officers from different nations into one working party had been tested in North Africa and Italy and had been found wanting; secondly, because of the far more important realization that any integration with a Russian staff was quite impossible except on the top level.[9]

Yalta and Potsdam

The conference of foreign ministers which met in Moscow during October, 1943, established the European Advisory Commission, which was given the task of preparing plans for the occupation of Germany as far as the tripartite level was concerned. Later, in 1944, the Provisional Government of France was invited to participate in these deliberations. But the Commission was not able to produce agreement, and thus a final decision had to be made on a higher level. This occurred at the Yalta conference, where it was decided that the United States, the U.S.S.R., and Great Britain should each occupy a zone in Germany, and that the French government should be invited to accept a similar zone for administration. It was also decided that the Soviet Union should occupy hitherto Polish land approximately as far as the so-called Curzon line, and that Poland should be compensated by "substantial accessions" of German territory. This latter provision was later implemented by the Potsdam conference in August, which handed over to Polish administration all Germany east of the rivers Oder and Neisse, plus the city of Stettin, except the northern part of East Prussia including the city of Königsberg (now renamed Kaliningrad) which was definitely ceded to the Soviet Union.[10]

All German authority actually came to an end as a result of the act of unconditional surrender of May 7 and 8, 1945.[11] The Doenitz government was dissolved and its members imprisoned. Despite vague threats about a Nazi underground movement (*Wehrwolf*), implying the possibility of an underground government or a government in exile, no traces of such subterranean authority have been found.

[9] A graphic and authoritative description of this lack of liaison between the Western Allies and the Soviet Union can be found in the book by Major General J. R. Deane, *Strange Alliance,* New York, 1947.

[10] *Department of State Bulletin,* Aug. 5, 1945.

[11] *The Axis in Defeat,* Department of State Publication 2423, pp. 23–25. This publication contains many other documents pertaining to the surrender and the establishment of Allied authority.

Allied control

The Allied powers took formal control of Germany on June 5, 1945, declaring that

> . . . the Governments of the United States of America, the Union of Soviet Socialist Republics, and the United Kingdom, and the Provisional Government of the French Republic, hereby assume supreme authority with respect to Germany, including all the powers possessed by the German Government, the High Command, and any state, municipal, or local government or authority.

At the same time, the four zones of occupation and the quadripartite regime of the city of Berlin were established. There was also constituted the supreme Allied authority for Germany, the Allied Control Council, and a similarly appointed quadripartite body to administer the city of Berlin, known by the Russian name of *Komandatura.*

The Allied Control Council, the *Komandatura* in Berlin, and the Allied zone commanders were the sole authority in Germany. Such German authorities as existed then existed by sufferance. Military-government law was the supreme law of the land.

4

From military occupation to the new republic

Military occupation and military government of Germany after her defeat were an inevitable, foregone conclusion. To this end, elaborate planning and training took place in the United States and Great Britain.[1] The Russians, on the other hand, thought that they could rely primarily on German Communists, many of whom had long been trained in Moscow and had become Soviet citizens.

The division of Germany into zones, and especially the establishment of a Russian zone in Eastern Germany, have often been criticized. That this presented a tragedy can hardly be denied. However, it is difficult to see what alternative

---

[1] There is a considerable literature on military government and its problems. Carl J. Friedrich and Associates, *American Experiences in Military Government in World War II,* New York, 1948; Harold Zink, *American Military Government in Germany,* New York, 1947; Hojo Holborn, *Military Government Organization and Politics,* New York, 1947; W. Friedmann, *The Allied Military Government of Germany,* London, 1947.

existed. Negotiations over the future occupation of Germany go back as far as 1943 and 1944. Before the invasion of Europe by the American and British forces it was by no means certain that the Russians would not occupy Germany before the Western forces arrived there. They had, after all, no ocean to cross, and their armies were on the march westward after the German defeat at Stalingrad in January, 1943. It seemed therefore imperative to come to some sort of understanding with the Russians. This meant the division of Germany into zones of approximately equal size and importance. No other basis of agreement with Moscow was feasible.

Allied, especially American, policy toward Germany went through a number of phases, some of which were in violent contradiction to one another. During the war and under the growing impact of Nazi brutalities of which the American public was becoming increasingly aware, ideas were current which envisaged the destruction of Germany as a nation. The most prominent ideas in that direction were contained in the famous "Morgenthau Plan," which proposed permanent division, subjugation, and deindustrialization of Germany.[2] The Morgenthau Plan never became reality, but it had its impact on official American policy as laid down in the directive of the United States Chiefs of Staff of April 26, 1945 (JCS 1067). This directive showed a very stiff attitude toward the Germans, perhaps natural at the end of a protracted war and in view of the universal loathing for the Hitler regime. Its guiding principles were stated in these terms:[3]

> It should be brought home to the Germans that Germany's ruthless warfare and the fanatical Nazi resistance have destroyed the German economy and made chaos and suffering inevitable and that the Germans cannot escape responsibility for what they have brought upon themselves.
>
> Germany will not be occupied for the purpose of liberation but as a defeated enemy nation. . . .
>
> The principal Allied objective is to prevent Germany from ever again becoming a threat to the peace of the world. . . .

To this end, (1) nothing was to be done to bring about the economic rehabilitation of Germany except in so far as that was necessary in the interest of military operation; (2) no relief was to be extended to the German people except as far as necessary to avoid disease and such disorder as might impede the Allied war effort; (3) denazification and demilitarization were to be carried out under all circumstances.

Whatever treatment one might wish to mete out to the Germans, the one thing which stands out in these directives is their totally negative character. Detailed instructions were given for the destruction of certain organizations and institutions, notably the Nazi party. But no guidance was offered to the harassed military gov-

---

[2] For the text, see facsimile reproduction in Henry Morgenthau's *Germany Is Our Problem,* New York, 1945.

[3] For the text, see *The Axis in Defeat,* Department of State Publication 2423, p. 40.

ernment officials concerning the encouragement of positive political and economic action with a view toward an eventual rehabilitation of Germany. In defense of JCS 1067, it should be stated that this document concerned itself primarily with the immediate postcombat phase and was therefore essentially short-range in nature. The military chiefs expected at that time that the long-range program for an administration of Germany would eventually be taken over by a civilian agency of the government, presumably the Department of State.

The negative attitude soon proved impractical and was finally abandoned in 1947. But it created a frame of mind which was not conducive to strong positive action on the top planning and operational levels. However, it was not so much the recognition that this policy was unwise which effected a change but rather extraneous causes, one of which was Soviet policy.

Soviet policy

The Soviet forces, being without a military-government organization, vested responsibility in their respective commanders of combat units, who had the help—if help it was—of the commissars and the NKVD, later MVD, men attached to their command. But from the very start, the Soviet Military Administration relied heavily on German Communists, many of whom they had brought with them.[4] While this was altogether in line with customary Soviet procedure, it was a less radical step than was expected by many observers.

Of all the belligerents on the Allied side, the Soviets were the only ones who consistently distinguished between the German people and the Nazis.[5] To emphasize this point, two significant organizations were formed in the Soviet Union during the war. One was the "Free Germany Committee," whose chief organizers were Wilhelm Pieck, veteran German Communist leader, and Erich Weinert, a Communist writer. Even more significant and certainly commanding far more prestige was the "Union of German Officers" founded by General Walter von Seydlitz and Lieutenant Count Otto von Einsiedel, and later headed by Field Marshal Friedrich von Paulus. All these were officers of the German sixth army which surrendered at Stalingrad. Von Paulus was its commanding officer, while Von Einsiedel achieved significance chiefly because he was a grandnephew of Prince Otto von Bismarck, the Iron Chancellor.

It was feared by many that the Soviet authorities were grooming the "Free Germany Committee" and the "Union of German Officers" as the future government of Germany, since the latter group especially could have appealed to a resurgent German nationalism, and since defeated nations seem to have a predilection

[4] Most important were Wilhelm Pieck and Walter Ulbricht.
[5] It is interesting that Dr. Joseph Goebbels, German propaganda minister, considered the failure of the Western Allies to concede such a difference as one of their worst psychological blunders, which greatly aided German propaganda. These remarks appear again and again in *The Goebbels Diaries* (trans. and ed. by Louis P. Lochner), New York, 1948.

for defeated generals. Contrary to such expectations, these two groups were not transplanted intact to German soil.

The Soviet authorities managed to turn the absence of Russian military-government machinery into an asset. Being without adequately trained personnel of their own, they relied from the very beginning on German help. And since there were not enough tested Communists around, other Germans were also used. This made the Russian zone appear in a more favorable light, at least in that instance, than the zones in the West. Moreover the Russians opened schools and places of amusement from the very start, while they remained closed in the West waiting for denazification to take place.

But most important of all was the Russian decision to license four political parties in their zone while the Western powers had forbidden all political activities until they could see clearly whom they could trust. There was danger that the Russian attitude might seem more liberal than that of the West, and to counter that danger the Western Allies were quickly forced to liberalize their own policies. Even so, the Russian policy might have gained considerable political success for the Soviet Union if it had not been for the savage conduct of so many Russian soldiers, which quickly nullified any favorable impression which the Soviet leaders might have wanted to create for their policies.

Even before Russian policy forced a different attitude on American military government, a gradual change had made itself felt. The military authorities, in their search for reliable Germans to be used in responsible positions, had frequently appointed men who had been prominent in anti-Nazi political parties before Hitler's rise to power. These men of course immediately contacted their friends and quickly rebuilt a measure of political life before it was officially permitted. American military-government officers were aware of this, but they needed the relatively few reliable people then available and closed their eyes to an inevitable development, if they did not aid it. Thus, at a time when the official policy was still stiff aloofness, cooperation between military government and Germans became more and more intimate. Later, when the need to build up Germany as a bulwark against Russia became official policy, this was very much more accelerated.

Zones of occupation

After the cessation of hostilities, the Allied Powers moved into their respective zones of occupation, and a separate zone, considerably smaller than the others, was cut out of the British and American areas and handed over to French administration. On June 5, 1945, was created the then supreme authority for Germany, the Allied Control Council, and a similar, quadripartite, authority was established for the city of Berlin, the *Komandatura* mentioned in Chapter 3.

At first military government confined itself to the local territorial units, namely municipalities and districts (*Kreise*). As communications were restored, larger units of government were rebuilt. However, the task of re-creating a completely collapsed governmental and administrative structure was tremendous, and American, British, and French military governments with all their faults accomplished an almost superhuman task.

As military government was established on higher levels, its problems multiplied, since it became increasingly clear that even the *Länder* were not able to exist economically without integration in a larger country. Moreover, relations were not always easy between the regular military commands and military government with their different organizational principles and overlapping authorities.

Denazification

A major stumbling block to successful military government was the monstrous problem of denazification. Denazification was primarily inaugurated by the American planners, and it constituted a problem chiefly in the American zone. This does not mean that there were more Nazis in that zone than in the others. But from the very beginning the American authorities took a more idealistic line toward the problems of Nazism than did the other three occupying powers. The issue itself was simple enough. The terrible brutality of the Nazi regime had become obvious to all. Perhaps the stories of concentration camps had not been entirely believed in America before, despite so much corroborating evidence. But the discovery and liberation of such infernos as Dachau, Buchenwald, and Bergen-Belsen left no doubt whatsoever about the nature of the Nazi regime, and consequently determination to eradicate once and for all every vestige of Nazism grew by leaps and bounds.

It was clear from the beginning that the initial momentum had to be furnished by military government. Moreover, it was well remembered how the Germans had been able to frustrate the desire of the Allied Powers in the First World War to punish German leaders accused of war crimes.[6]

The policy of the United States was first established as follows. All holders of a certain rank in Nazi party organizations were to be automatically arrested and made ineligible for office of any kind. Party members were to be purged from all but menial labor if their membership antedated 1937.[7] This policy was established by JCS 1067 and carried out by Military Government Law No. 8. Later, it was further amplified by various directives.

It is easy enough to see objections to this kind of policy. The denazification rules established in effect a presumption of guilt for certain categories of people; this was contrary to the well-established principle of Anglo-American justice by which a person is considered innocent until proved guilty beyond reasonable doubt.

---

[6] Articles 227 and 228 of the Treaty of Versailles provided for the extradition and trial of the ex-Kaiser and certain military leaders. The ex-Kaiser was never extradited because of the refusal of the Netherlands government; the generals received mock trials in Leipzig, if they were tried at all, and went free, with some minor exceptions.

[7] In 1937, the German Civil Service Code was promulgated, and from that time on great pressure to join the Nazi party was exerted, especially against public officials.

It provided for long periods of imprisonment without trial, as a great number of Germans were affected by this rule and the denazification mills ground only slowly; this was contrary to the Anglo-American tradition of habeas corpus, speedy trial, and fair bail. Besides, the denazification laws were clearly ex post facto laws. While certain other offenses committed by Nazis might have been considered criminal by direct application of law or by reasonable analogy, membership or the holding of office in the Nazi party per se were of course absolutely legal at the time. And finally, the denazification laws deprived many of the best-trained experts of their chance to participate in the rehabilitation of Germany. While many of them were guilty and incapable of fitting into a democratic order, many others had joined up for reasons of opportunism or fear.

But on the other hand, it is difficult to see what other policy military government could have pursued. The Allied forces were committed to the eradication of Nazism, which had just thrown the world into a holocaust of death and destruction. For reasons mentioned above, the task of eliminating Nazis could not be left to the Germans, at least not in the beginning, and the military-government officials, most of whom knew little about Germany and were only human, could not be permitted very much discretion in the matter. Consequently the directives which they received established a necessarily mechanical approach. It happened therefore that some real Nazis who had played a major role in the Hitler war machine were exonerated because for some reason or other they had never bothered to join the Nazi party, while others, who had joined under pressure or out of concern for their families, found themselves eliminated from all professional careers. On the whole, however, the denazification system was not intrinsically unfair. What made it unfair in effect was the number of cases involved. Over 11,000,000 people had to register. There were no authorities, American or German, who could have handled such a staggering number with any degree of expedition.

Then, as military government did not have the personnel to accomplish such a task, it was eventually turned over to the Germans, although this was not achieved without some initial difficulties. Upon request by the American military-government authorities, the Council of German Prime Ministers in the United States zone, the *Länderrat,* submitted a draft law for denazification and demilitarization. This was rejected by military government. There were fundamental differences between the German and American approach to the problem: the Americans wanted to judge former Nazis on the basis of their former positions in public and economic life, while the Germans wanted to confine trials to actual offenses committed. Moreover, in fining business leaders who had profited from their Nazi activities, the Germans wanted to extract much larger fines than the Americans were willing to grant. Finally the Germans wanted to enact legislation for the purpose of checking unproven accusations.[8]

[8] Carl J. Friedrich, "Denazification," in Friedrich et al., *op. cit.,* pp. 263–265. W. E. Griffith, "Denazification in the United States Zone of Germany," *Annals of the American Academy of Political and Social Science,* January, 1950, pp. 68–76.

The "Law for the Liberation from National Socialism and Militarism" was finally proclaimed by the Council of Prime Ministers and approved by military government on March 5, 1946. It recognized the supremacy of Military Government Law No. 8 and of the Allied Control Council Directive No. 24,[9] which established the over-all policy for the removal of Nazis from office. But the very fact that the final form of this law was determined to a considerable extent by the directives of American military government kept the Germans from considering it a really "German" law and thus deprived it of some of its psychological effect.

The law[10] established five classes of persons required to register as Nazis: (1) major offenders, (2) offenders, (3) lesser offenders, (4) followers, and (5) exonerated persons who upon investigation proved not to have been Nazis. The offenders were further subdivided into (*a*) activists (Art. 7), (*b*) militarists (Art. 8), and (*c*) profiteers (Art. 9). This portion of the law generally followed the preference of the German leaders for the principle of punishment for acts committed. But, upon insistence of the military-government authorities, there was appended to the law the principle contained in Control Council Directive No. 24, which embodied the American idea of punishment for positions held under the Nazi regime. This appendix referred not only to Nazi leaders of the upper ranks, but to virtually all functionaries, local or national. It also placed in the same category business and professional men of importance, higher ranking judges, all civil servants, and many more. All such persons were to be removed and made ineligible for future appointment.

The Prime Ministers refused to sign the appendix, which fortified the contention that this was an "American" law. They refused to accept the lumping together of Nazi party leaders with high civil servants and business leaders which, they felt, would only exonerate the real Nazis by placing them in one group with generally respected people. One of the keenest American observers has remarked that "no one reading the list . . . can help feeling that the men responsible for it sought a wholesale indictment of the German ruling class in all its branches."

The law established local denazification boards (*Spruchkammern*) and appeal boards, on which was now conferred major responsibility for carrying out the denazification program. This was a jump from one extreme to another. The American denazification authorities had had neither the staff nor the detailed knowledge necessary to accomplish this stupendous task. But in many respects it was even worse for the German tribunals. The type of work demanded from the members of the tribunal was such that leading citizens or first-line party leaders would not willingly indulge in it. Therefore some doubtful elements, although a minority, found their way to the bench or the prosecutor's table. Secondly, it was a case of

---

[9] *Occupation of Germany: Policy and Progress, 1945–46,* Department of State Publication 2783, pp. 20, 113 (excerpts).
[10] For the full text, see James K. Pollock and James H. Meisel, *Germany under Occupation,* Ann Arbor, Mich., 1947, p. 179. Excerpts may be found in *Occupation of Germany,* Department of State Publication 2783, p. 119.

neighbors trying and judging neighbors, and consequently strong pressure was brought to bear upon the tribunals. And while the Germans were able to mobilize more staff than the Americans, their number was still quite inadequate. Under the law of March 5, 1946, 11,674,152 persons had been obliged to register. By the end of 1946, only 125,738, that is, a little over 1 percent, had been tried.

The denazification system created a peculiar situation. A large number of people and their families lived under a shadow. Since they had been obliged to register with the denazification authorities, most of them were barred from their usual employment, and many of them faced financial ruin or a laborer's existence, considered degrading by the white-collar class. Yet most of these people were not deprived of their physical liberty. They were free to go about and spread disaffection. Moreover, the lighter cases were to be tried first, which was meant to favor the lesser offenders and followers, but frequently had the opposite result; the severity of the denazification procedure was eventually modified, and it was thus often the more dangerous cases who benefited from the new attitude, while many of the lesser offenders had already received more substantial punishment under the older system.

The magnitude of the denazification problem and the gradual reconsideration of the whole German issue eventually created a certain amount of relaxation of the law. In July, 1946, military government granted an amnesty to all German youth born between January 1, 1919, and March 5, 1928—the reason being that this generation had been entirely brought up under the Nazi regime and had had no opportunity to acquaint itself with democratic ways. Then on December 24, 1946, General McNarney extended an amnesty to approximately 800,000 lesser offenders and followers whose financial status was conclusive evidence that they had not profited from the Nazi regime.

The real breakdown of the denazification laws actually occurred in the German tribunals, which were far behind in their work and became more and more lenient.[11] Despite all attempts of the so-called "Special Branch" of military government's Public Safety Division, denazification became more and more of a mechanical process, something like delousing—unpleasant, but with clearly foreseeable results. Only prominent Nazis had to fear the tribunals, and even that was not always true, especially with numerous refugees from the East who were unknown in their new environment and frequently managed to hide their former identity.

Another major cause of the breakdown in the denazification procedure was the fact that only in the American zone was there any serious attempt at it. The British had a brief try but on the whole confined themselves to grave cases. They took great pains to investigate and if possible clear quickly those whom they wished to appoint to more important positions. In the French and Soviet zones there never was any denazification to speak of, although some former Nazi leaders were liqui-

---

[11] On Nov. 5, 1946, General Lucius Clay, the American commander, felt obliged to rebuke the Germans for this laxity. *The New York Times,* Nov. 6, 1946.

dated with or without trial. In July, 1947, Marshal Sokolovsky declared a virtual amnesty for all Nazis in the Soviet zone except for the most serious offenders.[12] Former Nazis who joined the Socialist Unity party (SED), the Communist-dominated official favorite of the Soviet authorities, were treated with indulgence and often even with considerable favor, as their bad past record put them at the mercy of the authorities, who knew that they could not afford to be disloyal to their new masters. Thus they were sometimes preferred over less pliable men of proven anti-Nazi convictions.

The isolation of the American denazification effort, the tremendous scope of the task, the inner conflicts over policy within the American element, and German reluctance to enforce a "foreign" denazification law deprived the program of much of its original meaning.

Toward a new German state

More and more responsibility was handed over to Germans, especially after local elections had produced more durable native authorities. Gradually active military government withdrew in stages, first from the local municipal and district levels, soon thereafter from the regional and provincial levels, and finally even from the *Länder.* On the lower echelon only liaison and security officers were left, who generally did not directly interfere in the administration but reported their observations to higher, zonal, headquarters. This process was fastest in the United States and U.S.S.R. zones, considerably slower in the British regions, and slowest in the French. Eventually, however, it was completed everywhere.

In principle the former *Länder* were reconstituted where possible. However, all of them had to submit to some surgery, partly in order to accommodate the carved-up pieces of Prussia, partly to settle within the zonal boundary lines, partly to eliminate enclaves and exclaves. A similar development took place in the Soviet zone, although there the *Länder* were later abolished in favor of a more centralistic government.

The combined territory of the Eastern and Western zones does not correspond to the area of former Weimar or Nazi Germany. The province of East Prussia has been absorbed by the Soviet Union and Poland. The vast and important area east of the rivers Oder and Neisse, including the city of Stettin, has been handed over to Polish administration, which considers this area as an integral part of Polish territory, in compensation for former Polish territory in the east ceded to the Soviet Union. The Western Allies have always insisted that Poland merely acts as administrator and that a final settlement is yet to be made at a future peace conference.[13] However, their aquiescence in the wholesale removal of 9,000,000 Germans from that area would indicate that the eastern frontier of Germany is already

[12] Law No. 201, Soviet Military Administration.
[13] Potsdam agreement, Item 9. *Occupation of Germany,* Department of State Publication 2783, pp. 74*f.*

effectively determined, short of another war. Germany has thus lost about one-third of her former territory as it existed after the Treaty of Versailles. At the same time she has maintained her former population despite this shrunken territory, as her war losses were more than made up by the influx of German refugees from such areas as the Sudetenland and the Balkans. The congestion of people in the remaining territory was therefore all the more serious. Moreover, apart from widespread war damage,[14] there was considerable dismantling and removal of industrial equipment under the provisions of the Potsdam agreement. Very serious was the loss of approximately 25 percent of Germany's food-producing land and 11 percent of her industrial area to Poland and the U.S.S.R.

When the European Advisory Commission and later the Potsdam conference established the crazy-quilt zone pattern of Germany, it was already apparent that Germany could not be governed through such small units as the *Länder* represented. The Potsdam agreement had stipulated (Item 14) that "during the period of occupation, Germany shall be treated as a single economic unit." It was also envisaged (Item 9, iv) that certain central administrative departments headed by state secretaries were to be created, particularly in the fields of finance, transport, communications, foreign trade, and industry.

It is now a matter of record that this plan did not work. The Soviet Union never permitted an economic integration of the zones, let alone a political one. The French were actually the first to object to a central German authority, but their reservations were quickly overshadowed by the widening split between Washington and London on the one side, and Moscow on the other.

Faced by the impossibility of creating larger administrative and economic units because of insurmountable Soviet obstruction, and confronted by a dangerous stagnation and decline of whatever German economy was left, the Western powers undertook such combinations as were available to them. First there was created in the American zone the Council of Prime Ministers, the *Länderrat,* whose chief architect was the noted American political scientist, James K. Pollock. Its experiences were very valuable in later developments.

The London conference of June, 1948, in which the United States, Great Britain, France, Belgium, the Netherlands, and Luxembourg participated,[15] provided for (1) eventual fusion of the three Western zones; (2) the establishment of a provisional Western German government; (3) an occupation statute which was to define the powers of the occupying states and of the Germans respectively; (4) an international authority of the Ruhr; and (5) minor territorial adjustments of Germany's western border.

The three military governors of the Western powers notified the German

---

[14] See United States Strategic Bombing Survey's *The Effects of Strategic Bombing on German Morale,* Washington, 1947.
[15] See the text of the agreement between the United States, the United Kingdom, France, and the Benelux countries (Belgium, Netherlands, Luxembourg), *Department of State Bulletin,* June 20, 1948, pp. 807–813.

Prime Ministers of the London decisions and outlined to them the procedure which was to be followed in calling a constituent assembly. The initial sailing was a bit rough, because the German party leaders composed their differences and issued a counterresolution to the request of the Allies.[16] They proposed to call the constituent assembly "Parliamentary Council," and they opined that the document to be drafted should not have the status of a full-fledged constitution but should rather be a basic law of provisional nature. The drafting of a permanent document was to be deferred until "the Allies are ready to return their sovereignty to the German people." Other objections were also stated, especially regarding the association of the occupation statute with the constitution.

The objections of the German leaders were a political maneuver caused by confusion. The Germans apparently did not realize that the proposals presented to them constituted the result of agreement between the Western Allies, not merely the policy of the military governors. They were prompted to their action by a fear of becoming vulnerable to the accusation of "splitting Germany" which was the propaganda line of the Communists and of some nationalist circles.

Reason eventually prevailed, and various face-saving devices were adopted in order to permit the Germans to accept the Allied plan without too much loss of face.

The occupation statute

The occupation statute itself brought on another battle. The Germans wanted the powers of the Allies more narrowly defined, wanted to limit Allied interference as much as possible, and wanted to broaden the guarantee of civil rights against Allied police action except when the purpose of the occupation itself was endangered.

Few of the German objections were permitted to survive, and on September 21, 1949, the occupation statute entered into force substantially as agreed upon by the three Western Foreign Ministers at the Washington conference of April 8, 1949.[17]

The occupation statute stipulated that the German government was to have all powers except those specifically reserved to the Allied powers. These reserved powers could be exercised in the following fields: (1) disarmament and demilitarization; (2) control of the Ruhr, restitution of property taken away by the Nazis, reparations, decartelization, anti-trust matters, foreign interests in Germany, and claims against Germany; (3) foreign affairs; (4) protection, prestige, and security

---

[16] For a detailed and revealing exposition of these and other developments leading to the adoption of the new constitution, see C. J. Friedrich, "Rebuilding the German Constitution," *American Political Science Review*, Vol. XLIII (1949), pp. 461–482, 704–720.

[17] The text of the occupation statute may be found in the *First Quarterly Report on Germany,* issued by the Office of the U.S. High Commissioner for Germany, Washington, 1950, Appendix IV. See also Edward H. Litchfield and Associates, *Governing Postwar Germany,* Ithaca, N.Y., 1953, pp. 616*ff.*

of the Allied forces, dependents, employees, and representatives, as well as occupation costs; (5) respect for the Basic Law (Constitution) and the constitutions of the *Länder;* (6) control of foreign trade and exchange; (7) control over internal action to a minimum extent and only so far as to ensure the use of food, funds, and other supplies in such manner as to reduce to a minimum the need for external assistance to Germany; and (8) authority over prisoners charged or sentenced before courts of the occupation powers or occupation authorities.

Technically these powers could be extended to every other field if conditions warranted. Section 3 of the statute reserves to the occupation authorities the right "to resume in whole or in part the exercise of full authority if they consider that to do so is essential to security or to preserve democratic government in Germany. . . ."

The area of the reserved powers was not closed to German legislation. The German federal government and the *Länder* could legislate and act after due notification to the occupation authorities. However, such action could not be contrary to occupation policy, and the Allied authorities could of course nullify all German action in the reserved fields. All amendments to the federal Constitution needed the approval of the occupation authorities.

A fair appraisal will show that the Allies used these reserved powers moderately and to an ever-decreasing extent. These prerogatives were further limited by the Petersberg Protocol of November 22, 1949.[18] On May 26, 1952, the Foreign Ministers of Britain, France, and the United States, as well as the Chancellor of Germany, signed a treaty on the relations between the three powers and the Federal Republic of Germany. This treaty restored virtually complete sovereignty to Germany, revoked the occupation statute, and abolished the Allied High Commission and offices of the *Land* commissioners.[19] However, this treaty, generally called the Bonn Treaty, was tied to the ratification of the treaty to create the European Defense Community which was signed in Paris on May 27, 1952. This treaty was defeated by the French National Assembly in 1954 but a substitute arrangement, known as the Western European Union, narrowly passed. France, Germany, and Italy ratified the agreement and other nations followed their example. Thus German sovereignty became an accomplished fact. The Allied High Commissioners, who upon the adoption of the German Constitution in 1949 had replaced the military governors, were transformed into Ambassadors, in June, 1953.

Another temporary limitation on German sovereignty was the Allied control over the Ruhr industries, which culminated in the creation of the International Authority for the Ruhr on December 28, 1948. This Authority, however, never achieved full effectiveness. Its power to allocate material in order to prevent discriminatory policies quickly became pointless since coal, coke, and steel were no longer in short supply. With the creation of the European Coal and Steel Com-

---

[18] *First Quarterly Report on Germany,* Appendix VII. Also Litchfield, *op. cit.,* pp. 619*ff.*
[19] *Ibid.,* pp. 622*ff. Department of State Bulletin,* June 16, 1952, p. 931.

munity (Schuman Plan), the Ruhr Authority was officially terminated in February, 1953.

Drafting the new Constitution

The German leaders had readily accepted the principle of establishing *Länder* constitutions,[20] but they raised fundamental objections to drafting a constitution for Western Germany. We have already mentioned that they were reluctant to undertake any action which could be interpreted as accepting or even approving the permanent division of Germany. But this was not all. Many German politicians felt that the *Länder* constitutions had been discredited in the eyes of the public by the occupation authorities and troops who disregarded them at will.[21] Now it was of course understood that the occupation authorities were not legally bound by the German constitutions, but since they had so often affirmed their devotion to democratic ideals, their arbitrary actions added no credit to their words. Where public safety was involved, the direct intervention of military authorities was easily understandable. But it was not so understandable why the American authorities stubbornly refused to permit a party press in their zone or why there were arbitrary arrests, even though some were justified. On these matters Germans and occupation authorities were bound to have different viewpoints, but it should be stressed that the fears of the German leaders were motivated by their desire to see a future constitution firmly established and accepted by their people without being first discredited. It is possible that the Germans were abnormally sensitive on this point, but that too is understandable.

The first difficulty was partly averted by avoiding the term *Verfassung* (constitution) and instead using *Grundgesetz* (basic law), which does not carry quite the same connotation of sovereignty in German usage. Secondly the preamble proclaims that it is the purpose of the Basic Law "to give a new order to political life for a *transitional* period" (author's italics). And the Constitution calls upon the entire German people "to accomplish, by free self-determination, the unity and freedom of Germany."[22]

This pacified the consciences of the German draftsmen, who were then able to undertake the actual task of writing a new constitution. A special commission was appointed by the Prime Ministers of the *Länder* to lay the groundwork for the con-

---

[20] R. G. Neumann, "New Constitutions in Germany," *American Political Science Review,* Vol. XLII (1948), pp. 448–468.

[21] C. J. Friedrich, "Rebuilding the German Constitution," *American Political Science Review,* Vol. XLIII (1949), cites numerous examples, p. 476. It should be said that in the majority of cases there was no intention on the part of the military authorities to flout German authorities; rather, there was lack of coordination and of mutual understanding. Frequently the military authorities felt that the German officials did not act vigorously enough, and a good case can be made for that contention.

[22] The term "basic law" was to denote both incompleteness and a transitional stage because of Germany's division. The *rapporteur,* Carlo Schmid, called Western Germany a "State-Fragment." Hermann von Mangoldt, *Das Bonner Grundgesetz,* Berlin and Frankfort, 1953, p. 25.

stitution, drafting those provisions on which there was agreement and presenting alternative suggestions concerning those on which no consensus could be reached. This document was submitted to the Parliamentary Council, which began to work on it on September 1, 1948. Chairman of the Council was the future federal Chancellor (Prime Minister) Konrad Adenauer.

The drafting process was not entirely smooth, not only because of disagreement between the two major political parties, the Christian Democrats and the Social Democrats, but also because military government injected itself. There were questions pertaining to the degree of federalism which the new state was to have. The Americans and French pressed for a federal solution, while the British favored a more centralized form of government. The problems of the emergency powers, the presidency, bicameralism, the stability of the government, the relationship between the *Länder* and the federation—all were the subject of considerable and able discussion.

On February 11, 1949, the executive committee of the Parliamentary Council submitted a draft to the military governors for their comments, prior to the final adoption of the draft. Then the fireworks began. The military governors found a long list of objections throughout the enitre document. Their justification cannot be examined here, but they provided an unprecedented intervention of military government in the drafting process; and although the military governors later retreated from many of their positions, they nevertheless furnished antidemocratic elements the argument that the constitution was not a "German" document. This accusation is quite unfounded in fact, for a substantial compromise was eventually reached, but it is debatable whether the gain achieved by the military governors' objections was worth the temporary "foreign" shadow thus cast on the Basic Law of the German Federal Republic.[23]

[23] The word "constitution" will be used henceforth in line with American usage.

5

Political life in Germany

In Germany, political life as it is understood in the occidental world came to an abrupt halt on January 30, 1933. Between that date and May 7, 1945, there was only the Nazi one-party state. In other countries occupied by German troops, and even to a certain small extent in Italy under the Fascist regime, some of the former political parties were able to lead a vestige of underground existence. Not so in Germany. There they were obliterated without exception, and only a fast-fading memory remained. The political opulence of party life during the Weimar regime had not equipped any of the parties for the hard realities of a hunted underground life. Nor were they prepared for the ruthlessness of the Nazis. Thus, party records and funds were easily seized by the police, membership lists confiscated, and all more or less prominent leaders imprisoned unless they had been prudent enough to seek exile.

Added to these events were the vigilance of the Gestapo and the heavy punishment meted out to suspected opponents of the regime. Consequently a non-Nazi political life could not exist even in nuclear form. The abortive attempt to overthrow the Nazi regime in June, 1944, was based on a hasty coalition of individuals of widely different political views. It had no grass-roots character, which it could not have afforded anyway for fear of discovery by the police, and it did not constitute the beginning of an alternative political movement.

Political vacuum

The elimination of the Nazi regime therefore created an absolute political vacuum. The German people were bitter, apathetic, hungry, and tired. For twelve long years their political leadership had told them about the glories of the Third *Reich* which they were creating for themselves. Now the ruins which surrounded them gave an eloquent commentary on these ambitions. Small wonder, then, that the speeches and promises of Germany's postwar political leaders were received with little enthusiasm, if not with aversion.

And finally there was the sheer effort to keep alive, the standing in line for hours, the necessity of dealing in the black market to avoid starvation, and the interminable jungle of both Allied and German bureaucracies which kept the Germans hopping from *Fragebogen* (questionnaire) to *Fragebogen*. In such an atmosphere, virile political life based on broad popular participation could not grow easily.

There was also a dearth of leadership. The political leaders who did reappear at first in Germany were for the most part relics of the Weimar period, where many of them had occupied minor posts. Now they came forth and offered themselves to the military-government authorities. They did not represent real parties at first, but rather political clubs which were to form the nucleus for mass parties later on. Some of them had formed so-called "Antifascist Committees" (*Antifa*), most of which were Communist-led. But they had no broad popular basis, and when they were dissolved their disappearance caused hardly a ripple.

Party life reborn

Nevertheless political leaders did obtain an early foothold. Military government needed responsible Germans to occupy positions as mayors, district chiefs, and heads of intermediate regions that were known as government districts (*Regierungsbezirke*). These former Weimar politicians and officials were logical choices, and on the whole they served loyally in positions where they had more of the form than the substance of power. However, as these leaders obtained places in the administrative machinery upon appointment by military government, they also began to organize their respective parties in a more or less overt manner.

It had been the plan of the Western occupation powers to make the establishment of political life a gradual, unhurried process. After careful screening, political parties, as well as unions and professional associations, were to be permitted on a local scale. After being tested, they were eventually to be permitted to broaden their basis. By that time, it was hoped, the German people would be a little more alert to their opportunities under a reasonable degree of political freedom, and the increased authority of political leaders would go hand in hand with a process of improved political maturity on the part of the people.

These carefully laid plans came to naught as a result of the policy adopted by the Soviet Military Administration. It has already been stated that the Soviet armies had no regular military-government apparatus and were therefore immediately dependent on native collaborators. The Soviet authorities managed to turn this apparent disadvantage into an advantage by licensing, almost immediately after the cessation of hostilities, four distinct political parties: the Communists, the Social Democrats, the Christian Democrats, and the Liberal Democrats. By this stroke the Russians achieved two things: they had an opportunity to pose as the most "liberal" occupation power, who gave the Germans political responsibility while the Western powers withheld it; and secondly, by permitting only four parties to organize, they took shrewd cognizance of the strong German aversion to a recurrence of the multitude of parties that marked the Weimar regime.

The creation of those four parties immediately caused such repercussions in Western Germany that military government found it necessary to follow the Russian lead. However, for some time to come, British, French, and United States military-government officials closely controlled the actions of German officeholders, while the Soviet Military Administration was generally content to give greater leeway to officials in its zone, holding them only strictly accountable for their results. As time went on, this process was reversed; the Western powers, especially the Americans, relaxed in their direct interference and gave the Germans a very substantial measure of self-government, while the strong hand of the Russians and their native handmaidens became increasingly evident in the East.

The party system today

It is a peculiar feature of Germany that most of its political history is not the history of its parties or party leaders. During the formative years of modern Germany—the period of empire (1871–1918)—the parties were strictly on the sidelines. The government of the country was in the hands not of party leaders but of personalities like Bismarck and his successors, who studiously avoided any partisan tinge. The political parties could talk, and even elect members of parliament, but the administration of the country remained outside their scope.

As we have seen, the experience of the Weimar Republic did little to bolster respect for the political party. Many Germans longed for strong leadership but, as Nazism in turn was discredited by its conduct and by its defeat, political parties were further discredited, even though the Nazi party had nothing in common with parties under a democratic system.

When parties sprang up again in 1945 and after, they were under the heavy supervision of military government. The business of government, while often entrusted to party leaders, was so strongly controlled and often directed by the Allied authorities that many politicians hesitated to take office for fear of appearing as the executive organs of a foreign state.

It was only after 1949, when Allied control had become nominal and had practically disappeared, that Germany's political profile began to take shape.

From this brief experience it is quite possible to draw a preliminary balance sheet and to point out several characteristic features of the contemporary German party scene.

1. In sharp contrast to the Weimar experience, the German Federal Republic has not produced the diversity of parties of its unfortunate precursor. After Allied control over the licensing of new parties relaxed its rigidity, there was a flurry of new parties; some special-interest groups and others formed around specific personalities. But this situation proved short-lived. The newer parties were unable to maintain themselves. Moreover, even some of the older parties have declined, with the result that Germany for the first time in her history is confronted by an approach to a two-party system. In fact, if Germany had voted solely under the direct-plurality system in single-member districts, a two-party system would actually exist. The decline of all parties except the Christian Democrats (CDU/CSU) and the Social Democrats (SPD) is very much in evidence.

2. The German public, by and large, does not quite understand the connection between political parties and government. It is inclined to look upon government as something impersonal, abstract (the term "state" is preferred to "government"), and to regard political parties as something separate, whose place in public life it cannot quite fathom. Parties are more likely to be regarded as a nuisance than as a necessity. The essentiality of political parties for the democratic process is not fully understood. Although Germans are wont to embrace very definite political philosophies, they have, by and large, little regard for political parties, even though these parties may be strong champions of the very same philosophy. Germany's younger generation has strong democratic inclinations but remains still reluctant to engage itself strongly in the day-to-day work of political parties. The high percentage of German voting participation (in the 1957 election, it was 88.2 percent) should be interpreted as a dedication to the exercise of a civic duty, rather than enthusiasm for a particular party.

3. The German political parties have strongly oligarchic tendencies. They are controlled by a small group of professional party bureaucrats or individual leaders, whose claim to prominence is more often based on party regularity and seniority than on exceptional qualifications. The CDU was long completely dominated by a single individual, the late Konrad Adenauer, and the same was true in the Social Democratic party while Schumacher was still alive. These, however, constitute unusual occurrences which are not likely to be repeated soon. Certainly no single person has been able to step into Schumacher's shoes in the Social Democratic party, and the same situation has prevailed in the CDU since Adenauer left the Chancellorship in 1963 and gave up the chairmanship of the party in 1966.

These oligarchic tendencies are not the result of any special rules or regulations but are based on habits and traditions. The German deputy and the German party member are conditioned to follow their leaders without too many questions. Moreover, the average German citizen is not conditioned toward the lively participation in civic activities which characterizes American life; even when he joins a party formally (which only a relatively small number of people will do), he does not expect to lay down the law to the party leaders.[1] Nevertheless, it should be noted that the disappearance or neutralization of overwhelmingly strong leadership personalities from all German political parties is likely to weaken these oligarchic tendencies in time.

4. German political leaders are still overaged. The average age of members of the fourth parliament (*Bundestag*) (1961–1965) was 52. Despite a much younger electorate, the fifth *Bundestag* (1965–1969) brought the average age down only to 50. Thus the German parliament remains the "oldest" in Europe.

5. Although controversy and occasional demagoguery have been no more lacking in Germany than in other countries, Germany's major parties have on the whole taken moderate and statesmanlike positions on both internal and external problems. The discipline and self-restraint of the German Trade Union Federation (*Deutscher Gewerkschaftsbund*) is particularly noteworthy in this connection.

The Christian Democrats

Germany's largest political party is the Christian Democratic Union (*Christlich demokratische Union,* CDU) which, together with its Bavarian sister party, the Christian Social Union (*Christlichsoziale Union,* CSU), has maintained an unbroken plurality throughout the life of the German Federal Republic. Beginning in 1949 with a head start over its nearest rival of less than 2 percent, it even achieved a majority in 1957. This it was not able to maintain, but its lead has remained sizeable.

When the CDU began its political life, it appeared to many to be the heir of the Center party of the Weimar Republic, for many of its leaders, especially Adenauer himself, were Catholics and former Center men. But the lessons of the past had been learned. Adenauer himself saw to it that the CDU remained interdenominational and that Protestants were given an appropriate share in the councils and the parliamentary representation of the party. There were delicate moments of both Catholic and Protestant suspicion, especially since the Catholics started with a more experienced leadership potential resulting from the Center party's experience and training. But this is now largely a matter of the past. The CDU has become strongly established in Protestant *Länder*—for instance, in Schleswig-Holstein, where it has consistently held a majority of the vote. By contrast, in largely Catholic areas like

---

[1] The classical work on the oligarchic nature of German parties, especially the Social Democrats, is Robert Michels' *Political Parties* (trans. by E. Paul and C. Paul), first published 1915, reprinted 1949.

Table 5. *Distribution of votes and seats in the Bundestag by party*

Parties	Percent of vote In 1949	Seats	Percent of vote In 1953	Seats	Percent of vote In 1957	Seats	Percent of vote In 1961	Seats	Vote in 1965	Percent of vote In 1965	Seats* In 1965
CDU/CSU	31.0	139	45.2	244	50.2	270	45.4	242	15,392,973	47.6	245
SPD	29.2	131	28.8	151	31.8	169	36.2	190	12,711,726	39.3	202
FDP	11.9	52	9.5	48	7.7	41	12.8	67	3,062,948	9.5	49
GB-BHE			5.9	27	4.6		2.8				
DP	4.0	17	3.3	15	3.4	17					
KPD	5.7	15	2.2								
Other splinter parties†									1,173,826	3.6	

* The nonvoting seats from Berlin are not listed.
† All splinter parties together. None of them received seats in the *Bundestag* under the 5 percent minimum clause.
They were:

AUD (*Aktionsgemeinschaft unabhängiger Deutschen*—Action group of independent Germans)   52,688 votes, 0.2 percent of total.
CVP (*Christliche Volkspartei*—Christian People's party)   19,904 votes, 0.1 percent of total.
DFU (*Deutsche Friedensunion*—German Peace Union)   432,221 votes, 1.3 percent of total.
FSU (*Freisoziale Union*—Free Social Union)   10,763 votes, 0.0 percent of total.
NPD (*Nationaldemokratische Partei Deutschlands*—National Democratic Party of Germany)   658,250 votes, 2.0 percent of total.
The CVP is confined to the Saarland. The DFU is said to be financed by the Communist East. The NPD is generally considered to be the latest of the Neo-nazi parties. Neither the DP nor the GB-BHE presented candidates in 1965. The KPD (Communist Party of Germany) was dissolved in 1956. In 1961 all nonrepresented parties polled 5.7 percent of the vote together, in 1965, only 3.6 percent.

Bavaria, not all Catholics vote CSU, and the CSU percentage of the Protestant vote is smaller than in the Protestant north.[2] Now that the CDU's leaders are all Protestants, the allegation of Catholic or clerical domination of the CDU can no longer be seriously maintained.

In contrast to the Social Democrats, the CDU does not possess a tight party organization. It sprang up in the beginning in different *Länder* simultaneously and with little coordination. Although an interzonal coordinating committee was formed in 1947, it was only in 1950 that the first real All-German (West Germany) Congress of the CDU could be held in Goslar. Since then the party organization has been firmed up but is still loose. However, its campaign techniques have become very refined and have developed a number of distinctly American features, which is not a surprise, since the party managers have avidly studied American campaign methods. The appointment of Herman Dufhues as "executive president" (*geschäftsführender Vorsitzender*) has contributed greatly to the strengthening of the party machinery.

The CDU lays far less stress on individual membership than does the SPD and as a result must rely on outside funds which, in practice, means fairly large donations from some important financial groups.

In Bavaria, the CDU's sister party, the CSU, was beset by serious internal difficulties at the beginning. Like its Weimar predecessor, the Bavarian People's party, the CSU is essentially more conservative than the CDU. Still, it has maintained a working relationship with the Social Democrats on the basis of a common insistence on "state's rights" and common suspicion of anything coming from north of the Main River.

For a long time the chief difficulty of the CSU was the serious split in its own ranks. At first it was led from its left wing by Dr. Josef Muller, former Bavarian Minister of Justice. Later an important section of the party, headed by Dr. Josef Baumgartner, seceded from the CSU and formed the Bavarian party (*Bayernpartei*) whose main platform was one of extreme Bavarian nationalism and of hostility to the Federal Republic. Much of the conflict was engendered by personal animosities. The Bavarian party obtained considerable success at first (in 1949) and almost balanced the CSU. But since then the Bavarian party has split, declined, and faded out of the picture.

For a while the CSU was dominated by Dr. Alois Hundshammer, a man of utter integrity but of almost medieval conservatism. Eventually leadership was won by Franz Josef Strauss. Strauss gave the CSU a more progressive note although it is somewhat to the right of the CDU. But the strong hold of the Catholic Church is not as strong as it was under Hundshammer, and some of the clergy have been wary of Strauss and his methods.

From the Center party the CDU has inherited the remnant of an intramural quarrel over social policy. The Center party, being a religious rather than a class

[2] F. von der Heidt and Sacherl, *Die Soziologie der Deutschen Parteien*, Munich, 1955.

party, combined several socially and economically heterogeneous groups, and in the CDU, too, a "left" and a "right" group are discernible. When the CDU was first organized, it seemed for a while as though the left might prove dominant.[3] However, it failed to take a firm hold. Its most important leader, Jakob Kaiser, was from Eastern Germany, and the iron curtain cut off his principal backing. Later the left wing was led by the able Karl Arnold, minister-president of North Rhine-Westphalia, who had once expressed himself in favor of the Social Democrats' demand for codetermination (*Mitbestimmungsrecht*) of the workers in industry. However, Adenauer's more conservative philosophy prevailed, although Arnold remained an important factor until his unexpected death in 1958. More recently the left wing, if that name is applicable, is represented and led by Hans Katzer, Minister of Labor in the 1965 cabinet of Ludwig Erhard.

The CDU belongs to the wide circle of Christian Democratic parties which includes the French MRP, the Italian Christian Democrats, the Belgian Christian Social party, and the Austrian People's party.[4] These and others share a common political philosophy without necessarily drawing the same political conclusions. The CDU's fundamental belief rests on the premise that the crisis of mankind and of civilization is primarily moral and spiritual and that a regeneration can take place only on a basis of Christian ethics. The same Christian principles lead the party to the conviction that human beings are bound to be imperfect and that it is therefore not safe to concentrate too much power in one person's hands whatever the field—social, economic, political, or administrative.

In its first party program, that of Ahlen in 1947, a balance between public and private enterprise was advocated. This somewhat socialistic tendency diminished rapidly when Konrad Adenauer ascended to the party's leadership and accepted the free-enterprise economic theories of Ludwig Erhard, who later became Minister of Economics and still later, Chancellor. Erhard, a former professor of economics, vigorously advocated a so-called "social market policy" (*Soziale Marktwirtschaft*), which is essentially free enterprise surrounded by safeguards for human welfare and social legislation. In the 1965 electoral campaign, Erhard coined the term "formed society" (*Formiertegesellschaft*) which is essentially the same as the "social market economy" and which constituted an attempt to apply the ideas of President Lyndon B. Johnson's "Great Society" to the German scene for German consumption.

This system has been extraordinarily successful. It is widely credited with the principal responsibility for Germany's recovery, the "economic miracle." To be sure, as in all model industrial states, this "free-enterprise" system is neither totally free nor totally enterprising but embraces a good many open and hidden government regulations. The constructive attitude of German business and labor and the

[3] Robert G. Neumann, "The New Political Parties of Germany," *American Political Science Review,* Vol. XL (1946), pp. 749–759.
[4] There is a loosely organized international association of Christian Democratic parties called *Nouvelles équipes internationales* (new international teams).

patience and frugality of the German people during the formative reconstruction days all deserve credit, which should go to more than one man or party. Nevertheless, Erhard's courageous decision to stick to his guns in difficult days, when many experts counselled a different course, was proven correct, and the credit which has therefore come to him is not undeserved.

In administrative theory, the CDU was traditionally anticentralist, favoring an emphasis on what Americans would call "states' rights"—a heritage from the old Center-party days when centralism meant northern, Prussian, and Protestant domination over the more Catholic south. However, once in power, the CDU discovered the advantages of centralism and much less is now being said in favor of decentralization.

Of special significance was the foreign policy advocated by the CDU's program. Under Adenauer's guidance it was unreservedly pro-Western, strongly supporting European integration and Atlantic partnership. Adenauer was determined that Germany should maintain the closest relations with the United States as indispensable protection against any attack or threat from the East. At the same time, he felt that the closest integration in the West was needed by Germany, not only to win back a place for Germany in civilized society, but also to shield and aid the renascent German democracy. When, as a result of the increasingly menacing cold war, the blockade of Berlin, and finally the Korean War, the rearmament of the West became indispensable, the question of a German contribution inevitably arose. Adenauer was not enchanted with the prospect of a new German army and warmly embraced the idea of the European Defense Community (EDC), first proposed by French Premier René Pleven. But when, after long and protracted discussion, this originally French idea was defeated in the French National Assembly in 1954, Adenauer reluctantly agreed to the establishment of a German army and its full integration into NATO. The West European Union Treaty of 1954, which made this possible, contained Germany's voluntary renunciation of the production of nuclear weapons.

On all these issues Adenauer faced considerable opposition, especially from those who feared that excessive German integration in the West would make reunification more difficult. Opposition was also voiced to Adenauer's consistent policy of trying to improve Franco-German relations, in which he sometimes made considerable concessions. Despite all this, his policy prevailed and has remained the CDU's policy.

The policy of Franco-German friendship played an important role in winning back a place for Germany, but went sour when the supposed crowning glory of Adenauer's career, the Franco-German Friendship Treaty of January 22, 1963, coincided with General de Gaulle's emphatic rejection of Great Britain's entry into the Common Market. Subsequent events deprived this treaty of almost all significance, but on the basic contention that Germany had to remain strongly tied to the West, there has been no wavering.

Both Adenauer and Erhard, as well as their Foreign Ministers, the late Heinrich von Brentano and Gerhard Schröder, were convinced that German reunification required Soviet concessions, possibly in the distant future, which would never be granted to a weak Germany negotiating in isolation, but would be granted, if at all, only to a strong Germany closely allied with a strong and united West. This is why Adenauer and his successors have always insisted that German unification must be tied to free all-German elections—a concession which the Soviet Union and the East German Communists have never been willing to grant because the outcome of such an election would be a foregone conclusion.

Few people would deny that the constancy in Adenauer's pro-Western attitude and the firmness of his objectives were largely responsible for the exceptional speed with which a defeated and despised Germany regained the respect of the world and a place among nations. Like most great historical figures, Adenauer had his eyes firmly fixed on broad objectives from which he was not deterred by the exigencies of the moment. His imperturbable calm, made even more extraordinary by a deeply lined face whose expression hardly ever changed, and an extraordinarily accurate sense of timing, marked him as a politician as well as a statesman. Added to this was an inexplicable physical stamina. When Konrad Adenauer became the first Chancellor of the new German Federal Republic, he was already seventy-three years old. When he resigned as Chancellor in 1963, still in fighting trim and seemingly unbroken vigor, he was eighty-seven. Not only was he indefatigable in campaigns, including that of 1965, where he was probably the liveliest fighter and able to outpace many a younger man (as this author can testify), but he could be a rough customer indeed. Being utterly sure of himself, he was prone to look with disdain upon those whom he did not consider his equals in ability—and there were mighty few of these.

If Adenauer's stewardship was fairly firm and smooth until 1959, it certainly declined after that date. Accusations against his allegedly excessive rigidity had mounted, and his age (then eighty-three) caused much behind-the-scenes debate and much speculation about his succession. There was also a lively press campaign, in which the weekly magazine *Der Spiegel* was particularly virulent, missing no opportunity to depict him as a man who had lived well beyond his time. That Adenauer himself did not relish such speculations can be easily understood. He obviously did not have the slightest intention of relinquishing the reins of power. If there was any senility or loss of faculties in *Der Alte* (the old man), as he was generally called, it was certainly not visible to this author, who had many opportunities to speak to Adenauer both before and after his retirement and who never saw the clarity and alertness of Adenauer's mind waver for a moment.

Why was Adenauer so determined to hold on to his job? For one thing, he did not believe that anyone else had the capability to steer a steady course for the German ship of state. Secondly, he had a profound distrust and disdain for the man who was the obvious choice as his successor and who did actually succeed him in the end, Ludwig Erhard. It was not that Adenauer did not consider Erhard to have been an excellent Minister of Economics, but he was certain that Erhard was not strong and particularly that he did not have "the political touch" and the sense of timing which a successful politician must have.

Thus in 1959 Adenauer embarked on an extraordinary set of maneuvers in order to block Erhard's path. In that year, the second term of President Heuss came to an end, and as the Constitution did not permit a third term, a successor had to be found. The Social Democrats advanced the candidacy of one of their most popular leaders, Carlo Schmid, a brilliant orator. The CDU found itself without a suitable candidate. For a short time, Adenauer pushed the candidacy of his intimate friend and collaborator, Heinrich Krone, Minister without portfolio, a highly respected conciliator within the CDU, but relatively unknown in the country at large. In view of Schmid's popularity and great public stature, there was danger that Krone's candidacy might not win out; hence Adenauer withdrew his support. Then Adenauer tried to kill two birds with one stone. He used extreme pressure to persuade Erhard to run for the presidency. This would have gotten him out of the way of the Chancellorship and would also have satisfied very well the requirements of the job of President, for Erhard was widely known and respected and would have been elected. Also he was a Protestant, and hence the then unwritten rule that the President should be a Protestant when the Chancellor is a Catholic would have been observed. However, the presidency is largely ornamental and powerless, and Erhard refused.

Adenauer, finding no acceptable candidate, then most reluctantly accepted the idea of becoming a candidate for the presidency himself. For a while he apparently considered ways and means of turning it into a more powerful position. Finally, he had to recognize that this was not possible without violating the Constitution. Thereupon, he again dramatically reversed himself and, in the late spring of 1959, decided to remain in the Chancellorship after all, and to propose the name of Heinrich Lübke, Minister of Agriculture, for the presidency. Erhard and his friends were badly upset by these maneuvers. But so strong was Adenauer's hold over his party that the uproar caused by his decision soon died down; Lübke was duly elected, and everything returned to "normal." There had been an outcry, which for a while seemed to seriously endanger the unity of the CDU/CSU and the position of the Chancellor, but once again Adenauer had correctly gauged the psychology of his party leaders and of parliament as a whole.

Two years later, in 1961, he once again led his party into an election campaign, stood through it with undiminished vigor, and again the CDU/CSU won a resounding victory with a combined total of 45.4 percent of the popular vote. To be sure, this was a decline from 50.2 percent in 1957 but nobody had expected that particular peak to be retained anyhow, and the 1961 figures still made a very respectable showing. Nevertheless the events of 1959 had opened the fissures of crisis within the party which would not soon heal again.[5] The crisis had begun over

[5] The succession crisis is described by Gerhard Braunthal in *Cases in Comparative Government,* Boston, 1965, pp. 207–240. Cf. also the broader study by Arnold J. Heidenheimer, *Adenauer and the CDU,* The Hague, 1960.

the succession to the presidency but turned into a much deeper dispute over the succession to the Chancellorship, involving, in addition to Erhard, younger and ambitious leaders such as the then Minister of the Interior Gerhard Schröder, and the Minister of Defense Franz Josef Strauss.

This internal crisis was exacerbated by a crisis in the foreign relations of the Federal Republic. Adenauer had made the closest possible relations with the United States the central factor of his government's policy. His relations with America, which were already excellent under the Truman-Acheson administration, became particularly intimate when General Dwight D. Eisenhower became President and when Adenauer entered into ties of deep personal friendship with Secretary of State John Foster Dulles. Undoubtedly, there was a great affinity of views and attitudes between those two statesmen, who shared not only militant opposition to communism but also a deep religious faith.

Dulles's death was a profound personal blow to Adenauer, who set aside all considerations of protocol and attended Dulles's funeral in Washington although the latter was no longer Secretary of State at the time of his death. With Dulles's passing, a new, and in Adenauer's eyes less desirable, period in American-German relations began. Between him and the new administration of President John F. Kennedy there were no longer the old, intimate ties. There was also the startling visual contrast between the young American President and the then eighty-five-year-old German Chancellor—a contrast to which Adenauer's enemies never failed to point. In addition, Adenauer became increasingly apprehensive about what he regarded as the altogether too optimistic view of the Kennedy administration regarding the evolution of East-West relations—a point of view which Adenauer's critics interpreted as further proof of his excessive rigidity and isolation from the main currents of world affairs.

In August, 1961, Germany and the Western world were shaken by yet another event. The exodus of refugees from Communist-controlled East Germany took on the proportions of a flood. The principal crossing point was Berlin. The Communists decided to take strong measures by erecting, suddenly, a wall which in West Germany became known as the "wall of shame" and which rigidly isolated East from West Berlin. For the Germans, this was a traumatic event, but neither the Chancellor nor his colleagues nor the Western allies had been prepared for this action; his reaction was neither immediate nor forceful, and added to the widespread rumor that he had "lost his touch."

After the election of 1961, Adenauer formed yet another government, his last. It proved to be an exceedingly difficult task. The Free Democratic party (FDP), which had been in steady decline and had polled only 7.7 percent of the vote in 1957, suddenly increased its forces to 12.8 percent. Clearly, the difference was made up of voters who would no longer accept Adenauer's leadership. Encouraged by this unexpected windfall, the FDP insisted on an unprecedented and humiliating "coalition agreement" in which Chancellor Adenauer was forced to promise that he would resign during the current term of the *Bundesrat*. His humiliation was made complete by the FDP's demand for the "head" of Foreign Minister von Brentano, if for no other reason than that this was the best way in which it could get back at Adenauer. With great dignity, von Brentano took himself out of this unsavory situation by resigning as Foreign Minister, but Adenauer's failure to stick by him did not make a favorable impression.

Adenauer's last term was beset by a number of problems and affairs. Most sensational among the latter was the "Spiegel affair." *Der Spiegel* is a sensational and corrosive but often well-informed weekly of mass circulation whose opposition to Adenauer and Strauss knew no restraint. In 1962 there appeared an article in *Der Spiegel* regarding Germany's military establishment which the government regarded as treasonable. It commenced prosecution. Strauss took the astonishing step of using the German military attaché in Madrid to pick up and bring home one of *Der Spiegel's* editors. This unprecedented action led to a general outcry which placed the government in a very difficult position but which spoke well for the degree of popular alertness in Germany's new democratic regime. Strauss first denied this action in parliament but later admitted it and was forced to resign. Prosecution of *Der Spiegel* dragged on, and eventually it was the government rather than the newspaper which lost the round. The government had clearly not covered itself with glory, and Adenauer himself did not remain untouched.

All these events contributed to a growing insistence that he make good his promise of resignation. The infighting was bitter and prolonged, for he was not only most reluctant to depart but was maneuvering desperately to prevent Erhard from succeeding him. But all the maneuvers which had proved successful in the past were unavailing this time. Finally, Adenauer accepted the inevitable and left the Chancellorship to Ludwig Erhard, though retaining the chairmanship of the CDU. Herman Dufhues was appointed "executive president" of the party to carry out practical administrative tasks. Otherwise, the first Erhard cabinet was not much different in composition from Adenauer's last one.

But Adenauer's retirement in 1963 did not end the crisis within the CDU/CSU; it merely precipitated a new phase. One of his last official acts was to sign the Franco-German Friendship Treaty of January 22, 1963. In other times, such a treaty would have been regarded as a major diplomatic triumph for the German government and as the fitting culmination of Adenauer's career, which had so long been dedicated to a rebirth of friendship between those hereditary enemies, France and Germany. But in politics, timing is the most important ingredient, and the timing of the Franco-German treaty was just about as bad as it could be. Only a few days before the treaty was signed, on January 13, De Gaulle exploded a bombshell by rejecting in a peremptory manner Great Britain's application to join the Common Market—an act which placed him in sharp opposition not only to the other five partners of the Common Market but also to the United States. Under those circumstances, the Franco-German treaty might have been interpreted as demonstrative support for De Gaulle and as opposition to the United States. The German debate over the ratification of the treaty proved to be very difficult. Adenauer succeeded only after accepting a preamble to the treaty which rankled De Gaulle without fully satisfying Adenauer's own critics.

The "changing of the guard" in 1963 did not heal the widening split within the CDU/CSU, but made it more evident. Neither the new Chancellor, Ludwig Erhard, nor the Foreign Minister, Gerhard Schröder, wanted to go as far as Adenauer had in pursuing a special relationship with France. They had come to the conclusion that the government of General de Gaulle was pursuing strictly French, nationalist policies which were not in Germany's best interests. They wanted to see Great Britain brought into Europe and they were convinced that Germany's precarious strategic position made necessary the closest possible relationship with the United States, the very opposite of what General de Gaulle's increasingly intense campaign against the United States spelled out.

The Erhard-Schröder foreign policy immediately came under heavy fire. This was not from the Social Democratic opposition, which was in general agreement with Erhard and Schröder as far as foreign policy was concerned; it came from within the CDU/CSU itself. The leader of this intra-party opposition was the former Minister of Defense, Franz Josef Strauss, strongly supported both behind the scenes and in front by the old master himself, ex-Chancellor Adenauer.

Many observers had written Strauss off, holding that his inauspicious departure from the government in 1962 marked the end of his political career. They were highly premature in this view. Franz Josef Strauss is one of Germany's most talented politicians; he is also a man of such ungovernable temperament that his high intelligence and his more primitive urges seem to be locked in a series of constant clashes. Strauss was born in Munich in 1915 and was preparing for a teaching career when the Second World War started and he was drafted. He had never been a Nazi and hence, immediately upon his return, he was appointed by the American military government to become chief administrator (*Landrat*) of his home county (Schongau). From there he rose rapidly. He helped to found the CSU in 1945, and in 1949 became its general secretary. In 1953 he became a minister without portfolio in the second Adenauer cabinet, and in 1955 he was placed in charge of scientific and nuclear problems—becoming Minister of Defense in 1956 at the age of forty-one. The newly reestablished German armed forces had had an inauspicious start under Theodor Blank, and now Strauss threw his enormous energy into building a great military instrument. Few critics would deny not only that he was very successful at this but also that he established firm civilian leadership and control over the new German armed forces—a feature which was particularly important in view of Germany's past. At the same time he proved an excellent campaigner and debater, having the rare ability to synthesize and explain complicated issues in a simple fashion.

It was not long after his resignation in 1962 that he began his comeback. He went on a visit to Israel which began with demonstrations against him but ended in a personal triumph when it was revealed that as Minister of Defense he had aided the Israeli army considerably. He returned to Bavaria, mobilized his considerable talents, and carried a *Land* election to a resounding victory. Then he was over-whelmingly reelected president of the CSU—a position which automatically made him deputy chairman of the CDU/CSU parliamentary group in the *Bundestag.* Since then, his command over the CSU, although not undisputed, has remained absolute.

When Strauss was Minister of Defense, his orientation had been extremely "Atlantic." Later, in the intra-party controversy, he emphasized more and more the need for a "European" policy based on close Franco-German collaboration. This gave him the reputation of being the chief German "Gaullist," and indeed he does support many of the General's contentions and criticisms—especially against the United States. However, while Strauss demanded a more "European" policy, his dedication to the principle of close Atlantic cooperation has never wavered.[6]

Although Strauss represents a minority element in the combined CDU/CSU, it is a powerful minority whose influence is growing. Its leaders are brought to-gether by a variety of motives, some sharing the views of Strauss, others merely distrusting Erhard and Schröder, still others wanting to take their places. Strauss and the young nationalist, Karl Theodor Freiherr zu Guttenberg, have been close associates and also intense rivals. Strauss frequently enjoys the support of Henrich Krone; the presiding officer of the *Bundestag,* Eugen Gerstenmaier, can also be found from time to time in his corner; and the chairman of the CDU/CSU parlia-mentary group, Dr. Rainer Barzel, who is nominally neutral, has at times shown a mild preference for Strauss' views. Following his retirement, Konrad Adenauer also sniped at the government from the sidelines with undiminished vigor.

It was not until the elections of September 19, 1965, that Erhard came into his own. It was the first election in which he led the CDU and it gave him a clear mandate at the end of a long road fraught with frustrations which at times must have seemed nearly unbearable. Ludwig Erhard was born in Fürth, Bavaria, in 1897 and was wounded in World War I. Later he became a professor of economics and directed several institutes of economic research. He played an important role in the German currency reform of 1948 and became Minister of Economics in 1952, a position in which he was highly successful but in which he also had to endure Adenauer's constant attempts to denigrate him. Even in the 1965 campaign, it seemed at times as though two elections were taking place—one in which Adenauer and Strauss ran in support of Erhard, and one in which they opposed him. In fact, the seemingly indestructible old ex-Chancellor proved the liveliest and perhaps the most interesting of all the campaigners of any party. But this time the people felt called upon to decide for or against Ludwig Erhard, not for or against Konrad Adenauer.

---

[6] Strauss has laid down his foreign policy concepts in a book written specifically for the English-speaking public, *The Grand Design: A European Solution to German Reunification,* London, 1965. An elaboration of these ideas can be found in a book by one of Strauss' asso-ciates, Karl Theodor Freiherr zu Guttenberg, *Wenn der Westen Will,* Stuttgart, 1965.

The outcome gave the CDU/CSU a greater victory than it had expected. With 47.6 percent of the vote, the party was once again clearly dominant. This underscored the pivotal significance of Erhard, who had in fact proven himself to be the "election engine" (*Wahllokomotive*) that he was reputed to be. Although it was by no means a one-man victory, he had clearly been "the engine which pulled the rest of the train." This had not been the result of a dynamic personality or of exceptional oratorical gifts or flair; that is not the figure which he cuts or attempts to cut. Actually, he tends often to be quite dull and pedantic in his speeches, and he became quite repetitive toward the end of the campaign. But it was his past reputation as the symbol of German recovery, of the economic miracle, of stability, which the German people wanted to retain.

At the same time, both the CDU and its rival the SPD became weaker in some of their habitual strongholds and gained strength in each other's strongholds. To many observers, this "weakening of the bastions" meant that both parties now had to contend with a larger floating vote and that if Erhard did not satisfy the voters there could be considerable shifting in the future.

The real conflict in German politics, however, was not between the CDU and the SPD but within the CDU/CSU, and this was in no way settled by the election. The voters had no opportunity to express themselves on the major issues of German foreign policy because on those the viewpoints of the Chancellor and his Foreign Minister on the one hand and of the Social Democratic opposition on the other hand were very much alike.

The bitter and prolonged infighting within the CDU/CSU and the coalition revealed serious cracks within the dominant party. In the bitter haggling over ministerial seats which preceded Chancellor Erhard's formal election in parliament on October 20, 1965, Strauss failed to unseat his principal targets in the cabinet— Foreign Minister Schröder and Vice Chancellor Erich Mende (FDP), but it is doubtful that he really expected this. What he did expect and did obtain was a highly reluctant but still adequate formal "declaration of rehabilitation" (*Ehrenerklärung*) by which the FDP retracted its previous declaration that he was morally ineligible for a cabinet post. Then Strauss revealed in a television interview on October 22, 1965, that Chancellor Erhard had offered him a cabinet post which he, Strauss, had declined. As this statement was never contradicted by Erhard, it must be taken at face value, although numerous observers saw in it a put-up job between the two men. The net effect of this and of the declaration of rehabilitation was that neither the CDU/CSU leadership including Erhard nor the FDP could ever again declare Strauss ineligible for a cabinet post. Besides, Strauss was able to unify the CSU behind him, burying his quarrels with other leaders like Freiherr zu Guttenberg and causing his close associate, Dr. Richard Jäger, to enter the cabinet as a fifth CSU minister (Justice), a gain of one. The real loser of the battle was Konrad Adenauer, who retired from the chairmanship of the CDU in 1966 at the age of ninety and died in 1967.

This, however, did not end the assault of the intra-party opposition on Erhard. There was growing dissatisfaction with the Chancellor's foreign and domestic policies. A sense of stagnation permeated the atmosphere. It gained intensity in 1966. In July of that year the *Land* election in North Rhine–Westphalia was the first of several contests to demonstrate that the vote-getting ability of Ludwig Erhard no longer existed. This was followed, later that year, by similar results in the *Land* Hesse. Only in Bavaria, where the redoubtable Franz Josef Strauss led the CSU, did the CDU/CSU hold its own.

In this situation of disarray, growing opposition, and apparent inability of the Chancellor to give his wavering flock strong leadership, the Free Democratic party (FDP) evidently decided that its continuation in the coalition government had become a liability and withdrew its support from Erhard. Thereby it unleashed the biggest cabinet crisis known to postwar Germany.

Ludwig Erhard finally came to the conclusion, in November, 1966, that his time had run out, and he declared his willingness to retire if agreement on a successor could be found. This was essential because it was by no means clear that the warring factions, which appeared to be in agreement only on the need for Erhard's retirement, could agree on a successor. The struggle was also confused by the disagreement between those who, like Erhard, wanted merely a restoration of the previous CDU/CSU-FDP coalition and those who sought a wider, so-called "great coalition" with the Social Democrats. A CDU/CSU minority government also remained a possibility.

After four weeks of uncertainty and crisis, the CDU was finally brought around to the "great coalition" view by the man who loomed increasingly as the strong man of the hour, Franz Josef Strauss. He had long been quietly busy building bridges to the Social Democrats. He had also begun to tone down his feud with Foreign Minister Gerhard Schröder. It was of course out of the question for Strauss to head the government. The cleavages and the criticism of his past conduct had been too great.

The near-ideal compromise candidate was found in Kurt Georg Kiesinger, a moderate leader of the CDU's southern wing and Prime Minister of Baden-Württemberg. A former chairman of the *Bundestag*'s foreign relations committee, Kiesinger had retired from Bonn when his further progress had been blocked by Adenauer, and had concentrated on *Land* affairs. There he had established a good record, and also a record of mutual respect with the Social Democratic opposition. Hence his candidacy was acceptable to all. Although it was revealed, at the last minute before the new government was formed, that Kiesinger had joined the Nazi party in 1933, there was no evidence that he had committed or was involved in any crimes, nor that he had ever been an officer. Nor could Kiesinger's assertion that he had soon become opposed to the Nazis be either proved or disproved.

At any rate, the Social Democrats refused to make an issue of the matter. Thus in December, 1966, the new government presented itself to the *Bundestag*. Prominently featured in it, next to the new Chancellor Kurt Georg Kiesinger, were the Social Democratic leader Willy Brandt, who became Vice Chancellor and Foreign Minister, the former Foreign Minister Gerhard Schröder, who became Minister of Defense, and Franz Josef Strauss, who returned as Minister of Finance.

Kiesinger had been selected, not because he was one of the principal leaders of the CDU, but because he was not, and therefore seemed to pose no serious obstacle to men like Strauss who vied for top billing but agreed that their time had not yet come. But, as so often happens in political history, this seemingly "transitory" figure surprised all. Kiesinger quickly asserted himself as the real, not merely the nominal leader, in spite of the presence of such strong figures as Strauss and Schröder in the cabinet. He was aided, of course, by the constitutionally strong position of the chancellor, but his own personality, competence, and knowledge were decisive factors. He managed to bind the wounds of the party and to lead it without becoming clearly identified with any faction.

In 1967 he took over the chairmanship of the CDU/CSU without serious opposition. He also managed to seem more independent toward America than his predecessors had been or had appeared to be, without permanently harming the good relations between the two countries. The partial misunderstandings and apprehensions which existed were largely removed or modified during Kiesinger's visit to Washington in 1967. The visit proved, in fact, a considerable personal and diplomatic success. At the same time he appeared friendlier to De Gaulle's aspirations than the more inflexible Erhard had, but made few real concessions to France; he appeared to open a more flexible policy toward the East, but again without undertaking any really substantial changes; and on the domestic front his attractive, calm personality seemed very reassuring, and he benefited from an upturn in the economic situation of Germany which began to appear early in his term of office.

All this helped not only to make Kiesinger the real leader of his again much more united party but also to make him the beneficiary of policies, many of which had actually originated with his Social Democratic coalition partners. Thus, in a dramatic and brief sweep, the CDU emerged from its doldrums with a firm hand at its helm and a new and brighter chapter opening in its fortunes.

The Social Democratic party

The reestablishment of the Social Democratic party organization was both prompt and effective. A number of factors contributed to this end. Among survivors of the Weimar regime, the Social Democrats usually had clean records which made them eligible for positions in the German administrative structure under military government. In their ranks there were a number of men who had seen previous service in administrative positions. As experienced and trustworthy civil servants and policymaking officials were not easily found, on account of the denazification policy, many of these Social Democratic relics from Weimar days were placed in positions of power and prestige which aided their efforts at reestablishing their party. Moreover, the long rule of the Weimar Social Democrats and the "Free

Trade Unions" by which they had dominated the German workers had created a kind of tradition which had often been passed on from father to son and to which the German workers now readily responded.[7]

The Social Democratic program also held considerable appeal. It placed the party squarely behind the democratic form of government. It advocated a democratic and moderate form of socialism, which appealed to many Germans as it did to other Europeans because of the general impoverishment of the population and the obvious need for some sort of state planning and initiative for the gigantic task of reconstruction. On the other hand, concerning questions of the class struggle and the relationship to religion, the party had become very moderate, a development which undoubtedly received its inspiration in the experience of the common suppression of all religions and classes by the defunct Nazi regime.

Because of their clean record as far as the Nazi period is concerned, the Social Democratic leaders were among the first who dared to stand up to such military-government orders as they considered unacceptable. Such criticism was often appreciated by military-government officers in the field, who understood the need for public criticism in a democracy, but it was sometimes resented back home by people whose concept of a loyal democrat was one who walks about draped in the Stars and Stripes, the Union Jack, or the *tricolore*.

Soon after the reestablishment of political parties, the Communists launched their vigorous campaign for a united workers' party. Their overtures were roundly turned down in Western Germany, but they found more receptive ears in the Eastern parts of the country.

The Communist fusion propaganda

It is of course easily understandable why the relatively small Communist party would want such a fusion with the much more numerous Social Democrats, especially since experience in the Soviet satellite countries showed that it could easily control its more moderate confreres. No such obvious advantage would seem to be on the side of the Social Democrats. Yet there were peculiar circumstances which exerted pressure in the direction of fusion. The greatest strength of the Social Democratic party in Weimar days had always been in those regions which became the Soviet zone of occupation, including the city of Berlin. Many of the party's leaders feared that, if they refused to make common cause with the Communists, Soviet pressure would sooner or later force them out of office, and perhaps even out of existence, in the regions where they expected to take their strongest hold. They also feared that such renewed pressure would cause many of their followers

---

[7] It must always be remembered that many political parties, but especially the Social Democrats, conducted large-scale programs of education and social affairs for their members. Membership therefore tended to become a way of life and a mold of social contacts which was often retained during the lifetime of the member.

to go over to the Communists, as that party would then be in a better position to give them what they wanted in social benefits and improvement of working and living conditions. Perhaps the Social Democratic leaders also dreaded a new period of illegality and suppression after they had emerged from the twelve long years of Nazi rule. Undoubtedly some of them genuinely believed the moderate and seemingly sincere assertions of the Communist leadership, and all of them were deadly afraid of any recurrence of Nazism, and remembered how the advent of Hitler had been made much easier by the fratricidal war between the two leftist parties.[8]

The influence of these considerations was strong. All these factors caused most of the Social Democratic leaders in Berlin and the Soviet zone, especially Otto Grotewohl, to accept fusion with the Communists. It was to be accomplished in May, 1946.

The SED

The Social Democrats of Western Germany, led by Kurt Schumacher, protested strongly against this decision. Even more violent opposition came from the membership itself. It was quite clear that this deal was one made by the leaders, not one in which the rank and file concurred. In the Soviet zone, the military-government authorities managed to prevent any plebiscite on the part of the party membership, but in Berlin, where the quadripartite arrangement prevailed, a party convention was held, and the leadership was repudiated by a majority of seven to one. However, the leaders had gone too far to recant, and they went ahead anyway. The Social Democrats of Western Germany and of Berlin repudiated this decision and expelled the renegades. The fusion was accomplished in June, 1946, in Eastern Germany, and the new united party gave itself the name of Socialist Unity party of Germany (*Sozialistische Einheitspartei Deutschlands*) and is commonly referred to as the SED, after its German initials.

The Berlin election, 1946

Since the old-line Social Democratic party (SPD) was outlawed in the Soviet zone, and since no SED existed in the Western zones,[9] the only place where a contest of popular strength was possible was Berlin, where both the SED and SPD were active. The SED went into this contest with high hopes. Not only did it receive the wholehearted support of the Soviet authorities, but it also counted on the "red"

[8] One of the most important Social Democratic leaders who was able to maintain some contacts with other Social Democrats was the former Hessian Minister of the Interior, Wilhelm Leuschner. He constantly preached the unity theme. On the day before his execution (September 29, 1944), he wrote "Remain united, rebuild!," and as he was led to the gallows, his lips formed the word *"Einheit"* (unity).

[9] The Communist party then operated in the Western zones although it was subsequently outlawed in the Federal Republic.

tradition of Berlin, a city in which the Nazis were never able to obtain a majority. But the Berliners went to the polls on October 20, 1946, and handed the now thoroughly Communist-dominated SED a resounding defeat.

Out of 1,945,981 votes cast, the SED obtained only 383,249, or slightly less than 20 percent. Strongest was the old-line Social Democratic party, which polled 948,851 votes, or just under 49 percent. The Christian Democratic Union, a middle-of-the-road to conservative party, occupied second place with 432,016 votes, or 22 percent; while the right-wing Liberal Democratic party was last with 181,875 votes, or a little over 9 percent.[10] Only in the Soviet zone outside Berlin was the SED able to obtain slim majorities and that by means which were far removed from the customary methods of the democratic process.

The Berlin election served as demonstration of a phenomenon which has now become widely recognized in all other countries as well, namely, that the Communists do not obtain majorities in fair and unfettered elections, and that the common people are seldom deceived about the true nature of the Communist program, no matter upon what fusion ticket it may appear. In Germany the Berlin election was a turning point insofar as it revealed to the Soviet authorities that Communism had little chance to gain the upper hand through regular elections. Consequently from that time onward the originally fairly mild SED regime in the Soviet zone became much harsher, political opponents were suppressed and even imprisoned in ever-increasing numbers, and the Soviet zone took on the appearance of a satellite state, where government is exercised not by the freely expressed will of the people but by the chosen instrument of the Soviet masters.

The forcible fusion of the Social Democrats and the Communists in the Eastern zone has not hurt the Social Democrats in the West because their strongly anti-Communist stand is well recognized by everyone. In contrast to the Christian Democrats, the Social Democratic party of Germany (*Sozialdemokratische Partei Deutschlands,* SPD) maintains an extremely strong organization. It has about 650,000 members (a decline from a high of 900,000), who are organized in 24 districts and over 9,000 local groups. The financial contributions of the membership make the solicitation of large funds less important for the SPD than for the CDU.

The main support for the SPD comes from the working classes, who have a traditional attachment to the party and have remained loyal to it. There is also considerable middle-class support, and for a while it looked as if the party would make large inroads into some rural regions, where in the meantime, however, it has declined. There is also little doubt that the SPD still has considerable support in the Eastern zone, where it can only lead an underground existence. If Germany were

[10] Percentages taken from total number of eligible voters. Of these, 89 percent cast valid ballots. It is significant that the SED was outclassed even in the Soviet sector of Berlin (SED 29.8 percent, SPD 43.6 percent). For a detailed breakdown, see Special Report of the Military Governor, United States Zone, *Statistics of Elections in Germany, 1946,* rev. ed., Mar. 15, 1947.

to be reunited, the effective strength of the SPD would probably be increased to a considerable extent. This explains in part the party's emphasis on the reunification theme.

According to the Dürkheim program (1950) the SPD favored planned credit and raw material policies, housing projects, the socialization of basic raw materials and key industries, as well as the reorganization of the social insurance system. However, the Bad Godesberg program of 1959 endorsed free enterprise, modified only by the demands of social justice. Nationalized enterprise is justified only as a counterweight to overly powerful private enterprises, but no new nationalization is advocated. The party endorses national defense and declares that "democratic socialism is rooted in Christian ethics" and denies that it is trying to proclaim "ultimate truths." Hence, the SPD can no longer be called socialist, but has become a liberal party of social reform.

Like the CDU, the SPD emerged after the war under the strong leadership of a remarkable man, Kurt Schumacher, who dominated the party completely. It was largely due to his personal influence that the social and economic policies of the SPD became increasingly overshadowed by questions of international policy. This is perhaps to be explained by the painful memories of the Weimar past in which the SPD was frequently accused of being too international-minded and of "betraying the national interest." Under Schumacher's leadership, the SPD acquired a strongly nationalistic line and concentrated on the problem of German reunification, one of the most popular political issues in Germany. The SPD vigorously rejected any compromise on the Saar question or any recognition of the Oder-Neisse frontier of Eastern Germany. It was very dubious about the Adenauer policy in favor of a "little Europe" composed of the six countries of the Schuman Plan (France, Germany, Italy, Belgium, Netherlands, Luxembourg) because it feared that the political composition of these countries would guarantee the perpetuation of private capitalism. Instead it wanted a larger European Union, especially with the inclusion of Great Britain.

At first, the SPD bitterly attacked Adenauer's policy of close political and military collaboration with the West. Its argument was that the reunification of Germany could be the result only of negotiations with Russia and that Russia would never consent to a united Germany if the latter were committed to a completely Western policy.

For a time this attitude produced political results, and the SPD steadily increased its votes in a number of *Länder* elections. It is not impossible that this success might have been continued if Schumacher had been able to lead his party with his tremendous dynamic ability and immense popularity. But he died in 1952 and his successor as chairman of the party, the colorless and mediocre Erich Ollenhauer, proved less successful. The greatest weakness of the party's position, however, lay in the inconclusive character of its central argument. While the SPD's critique of Adenauer's policy of close union with the West was perhaps well taken, its alternative suggestion of negotiating with the Russians carried little conviction since the

Germans had ample experience with the Russians and most of them did not believe that one can be successful in negotiating from a position of weakness.[11]

For five years after Schumacher's death there was no change in the party's negative policy line on foreign affairs. Nor did the party's political fortunes advance to any great degree. To be sure, it governed ably in several of the *Länder* having a large number of cities, where its administrations were generally efficient, frugal and quite conservative. Nevertheless, the historic suspicion of it as the "Red" party persisted among the middle classes, and its foreign policy, although clearly not Communist, did little to dispel that impression.

The foreign policy line came to a spasmodic end in the campaign of 1957 which the Social Democrats conducted under astonishingly demagogic slogans. Their principal motto in that campaign was "against atomic death," implying that Adenauer and the CDU were somehow leading Germany towards nuclear rearmament, which accusation was untrue and irresponsible. The result was a resounding defeat, even though the SPD's strength increased slightly from 28.8 percent to 31.8 percent, largely because of the disappearance of smaller parties. The CDU/CSU, however, reaped its greatest triumph by gaining a majority, with 50.2 percent of the vote. The defeat was all the greater as the Social Democrats had won a number of local and regional elections and had hoped for better fortunes at the national elections. Now, all these gains were wiped out and the Adenauer government, already in power for eight years, was clearly on the offensive.

It testifies to the maturity of the SPD leadership that they finally recognized these lessons and with resolution and courage undertook to remake their party. This effort was all the more impressive as it was conducted not by the new men but by those who had followed and advocated the unsuccessful line and who therefore demonstrated their courage in admitting their mistakes. At the party congress at Bad Godesberg in 1959, a virtual turnabout was executed. The last vestiges of Marxism and socialism were eliminated from the party's program, free enterprise was endorsed, with some qualifications in the name of social justice, and the nationalization of industries, never too popular among German Social Democrats, was virtually abandoned. More important, this party, which had voted against the reestablishment of any army, which had opposed the Council of Europe and the European Coal and Steel Community, now endorsed national defense and proclaimed its faith in European unification. And this once Marxist party now stated, "Democratic Socialism is rooted in Christian ethics." This turnabout was prepared and engineered by the party's most intelligent leader, Fritz Erler, and was carried through by the party's powerhouse, Herbert Wehner, who once, for a brief period, had been a Communist.

There remained the question of personalities. German elections had become

[11] Henry L. Bretton, "The German Social Democratic Party and the International Situation," *American Political Science Review,* Vol. XLVII (1953), pp. 980–996.

increasingly "American," that is, centering on personalities. This was an expression of the new election techniques imported from America and also indicated a diminishing of class lines and issues and a growing realization that the attitudes and abilities of individuals might be better indications of future actions than theoretical and abstract statements in a party program. Therefore, it had clearly become a matter of importance that the voter knew that by voting for the CDU he was in effect voting for a government under Konrad Adenauer, while by casting his ballot for the SPD he voted for the chancellorship of Erich Ollenhauer. This confrontation went all in favor of the CDU in 1957. Ollenhauer was a most honorable and dedicated man of moderation. But, compared to the "old master," he seemed pale.

Thus, after the disappointment of 1957, the Social Democratic leaders cast about for a standard-bearer with a better image. They saw him in the person of the mayor of Berlin, Willy Brandt. Brandt's good looks, his dynamic personality, his aura of a "fighting mayor" of Berlin, seemed better designed to challenge Adenauer than Ollenhauer's colorless personality. Brandt's selection was also designed to underline the basic changes in the party program of the SPD as he, together with other Social Democratic mayors (Max Brauer of Hamburg and Wilhelm Kaisen of Bremen) had been quite critical of the SPD's former foreign policy.

At first Brandt did not become much more than a standard-bearer. The party machinery remained in the hands of the real powers behind the throne, Herbert Wehner and Fritz Erler.

Wehner, probably the SPD's strongest personality, was born in 1906. He became a Communist for a short time in 1919, only to turn against communism later. He was active in the clandestine struggle against the Nazis and finally escaped abroad. After World War II, he devoted himself to the reestablishment of the SPD machinery and became strongly entrenched, especially in Hamburg. Although he shuns the limelight and has never been a candidate for a position demanding a great deal of public representation, he has the confidence even of his opponents both inside and outside the SPD.

The outstanding brain of the party and probably its most distinguished statesman was Fritz Erler. He was born in 1913, and his formal education did not go beyond the secondary stage, but he acquired a tremendous amount of knowledge through extensive reading, and learned to speak English and French to perfection. During the Nazi regime, he worked in the underground, was arrested, and spent many years in prison. He was the undisputed foreign-affairs and defense expert of the party and enjoyed universal respect among friend and foe alike. When he questioned cabinet ministers in *Bundestag* debates, his thorough knowledge of the subject matter was greatly feared. He was also well known and highly respected abroad.[12] When Ollenhauer died in 1964, Erler succeeded him as chairman of the

[12] A number of Erler's ideas were presented in English in the Jodidi Lectures at Harvard University and were published under the title *Democracy in Germany,* Cambridge, Mass., 1965.

SPD parliamentary group and if it had not been for his somewhat colorless image in public, he would probably have been the party's standard-bearer rather than Brandt.

The selection of Brandt came in for much criticism. Many observers felt that behind an impressive front of action and leadership, there was a personality full of doubt and lacking in depth. Certainly he had neither the party power of Wehner nor the intellectual clarity of Erler. And even the hope that his good looks (he was called *der schöne Willy*—handsome Willy) would attract the feminine electorate proved vain, as both the elections of 1961 and 1965 showed amply.

Ever since the turnabout of the Bad Godesberg party congress in 1959, the SPD tactics concentrated on one point; to win the confidence of the middle classes and to be fully accepted as a responsible party to whose hands the reins of government could be safely entrusted. The history of past electoral defeats as well as an analysis of Germany's social structure clearly indicate that no party can hope to win which is unable to attract middle-class votes.

At the beginning of the key election year 1965, it seemed as though this goal had come well within reach. The Social Democratic party's constructive and moderate attitude had been demonstrated on both the national and the international levels, and the party's record in *Länder* and local administrations had consistently been excellent. Its domestic and foreign policy was moderate and statesmanlike. The party's devotion to the Atlantic Alliance and to European integration was now unquestionable. Its congress at Karlsruhe in early 1965 was characterized by a rousing confidence that victory was now at hand. The Erhard government was in great difficulties, and the public opinion polls put the SPD ahead of the CDU/CSU for the first time although Brandt's personal popularity ominously continued to trail Erhard's by a very large margin. Even in those euphoric moments, few SPD leaders seriously expected to gain a majority, but there was a widespread belief that a plurality was now at hand and that the SPD would at long last come out of the opposition woods.

The elections of September 19, 1965, proved once more a cruel disappointment. To be sure, the vote for the SPD continued to rise, from 36.2 percent in 1961 to 39.3 percent in 1965, and the SPD group in the *Bundestag* gained 12 seats. But the CDU/CSU also increased its vote, by 2.2 percent. The gap between the two major parties remained large—8.3 percent—and was not closing very fast.

What was particularly disheartening to the SPD leaders was that they had done just about everything to win over the middle classes. What else could they have done? Not a note of radicalism had entered their campaign oratory. The party's campaign slogan had been truly astonishing for an opposition party, *Sicher ist sicher* ("safety first"—but a more idiomatic translation would be "don't rock the boat") which would have seemed more suitable for a government party than for the opposition. And in its habitual stronghold of Lower Saxony the SPD government had concluded a concordat with the Catholic church on which the CDU could hardly have improved. Some critical observers had opined that the SPD was trying to convince the voters that "it was the best CDU of them all."

All this had been to no avail. In the privacy of the polling booth, more Germans still preferred the CDU/CSU, despite the open disunity in CDU/CSU ranks, a number of government fumbles, and the beginnings of a fiscal crisis. The SPD was successful in marshaling an impressive number of intellectuals and seemed to have made some inroads among the youth. Yet this had not helped.

Under these circumstances it was understandable that a process of soul-searching commenced in the SPD. True, the party had made slow though steady progress since 1953, but in part at least this resulted from the decline of third parties. It was equally true that the distribution of votes in 1965 revealed some important inroads by the SPD in hitherto CDU/CSU strongholds such as Bavaria, Rhineland-Palatinate and the Saarland, but these were countered by losses in its own "fortresses." These trends had not been uniform: for instance, the SPD continued to make progress in the industrial Ruhr areas (North Rhine–Westphalia). But the CDU had also made advances in the traditionally CDU-voting *Land* of Bad Württemberg. In sum, these shifts were worrisome and a cause for considerable insecurity.

July of 1966 brought a sudden upturn of the SPD's fortunes. The already-mentioned elections in the *Land* North Rhine–Westphalia pulled the SPD even with the CDU, despite a relatively indifferent SPD *Land* ticket. The same pattern was repeated in the elections of Hesse later in 1966, where the SPD had long been dominant and where it now scored an even greater victory.

When the exodus of the FDP from the Erhard government in October, 1966, brought on a government crisis, the SPD suddenly found itself faced, not only with its first real opportunity to enter the government, but also with two possible ways of doing so—by leading a coalition government with the FDP or by joining one led by the CDU.

The choice was hard. There was pressure, especially from more impatient younger elements who pressed for a Brandt government with the FDP. However, the party leadership clearly saw the danger of such a volatile arrangement and preferred the safer, almost certainly more statesmanly, course of joining the CDU. By so doing, the SPD completed its return to "respectability"; by refusing to make an issue of Kiesinger's former Nazi-party membership, it made the new Chancellor beholden to it; by entering a government with Strauss, it gave evidence of a spirit of national union.

Of the party's top leadership, Brandt became Vice Chancellor and Foreign Minister, and Wehner became Minister for All-German Affairs. Erler, the party's top brain, was missing because his serious illness prevented his entering the cabinet. But even from his sickbed he gave his strong endorsement to the decision to enter the government. It was his last public act. He died in 1967.

There will be pressure on the foreign policy of the SPD. A younger German generation, which has become disappointed over the slowness of European integration and increasingly desirous of seeing some progress made toward German reunification, may be tempted to urge a more flexible attitude towards the Soviet Union. While this youth is certainly anti-communist, it has not had the same visual experience of the dismal reality of communism which has marked those Germans who fought on Russian soil or even those who remember the Berlin blockade and the airlift. Hence, among young Germans there is a somewhat greater willingness to experiment with East-West relations.

All these, however, are not likely to go too far. Where East-West relations are concerned, all concrete proposals for changes are up against the stone wall of the indisputable fact that the Soviet leaders from Stalin to Khrushchev to Kosygin and Brezhnev have unanimously refused to budge one inch on the German reunification issue. A considerable number of Social Democratic leaders visiting Moscow have been told in unmistakable terms that the U.S.S.R. would not consent to any form of reunification and that no concession on the part of Germany could change that. In the face of such realities, there are obvious limitations to any suggestions for flexibility.

Brandt and Wehner remain the principal leaders of the SPD since the death of Erler. Two other very able and respected Social Democratic leaders are Carlo Schmid, one of the best known, a vice chairman of the *Bundestag* and perhaps its most brilliant orator, and Helmut Schmidt, whom many regard as the SPD's "coming man," but who suffered reverses in 1966. Schmidt is an extremely intelligent man whose youthful appearance has identified him with the younger generation although he was born in 1918. As a member of the *Bundestag's* defense committee, he has acquired considerable knowledge of foreign and defense affairs and has steadily moved up in the party councils, being now one of its vice chairmen. For a while he concentrated his activities on the administration of the city of Hamburg as the head of one department in its government. This has not only enhanced his experience and reputation as an administrator, but has temporarily taken him out of the national limelight, with the result that he appears politically less "used up" than some of his elders. He has also made a reputation as a sharp, sometimes overly sharp debater.

The principal factor in the situation is that Erler's death makes it doubtful that anyone will replace Brandt as the standard-bearer of the party. Originally, as explained earlier, this position was created in response to the increasing Americanization of the electoral campaign and its emphasis on personalities. The voters were to be given a clear idea of the kind of government to expect should the party win. Now the experience with Brandt has raised serious doubts about its advantage, and there may arise younger contenders for the standard, like Helmut Schmidt. Thus, a struggle for leadership is a distinct possibility but it is not likely to materialize until the election of 1969 approaches.

The entry of the Social Democrats into the Kiesinger coalition government in 1966 was the logical end of an important development. The long road to "respectability" had now been completed. The Social Democratic ministers revealed themselves as highly responsible and able men—i.e., Brandt, Wehner, and Professor Karl Schiller, who proved to be a remarkable Minister of Economics. Perhaps most important of all, many of the Kiesinger government's ideas and tactical innovations originated with the Social Democrats.

And yet, in spite of all this, the fruits of this success seem once again to elude the Social Democrats. So strongly has Chancellor Kiesinger's personality impressed the German public that in its mind all the achievements of his government seem to have become his, despite the SPD's fine performance and despite the fact that his own modest personality has never permitted him to lay claim to achievements which were not his. Had Fritz Erler lived, his razor-sharp mind, the incisiveness of his concepts, and the great respect in which he was held everywhere might have created a more balanced and fairer picture of the respective contributions of the coalition partners. As it is, Brandt has proved no match for Kiesinger, and although Wehner's tactics in East-West relations have often proved brilliant, he is a man who does not love the limelight, and his achievements are not well known to the German public.

It would therefore seem that barring a major crisis or depression, the Social Democrats have not come substantially closer to majority or even to plurality status. However, their place as one of the two major parties as well as their claim to worthiness for governmental responsibility are thoroughly assured.

The Free Democratic party

The Free Democratic party (*Freie Demokratische Partei,* FDP) purports to be the heir to the liberal traditions of the Democratic party of the Weimar past, the party once headed by Gustav Stresemann. This ancestral claim is highly tenuous. By the time that the Weimar Republic came to an end, the Democratic party had already lost much strength and had even dropped the word "democratic" from its title. It had few cadres available in 1945 with whom a new beginning could be made. Hence, as a national phenomenon, the FDP is essentially a new creation. It does, however, have regional antecedents in the traditional liberalism of southwest Germany, especially in the regions of Württemberg and Baden, although these affect only one wing of the party.

The Free Democratic party appeared first in the Soviet sector of Berlin in 1945 under the name of the Liberal Democratic party, where its complete collaboration with the Communist regime soon discredited it. In West Germany it appeared first in Württemberg and Baden under the leadership of Professor Theodor Heuss who later became the first President of the Federal Republic. By 1946, the FDP had clearly established itself as the third-ranking party, but only in 1948 did the various independent party organizations of the different *Länder* unite into one organization and adopt the national title of Free Democratic party.

The national organization of the FDP did not automatically overcome deep-seated regional differences. In southern and southwestern Germany, it has remained an essentially liberal party in the nineteenth-century meaning of that word, while its northern organizations have oriented themselves further to the right. To complicate the picture further, the party tends to be anticlerical, despite the fact that several of its leaders are Catholics. This has helped it in the past to entice some votes away from the CDU, especially of those voters who had become opposed to Adenauer's ways but did not see their way clear to shift to the SPD.

In very general terms one might cautiously advance the generalization that in matters concerning religious problems, especially schools, the Free Democratic party stands closer to the Social Democratic party than to the Christian Democratic Union, while on economic problems it is closer to the latter and sometimes to the right thereof. However, any "philosophy" which the FDP might have is increasingly overshadowed by its desire for survival. In the past, this has led some of its leaders to nationalistic statements, and that opened the door to a period of infiltration by some former Nazis, who grouped themselves around the controversial personality of Friedrich Middelhauve. This gave the FDP much trouble, but shortly before the 1953 election, it finally purged that group from its ranks.

With one notable exception (1961), election figures have shown the unmistakable trend of a slow but steady decline of the Free Democratic party. It was constantly plagued under the strong governments of Konrad Adenauer by the difficult task of supporting the government positions enough to remain in the coalition and yet being sufficiently different to preserve its separate identity. This required some fancy footwork which was not always successful and which resulted in confused positions of semiopposition. One of the leaders, Dr. Thomas Dehler, the *enfant terrible* of the party, even took a nationalistic stance.[13]

Dehler became chairman of the FDP after 1953. Although he never carried the entire party with him, he and his friends became increasingly antagonistic toward Adenauer and the cabinet. In the debate over the statute of the Saar, the FDP voted against the government, except for the late vice chancellor Franz Blücher. Adenauer threatened the FDP's survival by proposing an electoral system which would have deprived it of a seat in parliament, but he was finally forced to retreat from this idea. Then the FDP counterattacked in the most populous *Land,* North Rhineland–Westphalia, overthrowing the coalition government there in February, 1956, (it was led by CDU Prime Minister Karl Arnold) and entering into a short-lived coalition with the Social Democrats.

Dehler gave up the party chairmanship in 1956, but the FDP continued to decline. An attempt by a group of "young Turks," led by the late Wolfgang Döring, to infuse new life into the party failed. Another attempt by two other FDP leaders, Walter Scheel and Erich Mende, to embark on a "private" foreign policy by mak-

[13] Even when Dehler was Minister of Justice in the first Adenauer cabinet, he delighted in making "Sunday speeches" which were frequently in conflict with government positions. Adenauer dropped him from the cabinet in 1953. Dehler's courageous anti-Nazi history made it possible for him to take this position without having his integrity questioned.

ing contact with Liberal Democratic party leaders in the Soviet zone, also came to nought. In fact it probably contributed to the further decline of the FDP in the elections of 1957. Only in Baden-Württemberg, the stronghold of liberal FDP leader Reinhold Maier, did the party advance slightly. It was a clear repudiation of both Dehler and the "young Turks."

After 1957, the Free Democratic party attempted to profit from the discontent with Adenauer's leadership which existed both on the left and on the right. It advanced the peculiar notion that a two-party system, toward which Germany seemed to be moving, was undemocratic because it did not offer the voter sufficient choice.

There is little doubt that the FDP would have continued to decline further had the 1961 elections not coincided with the then-recent memory of the presidential succession crisis and with other events which, in the opinion of a part of the electorate, put Adenauer in an unfavorable light. The FDP, having been on all sides of all questions, became a rallying ground for those who could no longer accept Adenauer but who were not ready to pass over to the Social Democratic party. As a result, the Free Democratic party, which had declined from 11.9 percent in 1949 to 7.7 percent in 1957, suddenly jumped in 1961 to an all-time high of 12.8 percent.

This success put the FDP in a rather strong position to impose its will on the last Adenauer government, including the demand that Adenauer should promise to retire after a suitable period. As a symbol of its resistance to Adenauer, the FDP entered the last Adenauer cabinet without its leader, Erich Mende.[14] Then it concentrated increasingly on German reunification, advocating a more positive approach towards the East and a more cautious approach towards the West, but both with restraint.

On its face, the 1965 election could be interpreted as a reverse for the FDP, which dropped from 12.8 to 9.5 percent of the vote. But this is neither accurate nor fair. As has been stated, the 1961 elections were a fluke; they were not typical of the long-term fortunes of the Free Democrats. It was fully expected in Germany that part at least, if not all, of the ex-CDU electorate which had become irritated with Adenauer in 1961 and had voted FDP would return to the CDU in 1965. Therefore, the fact that the FDP obtained 9.5 percent of the vote rather than dropping to or below its 7.7 percent figure of 1957 must be considered a limited success. In the long run, the FDP's chances for survival have perhaps not become brighter, but its decline has at least been retarded.

The 1965 election placed the FDP leadership in a real dilemma. In the first Erhard cabinet, its leader, Erich Mende, had occupied the Ministry of All-German Affairs. This ministry had a somewhat artificial origin, having been created by Adenauer to provide a ministerial home for the late Jakob Kaiser, and while it was not one of the most important, it had provided the FDP with a good platform for

---

[14] He reentered the government as vice chancellor in the first Erhard cabinet of 1963.

raising the reunification issue. Now the FDP was to be deprived of this office. At the same time Mende, who had declared the CSU leader Strauss to be personally obnoxious and unacceptable to him, now drew fire from Strauss, who returned the compliment. Knut von Kühlmann-Stumm, the FDP's parliamentary leader, and the always intractable Thomas Dehler urged a more independent course of action for the FDP, possibly a move into the opposition ranks. In the opinion of some observers, such a move might have made the FDP the center of a future "national opposition," insuring its own survival and swelling its ranks. Moreover, there was strong pressure on the FDP, which had so long had a reputation for taking strong positions only to give in meekly in order to stay in the government, to prove now that it had backbone, even at the cost of its place in the government. Yet the FDP had taken many contradictory positions, so there was real doubt as to its future reliability as a national opposition, especially when one compared it with other groups and people trying for that position, such as the CSU's Franz Josef Strauss and von Guttenberg.

In the end, a more moderate course prevailed under the influence of Erich Mende, who thereby emerged for the time being as a stronger leader than he had seemed in the past. Erhard, who had boxed himself in quite needlessly before the election by declaring himself opposed to a "great coalition," was now in no position to threaten the FDP with a turn toward the Social Democrats. Nor could he frighten the FDP with the threat of a change in the electoral law, which might deprive the FDP of its future but which could pass Parliament only with SPD support. Hence, the Free Democrats, despite their decreased strength, were able to hold their own. Mende returned to the government as Vice Chancellor and Minister of All-German Affairs. The assertion that that ministry's jurisdiction would be curtailed did not carry much weight, as it was never very important. But the FDP, because of its reduced parliamentary delegation, had to give up one ministry (Justice) and had to make the sacrifice of the declaration of rehabilitation (*Ehrenerklärung*) for Franz Josef Strauss.

After the Hesse elections in 1966, Mende and the FDP leadership decided that the coalition with Erhard and the CDU had become a liability. They left the government in October, 1966, and thus created the government crisis which led to Erhard's fall and the formation of the Kiesinger-Brandt coalition government.

Obviously Mende and the FDP would have preferred to join in a new coalition with the SPD in which the FDP's support would have been even more essential than it had been to Erhard. However, the SPD's decision to accept the CDU/CSU rather than the FDP as partners left the latter out in the cold.

At first the FDP leaders were quite pleased by their new opposition role because the coalition of CDU and SPD left the FDP with the role of the single opposition party and with the ability to capitalize on all the frustrations and shortcomings which normally are the lot of all governments.

However, as we have seen, the Kiesinger coalition government proved far more capable than the FDP leaders had anticipated, and the fruits of opposition status seemed sparse. This led to a certain corrosion in the FDP leadership which, in 1967, ended Erich Mende's leadership. He was succeeded by Walter Scheel who had been a member of the Adenauer and Erhard cabinets. However, the selection of this able young man appears unlikely to halt what appears to be Germany's slow transition to a two-party system.

The existence of a third party seems to please a number of Germans who prefer not having to choose between the CDU/CSU and the SPD. So the FDP is likely to continue as a minor but not insignificant factor in German politics for some time. But if it declines below the 5 percent limit, where parties are no longer represented in parliament, its further decline will then be rapid.

Other parties

The aforementioned three-party system has ruled the roost in Germany since 1957. True, the German party (DP) was represented in the *Bundestag* until 1961, but that was only because of the CDU's assistance. Since 1961, only the CDU/CSU, the SPD, and the FDP have had seats in the *Bundestag*. This is due to the operation of the electoral law which deprives parties of their seats in the parliament when they do not poll at least 5 percent of the national total or do not obtain at least three seats in direct elections in single-member districts.[15]

The fate of Germany's smaller parties is interesting, and it is encouraging in several ways for the stability of Germany's new democracy.

The BHE, GB/BHE, and DP.   It was not surprising that the tremendous influx of refugees and expellees into West Germany should make an impact on the political picture of the country. By 1950, over 9 million refugees and expellees had arrived in the Federal Republic; by 1954 they were estimated to have passed the 12-million mark. Most of them came without any possessions, but were in their best working years, since the very young and the very old had died in the fearful conditions under which they had been driven from their former homelands. Although the German federal government and the *Länder* and local governments made heroic efforts to absorb and settle these masses, a great deal of social and economic tension arose nevertheless. The Allied powers discouraged separate refugee parties in the beginning for fear that they would become a fertile field for extremism. It was hoped that the refugees and expellees would eventually be absorbed into the regular political parties and that this process would further tie them to their new homes.

But as soon as the Allied injunction was relaxed, a refugee party made its appearance. It called itself the League of the Expellees and Disenfranchised (*Bund der Heimatvertriebenen und Entrechteten,* BHE) and began operating in the *Land* of Schleswig-Holstein, which has an exceptionally large number of refugees and expellees. The BHE obtained 23.4 percent of the vote in the first election to that

[15] See page 462.

Land's legislature, and sizable votes in a few other *Länder* as well. In 1953 the BHE entered the election under the name All-German Bloc (*Gesamtdeutscher Block,* GB/BHE), but obtained only 5.9 percent of the vote. Its vote declined further in 1957. The ability of the national parties to absorb the refugees had thus been demonstrated.

In 1961 the GB/BHE attempted a fusion with the remnants of the German Party (DP) but the two of them, although in 1957 they had together polled 8 percent of the vote, now obtained only 2.8 percent and could no longer be represented in the *Bundestag.* The German party, which emerged from a regional historical party (the Guelphs) in the former state of Hanover, now part of Lower Saxony, has always maintained a close relationship with the CDU; it has in fact become absorbed into the CDU and its principal former leader, Dr. Joachim von Merkatz, has become one of the CDU leaders. In the 1965 election, the GB/BHE-DP combination made no further attempt to run candidates for office.

The SRP, DRP, and NPD.   As might have been expected, several attempts were made to refloat a neo-Nazi movement. In 1950 an openly neo-Nazi party called Socialist Reich party (*Sozialistische Reichspartei,* SRP) was organized under the nominal leadership of former Major Ernst Rehmer, who had been instrumental in suppressing the July, 1944, uprising in Berlin. The SRP caused some alarm in 1951 when it obtained 11 percent of the vote in the *Land* election of Lower Saxony. However, it did far less well elsewhere, was soon rent by internal dissension, and was outlawed in 1952 by the Federal Constitutional Court.

A successor party, the German Reich party (*Deutsche Reichspartei,* DRP) obtained only 1.1 percent of the vote in 1953, and 1 percent in 1957. In 1965 yet another successor presented itself, calling itself the National Democratic party of Germany (*Nationaldemokratische Partei Deutschlands,* NPD). It made a concerted effort, but to the keen disappointment of its leaders obtained only 2 percent of the total vote and of course fell far short of the minimum required for representation in the *Bundestag.*

In the *Länder* elections of 1966 the NPD did make significant gains, reaching around 7 percent, but rising even higher in a number of towns. No doubt a considerable number of former Nazis voted for the NPD, yet its relative success was undoubtedly due far more to general restiveness and unhappiness with the declining Erhard government than to an endorsement of either the NPD or of neo-Nazi principles. However in 1967 disastrous splits and scandals in the NPD all but eliminated it.

The Communist party and the DFU.   On the extreme left of the stage, the Communist party had polled 5.7 percent in 1949 and had sent 15 deputies to the *Bundestag.* By 1953, its share of the vote had dropped to 2.2 percent and it lost its representation. It was dissolved in 1956 by the Federal Constitutional Court. In 1965 a new party made its appearance, called German Peace Union (*Deutsche*

Friedensunion, DFU), composed of former Communists, ex-Socialists, and pacifists. This group was generally believed to receive much of its financial support from the Communist East. However, in the 1965 elections it received only 1.3 percent of the total vote.

Regional parties.   A few purely regional parties have remained, such as the Bavarian party (*Bayernpartei,* BP) or the Christian People's party (*Christliche Volkspartei,* CVP) which is in the Saarland. Before each election, a variety of tiny groups make their appearance, usually to disappear shortly thereafter. Among them are the Action Group of Independent Germans (*Aktionsgemeinschaft unabhängiger Deutschen,* AUD) which polled 0.2 percent of the vote in 1965, and the Free Social Union (*Freisoziale Union,* FSU) which polled even less.

Pressure groups

In the United States pressure groups are largely outside Congress and try to influence representatives, senators, and other legislators to follow their particular points of view. In Germany there are few such half-hidden special interests. There they sit right in parliament. Because of the operation of the proportional-representation system, it seems rather pointless to try to influence individual members of the *Bundestag.* Instead, pressure groups work directly upon the party leadership and seek direct representation in parliament. In the CDU/CSU, this means primarily business interests, and the situation is such that certain powerful ones are allotted certain seats and designate the man whom they wish to see elected. These men may be the leaders of the particular business group or industry or may be mere employees designated by them. In this open form, such "interest representation" is almost unique.

As far as the Social Democrats are concerned, the main outside group is that of the trade unions, although perhaps they put less pressure on the Social Democratic party than the party puts on them.

When German labor unions were revived after the war, considerable pressure was brought to bear upon them to amalgamate. In consequence thereof, the three different union groups which had hitherto existed in each of the occupation zones dissolved, and in October, 1949, formed the German Trade Union Federation (*Deutscher Gewerkschaftsbund,* DGB), which has about 6.4 million members. Although the DGB is officially nonpartisan, the overwhelming majority of its leaders and members are Social Democrats. The rest belong to the left wing of the CDU. There is virtually no Communist influence.

Under its first chairman, Hans Boeckler, the nonpartisan character of the German Trade Union Federation was maintained to a high degree. After his death, however, complaints were heard, and during the 1953 electoral campaign Chancellor Adenauer and the CDU leadership lodged a strong protest against some of the statements made by DGB leaders which seemed to favor the position of the Social

Democratic party. This irritated the Catholic trade-union group so much that it departed from the DGB once again and formed the Christian Labor Movement (*Christliche Gewerkschaftsbewegung, CGB*), which, with 200,000 members, has remained the smallest group outside the DGB.

In addition, two groups established their own separate organizations, the office workers and the civil servants (*Deutsche Angestelltengewerkschaft, DAG*, and the *Deutsche Beamtenbund, DBB*).

While the German Trade Union Federation (DGB) is not a political party, it nevertheless has legislative demands to make for which it relies mainly on the Social Democratic party. This was made quite clear in the bitter struggle over workers' codetermination resulting in the law of April 10, 1951, which applies to any enterprise in the mining, iron, and steel industries which employs more than 1,000 people. It provides for a board of directors of eleven people, five from management and five from labor (three from the shop stewards' committees and two from the national unions). The eleventh member is elected by a procedure which is said to favor management.

The enactment of this law created further demands for the enlargement of this system, which resulted in the bitterly contested law of July 19, 1952, which extended the right of workers' representatives on boards of directors but in a manner which maintains management in a two-thirds majority. The Trade Union Federation fought hard for a repeal or amendment to this act, which is not likely to occur. In the meantime the codetermination law has worked rather well, and even management has had occasion to express satisfaction. That this is so is largely due to the high degree of responsibility exhibited by German labor leaders. Some industrial circles would like to see the law repealed, but it is unlikely that this method will gain wider acceptance.

An entirely different type of pressure group has appeared in the form of the various German veterans' organizations. While veterans' organizations tend to be conservative in many countries and in some instances even reactionary, German veterans' organizations have been distinctly different for a number of reasons. In the first place all their leaders have traditionally been former high-ranking officers or staff officers. This makes a German veterans' organization something that is more like an army in civilian clothes than a real veterans' organization. It is often the continuation of the "state within the state" ideology which imbued the army before and after the Second World War. It also often carries within itself an outspoken or tacit contempt for civilians and an arrogant assumption that the military know best what is good for the state.

In recent years it has been notable that the veterans' organizations have not shown any clear, unified philosophy. On the whole they have been conservative and nationalistic. Some, like the veterans of Field Marshall Erwin Rommel's Afrika Corps, have declared themselves strong supporters of democracy, while parachutist General Wilhelm Ramcke made speeches which could hardly be bettered by an orator of the best Nazi period. Even the former black-shirted SS troopers have their organization, which, out of conviction or strategy, has been rather circumspect in its utterances.

A newspaper which began as a veterans' journal but is now a weekly of more general circulation is less reticent. It is the National Journal–Soldier's Journal (*Nationalzeitung–Soldatenzeitung*) which bears the iron cross on its masthead and is about as nationalistic and in fact neo-Nazi as one can get in print without running afoul of the law.

While these organizations bear watching, it should be noted that less than one-tenth of the surviving veterans have joined these organizations. The most renowned among the surviving generals of World War II have also remained aloof.

In Bonn are located offices of well over 200 various pressure groups and special interests. The coming and going of their representatives would fill many pages of a diary. One of the best known is the Federation of German Industries (*Bundesverband der deutschen Industrie*) whose chairman, Fritz Berg, is a well-known and highly influential public figure, and one of whose members is a leading banker, Herman J. Abs. In other countries the effectiveness of industrial pressure groups is often modified by the conflicting interests within industries; the German Federation, however, is in a very powerful position because of the dominant interests of heavy industry, especially iron and steel. Another pressure group of great significance is the German Farmers' Federation (*Deutscher Bauernverband*).

Yet another category of pressure groups are the representatives of refugees, organized generally by the areas from which their members came, such as the Sudetenland, Silesia, East Prussia, etc. These regional organizations, called *Landmannschaften,* hold annual public meetings where nationalist talks are intermingled with display of folklore and costumes. They are not so much concerned with Communist East Germany—the DDR—as with keeping alive the memory of the former German areas east of the Oder and Neisse Rivers and of the formerly German-speaking Sudeten area of Czechoslovakia. The manifestations of the *Landmannschaften* have, at times, reached a considerable noise level as when in 1965 they protested vigorously against a declaration issued by the German Federation of Protestant Churches which hinted at a possible future acceptance of the Oder-Neisse line. More often, however, these *Landmannschaften* do quiet legislative work in which they are more successful, since many of the *Bundestag* deputies of all political parties come from the eastern provinces.

It goes without saying that both Catholic and Protestant churches maintain a number of very powerful pressure groups. The most impressive outward manifestations are the annual Catholic Day (*Katholikentag*) and the Protestant Church Day (*Kirchentag*) which are attended also by delegates from East Germany if and when the Communist authorities permit.

Interest and pressure groups have played an important role in German politics for a long time. Nevertheless, study of them is relatively recent and largely due to the influence of American political science and sociology. The German public has generally reacted unfavorably to their activities. Since it is in the nature of things for pressure groups to act in the shadow and yet often influence decisions, appointments, and promotions, they have come in for a great deal of criticism.[16]

Outlook

Twenty years have passed since the end of the Hitler tyranny and the reestablishment of democratic political life in Germany. A comparison of that first twenty years with the equivalent period of the Weimar Republic is quite encouraging for the new German Federal Republic. Twenty years after the Weimar Republic was established, it had long since disappeared, Nazism was in full control, and Germany was at war. Twenty years after the end of World War II the prospects for democracy are very much brighter. The political party system of the Federal Republic has become well established, and no extremist movement agitating for the Republic's destruction is in sight. Extremist parties of the left and right are miniscule or have disappeared. Nor is there danger of a return to the multiple-party system of the Weimar Republic. Even if the Free Democratic party remains alive, the German party system is simplified, and clear majorities and stable governments are the results. To be sure, there were serious dissensions within the CDU/CSU. But while this menace to the Christian Democrats' control of the government might reappear and could cause considerable changes in the foreign policy of Germany, it does not affect the basic nature of the regime nor challenge its democratic foundations.

Germany enjoys extensive freedom of the press, speech, and assembly. Certainly one result of the famous *Spiegel* affair was that it produced a quick and angry reaction on the part of the German public in defense of press freedom. Of the 1,464 daily newspapers in the Federal Republic and in West Berlin, only a small number are affiliated with political parties. Most of them are independent, with varying shadings of tendencies. While radio and television are not private enterprises as in the United States, they are not centrally controlled agencies of the national government as in France, Italy, and most other continental European countries. Chancellor Adenauer proposed the establishment of a national television network but this measure was declared unconstitutional by the Federal Constitutional Court. After that decision, the *Länder* went ahead and established a second television chain on the basis of inter-*Länder* agreements.

While no serious challenge to the present political party system appears to exist, the younger German generation is not wholly sold on it, although it lacks a serious alternative. This is in part a German phenomenon but is also noted in many other countries. It is due partly to the break between generations, which is particularly keen in Germany, where the generation born after Hitler's death has never heard a satisfactory explanation from its elders as to what happened and why.

---

[16] See especially Theodor Eschenburg, *Herrschaft der Verbände?*, Stuttgart, 1963, 2d ed.; Rupert Breitling, *Die Verbände in der Bundesrepublik: Ihre Arten und ihre politische Wirkungweise*, Mannheim, 1955; Wolfgang Hirsch-Weber, *Gewerkschaften in der Politik*, Cologne, 1959.

In part it is due to the aging of German political leaders. Despite a number of younger deputies who entered parliament for the first time, the German parliament remains the oldest in the world in the average age of its members.

In German political life, there is now a far greater alertness to the danger of totalitarian activities than characterized the Weimar Republic. And the Germans, once so docile toward authority, are much more ready to challenge the authority of the state and the courts or of government in general than was customary in former days. Broad civic activities and citizens' participation in public affairs outside of party circles are still the exception rather than the rule, but they are slowly on the increase.

German political life appears, by all indications available to human sight, to be well integrated and stable. There are no indications of greater challenges and dangers than could normally be expected in the political ups and downs of any country. If there is still a certain reluctance of many Germans to identify themselves fully with the German Federal Republic, it has nothing to do with the regime or the political system, but pertains to the ever-present problem of Germany's unfulfilled desire, the desire for reunification. This is a much broader issue which will be discussed in the concluding chapter of this part.

6

Constitutional government

A. CIVIL RIGHTS

The Constitution opens with a declaration of civil rights which manifests considerable improvement over the Weimar and *Länder* constitutions. Article 1 declares the enumerated civil rights to be "directly valid law on legislation, administration, and judiciary." This lays to rest, once and for all, the assertion heard during the Weimar Republic that civil rights were only "declaratory" and did not constitute actual legal obligations. Nevertheless there are some "rights" in the Constitution which, because of their nature, cannot actually be "directly valid law," like the provision that "marriage and family are under the particular protection of the state" (Art. 6, Sec. 1).

There is a long list of rights: political, social, economic, moral, educational, etc. This is in line with other modern constitutions, as, for instance, those of France and Italy. However, the Weimar Constitution's example of including practically

446

every party program and promising every "right" under the sun has happily not been repeated, and the Bonn Constitution is in that respect more streamlined and realistic. Some of its sections are, naturally enough, projected against the experience of the Nazi regime, such as the first section of Article 1, which declares the dignity of man inviolable.

There is the customary protection of physical inviolability as well as of free speech, press, and assembly. There is also the equivalent of habeas corpus, which is made even more specific than is the case in the United States, for under the German provisions (Art. 104) it is not necessary that the accused apply for a writ of habeas corpus. On the day following his arrest he must be taken before a judge, who will then decide. However, under the German practice it is more difficult to be released on bail.

Censorship is specifically prohibited (Art. 5). Equality before the law and the legal equality of the sexes are also guaranteed. The Constitution not only guarantees the free exercise and profession of all faiths but also includes nonreligious ideologies (*Weltanschauungen*) and specifically recognizes the right to conscientious objection (Art. 4).

Property and the right to inheritance are guaranteed; the right of the government to take private property for public use with just compensation (eminent domain) is granted, and appeal to the regular courts is permissible in case of dispute.

Emphasis is placed on the right to join labor unions. Agreements not to join unions ("yellow-dog contracts") are declared null and void (Art. 9).

The problem of education is handled with special care because the controversy of private (parochial) versus public schools is well known in Germany's political history. Religious instruction has always been part of the regular curriculum of German schools, private and public (except in Bremen). The Constitution guarantees and perpetuates that system (Art. 7) in all state schools except in the so-called "nonconfessional schools." Private schools are also permitted to exist and are placed on an equal level with state schools, provided they meet the same standards. Recognition of private schools is a duty of the governmental authorities unless proper standards are not met, or segregation of students according to their means is encouraged, or the economic or legal status of the teaching staff is not sufficiently assured (Art. 7). Private elementary (grade) schools are permitted only under certain circumstances, when there is a specific need or when the parents of eligible children request it or when a public elementary school of the same type is not available.

The Constitution deems it necessary to declare that "arts and science, research and instruction are free" (Art. 5), but it is of course clear that the freedom of teaching pertains only to the university level, that is, to academic freedom in the generally accepted sense. In Germany as well as everywhere else, teaching on the primary and secondary levels is strictly subject to regulation by competent authority. The German Constitution adds a loyalty provision stating that "freedom of teaching does not absolve from loyalty to the Constitution." This is a provision which shows that the framers remembered the days when the German universities were centers of antirepublican and Nazi agitation.

One of the chief complaints against the Weimar Constitution and the constitutions of the *Länder* was the fact that all the civil rights which they contained existed only "within the framework of the law" or, in other words, could be set aside by law. Since civil rights are endangered in exceptional and critical times when legislatures are frequently willing to cloak governments with extraordinary powers and become rubber stamps, this type of "guarantee" seems a slender reed to lean upon. The Bonn Constitution repeats this process but with significant modifications. In the first place we have already seen that it declares all basic rights directly binding upon all courts and authorities. The law on the Federal Constitutional Court of March 12, 1951, also permits individuals whose civil rights have been injured to make a direct plaint (*Verfassungsbeschwerde*) to the Federal Constitutional Court. Secondly it decrees that limitations of basic rights by law must be general and must not apply to specific cases only. The basic nature of a civil right must not be changed. These limitations are somewhat vague because a law can be framed in such a way as to have general application in theory while it pertains only to specific cases or persons in actual practice. There is also a question as to what constitutes the basic nature of a civil right, especially as Article 18 provides that "whoever abuses the freedom of expression of opinion . . . in order to attack the free, democratic basic order, shall forfeit these basic rights." A corollary to this rule is also the provision of Article 21 which declares as unconstitutional "parties which, according to their aims and the behavior of their members, seek to impair or abolish the free and democratic basic order or to jeopardize the existence of the Federal Republic of Germany. . . ." The Federal Constitutional Court decides the application of both Articles 18 and 21. The reason for these sections is easy to see in view of the way in which the Nazis utilized the civil rights and guarantees of the Weimar Constitution to their own advantage. However, the definition of "abuse" is quite difficult and in itself subject to possible abuse. Moreover, the Federal Constitutional Court has considerable freedom in the definition of such an act because the forfeiture of these rights does constitute a penalty under the law.[1]

The Federal Constitutional Court has shown itself courageous and outspoken, and in dissolving the neo-Nazi Socialist Reich party it did not hesitate to condemn sharply all the racist and nationalistic neo-Nazi practices of that group.[2] The Communist party was also dissolved, for similar reasons. Interestingly enough, the verdict confined the application of the decree dissolving the Communist party to the territory of the Federal Republic ("to the area governed by the Basic Law in space and time")—*nur für den vom Grundgesetz zeitlich und sachlich beherrschten Raum*). Normally German legal theory holds the Basic Law applicable to all of

---

[1] Theodor Mounz and Günther Dürig, *Grundgesetz, Kommentar,* Munich and Berlin 1963, commentary on Article 18, p. 14.
[2] Decision of the Federal Constitutional Court establishing the unconstitutionality of the Socialist Reich party, *Bundesverfassungsgericht,* 1 BvB 1/51, Oct. 23, 1952.

Germany, including the Communist-controlled regions, although it can of course not be enforced there. But the reason for this verdict's departure from the general rule was the Court's desire not to complicate future reunification and the possible holding of all-German elections in which the Communist party would present candidates.

B. FEDERALISM

The new West German state is a federal union. The appropriate sections of the Constitution (Arts. 20–37, 50–53, 70–75, 105–109) are not too different from their counterparts in the Weimar Constitution, but the abolition of Prussia leaves the Federal Republic of Germany as a union of reasonably equal *Länder*. The smallest *Land* in respect to inhabitants, Bremen, has 750,000, while the largest, North Rhine–Westphalia, has 16,000,000. The crazy-quilt pattern of *Länder* created in the southwest corner of Germany by the artificial establishment of the French zone of occupation was greatly improved in 1952 when the former *Länder* of Württemberg-Baden, Württemberg-Hohenzollern, and Baden were united into one *Land* called Baden-Württemberg.

The Constitution establishes the principle of expressed and enumerated powers for the federation, with the *Länder* possessing all other (reserved) powers. The respective fiscal powers are precisely spelled out in Articles 105–109. Exclusive federal powers extend to foreign affairs, nationality, passports, migration and extradition, currency, customs, border control, railroad and air traffic, post and telegraph, trademark, copyright, cooperation with the *Länder* in matters of criminal police, protection of the Constitution, vice control, and federal statistics (Art. 73). The field of concurrent powers in which both the federation and the *Länder* may legislate is far more extensive. It covers the entire economy, all criminal and civil law as well as labor legislation, the control of associations and assemblies, railways, highway and water traffic, and many more subjects too numerous to mention (Art. 74). Of important fields, only education and police remain exclusively in the hands of the *Länder*. However, "in order to avert imminent danger to the existence or the free democratic basic order of the Federation or a *Land,* a *Land* may call for police assistance from other *Länder*." But if the *Land* concerned is not in a position to combat the danger, "the Federal Government may place the police in that *Land,* or the police forces of other *Länder* under its control" (Art. 91). This arrangement must be rescinded after the danger has passed or whenever the *Bundesrat* demands. This provision, which could be used in case of a neo-Nazi or Communist uprising, was written into the Constitution when the federal government had no police of its own and was solely dependent on that of the *Länder*. Since then, a Federal Border Police and a German army, navy, and air force have been created.

In the field of concurrent powers the *Länder* governments are presumably autonomous and may even conclude treaties with foreign countries concerning subjects under their control, although they may be overruled by superior federal law. However, the Constitution attempts to establish limits to federal legislation by the provision (Art. 72) that the federation shall legislate in the area of concurrent powers only under the following conditions: (1) when a matter cannot be effectively regulated by the *Länder*; (2) if the regulations of one *Land* prejudice the rights of another *Land* or *Länder*; or (3) if "the preservation of legal or economic unity demands in particular the preservation of uniformity of living conditions extending beyond the territory of an individual *Land*." The last condition is exceedingly broad and could, if rashly used, nullify all vestiges of federalism. However, this has not been the case in practice. Although there is thus an almost complete integration of federal and *Länder* administration, there is nevertheless a high degree of federal reality.[3]

Considerable power is also wielded by the federal government through the way in which it administers its policies. Just as in the Weimar Republic, the (Bonn) federal government relies on the *Länder* authorities to execute most of the federal regulations.[4] The *Länder* bureaucracies thus have two sets of functions: those which they exercise in their "autonomous" role, and those which devolve upon them as arms of the federal government. But this of course means federal control, and the Constitution provides that the federal government shall exercise supervision over the *Länder* governments to see to it that federal laws are faithfully executed. The federation may also establish certain uniform standards and practices and send supervisory commissioners to the *Länder* governments if the latter approve or, failing that, if the *Bundesrat* does. The federation may also issue specific, detailed orders (*Einzelanweisungen*). Under the Weimar Republic the *Reich* government (technically, the President) had the right to compel the *Länder* to obedience, even by use of armed might (*Reichsexekution*). Under the Bonn Constitution this right (*Bundeszwang*, federal compulsion) is much more circumscribed. Article 37 provides that if a *Land* does not fulfill its obligations under the Constitution or a federal law, the federal government may compel obedience by all means at its disposal and may also commandeer or direct the facilities of the *Länder*. However, and this is an important difference from the Weimar system, such action is possible only with the consent of the *Bundesrat,* which thus becomes the deciding authority. A less drastic form of intervention is a complaint of a *Land* or of the federal government to the *Bundesrat* charging a *Land* with the nonfulfillment of its obligations, provided such nonfulfillment has first been demanded directly by the federal government under its right of federal supervision (*Bundesaufsicht*). The *Bundesrat* then decides with finality (Art. 84). In either case, whether it is a case of federal compulsion or federal supervision, the *Land* concerned can appeal to the Federal Con-

---

[3] Cf. Thomas Ellwein, *Das Regierungssystem der Bundesrepublik Deutschland,* Cologne, 1963, pp. 24–26.

[4] Direct federal administration on all levels is provided for in the following fields: foreign service, finance administration, railways, and postal services, and conditionally for waterways and shipping (Art. 87).

stitutional Court. The federal government or any one of the *Länder* may also directly sue a *Land* for the nonfulfillment of its duties, before the Federal Constitutional Court (Art. 93).

Very detailed provisions exist concerning the respective fiscal responsibilities of the federation and the *Länder* (Arts. 105 to 109). Here the centralist tendencies of the Constitution are very much in evidence, as the federal authorities are charged with the principal responsibility for the collection of all taxes. These are then redistributed by a form of equalization (*Finanzausgleich*). The Constitution provides in great detail which taxes and revenues belong exclusively to the federal government, which belong to the *Länder,* and which lie in the joint domain. The more important taxes such as income taxes are collected centrally and distributed according to a complicated system roughly in the proportion of one-third to the federal government and two-thirds to the *Länder*. It is then up to the *Länder* to decide by *Land* law the amount of their income to devolve on the municipal administrations. But if all sources of public income are taken into consideration, the picture is reversed; thus for the fiscal year 1960 the federal authorities received 53.3 percent, the *Länder* 31.3 percent, the municipalities 12.4 percent, while 3 percent was reserved for the "equalization of burdens fund" (*Lastenausgleichsfonds*).

This system results in part from the fact that the federal government had to shoulder very heavy expenses, first with regard to the enormous influx of refugees and expellees, and later in the field of national defense. However it is a difficult system to administer and requires complicated agreements which sometimes materialize only as a result of prolonged annual negotiations. Experience has shown that in matters of this kind the *Länder* are likely to band together against the federal government regardless of their or its political composition.

Although this system appears to be heavily weighted in the direction of the federal government, the appearance is somewhat misleading because of the central role played by the Federal Council (*Bundesrat*). As will be elaborated later, members of the *Bundesrat* are not elected but are directly appointed by the *Länder* governments, and in all matters of legislation concerning federal relationships, the *Bundesrat* has an absolute veto. This is also true regarding amendments to the federal Constitution, because the *Länder* governments have a most important role to play in all aspects of federal legislation and even administration. The federal government, especially under former Chancellor Adenauer, tried to influence *Länder* elections in order to obtain a larger majority in the *Bundesrat*. In this it was never fully successful. Hence the Federal Council constitutes a very substantial bulwark for German federalism. Nor should the role of the Federal Constitutional Court be overlooked. When the federal government attempted to establish a system of radio and television networks controlled by the federal administration, the Federal Constitutional Court brought it to a determined halt. This has caused the *Länder* to organize regional associations in order to get the radio and TV chain under way.

Jealously guarded is the near-total sovereignty of the *Länder* on all levels of education. Nevertheless, it is true that the German educational system follows a more unified principle than has ever been the case before.[5] This is the result of the excellent work of the Conference of Ministers of Education, which has largely achieved the standardization of the German educational system on all levels without weakening the principle of *Land* control. There is flexibility in this system, which has permitted *Länder* to pioneer and experiment with various aspects of education and training. In this manner, more progress has probably been achieved than would have been brought about by a ponderous federal machinery. Also, healthy competition between *Länder* universities and other universities has added to the speed and excellence with which these institutions have made their comeback from the ravages of Nazism and war.

Economic prosperity in Germany has made it possible for a much larger percentage of young men and women to enroll in universities than was the case in previous generations. There they have often found inadequate facilities and faculty expansion hampered by an outdated system by which full professors could effectively throttle the newcomers when they saw fit to do so. Also, not all ministers of education of the *Länder* have been sufficiently liberal with requests for funds from their even less liberal ministers of finance. These conditions have led to sharp criticism.[6] Remedial measures have been planned or undertaken through the creation of new universities like those of Bochum, Regensburg, and Constance.

There is little doubt that the text of the Bonn Constitution shows a centralist tendency. But the practice has given German federalism a living reality and greater success than some critics originally assumed.

C. THE EXECUTIVE

As is normal in parliamentary regimes, the executive power in Germany is nominally shared by a federal President (*Bundespräsident*), a federal Chancellor (*Bundeskanzler*), and various federal ministers (*Bundesminister*).

The President

The nominal head of the Federal Republic of Germany is the federal President. His role is quite unlike that of his Weimar predecessors and similar to that of the French President during the late Fourth Republic. Under the Weimar Constitution the President was elected by the people and was the equal if not the superior of Chancellor and cabinet. His authority was real, not merely nominal. This arrangement has come in for general condemnation, and its evil results under Hindenburg are well known. But in all fairness it should be remembered that in the hands of a democratic president these powers might well have played quite a different role. The tragedy was the election and reelection of Hindenburg rather than the dualism

[5] Ellwein, *op. cit.*, p. 27, quoting the Hessian Minister of Education, Ernst Schütte.
[6] Georg Picht, *Die deutsche Bildungskatastrophe,* Freiburg i/B, 1964.

of presidency and cabinet. At any rate the fathers of the Bonn Constitution were not going to run a similar risk. The federal President is now elected by a special convention composed of the members of the *Bundestag* and an equal number of members elected by the popular representative bodies (legislatures) of the *Länder* (*Landtage*) according to the principle of proportional representation. The term of the President is five years, one more than that of the *Bundestag*. He is reeligible only once. If the President is incapable of performing his functions, his deputy is the presiding officer of the *Bundesrat*.

The official acts of the federal President require the countersignature of the federal Chancellor (Prime Minister) or of a competent minister and thus become the acts of the cabinet. Under the Constitution no countersignature is required when the President nominates or dismisses the federal Chancellor (Art. 58). However, this power is wholly theoretical. After the President's nomination the Chancellor must still be elected by the *Bundestag* (Art. 63), which means that the President can nominate only a man who can command the confidence of the majority of the legislature. Any other choice is impractical, since the President does not have general and unconditional dissolution power over parliament and he can therefore do nothing to keep in office a favorite who cannot command a majority. Nor can the President dismiss a Chancellor at will, for the *Bundestag* may refuse to accept any candidate other than the one dismissed. The President's function, like that of his French counterpart, is therefore to employ his skill in finding a government which stands a fair chance of being elected by the *Bundestag*. Otherwise his duties are nominal. Shortly after his election, the first federal President of the Bonn Republic, Theodor Heuss, exhibited certain illusions about his office when he attempted to force his federal Chancellor-designate, Konrad Adenauer, to change the proposed cabinet list in order to suit the preferences of the President. Adenauer, however, stood firm, and the President had to abandon his plan.[7] From the time of this issue, however, Theodor Heuss was involved in no further controversy and gained greatly in popularity and stature, as a result of great tact and personal charm as well as by his unassuming democratic comportment. His excellent literary style[8] and his thoughtful speeches (which he wrote himself) made him a fine representative of the best in German culture.

The federal Chancellor and the cabinet

The actual executive consists of the federal Chancellor (*Bundeskanzler,* Prime Minister) and the ministers (Art. 62). The federal Chancellor is nominated, as we have seen, by the federal President and must then be elected without debate by the *Bundestag*. If the person so nominated is not elected, the *Bundestag* may, two weeks later, elect a federal Chancellor without presidential nomination, but to be success-

[7] *The New York Times,* Sept. 15, 1949.
[8] Theodor Heuss, *Wündigungen: Reden, Aufrätze, und Briefe aus den Jahren 1949–1953,* Tübingen, 1955.

ful a candidate must receive an absolute majority of votes.[9] If there is still no Chancellor, another ballot shall be taken, in which plurality is sufficient. In the latter case the federal President may either appoint him or dissolve the *Bundestag* (Art. 63, Sec. 4), in which case new general elections must be held.

It is the principle of a parliamentary democracy that the government is responsible to the legislature. This is also the case in the Federal Republic of Germany, and the government may receive a vote of nonconfidence from the *Bundestag* at any time.[10] However, the government does not automatically fall in that case, but only if the *Bundestag* is able to elect a successor to the federal Chancellor by an absolute majority of its members and submits a request to the federal President to appoint the person so elected. The federal President must then comply. This unusual stipulation was adopted from the constitution of Baden-Württemberg (Art. 73),[11] where it has worked exceedingly well despite predictions to the contrary. It is designed to avoid the Weimar Republic's practice of frequent and sometimes frivolous overthrowals of cabinets.

Still another feature designed to strengthen the Chancellor is a conditional power to bring about the dissolution of the *Bundestag*. This may be accomplished in the following fashion: the Chancellor has the right to ask the *Bundestag* for a vote of confidence. If that is refused, the President may, upon the proposal of the Chancellor, dissolve the *Bundestag,* in which case new elections are held. If, however, the *Bundestag* were to elect a new Chancellor, the right of the old Chancellor to recommend dissolution would automatically lapse. Moreover, the President may presumably refuse the Chancellor's request for dissolution, in which case the latter would probably resign. This constitutes considerable discretion in the hands of the President, and the precedent of the Weimar presidency might have indicated that this discretion would be exercised. However, this has not been the experience of the German Federal Republic, and the Chancellor's power has remained generally unchallenged by the President.

President Heinrich Lübke differs in personality and style from his predecessor. Some observers, especially journalists, who rightly admired the literary style and intellectual brilliance of the late President Heuss, have tended to disparage Lübke. This, however, does him less than justice. President Lübke's honesty and probity have won him wide respect, which was demonstrated at his reelection in 1964 when the leadership of the Social Democratic opposition decided to vote for him, against opposition in their own ranks.

Like his predecessor, President Lübke has not been content with being a mere figurehead. In the difficult coalition negotiations of October, 1965, when the FDP advanced conditions for its participation which Chancellor Erhard was not yet pre-

---

[9] That is, an absolute majority of votes of all members entitled to vote in the *Bundestag.*
[10] The vote of nonconfidence is directed against the federal Chancellor personally.
[11] The Bavarian constitution attempted to achieve a similar effect by giving the cabinet a definite term (Art. 44, Sec. 1). However this is hedged with such conditions as to be probably unworkable.

pared to accept, Erhard considered facing a vote in the *Bundestag* without FDP support and thus being elected Chancellor by a plurality (on the third ballot, as explained below) rather than by majority. President Lübke's resistance to such a formula undoubtedly played a role in discouraging this approach and probably had an influence on the eventual outcome. Nevertheless, Lübke's known preference for a "great coalition" (CDU-SPD) and his well-known dislike of certain ministers did not prevail as long as Erhard could hold on to his office. When Erhard fell, it was for reasons other than Lübke's opposition.

There is still another power which strengthens the hands of the Chancellor. In the case envisaged above (Art. 63) in which the Chancellor has asked for a vote of confidence from the *Bundestag* and has failed to receive it, he may, instead of asking for dissolution, request the federal President, with the approval of the *Bundesrat,* to declare a "state of legislative emergency" (Art. 81) the details of which will be explained under "The Legislature."[12]

It has already become perfectly clear that the cabinet and especially the Chancellor dominate the scene and very definitely lead parliament. How difficult it is for a parliament to get rid of a Chancellor is well demonstrated by the fact that although Konrad Adenauer was elected to his post in 1949 by a majority of only one vote over the required minimum, he remained in office undisturbed throughout the legislative term of that *Bundestag.*

Whatever strength the Constitution gives to the head of the cabinet was immeasurably enhanced by the personality of the Federal Republic's first Chancellor, Konrad Adenauer, and by his conception of the job. Konrad Adenauer, although a firm democrat in principle, and an uncompromising foe of Nazism, was nevertheless something of a personal authoritarian who liked to run things his own way.[13] This meant that he would brook no interference from his party, let alone other parties, on whom to appoint to ministerial positions or on his policy. Frequent grumblings by parliament also usually went unheeded. In effect Adenauer transformed his position into something approximating the American presidency but without the checks and balances exercised by Congress.[14]

Certainly the personality and style of the second Chancellor, Ludwig Erhard, were quite different, and his political support was not as great as that enjoyed by his predecessor. And Chancellor Kiesinger differs from both. But that very difference illustrates the fact that even under such varied personalities the Chancellorship remains very strong. In constitutional law, the position of the Chancellor rests on Article 65, which provides that "the Federal Chancellor determines, and is responsible for, general policy." Although the same article goes on to say that "Each

---

[12] See pp. 471–473.
[13] Among the innumerable jokes surrounding the Chancellor's personality there was the mischievous one about "Konradolph and his Democraship" (*Konradolf und seine Demokratur*). For a good (and sympathetic) political biography, see Edgar Alexander, *Adenauer and the New Germany,* New York, 1957.
[14] The Constitutional Court has shown itself less pliable to the Chancellor's wishes.

Federal Minister conducts the business of his department autonomously and on his own responsibility," and that "The Federal Cabinet decides on differences of opinion between Federal Ministers," it is clear that the Chancellor sets the style and policy in reality as well as in theory. The Chancellor cannot be outvoted in the cabinet meeting, unless he deliberately permits such a course of events. Moreover, his resignation would bring down the entire cabinet, for he alone is elected by the *Bundestag,* and the other ministers obtain their positions legally from that fact.

Adenauer and Erhard reacted differently to the pressures applied on them. Erhard did not have an imperious disregard for men and proposals which displeased him, as did "the old man." But when the Chancellor puts down his foot, be he Adenauer, Erhard, Kiesinger, or someone yet to come, the rest of the cabinet is likely to fall in line. Under Adenauer this was, of course, standard procedure. But it also happened under Erhard as illustrated by the fact that he maintained his embattled foreign minister, Gerhard Schröder, who was not exactly popular in his own party despite an often impressive performance. Of course, individual ministers resign from time to time or are forced out as their views become incompatible with those of the Chancellor. But a general revolt in the cabinet remains unlikely.

Both Chancellors Adenauer and Erhard used strong right-hand men, whose power and influence by that very fact often exceeded those of other or regular cabinet ministers. Adenauer had two exceptionally able secretaries of state,[15] Otto Lenz and Hans Globke. The latter at times came closer to being a vice chancellor in fact than any vice chancellor by title. Chancellor Erhard's principal aide, until his resignation in 1966, was Ludger Westrick, who held the rank of Minister of State. His and Globke's positions were often compared to that of Sherman Adams in the earlier part of the Eisenhower administration in the United States.

Both Konrad Adenauer and Ludwig Erhard, in their different styles, clearly demonstrated the Chancellor's preeminence as a constitutional and political fact. Thus, the German chancellorship is one of the strongest positions in any constitutional regime in the West. The renowned German scholar, Theodor Eschenburg, has impressively summed up the situation in these penetrating words:

> Regardless of whether the Chancellor determines the guidelines for policy himself or takes them over from others, whether he accepts the majority view of the cabinet or overturns it—it is always he alone who bears responsibility. If the Chancellor is outvoted (in the cabinet) he must, symbolically, withdraw from the cabinet meeting into his study in order once again to decide for himself, and that decision is then final. "Lonely decisions" are not merely to be attributed to the peculiarity of Adenauer, but Article 65 of the Basic Law virtually asks for them. It is true that there has to be first deliberation and decision-making within the cabinet as a prior step. But from the sole responsibility of the Chancellor to Parliament may be deduced the justification for these "lonely decisions."[16]

---

[15] In European nomenclature, a secretary of state is roughly equivalent to an under-secretary. in the American sense.
[16] Theodor Eschenburg, *Staat und Gesellschaft in Deutschland,* Munich, 1963, p. 735.

The federal administration

There is a considerable difference, as has already been stated, between the federal ministries and their American, French, or British counterparts. The United States federal government uses its own agents and only rarely those of the states. Not so in Germany. In the German Federal Republic, as in the Weimar Republic and the German empire, many of the Federal ministries do not maintain their own branches and field agents either in the *Länder* or on the local administrative levels, but directly use the bureaucracy of the *Länder* governments and their subdivisions. Exceptions are the so-called "classical" Ministries of Foreign Affairs, Defense and Finance. The other two "classical" ministries, Interior and Justice, do rely on *Länder* agencies but it must be noted that the German Minister of the Interior does not possess the simple control over local and regional government which characterizes that ministry in most other European countries, especially in France.

Frequently called the "technical" ministries are those of Posts (including telephone and telegraph, which in Germany are government enterprises), and Transport (which also controls the nationalized railroad system). Furthermore, there are federal Ministries for Economics, Food, Agriculture and Forestry, for Labor and Social Affairs. As an outgrowth of the special conditions existing after World War II, there are Ministries for Housing and for All-German Affairs, as well as a Ministry for Refugees.

Peculiar to the German governmental structure is the Ministry for the Affairs of the Federal Council and the *Länder*. A relatively new addition is the Ministry for Science (formerly called Ministry for Nuclear Power.)[17]

Another new ministry is that for Family and Youth Affairs created in 1957 originally for political reasons but since fulfilling useful functions. Other specialized ministries are those for Health, for Economic Cooperation (originally an outgrowth of the Marshall Plan), and for Nationalized Property. Some ministers without specific departments or responsibilities have been called Ministers of State (like Ludger Westrick, who was principal assistant to Chancellor Erhard). The veteran CDU leader, Heinrich Krone, was given the designation "Minister for Special Tasks" and is also Chairman of the National Defense Council, though the two offices need not necessarily go together.

As already noted, there is no Ministry of Education, this being a responsibility which the Constitution vests exclusively in the *Länder*.

It must be obvious that these ministries are not equal in fact though they may be equal in protocol and status, as some functions are clearly more important than others. The Ministry of Finance serves as a kind of super-ministry, being both a ministry and a bureau of the budget, though it does not interpret its powers as broadly as does the United States Bureau of the Budget.

[17] The West European Union Treaty of 1954 prevents Germany from producing nuclear weapons but does not prohibit other nuclear research and activities. Technically the treaty does not prohibit German possession of nuclear weapons either, only their manufacture on German soil.

It is normal in democratic and parliamentary countries for ministers to be politicians and for no specific evidence of professional aptitude to be expected of them except, perhaps, success. Nevertheless, custom and political good sense have established certain rules which have been observed although without any statutory provisions. Thus, Ministers of Agriculture have invariably been former farmers or officials of agricultural associations, Ministers of Justice are always lawyers, and it would be surprising if a Minister for Family Affairs and Youth were a bachelor.

On the whole, German ministries are considerably smaller than their American, British, or French counterparts, relying as they do on the *Länder* bureaucracy in many instances. Much of the work of most of the ministries consists in determining the legal responsibility for the performance of certain acts because that is often determined by administrative law, as is the distribution of the work load. This explains the insistence on a legal education for the top civil service personnel. Within each ministry there are usually several divisions, which in turn are subdivided into individual functional units know as *Referate*. These *Referate* are grouped into divisions, each headed by a chief administrative officer known by the overwhelming title of Ministerial Bureau Director (*Ministerialbürodirektor*). A special *Referent* for organizational questions (*Organisationsreferent*) sees to the proper coordination of all service functions.

The civil service

The German professional civil service has always played a significant role in the governmental system. Under the empire and the Weimar Republic it had an enviable reputation for incorruptibility and efficiency, adhering strictly to professional standards (the *Berufsbeamtentum*). In a sense, its reputation for total political neutrality was never wholly accurate, but until 1914 a basically conservative attitude on the part of civil servants, professional and military men, was considered normal and not a demonstration of political bias. The Weimar Republic experienced a certain deterioration of the public service as an increasing number of civil servants interpreted their "neutrality" as implying even neutrality towards the existence and the survival of the Republic. The Nazi regime wrecked the system completely, imposing strictly political criteria for appointments, promotions, and dismissals, and dismissing a large number of officials on political or racial grounds. After the demise of the Nazi regime, the civil service class was further decimated by denazification and by the fact that between 1945 and 1949 no federal civil service existed.

Since the establishment of the German Federal Republic, there has been a conscious and on the whole quite successful effort to rebuild the civil service and to reestablish previous standards of excellence while avoiding the remoteness and authoritarian note which characterized it previously. Nobody will deny that much progress has been accomplished, nor that much more could be accomplished.

The Civil Service Act of 1953 did away with most of the changes or reforms instituted by the American, British, and French occupation authorities and in the main restored the previous system. It is in line with the long-standing characteristics of the system that the higher civil service career is still mainly reserved to people with legal education, a criterion which some observers consider unduly narrowing. One must remember, however, that the German universities of our day, like those of other countries, have now flung wide their doors to all qualified students; this fact and the general affluence of the country have gone far to remove a class label from those holding a university education. Also, the fact that the German educational system does not have the American and British institution of the undergraduate college, means that students go directly from the superior secondary schools to the professional and graduate schools which form the universities. In that system, the law schools constitute very broad divisions where many students go for motives not unlike those which would bring American students to a College of Letters and Science.

The German Civil Service is divided into four classes: (1) the higher service (*der höhere Dienst*) comprising the top positions where legal education is mandatory; (2) the elevated service (*der gehobene Dienst*) covering responsible positions of administrative assistants and the like; (3) the middle service (*der mittlere Dienst*) comprising the lower administrative jobs; and (4) simple service (*der einfache Dienst*) comprising largely secretarial, service, and menial jobs.

Law and regulations precisely prescribe access to these categories, with exact definitions of educational prerequisites and examinations. Promotion from one group into another is possible but infrequent. The entrance examinations are controlled by commissions, but the hiring of qualified candidates is left entirely to the government departments concerned. There is also a Federal Personnel Commission, but its sole function is to grant exemptions from certain rules and to issue general regulations. Technically, there are no political standards for appointments or promotion, but in the higher federal civil service Social Democrats are few; the reverse is true in some of the *Länder* long controlled by Social Democratic governments. This results largely from the conservative tradition of the public service, against which some of the *Länder* governments have reacted. In time, as qualified candidates without politically damaging pasts move to the higher ranks, this situation is likely to be ameliorated. For some time, much was made of the number of Catholics and Protestants in the service and whether they represented a duly balanced relationship, but this matter has declined in significance in recent years.

More interesting is the often quite intimate relationship existing between certain organized interests and the civil service personnel in certain ministries. Quite a number of appointments are "suggested" by pressure groups which also sometimes participate informally in the drafting of legislation. This does not mean that it is necessarily an improper relationship, as close contacts and personal interchange between professional associations and ministries dealing with the same subject matter, such as agriculture, often seem normal.

D. THE LEGISLATURE

The German parliament consists of two houses, the Federal Assembly (*Bundestag*) and the Federal Council (*Bundesrat*). Of the two, only the *Bundestag* is elected by the people. The *Bundesrat* is really a council of ambassadors of the *Länder*. Its members, as already stated, are delegates of the *Länder* governments who are appointed and removed by them at will and are subject to their instructions.

The terms *Bundesrat* and *Bundestag* are historical, the former going back to imperial Germany, the latter even earlier to the German Confederation of 1815–1866. In this sense the terms are perhaps somewhat misleading because these institutions carry historical memories which are not entirely justified in the light of their present composition and functions.

The electoral process

The Weimar Republic was characterized by a proportional-representation system of the most rigid variety. Its disastrous consequences in encouraging splinter parties and rule by party bureaucracy have already been discussed. The new Federal Republic wanted to modify this system but was not able to abandon proportional representation entirely because of Social Democratic insistence thereon. The reason for that was the heavy concentration of the Social Democratic following in industrial centers, which, under a single-member-district plurality system, would have meant that their urban deputies would have been elected by huge majorities but that the more evenly spread middle-class parties would have obtained a large number of deputies in the country.

The outcome of much discussion on the subject was a compromise system, first enacted by the electoral law of May 10, 1949, sometimes known as the "sixty-forty" law. Under its terms, 60 percent of the seats were filled through elections in single-member constituencies, and 40 percent by proportional representation of votes cast in each state. This law was superseded by another electoral law of 1953 and certain further modifications in 1957. The system works in the following fashion: 50 percent of the seats in the *Bundestag* are filled by proportional representation, the other 50 percent from single-member districts. Every German who goes to the polls casts, in effect, two votes, although he marks both of them on the same ballot. With his first vote (*Erststimme*) he votes for a particular person; with his second vote (*Zweitstimme*) he votes for a party list. The determination of election on the first vote is simple; it operates exactly as in Great Britain and the United States: all candidates run from single-member districts and whoever wins an absolute majority is elected. Determining the result of the second vote is more complicated since it follows the customary rules of proportional representation as generally applied in Europe. This system follows the methods of the Belgian mathematician D'Hondt by which seats in parliament are assigned to the various party lists roughly in proportion to the votes received.

Stimmzettel

für die Bundestagswahl im Wahlkreis **63 Bonn** am 19. September 1965

Sie haben 2 Stimmen

hier **Erststimme**
für die Wahl
eines **Wahlkreisabgeordneten**

hier **Zweitstimme**
für die Wahl
einer **Landesliste (Partei)**

	Erststimme			Zweitstimme		
1	**Dr. Adenauer, Konrad** Bundeskanzler a. D. Bad Honnef-Rhöndorf, Dr. Konrad-Adenauer-Straße 8 a	**CDU** Christlich Demokratische Union	◯	◯	**CDU**	Christlich Demokratische Union Dr. Adenauer, Dr. Barzel, Dr. Schröder, Frau Brauksiepe, Katzer	**1**
2	**Nellen, Peter** Regierungsrat a. D. Düren, Tivolistraße 38	**SPD** Sozialdemokratische Partei Deutschlands	◯	◯	**SPD**	Sozialdemokratische Partei Deutschlands Brandt, Dr. Heinemann, Dr. Arndt, Arendt, Figgen	**2**
3	**Dr. Rahn, Rudolf** Geschäftsführer Düsseldorf, Pempelforter Str. 10	**FDP** Freie Demokratische Partei	◯	◯	**FDP**	Freie Demokratische Partei Dr. Mende, Scheel, Zoglmann, Dr. Effertz, Frau Funcke	**3**
4	**Schwann, Hermann** Diplom-Landwirt Bergisch-Gladbach, Rommerscheider Str. 105	**AUD** Aktionsgemeinschaft Unabhängiger Deutscher	◯	◯	**AUD**	Aktionsgemeinschaft Unabhängiger Deutscher Schwann, Hartung, Frau Dr. Fritz, Dr. Manstein, Knaup	**4**
5				◯	**CVP**	Christliche Volkspartei Vollmer, Schulte-Kellinghaus, Lühnen, Frau Mühlhoff, Thielkes	**5**
6	**Kampkötter, Günter** **Inspek**tor der Berufsgenossenschaft Bonn, Hausdorffstr. 59	**DFU** Deutsche Friedens-Union	◯	◯	**DFU**	Deutsche Friedens-Union Behrisch, Frau Dr. Kirchhof, Lukrawka, Graf von Westphalen, Sanß	**6**
7				◯	**FSU**	Freisoziale Union Schacht, Wandel, Kokaly, Triebel, Spiecker	**7**
8	**Dr. Schulze-Rauschenbach, Arno** Oberregierungsrat a. D. Bonn, Wasserland 2	**NPD** Nationaldemokratische Partei Deutschlands	◯	◯	**NPD**	Nationaldemokratische Partei Deutschlands Prinz zu Salm, Schütz, Walendy, Dr. von Grünberg, Körner	**8**
9				◯	**UAP**	Unabhängige Arbeiter-Partei Kliese, Villmow, Planz, Daumann, Drees	**9**

FS-DRUCK-BONN Fritz Scheur · Bonn, Argelanderstraße 179 · Ruf 2 51 79

Photo credit: German Information Center

The votes are counted as follows: the *second votes* for each party list are counted and a preliminary allocation of seats is made in each *Land* as if *all* seats (and not only 50 percent) were to be allocated on the basis of proportional representation. From that figure are then *deducted* the number of seats which that party has already gained from single-member districts. The resulting figure determines how many seats each party receives under proportional representation (PR) in addition to the seats won in single-member districts. The names of the candidates finally elected by each party under PR are simply taken from the top of each party list down in the sequence indicated by the party presenting the list. Thus, the strength of a party's representation in parliament is determined by PR and the only effect of the single-member district elections is the internal ratio between directly elected and PR-elected deputies. A party cannot increase the number of its seats in parliament by doing exceptionally well in direct, single-member district elections. Only where a party has already won more seats in a *Land* from single-member districts than would have been allocated to it under PR does that party receive the larger number of seats. The necessary number are merely added to the total. Hence all *Bundestage* have actually had a few more members than was originally envisaged.

It is evident, therefore, that the German electoral system is still essentially a PR system. Had there been proportional representation pure and simple, each party would have received the same number of seats that it has now, but under this law some of each party's deputies have a closer relationship to their voters. On the other hand, had there been *only* single-member districts and plurality voting as in the United States, the outcome would have been quite different and would have favored the CDU/CSU.

In order to check the atomization of the political picture by the existence of too many parties—as was the case in the Weimar Republic—the electoral law states that a party cannot receive a seat in the *Bundestag* unless it meets one of the two following conditions: it must either (1) poll a minimum of 5 percent of the total vote cast in the Federal Republic or (2) elect at least three deputies from single-member districts. This measure cuts down considerably the number of parties represented in the *Bundestag*. Only four parties survived in 1957 and gained representation there. From 1961 on, there were only three.

In addition to the 497 elected members in the *Bundestag,* there are also 22 nonvoting members from Berlin. As Berlin is not fully incorporated into the German Federal Republic, in order not to provoke the Russians into more drastic measures than they have already taken, this method of representation was chosen.

The organization of the *Bundestag*

The organization of the *Bundestag* is regulated in general terms by the Constitution (Arts. 40–49) and in detail by the rules (*Geschäftsordnung*) adopted for each session[18] by the *Bundestag* itself. Its presiding officer, the president, is elected by secret ballot and has extensive powers. He is considered similar to the head of a household (*Hausrecht*) and has control over the housekeeping functions of the

---

[18] But the *Bundestag* may readopt the previous rules by tacit consent by merely continuing to apply them. Cf. Hermann von Mangoldt, *Das Bonner Grundgesetz,* Berlin and Frankfurt, 1953, p. 239.

Bundestag. He is also in charge of keeping order. The latter function gives him the right to exclude a deputy for as much as thirty days. The president is also endowed with police powers (*Polizeigewalt*) over which he is the final authority. Normally the local police[19] are not permitted to enter the premises of the *Bundestag,* but the president may call upon them for help if it becomes necessary.

The president is assisted by several vice presidents and a secretariat who, together with him, form the presidium. There is also a curious institution, the Council of Elders (*Ältestenrat*). It is composed of deputies of all major parties who are selected on the basis of age rather than seniority of service. The Council of Elders fulfills some of the functions of a steering committee by bringing about agreement among the different political groups concerning the distribution of the work load. It is also responsible for the selection of committee chairmanships, a good portion of which go to members of the opposition. This practice is in considerable contrast to the methods applied in the Congress of the United States.

The *Bundestag* may refuse to seat a prospective member for illegality of election, incompatibility, etc., but the person who is refused his seat may appeal to the Federal Constitutional Court.

The deputies enjoy the customary immunities to which is added an unusual one which was found in the Weimar Republic also, namely, that a deputy cannot be obliged to divulge information or documents which he has received in his capacity as a deputy. On the other hand there is a limitation in Article 46 which specifically excludes such immunity in cases of "defamatory libel" (*verleumderische Beleidigungen*) even when committed in the *Bundestag.*[20] This is undoubtedly a reaction to the abuse of the excessive immunities permitted under the Weimar Constitution. Otherwise the deputies enjoy immunity for their actions and utterances in the *Bundestag.* Before a deputy can be pursued for a criminal act, the *Bundestag* must give its consent. This is a right of the *Bundestag* and not of the deputy, who cannot voluntarily divest himself of his immunity, for the decisions of the *Bundestag* are presumably dictated by its concern for the public interest and the dignity of the house. Its consent is not necessary if the offender was arrested in the act of committing a crime or during the following twenty-four hours. However, the *Bundestag*'s consent would still be required for the serving of a sentence, and at any rate, any legal pursuit, imprisonment, or arrest of a deputy must be halted on the demand of the *Bundestag.*

[19] This means the police of North Rhine–Westphalia and of the city of Bonn.

[20] "Defamatory libel" is not a vague term to be defined by the *Bundestag* as is incorrectly implied in Harold M. Dorr and Henry L. Bretton, "Legislation," in *Governing Postwar Germany,* ed. by Edward H. Litchfield and Associates, Ithaca, N.Y., 1953. The term is precisely defined in Sec. 187 of the German Criminal Code (StGB) as the assertion of a fact which is capable of making a person appear contemptible or degraded in public opinion, if that assertion is proved to be untrue, and if its untruthfulness was known to the accused. To apply this rule was the unanimous intention of the framers. Cf. Mangoldt, *op. cit.,* p. 253. Even in that case, however, the *Bundestag* would have to vote that the accused member stand trial. Mounz and Dürig, *op. cit.,* Commentary to Art. 46, p. 10. This rule does not apply to lesser forms of libel under Secs. 185 and 186 StGB.

Fraktionen and committees

Any party whose deputies in the *Bundestag* number fifteen or more has the right to organize a parliamentary group, called *Fraktion*. This is in effect the party caucus, and its power was immense in the Weimar Republic. All decisions were made in the *Fraktionen,* in which the party leaders predominated and in which orders were received from a leadership outside parliament. It was possible to force deputies to toe the line by the imposition of compulsory obedience to caucus orders (*Fraktionszwang*). This was certainly one of the things which made the Weimar parliament appear unreal and consequently diminished its prestige.

The framers of the Bonn Constitution did not wish to return to this system. True, *Fraktionen* are again organized under the rules of the *Bundestag*. Their importance is stressed by the fact that only a *Fraktion* is entitled to have members on the committees of the *Bundestag,* including the Council of Elders. This means also that a party with fewer than fifteen deputies has no committee assignments. But Article 38 stipulates that the deputies "shall be representatives of the whole nation, not bound to orders and instructions and subject only to their conscience." This means that there is now *no legal Fraktionszwang.* Even deputies who are expelled from their parties remain members of the *Bundestag,* and if they had been required to deposit an undated letter of resignation with their party leadership, such "resignation" would not be legal.[21] Even if a party dissolves itself or is prohibited by a decision of the Federal Constitutional Court, its members do not thereby lose their seats in the *Bundestag.*

But words are one thing and deeds frequently another. The reference of Article 38 to the "unbound deputy" (*freies Mandat*) is unrealistic. The Weimar Constitution had a very similar provision in Article 21, which did not seem to prevent the imposition of *Fraktionszwang.*

It must of course be admitted that under a parliamentary system there ought to be a measure of party discipline in parliament, otherwise governments become too unstable. Too much "party regularity" is capable of making parliamentary debates seem staged and unreal. This can make an unfavorable impression on the public, enhanced by the fact that the pressure of work frequently forces the *Bundestag* to accept the recommendation of the Council of Elders and restricts debate on sometimes quite important questions to one hour. This allows ten minutes to the author of the bill and only a few minutes to a single representative from each *Fraktion.* Under these circumstances, the role of the individual deputy is even more curtailed than usual, when he would have at least the opportunity to make an individual speech.[22] It should be admitted that in the committees, where most of the real work is done, the expression of opinion is freer, but contrary to American practice German committee deliberations are not open to the press or the public and

[21] Mangoldt, *op. cit.,* p. 233.
[22] Normally a deputy may speak for one hour. The rule is liberally interpreted.

they do not therefore dispel the unfavorable impression created by the "debate," which is more like a reading of party dicta than an actual exchange of views. Even questions are curtailed by the fact that ten signatures are necessary (thirty for inter-pellations, which are less frequent than they were in the French Fourth Republic) before they can be admitted. This makes them a part of party strategy rather than of individual initiative. It is, however, noteworthy that the two major parties of Germany, the CDU/CSU and the Social Democrats, have different views and practices concerning party discipline in parliament. Despite the strong leadership of Chancellor Adenauer, the CDU/CSU members of the *Bundestag* were undivided in only about one-half of all votes taken in the *Bundestag,* whereas the Social Democrats voted as a bloc in virtually all of them.

The committee structure of the *Bundestag* follows the American and French systems, rather than the British. In this group must also be counted the already mentioned powerful steering committee, the Council of Elders. As already stated, it is this council which proposes committee chairmanships and memberships. The number of committee members is determined by the proportional strength of the *Fraktionen* represented in the *Bundestag.*[23] The choice of chairmen and committee members is a matter of informal agreement between the *Fraktionen.*

The committees of the *Bundestag* follow the customary categories of executive functions. Their importance is underlined by the fact that the first *Bundestag* of 1949 created thirty-nine standing committees. Because of the strong position of the respective party leaderships, however, the committees are less independent than those of the United States. The work is also hampered by the absence of anything like the legislative reference service in America. On the other hand the presence of many civil servants and university professors provides a reservoir of technical knowledge and experience which is reflected even more in the composition of the *Bundesrat.* Universities, especially the conveniently located universities of Bonn and Cologne, may also be counted upon to give a hand. In Germany as well as in most other countries, the bulk of legislative proposals originate in one of the government departments, although the *Bundestag* has used its right of initiative with increasing frequency. The members of the federal government have the right to attend all committee meetings and must be heard when they request it. They may also be summoned by the committees.

Besides the regular standing committees, the Bonn Constitution, like its Weimar predecessor, allows for investigating committees. These committees have a considerable standing and history in Germany. Perhaps one of the best known was the *Reichstag* committee which investigated the events that led up to the First

---

[23] For this reason several small parties united in one *Fraktion* in the first *Bundestag* of 1949. This was not possible in the second *Bundestag* of 1953 because of the reduced number of parties and the slaughter of the splinter groups. Sometimes small groups become "guests" of *Fraktionen* of other parties in order to obtain a measure of access to the more significant aspects of parliamentary life.

World War and published its findings in an edition of many volumes.[24] Article 44 of the Bonn Constitution entitles the *Bundestag* to organize investigating committees (*Untersuchungsausschüsse*) at any time. These committees are entitled to hold hearings and investigations on their own authority. They are obliged to proceed with an investigation when one-fourth of the committee's members demand it. Contrary to the American theory (but more like the American practice) these committees can hold investigations even if they have no bearing on any past, present, or future legislation. Traditionally four groups of cases have attracted the interest of investigating committees: (1) economic and social questions whose study might lead to legislation; (2) alleged mismanagement or misconduct in the administration; (3) contested elections; and (4) unusual criminal cases and instances of corruption. The investigating committees have quasi-judicial status inasmuch as they have a right to compel the rendering of certain evidence, but they may not themselves arrest or conduct searches. Apart from the fact that they cannot, of course, sentence a person, their powers are comparable to those of a criminal court. On the other hand the Constitution prescribes that the rules of criminal procedure in court are to be applied by the investigating committees as far as the nature of their work permits.

Finally there is the so-called "permanent committee" (*ständiger Ausschuss,* Art. 45). Unlike other committees, this one is not confined to the periods during which the *Bundestag* is in session. Its main task is to exercise the right of parliamentary supervision over the executive when the *Bundestag* is not in session, especially between the dissolution of one legislature and the convocation of its successor. The Permanent Committee has the same rights as all other committees, including that of conducting investigations. It may even interpellate the government, but it cannot cast a vote of nonconfidence against the government and it cannot participate in any administrative decision.

An unusual position was created by a constitutional amendment in 1956 (Art. 45b) which authorized the *Bundestag* to elect a Defense Commissioner (*Wehrbeauftragter*) "to safeguard the basic rights and to assist the *Bundestag* in exercising parliamentary control." This was designed as a further step to ensure that the army would not again become "a state within the state," and that its soldiers would remain "citizen soldiers." The Defense Commissioner was to be an independent agent of Parliament without any duties and obligations toward either the Ministry of Defense or the military establishment itself. He would report grievances and shortcomings to the Defense Committee and to the *Bundestag* as a whole.

This institution achieved some notoriety when a former Defense Commissioner, retired Admiral Hellmuth Heye, gave his views to a mass circulation weekly before presenting them to the *Bundestag*. Apart from this particular excess, however, the Defense Commissioners have done meritorious work in bringing out into the open undesirable practices, especially excessively hard training methods.

---

[24] *Die Grosse Politik der Europäischen Kabinette,* 1871–1914, Berlin, 1922, 40 vols.

However, it is to the Defense Committee of the *Bundestag* that principal credit belongs for safeguarding parliamentary control over the armed forces. The Ministers of Defense, Theodor Blank, Franz Josef Strauss, and Kai Uwe von Hassel, have also been careful in asserting civilian control. In this they were aided by intelligent and forward-looking military leaders, especially Generals Hans Speidel, Adolf Heusinger, Count Wolf von Baudissin, and Count Johann von Kielmansegg. The total incorporation of the German armed forces in the NATO defense and staff system was also undoubtedly of considerable value.

The organization of the *Bundesrat*

As already stated, the members of the *Bundesrat* are not elected, but are appointed by their respective *Länder* governments and are subject to their instructions and to removal by them. They are themselves members of the *Länder* governments. Since the latter are democratic governments responsible to their respective *Landtage,* this is not an undemocratic principle.

The number of seats in the *Bundesrat* assigned to each *Land* varies according to size and population of the *Länder* but is by means proportionate thereto. Bavaria, Baden-Württemberg, Lower Saxony, and North Rhine–Westphalia have five seats each. Hesse, Schleswig-Holstein, and Rhineland-Palatinate have four each; the Saarland, Bremen, and Hamburg have three each. Berlin has four nonvoting members. This constitutes then an almost equal representation of the *Länder* in the *Bundesrat,* very much in contrast to the situation in the empire and the Weimar Republic. Of course the reason why this is now possible is the disappearance of the gigantic *Land* of Prussia.

Another peculiarity of the *Bundesrat* is the fact that each *Land* delegation votes as a bloc. Party affiliations within the delegation are thus not adhered to, since the members often belong to different parties. But this should not lead to the erroneous assumption that party politics play no role. Quite the contrary; party politics play an important and increasing role, but it is the party politics of the respective *Länder* governments and not that of their delegates.

The work of the delegates is largely technical. They represent the cream of the crop of trained *Land* officials, and they are capable of making important contributions to legislation and administration. But their opinions have nothing to do with the way their votes are cast. Consequently party politics enter by the back door. For instance, Chancellor Adenauer's program for the ratification of the treaty to create the European Defense Community was endangered when the Social Democrats gained some success in one *Land* and thus were able to effect a shift in the *Bundesrat* vote. By the same token, Adenauer more than rectified the balance by throwing every support to his party and its allies in another *Land* election, the outcome of which modified the *Bundesrat* vote in the opposite direction. What is interesting to note here is that to an increasing extent the *Länder* governments cast their *Bundesrat* votes not according to *Land* interests but according to the partisan viewpoint of the national parties to which they belong. This political note tends to diminish the "expert" nature of the *Bundesrat*, without, however, nullifying it.

Like the *Bundestag*, the *Bundesrat* elects its president, but only for one year. There is of course no repetition of the imperial practice by which the chairmanship was always in the hands of one particular state (Prussia).

Since the *Bundesrat* is a very small body of 41 members plus 4 observers from West Berlin (in contrast to the *Bundestag*'s 497 plus 22 nonvoting members from Berlin), its organization is simple. It has 14 committees, of which 13 are standing committees and one is a conference committee to deliberate in joint session with the equivalent committee of the *Bundestag*. For the same reason the rules of debate are of course simple and there are no disciplinary problems.

In many respects the functions of the *Bundesrat* are quite different from those of the *Bundestag*. The Chancellor and his cabinet are not responsible to the *Bundesrat* as they are to the *Bundestag*, and there can therefore be no vote of confidence or censure in the *Bundesrat*. But on the other hand the government needs the *Bundesrat's* consent for certain administrative actions: for example, in order to issue executive orders concerning such matters as railroads, refugees, and the dismissal of certain public officials, or regulating the administration of certain federal matters by the *Länder* governments. We have already seen that the government needs the consent of the *Bundesrat* for the imposition of federal compulsion (*Bundeszwang*) and the emergency use of the *Länder* police forces. It is therefore conceivable that the *Bundesrat*, by refusing to give its consent to some of these measures which the government deems necessary, might actually force a government out of office. So far this has not occurred and is not likely to occur in the near future.

In the field of legislation the *Bundesrat* has, as we shall see below, only a suspensive veto in most issues, although it has an absolute veto in some.

The *Bundesrat* does not fall into any of the patterns of bicameral legislatures. It is not the equal of the *Bundestag*, but it has considerable power. It is both a legislative and an administrative body. It is part of a parliament, but it is also a council of ambassadors whose members represent other administrations.

Legislation

Bills may be introduced in the *Bundestag* by the government, by *Bundestag* members, or by the the *Bundesrat*. However, a government bill must first be introduced in the *Bundesrat*, which has three weeks within which it may comment on the bill before passing it on to the *Bundestag*. A bill, after being introduced, is subjected to a so-called "first reading." This is a discussion on the general principles of the bill and not on its details, although it may serve to bring some order into a complex subject. After a favorable vote on first reading, during which amendments cannot be considered, the bill is referred to committee, sometimes to several committees. Then follows a "second reading" at which details are again not discussed unless the *Bundestag* itself decides differently. The discussion follows certain main considerations such as principles, titles, etc. A vote terminates the discussion of each general topic. At this stage amendments may be introduced before the topic in question is put to the vote. Only international treaties must be discussed and decided without amendment.

The "third reading" begins again with the discussion of the general principles of the bill followed by a detailed discussion of the bill's component parts. Amendments may be considered but must be seconded by ten members. A vote ends the third reading and determines the fate of the bill.

This process can be considerably speeded up by unanimous consent of all members of the *Bundestag* present, which allows all three readings to be rushed through in a single day. Other rules may also be adjusted upon unanimous consent. Otherwise, no member may speak beyond one hour unless permission for extension is granted by a majority resolution. On the other hand, as already stated, the debate may be curtailed by decision of the Council of Elders.

Once a bill has passed the *Bundestag,* it is submitted to the *Bundesrat.*[25] The latter may, within two weeks of its receipt of the bill, demand that a conference committee of representatives of both houses be called in order to iron out differences. This conference committee is the only place where, according to the Constitution (Art. 77, Sec. 2), the members of the *Bundesrat* are not bound by instructions.[26] If this conference committee comes up with a new version of the bill, it is not necessary to start again with three readings thereof, but a single (fourth) reading is sufficient. However it is not always necessary that this formal step of the joint conference committee be taken. The role of the *Bundesrat* is essentially constructive, and since Article 43, Section 2, entitles its members to attend all meetings of the *Bundestag* and its committees with the right to be heard at any time, the *Bundesrat* has an opportunity to inject its views into the deliberation of the bill in the *Bundestag* before the three readings have run their course.

If the *Bundesrat* approves of a bill for which the Constitution *does not specifically require its consent,* either it may give its formal consent, in which case the bill becomes law immediately, or it may simply do nothing, in which case the bill becomes law two weeks after being sent to it if no joint conference committee has been demanded, or one week after the conference committee has terminated its deliberations. If the *Bundesrat* does not approve of a bill for which the Constitution does not specifically require its consent, it has the right to cast a suspensive veto. Conditions for exercising this right are (1) that a meeting of the joint conference committee has been demanded by the *Bundesrat* within two weeks after receiving the bill from the *Bundestag,* and (2) that the suspensive veto (*Einspruch*) is declared within one week after the deliberations of the conference committee have

---

[25] Even if the bill originated in the *Bundesrat* or was first submitted to it for its views, as is the case with government bills.

[26] But that would not protect *Bundesrat* members from being removed or dismissed by their respective *Länder* governments.

come to an end. No suspensive veto can be cast unless the conference committee has first considered the matter.

The suspensive veto can be overridden by the *Bundestag* by the simple act of repassing the bill with simple majority. If, however, the *Bundesrat* has cast its suspensive veto with a two-thirds majority of its members, it can be overridden by the *Bundestag* only by a two-thirds majority. It is sufficient if the two-thirds majority in the *Bundestag* constitutes two-thirds of the members *present,* provided this number is at least equal to a majority of all *Bundestag* members entitled to a seat in the house.

The *Bundesrat*'s suspensive veto is operative only against bills passed by the *Bundestag.* It is not operative against other measures taken by the lower house, such as, for instance, the establishment of an investigating committee.

There are, however, a number of bills for whose passage the consent of the *Bundesrat* is specifically required by the Constitution. This is especially the case with regard to constitutional amendments,[27] for which two-thirds majorities in both houses are required, and for legislation concerning changes in the territory of the *Länder* (Art. 29, Sec. 7), regulation of the execution of federal laws by *Länder* administrations (Arts. 84, Secs. 1 and 5; 85, Sec. 1), the enlargement of the federal administration by the creation of new agencies of direct administration (Art. 87, Sec. 3), a number of cases of fiscal legislation (Arts. 105, Sec. 3; 106, Secs. 3 and 4; 107; 108, Sec. 3), and for the disposition of property belonging to the former *Reich* (Arts. 134, Sec. 4; 135, Sec. 5). In these cases, no bill can become law without the express consent of the *Bundesrat.* Here it not only has an absolute veto, but is coequal with the *Bundestag.* Mere failure to object on the part of the *Bundesrat* would not allow the bill to become law. A positive act of consent is required.

The ratification of treaties follows the same procedure as legislation (Art. 59). This means that treaties concerning subjects in which the *Bundesrat* has an absolute veto can be ratified only with its express consent. In other ratifications it has the same suspensive veto as would apply to ordinary legislation.

If there is a dispute over the question whether a bill or a treaty requires the express consent of the *Bundesrat* or not, only the Federal Constitutional Court can decide.

After a bill has been passed by the legislature in the manner described above, it is certified by the federal President after countersignature by the federal Chancellor and the minister into whose field the bill falls. The President's certification is not an act of consent but a confirmation that the bill has been enacted in the manner prescribed by the Constitution, and that it is identical with the version adopted by the *Bundestag.* If the President finds that these conditions have been met, the law is certified and promulgated in the official journal (*Bundesgesetzblatt*). If the President finds that the bill was not enacted in the manner prescribed or that it is not the correct version, he should refuse certification until the error has

---

[27] As in France, constitutional amendments are regarded as special forms of legislation.

been remedied. The cabinet too may refuse its countersignature for these reasons; however, the President, before refusing his own certification, may ask for an advisory opinion of the Federal Constitutional Court.[28]

Dissolution and legislative emergency

The *Bundestag* is the only popularly elected national body of the German Federal Republic, and the question of dissolution and reelection pertains therefore only to it. The Weimar Constitution gave the *Reich* President and the Chancellor practically unlimited right of dissolution. Its exercise did not give the German government that stability which some advocates of dissolution expected; quite the contrary, for the right was frequently abused, especially toward the end of the Weimar regime, and served to keep in power minority governments that nobody wanted. It contributed considerably to the discredit of the ill-fated Weimar Republic.

The Bonn Constitution knows only a very limited right of dissolution which is not likely to be applied often, if at all. There is a remote possibility of dissolution under Article 63, Section 4. If the *Bundestag* does not elect as Chancellor a man nominated by the federal President, and if it does not elect another man within two weeks thereafter, another ballot is to be taken. If a candidate obtains an absolute majority, he must be appointed; but if a candidate obtains only a plurality, the President has the choice of either appointing him or of dissolving the *Bundestag* within seven days.

Normally the *Bundestag* is elected for a period of four years. If, however, the federal Chancellor, and he alone, asks the *Bundestag* for a vote of confidence and fails to receive it, he may propose to the federal President that the *Bundestag* be dissolved. The President may do so within twenty-one days. However, there is no dissolution when the *Bundestag* elects a new Chancellor. A few words of interpretation are in order here. It is a condition of dissolution that the Chancellor demand a vote of confidence, either directly or by tying the question of confidence officially to the passage of a given bill or measure. However, a vote of censure moved by a member of the *Bundestag,* even if successful, would not constitute grounds for dissolution. On the other hand, if the *Bundestag* fails to act within a reasonable period on the Chancellor's demand for a vote of confidence, that may be considered tantamount to a refusal. Since the President cannot act without the countersignature of the Chancellor, the President could not order dissolution on his own responsibility. But he is not bound by the Constitution to accede to the Chancellor's request.[29] The *Bundestag* may frustrate dissolution by simply electing a new Chancellor. This "new" Chancellor may of course be the same as the "old" one.

This provision, together with others, would prevent such events as the minority Papen and Schleicher governments. The Chancellor has to have a majority at one

[28] Art. 97, Sec. 2, Law on the Federal Constitutional Court, Mar. 12, 1951.
[29] The President's refusal would, however, create a conflict between President and Chancellor which might drag the President into a political controversy and make his position difficult, if not untenable.

time at least because he must be elected by the *Bundestag* (Art. 63). At the same time a government cannot escape a vote of confidence or censure by dissolving the *Bundestag*. The latter is thus placed squarely before its responsibilities. Either it may tolerate a minority government or it can elect a new Chancellor or it can create a situation which leads to dissolution and new elections. In no case, however, will there be a governmental vacuum.

The Weimar Constitution endowed the executive (President and Chancellor) with the exceptional and notorious emergency powers of the famous Article 48. Little of that is found in the Bonn Constitution. The Bonn government certainly has no right to set aside fundamental rights and rule by emergency decree "if the public safety and order . . . are seriously disturbed or endangered" (Art. 48, Weimar Constitution) as its predecessors could and did.

There is, however, a curious and involved residue of this situation in Article 81 of the Bonn Constitution. If the federal Chancellor has (1) asked for a vote of confidence by the *Bundestag* and has failed, and if (2) the *Bundestag* has elected no new Chancellor, and if (3) the *Bundestag* has refused to pass a bill which the government has declared to be "urgent,"[30] the government[31] may, instead of urging dissolution,[32] recommend to the federal President that he proclaim a "state of legislative emergency" (*Gesetzgebungsnotstand*). The federal President may or may not accept this recommendation, but he may proclaim a state of legislative emergency only (4) with the consent of the *Bundesrat*.

After the proclamation of the state of legislative emergency, the *Bundestag* has one more chance to avoid the actual carrying out of the proclamation by passing the bill for which the state of legislative emergency was proclaimed. If, however, it fails to do so, or passes it in a form which the government deems unacceptable, or fails to act within four weeks of the bill's resubmission after the proclamation, the bill will nevertheless be "deemed enacted" if the *Bundesrat* consents thereto. The Constitution itself may not be amended or modified in this way.

The state of legislative emergency can last only six months from the date of its proclamation. During that period other bills may also be enacted in the same manner, but in each case the procedure outlined above must be repeated. It is also understood that the *Bundestag* may not repeal these laws within the six-month period, though it may of course do so afterwards.[33] After the six months have passed, *no second* state of legislative emergency may be proclaimed during the same term of the same Chancellor.

---

[30] Step (1) and step (3) may be combined if the Chancellor ties the question of confidence to the bill.

[31] While dissolution may be recommended by the Chancellor alone (Art. 68), the state of legislative emergency must be recommended by the entire cabinet.

[32] The Constitution merely demands that there be no dissolution. Theoretically the Chancellor might have recommended dissolution and been refused by the President, after which the government recommended the proclamation of the state of legislative emergency. Politically such an eventuality is difficult to envisage.

[33] Mangoldt, *op. cit.*, p. 439.

What the framers of this provision had in mind is obviously a situation in which the government finds itself in a minority but the *Bundestag* is so badly divided as to be incapable of producing an alternative government. In that case the minority government which thus remains in office should be able to govern, at least for a time. The frequent governmental paralysis of the Weimar period is thus presumably avoided. At the same time it is clear that the state of legislative emergency can function only when the *Bundestag* meets and not when it is prevented from meeting by violence or other circumstances. Moreover, the time and "once in a term" limitations, but especially the need for the consent of the *Bundesrat*, would seem adequate safeguards against abuse, especially as the political composition of the *Bundesrat* is not likely to be totally different from that of the *Bundestag*. On the other hand, the way in which this right is circumscribed raises the question of whether it can actually operate. Up to now it has not been invoked, and in view of the comfortable majority of all German governments thus far, it is unlikely that it will be.

The experience with the ill-fated Weimar Constitution reveals that dangers to the democratic order come not only from the emergency decree power of the government, but also from the possibility that a rubber-stamp legislature might pass an enabling act transferring its legislative power to the executive. This is in fact the manner in which the Weimar Republic came to an end. Most important of all such measures, the infamous Enabling Act of March 24, 1933, was forced down the throat of a terrorized *Reichstag,* many of whose members were already in prison or concentration camps. Although legal niceties were observed in this case, it was essentially an act of violence rather than of law.

A specific prohibition against delegating legislative power was included in the draft of the new constitution elaborated by the Council of Experts meeting at Herrenchiemsee. A similar version was incorporated in later drafts, but in the fifty-seventh meeting of the Principal Drafting Committee (*Hauptausschuss*) it was unaccountably omitted without discussion.[34]

Nevertheless it goes too far to say that there are simply no limitations on delegated powers. Article 80 permits decree power to be vested by law in the federal or the *Länder* governments, and these decrees need not be confined to implementing laws but may go beyond that and create legal rules of their own. However, Article 80 stipulates that content, purpose, and extent of the delegated powers be specified in the law. A general, all-embracing enabling act would thus seem unconstitutional, to which must be added that, as already pointed out, decrees in a number of fields such as fiscal matters need the consent of the *Bundesrat*.

Realities of executive-legislative relationship

It is characteristic of all parliamentary forms of government that the constitution makes the powers of parliament appear more formidable than they actually

[34] Mangoldt, *op. cit.,* p. 380.

are. This is due to the fact that political realities and administrative practices do not always appear in the constitutional text. Nevertheless, although the greater power does lie with the executive, the German parliament is not a negligible quantity.

The lobbyists and special interest groups have recognized this situation and in a curious way have added to it by concentrating their activities on the executive rather than on the legislative branch of government. Ministries, in their turn, will deal only with national organizations. The result is that lobbyists deal primarily with civil servants and their political superiors, rarely with deputies.[35]

As long as the government has a majority in parliament, it has its way pretty much. The political parties are sufficiently disciplined for an upset in the house to be unlikely. Less political and more functional is the procedure in the committees, but this is possible only because committee hearings and deliberations are not open to the public. If they were, party control would be just as strong there as in the full house and the value of the discussions and contributions would cease. But there is a disadvantage, namely that the public does not have a full view of the contribution made by the opposition. This has faced the Social Democratic opposition with difficult problems. The German public tends to undervalue the opposition's role and to focus attention on the government. Under such circumstances, the opposition might have been strongly tempted to seek dramatic grandstand plays in order to attract attention. That the opposition has not done so is very much to its credit.

Other opportunities for the opposition and for sometimes dissident elements within the government coalition to put the government on the spot lie in the direct formal questions directed at the government. They may be "small" (*Kleine Anfrage*) or "large" (*Grosse Anfrage*) inquiries. They require fifteen and thirty signatures respectively. "Small" inquiries are usually answered in writing, while "large" ones are normally met by oral answers plus a subsequent debate which make them in fact an interpellation. Of course, the government may also organize an inquiry in order to bring certain matters before the public, but twice as many "large" inquiries are launched by the opposition as by the government parties.

A new institution was added in 1965. This is called the "Current Events Hour" (*Aktuelle Stunde*) and constitutes an hour-long debate. Each speaker is limited to five minutes. No statements may be read. Cabinet members have promised to adhere to the five-minute rule too, although the duration of their statements does not count against the hour time limit. This procedure is designed to make possible quick discussions of topics of immediate significance and timeliness.

In the executive-legislative relationship, the style, strength, and personality of the Chancellor are of central significance. The dominant role of Chancellor Adenauer was so great that at times the parliament seemed to shrink, although at no time did he have an altogether easy time with it. Under Chancellor Erhard there

---

[35] Theodor Eschenburg, *Herrschaft der Verbände?*, Stuttgart, 1963, 2d ed.

was a somewhat greater balance, and the role of the chairman of the parliamentary groups (*Fraktionsvorsitzender*) was therefore extremely important. In the CDU this role is ably exercised by Rainer Barzel; Fritz Erler of the SPD was a masterful performer; and the FDP's Knut von Kühlmann-Stumm is a man of considerable ability. These three men have contributed much to making the parliament of the Federal Republic vastly superior to its Weimar predecessor.

How much have personalities contributed to the success of German representative government and how much have institutions? A distinction is impossible to make. In the period of reconstruction strong personalities, deeply imbued with a fervor to make German democracy work, were indispensable. Whatever their faults, Germany owes a tremendous debt of gratitude to Konrad Adenauer and Kurt Schumacher, as well as to the discipline of its labor and the inventiveness of its management. With greater stability, the significance of institutional strength has increased and proved itself, particularly in the Chancellor crisis of 1966.

E. THE JUDICIARY

The reestablishment of a federal judiciary reflects the attempts to avoid some of the worst malpractices of the Hitler regime. The Nazis had destroyed the independence of judges and had abolished the principle that no one shall be tried except on the basis of law (*nulla poena sine lege*); they had abolished the provision that no one shall be deprived of trial before a competent and regular judge; they had established special courts, not bound by any kind of law; and they had proclaimed the principle that the will of the Führer was the supreme law. The Bonn Constitution contains specific safeguards against such contingencies—in so far as any constitution can accomplish such a feat. The principle of punishment solely on the basis of law is restored (Art. 103), and the death penalty is abolished. Procedural safeguards are established to assure a fair hearing, and double jeopardy is excluded. No one may be deprived of a trial before a lawful judge and extraordinary courts are prohibited. No ex post facto laws shall apply.

These are excellent principles, which were already included in the Weimar Constitution. But the record of the Weimar judiciary in living up to these high precepts was poor. Enemies of the Republic could usually count on mild judges, provided the offenders belonged to the right and not the left, and many judges and prosecutors took pains to demonstrate their hostility to democratic institutions.[36] Such an attitude would be dangerous in any country, but it was particularly disastrous in Germany, where the law of criminal procedure permits the judge a great deal of discretion and direct participation in the trial.

In view of these antecedents it is perhaps a little surprising to note that the Bonn Constitution has greatly extended the power of the judiciary; so much so, in

---

[36] See the evidence in the Nürnberg trial of the German justices. U.S. Military Government, *Information Bulletin* (1948) Nos. 138–142, quoted by Friedrich, *op. cit.*, p. 717.

fact, that some writers have used the term "judiciary state."[37] The explanation is perhaps that the fathers of the Constitution trusted parliament even less than the courts. This has turned out to be a dubious judgment.

Up to now, the record of the regular German judiciary is mixed and not always inspiring; there have been a number of decisions by inferior courts, dealing with Nazi criminals as well as with those who rebelled against them, which gave grounds for concern. Often, not so much malevolence as excessive formalism has been at fault, but even that is debatable.

In all fairness, it should be noted that the German federal government as well as the governments of the *Länder* have also been concerned about these events and have tried to remedy them. Also the press and a part of the public have reacted unfavorably to such judges.

One dramatic event threw a peculiar light on several sides of the controversy in 1964 and 1965. It was in the latter year that the statute of limitations would have prevented further prosecution of war crimes in as-yet-undiscovered cases.[38] The government and a majority in parliament realized that it was politically and morally wrong to let such criminals escape; yet there was hesitation to grant an exception to the general rule, partly because the Nazis had misused exceptional jurisdictions and rules so much, partly because a good part of the German public undoubtedly wanted to have the whole Nazi mess put behind them and done away with. In any case, there was a clear discrepancy between German and world opinion. The latter wisely prevailed. In the end, the *Bundestag* voted on March 25, 1965, to extend the statute of limitations for war crimes and Nazi atrocities for another five years, that is, until January 1, 1970. The vote was overwhelming, 344 to 96, with both CDU/CSU and all SPD votes in favor, while only the FDP was solidly opposed.

The ordinary court system

Only the top courts of the three judicial pyramids—ordinary, administrative, and constitutional—are federal courts. The lower echelons, inasmuch as they exist, are courts of the *Länder* and apply both federal and *Land* legislation.

There is no German equivalent to the American or British justice of the peace. The lowest step of the court hierarchy is therefore a regular court known as district court (*Amtsgericht*).[39] District courts are found in every town of any significance. Sometimes a single judge takes care of all business; sometimes in somewhat larger centers there are several judges, each one specializing in different categories of

---

[37] For quotations of references, see Mangoldt, *op. cit.,* p. 497.

[38] Where crimes had been discovered and prosecution started, even against fugitive offenders, the statute of limitations would not have applied, as such filing of formal charges automatically interrupts the statute of limitations.

[39] There are no proper translations for *Amtsgericht* and *Landgericht,* as neither term is descriptive. The translations "district court" and "regional court" have been chosen as descriptive of the courts' jurisdiction, but there are no agreed translations.

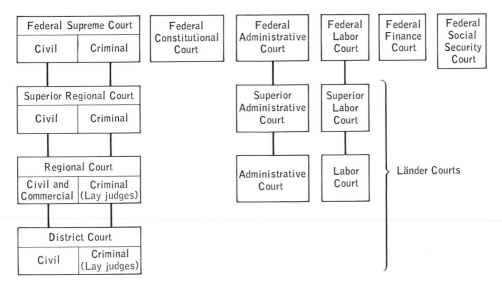

The German court system

cases. This type of court has jurisdiction in litigation involving sums under 1,000 German marks DM (about $250) as well as probate and similar cases. In criminal cases (other than minor infractions) the trial court is composed of one professional judge and two lay judges (*Schöffen*).

The next higher court, the regional court (*Landgericht,* in Berlin called *Kammergericht*), is both a court of first instance for more important matters and a court of appeals for cases decided by the district court. When engaged in civil cases, either on appeal or in original jurisdiction (amount unlimited), the court is composed of three regular judges. In criminal cases the court's composition is more complicated. If it is concerned with minor offenses on appeal from a single judge's verdict in the district court, it is composed of one regular judge and two lay judges. If concerned with an appeal case from a district court where a judge and two lay judges had decided, the regional court will be composed of three regular judges and two lay judges. The same composition prevails when the regional court holds trial for a more important offense (but not a capital crime) in original jurisdiction. When hearing a case of a grave offense or capital crime in original jurisdiction, the court (*Schwurgericht*) is composed of three professional judges and seven lay judges (*Geschworene*). Despite the difference in name, the smaller group of lay judges (*Schöffen*) and the larger one (*Geschworene*)[40] have the same functions. They are

---

[40] Literally translated, *Geschworene* means "sworn ones" or "jury." Until 1924 the *Geschworenen* were a true jury functioning very much like the American trial jury. Since then, however, they have become lay judges even though they have retained their old title.

selected by lot from a list of suitable people maintained by the respective city councils.

The distinction between both forms of lay judges (*Schöffen* and *Geschworene*) and the Anglo-American juries is considerable. In America the jury deliberates separately from the judge and usually deals only with questions of fact and not of law, although there are exceptions (as in Illinois). The German lay judges, however, deal with questions of both law and fact and deliberate together with the professional judges. Moreover, while unanimity is often required (or at least a large majority) in America, all German decisions are made by majority.

It is difficult to see much advantage to the German system. While the Anglo-American jury system occasionally leads to abuse, the German system leads nowhere. The lay judges, even where they outnumber the professionals, are completely under the thumb of the professional judges by whose learning and superior experience they are greatly impressed. The lay judges therefore can usually be relied upon to ratify the decisions of the professionals.

The lay-judge system does, however, have a considerable value and merit in the commercial chambers (*Kammern für Handelssachen*) of the regional courts[41] in which the lay judges are men of commerce and business who are chosen for their expert knowledge.

The next higher court, the superior regional court (*Oberlandesgericht*), is solely an appeals court and ordinarily has no original jurisdiction. It is also the highest ordinary court of the *Länder* except in Bavaria, which has a special *Land* supreme court (*Oberstes Landesgericht*). It is composed of a criminal and a civil section (called senates), each made up of three judges. It is the court of final resort for cases which had originally been heard by the district courts. For cases which originated in the regional courts, it is a court of second instance. It does not retry a case but either confirms the verdict of the inferior court or sends the case back for rehearing.

The apex of the ordinary court structure is the Supreme Federal Court (*Bundesgerichtshof*), which resides in Karlsruhe. Its composition is curious because its judges are chosen by an election committee composed of an equal number of people appointed by the *Länder* Ministers of Justice and elected by the *Bundestag*. The court began its function on October 8, 1950. It has both appellate and original jurisdiction. In civil cases it has only appellate jurisdiction for all cases originating in the regional courts. In its criminal section, the Supreme Federal Court has jurisdiction over cases which originated in the regional courts, but in those capital and other grave cases which were originally tried by the enlarged court of three judges and seven lay judges (*Schwurgericht*) the case goes up on appeal directly from the regional court to the Supreme Federal Court without first being reviewed by the superior regional court.

---

[41] Commercial chambers, like criminal chambers, may be established in places in which there is no regular regional court.

Strangely enough the Supreme Federal Court has original jurisdiction in the case of treason, which in German law comprises not only acts which aid a foreign power but offenses against the internal constitutional order of the state.[42]

The main purpose of the Supreme Federal Court is the unification of law through its jurisdiction. This is a vital task because the period between 1945 and 1950 saw the courts of each *Land* go their own ways and create great legal confusion which is still not quite overcome.

The administrative courts

Germany's administrative court system follows closely the French pattern from which it was originally adopted. Except for a supreme financial court, neither the German empire nor the Weimar Republic ever got around to establishing a supreme administrative court on the model of the Council of State in France. The Nazis established such a court in 1941, but because of war conditions and the collapse of the regime it amounted to little.

Under the present constitutional system, administrative courts (*Verwaltungsgericht*) were first reestablished in the *Länder* and, for a court of appeals, a superior administrative court (*Oberverwaltungsgericht*). In 1950 was established the Federal Finance Court (*Bundesfinanzgerichtshof*) with its seat in Munich, and in 1952 the Federal Administrative Court (*Bundesverwaltungsgericht*) was finally organized in West Berlin. In order to accept appeals from intra-service disciplinary tribunals, there was established a Federal Disciplinary Section (*Bundesdisziplinarhof*) at the Federal Administrative Court.

Administrative courts deal with controversies over rights which have been allegedly damaged by an act of public authority. However, claims resulting from the state's liability for its agents go before ordinary courts, and so do the salary claims of civil servants. Administrative courts also very frequently settle jurisdictional disputes between different public authorities. Their impact is not as great as that of the French Council of State, but nevertheless the German administrative courts can claim solid achievements in protecting individuals against administrative arbitrariness. Civil-rights cases, however, fall within the purview of the Federal Constitutional Court.

Labor courts and other specialized courts

Special courts for labor questions are known in many European countries. A good system existed under the Weimar Republic. It was abolished by the Nazi regime. With the reestablishment of the free trade-union system, it was again or-

---

[42] German law distinguishes between internal treason (*Hochverrat*), which is an attack by force against the internal security and integrity of the country and its constitutional order, and external treason (*Landesverrat*), which comprises aid and comfort to an external enemy or conspiracy to create an external danger to the country, espionage, etc.

ganized in the different *Länder,* all of which have labor courts and superior labor courts. In 1953 a Federal Supreme Court for Labor Affairs (*Bundesarbeitsgericht*) and a Federal Social Security Court (*Bundessozialgericht*) were created.

Labor courts are composed of judges representing both management and trade unions. They deal with disputes arising out of collective-bargaining agreements or the failure to arrive at such agreements; disputes concerning working conditions, health, and safety; and disputes arising out of agreements between management and shop-steward committees, as well as out of the new "right of codetermination" (*Mitbestimmungsrecht*), which gives labor a part in management. They have the same status as other courts. No appeal may be made except to a higher labor court, or if the case has a criminal or civil side, to the appropriate court.

The aforementioned Federal Finance Court (*Bundesfinanzhof*) is more than a court, having some of the functions of the American federal accounting office and also hearing appeals from the *Land* finance courts on fiscal and customs cases. The (federal) Patents Court in Munich is unique. It hears patents cases in first instance, but appeals may be heard by the Patents Section (*Patentsenat*) of the (supreme) Federal Court.

The Federal Constitutional Court

The summit of the entire German judicial system is a court which is essentially an innovation in the history of Germany although some of its functions were previously exercised by other courts. This is the Federal Constitutional Court (*Bundesverfassungsgericht*), whose seat is in Karlsruhe.

Because its jurisdiction penetrates manifestly into the political field, its composition is markedly different from that of all other tribunals. The Court is composed of two sections, called senates, which divide different categories of cases between them. They are equal and independent from one another and constitute a twin court. The judges are elected to the first or the second senate and do not change. Each senate is composed of twelve judges, one-third of whom (four) are judges of the highest courts (Supreme Federal Court, Federal Administrative Court, Supreme Federal Finance Court, etc.). They are elected for life. The other two-thirds of the judges are elected for eight years in such a way that half of them are elected every four years. Half of all the judges (lifetime and eight-year judges) are elected by the *Bundestag* and the other half by the *Bundesrat*. The *Bundestag* elects them indirectly, through an electoral college of twelve members who elect the judges by a three-fourths majority; the *Bundesrat* elects them directly by a two-thirds majority. The purpose of the large majority required, especially in the *Bundestag,* was to assure that there should be no political domination but a necessity for compromise. In actual practice, the rule led to a great deal of haggling and delayed quite unduly the establishment of the Court.[43]

---

[43] Some political influence in the composition of the two senates has been charged, which led to one being popularly called the "Black (Catholic) Senate" and the other, the "Red (Socialist) Senate." In fact, however, these implications are unfounded.

All judges must be fully trained jurists, and the lifetime judges, although outnumbered, have the task of guarding the legal continuity of the otherwise changing Court.

The jurisdiction of the Federal Constitutional Court is very considerable and extends to five groups of cases:

1. Most important is the right of judicial review. The Federal Constitutional Court decides whether a federal or a *Land* law is compatible with the federal Constitution, or whether *Land* law is compatible with federal law. To bring action in such cases, the Constitution requires a motion of the federal government or of a *Land* government, or of one-third of the members of the *Bundestag.* Far more frequently, however, another procedure is followed. In a case pending before some other court, the question of the constitutionality of a law may be invoked by the parties. When that happens, the court must suspend proceedings and refer the question of constitutionality to the Federal Constitutional Court for its decision, which is binding on the original court. The same is true when the question is raised as to whether a rule of international law is part of the law of the land and creates rights and duties for individuals. If the constitutional court of a *Land* intends to interpret the federal Constitution in a manner inconsistent with a past decision of the Federal Constitutional Court or of the constitutional court of another *Land,* it must apply for a decision of the Federal Constitutional Court.

2. The Law on the Federal Constitutional Court (*Bundesverfassungsgerichtsgesetz*) of March 12, 1951, extends the jurisdiction of the Court to the institution of the so-called "constitutional plaint" (*Verfassungsbeschwerde*). According to Article 90 of that law, an individual who feels deprived of the civil rights granted to him by the Constitution may appeal to the Federal Constitutional Court. Normally this is possible only after all other remedies have been exhausted, but exceptions are possible in case of irreparable damage. By far the greatest number of cases before the Federal Constitutional Court fall into this category. The complaint may be directed against any executive, legislative, or judicial act, but it can be raised only if the plaintiff's rights have been directly injured. A mere "taxpayer's suit" is not permissible.

3. The Federal Constitutional Court is responsible for the interpretation of the Constitution regarding disputes between the highest federal organs concerning their respective rights and duties. Obviously the Court does not decide all such disputes, most of which are political or administrative, but only those in which the interpretation of the Constitution is involved.

4. It decides controversies over the rights and duties of the federation and the *Länder* in their mutual relationships, especially with regard to the execution of federal law by *Länder* administrations and the federal supervision thereof.

5. It also has jurisdiction in other federation-*Länder* and inter-*Länder* controversies in public law, and may decide public law disputes even within a *Land* if that *Land* does not have an appropriate judicial authority of its own. The latter is the case in only one *Land.*

Finally the Constitution assigns to the Federal Constitutional Court a number of specific functions, most of which go beyond the usual scope of courts. These are (1) decisions over the loss of fundamental rights because of their misuse (Art. 18); (2) suppression of political parties because of their anticonstitutional attitude (Art. 21); (3) appeal against decisions of the *Bundestag* concerning the validity of an election (Art. 41); (4) impeachment of the federal President (Art. 61); (5) removal of a federal judge because of offenses against the constitutional order— this can be pronounced only by the Federal Constitutional Court with a two-thirds majority and upon the demand of the *Bundestag* (Art. 98, Secs. 2 and 5); (6) decisions about the continued validity of older law (Art. 126); and (7) decisions on an intra-*Land* controversy concerning the compatibility of *Land* law with that *Land*'s constitution, but only if the law of that *Land* specifically authorizes the Supreme Federal Court to render such a decision (Art. 99).

Despite its recent creation, the Federal Constitutional Court has already achieved an excellent record which greatly exceeds its expectations. It has not hesitated to act vigorously and courageously and has already fully justified its existence. Out of a growing practice, two widely separated decisions might be cited here. In the much discussed Southwest case,[44] the Federal Constitutional Court did not hesitate to declare an executive order unconstitutional because the *Bundestag* in delegating this right to the executive had failed to define the limits and the purpose of such delegation precisely as required by Article 80 of the Constitution. The Court thus reminded the parliament of its responsibility and helped to curtail sharply any possible return to a Weimar type of rule by decree.

In another case, the Court declared the Socialist Reich party unconstitutional and went into considerable detail in order to demonstrate what kind of political conduct it considers detrimental to the constitutional and democratic order of the state.[45] The same standards were applied to the Communist party, which was dissolved in 1957. In these cases the court attempted to define in significant fashion the "free basic democratic order" of Article 21:

> An order (system) which, excluding any form of violence and arbitrariness, establishes government under the rule of law based on the self-determination of the people according to the will of the majority at a given time and on the principles of freedom and equality. Minimal requirements of this system are: respect for the civil and human rights specified in the Basic Law, especially for the personal right to life and free development, popular sovereignty, the separation of powers, the responsibility of government, the legality of public administration, the independence of the courts, the principle of majority rule, as well as the equal chances for all political parties and the right to the or-

[44] Gerhard Leibholz, "The Federal Constitutional Court in Germany and the 'Southwest Case,'" *American Political Science Review,* Vol. XLVI (1952), pp. 723–731.
[45] Decision of the Federal Constitutional Court of Oct. 23, 1952, concerning the unconstitutionality of the Socialist Reich party, *Entscheidungen des Bundesverfassungsgerichts,* 1 BvB 1/51, Oct. 23, 1952.

ganization and the activities of an opposition within the framework of a constitutional order."

A significant decision protecting the *Länder* against federal encroachment halted an attempt by the federal government to establish a television network. The Court saw in this an encroachment on the rights of the *Länder,* particularly in the reserved field of education, and declared the attempt unconstitutional.[46]

These and other decisions have revealed the Federal Constitutional Court as one of the brightest spots in the constitutional fabric of the new Germany.

In view of the multiplicity of "supreme courts" the Constitution envisaged the creation of a "Supremest Federal Court" (*Oberstes Bundesgericht*). However, it was never established and it probably never will be.

F. *LÄNDER* GOVERNMENT

The German system of *Land* and local government has always been basically different from that of the United States. The traditional separation existing in the United States between federal, state, and local governments constitutes a marked contrast to the fundamental unity of the German system. The German national government, both under the Weimar Republic and the Third *Reich,* did not ordinarily employ its own local agents, but used the *Land* and local authorities for that purpose. Thus even where local government was autonomous it always had to act as a local agent of the national authorities in addition to its autonomous functions. So the citizen was usually confronted with only one system of bureaucracy, but on the other hand local government found itself fairly tightly controlled from above. However, this control was defined by detailed statutes which tended to prevent arbitrariness. It should also be mentioned that the civil service was thoroughly entrenched on the *Land* and local government level, even including the requirement that the mayor was to be a person endowed with high civil service qualifications. Technical efficiency was therefore of a high order, although the services were frequently more elaborate than economical.

Under the empire, the *Länder* had a very great degree of autonomy and considerable home rule prevailed in the municipalities. The centralist trend of the Weimar Constitution deprived the *Länder* of much of their autonomy, and while they did not become rubber stamps immediately, they were clearly moving in that direction. The extent to which centralization had taken place during the Weimar Republic can be gathered from the system of taxation. All taxes were collected by the national administration and then apportioned between the *Reich* and the *Länder.* Apportionment among the *Länder* was guided neither by size nor by number of population of the *Länder* but by the amount of income taxes collected in each *Land.*

---

[46] Verdict of the Second Senate, Feb. 28, 1961, *Entscheidungen des Bundesverfassungsgerichtes,* Vol. 12, pp. 205, 206.

This type of financial administration interfered with regional and municipal planning to a considerable extent, as taxes were standardized ánd could not be adjusted to the particular needs of the community. As an experienced observer has pointed out, it was through this type of fiscal management rather than through constitutional or statutory provisions that the last vestiges of German federalism became extinct.[47] This is why the Bonn Constitution spells out in such detail an equitable distribution of fiscal powers between the federation and the *Länder* (Arts. 105–115).

With the arrival of the Great Depression, German municipal government found itself saddled with staggering burdens which it could not carry, and more and more self-government was lost in the process of receiving additional aid from the national authorities. The poor financial position of the German communities provided the Nazis with a welcome excuse to "reorganize" the entire structure of local government, a task which was accomplished by means of a uniform code for all German municipalities, the German Municipal Act of 1935.

After the collapse of the Nazi regime and under Allied military government, German administrations were first established on the local level before *Länder* governments were reconstituted. This happened at different speeds in the Western zones of Germany. The American zone was the first in that respect; both the British and the French held on much longer to direct administration. Eventually *Länder* constitutions were written and adopted everywhere, with the British zone trailing far behind.

The *Länder* themselves were partly historical, partly artificial units. Bavaria, although it underwent some changes, mentions a 1,000-year history in its constitution, while Hesse was created out of three former units. The former *Länder* of Baden and Württemberg, after being artificially divided into three units in order to accommodate the creation of a French zone, were finally reunited in 1952, though with difficulty and much controversy,[48] into one *Land* which bears the name Baden-Württemberg. The Saar came under French control after the Second World War, but in accordance with the treaty of June 4, 1956, it rejoined Germany (the German Federal Republic) on January 1, 1957. Its economic link to France was ended in July, 1959.

The German Federal Republic is thus composed of ten *Länder:* Baden-Württemberg, Bavaria, Bremen, Hamburg, Hesse, Lower Saxony, North Rhine–Westphalia, Rhineland-Palatinate, Schleswig-Holstein and the Saar. West Berlin is in a category by itself as will be seen below.

The *Länder* are quite unequal in size although not nearly as much as was the case when Prussia existed. The most populated *Land* is North Rhine–Westphalia, which embraces the Ruhr industrial area and has over 13 million inhabitants. Bavaria is the largest state in area with over 27,000 square miles, but only a little over

---

[47] Arnold Brecht, *Federalism and Regionalism in Germany,* New York, 1945, p. 61.
[48] The religious conflict between the Catholic population of South Baden and the Protestant one of Württemberg played a significant role here.

9 million inhabitants (whereas North Rhine–Westphalia has a little over 13,000 square miles). The smallest *Land* in both population and area is the city-state of Bremen, which has over 700,000 inhabitants and 156 square miles.

All *Länder* are organized on the principle of parliamentary democracy. They have a popularly elected legislature which, except in Bavaria, is unicameral.[49] In most *Länder* it is called *Landtag,* but in Hamburg and Bremen it goes by the name of *Bürgerschaft* (literally translated, citizenry). These legislatures are elected by variously modified proportional-representation systems and their legislative term is usually four years. Despite strong Allied protest, civil servants may be members of the *Landtage* without retiring or even taking a leave of absence. Only the electoral law of North Rhine–Westphalia discourages this practice.

The executives of the *Länder* are cabinets headed by a minister-president (*Ministerpräsident*). In Bremen and Hamburg the cabinet is called a senate, and its chairman, the equivalent to the minister-president, is called mayor (*Bürgermeister*) and senate president in Bremen, lord mayor (*Oberbürgermeister*) in Hamburg.

Despite the fact that coalition governments are in power in most *Länder,* they have proved themselves very stable. This stability has been enhanced in several states by a provision similar to that in the federal Constitution, stipulating that a government which has received a vote of nonconfidence must resign only when a successor has been elected by the *Landtag.* The constitution of Bavaria has a curious provision in having the minister-president elected for four years, but stipulating somewhat vaguely that he must resign when cooperation between him and the legislature has become impossible. This provision has made little difference, and Bavaria is governed like the other *Länder.*[50]

Between the *Land* governmental level and that of local administration there is an intermediary authority in many *Länder* called a government district (*Regierungsbezirk*) and headed by a government president (*Regierungspräsident*) who is appointed by the *Land* government and subject to its direction.

On the whole the *Länder* of the German Federal Republic have more real self-government than they had under the Weimar Republic and of course under the Nazi regime. Contrary to the somewhat naïve and oversimplified assumptions of some Allied military-government policy makers, this does not in itself guarantee democracy or bring it necessarily any closer. Democracy and federalism are no more identical than are centralism and dictatorship. The German Empire of the Hohenzollerns was certainly a federal regime but equally certainly not a democracy. France is a unitary, centralist state, but also a democracy. Moreover, during the period of the Weimar Republic, the central government and the near-central government of Prussia were frequently more enlightened and democratic than some of

---

[49] The Bavarian senate is based on a corporative principle and has little significance.
[50] Robert G. Neumann, "New Constitutions in Germany," *American Political Science Review,* Vol. XLII (1948), pp. 448–468; Harold O. Lewis, *New Constitutions in Occupied Germany,* Washington, 1948.

the *Länder* governments. On the other hand, since the German people must educate themselves toward a democratic regime, the existence of *Länder* governments, which are much closer to the citizen than is the federal government, may be a good thing.

Germany has shown marked trends toward a more unitary regime. Partly this is political; the Christian Democrats, the chief spokesmen of federalism, are not nearly so keen on it now that they safely dominate the national government. More important has been the dire economic necessity which confronted the country after the Second World War and made extraordinary measures inevitable. The strong foreign policy and the rearmament of Germany all strengthen the centralist trend.

What protects the *Länder* from being submerged by the federal government is not so much their reserved powers under the Constitution, which, as we have seen, are few, but rather the important position of the *Bundesrat*. Also the vigorous attitude of the Federal Constitutional Court is likely to play an important role in the defense of "states' rights."

G. LOCAL GOVERNMENT

Just as the federal government exercises its regional functions through the *Länder* governments, so they exercise their local functions through local government. This makes for much streamlining but also for supervision.

Local government was the sector in which former German institutions were relatively satisfactory, at least before 1935. While not uniform, the prevailing system was that of an elected city council which elected a mayor, but the mayor had a very long term of office, certainly much longer than that of the council. In practice this meant that the mayor was a professional who had to blend with the directly elected councilors and did so with generally good results. The Nazis changed this in 1935, but the Allies did not go back to the preceding, generally satisfactory order. They attempted instead to impose the system to which they were accustomed at home. This was far less true of the Americans than of the British and the French. The British insisted on making both the mayor and the *Landrat* (head of the district, *Kreis*) purely political officials, while vesting the actual administration in a civil servant who, in the municipalities, became known as the city director (called, according to the importance of the city, *Gemeindedirektor, Stadtdirektor,* or *Oberstadtdirektor*). For the *Kreis* the British created an elected *Landrat* and a professional *Kreisdirektor*. The results of this reform were on the whole quite unsatisfactory. The Germans did not like the system; the separation between the political and the administrative worked against rather than for a democratic develoment and on occasion permitted politically doubtful elements to slip into the mayoralty who would have been kept out under the old and tried system.

In the French zone the French attempt to copy the *maire-adjoint* system in a totally foreign environment only raised complete incomprehension. The French system naturally disappeared as soon as the French no longer imposed it. The

British system has remained in North Rhine–Westphalia for the time being but has been eliminated elsewhere. The American zone went back to a modified version of the older system without too much difficulty.

Generally speaking, city government is not left to individual charters but is regulated by *Land* law along fairly uniform lines. There are, however, considerable differences between the various *Länder*.[51] Thus in Bavaria and Baden-Württemberg we find what corresponds to a mayor-council type of government, with the mayor in a strong position. He is elected directly by the people and in larger cities is a full-time official with a six-year term. In Hesse the same system prevails on the whole, but the law also permits a commission type of government; normally the *Bürgermeister* is elected by the council. In North Rhine–Westphalia, as already stated, the British type of system still prevails, but it is not likely to be adopted elsewhere and its future is uncertain.

A little more uniformity prevails on the district (*Kreis*) level. These districts are the main units of local government. In the case of more important towns, the town itself becomes a district, called urban district (*Stadtkreis*), in some ways comparable to the British county boroughs, and not subject to the jurisdiction of the district surrounding the city. The other, ordinary districts are called rural districts (*Landkreis*). There are no uniform rules about when a city is to become a *Stadtkreis*.

Except for North Rhine–Westphalia, the most important official of the *Kreis* is the rural councilor (*Landrat*), whose position is combined with that of the mayor in the *Stadtkreise*. The *Landrat* used to be appointed but is now elected by the legislative council of the *Kreis*, the *Kreistag*. Only in the area of the former French zone is he still appointed, subject however to confirmation by the *Kreistag*. The *Landrat* is the chief executive of the *Kreis*, who appoints all officials. His salary is paid by the *Land*, but that gives the *Land* government only limited control over him, as has been demonstrated by several unsuccessful attempts on the part of *Land* governments to get rid of a *Landrat*.

Unlike the city council, which meets frequently, the *Kreistag* meets only on occasion. In the interim, a committee of the *Kreistag*, the *Kreisausschuss*, carries on much of its business but also serves as something like a commission in a commission type of municipal administration.

Because the municipalities are frequently small and their problems many, they find it useful to undertake certain joint or cooperative operations. Inasmuch as this coordination takes place within the confines of the *Landkreis*, it is regulated by law although additional intermunicipal agreements may be made on a voluntary basis. Such agreements may involve joint handling of certain problems, contracting, purchasing, etc. A more permanent joint authority between municipalities has been established in certain *Länder* under the name of administrative office (*Amt*). These

[51] Roger H. Wells, "Local Government," in Litchfield and Associates, *op. cit.*, pp. 84–116.

Ämter are established for general governmental purposes, but there are also special, intermunicipal authorities for specific purposes, such as joint maintenance of utilities. These are called "common-purposes associations" (*Zweckverbände*).

The functions which local government has to perform are very extensive, especially on the city level. Apart from the usual tasks of planning, safety, health, and welfare, German municipalities usually own and run their utilities and transportation systems and maintain cultural institutions. A truly gigantic task has been added by the influx of refugees and expellees, who eventually numbered well over 12 million people in the German Federal Republic. These unfortunate people arrived with literally nothing to their names. Not only did they have to be housed and clothed but opportunities for work had to be found for them or, as often happened, they were encouraged to create such opportunities for themselves. Social problems of great gravity were created by the very mass of the influx, and these were all the more important as the habits of many of the refugees were quite different from those of the regular residents. There are now many towns and villages in which the refugees outnumber the original inhabitants and constitute the majority of the city administration. It is truly a miracle that under circumstances of this kind there has not been any major explosion.

The immense burden of administration and fiscal outlay which was placed on the shoulders of local government had the disadvantage that it encouraged encroachment by *Land* and federal authorities. It has meant that local government found its own sources of revenue insufficient and had to rely more and more on a share in *Land* and federal revenues. At the same time, local government has been made more rigid by the increasing number of mandatory tasks imposed upon it. In view of the emergency situation and the size of the problem, no other development could be expected. However, German local government is aware of these tendencies and watches them carefully, by no means in a spirit of submission.

H. THE GOVERNMENT OF WEST BERLIN

It is customary that capital cities of countries are administered differently from other municipalities. This also occurred in Berlin when in 1912 the city was detached, except for certain supervisory functions, from the province of Brandenburg and achieved the status of a province in its own right. The city charter of 1920 established the customary *Magistratsverfassung,* which implies something between a mayor-council and commission type of administration, especially as the position of the mayor was considerably strengthened later on. This city constitution also divided Berlin into twenty districts (*Bezirke*), each one with a charter similar to that of the city, and each with a district mayor and district council.

The Russians, who occupied the city first, revived the pre-Nazi constitution but infiltrated the government heavily with Communists. When the four-power occupation was established, the United States occupied six districts, the British four, the French two, and the Russians eight. Although the city constitution nominally remained in force, considerable divergences existed in the different sectors. This situation continued under the temporary charter of 1946.

The Russians walked out of the Allied Control Council on March 26, 1948, and on June 16, 1948, they left the *Komandatura.* Shortly thereafter the famous Berlin blockade began, and Communist pressure increased both inside and around the city. On June 23, 1948, a Communist mob stormed the city hall, which was located in the Russian sector; the city council moved to the Western sector, but the councilors of the Communist-controlled Socialist Unity party (SED) refused to go along; and the split into two Berlins became an accomplished fact.

In 1949 the three Western Allied Powers enacted a "little occupation" statute which was the Berlin corollary to the occupation statute for the German Federal Republic, and on August 29, 1950, the permanent constitution for Berlin was adopted.

Berlin is now both a city and a *Land,* somewhat comparable to the constitutions of Hamburg and Bremen. However, for reasons of international politics and out of fear of Russian retaliation, the Allies suspended that part of the constitution which would have incorporated Berlin into the German Federal Republic. Thus Berlin is a *Land* for internal purposes, but it is not fully a *Land* of the German Federal Republic. However, the German Federal Republic treats Berlin pretty much as if it were one of its *Länder,* and Berlin's hybrid status is underlined by the fact that it sends nonvoting delegates to both the *Bundestag* and the *Bundesrat.* Moreover, much of the city's income comes from federal government subsidies.

The constitution of the city-state of Berlin parallels that of other *Länder.* There is a popularly elected house of representatives composed of 200 members, of whom only 127 are actually functioning because 73 seats are reserved for East Berlin as a gesture to demonstrate that the West Berlin city government considers itself a government of the entire city. The house of representatives is elected by proportional representation for four years. It in turn elects the chief executive, who bears the title governing mayor (*Regierender Bürgermeister*). It also elects a cabinet of nineteen members. Mayor and cabinet must have the confidence of the house of representatives and must resign if that confidence is withdrawn.

Each district elects a district government called *Bezirksamt,* which is headed by a district mayor (*Bezirksbürgermeister*). These district mayors have established a council for mutual consultation and common action.

When the blockade ended the people of Berlin gave unmistakable proof of their solidarity with their government which, on December 3, 1950, was reelected by an unprecedented vote of 90.4 percent of the electorate. The same picture was repeated in all subsequent elections. This has enabled the city to stand firm against Russian and German Communist pressure during the many crises which have marked its recent history.

7

Government in Eastern Germany

It is difficult to imagine a greater contrast than that which exists between East and West Germany. While West Germany, the German Federal Republic, has been transformed into a democratic state with the usual accompaniments of such an institution—competing political parties, a press with divergent views, limitations imposed upon government by law and by the courts—Eastern Germany, now called the German Democratic Republic, has become a typical Soviet satellite which in every respect is following the model of the Soviet Union except that its "destalinization" is much less advanced.

In the economic sphere the contrast is equally drastic. While the living standard of West Germany is one of the highest in Europe, while its shops carry all conceivable goods in adequate supply, life in the Eastern zone is drab and impoverished. Only very limited amounts of consumers' goods are available for purchase, and both quality and variety are poor. In this region, which was once one of the chief food producers of Germany, many food varieties are now in short supply, although people do now have enough to eat. The mass exodus from the "Socialist paradise" continued until the Communists walled off East from West Berlin in August, 1961. The rest of the zonal border had become a death trap well before that. Even now, scarcely a week passes that some East German, including soldiers, does not try to escape despite grave risks. Many have been killed, maimed, or caught in the attempt. The East Germans are not able to vote freely as citizens of a democracy can, but they have already voted against their Communist regime—with their feet. Between 1954 and 1960, 1,500,000 persons fled from East to West Germany, half of them under twenty-five years old.[1]

Eastern Germany is the territory included in the Russian occupation zone. It thus does not include the areas east of the rivers Oder and Neisse, which are now administered as integral parts of Poland and the Soviet Union and from which nearly all German inhabitants have been expelled. As originally constituted, the Eastern zone, later the German Democratic Republic (*Deutsche Demokratische Republik,* DDR), comprised five *Länder:* Brandenburg, Mecklenburg, Saxony, Saxony-Anhalt, and Thuringia. The Eastern sector of Berlin is also included. The area comprises 30.2 percent of all German territory east of the Oder and Neisse Rivers. The population is 17 million (in contrast to the 55 million of West Germany).

It has never been and is probably not now Soviet policy to regard the East German state as a final creation. Rather Moscow expected to use it as a stepping-stone for the communization of all Germany. But, as has already been pointed out, this policy was a complete failure. Not only did Communism fail to attract West Germany, it failed even to attract strong support in East Germany, and the events of June, 1953, vividly proved that it requires only a small spark to disclose the real sentiments of the East German population.

This lack of popularity was first brought about by the conduct of the Russian soldiers in the waning months of the war and the initial period of occupation. It transferred easily to the native Communists and their cohorts, who carried out the orders of their Russian masters.

Nor is this situation likely to change. Although economic conditions have somewhat improved in the DDR, the gap between it and the Federal Republic is greater than ever, since progress in the West has been so much faster. What is probably much worse is the curious fact that the DDR has not even had its proper share of the destalinization and internal modifications which have made life somewhat more tolerable in the other East European countries, including the Soviet Union. In countries like Poland or Romania, a Communist regime which became more "Polish" or more "Rumanian" was obviously found more tolerable than one which was 100 percent Moscow-oriented. But while Poles may wish to be more "Polish," East Germans do not want to become more "East German"—they want

---

[1] These included 11,705 students, 4,600 physicians, 15,885 teachers, 738 university professors and lecturers, 15,536 engineers and technicians, and 41,300 farmers, both men and women. Between 1951 and 1960, 21,294 members of East Germany's armed forces and police fled to West Germany.

to be more "German." Hence the formula which tends to consolidate native Communist regimes elsewhere in eastern Europe would have the opposite effect in the DDR. This situation, curiously enough, creates a growing gap not only between the German Federal Republic and the DDR but also between the DDR and the other Communist countries of East Europe.

The political structure

Since the Communists could not have their way by persuasion, they set about to obtain it by force. The first avenue to that goal was their use of the political parties. It has already been described how the Communists forced the fusion of the much larger Social Democratic party with them into the Socialist Unity party of Germany (*Sozialistische Einheitspartei Deutschlands,* SED) although the great majority of the Social Democratic rank and file disliked the idea. The SED became the chosen instrument of the Soviet Military Administration and was quickly purged of the majority of Social Democratic holdovers. Even those Social Democratic leaders who had been completely loyal to the Communists in forcing the fusion were eliminated, including men like Max Fechner, who as Minister of Justice did not hesitate to persecute his erstwhile comrades in arms.[2] Only Otto Grotewohl, chief (former) Social Democratic architect of the fusion, held out in isolated splendor until his death in 1965, but he had long been reduced to the position of a figurehead.

A different approach was used toward the other parties. When the Soviet Military Administration licensed the Communists and the Social Democrats in 1946 (before the fusion) it also licensed the Christian Democratic Union and the Liberal Democratic party, the latter originally the Eastern version of the Free Democratic party. But beginning in 1946 these parties were subjected to increasing pressure and eventually terror. Registration and Soviet permission to organize were frequently withheld or delayed, paper allocation to non-SED newspapers was curtailed. When these relatively mild methods did not succeed and the non-Communist parties held their own surprisingly well, more drastic methods were used. More and more non-Communist party leaders would disappear. The parties were forced to purge themselves of all officers who failed to do the Soviet or SED bidding. Others again found their salvation in flight. Finally both the CDU and the LDP degenerated into mere instruments of Communist policy, to be used as the SED leaders saw fit. There is neither similarity nor contact between these shadow groups and their former sister parties in Western Europe. Nor is there any similarity between them and political parties as that term is generally understood.

The claim of these nominal "parties" to independent existence eventually became such a farce that the SED found it desirable to found two more parties which were to appeal especially to former Nazis. They were the National Democratic party

---

[2] Fechner was "liquidated" after the June, 1953, anti-Communist uprising.

and the Democratic Peasant party. In both cases the Communist wire pullers did not even bother to go through the motions of a genuine party establishment. The parties were organized from the top down by experienced SED bureaucrats with no more justification than "thousands and thousands of signatures," collected everywhere in the usual manner, "demanding the establishment of these parties."[3]

In addition to these "parties," Eastern Germany has a number of so-called "mass organizations." They are all solidly SED-controlled and are further instruments of Communist policy. There is the Free German Trade Union Federation (*Freie deutsche Gewerkschaftsbund,* FDGB). Like all Communist trade unions in Communist-controlled countries, this is a compulsory organization comparable to the Nazi "Labor Front." It is not a bargaining agent, since wages and conditions of work are fixed by the planning agencies. It is a political tool designed to mobilize the workers for special tasks. Another virtually compulsory organization is the Free German Youth (*Freie deutsche Jugend,* FDJ), the main instrument of the Communist leaders to educate youth in their image. In its intensely political and parliamentary training the FDJ is the spit and image of the Hitler Youth. There is also the Democratic League of Women (*Demokratischer Frauenbund Deutschlands,* DFD) which is the East German branch of a well-known international Communist women's organization whose true nature is often thinly camouflaged in other countries.

The coordination of these parties and mass organizations is the task of the National Front, another SED-dominated organization. Its prototype can or could be found in all the Soviet satellite countries, serving as a transition from the multiparty system to the one-party, totalitarian state. Actually, the National Front is merely a control device of the SED.

The SED's organization is very similar to that of the Communist party of the Soviet Union with all decisions being vested in the top. Moscow-trained Walter Ulbricht is the real leader of the SED and consequently of East Germany. But these things may change rapidly, within the hour, for neither Ulbricht nor Grotewohl nor any other German Communist really directs the SED. That direction lies neither in East Berlin nor in Pankow[4] but in Moscow.

The governmental structure

As early as July 27, 1945, Marshal Zhukov, then chief of the Soviet Military Administration in Germany, established twelve German central agencies. This was obviously an attempt to create Soviet-sponsored and Communist-infiltrated all-German government departments.[5] French opposition to any form of German cen-

---

[3] Richard M. Scammon, "Political Parties," in Litchfield and Associates, *op. cit.,* pp. 495–496. The best work on East Germany is J. P. Nettl, *The Eastern Zone and Soviet Policy in Germany, 1945–50,* London, 1951.
[4] Seat of the East German government.
[5] Kurt Glaser, "Governments of Soviet Germany," in Litchfield and Associates, *op. cit.,* p. 158.

tral government is primarily responsible for frustrating this scheme. On a zone-wide level these central agencies served as planning groups while orders were actually transmitted directly to the *Länder* administrations by the Soviet Military Administration.

These agencies exercised relatively little control. In 1947, when it became clear that the Western powers were going ahead with the consolidation of their zones regardless of Soviet objection, an Economic Commission was established which was to take tighter control but actually failed to function in that manner. Renamed German Economic Commission in 1948, it took on considerable administrative and legislative power. By the use of the newly drafted Economic Penal Law and the Requisition Law, the German Economic Commission (DWK) undertook the economic communization of the country, the expropriation of private enterprise, and the introduction of measures such as piecework in order to increase production. The expropriated industries and businesses in turn were combined into huge state-owned trusts.

Apart from economic problems, interior administration, justice, and education were administered by other central agencies, which, however, did not possess the vast powers of the German Economic Commission. Yet they held monthly meetings with the *Land* ministers, and their decisions, which actually emanated from the SED leaderships, were considered binding under the well-known Communist principle of "democratic centralism" by which the higher level unconditionally imposes its will on the lower one. By this device one-party rule and centralism were actually established while there was still the outward form of a multiparty system and federalism.

While the Council of Foreign Ministers was meeting in London for the purpose of finding a solution for the German problem, the central committee of the SED passed a resolution on November 26, 1947, calling for a "German People's Congress" (*Volkskongress*). It met in Berlin on December 6. Its delegates represented the Communist-dominated parties of the East as well as the mass organizations. There were also delegates from the West, but most of them represented either the Communist party or fellow travelers. At any rate the SED possessed absolute control and passed a resolution which was to be presented to the four Foreign Ministers. However, the Western Foreign Ministers refused to receive it.

In the spring of 1948 a second People's Congress met in Berlin and prepared the ground for a popular initiative in which signatures were collected on petitions for German unity.[6] A smaller committee, called People's Council (*Volksrat*), was elected by the Congress and posed as a kind of government, but its chief function was propaganda directed mainly against attempts to establish a government and a constitution for West Germany. The People's Council also proceeded to draft a constitution which was completed the same year. Actually this draft originated in

---

[6] H. B. Cox, "Establishment of the Soviet-sponsored East German Republic," *Department of State Bulletin,* Nov. 21, 1949, pp. 761–764.

the SED and was presented by Grotewohl. Final action on the constitution was postponed until the establishment of the German Federal (Bonn) Republic in order to place the blame for the split on the West.

Elections for a third People's Congress were held in May, 1949. The single slate of delegates—Soviet style—was presented to the people after a high-pressure propaganda campaign directed against widespread dissatisfaction with the constitutional draft. In spite of the pressure, the removal and arrest of opposition leaders, and the curb on any anti-Communist activities, 40 percent of the voters dared to reject the slate of delegates. The Congress, nevertheless, convened and ratified the draft constitution.

"Spontaneous appeals" and "demands" broke out all over Eastern Germany on October 2, 1949, which had been proclaimed "World Peace Day," calling for an all-German independent government. The authorities "acceded." The People's Council convened five days later and transformed itself into a People's Chamber (*Volkskammer*) to which the Soviet authorities transferred a number of administrative functions. The People's Chamber then proceeded to enact a number of laws which declared the Constitution to be in force and laid down rules for the appointment of a government as well as of *Länder* governments. Grotewohl was elected Minister-President, Ulbricht his deputy. The Soviet Military Administration transferred many of its functions to the German authorities, at least in theory, and on October 12, 1949, the structure of the East German State, now called German Democratic Republic (*Deutsche demokratische Republik,* DDR) was completed. Wilhelm Pieck, cofounder of the German Communist party in 1918, was elected President of the Republic, while Otto Grotewohl and Walter Ulbricht were elected co-chairmen of the government.

The Constitution of the DDR is centralist rather than federalist. The national parliament has the power to change *Land* boundaries at will, and the constitutional framework of the *Länder* (now abolished) was prescribed in the DDR Constitution. The national government could work through *Land* administrations or establish its own agencies. Where it did the former, it had an unlimited right of control and direction. It could also send its own emissaries into any *Land* agency with the power to give orders.

The parliament of the DDR is composed of the People's Chamber (*Volkskammer*), which has 400 members elected by proportional representation, and a Chamber of States (*Länderkammer*) whose members were elected by the *Landtage* from among their own members. But the *Länder* were abolished in the DDR, being replaced by fifteen regions (*Bezirke*), including East Berlin. The Chamber of States was dropped in 1952. A single slate of delegates was presented by the National Front and then adopted by the people in a Soviet-style polling process. Even under these circumstances the rulers did not feel entirely at ease, and in *Volkskammer* elections, the government exerted great pressure on the voters, demanding that they refrain from going into a voting booth and instead mark their ballots openly. It has been made abundantly clear that anyone going into a booth would be suspected of voting against the single slate of candidates and those few who dare to defy the government are often subject to arrest later on.

As a matter of fact, in most polling places there was no voting booth at all. The vote of 99.6 percent in favor of the National Front slate is therefore without significance. Most significant was the appeal of the city administration of West Berlin addressed to the people of the Soviet sector urging all those who were opposed to the regime in the East zone to mail the stubs of their September, 1950, ration books to the West Berlin administration. Although the Eastern government promised a special clothing ration in exchange for the stubs, more than 400,000 of the 600,000 voters of East Berlin sent in their stubs, or letters explaining that the stubs had been destroyed.[7]

The independence and irremovability of judges are not recognized, and there is a specific denial of the right of courts to review the constitutionality of laws.

The Constitution of the German Democratic Republic, like that of the Soviet Union, gives very little idea of how government is actually conducted. The federal structure of the state, which was only nominal to begin with, was made even more problematical by the introduction of central government commissioners (*Inspekteure*) very much on the model of the *Reichstatthalter* of Hitler Germany. Then in the summer of 1952 a law dissolved the five traditional *Länder* and replaced them by fifteen administrative districts. Without the Constitution having been amended in a formal way, the last outward vestige of federalism was thus removed and complete centralism instituted. This is further illustrated by the dissolution of the provincial committees of the East German political parties in favor of a more centralized party administration. The absolute dictatorship of the Communist rulers manifests itself in the customary *modus operandi* of totalitarian regimes: secret political police, imprisonment without trial or with mock trial, and concentration camps. Former Minister of State Security, General Wilhelm Zaisser, once known as General Gomez of Spanish Civil War ill fame, built up the paramilitary People's Police (*Volkspolizei,* Vopo), who even by their outward appearance remind one strikingly of the SS Elite Guard of Nazi days. Actually there are two distinct Vopo organizations. There is the blue-uniformed Vopo which carries out regular police duties and the so-called "garrisoned People's Police" (*Kasernierte Volkspolizei*) in Russian-style uniforms, which is a regular army. Although Zaisser was purged after the June, 1953, uprising, the regime has continued its oppressive policies. Indicative thereof is the dreaded law on the Defense of Peace of December 16, 1950,[8] which is so worded as to make any expression critical of the government and its policy punishable by up to life imprisonment and even death.

As in all totalitarian regimes, the administration of justice is that branch in which the inhuman nature of the system reveals itself most clearly. That the Pro-

---

[7] Glaser, *op. cit.,* p. 182.
[8] For the text of this law see *American Journal of International Law,* Vol. XLVI (1952), supplement, pp. 99–101. Practically identical laws were adopted by the U.S.S.R. and all satellites.

curator-General has the vast power which characterizes his position in the Soviet Union and that the secret police are all-powerful goes without saying. In addition the regular judiciary has been virtually abolished, as nearly all positions of judges and prosecutors have been taken by "people's judges" who receive little training in the law but a great deal of training in Marxism-Leninism and a special form of social science. They are often workers who have been trained in courses at special short-term academies. Best-known is the Walter Ulbricht Academy for Political and Legal Sciences.

Such democratic prejudices as the independence and irremovability of judges have, of course, no place in this Communist dictatorship. Judges are appointed for three years but may be dismissed whenever superior authority deems that necessary. A judge who does not impose the sentence desired "upstairs" is frequently punished, thus restoring a state of affairs which existed in the last years of the Nazi regime.

The economic sector of East Germany presents the customary picture of a Communist country with a completely nationalized industry. Whatever free enterprise existed has been successfully squeezed out, and the few independent business men who did not surrender voluntarily were either arrested or forced to flee to West Germany. The few private owners of small enterprises which remain are tightly controlled and have been largely forced into bogus 50–50 partnerships with the state. Sabotage trials await those who do not conform willingly enough. The workers are organized in the Free German Trade Union Federation (*Freie deutsche Gewerksschaftsbund*), the name once borne by the free trade unions of the Weimar Republic. But they are merely an adjunct of the SED organization, and the rulers of East Germany find it difficult to forget that in the 1953 uprising the workers of East Germany were in the forefront of the rebellion against the "worker's paradise."

It is not surprising that the agricultural sector in the DDR is the same total failure that it is in all Communist countries. The more the agriculture becomes collectivized, the worse it gets. The systematic expropriation and collectivization of agriculture was declared officially concluded in April, 1960. According to the DDR's Ministry of Agriculture, there had been established 19,345 "agricultural production cooperatives" (*Landwirtschaftliche Produktionsgenossenschaften,* LPG) with 945,000 members. The result, as always under such circumstances, has been an unending series of shortages, rationing, and a high cost of living, apart from the already mentioned wholesale flight of farm families.

In the industrial sector, great emphasis was placed on heavy industry, with the result that production rose about 150 percent from 1950 to 1960, at the expense and neglect of consumer goods. However, the DDR has become the most important supplier of machinery in the Eastern bloc. This constitutes progress, which is beginning to show some beneficial effects on living standards, but it is very little compared with the far greater progress achieved in the West. No Western visitor, touring the DDR's "showcase," East Berlin, or Leipzig at fair time, can fail to be startled by the enormous contrast between East and West, by the poverty, drabness, and emptiness of the East, and by the hopeless attitudes of its inhabitants, which contrast unfavorably even with those found elsewhere in the Communist East.

In spite of the complete paraphernalia of the totalitarian state, the so-called German Democratic Republic is nevertheless weak because it has not a single group of any size on which it can really rely. While the Soviet regime in the U.S.S.R. created an entirely new bureaucracy on which its control is primarily based, the government of the DDR has no equivalent. The bureaucracy of the state, the officers' corps of the police and paramilitary formations, even the staff of the SED itself, are permeated by bourgeois elements who, while not in open opposition, are nevertheless there to worry those in power.[9] The working class, which the regime has so strenuously tried to court, gave drastic evidence of its hostility to the regime in the bitter uprisings of the summer of 1953, which engulfed every industrial center in the entire Eastern zone of Germany. Although drastically repressive measures were taken under the fanatical guidance of the former Minister of Justice, Hilde Benjamin, the regime cannot be under any possible illusion about its lack of popular support. Even in a dictatorship, this is a matter of grave concern. However, the government of the DDR does not exist in its own right but as a satellite of the Soviet Union, by whose support alone it can maintain itself. The future of the DDR is therefore not merely a German problem but one which involves the entire complex of East-West relationships.

[9] Nettl, *op. cit.*, p. 312.

8

Germany and the world

More than twenty years have passed since the Nazi regime disappeared in the death and fire which it had created. The physical and psychological devastation of Germany was indescribable. For the first time in history, Germans had nothing to say about the future of their country. Many Germans doubted that it had a future or that it had become anything but a geographic and historical notion.

The road back has been swifter and more successful than anyone could have dreamed. Today Germany, the German Federal Republic, not only is restored physically and spiritually, but has regained a firm and respected place in the family of nations. Suspicions and apprehensions based on an unsavory past which the world will not easily forget, still exist; how could it be otherwise? Yet half the German population has no, or virtually no, recollection of the Hitler regime and can therefore not be expected to carry a sense of personal guilt. Nobody can or should pretend that the period 1933 to 1945 did not happen or that it was not as ghastly as in fact it was. Yet, as an American ambassador to Germany said in 1965:[1]

> The time has come, I say, for the world to make up its mind about the Germans. . . . For two decades the German goal has been to earn the world's acceptance. The Germans have worked hard for it. They expected that if they made good they could win from the world a final verdict in their favor. They have made progress, but what are their gains worth if the world takes all the Federal Republic offers— and still denies them the one thing they want most? If the world should ever force on the Germans the conviction that nothing they can do can ever gain them full acceptance—that there is no further use in their trying—then it will not be the Germans only who are the losers.

One should not expect the rest of the world simply to accept the say-so of the Germans. More evidence than that is clearly needed. But neither do the people of the world, and particularly of the West, have a moral right to act as though nothing has happened since 1945, as though the present were nothing more than the unbroken continuation of a twenty-year-old past. In the appraisal of any contemporary situation, men may legitimately differ. But certain facts stand out clearly.

Twenty years after the formation of the Weimar government, German democracy was dead, lost in the inflation of the Depression, in the fires of the *Reichstag,* and in the overthrow of the Versailles Treaty. The world stood poised on the brink of the worst war in modern history. Twenty years after the formation of the Bonn government, the German Federal Republic stands as a monument to the creative abilities of men. In every walk of life the contrasts between the Bonn and Weimar experiences are startling.

The lessons of the past have not gone unnoticed. The leading men of Bonn are profoundly, even painfully, aware of many of the mistakes of the past. Not all have been remedied. Not all Germans have fully accepted democracy, although few are implacably hostile. But the Bonn government and the Federal Constitutional Court have shown themselves alert to the danger of totalitarian activities. Among the German people, too, transformations are in evidence. There is a far greater readiness to challenge the authority of the state in the courts and elsewhere than was the custom in former days, and although broad civic activities and citizens' participation in public affairs in and out of parties are still the exception rather than the rule, their volume and intensity appear to be on the increase. Given time and stability, there is every reason to believe that these trends will continue.

The German Federal Republic was fortunate in that it encountered within its own boundaries none of the bitter resentments and hatreds which the Weimar Republic experienced. Once again democracy has come to the German people as a

---

[1] George C. McGhee, "A Time for Decision," address in Heidelberg, May 30, 1965, published in the *Department of State Bulletin,* July 26, 1965, pp. 157–160.

result of external events, not of its own achievements. Hence there is no folklore surrounding it, there is no German George Washington, no German Garibaldi or Mazzini, nor is there a German *Marseillaise*. German democracy was established because there was no alternative and no resistance; there was no mass conversion either. But it is quite possible that this new institution has become more solidly established in that form than if it had been the result of violent internal cleavages, of dramatic victories and defeats.

The German Federal Republic has been fortunate to have developed distinguished leaders and, on the whole, sensible and reasonable politicians and administrators who have administered the new Republic well. If the system had worked badly, the near-total absence of resistance to it would not have lasted long.

Germany is also fortunate in its new social structure. Although there are great differences in wealth, there is no real poverty. There are no really fundamentally opposed social forces, and the political parties are not irreconcilable; also they represent more and more a cross-section of the population rather than specific classes, groups, or regions.

Yet despite its progress and solidarity, Germany suffers from some serious problems. Internally it is experiencing a "generation break" greater than is normal. The factors that have brought this about are various. German youth never really received a satisfactory explanation of their country's recent past nor of some of the actions of their elders. This has intensified a feeling of rootlessness and alienation which otherwise might be considered standard for people of this age.

Also, while Germany's youth is welcomed into the political parties and a number of younger men have recently come to prominence,[2] politics remains the game of the older generation, with German politicians having the oldest average age in Europe. This fact helps to stigmatize politics as a dirty game played by the last generation. Therefore young men are even more reluctant to lower their standards by entering it, and thus a vicious circle is created in which politics remains the preserve of older men.

The alternative to the give-and-take of politics is naturally the purity of ideas unattached to the necessity for action. Possibly the most critical facet of the generation break is that Germany's young people have taken to one idea with particular enthusiasm and are in danger of being disappointed in it. This is the idea of a united Europe. There are several reasons why the European idea should have aroused such resonance in Germany, especially among the young. The reaction against the excessive, insane nationalism of the Nazi period created a desire for a new community to which loyalty could be attached. This is furthered by the feeling (now lessening) that the Federal Republic is a geographical and administrative entity rather than an emotional reality like Germany or Berlin. Finally, a somewhat contradictory idea, but one which leads in the same direction, is the realiza-

[2] Like Gerhard Stoltenberg, born 1928, appointed Minister of Scientific Research in 1965.

tion that the age of the superpowers has dawned and that Germany needs to be a part of something larger than itself if it is not to stagnate.

Unfortunately, Europe's move toward unity, which only a few years ago seemed secure, has become uncertain and at times even at best has been little more than treading water. This has led to a kind of "agonizing reappraisal" by many Germans, old and young, without any concrete results being produced other than uncertainty over the future.

This uncertainty is the result not only of the idealism of German youth but also of the unusually dependent condition in which Germany finds itself vis-à-vis its allies. This is seen in the realm of defense, where national planning has largely given way to joint planning, where the old general staff has disappeared to be replaced by the NATO general staff, and where ultimately German security must depend on the massive deterrent power of the United States.

By the same token, Germany has remained a strong partisan of European integration and of the European Communities, the Coal and Steel Community (Schuman Plan), the European Atomic Energy Community (EURATOM), and the European Economic Community (Common Market). Through these Germany has a far better chance of reaching its political and economic objectives than if it were to pursue purely national goals.

Beyond this, Germany has based its foremost goal, that of reunification, on its ties with a strong and united West. German leaders have staked their prestige and their country's future on the policies of nations which, while subject to German influence, are not subject to German control. Even when these allies, particularly the United States, are deeply sympathetic to German desires, they cannot be expected to make reunification the touchstone of all their foreign policy. Nor, for the present, are there any concrete steps which the allies could take in that direction.

All this does not diminish Germany's adherence to the Atlantic family of free nations, its policy being based both on national interest and on the needs of its own people (especially the young) for a new sense of identity. But this does make for a somewhat more delicate relationship, and this in turn makes it particularly imperative that Germany be accorded a place of equality and full partnership in both the European and Atlantic spheres. Obviously, this equality means more than just legal equality. It means essentially having a voice equal to that of countries of comparable population, size, and economic enterprise, such as Great Britain and France. It also means steady progress toward the time when German political or economic action is examined by the world on its merits and not viewed with apprehension merely because it is German.

If Germany were to be denied this place of full partnership, if the Germans were to come to the conclusion that they are to remain a suspect country no matter what they do, then the foundations of the Federal Republic might well be called into doubt. It is most unlikely that Germany would turn back to any form of Nazism, for the conditions of the world and of Germany are immensely changed since 1933. But even without that danger, if Germany were to choose to go adventuring, if in following nationalistic policies for its reunification (as was once debated) Germany were to turn its face and its concerns inward, the dangers to the stability and security of Europe would be increased a hundredfold.

Germany's start has been tremendous. More than just the start of a stable democratic regime has been made. But the course is far from run. The finish will depend at least as much on Germany's partners in the West as on the will and foresight of the German people.

part 4

The Union of Soviet Socialist Republics

No single man makes history. History cannot be seen, just as one cannot see grass growing. Wars and revolutions, kings and Robes-pierres, are history's organic agents, its yeast. But revolutions are made by fanatical men of action with one-track minds, geniuses in their ability to confine themselves to a limited field. They overturn the old order in a few hours or days, the whole upheaval takes a few weeks or at most years, but the fanatical spirit that inspired the upheavals is worshipped for decades thereafter, for centuries.

Boris Pasternak, Doctor Zhivago

In these years of the nuclear age, of space exploits, and of an "on again, off again" cold war, it is hardly necessary to emphasize the great importance of the Soviet Union, one of the two or three greatest powers in the world. Much if not everything may depend on our ability to understand correctly how the U.S.S.R. operates and what makes it tick.

Unfortunately such understanding is handicapped by a number of difficulties, for even though that vast country is no longer entirely an enigma or a riddle, it still has many elements of mystery. We have learned much, and we can piece together more. Certainly the pattern of Soviet power and policy can be ascertained with a fair degree of accuracy. But it is extraordinarily difficult to obtain reliable details even on major subjects.

We know, for instance, that all policy decisions are made by the leadership of the Communist party assembled in the Politburo, but we do not know for certain how the Politburo arrives at its decisions. Even when Stalin was alive, we were not quite sure to what extent he predominated in its deliberations, although it has since been disclosed by his successors that his word was indeed the final one. This pattern has been repeated under all Stalin's successors; long after the fact, we may learn how a decision was arrived at, but at this time the process of decision making remains a closely guarded secret. So too does the standing of many of the top members of the Politburo. Particularly during periods of transition, such as that following Lenin's and Stalin's deaths, the West was treated to the spectacle of apparently powerful men losing their positions and sometimes their lives almost overnight. Although less frequent, the same thing has happened when the person in power sought to strengthen his position. This gives rise to constant questioning about the nature and outlook of the Soviet government. Among the many difficulties which beset East-West relations and negotiations, not one of the least is this uncertainty about the nature of Soviet leadership.

Accurate and reliable answers to these and many other questions would greatly facilitate a better understanding of the U.S.S.R., because secrecy breeds fear, apprehension, and eventually hatred. The ancient Romans, wise in matters of state, understood this when they said *"damnant quod non intelligunt"* (they condemn what they do not understand).

But if we are inadequately informed about the Soviet Union, a major share of responsibility must be placed at the door of the Soviet government itself. A veil of secrecy surrounds even the most commonplace activities. No critical analysis of Soviet institutions or policy ever emerges from the Soviet Union except when the leaders themselves choose to express their displeasure concerning some aspect of the country's development or encourage such expression through their carefully controlled means of communication by selected spokesmen. All studies written by Soviet scholars present every phase of the regime in the most glowing colors, and although individuals may be criticized—after their ouster or reprimand has already been decided on by higher authority—the wisdom of policy and the excellence of major institutions have seldom been questioned. Foreign scholars are given no opportunity to gather detailed on-the-spot information except for very limited structural data on a low level, or if they study langauge or literature. Cultural exchanges produce practically no pertinent data in the social sciences from Soviet scholars.

It is easy enough to gather firsthand information in Great Britain or France; even in Nazi Germany it was possible for a foreign scholar to get about reasonably unmolested and to subject the regime and its governmental machinery to some scrutiny on the spot. But no such opportunities exist in the Soviet Union, where the movements of natives and especially of foreigners are strictly controlled and where occasional arrests of Western scholars, like that of Frederick C. Barghoorn in 1963, serve as a warning against inquisitiveness. That this attitude of excessive secrecy has its origins in the history of tsarist Russia and in the necessarily conspiratorial beginnings of the Communist party is not to be denied. But whether or not the Soviet government has good and sufficient reasons for its attitude, the fact remains that its official acts and attitude do not facilitate a better understanding of the U.S.S.R.

The foreign scholar and observer must therefore attempt to piece together a picture from three principal sources of information:

1. Official documents, journals, and newspapers. There is much valuable material here but it is difficult to use. No Soviet citizen is allowed to criticize basic policy decisions and is quickly called to order if he does. However, for reasons of efficiency, criticism of local and low-level officials is permitted. This may say much about the way in which a policy is working or the way living conditions are developing. Finally, when there are splits in the top leadership, this may be revealed, very obliquely, in contradictory articles in the leading journals. Such evidence is obviously shaky, and as one reaches the top of the Soviet power structure, it becomes exceedingly limited.

2. The "I was there" books written by foreigners. These are of very limited usefulness. Foreigners, as mentioned above, are given very little opportunity to conduct unescorted investigations.[1] Moreover, most of these writers are foreign correspondents, and few correspondents are trained political scientists or are otherwise equipped to undertake a detailed study of government. They are more likely to report general impressions and revealing personal experiences, which are very valuable for an understanding of the Russian scene but which are necessarily a far cry from a thorough, professional study. Moreover, some of these books contain some fantastic pieces of misinformation, which the author could easily have corrected by checking with his nearest public library and which cast some doubt on his entire work.[2]

3. The increasing number of refugees from the Soviet Union. There have always been some, but the aftermath of the war has supplied them in abun-

---

[1] See, for instance, Robert Magidoff, *In Anger and Pity,* New York, 1949. On this point all foreign correspondents are in agreement.
[2] A most amusing collection of such errors may be found in D. J. Dallin, *The Real Soviet Russia* (trans. by J. Shaplen), New Haven, Conn., 1944, pp. 1–9.

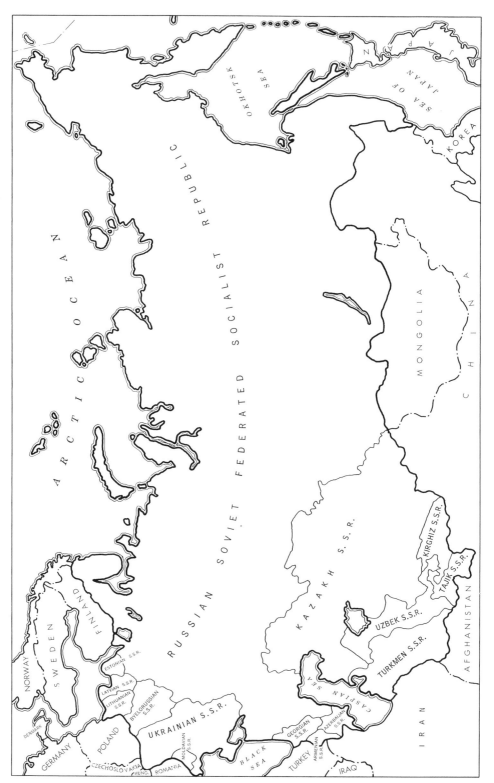

ARCTIC OCEAN

OKHOTSK SEA

SEA OF JAPAN

JAPAN

KOREA

RUSSIAN SOVIET FEDERATED SOCIALIST REPUBLIC

MONGOLIA

CHINA

NORWAY

SWEDEN

FINLAND

DENMARK

ESTONIAN S.S.R.

LATVIAN S.S.R.

LITHUANIAN S.S.R.

BYELORUSSIAN S.S.R.

GERMANY

POLAND

UKRAINIAN S.S.R.

CZECHOSLOVAKIA

HUNG.

ROMANIA

MOLDAVIAN S.S.R.

BLACK SEA

TURKEY

GEORGIAN S.S.R.

ARMENIAN S.S.R.

AZERBAIJAN S.S.R.

CASPIAN SEA

IRAQ

KAZAKH S.S.R.

KIRGHIZ S.S.R.

TAJIK S.S.R.

UZBEK S.S.R.

TURKMEN S.S.R.

IRAN

AFGHANISTAN

508

dant quantities. They are a very useful source, especially since their large number makes careful cross-checking possible. But three factors limit their usefulness: all of them are partisans; the picture they paint is done in unrelieved black, which sometimes fails to render a complete picture; and few of them were in positions where they had an opportunity to study the inner workings of the Soviet government. In fact, no Soviet official of top stature has fled to the Western side, and such is the centralization of control in the Soviet Union that an observer must be very near the top in order to get an over-all picture; there has as yet been no Russian Rudolf Hess.

Among secondary sources we find a growing number of studies undertaken by research institutions and scholars dedicated to the interpretation and analysis of available information and documents. Under the circumstances these studies often represent the most valuable source of information, but their accuracy and completeness are sometimes difficult to check.[3]

A major difficulty in utilizing these various sources of information lies in the intense partisanship which any discussion about Russia is likely to arouse. The Russian Revolution, like the earlier French Revolution, was not a purely national phenomenon but had and is still having repercussions in every country. Moreover, the ties between the Soviet Union and the Communist parties of all countries carry the controversy right into the discussion of domestic issues; hence the pervasiveness of the problem. Sober and balanced observations are even more difficult in such an atmosphere because there are extremists on both sides. To the Communist and Soviet sympathizers, all critical remarks about their ideal appear the result of stupidity, or more likely of fiendish design and propaganda. Facts which do not fit into their concept are simply ignored. Thus, despite the fact that overwhelming and carefully cross-checked information is available about the vast extent of forced labor in the Soviet Union, the "faithful" used to declare with a straight face and usually with conviction that such assertions were lies or that forced-labor camps were merely educational institutions, in which inmates received excellent treatment. The fact that the presence and the horror of such camps have now been revealed by bona fide Soviet writers and former inmates[4] seems hardly to have embarrassed them.

On the other side are those to whom nothing but evil can come from the U.S.S.R. and in whose view anybody who stated objectively that there had been considerable Soviet successes, as in the nationality question, would immediately fall under a shadow and be quickly suspected of being a card-carrying member of the

[3] Exceptionally valuable source material and commentary can be found in the bimonthly journal, *Problems of Communism*, published by the U.S. Information Office. One does not ordinarily look to government agencies of any country as publishers of objective and very scholarly material, but this periodical is an outstanding exception. Excellent also is the British periodical, *Survey*, a journal of Soviet and East European studies.

[4] *One Day in the Life of Ivan Denisovich* (trans. by Ralph Parker), New York, 1963, is one such illuminating book.

Communist party. The analyst must therefore expect attacks from both sides unless he confines himself to a purely descriptive role and refrains from any attempt at an explanation, which approach would make the whole exercise meaningless.

There is also the difficulty caused by the use of confusing terminology. The decisive element in the government of the Soviet Union is the Communist party, but there is little similarity between the parties which we discussed in the first three parts of this book and the Communist party of the Soviet Union. The former are parties of the masses, while the Communist party of the U.S.S.R. is a relatively small, elite organization. Moreover, there are many parties in the West, while the Communist party of the Soviet Union has a complete monopoly.

Even more controversial has been the use of the term "democracy," by which entirely different things are meant in the West and in the Soviet orbit.

Finally there are the theoretical aspects of the regime. Although the political theory of the Soviet Union has proved flexible and adjustable to changing conditions, the Soviet approach to all questions is dominated by the political theory of Marx, Lenin, and Stalin. No understanding of their country is remotely possible without a thorough comprehension of this theory, its methods, and its language. Unhappily, many Americans are unwilling to accept this point, because they are not theory-minded themselves and have long accepted the highly doubtful conclusion that all people are alike; consequently, since they do not hold with theory, they are prone to dismiss it as "propaganda" or worse and laugh it off as "silly." No greater error could be made.

Last, but not least, it is difficult to regard the U.S.S.R. as merely another country, though an immensely powerful and aggressive one. For the U.S.S.R. is also the center, the head, and the heart of a gigantic secular "world church" whose militant adherents all over the world are dedicated to it with fierce and unflinching devotion. This has not basically changed although the complete monolithism of the Stalinist period is a thing of the past and although Communist parties in Eastern Europe, especially in Romania, have often conducted policies not wholly countenanced by Moscow. And then the fierce Sino-Soviet[5] conflict has divided world Communism, but Moscow appears to be gaining the upper hand.

The actions of the Soviet Union and of its leaders must therefore be judged not solely in the light of its national interest, though that may predominate, but also in the light of this quasi-religious conviction of and dedication to a mission which encompasses the earth. What we have before us is thus not only a state, but also a wider force which a noted writer has, not inaccurately, called "the Islam of the twentieth century."[6]

---

[5] "Sino-Russian" would be a much better expression from a grammatical point of view but "Sino-Soviet" has become deeply ingrained, and I will therefore use it from here on.
[6] Jules Monnerot, *Sociologie du Communisme,* Paris, 1949, p. 10.

1

Historical antecedents

Isolation from the West

The historian Kliuchevsky[1] has stated that three elements dominated the early history of Russia: the steppe with its vast horizon, its dreamy atmosphere, and its constant danger; the great forest, which was home to most of Russia's early population and which forced them to eke out a miserable living at hard labor; and the rivers, the main highways of early days, the scene of constant movement. It is significant that these water roads lead away from Europe, chiefly to the Black Sea. And indeed Russia was unknown and considered to be a country of eternal darkness when ancient Greece and Rome were in bloom, and Russia has therefore no part in

[1] Vasily Kliuchevsky, *A History of Russia* (trans. by Hogarth), London, 1911–1931, Vol. I, pp. 2*ff*. See also G. Vernadsky, *Political and Diplomatic History of Russia,* Boston, 1936, pp. 25–36, and *History of Russia,* New Haven, Conn., 1951, 3d ed., pp. 1–59; Sir Bernard Pares, *A History of Russia,* New York, 1946, 4th ed., pp. 3–24; and Anatole G. Mazour, *Russia, Past and Present,* New York, 1951, pp. 1–22.

the heritage of Greco-Roman culture which is the foundation of Western civilization. There was some contact with the West later, but not until the beginning of the eighteenth century was that contact vital and constant to Russia.

Both historically and physically Russia found itself drawn both east and west. To the tensions caused by this pull were added those of the size and diversity of the Russian land mass and the growing inability of the tsarist[2] form of government to respond to the needs of the nineteenth and twentieth centuries. Russia's borders touched both China and Germany, both Afghanistan and Sweden. Russia's population included more than 100 nationalities and ran the cultural gamut from the Western urbanity of St. Petersburg to the barbarity of some of the tribes of the steppes. It was a country, remarked the historian Von Laue, "as vast as the face of the moon . . . and much of its territory was as useless as the moon."[3]

The linchpin in the system was the figure of the tsar. It was the tsars who had welded the country together and who personified it, who protected it from invasion, and who had raised it to the status of a great power. Surrounding and upholding the tsar were the aristocracy and the bureaucracy, and to a certain extent the church. Over time, the aloofness of these bodies, their lack of responsibility to those below them, and a certain sense of being unable to really change the character of the masses, bred arbitrariness and the corruption that comes with omnipotence.

Essentially, the system was so centralized that it became nearly immobile, particularly as it attempted to modernize and to respond to the demands of the modern era. Because the government was the principal mover, it became the sole mover. Without initiative from the center, little would change. Even with a strong ruler change was difficult because of the resistance of aristocracy, or of bureaucracy, or of church, or simply because of the lack of spontaneity of the Russian peasant. Reforms seemed to come drenched in the blood of Russia, as did those of Peter the Great, or to take long periods of time and then to be halfway measures, as were those of Alexander II. The successors of Alexander II (Alexander III and Nicholas II) were both essentially weak men. To this characteristic was added a deep conservatism strengthened by the memory of the assassination of Alexander II, which appeared to have resulted from his efforts at reform. Under these conditions the country slipped even further behind the human and material progress of the West.

The progress of the West was itself a source of strain for Russia, which since its emergence bloody but triumphant from the Napoleonic Wars, had been a force in European politics. With its huge land mass and large army, Russia could not avoid playing a part in the struggles of Europe. At the same time, the Crimean War had revealed dangerous lacks in the army, and as the technological gap grew larger between Russia and the West, so too did the deficiencies in Russia's might. The need to modernize the country was undeniable. But the difficulties were enor-

---

[2] The word came from "Caesar," but in Byzantium the title signified second rank, denoting suzerainty. The origin of the term is debated.
[3] Theodore H. Von Laue, *Why Lenin? Why Stalin?*, New York, 1964, p. 38.

mous. There existed very little in the way of a middle or an industrial class. Much of the large-scale industry that existed was owned by foreign capital (which also produced strains). Industrialization then could come only with a massive reorganization of the country from the top down. Tied as they were to the *status quo,* it is doubtful if the tsars could have done this. In any case, they were unwilling to seriously make the attempt. Farsighted ministers like Witte or Stolypin were either dismissed or assassinated. And though the country made some progress, by comparison with the West it stagnated.

The pressure of the West was not only material and political, it was also intellectual. The democracy and freedom of the West, as much as its industrial might, provided a model for the intelligentsia of Russia who saw all around them the cultural poverty of their own land. But this model too was a mixed blessing. For while the intellectual wanted greater freedom and democracy, he also wanted to remain Russian. Out of this ferment grew the myth of the "Russian spirit" destined to lead the world if only it could be liberated. It is a theme present in most of the writing of that period and best known in the works of Fyodor Dostoyevsky.

In these circumstances the political action of the intelligentsia developed in peculiar ways. Because they were cut off from effective participation in politics and from the practical realities of political life, they tended to be dreamers, builders of utopias. But since they were repressed, censored, watched, and distrusted by the authorities, their actions took the form of isolated terrorist attacks and assasinations. It was a development that has been characterized as a tradition of "conspiratorial activity, based on faith, fanaticism, and fratricide, and imbued with a strong dose of romanticism."[4] This disparity of means and ends, as well as the absence of experience, were to cause more than a few problems when these forces suddenly found themselves at liberty, with responsibility for the administration of a nation.

Yet in spite of all these strains, the system survived. In spite of short-lived peasant revolts, assassinations, several generations of revolutionaries, and the complete unfitness of Nicholas II,[5] the system held together. It would take four years of bloody war to finally complete the erosion of tsarism.

[4] Zbigniew Brzezinski and Samuel P. Huntington, *Political Power: USA/USSR,* New York, 1966, p. 26.
[5] Von Laue, *op. cit.,* p. 84, relates the following incident, which indicates how little Nicholas understood the world he lived in.

> On January 12, 1917, the British Ambassador, Sir George Buchanan, deeply perturbed over the turn of events, tried most tactfully to point out to Nicholas the need for public support. "Your Majesty, if I may be permitted to say so, has but one safe course open to you, namely to break down the barrier that separates you from your people and to regain their confidence."
>
> Whereupon Nicholas drew himself up and, looking hard at the embarrassed diplomat, replied, "Do you mean that *I* am to regain the confidence of my people or that they are to regain *my* confidence?"

The Revolution and consolidation

The Revolution of 1917 actually began in 1905. At that time the Russo-Japanese War had brought an unbroken series of defeats to Russia. The war was extremely unpopular. The issues were obscure, and the people could see no reason for the sacrifices demanded from them. The first demonstration took place in St. Petersburg, led by a priest, Gapon, who was by no means a revolutionary. The demonstrators were met by troops who turned the peaceful march into a terrible blood bath. The news of the massacre spread all over Russia, and a wave of strikes and sporadic fighting set in. Peasant revolts were common. Revolts broke out even in the army, and a mutiny of the fleet seized the battleship *Potemkin*. The rebellion was suppressed, and severe punishments meted out to those responsible. But the regime received a jolt from which it never quite recovered.

The Duma

An imperial manifesto of August 19, 1905, granted a Constitution which provided for a consultative assembly, the Duma. The reform was grudgingly made and

514

for the rest of his career the tsar worked to reclaim his prerogatives. Another document followed on October 30, which proclaimed civil liberties, more democratic election laws, and a promise of legislation by representative institutions. Moreover the cabinet system was introduced into Russia and the conservative but not reactionary Count Witte became the first Prime Minister. But these reforms came too late. Witte fell because of his inability to overcome the distrust of both liberals and reactionaries, and he was replaced by the reactionaries Goremykin and Stolypin.

The first Duma lasted only seventy days. After its dissolution, the deputies repaired to Vyborg (Viipuri) in Finland and proclaimed passive resistance against the government.

The second Duma was also dissolved unceremoniously after a few months. The Tsar announced new electoral laws which disenfranchised numbers of people and permitted the manipulation of the election.

Nevertheless the Duma's reputation increased, and it even achieved a measure of cooperation with Prime Minister Stolypin. But the latter, who had attempted some belated agrarian reforms, was assassinated, and with him passed the last able leader of imperial Russia. After his death in 1911, the ship of state remained adrift until it foundered in the Revolution of 1917.

The impact of Marxism

The works of Karl Marx and Friedrich Engels were translated into Russian although the complexity of their writing prevented wide circulation. In the chaotic situation created by the incapable tsarist regime, the Marxist solution had much appeal, especially among intellectuals and workers. Marx's principal expositor in Russia was Georgi Plekhanov. He and his colleagues united several revolutionary movements and in 1898 founded the Russian Social Democratic Workers' party. Among the leaders were Georgi Plekhanov, Pavel Axelrod, Vera Zasulitch, L. Martov, and Vladimir Ilich Ulyanov, better known as Lenin.

Lenin

Like most other Communist leaders, Vladimir Ilich Ulyanov, who called himself Lenin, was not a worker but a middle-class intellectual, the son of a civil servant. He became interested in revolutionary activities early in life and was deeply influenced by the execution of his older brother, Alexander, as a result of a Socialist Revolutionary plot against the life of Tsar Alexander III. He became convinced that isolated acts of terrorism were worse than useless, and the oppressive atmosphere of tsarist Russia led him to the unflinching belief that the revolutionary struggle could be won only if the party were dominated by a small, closely knit group of professional revolutionaries.

It is significant that Lenin was forced into exile and remained abroad for seventeen years with brief interruptions. Political leaders who remain in their country, even if underground, are often forced into compromise in order to solve a particular pressing problem. The exiled politician, on the other hand, is free from the moderating influence of responsibility. He is able to conceive his ideas in the abstract and to argue pure theory. This kind of atmosphere has proved deadly to many an exile who removed himself more and more from reality. It is evidence of Lenin's outstanding ability that he never lost sight of the practical side of the revolution and that he became its foremost tactician. At the same time, being away from Russia and seeing the broader picture, he was a determined opponent of compromise and gradualism. The party, as he saw it, was not to work for piecemeal reform but only for integral revolution. Its principal function was to be a strictly disciplined instrument of revolution. On this issue occurred the split of 1903 with the moderate wing of the party led by Plekhanov. The moderates wanted a broad-based party which would work for social reform. Lenin held that in a police state this was an impossibility. The two wings of the party were further divided over the ability of a basically agrarian state like Russia to move directly into a socialistic state, since Marx had seen this as coming only after a society had passed through the stage of capitalism. The issues were complex, but Lenin's group, rather accidentally, managed to gain a majority. Henceforth they called themselves Bolsheviks—from *bolshe,* meaning "greater," while the moderates were called Mensheviks—from *menshe* meaning "fewer."

The crumbling of the foundations of the Russian empire made it clear to Lenin that he could count only on the workers. The *bourgeoisie* would stop the revolution as soon as the autocracy of the tsar was removed, and the peasants would remain united only against the landlords and the tsar. After liberation and land reform they would break up into classes of their own. Lenin derived two conclusions from these theoretical concepts: first, the Bolshevik party had to remain clear of compromises and concessions to other groups in order to prevent the halting of the revolution halfway; second, the party had to keep its cadres intact in order to wage the inevitable civil war which was sure to follow the overthrow of tsarism. In that struggle the party with the better leadership and the better discipline was bound to win. During World War I he displayed contempt for those socialists who were inclined to cooperate with their governments. He saw in war merely the expression of the inner contradictions of the capitalist society, which ought to be turned into a civil war for revolutionary victory.

Lenin was never averse to taking great risks, which on occasion appalled some of his collaborators, but which were never taken in passion but only as part of a well-thought-out plan. For democracy, in the Western sense of the word, he had no use, although he would advocate participation in the formal process of democracy if that gave the party an opportunity for propaganda. Lenin was intellectually flexible, but single-minded. He was a man who, by the force of sheer intellect and great learning, knew precisely what he wanted. He had able lieutenants, but Lenin alone carried the Bolshevik Revolution to victory and beyond. Regardless of whether one agrees or disagrees with his ideas, he is one of the outstanding leaders of all times. The Communist regime of the Soviet Union cannot be understood without comprehension of his mind and personality.[1]

Trotsky

A great contrast existed between Lenin and his second-in-command, Leon (Leib) Davydovich Bronstein, who like many revolutionaries took on a fictitious name and chose that of Trotsky. Trotsky was an intellectual of dazzling and at times withering brilliance. He was immensely well read on a great number of subjects, but he was arrogantly conscious of his brilliance, which antagonized his associates, and his overconfidence made him an easy target for the far less brilliant but more calculating Stalin. Lenin called Trotsky the ablest man in the central committee but criticized him for his overconfidence and his attraction to the purely administrative side of problems. Up to the Revolution, Trotsky was a Menshevik. In 1905 he was vice president of the first Soviet in St. Petersburg and was deported to Siberia as a result. He lived abroad a good part of his life, was wholly international in outlook, and was at home in a number of languages.

Stalin

Iosif Vissarionovich Dzhugashvili was a Georgian, to whom Lenin gave the name "Stalin," the man of steel. He had an adventurous youth and, unlike Lenin and Trotsky, was almost completely confined to Russia in experience. His early services to his party were undertaken with exceptional daring, and he gave the impression of a man of unlimited determination who would remove anything that stood in his path. He had neither Lenin's broad and instant grasp of great problems nor Trotsky's theoretical brilliance or style. Endowed with a rough and popular sort of humor, he was easily rude and high-handed, although he was able to exercise a certain kind of charm on occasion. Lenin, who thought well of his ability and determination, nevertheless suggested in his political testament that Stalin be removed from the office of General Secretary of the Communist party and be replaced by a man "more patient, more loyal, more polite and more attentive to comrades, less capricious. . . ."[2] But Stalin was the organizer of the party and eventually of the state. It was he who built the originally secondary position of General Secretary into a powerhouse.

Stalin was patient and steady. Of all the Communist leaders of the first line,

[1] There are several collections of Lenin's works in many languages. Of special interest to an understanding of the Revolution and the Communist regime are *What Is to Be Done? State and Revolution, Imperialism: The Highest Stage of Capitalism, On Dual Power, Left Wing Communism, Letters on Tactics,* and *One Step Forward, Two Steps Backward.* There are numerous biographies of Lenin, e.g., D. S. Mirsky, *Lenin,* Boston, 1931; L. Trotsky, *Lenin,* London, 1925; N. K. Krupskaya (Lenin's wife), *Memories of Lenin* (trans. by E. Verney), New York, 1930; Louis Fischer, *The Life of Lenin,* New York, 1965.
[2] Sir John Maynard, *Russia in Flux,* ed. by S. H. Guest, 1948, p. 201.

he appears to be the most Asiatic, more reminiscent of the Great Khan than of Napoleon or Hitler. He was a poor speaker, although his earthy sentences were not without appeal, and he was mediocre as a theorist.[3] Yet there was a tremendous quality of energy, decisiveness, and indomitable will about him which elevated him over his environment and made him one of the outstanding personalities of the century.[4] Trotsky, with his restless energy, cosmopolitanism, and brilliant dialectical ability, was the type of the perpetual revolutionary; Stalin was essentially the man of postrevolutionary consolidation. Lenin, however, belonged to both camps, and it is this which raised him high above the field.

War and collapse

The First World War brought constant defeat to the Russian armies at the hands of the Germans. Not only were the Russian troops badly led, but the entire supply and production system was in scandalous condition. Although farseeing elements pressed for reforms and received some concessions, the prevailing sentiment at the court was for more autocracy and suppression. In this policy the neurotic Tsarina, who was long under the influence of the evil Rasputin, played a major role. Amidst general restiveness and a feeling of impending doom, the Tsar remained a melancholic fatalist who proved incapable of action.

The February and October Revolutions

When the food supply in St. Petersburg (renamed Petrograd) broke down in February, 1917, because of a faulty distribution system, bread riots commenced and increased despite suppressive measures. Soldiers, even regiments, of the Guards joined the demonstrators. The Duma appointed a provisional committee, composed of all parties except the Social Democrats,[5] to act as the government. One member, the most vigorous one, was a Socialist Revolutionary, Alexander Kerenski. The workers and their delegates had formed revolutionary councils (*soviet* in Russian) and refused to participate in the government, but Kerenski, who was also president of the Petrograd Soviet, persuaded them to change their minds.

The provisional committee and the army commanders finally convinced the Tsar on March 15, 1917, that only his resignation could remedy the situation. The Tsar at first wanted to resign in favor of his son, but when he learned that his son's

---

[3] J. V. Stalin, *Leninism,* New York, 1928–1933, 2 vols., and *Marxism and the National and Colonial Question,* New York, 1936.

[4] Isaac Deutscher, *Stalin: A Political Biography,* New York, 1949; B. Souvarin, *Stalin,* New York, 1939; I. D. Levine, *Stalin,* New York, 1931; L. Trotsky, *Stalin,* New York, 1946.

[5] Other parties were the Socialist Revolutionary party of agrarian reformist leanings; the Constitutional Democratic party, a liberal group known as Cadets (after the Russian pronunciation of the letters K.D., the initials of the Russian words for "constitutional democratic"); and the Octobrists, a moderate monarchist party (named for the foundation of the "Union of October 30").

illness was incurable, he abdicated in favor of his brother, the Grand Duke Michael. The Grand Duke declared the next day that he would accept the throne only if a constituent assembly invited him to do so. It did not, and with this act, or rather lack of action, the Russian empire and the Romanov dynasty came to an end.

The regime was not really overthrown; it caved in because of its own incapacity and lack of support. The events of March, 1917, have entered history as "the February Revolution" because the Old Style (Julian) calendar was still in force in Russia. If those events could be called "revolution," the Bolsheviks certainly had nothing to do with them. If it can be said at all that the Tsar was overthrown, then he was overthrown by a liberal-conservative government, not by Bolsheviks. When Nicholas II signed the abdication document, Lenin was in Switzerland, Trotsky in New York, and Stalin in Siberia.

The Provisional Government, headed by Prince Lvov and dominated by Kerenski, had a strong majority in the Duma, whereas the Bolsheviks did not even have a majority in the Soviet. However, revolutions are not made by majorities but, as Lenin pointed out, by energetic minorities led by professional revolutionists.[6]

The Provisional Government never was in full control. All the mainstays of authority crumbled with the end of autocracy. The people were not accustomed to ruling themselves, nor did the government contain experienced administrators. The dynamics of the situation were supplied by the easily swayed masses who responded to the passionate enthusiasm of the zealots. When the Provisional Government granted the notorious Army Order No. 1, which destroyed the authority of the officers of the armed forces, it was soon swamped by 2 million deserters and all local authority broke down.

Into this confusion came Lenin and the other Bolshevik leaders. Trotsky arrived from Canada a little later. They were able to do so by courtesy of the German High Command, especially General Ludendorff, who considered himself very clever for helping to plant the germ of collapse in the Russian body politic. Lenin and his colleagues quickly organized large demonstrations against those members of the Provisional Government who wanted to continue the war. Amidst rising Bolshevik agitation, Kerenski succeeded Prince Lvov on July 20, 1917, and with his eloquence brought a new fighting spirit to the troops. But the last military offensive collapsed, and many soldiers were won over by the Bolshevik agitation for immediate cessation of hostilities. At the same time, General Kornilov marched against Petrograd but bogged down, and General Krymov tried the same but also with disastrous results.

Lenin pressed for the immediate seizure of power, but was opposed in the Bolshevik Central Committee. The more moderate elements carried the day for a while, and the Bolsheviks agreed to enter the Constituent Assembly which was shortly to be elected. It is interesting to note that these elections, which actually took place after the Bolsheviks had seized power, gave an overwhelming majority

6 V. I. Lenin, *What Is to Be Done?*, New York, 1929, pp. 116*ff.* (first published in 1902).

to the Socialist Revolutionaries (16,500,000), while the Bolsheviks trailed far behind with 9,000,000. This was the first and only Russian election carried out under conditions of free, equal, and secret suffrage. But in a country which had never known responsible government, such elections were meaningless. The fact that the Bolsheviks did not have the majority of the people behind them by far did not disturb Lenin in the slightest.

The final seizure of power by the Bolsheviks took place on November 7, 1917. The government forces had evaporated. Only a women's battalion could be found to defend the Winter Palace in Petrograd, the seat of the government. There was a little more fighting in Moscow, but that too was quickly over.

At the same time the Congress of the Soviets was meeting. After learning of the capture of the Winter Palace and the imprisonment of almost the entire Provisional Government, the Congress declared itself to be the repository of all power and advocated immediate peace, the transfer of all land to the peasantry, and control over all production. It also established a government called Council of People's Commissars, composed solely of Bolsheviks and headed by Lenin, with Leon Trotsky in charge of Foreign Affairs, and with Joseph Stalin responsible for Nationalities.

The events of November 7, 1917, are known to world history as "the October Revolution" because of continued use of the Julian calendar in Russia.[7]

After their victory, the Bolsheviks renamed themselves Communists and thus made definite the separation between themselves and the more moderate Socialists. In a significant and symbolic act, they shifted the seat of government from Petrograd (later renamed Leningrad) to Moscow. Ever since Peter the Great, St. Petersburg-Petrograd had been the foreign city, the "window to the West." Moscow, on the other hand, is a far more Russian city and is imbued with the tradition of being the "Third Rome," the alternative center of the world. The world would never again be permitted to overlook that fact.

Consolidation

The situation faced by the new rulers of Russia was chaotic in the extreme. The peasants were in the process of producing their own land reform without help from the government. Urban-rural relations were at an all-time low, and without comunication food was not coming into the cities. Further, the whole question of the war remained to be settled, and on the sidelines the specter of civil war was

[7] The best and fullest account of the Revolution is W. H. Chamberlin, *The Russian Revolution 1917–1921*, New York, 1935, 2 vols. See also G. Vernadsky, *The Russian Revolution 1917–1931*, New York, 1932; A. Rosenberg, *History of Bolshevism*, Oxford, 1934. For significant partisan accounts, see Leon Trotsky, *History of the Russian Revolution*, New York, 1936, 3 vols.; Alexander Kerenski, *The Catastrophe*, New York, 1927; J. V. Stalin et al., *History of the Communist Party of the Soviet Union*, New York, 1939. See also E. H. Carr, *The Bolshevik Revolution 1917–1923*, London, 1950–1953, 3 vols.

becoming visible. That the Revolution survived at all is outstanding proof of the leadership which the party was able to bring to bear upon the situation. Particular credit must go to Lenin, who maintained the vision to see the broad picture despite the pressures of imminent dangers.

Above all, the Bolsheviks needed peace. This, however, was far from simple to achieve. Believing as they did in the imminence of revolution in the West, they were faced with the quandary of whether to make peace without waiting for the revolutions, which might thus be hindered, or to wait for the revolutions and then make peace, in which case they might be overthrown if the revolutions were delayed. The disintegration of the tsarist armies finally left them with little choice, so Trotsky led a delegation to Brest-Litovsk to see what terms could be obtained from the Germans. The answers they received were so bleak that Trotsky walked out, leaving the formula "no peace—no war," with the rather naïve notion that the Germans would not attack a country which refused to fight. Within days he was disabused of this misconception, as German armies struck into the Ukraine and Baltic provinces in what the German General Hoffman called "the most comical war I've ever known." Reasoning that at all costs the Revolution had to be protected, the Communists signed a treaty even more drastic than the one they had originally rejected.

With the situation on one front solved, the Bolsheviks could now turn their attention inward. Oblivious to the Russian incapacity to carry on the war, horrified by communism, and profoundly shocked at what they considered a betrayal of a sacred trust, the Allied powers had occupied Arkhangelsk, Murmansk, and Vladivostok. A Czech army composed mostly of former prisoners of war was strung along the Trans-Siberian Railroad and knifed through the country at will. Anti-Bolshevik armies known as "Whites" formed on the Don, in the Caucasus, and in Siberia. After the defeat of Germany by the Western powers, the Red Army was able to reconquer the Ukraine from the rule of a native government. In the south, however, the Communists failed after initial successes, and the Whites reached a line running through Tsaritsyn,[8] Voronezh, Orel, Kiev, and Proskurov on the Galician border. In the east the Red Army under Tukhachevski, Frunze, and Kamenev defeated the White army under Admiral Kolchak, and another White army under General Yudenich failed when it reached the outskirts of Petrograd.

The Communist survival must be partly accounted for by the brilliant organization of the Red Army under the direction of Trotsky. In two short years he expanded it from a few thousand to more than 5½ million men.[9] While not all of these were of equal value, they formed a striking force which gave a good account

---

[8] Tsaritsyn, the "Red Verdun," was the pivot and was held by Red troops under Voroshilov, despite great pressure from the Whites under General Deniken. Joseph Stalin was political commissar with the Red Army at Tsaritsyn. The city was later renamed Stalingrad.

[9] An interesting discussion of Trotsky's problems is contained in the first volume of Isaac Deutscher's three-volume biography of Trotsky, *The Prophet Armed: Trotsky 1879–1921,* New York, 1954.

of itself. Coming after the total breakdown of the tsarist army, this achievement must be reckoned one of the most outstanding of the early Revolution.

In addition to a centrally commanded army operating on interior lines of communication, the Communist government was assisted by the extraordinary incapacity of its enemies. The White generals openly championed the cause of the landlords instead of appeasing the peasants. Peasant uprisings were the result. In the fall of 1919 the entire region of the Siberian railway was in open revolt against the White troops of Admiral Kolchak, who was forced to retreat from the Urals. Moreover, the Whites stubbornly demanded a "united and undivided Russia" and could not come to terms with the new states of the Ukraine, Finland, Estonia, Latvia, Lithuania, and Poland. The Ukrainian army could not find common ground with General Denikin's army, and the halfhearted attempt at Allied intervention was abandoned under the pressure of public opinion at home. The Communists had their own hands full, too, but at least, thanks to Lenin's foresight, they possessed perfect discipline and were completely united.

After the retreat of the White armies had turned into a rout, the Poles attacked under Marshal Pilsudski, and in May, 1920, they occupied Kiev. A remaining White army under General Wrangel advanced to the Dnieper and the Don. But the Red Army, brilliantly led by General (later Marshal) Tukhachevski, counterattacked and drove the Poles back to the gates of Lvov and Warsaw. Poland was saved by the fact that Tukhachevski had outrun his supplies and that the other Red Army under General (later Marshal) Budënny did not make contact in time. The Poles, reorganized by the French General Weygand, drove the Red Army back to the Dnieper, but on September 14, 1920, an armistice was concluded between the Polish and Red armies. This rendered hopeless the position of the Whites under General Wrangel in the Crimea; and after extremely stubborn and bloody fighting their remnants were evacuated by ship.

The last White soldier left the soil of Russia on November 16, 1920. From that day on, the Communists were undisputed masters. This was of course highly gratifying to them, but it was not exactly what they had expected. They had hoped that the Russian Revolution would be only the clarion call to world revolution. Now they had been able to maintain themselves against a world of enemies, foreign and domestic, but the world revolution had not materialized. Socialism in one country, surrounded by a hostile world, was now the new problem which led to the deepest division in the ranks of the Communists and promoted the ascendancy of Stalin.

3

From Lenin to Stalin

By 1921 military operations were over. They had left Russia in weakened, almost chaotic condition. Large territories were lost; not only the ethnically different regions such as Finland and the Baltic states, but also about 10 million Ukrainians and White Russians[1] who came under Polish rule under the Treaty of Peace with Poland, of Riga, March 18, 1921.

The ruin of Russia was indescribable. Most industry was destroyed or had become useless. Transport equipment had worn out, and the civil war had eaten up the country's reserves. The drastic acts of "war communism" had further disrupted the economy, and the black market blossomed because of the suppression of retail trading. The peasants had taken over all the land, but they failed to produce more than they consumed, with the result that famine broke out in the cities. The government sent punitive collection expeditions to the villages, often causing famine there too, without appreciably lessening the burden of the cities.

[1] White Russians are natives of Russia's western section. They are also referred to as "Byelo-russians," from the Russian word *Belyi* meaning "white."

The NEP

Seeing the danger clearly, Lenin commanded a halt to further extension of the revolution in the economy and on March 21, 1921, inaugurated the New Economic Policy, the NEP. The peasants were now allowed to sell their surplus products after paying a stiff tax, private trade was licensed, factories were permitted in a number of cases to come under restricted private enterprise, and some foreign capitalists were admitted to manage a certain amount of business in Russia. Trade treaties with foreign countries followed, and Russian delegates appeared again at international conferences, culminating in the Treaty of Rapallo of 1922. The NEP marked the abandonment for the time being of plans for imminent world revolution and the retrenchment of the Bolshevik government. It lasted for seven years.

The NEP was a makeshift affair which Lenin called "a strategic retreat." Unlike the "Five-Year Plans" which followed it, the NEP was no plan, but rather experimentation and groping in the wilderness.

In the middle of these events, Lenin died in 1924. He was succeeded by a triumvirate composed of Stalin, Zinoviev, and Kamenev. Trotsky was excluded, and thereby hangs a tale.

The rise of Stalin

There had been opposition within the Communist party almost from its inception. Kamenev and Zinoviev had opposed Lenin on the issue of the revolutionary uprising. Bukharin, Radek, and Smyrnov published for a while a "left" opposition journal. Many Communists were unhappy about the temporary retreat of the NEP. It was Lenin's personality and skill which kept these divergent groups together. When he died, the conflicts came into the open. Trotsky was too sure of himself, too disdainful of lesser minds to build up his own position. He believed that his natural superiority would lay his opponents at his feet. Stalin was handicapped by no such illusion. He entrenched himself in the party as its General Secretary and made it a powerhouse which it had not been before. Together with Zinoviev and Kamenev he dominated the Communist International (Comintern) as well as the government. Lenin was ill for the last two years of his life and was unable to influence the course of events.

In the period between 1922 and 1929 Stalin gradually drew into his own hands all the reins of power in the party. As the party had become the sole ruler of the country, so Stalin became the sole ruler of the party. To understand how this was possible, one must consider several factors. The first is the nature of the so-called "dictatorship of the proletariat." Although this will be dealt with in more detail later on, it must be touched on here. In theory, lower branches of the party are supposed to elect those above them. Actually, what happened was that men on top were in the position of being able to put their own supporters into lower positions. These supporters could then be counted upon to back the man or men who had placed them in power. The key to this whole process was the Secretariat. It was through the use of this organ that Stalin built his power base, just as Khrushchev was to do in the 1950s.

These facts are, however, not sufficient to explain Stalin's rise. Much of the responsibility for his success goes to those he overthrew, Trotsky, Zinoviev, Bukharin, and the rest. Until much too late they failed utterly to understand the threat of Stalin. They remained divided almost until the end. Further, their adherence to the Leninist principle that there should be no factional challenge to party discipline often hindered their effective organization.

Finally, the time period occupied by these events should be remembered. The change-over took seven years, more than half of which were necessary to remove Trotsky from power. During that time Stalin maneuvered slowly and carefully, and much of what seems now so clear was far from clear then.

In the end, most of those who had fought Stalin were compelled to retract and were readmitted to the party for a few years until they were finally extinguished. Trotsky, however, never compromised. He was first deprived of his office as Commissar of War, later of all other official positions, and then was expelled from the party. He was exiled to Soviet Asia in 1927, and in 1929 was finally expelled from the Soviet Union.[2] In exile he continued the struggle against Stalin until he was killed by a Stalinist agent in 1940. That he had to be pursued even into his Mexican exile is proof of the formidable character of Trotsky's personality, although he never had as numerous a following as Stalin.

Building the new Communist society

We have seen that the NEP was a makeshift solution, a necessary but undesirable departure from communism, a strictly short-term solution. After Stalin had consolidated his position and the country had somewhat recovered from the worst effects of "war communism," he proceeded to direct it again toward its long-term goal, that of being the advance guard of communism. To this end the country had to be strong, and to be strong meant to be industrialized. This was to be accomplished by a series of Five-Year Plans which emphasized heavy industry and deemphasized light, or consumer-goods, industry. The laxity of the NEP was consigned to the past. More and more rigid controls were applied; sharper and sharper became the measures of punishment and suppression of real or imaginary opposition. The security police, the OGPU,[3] later renamed NKVD, MVD, and MGB, became the symbol of the regime. Within the confines of communist theory this was not without logic. Since industrialization had been decreed as a means of survival in a hostile world, all energy had to be devoted thereto. That meant the im-

---

[2] In 1923 Russia was officially renamed Union of Soviet Socialist Republics.
[3] The initial letters of the Russian words meaning "Unified Political Administration of the State." For an excellent study of the genesis and operations of the Soviet secret police, see A. Wolin and R. M. Slusser (eds.), *The Soviet Secret Police,* New York, 1957.

position of great austerity and the lowering of living standards until that goal was accomplished. In the meantime the fainthearted who might not wish to travel the long and arduous road to communism should be given no opportunity to upset the government plan; hence, strict control.

Although one finds it easy to criticize the Communists for their control and repression, one must remember that they were caught in the old dilemma of tsarist Russia; how to make of Russia a nation whose power was commensurate with its position. Like the tsars, although perhaps not for the same reasons, the Communists saw industrialization as the answer and organization as the method to accomplish the massive social tasks with which they were faced.

Thus the face of Russia and of the Russians was to be radically changed. A new generation of civil servants, engineers, workers, etc., was to be created, not in the image of the notoriously slow and inefficient Russian worker, but in an entirely new mold. The League of Communist Youth, the *Comsomol,* pioneered this development. A new type of administrator and bureaucrat arose, men who had no knowledge of the world outside the Soviet Union and who were single-mindedly devoted to the state.

Collectivization

While enormous plants sprang up all over Russia, Stalin turned his attention to the peasants. New classes had arisen under the NEP. Some peasants, termed *kulaks,* had been able to increase their holdings, although they were still far below Western European peasants in development and prosperity. Much of the surplus of food which went to the cities came from them, but on the whole the countryside failed to supply the surpluses needed for industrialization. Further, the distribution of land to the peasants that had occurred after the Revolution caused production to decline and made communal agriculture seem doubly attractive. The collectivization of the peasants, decided upon in 1928, was originally to have been a slow process. With the early successes that resulted, Stalin appears to have decided on a coup which would in one fell stroke remake the face of rural Russia.[4] He sent thousands of agents into the country with orders to "liquidate the kulaks as a class."[5] The rest of the peasants were either to be driven into collective farms or forced off the land altogether to form the new pool of labor for the industrialization of Russia. At the same time work discipline in the cities was tightened, absenteeism was severely punished, and freedom of travel within the country was restricted by the introduction of internal passports. Thus socialism was created in the steps that Marx had marked out for capitalism: the peasant was driven off the land, the workingman was paid only what would support him, and the surplus went to the

[4] I. Deutscher, *Stalin: A Political Biography,* New York, 1949, p. 317*ff.*
[5] Official statistics placed the number of *kulaks* at 5,859,000 (including family). Most, if not all, of them were deported. Cf. D. J. Dallin, *The Real Soviet Russia* (trans. by J. Shaplen), New Haven, Conn., 1944, p. 170.

plant owner to be plowed back into the firm—but in this case the firm was the Communist state.

Naturally the peasant resisted. If he could not fight, still he could slaughter his livestock and burn his land rather than deliver it up to the state. And this he did. Between 1929 and 1933 Russia lost 18 million horses, 30 million cattle—about 45 percent of the total, and nearly 100 million, or two-thirds, of all sheep and goats.[6]

Realizing that he had gone too far, Stalin placed the blame on his subordinates and called for a slowdown, but this was only a temporary measure. After a brief respite, the pace was stepped up again, and as before, those who would not cooperate were shipped off to forced-labor camps where both labor and lives were used recklessly and poorly.

Consolidation

In 1933 came the end of the first Five-Year Plan and a certain relaxation of repressive measures. One might also speculate whether the coincidence that Hitler came to power in Germany that same year had anything to do with it. At any rate, a little more emphasis was placed on persuasion and good example than before, and the new type of "shock workers," the Stakhanovites,[7] made their appearance. However, the process of strict coordination of all intellectuals was pursued, and large-scale purges were conducted among the luminaries and lesser lights of science, art, and letters. Together with this went the increasingly strong propaganda wave against religion, spearheaded by the Union of the Godless, which was under the leadership of Stalin's childhood friend Yaroslavsky.

The period of "relaxation" began in December, 1933, with the permission to certain peasant groups to acquire some privately owned cattle and receive private allotments. The management of cooperatives was also relaxed, and the peasants were given a greater voice in them.

Great improvements were noticed by 1936. "Life is better, life is brighter" was proclaimed from thousands of billboards, and there was some truth to it. Great progress was achieved in the process of industrialization, and an increasing quantity of consumer goods poured from the assembly lines. In foreign affairs Stalin propounded the possibility of peaceful coexistence between capitalistic states and the Soviet Union.[8] Diplomatic relations had been resumed between the Soviet Union and the United States in 1933, and in 1934 the U.S.S.R. had joined the League of Nations. The year 1935 saw the 1932 nonaggression pact between the Soviet Union and France blossom out into an alliance.

---

[6] Deutscher, *op. cit.,* p. 325.
[7] Named after a miner named Stakhanov.
[8] Stalin in his report to the 17th Congress of the Communist Party of the Soviet Union, quoted in Joseph Stalin, *Leninism,* New York, 1942, pp. 310–313.

The 1936 Constitution

The apex of this development was reached with the Soviet Constitution of 1936, often and quite correctly, as far as we know, referred to as the "Stalin Constitution" because Stalin was its principal architect. (There had been two previous constitutions, in 1918 and 1924.) On paper this Constitution, which established a federal form of government, was amazingly liberal, providing for free, equal universal, and secret suffrage, protection of certain types of private property, independent courts, a bicameral legislature, and many other items which will be discussed later. But no realistic analysis could pretend that all these provisions have become realities, and the lifeblood of a Western-type democracy, namely, the rival political parties which present a choice to the voter, is totally missing. Each constituency nominates only one candidate, who is then elected on a list of "party and nonparty" candidates. In the beginning there occurred considerable discussion about the candidate's fitness, although this touched only his personal qualifications and had nothing to do with politics as we would understand that term. This impression was confirmed by no less a person than Joseph Stalin himself, who commented on the Constitution as follows:[9]

> I must admit that the draft of the new Constitution does preserve the regime of the dictatorship of the working class, just as it also preserves unchanged the present leading position of the Communist Party of the U.S.S.R. If the esteemed critics regard this as a flaw in the Draft Constitution that is only to be regretted. We Bolsheviks regard it as a merit of the Draft Constitution.

The Stalin Constitution of 1936 was discussed in great detail and in innumerable meetings all up and down the country, and it gave rise to much hope for a softening of the regime. Unfortunately these expectations proved unfounded, largely as a result of events which had their origin two years earlier.

Kirov's assassination and the great purges

S. M. Kirov, secretary of the Communist party in Leningrad, was assassinated by a Communist in December, 1934. Kirov had been one of Stalin's closest associates. His murder was the first assassination of a major Communist official in sixteen years. Kirov had taken the place of Zinoviev when the latter fell from grace, and Stalin chose to see a link between the two events. It has even been plausibly suggested that Stalin had himself engineered the murder in order to provide himself with a pretext for eliminating all his former comrades. The sense of security which the party leaders had felt, on account of all the progress made, vanished. Their conspiratorial background made them especially sensitive to the possibilities of con-

---

[9] Report delivered at the Extraordinary Eighth Congress of the Soviets of the U.S.S.R., Nov. 25, 1936, quoted in Stalin, *ibid.*, p. 395.

spiracy when threatened by others. The increasingly arrogant attitude of the Hitler regime in Germany put them further on edge, and they were also influenced by the pall of heavy suspicion and apprehension toward outside influences which has always existed in Russia and which is understandable in a country that has never known the serenity which comes from a habit of freedom.

The perpetrators of the deed and 103 others were executed. Their connection with the murder was doubtful in many cases and not actually proved. But the NKVD,[10] the OGPU under a new name, was determined to wipe out all possible opposition in the bud.

This was the beginning of the "great purges" of the 1930s. Before they ended they were to decimate the Communist party and strike terror into the nation as a whole. Yet terror was new neither to Russia nor to the Communists. Under the tsars the notorious Ochrana became a symbol of the regime, and the rest of the civilized world looked upon it as an example of medieval barbarity. Today a far more callous world, which has experienced two world wars and the horrors of the Nazi Gestapo and concentration camps, may well look back to the Ochrana as a relatively mild form of coercion. The treatment of prisoners, while certainly not good, was usually tolerable. Trials in open court were the rule, not the exception, and the deportations to Siberia, while rigorous, were infinitely more humane than they became later under the Bolshevik regime. Deportees under the tsars were permitted a considerable amount of freedom—which is manifested by the sizable literary output of such men. They were able to keep in touch with their families and could even receive them as visitors or have them accompany them into exile. Escape was not too difficult, as evidenced by those who succeeded. Under Stalin, however, the person arrested by the police and sentenced to a term of forced labor usually disappeared without a trace. His family was fortunate if it heard from him at all. Escapes were very rare.[11]

During the Revolution and civil war there was established the Extraordinary Commission to Combat Counterrevolution, Sabotage and Speculation,[12] better known by its abbreviation as the Cheka. The Cheka, sometimes called "the unsheathed punishing sword of the Revolution," had absolute power over life and death, including individual and mass executions without trial. It was renamed Political Administration of the State, abbreviated OGPU, in 1922. The powers of the OGPU were almost as extensive as those of the Cheka. Its beginnings lay in the years of the NEP, but with the institution of the first Five-Year Plan in 1928 the scope of "economic crimes" was greatly enlarged, and the functions of the OGPU enlarged too. At the same time, mounting international tension tightened the administration of internal security.

[10] Meaning literally People's Commissariat for Internal Affairs.
[11] One of the few who escaped was V. V. Tchernavin, a professor of ichthyology, who described his experiences in *I Speak for the Silent,* Boston, 1935. See also Valentin R. Gonzalez (El Campesino), *Life and Death in Soviet Russia,* New York, 1952.
[12] When private trading was prohibited, it became "speculation," a criminal offense.

The OGPU was reorganized in 1934, presumably to curb its absolute power, and it became part of the Commissariat of Internal Affairs, NKVD. In this year also occurred the Kirov murder and the beginning of the purge. During the great purge wave of 1937–1938, the NKVD exercised as much absolute power as the Cheka and OGPU ever had. But it overreached itself, and its own leadership was purged twice. A new leadership was established under Lavrenti Beria in 1938, and after that it operated smoothly.

In 1935 Zinoviev, Kamenev, and ten others were tried for complicity and sentenced to various terms of imprisonment. But it is characteristic of the mounting fear which gripped the regime that they were retried in August, 1936, together with fourteen others, and executed. It was the first time that top Bolshevik leaders had been so treated. In January other distinguished leaders followed: Y. L. Pyatakov, former chairman of the State Bank and Assistant Commissar for Heavy Industry; Karl Radek, editor of *Izvestia* and President of the Chinese (Sun Yat-sen) University in Moscow; Grigori Sokolnikov, Ambassador in London and Assistant Commissar for Foreign Affairs. In June, 1937, the entire high command of the Red Army was liquidated. Among them were Marshal Tukhachevski, Chief of Staff of the Red Army, and Generals Yakir, Uborovich, and Putna, who had all rendered distinguished service to the Soviet Union. They were all shot after a secret trial. Marshal Gamarnik, Assistant Commissar of War and Chief of the Political Department of the Red Army, was said to have committed suicide in prison. The generals were accused of having conspired with Hitler's Germany to overthrow the Soviet regime,[13] and these extraordinary allegations were believed in many quarters in Russia and abroad.[14] However, in the voluminous files of the German government which were found by the Allies after the Second World War, no evidence was unearthed to support such a contention.

In 1938 another batch of former top Communists was arrested. Among them were Nikolai Bukharin, leading theoretician and former principal assistant to Stalin in the latter's fight against Trotsky. Terror, however, was not limited to the upper strata of the party and state organization. Once it had begun, it moved in steadily widening circles. Even the Webbs, whose work was usually friendly to the regime, were compelled to speak of a "reign of terror against the intelligentsia. Nobody regarded himself as beyond suspicion. Men and women lived in daily dread of arrest. Thousands were sent on administrative exile to distant parts of the country."[15] Thousands more were executed. Arrest could come at any time of the day or night. Although the show trials made a pretense of legal formalities, those arrested by the

[13] Quite apart from the absence of any evidence to sustain this accusation, there is also the fact that three of the executed generals, Gamarnik, Yakir, and Feldmann, were Jews.
[14] Joseph E. Davies, *Mission to Moscow,* New York, 1941. This is a completely uncritical book by the former United States Ambassador to Moscow, who swallowed the official Soviet version of the trials without blinking an eyelid.
[15] Sidney and Beatrice Webb, *Soviet Communism: A New Civilization?,* New York, 1936, Vol. II, p. 553.

secret police lacked even these rights.[16] Often people were arrested simply because they were members of a suspect group such as the engineers, or the intelligentsia, or because they had been associated with someone else who had been arrested. Above all, the purges were aimed at groups within the society, and particularly within the party, who opposed or seemed to oppose the regime. In at least one case in the Baltic states, orders were sent out to the local representatives of the Ministry of Internal Affairs to arrest and deport specified numbers of persons of given categories. The local officials picked the former officers of the Latvian army, estate owners, etc., within the given categories who seemed most likely to be enemies and proceeded to carry out instructions. After such a dose of arbitrary terror, one could well expect the community to be cowed.[17]

The great purge of the thirties was not the only purge of Stalin's career. During and after World War II the efforts of the NKVD, renamed Ministry of Internal Affairs (MVD), were again turned toward elements outside the party, toward the purge of whole nationalities who were accused of having collaborated with the enemy, like the Volga Germans, the Kalmucks, the Crimean Tartars, and others. Then followed the liquidation of the intelligentsia of Lithuania, Latvia, and Estonia[18] as well as the scrutiny and large-scale purge of former Russian prisoners of war and German slave laborers.[19] Toward the end of his life Stalin appeared to be beginning another series of purges which in the initial stages were concentrated on doctors and writers and which had strong anti-Semitic overtones. Death, however, cut short these plans.

These incredible waves of terror have provoked considerable speculation from the outside world, particularly from political scientists, historians, and philosophers. No authoritative answer to the "why" of terror is possible, but the question remains still vital, both because of the effects of the terror on the Soviet system of government to date and because of the necessity for understanding where the system may be heading in the future. The question, obviously, can be considered only in brief in this context.

[16] There is now ample evidence of the character and operation of the terror under Stalin. The outstanding work on NKVD-MVD-MGB-KGB procedure as well as forced labor is the survey of evidence submitted to the United Nations by the American Federation of Labor, *Slave Labor in Russia*, New York, 1949. See also P. Pirogov, *Why I Escaped*, New York, 1950, and especially J. Gliksman, *Tell The West*, New York, 1948, a most revealing work. See also T. S. Eliot (ed.), *Dark Side of the Moon*, New York, 1947; L. Fisher, *Thirteen Who Fled*, New York, 1949; V. Kravchenko, *I Chose Freedom*, New York, 1946; R. Magidoff, *In Anger and Pity*, New York, 1949; F. Utley, *The Dream We Lost*, New York, 1940; W. L. White, *Report on the Russians*, New York, 1945; John Scott, *Behind the Urals*, New York, 1942; S. Mora, *Kolyma*, Washington, 1949; O. J. Dallin and B. I. Nicolaevsky, *Forced Labor in the Soviet Union*, New Haven, Conn., 1947; and V. V. Tchernavin, *I Speak For the Silent*, Boston, 1935.
[17] John N. Hazard, *The Soviet System of Government*, Chicago, 1965, pp. 68–69.
[18] The massacre of 4,243 Polish officers in the forest of Katyn is now generally "credited" to the NKVD. See 82d Congress, 2d Session, House Report No. 2505, Dec. 22, 1952, *The Katyn Forest Massacre: Final Report of the Select Committee to Conduct an Investigation and Study of the Facts, Evidence, and Circumstances of the Katyn Forest Massacre.*
[19] Those who had joined the Vlassov army or other formations fighting with the Germans were executed.

One early explanation was that Stalin, fearful of treachery after the death of Kirov and foreseeing the impending crisis of World War II, felt it necessary to remove all those who might in any way be inclined to oppose him during a time of crisis, i.e., all the old Bolsheviks who had been removed from power but were still alive.[20] This argument probably has much truth to it, but it is insufficient. Stalin was certainly suspicious of those around him and may have felt the need to consolidate his position. For this end, the use of terror was an accepted weapon of the Bolshevik arsenal. Lenin had declared, "We have never rejected terror on principle . . . [it] is a form of military operation that may be usefully applied, or may even be essential in certain moments . . . [or] under certain conditions."[21] The change-over from Lenin's select use of terror against "class enemies" to Stalin's eventual use of terror against the party to consolidate his own position is not so great as to be difficult to understand. The difficulty is with the degree of terror used. Under Stalin the terror reached beyond "class enemies" and opposition forces in the party, to strike down vast numbers of the faithful for little reason. While the fear of those around him did put Stalin solidly in control, it is difficult to view these mass executions as sane, planned, power moves even though this may have been part of the rationale.

Two other theories have been offered to explain the extent and nature of the terror. The first of these rested largely on comparisons between the Nazis and the Communists and theorized that since both Hitler and Stalin had resorted to similar means it was probably the system itself which called forth these debauches of bloodletting to hold the top leadership in its position. In this view, terror was and is a permanent part of the totalitarian form of government. Hence, while it may recede at times, it is always there, in the background, waiting to rise to the surface.

The second, and in some ways the more compelling, theory sees the system as making some degree of terror possible but sees the personality of the dictator as being primarily responsible for the nature and scope of the terror.[22] In this theory both Hitler and Stalin are viewed as nearly perfect examples of the paranoid character, suspicious of all those around them and widening their fear of "enemies" from their own circle to include the entire outside world. Whether or not one accepts the paranoid view, there is considerable evidence to support the position that

---

[20] The near-total absence of a Russian fifth column during World War II is sometimes attributed to these purges. Deutscher, *op. cit.,* p. 357. However this story is true only to the extent that the Germans were unable to win over top leaders of the Soviet regime, the highest being merely a general, Vlassov. But German troops were welcomed as "liberators" in certain parts, especially in southern Russia, until Gestapo and SS methods destroyed whatever good will there was. This fact has been unquestionably established by Allied intelligence work in which the author participated. It was also borne out by the Soviet government, which deprived five Autonomous Republics and Regions of their status and deported their populations because of alleged collaboration with the enemy. They were the German Volga, Kalmyk, Chechen-Ingush, and Crimean Autonomous Soviet Socialist Republics and the Karachaev Autonomous Region. *The New York Times,* Nov. 30, 1945; June 27, 1946.
[21] Lenin, "Where to Begin?" *Selected Works,* Vol. III, p. 17.
[22] For a fuller treatment of this argument see Robert Tucker, *The Soviet Political Mind: Studies in Stalinism and Post-Stalin Change,* New York, 1963.

terror is a product of the character of the top leadership of the party, and that while the system encourages repression, it does not "call forth" the terror of a Stalin. This is a theme which will be pursued in more detail further on.[23] In any case, there can be little doubt that the great purges of the 1930s weakened the Soviet Union considerably as the Second World War drew closer, but that they left Stalin fully in control of the country and able to remain in power through the dark days of the first years of the war.

The Soviet-German Nonaggression Pact

Many of Stalin's decisions had been influenced, at least in part, by the expectation of war. The Munich agreement of 1938, from which the Soviet Union was excluded, apparently convinced Stalin of a British and French design to let the U.S.S.R. and Nazi Germany fight each other. With greater skill than Neville Chamberlain and Édouard Daladier, he turned the tables, and on August 23, 1939, the world was electrified by the news of the Soviet-German Nonaggression Pact. This was the green light for the Second World War,[24] which broke out a few days later. That Stalin was able to undertake this *volte-face* without any recorded opposition within the U.S.S.R. is proof positive of the absolute control which he had achieved.

The Soviet-German pact was fully obeyed by the Soviet government, and the Communist parties abroad, though weakened by Stalin's policy, promptly fell into line, branded the war as "imperialist," and worked against it wherever they could. During that period the Soviet Union occupied eastern Poland, the Baltic Republics of Lithuania, Latvia, and Estonia, parts of eastern Finland, Bessarabia, and northern Bukovina, all of which were incorporated into the Soviet Union. The native populations, in so far as they remained, were drastically reoriented.

War

But on June 22, 1941, Germany attacked the Soviet Union, and better relations ensued between Russia and the Western Allies. American lend-lease material arrived in great quantity,[25] although its impact was not felt until later in the war.

The Soviet government, realizing the extreme seriousness of the situation,

---

[23] See Chap. 4, pp. 535–544.

[24] Hitler's decision to attack Poland was made earlier, probably in May, but the Soviet-German Nonaggression Pact removed the last obstacle. It is impossible to believe that Stalin did not know this. The initiative to closer Soviet-German relations came from the U.S.S.R. See the memorandum of the German State Secretary for Foreign Affairs (Weizsäcker) about his conversations with the Soviet Ambassador (Merekalov) on Apr. 17, 1939. Cf. Department of State, *Nazi-Soviet Relations 1939–1941*, Documents from the Archives of the German Foreign Office, Washington, D.C., 1948, pp. 1–2.

[25] Out of a total lend-lease appropriation of $50,000,000,000, the Soviet Union received $11,000,000,000, including 6,800 tanks, 13,300 airplanes, 1,000 locomotives, 406,000 trucks and cars, 2,000,000 tons of steel, and 11,000,000 pairs of shoes. Cf. Edward R. Stettinius, *Lend-lease: Weapon for Victory*, New York, 1944.

conducted the war under national rather than Communist propaganda. Stalin called it the "Second Patriotic War."[26] The government relaxed its hitherto strongly anti-religious policy and gave some encouragement to the Orthodox Church, which it now controlled. As a means of gaining the confidence of the Western Allies, the Third Communist International was dissolved in 1943.

The U.S.S.R. suffered unprecedented devastation during the war. The German armies encircled Leningrad, took most of Stalingrad, and advanced to within 13 miles of Moscow. Seven million Soviet citizens died in battle or from other consequences of the war; 6,000,000 buildings, 1,700 cities, and 70,000 villages were destroyed.

While the Soviet marshals led the troops, the direction of the war rested securely in the hands of the Communist party leaders, and especially Stalin. A State Committee of Defense, composed of Stalin (chairman), Molotov (vice chairman), Beria, Malenkov, and Voroshilov, somewhat reminiscent of the British War Cabinet, was formed on July 1, 1941, and all internal security agencies were united under Lavrenti Beria.

During the war, national unity rather than party orthodoxy were stressed, and this gigantic conflict has become known in official Soviet history as the "Great Patriotic War." But as soon as victory approached, party discipline and ideological purity were stressed again, and special attention was focused on regions liberated from the Germans. And the party leadership clamped down hard.[27]

The Soviet Union emerged from the war with a tremendous increase in power. It had added much new territory: the Petsamo area, the Karelo-Finnish Soviet Socialist Republic, the Estonian, Latvian, and Lithuanian Soviet Socialist Republics, the Moldavian Soviet Socialist Republic, eastern Poland, northern east Prussia, Carpatho-Ruthenia,[28] Southern Sakhalin, and the Kurile Islands. Soviet troops occupied eastern Germany, eastern Austria, and strategic positions in China.[29] The whole of eastern Europe was under Russia's sway except for the unexpected defection of Tito's Yugoslavia. Russian armed forces were the largest in the world. Machinery for control of the Communist parties was reestablished in September, 1947, by the creation of the Communist Information Bureau (Cominform). Never in her entire history had Russia wielded such power. Peter the Great would have been pleased with his successors.

But as a result of this expansion and of Russia's threatening pose in Berlin and on the Balkans, Western resistance grew, culminating in the Truman Doctrine and the 1949 North Atlantic Treaty. This in turn led to further assertions by the party leadership that still greater sacrifices and discipline were necessary because the U.S.S.R. was "encircled" by hostile, capitalist powers.

---

[26] The first was the war against Napoleon in 1812. J. V. Stalin, *The Great Patriotic War of the Soviet Union,* New York, 1945.

[27] Merle Fainsod, *How Russia is Ruled,* Cambridge, Mass., 1963, rev. ed., pp. 113–116.

[28] Formerly part of Czechoslovakia. Also known as Carpatho-Russia and Carpatho-Ukraine.

[29] Especially Dairen and Port Arthur, as well as the control of the Manchurian Railroad.

4

The U.S.S.R. after Stalin

The death of Joseph Stalin occurred on March 5, 1953. But during the year prior to his death there were numerous indications that many changes were in the offing. The 19th Congress of the Communist party met in October, 1952, after an interval of thirteen years, and enacted a new statute (rules) of the Communist party of the Soviet Union.[1] Instead of the old Politburo, the new statute provided for a Presidium (of the central committee) composed of twenty-five members and eleven candidates—twice as many as had been in the old Politburo. Most of the new members had not previously been close to the chief luminaries of the Politburo. Simultaneously, the former Orgburo was abolished and its functions taken over by the Secretariat.

In December, 1952, an ominous discussion started about Nikolai Voznesensky, a former deputy premier, Politburo member, and chief of the State Plan-

---

[1] For the text of the Party statute see James S. Meisel and Edward S. Kozera, *Materials for the Study of the Soviet System,* Ann Arbor, Mich., 1953, pp. xliii-lxi.

ning Commission, who had disappeared years ago. Then in January, 1953, several doctors were arrested on fantastic charges of having killed Georgi Malenkov's great rival, Andrei Zhdanov, in 1948. The accusing finger seemed to point in the direction of police chief Lavrenti Beria, but Malenkov also appeared threatened. In February, 1953, an especially bitter campaign for "vigilance against spies and saboteurs" swept over every corner of the Soviet Union.[2] It was easy to see that a gigantic purge was in the making, perhaps an even bigger one than occurred in the thirties. But when Stalin died in March, his successors lost no time in making their own changes. The Presidium was immediately reduced to the size and the membership of the former Politburo. The accusation against the doctors was dropped, and they were reinstated—an almost unheard-of thing—while their accusers were purged, among them N. G. Ignatiev, a candidate for the Presidium and the man Stalin had apparently groomed for Beria's job.

Stalin was of course buried with the customary ceremonies, but soon thereafter the Stalin cult of Byzantian veneration ceased. After a few weeks little was heard of "the great and wise leader and teacher," the "greatest scientist, artist, linguist, strategist, etc.," who ever walked the face of the earth. In his order of the day of May 9, 1953, Marshal Bulganin declared that the Soviet army had won its victory under the leadership of the "glorious Communist Party"; no mention of the name of Stalin, so common in previous years. On the contrary, there was begun a determined campaign against the leadership cult. Soon the following words appeared in the Communist party's chief theoretical journal:[3]

> Sometimes the acts and the will of outstanding personalities are presented as the determining factor of historical development and are alleged to decide the outcome of class struggles and wars. In the interest of the correct education of cadres, communists, and all toilers, it is necessary to overcome determinedly such errors and distortions of Marxism-Leninism.

And F. B. Konstantinov went so far as to term the overestimation of strong personalities "one of the most characteristic features of fascism."[4]

The condemnation of the personality cult which so characterized the Stalin regime was obviously meant to herald the coming of a collective leadership rather than an individual one. In fact the new rulers of Russia generally avoided the limelight. The new "leader" was supposed to be the Communist party rather than a single individual. This policy was also carried out in the Union Republics and among the lower echelons of the party.

After Stalin's death it appeared that his place had been taken by a team of three (*troika*) composed of Georgi Malenkov, Lavrenti Beria, and Nikita Khrush-

---

[2] Klaus Mehnert (K.M.), *"In Bewegung Geraten," Osteuropa,* Vol. III (1953), p. 241.
[3] *Kommunist* (formerly, *Bolshevik*), May 2, 1953.
[4] *Pravda,* June 28, 1953.

chev, with Vyacheslav Molotov in an uncertain role.[5] That Khrushchev's star was rising was seen by the fact that he became Stalin's successor as First (General) Secretary of the Communist party. But Beria too fortified his position greatly and worked his MVD (secret police) henchmen into the top administrative positions in such regions as Georgia, Azerbaijan, and Uzbek. At the same time Beria became identified—whether justified or not is not known—with a more permissive policy toward the different non-Russian nationalities and local interests, a policy which appears to have brought him into conflict with Khrushchev, a representative of the Great Russian claim of preeminence.

It seems likely that Beria's increasing power threatened not only Khrushchev but also Malenkov. It is, however, probable that the decisive element in the situation was the development of the foreign political situation which brought about the fall of Beria, just as it had caused the eclipse of Zhdanov. The policy of the more loosely held reins, associated with Beria, did not lead to positive results favorable to the Soviet Union but instead to an eruption of pent-up feeling in the revolt of the workers of East Berlin and the Soviet zone of Germany on June 17, 1953. Ten days later the Presidium of the Central Committee attended the opening performance of the opera *The Decembrists* at the Bolshoi Theater in Moscow. All members except Beria and M. Bagirov, a candidate and Beria henchman, were present.[6] In other countries such an event would have little significance, but in the Soviet Union the presence or absence of a man at such a function, his place at the center or the side, are all highly significant and duly noted. The removal and arrest of Beria was announced only on July 9,[7] but it is likely that he was already in custody at the time of the opera performance.

The accusations against Beria followed the usual pattern. He was accused of having sought to make himself the sole master of the country, of having wanted to undermine the collective-farm system, of having tried to strengthen bourgeois nationalism, of undertaking illegal administrative acts, and of attempting to replace revolutionary methods with evolutionary ones.[8] The wording of these accusations would indicate that the policy of the looser reins was attributed to Beria and condemned. But this did not exclude its continuation. After all, Stalin too condemned policies of Trotsky's—which he then proceeded to carry out.

In assessing the reasons for the downfall of a Soviet leader, it needs to be borne clearly in mind that power and policy are twins. That is to say that power struggles are fought, not in terms of personalities, but in terms of policies and ideo-

---

[5] Collective leadership was also the aim of Lenin for his succession. See Robert G. Daniels, "The Soviet Succession: Lenin and Stalin," *The Russian Review*, Vol. XII (1953), pp. 153–172.

[6] *The New York Times*, June 29, 1953.

[7] *Ibid.*, July 9, 1953.

[8] According to the report of *Pravda*, July 10, 1953. See also *The New York Times*, July 10, 1953.

logical positions. It was this which allowed Stalin to outmaneuver first the "left" and then the "right" opposition without their realizing until too late that they were actually faced by a drive for control of the party. Thus, while a foreign policy debacle may have weakened Beria's position, there is considerable evidence to suggest that the real reason for his overthrow was the danger that he was becoming too powerful; was, in short, on the point of becoming another Stalin.

The theory that the top leadership was afraid of another Stalin is supported by the fact that within two weeks after Stalin's death, the man who had seemed ready to succeed him, Malenkov, was forced to yield one of his two top posts, the Prime Ministership and the Party Secretaryship. He chose to yield the Party Secretaryship to Khrushchev, probably the worst mistake he ever made from a personal standpoint.[9]

It is more important to note that the removal of the seemingly all-powerful master of the police proceeded more easily than might have been expected, and the unconfirmed reports that Beria was lured into a trap may well be correct. It has since been made clear that the army, and notably Zhukov himself, played an extremely important role in his removal, as had been at first conjectured. Furthermore, the presiding officer of the tribunal which tried Beria's case post-mortem and found him guilty of the crimes for which he had already been executed was, significantly, Marshal Ivan Koniev.[10]

The liquidation of Beria left Malenkov and Khrushchev at the top. The secret police, now headed by a relative underling, was detached from the Ministry of the Interior (MVD) and placed under a Committee for State Security under the Council of Ministers, headed by another relative underling. In 1962 a new joint Party-State Control Commission was established holding, for the first time, authority to investigate all phases of both governmental and party activities.[11] The security services were consistently downgraded and gradually eliminated as a possible independent contender for power.

While the "collective leadership" seemed to continue with Malenkov and Khrushchev at the top, Vyacheslav Molotov and Nikolai Bulganin next in line, and Lazar Kaganovich, the man with the passion for anonymity, farther in the background, some signs of change appeared. *Pravda*, the party organ, began to criticize ministries under Malenkov's control, while *Izvestia*, the government organ, passed this campaign over with silence. Khrushchev headed the vital mission to Peking, while Malenkov stayed at home and Molotov went to relatively unimportant East

---

[9] See Zbigniew Brzezinski and Samuel P. Huntington, *Political Power: USA/USSR*, New York, 1964, p. 240; and Robert Conquest, "De-Stalinization and the Heritage of Terror," in *Politics in the Soviet Union,* ed. by Alexander Dallin and Alan F. Westin, New York, 1966, p. 42.
[10] *The New York Times,* Dec. 24, 1953. Beria's trial was held in secrecy, and the accuracy of the reports cannot therefore be tested. It would seem from presently available evidence that there never was a trial of Beria per se. He seems to have been executed and then a mock trial seems to have been held in which he was found guilty of all the charges of which he had been accused.
[11] Herbert Ritvo, "Party Controls Reorganised," *Survey* (October, 1963), No. 49, p. 87.

Berlin. To foreign visitors voluble Khrushchev presented himself increasingly as "the boss."

But the outside world learned the facts only on February 9, 1955, when, at a meeting of the Supreme Soviet, its chairman, Alexander Volkov, read a letter from Premier Malenkov asking to be relieved of his job because of "inexperience." In his stead was nominated and elected Nikolai Bulganin, a political marshal who began his work in the Cheka and gained prominence as chairman of the Moscow Soviet (mayor) before and during World War II. Everybody assumed that Bulganin was mainly a figurehead and Khrushchev the real leader, and this was accurate, as subsequent events showed.

Certain new features surrounded this change of command. Malenkov sat at the rostrum while his letter of resignation was being read, instead of being in prison. Instead of being tried and shot in the approved Stalinist style, he was made Minister of Electric Power Stations. Instead of being denounced in the classical style as a "traitor, saboteur, and foreign hireling," he merely admitted certain errors and shortcomings, including the failure of Soviet agriculture, which was actually Khrushchev's department.

Khrushchev's rise to power revealed both similarities to and differences from that of Stalin. Like Stalin, he used the position of Party Secretary to control the party. The tools of the struggle for power were also the same, i.e., division of the Presidium over questions of policy, with Khrushchev taking the line that would win power rather than the line he necessarily felt was best. Thus, while he later showed himself heavily committed to increasing consumer goods, he became a proponent of the predominance of heavy industry in order to topple Malenkov from power.

Two significant differences also appear. One was the absence of physical violence. Whatever the reasons, the plain fact is that after the execution of Beria, no major party figure paid the supreme penalty for the loss of a political battle, nor did Khrushchev's opponents attempt violence against him, as will be noted further on. Secondly, there is considerable evidence to indicate that Khrushchev never enjoyed the total control that Stalin did. Although he was unquestionably the "boss," he consistently had to bargain with strong countercurrents in the top leadership of the party.[12]

The period of Khrushchev's rule was significant in other respects as well. He was the first of the Soviet leaders to recognize and publicly acknowledge the total failure of communism in the agricultural sector and he advocated limited incentives to collective farmers. In 1954, he obtained the approval of the Central Committee for a daring but dubious venture in cultivating virgin lands. On this scheme Khrushchev virtually gambled his political future. In many ways his enterprises were marked by boldness and experimentation. Perhaps his most startling venture was the famous "secret speech" made at the Twentieth Party Congress in February,

---

[12] This argument is made with great force and scholarship in Carl A. Linden's *Khrushchev and the Soviet Leadership 1957–1964,* Baltimore, 1966.

1956, in which he revealed a wide range of crimes committed by Stalin. It is still a matter of conjecture as to what caused Khrushchev to make these revelations and thus publicly condemn and repudiate twenty years of Communist life. Some have felt that this was Khrushchev's personal guarantee that the violence of Stalin would not be repeated.[13] Others have viewed it as a tactical maneuver designed to put Khrushchev's foes in a bad light and to build support for him in the ranks of those weary of Stalin's purges.[14] This view is somewhat supported by the cresting and falling of waves of destalinization at times of crisis. Both views probably have truth in them and it is certain that forces have been released which it will be extremely difficult to harness again.

The bloody repression of the Budapest uprising in 1956 dented his credibility as a more tolerant Soviet leader, but subsequent events restored it—at least in part. But a crisis brewed for Khrushchev, and in May, 1957, he found himself with a 7 to 4 majority against him in the Presidium of the Central Committee, the former Politburo of the Communist party of the Soviet Union. Khrushchev weathered this storm by shifting his basis of operation from the Presidium to the full Central Committee, in which his followers had a majority, and in October of 1957 he further strengthened his position by ousting a too powerful friend, Marshal Grigory Zhukov. In all these cases, and from all sides, the absence of physical violence and terror was noticeable. The simultaneous launching of Sputnik I and Russia's giant venture into the space age further consolidated Khrushchev's power. Quickly he attempted to exploit his newfound strength by launching, in November, 1958, another Berlin crisis. However, the Western powers stood firm, and eventually Khrushchev's bluster, revealed as empty threat, evaporated, and he had to back down.

Great as was Khrushchev's power, he nevertheless had to face considerable problems and difficult alternatives. The U.S.S.R. became a major nuclear power, but the United States was and remained far ahead. Although the successes of the first Sputniks had revealed Russia's superiority in the field of propulsion, the U.S.S.R. proved unable to convert this advantage into the production of a large arsenal of intercontinental ballistic missiles (ICBMs), and the United States continued not only to produce a much larger number of nuclear weapons and missiles but also to forge well ahead in the dispersal and hardening of missile sites and in the development of Polaris-type submarines.[15] Moreover, Khrushchev's boastful promise of overtaking the United States in economic production proved an empty

---

[13] An excellent summary of the Khrushchev period and of Khrushchev's downfall may be found in Merle Fainsod, "Khrushchevism in Retrospect," *Problems of Communism,* January-February, 1965, pp. 1–9.

[14] Conquest, *op. cit.;* Linden, *op. cit.,* particularly Chap. 5; and Brzezinski and Huntington, *op. cit.,* pp. 246–247.

[15] Russia's initial advantage in the propulsion field and its potential capability of getting a head start in the production of ICBM's created the fear of a "missile gap" which played quite a role in the American presidential campaign of 1960. However, the U.S.S.R. was either not willing or not able to take full advantage of these possibilities, America's nuclear superiority remained on a high level, and the missile gap never developed.

threat, although the Soviet Union's economic growth rate was ahead of that of the United States for a time (if Russian statistics are to be believed—always a dubious assumption). The fact that the American gross national product (GNP) remained approximately twice as large as that of the Soviet Union meant that the gap between the two countries actually increased. This difficult situation was made worse by the continued failure of Soviet agriculture. The year 1958 produced a large harvest due to uncommonly favorable weather. However, nothing of the like occurred later, production went into a tailspin, and 1963 was a year of unmitigated agricultural disaster, in which the Soviet Union was compelled to buy 12 million tons of grain abroad in order to meet minimal needs. Only 1966 finally produced a bumper crop.

It was clear that the U.S.S.R. had a strong interest in stopping or at least slowing down the arms race and entering into a period of international tranquility in order to devote its resources to the repairing and building up of the domestic economy. This, however, meant the assignment of low priority to support of the rapid industrial and military buildup of Communist China, and the discouragement of the latter's expansionist aims.[16] This has been viewed as the basic cause for the bitter conflict between the Soviet Union and Communist China.[17] This deviation from the historic Communist practice of putting heavy industry ahead of all else was the source of considerable tension within the ranks of the party leadership.[18]

As unsolved problems kept piling up, as the agricultural picture became darker in the Soviet Union, some steps were taken to reorganize an obviously rickety structure. A previously decreed drastic reorganization of the party and governmental system into parallel industrial and agricultural hierarchies was cancelled. Steps were taken to free Soviet agriculture from the bonds of fanciful theories propagated by a party genealogist, Trofim Lysenko. Some limitations on the private plots cultivated by collective farmers were removed. And in industry, under the influence of a veteran economist, Professor Liebermann, an incentive system was propagated. This did not mean the introduction of capitalism into Russia, but rather the recognition that certain features of the free-enterprise system worked better and might be adapted to Communist views.

Certainly it would go too far to say that Khrushchev's record showed no achievements. Under his rule, the rate of growth in Soviet production had increased for a while, although later it slumped and dropped below the growth rate of the United States. Life became a good deal more tolerable, there was a reduction in working hours, there were larger social security benefits, consumer goods became more available although still in irregular supply, and the always difficult housing situation improved somewhat. Under Khrushchev, the Soviet Union remained a police state and a dictatorship, but at least the consequences of running afoul of the authorities or of official doctrine became much more moderate than they had been

---

[16] Fainsod, *op. cit.*, p. 5.
[17] Donald S. Zagoria, *The Sino-Soviet Conflict, 1956–1961,* Princeton, N.J., 1962.
[18] Linden, *op. cit.*, sees this as a constant theme of Khrushchev's period of primacy.

under Stalin. The huge forced-labor camps were greatly reduced, justice, while still harsh and arbitrary, was meted out in a relatively mild fashion; men like Vyacheslav Molotov and Lazar Kaganovich, formerly Stalin's henchmen, were denounced as "enemies of the party," and banished to minor positions or retirement but did not disappear into prisons and were not stood up before firing squads. To citizens of a free country, that might seem little indeed, but for those whose ears had become attuned to the dreadful knock of the secret police and the disappearance of thousands and thousands of people without a trace and without a trial, these were nevertheless measures of solid progress.

However, in foreign affairs there were either setbacks or standstills. Cuba had joined the Communist camp but that was more than offset by the Cuban missile crisis in October of 1962, in which American determination forced Khrushchev to back down and pull his missiles out of Cuba—a startling demonstration of American military superiority and Russian miscalculation. Nor were there any Russian victories in Africa or Asia. In a sense the disintegration of the rigid unity of the Communist empire was Khrushchev's greatest and possibly most lasting achievement. Yet he obtained little thanks for this, least of all from those East European Communist leaders who profited from it.

By October, 1964, Khrushchev had apparently used up his capital. His many unfulfilled promises, the failure of his agricultural venture, the deepening rift with China, also his blustering personality and his deportment, which seemed ill-suited to the head of a powerful nation, and the ever-present envy of his colleagues and associates, all contributed to his downfall.

The plot must have been well prepared because everything points to the conclusion that Khrushchev was in the dark and that it was only at the very last moment that he realized that he was facing a hostile majority in the Central Committee of the Communist party which had hitherto been the mainstay of his power. Nobody knows exactly what went on except that an official announcement was issued on October 17, 1964, to the effect that three days earlier, on October 14, the Central Committee had removed Nikita Khrushchev as First Secretary of the Central Committee. The largely ornamental Presidium of the Supreme Soviet went through the motions a day later of removing him from all government offices, in particular from that of Prime Minister. It was a bloodless coup and everything indicates that Khrushchev has been permitted to live a quiet and not uncomfortable life of retirement although it is unlikely that he can travel at will. He has been seen on a few occasions since his enforced retirement, but his contacts—especially with foreigners—appear to be practically nil.

It is interesting that Khrushchev was removed, not by long-standing adversaries, but by his closest associates, who by and large appeared to continue his policies. The fact that he has been replaced by two men rather than one would, on first impression, appear to be a repetition of his own rise to power, when he shared billing with Nikolai Bulganin for a short time. Of course, it is not impossible that one man should again take over eventually; however, for the time being, there seems to be an actual division of power and responsibilities between the new top men, Leonid Brezhnev and Alexei Kosygin. By contrast, nobody was in the slightest doubt, when the Khrushchev-Bulganin tandem existed, that Bulganin's role was purely ornamental.

Leonid Ilyich Brezhnev, Khrushchev's successor as First Secretary of the party, was born in the Ukraine in late December, 1906, as the son of a miner, and he himself worked in the mines from his fifteenth year on. He improved his education through evening courses and eventually became an engineer. A party member since 1931, he became a party official in the Ukraine, where he became acquainted with and worked closely with Nikita Khrushchev. He was a colonel in the army during World War II. As Khrushchev's protegé, he became deputy chief and eventually chief of the political division of the Fourth Ukrainian Front, was given the rank of major general and later lieutenant general. From 1946 to 1947 he supervised the reconstruction of various areas in the Ukraine until he became first secretary of the Communist party in the Moldavian Soviet Republic (Bessarabia). In 1952 he became a member of the Central Committee and candidate member of the Presidium. He briefly lost these offices after the death of Stalin, but at the Twentieth Party Congress in 1956 he again became candidate member of the Presidium and also a secretary of the Central Committee. The trust Khrushchev placed in him was shown by his selection as director of Khrushchev's virgin lands project during its critical opening phase from 1954 to 1955. In the struggle within the Presidium in 1957, he sided with Khrushchev and was rewarded with full membership, becoming Chairman of the Presidium of the Supreme Soviet in 1960 and thus nominal head of the state. In this he was replaced by another star, Anastas Mikoyan, on July 15, 1964, but he retained his other high party offices.

Not quite three years younger, Alexei Nikolajevich Kosygin was the son of a St. Petersburg (later Leningrad) metalworker. He joined the Red Army at age fifteen and participated in the civil war, and later studied and became a textile engineer. He occupied a number of minor party posts, becoming the director of a textile factory in 1938. Then he became one of Stalin's principal advisors on questions of economic and fiscal policy. In 1938 he was made chairman of the city administration of Leningrad, and in 1939 People's Commissar (minister) for the textile industry, in the same year being elected member of the Central Committee of the party. He advanced rapidly, rising in 1943 to Prime Minister of the Russian Socialist Federated Soviet Republic. In 1946 he became candidate member of the Politburo while at the same time advancing to the position of Deputy Prime Minister to Stalin in the U.S.S.R. government. In 1948 he became Minister of Finance and full member of the Politburo. He lost the Finance Ministry, but occupied other ministries under Stalin, Malenkov, and Khrushchev, advancing again under the latter to the position of Deputy Prime Minister. Curiously enough, after having become a member of the Presidium of the Central Committee, he was demoted to candidate level. But this does not seem to have handicapped his career on the purely governmental side. After the fall of Molotov, Malenkov, and Kaganovich, he rose again to Deputy Prime Minister, and in May, 1960 he became First Deputy Prime Minister in the place of Frol Koslov, who had been Khrushchev's heir apparent but who was cut down by illness.

One can clearly see not only that both Brezhnev and Kosygin were "survival specialists" since they rose steadily under both Stalin and Khrushchev, but that they became strictly "Khrushchev men," supporting him in every one of his moves until they finally overthrew him. Among the qualities which permitted men to survive the Stalin holocaust and rise to the top of the heap have been considerable ability plus ruthlessness, shrewdness, and a total lack of sentimentality. These qualities were typical of both these men.

When the take-over occurred in October, 1964, an early demise of the "duumvirate" of Brezhnev and Kosygin was predicted, with Brezhnev generally considered as the one most likely to emerge on top. To date, however, the two have seemed to work well together although it is difficult to tell whether this is the result of agreement on essentials or of a balance of power in the Politburo. The fact that in the Soviet system of government, policy struggles tend to turn into struggles for the control of power mitigates against the continued working of their arrangement. However, the manifest desire of the party leadership not to find themselves faced by another Stalin may serve as a countervailing tendency. Much will depend on the nature of new problems, the solutions found for old and persistent difficulties, and the desire of one or more of the upper leadership to succeed to the "throne."

5

Marxism-Leninism: the theoretical foundations of the state

Every state, every social organism composed of thinking human beings, has a political theory. In fact it is this theory which holds it together. The club, the labor union, the Rotary Club—all have certain ideas which their members hold in common which give them a purpose and make them want to remain in the organization. An association without common concepts would merely be a roomful of people incapable of acting as a group.

Clubs and similar organizations occupy only a limited field in our lives; their purposes are therefore limited, as are the ideas which underlie their existence. But it is different with the state. Aristotle wrote that man was a "political (social) animal," by which he meant that man had to live in organized society in order to be fully himself. Today there are few people in the world who are not subjects or citizens of a state, and the conditions which surround them there determine to a large extent their existence and their aspirations.

Because living in a state is so much more pervasive than mere membership in a club, the underlying ideas which all citizens are supposed to hold in common cover a good deal of ground. Some states have been fortunate and have settled their fundamental differences before their people entered into the Industrial Revolution. Other newer states found that their citizens largely agreed on fundamentals when the basic framework of their structure was established. England is an example of the former, and the United States of the latter. The political life of these two countries has therefore evolved around ways and means, rather than fundamentals, for such a long time that their inhabitants have come to regard the controversy over ways and means as the principal, perhaps the sole, basis for political action. Americans are inclined to be distrustful of political theory as a basis for political action, and we sometimes disparage theory as a key to the understanding of other people's political action. We are sometimes wont to consign political theory to the realm of "propaganda"—the useful little word which gives some of us the illusion of shrewdness when we are merely ignorant.

Much of the world has been less fortunate than we were. Questions of a fundamental nature still play their tortuous role, and answers are debated on the basis of their agreement with certain doctrines rather than in relation to their practical application. In old Russia there was a time when young intellectuals greeted each other with the words "In what do you believe?"

The question which has continually been raised is to what degree both the Soviet citizens and the more dedicated members of the Communist party really operate within the framework of their doctrine. It is probable that many "men in the street" regard the official doctrine with a certain degree of cynicism, in the same way that many Americans regard the basic tenets of Americanism. But, as Carew Hunt has remarked,[1]

> . . . between total commitment and total disillusionment there are many intermediate positions. It is quite possible for a man to regard much of what he is told as nonsense while still believing that there is something of value behind it, especially if he identifies that "something" with the greatness of his country.

The question of leadership is more difficult. Doctrine serves neither as a prison nor as an absolute blueprint for the future. Neither is it a totally cynical facade put on to justify the retention of power. It is a framework in which the leaders see and understand the world and which serves essentially to order their thinking. It is a system in which they have been nurtured for a considerable period of time and it would be strange if they were not affected by it. Besides, Marxism-Leninism serves some very useful functions.

Like a spiritual religion, it purports to possess the *truth,* although communism

[1] R. N. Carew Hunt, "The Importance of Doctrine," *Russia Under Khrushchev, An Anthology,* an issue of the publication *Problems of Communism,* ed. by Abraham Brumberg, New York, 1964, p. 8.

speaks of "scientific accuracy" which amounts to the same thing. Communism, like religion, demands unqualified allegiance to the tenets of the "faith" and stands ever ready to excommunicate the apostate. Like religion it has a kind of "scripture," the writings of the masters, Marx-Engels-Lenin and, for a while, Stalin, which is subjected to ceaseless exegesis. Like some religions it has a tightly organized quasi-church, the body of the elect, the party. Communism also has a hierarchy which demands obedience, and it shows little liking for opposite views which, being "untrue" by definition, cannot be tolerated.

As a quasi-religion, communism provides its followers with an intellectual home in which all questions have an answer—not an inconsiderable attraction in troubled times. It gives them a sense of superiority, because they are supposedly the repositories of the "truth." It gives them a sense of mission, raises them above the confines of their own lives, and imbues them with great courage and devotion. It enables them to justify anything—and there is much to justify. But it also tends to make them peculiarly blind to the outside world, which they view through their party spectacles and which they believe they understand thoroughly and "scientifically" when in reality they are often woefully ill informed. Such is the frame within which political action originates in the Soviet Union. It is a flexible frame, and much can be seen through it, but like all frames it has its limitations.

Karl Marx

The founder of the school and one of the most creative and original personalities of all time was a German, Karl Marx (1818–1883), who lived in London most of his life. His writings were voluminous, and the literature about his work is immense. The following lines are in the nature of a brief survey of Marxism-Leninism which can hope only to scratch the surface.[2]

Historical materialism

The foundation of the Marxist system is the concept of historical materialism. Marx contends that human life and aspirations are the result of economic factors, especially the production process, which form them. All spiritual, idealistic, and intellectual processes are the result of economic conditions and therefore molded by them. Marx formulated this thought in the following way:[3]

---

[2] Among Marx's own works the most important for our purposes is his *Critique of Political Economy;* also *Manifesto of the Communist Party, The Class Struggles in France,* and *Capital* (especially Vol. I), as well as his correspondence. Among Engels's works, note especially *Herr Eugen Dühring's Revolution in Science* (known as the "Anti-Dühring") and his correspondence. Note also G. D. H. Cole, *What Marx Really Meant,* London, 1934; Sydney Hook, *Towards an Understanding of Karl Marx,* New York, 1933, and his *From Hegel to Marx,* New York, 1936; H. J. Laski, *Karl Marx: An Essay,* London, 1922; and Paul M. Sweezy, *Socialism,* New York, 1949.

[3] Karl Marx, *Critique of Political Economy* (trans. by N. I. Stone), New York, 1904, p. 11.

In the social production which men carry on they enter into definite relationships that are indispensable and independent of their will; these relations of production correspond to a definite stage of development of their material powers of production. The sum total of these relations of production constitutes the economic structure of society—the real foundation on which rise legal and political superstructures and to which correspond definite forms of social consciousness. The mode of production in material life determines the general character of the social, political, and spiritual processes of life. It is not the consciousness of men that determines their existence, but, on the contrary, their social existence determines their consciousness.

The above quotation crystallizes several essential concepts of Marxism. All society is formed by its economic basis, in particular by the production process. Change that and you change society. Historical materialism thus appears in a twin role: it provides a scientific, logical (dialectic) method by which the course of history can be accurately discovered, and it is a tool through which the course of history can be changed by changing the production process.

The "dictatorship of the proletariat"

Social history so viewed becomes a dynamic process. Each stage of history is dominated by a class—namely, the class which owns the means of production and thus controls the production process. In modern times, in the era of capitalism, the ruling class which controls the means of production is the *bourgeoisie*. But this class system bears the seed of its own destruction within itself, according to Marx, for at a certain stage in its development new production methods conflict with existing property relationships; the result is ever-widening crises and a transformation of the social order. Thus capitalism forges the weapons which destroy it, but it also "calls into existence the men who are to wield those weapons—the modern working class —the proletariat."[4] This is the class which must sell its labor in order to live, but as a result of technological advance there is created an industrial "reserve army" of unemployed which helps to keep wages down to the bare existence level. Because of this condition, the *bourgeoisie* makes greater and greater profits, while the proletariat becomes increasingly impoverished. This development leads to ever-widening crises, which deprive more and more groups of property and force them to merge with the proletariat. But in this way it also strengthens the proletariat, which eventually overthrows the regime and establishes its own dictatorship and a new social order. It should be emphasized that according to this theory the proletariat encompasses the overwhelming majority of the people, and its "dictatorship" may therefore be "democratic." To Marx and Engels the "dictatorship of the proletariat" is more "democratic" than the rule of the *bourgeoisie,* because the former is rule by majority while the latter is rule by a small minority.

---

[4] Karl Marx and Friedrich Engels, *Manifesto of the Communist Party* (generally known as the Communist Manifesto), New York, 1932, p. 15 (first published in 1848).

The "withering away" of the state

The dictatorship of the proletariat is not supposed to be the final development. It is still a "state," and a "state" is by definition a machinery for suppression, i.e., suppression of classes.[5] True, according to Marx this is better than "bourgeois democracy,"[6] because the former constitutes force exercised by the majority against the minority while the latter means presumably force by the minority against the majority. Yet according to Marx and Engels this is merely a transitory stage:[7]

> The proletariat seizes state power, and then transforms the means of production into state property. But in doing this, it puts an end to itself as the proletariat, it puts an end to all class differences and class antagonism, it puts an end to the state as the state. . . . As soon as there is no longer any class of society to be held in subjection; as soon as, along with class domination and the struggle for individual existence based on the former anarchy of production, the collisions and excesses arising from these have also been abolished, there is nothing more to be repressed and a special repressive force, a state, is no longer necessary.

Thus the state withers away because there is no further need for it, and the end of the state ushers in a society without antagonism, without exploitation, in which "people will become gradually accustomed to the observance of the elementary rules of social life . . . without compulsion, without subordination, without the special apparatus for compulsion which is called the state."[8]

This is still the general framework within which Communist political theory develops, but there have been a number of significant modifications. Marx oversimplified society. He presented the picture of a world with two poles called *bourgeoisie* and proletariat. He ignored the peasants and the middle class, whose members he assumed would join the one or the other of the two main classes. In fact, it was the very assumption of the greater part of these two classes joining the proletariat which was to give the latter its overwhelming numerical superiority. Moreover, the proletariat was to become increasingly impoverished and under the theory of economic determinism was to act as a class in accordance with its economic interest. But contrary to these expectations the peasants and the middle class did not cease to exist. In many instances they became stronger. Nor did the proletariat become increasingly impoverished. Social legislation, trade-union activities, adjustments within the capitalistic machinery, and the power of democratic labor parties improved their lot in all industrial countries. The First World War finally revealed that the proletariat did not act in accordance with its alleged interest but proceeded to support its respective bourgeois governments and the war. It became necessary to make adjustments for these events, and this was primarily Lenin's contribution.

[5] Lenin, *State and Revolution*, New York, 1929, p. 74.
[6] This concept, of course, ignores the fact that majority rule is not the only essence of democracy and that it also includes civil rights for minorities.
[7] Friedrich Engels, *Herr Eugen Dühring's Revolution in Science* (trans. by E. Burns), London, 1935, p. 306.
[8] Lenin, *op. cit.*, p. 74.

Lenin and the theory of imperialism

Lenin stressed the theory that imperialism was the highest stage of capitalism.[9] He maintained that the enormous expansion of the capitalist economy has led to an imperialistic development from which certain parts of the proletariat, especially the skilled workers, profit. This era of imperialism is characterized by the export of finance capital and the control of the banks over industry. It is also characterized by the growth of gigantic monopolies. Again, however, the "inevitable" economic forces throw these monopolies into a savage struggle for markets which culminates in war. Such a war, according to Lenin, is nothing but a war between trusts in which the workers have no stake. The worker must therefore see that he ought not to strive for temporary advantage through the rivalry of one monopolist with another but should realize his opportunity by acting in the ultimate interest of his class, by turning the imperialist war into a civil war.

The role of the Communist party

In contrast to Marx, who believed in the critical faculty of the proletariat and therefore expected revolutionary fervor and action to become the spontaneous reactions of the masses, Lenin believed that the masses of the proletariat were not always aware of their "true" interests. Therefore the proletariat had to be guided by "its most advanced part, the Communist party." This meant in effect that the "dictatorship of the proletariat" became in effect the dictatorship of the Communist party. Lenin justified this as follows:[10]

> . . . in the era of capitalism, when the masses of the workers are constantly subjected to exploitation and cannot develop their human faculties, the most characteristic feature of working class political parties is that they can embrace only a minority of their class. . . . That is why we must admit that only this class-conscious minority can guide the broad masses of the workers and lead them.

Stalin later tried to minimize Lenin's frank admission by asserting that Lenin merely meant that the Communist party leads the proletariat and that it does not share that role with any other party. But since the will of the proletariat is clearly established by its leadership and since there is on record no single, solitary instance in which the proletariat or members thereof have expressed themselves in opposition to the party or even differed therefrom, and lived, the difference between Lenin's words as we would ordinarily understand them and Stalin's interpretation thereof is not visible to the naked eye. Under Communist theory there can actually be no such difference between the proletariat and the party. The "dialectical

[9] Lenin, *Imperialism: The Highest Stage of Capitalism,* New York, 1939.
[10] Lenin in a speech before the second congress of the Communist International, quoted by Hans Kelsen, *The Political Theory of Bolshevism,* Berkeley, Calif., 1949, p. 52.

method" according to Communist doctrine is a scientific process by which "correct" policy may be accurately determined.[11] "Destalinization" has in no way affected this argument. Hence disagreement would only indicate ignorance or worse. In this formulation disagreement becomes "deviation," which is tantamount to mortal sin. It is only natural that the exposition of the "correct" policy must be the task of the "most advanced part" of the proletariat, the Communist party. The position of the party was clearly stated by Stalin:[12]

> A party is a part of a class, its most advanced part. Several parties, and consequently, freedom for parties, can exist only in a society in which there are antagonistic classes whose interests are mutually hostile and irreconcilable. . . . But in the U.S.S.R. there are no longer such classes as the capitalists, the landlords, the kulaks, etc. In the U.S.S.R. there are only two classes, workers and peasants, whose interests—far from being mutually hostile—are, on the contrary, friendly. Hence there is no ground in the U.S.S.R. for the existence of several parties, and consequently, for freedom for these parties. In the U.S.S.R. there is ground only for one party, the Communist Party.

Naturally, total unity within that party is an absolute postulate. This is not a Stalinist innovation. At the Tenth Party Congress in 1921, Lenin vigorously proposed a resolution entitled "On the unity of the Party" which inveighed against "factionalism" and in fact meant that henceforth party members were forbidden, on penalty of expulsion, to meet in informal groups and discuss public or party affairs. As a result, almost one-third of all party members were expelled in the first major purge of 1921.[13]

The justification of the single-party state is thus based on the contention that opposing classes have disappeared in the Soviet Union. But did not Engels and Lenin say that when that happens the state withers away? No, says Stalin, because the Soviet Union is encircled by capitalist states. According to Stalin, Engels's position can be understood only under two assumptions: (1) by studying the socialist state solely from the angle of its internal development; or (2) if one assumes that socialism (communism) has already become victorious in all or the majority of countries and that therefore there is no danger of foreign attack and therefore no need for the state and the army.[14]

> But it follows from this that Engels' general formula about the destiny of the Socialist state in general cannot be extended to the partial and specific case of the victory of Socialism in one country alone, a country which is surrounded by a capitalist world, is subject to the menace of foreign military attack, cannot there-

[11] Stalin, *Dialectical and Historical Materialism,* New York, 1940.
[12] Stalin, *Leninism,* New York, 1942, p. 395.
[13] Alfred G. Meyer, *The Soviet Political System: An Interpretation,* New York, 1965, pp. 159–160.
[14] *Ibid.,* p. 471.

fore abstract itself from the international situation, and must have at its disposal a well-trained army, well-organized punitive organs, and a strong intelligence service—consequently must have its own state, strong enough to defend the conquests of Socialism from foreign attacks.

Thus, as long as all the world is not dominated by communism, the Soviet "state" does not wither away but on the contrary becomes stronger. This is so because the capitalistic "encirclement" is considered hostile by definition, since the economic interests of capitalist powers require them to fear the alleged attraction of the Soviet Union.

Thus in the theory and the pronouncements of communism the shape of the Soviet state can already be perceived. It is a state whose leaders believe they possess a "scientific" method for determining "correct" policy. It is a state whose leaders believe in the inevitability of communist triumph everywhere in the world and who believe that this end can be achieved by an uncompromising revolutionary policy.[15] It is a state which is dominated and guided by a single political party, the Communist party, from which all policy emanates. The Communist party is everything. And it is no less everything because the rules for the discipline of party members have been somewhat relaxed since the Twenty-second Party Congress of 1961. The institutions of the state are merely tools to be used as the party sees fit, to be picked up or discarded at will. Since the party is presumably the custodian of an inevitable, historical development,[16] it cannot be limited by any institutional or constitutional factors. Consequently in the Soviet Union constitutions and legal documents are as secondary in importance as are the formal institutions of the state. The living constitution, the actual government, is the Communist party. A study of that Communist party must therefore be the first step in the investigation of the institutions of government in the Union of Soviet Socialist Republics.

---

[15] Stalin, *Dialectical and Historical Materialism,* p. 14. Hence, in order not to err in policy, "one must pursue an uncompromising proletarian class policy, not a reformist policy of harmony of the interests of the proletariat and the bourgeoisie."
[16] Waldemar Gurian, *Bolshevism: An Introduction to Soviet Communism,* Notre Dame, 1952, p. 15.

6

The Communist party

The Communist party of the Soviet Union is not an open mass party like Western political parties but a closed society of the new "elite." Only the most rigorous tests will admit a new member, and even after admission he must be constantly prepared to prove his devotion to the "party line" or to face a purge. A party member thus accepts a heavy burden of supervision and uncertainty as a price for the coveted position which party membership confers. The party constantly strives to recruit into its ranks the leading members of all elements of society. At the same time, positions of significance are difficult to obtain without party membership although this is no longer as strict a rule as it once was, particularly in the sciences, where the party has retreated considerably since the days of Stalin.[1]

The pivotal and monopoly position of the party is well recognized. "Here in the Soviet Union, in the land of the dictatorship of the proletariat," said Stalin, "the fact that not a single important political or organizational question is decided

[1] This is a central theme in Albert Parry's *The New Class Divided,* New York, 1966.

by our Soviet and other mass organizations without directions from the Party must be regarded as the highest expression of the leading role of the Party. . . . In this sense it could be said that the dictatorship of the proletariat is in essence the dictatorship of its vanguard, the dictatorship of its Party."[2] The Soviet Constitution of 1936 (Art. 126) states that

> The most active and politically-conscious citizens in the ranks of the working class and other sections of the working people unite in the Communist Party of the Soviet Union (Bolsheviks), which is the vanguard of the working people in their struggle to strengthen and develop the socialist system and is the leading core of all organizations of the working people, both public and state.

And Andrei Vyshinsky, Soviet diplomat and former leading jurist of the U.S.S.R., wrote, "The political basis of the USSR comprises—as the most important principle of the working class dictatorship—the leading and directing role of the Communist Party in all fields of economic, social and cultural activity."[3] "The workers themselves," said Lenin, "do not know as yet how to rule and would first have to go through years of schooling. Hence, in order to rule, an army of revolutionaries—Communists hardened in battle—is necessary. We have such; it is the Party." Thus, in the clear words of the Communist leaders themselves, the "dictatorship of the proletariat" is in effect the dictatorship of the Communist party.

The monolithic party and "democratic centralism"

The monopoly position of the party excludes all possibilities that the formulation of its policy might be challenged by outside forces. Can there be challenge within? The Communist party[4] is a single, unified, and centralized structure, a "monolith." Only one will, one direction, may prevail. Factionalism is strictly prohibited. But at the same time Communists claim that their party is endowed with what they are pleased to call "democratic centralism." This term implies a combination between the principle of mass participation at the bottom and the concentration of leadership at the top. According to the party rules, this means:

1. The election of all party bodies, from the lowest to the highest.

2. Periodical reports by the party bodies to their party organizations.

3. Strict party discipline and subordination of the minority to the majority.

4. The absolutely binding character of the decisions of higher bodies upon lower bodies.[5]

---

[2] J. V. Stalin, *Problems of Leninism*, New York, 1934, p. 34.

[3] Andrei Y. Vyshinsky, *The Law of the Soviet State* (trans. by H. R. Babb), New York, 1948, p. 159.

[4] J. Towster, *Political Power in the U.S.S.R.*, New York, 1948, p. 120. This is one of the most detailed and authoritative works on the Soviet Union.

[5] Rule 21, Statute (rules) of the Communist Party of the Soviet Union of 1952.

However the twenty-second Party Congress of 1961 strengthened the role of the larger party assemblies and committees, decreased the size of the party bureaucracy, and curtailed the reeligibility of members to the same post for more than three successive terms, although exceptions were made for those with "exceptional qualities."[6]

What is the reality of "democratic centralism"? There will be little dispute about the word "centralism," which means essentially two things in the Communist party: the absolute concentration of power at the top, and the total absence of a federal principle within the party. The term "democratic centralism" implies that there is democracy within each level of the party but that there is no democracy between levels. Thus the upper levels dictate absolutely and without restraint to the lower levels. The area organization dictates to the town organization and is in turn dictated to by the regional organization, and that goes all the way up to the Politburo, which dictates the entire policy of the party and thus of the state.

As all power is concentrated at the top, it is clear that no reserved powers remain in the hands of the party organizations for the various territorial subdivisions. As far as the Communist party is concerned, the guiding principle is thus clearly unitary and not federal.

Despite this admitted concentration of all power at the top, it is still claimed that there is intra-party democracy because (1) all organs of the party are elected, (2) each organ is accountable to the larger body electing it, and (3) the party practices "self-criticism."

The reality, however, is that the usual way in which party officers are chosen is by co-option, that is, for instance, by members of a committee or presidium deciding who shall fill a given vacancy, or by appointment from high authority.[7] Where there are elections, they are pure formalities, pure ratification of decisions already made at a higher level. There is not on record a single instance at which a contest developed between rival candidates for office. It is of course impossible to gauge accurately the nature of the informal discussions which precede the formal election of officers. Undoubtedly there are many instances, especially at the lower level, where the qualifications of several people are discussed. However, these discussions concern themselves solely with the personal fitness of a man or woman for a specific task, and never involve difference of policy. The more important the office is, the more evident is the will of the party leadership—a will which is clearly and immediately understood and never disobeyed.

The accountability of officers to larger bodies is purely theoretical and has no relation to reality. Meetings of party congresses and conferences have become more and more irregular and infrequent, despite the provisions of the party rules which demand periodic conferences at given intervals. Nor is there ever feasible, under existing conditions, a ground swell which would oust an officer or committee. The

[6] For the text of the 1961 party program, see Jan F. Triska (ed.), *Soviet Communism, Program and Rules*, San Francisco, 1962.
[7] Merle Fainsod, *How Russia Is Ruled*, Cambridge, Mass., 1953, p. 181.

party may give in to popular dissatisfaction against an officer and have him removed, but this occurs only when the bone of contention is the efficiency with which the individual executes official policy. The policy itself may not be questioned. In all such instances the actual ouster is the result of a decision by the party leaders and is always well known to the congress membership before the meeting gets under way. Frequently officials marked for disciplinary action are criticized in the party press, and this serves to give a hint to party members and delegates concerning the attitude and action expected of them. The literature of analysts and eyewitnesses is full of graphic descriptions showing how such "marked men" suddenly find themselves isolated and attacked from all sides. Only in disputes over literature did some opposition appear, in 1965 and 1966. Since such literary quarrels are fraught with political implications, their significance should not be underrated. However, they are at best a small beginning.

"Self-criticism"

Most interesting among arguments purporting to show the existence of intra-party democracy is that of self-criticism. Self-criticism undoubtedly exists within the party, sometimes on a fairly large scale, but there are significant limitations to the exercise thereof. The would-be critic must never attempt to organize the supporters for his views, for to do so would make him guilty of "factionalism,"[8] a severe breach of discipline and of the principle of party unity. Nor must self-criticism ever attack policy, which as we have seen is laid down to lower bodies by higher ones and originates in the Presidium. To attack the party line constitutes the offense of "deviationism," a most serious error involving danger to the perpetrator.

What is then the purpose of "self-criticism"? In the first place, it is a method by which broad attention can be focused on the implementation and execution of a policy already decided upon at high levels. Thus a wide array of talent may be brought to bear upon the mechanics of carrying out orders, a process which adds to efficiency and diverts possible criticism from the merits of the policy itself.

Secondly, it is an important means of disciplining inefficient, corrupt, or negligent officials. It allows citizens to vent at least some of their frustrations on low-level officials, and at the same time it adds to efficiency of operations by adding hundreds of extra eyes and ears to the reguar means of control and keeping officials on the alert.

Thirdly, it is a method of throwing an official to the wolves in order that pent-up feelings may concentrate on him and be diverted from higher levels.

Fourthly, it serves to demonstrate the all-important and all-powerful character of the party from whose avenging sword no one, not even formerly powerful leaders, is ever exempt.

Fifthly, self-criticism is a peculiar, and to the Western mind, a particularly

---

[8] "Factionalism" has been defined by Stalin as "the rise of groups with special platforms and with the aim of shutting themselves off to a certain extent and creating their own group discipline" (13th Congress of the Communist party).

repulsive part of the Communist ritual. A party member, no matter how high, must, when criticized, immediately confess his errors in a most abject fashion. Since a member, especially a high official, is publicly criticized only when his downfall or at least his diminution has already been decided upon by the powers that be, this complete self-debasement is the only way in which the victim can save himself from the worst—and even then he may not succeed. This ritual is typical not only for the Communist party of the Soviet Union but also for all the Communist parties in the world. It serves again to demonstrate the infallibility of the party and the official doctrine. All difficulties are the result of personal error of individuals, of their inability to understand the gospel of Marxism-Leninism "correctly." The party, the doctrine, are never in error.

Thus "self-criticism," far from being an expression of an imagined "intra-party democracy," is only an instrument to help shape the completely obedient party member, who will labor day and night to carry out the party's directives without ever questioning their wisdom or validity, who can be turned in any direction—the perfect human robot.

The question of what constitutes a fit subject for self-criticism lies solely with the Central Committee of the party, which means the Presidium. Although the exceptionally harsh form of oppression practiced under Stalin appears to be now a matter of the past, Stalin's statement on the limitation of intra-party democracy is still valid. Replying to a certain Lutovinov, he stated:[9]

> He [Lutovinov] wants real democracy, that all, at least the most important questions should be discussed in all the cells from bottom up, that the whole party should get going on every question and should take part in the consideration of that question. But, comrades, . . . with such an arrangement our party would be transformed into a discussion club of eternally jabbering and never-deciding [people], while our party must, above all, be an acting one, because we are in power.

The functions of the Communist party emerge clearly from its role as the "guide" of state and people. It is the spark plug of all action in the public and sometimes the private sector of Soviet life. All important actions originate in the party and are pressed by the party, but because of the frequent identity of state and party officials, it is not always easy to distinguish between government and party affairs.

Propaganda

The Communist party is also in charge of the ideological education of the people. No regime can get along without a measure of support on the part of the people, and the Soviet leaders are well aware of that. Consequently Marxist-Leninist-

[9] J. Stalin before the 12th Congress of the Russian Communist party, April, 1923; cf. Towster, *op. cit.,* p. 157.

Stalinist doctrine is propagated by all organs and sections of the party. Since Communist theory holds that every field of human endeavor is an expression and instrument of class warfare, the party makes use of every available instrument. Thus not only is all political thought strictly streamlined according to the accepted doctrine, but music, art, science, and every other conceivable activity must reflect a proper Communist attitude. Before Stalin's demise this proper attitude had a strongly nationalistic note, which included the claim that Russians had originated and invented all kinds of things which are ordinarily attributed to such people as Edison, Rutherford, and Marconi. These endeavors to strengthen national pride and to combine it with Communist loyalty may have taken their cue from the experience with patriotic propaganda during the war. They were undoubtedly quite successful. At present the nationalistic element is less in evidence; rather than dwell on imaginary scientific triumphs the Soviet leaders have now concentrated their efforts on propagandizing and exploiting the very real Soviet successes in the realm of science in order to prove the superiority of their system.

The reverse side of the party's teaching function is the duty of eliminating impurities. Failure to follow the party line may, under certain circumstances, be considered "wrecking," and writers who fail to observe the strict confines of Marxism-Leninism as expounded by the party have found themselves termed "enemies of the people."[10] Similarly, internecine power struggles between rival factions for leadership in the country have always been represented by the victorious group as a fight against anti-party elements and for the correct party line, never as a personal feud; opponents, whether of Stalin, Khrushchev, or Brezhnev and Kosygin, have always gone to their downfall under the label of enemies of the party and the people.

The Communist party also serves as a device by which the government and the party keep the people informed about their activities. Since the party and the government have a monopoly on all information channels, this is a highly effective means of control. No single organ of information carries as much authority as the chief newspaper of the Communist party, *Pravda* (Truth). Opposing papers, foreign or domestic, are of course prohibited. Apart from underground literature, which probably exists in some measure, foreign radio broadcasts are the only possible source of non-Communist information. Listening to foreign stations is not punishable by law at the present time, though repeating what has been heard is. But short-wave radios are not numerous in the Soviet Union, and Soviet stations have been "jamming" such Russian-language programs as the "Voice of America."

As the party carries down to the people what the government does, it also attempts to stimulate them for such action as the government and the party may deem desirable. Meetings are held, speeches heard, and resolutions passed. A special device is the so-called "organized discussion," by far the most frequently heard

---

[10] See S. N. Harper and R. Thompson, *The Government of the Soviet Union,* New York, 1949, 2d ed., pp. 76*ff*. Art. 131 of the Soviet Constitution terms public, socialist property "sacred" and calls persons who commit offenses against it "enemies of the people."

discussion of public issues in the Soviet Union. This is not an ordinary, free debate exposing different points of view, but rather the exploration and dramatization of the best ways and means by which the given policy may be carried out most efficiently.

Not only does the Communist party report to the people about the activities of the government, but it also reports to the government and party leadership about sentiments among the people. In so far as this is a security function, it is carried out by the secret political police, now the MGB, but it is the duty of the party to report significant changes in public opinion in order that party and government may take the necessary action.

Membership

As of 1965, the members and candidate members of the Communist party numbered 11,785,000 out of a population of more than 200,500,000.[11] Rigorous standards of loyalty, efficiency, and personal conduct must be observed by those who wish to be admitted to the new aristocracy, but once admitted the Communist is by no means safe. He must submit to far greater supervision and control than will be imposed on nonmembers, and in his work as well as his deportment he is supposed to be a model. Failure to live up to these standards as well as any kind of "deviation" or "wrecking"[12] will be met with disciplinary punishment, which may include expulsion and worse. Communists are therefore likely to work under considerable strain. Usually they are extremely hard-working, devoted men of unquestioning obedience. Whatever talent and ability the country possesses may be found in the present or former ranks of the Communist party.

Finally, the Communist party exercises a "tutelage" over the people with the avowed purpose of educating them toward the goal of general participation in the processes of government. This is to be achieved by including most Soviet citizens in a great variety of voluntary and compulsory organizations among which the Communist party is the apex. In that way the citizenry is to learn "by doing" the functions of government. In reality, however, little progress appears to have been made in that direction. The Webbs[13] saw in the Soviet Union a pluralistic, multiform society in which all governmental functions were shared by a number of interacting "pyramids," i.e., mass organizations, rising from level to level and culminating in the Kremlin. According to the Webbs, every citizen has a distinctive part in this structure because he participates directly or indirectly on some level or other.

The developments in the Soviet Union and the statements of the Communist leaders themselves have definitely refuted this analysis. The Soviet state, and the

[11] "CPSU in Figures (1961–1964)" *Partiinaya Zhizn (Party Life),* May, 1965, No. 10, pp. 8–17.
[12] A person who fails to take proper measures against inefficiency and waste, or who fails to report such negligence, may be guilty of "wrecking."
[13] Sidney and Beatrice Webb, *Soviet Communism: A New Civilization?* New York, 1936, Vol. I, Introduction.

all-pervasive Communist party which "leads" it, is monolithic, not pluralistic. There is no doubt that the Communist party occupies the "leading and directing role" in every field. There are not many "pyramids," but only one. The people who participate in the various mass organizations—and even in the membership of the Communist party below the top level—do not really participate in the process of decision making, of policy, but merely fill an assigned place in a prescribed manner. This kind of "mass participation" does not constitute democracy, but quite on the contrary is the typical mark of totalitarian regimes, which it serves as an effective propaganda device.

Since the Communist party of the Soviet Union is an organization of the governing elite, it is also concerned with the continued supply of future elite material. The party therefore tends more and more to represent the better-educated and urban classes.[14] This development was interrupted during and shortly after the war when the doors of the party were thrown open to the members of the armed forces, among whom the rural and less educated elements predominate. But in recent years the long-range elitist trend has been clearly resumed and intensified. This means that workers contribute a decreasing number of party members, while peasant representation is extremely small, although it is by far the largest population group in the Soviet Union. In other words, the basis of Communist rule is not the workers, let alone the peasants, as Communist propaganda might indicate, but the managerial personnel, the bureaucracy. This tendency sharpens the gulf between the governors and the governed, and the Soviet rulers find it, therefore, expedient to widen the doors of the party from time to time in order not to lose contact with the masses of the people. But after a while, in order to fulfill its proper role as the directing center the party must return to its elitist tendencies. That such a situation produces considerable tensions is clear, but how strong they are is difficult to gauge. Evidence would indicate that they do not threaten the regime seriously, but this might change if the Soviet citizens, including the party members, had continuous contact with countries and civilizations outside the iron curtain. This is why the long-maintained isolation of the U.S.S.R. from the West is loosening up only gradually, and while the situation has materially improved, it is still a far cry from the type of contacts which are customary among Western countries.

Organization

The vast network of functions which the Communist party of the Soviet Union carries out can be put into operation only through well-organized machinery.[15] At the bottom of the ladder stand the primary party organs, formerly known

[14] For an excellent analysis of the Party's composition, see Fainsod, *op. cit.,* pp. 209–239, and Alfred G. Meyer, *The Soviet Political System,* New York, 1965, pp. 179–193.
[15] Georg Brunner, "Bylaws of the Elite: The Party Statutes," in *Problems of Communism,* March–April, 1965, pp. 48–52.

as "cells." They are to be found in every factory, shop, office, school, army, etc., wherever there are at least three party members. Each primary organization elects an executive committee or "bureau" and a secretary who is in reality the chairman and most significant officer. Even at that low level, the exalted position of the Communist party is recognized by the party rules, which provide that the primary organs "have the right of control over the activity of the administration of the enterprise" (rule 59, as of Twenty-second Party Congress, 1961).

If the primary unit is large, it has a party bureau, but in any case its central figure and director is the party secretary. He has his hand in every activity of the unit and gives the orders. He also bears the responsibility for the unit's performance and will be severely taken to task by higher headquarters for any failings.

According to the party statute (rule 57), the responsibility of primary party units comprises agitation and propaganda among the masses, conducting and supervising the political education of party members and candidates, recruiting new members, assisting higher levels of the party, mobilizing all efforts for the fulfillment of production plans, combating negligence, showing proper regard for the improvement of cultural and living conditions of the workers and peasants, developing "criticism" and "self-criticism," and inculcating Communists with "the spirit of an uncompromising attitude toward shortcomings."

Among those functions of particular significance are the recruitment of new members, their screening, and their introduction to their party responsibilities. As for the party's duty of supervising management, the secretary is not to interfere with the channel of command between the factory management and their technical superiors. But in actuality party secretaries frequently interfere in everything and cause confusion which sometimes meets with criticism from higher levels of command.

It is essential for party control over all enterprise that strictest efficiency and dedication to the task at hand should prevail. Personal influence and cliques are severely condemned. But there are probably few countries in the world where such influences and cliques are more important. Where there is so much power residing in certain positions, people with ambition naturally gravitate thereto. These cliques in turn have their significance in the power struggle which goes on unceasingly. Important party members surround themselves with their "people," and if they fall down, their "people" fall with them. Thus not long after the death of Andrei Zhdanov in 1948, all the Zhdanovites throughout Russia and even in other Communist parties were quickly liquidated. The same happened to the henchmen of Lavrenti Beria after he was executed. Thus to have fair longevity, a party member must not only be unquestioningly obedient, diligent, and efficient, but he must also have learned the art of sensing in good time every change in the power balance of the leadership. Consequences of "wrong associations" are now less drastic, but the removal of persons for such reasons still goes on, though now it is merely from their positions, not from life itself. A good example is the formerly highly influential

Alexei Adjubei, Khrushchev's son-in-law, who lost his positions in the press and radio soon after Khrushchev's ouster and was relegated to a minor position in a publishing house.

The primary organs elect delegates to the city or district conference of the party. This conference elects a committee which in turn elects a bureau and a secretary. This form of organization is then maintained by all other, higher echelons. Above the city or district conference are the organizations for the areas, regions, territories, and Union Republics.[16] They in turn elect delegates to the All-Union Congress of the party on the basis of 1 delegate per 1,000 members. At the sixteenth party Congress there were 2,159 delegates, but at the eighteenth Congress in 1939 there were only 1,574, and at the nineteenth there were 1,359 delegates. At the twenty-first party Congress in 1959 there were 1,269 delegates with voting rights, representing the members on a scale of 1 to 6,000, and 106 delegates without voting rights, representing the candidate members on the same scale. At the twenty-second party Congress of 1961, there were an unprecedented 4,408 full delegates and 405 alternates; or approximately 1 full delegate for 2,500 members. The figures were even slightly higher at the twenty-third party Congress in 1966, where 4,620 full delegates and 323 alternates were reported. Of course none of these elections is contested. Higher party echelons usually let it be known whose election is desired, and the person concerned is then elected without fail.

All Union Republics, except the largest, the Russian Socialist Federated Republic (R.S.F.S.R.), which comprises two-thirds of the territory of the Soviet Union, have their own party organizations which are modeled on the national organization. Until 1956 the territorial units of the R.S.F.S.R. reported directly to the national party organization, but the 20th Congress established for the first time a bureau of the Central Committee on party work in the R.S.F.S.R., a purely appointive and instrumental body in no way comparable with the structure existing in the other Republics. This is not actually a discrimination against the R.S.F.S.R. but is in its favor. The Communist party of the Soviet Union is, in fact, the Russian Communist party, and the Communist parties of the other republics are its branch organizations.[17] In the R.S.F.S.R. the party organization is divided into eight territories which in turn are divided into regions and areas. The other Union Republics have only regions and lower units. Below the areas are the city and district organizations, and at the lowest level are the already mentioned primary organizations, whose average membership is twenty.

At the head of each level of the party hierarchy is an executive committee (bureau) in which the first secretary plays the key role. In addition a representative of the All-Union Central Committee is attached to each Union Republic in order to

---

[16] In 1952, at the 19th Congress, the mandate commission reported the existence of 15 central committees (headed by the Central Committee of the Communist party of the Soviet Union), 8 territorial committees, 167 regional committees, 36 area committees, 544 city committees, 4,886 district committees, and 350,304 primary party organizations.

[17] D. J. R. Scott, *Russian Political Institutions,* New York, 1957, p. 137.

supervise the performance of its task. Moreover, party discipline is enforced by a "party Collegium," which is responsible directly to the national party Control Committee.

Sessions of the All-Union Congress are called by the Central Committee. The party rules of 1961 (rule 31) provide that a Congress shall be convoked every four years, though under the rules of 1939 the interval was to be three years. Until now, however, party congresses were most infrequent, and the convocation of the 20th Congress on time in 1956 was the first time that the party had obeyed its own rules on the subject. Its predecessor, the 19th Congress, was held in 1952 after an interval of more than thirteen years. Former party rules also provided for a party Conference to meet more frequently,[18] but the last such Conference met in 1941, and the institution was abolished by the party statute of 1952.

In the earlier period of the Soviet regime, congresses were held frequently and saw spirited discussions, but this development ended in 1927 after Stalin had consolidated his power. Membership in the Congress increased enormously, and discussion became "organized" as indicated above. Instead of debating and ratifying party policy, the Congress heard a large number of reports which were solemnized by being read to the delegates. Beyond that the sole function of the Congress became the lending of its prestige to government policy. This process was completed at the 17th Congress in 1934, when Stalin remarked that "no objections whatever have been raised against the report. Hence it has been revealed that there is extraordinary ideological-political and organizational solidarity in the ranks of our Party."

The Central Committee

The most important organism in the Communist party is nominally the Central Committee, within which operates the real ruling force of the Soviet Union, the Political Bureau (Politburo). "Not one important political or organizational question is decided by any one state institution in our republic without guiding instructions of the Central Committee of the Party," said Lenin,[19] and the Communist party rules provide that "the Central Committee directs the work of the central Soviet and Public organizations through the Party groups in them."[20]

The Central Committee, as elected in 1966, is composed of 195 members and 165 candidates. They are elected by the party Congress. All the important Communist leaders are among them. Meetings were originally required to be held twice monthly, and then from 1921 once in two months, from 1934 once in four months, and from 1952 once in six months. However, in his secret speech at the twentieth party Congress, Khrushchev declared that during the last fifteen years of Stalin's

[18] The party Conference was abolished in 1934 but was reinstated in 1939.
[19] Towster, *op. cit.*, p. 153n.
[20] Party statute of 1952, rule 36.

life plenary sessions were hardly ever called, and during the entire war there had not been a single one. The proceedings of the Central Committee were not made public, but individual speeches and reports were often published. In this respect, a unique precedent was set by the publication of the stenographic minutes of the December, 1957, Central Committee session and the publication therein of the speeches made during the conference itself.

For a number of years the Central Committee was the forum within which were carried out the major factional fights within the party. Trotsky called the doctrine that Bolshevism did not tolerate factionalism "a myth of the epoch of decline."[21] He wrote that the "history of Bolshevism is a history of the struggle of factions. . . . The Central Committee relied upon this seething democratic support. From this is derived the audacity to make decisions and give orders."

With the increasingly monolithic and Stalinist character of the Communist party, however, and the revelation that even the heroes of the Revolution were not safe from sudden downfall and execution, factionalism came to an end in the Central Committee.

Very little is known about its actual work. A great number of orders are published as emanating from it, but in view of its infrequent meetings they must come from the Politburo or the Secretariat. All indications point to the correctness of the assumption that the Central Committee had little real significance for a long time and that its theoretically enormous powers were wielded, often in its name, by the Politburo. It would appear, however, that the Central Committee may now be undergoing a resurrection as an operative organ. It was the scene of Khrushchev's triumph over his enemies after his defeat in the Politburo and was probably the scene of his downfall in 1964.

The Presidium-Politburo

The principle of centralism places a tremendous amount of responsibility and work on the shoulders of those on top. This means a large number of daily decisions on a great variety of subjects. A body like the Central Committee which meets in plenary session only three to six times a year is, of course, quite unable to carry such a load. The overwhelming majority of these decisions are therefore made by a smaller, permanent committee of the Central Committee, the Politburo. In the course of years the Central Committee has thus become primarily an organ of ratification for decisions of the Politburo. When the Central Committee opens its mouth, it is the voice of the Politburo which comes out.

In the entire history of the Soviet Union it has always been this small committee which wielded the decisive power in the state. Under the name of Political Bureau, but better known by its abbreviation as Politburo, it was already established in 1917. The 8th Congress of the Communist party in 1919 established the

---

[21] L. Trotsky, *The Revolution Betrayed* (trans. by M. Eastman), New York, 1937, p. 95.

system which was to last, essentially, until 1952. It placed supreme direction in the Politburo, and organizational work in the Organizational Bureau, better known as Orgburo. The functions of the Secretariat were not clearly defined at that time. It was only through Stalin's use of the Secretariat as a vehicle for his own road to power that it became all-important. In fact, until 1941 Stalin held no official post other than that of General Secretary of the Communist party and member of the Politburo. It was largely due to war exigencies that he assumed officially the post of Premier, whose actual title was Chairman of the Council of People's Commissars, later Council of Ministers.

As early as 1925 Stalin characterized the enormous power of the Politburo as follows: "The Politburo is the highest organ not of the State but of the Party and the Party is the highest directing force of the State."[22]

The 19th Congress of the Communist party of the Soviet Union brought certain changes. Both Politburo and Orgburo were abolished. In their stead was created the Presidium of the Central Committee. As elected in October, 1952, it contained twenty-five members, fourteen more than the former Politburo, and eleven alternates. Stalin's design appeared to be that of making the group too large and divided to be efficient. Since he was the one arbiter of disputes, he retained firm control.

But within twenty-four hours after Stalin's death on March 5, 1953, further and abrupt changes were made. The Presidium was reduced to ten members, one less than the number which had comprised the Politburo. Eight of the ten members had been in the Politburo. In 1966 the name "Politburo" was restored.

To trace the expansions and contractions in the size of the Politburo and the Secretariat in the years after 1953 is a bewildering process, complicated by the fact that identification between the two bodies is not fixed, being complete at times, incomplete at others. For instance, at present only four of the eleven permanent members of the Politburo are also members of the Secretariat (Brezhnev, Kirilenko, Shelepin, and Suslov). Suffice it to say that for Westerners, often the first clear sign of a shift in power at the top is when members are raised to, or dropped from, the Politburo.

No organ of government remains without change over time, nor does any institution look from the inside as it does from the outside. These broad generalizations are particularly true of a body as centrally powerful in a changing society as is the Politburo, whose role and power have altered considerably through the years. In its early days, it was dominated more than anything else by the personality of Lenin. Then followed a period of gradually diminishing collective leadership until Stalin completely gained the upper hand. Under Stalin, as Khrushchev himself complained, the Politburo was reduced to a completely subordinate position with all important, and most minor, decisions being made by the dictator himself.

The reaction against this total one-man control has left a firm impression on

---

[22] To the 14th Congress of the Communist party, 1925. Towster, *op. cit.*, p. 160*n*.

the party's upper echelons, with apparently a real reluctance to let one man become too strong. Thus, as already noted, Beria was quickly cut down after Stalin's death, and Malenkov was forced to loosen his grip on the reins of power. The same sentiment nearly pitched Khrushchev out of the saddle in 1957 and played a part, although how great it is not possible to determine, in his overthrow in 1964.

The present condition of the Politburo is a subtle combination of unity and diversity which no outsider can ever hope to understand completely. Yet, several general statements are possible. No matter how united it appears to the outside world, and no matter how unified it may actually be on certain points, it is a body under great strain. A leading Kremlinologist described the situation in these words:[23]

> Most Soviet leaders have risen to the top through one or more of the centralized bureaucratic apparatuses that make up the political, administrative, and economic institutions of the Soviet regime. They have gathered personal followings around themselves during their rise by rewarding the faithful and punishing the disloyal. They confront each other in the no man's land at the apex of the bureaucratic pyramid of party and state where . . . the lack of any political arrangements of a genuinely constitutional character makes the enterprise of leadership especially difficult for those who venture to undertake it.

Part of the tension under which the Politburo must labor is the result of the doctrinal supposition that for every problem there is, and can only be, one right (i.e., "scientific") answer. Thus, major differences over policy tend to harden into differences over doctrine which obviously are much harder to resolve through compromise.

Two further problems are the lack of institutional arrangements for making decisions and holding power and the impossibility of the existence of a "loyal opposition." This being the case, differences over policy tend toward expression as a struggle over the control of power. And this in turn provides an always open road to further dictatorship. This paradox of a desire for collective leadership with its implications of diversity, and the equally strong desire for unity is a source of constant tension in the party leadership. Within the present framework of Communist government, it is not subject to permanent resolution.

It is interesting that, with the exception of a very short time, not a single professional military man has risen to Politburo rank except for Marshal Klementi Voroshilov and Nikolai Bulganin, and they must be classed with the politicians rather than with the generals, for they owed their rise to political and not military achievements. The only exception was the short-lived tenure of Marshal Zhukov as candidate and then full member of the Politburo and Minister of Defense (1956–1957). He has since been forcibly retired, and his successor, Malinovski, is not a member of the party's top organs. None of the other real military leaders of

[23] Linden, *Khrushchev and the Soviet Leadership,* Baltimore, 1966, p. 13.

the country has been so elevated before or since, not Konev, Timoshenko, or any other. Zhukov's appointment was probably the result of his assistance to Khrushchev at the time of the 1957 attempt to oust the former First Secretary. His power menaced Khrushchev's, however, which caused his early downfall. The rule would seem to hold, then, that the party regards the army with suspicion and makes every effort to keep it subservient, denying it a significant voice or even effective representation in the decision-making bodies of the Soviet Union. This does not mean that the Soviet Army does not have considerable influence, but there is no evidence that it enjoys anything like a dominant position or that it is even a regular participant in top-level policy-making decisions.

In order to carry out its vast functions the Politburo has a series of well-staffed functional departments which keep its members informed on all developments.[24] This staff is something more than a cabinet secretariat and something less than a supergovernment. It is, as Nemzer points out, only one of the agencies which serve the men in command. But it concentrates and channelizes the flow of information on which the members of the Politburo must depend in order to reach their decisions. But efficiency, while desirable, is not the principal purpose of government, whether democratic or totalitarian. In the Soviet Union, control by the party and the responsibility of the government bureaucracy are indispensable concomitants of the control mechanism through which the Communist leaders rule.

Such a concentration of powers is, contrary to a widespread impression, not necessarily a very efficient method. In a country in which error and failure become treason and sabotage, subordinate levels of the administration are fearful of making decisions and are inclined to refer everything to higher headquarters, where, as a result, a terrific jam piles up. That this is quite a problem in the Soviet Union is attested by frequent critical remarks in the Soviet press. At the same time there is also an inclination on the part of lower levels and agents abroad to report what corresponds to the official bias rather than objective facts. The desire to please rather than to send unvarnished reports clearly enters into the picture.

The Secretariat

Even when the Orgburo still existed, it had lost some of its functions to the Secretariat, which had become the real director of party activities. The first secretariat of the Communist party was a small office with an essentially technical and service character. That it developed into something quite different is due solely to the personality of Joseph Stalin, who as General Secretary transformed it completely. Because many problems concerned both the Politburo and the Orgburo, it was decided at an early period that the General Secretary should be a member of

[24] Louis Nemzer, "The Kremlin Professional Staff: The 'Apparatus' of the Central Committee, Communist Party of the Soviet Union," *American Political Science Review*, Vol. XLIV (1950), pp. 64–85.

both groups and thus serve as a coordinator. In that and in every other function he was supposed to be solely the executor of the will of the Central Committee and of the Politburo and Orgburo.

Stalin became General Secretary in 1922. He came to this office with a rich experience in organizational matters and a considerable study of nationality problems.[25] His position gave him an exceptional opportunity to be in contact with every branch of party activities, and as the coordinator of Politburo and Orgburo he became the vital center of party and state activities.

As the Secretariat was thus gradually transformed from an executor to an executive, considerable resistance appeared, and Zinoviev submitted plans which would have reduced its status. Stalin was able to thwart this, and when the opposition tried it in 1925, its plans were frustrated.

It is extremely important to understand clearly the workings of the Secretariat because of its central importance, past, present, and future in Soviet government. From the Central Committee of the Soviet Union down to lowly primary party organizations, each rung is organized in essentially the same way, that is, with a general conference of members or representatives of members, a central committee, and a secretary. In theory the members elect the conference, which in turn elects the committee, which in turn elects the secretary. In reality it is the local secretary who has control over the committee and the conference. The election of the secretary is a mere formality since he is appointed from Moscow. And the man who appoints the local secretaries is the First Secretary of the Communist party.

If it is remembered that the local secretaries are the real key to power at each level, the line of power control should now be clear: the First Secretary controls the local secretaries, they in turn control who will be elected from their level of power to the next level and so on, up to the election of the members of the Central Committee and the Politburo of the Communist party of the Soviet Union. It is in this manner that Stalin and Khrushchev took power. It was by packing the Central Committee that Khrushchev was able to withstand the 1957 onslaught when he was outnumbered in the Presidium.

Naturally, it takes a strong man to make this system work, since many individuals must be rooted out of their positions in local secretariats if supporters of the new Secretary are to take over. But then, few weak men rise to the top in Communist politics. One man who did not rise to power from the First Secretaryship was Malenkov: he had the position for only a period of weeks after Stalin's death and was then forced to drop one of his two positions of power—the other being the Premiership. If he had kept the Secretary's job and yielded the Premiership, Soviet history might have taken rather a different turn, but that is one of the great "ifs" of history.

After Khrushchev's fall, party and governmental leadership were once more divided, as we have seen, with Leonid Brezhnev becoming First Secretary and

---

[25] Stalin, *Marxism and the National Question,* New York, 1942 (first published in 1913).

Alexei Kosygin Prime Minister. In contrast to the short-lived Bulganin-Khrushchev tandem, in which from the very start Bulganin was clearly relegated to the position of a figurehead, Kosygin's position is quite real and significant, although Brezhnev is clearly the senior partner. As these lines are written, this combine has every appearance of stability. However, observers have noted that the Soviet system is not well geared to dual controls at the top, and its further evolution is therefore watched with great interest by the outside world and the army of "Kremlinologists."[26]

The Control Committee

This is a committee ostensibly elected by the Central Committee; as its chief function it watches over the strict ". . . observance of Party discipline by Party members and candidate members of the CPSU, and takes action against Communists who violate the program and the rules of the Party, . . . Party or state discipline, or are violators of Party ethics."[27]

The Committee of Party Control works with all the security agencies of the government, especially with the secret police. The 1952 party rules gave it the right and duty to have its own authorized representative in all Republics, Regions, and Territories, independent of all local party organs and responsible only to the Committee of Party Control. However, this rule was abrogated in 1956, perhaps in realization of the excessive duplication of the proliferating channels of control within the Soviet system and as a result of Khrushchev's attempts to decentralize and streamline somewhat the apparatus of his rule. That such an organ with such extensive powers is deemed necessary despite the existence of the ordinary organs of state security, above all the secret police, is evidence that the cross-checking and one-watch-the-other attitude which characterize dictatorships are far from unknown in Russia. The old proverb, "Who watches the watchers?" holds particularly true in a dictatorship.

However, by 1962 the importance of the Central Control Commission, then called Central Auditing Commission, had considerably declined. But in November, 1962, the Commission was merged with a governmental body, the Commission for State Control, an outstanding example of the complete control of the state by the party. The new body was renamed the Committee for Party and State Control and was placed under both the party's Central Committee and the Council of Ministers. Alexander Shelepin, a rising star, became its chairman. Then in December, 1965, there took place another one of those oblique moves whose full significance is not

---

[26] In a somewhat popularized version, a "Sovietologist" is a specialist on general aspects of the Soviet Union, while a "Kremlinologist" is concerned primarily with the intricate power relationships between the men at the top and with their rise to and fall from power. The preoccupation with the latter "branch" is the normal result of a closed society in which important information which would be available in open societies through normal channels and ordinary methods of social science research, can be obtained only obliquely and in a manner which relies mainly on informed, high-level guesswork.

[27] Party statute of 1961, rule 40a.

clear. Shelepin was removed from this position—but remained an important member of the Presidium-Politburo. These moves and countermoves have been seen by some as reflecting a continuing struggle in the Presidium, where Khrushchev by no means kept the upper hand at all times.[28] The issue of how much control should be exercised by the party as opposed to the state is an ongoing one.

Youth organizations

In addition to the regular cadres of the Communist party, there are certain auxiliaries, among which the youth organizations are by far the most significant. Closest to the party is the All-Union Leninist Communist League of Youth, known by its Russian abbreviation as *Comsomol,* and officially termed "the assistant of the Communist Party of the Soviet Union (Bolsheviks) and its reserve." It is the great organization which connects the youth of the country with the Communist party. Closely patterned on the party, it is nevertheless a mass organization numbering, in 1949, 9,300,000 members. By 1963, membership had reached 19 million. The regime knows well that its future depends on the support of the youth, the coming generation, and much care is spent thereon.[29]

The Communist youth are organized according to age into three groups, Comsomols (fourteen to twenty-six), Pioneers (nine to sixteen), and Little Octobrists (seven to eleven). The aim of the Comsomols and the other youth organizations is both political and nonpolitical. The indoctrination of youth with Marxist ideas and the firm establishment of Bolshevik and Stalinist loyalties are among their foremost goals. The Comsomols also undertake to root out all vestiges of religious feelings.

In order to create an *esprit de corps,* a number of specific tasks were given the Comsomols, by command of the party. In the early years of the regime they mobilized thousands of men for war. Later they sent thousands of members to distant places in order to establish factories, railroads, etc., and to help rebuild the shattered economy.

Special emphasis was placed on the role of the Comsomols to give the Soviet Union a new generation of scientists and specialists, and they played a crucial role in the collectivization program. With the advent of war, a great deal of stress was placed on the necessary increase in military strength. The Comsomols took a special interest in the air force, sending many members into its ranks and performing a number of services for it. In return the armed forces furnished instructors for paramilitary training. The Comsomol organization is thus an important conveyor belt for the party, which it furnishes with young activists; it also spearheads those drives

[28] Grey Hodnett, "Khrushchev and Party State Control," in *Politics in the Soviet Union,* ed. by Alexander Dallin and Alan Westin, New York, 1966, pp. 113–163.
[29] Revealing chapters from Soviet schoolbooks were published by G. S. Counts and N. P. Lodge under the title *I Want to Be like Stalin,* New York, 1947.

which the party considers especially important and seems to have played a major role in Khrushchev's plans for the reclaiming of virgin lands in central Asia.

The Pioneers and the Little Octobrists naturally have less ambitious roles to play. For many years the party and the Comsomols made it difficult for sons and daughters of the former *bourgeoisie* and the intelligentsia to join, but the Pioneers always kept their ranks open. The principal task of the Pioneers is education. They are supposed to inculcate in their members a "socialist attitude toward study, labor, and communal activities,"[30] and they are supposed to emulate the Comsomols in every respect.

The Little Octobrists engage in constructive supervised play and on occasion help the Pioneers in certain campaigns and work for which they are fitted. Even at that early age military skills are stressed, as are clean and wholesome living habits which will make the young Communist a model to his environment. Further cooperation between party and Comsomols is intimate, and through them the entire youth movement is closely integrated with the party structure.

As in the party, the backbone of the Comsomol organization is the secretaries, who are nominally elected but in actuality are designated by higher headquarters. This is confirmed by the fact that almost all Comsomol secretaries are Communist-party members.

The Communist rulers of the Soviet Union obviously lay great stress on the education of youth for the formation of the future cadres of the Soviet regime. For that reason the activities of youth organizations, especially of the Comsomols, concentrate on political indoctrination, military and para-military training, and leadership in carrying out the orders and directives of the party. School and youth-organization activities are intimately connected. No subject of instruction is without some political significance. Even the examples in elementary instruction in mathematics carry political symbols. Comsomol members must further instruct the young Pioneers under their care and serve as models and examples for them in every way. To further these objectives there is also an extensive press especially written for and by these youth groups, among which *Komsomolskaya Pravda* is the best known.

How effective is this system? Many people in the West are inclined to believe that such complete indoctrination is bound to make totally devoted and obedient robots out of the entire Soviet youth. There are many indications, however, that this pessimistic view is greatly exaggerated. In the first place every teacher knows that the degree to which he can influence his students is, after all, limited. Moreover a study of the effects of Nazi indoctrination on the Hitler Youth—a very comparable situation—reveals that excessive indoctrination often leads to a reaction of being overfed with propaganda and, after the young people have seen the contrast between propaganda and reality, to disillusionment, as was amply demonstrated by

---

[30] John N. Hazard, "The Socialist State: The Soviet Union and Its Orbit," in *Foreign Governments,* ed. by F. M. Marx, New York, 1949, p. 433.

the events in Poland and Hungary, where youth was everywhere in the very forefront of the resistance to the regime.

It is true that these parallels must be drawn with caution as far as the Soviet Union is concerned. The Communists have been in power much longer than the Nazis were, and the geographic situation of Russia has permitted them to isolate their people more effectively than would have been possible in central or western Europe. Nevertheless there is impressive testimony to a spirit among Soviet youth which is not totally satisfactory from the standpoint of the Soviet leaders.[31] It has been stated on good authority that children are often bored with their daily dose of propaganda rather than infatuated with it. Those who become inspired at first often become disillusioned at the first contact with reality.[32]

Perhaps the most telling proof of this is the fact that nearly 4 million Soviet soldiers surrendered to the Germans in the first half year of the war or were easily captured. Of those, many thousands volunteered for service against the Soviet Union. Only when German terrorism began the wholesale slaughter of Russians and the Nazi doctrine of racial superiority was applied in the East did this widespread source of collaboration cease.[33] Other, more recent, indications may be found in numerous complaints in the Soviet press and in official speeches about the attitude of youth and the supposedly still strong bourgeois influence in their midst.

The Comsomol is a selective organization, but it is not nearly so selective as the Communist party. During the war, membership in the Comsomols rose to 15 million, but by 1949 this was down to somewhat more than 9 million. This decline was the result not of purges, but of nonpayment of dues, nonattendance at meetings, and other evidence of a lack of interest. An intensive campaign waged after the 11th Congress of the Comsomols in 1949 brought the figure to the presently enrolled 19 million, but the initial postwar loss remains significant.

It would be foolhardy and unsupported by evidence to regard Soviet youth as a hotbed of rebellion against Communism. But neither is it that mass of automatons, that "lost" generation, which some see. Undoubtedly there are many fanatics in the Communist youth organizations, but the majority join because the Comsomols in particular are a road to the party and hence the almost exclusive avenue to a higher career.

---

[31] 83d Congress, 1st Session, Senate Document No. 69, *Tensions within the Soviet Union,* July 28, 1953, pp. 10–16.

[32] Merle Fainsod, "Controls and Tensions within the Soviet System," *American Political Science Review,* Vol. XLIV (1950), pp. 275f.

[33] It was one of the great tragedies of the war that the Western Allies apparently never realized the depth of this movement and that these Russians were acting primarily for reasons of anti-Communist rather than pro-Nazi sentiments. After the war and even as late as 1947 these Russians were handed over to the Soviet authorities, who liquidated them by mass execution and deportation. See George Fischer, *Soviet Opposition to Stalin,* Cambridge, Mass., 1952. He sees the explanation for so much collaboration with the Germans primarily in an inertness of the Russian masses, which according to him made them prone to go with the master of the hour. This interpretation of this otherwise very valuable book is open to considerable dispute. See the excellent study by A. Dallin, *German Rule in Russia, 1941–1945,* New York, 1957.

Labor unions

There was a dispute between Lenin[34] and Trotsky concerning the place of labor unions in the Communist state. Trotsky wanted to integrate them with the organization of the state, while Lenin wanted to keep them separate. During the NEP, when a limited amount of free enterprise was permitted, the unions performed the traditional functions of collective bargaining and general maintenance of the workers' interests. But when that phase was over, the role of labor unions had to be redefined. Tomski, the leader of the union movement, advocated continued independence and opposed the idea that labor unions should press the workers for higher production. He was removed and eventually committed suicide during the purge.

Under a planned socialist economy the setting of wages could no longer be left to the tug of war of collective bargaining but had to be fixed by the state planners in accordance with the national economy. Higher wages could come only from higher production, and that became the principal goal of the labor unions, which joined forces with the state agencies for that purpose. A leading Soviet book on labor law explains: "The amount of wages and salaries is at the present time fixed by the decisions of the Government (or on the basis of its directives) by means of governmental planned regulation of wages and salaries for separate groups and categories of workers." The author continues that wage fixing is done by negotiation between the labor unions and management only where the regulations provide for a span rather than a precise sum.[35]

Stalin defined the role of labor in these words:[36]

(*a*) the fight—by means of self-criticism—against bureaucracy, which shackles the labor initiative and labor activities of the masses;
(*b*) the fight—by means of socialist emulation—against the labor shirkers and disrupters of proletarian labor discipline; and finally
(*c*) the fight—by introduction of the uninterrupted week—against routine and inertia in industry.

Labor unions in the Soviet Union are organized industry-wide rather than on the craft principle. The Soviet unions, organized in the All-Union Central Council of Trade Unions (VTsSPS), number over 30 million members and in this they are the largest in the world. Their organization follows the well-known principle of "democratic centralism," which means here as in all other respects that all orders emerge from the top. Basic units of the labor unions exist in every factory and elect, at least nominally, their executive committees. In larger factories, shop com-

[34] For Lenin's views on trade unions, see the study by Thomas T. Hammond, *Lenin on Trade Unions and Revolution, 1893–1917*, New York, 1957.
[35] I. T. Gelyakov (ed.), *Zakonodatel 'stvo o trude*, Moscow, 1947, p. 65, quoted in *Tensions within the Soviet Union*, p. 67n.
[36] Stalin, *Leninism*, p. 135.

mittees are organized to handle different tasks. There are also "norms and conflicts commissions," but their jurisdiction is limited by the provisions of the law and actually does not extend much beyond the interpretation and application of the law. As to the effectiveness of this grievance machinery, there seems to be a difference of opinion,[37] but its scope seems to have gradually increased.

Factory unions elect delegates to city and district conferences. They in turn elect delegates to higher-level congresses. The pattern of labor-union organization follows closely the pattern of the party organization, and the former is completely dominated by the latter. This is made clear by the by-laws of the labor unions of the U.S.S.R., which state: "Soviet labor unions conduct all their work under the direction of the Communist Party—the organizing and directing force of socialist society. The trade unions of the U.S.S.R. rally the working masses around the party of Lenin and Stalin.[38]

In reality then the Soviet labor unions represent not the workers, but the state and the party. Their task is not the improvement of the worker's lot but the improvement of the worker's labor and the increase of production. In addition they serve as one of the several mass organizations which the regime uses from time to time in order to mobilize the people for a given task.

The labor unions function in a number of fields. The wage commission has nothing to do with wages but rather with the institution of piecework rates in factories—a practice against which the free labor unions of the world have waged an unceasing battle since the latter part of the nineteenth century. Other commissions look after the observance of safety rules, the most rational use of supplies and labor, cultural enterprise, and housing. In the housing field the commissions have, however, little influence and no funds. The grievance machinery under the norms and conflicts commissions has already been mentioned. Most important of all is, however, the administration of the social security system. But even that is used for speed-up purposes, since it grants markedly higher benefits to labor-union members, people who stay long on their jobs, and members of the Communist work brigades (which in recent years have taken over the role of the Stakhanovites), in which one-third of the union membership is said to be engaged.[39] They are supposed to compete with each other and generally boost labor's output and quality.

If the labor unions did not succeed in increasing the individual performance of the workers, the extremely harsh penalties of the Soviet labor law until a few years ago, would. Workers were subjected to extremely severe penalties for absenteeism, for giving up work without permission, and even for laziness.[40] Fines of 25 percent of six months' wages and six months' imprisonment were provided for

[37] Fainsod, *How Russia Is Ruled*, pp. 522f.

[38] *Trud*, May 11, 1949, quoted in *Tensions within the Soviet Union*, p. 67n.

[39] *Trud*, Oct. 22, 1961, as quoted in Meyer, *op. cit.*, p. 431.

[40] Barrington Moore, Jr., *Soviet Politics—The Dilemma of Power*, Cambridge, Mass., 1950, pp. 257f.; Vladimir Gsovski, "Elements of Soviet Labor Law," *Monthly Labor Review*, Mar., 1951, p. 258.

absenteeism. Repeated instances of tardiness could involve imprisonment of not less than one year; leaving or changing jobs without permission could result in imprisonment up to three years. The labor law also gave the management of an enterprise the right to transfer workers anywhere in the Soviet Union without regard to their personal preferences. Being tied to the job and under the constant threat of severe penalties for even minor infractions, labor in the Union of Soviet Socialist Republics had reached the state of near serfdom.

Since Stalin's death, some relaxation of controls has occurred. Apart from annulment of most of the extreme criminal punishments applicable to the enforcement of labor discipline and of the former restrictions against free movement of individuals from one enterprise to another of their choice, there has been a considerable humanization in Soviet legislation on the subject. Under the new measure, minor negligence and other so-called "administrative offenses" are no longer to be considered violations of the criminal code. Acts "analogous" to illegal acts are no longer to be punishable under the criminal code either. On the whole, most labor offenses which were formerly criminally punishable are now handled through administrative channels; instead of prosecutions, fines of less drastic proportions than those of Stalin's era are meted out.[41]

Forced labor

Considering the circumstances under which "free" labor existed under Stalin, one might have said that there was no great difference between free and forced labor.[42]

It is true that all countries have forced labor as part of their penal systems. But in most countries prisoners under sentence of forced (or hard) labor comprise an infinitesimal proportion of the population and are only hardened, common criminals. It remained for the Nazi regime, and to an even larger extent to the Soviet Union, to make forced labor an industry. Estimates vary greatly and range somewhere between 10 and 20 million men and women engaged in forced labor in the Soviet Union. One of the most careful and reliable studies has stated that the total ranged, in different periods, from 7 to 12 million.[43]

Forced labor is not merely a penal measure in the U.S.S.R.; it is also an industry which at one time became so big that the original Commissariat (Ministry)

[41] E.g., *The New York Times*, Apr. 24, 1956, pp. 1, 6. On the problem of the wide-scale re-evaluation and reexamination of Soviet legal theory and practice, see G. Ginsburgs, " 'Socialist Legality' in the U.S.S.R. since the XXth Party Congress," *American Journal of Comparative Law*, Vol. 6, No. 4 (Autumn, 1957), pp. 546–559.

[42] In interviews with numerous German prisoners of war (not Germans condemned to forced labor in Russia) lately returned from the U.S.S.R., the author was told repeatedly that there was no great difference between the treatment and food given to prisoners of war and those given to Russian "free" labor.

[43] David J. Dallin and Boris I. Nicolaevsky, *Forced Labor in the Soviet Union*, New Haven, 1947, p. 86.

for Internal Affairs (NKVD) had to be split into two organizations: the Ministry for Internal Affairs (MVD) in charge of the administration of forced labor, and the Ministry of State Security (MGB). After Stalin's death they were reunited under the title MVD but were again separated in 1955. State security was placed under a committee (KGB) under the Council of Ministers to underline its lesser status. Shortly thereafter the chairman of the committee was admitted to the Council of Ministers, with the result that the KGB again became a ministry in fact though not in theory.

The extent of these operations has become clearer from a remarkable document, dated 1941, which eventually came into Western hands.[44] It shows that percentages ranging from 12 to 40 percent of a large number of construction and industrial projects were to be supplied from forced labor contributed by the NKVD. It has been estimated that an over-all average of 17 percent of the labor engaged on construction projects in 1941 was to be supplied by the NKVD, i.e., forced labor.[45] According to this there would have been, very conservatively estimated, 3½ million prisoners in camps under direct NKVD administration and supplied to these projects. This figure does not include other types of prisoners: those held in ordinary prisons, those contracted out to other enterprises, etc. An accurate estimate of forced labor is made difficult not only by the paucity of available information but also by the different categories of such labor, ranging from prisoners in concentration camps to workers compelled to remain at their previous jobs at sharply reduced wages as a penalty for the infraction of labor discipline. The last-mentioned category is already close to "free" labor, and the figure of forced labor will depend partly on the groups included in that term.[46]

The era of post-Stalin reforms witnessed a considerable relaxation in the slave-labor situation. The thaw in the dictatorship of the regime and the serious downgrading of the secret police, the ferment in Soviet society on the death of the old dictator, and the campaign for a strengthening of "socialist legality" and against the excesses of the police (necessitated in part by the campaign to explain the death of Beria and smear his memory) brought about considerable changes in the forced-labor situation. Some of the more infamous of the camps—Vorkuta, for example,

[44] Department of State, *Forced Labor in the Soviet Union,* Washington, 1952, p. iv.
[45] Naum Jasny, "Labor and Output in Soviet Concentration Camps," *Journal of Political Economy,* Vol. 59 (1951), pp. 409*f.* For a summary see Fainsod, "Controls and Tensions within the Soviet System" and *Tensions within the Soviet Union,* p. 80.
[46] Authoritative and richly documented accounts of forced labor and concentration camps in the Soviet Union are now available in considerable quantity. Apart from Dallin and Nicolaevsky, *op. cit.,* see American Federation of Labor, *Slave Labor in Russia,* New York, 1949; Elinor Lipper (a Dutch Communist), *11 Years in Soviet Prison Camps,* Chicago, 1951; Jerzy Gliksman, *Tell the West,* New York, 1948. See also Simon Wolin and Robert M. Slusser (eds.), *The Soviet Secret Police,* New York, 1957. Many former inmates of Soviet concentration camps also testified in the suit of Victor Kravchenko against the French Communist weekly, *Les Lettres Françaises,* in Paris, 1949. Further evolution of destalinization and Khrushchev's open admission of Stalin's terror produced eyewitness reports published in the Soviet Union. One of the most moving is Alexander Solzhenitsyn's *One Day in the Life of Ivan Denisovich* (trans. by Ralph Parker), New York, 1963.

which had been the scene of a bloody uprising after Stalin's demise—were reported to have been closed, many of the inmates of those camps were gradually released and permitted to return to their homes, and the regime pledged itself to end mass forced labor and the prison camps.[47] This is not to say that all forced labor in the Soviet Union has now been abolished by any means, but it does seem that forced labor is no longer subject to quite the same abuses and excesses as it had been under Stalinism and that its scope has been narrowed. The political character of much of this population in exile seems to have greatly diminished. The abolition, in 1953, of the extraordinary quasi-judicial powers of the secret police, which permitted it to seize and exile people by simple administrative order, permits some cautious optimism and hope for a continuing diminution in the numbers of the unfortunate victims of Soviet terrorism.

However, as Professor Fainsod stated, it cannot be assumed that the abatement of the terror means that it will never be revived. This much can probably be said—that the longer the period of relative relaxation lasts, the harder it will be for the government to return to the repressive methods of the Stalin era.

Collective farms and party leadership

The first step toward the mass organization of the peasants was the cooperatives, which reached many millions of families. But the older form of consumers' and producers' cooperatives has been superseded among the peasantry by the collective farms, the *kolkhozi*. The kolkhoz is more than a cooperative; it is an entire way of life, embracing every facet of peasant existence. Kolkhoz members pool all their resources, and only very little is left to personal ownership. Through the Machine Tractor Stations (MTS) which were abolished in 1958, the state contributed mechanized equipment and exercised strict control. Theoretically the kolkhoz is self-governing, but that self-government has become increasingly theoretical since the thirties.[48] Unlike the unions, the kolkhozi have no regional or national organization, but each one maintains direct relations with the village soviet in its area. Through it, the agricultural departments of the state administration exercise direct control over the kolkhoz administrations, whose acts and decisions they may set aside at any time.

Through the tight organization of the kolkhoz, and since the abolition of the older *mir,* party and state are in a position to reach every peasant and to mobilize him for such purposes as may be necessary. It is also through the kolkhoz organization that the ideological indoctrination of the peasants is accomplished. In this work party members and especially trained Comsomol members are in the forefront, since they fill many posts of kolkhoz chairmen.

[47] E.g., *The New York Times,* May 14, 1956, p. 1.
[48] See Gregory Bienstock et al., *Management in Russian Industry and Agriculture,* New York, 1944.

Originally it was thought that the state farm, the *sovkhoz,* was the ideal form of agricultural enterprise from the Communist standpoint. But the performance of the sovkhoz left much to be desired. The peasants shied away from them, and the personnel of the state farms were usually of inferior quality and found more land assigned to them than they could handle. Much equipment was mishandled or worn out in the process, and in 1934 Stalin openly acknowledged the failure of the system.

The question of the size of agricultural enterprises is not merely an economic and administrative question in the Soviet Union; to a very considerable extent it is also a political one. Although the great majority of the population is rural, it plays a disproportionately small role in the Communist party and has offered the greatest resistance to communization. In 1947, only 27 percent of the total party membership was rural. Actually this figure is probably too large because it includes a considerable number of administrators who were not peasants.[49] Moreover, Communist leaders had frequent occasion to complain that many collective farms had no party organizations. A major drive by the party succeeded in increasing somewhat the proportions of the party's membership in the countryside, and by the time of the 1956 Congress, Khrushchev reported more than 3 million members and candidates of the party in agricultural districts. However, by his own admission, less than half of these were working directly in the collective farms, the machine-tractor stations, or the state farms.

There are a number of factors which contribute to this situation. From the very beginning the Communists have waged a ceaseless war against the peasants, which culminated in the forced collectivization of the thirties and cost approximately 5 million peasants their lives. Then there were the numerous forays to "liquidate the kulaks as a class," which resulted in mass confiscation and mass deportation, for kulaks were not large landowners—who had long since disappeared —but small holders who had as many as three horses and employed fifty days of labor per year.[50]

The hostility of the peasants to Communism is understandable. In all countries of the world farming is not merely a way to earn a living but a way of life. Farmers and peasants are essentially conservative and have an owner's mentality. To own the land they till is their ambition. In other words, peasants have a capitalistic outlook. Unless their bourgeois inclinations are held under control they may become a menace to the entire system.

The stubborn persistence of peasant resentment forced the Communist leadership to reconsider its methods. It came to the conclusion that in view of the sparsity of party organizations on the collectives, the latter themselves would have to be consolidated in order to produce tighter control and to make the available supply

[49] Fainsod, *How Russia Is Ruled,* p. 270.
[50] M. K. Bennett, "Food and Agriculture in the Soviet Union, 1947–48," *Journal of Political Economy,* Vol. LVII (1949), pp. 194f.

of Communist-party manpower cover more ground. Before the war the official line was that work in small groups (*zveno*) of about twenty people to cultivate a given plot was most effective. Politburo member Andrei Andreyev was particularly identified with that system. But in 1950 it was condemned, Andreyev got the axe, at least for the time being, and emphasis was now placed on the much larger brigade. A campaign for the consolidation of collective farms was undertaken in the same year under the leadership of Nikita Khrushchev, Andreyev's successor as the chief agricultural specialist of the Politburo. In October, 1952, Georgi Malenkov reported to the 19th Congress of the Communist party of the Soviet Union that the number of collective farms had been reduced from 254,000 to 97,000. Much of that consolidation remained, however, on paper.

While the consolidation campaign was in full swing, Khrushchev proposed an even more ambitious scheme. He advocated the creation of large agricultural settlements—so-called "agro-cities"—around which the collective farms were to stretch. Private plots were to be diminished and tilled in common. The aim of this plan was clear. It was to transform the peasants into a vast proletariat without the vestige of any independent production. The creation of agro-cities, even more than the consolidation of collective farms, would create an administrative bureaucracy and make possible the organization of strong party units. However, this scheme was soon repudiated and officially condemned. In his speech to the 19th Congress, Malenkov strongly criticized it by reminding his listeners that the primary task was the increase of production. Although Khrushchev's plan of agro-cities was repudiated, it does indicate the direction in which Communist thinking goes.

The problems of Soviet agriculture are extremely complicated and are made more so by their dual political and economic nature.[51] Much of the land in the U.S.S.R. is not good farm land.[52] This, and the undeniable backwardness of the Soviet peasants at the time of the Revolution were problems with which any regime would have had to deal. The Communists complicated this in a number of ways. They placed industrialization ahead of improvement in the agricultural sector, a position which it still holds, but at the same time they demanded that the rural sections of the country foot much of the bill for this industrialization in both human and material terms. Hence, while the state constantly demands more from the farmer, it is unwilling to make the large-scale investments in fertilizer, irrigation, and intensive labor which would make this possible. Some of the gap has been filled by mechanization, but many more resources are needed really to move the countryside forward.

[51] One should not, however, forget that the rational solution of farm problems is hindered in the United States as well as in the Soviet Union by the presence of an "ideology" of the "yeoman farmer." For an interesting discussion of the similarities and differences of the two, see Zbigniew Brzezinski & Samuel P. Huntington, *Political Power: USA/USSR,* New York, 1966, pp. 301–330.

[52] Alec Nove, "Soviet Agriculture Marks Time," in *The Soviet Economy,* ed. by Harry B. Shaffer, New York, 1963, pp. 155–172.

Further complications have resulted from the desire to collectivize the country-side. Part of the rationale for this lies in the ideological-demand that Communism be brought to all rural areas. That strong ideological motivation is reinforced by the political fact that collectivization makes the gathering of goods much easier than was the case in the early days of the Revolution when the local commissars had to search thousands of individual farms for goods which the peasants became experts at hiding. This desire for ease in management and political control has led to a steady increase in the size of collective farms, as has been noted.

The regime, however, has been forced time and time again to recognize that on a purely collective farm the peasant feels no incentive to work, and yield falls. Hence the party has allowed the peasant to retain a small private plot which he may cultivate in his spare time, the produce from which he may sell on the open market. The peasant, in turn, cultivates his "bourgeois mentality" by spending most of his time on his private plot instead of in the collective fields, and indeed this small private sector, only 3 percent of the cultivated land, produces one-third of the gross agricultural output.

The party is faced with the dilemma that while it dislikes the private plots, it needs the goods which are produced thereon. Further, since the death of Stalin, the party has appeared unwilling to unsettle the country-side with a direct attack on private plots. As a result, the sternness of party policy toward private plots has swung back and forth, depending on how much they are needed in a given year. The party is quite sensitive to its agricultural failings, for as Khrushchev once re-marked, "It is understood not only by the educated Marxist or the educated man in general, but by everyone who has learned how to eat."[53]

In recent years the Soviets have launched two major efforts to overcome farm problems. The first was a pet project of Khrushchev's, and its failure no doubt con-tributed to his downfall. This was the virgin lands scheme, an attempt to bring under cultivation vast areas of semiarid land which had not previously been settled. The work was to be done by the sovkhozi, state farms, which, like factories, have a guaranteed minimum wage, so that the problem of private plots and incentives is not so great as on the kolkhozi, or collective farms. Aided by an unusually heavy rainfall, the project produced a bumper crop in 1958 which led to a massive ex-pansion of the program and great hopes for future production which were written into the 1959 seven-year plan. The joint factors of more normal weather and the regime's failure to provide the irrigation and the chemical fertilizers that were needed soon caused a massive collapse of that program. Several of the newly plowed areas had to be abandoned, and, while the work continues, it is at a much reduced rate and without the former expectations for a complete solution to the agricultural problem.

The second effort is being particularly stressed by the Brezhnev-Kosygin team.

[53] Speech to a conference of S.F.S.R. Agricultural Workers, March 12, 1963, quoted in Nancy Nimitz, "The Agricultural Scene: The Lean Years," *Problems of Communism,* May–June, 1964, p. 13.

This is the attempt to add greatly to the incentives of the collective farmer. These incentives have been of four kinds: (1) the amounts of goods which the collective farms must turn over to the state have been much reduced, (2) prices for these goods have been increased, (3) there is an additional 50 percent premium paid for goods sold to the state over and above the quota, and (4) the part of these proceeds going to the individual farmer has been aligned more with the individual's performance than with his job qualifications. These reforms do seem to be having an effect, and the harvests have increased considerably—witness the bumper crop in 1966.

Nevertheless, the problem is far from solved, and solution is constantly hindered by the party's insistence on centralized control in an area that is simply not suited to such control.[54] Farm problems are generally local—deciding which crops are best for which soils, which field should lie fallow at a given time, and the like. Demands for uniformity on all farms in all locations leads to constant mistakes, wastes, inefficiencies. Khrushchev, for example, may well have been right on the whole when he demanded that fewer fields be allowed to lie fallow at one time. Nevertheless, in some locations this certainly helped to destroy the soil. Such control is worsened by the fact that a command from the center to let fewer fields lie fallow may well be interpreted by an overzealous administrator as a command to let no field lie fallow. To surrender this central control would, however, mean to surrender a degree of political control over a sector of the population which is viewed with great suspicion. This the party is unlikely to do.

Instead, the party continues to send loyal party men out to manage farms despite the fact that such men often know little about farming and are usually transferred before they can learn. Thus the interweaving of political and economic factors forms a matrix from which it is unlikely that the regime will be able wholly to extricate itself.

The Soviet Army and the Communist party

The control and political loyalty of the armed forces have been matters of primary consideration for the Soviet leaders from the very beginning of the regime. In this they were aided by the fact that the tsarist army went to pieces and that an entirely new instrument had to be forged by the Bolsheviks. It was clear that if the army were to stand aloof from the regime, and show an "unpolitical" or even hostile attitude, the very existence of the regime would then be in danger. Apart from the general tendency of the regime to permeate all institutions with its spirit, it was of particular importance to do so in the army. As a result the political control and the political education of the soldiers were vested in a system of commissars who, together with the military commanders, bore co-responsibility for their respective units. At the same time care was taken that as many officers and men as possible

[54] *Ibid*, p. 21.

should be party members and that promotions should be open as far as possible only to party members or to Comsomols.

As the dark clouds of coming war began to form on the horizon, it became necessary to increase the efficiency of the Red Army. Military discipline was heightened, and the social and economic contrast between officers and enlisted men was increased beyond what is customary in the so-called "capitalistic" armies in order to increase the men's desire for promotion.

The institution of the commissars saw its ups and downs. After the great army purge in 1937, which culminated in the execution of Marshal M. N. Tukhachevski and the suicide of Assistant People's Commissar for War, Jan Gamarnik, party control was tightened. Political commissars were made co-equal with the respective commanding officers. But this system worked very badly in the Finnish war and contributed to a great deal of confusion. Hence the commissars were abolished in 1940 and replaced by Assistant Commanders for Political Affairs (*zampolits*). The surrender *en masse* of Red soldiers and officers in the first few months after Russia's invasion by the German army was a danger signal to the party leadership, and it responded by the reinstitution of the commissar system shortly afterward. But when the situation again became consolidated and the large-scale defections ceased, there was again a return to the zampolits in October, 1942.

It is noteworthy that the party regards political control of the army as so important that it takes direct responsibility for this task. The army is honeycombed with a system of primary party and Comsomol organizations which are supervised, directed, and advised by the Main Political Administration (MPA). It is interesting to note that the MPA is a department in the U.S.S.R. Ministry of Defense *but at the same time* is also the military department of the Central Committee of the Communist party, or in reality of its Politburo.[55] MPA representatives are attached to every level of command. From the army corps down they work through the zampolits and on the company level through the chief party worker, the *politruk*. These different levels of party officers work not only on the improvement of the political education and loyalty of officers and soldiers, but also report periodically to their political superiors on such questions as army morale, the personal reliability of certain officers, the effectiveness of the work of the zampolits, etc. In addition the zampolits control the clubs and recreation facilities for the soldiers and thus have an opportunity to be doubly effective. In addition to the party organizations, the primary Comsomol groups in the army reinforce the party's work. These are also under the control of the MPA.

The MPA, the zampolits, and politruks, as well as the party and Comsomol organizations in the army, may be called the positive instruments of party control. The negative instruments are in the special security organization of the Ministry of Internal Affairs, the MVD, and the Committee of Party and State Security (KGB). The latter maintains its own chain of command within the army. All levels of com-

[55] Nemzer, *op. cit.*, pp. 78*f*.

mand down to the battalion have their attached special sections of MVD men who are in charge of all aspects of security. Files are maintained on every soldier and officer, mail is spot-checked, and denunciations are encouraged.[56] This seems to be the institution most resented, especially by the officers; at any rate that is the story of every officer-escapee from the Soviet Army[57] who has reached sanctuary in the West.[58]

In this system of tensions produced by the party machinery on one side and the MVD-KGB on the other, a third factor enters. The soldier, and especially the officer, knows that the road to promotion and thus to a very considerable improvement of both his personal comfort and his social standing goes through the party. Not only will he have to aspire to party or at least to Comsomol membership—and thus submit to further checks and controls—but he must have a good record with his zampolits and a clean slate with the KGB. Out of this interlocking system of positive and negative controls, of threats and inducements, it is hard to imagine that the army could emerge as an independent force against the party. Only in an intra-party quarrel could the army lend weight to one side, but even that is not easy to envisage because it presupposes the army as a unit defining its own political line, whereas the above-mentioned system makes that virtually impossible.

Lest the army become a popular symbol for something opposed to the political leadership, the party has consistently played down the famous contemporary military leaders of the country. Marshal Georgi Zhukov was soon after the war shifted to a relatively secondary command and then retired altogether. After Stalin's death he became Deputy Minister of Defense under Bulganin. When Bulganin became head of the government, Zhukov became Minister of Defense, which to many observers indicated the growing importance of the army. He also broke with precedent by becoming the first professional soldier ever to sit as a full member of the Politburo. It is a conclusive measure of the party's control over the armed forces, however, that such a popular and seemingly powerful figure, who had been credited with playing the vital role in Khrushchev's rise to power and in the downfall of such men as Beria and then the Malenkov-Molotov-Kaganovich group, could have been ousted so easily and unresistingly from all his posts and again relegated to an oblivion even deeper than that which he suffered under Stalin. Since then there is little doubt in anybody's mind concerning the party's paramountcy over the army, a fact proved time and again since Zhukov's disgrace and the Red Army's meek acceptance of all party measures designed to strengthen the party's hold over it.

There are some indications that the army and Defense Minister Marshal Rodion Malinovski may have asserted themselves in matters of defense budgets and the problem of missiles versus manned aircraft and ground forces. However, on the question of party control there does not seem to have been any challenge

---

[56] Fainsod, "Controls and Tensions within the Soviet System."
[57] The Red Army is now officially renamed Soviet Army.
[58] *The Soviet Union as Reported by Former Soviet Citizens,* Department of State, Report No. 3, May 15, 1952, p. 2.

since the Zhukov affair.[59] It might also be noted in passing that in modern Russian history the army has never played an important political role and has no tradition of so doing. While the army is therefore full of tensions as the result of the tight network of political and security controls which permeate it, there is little to suggest that it could emerge as an alternative or a threat to the present Communist leadership of the country.

The Communist party and religion

The most important religious denomination in the Soviet Union is the Russian Orthodox Church. Complete separation of state and church is ordained (Art. 124). There is also guaranteed "freedom of religious worship and freedom of antireligious propaganda," but presumably not freedom for religious propaganda. The basic attitude of the Soviet government and the Communist party has been dominated by the famous Marxist assertion that "religion is opium for the people." In the earlier periods of the Soviet regime, this principle was vigorously pursued. Hostile feelings were mutual, and Patriarch Tikhon in his message to the Orthodox Church on January 18, 1918, warned all believers "not to enter into any kind of association with these monsters of the human race."[60]

The government suppressed the church vigorously; churches were burned or transformed into club homes for the Society of the Godless, altars and icons were desecrated, and other items of worship were carted away. Then followed a relatively quiet period during which the church was pretty much left alone within the confines of the narrow restrictions placed upon it. But the Second World War brought about a spectacular change. The war was fought as a great patriotic adventure, not as a struggle of the Communist party. The church proved itself loyal to the regime, and the sight of masses of worshippers who thronged the cathedrals convinced the government that it had in the church an instrument which could be used for the greater mobilization of the population. This ushered in a reconciliation of church and state in which the former placed itself fully at the disposal of the latter. The government in turn suspended the two principal atheist publications and in 1942 appointed the Metropolitan of Kiev and Galicia, Nicolai, as a member of the "Extraordinary State Commission for the Investigation of German War Crimes."

Since the war this relationship has continued. A new patriarch was elected by a national assembly of the Russian Orthodox Church. The church is under the administration and supervision of the State Council on Affairs of the Orthodox Church, in which the church is not represented, and which is headed by a professed atheist. In return for this relative freedom, the Orthodox Church, inasmuch as it is

[59] For a detailed account of army-party relationships, see Fainsod, *How Russia Is Ruled,* pp. 463–500.
[60] Julius F. Hecker, *Religion and Communism,* New York, 1934, pp. 200f.; Paul B. Anderson, *People, Church and State in Modern Russia,* New York, 1944. See also interview with Gyorgy G. Karpov, Chief of the State Council, in *Christian Science Monitor,* Sept. 30, 1944.

controlled by Moscow, has become one of the vanguards of the Communist regime, especially outside the Soviet Union.

Communist doctrine is still hostile to religion, and party members are expected not to be believers. One editorial in an official paper claimed that religion was "harmful to the Communist Party and fertilizes the soil for hostile, anti-Soviet elements."[61] At the present time the *modus vivendi* between state and Orthodox Church continues. Other churches, however, are vigorously suppressed, especially the Roman Catholic Church, which the Communists regard as their principal enemy.

If at the present time there is a degree of toleration of the Russian Orthodox Church, it must be emphasized that this toleration extends only to the church as an institution and not to its doctrine as a religion. "Dialectical materialism," states an official paper, "the philosophy of Marxism-Leninism and the theoretical foundation of the Communist party, is incompatible with religion."[62] The official organ of the Comsomols, *Komsomolskaya Pravda* of October 18, 1947, had this to say: "The party cannot be neutral regarding religion and it conducts antireligious propaganda against all religious prejudices because it stands for science and religious prejudices are opposed to science since any religion is contrary to science."[63]

Although the leadership of the Russian Orthodox Church in the Soviet Union has furthered the Communist objectives in every way and has been particularly active in espousing the Communist "peace" propaganda line, the party has few kind words for it. In a widely distributed official Soviet propaganda pamphlet, the author, P. F. Kolonitsky, writes as follows:[64]

> It is true that, complying with the will of the Soviet churchgoers and also with their duty as citizens, the clergymen of the Orthodox Church stand for the cause of peace. . . . But religion remains religion. . . . Religion itself was and is a reactionary ideology. In that they preach faith in God, the clergy does harm, implants ignorance in believers' minds and, consciously or unconsciously, opposes the cause of the struggle for communism. . . . Therefore, an indivisible part of the communist education of the working people is the exposure and rout of the religious ethic.

All this adds up to the following situation. For the public at large the Russian Orthodox Church is tolerated, although religion is discouraged whenever possible. But even the slightest demonstration of religious sentiment on the part of party members is severely criticized and the official party line is that religious belief and party membership are incompatible. Even so slight an act as a local Comsomol sec-

---

[61] Editorial in the official organ of the Byelorussian government, reported in *The New York Times*, Sept. 28, 1948.
[62] *Molodoi Bolshevik*, Nos. 5–6, 1946, p. 58, quoted in *Tensions within the Soviet Union*, p. 33.
[63] *Ibid.*
[64] P. F. Kolonitsky, *Moral Kommunisticheskaya i Moral Religionznaya* (Communist Ethic and Religious Ethic), Moscow, 1952, translated in excerpts in *Current Digest of the Soviet Press*, Vol. IV, Aug. 23, 1952, pp. 5f.

retary's participation in a wedding ceremony in which an icon was held over the bride's head aroused the ire of *Komsomolskaya Pravda,* which condemned the attitude that religion was a private affair. Not so, says that paper. "For the Young Communist League member, just as for the Communist, the attitude to religion can in no way be a 'personal matter,' since religious conceptions are foreign to our communist outlook."[65]

Since all roads to a significant career and promotion lead through membership in the Communist party or at least in the Comsomols, religion is effectively cut off from the more important parts of the Soviet population. It is nevertheless remarkable that so many people are still stubbornly clinging to their beliefs and that religion is not entirely expunged from the hearts of the young, although few young people can be seen in Russian churches.[66]

The special ire of the party is reserved for the Roman Catholic Church, not only because of its frankly anti-Communist attitude, but also because its center lies outside the Soviet Union and thus cannot be controlled by Moscow. Today Roman Catholic services are practically extinct in the Soviet Union. Foreign Catholic priests can minister to the faithful in one Moscow church.

The Roman Catholic Church, as such, never counted a large congregation in the Soviet Union. However, the cession to the U.S.S.R. of former Polish territory brought into the Soviet Union large numbers of members of the Uniate Church, which recognized the spiritual authority of Rome. Immediately after the occupation of those territories the bishops of this church were deported and never seen again. In 1946 the Uniates were forced to break with Rome and reunite with the Russian Orthodox Church, but the assassination in 1948 of Dr. Kostelnik, who was held responsible for this, is evidence of resentment.

Next to the Catholics, the Jews are one of the most distrusted groups in the Soviet Union. Anti-Semitism had a long history of semiofficial encouragement under the tsars. In its early days the party opposed this idea, and when the White armies during the civil war unfurled the banner of "Beat the Jews and Save Russia"[67] the Bolsheviks came out strongly for equal rights for all. Indeed the Red Army was viewed as a savior and liberator by most Jews.

Later, as Stalin proceeded to revive the idea of Russian nationalism, the Jews began to find themselves once again on the very short end of a very long stick. Essentially this phase of anti-Semitism was motivated by the desire to gain support among the peasantry rather than by a real feeling of hostility toward the Jews. The hostility came only with the founding of the state of Israel when the enthusiasm shown by the Jews for the newly created state made them extremely

---

[65] *Komsomolskaya Pravda,* Apr. 25, 1951, in *Current Digest of the Soviet Press,* Vol. III, June 2, 1951, p. 8.

[66] Alex Inkeles, "Family and Church in the Postwar U.S.S.R.," *Annals of the American Academy of Political and Social Science,* May, 1949, pp. 33–37.

[67] Erich Goldhagen, "Communism and Anti-Semitism," *Russia Under Khrushchev,* an anthology from *Problems of Communism,* ed. A. Brumberg, New York, p. 328.

suspect in the eyes of the regime. Almost overnight all Jewish cultural institutions were abolished, Jewish writers were arrested and shot, and "all organized Jewish endeavor came to an abrupt end."[68]

The worst aspects of Stalinist repression came to an end with the death of the old dictator. The Jews, however, were not really rehabilitated, and the party has continued to pursue a policy of assimilation through attrition. The Jews are still denied any institutional way of training their children in the religion, and the regime, while not overtly hostile, continues to exert a steady pressure on the Jews to assimilate with the general population. Khrushchev summed up his feelings toward the Jews in these words: "They do not like collective work, group discipline. . . . They are individualists. . . . Jews are interested in everything, they want to probe into everything, they discuss everything, and end up by having profoundly different opinions."[69]

Although other religious groups are far less numerous than the Christians and Jews, the Soviet attitude toward them is more or less similar. True, Islam at times enjoyed a degree of toleration for its religious and cultural practices, but the Communist party has run into repeated difficulties with Moslem Russians which in some respects have been greater than those it has had with the Orthodox Church.

The party and the bureaucracy

Large and indeed growing bureaucracies are characteristic of all modern states, but this trend is greatly accentuated in totalitarian countries, where hardly any human activity is completely unrelated to the control and the management of the government. There is also another element in the nature of bureaucracy which is particularly typical of modern totalitarian regimes and which has been developed farthest in the Soviet Union. It consists of the fact that there is no such thing as a "neutral" or "unpolitical" civil service, but that on the contrary the primacy of the political element is firm dogma.

This means first of all that there is an increasing degree of personal union between party and governmental leadership. Unlike earlier years when the party leadership, especially Stalin himself, occupied no formal place in the government, after Stalin's death all the members of the Presidium of the Central Committee except two were cabinet ministers, and except for Bulganin, who was Premier (Chairman of the Council of Ministers), they all bore the title of Deputy Premier. The two Presidium members who were not cabinet ministers were Voroshilov, the nominal head of the state, and Khrushchev, the First Secretary of the Communist party. Under the latter's ascendancy, the pendulum swung sharply in the other direction. Only four full members of the party Presidium held ministerial positions. Khrushchev was both Premier and First Secretary of the Central Committee. As

[68] *Ibid,* p. 331.
[69] Interview with Serge Goussard, correspondent of *Le Figaro,* Paris, Apr. 9, 1958.

reconstituted at the 23d Congress of the Communist party, the Politburo, as the Presidium was once again renamed, contained a majority of members who were not ministers. Brezhnev is not in the cabinet at all, while Kosygin is Prime Minister (Chairman of the Council of Ministers).

Secondly, as already mentioned, the road to positions of any significance goes through party membership. This means that the party has a direct hand in the selection of future managerial personnel whom it can test by various assignments before the candidate receives a post in the most sensitive echelons of the governmental hierarchy.

Thirdly, the emphasis on the "political" means that every governmental function, whatever its nature, has to serve a political purpose. It is not sufficient that a given administrative task is carried out in an efficient manner. Also, the official in charge must be keenly away of its political significance and unceasingly emphasize it, thus becoming a part of the party propaganda machine.

This total permeation of the atmosphere with political considerations, this never-ending insistence on the political significance of the most minor task, leads inevitably to the conclusion that failure to perform such a task properly is not merely a human error but political sabotage, wrecking, or treason. And in a dictatorship of this kind there are no graver offenses.

The Soviet official is thus subjected to a system of cross pressures of fantastic proportions. His superiors and a long chain of command and control agencies watch over the proper performance of his task; the party through its multiple channels watches over his political orthodoxy, his party work, and the proper emphasis of the political element in his work. And the KGB watches over everything, not only his deeds and omissions, but also his associations, for to have chosen friends who later turn out to be purged or are friends of those who are purged is to invite oblivion.

The experiences of both the Nazi and Soviet regimes suggest that the pressure of such cross tensions is extremely severe and that practically the only way to get a little elbow room is to make deals with those assigned to watch—in other words, corruption, which in the Russian press has received the name "family groups." But even though corruption is the only way to obtain some freedom of operation, it is also an extremely dangerous method in an atmosphere so heavily loaded with denunciations. Consequently, this method, which is designed to relieve tension, produces tension in its turn. Professor Merle Fainsod hardly exaggerates when in a brilliant book he characterizes this network of controls as "a system of power founded on institutionalization of mutual suspicion."[70]

We have seen that all activities are "public" in the Soviet Union. There is no such thing as a "private" sector, no activity which escapes the vigilance and, where necessary, the direction of the state. All activities, whether economic, scientific,

---

[70] Fainsod, *How Russia Is Ruled*, p. 388. See also by the same author, "Recent Developments in Soviet Public Administration," *Journal of Politics*, Vol. XI (1949), pp. 679–714.

intellectual, or even highly personal, are therefore somehow related to governmental activities and control. In a sense, this control is made more plausible and more complete by the fact that it is not the governmental machinery which controls in the last analysis, but the Communist party. For it is more natural for a political party, especially for *the* political party in a totalitarian regime to concern itself with the mental attitude, the cultural activities, and where necessary, even highly private and personal acts of the citizen. The party governs the state in the name of purity of the doctrine and "scientific correctness" of all its actions.

Although the control of the party, i.e., of the Politburo, over the entire governmental machinery is total and absolute, the organization of that relationship varies from time to time and will continue to vary in the future. In the earlier period of the Stalinist regime, the membership of the Politburo and the government were kept separate on the whole. Even Stalin himself did not take a governmental position until the advent of war. Yet even when he was "only" General Secretary of the Communist party, there was no doubt as to where the center of power lay. Influential foreign statesmen and diplomats, if they wanted to get "the word," always tried to see Stalin; whoever was Chairman of the Council of Ministers or minister of this or that was highly irrelevant. Later on, Stalin not only became Chairman of the Council of Ministers, but toward the end of his life appeared to diminish the significance of the Politburo, then already renamed Presidium, of the Central Committee of the Communist party by greatly enlarging its membership, an act which some interpreted not only as a denigration of the institution but as a preparation for the liquidation of its best-known members.

Under Khrushchev and his successors, Brezhnev and Kosygin, the tendency reverted to only a handful of ministers being members of the Presidium, which was again reduced to eleven members. Because the Soviet government is exceedingly large, and the number of ministers far greater than in any Western government, the possibility of the Politburo acting as a "board of directors" is thereby enhanced. On the other hand, a short-lived attempt under Khrushchev to divide the control functions of the Politburo into an industrial and an agricultural sector proved unsuccessful and was reversed.

Under Stalin it was obvious that the institutions of government and of the party were designed to check each other constantly and thereby protect the dictator from being overthrown.[71] Under Khrushchev and, later, Kosygin, these multilayered checks and balances were reduced in number and intensity. Nevertheless there is ingrown and inbred in the Soviet governmental system a permanent system of duplicate controls at every level—from the lowest to the highest—which ensures that party dictates are observed. At times, when stupid party bureaucrats, especially on local levels, became particularly irksome and hindered output of needed goods, they were dammed back. But they were never eliminated and can not be eliminated if party control is to continue to function. Although no government in the world is

---

[71] Meyer, *The Soviet Political System*, p. 200.

really efficient or, for that matter, designed to be efficient, the inefficiency built into the dual Soviet control system is excessive and has more than once prevented the Soviet Union and Soviet production from reaching their goals. As the experience of Soviet agriculture has demonstrated with particular clarity, when everything is centrally planned and centrally controlled, errors in judgment and foresight are bound to produce monumental results.

Culture, science, and the party

Although Communism was supposed to free all creative talents to reach ever greater heights, the hard fact is that the relationship between culture and Communism has been a troubled one in the Soviet Union. As Barrington Moore said,[72] the Communist party has never been able quite to make up its mind whether to coddle the intellectuals or to shoot them.

This is not surprising. It is a basic tenet of any totalitarian state that there can be nothing outside the control of the state and its leadership. It is a further tenet that mere obedience is not enough but that everybody must take a positive view of the regime. There can be no "unpolitical" branch of human endeavor.

The logical extension of this doctrine is that there can be no objective science and that there is a party line even in such seemingly unpolitical subjects as physics and horticulture. Thus S. Vavilov, at one time President of the Academy of Science of the U.S.S.R., and an internationally respected physicist, wrote: "The task of Soviet physicists is to exploit unreservedly the dialectical materialism of Marx, Engels, Lenin, and Stalin, as a powerful weapon also in the field of physics."[73]

While these tendencies had been quite noticeable throughout the Soviet regime, they shifted into high gear after the end of the Second World War. Their chief protagonist and spokesman was Andrei Zhdanov, and he began with a purge of Soviet literature in September, 1946, and quickly extended it to all other fields. "Objectivism," "cosmopolitanism," "failure to stress properly Russian achievements," and "lack of ideology" are the accusations directed against those who are to be condemned.

Those who become the victims of this process are by no means open or hidden resisters, but rather people who have missed a turn of the party line. The Zhdanov purge reached its heights in 1947 with the condemnation of G. F. Alexsandrov's book on the history of Western European philosophy. Alexsandrov had applied Engels's formula of the jump from the realm of necessity to the realm of freedom in the hitherto conventional form when he found himself condemned by Zhdanov. In the interest of the continuity of the Soviet Union, it was no longer proper to speak of "jumps." Only "continuity" was now officially permitted.

The case most widely publicized was the rise of Trofim Lysenko to leadership

---

[72] Quoted in Meyer, *op. cit.,* p. 448.
[73] Quoted in *Tensions within the Soviet Union,* p. 18.

in the field of genetics. This man, although of more than doubtful scientific knowledge, and on the basis of experiments which practically all Western scientists regarded as fraudulent, upheld and developed the Michurin theory of environmental transmutation of genes and condemned the traditional Mendelian school of the chromosome theory of heredity. Although the weight of scientific opinion was against him, Lysenko overcame all opposition at the August, 1948, meeting of the Lenin Academy of Agricultural Science by declaring, "The Central Committee of the party has examined my report and has approved it."[74]

As those Soviet geneticists who wished to retain their positions and perhaps even their lives and freedom[75] rushed forward to surrender, one specialist, A. R. Zhebrak, wrote with a frankness which might have been intended irony: "Now that it has become clear to me that the basic postulates of the Michurin tendency in Soviet genetics have been approved by the Central Committee of the Communist party, I, as a member of the party, do not consider it possible for me to retain a position that has been recognized as erroneous by the Central Committee."[76]

One intervention of the party was carried out by Stalin himself when he condemned the hitherto authoritative (in the U.S.S.R.) school of N. Ya. Marr in linguistics.[77] This and other interventions by Stalin netted him such accolades as these remarks of a military judge in a law journal: "All the most important questions of scientific socialism, political economy, philosophy, law, governmental, economic and cultural construction, military affairs, literature, and art have received the utmost development in the works of Comrade Stalin."[78]

After Stalin's death there was a temporary shift. Criticized composers like Shostakovich and Khachaturian returned and even made some mild snide remarks against "bureaucratic control of creative composition." Michael Sostchenko, one of the victims of Zhdanov's literary purge in 1946, reemerged and started to publish again. And G. F. Alexsandrov, the butt of Zhdanov's ire in 1947, returned to become Minister of Culture. And then the powerful First Secretary of the Communist party of the Soviet Union, Nikita Khrushchev, launched a sharp attack obviously aimed at Lysenko.

But soon the pendulum swung again the other way. At the Congress of Soviet Writers of 1955 Ilya Ehrenburg, one of the most faithful followers of the party line, was bitterly criticized for a novel which contained some mild satire on the bureaucratic features of Soviet life. Dudintsev, the author of the controversial novel, *Not by Bread Alone*, was vociferously denounced and forced to do penance and admit his guilt. And too well known to need description is the fate visited on the world-renowned figure of Boris Pasternak for his *Doctor Zhivago*, in which he pre-

[74] Bertram D. Wolfe, "Science Joins the Party," *Antioch Review*, Spring, 1950, pp. 47–60.
[75] Lysenko's predecessor, Professor Vavilov, a world-renowned authority, was sent to a forced-labor camp and died there.
[76] *Pravda*, Aug. 15, 1948, quoted in *Tensions within the Soviet Union*, p. 21.
[77] *Pravda*, June 20, 1950, quoted in *Current Digest of the Soviet Press*, Vol. II, July 8, 1950, p. 8.
[78] Quoted in *Tensions within the Soviet Union*, p. 27.

sumed to express views diverging from the official ones. In many respects this reminds one of the more objectionable aspects of Stalinism.[79]

The life of intellectuals, writers, and artists is not easy in the Soviet Union. In the first place, there are no "free professions." They are all totally dependent on the state and the party for income, research funds, assistance, laboratory equipment, and permission to publish or exhibit. Secondly, the regime never tires of educating and reeducating intellectuals, writers, and artists to the fact that they are servants of the state and the party and that their works must show, and will be judged by the presence of, party enthusiasm, ideological dedication, civic-mindedness, and several other proofs of loyalty and devotion.[80] The party has never tired of using its power; an unending flow of directives, admonitions, and warnings has descended upon artists and writers.

However, in the exercise of control, the party and state authorities have not been uniform. After the nightmarish oppression of the Stalin era, controls were substantially relaxed. After a while critical writing reached a point that seemed to have given the Soviet leaders reason for concern, and the controls were once again tightened, as we have seen particularly dramatically in the Pasternak case. But such is life in a dictatorship that, once there is the slightest relaxation, people who are hungry for liberty flock to the writers and poets who dare walk a more independent course. This tendency is all the greater and hence more dangerous to the regime since literature and poetry have always held a particularly high place of esteem in Russian culture, in both the tsarist and Communist days. Hence, the shock over the Pasternak affair was deep, both in the Soviet Union and abroad, and probably contributed to yet another period of relaxation. However, the party watched this with growing irritation, and various disciplinary measures were imposed on writers and poets, sometimes in a haphazard and arbitrary fashion. It is difficult to see exactly why one writer may be barely tolerated while another may be hauled off to prison. The first of the "young lions" among poets, Evginy Evtushenko, one of the best-known of the poets, was in and out of trouble, while another rising star, poet Andrey Voznesensky, came in for greater restraint and was sent to Siberia for several months. Forced to indulge in "self-criticism," he showed great courage in merely promising to work harder, and he did indeed return from exile loaded with poems. His poetry readings have become first rate events in Moscow.[81] A much harsher fate, however, befell another young poet, Osip Brodsky, who in 1964 was condemned to five years of corrective labor for being a "loafer." The reasons for this particular sentence are still unclear.[82]

The zigzagging course of relative tolerance and crackdown has evidently en-

---

[79] For the fate of lesser figures and the regime's struggle against any expression of originality or creativity or any deviation from the party line in literature, see, for example, E. Alexander, "The Ferment in Soviet Armenian Literature," *American Slavic and East European Review,* Vol. XVII, No. 4 (December, 1958), pp. 495–508.

[80] Meyer, *op. cit.,* p. 454.

[81] *Life,* Apr. 1, 1966, pp. 69–72.

[82] Pierre Forgues, "Russian Poetry, 1963–1965," *Survey,* July, 1965, pp. 54–70.

couraged some of the more courageous writers and poets to resist. In 1962, Khrushchev attacked sculptor Ernst Neizevstny in a series of brutal public statements which were followed by seven months of public meetings in which dogmatists in factories and universities all over the country tried to get errant writers and artists to recant, to revise their critical works, and to support the party in the construction of Communism. Some did pull in their horns, including Evtushenko, who altered some lines of his famous poem, "Babi Yar." However, after Khrushchev's fall, there was again a period of relaxation, lasting from 1963 through most of 1965. In October, 1965, another crackdown began, led by P. N. Demichev, a candidate member of the Presidium of the Central Committee and a member of its powerful Secretariat. Now there was resistance, especially in a magnificent poem by Evtushenko called "Letter to Esenian."[83] But evidently the authorities considered the general evolution of literary criticism to be getting out of hand. Hence they made an example of two Soviet writers: Andrei Synyavesky and Yuli Daniel were arrested on October, 1965, and accused of the "crime" of having published abroad under the names of "Abram Tertz" and "Nikolai Arzhak." On February 14, 1966, they were sentenced to seven and five years of hard labor respectively. Yet at the very same time, another writer who had published abroad, Valery Tarsis, whose work *Ward Seven* had shocked readers in the West, was allowed to leave the Soviet Union and seek exile in the West. In his book, Tarsis had depicted conditions in a psychiatric hospital in Moscow populated with critics of the Soviet system who, by definition, had been considered insane. Tarsis himself had been confined, and perhaps this was the reason why he was permitted to leave. But a logical explanation for the contrast between the treatment of Synyavesky and Daniel on the one hand and of Tarsis on the other is hard to find.

The condemnation of the two writers, who were not even accused of treason but merely of having criticized the Communist regime, aroused a wave of protest, perhaps the first which could be heard even inside the Soviet Union. Abroad, it ringed the world and found echoes even among leading Communist intellectuals and Communist party newspapers like the French *Humanité*. But it appears that this merely increased the apprehensions of the Soviet leadership, for at the 23d Congress of the Communist party of the Soviet Union, a number of speakers (with the blessing of party Secretary Brezhnev) berated the rebellious writers and thereby raised the ominous possibility of another crackdown. That it will reach the depths of depravity of the Stalinist period is unlikely, but as these lines are written, trouble is clearly once more ahead for the Soviet Union's embattled writers and poets.

The result of the struggle between knowledge and politics has been rather different on the scientific front. There the party has gradually had to pull back from its extreme of forcing science to coincide with the party view of life. This was

---

[83] Sergei Esenian was a much-loved lyrical poet who committed suicide over the persecution to which he was subjected. This poem has been translated and published in John Scott's "The Soviet World," a report to the publisher of *Time* which was published for limited circulation in 1966.

necessary largely because the regime was forcing the scientists into a position where creative work was becoming more and more difficult. No matter how much the party hated to swallow its pride, it had to back down in certain fields if the West was to be matched in technological achievements. These developments have gone far and have even led some writers to believe that a new age of political pluralism is about to dawn in the Soviet Union.[84] That seems unlikely, since the party has only retreated in areas which are as nearly nonpolitical as possible. The power of decision making rests as firmly as ever in the grip of the upper strata of the party leadership. These men are firm party members and "generalists," while the majority of scientists are specialists and more or less nonpolitical. It is most unlikely that members of the scientific community will pose a serious threat to the political control of the party in the near future.

[84] Albert Parry, *New Class Divided,* New York, 1966.

7

Soviet federalism

The existence of over 150 different races and nationalities in the Soviet Union has confronted that country with exceptionally difficult problems. Accidental and often forceful absorption into the Russian empire, as well as a rigorous Russification policy of the tsars, especially harsh under some of them, left a legacy of hate against the "Great Russians."[1]

The nationality problem attracted Stalin's attention at an early time, and Lenin too considered it of prime significance. The views of the founders Marx and Engels were of little help. They regarded nationalism as a possible tactical weapon of the proletariat, but never as a genuine political force per se. For federalism they had no use at all. "The proletariat can use only the form of the one and indivisible republic," wrote Engels.

But Lenin quickly grasped the nature of Russian realities and at an early date embraced the principle of national self-determination. This concept he later en-

---

[1] Essentially the people now living in the Russian Soviet Federative Socialist Republic, in contradistinction to the "Little Russians," i.e., the Ukrainians.

larged to include the right of individual states to secede from the Union,[2] which is still a full-fledged part of Soviet constitutional theory, although as we shall see it has no place in practice. Lenin attempted to establish certain limitations by his pronouncements against nationalism; while he was for the *right* of secession he was very much opposed to the *reality* of secession.[3] Federalism and the maintenance of national autonomy, political or cultural, was thus in Lenin's eyes a necessary concession to the tactical situation, not a stipulation of deep conviction. But Lenin was aware of the great strength of nationalism and wanted to establish his unitary ideal of the state by voluntary rather than coercive measures, because he believed the former to have more durable results than the latter.

However, every question of national independence was to be studied on the basis of the class angle. In other words, national self-determination which suited Soviet policy was all right, but other types were not.[4]

If Lenin and Stalin accepted national self-determination only with reservations, this was even more the case with federalism, which they considered detrimental to the economic development of the socialist state. "Only in individual, exclusive cases can we advance and actively support . . . the replacement of the complete political unity of the state with the weaker, federal unity. . . ."[5]

The federal form of government was established right after the Revolution,[6] however, and has remained a salient feature of government in the Soviet Union. It would be a mistake to see in this development a reversal of earlier policies. The Communist ideal is still one of absolute unity, but the Soviet leaders have learned that this goal can be reached only by indirect means. The idea of unity is condemned to failure without the thorough integration of the non-Russian masses. The federal form of government, together with an emphasis on the preservation of national culture and the economic development of non-Russian areas, is more likely to win over these masses and thus pave the way to a fuller unity. The aim of federalism in the Soviet Union is therefore the establishment of a truly unitary system.

The Union Republics and their subdivisions

Article 13 of the Soviet Constitution of 1936 defines the U.S.S.R. as a "federal state, formed on the basis of a voluntary union of equal Soviet Socialist Republics." These are now the following:

---

[2] V. I. Lenin, *Collected Works*, New York, 1945, Vol. XVI, p. 507.

[3] "We on our part, do not want separation at all. We want as large a state as possible." *Ibid.*, Vol. XXI, p. 316. In another context Lenin said, "There is *nothing,* absolutely nothing here, and there must be nothing here, but the *right* to secede." Quoted in Alex Inkeles, "Soviet Nationality Policy in Perspective," *Problems of Communism*, May–June, 1960.

[4] Stalin said: "There are instances when the right of self-determination comes into conflict with another, higher right—the right of the working class . . . to fortify its power." 12th Congress of the Russian Communist party (1923). J. Towster, *Political Power in the U.S.S.R.*, New York, 1948, p. 61.

[5] Lenin, *op. cit.*, Vol. XVII, pp. 154–156.

[6] See the *Charter of the Nations of Russia*, 1917, signed by Lenin and Stalin. M. W. Graham, *New Governments of Eastern Europe*, New York, 1927, pp. 594f.

The Russian Soviet Federative Socialist Republic
The Ukrainian Soviet Socialist Republic
The Byelorussian (White Russian) S.S.R.
The Uzbek S.S.R.
The Kazakh S.S.R.
The Georgian S.S.R.
The Azerbaidzhan S.S.R.
The Lithuanian S.S.R.
The Moldavian S.S.R.
The Latvian S.S.R.
The Kirghiz S.S.R.
The Tadzhik S.S.R.
The Armenian S.S.R.
The Turkmen S.S.R.
The Estonian S.S.R.

The aforementioned are the so-called "Union Republics." Theirs is the highest form of statehood that nations may obtain in the Union of Soviet Socialist Republics. Theoretically these Republics are equal to one another, but that equality is neither true nor possible. One of them, the Russian S.F.S.R., comprises over three-fourths of the territory of the U.S.S.R., contains more than three-fifths of its population, and extends from the Baltic to the Pacific. To maintain that any real equality can exist between this colossus and, say, the Kirghiz S.S.R. is to state an obvious absurdity.

The Union Republics are subdivided into Territories (6), Regions (121), Autonomous Republics (19), Autonomous Regions (9), and national areas (10). These are again subdivided into districts (*raions*), except for the Baltic republics (Lithuanian, Latvian, Estonian S.S.R.'s), which have retained their traditional *uyezds* and *volosts* from the days of the tsars. Not all Union Republics have all of these subdivisions.

The federal relationship extends only from the Union to the Union Republics; all lower units are creatures of the Union Republics.[7]

Each Union Republic has its own constitution, which must be in conformity with the Constitution of the U.S.S.R. Its territory cannot be altered except with its consent (Art. 18), and it has the right "freely to secede from the U.S.S.R." Technically the U.S.S.R. has only expressed and enumerated powers (Art. 14), while all others are reserved to the Republics.

Federalism: true or false?

If one were to confine oneself to the constitutional text one would indeed be forced to conclude that true federalism exists in the Soviet Union, and this impres-

---

[7] For an interesting commentary, see V. V. Aspaturian, "The Theory and Practice of Soviet Federalism," *Journal of Politics*, Vol. XII (1950), pp. 20–51.

sion would be increased by two amendments enacted in 1944 (Arts. 18*a* and 18*b*). One of them grants the Union Republics the right to enter into direct relations with foreign states, to exchange diplomatic and consular representatives with them, and to conclude treaties with them. The other gives the Union Republics control over their own armed forces.[8] These amendments paved the way for the inclusion of the Ukrainian and Byelorussian Soviet Socialist Republics in the United Nations.

Yet a closer examination of the issue will place Soviet federalism in a more debatable category. Federalism, if it is to be real, is based on two conditions: (1) the existence of a constitution, written or unwritten, which actually limits the powers of government, and (2) a substantial division of powers between central and regional governments, leaving considerable and significant powers to the latter.

All Soviet writers refer to the Constitution as the "fundamental law" to which all other law is subordinate. But another concept proves that this idea can be accepted only with very serious reservations. It is stated that "the dictatorship of the proletariat is authority unlimited by any statutes whatever."[9] It is not the Constitution which lays down the course of the dictatorship of the proletariat, but it is the dictatorship of the proletariat which lays down the legal forms of conduct of which the Constitution is the foremost but by no means the only expression. The Soviet Constitution therefore emerges as a tool of the "dictatorship of the proletariat" or of the political forces which control it, not as a limitation upon that dictatorship. This principle is also borne out by the well-known comment of Stalin that the Constitution (1936) is an expression of what has been achieved, which implies that further changes will, of course, take place and be eventually recorded in the Constitution but that until that is done the Constitution does not prevent those changes. "The forms of our state will again change in conformity with the changes in the situation at home and abroad," said Stalin. But Molotov put it even more clearly when he said that the Communist party was always "subordinating the forms of the state structure to the fundamental interests of socialism and to the task of strengthening the proletarian dictatorship."[10]

The relationship between the Union and the Union Republics

Let us now turn to an examination of the relationship between the Union (central) government and the governments of the Union Republics. The Soviet Constitution distinguishes between All-Union and Union-Republican ministries. The All-Union ministries exercise their functions directly throughout the entire territory of the U.S.S.R., while the Union-Republican ministries "direct the branches of the state administration entrusted to them through corresponding Ministries of

---

[8] However, these rights are limited by the powers of the central government as outlined in Art. 14.

[9] Andrei Vyshinsky, *The Law of the Soviet State* (trans. by H. R. Babb), New York, 1948, p. 48.

[10] V. Molotov, *The New Soviet Constitution*, New York, 1937, p. 21.

the Union Republics" (Constitution, Art. 76). In other words, the power of the Union government is supreme in the fields of both the All-Union and the Union-Republican ministries, although the form of administration differs. An examination of the pertinent articles in the Constitution (Arts. 77, 78) before a wave of amendments was enacted reveals that every conceivable manifestation of political and especially economic life was long under the control of the central government through either All-Union or Union-Republican ministries, leaving to the authority of the republican governments only limited matters—and those only theoretically.

Moreover, a study of the developments in that area since the Bolshevik Revolution shows conclusively that the trend long ran unmistakably in the direction of greater centralism. Until very recently, of the six fields which were once under the exclusive control of the Republics, only two, education[11] and social security, remained. A number of Union-Republican ministries became All-Union ministries.[12] Two ministries, those for Foreign Affairs and the Armed Forces,[13] went the other way, being transformed from All-Union to Union-Republican rank, but a parallel amendment to Article 14 gave the Union government the right to deal with the "establishment of general procedure governing the relations of Union Republics with foreign states" and with the "determination of directing principles governing the organization of the military formations of the Union Republics."

After the death of Stalin, however, the picture altered profoundly. Besides drastic consolidation of ministries and wholesale abolition of many of them, the Khrushchev regime made a vigorous attempt to effect a decentralization of the political and especially of the economic life of the country. A thorough reorganization of the ministerial system of the U.S.S.R. began in 1956, marked by elimination of independent industries, merging of two or more into one agency, and numerous transfers of ministries from the All-Union to the Union-Republican level. The overhauling of the administration has resulted in the increase of the Republics' role in administration and in their administrative powers. At present the following agencies have been turned over completely to the Republics' jurisdiction: Motor Transport and Highways; Paper and Wood Products Industry; Municipal Economy (local public works); Lumber Industry; Popular Instruction (basic education); River Fleet; Social Security; Building, Internal Affairs and most important, Justice. With regard to two of these there still remain vestiges at the federal level, though no longer those that used to exist. There is still the Chief Administration for the Building of Motor Roads and a Juridical Committee, both attached directly to the Council of Ministers.

---

[11] But not higher education, which is under a Union-Republican ministry (Art. 78).
[12] In 1936 the Constitution listed 8 All-Union and 10 Union-Republican ministries. In 1955 there were listed 36 and 22 respectively, indicating a strong tendency toward specialization. The former Commissariat for Heavy Industry was the parent body for no less than 27 new ministries. At the May, 1957, meeting of the Supreme Soviet, there were listed 11 All-Union and 14 Union-Republican ministries. Shortly thereafter, the number of the latter dropped to twelve. By December, 1958, there were only 6 All-Union and 10 Union-Republican ministries.
[13] In March, 1950, a new Ministry of the Navy was created.

By January 1, 1964, the enormously cumbersome U.S.S.R. Council of Ministers comprised over fifty members, namely, one Chairman (Prime Minister), three first vice chairmen, eight vice chairmen, three All-Union ministers, eight Union-Republican ministers, and thirty-one heads of committees, commissions, and agencies, among which the most important is that of the State Planning Committee (*Gosplan*).

In addition, the fifteen chairmen of the Councils of Ministers (Prime Ministers) of the Union Republics are ex-officio members of the U.S.S.R. Council of Ministers.

In addition there are other manifestations of actual centralism over apparent federalism. The Presidium of the Supreme Soviet has the power to annul decisions and orders of the Councils of Ministers of the Union Republics if they do not conform to law (Art. 49*f*). Also peculiarly centralistic is the position of the Procurator-General of the U.S.S.R., who supervises the strict execution of the laws throughout the entire territory of the Soviet Union.

It also appears that the central authorities have a heavy hand in the incorporation and elimination of lesser units of government. This was evident in the establishment of an autonomous region out of territory ceded by China and other areas taken from Germany and Japan, as well as in the elimination of five units during the war for treasonable activities.[14] It is noteworthy that in 1957 the central authorities surrendered their former right to confirm any territorial changes within the Republics without which such amendments were not valid. At present internal modifications of any territorial administrative order are exclusively within the jurisdiction of the Republic concerned, although any changes between two Republics must still be sanctioned by Moscow, as must the creation of new Autonomous Republics and Autonomous Regions within Union Republics.

Most important of all, however, is the pervasive position of the Communist party, which is strictly centralist and without a spark of federalism. Since all policy emanates from the Communist party, it actually matters little whether there exists a federal form of government or not. The Politburo of the party determines all policy for the entire Union, and this policy is carried out by all state authorities, federal or central. A federal structure, governed by a unitary, monolithic party, provides merely a table of organization of the distribution of the work to be done. Federalism, in order to be real, must reserve to the component parts at least some autonomy in the realm of policy; but that is quite impossible in the one-party state of the Soviet Union.

This is perhaps not unnatural, because the Soviet Union is a state with a

---

[14] Since Stalin's death, three of the latter have been revived: the Kalmyk and Chechen-Ingush as Autonomous Republics of the R.S.F.S.R., and the Karachai-Cherkess as an Autonomous Region of the R.S.F.S.R. In 1956, the Karelo-Finnish S.S.R. was absorbed into the R.S.F.S.R. as an Autonomous Republic, and Crimea was ceded by the R.S.F.S.R. to the Ukrainian S.S.R. in 1955. Periodically there have been other cessions or exchanges of territory between various "sovereign" components of the U.S.S.R.

strictly and integrally planned economy. The Communists and also most non-Communist socialists have always recognized that federalism and state planning are in fundamental conflict. Because of the close connection between political and economic direction in the Soviet Union, unitarism rather than federalism is the real nature of the regime. When Lenin inaugurated the NEP and the strategic retreat from war communism, federalism, although never a working system, was part of that retreat. Since the return to uncompromising communism, federalism has steadily lost more and more of whatever ground it had. In fact the supreme, directive function of the state national economic plan is specifically recognized in the Constitution (Art. 11). Moreover, the creation of the National Economic Councils is a further centralizing device in the economic sphere.

Cultural autonomy

Any discussion of Soviet federalism will eventually lead to the topic of "cultural autonomy." From the beginning of the regime, the Communist leaders have emphasized the equality of all races and nationalities of the Soviet Union. Much effort has been expended on the furtherance, and at times the revival, of language and culture of the various nationalities. All Soviet languages may be used in the courts and government offices of the U.S.S.R., a tremendous increase in the literature of many Soviet nations has taken place, and the availability of schools in the native language of all citizens has helped to reduce greatly the rate of illiteracy. Compared with the persistent and at times forceful "Russification" attempts by the tsars, this is indeed great progress. But one must never lose sight of the fact that the eventual aim of these cultural activities is unity, not diversity. Stalin felt that national languages and cultures would and should come to an end, but not before the victory of socialism all over the world.[15] Until then cultural diversity is used as a tool for national unity. The form of expression is left to native tongues and cultures, but the meaning and direction of these expressions are as tightly controlled from the top as are all other activities of Soviet citizens. The Politburo lays down the precise line for music, drama, art, etc., and any citizen who disregarded such direction would do so at his dire peril. In the economic and social fields, and with the exception of the Jews, the party works hard to see that the various nationalities are treated equally. In the political field, however, it is clear that the high party positions are overwhelmingly held by Great Russians. This is only one more way in which the various nationalities are cut off from effective control of their own destinies. But that was only natural in view of the prominent role of the "Great Russians" among the peoples of the Soviet Union, and it furthered the purpose of uniting all in a common pride.

In its particular chauvinistic manifestation, this aberration of Stalinism was abandoned after its creator's death. However, the campaign to glorify the Soviet

---

[15] Stalin, *Marxism and the National and Colonial Question*, pp. 265f.

Union and its achievements has continued unabated. Currently it takes the form of magnifying all the successes of Soviet science in the field of rocketry and atomic development and claiming preeminence for Soviet society in every aspect of technical and cultural development. The emphasis on the excellence of things Soviet as opposed to things "Russian" or "Great Russian" is again very much in evidence.

Secession?

The official doctrine still insists that the association of nations, especially of the Union Republics, is free and voluntary and that the right of secession is a reality.[16] In fact Stalin, commenting on the 1936 Constitution, stated that a Union Republic would have to be a border republic "because, since the Union Republics have a right to secede from the U.S.S.R., a republic . . . must be in a position logically and actually to raise the question of secession from the U.S.S.R." But at the same time he admitted that "of course none of our republics would actually raise the question of seceding from the U.S.S.R. But since the right to secede from the U.S.S.R. is reserved to the Union Republics, it must be so arranged that this right does not become a meaningless scrap of paper [!]." This bit of dialectics fits well into the general pattern. Just how would a Union Republic go about the business of seceding, the policy of the Communist party being clearly against secession? This right is highly theoretical and actually could not be exercised without a breakup of the party.

This emphasis on the unreal right of secession is part of the larger picture which tends to grant the component parts of the Soviet Union more prestige and status while depriving them of substance, thus amassing even greater power and control at the top. That this is a trend which is entirely in conformity with the classical Communist position may be surmised from this statement by Lenin: "In the example of the Russian Soviet Republic we see most graphically that the federation we are introducing will serve now as the surest step to the most solid unification of the different nationalities into a single, democratic, centralized Soviet State."[17]

In another exercise in dialectics Vyshinsky declared[18]

The Soviet Union State is a federative state. Both by its class essence and by its organizational structure it is sharply distinguished from all existing forms of federation, confederation and unitarism formerly or now existing in the capitalist world. It is a type of state without a precedent in history. It emerges from the problems of the worker class dictatorship in a multinational country. It is the

---

[16] Vyshinsky, *op. cit.*, pp. 214–217. The American doctrine of federalism does not recognize the right of secession. Texas v. White, 2 Wall., 700 (1869).

[17] Lenin, *op. cit.*, Vol. XXII, pp. 415f.

[18] Vyshinsky, *op. cit.*, pp. 228f. Despite the fact that Vyshinsky is now posthumously discredited, the above quotations from his book still reflect official doctrine as it is today.

realization and expression of the general will and mutual confidence of the toilers of nations with equal rights.

Trained Leninist-Stalinist dialecticians might perhaps be able to find evidence of a Soviet federalism, since such dialectics appear to outsiders only too often as the art of declaring that contradictions are not contradictions and that those who see them are blind. By the generally accepted Western standards of political science, Soviet federalism is as real as the Emperor's new clothes in Hans Christian Andersen's famous tale.

8

The soviets

The Soviet Constitution provides that "The political foundation of the U.S.S.R. are the soviets of working people's deputies, which grew and became strong as a result of the overthrow of the power of the landlords and capitalists and the conquest of the dictatorship of the proletariat" (Art. 2).

Literally the Russian word *soviet* means "council," but the form of council which has given the regime its name is the result of historical development in Russia and of the use which the Communist leaders managed to make of it. The first soviets were strike committees which sprang up in the factories during the revolution of 1905. Soon city-wide soviets were formed, composed of factory delegates. Some leaders like Trotsky obtained political fame in those assemblies.

These soviets were revolutionary bodies, composed of activist elements. To what extent they represented the workers might be an interesting though futile topic of discussion, but that they were not elected by standardized, orderly procedure was common knowledge. If they represented the workers it was certainly a small minority of them, but revolutionaries are not easily deterred by such technicalities. There were no such things as labor unions in those days, and the soviets were a makeshift which was possible only amid the confusion of a revolutionary period. There was, however, one significant element in this situation. The authority of the government was wholeheartedly on the side of the employers and against the workers. Consequently the workers' councils, the soviets, directed their activities against the state authorities and were essentially political bodies. When the strike wave became larger, delegates from various factories were elected to a "soviet of workers' deputies." This was a large body, but between sessions a small executive committee took care of current business. This type of organization became best known in St. Petersburg, the capital city, but quickly spread to most other major industrial towns. The left-wing parties were, of course, not slow in seeing possibilities in this development, and they began to organize the soviets for political action. Lenin especially pointed to the soviets as a "government in embryo" and an appropriate tool through which the dictatorship of the proletariat could be achieved.

During the revolutionary period of 1917 there existed a parliament of sorts, the Duma, but simultaneously the soviets were revived, thus creating a picture of "dual power." Soldiers' representatives were sent to the soviets, which became known as "Soviets of Workers' and Soldiers' Representatives." There were also peasants' soviets, but they never acquired the same status as the soviets of workers' and soldiers' representatives mainly because the Bolsheviks saw little chance of dominating them.

The Congress of Soviets

In June, 1917, an All-Russian Congress of Soviets of Workers' and Soldiers' (later also Peasants' and Cossacks') Representatives was called to St. Petersburg and elected a central executive committee.

The Bolsheviks were able to take control, first of the St. Petersburg and Moscow Soviets, later of the second All-Russian Congress of Soviets. Previously Lenin had advanced the slogan "All powers to the Soviets"; now the Congress of Soviets prepared to take all power and appointed a cabinet, the so-called "Council of People's Commissars," which was to be subordinate to the Congress. This was the form of administration which the Communist leaders found eminently suitable and which they have retained with some variations.

The earlier Congresses of Soviets were of enormous size. The last ordinary Congress had 2,562 members, and the last one held, the Extraordinary Eighth Congress of 1936, which enacted the new Constitution, had 2,016 members. Under these circumstances any legislative work was impossible. The Congresses actually became mass meetings. There was a central executive committee, but it was too numerous (at one time, 757) and met too infrequently. As a result a smaller body, a Union Presidium of twenty-seven members, did most of the work.

The Supreme Soviet

The central executive committee had been a bicameral body. This was essentially the model underlying the Constitution of 1936, which created a Supreme Soviet of the U.S.S.R., described as "the highest organ of state power" (Art. 30). The Supreme Soviet is divided into a Soviet of the Union and a Soviet of Nationalities. The members of the Soviet of the Union are elected on the basis of one deputy for every 300,000 people, while the members of the Soviet of Nationalities are elected by the citizens voting by component parts, with the result that each Union Republic is entitled to twenty-five delegates, each Autonomous Republic to eleven, each Autonomous Region to five, and each national area to one. Each Union Republic is represented by one deputy chairman on the Presidium of the Supreme Soviet.

The Supreme Soviet is large. The one elected in 1962 had 1,443 members, 791 as deputies to the Soviet of the Union and 652 as members of the Soviet of Nationalities.[1] The Supreme Soviet is elected for a term of four years. In the event of insoluble disagreement between the two houses, the Supreme Soviet is to be dissolved by its Presidium and new elections are to be organized.

Similar soviets exist on all other levels of government, down to the village, but only the Supreme Soviet is bicameral.

Elections

All Soviet citizens of eighteen or older may vote, and any citizen over twenty-three may be elected. No difference is made as to class, and no group is excluded from the universal, equal, direct, and secret suffrage.[2] Once elected, a deputy may be recalled at any time by a majority of his electors.

For the purpose of elections the country is divided into appropriate election districts, while the local government authorities (executive committees of city and village soviets) compile the voters' lists. Candidates are nominated for their respective electoral districts. There are approximately 300,000 voters to one deputy.

Article 141 of the Constitution provides that the right to nominate candidates

---

[1] A survey of the Soviet elected in 1957 shows the following breakdown: 348 women, 1,050 members and candidate members of the Communist party, 297 non-party individuals, 318 workers, 220 peasants, and 809 representatives of the intelligentsia. In the 1958 Supreme Soviet, 614 of the 1,378 members (44.6 percent) were workers and peasants directly employed in industrial and agricultural pursuits. In social status, 60 percent of all elected personnel were workers and peasants, the others, "representatives of the working intelligentsia." Over 26 percent of the membership were women. Ministry of Higher Education of the U.S.S.R., *Izvestiia vysshykh uchebnykh zavedenii, Pravovedenie* (Bulletin of the Higher Educational Institutions, Jurisprudence), No. 1 (1958), p. 3.

[2] Before 1936 certain groups, *bourgeoisie*, kulaks, etc., were disfranchised. In addition, workers sent deputies at the rate of 1 to 25,000 while the rural areas were entitled only to 1 to 125,000. The urban population was also directly represented on all levels, while the rural inhabitants were represented only indirectly in the assemblies of the higher levels.

on all levels "is secured to public organizations and societies of the working people: Communist Party organizations, trade unions, cooperatives, youth organizations and cultural societies." Election regulations have extended this to general meetings of workers, employees, servicemen, collective farmers, and general rural meetings. Since every Soviet citizen belongs to one of these groups, his right to participate is assured.

The process by which candidates are nominated is quite informal. The exercise of considerable initiative is encouraged because it shows the existence of potential leaders. However, there are also instances in which the party organization makes it quite clear from the beginning whom it wants, and instances have been recorded by (hostile) eyewitnesses in which candidates were presented who were totally unknown to their nominators. More often, however, the party remains in the background at this stage. If and when different candidates are proposed by various organizations, informal conference committees are appointed which narrow down the choice to one person. It is at that stage that the party exercises its role of leadership and guides the choice which will eventually be made. Not all candidates are Communist party members, but those who are not must be persons who are devoted to the cause.[3] Those nominated are usually distinguished by superior performance in their professions or constitute the elite in some other way. Never is nomination or election a question of policy, as all candidates are supposed to be devoted to the party line and the policy of the government whether they are Communists or not.[4] That an actual opponent of the regime, or even a slightly dissident person, could be nominated is quite out of the question. Not only would such a person be eliminated by the Election Commission (if he had not already been eliminated by the police), but he could hardly get by the scrutiny of the party organization which "guides" the nominations. The extent to which such guidance is effective may be seen from the fact that, although less than 5 percent of the population are members of the Communist party, about three-fourths of all deputies (on all levels) are party members; most deputies are also men who have been the recipients of special honors in the form of decorations, awards, or other distinctions.

Thus on election day the voter has no choice: he has only one candidate on the "List of Communists and Nonparty People." He may vote against the bloc, but only an infinitesimal number choose to avail themselves of this opportunity. Despite the Constitution, people vote "openly" in many polling places, thus putting an onus on those who enter the booth. This practice, although not officially sanctioned, helps to discourage the "no" vote. Nevertheless a great deal of propaganda and agitation goes into the campaign. Enormous numbers of propaganda workers are trained and put to work. Meetings are held, some questions are answered, and the attention and excitement could not be much greater if there were a real contest. Actually there is a contest in a way: the problem is that of getting out the vote. A

[3] J. Towster, *Political Power in the U.S.S.R.*, New York, 1948, p. 193, quoting A. Gorkin, *The Electoral Law of the Soviet State* (in Russian), Moscow, 1945, p. 32.
[4] John N. Hazard, *The Soviet System of Government*, Chicago, 1964, p. 51.

100 percent record is the goal, and in Stalin's district in Moscow it was regularly achieved when he was alive. In the 1954 election to the Supreme Soviet, participation reached an all-time high of 99.98 percent of all voters. In 1962 it was not much smaller—99.95 percent.

There is no similarity whatsoever between Soviet and Western elections. All candidates are of one political conviction, only one party exists, and only one candidate is presented at the final election.[5] The idea that a voter decides for or against a policy, for or against a government, is totally absent in the Soviet Union. Nevertheless, it would be a mistake to view Soviet elections as a waste of time. Actually, they serve several distinct functions. "The Soviet election system," writes Vyshinsky, "is a mighty instrument for further educating and organizing the masses politically, for further strengthening the bond between the state mechanism and the masses, and for improving the state mechanism and grubbing out the remnants of bureaucratism." Elections afford the party an opportunity to fill the people with its spirit, to get into direct touch with every layer of the population. Speakers exhort the people to make still greater efforts in production, etc., and things are generally stirred up. Elections are also kinds of "command-post exercises" for the cadres of the Communist party, which have an opportunity to show their organization and agitatorial skill. Only on a few occasions do enough voters get up the considerable courage needed to vote against a candidate and thus deny him election for which a majority is required. In such a case, the election is declared invalid, and another full round of nominations and elections is required, usually with a different candidate.

Such courage is indeed infrequent. In fact, abstaining from voting and even going to the polls late have been frowned upon.[6]

For internal and external consumption, Soviet elections are also plebiscites in which the people endorse the regime from time to time. This is another manifestation of the concept of mass participation which the Communists like to call "democracy."[7]

Both Soviet elections and Soviet governmental institutions serve the function of bringing wide numbers of people into the governmental service without diluting the elitist and leadership roles of the party. Thus, for example, in 1957, 1,200,000 Soviet citizens (not all party members) worked on electoral commissions to select over 1,500,000 candidates (not all party members) for national, republic, and local soviets. In 1962, 1,823,500 citizens served as deputies to various soviets. In addition it is estimated that some 20 million citizens participate in the work of local soviets by serving on commissions and other such bodies. The party makes sure

---

[5] On the "List of Communists and Nonparty People."

[6] Alfred G. Meyer, *The Soviet Political System,* New York, 1965, p. 271.

[7] "Under the new Stalin Constitution elections to the Supreme Soviet of the U.S.S.R. . . . have shown that the entire population of the land of the Soviets are completely united in spirit, have demonstrated an unprecedented democracy." Andrei Vyshinsky, *The Law of the Soviet State* (trans. by H. R. Babb), New York, 1948, p. 722.

that a broad cross section of the population is drawn into these activities, but at the same time the party carefully organizes and controls the entire process.[8]

This is the manner in which all soviets are elected, but the greatest effort and most persistent agitation are reserved for the election of the Supreme Soviet.

Deputies are men and women from all walks of life, but all of them are people who have gained distinction in their group or profession. The Constitution grants them the customary immunities of members of parliament—to which little attention is paid in practice—and they enjoy a number of other privileges such as free travel. While their legislative duties are light, other obligations burden them considerably. In particular they are supposed to be a link between their electors and the government, and they become therefore the recipients of numerous complaints and other grievances from their constituents, which often give the government an idea where the shoe pinches.

Power and organization

Sessions of the Supreme Soviet are regularly convoked twice each year, although extra sessions have been called repeatedly. Each session lasts for about one week. This fact alone, together with the very large number of deputies, demonstrates that the legislative functions of the Supreme Soviet are a myth, even though the Constitution says that "the legislative power of the U.S.S.R. is exercised exclusively by the Supreme Soviet of the U.S.S.R." (Art 32). The vast amount of laws which a modern state needs could not possibly be ground out by over 1,400 people, meeting for a week twice per year. Actually most laws, although they may be called decrees, ordinances, etc., are issued by the Council of Ministers (government) or the Presidium of the Supreme Soviet, as we shall see.

There are but few committees. Credentials Commissions operate in each house in order to examine the deputies' election papers. There are three committees which work through the bills which fall in their fields of competence: the Legislative Commission, the Budget Commission, and the Foreign Affairs Commission. Furthermore, in line with the reorganization of the Soviet governmental, administrative, and economic machinery in the direction of decentralization and emphasis on local initiative, the Soviet of Nationalities at its February, 1957, session created an Economic Commission composed of one chairman (one of the secretaries of the Central Committee of the Ukrainian party) and thirty members (two from each Union Republic). The Commissions prepare the laws for submission to the two houses which then pass upon them. Consent of both houses is necessary for enactment of laws. The activities of the Commissions are now more publicized than formerly.[9]

The Supreme Soviet, being the "highest organ of state power in the U.S.S.R.,"

---

[8] Zbigniew Brzezinski and Samuel P. Huntington, *Political Power: USA/USSR,* New York, 1964, pp. 94–95.
[9] Derek J. R. Scott, *Russian Political Institutions,* New York, 1957, p. 103.

has power to legislate in all fields over which the Union government as a whole has jurisdiction. This field is outlined in Article 14.

Article 31 stipulates that these powers are to be exercised in so far as their execution is not reserved for other authorities such as the Presidium, the Council of Ministers, or the governments of the Union Republics. But in practice the Supreme Soviet may set aside these limitations. This was demonstrated in 1939 and 1942 when the Supreme Soviet and not the duly constituted authority for that purpose, namely, its Presidium (Art. 49), ratified the Soviet-German and Anglo-Soviet treaties—presumably to give them a more solemn character.

In addition to the general Union powers in which the Supreme Soviet may legislate, it also may amend the Constitution (by a two-thirds majority in both houses, Art. 146); elect the Presidium (Art. 48) and the Supreme Court (Art. 105); and appoint the Council of Ministers (Art. 560) and the chief law-enforcement and prosecuting officer, the Procurator-General of the U.S.S.R. (for a term of seven years, Art. 114).

The reality of power

On paper these powers are as formidable as those of any Western parliament. In practice the difference could not be greater. We have already seen the striking discrepancy between the vast amount of work a full-fledged national legislature has to do, and the short and infrequent sessions of the Supreme Soviet. In addition to that, there is the fact that all bills originate with the government, and considering the method by which deputies are selected, no differences of opinion are likely to occur. This was not always the case in past Soviet history, but it has been the case since 1936. The regular procedure is that government members make their report or submit their bills,[10] and the deputies shout their approval or signify assent by a show of hands. The formula frequently applied now is to state that the report or proposal of the government was presented with such admirable clarity that no debate was necessary. At the infrequent instances where a bill is debated, all speakers argue in favor of the measure. There are, however, general debates in which deputies bring up shortcomings in performance and tardiness in operation and suggest measures for improvement. Here again, it is never policy that is debated or at stake, but rather the most efficient implementation of a policy already laid down.

When it is time for the vote, it is invariably unanimous. There is no instance recorded in which a deputy of the Supreme Soviet failed to vote in favor of a measure introduced or endorsed by the government.

Contrary to official insistence both in the constitutional text and in the opinion of Soviet writers, it is impossible to accept the view that the Supreme Soviet is in fact "the highest organ of state power" or that it exercises legislative power exclusively. An institution which does not determine policy, which in fact has no hand in the determination of policy, cannot easily be held to possess "power." It is

[10] Sometimes bills also originate in the Commissions.

also a fact that the overwhelming majority of enactments come not from the Supreme Soviet, but from its Presidium in the form of "decrees" or from the government in the form of "decisions and ordinances." Soviet writers insist that there is a difference and that statutes enacted by the Supreme Soviet are of a higher order than decrees, decision, or ordinances, but since such decrees, etc., have never been revoked except on government initiative, and since they come into operation at once without waiting for any Supreme Soviet confirmation, it is difficult to see any practical difference except one of names and totally abstract distinction.

The Presidium of the Supreme Soviet

The Supreme Soviet, at a joint session of both houses, elects the Presidium of the Supreme Soviet of the U.S.S.R. (Art. 48). It is composed of a Chairman, fifteen vice chairmen (one for each Union Republic), a secretary, and sixteen other members, thirty-three in all. For a long time, there was one less, because the former Chairman of the Presidium, Marshal Klementi Voroshilov, was also chairman of the Presidium of the Supreme Soviet of the Russian Soviet Federative Socialist Republic.

The Presidium is a unique institution, indigenous to the Soviet system and without parallel anywhere else except in the satellite states which have copied the Russian model. It has its antecedents and roots in many European institutions: in the nominal presidency of the French type, in the principal standing committee of several European legislatures, in the constitutional review board which the Abbé Sieyès envisaged in the French Revolution and which the French Constitution of 1946 instituted. Nevertheless, it is an original contribution of the Soviet state. The Presidium has a combination of representative, executive, legislative, and even some judicial functions, totally rejecting thereby the concept of the separation of powers.

Stalin described the Presidium as a "collegiate president"—a term which depicts one of its functions quite well. Some of these "presidential" functions are exercised by the chairman of the Presidium, despite the fact that neither the law nor the Constitution gives him any special powers. Nevertheless the statutes enacted by the Supreme Soviet are promulgated with his signature, and he also signs the decrees of the Presidium itself. He receives foreign envoys and ministers, and he exchanges messages with other heads of state as an equal among equals. All his acts, however, are in the name of the Presidium.

The importance of the Presidium goes far beyond these purely formal functions, a fact which is demonstrated by the presence of several members of the Politburo therein. It puts out a steady stream of decrees and edicts touching on many important aspects of Soviet life such as declaring war when the Supreme Soviet is not in session, appointing and relieving ministers of the U.S.S.R., exercising the right of pardon, conferring decorations, ratifying or denouncing international treaties, and so on. But any long delineation of its powers really misses the central elements of the functions it performs, because dwelling on its powers is to ignore what must never be ignored in the study of Soviet government; that true policy making rests in the hands of the Politburo of the Communist party.

Thus the Presidium of the Supreme Soviet has broad powers, but its essential task is administration. Of course it may recommend policy to the Politburo, and since there is a certain overlapping in the membership of the two bodies, these recommendations may be well received. In the final analysis, however, real power continues to be centered in the party.[11]

The interpretation of law

Very substantial also is the right of the Presidium to interpret laws, which is accomplished in the form of commentary and directive upon the execution of operative laws.[12] Moreover the Presidium may invalidate executive decrees of the Union and Union-Republican governments if they are not in conformity with the laws (including the Constitution) of the U.S.S.R., but it may not set aside laws passed by the Supreme Soviets of the U.S.S.R. or of the Union Republics, which cannot be vetoed and which go into operation without further ado. The right to annul executive decrees for illegality was shared by the Presidium and the Supreme Court of the U.S.S.R. under the 1924 Constitution, but the 1936 Constitution reserved the right exclusively to the Presidium. There is no judicial review in the Soviet Union.

Soviet writers emphasize the point that the Presidium is responsible to the Supreme Soviet and that it may be removed as a whole or in part at any time. However, if such removals take place the decision, as in every other instance, is not actually taken in the Supreme Soviet but, being a matter of highest policy, emanates from the Politburo.

The Presidium thus emerges as an extremely important and fully occupied[13] administrative device which participates in every branch of the government. Unlike the Supreme Soviet, it is in permanent session and is therefore able to discharge its functions continually.

Other soviets

The soviet form of government is not confined to the top but is followed all the way down to the local level. Both the Union Republics and the Autonomous

---

[11] Merle Fainsod has noted that the control of state administration by the party is enhanced by the fact that leaders like Stalin and Khrushchev appointed their own people (who were necessarily party people) to high positions in the state administration in order to protect their own positions of leadership. How much party control has continued under Brezhnev and Kosygin is difficult to judge, but it is likely that it still goes on. "The Party in the Post Stalin Era," *Problems of Communism,* January-February, 1958, pp. 7–13.

[12] Continental countries have always known the practice of "authentic interpretation," i.e., interpretation of laws by the legislature. The prerogative of the Presidium is a considerable broadening of that right.

[13] Nine-tenths of the Presidium's publications deal with honors, medals, and decorations.

Republics have unicameral Supreme Soviets who elect their Presidia (Arts. 57–63, 89–93), which operate in conformity with the U.S.S.R. Constitution as well as with their own constitutions.[14] On the lower levels—namely, the Territories, Regions, Autonomous Regions, areas, districts, cities, and villages—there are Soviets of Working People's Deputies (Arts. 94–101) which operate in conformity with the Constitution of the Union Republic in which they are located. Actually the most common soviets are for Territories or Regions, districts, cities, and villages.

The Union Republics and the Autonomous Republics have Councils of Ministers as their chief executive and administrative organs, but the lower levels have executive committees of their respective soviets composed of a chairman, a vice chairman, a secretary, and varying numbers of members (Art. 99). In very small localities, the chairman, the vice chairman, and the secretary of the local soviet are the executive and administrative organs (Art. 100). These executive committees, chairmen, etc., are responsible to their respective soviets and to the soviet of the next higher level (Art. 101).

It is said that the local executives operate under the strict direction of their soviets. But the hand of higher levels is strongly felt, and there is always the ubiquitous secretary of the Communist party in the village, town, or other unit of government, who cannot be ignored. In recent years these men have taken on overt administrative responsibilities to an increasing extent. The soviet form of government, with the strict accountability of lower to higher levels of governments, lends itself well to the close integration and control of the country which is deemed necessary in order to assure the success of the political and economic aspirations of the regime.

[14] Union Republic and Autonomous Republic constitutions must be in conformity with the Constitution of the U.S.S.R. Amendments to the U.S.S.R. Constitution which concern the Union or Autonomous Republics result, therefore, in amendments to those constitutions as well.

9

The administration

"The highest executive and administrative organ of the state power of the Union of Soviet Socialist Republics is the Council of Ministers[1] of the U.S.S.R.," states the Constitution (Art. 64). It stands at the head of a vast and ever-increasing bureaucracy which administers the machinery of the state. In our times, when all states have taken upon themselves many functions and services, all governmental machineries have increased their staffs. But in the Soviet Union, where every economic, social, scientific, or artistic activity is controlled and administered by the state and the party, the bureaucracy is of truly formidable size. This has resulted in a mushrooming of bureaus and agencies bewildering even to the casehardened student of public administration. From time to time new bureaus are created in order to investigate why there are so many bureaus, but old bureaucrats never die and the new bureaus

---

[1] Until Mar. 19, 1946 the government was known as the Council of People's Commissars, often referred to as *Sovnarkom,* an abbreviation from the Russian *Sovyet Narodnykh Komiss-arov.*

continue to exist more or less peacefully side by side with those which they were designed to eliminate.

These 11,000,000 to 12,000,000 clerks, analysts, planners, and administrators are the new "middle and upper classes" of the Soviet Union. They are far more representative of the modern U.S.S.R. than the old-fashioned revolutionaries.

From time to time attempts are made to put new spirit and soul into the machinery of government. Inefficient bureaucrats are pilloried in such journals as *Pravda, Izvestia, Kommunist, Trud,* etc. Red tape and inefficiency are ridiculed in *Krokodil* and on the stages of cabarets. At public meetings, party conferences, etc., speakers inveigh against the "soulless bureaucracy." Party members point their accusing fingers at certain cases, and the offenders are then removed or demoted, but like quicksand the immense machinery quickly fills every hole that removal may have created, and matters stand pretty much as they were before.

While Russians are not generally known as speedy operators, the cause of this state of affairs does not lie in national characteristics. The size of the machinery itself virtually excludes a high degree of efficiency, because effective direction and supervision become extremely difficult. Worse, however, is the excessive degree of centralism which deprives the working levels of the administration of sufficient authority and places an intolerable burden upon higher authorities. It also facilitates the habit, known colloquially (in America) as "passing the buck," i.e., of letting others, in this case higher authority, take responsibility even when authority exists on the lower levels. Moreover, there is the stultifying desire to please, so characteristic of all authoritarian regimes, where civil servants report to their superiors frequently that "everything is going according to plan" when in reality nothing of the kind is true. Soviet publications have frequently criticized directors of plants and managers of state enterprise who reported fulfillment of production quotas and other glowing results when the reality of the situation was quite the reverse. But in a country in which a wrong decision or a failure to see deficiencies may easily be interpreted as "wrecking," which would result in long terms of forced labor and imprisonment for those held responsible, civil servants and managerial personnel prefer to be safe rather than to strike out boldly and to institute innovations. It cannot be said that the Soviet leaders are not aware of this, but all they can do is to change personnel and to inculcate better morale in their services. Inasmuch as the faults are inherent in the system the leaders are powerless to effect lasting improvements without very substantial alterations in the structure and the concepts of the Soviet regime.

It is therefore not surprising that the role of the Communist party in watching over the efficiency of production and service is exceptionally important and absorbs much of the party's efforts. Other organizations, especially trade unions, also take part in this work. Since effective control from the inside is difficult and often impossible, as the criticism of a superior may result in worse than dismissal, outside inspection is necessary.

Under the contitutional regime of 1924 the government was regarded as both executive and legislative, having the power to issue decrees which were binding in the entire Soviet Union.[2] The Constitution of 1936 places all legislative power exclusively in the hands of the Supreme Soviet, but the Council of Ministers has the power to issue decisions and orders (Art. 66). However, legal and constitutional doctrine demands that these remain within the confines of the law as set out by the Supreme Soviet, to which the Council of Ministers is responsible. That is the theory. In practice the Council of Ministers is the foremost legislator of the country. By far most of the rules which guide everybody's conduct and are enforced in the entire territory of the Soviet Union are issued by the Council of Ministers. Especially the economic life of the country is regulated almost exclusively by ordinances and decisions of the Council of Ministers.[3] Any subordination of these decisions and ordinances to the will of the Supreme Soviet is wholly theoretical and academic.

The Council of Ministers

The authority of the Council of Ministers covers the entire field of executive functions, but a major portion of its activities is taken up by economic affairs. In these it has the aid of certain agencies such as the State Planning Commission, the Central Statistical Administration, the Bureau of Administrative Affairs, and the Secretariat.[4]

A good part of executive business is performed by the individual ministries, but the Council of Ministers now requires to an increasing degree that ministerial orders and activities be submitted to the whole Council for information, and in a number of instances individual acts have been annulled.[5] If a ministry submits an edict to the Council of Ministers for confirmation prior to issue, it becomes an ordinance or decision of the Council and has greater authority than a purely departmental directive.

Ordinarily the Council of Ministers also coordinates the armed forces and the economic activities pertaining thereto. But after the German invasion the Soviet government adopted the British device of the War Cabinet, in the form of the State Defense Committee. It is interesting that this agency was created in 1941 by a joint decree of the Presidium of the Supreme Soviet, the Central Committee of the Communist Party, and the Council of People's Commissars (ministers). As in Britain, the entire power of government and especially the conduct of the war were placed in the hands of this group. Actually all real power was vested in Stalin personally. He combined the chairmanship of the State Defense Committee and of the Council

---

[2] Constitution of 1924, Art. 38.

[3] For a revealing comparison of the number of "laws" issued by the Council of Ministers as compared with other agencies, see J. Towster, *Political Power in the U.S.S.R.*, New York, 1948, p. 260*n*.

[4] Until 1955 the Economic Council issued quite a number of orders under its own authority, but it was abolished in that year.

[5] It will be noted that, while the Presidium annuls acts of the Council of Ministers, the Council of Ministers annuals acts of individual ministers.

Central agencies for economic management

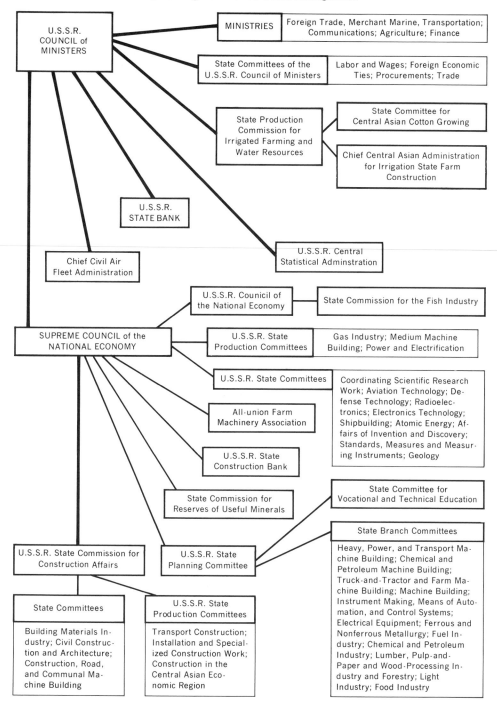

of People's Commissars (ministers) with the Commissariat of War and the position of commander in chief of the armed forces.

The Council of Ministers (cabinet) consists of the Chairman, 3 first deputy chairmen, 8 deputy chairmen, 11 ministers, and 51 agency heads and chairmen of administrative committees with the rank of minister,[6] as well as the 15 chairmen of the Councils of Ministers of the Union Republics—88 altogether. Under Bulganin's chairmanship of the Council of Ministers, he and several first deputy chairmen constituted a presidium of the Council, a kind of inner cabinet. Then for a few months the title of "first deputy chairman" was dropped and "deputy chairman" substituted. It later reappeared under both Khrushchev and Kosygin. The ministers are the heads of departments. Until 1947 there occurred an increasing proliferation of ministries, most of them being in charge of an economic sector like the aircrafts industry, machine and instrument making, etc.

By April, 1960, the Council of Ministers contained 15 ministries in addition to 19 state committees. The majority are concerned with economic matters.

The ministries are classified as All-Union and Union-Republican. The All-Union ministries (three on January 1, 1964) direct their affairs throughout the entire territory of the Soviet Union through their own agents;[7] the Union-Republican ones operate through the corresponding ministries of the Union Republics.[8] In addition to the regular ministers, there are also ministers without portfolio, that is, without specific departmental responsibility.

The ministers are department heads like their Western counterparts, but there are substantial differences. Western ministers are almost always politicians and amateurs; Soviet ministers often remain for long terms and become professionals. They are not necessarily party leaders, although they are all party members. Unlike Western ministers, however, Soviet ministers do not make policy decisions on the highest level; that is the function of the Political Bureau of the Central Committee of the Communist party.

Ministers are theoretically appointed by and responsible to the Supreme Soviet, but in actuality they are appointed and removed by the party Politburo, to whose policies they are completely subservient and sensitive. Just how the procedure of removal works in detail is unknown, but from time to time the ministers are suddenly removed or shuffled around. Sometimes they also disappear.

It appears, therefore, that Soviet ministers, especially when they are not mem-

[6] The State Planning Committee, the Control Commission of the Council of Ministers, the State Committee for Labor and Wages, the State Scientific and Technical Committee, the State Committee for Aviation Engineering, the State Committee for Defense Engineering, the State Committee for Radio and Electronics, the State Committee for Shipbuilding, the State Committee for Construction, the State Committee for Foreign Economic Relations, the State Security Committee, and the State Bank.

[7] All-Union ministries deal with foreign trade, merchant marine, and transportation.

[8] Union-Republican ministries now deal with the following: higher education, geology and conservation of mineral resources, health protection, foreign affairs, culture, defense, communications, agriculture, and finance.

bers of the party Politburo, are highly placed administrative assistants rather than policy-making chiefs like British or French cabinet members. The party Presidium may decide every detail of policy, or it may merely lay down the outlines, leaving the details to the Council of Ministers, but there is never any question where the final authority lies.

The pattern of administration

Within each department the "single-manager principle" is in operation, although there are high councils (*collegia*), composed of the minister, his deputies, and several others in each department. The single-manager principle makes for clear lines of authority, but it also works swift retribution on the inefficient or disloyal individual once he is discovered.

This pattern of administration is followed in the Union Republics, whose cabinets are composed of Union-Republican and Republican ministers, but as we have seen, very little is now left to purely Republican administrations.

The use of advisory councils has been widespread and is designed to promote close relationships between the nerve center and the field operations of the various ministries. Different from them are the collegia of high ministerial officials with whom the minister meets from time to time to seek advice. The minister's decision is final, and although the members of the collegia may theoretically appeal to the Council of Ministers, this may turn out to be an extremely ill-advised act unless the collegia maintain unusually close relations to the party leadership and are satisfied that the minister's liquidation is already under way.

All-Union and Union-Republican ministries are generally organized in nearly the same fashion. The difference, that the former operate their own field services while the latter act through the staffs of their opposite numbers in the governments of the Republics, affects the choice of subordinate officials only. The power of final decision, in either group, rests at the top.

In each one of the fifteen Republics of the Soviet Union there is a council of ministers which, like the national government, has two types of ministries: those which correspond to ministries of the national government and are subordinate thereto, and those which are concerned with the "exclusive" powers of the Republican government. Among the latter group of Republican ministries one finds motor transport and highways, paper and wood products industry, municipal economy (local public works), lumber industry, lower education, river fleet, social security, building, justice, and internal affairs.

A simpler form of administration prevails on lower levels. Below the Union Republics we find the Autonomous Republics [and in the R.S.F.S.R. the Territory (*krai*) as well as the Region (*oblast*) and the city and district (*raion*).] Larger cities are divided into several raions. Smaller towns are directly under the oblast or krai, while quite small ones are subordinate to a raion. But while degrees of centralization differ in the administration, this extends only to the purely technical carrying out of functions. All decisions emanate from the party, and the party organization on all levels watches over the execution of this policy.

The Control Committee

The Ministry of State Control was created in 1940 as a successor to the Commission of Soviet Control. It served as general administrative watchdog. Together with the Ministry of Finance, it had control over expenditures, but its functions went much further. It was charged in general with seeing that the government's decisions were carried out. Its organization paralleled that of all the ministries, and its agents were installed in all important offices and enterprises. In the Union Republics there were ministries of state control which followed the same model as the central ministries. Their chief personnel were appointed by the Council of Ministers of the Republics with the consent of the Minister of State Control of the Soviet Union. Thus, despite the Union-Republican form of organization, there was actually strict centralization.

In May, 1957, Khrushchev warned the Supreme Soviet that the Ministry, then under Molotov, had gone too far in the direction of duplicating the work of other institutions, particularly that of the Finance Ministry. Whether this was true or only part of the campaign then being waged by Khrushchev against Molotov is not known; however, in August, 1957, the Ministry of State Control was again downgraded into a Commission of State Control. But in November, 1962, the jurisdiction of the Commission was widened to include both the party and the government. It was now called Committee for Party and State Control.

In case an error or worse is found, the Committee has extensive powers to deal with the situation. It may hand down an administrative decision or hand over the culprit to punishment by the courts. It may also direct agencies of the party or government to remove shortcomings.

The Committee has considerable importance, as it not only controls the secret police but can also initiate any investigating or punitive action throughout the vast network of the party and the government administration. Its organization, however, reflects the care of the party leadership, which wishes to preserve this finely-honed instrument of control and, if need be, of power, but wants to make certain that it does not fall into the hands of another Beria. Thus, on December 6, 1965, the Committee for Party and State Control was once again renamed, this time Committee for People's Control, and its powerful head, Alexander N. Shelepin, was removed and was confined to his party duties.

The ups and downs of this Committee are a central example of the party's wavering between its desire to lead but leave administration to the state, and its desire to control and watch all aspects of political activity.[9]

[9] For an illuminating essay on this, see Grey Hodnett, "Khrushchev and Party State Control," in *Politics in the Soviet Union,* ed. by Alexander Dallin and Alan F. Westin, New York, 1966, pp. 113–164.

The Five- and Seven-Year Plans

A further factor which tends to limit the scope of activities for most ministries is the need for conformity with the over-all economic plan. In the Soviet Union the socialist aim of taking over the means of production has been fully realized, and they are all administered and owned by the state. Their operation is planned with a view to over-all efficiency rather than to the individual performance of any single industry or branch.

The direction of economic policy lies, of course, within the party Politburo as usual. The chief planning agency is the State Planning Commission (*Gosplan*), which in 1948 was renamed the State Planning Committee. At the same time there was created a Committee for the Material-Technical Supply of the National Economy (*Gossnab*), which took over the task of rendering more efficient the allocation and distribution of materials and machinery. Thus *Gosplan* is confined to its responsibility of planning the national economy. It drew up the economic plan, known as the Five-Year Plan, until the sixth one, scheduled to run from 1955 to 1960, was superseded in 1958 by Khrushchev's Seven-Year Plan for the period 1959–1965. It also draws up the annual and quarterly plans and supervises their execution. These plans are further broken down by territorial units. They are then carried out by the respective ministries, the coordinating units below the departmental level (*glavks*), the combines, and the trusts. These in turn have their own planning departments in which the general blueprints are spelled out in greater detail.

Each economic enterprise is part of a state trust. Several trusts are organized into industrial combines, and over them is the ministry in charge of that particular type of production. Further coordination is effected by interdepartmental councils and formerly by the now inoperative Economic Council.

The *Gosplan* organization is very elaborate. The national *Gosplan* has its counterparts in the various Union Republics, and they in turn have their planning committees in all areas down to the regions, districts, and towns. Although the *Gosplan* is thus organized on the model of a Union-Republican ministry, it is even more centralized than they usually are. The territorial subdivision is balanced by an elaborate structure of sectional organization which deals directly with every aspect of ministerial and governmental activity, and there is yet another, functional structure of sections designed to coordinate the first and the second subdivisions.

There are altogether twelve state branch committees, each representing the principal industries. The chairmen of these committees have ministerial rank and are members of the U.S.S.R. *Gosplan*. In addition, two more committees are attached to *Gosplan,* the State Committee for Vocational and Technical Education, and the State Committee for Central Asian Cotton Growing, which later was placed under another state committee, that for Irrigation Farming and Water Resources.[10]

While *Gosplan* is responsible for the elaboration of the economic plan which determines in detail every economic activity of the country, its policy and objectives

[10] G. Mironev, in *Ekonomicheskaya Gazeta,* Nov. 23, 1963, p. 30.

emanate from the party Presidium, which decides the general direction and emphasis of the plan. Then *Gosplan* implements it and works it out in detail, always subject to such revisions or adaptations as the party leadership may decide.

A drastic revision of the economic planning and administrative system of the
Soviet Union was launched by Khrushchev in 1956, culminating in the May, 1957,
decisions to reorganize Soviet economy on the basis of economic regions. The entire
U.S.S.R. was subdivided into 105 economic administrative regions (70 for the
R.S.F.S.R., 11 for the Ukraine, 9 for Kazakhstan, 4 for the Uzbek Republic, and
1 for each of the other 11 Republics). These were later drastically curtailed in
number when it appeared that too much "regionalism" was developing. In general,
in the R.S.F.S.R. each region (*oblast*) became an economic administrative region,
but in outlying territories where industrial development was not as advanced, two or
more oblasts were sometimes fused into one economic administrative region. To
administer the new system, the Supreme Soviets of the Union Republics were
charged with the creation of these regions and the Councils of Ministers of the
Union Republics had to appoint their respective economic councils:[11]

> The economic councils, through their subsidiary departments, industrial adminis-
> trations, combines, and trusts, and with the aid of their affiliated consultative
> bodies, the technical-economic councils, are to manage most industrial enterprises
> within their respective regions, except for those enterprises controlled by "local"
> industry and cooperatives and a few other specified enterprises.

The economic councils are responsible directly to the Republican Council of
Ministers and through them to the federal Council of Ministers: their internal structure was left to the discretion of the respective Republican Councils of Ministers
and varies according to local criteria. In some instances, former institutions which
have proved particularly efficient have been left outside the new structure.[12]

Only the management of industry and construction has been thus reorganized.
All other sectors of the economy, such as agriculture, transport, domestic and foreign trade, have been left as before. The result has been a certain decentralization
of administrative responsibilities and apparently an attempt to increase local initiative and improve the efficiency of the economy. However, at the same time, it is
clear that the decision-making authority still lies at the center; the most obvious
result of Khrushchev's plan was primarily an increase in the number of administrative organs and a more complex structure of the economic administration.[13]

[11] Paul E. Lydolph, "The Soviet Reorganization of Industry," *American Slavic and East European Review*, Vol. XVII, No. 3 (October, 1958), p. 296.
[12] E.g., the Chief Leningrad Construction Trust, the Azerbaidzhan Republic Ministry of Oil
Industry. In many cases, enterprises of local, cooperative, baking, and some other industries
would remain under the jurisdiction of local soviets rather than be incorporated into the
economic-region system.
[13] See the doubts expressed by N. Laskovsky on this matter, "Reflections on Soviet Industrial
Reorganization," *American Slavic and East European Review*, Vol. XVII, No. 1 (February,
1958), pp. 47–58.

Gosplan was originally intended to be only a planning agency. In the course of time, however, it has developed more and more in the direction of supervising the detailed execution of the plan. The managerial personnel which has to operate under these circumstances is strictly controlled and supervised. And the details of instructions received from above, as well as their lack of freedom in selecting their assistants, delimit their field of operations considerably.

The total emphasis in this gigantic operation is on fulfilling "the plan." By directives, speeches, newspaper articles, factory resolutions, praise of the diligent, and blame for the tardy, an atmosphere of competition is created. Among the workers, the work brigades are to set an example for others to follow, while "socialist competition" is the name for a slightly less stringent speedup system.[14] With these "shock troops" of labor setting the pace, the daily output quota, the "norm," is constantly moved upward. Considerable wage differentials[15] and other advantages for the elite strengthen the system.

While it is the obvious intention of this method to improve output and efficiency by creating an artificially competitive system, it also creates its own counter-forces. The almost frantic emphasis on the fulfillment and overfulfillment of the plan makes for "paper fulfillment"—attempts by plant managements and other subordinate authorities to juggle figures or worse in order to report a triumph when the truth of the situation is quite different. It also produces mutual-protection relationships between administrative organs designed to watch one another; these are the so-called "family relationships" which have already been mentioned. It makes for overbureaucratization and a great use of papers and forms. It produces constant production breakdowns and acute shortages in all kinds of products. The Soviet press is full of such instances, tales of fraudulent reporting, of "family relationships," of bureaucratic boondoggling. *Krokodil,* the Soviet humor magazine, has shown the type of manager who storms and rages on the last of the month in order to get his quota fulfilled, only to relax into inactivity on the first. It would seem that Communism too has its "inner contradictions" which Marxists like to ascribe only to capitalism.

It would certainly be a gross error to infer that the Soviet economy is breaking down. The relatively low standard of living and the constant shortages of consumer goods are caused primarily by a long-asserted emphasis on heavy industry to the detriment of consumer goods. But the flood of complaints which sweep

[14] For an authoritative exposition, see Margaret Miller, *Labour in the U.S.S.R.,* London, 1942. Also G. Bienstock et al., *Management in Russian Industry and Agriculture,* New York, 1944; A. Baykov, *Development of the Soviet Economic System,* Cambridge, England, 1946; L. E. Hubbard, *Soviet Labor and Industry,* London, 1942. For a Communist view, see M. Dobb, *Soviet Planning and Labor,* New York, 1943, and N. A. Voznesensky, *Economy of the U.S.S.R. during World War II,* Washington, 1948. For a brief summary, based largely on the above works, see *Communism in Action,* prepared by the Legislative Reference Service of the Library of Congress, Washington, 1946, 79th Congress, 2d Session, House Document No. 754. For a bibliography of books and articles, see Harry Schwarz, *Soviet Economy,* Syracuse, N.Y., 1949.
[15] A. Bergson, *Structure of Soviet Wages,* Cambridge, Mass., 1944.

through the Soviet press indicate that the totally state-owned and planned economy of the Soviet Union is far from achieving the clocklike precision which was expected for it.

On the other hand the complete concentration of the entire Soviet economic machinery on heavy industry and other activities of special strategic importance—to the detriment of consumer goods—has produced significant results. Especially spectacular are Soviet advances in the field of atomic energy and space technology. In spite of relatively low output per man the total industrial achievement of the Soviet Union is therefore quite impressive and constitutes a real challenge to the democratic world.

This challenge should, however, not be exaggerated. Percentage-wise, a country's growth rate is always greater when it is underdeveloped, and it slows down as the economy proliferates and becomes more sophisticated. This is the case in the Soviet Union, whose growth rate has declined to somewhere between 3 and 4 percent and at times has sunk below that of the United States. Considering that the gross national product (GNP) of the United States is twice as large as that of the Soviet Union, this means that the gap between the two countries is actually widening steadily in favor of the United States. This has given further impetus to the acceptance of such theories as those proposed by Professor Y. Liebermann, who urged the introduction of an incentive system, among other reforms. This should not be regarded as anything like private enterprise, since state control would be in no way affected thereby. But it would tend to lessen the possibility of major planning deficiencies being created by an ignorant bureaucracy far removed from the place of action. There is every reason to believe that the Chairman of the Council of Ministers (Prime Minister) Kosygin is giving some attention to these suggestions while assuring the party's ideologues that he continues to support centralized planning. As one informed observer put it, "Centralized but rationalized management, depending more strictly on the laws of the market, seems to have been his objective."[16]

These reforms, as well as a somewhat greater emphasis on consumer goods, have apparently met with some resistance within the party machinery, and the outcome is not yet certain as these lines are written. At any rate, it was noticeable that when the 23d Congress of the Communist party of the Soviet Union convened in Moscow in March and April, 1966, bombastic statements of the Khrushchev era about catching up and overtaking the United States economic achievement were conspicuous by their absence.

[16] Michel Tatu, "Economics and Politics; Soviet Reforms: The Debate Goes On," *Problems of Communism*, January–February, 1966, p. 29.

10

Law and justice

The Soviet concept of law is intimately associated with its idea of the nature of the state. According to Marx, Lenin, and Stalin, the state is, as we have previously seen, a coercive machinery designed to establish and uphold a particular type of social organization. The state of capitalistic society and of the transition to socialism in particular is looked upon as an expression of the domination of one class over others, and the law of that state is therefore considered a tool for the maintenance of that domination.

We have also learned that according to Marx, the form of the state results from productive relationships and that these economic considerations are the basis on which the "physiological superstructure is erected." Naturally law must follow in the same groove. "Marxism-Leninism," writes Vyshinsky, "gives a clear definition (the only scientific definition) of the essence of law. It teaches that legal relationships (and, consequently, law itself) are rooted in the material conditions of life, and that law is merely the will of the dominant class, elevated into a statute."[1] Soviet legal science therefore utterly rejects the concept of an independent "idea of the law" which may exist separate from the economic and class structure of the state. Law is merely an expression of the will of the state, an expression of the material form of life in that state, and in a class society it is the will of the ruling class.

With the eventual withering away of the state, the law too will eventually disappear. But until that happens, the strengthening and intensification of Soviet law is necessary, not in the interest of abstract justice, but as a tool for the accomplishment of the Communist aim. The standards of justice are therefore directly derived from this consideration and are not apart therefrom. Law is in essence that which furthers the aims of the Socialist revolution. Impartiality, due process of law, and similar embellishments of the "bourgeois" types of law are of secondary consideration. "Law is a political measure, law is politics," said Lenin. A Soviet authority, P. Romashkin, writes: "Soviet law is a system of rules established by the state to promote the consolidation of the social order which helps society advance towards Communism."[2] This approach to law is bound to produce arbitrariness. Commenting on recent experience, a noted specialist shows that ". . . once the authorities are determined to do so, there is nothing to prevent them from flagrantly flouting their own laws."[3]

The character of Soviet law as a "tool" of the regime also has another facet. In the period of "capitalistic encirclement," the defense of the Soviet state is a matter of paramount importance. Soviet law, therefore, being a tool of that state, has a special role to play in the wiping out of all enemies of the regime, domestic or foreign. Forced labor and police (KGB) detention are consequently merely continuations of the regular judicial machinery, although they exist quite apart administratively.

The judges

There are certain principles common to all regular Soviet courts. All judges are elected for a special term. The judges of the Supreme Court and the Special Courts of the U.S.S.R., as well as the Supreme Courts of the various Union and Autonomous Republics, are elected by their respective Supreme Soviets for a term of five years. The courts of lesser territorial units are elected for the same term by their respective soviets, while the judges of the lowest courts, the People's Courts,

---

[1] Andrei Vyshinsky, *The Law of the Soviet State* (trans. by H. R. Babb), New York, 1948, p. 13. See also, Harold J. Berman, *Justice in Russia: An Interpretation of Soviet Law,* Cambridge, Mass., 1950; Vladimir Gsovski, *Soviet Civil Law,* Ann Arbor, Mich., 1948–1949, 2 vols.; René David and John N. Hazard, *Le Droit Soviétique,* Paris, 1954, 2 vols.; Eugene Kamenka, "The Soviet View of Law," *Problems of Communism,* March–April, 1965, pp. 8–16; and Klarus Westen, "The New Codes of Civil Law," *ibid.,* pp. 34–41.
[2] P. Romashkin, *Fundamentals of Soviet Law,* Moscow, 1962, p. 20, as quoted by Afred G. Meyer, *The Soviet Political System,* New York, 1965, p. 303.
[3] Leonard Schapiro, "Prospects for the Rule of Law," *Problems of Communism,* March–April, 1965, p. 3.

are elected by the inhabitants of their districts for a term of three years (Arts. 105–109). But a constitutional amendment in 1958 made judges of the People's Courts eligible for five-year terms and assessors of those courts for two years.

The courts consist of both professional and lay judges (assessors). Actually the law does not provide that the regular judge must be learned in the law, but that is the rule. The lay judges, of course, are not so trained. Ordinarily there are two lay judges and one professional judge (chairman) in cases involving original jurisdiction, while a larger number of judges is the rule in appeals cases.

Lay judges are people from every walk of life who continue to pursue their professions but are selected for special court duty. They must not be confused with jurors, who do not exist in the Soviet system. The juries of other systems decide only specific questions of facts specially submitted to them, while questions of law are generally reserved to the judge; also, judge and jury deliberate and decide quite separately from each other. In the Soviet Union, however, the lay judges are full-fledged judges and temporary members of the bench as in Germany, and they deliberate and decide all questions of both law and fact together with the professional judge. Decisions are reached by majority vote, although as a rule the view of the professional judge prevails.

According to the Constitution, all court proceedings are public and all languages are permitted, either directly or through interpreters. The Constitution also guarantees the right of counsel and the independence of the judges. However, an attorney who did his best for a defendant accused of a political offense would find his future in jeopardy. If some lawyers have nevertheless been slightly more vigorous in the defense of their clients in recent years, this has been a very small improvement, and they have a long way to go before reaching anything like the independence and vigor of Western attorneys. The "independence" of judges will be discussed later.

The court system

Except for the People's Courts, all Soviet courts have both original and appellate jurisdiction, including the Supreme Court of the U.S.S.R. Appeal is permissible from any court to the next higher court, but except for rare incidents appeals do not go any higher. Only the decisions of the Supreme Court in *original* jurisdiction cannot be appealed to any higher authority. Appeals may originate with either party to a suit, or in criminal cases with both the accused (and his attorneys) and the prosecutor.

The lowest level of the judicial hierarchy is occupied by the People's Courts. These are exclusively courts of original jurisdiction, and they absorb the great majority of cases, civil and criminal.

A peculiarity are the so-called "comradely courts,"[4] which might better be

---

[4] Albert Beiter, "Comradely Justic: How Durable Is It?," *Problems of Communism*, March–April, 1965, pp. 82–92.

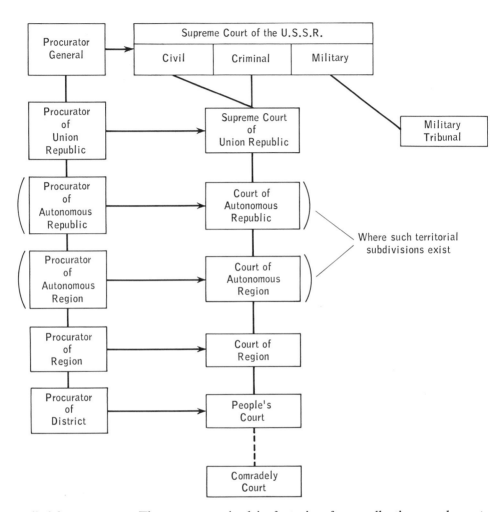

called honor courts. They are organized in factories, farm collectives, and apartment houses to deal with petty theft, libel, etc., and can impose fines and reprimands. They may be elected for each case or consist of all those present at a meeting.[5] The "comradely courts" are under the supervision of the People's Court, which can annul their decisions. In 1959 a new draconic form of "comradely courts" was instituted in most of the Union Republics to deal with "speculators, hooligans, unemployed elements, etc." Judgment up to banishment from the place of residence may be meted out at meetings of "friends and neighbors." There is a review of this judgment by the local soviets, but not by the courts.

[5] Berman, *op. cit.*, pp. 266–269.

The courts of the areas, Regions, Autonomous Regions, and Autonomous Republics, serve as courts of appeal in cases coming up from the People's Courts of their respective areas. They also have original jurisdiction in cases involving "counterrevolutionary activities, crimes against administrative orders when they involve particular danger to the state, the pillaging of socialist property, and other important economic crimes." Original jurisdiction pertains also to civil cases between state and social institutions, enterprises, and organizations.

The supreme courts of Union and Autonomous Republics and regional courts in the person of their newly created presidia (composed of the president of the court, the deputy presidents, and two rank-and-file members of the court, named by the Presidium of the Supreme Soviet of the Republic concerned, or by the executive committee of the regional soviet having jurisdiction over the court) also have had the power of review since 1954.[6]

The highest judicial authority in each Union Republic is its supreme court. It supervises all inferior courts in the Republic by examining all protests coming from the Procurator-General or Chairman of the Supreme Court of the U.S.S.R., or the procurator or chairman of the supreme court of the Republic. It also examines on appeal the judgments and verdicts of courts which are one step in rank below that of the supreme court.[7] The supreme court may set aside the decision of any inferior court in the Republic. It also has original jurisdiction in cases of exceptional gravity and in crimes involving the top officials of the Republic. But the Presidium of the (Republic's) Supreme Soviet, the Procurator, the KGB, and the full court itself may place other cases directly before the supreme court of the Republic.

The apex of the whole judicial structure is the Supreme Court of the U.S.S.R. (Art. 104). It consists of a Chairman, two vice chairmen, nine judges, and 20 lay judges (people's assessors). It is organized in three divisions or panels, for criminal, civil, and military affairs. The former panels, or collegia, for railroad-transport and water-transport affairs were first merged and then totally abolished. The Chairman of the Supreme Court may preside over any case before the court. He may also remove any case from any court in the U.S.S.R. and submit a protest about it to a full session of the Supreme Court.

The Supreme Court is primarily a court of appeals and review, but it also has original jurisdiction in criminal and civil matters of All-Union importance. Its verdicts are final and have the force of law. Its entire plenum convenes not less than once every three months to consider protests against acts of inferior courts and to issue instructions concerning general court practice and procedure which ensure uniformity throughout the country. There are also State Arbitration Boards (*GosarbiArazh*) to solve conflicts between state economic enterprises.

[6] John N. Hazard, "Governmental Developments in the USSR since Stalin," *Annals of the American Academy of Political and Social Science,* January, 1956, pp. 20–21.
[7] Because of the great variety in size among the various Union Republics, the territorial subdivisions thereof differ; some have regional subdivisions which others lack.

No independence of judges

The Constitution of 1936 has given the judiciary a higher status and a more independent existence than was the case before. However, the stipulation that judges are "independent and subject only to the law" (Art. 112) must be understood with some qualifications. As we have seen, the Soviet concept of government rejects the notion of an independent law or justice. This principle used to be stated quite frankly. In 1927, the then Commissar of Justice, N. V. Krylenko,[8] wrote,

> The . . . principle is the dependence and removability of our courts. Whereas the basic principle of the bourgeois court is its independence, the irremovability of the judge . . . we say plainly that our judge is both removable and dependent; inasmuch as he is an organ of state power . . . he is, therefore, both removable and dependent upon the proletariat, the state, the toiling class, whom he is called upon to serve.

This principle was officially discarded in the 1936 Constitution. But in the same year that Vyshinsky and others were extolling complete independence of the judge, the then Commissar of Justice, N. M. Rychkov, stated that the men to be advanced to judicial positions should be party and non-party Bolsheviks, devoted to the cause of socialism, and that all local party and Soviet organs must properly organize the work of the judiciary. Another writer, N. Poliansky, stated even more clearly that "the independence of judges does not at all exclude the duty to follow the general policy of the government. The judiciary is an organ of state power and cannot be outside politics."[9]

It has already been noted that there is, of course, no judicial review in the U.S.S.R. Nor does the judiciary possess the power to annul decisions and decrees of the Presidium of the Supreme Soviet or of the Council of Ministers. On the contrary, the Council of Ministers has established the organization of the courts, including the Law on the Judiciary of 1938, which governs the courts. These changes were largely ratified by a law in 1958. The Minister of Justice was formerly charged with supervising the administrative part of the Supreme Court's work, and he participated regularly in the deliberations of the Supreme Court when it was meeting in full session.[10] The Ministry has now been abolished at the federal level.

In addition to the regular court hierarchy, there is also a military court structure; this is subordinate to the Supreme Court of the U.S.S.R., which acts as its court of appeals. Its jurisdiction depends on the nature of the crime as well as the status of the accused. Formerly the military tribunals were also empowered to try civilians in certain cases, but this has now been abolished.

In contrast to the conflict system to which Western lawyers, especially Anglo-

---

[8] Quoted by J. Towster, *Political Power in the U.S.S.R.*, New York, 1948, p. 303n.
[9] *Ibid.*, pp. 302, 304.
[10] When the Supreme Court meets in full session, the Procurator-General must attend, while the Minister of Justice may also be present.

American attorneys are accustomed, Soviet justice adopts a more summary system in which the distinction between judges, prosecutors, and attorneys is not nearly as sharp as it is in our courts. Theoretically, the Soviet system is designed to do justice as cheaply and summarily as possible, justice in the interest of the state and of society rather than the rights of the individual. From a Western point of view, this is a highly unsatisfactory system. However, one should note that attempts have been made in recent years, with some results, to humanize proceedings and to be less brutally unmindful of the rights of individuals. In ordinary criminal cases this has definitely had results, and while sentences still tend to be harsh by Western standards, they are less harsh than they used to be only a few years ago.

In political matters, however, the expediency and the wishes of the government rather than the letter of the law, clearly prevail. This was demonstrated once again in 1966 in the case of a young American, Bernard Mott, who innocently crossed into the Soviet Union from Norway at a place where Norwegians can pass freely and where others have passed and have merely been asked to leave the Soviet Union. For some reason unknown to the world, Mott was condemned to the brutal punishment of ten years of forced labor, from which he was released only by his suicide—if suicide indeed it was.

The Procurator-General

A unique position in the judicial machinery is maintained by the Procurator-General of the U.S.S.R. This officer is appointed by the Supreme Soviet for a term of seven years (Art. 114). His office is a strictly centralized one because he appoints all the procurators of the Republics, Territories, Regions, etc. (Art. 115). The procurators of the lowest units of government, areas, districts, and cities, are appointed by the procurators of their respective Union Republics, subject to the approval of the Procurator-General (Art. 116). All members of the procuratorial staff are completely independent from all local organs whatsoever and are subordinate solely to the Procurator-General (Art. 117).

The independence of the Procurator-General does not, of course, mean that he is independent of the Communist party and its Presidium. But his freedom from possible local pressure helps materially in establishing uniform standards of law enforcement through the entire territory of the U.S.S.R.

The powers of the Procurator-General are vast and important. In him is vested supreme supervisory power to ensure the strict observance of the law by all ministries and institutions subordinate to them, as well as by officials and citizens of the U.S.S.R. generally (Art. 113). This is a greater power than that vested in the Supreme Court of the U.S.S.R., which supervises only the judicial activities of subordinate courts. But it is a power which follows strictly the command of the party leadership as evidenced in the numerous purge trials. The Soviet concept of legality is thus markedly different from that customary in the West.

In pursuit of his functions the Procurator-General has developed a unique, because official, organization of informers. Vyshinsky, a former Procurator-General, wrote, "All the organs of Soviet Community, the Young Communist League, the trade unions, worker correspondents and peasant correspondents, and so on, take an active part in the work of the Soviet Prosecutor's office, in its struggle to strengthen socialist legality."[11] These groups are well organized and meet regularly under specific leaders. They "signal" cases to the Procurator's office, including cases involving their associates, friends, and parents. Their services have been found most effective by the Soviet authorities.[12]

The regular court system is only one part of the vast organization which controls those who step out of line. In fact, as far as penal justice is concerned, the regular courts are comparable to the visible peaks of an iceberg; much more lies underneath: the secret police, the deportations, and the forced-labor camps.

---

[11] Vyshinsky, *op. cit.*, p. 528.
[12] S. N. Harper and R. Thompson, *The Government of the Soviet Union,* New York, 1949, 2d ed., p. 237. For a survey of the Procuracy's role in the Soviet system and its *modus operandi, see* G. Ginsburgs, "The Soviet Procuracy and Forty Years of Socialist Legality," *American Slavic and East European Review,* Vol. XVIII, No. 1 (February, 1959), pp. 34–62.

11

The position of the individual

The Soviet Constitution establishes and "guarantees" a considerable number of civil rights. The list of liberties (Arts. 118–133) contains all those which are customary in Western democracies and many more. This development emerged in the 1936 Constitution. Previous documents had conferred personal rights only with considerable restrictions and on an unequal basis and had given civil rights only to the workers. The Constitution of 1936 placed everyone on the same level. Lest the reader should come to the hasty conclusion that Stalin had unfurled the banner of Jeffersonian democracy, let us examine the theory and practice of civil rights in the U.S.S.R.

Soviet theorists assert that in the so-called "bourgeois" states democracy is a sham and an illusion. The people may go through the motions of electing "their" representatives, but in reality they are merely permitted to choose between different representatives of their oppressors. Civil rights, assert the Soviet theorists, are meaningless without economic freedom. They say,[1]

[1] Stalin in an interview with Roy Howard, 1937.

What can be the "personal freedom" of an unemployed person who goes hungry and finds no use for his toil? Only where exploitation is annihilated, where there is no oppression of some by others, no unemployment, no beggary, and no trembling for fear that a man may on the morrow lose his work, his habitation, and his bread—only there is true freedom found.

The Communist concept of personal freedom is thus derived from two principal assumptions: (1) that freedom is possible only when there is complete economic security and abundance; and (2) that only the Communist state can achieve and safeguard this economic goal. Said Stalin, "There neither is nor should be an irreconcilable contrast between the individual and the collective. . . . There should be none forasmuch as collectivism-socialism does not deny individual interests. It amalgamates them with the interests of the collective."[2]

Since a conflict between the state and the individual is "unnatural" under socialism, as that term is understood in the Soviet Union, any such "perversion" can only be the result of criminal tendencies on the part of the individual. Vyshinsky makes this point abundantly clear:[3]

In our state, naturally, there is and can be no place for freedom of speech, press, and so on for the foes of socialism. Every sort of attempt on their part to utilize to the detriment of the state—that is to say, to the detriment of all the toilers— these freedoms granted to the toilers must be classified as a counterrevolutionary crime to which Article 58, Paragraph 10, or one of the corresponding articles of the Criminal Code is applicable.

The Constitution underscores this point. Articles 125 and 126 grant the rights of free speech, press, and assembly, "in conformity with the interests of the working people, and in order to strengthen the socialist system." All other personal rights are granted unconditionally.

The principle that certain economic conditions must precede the establishment of real freedom is graphically demonstrated in Chapter 10 of the Constitution, entitled "Fundamental Rights and Duties of Citizens" (Arts. 118–133), which begins with an enumeration of economic rights, relegating the civil liberties of the Western type to a later, less conspicuous position.

Another characteristic of the Soviet Constitution is the fact that it unites in one section and usually in the same articles both rights and corresponding duties and outlines the machinery through which they may be accomplished. Likewise rights, especially economic rights, call for intervention on the part of the state and the rendering of certain services on the part of the state. All these rights are by Communist doctrine the result of the (socialist) economic and social order. The concept of "natural right" is, of course, rejected.

[2] Quoted by Andrei Vyshinsky, *The Law of the Soviet State* (trans. by H. R. Babb), New York, 1948, p. 540.
[3] *Ibid.,* p. 617.

The joining together of concepts of rights and of duties is by no means accidental, nor is it a result of careless thinking. Rather, it represents a highly important characteristic of the Communist form of totalitarianism which is quite different from, say, the dictatorship of a Franco. Control of the population is not enough for the Soviets. What they want and constantly work for is control with mobilization. Individuals are not only asked to accept the regime, they are expected to support it wholeheartedly and to strive continually for its success and improvement. The duties required of party members are simply those that the regime would like to see performed by all citizens if only that were possible. Looked at in this light, such institutions as comradely courts, "discussion" of some types of draft legislation (such as the 1936 Constitution), and the Soviet "election," all form part of the pattern of mobilizing the population.

Work

The first right (Art. 118) which the Soviet Constitution confers on its citizens is the "right to work." This means that the state furnishes jobs to everybody, and that is only natural, because practically all enterprise is owned and operated by the state. The Constitution declares that "the right to work is ensured by the socialist organization of the national economy, the steady growth of the productive forces of Soviet society, the elimination of the possibility of economic crises, and the abolition of unemployment."

What the state gives, the state can take away. The combining of all political and economic power in the hands of the state therefore serves to control the citizen all the more securely, since none of his activities are outside the purview of governmental authority. Unemployment does not exist in the Soviet Union, although a large number of citizens work in forced-labor camps. However, wages in terms of purchasing power are extremely low except in the highest ranks of the hierarchy, and the wage differential between executive positions and unskilled labor is as great as in any "capitalistic" country, and frequently greater. This is also reflected in the armed forces, in which a colonel's pay is thirty times that of a private.

The factory or shop in which the Soviet citizen works is a more or less self-contained unit, inasmuch as it satisfies his cultural, medical, and social needs. Often it also furnishes his living accommodation (graded strictly according to rank) and his food and clothing requirements. Exceptionally good work as well as excess profits on the part of the enterprise may lead to bonuses and increase of services. The money which he does not need he may put aside in a state bank. But the government sees to it that these funds are drained off on occasion, thus eliminating the danger of a new capitalistic or "speculator's" class. This drainage is largely accomplished by the "gray market," the state stores which sell goods at prices very much above the controlled prices in other types of stores. Since Soviet citizens may purchase only a limited quantity of rationed goods at controlled prices, the additional expenditure at inflated prices is difficult to avoid. Another method by which money may be drained off is devaluation, which appeared in the Soviet Union as a post-war phenomenon as it has in other countries.

Housing and health

Perhaps the greatest problem of the Soviet worker is housing. Not even in the slum areas of the Western capitals is there such congestion as is commonly found in the industrial centers of the Soviet Union. One room to a family is still a common occurrence. Private cooperatives for the building of houses and apartments are possible under Soviet law. By decree, a Soviet citizen is now permitted to own or build a home, although it appears that this is permissible only if he does so for his own use and not for the purpose of resale or renting. However, private construction is not practicable in the large urban centers, where the greatest shortage exists, and it is difficult to save enough money for the purpose.

Public health services are furnished, and medicine has been largely socialized, yet private medical practice is permissible in view of the shortage of public health facilities. It is interesting to note that Stakhanovites and other shock workers are frequently given permission and compensation for undergoing private treatment as a reward for exceptional merit.

Other benefits

The Soviet citizen is insured against the loss of earning power through sickness, disability, or old age (Art. 120). But absenteeism or tardiness may lead to severe fines and punishment. He is also entitled to rest and leisure (Art. 119), which means the establishment of the eight-hour day for ordinary work, with reduction to seven or even four hours where labor is especially arduous. He is also entitled to paid vacations and to the use of rest homes and other recreational facilities, all of which the state furnishes. The "parks of culture and rest" and the "workers' clubs" are common in all cities. Vacation spots of great desirability, however, are reserved for especially meritorious cases and for the higher bureaucracy, the new elite of the Soviet society, which is as class-conscious, as superior in deportment, and as removed financially and psychologically as any "upper class" in the despised "bourgeois" states ever was.

In the U.S.S.R. women are accorded equal rights with men in all spheres and levels (including such dubious "rights" as the privilege of running a jack hammer or doing heavy field work), but they are not much in evidence now on the highest party level. Only recently did a woman become a Politburo member. Women receive aid for maternity and similar occasions, and the Soviet government has copied the Nazi and Fascist custom of awarding decorations, titles,[4] and monetary compensation to women who bear an exceptional number of children.

---

[4] A woman bearing ten children or more is awarded the title of "Mother Heroine."

The family

In the beginning of the Soviet regime family ties were taken lightly, and it was assumed that the state would accept much of the burden of rearing children and maintaining households.[5] Marriage with or without official registration was little restrained, since divorce was easy and could be accomplished unilaterally by simple notification on the part of one spouse.

All this has changed very substantially. Marriage must now be registered, and divorce can be obtained only through litigation, which may be quite complicated and costly.[6] In fact, the general Soviet attitude now is one of extolling the virtues of the family and the sanctity of marriage.

Education

The Constitution guarantees the right to education (Art. 121). The original version of that article provided for free education, including higher education. In 1947 this was amended to make education free only up to the seventh grade. However, tuition fees are not exorbitant, and stipends and scholarships are available for capable students.

The Soviet government fully realizes the importance of education and the need for controlling the minds of the future generation. This is accomplished in the Soviet schools, where the slightest vestige of foreign ideology has been exterminated. The Communist party is forever vigilant in supervising education and research, not as an instrument for the discovery of truth but to further the purposes of the Soviet state. This point of view was well illustrated in an article in the official *Voprosy Istorii (Questions of History)*, September, 1948, which finds it alarming that there are still historians who interpret historical problems in the light of "bourgeois objectivism" and not from the party point of view.[7]

The Soviet schools have substantially reduced the illiteracy of prewar days. During the revolutionary period heavy emphasis was placed on technical instruction to the almost total exclusion of cultural subjects. Later this trend was criticized and reversed. Likewise the equalitarian tendency of earlier days has been modified. There is now recognition of individual and regional differences. Moreover, a compromise is made between the principle of the common secondary level and the need for university preparation. The basis of the school system is compulsory, basic in-

---

[5] Friedrich Engels, *The Origin of the Family, Private Property, and the State,* New York, 1942; Alexandra Kollontai, *Communism and the Family,* San Francisco, no date (Russian ed., 1919).

[6] Alex Inkeles, "Family and Church in the Post-war U.S.S.R.," *Annals of the American Academy of Political and Social Science,* May, 1949, pp. 33–44; John N. Hazard, "Law and the Soviet Family," *Wisconsin Law Review,* 1939, pp. 224–253; Vladimir Gsovski, "Marriage and Divorce in Soviet Law," *Georgetown Law Journal,* Vol. XXXV (1947), pp. 209–223.

[7] Sergius Yakobson, "Post-war Historical Research in the Soviet Union," *Annals of the American Academy of Political and Social Science,* May, 1949, p. 130.

struction lasting seven years (ages seven to fifteen), after which students either complete their education in vocational schools (for four more years) or transfer to specialized technical, medical, or other preparatory schools.[8]

Race relations

The Constitution forbids all discrimination on the basis of nationality or race (Art. 123). In this field the Soviet government can claim certain accomplishments in comparison with the situation under the tsars. The vigorous Russification and the virulent anti-Semitism which marked the imperial regime are not so much in evidence today. On the other hand, it cannot be denied that the individual has much less freedom under Communism than even under the tsar, although this system controls all equally without regard to race or color.

But even with these qualifications, the Soviet claim that there are no racial distinctions and discriminations in the U.S.S.R. cannot be accepted at face value. Although the forceful Russification policy of the tsarist regime has not been repeated, there is little doubt that the Great Russians, essentially the inhabitants of the western part of the Russian Soviet Federated Socialist Republic (R.S.F.S.R.)—the Russians in the narrow sense of the word—occupy the leading positions in the state and are regarded, in Stalin's own words, as "the leading force of the Soviet Union among all the peoples of our country."[9]

The leading position of the Great Russians was assured even under Stalin, a Georgian and under Khrushchev, a Ukrainian. The same was true of the governmental and industrial administrations of the Union Republics, where Great Russians had the lion's share of influential positions.[10] This trend was of course particularly strong among the Asiatic republics because of the greater reservoir of educated and trained manpower which the Russians had at their disposal. Currently, this discrepancy is less obvious. Similarly, there appears to be greater stress on local representation and local self-administration since the death of Stalin, thus giving non-Russian groups a greater share in the party and governmental machinery.

Observers agree in general that Russia's trouble spot is the Ukraine, which has been the target of repeated accusations of "bourgeois nationalism," an accusation which has never been directed against the Great Russians.[11] There is also the fact that the invading German armies found a degree of collaboration in the Ukraine and among other non-Russian people which they did not find among the Great Russians.

---

[8] Nicolas Hans, "Recent Trends in Soviet Education," *ibid.,* pp. 114–122.
[9] Quoted in 83d Congress, 1st Session, Senate Document No. 69 (1953), *Tensions within the Soviet Union,* p. 43.
[10] *Ibid.,* pp. 43–45.
[11] John S. Reshetar, Jr., "National Deviation in the Soviet Union," *American Slavic and East European Review,* Vol. 12 (1953), p. 173.

Speech, press, assembly, and asylum

We have already mentioned the limitations imposed on the rights of free speech, press, and assembly. The corollary to these rights is the statement (Art. 125) that these rights are ensured by placing at the disposal of the working people printing presses, needed supply of paper, and other facilities—over which, however, the state retains complete control, thereby possessing an additional method to prevent the possibility of free speech, press, and assembly from getting out of hand.

The Constitution affords the right of asylum to foreign citizens "persecuted for defending the interests of the working people . . ." (Art. 129), which in practice applies primarily to Communists.

Duties

Finally the section on the fundamental rights and duties of citizens contains an enumeration of duties which appear to be specially significant. Article 130 admonishes every citizen "to abide by the Constitution, to observe the laws, to maintain labor discipline, honestly to perform public duties, and to respect the rules of socialist intercourse." Article 131 instructs every citizen "to safeguard and fortify public, socialist property as the sacred and inviolable foundation of the Soviet system . . ." and declares that all persons "committing offenses against public, Socialist property are enemies of the people."

The Constitution further establishes universal military service, which helps to make the Soviet army by far the largest army of the world, and declares it to be "the sacred duty" to defend the country. "Treason to the motherland—violation of the oath of allegiance, desertion to the enemy, impairing the military power of the state, espionage,—is punishable with all the severity of the law as the most heinous of crimes" (Art. 133).

Behind the facade of civil rights there looms the secret political police, with far-reaching rights to arrest any citizen and to confine him in prison or forced-labor camp for any length of time. This is probably the most feared and hated Soviet institution, and many citizens would undoubtedly like to see it further modified or abolished. But as far as civil rights in general are concerned, the Soviet citizen who has not lived abroad has never enjoyed civil liberties and therefore has only a dim idea of what he misses. There appears to be little evidence of a "ground swell" in the Soviet Union demanding a bill of rights and the enforcement of real civil liberties.[12]

Among intellectuals, and especially writers, there seems to be something of an awareness of what is amiss. None of this, however, is likely to have very concrete results, especially as the regime sees to it that critical trees do not grow into the sky.

[12] George Ginsburgs, "Rights and Duties of Citizens," *Problems of Communism*, March–April, 1965, pp. 22–28.

12

The Soviet Union and the world

This is not the place to examine the foreign relations of the Soviet Union, to which obviously much more space would have to be devoted than is available here.[1] This chapter merely is to point out certain features of international relations which are peculiar to the Soviet orbit and which are derived directly from the nature of the Communist regime.

Communists believe, as we have seen, in a form of economic determinism. Applied to the field of international relations, this would mean that the cleavage

[1] See M. Beloff, *Foreign Policy of Soviet Russia,* Oxford, 1947–1949, 2 vols.; and *Soviet Foreign Policy after Stalin,* Philadelphia, 1961; D. J. Dallin, *Soviet Russia's Foreign Policy, 1939–1942,* New Haven, Conn., 1942; L. Fischer, *The Soviets in World Affairs,* New York, 1930, 2 vols.; also his *Trends in Russian Foreign Policy since World War I,* Washington, 1947, Senate Committee on Foreign Relations, 80th Congress, 1st Session; Frederick C. Barghoorn, *Soviet Foreign Propaganda,* Princeton, N.J., 1964; Zbigniew Brzezinski, *Ideology and Power in Soviet Politics,* New York, 1962 and *The Soviet Bloc, Unity and Conflict,* New York, 1961; J. M. Mackintosh, *Strategy and Tactics of Soviet Foreign Policy,* New York, 1962; and Alvin Z. Rubinstein, *The Foreign Policy of the Soviet Union,* New York, 1955.

between the capitalistic and the communist worlds is the direct result of their economic differences and is therefore inherent in the era of coexistence of both. Lenin, in emphasizing the role of imperialism as the "highest stage of capitalism," spoke of an "inevitable struggle between the capitalist and the socialist world" and of a "series of frightful clashes" which would result. Stalin echoed these sentiments.[2] Stalin and other Soviet leaders have spoken of the possibility of a "peaceful coexistence" of the "two worlds," but there is not necessarily a contradiction between the two approaches; presumably the struggle—which need not take military forms —is still inevitable and in fact upon us now because of the "inner contradictions" of capitalism and the "predatory nature" of imperialism. The capitalist leaders, we are told, look to the Soviet Union with hatred because of that country's alleged attraction to the workers of the world, and they therefore regard the U.S.S.R. as an enemy. Moreover, they are "warmongers" because they allegedly hope to incite a war in order to divert the masses from domestic difficulties.[3] The very fact of "coexistence" spells danger to the Soviet Union, which must be strong and vigilant in order to avoid disaster. It therefore maintains the largest army and air force in the world and has anchored the system of universal military service in its Constitution.

Despite that fact, the Soviet Union poses as "the camp of peace" while the "capitalistic" countries are, by definition, called "warmongers." Personal and idealistic (in contrast to materialistic) factors such as "good will" have little room in Communist thinking. This does not mean that the Soviet government is necessarily and at all times a deceiver. During periods of good diplomatic relations the Soviet government has been found to take great care in its treaty obligations, but otherwise clear violations of treaties are frequent.[4] However, the Communist leaders believe they are "realistic" in utterly rejecting the possibility of good will on the part of representatives of countries whose economic interests they believe must be at variance with that of the Soviet Union. The alleged belief in hostile environment is fundamental to Soviet foreign policy, but as we have seen it is also a justification for certain domestic measures of the regime.

In one of his last declarations, Stalin spoke of the inevitability of war between capitalist countries and again predicted the downfall of capitalism,[5] but this return to Leninist doctrine would seem to be primarily an attempt to show why capitalism had not yet collapsed. It was a direct slap against those more realistic Soviet economists, like Eugene Varga, who had maintained that capitalism had learned from the

[2] N. A. Voznesensky, *The Economy of the U.S.S.R. during World War II* (trans. under the auspices of the American Council of Learned Societies), Washington, 1948, p. 105.
[3] "X" (George F. Kennan), "The Sources of Soviet Conduct," *Foreign Affairs,* July, 1947.
[4] "Soviet Violations of Treaty Obligations: Document Submitted by the Department of State to the Senate Committee on Foreign Relations," *Department of State Bulletin,* June 6, 1948, pp. 738–744.
[5] J. V. Stalin, "Economic Problems of Socialism in the U.S.S.R.," *Bolshevik,* Oct. 2, 1952, reprinted in J. S. Meisel and E. S. Kozera, *Materials for the Study of the Soviet System,* Ann Arbor, Mich., 1953, p. xiv.

past and had adapted itself to the present situation and thus avoided the depression-war cycle, hitherto claimed as inevitable.

International law

This naturally colors the Soviet government's attitude toward international law. Communist legal science considers international law the law of the dominant states, therefore as "bourgeois international law," as stated by Vyshinsky. The outstanding Soviet authority on the subject, E. A. Korovin, wrote a book to which he gave the revealing title *The International Law of the Period of Transition,*[6] meaning the transition from a capitalistic to a socialist world. This is merely a method of adaptation to the realities in international life, not a matter of conviction or belief in common legal norms. Two later works, one by V. N. Durdenevski and S. B. Krylov[7] and one by F. I. Kozhevnikov,[8] follow a more traditional course by recognizing the existence of international law which, because of the important role of the U.S.S.R., can no longer be considered purely bourgeois; but their views were roundly denounced by Korovin,[9] who appeared to be again on top. It must be presumed, therefore, that the earlier views of Korovin are dominant and that international law is not accepted in principle except when convenient. This has been stated clearly in a later work by F. I. Kozhevnikov,[10] who accepts only those institutions which serve Soviet policy while he rejects those that do not. In contrast to Korovin, Kozhevnikov had a few kind words to say about arbitration and, with some reservations, about the International Court of Justice. But that was before Korovin's chilling blast, and the present standing of such moderate views must seriously be doubted. This is also in line with the views of the late Andrei Vyshinsky who, at the occasion of the Belgrade Conference on Navigation on the River Danube, rejected categorically the suggestion that disputes over the treaty should be submitted to the International Court of Justice.[11] Both Korovin and the (re-

---

[6] E. A. Korovin, *Mezhdunarodnoe Pravo Perekhodnovo Vremeni,* Moscow-Petrograd, 1923.

[7] V. N. Durdenevski and S. B. Krylov, *Mezhdunarodnoe Pravo* (International Law), Moscow, 1947.

[8] F. I. Kozhevnikov, *Uchebnoe Posobie po Mezhdunarodnomy Publichnomu Pravu* (Study Aid for International Public Law), Moscow, 1947.

[9] Review in *Sovetskoe Gosudarstvo i Pravo* (Soviet State and Law), August, 1948. Reprinted in *The American Journal of International Law,* Vol. XLIII (1949), pp. 387–389. The tenor of the criticism is revealed in comments like the following. Kozhevnikov refers to Grotius as the founder of international law. Korovin replies: "It would seem that the title of 'founder' is applicable only to the four great names of Marx, Engels, Lenin and Stalin. They are founders of all contemporary science relating to society and the state." Or: "Those [Soviet contributions] which he has set forth he sometimes treats, not in a militant fashion, but with an objective tone, when they are the very points which should be presented not objectively, but with the full force of Soviet patriotic pathos."

[10] F. I. Kozhevnikov, *Sovetskoe Gosudarstvo i Mezhdunarodnoe Pravo 1917–1947* (The Soviet State and International Law 1917–1947), Moscow, 1948.

[11] Walter A. Radius, "The Issues at Belgrade Were Clearly Drawn," *Department of State Bulletin,* Sept. 19, 1948, pp. 348ff.

formed) Kozhevnikov agree now that a "new form of international law has emerged from the relationship between the U.S.S.R. and the 'People's Democracies.'"[12]

The above problems belong primarily in the traditional field of foreign policy, which is not our principal concern. There is, however, another side of Moscow's international relations. Ever since its rise to power, the Communist party of the Soviet Union—and that means the Soviet government—has been the head and the heart of an international movement with a powerful following in every country.

The Communist International

The existence of international political associations is not peculiar to communism, nor did it originate with it. The forerunner of later Internationals was the Communist League, which was founded in 1836 and for which Marx and Engels wrote the Communist Manifesto in 1848. The so-called First International was founded in London in 1864; it was the first thoroughly organized international organization of socialist parties, and Marx wrote its bylaws. The First International soon disintegrated and was officially dissolved in 1876, but a similar organization was established in Paris in 1889 as the International Working Men's Association, better known as the Second International.

The Second International was revived after its dormant period in the First World War and retained its status as the international organization of socialist (non-Communist) parties. It disappeared in the Second World War and has now been officially revived. There is also a loose international association of Christian Democratic parties.

But all these organizations were and are free associations of equals. Decisions are taken by majority vote and no one party or country is dominant. The Communist International, however, which was organized in Moscow in 1919 and which became known as the Third International, or Comintern (Communist International), as well as its successor the Cominform (Communist Information Bureau), which was founded in 1947, took a different course.

The Bolshevik Revolution had an international character from the very beginning. Its leaders saw it as the first step of the world revolution, and the preamble to the Constitution of 1924 proclaimed that the federation of the Soviet Republics was merely the first step toward a soviet world republic.[13] To this end the Communist International, Comintern, was founded in March, 1919. It is interesting to note that this brain child of Lenin's was not greeted with any great enthusiasm by the communist parties of Central and Western Europe. The leaders of

[12] For a fuller treatment, see T. A. Taracouzio, *The Soviet Union and International Law,* New York, 1935; E. A. Korovin, "The Contribution of the U.S.S.R. to International Law," *Soviet Press Translations,* Vol. III (Dec. 1, 1948), pp. 655*ff.;* Harold J. Berman, *Justice in Russia,* Cambridge, Mass., rev. ed., 1963.

[13] L. H. Laing, M. C. Vernon, S. Eldersveld, J. S. Meisel, J. K. Pollock, *Source Book in European Governments,* New York, 1950, p. 227.

the German Communists, especially their most outstanding personality, Rosa Luxemburg, opposed this step. They distrusted the Bolshevik (Russian) leaders and wanted to establish strong communist parties in the West first.[14] However Lenin went ahead and perhaps inadvertently showed his hand by leaving the preparation for the organization of the Comintern in the hands of the Soviet Foreign Office. Because of the disturbances of the time, few genuine foreign delegations reached Moscow. The delegate of the German Communists, Eberlein, allowed himself to be persuaded to abstain from voting, in direct contradiction to the German Communist leadership, which had instructed him to vote against the formation of the International. The Third (Communist) International was thus from the beginning a Russian creation, dominated completely by the Communist party of the Soviet Union. Its first president was Grigori Zinoviev, and Moscow became its headquarters.

The organization of the Comintern was a replica of the Communist party in the Soviet Union. Nominally, supreme authority was vested in a World Congress, in which all national parties were to be represented and which was to meet every two years. The Congress elected an Executive Committee, which was supposedly responsible to it but which in actuality assumed all the functions of the Congress. There was also elected an International Control Commission. The Executive Committee elected a Presidium (the counterpart of the Politburo) which appointed a Political Secretariat. The Communist party of each country was constituted as a "section" (branch) of the Comintern. Article 13 of the Statute of the Communist International of 1928 provided as follows: "The decisions of the Executive Committee of the Communist International are obligatory for all the sections of the International and must be promptly carried out." And Article 14 ruled that the executive committees of the various communist parties of the world were responsible to their respective national congresses and to the Executive Committee of the Communist International.[15] No secrecy prevailed concerning the actual leadership of the Executive Committee. Article 8 of the Statute of the Communist International of 1920 read as follows:

> The bulk of the work and responsibility in the Executive Committee of the Communist International lies with the Party of that country, where, in keeping with the resolution of the World Congress, the Executive Committee finds its residence for the time being. The Party of the country in question sends to the Executive Committee not less than five members with a decisive vote. In addition to this one representative with a decisive vote is sent to the Executive Committee from each of the other ten to twelve largest Communist Parties. . . .

The country in which the Executive Committee found its residence was, of course, the U.S.S.R.

[14] Franz Borkenau, *World Communism,* New York, 1939, p. 161. This is without doubt the most authoritative work on the Communist International.
[15] *Blueprint for World Conquest as Outlined by the Communist International,* with an introduction by W. M. Chamberlin, Washington, D.C., 1946.

While the domination of Russian Communism over the Comintern was established from the beginning, it was only under Stalin that the Comintern became the conveyor belt, first of Stalin's domination over Communism at home and abroad, and later of the aspirations of Soviet foreign policy. A former leader of the German Communist party has described graphically and in detail how the Comintern was employed in order to change the leadership of the party in Germany and to help strengthen Stalin's hand at home,[16] and a former leader of Italian Communism has told how the members of the Executive Committee of the Communist International were once cajoled into issuing a violent protest against a letter by Leon Trotsky—a letter which none of them was permitted to see or read.[17]

The absolute and unquestioned domination of the Comintern by the Soviet leadership became an accomplished fact long before the outbreak of the Second World War. Whenever the Moscow party line changed, the policies of all other communist parties changed likewise. All of them pursued the ever-increasing hate campaign against the democratic socialists, who were regarded as "social fascists" and the "principal enemy of the workers." All of them suddenly reversed themselves in the thirties when the call went out from Moscow for a united front with the socialists and later for a popular front with all moderate and democratic parties. Similarly it is still well remembered how the Communists of all countries inveighed against the "imperialist war" and how criticism of Nazism and Fascism disappeared from the Communist press—until the German attack against the Soviet Union changed everything, and the same parties which had hitherto condemned the war could hardly get enough of it now and demanded an immediate opening of a second front.

After Russia's entry into the war a period of fairly good relations with other nations ensued, and as a gesture of good will the Comintern was officially dissolved in 1943. However, there is ample proof that the intimate contact between communist parties did not cease and that they continued to take orders from the same headquarters.[18]

The early postwar years showed the Soviet Union in a position of unprecedented power. Not only had it added vast territories to its domain—the only belligerent of the Second World War to reap such a reward—but Communist regimes were set up in Poland, Czechoslovakia, Hungary, Yugoslavia, Bulgaria, Romania,

---

[16] Ruth Fischer, *Stalin and German Communism*, Cambridge, Mass., 1948. Ruth Fischer, who together with Paul Maslov was once a principal leader of the German Communist party, is the sister of Gerhard Eisler.

[17] Ignazio Silone, "Farewell to Moscow," *Harper's Magazine*, Nov., 1949, pp. 93–99.

[18] In the United States this was most spectacularly revealed when Earl Browder, who had become identified with the policy of good relations between East and West, was criticized during the summer of 1945 by the French Communist leader Jacques Duclos in a French Communist publication, *Les Cahiers du Communisme*. Duclos was generally regarded as a Comintern agent, and his article was reprinted verbatim in the New York edition of the *Daily Worker*, which still carried Browder's name on its masthead as editor in chief. As usual in such cases, Browder suddenly found himself attacked on all sides and was first demoted and then expelled from the party.

and Albania. Communist armies fought in Greece, China, and Indochina. Communist parties of great strength developed elsewhere in Europe, especially in France and Italy.

The Communist Information Bureau

The closer coordination of those forces was effected by the creation in September, 1947, of the Communist Information Bureau, generally known as the Cominform, whose headquarters were first established in Belgrade and later in Bucharest. It published a journal with the title *For a Lasting Peace, for a People's Democracy*.

The Cominform was, more clearly than the Comintern, an instrument of Soviet foreign policy, whose interests it served without exception. The Cominform had no published statute, and its organization was a good deal looser than that of the Comintern. Its basis was primarily the Soviet Union and its satellites, while the most powerful communist parties in the West, especially those of France and Italy, were regularly represented. It was originally designed only "to exchange experiences and coordinate activities," but the expulsion of Tito's Yugoslav Communist party revealed that it was supposed to have disciplinary power over its members. The strict nature of this conveyor belt of orders from the Kremlin was revealed fully in the exchange of acrimonious notes between the Cominform and the Communist party of Yugoslavia.[19] ". . . the Cominform accepts the process of the Central Committee of the All-Union Communist of Bolsheviks . . . ," stated the manifesto which accused Tito of having conducted a "hateful policy in relation to the Soviet Union and the All-Union party of Bolsheviks" and of "an undignified policy of underestimating Soviet military specialists. . . ."

The Cominform met but rarely; when it did, it appeared to be primarily concerned with some specific issue of Soviet foreign policy[20] and, in its closing years, especially with the struggle against the danger of Titoism. With Khrushchev's 1955 decision to reestablish friendly relations with Yugoslavia, the Cominform was abolished, apparently as the price of the *rapprochement*.

The absence of an institutional framework for the Kremlin's control of its subordinates in no way means a relaxation of that control or a diminution of its intensity. Periodic brotherly conferences and a multitude of other methods perpetuate Moscow's predominance.

The existence of a world-wide system of foreign agents, in the form of the various communist parties and the Comintern-Cominform, is usually regarded as a

[19] For the text of the Cominform manifesto, see *The New York Times,* June 29, 1948. For the Yugoslav reply, see *Statement of the Central Committee of the Communist Party of Yugoslavia,* Belgrade, 1948. Also, Royal Institute of International Affairs, *Soviet-Yugoslav Dispute,* London, 1948, containing the texts.

[20] See the statement by the late Bulgarian Premier Georgi Dimitrov, that internationalism is "international collaboration under Comrade Stalin," speech delivered before the 5th Congress of the Bulgarian Communist Party, Dec. 19, 1948, Georgi Dimitrov, *Political Report,* Sofia, 1948.

great tactical advantage for the Soviet Union. However, this is true only to a limited extent. In war the communist parties may be counted upon to furnish aid to the U.S.S.R. regardless of their countries' policies—on that we have the word of all the Communist leaders of the world. But on the other hand the existence of these parties isolates Moscow from the rest of the world. Every bit of information carried there is seen through the narrow spectacles of party doctrine. A strike in America becomes an expression of the "class struggle"; business difficulties become the beginning of capitalism's inevitable and long-predicted depression. The outside world is consistently misrepresented, and there are many indications that the Soviet leaders, despite an enormous intelligence machinery, are actually poorly informed about the democratic world. The policies of the Cominform have been an unbroken chain of failures. The postwar period has handed communism spectacular successes, the latest of which is China. But these victories were accomplished through various forms of violence. In Western Europe, where "Action Committees" and similar trappings of impending "People's Democracies" are not tolerated, the Communist parties have suffered considerable reverses as their ties to Moscow become ever more apparent.

The Communist parties of the world and the Soviet Union

During Lenin's and especially during Stalin's rule, the communist parties of the world were expected to maintain the strictest obedience to the interests and the commands of the Soviet Union. In those days, it was said of Maurice Thorez, then leader of the French Communist party, that "when Stalin has a cold, Thorez sneezes!"

However, starting under Khrushchev and still going on, there has been a double evolution. The deliberate destalinization started by Khrushchev undermined and destroyed the foundation for absolute and unquestioning obedience to Moscow. To a slowly growing extent, the communist parties in eastern Europe outside the U.S.S.R. began to develop policies on their own, first Poland, followed by Hungary and Rumania, with Bulgaria and Czechoslovakia joining later. Tito in Yugoslavia had of course done so long before. As these lines are written, this development has gone perhaps farthest in Romania.

Only the East German puppet regime of Walter Ulbricht remains relatively Stalinist, partly because of its total dependence on Moscow's support, partly because it is in a different position from the regimes in the other communist East European countries. In the latter, a more national communism is capable of strengthening the regime, because Poles, Rumanians, Hungarians, etc., would rather be more Polish, more Hungarian, more Rumanian, than Russian. But for the inhabitants of East Germany, nationalism is not a question of being more "East German"; it is a question of being more "German." Hence, in the so-called "German Democratic Republic," the Soviet Zone, a more "national" trend would not strengthen the regime but would weaken it.

Yet another but very important factor is the growingly bitter and now seemingly irreparable rift between Communist China and the Soviet Union. In this struggle, the overwhelming majority of communist parties in the world have now sided with the Soviet Union, as was clearly indicated at the 23d Congress of the Communist party of the Soviet Union when it convened in Moscow in March, 1966.[21]

However, in agreeing to be present at the Congress, the Communists of other nations had played a long and coy game and had used every opportunity to gain advantages for themselves and to preserve a maximum degree of independence. Strangely enough the communist parties of Western Europe had been slower in asserting themselves than had been those of the East European Communist regimes.[22]

It is well not to exaggerate the degree of communist independence. The Communist leaders outside the Soviet Union and especially in Eastern Europe know very well that their regimes are resented by their people and would not last one day if the umbrella of the Soviet army were to be withdrawn. This limits their independence materially. Moreover, the success or failure of the oldest and most important Communist experiment, the Soviet Union itself, reflects on the future of communism everywhere. Thus it was again proclaimed at the 23d Congress of the Communist party of the Soviet Union that a Communist's devotion to his ideal can still be measured by his attitude toward the Soviet Union. But it would be very difficult now to reverse the direction in the relationship between Moscow and the other communist countries of Eastern Europe. In the economic field in particular, neither the one-sided relationships to the Soviet Union, nor the overly rigid network of bilateral relationships known as the Council of Mutual Economic Assistance (COMECON),[23] were able to diminish the lure of greatly expanded economic relationships with the West and of somewhat closer relations to the European Economic Community (Common Market).[24]

Contemporary Soviet foreign policy

The Soviet Union emerged from the Second World War with its power immensely increased and its frontiers greatly extended both in Europe and in Asia. Moreover other Communist regimes had pushed into the heart of the European continent and covered a good part of the Asiatic mainland. But all this was achieved by force. In Europe every Communist victory, except in Czechoslovakia and pos-

---

[21] Although only the communist parties of Albania, New Zealand, and of course China, remained absent, it should not simply be taken for granted that all the others represented there had fully accepted the Moscow line. The Communist party of North Vietnam was represented in Moscow, but this did not mean that they had broken with Peking.

[22] With the exception of the Italian Communist party, which had conducted a fairly independent course even while Stalin was alive, and even more so later.

[23] See Andrzej Korbonski, *COMECON,* Carnegie Endowment for International Peace, International Conciliation Pamphlet 549, September, 1964.

[24] It may be expected that several Communist countries will attempt to establish formal or informal relations with the Common Market. They are of course excluded from membership.

sibly in Yugoslavia, was achieved by Soviet troops; native Communists merely took over from them. Even in Czechoslovakia and Yugoslavia Communist force was decisive. In Asia, too, Communist expansion was the result of armed might. The Communist hope that the masses would rise and overthrow their own regimes was not realized anywhere in the world.

As the hope of turning the masses against their governments with slogans of world revolution was obviously hopeless, Moscow evolved a new and different slogan—of peace. And one must credit its enormous propagandistic skill, that the country which has most consistently disturbed the peace of the postwar world, should succeed in convincing so many people that it was the champion of peace. One of the principal reasons for its success is the fact that the war-ravaged countries of Europe and Asia have a deep longing for peace to which this slogan appeals in a powerful manner. It is doubtful that the slogan and the numerous declarations like the Stockholm declaration or the many "peace congresses" organized by the Communists have actually converted many to Communism, but they have often been able to enlist the services and cooperation of non-Communists who allowed themselves to be convinced of the sincerity of the "peace" aim of the organizers of these meetings. Thus the slogan has received a wider reception than any purely Communist idea could have gained.

To those who feel that the communists have proved themselves more skillful at propaganda than the West, several facts should be pointed out. In the first place, it must be admitted that the Soviet leaders enjoy one advantage which the West cannot possibly acquire. They have, in every country of the world, an often numerous, and always militant and zealous, group of devoted people who will still carry out instructions given them. In other words, the U.S.S.R. has native advocates in every part of the world. The West does not. The idea of an "American," "British," or "French" party in another country, sworn to obedience to the commands of Washington, London, or Paris, is an obvious absurdity and a direct contradiction to the democratic ideals which those countries profess. The West has of course many friends, but friends do not always agree and certainly do not obey orders. As a result, Western ideas and policies sometimes appear as "foreign," especially in countries with a colonial past and an anti-Western sensitivity, while communist ideas are presented as "native" and directed toward "national liberation." Of course not all national liberation movements are communist by any means, but some are, and others have had periods in which they were not vigilant against penetration. Yet, despite this enormous advantage, communism has achieved no new laurels, and since the fall of China to communism, the East-West fronts have remained in a state of uneasy stability. The Korean conflict served unmistakable notice that new communist military aggression would not be tolerated, and this is also United States policy in Vietnam.

And yet no lesson is going to last forever. It was not long after Russia had demonstrated its scientific achievements in space by launching Sputnik I in 1957 that another Berlin crisis was unleashed by Khrushchev. This was, however, warded off by the West's firmness and unity. Then in 1962 Khrushchev engaged in another, more dangerous, maneuver by placing intermediate and medium-range missiles on Cuba within 90 miles of America's shores. Had they been permitted to remain there, America's advantage in nuclear weapons and delivery systems would have been effectively cut, and the balance of power would have changed abruptly. However, the determination of President John F. Kennedy and the United States government forced Khrushchev to withdraw his missiles, an event which undoubtedly contributed to his downfall two years later.

In subsequent years the foreign policy of the Soviet Union became increasingly overshadowed by the growing conflict with Communist China and to a lesser extent by the war in Vietnam.[25]

The Soviet leaders became increasingly concerned over the belligerent and dangerous policies of Peking's leadership, while they resisted the constant demands of Peking that they give second place to their own internal revolution and siphon far greater amounts of aid to the revolutionary struggle abroad, especially when that was likely to strengthen Peking and not Moscow. This resistance was branded by the Peking leadership as a base form of betrayal. By the time the 23d Congress of the Communist party met in Moscow in 1966, the breach had become unbridgeable and was rapidly growing worse.

In this situation the Soviet government is in a dilemma, or at the least in a very delicate spot. It is engaged in a double struggle with Peking. One is of the old-fashioned nationalist type, involving China's ill-concealed appetite for the U.S.S.R.'s maritime provinces (especially Vladivostok) and much of Soviet Asia. The other is the international struggle for predominance within the world communist family. From the standpoint of territorial integrity the Soviet Union undoubtedly has far less to fear from the United States than from China, and were it only for this side of the conflict, the two mightiest world powers might indeed have a good deal in common. But too close a relationship with the United States would only add fuel to the flames of Peking's propaganda line that Moscow has betrayed the Communist revolution and is making common cause with the capitalists of the United States. The situation has become complicated even further by the war in Vietnam, in which China obviously seeks the humiliation not only of the United States but also of the Soviet Union—proofs that both the United States and the U.S.S.R. are in a sense "paper tigers." This obliges the Soviet Union to maintain an atmosphere of belligerency toward the United States, although it is clear that neither an outright Communist victory nor a similar success by the United States is in Moscow's best interest as the Russians see it.[26]

This dilemma has stalled a number of attempts at East-West agreements, but there is no reason to believe that the standstill must last indefinitely.

---

[25] Donald S. Zagoria, *The Sino-Soviet Conflict, 1956–1961,* Princeton, N.J., 1962.

[26] Even if one were to accept the thesis that the government of Hanoi and the Viet Cong are quite separate and distinct from Peking, a victory of the Communists in Vietnam would still be regarded as proof of the correctness of the Chinese, not the Moscow, thesis.

In Europe it has been the Soviet Union's policy to keep the West from consolidating its unity. The Soviet Union has consistently and persistently fought the Marshall Plan, the North Atlantic Treaty Organization (NATO), and similar pacts elsewhere. Soviet propaganda has, moreover, made Germany (that is, the German Federal Republic) its particular target, knowing that a fear of Germany persists in many countries which were ravaged in World War II. If General de Gaulle's endeavors to unravel the Common Market were successful, further opportunities for deepening the division within Western Europe would undoubtedly be utilized by Moscow. However, it is a mistake to believe that East-West relations can become better only if the West is weaker. The Soviet government can be counted upon to do everything possible to strengthen its position, especially in the face of increasing Chinese pressure. If the West is divided, Russia will no doubt endeavor to strengthen its hand by playing on such dissensions there as it can. But for the same reasons, if the West is united, the Soviet Union will have to come to terms with it.[27]

It is reassuring to realize that the Soviet leaders have thoroughly grasped the immense significance of nuclear weapons and the universal destruction which would follow the outbreak of a general war. Thus their policy, while often belligerent in tone and at times potentially dangerous, as in the 1962 Cuba crisis, has nevertheless been cautious on the whole and has not taken positions from which it might have been impossible to retreat. This is also the policy which appears to be followed by Khrushchev's successors, Brezhnev and Kosygin. But nowhere does this promise great changes or breakthroughs in the direction of international peace and understanding. Thus, that which is sometimes called the cold war is likely to continue, sometimes colder, sometimes warmer, sometimes a little more dangerous than at other times, but never really going to the brink. But nothing, absolutely nothing is there to indicate that the Soviet leaders have modified their aims and aspirations. What has been modified is their action, because of their realistic appraisal of the power at their disposal and of that at the disposal of their possible opponents.

Yet in this fast-moving world nothing is totally impossible; and eventually better relations between the Soviet Union and the West are not inconceivable.

[27] Dean Acheson, "Europe: Decision or Drift," *Foreign Affairs,* January, 1966, pp. 198–205.

13

Conclusions

The Bolshevik Revolution was without doubt one of the most outstanding events of the twentieth century, comparable in its impact only to the French Revolution of 1789. Since the day when Lenin and his associates seized power in Russia, men of intelligence all over the world have hotly debated the merits and demerits of the Soviet regime. Some have seen in it the fulfillment of men's highest aspirations, the great hope of mankind, while others have regarded it as the foulest blow to Occidental civilization and the incarnation of all evil. The heat of the debate itself indicates the importance of the subject, quite apart from the great power which the U.S.S.R. wields in international affairs.

In an atmosphere of this kind, cool analysis has always been difficult; too many people have already made up their minds long ago, often on purely emotional grounds, and facts presented to them are evaluated solely on the basis of their agreement or disagreement with preconceived notions, not on the basis of intrinsic value. Any writer or analyst who tries to be calm and objective is confronted with the question, "What is objectivity?" A purely factual description of the Soviet government might be objective but would remain completely meaningless, because there is little point in enumerating the powers of the Supreme Soviet or the right of election unless one also states what those powers and rights mean. But that goes into the field of analysis and therefore of controversy.

Some extricate themselves from this dilemma of either giving meaningless facts or becoming the target of attacks, by escaping into a fairyland in which all facts are equal. Such writers believe it to be "objective" to criticize in equal measure the admittedly reprehensible chain gangs that formerly existed in Georgia in the United States and the forced-labor camps that existed in the Soviet Union under Stalin, completely ignoring the total differences in the moral and physical dimensions thereof. That type of objectivity conjures up before the eyes of the reader a very incorrect and misleading picture and encourages him to minimize very important differences between his own and certain foreign institutions and approaches.[1]

In our day there is much talk, in the author's view much superficial talk, about a "convergence" of the Soviet and the Western, especially the American, political systems. Now it is of course true that in American life there is far more planning, far more public ownership, far more government intervention and government-sponsored services than would have seemed conceivable even a few decades ago. On the other hand, terror stalks the Soviet citizen far less today than was the case under Stalin. There is a growing realization in the Soviet Union that personal incentive plays an important role in economic enterprise and that industries must, in a certain sense, be profitable even in a "socialist" economy. And there are the already mentioned realities of the nuclear age which are as fully comprehended in the Soviet Union as in the United States, plus an apparently growing awareness that instability and disorder may in time become a menace to the Soviet Union, not merely to the "capitalist" West.

But these parallel modifications, profound and significant as they may be, cannot hide the fact that the two regimes are and remain fundamentally different in nature and purpose. As has been brilliantly stated by Brzezinski and Huntington,[2] the Soviet Union represents an essentially political system designed exclusively to establish and perpetuate Communist rule. To this central purpose, all others are subordinate. Further, the Soviet society has been created from the center out. It not only is, but has always been, a highly centralized society in which all real opposition to the Communist party has been rigorously crushed. Despite certain liberalizing traits, *political power* remains firmly fixed in the hands of top party leaders.

By contrast, the American system constitutes a loose governmental framework within which the forces of American society may develop in reasonable freedom. Thus, while the Soviet system has a maximal political purpose, the American system has a minimal political purpose.

[1] A good illustration of this type of presentation is *The United States and the Soviet Union: Some Quaker Proposals for Peace,* New Haven, Conn., 1949.
[2] Zbigniew Brzezinski and Samuel P. Huntington, *Political Power: USA/USSR,* New York, 1964, page 409.

On the operational level, the Soviet system may appear more vigorous and certainly often more skilled, since its leaders are professional practitioners in the art of wielding political power; by contrast, the American system is essentially diffuse, pluralistic, geared to an unending process of adjustment and compromise between divergent forces.

The goals of the Soviet system remain firm and precise even if in practice some modifications take place, while the goals of the American system are difficult to define, revealing constant modification, and attempts to define them as a definite pattern or even to create an American ideology have almost uniformly ended in failure.[3] American goals can be seen more clearly in retrospect but even there they are diffuse, many-sided.

The unity of theory and action plus the professionalism of Soviet leaders has frequently given the Soviet system a temporary tactical advantage and has at times exerted an attraction for leaders of newly emerging nations who were looking for systems which would give them effective control while they went about the business of developing their countries.

But it is equally clear that there are two sides to the medal: the doctrinal unity of the Soviet system makes for a rigidity which produces strains that the more loose-jointed American system can overcome far more easily; and the problem of succession can easily become a crisis of the regime in the Soviet system, which is not the case in the United States. Moreover, in the long run the prospects remain brighter for the West because, as Brzezinski and Huntington wisely remark, it is easier to turn amateurs into professionals than to repair basic shortcomings in the political system.

Perhaps most important of all is the fact that the Soviet Union is and remains a dictatorship. Nothing can hide or modify that fact. Even though the Soviet citizen may now sleep more calmly in his bed—though not as yet with complete assurance—and even though the Soviet leader must pay some attention to widely held grievances, the Soviet citizen has precious little influence on his government, and elections remain a means for mobilizing the masses in support of official policy and have absolutely nothing to do with sharing the power of decision making. There is no indication whatsoever that these basic characteristics are about to change.

Finally, despite greatly enhanced travel opportunities for Westerners and even now for Soviet citizens, the U.S.S.R. remains an essentially closed society. The freedom of foreign scholars to undertake meaningful political science, sociological, or economic research in the Soviet Union remains severely circumscribed. The late, unlamented Nazi regime was more accessible on that score than is the Soviet Union today. Cultural exchanges between the Soviet Union and the West have made considerable progress but are still far from free. In fact, occasional arrests and trials of foreigners and Russians alike as well as comments in the Soviet press from time to

---

[3] *Goals for Americans: Report of the President's Commission on National Goals,* New York, 1960; and Paul Campbell and Peter Howard, *America Needs an Ideology,* London, 1957.

time that foreigners are all spies and must be treated with caution, serve as a reminder to the Soviet citizenry not to draw excessive conclusions from the "thaw" of East-West relations and not to forget that "big brother" continues to watch vigilantly.

What of the stability of the Soviet regime? Everything indicates that it remains very high, despite the great strains caused by ideological rigidity and a high degree of centralization. There are indications that young Russians, in particular, have become increasingly critical of their regime, but nothing points to any serious internal danger to the Soviet regime's survival.

Further, a number of succession problems have been successfully overcome. The transfer of power from Stalin to Malenkov and Khrushchev still was somewhat precarious. That from Khrushchev to Brezhnev and Kosygin, although carried out with customary conspiratorial secrecy, operated smoothly. It should also be noted that Khrushchev was overthrown, not by his adversaries, but by his longtime adherents and supporters. Hence one may assume that it was his adventurous style, his erratic behavior, and the fiasco of the Cuban missile crisis which led to his downfall, and not basic opposition to his policies. Even those Russians who dislike their regime are apparently on the whole not conscious of any possible alternative.

The Soviet regime demonstrates a completely managed state in which a few men determine, in accordance with a definite political theory, what should or should not be done by all organs of the state down to the lowest branch and by all citizens. It demonstrates a political organism in which every action is designed in some manner to serve the state and the party, and nearly perfect techniques through which the enthusiastic support of the citizen is to be marshaled. It also manifests equally efficient methods by which any lack of enthusiasm among the citizens may be rendered harmless to the state and to the party.

But that works only in the Soviet Union proper. In the relations between the U.S.S.R. and the other Communist countries, Moscow's control has been loosening increasingly. No longer can the Soviet leadership assume unqualified and unquestioned support from the other Communist nations. Only East Germany, the so-called German Democratic Republic (DDR), remains a close copy of the previous type of the true satellite regime. Yugoslavia has completely broken away from Soviet control. Relations between Moscow and Belgrade are now cordial, while those between Moscow and Peking seem to worsen by the hour, so much that if there is any real danger of armed conflict involving the Soviet Union, it is now much more likely between the U.S.S.R. and Communist China than between the U.S.S.R. and the United States. Once again it is demonstrated that the similarity of domestic regimes does not in itself guarantee the continuation of cordial relations in the realm of foreign affairs.

Even after an existence of fifty years, the Soviet system cannot overcome its revolutionary and conspiratorial origin. It is a system built on the assumption of an ever-present conflict. This, as well as the legend of Western encirclement and of "scientifically inevitable" Communist victory, forms the justification for the constant demand for sacrifice and for the privation which is imposed on Soviet citizens. But both the exigencies of the nuclear age and the success of the "capitalistic" regimes have made clear that coexistence is a reality. As living standards in the Soviet Union increase, upheaval and instability in the world—although doctrinally a revolutionary necessity—become increasingly a menace to the U.S.S.R. just as much as they are to the Western world. To these realities the Soviet system has not yet adjusted, and further modifications would therefore seem to be in order. When they occur, they will, as is customary in Communist regimes, be clothed in profound doctrinal discussions and reinterpretation of the sacred Marxist-Leninist doctrine. However, they are unlikely to come quickly and the Brezhnev-Kosygin team seems to be particularly disinclined toward rash or exceptionally imaginative moves.

Although Soviet Communism affects a pose of being young and of being "the wave of the future," it is already half a century old and shows signs of stagnation and attachment to methods which are outdated. The rather mediocre success which the Communist leaders have had in the newly emerging countries, where many factors initially seemed to favor them, is a clear revelation of this. Soviet tactics have often shrewdly played down the Communist element and attempted to attach themselves to native nationalism, but it always becomes apparent, sooner or later, that Communism cannot in the long run tolerate any nationalism other than its own.

Neither the Soviet Union nor the other Communist countries have remained immune from the malaise which has swept the youth of the world and which has created a widespread feeling of alienation that Marx believed was confined to the capitalistic system. To a tightly controlled system like the Communist one, such a "long-haired" malaise must seem even more serious than it does to the more loosely organized Western systems which are geared to the absorption of divergent and contradictory moods.

Hence, the problem of adjustment to realities in the second half of the twentieth century has turned out to be no less great for the Soviet Union than for the rest of the world, and in some respects, greater. Khrushchev realized this clearly and went about it with imagination but in a boorish, uneven, and bull-in-the-china-shop manner. His successors, while avoiding his most obvious errors, have also acted thus far without his imagination and vigor. Thus the problem of adjustment remains, and the world will continue to watch Soviet endeavors with the fascination and attention due a powerful country trying to find its proper role in a rapidly changing world.

Toward a more united Europe and Atlantic partnership: the emergence of community

Political frontiers are the results of a respectable, historical and ethnic evolution, of a long effort towards national unification; one should not even attempt to erase them. In other periods, they were changed by violent conquest or by fruitful marriages. Today it is sufficient to devaluate them. Our frontiers in Europe should become less and less barriers to the exchange of ideas, of persons and of goods. The sentiment of solidarity among nations will win out over the nationalisms which are now outdated.

Robert Schuman[1]

[1] Robert Schuman, *Pour l'Europe,* Paris, 1963, p. 23; a slender volume, planned and put together by him shortly before his death and published posthumously.

General introduction

The reader may be somewhat surprised to find a part of this book devoted to European integration and a smaller part, to Atlantic partnership. In most instances these subjects are taken up within a context of general or regional international relations, and they may therefore be unexpected as additions to a book primarily devoted to the political life and the governmental system of major European states.

In my view, the idea that the institutions of European integration are just special forms of international organization is outdated and ought to be subjected to a searching review.

International organizations such as the United Nations and the Organization of American States have been set up by states wishing to act together with regard to a number of matters of common concern, among which the preservation of peace and the settlement of disputes are, without doubt, the most important. These organizations are essentially conveniences, established in order that the common purposes may be more effectively pursued. But the member states have not limited their sovereignty and their prerogatives any more than they have in numerous other international treaties. In particular, they have not transferred to these international organizations any part of their national sovereignty and governmental prerogatives, nor have they empowered the secretariats and other organs of these international organizations to act for them except in a few instances, where for a specific cause, place, and time, such authority was specifically granted.

In other words, these international organizations are governed entirely by their member states, who at all times continue to pursue their national interests within the international organization. Strictly speaking, there is no such thing as a "United Nations policy" except those general principles stated in the Charter, to which a certain number of resolutions may be added, many of them unenforced and perhaps unenforceable. In part this is because there are no true United Nations organs charged with the responsibility of enforcing the principles. Only to a very limited extent could the United Nations peacekeeping forces be placed in this category, and their very existence and financial support are questioned by important members, among them the U.S.S.R. and France. The Secretariat of the United Nations, like similar organs of the other international organizations, is strictly a service organization, designed and equipped to aid the member nations in making those decisions and undertaking those actions envisaged by its Charter and resolutions. The secretariats of international organizations are not authorized to act and do not act *for* the members in any significant fashion. They do not negotiate in their name, they do not make rules, they do not regulate the conduct of the members nor issue licenses for their business or other activities. To be sure, the United Nations has a court, the International Court of Justice, but although technically termed "the principal judicial organ of the United Nations," it is really a quite separate and distinct organization which, under the name of "Permanent Court of International Justice" and with a virtually identical statute, antedated the United Nations by many years. Its principal role has been aptly described as that of seeking "to strengthen the role of law among the sovereign states,"[2] and it serves the United Nations as such only on infrequent occasions. Moreover individuals have no standing before the Court and their cause can be taken up only if it is presented by one of the member states.

The above remarks are not intended to be critical of international organizations in general or of the United Nations in particular. On the contrary, if it is the principal and most noble task, especially of the United Nations, to preserve the peace and to settle disputes which, if left unattended, might lead to dangerous conflagrations, then it is important that the organization be as universal as possible and that it include among its members countries with the most diverse political systems and aspirations. But the more diverse states are in their aspirations, the less are they likely to confide important functions to common organs on a long-range or permanent basis, or indeed to agree even to the establishment of such organs. Therefore, those countries which seek continuous, common, and collective action on a number of important matters of common concern will find this possible to attain only if their association is confined to states holding reasonably common views and outlooks, with economic, social, and political systems sufficiently similar to permit them to undertake such common actions.

Since the preservation of peace and progress on important political, economic, and social issues are of great importance to millions of people, the parallel existence of both forms of organization described above creates the greatest possible benefit for mankind. It is, however, well not to confuse these two types of groups. Here we are concerned with the more *integrated* organizations which (in contradistinction to the *international* ones) are often called *supranational*. They are especially the three European Communities: the European Coal and Steel Community (ECSC), during its formative phase often called the Schuman Plan;[3] the European Atomic Energy Community (EURATOM); and the European Economic Community (EEC), better known as the Common Market. Having a lesser degree of integration, with a form of community organization that places it closer to the UN type of organization, is the North Atlantic Treaty Organization (NATO). Here the integrated features are largely confined to the military staff levels.

To use the example of the European Economic Community (Common Market), here we find a major administrative and executive body, the Commission, the very pivot around which turns the work of the EEC. To be sure, there is also a Council of Ministers which is the supreme policy-making body of the Community, and which is organized like the councils in international organizations, with one delegate from each member country. But the Commission is not merely a secre-

[2] L. Larry Leonard, *International Organization*, New York, 1951, p. 68.
[3] The principal outlines of this plan were the work and the brainchild of Jean Monnet, but it was the merit of Robert Schuman, then French Foreign Minister, that he grasped the significance of this plan and made it the principal objective of government policy. It has entered into history as the Schuman Plan.

tariat, not merely the executive organ of the Council of Ministers; it is a separate and independent body representing the Community as a whole, not the individual member states, and it acts for the Community in an executive fashion. Thus, for instance, in a series of international negotiations designed to effect large cuts in tariffs and carried out under the auspices of the General Agreement on Tariffs and Trade (GATT), the most recent phase of which was called the "Kennedy Round," the Commission negotiated for the Community as a whole. When the United States negotiates tariff cuts with the Community, it deals exclusively with the Commission and not with the individual member states (France, Germany, Italy, Belgium, the Netherlands, Luxembourg).

In like manner, the Court of Justice established for the European Communities acts as a general administrative and constitutional court as well as an arbitrator and may set aside both national and supranational acts which it finds to be violating the treaties that established the Communities.

Hence these Communities have become realities, not only on a high political level, but also in the daily business life of the countries concerned. Innumerable economic and business activities are carried out within the purview of the Commission's regulations, and numerous cases are placed before national and international tribunals dealing with interpretation of the regulations.

It would be going much too far to call these Communities "states" or "super-states." They are not. But neither are they international organizations like the OAS and the UN. They are essentially new types of organisms exercising defined functions which in nonmember states are considered part of the traditional functions of a sovereign government, and they have begun to have both a constitutional and a political life of their own. Originally it was envisaged that directly elected legislative assemblies would also be established. Failure to make this explicit in 1950 and in 1955 is now seen as an error. Thus far this has been prevented, largely but not exclusively by France, and the present European Parliament is merely a body of delegates from the respective national parliaments. It may, however, be confidently expected that once the present difficulties are overcome, a parliament whose members will be directly elected in the respective countries will make its appearance. In that case, "Community politics" will take on a new form which at present cannot even be imagined. However, even now there is a political content to these Communities, and they are therefore fully entitled to be considered within the framework of the comparative study of government.

1

The evolution of an idea: concepts of European unity, old and new

Since time immemorial, mankind has stubbornly and persistently had dreams and visions of unity. Ravaged by war, joined and rent apart by the ambitions of princes and potentates, made fearful by the uncertainty of fate and long periods of lawlessness and desolation, the people of Europe have revived time and again a vision of unity in which law rather than force would prevail and in which people might live in peace.

This dream has had several roots. One without doubt was a somewhat glorified memory of the Roman Empire which, despite its wars and shortcomings, left a memory of a thousand years of relative stability, peace, and law. The contrast between it and the dark ages which followed made this memory appear particularly bright.[1]

[1] It is not my intention to dismiss the Middle Ages simply as the "dark ages." This would not be fair in view of the many important cultural and spiritual achievements of that period. However, from the standpoint of statecraft, it was a period much of which was characterized by an uncommon degree of lawlessness and arbitrariness, in which few institutions of lasting value were created, and which therefore compares unfavorably with both the preceding and the following periods. In that sense the derogatory term, "dark ages" has its justification.

Another important root may be found in the tenets of Christianity, which, being a universal and not a tribal or national religion, called all mankind to a code of ethics and morality on which a stable society could conceivably be built. The fact that many concepts of the Roman law had been preserved in the canon law of the church enhanced this impression.

Of course, these ideas were not specifically "European." It would be more accurate to call them "Christian" or perhaps "Occidental." With perhaps dubious justification,[2] Europeans regarded themselves and their civilization as far superior to all others, and as we have already seen, Christianity had a universal appeal. Hence the earlier European ideas of unity or, as it was often thought of, "Christian unity," were in effect appeals to a world state.

The great Italian poet, Dante Alighieri, viewing with sadness the "endless strife of princes and cities," wrote around 1310 *De monarchia,* in which he proposed that a new monarch revitalize Roman law within a Christian world empire. His rationale was ageless: "Since the one may not take cognizance of what concerns the other, the one not being subject to the other (for a lord has no rule over his peer), there must needs be a third, or wider jurisdiction which has princedom over both."

About the same time, in 1306, Pierre Dubois wrote *De recuperatione terrae sanctae* (On the Regaining of the Holy Land), suggesting a looser federation of states, with the rulers meeting in council, and the establishment of a court with the Pope as the principal arbiter. Other ideas of European union or federation are associated with the names of Emeric Crucé (*Le Nouveau Cynèe,* 1623); of the French King Henry IV, who presented a plan, "The Grand Design," really the work of the Duke de Sully; of William Penn, who in 1693 wrote his essay *Toward the Present and Future Peace of Europe,* in which he suggested a "parliament of Europe;" of the Abbé de Saint-Pierre who in 1712 wrote his memorandum *To Restore Perpetual Peace to Europe;* and of the great German philosopher Immanuel Kant who, in 1795, in his celebrated essay *Zum ewigen Frieden* (On Perpetual Peace), advocated a confederation but recognized that this would be possible only if people first accepted for themselves a free form of government in their respective countries.

Before World War I none of these ideas assumed any practical significance. The rivalry among European states was far too great and overshadowed all other considerations. Yet after World War I, for the first time, the idea of a United Europe ceased to be the exclusive province of esoteric thinkers or the occasional and usually meaningless subject of somebody's grandiloquent statement at a suitably festive occasion, and moved closer to the political level. This development was largely due to three men, two of them statesmen of the first magnitude—Aristide Briand and Gustav Stresemann, Foreign Ministers of France and Germany respec-

---

[2] In the Middle Ages Arab civilization could, in many respects, be considered the equal if not the superior of that of Europe. The Crusades and trade relations had afforded numerous contacts between the two cultures. However, the civilizations of the Far East remained largely unknown in Europe at that time.

tively during much of the interwar period—and one the founder and animator of the Pan-Europe movement, Count Richard Coudenhove-Kalergi. Although no concrete steps toward greater European unity could be taken during that troubled period and under the shadows of Italian fascism and German national socialism, the idea was becoming more firmly rooted, especially among the younger generation.

But when the movement toward European unification took its first small but significant and concrete steps after the end of World War II, it was under the inspiration of other men and of vastly changed realities.

World War II had left large parts of Europe devastated and exhausted. Of all the European powers which had participated in the war, only Great Britain might be considered genuinely among the victors. But the long and costly struggle had left it exhausted. The true victors of the war were the new superpowers, the United States and the Soviet Union. It was clear that for the first time in Europe's recorded history the power centers of the world had moved away from Europe. No longer was the struggle between European powers tantamount to a struggle for world leadership. In effect, such a struggle had lost all sense and meaning. One could even say with the wisdom of historical hindsight that the bloody wars that had devastated Europe had been civil wars within the European and later the Atlantic civilization.

In view of these conditions and the emergence of superpowers, one might have expected the idea of a more unified Europe to be in the air. Nevertheless, it is highly doubtful that anything would have come of it had it not been for two other important factors. One was the role played by the United States, the other the presence on each side of the Atlantic of a number of inspired and at the same time hardheaded and practical statesmen.

What prompted the United States to embrace so warmly the idea of European unification? A former Dutch minister, a distinguished diplomat and business leader, who was prominently associated with the European side of the Marshall Plan, has put his impressions in these words:[3]

There was the economic concept of the large single market, which in American eyes was indispensable for a better division of labor and a higher standard of living. There was the political feeling that only a strong and unified Europe could resist Communist and internal and external pressures. There was the irritation about the fragmentation of the European continent and the fear of conflicts between European nations which had brought the U.S. twice into a world war. There was a genuine desire to transplant the blessings of the politically and economically unified state on a continental scale to the old mother countries with which the average Americans still felt such close links.

[3] E. H. Van der Beugel, "The United States and European Unity," *International Spectator*, The Hague, Apr. 8, 1965, p. 449. See also by the same author, "From Marshall Aid to Atlantic Partnership," *The Atlantic Community Quarterly*, Spring, 1966, pp. 5–16, as well as a larger study, *European Integration as a Concern of U.S. Foreign Policy: From Marshall Aid to Atlantic Partnership*, New York, 1966.

Whatever one may think of this American policy, only a very peculiar form of logic could manage to interpret it as having been primarily motivated by a desire to dominate Europe. If that had in fact been America's motivation, it would obviously have been far better to keep Europe disunited and hence weak. Nor could one say that America simply accepted the inevitable and tried to dominate it. Without America's active encouragement and cooperation, it is highly doubtful that the European Communities as they exist now would ever have seen the light of day.

It is a strange though by no means infallible rule of international politics and diplomacy that one can sometimes create a situation by acting as though it already existed. This was demonstrated by the then Secretary of State George C. Marshall at his famous Harvard University speech on June 5, 1947, in which he said: "There must be some agreement among the countries of Europe as to the requirements of the situation and the part these countries themselves will take in order to give proper effect to whatever action might be taken by this government. . . . The initiative must come from Europe."[4] The Secretary, addressing himself to "Europe" and assuming the ability of that "Europe" to act in concert in the manner he indicated, set in motion a series of activities in Europe which showed that his words had been well understood and that they had fallen on fertile soil. The immediate result was the establishment in 1948 of the Organization for European Economic Cooperation (OEEC). The pivotal significance of the OEEC for the later development of the European Community can hardly be exaggerated. Let us quote once again Van der Beugel:[5]

> The OEEC achieved remarkable results. One was a new method of cooperation. For the first time in the history of cooperation between sovereign nations, the economic policies of countries were studied, screened and criticized for an international forum. Governments learned to take into account the impact of their economic policies on neighbor countries. Government officials learned to work closely together and to approach problems not only from a national but also from a common point of view. It is not by chance that so many of the civil servants who were active in the first years of OEEC were later the prominent figures in the process of further European unification.

At that stage, American cooperation and participation were at their most intense and intimate. In inspiring and signing the North Atlantic Treaty[6] in 1949, the United States clearly identified itself fully with the defense of Europe and thus established a shield behind which European reconstruction could take place. In OEEC and the various branches of the Marshall Plan Organization, Americans were playing an important role, formally or informally. In fact, there was such easy cooperation between Americans and Europeans that it would have been difficult to

[4] U.S. *Department of State Publication 2882,* European Series, No. 25, 1947.
[5] Van der Beugel, *op. cit.,* p. 448.
[6] See pp. 727ff.

specify precisely what was an American and what was a European contribution. The American policy makers and planners were by no means unmindful of the probability that a strengthened and united Europe would inevitably become a competitor of formidable proportions. Nevertheless, there was an almost universal conviction that the benefits to be gained in stability and security as well as in a larger fashion from economic and political cooperation would far outweigh these problems. In both the Truman and the Eisenhower administrations there was no doubt that great cohesion among European countries had a very high priority. Beyond that, it was a goal broadly supported by the American people and the United States Congress.

The American initiatives were fully reciprocated by equally important European moves. Europe was fortunate to have in those days a number of distinguished, in fact great, men who understood the needs of the hour and who had grasped immediately the significance and the possibilities in Secretary Marshall's statement. Winston Churchill, then leader of the Opposition in Great Britain, had already made his famous speech at Zurich on September 19, 1946, in which he advocated "recreating the European family, or as much of it as we can, . . . a kind of United States of Europe." But later, when he returned to head the British government, he pulled back from that statement, at least as far as Britain itself was concerned, by saying that "Britain was in Europe but not of it." On the other hand, Foreign Secretary Ernest Bevin had been the quickest in responding to Secretary Marshall's invitation and had been instrumental in organizing the European response, although the full implication of greater European unity was no more welcome to him, as far as Britain was concerned, than it later became to Churchill. In that fact one could see once more that the British do have a truly national policy in foreign affairs, in force whichever party happens to be in power and even if, as is quite possible, that policy may be wrong.

More significant with regard to European unification was the response on the European continent. In France it was expressed especially by Robert Schuman and Jean Monnet, in Germany by Konrad Adenauer, in Italy by Alcide de Gasperi, and in Belgium by Paul-Henri Spaak. They had much in common. Three of them, Schuman, Adenauer, and De Gasperi, were devout Catholics and keenly aware of the transnational significance of their religion. For a while, some of their more intractable opponents referred to their idea as the "international of the Vatican." But this unjust and supercilious characterization never took hold and was soon forgotten, because there were too many non-Catholics equally interested in the idea of a unified Europe. The same three men have often referred to themselves as "men of the border." Robert Schuman was born in Lorraine when that province was under German rule, and he obtained his legal education at the University of Strasbourg when it was a German university.[7] He was bilingual, speaking French and German

---

[7] There is a widespread belief that Schuman served in the German army in World War I. This was not the case. He avoided military service altogether in order not to fight his country, France.

with equal fluency. Alcide de Gasperi was born in the Trentino region when it belonged to Austria-Hungary and served for a while as a deputy in the Austrian parliament before World War I. He too was bilingual, speaking German as fluently as his native Italian. Although Adenauer was never anything but a German, he was born and lived all his life in the Rhineland, where French cultural influence has always been strong. Shortly after World War I he was even implicated, though without definite proof, in some of the separatist activities, i.e., local moves tending to separate the Rhineland from Germany. He always felt a strong kinship toward France. Spaak is not a borderlander in the same sense of Schuman, Adenauer, or De Gasperi. However, he comes from Brussels, which straddles the deep language conflict between the French-speaking Walloons and the Dutch-speaking Flemings. All these men had an outlook that went well beyond national concerns, although they were all patriotic citizens and leaders of their respective countries.

Of course, like all political leaders, these men were moved by mixed motives. In particular, Adenauer could conceive of Germany's return to a respected place in the family of nations only through a closely interwoven European combination. Thus, by pursuing a policy of European integration, he was also directly advancing German interests. It is this very combination of interests which made the integration policy both stronger and more realistic.

Another important factor was the role played by Jean Monnet. This owner, until recently, of a well-known cognac firm which bears his family name had been first deputy secretary-general of the League of Nations, chairman of the Franco-British Economic Coordination Commission in 1939, member of the British Supply Council in Washington during the earlier part of the war, 1940–1943, and Commissioner (minister) for Armaments, Supplies and Reconstruction of the French Commission of National Liberation, 1943–1944 (General de Gaulle's government-in-exile, later government in Algiers). As chairman of the French Planning Commission during the critical postwar years, he was in an excellent position to launch many significant ideas and to backstop many others. Perhaps most significant was the unique influence which Monnet exerted in Washington. He was particularly close to both the Truman-Acheson and the Eisenhower-Dulles administrations;[8] also Secretary of State Christian Herter, as head of an important Congressional committee instrumental in the preparation of the Marshall Plan, and Under Secretary George Ball, as a private attorney, had had close relations with him. Monnet's influence was not the result of a mesmeric personality nor of impassioned pleas. He is a soft-spoken, undramatic, matter-of-fact person. As one European observer put it,[9]

It was not only because Monnet's concepts and plans fitted so well into the aims and objectives of American policy towards Europeans, it was also because he knew the secret of presenting his case in words and in a way which always convinced

[8] Van der Beugel, *op. cit.,* p. 450.
[9] *Ibid.,* p. 450.

his American friends. Whether one always agreed with Monnet or not, it is a fact that no single European has had such an impact on relations between Europe and America during these rather crucial years.

But perhaps the principal reason for the great influence and impact of Monnet and of the great European leaders lay in their intensely practical and politically realistic approach. Previous apostles of a united Europe had usually capped their plans with a blueprint and sometimes a kind of draft constitution for a politically united Europe, federal, confederal, or otherwise. Such an approach, while intrinsically logical and laudable, hurls itself against political realities and is likely, therefore, never to see fruition. To ask old and proud nations to relinquish their nationhood or at least their governmental structures, their accustomed political ways, and their independence in decision making in one gigantic leap forward, is to ask a great deal. Even for the nations of the Benelux group (Belgium, Netherlands, Luxembourg), who are so close to each other in history, economic and social composition, and forms of government, a "one leap" move to political union proved too big a step to accomplish. True, the foundation of the American union proves that such an event is not intrinsically impossible. But history knows only a very few examples where this approach succeeded and many more where it did not.

All previous plans had culminated in the drafting of a constitution for a federated Europe, had in a sense tried to build Europe from the top down. Schuman, Monnet, and the others wanted to build it from the bottom up. In that lay one of the principal innovations.

Like all great ideas, this one was essentially simple. Its proponents refrained from writing grandiloquent memoranda, or drafting constitutional documents with juridical perfection. They began with the fact that Europe had to find a way of getting on with the job of reconstructing itself, of overcoming ancient hatreds and barriers, and now that it was no longer the hub of the universe, of finding a role and a mission for itself. This clearly could no longer be undertaken by individual European countries pursuing their own exclusively national aims. The experience of the Marshall Plan, and in particular of the OEEC, had shown the benefit of collective action and had proved that it was indeed possible to work together, to pool resources, and to act in the common interest and not merely in several separate interests. The idea, then, was to start with a very modest undertaking. Let the countries concerned identify some of their most pressing problems, let them decide which could best be solved in common, let those who would, go ahead, perhaps without a detailed blueprint of action, but in the conviction that the very act of working in concert and in mutual confidence would teach the participants ways to act and how best to identify their common interests. Let those who did not feel that they could go along with this stay behind, but let them not prevent those who would go ahead from doing so. If the latter were proven right, the logic of facts would prove stronger than the logic of talk.

With that luminous simplicity which characterized his life and his words,

Robert Schuman described some of the basic ideas which inspired him and his colleagues. One thought is quoted at the beginning of Part V, another was as follows:[10]

> I repeat again, it is not a matter of erasing ethnic and political frontiers. They are given factors of history; we do not hold the pretensions of correcting history, nor of inventing a streamlined and directed geography. What we want is to take away from the frontiers their rigidity, I would even say their intransigent hostility.

So far these were merely ideas, and ideas, no matter how wonderful and sublime, do not often change the course of events unless they can be translated into action and in particular into institutions. In their determination to deal with this fact is where the great strength of the founders of the European Communities lay. Monnet, quoting another writer, Amiel,[11] said that "it is institutions which control the relations between men, it is they which are the true support of civilization."[12]

The first and indispensable institutional step was the creation of the European Coal and Steel Community, the so-called Schuman Plan. Robert Schuman himself has frankly and with characteristic modesty given all the credit for the inception of this idea to Jean Monnet.[13]

> May I be permitted to underline here the exceptional merits of a man who himself is exceptional, of my friend Jean Monnet. It was Jean Monnet who, with his collaborators, sketched out in a few months, in a small hotel in the Rue Martignac, the ideas of the Coal and Steel Community, without publicity, unknown to the public and even to the government.

To this author Schuman once described how Monnet had made two copies of his proposal, handing one to the Prime Minister, Georges Bidault, who did not grasp its significance, and the other to Schuman, who immediately was electrified. The American Secretary of State at the time, Dean Acheson, has described how this project was first broached to the American government, without whose support Schuman did not think he could approach his future partners.[14]

> But to return to Paris in 1950, on the drive into town Bruce[15] told me that Schuman would call on me at the Ambassador's residence. Only Bruce, Schuman, his interpreter and I were to be present. This was puzzling. . . . We racked our brains to think of any reason for a Sunday call. We soon found out. After a few words of greeting and appreciation for my coming to Paris, Schuman began to expound what later became known as the "Schuman Plan," so breathtaking a step toward

---

[10] Schuman, *op. cit.*, p. 33.

[11] Henri-Frédéric Amiel, *Fragments du journal intime,* Geneva, 1897, 12th ed.

[12] Michael Curtis, *Western European Integration,* New York, 1965, p. 16.

[13] Schuman, *op. cit.*, p. 164.

[14] Dean Acheson, *Sketches From Life of Men I Have Known,* New York, 1959, pp. 36–37.

[15] David K. Bruce, then American Ambassador to Paris.

the unification of Western Europe that at first I did not grasp it. The whole French-German production of coal and steel would be placed under a joint high authority, with an organization open to the participation of other European nations. . . . Back he went to the central theme, the unity of Europe, the end of national rivalries in a new, spacious and vastly productive Europe. As he talked, we caught his enthusiasm and the breadth of his thought, the rebirth of Europe, which, as an entity, had been in eclipse since the Reformation.

The Schuman Plan was designed to meet a number of vital objectives. There was the indispensable, yet difficult task of establishing Franco-German friendship and collaboration without which no collective action and progress were possible. And that, only a few years after the harsh German occupation of France had ended. There was the task of pooling the European coal and steel resources, in particular those of France and Germany, and making them intertwine in such a way that they could no longer be separated and help drive nations apart. Within this broader settlement the poisonous issue of the Saarland, which had twice endangered Franco-German relations, was to be defused, subject to a later, permanent settlement. The plan also provided for a relatively painless end to Allied control over the German economy and in particular over the rich Ruhr Basin and for replacing it in fact with Franco-German control.

What was planned here was more than a free-trade area, more than a cooperative enterprise, or an international committee, many of which were in existence. What was planned here was no less than the creation of an international authority with power to fix prices, control the flow of labor, assure the flow of raw materials, settle disputes, and assess penalties. In other words, a supranational authority was proposed which, within a limited but important sector, was to regulate the conduct of the citizens and enterprises of its member countries, to exercise vast rights which hitherto no government had allowed to escape from its sole and exclusive control. To say that these functions were economic and not political misses the point. The exercise of such rights even, or perhaps particularly, when concerned with economic subjects is in itself a political act.

Nevertheless, Schuman and Monnet saw very clearly that the success of their venture would produce the demand and need for further collaborative action and regulation and that the result of that in turn would be further and growing political integration. This still did not mean the creation of superstate blueprints. What it did mean was that as each stage was tested, as the participants saw the necessity and the wisdom of further and more sophisticated cooperation, as they learned in the doing how to work with one another and how to gain a better understanding of their common interests, they would, by the logic and the necessity of this evolution, approach one integrative stage after another in due time. Each stage therefore would first be tested, and by its success create the readiness for the next step. Nobody would know exactly where the road would end, but its general direction would be clear.

The treaty establishing the European Coal and Steel Community was signed in 1951, and that institution will be discussed more fully in Chapter 3 of this section. How Robert Schuman saw the future of a few years later applies equally well to his vision of the future from the year 1951:[16]

> The economic integration which we are now about to put into reality is, in the long run, not conceivable without a minimum of political integration. This is a logically necessary complement. The new Europe must have a democratic base; the councils, the committees and the other organs should be placed under the control of public opinion—an effective control but without paralyzing action nor useful initiative. European integration should in a general manner avoid the errors of our national democracies, in particular the excesses of bureaucracy and of technocracy.

Schuman looked even farther.

> Another stage which is not mentioned in the present treaties would be more important and more difficult. It is a matter of integrating not only voters but politics. Decisions of international impact can be taken by the associated states only in common action.

What he had in mind was more than consultation, more than occasional collective diplomatic action; he was thinking of collective decisions binding on all member states and citizens. But he immediately added that he did not think Europe was ready to take such a step. To do so prematurely would be imprudent and counterproductive. What he hoped to achieve in some future time was a state of affairs where "foreign policy would no longer be the juxtaposition of antagonism but the friendly conciliation and the prevention of divergences which can be admitted and discussed without aggravation."

Just how important it was not to push matters too quickly was being illustrated through the early 1950s by the fate of the European Defense Community (EDC). The North Atlantic Treaty of 1949 had been the first collective response to Soviet belligerency and threats. As the threats did not abate, it rapidly became increasingly necessary to put Europe's defense on a firmer basis, and to raise the necessary forces, not only in America, but above all in Europe itself. It was clear that the largest reserve of manpower was to be found in Germany, but memories of German soldiers striding across Europe were still fresh and painful, and an outright call for German rearmament would be bound to run into heavy opposition and apprehension. This situation led to the proposal of an integrated European army. Although Winston Churchill had earlier proposed the creation of such an army, it was the plan of the then French Prime Minister René Pleven which accomplished the initial "squaring of the circle." He proposed a European army, integrated down

[16] Schuman, *op. cit.,* pp. 145–146.

to the battalion level, which would produce German soldiers but not a German army. Armies are prime instruments of national sovereignty, and hence such an ambitious plan clearly demanded a degree of political unity that hitherto had not been achieved. The Treaty for a European Defense Community (EDC) was signed in May, 1952, following this plan, providing for common institutions, common armed forces, and a common budget. Twelve German divisions were to be integrated into a European force under the NATO Supreme Commander. So great was the confidence that this treaty would be signed that plans were made for a European Executive Council, a Council of Ministers, a Court, a bicameral Assembly, and an Economic and Social Council. A giant step seemed to have been taken toward a supranational European community.

But this was not to be. Britain did not intend to join EDC, despite Churchill's earlier proposal, as noted previously. Germany and Italy were bound to gain greatly from the proposal and were of course for it. France proved the real stumbling block. For two years the debate dragged on under one French government after another until the summer of 1954, when the French National Assembly definitively torpedoed the treaty's ratification. Premier Pierre Mendès-France, head of the French government then in power, had introduced the measure in a lukewarm fashion clearly indicating his reservations, and had refused to fight for ratification. The adamant opposition of the Gaullists also played a significant role. Much of the opposition both in the French parliament and in the press centered on the real or imagined threat of the revival of German militarism, and had therefore strong support from the left.[17] However, only a very few months later, the same French National Assembly without great difficulty passed the West European Union Treaty, which permitted the establishment of a national German army in the strength of the same twelve divisions which had been envisaged for EDC. This clearly shows that French nationalism, rather than fear of German militarism, was the true cause of the defeat of this most ambitious effort toward European unification.

The defeat of EDC seemed like a crushing blow to those who thought that European unification had come near to accomplishment. To many contemporary observers, it seemed as though a great and hopeful movement had come to a grinding halt.

But that was underestimating the resilience and determination of the new "Europeans." Paul-Henri Spaak has been quoted as saying that "those working for European unity are fated to be constantly on the verge of either triumph or disaster."[18] And in truth, the founding fathers of European unity did not give up. They accepted the fact that the attempted leap toward military and political unity had perhaps been too great, and they settled for the somewhat less ambitious but nevertheless highly significant goal: the creation of a common European market.

The preamble to the treaty establishing the European Coal and Steel Com-

---

[17] But not from the entire left.
[18] Curtis, *op. cit.,* page 19.

munity in 1951 had already envisaged a fuller European economic community in these words: "Conscious of the fact that Europe can be built only by concrete actions which create a real solidarity and by the establishment of common bases for economic development. . . ." The treaty went even further because it laid plans for establishing a common external tariff on coal and steel imports after a five-year transitional period ending in February, 1958. Now, after the disappointment of EDC, the six countries of France, Germany, Italy, Belgium, Netherlands and Luxembourg made a new stab at European integration. The curtain raiser was a conference of their six foreign ministers in Messina, Italy, in June, 1955. Remembering that one of the reasons for the EDC's failure had been the narrowness of its objective, they decided to try for a broader approach.[19] They resolved to "pursue the establishment of a united Europe by developing common institutions, by the progressive fusing of national economies, by creating a common market and by the progressive harmonizing of social policies." A drafting committee was appointed, headed by the Belgian Foreign Minister, Paul-Henri Spaak, and it worked rapidly and submitted its report on April 21, 1956. The report was divided into three sections: the first dealt with the common market; the second with an atomic energy community; and the third with "areas requiring immediate attention" which included sources of power other than nuclear, air transport, postal services, and telecommunications.

Regarding the third area there has been little progress. However, the Spaak reports laid the foundation for two of the present Communities, the European Economic Community—Common Market, and the European Atomic Energy Community—EURATOM.

The Spaak report also spelled out a number of principles: the common market was to be a real customs union and not merely a free-trade area; it was to be more than just the abandonment of internal tariff barriers; it was to establish a common external tariff; and its development would go through a number of clear stages over a period of fifteen years. In addition, France demanded and received a number of important concessions. These involved special provisions for its overseas territories, the harmonization of social benefits, and a rather rigid timetable.

Principles and concessions alike were written into a treaty which was signed in Rome on March 25, 1957, and which created both the Common Market and the EURATOM organization. In view of their experience with France's failure to ratify the EDC treaty, the other nations delayed their ratifications until the French had decided. There was a lively debate in France with opposition coming from the Communists, who obviously opposed all action tending toward European consolidation, from the Gaullists and other nationalists who were fearful of limitations to France's sovereignty, and from other leaders such as former Premier Pierre Mendès-France who felt that the French economy was not sufficiently modernized to face

---

[19] Serge Hurtig, *The European Common Market*, Carnegie Endowment for International Peace, International Conciliation Pamphlet, March, 1958, p. 326.

foreign, especially German, competition. However, all these arguments were overcome. In the long run they were proven groundless, for it was not long before the vitality of French industry proved itself well in the new competitive situation.

Once the Treaty of Rome had been ratified by France, the other member countries soon ratified also, and the treaty came into effect on January 1, 1958.

Before we turn to an analysis of these three important European Communities—Coal and Steel, Atomic Energy, and the Common Market—let us take a look at the idea of European consultative assemblies and particularly at the Council of Europe.

2

The Council of Europe

The trend toward greater European cooperation and cohesion has manifested itself at all levels of governmental activities, the executive, the judiciary, and the legislative. It is therefore not surprising that the creation, and even proliferation, of European assemblies has been a post-World War II phenomenon.

Two principal and quite different concepts inspired those who created these assemblies. The one, more ambitious idea was that of a great European assembly in which all problems of common concern would be discussed, in which inspiration would strike and create new common institutions, and in which the foundation for settlement of differences would be laid in grand debates.

The second, more modest hope was tied to the growth of the executive authorities of the new European Communities, especially the High Authority of the European Coal and Steel Community and the Commission of the European Economic Community. Here the function of the assemblies was to be similar to that which national parliaments exercise regarding their governments: appointing and confirming members of the executive authorities, discussing and debating the budgets, enacting legislation, and dealing with quasi-legislative matters.

Although the aims of the second type of assembly have come slightly closer to fruition, neither of these aspirations has as yet been fulfilled. But international assemblies have nevertheless played an important role in the growing development of European cooperation.

The first of these assemblies was the Council of Europe, whose statute was signed in London on May 5, 1949, on behalf of the governments of Belgium, Denmark, France, Ireland, Italy, Luxembourg, the Netherlands, Norway, Sweden, and the United Kingdom (Great Britain). Since then, seven other countries have joined: Germany, Turkey, Greece, Austria, Switzerland, Sweden, and Cyprus. One of its remarkable and significant features was Britain's membership, which seemed at that time a significant step of Britain "toward Europe." There had been a number of important statements favoring such a step from British leaders, especially Winston Churchill who had already declared during the war, "Hard as it is to say 'no,' I trust that the European family may act unitedly as one under a Council of Europe."[1] Later, in his famous Zurich speech of September 19, 1946, he once again affirmed these ideas. His Labor-party opposite number, Clement Attlee, had already declared in 1939 that "Europe must federate or perish,"[2] and later the Attlee government's Foreign Secretary, Ernest Bevin, had said on January 22, 1948, "I believe the time is ripe for a consolidation of Western Europe," but all these hopeful British statements proved somewhat less than decisive when it came time to act.

Paul-Henri Spaak of Belgium, Georges Bidault of France, and Count Carlo Sforza of Italy, Foreign Ministers of their respective countries, had lent their weight to the creation of a consultative assembly, supported by the Treaty of Brussels of 1948, in which the governments of Britain, Belgium, France, Holland, and Luxembourg had provided for "economic, social and cultural collaboration, and collective self-defense." Yet when Bidault made the first official proposal for such a European parliament, the British government first introduced a counterproposal for a purely governmental body. Then, when they realized the strength of feelings on the Continent, they did accept the idea of a European assembly and proposed to take part in it. Their determination was probably enhanced by the fact that the subsequent agreement establishing the Committee of Ministers as well as the Consultative Assembly, which together form the Council of Europe, very nearly coincided with the signing of the North Atlantic Treaty on April 4, 1949. No doubt the fact that America strongly favored such a development also played its role.[3]

The work of the Council of Europe began with a split between two tendencies. On one side there were continental federalists, like France's André Philip, who wanted to progress immediately to the drafting of a supranational charter outlining the structure of a strong political organization. On the other side there were individualists like those in Great Britain who were highly dubious of any such approach

---

[1] George Lichtheim, *The New Europe Today and Tomorrow,* New York, 1963, p. 17.
[2] A. H. Robertson, *The Council of Europe: Its Structure, Functions, and Achievements,* New York and London, 1961, 2d ed., pp. 2–3.
[3] Robertson, *ibid.,* pp. 5–6.

and who favored cooperation of governments and citizens, as well as parliaments, regarding matters of common concern. The actual nature of the Council of Europe was far closer to the British concept, having the power of recommendation only and including only a nonpermanent or semipermanent Committee of Ministers.

The Consultative Assembly of the Council of Europe is composed of representatives chosen, since 1951, by the parliaments of the member countries.[4] All the representatives are members of their respective national parliaments. The number of delegates assigned to each country reflects the size of its population without being exactly proportionate.[5] The largest delegations, those of Great Britain, France, Germany, and Italy, have eighteen members each. In Britain the delegation is appointed by the government, but only after informal consultations and agreement between the party leaders. In all other countries the delegates are elected by the respective national parliaments. Politically, they divide approximately on the same basis as do the various political parties in each member country. However, this is not completely the same, as no parliament has elected or appointed Communists to the Council in view of their total opposition to the institution of the Council. There has also been a tendency to exclude those parliamentarians whose views are completely opposed to all concepts of European cooperation.

Since the delegates to the Consultative Assembly of the Council of Europe have been elected to their seats in their respective national parliaments on the basis of national, not European, issues, they represent only themselves and their consciences when they come to the European Assembly. An interesting innovation is that they are seated in the Assembly chamber (which is built like that of other parliamentary assemblies in Europe) in alphabetical order, not by national groups nor by party groups. This was done deliberately to deemphasize both political and national divisions and to focus on the common problems of Europe. Understandably, the noble aspirations of this principle were not wholly fulfilled; delegates tended to be conscious of their national origin although formal groups were not organized along national lines. The formal groups are organized along political lines which, because of the similarity of political parties on the European continent, are Christian Democrat, Liberal,[6] and Socialist.

On paper the competence of the Council of Europe is very large, including economic, social, cultural, scientific, legal, and administrative matters, as well as "the maintenance and further realization of human rights and fundamental freedom," in fact, almost everything except defense, although that too has come in for

---

[4] The first delegates were chosen by their respective governments.
[5] Compare the similar system of the Federal Council (*Bundesrat*) in Germany.
[6] The word "liberal" is to be understood in the European, not the American sense. It generally connotes a party of somewhat progressive intellectual orientation, often anticlerical, but tending to favor free enterprise and government nonintervention in the national economy. Examples of such parties are the Liberal party of Britain, the Radical party of France, and the Free Democratic party of Germany.

debate very frequently.[7] Its membership is the largest of any European assembly. But in reality the Council lacks power. This absence of power is noticeable in both the Committee of Ministers and the Consultative Assembly. The Committee of Ministers may make recommendations to member governments, but only on a unanimous vote, and its decisions are not binding; nor are those of the Consultative Assembly, whose position is already clearly indicated by the word "Consultative." This has virtually vitiated the functions of the Committee of Ministers, since its lack of power stands in contrast to the strength of all the other Councils of Ministers in the various other European organizations and Communities.

The Committee of Ministers meets twice a year for brief periods, but actually most of the work is done by deputies who meet once a month and who are senior officials. Some of them are also the permanent representatives of their countries at the seat of the Council of Europe in Strasbourg, while others come specially for meetings from their respective national capitals.

Both the Committee of Ministers and the Consultative Assembly are aided by an able Secretariat, headed by a Secretary-General and a Deputy appointed by the Consultative Assembly on the recommendation of the Committee of Ministers. The role of the Secretary-General has varied with time and the personality of the incumbent, but in no case has it approximated the role of comparable offices in other European organizations.

In a series of controversies with the Committee of Ministers, the Consultative Assembly has been able to increase its functions, but such gains as it has been able to make have been largely with regard to its procedure, its agenda, and its budget. Annual joint colloquia, attended by almost all the foreign ministers and some of the members of the Consultative Assembly, have also been held and there has been a good deal of frank discussion in them.

Those who hoped that the progressive unification of Europe would be the principal task of the Council of Europe have not seen their hope fulfilled. For that task, the Council was too large, the interests of its members too diverse, the unanimity rule scarcely conducive to concrete progress, and the Secretariat too weak to act as a true common organ of the Council toward the outside. The presence of the three neutral powers of Europe, Austria, Sweden, and Switzerland, sometimes has made discussion of certain disputed political affairs difficult. Moreover, with such countries as Great Britain, Switzerland, Turkey, Norway, and Denmark as members, there never was much hope for agreement on a structurally unified Europe. As a case in point, although the Council of Europe could have played a very useful role in the settlement of the Cyprus dispute, since it was the only organization outside the United Nations of which all contestants were members, the Council did not concern itself with this problem.[8]

[7] Kenneth Lindsay, *European Assemblies: The Experimental Period, 1949–1959,* London and New York, 1960, pp. 17–18.
[8] Michael Curtis, *Western European Integration,* New York, 1965, p. 34.

But although the Council of Europe has not moved Europe toward greater organic unity or federalism, it has nevertheless made significant contributions in other and important ways. First and foremost, it has been the principal platform for the discussion of European ideas, especially in the period before the formation of the three European Communities. It was the forum before which all the great ideas of European integration were widely debated, the Schuman Plan, the plan for a European army, and others. In their development the Consultative Assembly has not only played a significant role as an important way station, but has also functioned as an eminently important educational device. Because of their very absence of power, the delegates were able to speak with considerable freedom. They returned to their respective national parliaments with a keener understanding of common interests and with greater appreciation for the concerns of other countries. This recognition often resulted in various forms of national legislation, on which those parliamentarians who had served in the Consultative Assembly could now speak with greater knowledge and understanding.

Second, the Council of Europe has attempted to act as a connecting link between the growing number of European organizations and has been frequently the cause of, or an important contributor to, common action.

Third, the Council of Europe performs an important liaison function between itself and a large number of world-wide organizations, as well as nongovernmental groups such as labor unions. Sixty-four nongovernmental international organizations now have consultative status with the Council of Europe. Also, certain states which are not members either because of political objections, such as Spain, or because they are not European countries, such as Israel, have sent observers and participate in certain aspects of the Council's work.

Fourth, the Council has proposed and stimulated a considerable number of international conventions and treaties, not all of which of course have been ratified or adhered to by all the members. A particularly important document of this kind was the European Social Charter which was signed in Turin in 1961. Its objective was to promote the social welfare and increase the standard of living of the peoples of Europe. It concerns itself with general social policy including certain fundamental rights such as the right to work, to form labor unions, to social security, and to social and medical assistance. It establishes minimum standards to be raised gradually.

Fifth, the Council for Cultural Cooperation was created on January 1, 1962, taking on the cultural work hitherto conducted by several bodies within the Council of Europe framework. Its work has been primarily in the field of education. The progress achieved is indicated by the growing tendency within the European family to regard cultural and educational affairs as more than mere appendanges of foreign policy, and to transfer them to officials specializing in various technical fields.[9]

There have also been a number of studies in cultural affairs and endeavors to

[9] Curtis, *op. cit.,* p. 41.

arrive at mutual recognition of university degrees, to stimulate university exchanges, and university courses on European problems. In addition, important efforts are underway to produce textbooks on European history which will be free from the national biases and recriminations which have characterized such books in the past.

Sixth, the Council of Europe system has made significant contributions to Europe's legal unification by its work on human rights and its establishment of a European Court of Justice. Europeans had been appalled by the violation of the most elementary human rights and requirements for human dignity committed by the Nazis and by others, especially the Communists. Many Europeans wanted a charter of human rights which would form a foundation both for improvement of conditions and for the prosecution of offenders. But the Universal Declaration of Human Rights drafted by the United Nations disappointed many people, and their disappointment gave impetus to a congress called in the Hague in 1948 which urged a stronger and more detailed European declaration of human rights and a court of justice to watch over its implementation. The Consultative Assembly, in September, 1949, recommended a draft convention, following the British concept of precise definitions rather than the Continental tradition of general principles. In November, 1950, the European Convention for the Protection of Human Rights and Fundamental Freedoms was signed in Rome, and it came into effect in September, 1953, after ten countries had ratified it. There are now seventeen signatories, though France and Switzerland are not among them. Particularly significant is the willingness of ten countries to permit individuals to make application to the Court of Justice, and of eight countries to recognize the Court's compulsory jurisdiction. Thus, in contrast to the United Nations, the Council of Europe and especially the Court of Justice have concrete responsibilities and powers in the field of human rights.[10]

The European Commission of Human Rights is composed of seventeen members, one from each ratifying nation, mostly jurists of high repute, who are appointed for a term of six years and who are supposed to act as individuals rather than as representatives of their respective countries. The Commission has both a quasi-judicial and a conciliatory role to play.

The Court of Justice is composed of fifteen judges elected by the Consultative Assembly for a period of nine years. The judges are nominated by their governments but, like the judges of the International Court of Justice, are independent and include some of the most distinguished jurists of Europe. Individuals cannot present cases to the Court, although with the permission of their governments, they can present cases to the Commission. The relationship between the Commission and the Court is a unique and interesting one, with the former acting as an advisor to the latter.

---

[10] In several European countries, domestic courts have made reference to the European Convention on Human Rights in their decisions. Eight countries, among them Germany, have reenacted the Convention as part of their national legal system.

Although this setup provides interesting innovations, it is a rather cumbersome system, in which the lines of jurisdiction are not always clearly drawn. In particular the Commission has extended its role to become a quasi-judicial body, while the Court has acted much more restrictively on its own jurisdiction. The Committee of Ministers has also been called upon to act in this field because not all members of the Council of Europe have accepted the Court's jurisdiction.

The Court of Justice of the Council of Europe has been overshadowed by the Court of the European Communities. Moreover, the facts that France did not ratify the Convention for the Protection of Human Rights and that Britain and Italy have placed considerable limitations on the Court's jurisdiction have hampered it. Nevertheless, the establishment of the European Convention on Human Rights and the organization of the Commission and of the Court have been important milestones.

The proposal by the Consultative Assembly that a European supreme court should be established in order to interpret the numerous European conventions formulated under the auspices of the Council of Europe has not been adopted. Nevertheless the various organs and conventions described above have contributed greatly to a measure of legal unification and have provided the indispensable preparation for the more far-reaching legal setup established by the European Communities.

One might sum up by saying that the significance of the Council of Europe has been more historical than contemporary. Some of its hopes have not been realized; some of its functions have been taken over within a more limited area but with greater power by the Communities. Nevertheless, the Council of Europe continues to provide a forum and an organizational framework which function and which can be called upon again as further steps are taken toward European common action beyond the confines of the Communities.

3

The dawn of Community: the European Coal and Steel Community — Schuman Plan

The birth of the European Coal and Steel Community constituted a tremendous step forward for Europe. A leading authority sums it up in these words:[1]

> The Coal and Steel Community is empowered to make policy binding on the governments as well as the coal and steel industries directly under its sway. It has a taxing, lending, borrowing, planning and rule-making capacity in excess of any other existing international agency. Within its framework, national trade associations, trade unions, political parties and civil servants constantly meet, debate, and seek to influence policy.

[1] Ernst B. Haas, *The Uniting of Europe: Political, Social and Economic Forces, 1950–1957*, Stanford, Calif., 1958, p. 29.

But all this was not easily achieved. There were some German apprehensions, especially in conservative quarters, but the prospect that the Schuman Plan would abolish the degrading and unworkable control of the International Ruhr Authority compensated very largely for that.[2] There was also a bitter personal struggle between the German Chancellor, Konrad Adenauer, and the leader of the Social Democrats, Kurt Schumacher. Under the latter's influence, and as long as Schumacher lived, Germany's opposition party consistently opposed the Schuman Plan and the Coal and Steel Community, although a more positive view existed among its rank and file, especially in labor unions, which eventually exerted itself.

In Italy, opinion was generally favorable, despite opposition on the left, largely because of a hope that the Schuman Plan would make for bigger markets and alleviate Italy's unemployment.

A great disappointment but hardly a surprise to the initiated was Britain's refusal to go along. Although it was a Labor government which refused adherence, the refusal reflected without doubt the attitude most generally shared by Britons of both political parties. In particular there was an unwillingness to accept the idea of a supranational authority. But this was precisely the point on which Schuman and Monnet did not yield.[3] The British decision did not substantially delay or hamper the work of the six governments who decided to go ahead without Britain. The only loser was Britain itself, which much later found it necessary to apply for membership under infinitely more difficult conditions and thus far without success.

In France, however, the very cradle of the Schuman Plan, this scheme for a Coal and Steel Community came under a great deal of fire. General Charles de Gaulle, then out of power, condemned the plan with the scathing remark, *"un méli-mélo de charbon et d'acier"* (a hodge-podge of coal and steel),[4] and his principal lieutenant in parliament, Michel Debré, mounted one of his customary furious attacks against the plan. But at that time the Gaullists did not have much influence in France, and hence the main attack came from the extreme left and was orchestrated on an all-European basis. Representatives of the Communist parties of the prospective member countries of the Coal and Steel Community, Germany, France, Italy, Holland, Belgium, and Luxembourg, attacked the proposal furiously on July 4, 1950, on the grounds that it was "dictated by American imperialists in preparation for war against the Soviet Union and the people's democracies." This was the general line. Apart from that, the tune varied. In France, where the Communists operated in edifying conjunction with the Gaullists, they conjured up the

---

[2] Hans A. Schmitt, *The Path to European Union: From the Marshall Plan to the Common Market,* Baton Rouge, La., 1962, pp. 63–67.

[3] In a conversation Robert Schuman told this author that he felt that if the British had joined, it would only have been for the purpose of slowing down or delaying the authority of the supranational body.

[4] John Goormaghtigh, *European Coal and Steel Community,* Carnegie Endowment for International Peace Conciliation Pamphlet, May, 1955, p. 351.

spectre of German economic domination. The Belgian Communists predicted the wholesale deportation of unemployed miners to the Aachen pits.[5]

Next to the attack by the enraged, there was the attack by the timid. Some labor unions criticized the plan for failing to give equal weight to social and economic problems. More conservatively inclined critics felt that a free-enterprise country, like Belgium, for example, could not join such an elaborately planned economic design without disaster. And in every country there were special interests who felt that their particular industry had to become substantially stronger before it could successfully stand up to the competition of the others.

Against all these counsels of hostility, timidity, and despair, the "founding fathers" led by Robert Schuman and Jean Monnet stood firm, like rocks. They and their equally determined colleagues, Adenauer, De Gasperi, and Spaak, proved the valuable lesson of politics that in a crisis, character and vision are the decisive qualities which separate the statesmen from the politicians. Robert Schuman put it this way:[6]

> The hard lessons of history have taught the man of the border that I am, to be suspicious of hasty improvisations, of too ambitious projects, but they have also taught me that when an objective judgment, seriously thought through and based on the realities of facts and of the higher interests of men, leads to new initiatives, even revolutionary ones, it is imperative—even if they hurt established customs, worldly antagonisms and ancient routines—to hold firm and to persevere.

There were a number of difficult issues for which solutions had to be found. Among them was the demand of the Belgian mine industry for subsidies to gear their mines to a more competitive position. Another controversy developed over antitrust provisions of the draft treaty. The attitude of these provisions, which were modeled on American theory and practice, was new to most Europeans, but it was sternly upheld by Monnet, who reminded his colleagues that in the past cartels had reduced production whereas the Schuman Plan proposed to increase it.[7] The French point of view won, aided by some American pressure.

There was also a dispute over the geographic scope of the treaty, especially since Italy was dependent on Algerian iron ore; and there was a debate about the authority of the new supranational executive over setting wages. The latter issue was not really resolved, but labor's claims received indirect recognition when it was decided in a "gentlemen's agreement" (not incorporated in the treaty), that one of the members of the supranational High Authority would be nominated by labor. Even the seat of the Community remained in dispute. Luxembourg was chosen pro-

---

[5] Schmitt, *op. cit.*, pp. 64–65; H. W. Ehrmann, "The French Trade Associations and the Ratification of the Schuman Plan," *World Politics*, Vol. VI (1954), pp. 453–481.
[6] Robert Schuman, *Pour l'Europe*, Paris, 1963, p. 14.
[7] Schmitt, *op. cit.*, p. 72.

visionally. (It became in time the Community's permanent seat although no formal decision was made.)

Finally the treaty was signed, on April 18, 1951. It was as "European" in form as possible. It was printed in Louis XIV type with German ink on Dutch vellum, bound in Belgian parchment, and adorned with a marker of Italian silk.[8] It was to be symbolic of European unity and collaboration.

THE INSTITUTIONS OF THE EUROPEAN COAL AND STEEL COMMUNITY

The institutions of the European Coal and Steel Community (ECSC) are: (1) the High Authority; (2) the Special Council of Ministers; (3) the Common Assembly; and (4) the Court of Justice. The French government, then more supranationally inclined than later, wanted a small High Authority responsible only to the Common Assembly and was reluctant to accept a Council of Ministers favored by the Benelux countries, who were concerned over possible big-power domination of the High Authority. There was no need for a special decision on the official language or languages to be used; all four languages of the six member countries, French, German, Italian, and Dutch,[9] were equally admissible.

The ECSC established a special form of double executive which became also the form later adopted by the Common Market and EURATOM. One might speak of a "national" and of a "supranational" part of the executive. The "national" executive is the Council of Ministers. The "supranational" executive is the general executive arm of the Community, the High Authority. It has a good deal of legislative and judicial power also. Article 8 of the Treaty of Paris stipulates that the High Authority is "responsible for showing the fulfillment of the purposes stated" in the treaty.[10]

The High Authority is composed of nine members chosen for their "general competence" (Art. 9), which may be presumed to mean that they need not be experts, and which in fact means that political considerations play a large role in their selection. This is not unjust, since their political skill and understanding will largely determine their success or failure. Eight of the nine members of the High Authority (called High Commissioners) are appointed by the member governments by agreement among them. These High Commissioners in turn elect a ninth, who is, by tacit agreement as we have seen, a man nominated by the labor movements. The members of the High Authority are elected for a period of six years.

An unusual feature of the treaty provided for a slightly different mode of election for the first slate of High Commissioners than for their successors. Complete agreement was required among the member countries at the outset—presum-

[8] *The Times,* London, Apr. 18, 1951, quoted by Schmitt, *op. cit.,* p. 76.
[9] Belgium is linguistically divided between French-speaking Walloons and the Flemings, whose language is virtually identical with Dutch.
[10] For the partial text of this and other European regional treaties, see Ruth C. Lawson, *International Regional Organizations: Constitutional Foundations,* New York, 1962.

ably in order to give the Community a good start. Since then three High Commissioners retired every other year, and the vacancies were alternately filled by cooption and by election. In the latter case, a five-sixth majority was sufficient. One-third of the membership of the High Authority is reviewed every two years. However, if a government has already voted against two persons for individual appointment and against four persons when there is a general or biennial renewal of membership, its further attempt to veto may be referred to the Court of the Community by another government, and that Court may declare the veto to have been abused and may declare it null and void.

The President and Vice President of the High Authority are chosen for two years and by the same procedure as prevails for the election of members, that is, by the governments. As these lines are written the High Authority has had four presidents, Jean Monnet, René Meyer, a former French Prime Minister, Piero Malvestiti, a former Italian minister, and Dino Del Bo, a former Italian professor and political personality. In this method of selection, care for both the autonomy of the High Authority and for the rights of national governments is in evidence.

The High Authority operates as a collegiate body under a quorum which must be more than half its membership. It issues decisions which are binding in all their details; recommendations which are binding with regard to their objectives, leaving open the specific means for meeting them; and opinions which are not binding (Art. 14). When decisions and recommendations have an individual character, they are binding upon notification of the interested person, group, or authority; in all other cases they become effective upon publication.

In order to exercise these vast functions, the High Authority operates through a system of working parties, each of which consists of two men concerned with one of the specific fields under the jurisdiction of the High Authority, to wit, transport, external affairs, social affairs, economic affairs, coordination of energy, the common market of coal and steel, finance, and rules of competition. Each member of the High Authority has a special field of responsibility but is also a member of one or two other working parties. These working parties meet at least once a week and present their recommendations to the High Authority as a whole, which then acts by majority vote.

Within its general responsibility for establishing a common market for coal, iron ore, and scrap metal for ordinary and special steels, the ECSC is responsible for the elimination of import restrictions, tariff barriers, and open and hidden subsidies to industries including tax concessions, the ending of the discriminatory freight-rates, the guaranteeing of conditions of equality to producers for the supply of raw materials, the publication of prices and their maintenance, the free choice by consumers of their suppliers and carriers, decartelization, and the suppression of other practices which interfere with competition, such as undue price-fixing through fusions and production or distribution control.

Among other functions under the special responsibility of the High Authority are the promotion of technical and economic research concerning coal and steel industrial safety, the financing of programs to eliminate featherbedding, the granting or guaranteeing of loans for industrial investment, and financial aid for the purpose of maintaining workers' earning capacity or for retraining, housing, and the like. Should there be serious under- or over-production, quotas may be allocated which may be correspondingly large or small. The High Authority may undertake plans for compensation against price differential and it may supervise the issuance and control of export and import licenses for coal and steel trade. A number of studies are constantly being carried out to supervise existing trends.

In many direct and indirect ways, the High Authority can also affect investment by providing useful information and advice as well as financial aid. The High Authority must be notified three months in advance of an investment program. If its advice is negative, the chances of an enterprise obtaining the necessary investments are materially reduced. The High Authority has played an important role here, granting investment aid for industrial development and modernization, of which Germany has received approximately one-half. However, the High Authority has been criticized for its habit of channeling investments largely to the industries of the country in which the funds were raised.[11] The High Authority has labored significantly to aid depressed areas and has helped through housing and social welfare to increase labor mobility. While it cannot raise social security provisions of national laws, it can prevent the payment of substandard wages. The High Authority has also undertaken useful studies in the field of industrial hygiene and mine safety, and has generally contributed to the improvement of the conditions of work.

In order to accomplish all these things, the High Authority is granted considerable powers. We have already seen the forms of directives which it may issue. It can fine industries which have unfairly reduced wages, it can fix production quotas, it can approve price-compensation schemes, it can issue rules concerning trusts and can establish maximum or minimum prices under certain conditions of shortage or crisis.

These powers are indeed formidable, and what is more important, they are truly supranational. However, it would not be accurate to say that the High Authority has always exercised them to their fullest extent. Subsidies are outlawed, but they have in fact found their way back into use in a number of cases, in both direct and indirect forms. In fact, the situation has gotten out of hand to such an extent that the High Authority has proposed legal control of national subsidies and the necessary revision of the Treaty of Paris to that effect. In the field of price publicity and price alignment, the High Authority has also fallen short of full success. A number of governments have not fully complied with the decision of the High Authority calling for the publication of information about certain tariffs and prices. An initial decision by the High Authority to allow a 2.5 percent variation of prices above and below the published figures[12] was outlawed by the Court in December,

---

[11] Curtis, *op. cit.,* p. 130.
[12] The so-called "Monnet rebates."

1954. The price system within the ECSC regarding steel broke down almost completely in 1963 as a result of drastic price reductions and considerable increases in imports.

The provisions of Articles 65 and 66, on decartelization, have also not been fully observed—have, in fact, been more often violated. This has been evident in both the Ruhr industry and the French management of nationalized mines, the *Charbonnages de France*. Moreover the High Authority has approved over 200 mergers and so far has refused none. It has been argued that the industries primarily under control of the High Authority are not actually competitive by virtue of their technical needs, methods of financing, and market conditions.[13] Then, too, other sources of energy are competing and there are the familiar problems of instability of employment and resistance of workers to retraining.

In its work, the High Authority is assisted as well as controlled by the Council of Ministers, which in turn is assisted by a permanent group of deputies, the so-called Coordinating Committee (COCOR), who prepare the work and decisions of the Council and coordinate the work of the various committees and groups of experts. The voting rules of the Council are highly complicated (Art. 28). The Council makes its decision by a simple majority (plurality), a qualified majority ($\frac{2}{3}$ or $\frac{5}{6}$), or unanimously, depending on the subject matter. In addition, the votes are weighted: the vote of states producing at least 20 percent of the coal and steel of the Community—that is to say, France and Germany—is treated in a special way. For instance, in cases where concurrence of the Council is required by plurality, this may be obtained either (1) by a majority of states including the vote of one of the countries producing at least 20 percent, or (2) if the vote is equally divided and if the High Authority maintains its proposal after a second reading, by the representatives of two member states, each of which produce at least 20 percent. Decisions of the Council requiring a qualified majority or a unanimous vote also must include the vote of one of the states producing at least 20 percent.

There is also a Consultative Committee which is essentially an advisory committee to the High Authority (Art. 18). This committee consists of no less than thirty and no more than fifty-one members serving for two years and is supposed to include an equal number of producers, workers, consumers, and dealers. It has proved rather cumbersome and its usefulness has declined.

The Treaty of Paris furthermore created a parliamentary body, the Common Assembly. Later on, when the Common Market and EURATOM were created, the Common Assembly was enlarged to become the assembly for all three Communities. In 1962 it emphasized its role further by changing its name to the European Assembly though it is commonly called the European Parliament. The Common Assembly was organized with a membership of 78: 18 each from Germany, France, and Italy, 10 each from Belgium and Holland, and 4 from Luxembourg. Each country may decide how to choose its delegates, but in effect they are elected by

[13] Curtis, *op. cit.*, p. 138.

their national parliaments. The Treaty of Paris envisages a directly elected parliament in the future, but such a development remains blocked by resistance especially from France. Most of the members are members also of the Consultative Assembly of the Council of Europe, and the organization of the European Parliament follows largely the model of the Consultative Assembly, with Christian Democrat, Socialist, and Liberal groups. However, in contrast to the Consultative Assembly, the European Parliament's members are grouped physically by party caucuses and do not sit in alphabetical order.

Monnet and Schuman had hoped that the Common Assembly would become a real European parliament. It does have control over its own budget, but not over that of the ECSC as such. It also has a role to play in amendments to the Treaty of Paris and it may pass a vote of censure against the High Authority—a power which has never been used to date. In fact, thus far the endeavor of the European Parliament has been to strengthen the supranational executive rather than to weaken it. In general it discusses the policies of the Council of Ministers and of the High Authority and has been consulted on appointments.

The Treaty of Paris established a Court of Justice which in 1958, after the creation of the Common Market and EURATOM, was extended to cover all three European Communities. The Court is composed of seven judges appointed by common agreement among the governments. They hold office for six years and are reeligible. Elections occur every three years, of alternately three and four members of the Court. The Treaty does not specify the nationality of the judges, but it is unlikely that judges will be chosen from nonmember nations. The presiding judge is chosen by the other judges for a three-year term. The Court is assisted by two advocates-general who are appointed in the same manner as the judges.

Article 31 of the Treaty of Paris stipulates the functions of the Court. It deals with conflicts between member states, between the states and the organs of the Community, and between those organs. States, business enterprises, or their associates may sue the organs of the Community before the Court on certain specified grounds. A person or business which has been fined by the High Authority may appeal to the Court. Any dispute concerning interpretation of the treaty may be submitted to the Court and it may decide on the removal from office of a member of the High Authority. Significantly, the judgments of the Court must be executed in the territory of the member state and are enforced through the regular procedures of the countries concerned. To be so enforceable, the judgments of the Court have to be certified as authentic by a cabinet minister of the government concerned, but that is merely a formality.

THE RECORD OF THE EUROPEAN COAL AND STEEL AUTHORITY

In the evolution of the European Communities and in Europe's difficult progress toward greater unity, the European Coal and Steel Community has played a highly important role. Nevertheless, its record of success has been somewhat mixed. In part this is the result of the fact that ECSC was originally designed as part of a triangular system whose other two parts, the European Defense Community and an eventual political authority, have not materialized. In part it results from the fact that in recent years it has been increasingly overshadowed by the European Economic Community. And moreover it has been beset by a number of exceptionally difficult economic problems.

In particular, ECSC has labored under the disadvantage that the Treaty of Paris does not really provide for a common commercial policy, and that the right of the High Authority to affect national commercial policies is very limited indeed. In contrast to the Common Market, which is empowered by the Treaty of Rome to *establish* a common external tariff and which envisages a common foreign-trade policy, the ECSC is empowered by the Treaty of Paris only to *harmonize* external tariffs.

The ECSC organization is also deficient in transport and energy policies. In the field of transport, the work of the High Authority has concerned itself primarily with preventing rate discrimination. This has been done especially by imposing tapering rates, i.e., rates to be payable over the whole run, avoiding the more expensive separate charges for crossing parts of national territories. But the jurisdiction of the ECSC does not extend to direct control over carriers. Hence progress toward harmonization of different transport policies and railroad rates has been small, while there has been none to speak of for road and inland waterway transportation. Also there are no uniform schedules, and there still remain some special rates and discriminatory practices by indirect means.

In the field of energy policy the assumption generally held when the Treaty of Paris was signed was that coal would be in short supply while oil would be plentiful. But this picture changed. High-priced European coal became a glut on the market, while the percentage of coal utilized in the production of energy declined steadily. Other sources—oil, natural gas, water power—have risen in significance. The fact that energy control is divided among the three European Communities and that interests differ in the member countries, has made for difficulties. A common energy policy has been under discussion for some time but agreement has not been achieved. Since 1959, an interexecutive working group including representatives of the three Communities has been established, with the High Authority in the position of responsibility for preparing proposals. To date, it has succeeded only in establishing general principles by an agreement concluded in April, 1964.

There have been other crises. The steel industry found itself in need of vast investments for the purpose of modernization. In the opinion of some observers, solutions would be facilitated by granting the High Authority the right to relax certain antitrust provisions of the Treaty of Paris. Such a request was, however, denied by the Court in 1961. Similarly the coal industry, especially in Belgium, has been ailing. The High Authority's request for powers under Article 95 of the treaty to permit the relaxation of rules was denied by the Council of Ministers. The High

Authority was able, therefore, to authorize only palliatives under the more restrictive Article 37.

The steel industries have been more and more handicapped by rising costs and diminishing labor productivity, rising foreign competition, and the need for the use of expensive but low-grade iron ore, as well as structural problems. A conflict grew between groups of steel producers using higher and lower grades of ores and having varying degrees of productivity. France's demands for the increase of tariffs and of minimum price levels, and for the import of foreign coal, divided the Community. Agreement was reached when the High Authority showed unusual energy, but the long-range problem of surplus production and insufficient plant utilization remains. Moreover, the appearance of additional overseas suppliers of high-grade ore, and lowering of transoceanic transport rates due to the introduction of large cargo ships, have contributed to the reduction of iron ore production within the Community. All this has created a major problem for the retraining and relocation of approximately 200,000 miners.

Despite the above difficulties and drawbacks, the European Coal and Steel Community has definite achievements to its credit. During the first ten years of its existence, steel output expanded at an unprecedented rate—74 percent—from 42 million metric tons in 1952 to 73 million tons in 1961. In 1964 steel production increased further to 82.8 million metric tons, a 13.1 percent increase over the 1963 production figures.[14] Steel prices held relatively stable although in the 1962–1963 crises they fell by 15 percent.

In the coal sector, the Community had to take note of the fact that after an initial expansion because of an acute energy shortage, a growing share of the energy market was being won by oil: in 1962 coal provided only 47.5 percent of total energy consumption compared with 52.9 percent in 1960 and 72.5 percent in 1950. In this situation, the High Authority's task was to ensure the orderly retreat of coal at a pace which would preclude social or economic dislocation. Uneconomic pits are being closed and others regrouped and reorganized. Over 250,000 miners have left the Community's coal industry, aided by numerous programs encouraged or furthered by the High Authority.

Intra-Community trade has soared. If one fixes the volume of such trade in 1952 at an index figure of 100, then ten years later scrap increased to nearly 800 and then descended slightly to about 700, steel increased to 500, and iron ore to 300.

The record of the Authority in sponsoring housing, resettlement, and retraining programs is impressive. In the same ten-year period the High Authority's housing program covered roughly 100,000 homes for coal and steel workers at a

---

[14] *European Community Bulletin,* February, 1965. In fact, the President of the ECSC High Authority, Dino Del Bo, warned in a press conference in Japan that steel output throughout the world was tending to outstrip demand, and pointed out the need for maximum efforts by countries to increase industrial steel consumption. *European Community Bulletin,* December, 1965.

total cost of $620,000,000, of which the High Authority contributed in direct grants, loans, and funds raised, $154,000,000. In the same period resettlement and retraining programs covered 130,000 workers at an expenditure of $47,000,000.

Investments over the same ten-year period reached 9 billion dollars, toward which the High Authority provided $400,000,000. The High Authority has contributed to this record by reducing trade barriers, by combating numerous forms of national discrimination in transport rates, by abolishing special administrative taxes and by abolishing tax exemptions granting unfair advantages. The High Authority has also facilitated transport agreements and has represented members in negotiations concerning tariff concessions with outside countries, notably the United States.

The High Authority has taken the initiative in numerous dealings even where statutory authority was not completely clear. In many instances, the six governments went along with it, but not always. Especially since the advent of General de Gaulle in France, there have been growing attempts to curtail the supranational activities of the High Authority. During the 1963 steel crisis, French industrialists actually attempted, with obvious support from the French government, to abolish the High Authority and replace it by a loose association among European steel companies. This was not successful. But there has been other opposition to control by the High Authority, notably in Germany with regard to the regulation of its industry, and even in Holland, normally a country marching in the forefront of supranationalism. It is interesting to note, however, that as business and governments have become increasingly critical of the European Coal and Steel Community, labor unions have rallied more strongly in support. In April, 1967, the High Authority was merged with the Commissions of the Common Market and of EURATOM into a single European Commission. The different Community organisms, however, remained intact.

Being engaged in a pioneering venture, the men of the ECSC sometimes had to bend to the political wind in order to preserve their authority for more important issues. Perhaps one might sum up by saying that the High Authority has not always made full use of its very extensive powers, and it has been overly cautious regarding its relationship to the Council of Ministers, but that nevertheless it was the European Coal and Steel Community that established firmly the principle of European community life. Even though the ECSC has since been overshadowed by the more comprehensive EEC (the Common Market), the pioneering role of the Schuman Plan and the European Coal and Steel Community deserve praise and attention.

4

The European Economic
Community—the Common Market

The European Economic Community (EEC) is so far the most far-reaching and most important step toward European integration. It is the institution which comes first to mind when "European unity," "European integration," and their like are discussed. It is part of a concerted effort by farseeing and dedicated statesmen in Europe to guide Europe toward greater cooperation and unity. It is also the result of experience, involving both successes and failures of the past.

We have seen how the creation of the European Coal and Steel Community engendered an optimism which carried its authors forward to the far more ambitious plan of military and political integration of the European Defense Community. The failure of that plan in 1954 was a heavy blow to their hopes. Paul-Henri Spaak wrote: "The failure of EDC was a terrible blow to the idea of European integration . . . it was a blow to the whole European idea, and at that moment it was a question as to whether the efforts in this direction, which had been constant since 1948, would not be halted once and for all."[1] The Western European Union treaty (WEU) which took the place of the defunct EDC treaty, and which provided the basis for Germany's rearmament and eventual entrance into NATO seemed then "not so much a tribute to successful salvaging as a symbol of supranational failure."[2]

WEU possibly saved the Atlantic Alliance and laid the foundation for a vital German contribution to the common defense which the cold war and the consequences of the Korean War had made necessary. But it did not revive the sagging efforts for a new initiative toward further European unity. At the Messina meeting of foreign ministers in May, 1955, the representatives of the smaller European countries pressed for a further effort, but both France and Germany seemed reluctant. No doubt the High Authority of the European Coal and Steel Community played an important, dynamic part in the discussions, but once again it was Jean Monnet who, as President thereof, played a pivotal role. It is widely believed that he inspired the Spaak resolution which laid the foundation for the later Common Market by demanding "appropriate institutional means for the realization and operation" of the new organism.[3]

After the Messina meeting, Jean Monnet resigned from the presidency of the High Authority, as he had said he would, in order to devote himself to the cause of European unification under conditions which would grant him greater independence of action. Choosing carefully the men with whom he wanted to work, he founded the "Action Committee for the United States of Europe" and invited as its members a limited and highly select circle of men representing the Socialist, Christian Democratic, and Liberal parties, as well as the labor unions of the six members of the ECSC. He intended to "make the Messina resolution of June 2 a real way station on the road to a United Europe," and accepting membership on the Committee was tantamount to accepting the principle of supranational integration.[4]

The method of this Action Committee was not mass appeal or propaganda but rather close liaison with highly influential persons who had the "inside track" and who could quietly move their respective parties, labor unions, and countries along the path of European unity. When one looks over the list of the original members of the Action Committee, one sees once again Monnet's deft touch. Among the Socialist leaders were Guy Mollet of France and Erich Ollenhauer, the president of the German Social Democratic party, who together with Kurt Schumacher and then as Schumacher's successor had originally strongly attacked the European Coal and Steel Community. There were such Christian Democratic leaders as Amintore Fanfani, who later became Italian Prime Minister and Foreign Minister; Kurt Georg Kiesinger, later Chancellor of the German Federal Republic; and Theo Lefebvre, President of the Belgian Christian Social party and later Prime

---

[1] Paul-Henri Spaak, "The New Europe," *Atlantic Monthly,* September, 1958, p. 39.
[2] Hans A. Schmitt, *The Uniting of Europe: Political, Social and Economic Forces, 1950–1957,* Stanford, Calif., 1958, p. 231.
[3] *Ibid.,* pp. 232–233.
[4] Schmitt, *op. cit.,* p. 233.

Minister. There were such important Liberals and Conservatives as Maurice Faure and René Pleven of France, who had been ministers and, in the case of Pleven, Prime Minister, as well as Italy's Giovanni Malagodi and Ugo La Malfa. There were also Europe's most important labor union leaders.

The role of this Action Committee, guided by Jean Monnet and his able Dutch vice president, Max Kohnstamm, cannot possibly be overestimated. A close observer[5] described this operation as follows:

> At the same time, the Action Committee was no shapeless coalition of all parties and interests. There was no courting of the extreme right or the Communist left. Monnet recruited the men and forces he needed, no more. Remembering the opposition of big business to his projects in the past, he invited no trade association representatives. He did not splinter his phalanx with potential dissidents. As a bold, supremely confident strategist, strengthened by a cause whose success was to be his only reward, Monnet wasted no time building up pressure obliquely and by stealth. He went straight to his goal by approaching the men who counted and on whom he could count. He proselyted neither his enemies nor the masses. The former he discounted, the latter he left to the individual members of the committee.

The European Economic Community was created by the Treaty of Rome on March 25, 1957. It is commonly called the Common Market. I shall use this popular designation here frequently, but it should be remembered that this term is not entirely accurate: the European Economic Community is both more than that and less than that. It is less than a complete common market in that it does not establish a common currency, but it is more in that it has economic objectives that go well beyond those of a simple common market. They include various responsibilities to increase prosperity and expand industry, raise the standard of living, remove and prevent discrimination in economic competition, encourage the free movement of labor and capital and the free establishment of business, achieve a common agricultural policy and a common foreign-trade policy, harmonize monetary policies as well as legislation in a large number of areas, retrain and look after the employment of workers, arrive at common transportation and energy policies (except those already covered by ECSC), and aid in the development of overseas regions associated with member countries.

When the ECSC treaty was being written, its framers were anxious to establish definite rules of supranationality and specifically wrote those policies into the Treaty of Paris to benefit the High Authority. This did not seem prudent to the founding fathers of the EEC; the Treaty of Rome is therefore in some respects an enabling act designed to make it possible for the EEC to arrive at those policies more gradually. But the EEC's responsibilities are very vast, dealing with the whole range of economic activities, unlike the responsibilities of ECSC which were confined to specific industries.

[5] Schmitt, *op. cit.*, p. 235.

The European Economic Community has the following objectives:

1. To free the movement of labor, capital, and enterprise within the Community;

2. To place restraints on governmental or private actions which have discriminatory or restrictive effects, which might be used to circumvent the effects of antitrust regulations, or which would "distort competition within an area," i.e., create unfair competition;

3. To harmonize economic and social policies such as monetary and employment practices, social security policies, minimum wage lines, etc.;

4. To establish common agencies including development and adjustment funds and to share responsibility for the development of overseas territories, particularly those having "special relationships" with member countries;

5. To move toward political unity involving at least the recognition of a high degree of mutual interests, underlining an aspiration toward increasingly closer association.[6]

A leading specialist has summarized these functions in the following fashion:[7]

> The EEC has as its primary goal the creation of an area in which goods, people, services and capital will be able to circulate freely. To achieve this a customs union is created but a customs union in which attention is devoted not only to barriers between states, but to economic, financial, and social reactions that may take place in the member states. The main purpose is the abolition of trade barriers, tariffs, and quotas which is to be accomplished more or less automatically during a 12–15 year transition period, divided into three four-year stages. A series of targets is assigned to each stage, and these relate not only to progress in removal of trade barriers, but also to parallel measures of economic and social alignment. This process is to be accompanied by the establishment of a common external tariff, within which an alignment of the several economies is to go on in order to adjust differences in price and working conditions, and in productive resources. Advancement from one stage to another is dependent upon achieving these respective targets. All this is to be supervised by institutions specially set up by the treaty.

The stated objectives are economic and so are the means. The deeper motives are political and are stated clearly in the preamble to the Treaty of Rome in which the European signatory powers declared themselves "determined to establish the foundations of an ever-closer union among the European peoples."

[6] Emile Benoît, *Europe at Sixes and Sevens: The Common Market, The Free Trade Association and the United States,* New York, 1961, pp. 30–31.
[7] Leonn Lindberg, *The Political Dynamics of European Economic Integration,* Stanford, Calif., 1963, p. 4; G. F. Deniau, *The Common Market: Its Structure and Purpose,* London, 1960, pp. 59–61.

THE INSTITUTIONS OF THE EUROPEAN ECONOMIC COMMUNITY

The organizational structure of EEC follows closely that of the ECSC and was repeated by EURATOM. We find again the double executive composed of a Council of Ministers and a Commission, the Court, and the Assembly (European Parliament). The last two institutions, as we have seen, serve all three Communities.

A. The Council of Ministers

In contrast to the Council of Ministers of ECSC, the Council of Ministers of EEC consists of one delegate from each member state. However, "delegate" does not mean one person designated to serve continuously on the Council. In many instances, the delegate from each member state will be the Foreign Minister. At other times, depending on the agenda, the delegates are the Ministers of Finance or the Ministers of Economics, or the Ministers of Agriculture, and so on. In practice, the Foreign Ministers meet quite frequently, as much as two or three times a month during certain peak periods, but each meeting is likely to be relatively brief, while the Ministers of Agriculture, for instance, may meet as often or oftener, but since their responsibilities at home are usually less pressing, they may meet for a longer period. This sometimes gives them a temporary advantage over their foreign-affairs colleagues. Naturally the minister may be represented by another high official, usually a secretary of state.[8]

Although the Council of Ministers is a national body in the sense that its members each individually represent their own countries and interests, it is a supranational body at the same time because its decisions are immediately binding and applicable on all members and individual citizens within the Community.

The voting procedure in the Council of Ministers reflects both the experience of the Coal and Steel Community and the more generalized significance of the Common Market. It also reflects a determination to achieve a steady rate of progress which has been retarded but not stopped by the recent policies of the French government. The voting procedure is exceedingly complicated and is directly tied to the relationship between the Council and the Commission. On some matters the Council has the sole decision, on others the Commission can act alone. Where the Council has the right of decision, its voting procedure varies depending on the nature of the question. During the transitional period, unanimity has been required in a number of categories (although most of them were supposed to be transferred to majority voting on January 1, 1966). Unanimity is defined by Article 148, Section 3 of the Treaty of Rome to mean the unanimity of those voting. Abstentions do not prevent the adoption of Council decisions requiring unanimity.

Where a majority is sufficient, it may be a simple majority or a plurality or

---

[8] In continental Europe, where heads of the principal government departments are called ministers, their principal deputies usually carry the title of secretary of state. They are equivalent to the Under Secretary of State in the American system.

one of several types of qualified majorities. Although the treaty states that where not specifically otherwise provided for, decisions of the Council shall be reached by a simple majority vote, the fact is that most types of activities likely to come before the Council have their majority specified in the treaty. Thus a simple majority suffices in only six cases in the treaty.

There is also the practice of weighted voting, which is designed to conciliate the juridical equality of states with their functional inequality.[9] And weighted voting plays its principal role in qualified majority voting. It functions in this fashion: Germany, France, and Italy have four votes each, Holland and Belgium two each, Luxembourg one. A qualified majority means twelve votes out of seventeen. Where the Council of Ministers acts upon a Commission proposal, any combination of states may produce this majority, but in all other cases at least four states must give their assent.[10] In effect, this means that the smaller states have considerable strength unless the larger ones agree with each other and with the Commission. But no single big power can block the work of the Council. Two big powers alone cannot do so either and must obtain the support of two smaller ones. However, a single big power can further the work of the Commission because its assent to a favorable proposal from the Commission produces a more liberal voting rule, in that any combination of states may then produce a majority. This is, however, a unique innovation in this treaty.

Another interesting feature is that even when the Council acts by a qualified majority, it must reject or accept the Commission proposals in their entirety. Only by a unanimous vote can the Council formally amend proposals of the Commission. The Commission, on the other hand, can change its proposal if it wishes.

Especially specified majorities are required in a number of cases involving budgetary affairs. Here the weighting is based on the relative size of the financial contribution of the member states to the respective funds under consideration. Here again, however, care is taken that a single big power cannot block or force decisions.

On first examination, this system may seem unnecessarily complicated. Further reflection will reveal some very good reasons for it. One, already mentioned, is to prevent groups of big countries from lording it over small countries. Another is to force all countries to seek the Community interest rather than simply to trade off national interests with each other. Another is to push and facilitate collective action, the very core of the spirit of a Community.

The Council is assisted in its work by a Secretariat of some 400 people at the Community's headquarters in Brussels, headed by five directors-general who are responsible for external affairs, general affairs, internal market affairs, energy, and administration. The Council is further assisted by an unusual organization, the Committee of Permanent Representatives. Each member country keeps a perma-

---

9 Lindberg, *op. cit.,* p. 32.
10 There is one exception to this rule—Art. 44, Sec. 6.

nent delegation in Brussels whose resident head has the rank and title of Ambassador and is a member of the Committee of Permanent Representatives.[11] This group carries on the same work as the Council, meeting regularly, whereas the Council meets only at specific intervals, as explained earlier.

B. The Commission

The pivot of the entire organization of the European Economic Community is the Commission. It consists of nine members chosen for four-year terms. France, Germany, and Italy provide two commissioners each, while the remaining three member states have one each. The President and three Vice Presidents are chosen from among the members of the Council for two-year terms.

The Commission's members are appointed by the governments of the member states acting in common agreement (Art. 158) and are elected for four-year terms which may be indefinitely renewed. The unanimity provision may block the election of a new Commissioner, but it cannot be used to remove one who is already elected, even if his term has expired. Article 159 stipulates that a member of the Commission shall remain in office until provision has been made for his replacement. Only where a Commissioner can "no longer fulfill the conditions required for the performance of his duties" or where he has committed serious offenses, may he be declared removed by a judgment of the Court of Justice acting on a petition of the Council or of the Commission.

The Commissioners are selected for their "general competence," as in the case of the High Authority of the ECSC, and for their "indisputable independence" (Art. 157). That these criteria have been followed is amply witnessed by the performance of the Commission to date. The Commission is responsible to the Assembly to the extent that its members must reply to questions, and if the Assembly adopts a motion of censure against the Commission by a two-thirds majority of those voting (representing a majority of all members of the Assembly), the entire Commission must resign (Art. 144).

The Commission is aided by an executive secretariat of about sixty persons and is responsible for the recruitment and general administration of a staff of slightly under 3,000. The quality of these staffs has been extraordinarily high; in fact the equal in talent, knowledge, and devotion of those "Eurocrats" would be difficult to find anywhere in the world. Unfortunately, national governments have tended to be reluctant to let some of their people enter the European service and have prevented necessary expansion of the Community staffs by keeping the purse strings rather taut. Each Commissioner in addition has a personal cabinet, as is

---

[11] Nonmember countries, among them the United States, also maintain full missions in Brussels accredited to the three European Communities. The heads of these missions are also Ambassadors but, not being from member states, they do not sit on the Committee of Permanent Representatives.

customary in France and several other European countries, composed of close and essentially political advisors.

The EEC Commission is specifically charged with the supervision and the application of the Treaty of Rome and of the measures adopted by the organs of the Community. To these ends it can formulate recommendations or opinions, it can correct information, and it has the right to address the Council of Ministers with precise proposals for action. We have already seen that the Council cannot amend these but must accept or reject them by unanimous vote, although the Commission may alter them if it chooses.

Theoretically the Commission makes decisions by majority vote. In actual practice, unanimity is sought, especially for important decisions. However, the work of the Commission has become so complex and many faceted that individual Commissioners have had to adopt a "written procedure," i.e., unilateral rulings, submitted in writing to their fellow Commissioners and assumed adopted if no objection is heard within an agreed time span.

The Commission may lay down four different kinds of rules:

1. It can issue quasi-legislative rules which have the effect of legislation, are binding on states, become part of their law, and do not have to be ratified by their national parliaments.

2. It can issue directives of a more general nature, but the manner of enforcement may be decided by national governments and administration.

3. It may issue directives to particular persons, business enterprises, or states, which are binding on these states, groups, or individuals concerned.

4. It may make recommendations or give opinions to the Council of Ministers or publish its views, even where it may not have the power to go further.

In addition, the Commission may ask a state to justify its action within a specified period and may, if it is refused, issue a statement giving its reason for having done so. If the state concerned still does not comply, the Commission may bring a case of this kind to the Court, which it has done in a number of cases. The Commission applies the rules of the treaty to individual cases and may allow or disallow safeguard clauses on behalf of states or business enterprises. In the implementation of decisions taken, the Commission may suspend or modify the common external tariff, issue import quotas, approve agreements between business firms, investigate and fine firms, issue regulations concerning the application of the antitrust provisions, and apply agricultural regulations especially determining variable levies designed to alleviate inequality. As the European Economic Community moves further along, the power of the Commission is designed to increase.

Perhaps its most important power is that of initiating proposals, since the Council of Ministers cannot act without them. It was designed that after January 1, 1966, when the Council was to make nearly all its decisions by simple or qualified majority, the influence of the Commission would increase further.

Even more than the Council, the Commission acts as the true spokesman for the Community interest, and this is an obligation which the Commissioners have carried out to an extraordinarily high degree. They have managed to act in such a way that their individual nationalities have become virtually a matter of indifference. Even in the bitter complaint of General de Gaulle about the "stateless Aereopags" lies an unintended confirmation that the Commissioners have indeed done their duty.

Another very important aspect of the role of the Commission is that it can not only mediate and conciliate differences within the Community but can also act externally on behalf of the Community as a whole. Notable are the negotiations of the Community with Greece, Turkey, and certain African states, as well as with Austria for a possible future associate status for the latter. Perhaps most significant is the task of the Commission to negotiate generalized reductions of tariffs and restraints of trade on behalf of the Community. This was done within the General Agreement on Tariffs and Trade (GATT), the first phase of which was called the Dillon Round (1960–1962), the second, which was concluded in 1967, the Kennedy Round. In April, 1967, the Commission was enlarged to fifteen members and absorbed both the High Authority of the ECSC and the Commission of EURATOM into a single European Commission.

The special relationship between the Council of Ministers and the Commission forms both the strength and the weakness of the Common Market organization. The economy of Western Europe has become so interwoven that in a sense it can only go forward. To this end, the continued and imaginative exercise of initiatives by the Commission is essential. However, ultimate power still resides in the states, and the ministers are dependent on the national policies in their respective countries. If one government, like that of France, is determined to stop this process, the Community cannot simply remain where it is: if stagnation were to be forced on it for a prolonged period, it might deteriorate and possibly even die. But so much is at stake now for every country that such a danger, while not totally excluded, is increasingly unlikely.

C. The Court of Justice

We have already seen that the Court originally created for ECSC now serves all three Communities, and we have discussed its composition and mode of selection.[12] In the Court, all four official languages are permitted, although French is the one most widely used. Interesting is the role of the two Advocates-General who participate in the hearing and in the questioning and then write their conclusions and recommendations. Then the Court retires and deliberates and decides by itself. It is not bound to follow the advice of the Advocates-General and often does not. However, the views of the Advocates-General are often very interesting and for-

[12] See page 688.

ward-looking, and it seems likely that some of their views, while possibly rejected at first, may find their way into future decisions.

As in the case of the ECSC, the Court hears suits of member states against each other, although the Commission usually tries to settle the dispute first. The Court may hear cases between Community institutions, and appeals against states accused of having defaulted on their treaty obligations. It may also hear appeals by private persons against the acts or omissions of the Commission or the Council. Moreover, national courts may certify to the Court the question of the interpretation and validity of executive acts of the Community, and in that case the national court is bound by the decision of the European Court. However, the latter is powerless to compel national courts to certify cases to it even if Community law is involved; nor may it review the judgment of national courts if no certification has taken place.[13]

The Court's record is impressive. It has not tried to "quasi-legislate," but it has helped states and individuals to adhere strictly to the treaties and regulations. Thus far the Court has made nearly 200 decisions, while about as many are still pending. It has aided the uniform application of the Treaty of Rome by national courts and it has upheld private rights of individuals against national authority and national courts. In all six member countries, the validity of Community law and Community judicial decisions has become firmly established. The Court has even gone so far as to stipulate that "the Community constitutes a novel juridical order of international legal character, for the benefits of which the states, though only in limited areas, have limited their sovereign rights."[14]

D. The European Parliament

As we have already seen, the Assembly created by the Treaty of Paris for the European Coal and Steel Community also serves the European Economic Community. Its membership was increased from the original 78 to 142, with Germany, France, and Italy contributing 36 members each, Belgium and the Netherlands 14 each, and Luxembourg 6. We have already discussed the general political composition of the Assembly, which changed its name to European Assembly but is generally known as the European Parliament.

The Parliament elects its President and eight vice presidents who are to represent all nations and all political groups. We have already seen that the members sit together in political groups, not in alphabetical order as in the Consultative Assembly of the Council of Europe and in the Assembly of the West European Union. There is one interesting and increasingly awkward phenomenon: since Communists have thus far not been elected to the European Parliament, there is one group and

---

[13] The Costa Case, Court of Justice of the European Communities, Case No. 6/64, July 15, 1964.
[14] Case of N. V. Allgemeine Transport, 1963.

one group only which stands out in opposition to the rest. That is the group of French deputies from the Gaullist Union for the New Republic (UNR). This is so because all the other members usually represent viewpoints generally favorable to European integration, much as they may differ on other issues. Hence to an increasing extent, debates in the European Parliament are often overshadowed by sharp disputes over the policies of General de Gaulle and recriminations over whatever is the latest act in the game of French solitaire. This sort of debate may underline the basic isolation of the French Gaullists and the equally basic unity among those who wish to proceed to a more united and integrated Europe, but it does not enhance the work of the Assembly, its questioning of the executive bodies of the Communities, and its drive toward greater independence.

The three main political groups, Socialist, Christian Democratic, and Liberal (Conservative) have worked in different ways and through different subgroups or working parties. Cohesion is greatest among the Socialists and least among the Liberal-Conservatives. But these lines of division are by no means permanent, and the vote is quite often cast along national rather than political or ideological lines.

Legally the European Parliament is an essentially consultative group which also, as we have seen, holds the so-far theoretical right of censure against the Commission. It is consulted a great deal, as the Commission in particular and other executive bodies too, seek and welcome opportunity to bring their views and ideas up for discussion. In fact, all three executive commissions are in the habit of informally consulting parliamentary committees before formulating their proposals with finality.

Discussions on the work of the Communities arise from either oral or written questions directed to the Commission or to the High Authority or to the Councils of Ministers. A general debate is also held on each Community and on the report by the Commission of the EEC re the economic situation and the biennial Council summaries of its activities. Once a year there is also held a "colloquy," which is a debate on specific subjects in which the Chairman of the Council of Ministers and members of the Commissions participate. However, this is for better understanding, and no vote is taken.

It is natural for a parliamentary body to be restive if it does not have as much power and influence as its members think is its due. This, without doubt, is true of the European Parliament. Various attempts have been made to remedy the situation. The most recent was a proposal by the Commission of the EEC which would have given it a separate budget to be approved by the Parliament. Whether this proposal was ever likely to see acceptance is difficult to say, but at any rate the interruption of Community activities by the action of the French government of June 30, 1965, brought this move to an at least temporary end.

Among the demands raised by the Parliament in 1963 were: participation in the appointment of Community executives, consultation between the Parliament and the Council of Ministers on all important questions, motions adopted by a two-thirds majority to be binding upon the Council unless opposed by unanimous decision, ratification of international agreements by the Community, greater parliamentary control over finances, and nomination of judges for the Court of Justice from lists submitted by the member states. None of these demands have been acted upon thus far.

The inability of the European Parliament to obtain greater power is serious in so far as it makes for an imbalance in the relationship between an increasingly powerful executive and a powerless quasi-legislature. In the interests of harmonious democratic development, this is not a desirable situation and it ought to be remedied. This, however, is unlikely to happen because the present Parliament is not directly elected, i.e., elected by the people with a view toward their European responsibilities, but is only an assembly of appointed delegates whose responsibilities to their voters cover only national affairs. This was recognized both by the Treaty of Paris and by the Treaty of Rome, which provided for direct popular election of the Parliament. In 1960, a study group of the European Parliament unanimously proposed a project for a parliament elected by direct and universal suffrage. The French government has, however, consistently blocked such a development, and as long as General de Gaulle rules in France this policy is not likely to change.

E. Advisory bodies

The Treaty of Rome provides for an *Economic and Social Committee* to advise the Council and the Commission. The Economic and Social Committee is composed of 101 representatives of "various categories of economic and social life, in particular, representatives of producers, agriculturists, transport operators, workers, merchants, artisans, the liberal professions and of the general (public) interest" (Art. 193). They are elected by unanimous vote of the Council for a four-year term. Each government submits to the Council a list of twice as many candidates as it is entitled to have members. Before making its decision, the Council must consult the Commission, and it may also obtain the advice of other European organizations representing various economic and social interests. The treaty provides, in particular, that agriculture and transport must be adequately represented.

The Economic and Social Committee must be consulted by the Council and by the Commission in a number of cases specifically stipulated in the treaty. They meet in three main groups—industry, labor unions, and others—but they also divide into nine sections, each one charged with a different subject and subdivided into three working groups which prepare the initial working papers.

Although the Treaty of Paris does not oblige the High Authority of the ECSC to consult this Committee, this is nevertheless done frequently.

The Economic and Social Committee has some influence and its role has been generally beneficial. However, it has no right of initiative and it is not permitted to give an opinion on the implementation of the treaties unless such a question is submitted to it. Moreover, it can meet only at the request of the Commission or of the Council of Ministers. However, it has been frequently and regularly consulted and has given a number of reports and opinions which have had a fair amount of influence. It has also taken to an informal exchange of documents and views with the European Parliament, which normally awaits the opinion of the Committee before it discusses the items under consideration.

Not strictly speaking an advisory committee, but a separate autonomous agency, is the *European Investment Bank*. It was organized with a subscribed capital of 1 billion dollars to aid investment within the Six and to furnish guarantees to private lenders. The Bank is headed by a Board of Governors made up of the Ministers of Finance of the six member countries, who meet annually and establish general policy. There is also a Board of Directors composed of twelve members and twelve alternates, three each from France, Germany, and Italy, two from Belgium, Netherlands, or Luxembourg, and one from the EEC Commission. The day-by-day activity is carried out by a management committee consisting of the president and two vice presidents of the Bank.

The Bank has been active in three main types of cases:

1. Aid to underdeveloped regions of member countries, such as the Massif Central in France, certain parts of France's south, and the "Mezzogiorno" in southern Italy.

2. Modernization in areas of intrastate significance such as railroads and road transport.

3. The retraining and reintegration of workers who have lost their employment as a result of tariff reductions and similar measures undertaken by the Community.

Of the 1 billion dollars subscribed, only one-fourth has actually been paid in, and the Bank has been forced to borrow an approximately equal amount from the general capital market. The largest amount of investment has gone to Italy, which probably had the most need of it. Although loans are mainly for the territories of the member countries, they may also be granted to outside states provided the Board of Governors approves them unanimously.

PROGRESS AND PROBLEMS OF EEC

A. The Common Market forges ahead

Tariffs between Community member countries were reduced by 50 percent during the first four and one-half years of the Common Market's existence. So speedy and successful was this operation that the Commission recommended the abolition of the remaining 50 percent in a similar period. It was envisaged that by July 1, 1968, all tariffs between member countries would be completely abolished, three years ahead of schedule. This development has been constantly pushed along by the Commission, but it has undoubtedly also profited from the trade rivalries arising between EEC and the so-called "Outer Seven," the members of the European Free Trade Association (EFTA).

The Commission also proposed that the common external tariff should be established in three stages: the first by January 1, 1961; the second by July 1, 1963; and the third by January 1, 1967. This last date was later changed to July 1, 1968. Thus, both the total abolition of internal tariffs and the establishment of the common external tariffs were to be accomplished by the middle of 1968. The Commission also believed that all national equalization taxes on imports and all national quota arrangements should have been abolished by the same date. However, Community quotas were to be imposed where necessary in order to protect specific Community industries which were faced with special problems. The latter meant that a member country which found it had balance-of-payments difficulties could place restrictions on imports, even (to a lesser extent) those from other member countries. Italy in particular made use of these provisions, but all the other countries also made use of these escape clauses in different degree. Against that, one has to underline the extraordinary speed and considerable ease with which tariffs were lowered and industrial quotas were reduced, especially in the industrial sector. The Community has also borne in mind the apprehension of outsiders lest it become a high-tariff, protected area, since the members of the Community are important markets for many other countries, especially Scandinavia, the United States, and Japan. Thus, on January 1, 1959, the tariff cuts within the Common Market were extended to all members of the General Agreement on Tariffs and Trade (GATT), and quota increases were extended to members of the Organization for Economic Cooperation and Development (OECD).

However, the quintessence of the Common Market policy is the common external tariff. It is this which distinguishes it from a mere free-trade area such as EFTA. Beginning in February, 1960, the common tariff was established for a list of nearly 3,000 items which in itself was a condensation of innumerable tariff positions. This was done on the basis of the arithmetical average of national duties as of January 1, 1957, the year in which the Treaty of Rome was signed. A number of items, about seventy, known as "List G," and a few others added later by the Council of Ministers, were excepted and reserved for special negotiation among the member states.

The common external tariff was established at a rate of approximately that of Germany, double those of the Benelux nations, and half those of France and Italy. In its policy the common external tariff conformed to the rules of GATT according to which the average level of the common tariff was not to be higher than the average of the various national tariffs which it replaced. Critics have argued, however, that in these figures the volume of trade was not taken into account and that the simple application of an arithmetical rule actually led to a generally higher tariff rate.

Again mindful of concerns outside the Common Market area, the first alignment of national tariffs into the common external tariff was made with a 20 percent reduction. In general it was done in this fashion: where national tariffs were not out of line with the common external tariff by more than 15 percent, the alignment would take place immediately; otherwise the difference would be reduced by 30 percent. A second 30 percent alignment was undertaken on July 1, 1963, and the alignments were to be completed by January 1, 1967. Actually, July 1, 1968, was the date agreed upon later—in May of 1966. However, there are a number of exceptions and qualifications if the Community production of certain products is insufficient or if the members of the country concerned depend on imports from nonmembers.

It is natural that even fairly liberal policies on the part of the Commission have not dispelled all the fears of outsiders. True, tariffs were generally reduced, including those in the high categories. Even the tariffs on List G were fixed at lower levels than some had expected. But the Community retained powerful weapons in its hands to protect what it considered its interests. When, early in 1962, the United States government raised duties on Belgian carpets and glass[15] (although it had a policy of lowering tariffs and was planning to give the President exceptional authority to do so under the Trade Expansion Act of that year), the Community retaliated quickly by raising duties on plastic products, paint, and synthetic textile fibers. Particularly long remembered on both sides, perhaps because of its excesses and vagaries, was the so-called "chicken war," over the continued movement of American poultry to the Community markets.

The Commission has vigorously rejected accusations of protectionism. It points to the fact that the trade deficit of the Common Market rose twelve times in the first five years of the Common Market's existence, and its deficit with the United States rose from $712,000,000 to $2,500,000,000 in the same period. Agricultural imports increased 21 percent, while world trade in agricultural products during the same period rose only by 11.6 percent. As we have already mentioned, the general tariff reductions were extended to all GATT members. The Community has also liberalized its import policies regarding tropical products, but many of these are raw materials which are duty-free in any case.

It is, however, true that a common market is in itself not necessarily a guarantee of the liberalization of trade. Everything depends on its policies. In that respect, the big push came in the greatest endeavor at world-wide tariff cutting yet seen, the so-called Kennedy Round. Here, under all circumstances, tough bargaining was carried on. Here were numerous highly complex problems. To name only one which gave rise to controversy: the United States proposed lineal, across-the-board tariff cuts of 50 percent. This was done in response to European complaints that the old method of handling each tariff separately on hundreds of items was too slow and cumbersome.[16] Community representatives, on the other hand, pointed to the fact that American tariffs tend to have greater differentials than European

---

[15] This was a tactical move by the United States government to disarm critics of the Trade Expansion Act. In the opinion of this author, it was of doubtful necessity and questionable wisdom.

[16] For instance, the following items were listed separately: linen handkerchiefs, cotton handkerchiefs, cotton handkerchiefs with lace edges, cotton handkerchiefs with rolled edges, cotton handkerchiefs with silk embroidery, etc.

tariffs and that some United States tariffs are very high while others are quite low. European tariffs, they said, tend to be more in the intermediate class. This meant that certain high American tariffs, even if they were cut 50 percent, would remain high and would retain their protective value, while many more European tariffs, were they to be cut 50 percent, would cease to be protective. Hence, the Commission tended to favor a more differentiated rather than a simple across-the-board system.[17] Agreement was finally reached in 1967.

The fate of the Kennedy Round was tied up with two even more difficult and uncertain questions. One was the evolution of the common agricultural policy of the Common Market; the other was the policy of the French government.

The Treaty of Rome dealt with agriculture in only a very general fashion. The details were to be filled in as the Community progressed. The mechanism and institutional bases for Common Marketing organizations were established by Community regulations for grains, pork, poultry, eggs, wine, fruit, and vegetables. Some additional provisions for wine were to be worked out later. For milk and dairy produce, beef and rice, similar mechanisms and institutions were expected to come into force in 1963 in accordance with proposals which the Commission had already presented to the Council of Ministers. The Commission further intended to put forward proposals for the common organization of the markets for sugar, potatoes, oils and fats, ethyl alcohol, tobacco, and nonedible horticultural products. It also endeavored to find common policies for fisheries and forestries. When all this had been accomplished, about 90 percent of the agricultural produce of the member countries would have been subject to market organization on a Community basis.

Particular difficulty lay in a common price policy. Without a harmonization of prices, the establishment of a common agricultural market was obviously difficult if not impossible. Moreover, the levels eventually to be fixed for agricultural target prices would determine to a large extent the degree of protection which had to be given to the Community's agriculture. The Commission also intended to make proposals to establish levels of farmers' and farm workers' incomes and to guide the production of meat in order to gear it to demand, and all this was to be in implementation of Articles 39 (and 110) of the Treaty of Rome. Article 39 states:

> The Community, by adopting measures designed to raise the individual incomes of those engaged in agriculture and encouraging the rational development of agricultural production, will make its contribution to the harmonious development of world trade by insuring a satisfactory level of trade between the Community and non-member countries.

We are confronted here with two sets of interrelated problems: one set deals

[17] The facts are exceedingly complex and are in dispute because, while the charge of greater differences in the height of American tariffs is correct, the number of such high tariffs is not so great. Naturally, a decisive point is the volume of trade, not the number of tariffs in the one or the other class.

with harmonization of prices between the countries of the Community, the other with determination of the relationship between Community agriculture and outside producers, especially those overseas. These relationships are made difficult by considerable disparities. Within the Common Market there is one agricultural worker per 2.7 acres, while in the United States there is one for every 53 acres. The enormous disparity of productivity immediately becomes apparent. But disparity also exists within the Common Market itself, especially between the agriculture of France, which is the most efficient in the Common Market and which has half of the arable land within the Community, and Germany, whose agriculture is relatively inefficient and produces at high cost. For France, the situation is one of wishing for uniform but relatively low prices within the Community which would enable its efficient agriculture to have a large market, while at the same time it would like to see this market protected against products of the still more efficient agriculture of America and other overseas producers. For Germany, the situation is one of needing high wheat prices to sustain its agriculture, and also of needing to export in order to pay for its food. Moreover, in all Common Market countries, the agricultural sector is politically important, and hence there is considerable pressure in each for that kind of agricultural policy which seems to favor that country the most. One might say that the agricultural sector is the most nationalist and the most difficult to "communalize."

It had been the argument of France that a favorable solution of the agricultural question was imperative, not only because this had clearly been agreed upon, if only in general terms, but also because it was to compensate France for the concessions it had made in the industrial alignments. This argument was somewhat exaggerated because the French, although perhaps believing that they were making sacrifices, actually found that they were able to adjust their industrial sector to the Common Market very well, and have proved themselves efficient industrial producers. At the same time, from the standpoint of an efficient agricultural policy, German concessions were clearly called for and had already partially emerged. However, the Germans did not want to agree on a price policy alone without knowing more about the general common agricultural policy, and furthermore they wanted to make certain that the French would agree to concessions under the Kennedy Round in which Germany had a particular interest. All this took place under the pressure of the United States Senate's Trade Expansion Act, which was due to expire in 1967, since with it, unless renewed, would expire the authority of the American representatives to make the large-scale tariff reductions necessary if the Kennedy Round were to succeed. Intricate and complex compromise solutions were finally found just in time.

On all the differences between France and Germany and among the other members of the Community, innumerable papers have been written, and slow progress has been made. A common pricing and marketing and competitive policy was supposed to be harmonized by 1970. During the transitional period, variable levies were to be adopted in order to prevent hardships, equalize sacrifices, provide adequate guarantees to farmers and consumers, and guarantee free circulation of produce. Levies and subsidies were to be gradually reduced and to end in 1970. Another system of levies was directed at producers and importers from outside the Community and were higher than those for intra-Community trade. These levies against outsiders were to be abolished by 1970, but by then there should be a common variable levy against outside countries as well as a common finance support system to go together with a common price for agricultural commodities within the Common Market. The variable tariff levies against outsiders were designed to protect the internal market and in effect permit imports only where there are internal shortages. Since the levies are the difference between the Common Market price and the world price, Common Market agriculture would in effect be protected.

There were many delays. One set of delays came from the negotiations between the EEC and Britain which came to an end abruptly when General de Gaulle declared, on January 14, 1963, that Great Britain was not "sufficiently European" to be permitted entry. In another way, the German resistance to a common price level for cereals caused further delay. There were a series of "marathons" in which the French government threatened to walk out on the Common Market if its demands were not met and where last-minute agreements were reached, especially in December, 1964.

There was also disagreement about what should be done with the very considerable funds which were collected from the levies and which were to go to the Agricultural Guidance and Guarantee Fund to partially finance export rebates, price supports, and structural readjustments. There was disagreement over the idea proposed by the Commission that the funds would underwrite the budget of the Community itself.

Agreement on agricultural policy would have been difficult enough even if political harmony had continued to exist. However, the increasingly anti-integrationist policies of the French government and of General de Gaulle himself, transformed the agricultural crisis of the Common Market into a full-scale political crisis which, for a while at least, seemed to threaten the very existence of the entire European Community system.

Fortunately, the logjam was finally broken in July, 1966. A fund of $1,006,000,000 was established for switching from national control to the Common Market by mid-1968. Half of the money was to come from Common Market levies on food imports from nonmember countries (which brought their prices up to Common Market levels) and the other half directly from the treasuries of the member countries. The fund was to be used mainly to support farm-product exports to nonmember countries, while the rest was to be spent on internal market support and on farm modernization in the Community. As part of a Community-wide farm control program, uniform marketing and quality standards were to be imposed in rapid succession on a series of products. Community-wide common prices for each commodity were yet to be established except for grain, on which agreement had been reached.

The importance of this series of decisions, which set deadlines for the implementation of the industrial as well as agricultural customs unions well in advance of the treaty deadline of January 1, 1970, was that it proved the viability of the Community institutions. Their ability to survive, relatively unaltered, the attack of their strongest member and, immediately after this attack failed, to take decisions to achieve these goals demonstrated the degree of solidity which the institutions had attained. It also illustrated the importance of the agricultural decisions for France, which accepted its failure to obtain agreement on its major stated policy objectives in order to assure agreement on early implementation of the common agricultural policy.

B. The free flow of persons, services, and capital

Community regulations have prescribed rules guaranteeing the free stay and working permits within the Community of all citizens of Community countries. At first, priority was to be given to nationals, and only remaining vacancies were to be filled by other Community citizens. But since 1964 that rule has been rescinded, and all vacancies may be filled immediately by any citizen of a Community country. These rules are important in the long run. At the present they have little significance because there is such a tremendous labor shortage in all the countries of the Common Market that increasing numbers of workers have to be imported from non-Community countries, and increasingly from Asia and Africa.

The capital market was also to be freed, and all restrictions of capital movements were to be ended by 1967. There are still controls, but progress is considerable, and governments cannot restrict the purchase and sale of foreign stock. Differences in banking systems add to the complexity, and governments have their own ways, including preferential taxes, for siphoning capital into national investments. The picture is made even more complicated by the increasingly tight European money market. This has encouraged opportunities for American investment, and yet American investment is not always welcomed. Several European countries try to make a difference between investments from abroad which tend to dominate and control European companies, and those which do not. In certain industries, especially those related to national defense, foreign domination is often resented, especially in France. Also the building of plants by foreign companies, although often welcome, has sometimes caused difficulty in an already tight labor market. At the same time, attempts to stop foreign investment and control have often been a failure—especially where large investments were needed, which could not be found in the local or the European money market. An example of this is the affair of the *"Machines Bull"* industries in France, where the French government intervened, but unable to provide the necessary funds, finally could not prevent the enterprise from coming under the domination of the General Electric Company of America. Some Europeans also fear that the increasing domination by foreign companies will lead to the continuation of the "brain drain," and the siphoning off of European scientists into American laboratories.

The problem is not acute in an over-all sense, because American investments in Europe represent only about 8 percent of capital invested in Western Europe.

But it is acute in certain branches of industry where American domination increases rapidly. Moreover, American direct investments in the Common Market countries increased more than eightfold in the period from 1950 to 1964, as most American investments abroad find their way into the Common Market countries. Of some 3,000 direct investment operations carried out by American firms and individuals in Western Europe between 1958 and 1965, approximately four-fifths were in EEC countries, with Western Germany being the principal pole of attraction.

This book is not the place to go deeply into this very complex field. Suffice it to say that at some time it will be necessary for America and the Common Market to reach an understanding about some regulation of the flow of investment, perhaps discouraging certain ill-considered or inexperienced foreign industrial operations.

In other fields, such as freeing other activities, less progress has been made. The Treaty of Rome calls for the removal of all obstacles to the operation of services, insurance, banking, finance, distribution, personal services, and to the exercise of the liberal professions (doctors, attorneys, etc.) inside a Community. This was to be achieved by 1969. Initial regulations were approved by the Council of Ministers in 1961, but since that time there has been rather slow progress. These services and businesses are used to operating within a national context, and members of the liberal professions are known to be not very liberal to their competitors.

There are differences of opinion about the success of the Community's antitrust policy. There has been from the outset a difference of attitude between Germany and the other countries, and there is a difference of philosophy between Americans and Europeans in general. The American antitrust philosophy usually tends to oppose "bigness" per se, while Europeans consider trusts and cartels undesirable only when they impose unfair restraint, and the Germans are even more reluctant than other Europeans to see any interference.

The Commission has been applying regulations tending to prevent fixing of prices, restriction of production, and dividing of markets. When it has to make a decision in an antitrust matter, it must consult the governmental authorities of the countries concerned as well as the Advisory Committee composed of one official from each of the member countries. Because the provisions of the treaty are considered to be directly applicable to the parties in most instances, the practice has evolved of allowing business enterprises to apply to the Commission for "negative clearance," i.e., to get a binding ruling from the Commission that certain activities are not in violation of the treaty. Requests for negative clearances became so numerous by 1964 that the Commission in that year proposed a system of group exceptions which would permit rulings by several broad categories. However, the Council of Ministers did not accept the simplifying procedure.

Most observers would agree that the antitrust controls of the European Economic Community leave something to be desired. Though competition is quite brisk within the Community, this has been due more to the rapid growth of business, especially of such price-depressing enterprises as supermarkets and discount houses, than to the efficiency of Community antitrust policy and enforcement.

The harmonization of commercial policy has been very slow. This involves commercial policy not only within the Community but also with outside countries including the Communist countries of Eastern Europe.

Theoretically, the Community has the right to act in the field of general economic and monetary policy, but as far as regulations controlling the general economy are concerned, the Commission has been reluctant to incur the displeasure of industry, especially of German industry. The opposition to planning on the part of Germany is particularly great (even if the word "programming" is used, as is done frequently to avoid at least verbal difficulties).

The Community also recognizes the impact of monetary questions on trade and the relationship between tariffs and inflation or deflation. A Monetary Committee has been concerned with these problems. It is composed of two representatives of each member state taken from the central banks and the Ministries of Finance plus two members from the Commission. This committee has met frequently, but it has not often been able to assert itself. Countries have acted without consulting either the Monetary Committee or the Commission. However, the growing inflationary peril has brought national governments to consider more seriously their common responsibilities. If one of the member countries finds itself in financial difficulties, an initiative to help it must come from the Commission, which then proposes action to the governments concerned. If this does not remedy the situation, the Commission, after consultations with the Monetary Committee, can then propose mutual aid to the Council of Ministers. If help is refused or if it is inadequate, a member has the right to invoke the exceptions procedure in the treaty, and the Commission may then fix such safeguards and exceptions as may assist the country concerned to emerge from its difficulties.

The logic of Community policy should lead to a single monetary system and monetary authority as well as to a pooling of gold and foreign-exchange reserves. However, this type of step has never been approved by the Council of Ministers, and countries concerned are inclined to take their separate ways, often applying for help to the United States rather than relying on Community remedies. Moreover, an informal arrangement of periodic meetings of representatives of ten major nations, rather than of the six of the Common Market alone, has often been more potent in the solution of fiscal and monetary problems.

Although the Commission has undertaken some fruitful measures to avoid discrimination due to transportation rates and policies, the harmonization of transport policy itself has been slow. In part, this is the result of the very different and strictly national origins of the transportation systems; in part it is due to the ease with which control over transportation lends itself to discriminatory policies or encouragement of industry and development in certain parts of a national territory. At any rate, transportation policy is an important area for development of the Community, but also one to which progress comes more slowly.

The Commission has taken seriously its obligations to harmonize social policies. It has looked upon its task as going beyond that of simply harmonizing conditions or reducing imbalances or improving production and lowering costs, and has considered social policy as a means to achieve greater social justice, thus moving toward the larger political objectives of the Community. The Commission has pressed for the full application of Community regulations regarding the free flow of labor, has emphasized social security equalization for migrant workers, has pushed for more equitable national legislation, and has urged the extension of the operation and the contents of the European Social Fund. The Commission has also taken responsibility for aiding vocational training and employment and for harmonizing living and working conditions with a view to their steady improvement.

However, on the enormous agenda of the Commission and of the Community in general, social policy has not always been able to attain the highest priority. Nevertheless, the labor shortage has necessitated many measures of improvement without Community or Commission pressure. Thus, a good deal of progress has been made. There has been an agreement to allow migrant workers to participate in the national social security systems of the countries in which they happen to work and to carry over rights accrued in another country. There has been progress in a common policy toward vocational training. There has been a good deal of consultation and study. But the Commission has generally avoided questions of income, which have been left largely to national policy.

The European Social Fund was organized to insure workers against temporary loss of employment arising from economic integration and to promote the creation of jobs in general. It has aided in the settlement and retraining of workers and has improved the mobility of labor.

Since all three Communities deal with energy problems, some coordination of policy has been necessitated. The demand for energy rose by 62 percent between 1950 and 1960, and by 1970 it is expected to reach 140 percent over 1950. But the relative importance of coal in the over-all energy production of the six member countries has fallen, as we have already seen, while the importance of oil has increased. With the decline of coal and the growing dependence on outside suppliers for oil, the Communities have become sensitive in the energy field and have tended to keep the domestic production of coal at a higher rate than purely economic considerations would justify.

There is an Inter-Executive Energy Committee consisting of three representatives of the EEC Commission, three from the ECSC High Authority, and two from the EURATOM Commission. Numerous recommendations for the coordination of national policies on energy have flowed from this source. However, strong national differences persist, and it has been exceedingly difficult to find a common denominator for diverse special interests like high-cost Belgian and low-cost German mines, different policies toward imports from the Communist countries, etc. Agreement was finally reached in 1964 on the outlines of a common energy policy intended to produce inexpensive power and a secure supply combined with free choice for the consumer, fair competition in a single market, and price stability.

C. The political challenge

A major political challenge to the very nature of the European Economic Community in particular and to the Community system in general has arisen from the policies of the French government of General de Gaulle. This has manifested itself primarily in two instances, the exclusion of Great Britain from the Common Market in 1963, repeated in 1967, and the crisis which began on June 30, 1965, and partially ended on February 28, 1966.

Before coming to power, General de Gaulle and his lieutenants never left any doubt about their hostility to the Community system. The Gaullists consistently voted against all Community treaties when they were in the opposition. When General de Gaulle came to power, he accepted all the obligations of France but still was clearly dissatisfied with the Community system and determined to pursue his general policy of freeing himself from any kind of integration or supranational commitment or restraint.

At first, De Gaulle attempted to divert the desire for greater political union in Europe from the supranational form of the Communities to a concept more in tune with his idea of a "Europe of fatherlands" (*l'Europe des patries*). The Foreign Ministers of the member countries began in November, 1959, to hold meetings every three months on the "political extension of the European Communities." A committee was eventually set up with the task of drawing up concrete proposals for the consideration of heads of state and government. A French diplomat and later minister, Christian Fouchet, became chairman. The Fouchet Committee reported out a plan[18] in November, 1961, providing for a council of heads of state acting by unanimity, an intergovernmental European political commission responsible for assisting the Council, and an advisory European parliament. This proposition not only shifted weight very considerably from the Commission to the Council of Ministers but also tended to abandon the weighted-voting concept and replace it by unanimity rule. This plan met with considerable opposition and was abandoned.

The next stage began with the negotiations for Great Britain's entry into the Community, and it had been preceded by one of the greatest miscalculations undertaken by a government. When the Community system began with the European Coal and Steel Community, Great Britain opposed and rejected not only its own entry but the idea as such, and British voices ridiculing or belittling this approach were not rare. Had Great Britain taken a different attitude from the beginning, the entire history of the European Communities might have been quite different. However, this was not the case. As the Community system began to show its unquestionable success, as its production soared while British industry made a much slower and more difficult recovery, there was a change of heart in Britain or at any rate, the need to join became almost overwhelming, although the British public did not favor the idea and only recently has shifted to strong support.

The negotiations between Britain and the Common Market proved long and

---

[18] There actually were two Fouchet plans, quite different from each other, because General de Gaulle had objected, somewhat unexpectedly, to the first version.

quite difficult. They were carried out with great skill by Edward Heath for Britain. Progress was slow but steady. Then suddenly, on January 14, 1963, General de Gaulle, in one of his peremptory and totally unilateral steps, declared in a so-called "press conference"[19] that Britain was not sufficiently "European" to enter the EEC and was too closely tied to America. It would not be correct to say that all difficulties had been overcome in the negotiations between Britain and the Common Market when the General unleashed this cold blast, but neither could it be said that any impasse or any particularly difficult point had been reached or that any particular justification existed for the timing of his ban. One might surmise that he wished to prevent Britain's entry, that he had expected negotiations to fail, and that when they did not, he stepped in to achieve his object.

General de Gaulle's declaration of January 14, 1963, constituted the first assault of nationalism on the thus-far-developed Community system. This resulted not so much from the rejection of Britain's entry in itself—for many good "Europeans" had been dubious about the wisdom of that move—but rather from the totally unilateral manner in which the French chief of state acted, because unilateral, wholly national moves are contrary to the idea and spirit of the Community.

The situation was then further aggravated by the Franco-German Friendship Treaty of January 22, 1963. In politics, whether domestic or international, timing is a matter of the utmost significance. Nobody could but rejoice at the moves toward Franco-German friendship, and at any other time such a treaty would have been hailed by all. But within the Community system, a special treaty of friendship and consultation between two members was a dubious step, and since it happened only a week after the bombshell of January 14, 1963, it had the possibly unintended (at least as far as the Germans were concerned) effect of seeming to endorse De Gaulle's declaration of January 14. The deplorable effects of this treaty were quickly recognized in Germany, and the *Bundestag* adopted a preamble to the treaty countermanding its bilateral impact. (This preamble was never accepted by France.) The treaty was one of the last acts of Chancellor Konrad Adenauer before he retired from the German chancellorship. His successor, Ludwig Erhard, was much less keen on pursuing the special relationship between France and Germany.

In Community circles, the Franco-German Treaty was interpreted as an attempt to weaken the Community's authority, and this interpretation was probably correct—at least as far as the French were concerned. At any rate, because of its unfortunate effect and because of France's increasingly anti-Community policies, the Franco-German Treaty lost much of whatever consequence it ever had and is now little more than an empty shell calling for periodic but usually quite perfunctory and formal consultations.

[19] General de Gaulle's press conferences have little in common with such institutions elsewhere. They are completely organized, prearranged affairs—public spectacles designed to give him a dramatic opportunity to say what he wants to say. Questions are used only to present him with openings for his statements. Questions designed to elicit information on other points are either discouraged in advance or are ignored.

Nothing was ever quite the same after January 14, 1963. Nationalism had raised its head again, and had challenged the Community spirit. Stripped of mutual confidence, in which so much progress had been achieved, the Community system had received a severe blow.

After that came several skirmishes, but the next great encounter occurred on June 30, 1965. The Commission of the European Economic Community had undertaken a daring step whose wisdom will long be debated, both as to its substance and, especially, as to its timing. The time for a settlement of the agricultural policy had come, and the Commission presented an ambitious program, not only for settling these agricultural issues, but also for providing an independent budget for the Community to be based on the funds received from the agricultural levies, with control over those funds to be exercised by the European Parliament. It is not certain whether the Commission really expected the French government to accept this far-reaching plan, which would have greatly enhanced the power of the Community, especially of the Commission and the Parliament, or whether it merely wanted to launch the idea for later discussion, perhaps achieving a compromise in the meantime. Undoubtedly the Commission also believed that the French had such a strong political interest in the settlement of the agricultural crisis that they might not prove too difficult.

That, however, was a miscalculation. The French government chose to take the project of the Commission as a direct challenge, rejected it, and even proved adamant on the agricultural issues. In similar situations in the past when deadlines had approached, the clock had been stopped and the Ministers had gone into a "marathon" of work and consultation until some settlement, usually favorable to the French, had been reached. This time, the French Foreign Minister, Maurice Couve de Murville, the chairman (by rotation) of the Council of Ministers, refused to negotiate beyond the midnight deadline of June 30, and adjourned the meeting. The crisis was on. If anyone had doubted that the crisis was a political one, had thought it merely over the Commission's proposals or over the reluctance of France's partners to accept an agricultural settlement on lines acceptable to France, the illusion was quickly dispelled by a speech of Foreign Minister Couve de Murville in the National Assembly of France. Besides, if the French had really been concerned only with the failure of their partners to come to an agreement on the agricultural problems, they would obviously have tried to negotiate harder and longer as they had in previous years. The fact that Couve de Murville refused to let the meeting go on beyond June 30 indicated that a political rather than an agricultural crisis had broken out, and had in fact been planned.

There followed a sharp condemnation by France of the Community approach and an immediate withdrawal of France's representatives, not only from the European Economic Community where the crisis had actually broken out, but from the other two Communities as well. The French government made no bones about the fact that it desired to lower the status of the Commission considerably, make it far more subservient to the Council of Ministers, and remove Commissioners who had proved particularly recalcitrant, especially the President, Walter Hallstein of Germany, and the Vice President and Commissioner in charge of agriculture, Sicco Mansholt of Holland.

There is little doubt that France would have remained adamant had it not been for the French presidential elections of December 5 and 19, 1965, in which General de Gaulle failed to receive a majority on the first ballot and was generally jolted in his certainty of victory. Although the elections turned primarily on domestic issues and the nature of the Gaullist regime, widespread concern over France's policies toward the Common Market also made an important and deep impression on many worried French voters.[20]

From the French domestic political point of view, and in view of the National Assembly elections in 1967, a more flexible policy toward the Common Market now seemed to be in order. Thus, after much wrangling and after a pause of eight months, France agreed to another meeting of the Council of Foreign Ministers, to be held in Luxembourg on January 18, 1966. By insisting on a place other than Brussels, the French government wanted to demonstrate its opposition, especially opposition to the Commission of the EEC. If anyone had expected the French delegation to come to the Luxembourg meeting in a contrite, or at least conciliatory, spirit, he would have been quite mistaken and would have misjudged the nature of General de Gaulle.

France presented ten demands which were rather unequivocal in their intentions. The Commission was to be deprived of its right of initiative, perhaps its single most important right, and, in fact, duty. All decisions were to be made by the Council of Ministers, and the Commission was to act only on the Council's instructions. The Commission was to cease all activities and do away with all paraphernalia or protocol which would make it appear like a government. Moreover, rapid progress was to be made toward the unification of all three Communities and the election of a new Commission from which presumably (although this was not openly mentioned) most of the old Commissioners—and definitely Hallstein and Mansholt—were to be removed. In fact, it was clearly intended that the Commission should become a group of high-level civil servants useful for carrying out instructions rather than for developing initiatives. Most important of all, however, was the French insistence that the change to majority voting on most issues in the Council of Ministers, scheduled for January 1, 1967, was to be suspended and in fact rescinded—not by a formal amendment to the treaty, which the French recognized as clearly out of the question, but at least by a written declaration.

The French proposal specified a tight time schedule that made some delegates regard it as an ultimatum. It was met with stony rejection by the other five countries, who acted in complete solidarity. The meeting was short and heated; for a while the other delegations walked out on the French, and the meeting broke up in an atmosphere which was described by the French press agency as "one that

[20] See page 358.

could perhaps not be called rupture, but which was nevertheless heavy with menace."

The Council resumed its deliberations on January 28, again in Luxembourg, and this time the French government was obliged to retreat. It dropped the timetable. The serious limitations that were to be placed on the Commission's activities were not enacted. Only in a few minor and protocol points were some concessions made by the five, such as the decision that henceforth ambassadorial heads of foreign missions to the Community would present their letters of credence not to the President of the Commission alone but to the President of the Council of Ministers *and* the President of the Commission meeting separately.

Most important of all was an "agreement to disagree" on the majority voting formula prescribed by the Treaty of Rome: in case no agreement on this matter could be found in the Council of Ministers, they would continue to negotiate in the hope of achieving agreement. In the view of the five, if no agreement could be achieved, a vote by the majority as set forth in the treaty would take place. But in the French view, one would have to continue to negotiate.

With this series of decisions, the Community resumed its life that had been interrupted for eight months, and moved forward toward settling the agricultural question and the Kennedy Round, which were now under great pressure of time, as we have seen. But although the French had failed to gain their objectives, and although the European Economic Community could once again resume its activities, the crisis was far from over. Because of the agreement to disagree on the majority formula, the French government was in a position to turn any future disagreement into a full-fledged crisis. True, the majority formula was in many respects symbolic. All members realized that important measures could not simply be forced down the throat of an important country. Attempts to find agreement would go on in any case. But the majority formula was at least a point of pressure urging, so to speak, agreement. By rejecting this formula, the French delegates were in effect saying that they were keeping free to resist agreement and to choose crisis instead.

This had been a great challenge to the Community. It had also been its baptism of fire, from which it emerged shaken but in the long run quite possibly strengthened, for the five other countries had stood firm and had manifested their determination to resist the French government's endeavor to change substantially the nature and impact of the Community. It is not certain that this degree of unity and determination to remain together could have been achieved except by the unifying force of General de Gaulle's brusque and unilateral action. The opposition, if not to say the bitterness of the five, was directed not solely at the French policy but also at the methods employed by General de Gaulle. In bilateral relationships, forceful dealings are common, yet when an agreement is reached, the irritations of the negotiations are quickly forgotten. But in a multilateral relation like the Community, no real progress can be achieved if each nation acts solely in its own interest and shows nothing but disdain and contempt for the existence and the pursuit of the Community interest. Hence, General de Gaulle's style was more than just an abrupt manner of acting; it was detrimental to the entire nature of the Community.

Moreover, the elections of December, 1965, had shown that the France of Robert Schuman and Jean Monnet was still alive. Whether and when this other France would again be able to assert itself was not certain. But the idea of European Community certainly had many faithful and powerful allies in France, and it was clear that France would lose a great deal were it to turn against the Communities. Thus the constant threat of a walkout has lost much of its effectiveness, whether or not the Frenchmen who are faithful to the Community idea are ever able to lead France back to full Community participation or not.

In fact, by June of 1966 the Community system had proved of such extraordinary importance and advantage to all, including France, that to leave or to destroy it seemed now almost inconceivable. Some measure of the importance of the Common Agriculture Policy to France is that France stands to gain $300,000,000 annually in *net* revenues from the Common Agriculture Policy beginning in 1970.

Yet another crisis moved toward its climax in 1967. The High Authority of the ECSC, the Commissions of the EEC and EURATOM were to be combined into one, single fifteen-member Commission. That action itself was supported by all member states. However, the French saw this occasion as an opportunity to remove the Chairman of the EEC Commission, Walter Hallstein, who appeared too "supranational" and independent to them. Other unpopular (to the French) Commissioners, like the Dutch Sicco Mansholt, might also be dropped. For a while there was an impasse; the French on one side and all the rest on the other side stood adamant. However, the new German Kiesinger government wanted to appease De Gaulle, at least in form, and agreed to a "compromise" formula by which Hallstein would have been reelected but only for six months, after which there would have been rotation. It was Hallstein himself who put a quick end to this proposal, which would have weakened not only himself but his successor as well. He refused to be a candidate for reelection, either as Commissioner or as President.

Hallstein's honorable and dignified exit opened the way to the election of the Belgian Jean Rey, a former Minister and Commissioner who had conducted the Kennedy Round negotiations on behalf of the EEC Commission.

Rey, probably more subtle a tactician than the stern Hallstein, may be able to avoid some of the friction, especially over protocol, which marked the Hallstein era. But Rey is no less a convinced European integrationist than Hallstein and will be no pushover for the French by any means. His more flexible tactics and his more ingratiating personality may, however, be an advantage for the Communities in their endeavor to "survive De Gaulle."

5

The European Atomic Energy Community

Although the Treaty of Rome created two Communities, the European Economic one (EEC) and the European Atomic Energy one (EURATOM), the latter has become almost completely overshadowed by the former. This was not always the case. Prior to the Treaty of Rome, there was considerable excitement over the possibility of harnessing and exploring the atom on a European basis. In a speech before the Consultative Assembly of the Council of Europe, Paul-Henri Spaak said "The atom and automation are the future."[1]

There were a number of reasons for this excitement. For one, atomic energy was a new and mysterious force in whose exploration the United States and the U.S.S.R. were obviously far ahead of the rest of the world. Now Europe was to play its role and receive its share, especially in the nonmilitary field. There was

---

[1] Oct. 21, 1955, quoted by Richard Mayne, *The Community of Europe,* New York, 1963, p. 111.

also the belief that the Western world, and Europe in particular, was heading for a fuel shortage, and many considered nuclear energy the way out. The necessity for such a way out was also illustrated politically by the ill-fated Suez venture, in which the possibility that Egypt's President Gamal Abdel Nasser might cut Europe off from Middle Eastern oil supplies played a very important role.

To those who planned the development of a European Atomic Energy Community, it was axiomatic that the Western European nations had to develop their own atomic industry. In this they had a basic choice between pooling their resources and developing their national enterprises. They could be aided through the International Atomic Energy Agency and through bilateral agreements with the United States, possibly Great Britain, and perhaps even the Soviet Union. Whichever plan was chosen, serious difficulties existed because of a shortage of qualified manpower and capital, which made some kind of pooling appear imperative. Also, with pooling, the costly training of scientific and technical personnel could be undertaken with far greater economy, while specialization and coordination of technological development would permit more experimentation with different types of reactors and other processes.[2]

There were numerous differences of views. On the one hand, it was felt that a rapid development of nuclear energy would have a "spill-over effect" on industrial development in general, and if pushed ahead speedily, would accelerate the development of qualified personnel and technological knowledge. Rapid development of nuclear power would also mean the equally rapid development of assorted equipment and associated industry.

But on the other hand, there were some voices which warned against the excessive concentration of scarce resources in this new technology. There was also a question of whether European industry would not benefit if it waited out earlier developments and then tried to join in later. There were also differences in views about the amount of electric power required, although the balance of opinion believed that a shortage was imminent.

Rather strong differences also appeared between the German government, which favored private industry as a principal developer, and the French, which (it might seem ironical now) insisted on development under public authority in an integrated European fashion. But while the French wanted to "Europeanize nuclear energy," they made a very careful distinction between military and peacetime use. Having started a nuclear program of their own,[3] the French were jealous of France's status as a great power and rejected supranational controls over their military nuclear programs. To many French nationalists, the attempt to establish European controls over France's entire nuclear program was an effort to reestablish the European Defense Community through the back door. However, the France

---

[2] Klaus E. Knorr, *EURATOM and American Policy: A Conference Report,* Princeton, N.J., 1956, p. 6.
[3] Lawrence Scheinman, *Atomic Energy Policy in France under the Fourth Republic,* Princeton, N.J., 1965, chap. 5, *passim.*

of 1959 did not in any way object to strong political controls over EURATOM's program.

Just how much special nuclear material EURATOM or European nations were to develop themselves and how much they were to purchase, especially from the United States, remained a matter of contention. The gaseous diffusion plants used in the United States for production of fuel are extremely complex and expensive, and require enormous amounts of electrical energy to operate. It was said that each of the American plants absorbed two million kilowatts. Some critics were heard to remark that a gaseous diffusion plant was likely to consume in ten years more electricity than atomic power could contribute to the energy supply of Western Europe.[4] On the other hand, they are capable of both military and peaceful development, and the less expensive process using enriched uranium purchased from the United States was not so interesting to nations seeking to acquire dual (peace and war) capabilities, whether they admitted it or not.

The new Community was given the exclusive right to own special fissionable materials and the right of option to other nuclear materials. In general, EURATOM was set up to help develop a peaceful nuclear industry in Europe and thereby raise living standards, which are closely linked to the level of energy consumption. It was estimated that electricity consumption in Western Europe, now little more than one-third of that in the United States, was doubling every ten years. It was further estimated that at that rate of growth, by 1980 the countries of the Community might have to produce roughly as much additional electricity by nuclear means as they now produce in conventional power plants.[5]

By a unified process, EURATOM was to help the modernization of Europe's technical evolution at a high rate of economy in manpower and fiscal outlays. At the same time, by collaborating in such a vital activity, EURATOM was to do its share in leading Europe toward greater unity. Besides giving aid in research and development, it would buy nuclear fuel and supervise the flow of a regular and equitable supply to all the member states, thus preventing discrimination, and at the same time imposing controls adequate to prevent the misuse of these materials. EURATOM was also to be a clearing house for nuclear information on industrial problems and was to supervise the exchange of information between member and nonmember states.

The institutions of EURATOM are closely modeled on those of the Common Market and the Coal and Steel Community. There is, once more, a Council of Ministers, whose members are usually Ministers of Science, Finance, or sometimes Foreign Affairs. Because of the close identity between the Common Market and EURATOM, the latter's Council meetings are usually held immediately preceding meetings of the Council of Ministers for the EEC. Most decisions are reached by unanimity.

---

[4] Knorr, *op. cit.,* p. 10.
[5] European Community, *The Facts,* Brussels, 1961.

The EURATOM Commission, like the Commission of the Common Market, is the main supranational body of the organization. It is relatively small, consisting of five members, who are chosen by the respective governments, by unanimity, for four-year terms. The president and vice president are chosen from among the five for a two-year period which can be renewed. There is no written or unwritten law as to the nationality of the president, as such. But since the creation of EURATOM the nationality of the heads of the other two Communities has been rather steady, with the Common Market headed by a German and the Coal and Steel Community by an Italian. Hence, for the sake of balance and by tacit agreement, the presidents of EURATOM have thus far always been Frenchmen. First was Louis Armand, who was succeeded by one of the outstanding figures of the struggle for European unity, Etienne Hirsch. Hirsch fell afoul of General de Gaulle's anti-integrationist tendencies and was forced out. He was succeeded by Pierre Chatenet, a former Minister of the Interior in De Gaulle's government.

Under the Commission, there are nine directorates into which the work of the Commission is divided, and each Commissioner is responsible for supervising one or two of them. The methods of the Commission's work closely parallel those of the Common Market Commission. However, the composition of the EURATOM Commission's staff is quite different: of its 2,700 employees, 2,100 are scientific researchers working in the various research centers of the Community. In April, 1967, the new, enlarged European Commission absorbed the functions of the EURATOM Commission.

The Commission is aided by a Scientific and Technical Committee, an advisory body composed of twenty scientists appointed by the Council of Ministers after consultation with the Commission. It functions as a research council, ruling on research proposals for a fiscal year. Since 1961 there has also been a Consultative Committee for Nuclear Research which brings together high-ranking national civil servants and members of the Commission in order to explore common problems. A number of valuable studies and reports have emanated from that body. In addition, there exists a Supply Agency which has a prior right of option for all nuclear ores, raw materials, and fissionable materials that could be used within the Community. It is to implement the principle of equality of access and absence of discrimination. This Agency, which is advised by a Consultative Committee, is technically independent, but is composed entirely of EURATOM officials and may thus be considered an instrument of EURATOM policy.

The Commission is charged with the responsibility of forecasting the energy needs of the Community, and interested firms and governments must file, three months in advance, notice of investment projects in the field of nuclear energy. As already mentioned, the Information and Documentation Center acts as a clearing house for information for both members and nonmembers. EURATOM has a choice of conducting its own research programs or of assisting national nuclear research programs, financially or otherwise. It does both.

In particular, EURATOM promotes research in its own research centers, notably those of Ispra (north of Milan, Italy), where work is concentrated around the ORGEL heavy-water reactor; of Mol, Belgium, the Central Nuclear Measurements Bureau; of Karlsruhe, Germany, the European Transuranian Institute; and the general-purpose establishment at Petten, Holland. In addition, EURATOM has well over 300 contracts involving over $200,000,000, under which it contributes both financial and personnel resources. It has also joined in international projects with the European Nuclear Energy Agency (ENEA) located in Winfrith, England, and known as the Dragon Project.

EURATOM has also played an important role in industry. It has brought into being a common market for all nuclear materials and equipment, has put into force a plan for the free movement of qualified atomic workers, has elaborated an insurance convention providing joint Community coverage (supplementary to that of OECD) for large-scale atomic risks, and has earmarked considerable funds for help to power plants which are of especial importance to the Community.

EURATOM has also established basic standards for health protection of nuclear workers which have been incorporated into the laws of the Community's member states; it maintains a constant check of the level of radioactivity in the atmosphere, water, and soil; and it watches over the security control procedure designed to prevent the misuse of nuclear material under Community authority.

It had been expected that EURATOM would use the considerable resources at its disposal to establish central, supranational facilities, and to prevent the production of nuclear weapons through its control over the supply of uranium and key production plants. These hopeful expectations generally have been fulfilled but France, which had embarked on a nuclear weapons program *before* EURATOM came into being has gone its own way. By and large, EURATOM has preferred to sponsor research into commercial developments of nuclear power and to supplement all on-going nuclear research in its member countries. While the attitude of France has been partly responsible for this, there has been a decreasing willingness to make EURATOM the single control agency for nuclear developments in Europe, and thus its quite significant contributions have been more in the technical field and in aid to research, than in general development.

Much research has been undertaken for the purpose of reducing the cost of producing power from nuclear sources. In this, the United States–EURATOM joint power program and EURATOM's own reactor participation program have played a very important role. The United States–EURATOM agreement was instrumental in the creation of three reactors of American design, two of which were built with American loans. They are located in Italy (SENN), and Germany (KRB). A Franco-Belgian cooperation plan (SENA), a Dutch project (SEP), and an Italian one (SIMEA) were also aided. The United States–EURATOM Joint Research and Development Board has authorized around thirty contracts per year in the Community countries, and a slightly lesser number in the United States. These projects contributed to lowering the cost of production of nuclear energy.

But it is notable that EURATOM also made a contribution to United States research. Under a contract signed on May 14, 1964, fast-breeder-reactor research in the United States was financed by EURATOM under a contract signed with the United States Atomic Energy Commission, and seventeen private power companies joined in the Southwest Atomic Energy Associates (SAEA).

The Community has encouraged the development of three types of reactors, conventional, advanced, and fast. Considerable hope is placed in the fast breeder reactor because of its ability to produce vastly more energy than it consumes. It is hoped that by the 1970s this type of reactor will reach full use. Under the revised United States–EURATOM Agreement of 1963, cooperation has been extended to that important sector. The considerable assistance by the United States to this program has followed general policy encouraging European unity, but was undoubtedly also motivated by a desire to avoid individual national nuclear capabilities as part of a proliferation process. Moreover, it was hoped that the United States would be able to induce Europe to develop American-type atomic power stations. These objectives have been only partially reached. The United States has constantly urged use of the enriched-uranium type of reactors because of their greater economy and also because they do not produce plutonium as do natural uranium reactors.

There is no doubt that EURATOM has played a significant role in stimulating nuclear research and production in Europe and has established important links with many countries outside the Community. But the perhaps excessive hopes originally placed on it have not been fulfilled. In part this resulted from the fact that the expected dramatic power shortage in Europe did not occur, and that far from being squeezed in its supply of oil, Europe benefited from the discovery of many more oil deposits, so that there was actually a glut on the oil market. This somewhat diminished interest in the speedy development of nuclear power.

But it is in the field of European integration that the great hopes for this institution have failed. Since the removal of Etienne Hirsch as president of the EURATOM Commission, it has not taken a leading role in this direction. The EURATOM Commission has been pliable in the face of French pressure, more so than the EEC Commission. Moreover, the decision of EURATOM to rely largely on American reactors increased French opposition.

One noble effort planned by EURATOM seemed at one time to approach fruition, but has since receded into the background. This was the project of creating a European University to be located in Florence, Italy. Two groups of experts from member countries were instructed by an intergovernmental committee on May 27, 1964, to begin drafting an international agreement creating the university and proposals for its operation. This agreement provided for contributions to the university's budget from the member countries. Initially, the university was conceived as a two-year, postgraduate institution for research on European integration, not merely EURATOM affairs. It was expected to develop faculties (schools or departments) of law, economics, political and social sciences, history, and possibly sociology and mathematics. Approximately 300 students were to be admitted during its first year, and enrollment was to increase to 500 after three years. A highly favorable teacher-student ratio was envisaged, one professor per ten students.

The project was warmly supported by the European Parliament and has enjoyed the constant encouragement of the Italian government. Several times agreement has seemed near but has then again receded into the background. Although the project is kept alive, the climate, as these lines are written, is not favorable for this ambitious and promising project ever to see the light of day.

In the quest for European unity EURATOM has not fulfilled its expectations. It has proved an important tool in the encouragement of scientific development and nuclear progress, but in the political field has left the principal role to the Common Market. It is in the arena of the latter that the battle for and against further European integration will be conducted.

6

A partial Atlantic community? the North Atlantic Treaty Organization

In a book dedicated to European government and European communities, one might not necessarily expect a chapter on Atlantic partnership. Yet there is a relationship between the two: neither European union nor Atlantic partnership is feasible without the other. An Atlantic partnership between an overwhelmingly strong America and a weak, divided Europe would be characterized by such a degree of inequality that a true partnership would be difficult to achieve, even with the best will in the world on the part of all concerned. At the same time, in the era of superpowers in the technological, particularly the nuclear, field it is difficult to see how even a united Europe could realize its full potential except in close cooperation with the United States.

The partial Atlantic community formed in the North Atlantic Treaty Organization has profited from the lessons of the European Communities. On the other hand, the crisis in NATO's existence is intimately tied to the crisis in the European

Communities and stems largely from the same source, the policies of General de Gaulle. The outcome of the crisis in the one sphere is very likely to affect the outcome in the other. That one system will triumph while the other founders is most unlikely.

The purpose of this chapter is, then, not to give a detailed view of the North Atlantic Treaty Organization's functions and operations, but to analyze its basic purpose and procedures and relate them to the process of European integration.

We have seen that the European Communities began as a deliberate attempt at European integration, an attempt to lead Europe toward greater unity, especially political unity. No such intention overshadowed the origin of the North Atlantic Treaty Organization. It started as an alliance, or more accurately as a treaty of mutual assistance, designed primarily to demonstrate America's determination not to allow Europe to be overrun by menacing Soviet might.

At the time of Germany's surrender in 1945, the Allied forces in Europe were about 5 million strong. One year later, following demobilization, the armed strength had been reduced to 880,000 men. The Soviet Union, on the other hand, continued to keep its armed forces on a wartime footing: in 1945 they amounted to more than 4 million men. It also kept its war industries going at full blast.[1]

There followed quickly a series of incidents and a general worsening of the relationship between the Soviet Union and the West, especially the United States, which is generally referred to as "the cold war." There was the dispute in 1945 over the composition of the Polish provisional government. There was a situation in Romania and Bulgaria and the seizing of power by the Communists in Prague. In the spring of 1948 everything pointed to the determination of the Soviet Union to seize as much of Western Europe as possible, by political infiltration and subversion on the model of the Czechoslovak coup. Countermoves through the Marshall Plan and the Brussels Treaty of March 17, 1948—a forerunner of the North Atlantic Treaty—merely increased the determination of the Soviet Union to destroy the opposing bloc "in order to make the world safe for Soviet Communism."[2] Further straws in the wind were Communist-inspired uprisings in Greece with open intervention and support coming through Bulgaria and Albania.

But perhaps the most dramatic event was the blockade of Berlin in 1948 which produced the extraordinary Allied airlift.[3] Although the airlift was primarily an American enterprise, it was conducted with full British and French participation. It may, therefore, be considered the first of the "NATO exercises" although NATO, the North Atlantic Treaty Organization, had not yet come into existence.

What had stopped the blockade and dissuaded the Soviet Union from further aggressive action had not been the physical might of the alliance. There were only about a dozen scattered, understrength Western divisions in Europe, while Russia

[1] Lord Ismay, *NATO: The First Five Years,* New York, 1956; *NATO: Facts about the North Atlantic Treaty Organization,* Paris, 1965, p. 4.
[2] Robert E. Osgood, *NATO: The Entangling Alliance,* Chicago, 1962, p. 28.
[3] W. Phillips Davison, *The Berlin Blockade,* Princeton, N.J. 1958.

maintained twenty-five fully armed divisions in Central Europe, and over all had at least 140 divisions of battle strength (not counting the numerous satellite divisions).[4] Nor was the nuclear monopoly of the United States much of a deterrent, as there seemed to be little inclination to use it except in case of a massive Soviet assault on Europe. But the airlift was a demonstration of American and Western European determination which heralded the North Atlantic Alliance. Not that the combined Western might could have stood up very successfully to a really serious Soviet onslaught. But what the Russians probably had in mind was not a Hitlerite *blitzkrieg* but a breaking of the will to resist by incessant threats and incursions. The standing up to this threat and the beginning of organizing the common resistance, constituted an effective countermeasure.

Now let us backtrack from 1948 to the situation in the United States in the spring of 1947. Those Americans who had hoped to return from World War II to a world of peace and tranquility had been disappointed. A series of countermeasures had to be taken against the aggressive acts of the Soviets. On March 12, 1947, President Harry S. Truman called upon the Congress of the United States to help other nations resist attempted subjugation by armed minorities or by outside pressure. Following the announcement of what was to become the Truman Doctrine, the Congress of the United States authorized the appropriation of $400,000,000 for aid to Greece and Turkey.

On June 5, 1947, in a speech at Harvard University, the then Secretary of State, George C. Marshall, initiated a program for European recovery which was to be named after him. He proposed that the United States should come to the help of Europe and suggested that the European countries should agree on their requirements and on the manner in which they could assist one another. He underlined that this policy was "directed not against any country or doctrine but against hunger, poverty, desperation, and chaos. . . ."[5]

This offer of economic assistance did not exclude the Soviet Union or the Communist satellite countries. However, it was rejected by Stalin. Such countries as Czechoslovakia and Poland inside the Iron Curtain, and Finland at the edge, who had shown some interest in participating, were forced to pull out. Eventually the Communists set up their Communist Information Bureau (Cominform), a revival of the former Communist International, in order to fight the Marshall Plan as an "instrument of American imperialism."

Thus the European world was effectively split into two blocs. A few months later, on January 22, 1948, Ernest Bevin, then British Foreign Secretary, suggested a formula for a Western union, building on the model of the Dunkirk Treaty of Mutual Assistance which had been signed by France and Great Britain on March 4, 1947. Exactly a year after that signing, on March 4, 1948, the representatives of Belgium, France, Luxembourg, the Netherlands, and the United

[4] Osgood, *op. cit.,* p. 29.
[5] *U.S. Department of State Publication 2882,* European Series, No. 25, 1947.

Kingdom met in Brussels to consider the terms of a treaty of mutual assistance. The result was the Brussels Treaty of March 17, 1948.

The ink was scarcely dry on the Brussels Treaty when the Russian blockade of Berlin began, in June, 1948. It was to last for 323 days. In September of 1948 a military organ was created under the Brussels Treaty known as the Western Union Defense Organization, and Field Marshal Montgomery was appointed chairman of its Commanders-in-Chief Committee.

Meanwhile, on April 11, 1948, Secretary of State George Marshall and Under Secretary of State Robert M. Lovett had opened preliminary talks with the chairman of the United States Senate Foreign Relations Committee, Senator Tom Connally, and with the ranking Republican member, Senator Arthur H. Vandenberg, about possible participation in a mutual defense system. The idea of a single mutual defense system was proposed by Louis St. Laurent, the Canadian Prime Minister, on April 28 of that year in the Canadian House of Commons. Then on June 11, 1948, the United States Senate passed the so-called Vandenberg Resolution, recommending "the association of the United States, by constitutional process, with such regional and other collective arrangements as are based on continuous and effective self help and on mutual aid." Now the coast was clear for the elaboration of a treaty of mutual assistance. This was done by the signatory powers of the Brussels Treaty plus Canada and the United States. Denmark, Iceland, Italy, Norway, and Portugal also proclaimed their adherence.

Despite the pressure brought to bear by the Soviet Union on the parties to the treaty, there was no turning back. On April 4, 1949, the North Atlantic Treaty was signed in Washington by the foreign ministers of Belgium, Canada, Denmark, France, Iceland, Italy, Luxembourg, Netherlands, Norway, Portugal, the United Kingdom, and the United States. The parliaments of the member countries ratified the treaty within five months, as did the United States Congress. Subsequently, Greece and Turkey joined, in 1951 and 1952 respectively.

When the North Atlantic Treaty was signed, nobody had mentioned German rearmament. Clearly the time was not ripe. But equally clearly, the necessary strengthening of Europe was not going to be accomplished without this principal reservoir of manpower. A first attempt to tackle this problem was the previously mentioned Pleven Plan which later became the project called "European Defense Community," providing for an integrated European army down to the battalion level, at least in its initial stage. But as we have seen, the plan, after much delay, was finally defeated in the French National Assembly.

There followed a few months of intense diplomatic activity seeking an alternative solution. At the initiative of the British government, a conference was held in London from September 28 to October 3, 1954, bringing together the foreign ministers of the five Brussels Treaty powers as well as those of Germany, Italy, the United States, and Canada. Their resolutions were further confirmed at a meeting held in Paris in late October of the same year, which created the Western European Union (WEU). This opened the road to the reestablishment of German armed forces, but Germany undertook voluntarily to forego the production of "ABC weapons."[6]

Accession to the Western European Union treaty by both Germany and Italy paved the way for the inclusion of Germany in NATO, which became official on May 5, 1955. The German armed forces, thus added to those of other NATO powers, became fully integrated into the North Atlantic Treaty Organization.

As originally conceived, the North Atlantic Treaty did not establish an alliance. In form it was a pact of mutual assistance. In substance, it demonstrated and documented the determination of the United States to use its might in the defense of Europe to establish a protective umbrella under which Europe could reconstruct its shattered economies and cities. The principal factor in the guarantee of Europe's security by the United States was its Strategic Air Command (SAC) which carried nuclear weapons and which remained outside the NATO structure. But for the United States, the establishment of a peacetime alliance was an absolutely unprecedented event.

THE STRUCTURE OF NATO

The North Atlantic Treaty is a very brief document. Its heart is the mutual assistance provision of Article 5 and the pledge of Article 3 to "maintain and develop their individual and collective capacity to resist armed attack." The treaty itself mentions only a Council and a Defense Committee. The entire subsequent structure is the result of protocols, Council decisions, and bilateral and multilateral agreements.

NATO has both a civilian and a military side. On the civilian side, the highest authority is the North Atlantic Council (NAC). It is composed of permanent representatives of the fifteen member countries who hold the rank of ambassador from their respective governments, and whose decisions are unanimous. In that form, the North Atlantic Council ordinarily meets two or three times a week. In addition, twice a year the Council meets at the ministerial level, that is, the member countries are represented by their Foreign and Defense Ministers.

The Council is assisted by an international staff/secretariat, headed by a Secretary-General who is chairman of the North Atlantic Council.[7] NATO has been fortunate in attracting outstanding statesmen as its secretaries-general. The first Secretary-General was Lord Ismay, who had been personal chief of staff to Winston Churchill. He was succeeded by the former Belgian Foreign Minister, Paul-Henri Spaak, and he in turn by the former Dutch Foreign Minister, Dirk U. Stikker. Since August 1, 1964, former Italian Ambassador Manlio Brosio has served as Secretary-General.

The international staff/secretariat has a number of divisions: the Division of

---

[6] Atomic, bacteriological, and chemical.

[7] Each year the foreign minister of a member state is elected President of the Council. The presidency rotates annually according to the alphabetical order of the NATO countries.

Political Affairs, the Division for Information Service, the Press Service, the Division of Economics and Finance, the Division of Production, Logistics, and Infrastructure, and the Division of Scientific Affairs. There are also auxiliary offices such as the Civil Emergency Planning Bureau, and administrative offices. These principal civilian agencies of NATO were originally established in Paris at the request of the then French government. In 1967 they moved to Brussels.

In the last few years the North Atlantic Council has created a number of subsidiary bodies, each one responsible for specific tasks: the organization of the NATO pipeline system in the Central Europe region, the NATO maintenance and supply organization, a number of production organizations for specific weapons systems, and a NATO supply center.

On the military side, the highest organizational strata comprise the Military Committee, the Area Commands, and a Regional Planning Group.

The Military Committee is the senior military authority within NATO. It is composed of a chief of staff from each member country.[8] The presidency of the Military Committee rotates annually in alphabetical order of countries. The chairmanship is held by a permanent chairman elected by the Military Committee. The Military Committee meets regularly at least twice a year, and whenever else it finds it necessary. It is responsible for making recommendations and giving guidance on military questions. In order that it may function on a continuous basis, each chief of staff appoints a permanent military representative to the Committee.

The Standing Group was originally designed to be the principal executive agency of the Military Committee. It was composed of the military representatives of the chiefs of staff of France, Great Britain, and the United States, with their supporting officers. It was served by an international planning staff which was open to members of all NATO nations having military forces, and it was headed by a director who was selected from the nations not represented on the Standing Group.

Under the Director, the Standing Group International Planning Staff consisted of four staff divisions, each headed by a Deputy Director, and the Assistant Director for Meteorology and a Chairman of the Communications Electronics Committee. Two Deputy Directors were selected from Standing Group nations, and the other two from non-Standing Group nations on a rotating basis.

Originally set up as the executive agent of the Military Committee, the Standing Group was intended to be the superior military body responsible for strategic guidance in all the areas of NATO responsibility, and the NATO commanders were to be responsible to it. As a matter of fact, the Standing Group has not performed the role for which it was intended. The Military Committee—and SACEUR in particular—have taken over the central role.

As originally conceived, the Standing Group had the task of coordinating defense plans that originate in NATO commands and in the Canada–United States Regional Planning Group, and of making appropriate recommendations to the

---

[8] Iceland, having no military forces, may be represented by a civilian.

Military Committee and ultimately to the North Atlantic Council. Its structure was as follows: the Standing Group met in Washington; at the North Atlantic Council it was represented by a general officer assisted by an allied staff; it had a number of military agencies under its authority such as the Military Agency for Standardization (MAS) in London; the Advisory Group of Aerospace Research and Development (AGARD) and the NATO Defense College, both located in Paris but later relocated; the Allied Military Communications and Electronics Committee (AMCEC), the Allied Long-Line Agency (ALLA), the Allied Radio Frequency Agency (ARFA), and the Allied Naval Communications Agency (ANCA) as well as the Allied Communication Security Agency (ACSA).

The Standing Group had long been under considerable criticism, and many observers recommended its abolition. Its composition, which excluded Germany, had clearly become outdated. Moreover, its location and that of the Military Committee in Washington, away from all the other headquarters, which was quite justified in the beginning, became distinctly awkward. Its abolishment in 1966 was a useful improvement in the NATO command structure. Its subordinate organs were taken over by the Military Committee.

The strategic area covered by the North Atlantic Treaty is divided into three commands and a regional planning group. The most important is the European Command, which extends from the North Cape to North Africa, and from the Atlantic to the eastern border of Turkey, excluding Great Britain. This area is under the Supreme Allied Commander, Europe (SACEUR), whose headquarters were established in the vicinity of Paris and are designated as Supreme Headquarters Allied Powers Europe (SHAPE). It has now moved to Belgium. The Supreme Allied Commanders in Europe have always been Americans; the first one so appointed was General Eisenhower, who was succeeded by General Matthew Ridgway, who was followed by General Lauris Norstad. The present Commander is General Lyman L. Lemnitzer.

There are four subordinate commands directly responsible to SACEUR, the Northern European Command, the Central European Command, the Southern European Command, and the Mediterranean Command.

Coequal with SACEUR are the other two area commands—the Supreme Allied Commander at Atlantic (SACLANT) and the Channel Committee and Channel Command—and the Canada–United States Regional Planning Group.

Other NATO military agencies are the NATO Defense College, which was also established in Paris and later moved to Rome, the Military Agency for Standardization in London, and various communications agencies.

There is no parliamentary control over the civilian or military agencies governing NATO. However, since 1955, an informal Parliamentarians' Conference has met once a year for a few days. Each national legislature designates delegates to attend, and each nation is assigned a certain number of votes, although the number of people in its delegation can be larger. Out of a total of 175 votes, the United States has 36, while Great Britain, France, Germany, and Italy have 18 each.

The meetings of the Parliamentarians' Conference are somewhat formal. They are addressed by military and civilian leaders, but relatively little debate takes place. These conferences are valuable because of the contact they provide, but there is little continuity, and time is far too short to permit any probing in depth. There have been various proposals for a more powerful and significant Atlantic Assembly, but they have come to naught and have been, at least for the present, swept away under the avalanche of more significant and serious problems.

THE PERILS AND TRIBULATIONS OF NATO

NATO is unique not only in that it is the first integrated alliance system to exist in peacetime, but even more in the political implications of this fact: namely, that its members have come to the conclusion that they have permanent interests in common which they are resolved to pursue in common. Basically, this provides a foundation on which a community type of structure might be established. However, the community spirit is not nearly as far advanced in the Atlantic area as it is in Europe, and there are a number of difficult problems which emerge from the nature of the alliance, its military character, the facts of life of the nuclear age, and the great inequality in the power and variety in outlook of NATO's members.

Because NATO is in the midst of a deep crisis as these lines are written, confusion over the various causes of the crisis, which stem from many origins, can easily occur. Some causes may be attributed to the nature of the alliance itself. Others come from the highly personal views of General de Gaulle, which are diametrically opposed to the NATO concept. Because French diplomacy has, in the pursuit of its policies, used the arguments of other European critics, a picture has arisen in the minds of many observers fusing and confusing the French viewpoint with the general European criticism. However, this is an error against which it is necessary to guard; for most European critics of NATO's structure and policies believe nevertheless in the continuation of the integrated Atlantic defense system and merely wish to make it more effective. The French policy, as we shall see, is directed to a quite different end.

There are good reasons why, for the first time in history, an integrated alliance should exist in peacetime. It emerges from the changed conditions of the nuclear age. In past efforts, in the so-called "conventional weapons" age, it was the function of general staffs to prepare for wars under any, even unlikely, contingencies. However, the decision to resort to arms, then as now, lay in the hands of the political leadership. If that leadership decided to go to war, or was forced into war by aggression, it was the purpose of military planning and eventually of military command to conduct the war as successfully as possible. In other words, the essence of strategy in the conventional age was the conduct of war and the attainment of victory.

In the nuclear age, on the other hand, wars have become such tremendously destructive affairs that victory has become a difficult, perhaps impossible, enterprise.

Moreover the destruction on both sides could be so great that the difference between victory and defeat would not be discernible. Under these circumstances the purpose of strategy is to prevent war, not to conduct war successfully. This is to be done by the strategy of deterrence, that is to say, a potential aggressor is to be confronted with such overwhelming force, or rather with the certainty of such huge and unacceptable destruction, that he will prefer not to resort to arms to begin with. If an alliance is to be a part of this deterrent strategy, it is important that it be so closely integrated and so well planned, its targets of actions selected and assigned in peacetime, that it is able to act instantaneously. Or, in other words, while traditional, conventional alliances were planned for the event of war and only rudimentary agreements were necessary in times of peace, the alliance system of the nuclear age has to fulfill its role entirely in peacetime. If war does come, the alliance system and the general strategy have, in one sense, failed, for the prevention of war was their major function.

This means for Europe that all deterrent strategies must in some way be integrated with the nuclear power of the United States, because that power alone is in a position to constitute a credible deterrent. Ninety-seven percent of Western nuclear strength is in the hands of the United States. In the opinion of American and most European strategists, a small, independent, national nuclear force of a European power could not organize a credible deterrent, because even if such a force were able to reach its target, the subsequent total destruction of its homeland would make it extremely dubious that its planes or missiles would ever be ordered to leave the ground, the sea, or the launching pad.[9]

Nuclear strategy

In the days when the United States had a nuclear monopoly, it coined the theory of "massive retaliation." This meant that any kind of aggression in Europe would immediately bring about massive destruction of the enemy by strategic nuclear weapons. Although in those days the United States possessed relatively few, and by present standards crude, nuclear weapons and although it was never at all certain that such massive retaliation would actually be applied if an enemy foray were less than a wholesale invasion, the doctrine of massive retaliation was nevertheless credible because of the American monopoly and because a potential opponent could not incur the risk of having his bluff called. Since this was the period in which the basic tenets of NATO strategy were established, massive retaliation, or to be more precise, an almost immediate nuclear escalation remained the official doctrine of NATO. Due to certain European objections, it could never be changed, although the United States, the principal nuclear power, did in fact change its strategy.

[9] Albert Wohlstetter, "Nuclear Sharing: NATO and the N plus I Country," *Foreign Affairs,* Vol. 39, April, 1961, pp. 372–37. For an opposite view, see General Gallois.

Contrary to frequently heard views, this change was not arbitrary or capricious.[10] It developed in the following manner. Although the United States was still very far ahead of the Soviet Union in all forms of nuclear weapons and delivery systems, the Soviet Union, the only potential enemy capable of indulging in nuclear warfare in the foreseeable future, was nevertheless increasing its nuclear power, hardening its sites[11] and dispersing them, and developing an undersea missile fleet. Hence, an increasing number of Soviet targets would escape the destruction wrought by an American second-strike attack.[12] The resulting damage to the United States was bound to increase with time. Under these circumstances, a threat of massive retaliation to even a relatively limited enemy attack would be increasingly lacking in credibility. It seemed better to the authors of that theory to plan to do two things: (1) engage the enemy with forces only commensurate to those that he had employed, making sure that he would not win an easy victory and would be certain of incurring serious involvement which would carry with it the very real danger of nuclear escalation; but at the same time (2), by this involvement give him one more chance to think before the ultimate weapons were used.

In the opinion of American planners, this theory was more credible and hence increased rather than decreased the deterrent force of America's and the West's nuclear arsenal. However, in the opinion of many European specialists, the possibility that an opponent could invade Western Europe without being certain of drawing immediate nuclear counterstrikes, would make Europe more vulnerable, not less so.[13] Some other critics also expressed the opinion that this theory made Europe "expendable" and that nuclear weapons would be used only in defense of the American homeland.

Although these European critics have little support in actual American strategic thought, they have never been stilled. Their irritation came not so much from the difference in strategic concepts as from the fact that the NATO authorities had never officially changed their nuclear doctrine although America had in fact done so and by so doing had established a *fait accompli*. This fact, more than the validity or invalidity of the doctrine, tended to remind Europeans of the inequality of their position and of the absurd situation, imposed by the technology of the nuclear age, in which this now rich and resurgent Europe was still forced to rely almost entirely on American nuclear power for its defense.

---

[10] The basic doctrine of the new theory of flexible response may be found in the book by General Maxwell D. Taylor, *The Uncertain Trumpet,* New York, 1959.

[11] A "hardened site" is a highly protected underground installation which can be destroyed only by a direct or near direct nuclear hit.

[12] In the nomenclature of nuclear theory, a first strike is the initial attack, the riposte thereto constitutes a second strike. Strikes may be counterforce, i.e., against military targets, missile sites, etc., or countercity, i.e., against population centers.

[13] A good summary of European objections and fears may be found in the book by Raymond Aron, *The Great Debate: Theories of Nuclear Strategy* (trans. by Ernst Pawel), New York, 1965.

Nuclear sharing

This inequality gave rise to various thoughts about ways in which Europe might share in nuclear decision making. This problem, which is rather technical and cannot be explored in detail here, was complicated by several factors. One was that America was, and remains, convinced of the ineffectiveness of small national nuclear forces. Another was the problem of giving a share in nuclear decisions not only to European powers which had already gone nuclear, such as France and Great Britain, but also to nonnuclear countries like Germany, whose acquisition of nuclear weapons would have caused a great deal of difficulty and would have had explosive political potentialities.

A number of plans have been proposed in order to grapple with this difficult problem. One was for the Multilateral Nuclear Force (MLF), an integrated multilateral force of surface ships with a considerable nuclear punch to be managed by an integrated multilateral authority. Another plan was a British modification which envisaged both multinational, i.e., national but coordinated, units, and multilateral, i.e., integrated, components. Further attempts to arrive at a solution were made through the establishment of a committee, first called select and then special, proposed by Secretary of Defense McNamara in 1965. So far, however, the complex problem arising from the huge inequality of nuclear weaponry has eluded solution.

The degree of American influence

At the bottom of the uneasiness, is, possibly, the fact that the NATO structure has always been heavily dominated by American personnel, forces, and weapons. Many Europeans have felt, rightly or wrongly, that NATO strategy meant that they were pulling an oar in the American boat. Perhaps this situation might have been better balanced if Europe had been willing to make greater sacrifices in the common defense. But in the absence of powerful European nuclear weapons, such contributions would have had to be made primarily in ground forces or through other forms of financial contributions which in the opinion of many Europeans would still not have been certain of giving Europe a significantly greater voice. Many Europeans felt, probably correctly, that if Europe were united, its combined voice would certainly be very much stronger. This idea has always been warmly supported by United States policy but, as we have seen in preceding chapters, many obstacles appear to block the path of greater political European integration.

Political consultation

The word "consultation" covers a great many possibilities. They range all the way from merely informing one's allies of a decision already taken (as the U.S. did in the case of the Cuban missile crisis) to forms of joint decision making. This has been earnestly attempted but has proven enormously difficult. Several members of NATO have had interests going well beyond the NATO area. Thus many European countries, especially Britain and France, as earlier the Netherlands and Belgium, have complained that the United States did not support their policies in Africa and Asia. In more recent years, the United States has made similar complaints with regard to its policies in the war in Vietnam. Doubtless, this is one area in which further progress needs to be made, and the crisis of NATO unleashed by General de Gaulle's policies has thrown a spotlight on this problem.

THE CRISIS OF 1966

We have seen that however military are the organization and the immediate purpose of NATO, the underlying assumption is political: namely, that the members of NATO have permanent common interests and that they would and should solve them in some form of common action. On this there is little difference between the United States and thirteen of the other fourteen members of NATO. The French government of General de Gaulle, however, has fundamentally different views.

In his war memoirs General de Gaulle defines the desirable policy for France in these terms: "To collaborate with the West or the East, to contract if necessary with the one or the other side necessary alliances, without ever accepting any form of dependence."[14] Although he was writing of his sentiments at the end of World War II, there is little doubt that these thoughts constitute his present ideas, for this volume of his memoirs was published in France in 1959 and in an English translation in 1960, well after his return to power, and if he had found these thoughts embarrassing, he could easily have expunged them from his book. This idea of contracting with either side for the sole purpose of furthering the national interest of France is fundamentally incompatible with the idea of a permanent alliance or any other permanent relationship, be it European or Atlantic.

Even before he came to power, General de Gaulle and his followers scarcely hid their distaste of the NATO system. His true objection was not to the way in which NATO was organized, but to its fundamental concept. It is therefore entirely consistent that General de Gaulle, although highly critical of NATO, has never made any formal proposal for its reform. In 1958 he did make an informal proposal for a directorate to be established, composed of Britain, France, and the United States, which in addition to world-wide responsibilities would have given NATO informal direction. General Eisenhower rejected this proposal on the grounds that it was a matter concerning all fifteen members and not just three. Since 1958, no further proposal, formal or informal, has been made by the French government for reform of NATO.

During 1964 and 1965 increasing signs appeared that General de Gaulle

---

[14] General de Gaulle, *Mémoires de guerre, Paris,* 1959, Vol. III, Le Salut, 1944–1946, p. 179.

intended to pull out of NATO. In fact, the degree to which French forces were subject to NATO disposition was increasingly reduced. There were also numerous statements indicating that the key year might be 1969 when, according to the North Atlantic Treaty, countries may withdraw from NATO after giving one year's notice.

However, for various reasons which can only be surmised and which may possibly be attributed either to General de Gaulle's age or the possibility of a loss of his majority in the National Assembly, the timetable for France's withdrawal was greatly accelerated in 1966, beginning with a press conference on March 8. In a rapid series of statements and letters the Allies, especially the United States, were notified that foreign installations would have to be removed from the soil of France or be placed under French command in a way which was clearly unacceptable. This was all the more unacceptable as at the same time it was announced that by the summer of 1966 all French forces and personnel still at the disposal of NATO would be withdrawn.

These measures could hardly be interpreted in any way other than as being aimed at NATO's very existence, for the integrated organization and staffs, the common planning and collective action constitute the nature of the Atlantic Alliance. NATO without the "O" makes little sense in the opinion of the United States and the other thirteen NATO members other than France, because it is in the organization and its ability to act instantly that the deterrent value of the alliance lies.

Just what alternative arrangement General de Gaulle has in mind, has never been made clear. One authoritative article published by a study group of the French Center for the Study of Foreign Affairs probably comes close to revealing his thoughts.[15] This article envisaged a European continental defense system in which France alone would have nuclear weapons and in which France therefore would be the leader. Germany would participate but, being removed from any participation in the decision over weapons, would have to maintain a secondary position. This unintegrated defense system then might enter into a bilateral relationship with the United States.

Whatever the true intentions of General de Gaulle about the future of Europe's defense, there is little doubt that it is and has always been his intention to unravel the existing structure of NATO.

The reaction to his proposals has been interesting. Not only America, but the other thirteen members of NATO other than France, showed considerable unity. The effort to move to a common strategy was led actively by Great Britain. In part this resistance might have been influenced by the previous attack of General de Gaulle on European integration and the test of the two Luxembourg meetings of the Council of Ministers of EEC in January, 1966, in which the French had been confronted by unanimous opposition and had been forced to back down.

---

[15] X X X, "Faut-il Reformer l'Alliance Atlantique?" *Politique Etrangère*, 1965, No. 3, pp. 230–244.

But perhaps more important was another factor. Under the impact of somewhat improved relations between the Soviet Union and Western Europe and the United States, and the U.S.S.R.'s preoccupation with its growing struggle with China, the problems of NATO had, in the opinion of many Europeans, lost some of their relevance. Alliances are always in danger when the external threat against which they were created diminishes. However, the French-caused NATO crisis of 1966 forced all NATO members to reconsider their principal assumptions. In that process they discovered that NATO was in effect a political association designed to cope with the two principal problems of Europe, i.e., how to deal with the Soviet Union from a basis of strength, and how to keep Germany firmly tied to the West. In the event of NATO's disappearance, the German armed forces would have to reestablish their national general staff and pursue national rather than NATO aims. While nobody would say that under those circustances Germany would necessarily fall into former patterns, Germany's political structure was based very much on the assumption of close integration with the West, and if there were an absence of this integration and of these assumptions, nobody, not even most Germans, could say with finality just where Germany's road would go. At any rate, that seemed too much of a risk to take and has contributed to the solidarity of the Western position.

This is not the place to discuss in detail the specifics of a fast-moving crisis, of the replacement of depots and headquarters from France, of the rearrangement of the early warning system, of the overflight rights over French territory whose cessation would cut Italy off from the rest of the Alliance, and of many more problems.

The issue is more fundamental. Two basic conceptions confront each other. One is the belief in a common Atlantic destiny, in an Atlantic political civilization capable of confronting the many problems of our age through increasingly common, collective action. The other is a belief in a return to nationalism, the complete freedom of states to pursue their own and only their own interests.

General de Gaulle is unlikely to win his goal of dominating an unintegrated Europe if for no other reason than that Germany is unwilling to accept the secondary role assigned to her in his scheme. Only if he were able to persuade the Soviet Union to make a really meaningful gesture in the direction of German reunification is Germany likely to accept such a position, and even then only temporarily. However, the Soviet Union does not appear likely to take such a step in the foreseeable future. But General de Gaulle may succeed in destroying NATO, for his withdrawal, and the brusque manner in which he denies the French territory and communication lines to NATO cause not only grave inconvenience but also great expense.

Nevertheless, the crisis revealed that the overwhelming majority of NATO members believe that NATO is necessary and must be maintained. In that lies not only hope, but the possibility of new vitality. That in turn, however, will come about only if NATO members are not content merely to return to the point of departure to patch up the existing structure. For indeed, if NATO is to survive and prosper, membership must become even more worthwhile, not just in military but also in political terms. This requires that participation in common decision making must be more meaningful for all concerned.

This is not a simple matter, and changes are necessary in the attitude of both Europeans and Americans. First of all, a close association between separate European states and an overwhelmingly powerful America always bears the danger, even with the best will in the world, of turning into a satellite relationship, or into a relationship of such inequality that it turns sour and fails. European unity, or at least the progressive unity of the Six, would make possible a more equal relationship and would enhance both European unity and Atlantic partnership. To this desirable relationship of equals, America can make some contributions, but essentially it can only be the work of the Europeans themselves.[16]

Secondly, new vitality for NATO requires that in time the Europeans accept greater responsibilities in world affairs, even outside the Atlantic area. In the past, such world responsibilities were carried essentially as part of an imperial or imperialist policy. Since most European countries have lost their former colonial possessions, and have overcome the psychological shock of the change, Europeans have come to enjoy their freedom from responsibility and are reluctant to shoulder old burdens again. Nobody requests a return to colonialism. But the Atlantic area is too powerful, too rich, too influential an area to escape involvement in the affairs of the world, in the evolution of underdeveloped countries, and the like. To pretend that these matters do not concern the Alliance is unrealistic, for some Alliance members will be concerned while others may withdraw into disagreement, thereby endangering the partnership.

But America will have to recognize that in order to have partners she has to be one, or in other words, that an Atlantic partnership cannot mean simply adding an Atlantic weight to American policy any more than France will succeed in adding a European weight to French national policy. As the European Communities have demonstrated, what is needed is a search for ways of acting in common after having sought in common for common policies and common outlooks. Raymond Aron has wisely stated that "in the thermonuclear age alliances transform themselves into Communities or they cease to exist."[17]

It inspires the imagination to contemplate what a true Atlantic Community could accomplish. In the United Nations, in aid to less developed countries, in international trade, an Atlantic partnership could accomplish outstanding results beneficial to all concerned. This is not to say that we should impose our ideas and our images on other nations and cultures. But the values, experience, and institutions of the Atlantic world are not just regional achievements, they have universal values and applicability. Ideally it would be better to wait for greater European unity before taking steps toward an Atlantic Community lest European countries

---

[16] Jean Monnet, "Des Partenaires égaux," *La Nef*, February–April, 1966, pp. 7–17.
[17] In François Duchêne, *Beyond Alliance*, Paris, 1965.

be dissolved in an American cup of tea. But at this time when both the European Communities and NATO face mortal danger to the very principle on which they are established, each type of organization for collective action gains from the strength of the other, especially since the attack on both comes from the same source. The road of the future does not depend on meticulously drafted legal blueprints; of those there is no shortage. Rather it depends on the will of men to decide which way the nations of the Atlantic region should go.

It is important to keep in mind the lesson of states such as we have discussed in the first four parts of this book as well as the lessons of the European Communities. Concrete collaboration and collective action in a spirit of accepting permanent common interests cannot live on good intentions alone, but must be based also on the forging of common institutions. This is the lesson which Britain and the English-speaking nations especially have taught on the national level. This lesson has once again been reconfirmed in the supranational sphere in the European Communities. Time will tell whether we shall eventually be permitted to apply these lessons also to the Atlantic partnership.

The Constitution of France adopted by the referendum of September 28, 1958

Promulgated October 4, 1958

PREAMBLE

The French people hereby solemnly proclaims its attachment to the Rights of Man and to the principles of national sovereignty as defined by the Declaration of 1789, confirmed and complemented by the Preamble of the Constitution of 1946.

By virtue of these principles and that of the free determination of peoples, the Republic hereby offers to the overseas territories that express the desire to adhere to them, new institutions based on the common ideal of liberty, equality, and fraternity and conceived with a view to their democratic evolution.

Art. 1—The Republic and the peoples of the overseas territories who, by an act of free determination, adopt the present Constitution thereby institute a Community.

The Community shall be based on the equality and the solidarity of the peoples composing it.

Title I: ON SOVEREIGNTY

Art. 2—France shall be a republic, indivisible, secular, democratic and social. It shall ensure the equality of all citizens before the law, without distinction of origin, race or religion. It shall respect all beliefs.

The national emblem shall be the tricolor flag, blue, white and red.

The national anthem shall be the "Marseillaise."

The motto of the Republic shall be "Liberty, Equality, Fraternity."

Its principle shall be government of the people, by the people and for the people.

Art. 3—National sovereignty belongs to the people, which shall exercise this sovereignty through its representatives and through the referendum.

No section of the people, nor any individual, may attribute to themselves or himself the exercise thereof.

Suffrage may be direct or indirect under the conditions stipulated by the Constitution. It shall always be universal, equal and secret.

All French citizens of both sexes who have reached their majority and who enjoy civil and political rights may vote under the conditions to be determined by law.

Art. 4—Political parties and groups may compete for votes. They may form and carry on their activities freely. They must respect the principles of national sovereignty and of democracy.

Title II: THE PRESIDENT OF THE REPUBLIC

Art. 5—The President of the Republic shall see that the Constitution is respected. He shall ensure, by his arbitration, the regular functioning of the public powers, as well as the continuity of the state.

He shall be the guarantor of national independence, of the integrity of the territory, and of respect for Community agreements and for treaties.

Art. 6—The President of the Republic shall be elected for seven years by an electoral college comprising the members of parliament, of the general councils and of the assemblies of the overseas territories, as well as the elected representatives of the municipal councils.

These representatives shall be:

the mayor for communes of fewer than 1,000 inhabitants;

the mayor and the first deputy mayor for communes of from 1,000 to 2,000 inhabitants;

the mayor, first deputy mayor and a municipal councilor chosen according to the order of appearance on the council list for communes of from 2,001 to 2,500 inhabitants;

the mayor and the two first deputy mayors for communes of from 2,501 to 3,000 inhabitants;

the mayor, the two first deputy mayors and three municipal councilors chosen according to the order of appearance on the council list for communes of from 3,001 to 6,000 inhabitants;

the mayor, the two first deputy mayors and six municipal councilors chosen according to the order of appearance on the council list for communes of from 6,001 to 9,000 inhabitants;

all the municipal councilors for communes of more than 9,000 inhabitants;

in addition, for communes of more than 30,000 inhabitants, delegates appointed by the municipal council at the rate of one delegate for every 1,000 inhabitants above 30,000.

In the overseas territories of the Republic, the elected representatives of the councils of the administrative units shall also form part of the electoral college under the conditions to be determined by an organic law.

The participation of member states of the Community in the electoral college for the President of the Republic shall be determined by agreement between the Republic and the member states of the Community.

The modalities implementing the present article shall be determined by an organic law.

Art. 7—The President of the Republic shall be elected by an absolute majority on the first ballot. If this is not obtained, the President of the Republic shall be elected on a second ballot by a relative majority.

The voting shall be opened upon summons by the government.

The election of the new President shall take place twenty days at the least and fifty days at the most before the expiration of the powers of the President in office.

In the event of a vacancy in the presidency of the Republic, for any cause whatsoever, or in case of prevention officially noted by the Constitutional Council, to which the matter has been referred by the government, and which shall rule by an absolute majority of its members, the functions of the President of the Republic, with the exception of those provided for by Articles 11 and 12 below, shall be temporarily exercised by the president of the Senate. In the case of a vacancy, or when the prevention is declared definitive by the Constitutional Council, the voting for the election of a new President shall take place, except in case of *force majeure* officially noted by the Constitutional Council, twenty days at the least and fifty days at the most after the beginning of the vacancy or the declaration of the definitive character of the prevention.

Art. 8—The President of the Republic shall appoint the Premier. He shall terminate the functions of the Premier when the latter presents the resignation of the government.

At the proposal of the Premier, he shall appoint the other members of the Government and shall terminate their functions.

Art. 9—The President of the Republic shall preside over the Council of Ministers.

Art. 10—The President of the Republic shall promulgate the laws within fifteen days following the transmission to the government of the finally adopted law.

He may, before the expiration of this time limit, ask Parliament for a reconsideration of the law or of certain of its articles. This reconsideration may not be refused.

Art. 11—The President of the Republic, on the proposal of the government during [parliamentary] sessions, or on joint motion of the two assemblies, published in the *Journal Officiel,* may submit to a referendum any bill dealing with the organization of the public powers, entailing approval of a Community agreement, or providing for authorization to ratify a treaty that, without being contrary to the Constitution, might affect the functioning of the institutions.

When the referendum decides in favor of the bill, the President of the Republic shall promulgate it within the time limit stipulated in the preceding article.

Art. 12—The President of the Republic may, after consultation with the Premier and the presidents of the assemblies, declare the dissolution of the National Assembly.

General elections shall take place twenty days at the least and forty days at the most after the dissolution.

The National Assembly shall convene by right on the second Thursday following its election. If this meeting takes place between the periods provided for ordinary sessions, a session shall, by right, be opened for a fifteen-day period.

There may be no further dissolution within a year following these elections.

Art. 13—The President of the Republic shall sign the ordinances and decrees decided upon in the Council of Ministers.

He shall make appointments to the civil and military posts of the state.

Councilors of State, the Grand Chancellor of the Legion of Honor, ambassadors and envoys extraordinary, master councilors of the Audit Office, prefects, representatives of the government in the overseas territories, general officers, rectors of academies [regional divisions of the public educational system] and directors of central administrations shall be appointed in meetings of the Council of Ministers.

An organic law shall determine the other posts to be filled in meetings of the Council of Ministers, as well as the conditions under which the power of the President of the Republic to make appointments to office may be delegated by him to be exercised in his name.

Art. 14—The President of the Republic shall accredit ambassadors and envoys extraordinary to foreign powers; foreign ambassadors and envoys extraordinary shall be accredited to him.

Art. 15—The President of the Republic shall be commander of the armed forces. He shall preside over the higher councils and committees of national defense.

Art. 16—When the institutions of the Republic, the independence of the nation, the integrity of its territory or the fulfilment of its international commitments are threatened in a grave and immediate manner and the regular functioning of the constitutional public powers is interrupted, the President of the Republic shall take the measures required by these circumstances, after official consultation with the Premier and the presidents of the assemblies, as well as with the Constitutional Council.

He shall inform the nation of these measures in a message.

These measures must be prompted by the desire to ensure to the constitutional public powers, in the shortest possible time, the means of accomplishing their mission. The Constitutional Council shall be consulted with regard to such measures.

Parliament shall meet by right.

The National Assembly may not be dissolved during the exercise of exceptional powers.

Art. 17—The President of the Republic shall have the right of pardon.

Art. 18—The President of the Republic shall communicate with the two assemblies of parliament by means of messages, which he shall cause to be read, and which shall not be the occasion for any debate.

Between sessions, the parliament shall be convened especially to this end.

Art. 19—The acts of the President of the Republic, other than those provided for under Articles 8 (first paragraph), 11, 12, 16, 18, 54, 56 and 61, shall be countersigned by the Premier and, should circumstances so require, by the appropriate ministers.

Title III: THE GOVERNMENT

Art. 20—The government shall determine and conduct the policy of the nation.

It shall have at its disposal the administration and the armed forces.

It shall be responsible to the parliament under the conditions and according to the procedures stipulated in Articles 49 and 50.

Art. 21—The Premier shall direct the operation of the government. He shall be responsible for national defense. He shall ensure the execution of the laws. Subject to the provisions of Article 13, he shall have regulatory powers and shall make appointments to civil and military posts.

He may delegate certain of his powers to the ministers.

He shall replace, should the occasion arise, the President of the Republic as the chairman of the councils and committees provided for under Article 15.

He may, in exceptional instances, replace him as the chairman of a meeting of the Council of Ministers by virtue of an explicit delegation and for a specific agenda.

Art. 22—The acts of the Premier shall be countersigned, when circumstances so require, by the ministers responsible for their execution.

Art. 23—The functions of members of the government shall be incompatible with the exercise of any parliamentary mandate, with the holding of any office, at the national level in business, professional or labor organizations, and with any public employment or professional activity.

An organic law shall determine the conditions under which the holders of such mandates, functions or employments shall be replaced.

The replacement of the members of parliament shall take place in accordance with the provisions of Article 25.

Title IV: THE PARLIAMENT

Art. 24—The parliament shall comprise the National Assembly and the Senate.

The deputies to the National Assembly shall be elected by direct suffrage.

The Senate shall be elected by indirect suffrage. It shall ensure the representation of the territorial units of the Republic. Frenchmen living outside France shall be represented in the Senate.

Art. 25—An organic law shall determine the term for which each assembly is elected, the number of its members, their emoluments, the conditions of eligibility and the system of ineligibilities and incompatibilities.

It shall likewise determine the conditions under which, in the case of a vacancy in either assembly, persons shall be elected to replace the deputy or senator whose seat has been vacated until the holding of new complete or partial elections to the assembly concerned.

Art. 26—No member of parliament may be prosecuted, sought, arrested, detained or tried as a result of the opinions or votes expressed by him in the exercise of his functions.

No member of parliament may, during parliamentary sessions, be prosecuted or arrested for criminal or minor offenses without the authorization of the assembly of which he is a member except in the case of *flagrante delicto*.

When parliament is not in session, no member of parliament may be arrested without the authorization of the secretariat of the assembly of which he is a member, except in the case of *flagrante delicto,* of authorized prosecution or of final conviction.

The detention or prosecution of a member of parliament shall be suspended if the assembly of which he is a member so demands.

Art. 27—Any compulsory vote shall be null and void.

The right to vote of the members of parliament shall be personal.

An organic law may, under exceptional circumstances, authorize the delegation of a vote. In this case, no member may be delegated more than one vote.

Art. 28—Parliament shall convene by right in two ordinary sessions a year.

The first session shall begin on the first Tuesday of October and shall end on the third Friday of December.

The second session shall open on the last Tuesday of April; it may not last longer than three months.

Art. 29—Parliament shall convene in extraordinary session at the request of the Premier, or of the majority of the members comprising the National Assembly, to consider a specific agenda.

When an extraordinary session is held at the request of the members of the National Assembly, the closure decree shall take effect as soon as the parliament has exhausted the agenda for which it was called, and at the latest twelve days from the date of its meeting.

Only the Premier may ask for a new session before the end of the month following the closure decree.

Art. 30—Apart from cases in which parliament meets by right, extraordinary sessions shall be opened and closed by decree of the President of the Republic.

Art. 31—The members of the government shall have access to the two assemblies. They shall be heard when they so request.

They may call for the assistance of commissioners of the government.

Art. 32—The president of the National Assembly shall be elected for the duration of the legislature. The president of the Senate shall be elected after each partial re-election [of the Senate].

Art. 33—The meetings of the two assemblies shall be public. An *in extenso* report of the debates shall be published in the *Journal Officiel.*

Each assembly may sit in secret committee at the request of the Premier or of one-tenth of its members.

Title V: ON RELATIONS BETWEEN PARLIAMENT AND THE GOVERNMENT

Art. 34—The law shall be voted by parliament.

The law shall establish the regulations concerning:

civil rights and the fundamental guarantees granted to the citizens for the exercise of their public liberties; the obligations imposed by the national defense upon the person and property of citizens;

nationality, status and legal capacity of persons, marriage contracts, inheritance and gifts;

determination of crimes and misdemeanors as well as the penalties imposed therefor; criminal procedure; amnesty; the creation of new juridical systems and the status of magistrates;

the basis, the rate, and the methods of collecting taxes of all types; the issuance of currency.

The law likewise shall determine the regulations concerning:

the electoral system of the parliamentary assemblies and the local assemblies;

the establishment of categories of public institutions;

the fundamental guarantees granted to civil and military personnel employed by the state;

the nationalization of enterprises and the transfers of the property of enterprises from the public to the private sector.

The law shall determine the fundamental principles of:

the general organization of national defense;

the free administration of local communities, of their competencies and their resources;

education;

property rights, civil and commercial obligations;

legislation pertaining to employment, unions and social security.

The financial laws shall determine the financial resources and obligations of the state under the conditions and with the reservations to be provided for by an organic law.

Laws pertaining to national planning shall determine the objectives of the economic and social action of the state.

The provisions of the present article may be detailed and supplemented by an organic law.

Art. 35—Parliament shall authorize the declaration of war.

Art. 36—Martial law shall be decreed in a meeting of the Council of Ministers. Its prorogation beyond twelve days may be authorized only by parliament.

Art. 37—Matters other than those that fall within the domain of law shall be of a regulatory character.

Legislative texts concerning these matters may be modified by decrees issued after consultation with the Council of State. Those legislative texts which shall be passed after the entry into force of the present Constitution shall be modified by decree, only if the Constitutional Council has stated that they have a regulatory character as defined in the preceding paragraph.

Art. 38—The government may, in order to carry out its program, ask parliament for authorization to take through ordinances, during a limited period, measures that are normally within the domain of law.

The ordinances shall be enacted in meetings of the Council of Ministers after consultation with the Council of State. They shall come into force upon their publication, but shall become null and void if the bill for their ratification is not submitted to parliament before the date set by the enabling act.

At the expiration of the time limit referred to in the first paragraph of the present article, the ordinances may be modified only by law in those matters which are within the legislative domain.

Art. 39—The Premier and the members of parliament alike shall have the right to initiate legislation.

Government bills shall be discussed in the Council of Ministers after consultation with the Council of State and shall be filed with the secretariat of one of the two assemblies. Finance bills shall be submitted first to the National Assembly.

Art. 40—The bills and amendments introduced by the members of parliament shall be inadmissible when their adoption would have as a consequence either a diminution of public financial resources, or the creation or increase of public expenditures.

Art. 41—If it shall appear in the course of the legislative procedure that a parliamentary bill or an amendment is not within the domain of law or is contrary to a delegation granted by virtue of Article 38, the government may declare its inadmissibility.

In case of disagreement between the government and the president of the assembly concerned, the Constitutional Council, upon the request of one or the other, shall rule within a time limit of eight days.

Art. 42—The discussion of bills shall pertain, in the first assembly to which they have been referred, to the text presented by the government.

An assembly, given a text passed by the other assembly, shall deliberate on the text that is transmitted to it.

Art. 43—Government and parliamentary bills shall, at the request of the government or of the assembly concerned, be sent for study to committees especially designated for this purpose.

Government and parliamentary bills for which such a request has not been made shall be sent to one of the permanent committees, the number of which shall be limited to six in each assembly.

Art. 44—Members of parliament and of the government shall have the right of amendment.

After the opening of the debate, the government may oppose the examination of any amendment which has not previously been submitted to committee.

If the government so requests, the assembly concerned shall decide, by a single vote, on all or part of the text under discussion, retaining only the amendments proposed or accepted by the government.

Art. 45—Every government or parliamentary bill shall be examined successively in the two assemblies of parliament with a view to the adoption of an identical text.

When, as a result of disagreement between the two assemblies, it has been impossible to adopt a government or parliamentary bill after two readings by each assembly, or, if the government has declared the matter urgent, after a single reading by each of them, the Premier shall have the right to bring about a meeting of a point committee, composed of an equal number from both assemblies, charged with the task of proposing a text on the matters still under discussion.

The text elaborated by the joint committee may be submitted by the government for approval of the two assemblies. No amendment shall be admissible except by agreement with the government.

If the joint committee does not succeed in adopting a common text, or if this text is not adopted under the conditions set forth in the preceding paragraph, the government may, after a new reading by the National Assembly and by the Senate, ask the National Assembly to rule definitively. In this case, the National Assembly may reconsider either the text elaborated by the joint committee, or the last text voted by it, modified when circumstances so require by one or several of the amendments adopted by the Senate.

Art. 46—The laws that the Constitution characterizes as organic shall be passed and amended under the following conditions:

A government or parliamentary bill shall be submitted to the deliberation and to the vote of the first assembly notified, only at the expiration of a period of fifteen days following its introduction.

The procedure of Article 45 shall be applicable. Nevertheless, lacking an agreement between the two assemblies, the text may be adopted by the National Assembly on final reading only by an absolute majority of its members.

The organic laws relative to the Senate must be passed in the same manner by the two assemblies.

The organic laws may be promulgated only after a declaration by the Constitutional Council on their constitutionality.

Art. 47—The parliament shall pass finance bills under the conditions to be stipulated by an organic law.

Should the National Assembly fail to reach a decision on first reading within a time limit of forty days after a bill has been filed, the government shall refer it to the Senate, which must rule within a time limit of fifteen days. The procedure set forth in Article 45 shall then be followed.

Should parliament fail to reach a decision within a time limit of seventy days, the provisions of the bill may be enforced by ordinance.

Should the finance bill establishing the resources and expenditures of a fiscal year not be filed in time for it to be promulgated before the beginning of that fiscal year, the government shall urgently request parliament for the authorization to collect the taxes and shall make available by decree the funds needed to meet the government commitments already voted.

The time limits stipulated in the present article shall be suspended when the parliament is not in session.

The Audit Office shall assist parliament and the government in supervising the implementation of the finance laws.

Art. 48—The discussion of the bills filed or agreed upon by the government shall have priority on the agenda of the assemblies in the order determined by the government.

One meeting a week shall be reserved, by priority, for questions asked by members of parliament and for answers by the government.

Art. 49—The Premier, after deliberation by the Council of Ministers, shall make the government responsible, before the National Assembly, for its program or, should the occasion arise, for a declaration of general policy.

When the National Assembly adopts a motion of censure, the responsibility of the government shall thereby be questioned. Such a motion is admissible only if it is signed by at least one-tenth of the members of the National Assembly. The vote may not take place before forty-eight hours after the motion has been filed. Only the votes that are favorable to a motion of censure shall be counted; the motion of censure may be adopted only by a majority of the members comprising the assembly. Should the motion of censure be rejected, its signers may not introduce another motion of censure during the same session, except in the case provided for in the paragraph below.

The Premier may, after deliberation by the Council of Ministers, make the government responsible before the National Assembly for the adoption of a given text. In this case, this text shall be considered as adopted, unless a motion of censure, filed during the twenty-four hours that follow, is carried under the conditions provided for in the preceding paragraph.

The Premier shall have the right to request the Senate for approval of a declaration of general policy.

Art. 50—When the National Assembly adopts a motion of censure, or when it disapproves the program or a declaration of general policy of the government, the Premier must hand the resignation of the government to the President of the Republic.

Art. 51—The closure of ordinary or extraordinary sessions shall by right be delayed, should the occasion arise, in order to permit the application of the provisions of Article 49.

Title VI: ON TREATIES AND INTERNATIONAL AGREEMENTS

Art. 52—The President of the Republic shall negotiate and ratify treaties.

He shall be informed of all negotiations leading to the conclusion of an international agreement not subject to ratification.

Art. 53—Peace treaties, commercial treaties, treaties or agreements relative to international organization, those that commit the finances of the state, those that modify provisions of a legislative nature, those relative to the status of persons, those that call for the cession, exchange or addition of territory may be ratified or approved only by a law.

They shall go into effect only after having been ratified or approved.

No cession, no exchange, no addition of territory shall be valid without the consent of the populations concerned.

Art. 54—If the Constitutional Council, the matter having been referred to it by the President of the Republic, by the Premier, or by the president of one or the other assembly, shall declare that an international commitment contains a clause contrary to the Constitution, the authorization to ratify or approve this commitment may be given only after amendment of the Constitution.

Art. 55—Treaties or agreements duly ratified or approved shall, upon their publication, have an authority superior to that of laws, subject, for each agreement or treaty, to its application by the other party.

Title VII: THE CONSTITUTIONAL COUNCIL

Art. 56—The Constitutional Council shall consist of nine members, whose mandates shall last nine years and shall not be renewable. One-third of the membership of the Constitutional Council shall be renewed every three years. Three of its members shall be appointed by the President of the Republic, three by the president of the National Assembly, three by the president of the Senate.

In addition to the nine members provided for above, former Presidents of the Republic shall be members ex officio for life of the Constitutional Council.

The president shall be appointed by the President of the Republic. He shall have the deciding vote in case of a tie.

Art. 57—The office of member of the Constitutional Council shall be incompatible with that of minister or member of parliament. Other incompatibilities shall be determined by an organic law.

Art. 58—The Constitutional Council shall ensure the regularity of the election of the President of the Republic.

It shall examine complaints and shall announce the results of the vote.

Art. 59—The Constitutional Council shall rule, in the case of disagreement, on the regularity of the election of deputies and senators.

Art. 60—The Constitutional Council shall ensure the regularity of the referendum procedure and shall announce the results thereof.

Art. 61—Organic laws, before their promulgation, and regulations of the parliamentary assemblies, before they come into application, must be submitted to the Constitutional Council, which shall rule on their constitutionality.

To the same end, laws may be submitted to the Constitutional Council, before their promulgation, by the President of the Republic, the Premier or the president of one or the other assembly.

In the cases provided for by the two preceding paragraphs, the Constitutional Council must make its ruling within a time limit of one month. Nevertheless, at the request of the government, in case of urgency, this period shall be reduced to eight days.

In these same cases, referral to the Constitutional Council shall suspend the time limit for promulgation.

Art. 62—A provision declared unconstitutional may not be promulgated or implemented.

The decisions of the Constitutional Council may not be appealed to any jurisdiction whatsoever. They must be recognized by the public powers and by all administrative and juridical authorities.

Art. 63—An organic law shall determine the rules of organization and functioning of the Constitutional Council, the procedure to be followed before it, and in particular the periods of time allowed for laying disputes before it.

Title VIII: ON JUDICIAL AUTHORITY

Art. 64—The President of the Republic shall be the guarantor of the independence of the judicial authority.

He shall be assisted by the High Council of the Judiciary.

An organic law shall determine the status of magistrates.

Magistrates may not be removed from office.

Art. 65—The High Council of the Judiciary shall be presided over by the President of the Republic. The Minister of Justice shall be its vice-president ex officio. He may preside in place of the President of the Republic.

The High Council shall, in addition, include nine members appointed by the President of the Republic in conformity with the conditions to be determined by an organic law.

The High Council of the Judiciary shall present nominations for judges of the Court of Cassation [supreme court of appeal] and for first presidents of courts of appeal. It shall give its opinion under the conditions to be determined by an organic law on proposals of the Minister of Justice relative to the nomination of the other judges. It shall be consulted on questions of pardon under conditions to be determined by an organic law.

The High Council of the Judiciary shall act as a disciplinary council for judges. In such cases, it shall be presided over by the First President of the Court of Cassation.

Art. 66—No one may be arbitrarily detained.

The judicial authority, guardian of individual liberty, shall ensure the respect of this principal under the conditions stipulated by law.

TITLE IX: THE HIGH COURT OF JUSTICE

Art. 67—A High Court of Justice shall be instituted.

It shall be composed, in equal number, of members elected, from among their membership, by the National Assembly and by the Senate after each general or partial election to these assemblies. It shall elect its president from among its members.

An organic law shall determine the composition of the High Court, its rules, and also the procedure to be applied before it.

Art. 68—The President of the Republic shall not be held accountable for actions performed in the exercise of his office except in the case of high treason. He may be indicted only by the two assemblies ruling by identical vote in open balloting and by an absolute majority of the members of said assemblies. He shall be tried by the High Court of Justice.

The members of the government shall be criminally liable for actions performed in the exercise of their office and rated as crimes or misdemeanors at the time they were committed. The procedure defined above shall be applied to them, as well as to their accomplices, in case of a conspiracy against the security of the state. In the cases provided for by the present paragraph, the High Court shall be bound by the definition of crimes and misdemeanors, as well as by the determination of penalties, as they are established by the criminal laws in force when the acts are committed.

Title X: THE ECONOMIC AND SOCIAL COUNCIL

Art. 69—The Economic and Social Council, at the referral of the government, shall give its opinion on the government bills, ordinances and decrees, as well as on the parliamentary bills submitted to it.

A member of the Economic and Social Council may be designated by the latter to present, before the parliamentary assemblies, the opinion of the Council on the government or parliamentary bills that have been submitted to it.

Art. 70—The Economic and Social Council may likewise be consulted by the government on any problem of an economic or social character of interest to the Republic or to the Community. Any plan, or any bill dealing with a plan, of an economic or social character shall be submitted to it for its advice.

Art. 71—The composition of the Economic and Social Council and its rules of procedure shall be determined by an organic law.

Title XI: ON TERRITORIAL UNITS

Art. 72—The territorial units of the Republic shall be the communes, the departments and the overseas territories. Any other territorial unit shall be created by law.

These units shall be free to govern themselves through elected councils and under the conditions stipulated by law.

In the departments and the territories, the delegate of the government shall be responsible for the national interests, for administrative supervision, and for seeing that the laws are respected.

Art. 73—Measures of adjustment required by the particular situation of the overseas departments may be taken with regard to the legislative systems and administrative organization of those departments.

Art. 74—The overseas territories of the Republic shall have a particular organization, taking account of their own interests within the general interests of the Republic. This organization shall be defined and modified by law after consultation with the territorial assembly concerned.

Art. 75—Citizens of the Republic who do not have ordinary civil status, the only status referred to in Article 34, may keep their personal status as long as they have not renounced it.

Art. 76—The overseas territories may retain their status within the Republic.

If they express the desire to do so by decision of their territorial assemblies taken within the time limit set in the first paragraph of Article 91, they shall become either overseas departments of the Republic or, organized into groups among themselves or singly, member states of the Community.

Title XII: ON THE COMMUNITY

Art. 77—In the Community instituted by the present Constitution, the states shall enjoy autonomy; they shall administer themselves and, democratically and freely, manage their own affairs.

There shall be only one citizenship in the Community.

All citizens shall be equal before the law, whatever their origin, their race and their religion. They shall have the same duties.

Art. 78—The Community shall have jurisdiction over foreign policy, defense, the monetary system, common economic and financial policy, as well as the policy on strategic raw materials.

In addition, except by special agreement, control of justice, higher education, the general organization of external and common transport and of telecommunications shall be within its jurisdiction.

Special agreements may establish other common jurisdictions or regulate the transfer of jurisdiction from the Community to one of its members.

Art. 79—The member states shall benefit from the provision of Article 77 as soon as they have exercised the choice provided for in Article 76.

Until the measures required for implementation of the present title go into force, matters within the common jurisdiction shall be regulated by the Republic.

Art. 80—The President of the Republic shall preside over and represent the Community.

The Community shall have, as organs, an Executive Council, a Senate and a Court of Arbitration.

Art. 81—The member states of the Community shall participate in the election of the President according to the conditions stipulated in Article 6.

The President of the Republic, in his capacity as President of the Community, shall be represented in each state of the Community.

Art. 82—The Executive Council of the Community shall be presided over by the President of the Community. It shall consist of the Premier of the Republic, the heads of government of each of the member states of the Community, and of the ministers responsible for the common affairs of the Community.

The Executive Council shall organize the cooperation of members of the Community at government and administrative levels.

The organization and procedure of the Executive Council shall be determined by an organic law.

Art. 83—The Senate of the Community shall be composed of delegates whom the parliament of the Republic and the legislative assemblies of the other members of the Community shall choose from among their own membership. The number of delegates of each state shall be determined, taking into account its population and the responsibilities it assumes in the Community.

The Senate of the Community shall hold two sessions a year, which shall be opened and closed by the President of the Community and may not last more than one month each.

The Senate of the Community, upon referral by the President of the Community, shall deliberate on the common economic and financial policy before laws in these matters are voted upon by the parliament of the Republic and, should circumstances so require, by the legislative assemblies of the other members of the Community.

The Senate of the Community shall examine the acts and treaties or international agreements, which are specified in Articles 35 and 53, and which commit the Community.

The Senate of the Community shall take enforceable decisions in the domains in which it has received delegation of power from the legislative assemblies of the members of the Community. These decisions shall be promulgated in the same form as the law in the territory of each of the States concerned.

An organic law shall determine the composition of the Senate and its rules of procedure.

Art. 84—A Court of Arbitration of the Community shall rule on litigations occurring among members of the Community.

Its composition and its competence shall be determined by an organic law.

Art. 85—By derogation from the procedure provided for in Article 89, the provisions of the present title that concern the functioning of the common institutions shall be amendable by identical laws passed by the parliament of the Republic and by the Senate of the Community.

Art. 86—A change of status of a member state of the Community may be requested, either by the Republic, or by a resolution of the legislative assembly of the state concerned confirmed by a local referendum, the organization and supervision of which shall be ensured by the institutions of the Community. The modalities of this change shall be determined by an agreement approved by the parliament of the Republic and the legislative assembly concerned.

Under the same conditions, a member state of the Community may become independent. It shall thereby cease to belong to the Community.

Art. 87—The particular agreements made for the implementation of the present title shall be approved by the parliament of the Republic and the legislative assembly concerned.

Title XIII: ON AGREEMENTS OF ASSOCIATION

Art. 88—The Republic or the Community may make agreements with states that wish to associate themselves with the Community in order to develop their own civilizations.

Title XIV: ON AMENDMENT

Art. 89—The initiative for amending the Constitution shall belong both to the President of the Republic on the proposal of the Premier and to the members of parliament.

The government or parliamentary bill for amendment must be passed by the two assemblies in identical terms. The amendment shall become definitive after approval by a referendum.

Nevertheless, the proposed amendment shall not be submitted to a referendum when the President of the Republic decides to submit it to parliament convened in congress; in this case, the proposed amendment shall be approved only if it is accepted by a three-fifths majority of the votes cast. The secretariat of the congress shall be that of the National Assembly.

No amendment procedure may be undertaken or followed if it is prejudicial to the integrity of the territory.

The republican form of government shall not be the object of an amendment.

Title XV: TEMPORARY PROVISIONS

Art. 90—The ordinary session of parliament is suspended. The mandate of the members of the present National Assembly shall expire on the day that the Assembly elected under the present Constitution convenes.

Until this meeting, the government alone shall have the authority to convene parliament.

The mandate of the members of the Assembly of the French Union shall expire at the same time as the mandate of the members of the present National Assembly.

Art. 91—The institutions of the Republic, provided for by the present Constitution, shall be established within four months counting from the time of its promulgation.

This period shall be extended to six months for the institutions of the Community.

The powers of the President of the Republic now in office shall expire only when the results of the election provided for in Articles 6 and 7 of the present Constitution are proclaimed.

The member states of the Community shall participate in this first election under the conditions derived from their status at the date of the promulgation of the Constitution.

The established authorities shall continue in the exercise of their functions in these states, according to the laws and regulations applicable when the Constitution goes into force, until the establishment of the authorities provided for by their new regimes.

Until its definitive constitution, the Senate shall consist of the present members of the Council of the Republic. The organic laws that shall determine the definitive constitution of the Senate must be passed before July 31, 1959.

The powers conferred on the Constitutional Council by Articles 58 and 59 of the Constitution shall be exercised, until the establishment of this Council, by a committee composed of the Vice-president of the Council of State, as Chairman, the First President of the Court of Cassation, and the First President of the Audit Office.

The peoples of the member states of the Community shall continue to be represented in parliament until the entry into force of the measures necessary to the implementation of Title XII.

Art. 92—The legislative measures necessary to the establishment of the institutions and, until they are established, to the functioning of the public powers, shall be taken in meetings of the Council of Ministers, after consultation with the Council of State, in the form of ordinances having the force of law.

During the time limit set in the first paragraph of Article 91, the government shall be authorized to determine, by ordinances having the force of law and passed in the same way, the system of elections to the assemblies provided for by the Constitution.

During the same period and under the same conditions, the government may also adopt measures, in all domains, which it may deem necessary to the life of the nation, the protection of citizens or the safeguarding of liberties.

appendix **B**

Basic law for the Federal Republic of Germany, 1949, as amended

PREAMBLE

The GERMAN PEOPLE in the *Länder* of Baden, Bavaria, Bremen, Hamburg, Hesse, Lower Saxony, North Rhine-Westphalia, Rhineland-Palatinate, Schleswig-Holstein, Württemberg-Baden and Württemberg-Hohenzollern,

Conscious of its responsibility before God and Men,

Animated by the resolve to preserve its national and political unity and to serve the peace of the world as an equal partner in a united Europe,

Desiring to give a new order to political life for a transitional period, has enacted, by virtue of its constituent power, this Basic Law of the Federal Republic of Germany.

It has also acted on behalf of those Germans to whom participation was denied.

The entire German people is called on to achieve by free self-determination the unity and freedom of Germany.

I: BASIC RIGHTS

Art. 1—(1) The dignity of man is inviolable. To respect and protect it is the duty of all state authority.

(2) The German people therefore acknowledge inviolable and inalienable human rights as the basis of every community, of peace and of justice in the world.

(3) The following basic rights bind the legislature, the executive and the judiciary as directly enforceable law.

Art. 2—(1) Everyone has the right to the free development of his personality insofar as he does not violate the rights of others or offend against the constitutional order or the moral code.

(2) Everyone has the right to life and to inviolability of his person. The freedom of the individual is inviolable. These rights may only be encroached upon pursuant to a law.

Art. 3—(1) All persons are equal before the law.

(2) Men and women have equal rights.

(3) No one may be prejudiced or favored because of his sex, his parentage, his race, his language, his homeland and origin, his faith or his religious or political opinions.

Art. 4—(1) Freedom of faith and of conscience, and freedom of creed, religious or ideological, are inviolable.

(2) The undisturbed practice of religion is guaranteed.

(3) No one may be compelled against his conscience to render war service as an armed combatant. Details will be regulated by a Federal law.

Art. 5—(1) Everyone has the right freely to express and to disseminate his opinion by speech, writing and pictures and freely to inform himself from generally accessible sources. Freedom of the press and freedom of reporting by radio and motion pictures are guaranteed. There shall be no censorship.

(2) These rights are limited by the provisions of the general laws, the provisions of law for the protection of youth and by the right to inviolability of personal honor.

(3) Art and science, research and teaching are free. Freedom of teaching does not absolve from loyalty to the constitution.

Art. 6—(1) Marriage and family enjoy the special protection of the state.

(2) Care and upbringing of children are the natural right of the parents and a duty primarily incumbent on them. The state watches over the performance of this duty.

(3) Separation of children from the family against the will of the persons entitled to bring them up may take place only pursuant to a law, if those so entitled fail in their duty or if the children are otherwise threatened with neglect.

(4) Every mother is entitled to the protection and care of the community.

(5) Illegitimate children shall be provided by legislation with the same opportunities for their physical and spiritual development and their position in society as are enjoyed by legitimate children.

Art. 7—(1) The entire educational system is under the supervision of the state.

(2) The persons entitled to bring up a child have the right to decide whether it shall receive religious instruction.

(3) Religious instruction forms part of the ordinary curriculum in state and municipal schools, except in secular schools. Without prejudice to the state's right of supervision, religious instruction is given in accordance with the tenets of the religious communities. No teacher may be obliged against his will to give religious instructon.

(4) The right to establish private schools is guaranteed. Private schools, as a substitute for state or municipal schools, require the approval of the state and are subject to the laws of the *Länder*. This approval must be given if private schools are not inferior

to the state or municipal schools in their educational aims, their facilities, and the professional training of their teaching staff and if a segregation of the pupils according to the means of the parents is not promoted. This approval must be withheld if the economic and legal position of the teaching staff is not sufficiently assured.

(5) A private elementary school shall be admitted only if the educational authority finds that it serves a special pedagogic interest or if, on the application of persons entitled to bring up children, it is to be established as an inter-denominational or denominational or ideological school and a state or municipal elementary school of this type does not exist in the community.

(6) Preparatory schools remain abolished.

Art. 8—(1) All Germans have the right to assemble peacefully and unarmed without prior notification or permission.

(2) With regard to open-air meetings this right may be restricted by or pursuant to a law.

Art. 9—(1) All Germans have the right to form associations and societies.

(2) Associations, the objects or activities of which conflict with the criminal laws or which are directed against the constitutional order or the concept of international understanding, are prohibited.

(3) The right to form associations to safeguard and improve working and economic conditions is guaranteed to everyone and to all trades and professions. Agreements which restrict or seek to hinder this right are null and void; measures directed to this end are illegal.

Art. 10—Secrecy of the mail and secrecy of posts and telecommunications are inviolable. Restrictions may be ordered only pursuant to a law.

Art. 11—(1) All Germans enjoy freedom of movement throughout the Federal territory.

(2) This right may be restricted only by a law and only in cases in which an adequate basis of existence is lacking and special burdens would arise to the community as a result thereof or in which the restriction is necessary for the protection of youth against neglect, for combatting the danger of epidemics or for the prevention of crime.

Art. 12—as amended March 19, 1956—(1) All Germans have the right freely to choose their trade or profession, their place of work and their place of training. The practice of trades and professions may be regulated by law.

(2) No one may be compelled to perform a particular work except within the framework of a traditional compulsory public service which applies generally and equally to all. Anyone who refuses on conscientious grounds to render war service involving the use of arms, may be required to render an alternative service. The duration of this alternative service shall not exceed the duration of military service. Details shall be regulated by a law which shall not prejudice freedom of conscience and shall provide also for the possibility of an alternative service having no connection with any unit of the armed forces.

(3) Women shall not be required by law to render service in any unit of the armed forces. On no account shall they be employed in any service involving the use of arms.

(4) Forced labor may be imposed only in the event that a person is deprived of his freedom by the sentence of a court.

Art. 13—(1) The home is inviolable.

(2) Searches may be ordered only by a judge or, in the event of danger in delay,

by other organs as provided by law and may be carried out only in the form prescribed by law.

(3) Otherwise, this inviolability may be encroached upon or restricted only to avert a common danger or a mortal danger to individuals, or, pursuant to a law, to prevent imminent danger to public security and order, especially to alleviate the housing shortage, to combat the danger of epidemics or to protect endangered juveniles.

Art. 14—(1) Property and the rights of inheritance are guaranteed. Their content and limits are determined by the laws.

(2) Property imposes duties. Its use should also serve the public weal.

(3) Expropriation is permitted ony in the public weal. It may take place only by or pursuant to a law which provides for kind and extent of the compensation. The compensation shall be determined upon just consideration of the public interest and of the interests of the persons affected. In case of dispute regarding the amount of compensation, recourse may be had to the ordinary courts.

Art. 15—Land, natural resources, and means of production may for the purpose of socialization be transferred into public ownership or other forms of publicly controlled economy by a law which provides for kind and extent of the compensation. With respect to such compensation Article 14, paragraph 3, sentences 3 and 4, apply *mutatis mutandis*.

Art. 16—(1) No one may be deprived of his German citizenship. Loss of citizenship may arise only pursuant to a law, and against the will of the person affected it may arise only if such person does not thereby become stateless.

(2) No German may be extradited to a foreign country. Persons persecuted for political reasons enjoy the right of asylum.

Art. 17—Everyone has the right individually or jointly with others to address written requests or complaints to the competent authorities and to the representative assemblies.

Art. 17a—*as amended March 19, 1956*—(1) Laws concerning military service and alternative service may, by provisions applying to members of the armed forces and of alternative services during their period of military or alternative service, restrict the basic right freely to express and to disseminate opinions by speech, writing, and pictures (Article 5, paragraph 1, first half-sentence), the basic right of assembly (Article 8), and the right of petition (Article 17), in so far as it permits to address requests or complaints jointly with others.

(2) Laws for defense purposes, including the protection of the civilian population, may provide for the restriction of the basic rights of freedom of movement (Article 11) and inviolability of the home (Article 13).

Art. 18—Whoever abuses freedom of expression of opinion, in particular freedom of the press (Article 5, paragraph 1), freedom of teaching (Article 5, paragraph 3), freedom of assembly (Article 8), freedom of association (Article 9), the secrecy of mail, posts and telecommunications (Article 10), property (Article 14), or the right of asylum (Article 16, paragraph 2) in order to attack the free democratic basic order, forfeits these basic rights. The forfeiture and its extent are pronounced by the Federal Constitutional Court.

Art. 19—(1) Insofar as under this Basic Law a basic right may be restricted by or pursuant to a law, the law must apply generally and not solely to an individual case. Furthermore, the law must name the basic right, indicating the article.

(2) In no case may a basic right be infringed upon in its essential content.

(3) The basic rights apply also to corporations established under German public law to the extent that the nature of such rights permits.

(4) Should any person's right be violated by public authority, recourse to the courts shall be open to him. If no other court has jurisdiction, recourse shall be to the ordinary courts.

II: THE FEDERATION AND THE *Länder*

Art. 20—(1) The Federal Republic of Germany is a democratic and social federal state.

(2) All state authority emanates from the people. It is exercised by the people by means of elections and voting and by separate legislative, executive and judicial organs.

(3) Legislation is subject to the constitutional order; the executive and the judiciary are bound by the law.

Art. 21—(1) The political parties participate in the forming of the political will of the people. They may be freely formed. Their internal organization must conform to democratic principles. They must publicly account for the sources of their funds.

(2) Parties which, by reason of their aims or the behavior of their adherents, seek to impair or destroy the free democratic basic order or to endanger the existence of the Federal Republic of Germany are unconstitutional. The Federal Constitutional Court decides on the question of unconstitutionality.

(3) Details will be regulated by federal legislation.

Art. 22—The federal flag is black-red-gold.

Art. 23—For the time being, this Basic Law applies in the territory of the *Länder* of Baden, Bavaria, Bremen, Greater Berlin, Hamburg, Hesse, Lower-Saxony, North Rhine–Westphalia, Rhineland-Palatinate, Schleswig-Holstein, Württemberg-Baden and Württemberg-Hohenzollern. In other parts of Germany it shall be put into force on their accession.

Art. 24—(1) The Federation may, by legislation, transfer sovereign powers to international institutions.

(2) For the maintenance of peace, the Federation may join a system of mutual collective security; in doing so it will consent to such limitations upon its sovereign powers as will bring about and secure a peaceful and lasting order in Europe and among the nations of the world.

(3) For the settlement of disputes between nations, the Federation will accede to agreements concerning a general, comprehensive and obligatory system of international arbitration.

Art. 25—The general rules of public international law form part of the federal law. They take precedence over the laws and directly create rights and duties for the inhabitants of the federal territory.

Art. 26—(1) Activities tending and undertaken with the intent to disturb peaceful relations between nations, especially to prepare for aggressive war, are unconstitutional. They shall be made a punishable offense.

(2) Weapons designed for warfare may be manufactured, transported or marketed only with the permission of the Federal government. Details will be regulated by a federal law.

Art. 27—All German merchant vessels form one merchant fleet.

Art. 28—(1) The constitutional order in the *Länder* must conform to the principles of republican, democratic, and social government based on the rule of law, within the meaning of this Basic Law. In each of the Länder, counties, and communities, the people must be represented by a body chosen in universal, direct, free, equal, and secret elections. In the communities, the assembly of the community may take the place of an elected body.

(2) The communities must be guaranteed the right to regulate on their own responsibility all the affairs of the local community within the limits set by law. The associations of communities also have the right of self-government in accordance with the law within the limits of the functions given them by law.

(3) The Federation guarantees that the constitutional order of the Länder conforms to the basic rights and to the provisions of paragraphs 1 and 2.

Art. 29—(1) The federal territory shall be reorganized by a federal law with due regard to regional ties, historical and cultural connections, economic expediency and social structure. Such reorganization should create Länder which by their size and capacity are able effectively to fulfill the functions incumbent upon them.

(2) In areas which upon the reorganization of the Länder after May 8, 1945, became, without plebiscite, part of another Land, a specific change in the decision then taken regarding the Land boundaries may be demanded by popular initiative within a year from the coming into force of the Basic Law. The popular initiative requires the assent of one-tenth of the population entitled to vote in Landtag elections. If the popular initiative receives such assent, the Federal government must include in the draft of the reorganization law a provision determining to which Land the area shall belong.

(3) After the law has been passed, such part of the law as provides for the transfer of an area from one Land to another must be submitted to a referendum in that area. If a popular initiative received the assent required under paragraph 2, a referendum must in any event be held in the area concerned.

(4) Insofar as the law is rejected in at least one area, it must be reintroduced into the Bundestag. After it has been passed again, it requires to that extent acceptance by a referendum in the entire federal territory.

(5) In a referendum the majority of the votes cast decides.

(6) The procedure shall be established by a federal law. The reorganization should be concluded before the expiration of three years after promulgation of the Basic Law and, should it become necessary as a result of the accession of another part of Germany, within two years after such accession.

(7) The procedure regarding any other change in the territory of the Länder shall be established by a federal law which requires the consent of the Bundesrat and of the majority of the members of the Bundestag.

Art. 30—The exercise of governmental powers and the discharge of governmental functions is incumbent on the Länder insofar as this Basic Law does not otherwise prescribe or permit.

Art. 31—Federal law overrides Land law.

Art. 32—(1) The conduct of relations with foreign states is the concern of the Federation.

(2) Before the conclusion of a treaty affecting the special interests of a Land, this Land must be consulted in sufficient time.

(3) Insofar as the Länder have power to legislate, they may, with the consent of the Federal government, conclude treaties with foreign states.

Art. 33—(1) Every German has in every Land the same civic rights and duties.

(2) Every German is equally eligible for any public office according to his aptitude, qualifications and professional achievements.

(3) Enjoyment of civil and civic rights, eligibility for public office, and rights acquired in the public service are independent of religious denomination. No one may suffer disadvantage by reason of his adherence or non-adherence to a denomination or ideology.

(4) The exercise of state authority as a permanent function shall as a rule be entrusted to members of the public service whose status, service and loyalty are governed by public law.

(5) The law of the public service shall be regulated with due regard to the traditional principles of the permanent civil service.

Art. 34—If any person, in the exercise of a public office entrusted to him, violates his official obligations to a third party, liability rests in principle on the state or the public authority which employs him. In the case of willful intent or gross carelessness the right of recourse is reserved. With respect to the claim for compensation or the right of recourse, the jurisdiction of the ordinary courts must not be excluded.

Art. 35—All federal and *Land* authorities render each other mutual legal and administrative assistance.

Art. 36—as amended March 19, 1956—(1) Civil servants employed in the highest federal authorities shall be drawn from all *Länder* in appropriate proportion. Persons employed in other federal authorities should, as a rule, be drawn from the *Land* in which they serve.

(2) Military laws shall take into account the division of the Federation into *Länder* and the latter's particular ethnic conditions.

Art. 37—(1) If a *Land* fails to comply with its obligations of a federal character imposed by the Basic Law or another federal law, the Federal government may, with the consent of the *Bundesrat,* take the necessary measures to enforce such compliance by the *Land* by way of federal compulsion.

(2) To carry out such federal compulsion the Federal government or its commissioner has the right to give instructions to all *Länder* and their authorities.

III: THE LOWER HOUSE OF PARLIAMENT (*Bundestag*)

Art. 38—(1) The deputies to the German *Bundestag* are elected in universal, direct, free, equal and secret elections. They are representatives of the whole people, are not bound by orders and instructions and are subject only to their conscience.

(2) Anyone who has attained the age of twenty-one is entitled to vote; anyone who has attained the age of twenty-five is eligible for election.

(3) Details will be regulated by a federal law.

Art. 39—(1) The *Bundestag* is elected for a four-year term. Its legislative term ends four years after its first meeting or on its dissolution. The new election takes place during the last three months of the term or within sixty days after dissolution.

(2) The *Bundestag* assembles within thirty days after the election, but not before the end of the term of the previous *Bundestag*.

(3) The *Bundestag* determines the termination and resumption of its meetings. The President of the *Bundestag* may convene it at an earlier date. He must do so if one-third of the members, the federal President, or the federal Chancellor so demand.

Art. 40—(1) The *Bundestag* elects its president, vice-presidents and secretaries. It draws up its rules of procedure.

(2) The President exercises the proprietary and police powers in the *Bundestag* building. No search or seizure may take place in the premises of the *Bundestag* without his permission.

Art. 41—(1) The scrutiny of elections is the responsibility of the *Bundestag*. It also decides whether a deputy has lost his seat in the *Bundestag*.

(2) Against the decision of the *Bundestag* an appeal can be made to the Federal Constitutional Court.

(3) Details will be regulated by a federal law.

Art. 42—(1) The meetings of the *Bundestag* are public. Upon a motion of one-tenth of its members, or upon a motion of the Federal government, the public may, by a two-thirds majority vote, be excluded. The decision on the motion is taken at a meeting not open to the public.

(2) Decisions of the *Bundestag* require a majority of votes cast unless this Basic Law provides otherwise. For the elections to be made by the *Bundestag* the rules of procedure may provide exceptions.

(3) True and accurate reports of the public meetings of the *Bundestag* and of its committees shall not give rise to any liability.

Art. 43—(1) The *Bundestag* and its committees may demand the presence of any member of the Federal government.

(2) The members of the *Bundesrat* and of the Federal government as well as persons commissioned by them have access to all meetings of the *Bundestag* and its committees. They must be heard at any time.

Art. 44—(1) The *Bundestag* has the right, and upon the motion of one-fourth of its members the duty, to set up a committee of investigation which shall take the requisite evidence at public hearings. The public may be excluded.

(2) The rules of criminal procedure shall apply *mutatis mutandis* to the taking of evidence. The secrecy of the mail, posts and telecommunications remains unaffected.

(3) Courts and administrative authorities are bound to render legal and administrative assistance.

(4) The decisions of the committees of investigations are not subject to judicial consideration. The courts are free to evaluate and judge the facts on which the investigation is based.

Art. 45—(1) The *Bundestag* appoints a Standing Committee which shall safeguard the rights of the *Bundestag* as against the Federal government in the interval between two legislative terms. The Standing Committee has also the powers of a committee of investigation.

(2) Wider powers, such as the right to legislate, to elect the federal Chancellor, and to impeach the federal President, are not within the province of the Standing Committee.

Art. 45a—added March 19, 1956—(1) The *Bundestag* shall appoint a Committee on Foreign Affairs and a Committee on Defense. Both committees shall function also in the intervals between any two legislative terms.

(2) The Committee on Defense shall also have the rights of a committee of investigation. Upon the motion of one-fourth of its members it shall have the duty to make a specific matter the subject of investigation.

(3) Article 44 paragraph (1) shall not be applied in matters of defense.

Art. 45b—added March 19, 1956—A Defense Commissioner of the *Bundestag* shall be appointed to safeguard the basic rights and to assist the *Bundestag* in exercising parliamentary control. Details shall be regulated by a federal law.

Art. 46—(1) A deputy may not at any time be prosecuted in the courts or subjected to disciplinary action or otherwise called to account outside the *Bundestag* on account of a vote cast or an utterance made by him in the *Bundestag* or one of its committees. This does not apply to defamatory insults.

(2) A deputy may be called to account or arrested for a punishable offense only by permission of the *Bundestag,* unless he is apprehended in the commission of the offense or during the course of the following day.

(3) The permission of the *Bundestag* is also necessary for any other restriction of the personal freedom of a deputy or for the initiation of proceedings against a deputy under Article 18.

(4) Any criminal proceedings and any proceedings under Article 18 against a deputy, any detention and any other restriction of his personal freedom shall be suspended upon the request of the *Bundestag.*

Art. 47—Deputies may refuse to give evidence concerning persons who have confided facts to them in their capacity as deputies or to whom they have confided facts in such capacity, as well as concerning these facts themselves. To the extent that this right to refuse to give evidence exists, no seizure of documents may take place.

Art. 48—(1) Any person seeking election to the *Bundestag* is entitled to the leave necessary for his election campaign.

(2) No one may be prevented from accepting and exercising the office of deputy. He may not be dismissed from employment, with or without notice, on this ground.

(3) Deputies are entitled to compensation adequate to ensure their independence. They are entitled to the free use of all state-owned transport. Details will be regulated by a federal law.

Art. 49—*as amended March 19, 1956*—In respect of the members of the Presidency, the Standing Committee, the Committee on Foreign Affairs and the Committee on Defense, as well as their principal substitutes, Articles 46, 47 and paragraphs 2 and 3 of Article 48 shall apply also in the intervals between any two legislative terms.

IV: THE UPPER HOUSE OF PARLIAMENT (*Bundesrat*)

Art. 50—The *Länder* participate through the *Bundesrat* in the legislation and administration of the Federation.

Art. 51—(1) The *Bundesrat* consists of members of the *Länder* governments which appoint and recall them. Other members of such governments may act as substitutes.

(2) Each *Land* has at least three votes: *Länder* with more than two million inhabitants have four, *Länder* with more than six million inhabitants, five votes.

(3) Each *Land* may delegate as many members as it has votes. The votes of each *Land* may be cast only as a block vote and only by members present or their substitutes.

Art. 52—(1) The *Bundesrat* elects its President for one year.

(2) The President convenes the *Bundesrat.* He must convene it if the members for at least two *Länder* or the Federal government so demand.

(3) The *Bundesrat* takes its decisions by at least a majority of its votes. It draws up its rules of procedure. Its meetings are public. The public may be excluded.

(4) Other members of, or persons commissioned by, *Länder* governments may serve on the committees of the *Bundesrat.*

Art. 53—The members of the Federal government have the right, and on demand the duty, to take part in the debates of the *Bundesrat* and of its committees. They must be heard at any time. The *Bundesrat* must be currently kept informed by the Federal government of the conduct of affairs.

V: THE FEDERAL PRESIDENT

Art. 54—(1) The federal President is elected, without debate, by the Federal Convention. Every German is eligible who is entitled to vote for the *Bundestag* and who has attained the age of forty.

(2) The term of office of the federal President is five years. Reelection for a consecutive term is permitted only once.

(3) The Federal Convention consists of the members of the *Bundestag* and an equal number of members elected by the representative assemblies of the *Länder* according to the rules of proportional representation.

(4) The Federal Convention meets not later than thirty days before the expiration of the term of office of the federal President or, in the case of premature termination, not later than thirty days after this date. It is convened by the president of the *Bundestag*.

(5) After expiration of the legislative term, the period specified in paragraph 4, first sentence, begins with the first meeting of the *Bundestag*.

(6) The person receiving the votes of the majority of the members of the Federal Convention is elected. If such majority is not obtained by any candidate in two ballots, the candidate who receives the largest number of votes in a further ballot is elected.

(7) Details will be regulated by a federal law.

Art. 55—(1) The federal President may not be a member of the government or of a legislative body of the Federation or of a *Land*.

(2) The federal President may not hold any other salaried office, nor engage in a trade, nor practice a profession, nor belong to the management or the board of directors of an enterprise carried on for profit.

Art. 56—On assuming his office the federal President takes the following oath before the assembled members of the *Bundestag* and the *Bundesrat:*

"I swear that I will dedicate my efforts to the well-being of the German people, enhance its benefits, ward harm from it, uphold and defend the Basic Law and the laws of the Federation, fulfill my duties conscientiously, and do justice to all. So help me God."

The oath may also be taken without religious affirmation.

Art. 57—If the federal President is prevented from exercising his powers, or if his office falls prematurely vacant, his powers will be exercised by the President of the *Bundesrat*.

Art. 58—Orders and decrees of the federal President require for their validity the countersignature of the federal Chancellor or the appropriate federal minister. This does not apply to the appointment and dismissal of the federal Chancellor, the dissolution of the *Bundestag* under Article 63 and the request under Article 69, paragraph 3.

Art. 59—(1) The federal President represents the Federation in its international relations. He concludes treaties with foreign states on behalf of the Federation. He accredits and receives envoys.

(2) Treaties which regulate the political relations of the Federation or relate to matters of federal legislation require the consent or participation, in the form of a federal law, of the bodies competent in any specific case for such federal legislation. For ad-

ministrative agreements the provisions concerning the federal administration apply *mutatis mutandis.*

Art. 59a—added March 19, 1956—(1) The *Bundestag* shall determine when a case of defense has occurred. Its decision shall be promulgated by the federal President.

(2) If insurmountable difficulties prevent the *Bundestag* from assembling, the federal President may, when there is danger in delay, make and promulgate this determination, subject to countersignature by the federal Chancellor. The federal President should previously consult the presidents of the *Bundestag* and the *Bundesrat.*

(3) Statements concerning the existence of a case of defense which involve international relations shall not be issued by the federal President until after such promulgation.

(4) Any decision on the conclusion of peace shall be taken by means of a federal law.

Art. 60—as amended March 19, 1956—(1) The federal President appoints and dismisses the federal judges, the federal civil servants, the officers, and noncommissioned officers, unless otherwise provided for by law.

(2) He exercises the power of pardon on behalf of the Federation in individual cases.

(3) He may delegate these powers to other authorities.

(4) Paragraphs 2 to 4 of Article 46 apply *mutatis mutandis* to the federal President.

Art. 61—(1) The *Bundestag* or the *Bundesrat* may impeach the federal President before the Federal Constitutional Court for willful violation of the Basic Law or any other federal law. The motion for impeachment must be brought forward by at least one-fourth of the members of the *Bundestag* or one-fourth of the votes of the *Bundesrat.* The decision to impeach requires a majority of two-thirds of the members of the *Bundestag* or of two-thirds of the votes of the *Bundesrat.* The prosecution is conducted by a person commissioned by the impeaching body.

(2) If the Federal Constitutional Court finds the federal President guilty of a willful violation of the Basic Law or of another federal law, it may declare him to have forfeited his office. After impeachment, it may issue an interim order preventing the federal President from exercising the powers of his office.

VI: THE FEDERAL GOVERNMENT

Art. 62—The Federal government consists of the federal Chancellor and the federal ministers.

Art. 63—(1) The federal Chancellor is elected, without debate, by the *Bundestag* on the proposal of the federal President.

(2) The person obtaining the votes of the majority of the members of the *Bundestag* is elected. The person elected must be appointed by the federal President.

(3) If the person proposed is not elected, the *Bundestag* may elect within fourteen days of the ballot a federal Chancellor by more than one-half of its members.

(4) If there is no election within this period, a new ballot shall take place without delay, in which the person obtaining the largest number of votes is elected. If the person elected obtained the votes of the majority of the members of the *Bundestag*, the federal

President must appoint him within seven days of the election. If the person elected did not receive this majority, the federal President must within seven days either appoint him or dissolve the *Bundestag*.

Art. 64—(1) The federal ministers are appointed and dismissed by the federal President upon the proposal of the federal Chancellor.

(2) The federal Chancellor and the federal ministers, on assuming office, take before the *Bundestag* the oath provided in Article 56.

Art. 65—The federal Chancellor determines, and is responsible for, general policy. Within the limits of this general policy, each federal minister conducts the business of his department autonomously and on his own responsibility. The Federal government decides on differences of opinion between the federal ministers. The federal Chancellor conducts the business of the Federal government in accordance with rules of procedure adopted by it and approved by the federal President.

Art. 65a—added March 19, 1956—(1) Power of command in respect of the armed forces shall be vested in the federal Minister of Defense.

(2) Upon promulgation of the determination concerning the case of defense, the power of command shall devolve on the federal Chancellor.

Art. 66—The federal Chancellor and the federal ministers may not hold any other salaried office, nor engage in a trade, nor practice a profession, nor belong to the management or, without the consent of the *Bundestag,* to the board of directors of an enterprise carried on for profit.

Art. 67—(1) The *Bundestag* can express its lack of confidence in the federal Chancellor only by electing a successor by the majority of its members and by requesting the federal President to dismiss the federal Chancellor. The federal President must comply with the request and appoint the person elected.

(2) Forty-eight hours must elapse between the motion and the election.

Art. 68—(1) If a motion of the federal Chancellor for a vote of confidence is not assented to by the majority of the members of the *Bundestag*, the federal President may, upon the proposal of the federal Chancellor, dissolve the *Bundestag* within twenty-one days. The right to dissolve lapses as soon as the *Bundestag* by the majority of its members elects another federal Chancellor.

(2) Forty-eight hours must elapse between the motion and the vote thereon.

Art. 69—(1) The federal Chancellor appoints a federal minister as his deputy.

(2) The tenure of office of the federal Chancellor or a federal minister ends in any event on the first meeting of a new *Bundestag;* the tenure of office of a federal minister ends also on any other termination of the tenure of office of the federal Chancellor.

(3) At the request of the federal President, the federal Chancellor, or at the request of the federal Chancellor or of the federal President, a federal minister is bound to continue to transact the business of his office until the appointment of a successor.

VII: LEGISLATIVE POWERS OF THE FEDERATION

Art. 70—(1) The *Länder* have the power to legislate in so far as this Basic Law does not confer legislative powers on the Federation.

(2) The division of competence between the Federation and the *Länder* is determined by the provisions of this Basic Law concerning exclusive and concurrent legislative powers.

Art. 71—On matters within the exclusive legislative powers of the Federation the *Länder* have authority to legislate only if, and to the extent that, a federal law explicitly so authorizes them.

Art. 72—(1) On matters within the concurrent legislative powers the *Länder* have authority to legislate as long as, and to the extent that, the Federation does not use its legislative power.

(2) The Federation has the right to legislate on these matters to the extent that a need for a federal rule exists because

1. a matter cannot be effectively dealt with by the legislation of individual *Länder,* or
2. dealing with a matter by *Land* law might prejudice the interests of other *Länder* or of the entire community, or
3. the maintenance of legal or economic unity, especially the maintenance of uniformity of living conditions beyond the territory of a *Land,* necessitates it.

Art. 73—*as amended March 27, 1954*—The Federation has the exclusive power to legislate on:

1. Foreign affairs as well as defense, including both military service for males over 18 years and the protection of the civilian population;
2. Citizenship in the Federation;
3. Freedom of movement, passports, immigration and emigration, and extradition;
4. Currency, money and coinage, weights and measures, as well as computation of time;
5. The unity of the customs and commercial territory, commercial and navigation agreements, the freedom of movement of goods, and the exchanges of goods and payments with foreign countries, including customs and frontier protection;
6. Federal railroads and air traffic;
7. Postal and telecommunication services;
8. The legal status of persons employed by the Federation and by federal bodies-corporate under public law;
9. Industrial property rights, copyrights and publication rights;
10. Cooperation of the Federation and the *Länder* in matters of criminal police and of protection of the Constitution, establishment of a federal office of the criminal police, as well as international control of crime;
11. Statistics for federal purposes.

Art. 74—Concurrent legislative powers extend to the following matters:

1. Civil law, criminal law and execution of sentences, the system of judicature, the procedure of the courts, the legal profession, notaries and legal advice;
2. Registration of births, deaths, and marriages;
3. The law of association and assembly;
4. The law relating to residence and establishment of aliens;
5. The protection of German cultural treasures against removal abroad;
6. The affairs of refugees and expellees;
7. Public welfare;
8. Citizenship in the *Länder;*
9. War damage and reparations;

10. Benefits to war-disabled persons and to dependents of those killed in the war, assistance to former prisoners of war, and care of war graves;

11. The law relating to economic matters (mining, industry, supply of power, crafts, trades, commerce, banking and stock exchanges, private insurance);

12. Labor law, including the legal organization of enterprises; protection of workers, employment exchanges and agencies, as well as social insurance, including unemployment insurance;

13. The promotion of scientific research;

14. The law regarding expropriation, to the extent that matters enumerated in Articles 73 and 74 are concerned;

15. Transfer of land, natural resources, and means of production into public ownership or other forms of publicly controlled economy;

16. Prevention of the abuse of economic power;

17. Promotion of agricultural and forest production, safeguarding of the supply of food, the import and export of agricultural and forest products, deep-sea and coastal fishing, and preservation of the coasts;

18. Dealings in real estate, land law and matters concerning agricultural leases, housing, settlements and homesteads;

19. Measures against epidemic and infectious diseases of humans and animals, admission to medical and other professions, and practices in the field of healing, traffic in drugs, medicines, narcotics, and poisons;

20. Protection with regard to traffic in food and stimulants as well as in necessities of life, in fodder, agricultural and forest seeds and seedlings, and protection of trees and plants against diseases and pests;

21. Ocean and coastal shipping as well as aids to navigation, inland shipping, meteorological services, sea waterways and inland waterways used for general traffic;

22. Road traffic, motor transport, and construction and maintenance of long-distance highways;

23. Railroads other than federal railroads, except mountain railroads.

Art. 75—Subject to the conditions of Article 72 the Federation has the right to enact general rules concerning:

1. The legal status of persons in the public service of the *Länder*, communities, and other bodies-corporate of public law;

2. The general rules of law concerning the status of the press and motion pictures;

3. Hunting, protection of nature, and care of the countryside;

4. Land distribution, regional planning, and water conservation;

5. Matters relating to registration and identity cards.

Art. 76—(1) Bills are introduced in the *Bundestag* by the Federal government, by members of the *Bundestag*, or by the *Bundesrat*.

(2) Bills of the Federal government shall be submitted first to the *Bundesrat*. The *Bundesrat* is entitled to state its position on these bills within three weeks.

(3) Bills of the *Bundesrat* shall be submitted to the *Bundestag* by the Federal government. In doing so the Federal government must state its own views.

Art. 77—(1) Federal laws are adopted by the *Bundestag*. Upon their adoption, they shall, without delay, be transmitted to the *Bundesrat* by the President of the *Bundestag*.

(2) The *Bundesrat* may, within two weeks of the receipt of the adopted bill, demand that a committee for joint consideration of bills, composed of members of the *Bundestag* and the *Bundesrat,* be convened. The composition and the procedure of this committee are regulated by rules of procedure adopted by the *Bundestag* and requiring the consent of the *Bundesrat.* The members of the *Bundesrat* on this committee are not bound by instructions. If the consent of the *Bundesrat* is required for a law, the demand for convening this committee may also be made by the *Bundestag* or the Federal government. Should the committee propose any amendment to the adopted bill, the *Bundestag* must again vote on the bill.

(3) Insofar as the consent of the *Bundesrat* is not required for a law, the *Bundesrat* may, if the proceedings under paragraph 2 are completed, enter a protest within one week against a law adopted by the *Bundestag.* This period begins, in the case of paragraph 2, last sentence, on the receipt of the bill as re-adopted by the *Bundestag,* in all other cases on the conclusion of the proceedings of the committee provided for in paragraph 2.

(4) If the protest is adopted by a majority of the votes of the *Bundesrat,* it can be rejected by a decision of the majority of the members of the *Bundestag.* If the *Bundesrat* adopted the protest by a majority of at least two-thirds of its votes, the rejection by the *Bundestag* requires a majority of two-thirds, including at least the majority of the members of the *Bundestag.*

Art. 78—A law adopted by the *Bundestag* is deemed to have been passed if the *Bundesrat* consents to it, does not make a demand pursuant to Article 77, paragraph 2, does not enter a protest within the time limited by Article 77, paragraph 3, or withdraws such protest, or if the protest is overridden by the *Bundestag.*

Art. 79—as amended March 27, 1954—(1) The Basic Law can be amended only by a law which expressly amends or supplements the text thereof.

With respect to international treaties the subject of which is a peace settlement, the preparation of a peace settlement or the abolition of an occupation regime, or which are designed to serve the defense of the Federal Republic, it shall be sufficient, for the purpose of a clarifying interpretation to the effect that the provisions of the Basic Law are not contrary to the conclusion and entry into force of such treaties, to effect a supplementation of the text of the Basic Law confined to this clarifying interpretation.

(2) Such a law requires the affirmative vote of two-thirds of the members of the *Bundestag* and two-thirds of the votes of the *Bundesrat.*

(3) An amendment of this Basic Law affecting the division of the Federation into *Länder,* the participation in principle of the *Länder* in legislation, or the basic principles laid down in Articles 1 and 20, is inadmissible.

Art. 80—(1) The Federal government, a federal minister, or the *Land* governments may be authorized by a law to issue ordinances having the force of law. The content, purpose and scope of the powers conferred must be set forth in the law. The legal basis must be stated in the ordinance. If a law provides that a power may be further delegated, an ordinance having the force of law is necessary in order to delegate the power.

(2) The consent of the *Bundesrat* is required, unless otherwise provided by federal legislation, for ordinances having the force of law issued by the Federal government or a federal minister concerning basic rules for the use of facilities of the federal railroads and of postal and telecommunication services, or charges therefor, or concerning the

construction and operation of railroads, as well as for ordinances having the force of law issued on the basis of federal laws that require the consent of the *Bundesrat* or that are executed by the *Länder* as agents of the Federation or as matters of their own concern.

Art. 81—(1) Should in the circumstances of Article 68 the *Bundestag* not be dissolved, the federal President may, at the request of the Federal government and with the consent of the *Bundesrat*, declare a state of legislative emergency with respect to a bill, if the *Bundestag* rejects the bill although the Federal government has declared it to be urgent. The same applies if a bill has been rejected although the federal Chancellor had combined with it the motion under Article 68.

(2) If, after a state of legislative emergency has been declared, the *Bundestag* again rejects the bill or adopts it in a version declared to be unacceptable to the Federal government, the bill is deemed to have been passed insofar as the *Bundesrat* consents to it. The same applies if the bill is not adopted by the *Bundestag* within four weeks of its reintroduction.

(3) During the term of office of a federal Chancellor, any other bill rejected by the *Bundestag* may be passed in accordance with paragraphs 1 and 2 within a period of six months after the first declaration of a state of legislative emergency. After expiration of this period, a further declaration of a state of legislative emergency is inadmissible during the term of office of the same federal Chancellor.

(4) The Basic Law may not be amended nor be repealed nor suspended in whole or in part by a law passed pursuant to paragraph 2.

Art. 82—(1) Laws passed in accordance with the provisions of this Basic Law will, after countersignature, be signed by the federal President and promulgated in the *Federal Gazette*. Ordinances having the force of law will be signed by the agency which issues them, and unless otherwise provided by law, will be promulgated in the *Federal Gazette*.

(2) Every law and every ordinance having the force of law should specify its effective date. In the absence of such a provision, it becomes effective on the fourteenth day after the end of the day on which the *Federal Gazette* was published.

VIII: THE EXECUTION OF FEDERAL LAWS AND THE FEDERAL ADMINISTRATION

Art. 83—The *Länder* execute federal laws as matters of their own concern insofar as this Basic Law does not otherwise provide or permit.

Art. 84—(1) If the *Länder* execute federal laws as matters of their own concern, they provide for the establishment of authorities and the regulation of administrative procedures insofar as federal laws consented to by the *Bundesrat* do not otherwise provide.

(2) The Federal government may, with the consent of the *Bundesrat*, issue general administrative rules.

(3) The Federal government exercises supervision to ensure that the *Länder* execute federal laws in accordance with applicable law. For this purpose the Federal government may send commissioners to the highest *Land* authorities and, with their consent or, if this consent is refused, with the consent of the *Bundesrat*, also to subordinate authorities.

(4) Should any shortcomings which the Federal government has found to exist in

the execution of federal laws in the *Länder* not be corrected, the *Bundesrat* decides, on the application of the Federal government or the *Land*, whether the *Land* has acted unlawfully. The decision of the *Bundesrat* may be challenged in the Federal Constitutional Court.

(5) For the execution of federal laws, the Federal government may, by federal law requiring the consent of the *Bundesrat*, be authorized to issue individual instructions for particular cases. They must be addressed to the highest *Land* authorities unless the Federal government considers the matter urgent.

Art. 85—(1) Where the *Länder* execute federal laws as agents of the Federation, the establishment of the authorities remains the concern of the *Länder* insofar as federal laws consented to by the *Bundesrat* do not otherwise provide.

(2) The Federal government may, with the consent of the *Bundesrat,* issue general administrative rules. It may regulate the uniform training of civil servants and salaried government employees. The heads of authorities at intermediate level shall be appointed with its agreement.

(3) The *Land* authorities are subject to the instructions of the appropriate highest federal authorities. The instructions shall be addressed to the highest *Land* authorities unless the Federal government considers the matter urgent. Execution of the instructions shall be ensured by the highest *Land* authorities.

(4) Federal supervision extends to the conformity with law and appropriateness of the execution. The Federal government may, for this purpose, require the submission of reports and documents and send commissioners to all authorities.

Art. 86—Where the Federation executes laws by federal administrative agencies or by federal bodies-corporate or institutions under public law, the Federal government issues, insofar as the law contains no special provision, the general administrative rules. It provides for the establishment of authorities in so far as the law does not otherwise provide.

Art. 87—(1) The foreign service, the federal finance administration, the federal railroads, the federal postal service and, in accordance with the provisions of Article 89, the administration of the federal waterways and of shipping are conducted as matters of federal administration with their own subordinate administrative structure. Federal frontier protection authorities and central offices for police information and communications, for the compilation of data for the purpose of protecting the Constitution and for the criminal police may be established by federal legislation.

(2) Social insurance institutions whose sphere of competence extends beyond the territory of one *Land* are conducted as federal bodies-corporate under public law.

(3) In addition, independent federal higher authorities and federal bodies-corporate and institutions under public law may be established by federal law for matters on which the Federation has the power to legislate. If new functions arise for the Federation in matters on which it has the power to legislate, federal authorities at intermediate and lower level may be established, in case of urgent need, with the consent of the *Bundesrat* and of the majority of the members of the *Bundestag*.

Art. 87a—*added March 19, 1956*—The numerical strength and general organizational structure of the armed forces raised for defense by the Federation shall be shown in the budget.

Art. 87b—*added March 19, 1956*—(1) The administration of the Federal Defense Forces shall be conducted as a federal administration with its own administrative substructure. Its function shall be to administer matters pertaining to personnel and to the immediate supply of the material requirements of the armed forces. Tasks connected with benefits to invalids or construction work shall not be assigned to the administration of the Federal Defense Forces except by federal legislation which shall require the consent of the *Bundesrat*. Such consent shall also be required for any legislative provisions empowering the administration of the Federal Defense Forces to interfere with rights of third parties; this shall, however, not·apply in the case of laws concerning personnel.

(2) Moreover, federal laws concerning defense including recruitment for military service and protection of the civilian population may, with the consent of the *Bundesrat,* stipulate that they shall be carried out, wholly or in part, either under federal administration with its own administrative substructure or by the *Länder* acting as agents of the Federation. If such laws are executed by the *Länder* acting as agents of the Federation, they may, with the consent of the *Bundesrat,* stipulate that the powers vested by virtue of Article 85 in the Federal government and appropriate highest federal authorities shall be transferred wholly or partly to higher federal authorities; in such an event it may be enacted that these authorities shall not require the consent of the *Bundesrat* in issuing general administrative rules as referred to in Article 85, paragraph 2, first sentence.

Art. 88—The Federation establishes a note-issuing and currency bank as the federal bank.

Art. 89—(1) The Federation is the owner of the former *Reich* waterways.

(2) The Federation administers the federal waterways through its own authorities. It exercises the public functions relating to inland shipping which extend beyond the territory of one *Land* and those relating to maritime shipping which are conferred on it by law. Upon request, the Federation may transfer the administration of federal waterways, in so far as they lie within the territory of one *Land,* to this *Land* as an agent. If a waterway touches the territories of several *Länder* the Federation may designate as its agent one *Land* if so requested by the *Länder* concerned.

(3) In the administration, development and new construction of waterways the needs of soil cultivation and of regulating water supply shall be safeguarded in agreement with the *Länder*.

Art. 90—(1) The Federation is the owner of the former *Reich* motor roads and *Reich* highways.

(2) The *Länder*, or such self-governing bodies-corporate as are competent under *Land* law, administer as agents of the Federation the federal motor roads and other federal highways used for long-distance traffic.

(3) At the request of a *Land*, the Federation may take under direct federal administration federal motor roads and other federal highways used for long-distance traffic, in so far as they lie within the territory of that *Land*.

Art. 91—(1) In order to avert any imminent danger to the existence or to the free democratic basic order of the Federation or of a *Land*, a *Land* may request the services of the police forces of other *Länder*.

(2) If the *Land* in which the danger is imminent is not itself willing or able to fight the danger, the federal government may place the police in that *Land* and the police forces of other *Länder* under its own instructions. The order for this shall be rescinded after the danger is past, or else at any time on the demand of the *Bundesrat*.

IX: THE ADMINISTRATION OF JUSTICE

Art. 92—The judicial authority is vested in the judges; it is exercised by the Federal Constitutional Court, by the Supreme Federal Court, by the federal courts provided for in this Basic Law and by the courts of the *Länder*.

Art. 93—(1) The Federal Constitutional Court decides:

1. on the interpretation of this Basic Law in the event of disputes concerning the extent of the rights and duties of a supreme federal organ or of other parties concerned who have been endowed with independent rights by this Basic Law or by rules of procedure of a supreme federal organ;

2. in case of differences of opinion or doubts on the formal and material compatibility of federal law or *Land* law with this Basic Law, or on the compatibility of *Land* law with other federal law, at the request of the Federal government, of a *Land* government or of one-third of the *Bundestag* members;

3. in case of differences of opinion on the rights and duties of the Federation and the *Länder*, particularly in the execution of federal law by the *Länder* and in the exercise of federal supervision;

4. on other disputes of public law between the Federation and the *Länder*, between different *Länder* or within a *Land*, unless recourse to another court exists;

5. in the other cases provided for in this Basic Law.

(2) The Federal Constitutional Court shall also act in such cases as are otherwise assigned to it by federal law.

Art. 94—(1) The Federal Constitutional Court consists of federal judges and other members. Half of the members of the Federal Constitutional Court are elected by the *Bundestag* and half by the *Bundesrat*. They may not belong to the *Bundestag*, the *Bundesrat*, the Federal government or the corresponding organs of a *Land*.

(2) Its constitution and procedure will be regulated by a federal law, which will specify in what cases its decisions shall have the force of law.

Art. 95—(1) To preserve the uniformity of application of federal law a Supreme Federal Court will be established.

(2) The Supreme Federal Court decides cases in which the decision is of fundamental importance for the uniformity of the administration of justice by the higher federal courts.

(3) The judges of the Supreme Federal Court are selected jointly by the Federal Minister of Justice and a committee for the selection of judges consisting of the *Land* Ministers of Justice and an equal number of members elected by the *Bundestag*.

(4) In other respects, the constitution of the Supreme Federal Court and its procedure will be regulated by federal legislation.

Art. 96—*as amended March 19, 1956*—(1) Higher federal courts shall be established for the fields of ordinary, administrative, finance, labor and social jurisdiction.

(2) Article 95, paragraph 3, applies to the judges of the higher federal courts, provided that the ministers competent for the particular matter take the place of the federal Minister of Justice and the *Land* Ministers of Justice. The terms of service of these judges shall be regulated by special federal legislation.

(3) The Federation may establish federal disciplinary courts for disciplinary proceedings against federal civil servants and federal judges, as well as federal service courts for disciplinary proceedings against soldiers and for proceedings concerning complaints of soldiers.

Art. 96a—added March 19, 1956—(1) The Federation may establish military criminal courts for the armed forces as federal courts. They shall not exercise criminal jurisdiction except in the case of defense or over members of the armed forces serving abroad or on board warships. Details shall be regulated by a federal law.

(2) The military criminal courts shall be within the sphere of business of the federal Minister of Justice. Their full-time judges must be professional judges.

(3) The Federal Supreme Court shall be the superior federal court for the military criminal courts.

Art. 97—(1) The judges are independent and subject only to the law.

(2) Judges appointed permanently on a full-time basis to an established post can, against their will, be dismissed, or permanently or temporarily suspended from office, or transferred to another post, or retired before expiration of their term of office only under authority of a judicial decision and only on grounds and in the form provided for by law. Legislation may set age limits for the retirement of judges appointed for life. In the event of changes in the structure of the courts or their areas of jurisdiction, judges may be transferred to another court or removed from their office, provided they retain their full salary.

Art. 98—(1) The legal status of the federal judges shall be regulated by a special federal law.

(2) If a federal judge, in his official capacity or unofficially, infringes upon the principles of the Basic Law or the constitutional order of a *Land*, the Federal Constitutional Court may decide by a two-thirds majority, upon the request of the *Bundestag*, that the judge be transferred to another office or placed on the retired list. In a case of an intentional infringement, his dismissal may be ordered.

(3) The legal status of the judges in the *Länder* shall be regulated by special *Land* laws. The Federation may enact general rules.

(4) The *Länder* may provide that the *Land* Minister of Justice together with a committee for the selection of judges shall decide on the appointment of judges in the *Länder*.

(5) The *Länder* may, with respect to *Land* judges, enact provisions corresponding with paragraph 2. Existing *Land* constitutional law remains unaffected. The decision in a case of impeachment of a judge rests with the Federal Constitutional Court.

Art. 99—The decision on constitutional disputes within a *Land* may be assigned by a *Land* law to the Federal Constitutional Court, and the decision of last instance in matters involving the application of *Land* law, to the higher federal courts.

Art. 100—(1) If a court considers a law unconstitutional, the validity of which is relevant to its decision, the proceedings shall be stayed, and a decision shall be obtained from the *Land* court competent for constitutional disputes if the matter concerns the violation of the constitution of a *Land*, or from the Federal Constitutional Court if the matter concerns a violation of the Basic Law. This also applies if the matter concerns the violation of this Basic Law by *Land* law or the incompatibility of a *Land* law with a federal law.

(2) If, in the course of litigation, doubt exists whether a rule of public international law forms part of the federal law and whether such rule directly creates rights and duties for the individual (Art. 25), the court shall obtain the decision of the Federal Constitutional Court.

(3) If the constitutional court of a *Land*, in interpreting the Basic Law, intends to deviate from a decision of the Federal Constitutional Court or of the constitutional court of another *Land*, it must obtain the decision of the Federal Constitutional Court; if, in interpreting other federal law, it intends to deviate from the decision of the Supreme Federal Court or a higher federal court, it must obtain the decision of the Supreme Federal Court.

Art. 101—(1) Extraordinary courts are inadmissible. No one may be removed from the jurisdiction of his lawful judge.

(2) Courts for special fields may be established only by a law.

Art. 102—Capital punishment is abolished.

Art. 103—(1) In the courts everyone is entitled to a hearing in accordance with the law.

(2) An act can be punished only if it was a punishable offense by law before the act was committed.

(3) No one may be punished for the same act more than once in pursuance of general penal legislation.

Art. 104—(1) The freedom of the individual may be restricted only on the basis of a formal law and only with due regard to the forms prescribed therein. Detained persons may be subjected neither to mental nor to physical ill-treatment.

(2) Only judges may decide on admissibility or extension of a deprivation of liberty. Where such deprivation is not based on the order of a judge, a judicial decision must be obtained without delay. The police may hold no one on their own authority in their own custody longer than the end of the day after the arrest. Details shall be regulated by legislation.

(3) Any person provisionally detained on suspicion of having committed a punishable offense must be brought before a judge at the latest on the day following the arrest; the judge shall inform him of the reasons for the detention, examine him and give him an opportunity to raise objections. The judge must, without delay, either issue a warrant of arrest setting forth the reasons therefor or order the release from detention.

(4) A relative of the person detained or a person enjoying his confidence must be notified without delay of any judicial decision ordering or extending a deprivation of liberty.

X: FINANCE

Art. 105—(1) The Federation has the exclusive power to legislate on customs and fiscal monopolies.

(2) The Federation has concurrent power to legislate on:
1. excise taxes and taxes on transactions, with the exception of taxes with localized application, in particular of the taxes on the acquisition of real estate, on increments in value, and for fire protection;
2. taxes on income, on property, on inheritances, and on donations;
3. taxes on real estate and businesses, with the exception of the fixing of the tax rates;

if it claims the taxes in whole or in part to cover federal expenditure or if the conditions laid down in Article 72, paragraph 2, exist.

(3) Federal laws relating to taxes the yield of which accrues in whole or in part to the *Länder* or the communities (community associations) require the consent of the *Bundesrat*.

Art. 106—as amended December 23, 1955 and December 24, 1956—(1) The yield of fiscal monopolies and receipts from the following taxes shall accrue to the Federation:

    1. customs duties,
    2. such excise taxes as do not accrue to the *Länder* in accordance with paragraph 2,
    3. turnover tax,
    4. transportation tax,
    5. nonrecurrent capital levies, and equalization taxes imposed for the purpose of implementing the equalization of burdens legislation,
    6. Berlin emergency aid tax,
    7. supplementary levies on income and corporation taxes.

(2) Receipts from the following taxes shall accrue to the *Länder:*

    1. property tax,
    2. inheritance tax,
    3. motor-vehicle tax,
    4. such taxes on transactions as do not accrue to the Federation in accordance with paragraph 1,
    5. beer tax,
    6. levies on gambling establishments,
    7. taxes with localized application.

(3) Receipts from income tax and corporation tax shall accrue: until 31 March, 1958, to the Federation and the *Länder* in a ratio of 33⅓ percent to 66⅔ percent, and from 1 April 1958, to the Federation and the *Länder* in a ratio of 35 percent to 65 percent.

(4) The ratio of apportionment of the income and corporation taxes paragraph 3 should be modified by a federal law requiring the consent of the *Bundesrat* whenever the development of the relation of revenues to expenditures in the Federation differs from that in the *Länder* and whenever the budgetary needs of the Federation or those of the *Länder* exceed the estimated revenues by a margin substantial enough to call for a corresponding adjustment of the ratio of apportionment in favor of either the Federation or the *Länder*. Any such adjustment shall be based on the following principles:

    1. the Federation and the *Länder* shall each bear the expenditures resulting from the administration of their respective tasks; Article 120, paragraph 1, shall not be affected;
    2. there shall be equality of rank between the claim of the Federation and the claim of the *Länder* to have their respective necessary expenditures covered from ordinary revenues;
    3. the requirements of the Federation and of the *Länder* in respect of budget coverage shall be coordinated in such a way that a fair equalization is achieved, any overburdening of taxpayers precluded, and uniformity of living standards in the federal territory ensured.

The ratio of apportionment may be modified for the first time with effect from 1 April, 1958, and subsequently at intervals of not less than two years after the entry into force of any law determining such ratio; provided that this stipulation shall not affect any modification of such ratio effected in accordance with paragraph 5.

(5) If a federal law imposes additional expenditures on, or withdraws revenues from, the *Länder,* the ratio of apportionment of the income and corporation taxes shall be modified in favor of the *Länder,* provided that conditions as envisaged in paragraph 4 have developed. If the additional burden placed upon the *Länder* is limited to a period of short duration, such burden may be compensated by grants from the Federation under a federal law requiring the consent of the *Bundesrat* and which shall lay down the principles for assessing the amounts of such grants and for distributing them among the *Länder.*

(6) For the purposes of the present Article, revenues and expenditures of communes (associations of communes) shall be deemed to be *Land* revenues and expenditures. Whether and to what extent receipts from *Land* taxes are to accrue to communes (associations of communes), shall be determined by *Land* legislation.

Art. 107—as amended December 23, 1955—(1) Receipts from *Land* taxes shall accrue to the individual *Länder* to the extent that such taxes are collected by revenue authorities within their respective territories (local receipts). Federal legislation requiring the consent of the *Bundesrat* may provide in detail for the determination and allotment of local receipts from specific taxes (tax shares).

(2) A federal law requiring the consent of the *Bundesrat* shall ensure a reasonable financial equalization between financially strong *Länder* and financially weak *Länder,* due account being taken of the financial capacity and requirements of communes (associations of communes). Such law shall provide for equalization grants to be paid to financially weak *Länder* from equalization contributions made by financially strong *Länder;* it shall furthermore specify the conditions governing equalization claims and equalization liabilities as well as the criteria for determining the amounts of equalization payments. Such law may also provide for grants to be made by the Federation from federal funds to financially weak *Länder* in order to complement the coverage of their general financial requirements (complemental grants).

Art. 108—(1) Customs, fiscal monopolies, the excise taxes subject to concurrent legislative powers, the transportation tax, the turnover tax, and the nonrecurrent capital levies are administered by federal finance authorities. The organization of these authorities and the procedure to be applied by them will be regulated by federal law. The heads of the authorities at intermediate level shall be appointed after consultation of the *Land* governments. The Federation may transfer the administration of nonrecurrent capital levies to the *Land* financial authorities as its agents.

(2) If the Federation claims part of the income and corporation taxes for itself, it is entitled to administer them to that extent; it may, however, transfer the administration to the *Land* finance authorities as its agents.

(3) The remaining taxes are administered by *Land* finance authorities. The Federation may, by federal laws which require the consent of the *Bundesrat,* regulate the organization of these authorities, the procedure to be applied by them and the uniform training of the civil servants. The heads of the authorities at intermediate level shall be appointed in agreement with the Federal government. The administration of the taxes

accruing to the communities (community associations) may be transferred by the *Länder* in whole or in part to the communities (community associations).

(4) In so far as taxes accrue to the Federation, the *Land* finance authorities act as agents of the Federation. The *Länder* are liable to the extent of their revenues for an orderly administration of such taxes: the federal Minister of Finance may supervise the orderly administration, acting through authorized federal agents who have a right to give instructions to the authorities at intermediate and lower levels.

(5) The jurisdiction of finance courts will be uniformly regulated by federal law.

(6) The general administrative rules will be issued by the Federal government and, in so far as the administration is incumbent upon the *Land* finance authorities, will require the consent of the *Bundesrat*.

Art. 109—The Federation and the *Länder* are autonomous and independent of each other as regards their budgets.

Art. 110—(1) All revenues and expenditures of the Federation must be estimated for each fiscal year and included in the budget.

(2) The budget shall be established by a law before the beginning of the fiscal year. It must be balanced as regards revenue and expenditure. Expenditures will as a rule be authorized for one year; in special cases, they may be authorized for a longer period. Otherwise no provisions may be inserted in the federal budget law which extend beyond the fiscal year or which do not relate to the revenues and expenditures of the Federation or its administration.

(3) The assets and liabilities shall be set forth in an appendix to the budget.

(4) In the case of commercially operated enterprises of the Federation the individual receipts and expenditures need not be included in the budget, but only the final balance.

Art. 111—(1) If, by the end of a fiscal year, the budget for the following year has not been established by a law, the Federal government may, until such law comes into force, make all payments which are necessary:

a. to maintain institutions existing by law and to carry out measures authorized by law;

b. to meet legal obligations of the Federation;

c. to continue building projects, procurements, and other services or to continue the grant of subsidies for these purposes, provided amounts have already been authorized in the budget of a previous year.

(2) In so far as revenues provided by special legislation and derived from taxes, levies, or other sources, or the working capital reserves, do not cover the expenditures set forth in paragraph 1, the Federal government may borrow the funds necessary for the conduct of current operations to a maximum of one-quarter of the total amount of the previous budget.

Art. 112—Expenditures in excess of budget items and extraordinary expenditures require the consent of the federal Minister of Finance. The consent may only be given if there exists an unforeseen and compelling necessity.

Art. 113—Decisions of the *Bundestag* and of the *Bundesrat* which increase the budget expenditure proposed by the Federal government or involve new expenditure or will cause new expenditure in the future, require the consent of the Federal government.

Art. 114—(1) The federal Minister of Finance must submit annually to the

Bundestag and to the *Bundesrat* an account of all revenues and expenditures as well as assets and liabilities.

(2) This account shall be audited by an Audit Office, the members of which shall enjoy judicial independence. The general account and a summary of the assets and liabilities shall be submitted to the *Bundestag* and the *Bundesrat* in the course of the following fiscal year together with the comments of the Audit Office in order to secure a discharge for the Federal government. The audit of accounts will be regulated by a federal law.

Art. 115—Funds may be obtained by borrowing only in case of extraordinary need and as a rule only for expenditure for productive purposes and only pursuant to a federal law. The granting of credits and the provision of security by the Federation the effect of which extends beyond the fiscal year may take place only pursuant to a federal law. The amount of the credit, or the extent of the obligation for which the Federation assumes liability, must be fixed in the law.

XI: TRANSITIONAL AND CONCLUDING PROVISIONS

Art. 116—(1) Unless otherwise provided by law, a German within the meaning of this Basic Law is a person who possesses German citizenship or who has been admitted to the territory of the German *Reich,* as it existed on December 31, 1937, as a refugee or expellee of German stock or as the spouse or descendant of such person.

(2) Former German citizens who, between January 30, 1933, and May 8, 1945, were deprived of their citizenship for political, racial or religious reasons, and their descendants, shall be re-granted German citizenship on application. They are considered as not having been deprived of their German citizenship if they have established their domicile in Germany after May 8, 1945, and have not expressed a contrary intention.

Art. 117—(1) Law which conflicts with Article 3, paragraph 2, remains in force until adapted to this provision of the Basic Law, but not beyond March 31, 1953.

(2) Laws which restrict the right of freedom of movement in view of the present housing shortage remain in force until repealed by federal legislation.

Art. 118—The reorganization of the territory comprising the *Länder* of Baden, Württemberg-Baden and Württemberg-Hohenzollern may be effected nothwithstanding the provisions of Article 29, by agreement between the *Länder* concerned. If no agreement is reached, the reorganization will be regulated by a federal law which must provide for a referendum.

Art. 119—In matters relating to refugees and expellees, in particular as regards their distribution among the *Länder*, the Federal government may, with the consent of the *Bundesrat,* issue ordinances having the force of law, pending settlement of the matter by federal legislation. The Federal government may in this matter be authorized to issue individual instructions for particular cases. Except where there is danger in delay, the instructions shall be addressed to the highest *Land* authorities.

Art. 120—(1) The Federation bears the expenditure for occupation costs and the other internal and external burdens caused as a consequence of the war, as provided for in detail by a federal law, and the subsidies toward the burdens of social insurance, including unemployment insurance and public assistance for the unemployed.

(2) The revenues are transferred to the Federation at the same time as the Federation assumes responsibility for the expenditures.

Art. 120a—added August 14, 1952—(1) Laws concerning the implementation of the Equalization of Burdens may, with the consent of the *Bundesrat,* stipulate that in the field of equalization benefits, they shall be executed partly by the Federation and partly by the *Länder* acting as agents of the Federation, and that the relevant powers vested in the Federal government and the competent highest federal authorities by virtue of Article 85, shall be wholly or partly delegated to the Federal Equalization Office. In the exercise of these powers the Federal Equalization Office shall not require the consent of the *Bundesrat;* with the exception of urgent cases, its instructions shall be given to the highest *Land* authorities (*Land* Equalization Offices).

(2) The provisions of Article 87, paragraph 3, second sentence, shall not be affected hereby.

Art. 121—Within the meaning of this Basic Law, a majority of the members of the *Bundestag* and of the Federal Convention is the majority of the number of their members established by law.

Art. 122—(1) From the time of the first meeting of the *Bundestag,* laws shall be passed exclusively by the legislative organs recognized in this Basic Law.

(2) Legislative bodies and bodies participating in legislation in an advisory capacity whose competence ends by virtue of paragraph 1, are dissolved from that date.

Art. 123—(1) Law in force before the first meeting of the *Bundestag* remains in force, in so far as it does not conflict with the Basic Law.

(2) Subject to all rights and objections of the interested parties, the state treaties concluded by the German *Reich* concerning matters for which, under this Basic Law, *Land* legislation is competent, remain in force, if they are and continue to be valid in accordance with general principles of law, until new state treaties are concluded by the agencies competent under this Basic Law, or until they are in any other way terminated pursuant to their provisions.

Art. 124—Law affecting matters within the exclusive power to legislate of the Federation becomes federal law wherever it is applicable.

Art. 125—Law affecting matters within the concurrent power to legislate of the Federation becomes federal law wherever it is applicable:

1. in so far as it applies uniformly within one or more zones of occupation.
2. in so far as it is law by which former *Reich* law has been amended after May 8, 1945.

Art. 126—The Federal Constitutional Court decides disputes regarding the continuance of law as federal law.

Art. 127—Within one year of the promulgation of this Basic Law the Federal government may, with the consent of the governments of the *Länder* concerned, extend to the *Länder* of Baden, Greater Berlin, Rhineland-Palatinate, and Württemberg-Hohenzollern any legislation of the Bizonal Economic Administration, in so far as it continues to be in force as federal law under Articles 124 or 125.

Art. 128—In so far as law continuing in force provides for powers to give instructions within the meaning of Article 84, paragraph 5, these powers remain in existence until otherwise provided by law.

Art. 129—(1) In so far as legal provisions which continue in force as federal law contain an authorization to issue ordinances having the force of law or general administrative rules or to perform administrative acts, the authorization passes to the agencies henceforth competent in the matter. In cases of doubt, the federal government will decide in agreement with the *Bundesrat;* the decision must be published.

(2) In so far as legal provisions which continue in force as *Land* law contain such an authorization, it will be exercised by the agencies competent under *Land* law.

(3) In so far as legal provisions within the meaning of paragraphs 1 and 2 authorize their amendment or supplementation or the issue of legal provisions in place of laws, these authorizations have expired.

(4) The provisions of paragraphs 1 and 2 apply *mutatis mutandis* whenever legal provisions refer to regulations no longer valid or to institutions no longer in existence.

Art. 130—(1) Administrative agencies and other institutions which serve the public administration or the administration of justice and are not based on *Land* law or treaties between *Länder,* as well as the Association of Management of Southwest German Railroads and the Administrative Council for the Postal Services and Telecommunications of the French Zone of Occupation are placed under the Federal government. The Federal government provides with the consent of the *Bundesrat* for their transfer, dissolution or liquidation.

(2) The highest disciplinary superior of the personnel of these administrations and institutions is the appropriate federal minister.

(3) Bodies-corporate and institutions of public law not directly under a *Land,* and not based on treaties between *Länder,* are under the supervision of the appropriate highest federal authority.

Art. 131—Federal legislation shall regulate the legal status of persons, including refugees and expellees, who, on May 8, 1945, were employed in the public service, have left the service for reasons other than those arising from civil service regulations or collective agreement rules, and have not until now been employed or are employed in a position not corresponding to their former one. The same applies *mutatis mutandis* to persons, including refugees and expellees, who, on May 8, 1945 were entitled to a pension or other assistance and who no longer receive any assistance or any commensurate assistance for reasons other than those arising from civil service regulations or collective agreement rules. Until the federal law comes into force, no legal claims can be made, unless otherwise provided by *Land* legislation.

Art. 132—(1) Civil servants and judges who, when the Basic Law comes into force, are appointed for life, may, within six months after the first meeting of the *Bundestag,* be placed on the retired list or waiting list or be transferred to another office with lower remuneration, if they lack the personal or professional aptitude for their office. This provision applies *mutatis mutandis* also to salaried employees whose service cannot be terminated by notice. In the case of salaried employees whose service can be terminated by notice, periods of notice in excess of the periods fixed by collective agreement rules may be cancelled within the same period.

(2) This provision does not apply to members of the public service who are not affected by the provisions regarding the liberation from National Socialism and militarism or who are recognized victims of National Socialism, unless there exists an important reason with respect to their personality.

(3) Those affected may have recourse to the courts in accordance with Article 19, paragraph 4.

(4) Details will be regulated by an ordinance of the Federal government which requires the consent of the *Bundesrat.*

Art. 133—The Federation succeeds to the rights and obligations of the Bizonal Economic Administration.

Art. 134—(1) *Reich* property becomes in principle federal property.

(2) In so far as the property was originally intended to be used predominantly for administrative tasks which, under this Basic Law, are not administrative tasks of the Federation, it shall be transferred without compensation to the authorities now charged with such tasks, and to the *Länder* in so far as it is being used at present, and not merely temporarily, for administrative tasks which under the Basic Law are now within the administrative functions of the *Länder*. The Federation may also transfer other property to the *Länder*.

(3) Property which was placed at the disposal of the *Reich* by the *Länder* and communities (associations of communities) without compensation shall again become the property of the *Länder* and communities (community associations), in so far as it is institution under public law which now discharges these tasks.

(4) Details will be regulated by a federal law which requires the consent of the *Bundesrat*.

Art. 135—(1) If after May 8, 1945, and before the coming into force of this Basic Law an area has passed from one *Land* to another, the *Land* to which the area now belongs is entitled to the property located therein of the *Land* to which it formerly belonged.

(2) Property of *Länder* and other bodies-corporate and institutions under public law, which no longer exist, passes in so far as it was originally intended to be used predominantly for administrative tasks or is being used at present, and not merely temporarily, predominantly for administrative tasks, to the *Land* or the body-corporate or institution under public law which now discharges these tasks.

(3) Real estate of *Länder* which no longer exist including appurtenances, passes to the *Land* within which it is located in so far as it is not included among property within the meaning of paragraph 1.

(4) If an overriding interest of the Federation or the particular interest of an area so requires, a settlement deviating from paragraphs 1 and 3 may be effected by federal law.

(5) For the rest, the succession in law and the settlement of the property, in so far as it has not been effected before January 1, 1952, by agreement between the *Länder* or bodies-corporate or institutions under public law concerned, will be regulated by a federal law which requires the consent of the *Bundesrat*.

(6) Interests of the former *Land* of Prussia in enterprises under private law pass to the Federation. A federal law, which may also deviate from this provision, will regulate details.

(7) In so far as, on the coming into force of the Basic Law, property which would fall to a *Land* or a body-corporate or institution under public law pursuant to paragraphs 1 to 3 had been disposed of through or under authority of a *Land* law or in any other manner by the party thus entitled, the passing of the property is deemed to have taken place before such disposition.

Art. 135a—*as amended October 22, 1957*—By the legislative power reserved to the Federation in Article 134, section 4 and Article 135, section 5 it may be determined that the following obligations need not be fulfilled entirely or partly:

1. Obligations of the *Reich* and obligations of the *Land* Prussia and of other public corporations and institutions which do not exist any longer.
2. Obligations of the Federation or of other public corporations or institutions in

connection with the transfer of title according to Articles 89, 90, 134, and 135 and obligations of the above-mentioned corporations and institutions which arise from acts of institutions mentioned in section 1.

3. Obligations of the *Länder* and municipalities (associations of municipalities) which have arisen from measures which these units undertook prior to August 1, 1945 in the execution of orders of the occupation powers, or for the purpose of remedying an emergency situation created by acts of war within the scope of administrative tasks which were incumbent on those units of government within the framework of administrative duties devolved from or delegated by the *Reich*.

Art. 136—(1) The *Bundesrat* assembles for the first time on the day of the first meeting of the *Bundestag*.

(2) Until the election of the first federal President his powers will be exercised by the president of the *Bundesrat*. He has not the right to dissolve the *Bundestag*.

Art. 137—as amended March 19, 1956—(1) The right of civil servants, of salaried employees of the public services, of professional soldiers, of temporary volunteer soldiers and of judges to stand for election in the Federation, in the *Länder,* or in the communes may be restricted by legislation.

(2) The Electoral Law to be adopted by the Parliamentary Council applies to the election of the first *Bundestag,* of the first Federal Convention and of the first federal President of the Federal Republic.

(3) The function of the Federal Constitutional Court pursuant to Article 41, paragraph 2, shall, pending its establishment, be exercised by the German High Court for the Combined Economic Area, which shall decide in accordance with its rules of procedure.

Art. 138—Changes in the rules relating to notaries as they now exist in the *Länder* of Baden, Bavaria, Württemberg-Baden and Württemberg-Hohenzollern, require the consent of the governments of these *Länder.*

Art. 139—The provisions of law enacted for the liberation of the German people from National Socialism and militarism are not affected by the provisions of this Basic Law.

Art. 140—The provisions of Articles 136, 137, 138, 139 and 141 of the German Constitution of August 11, 1919, are an integral part of this Basic Law:

Art. 136—Civil and political rights and duties are neither dependent upon nor restricted by the practice of religious freedom.

The enjoyment of civil and political rights, as well as admission to official posts, is independent of religious creed.

No one is bound to disclose his religious convictions. The authorities have the right to make enquiries as to membership of a religious body only when rights and duties depend upon it, or when the collection of statistics ordered by law requires it.

No one may be compelled to take part in any ecclesiastical act or ceremony, or the use of any religious form of oath.

Art. 137—There is no state church.

Freedom of association is guaranteed to religious bodies. There are no restrictions as to the union of religious bodies within the territory of the Federation.

Each religious body regulates and administers its affairs independently within the limits of general laws. It appoints its officials without the cooperation of the *Land*, or of the civil community.

Religious bodies acquire legal rights in accordance with the general regulations of the civil code.

Religious bodies remain corporations with public rights in so far as they have been so up to the present.

Equal rights shall be granted to other religious bodies upon application, if their constitution and the number of their members offer a guarantee of permanency.

When several such religious bodies holding public rights continue to form one union this union becomes a corporation of a similar class.

Religious bodies forming corporations with public rights are entitled to levy taxes on the basis of the civil tax-rolls, in accordance with the provisions of *Land* law.

Associations adopting as their work the common encouragement of a world philosophy shall be placed upon an equal footing with religious bodies.

So far as the execution of these provisions may require further regulations, this is the duty of the *Land* legislatures.

Art. 138—*Land* connections with religious bodies, depending upon law, agreement or special legal titles, are dissolved by *Land* legislation. The principle for such action shall be laid down by the Federal government.

Ownership and other rights of religious bodies and unions to their institutions, foundations and other properties devoted to purposes of public worship, education or charity, are guaranteed.

Art. 139—Sundays and holidays recognized by the *Land* shall remain under legal protection as days of rest from work and for the promotion of spiritual purposes.

Art. 141—Religious bodies shall have the right of entry for religious purposes into the army, hospitals, prisons, or other public institutions, so far as is necessary for the arrangement of public worship or the exercise of pastoral offices, but every form of compulsion must be avoided.

Art. 141—Article 7, paragraph 3, first sentence, has no application in a *Land* in which different provisions of *Land* law were in force on January 1, 1949.

Art. 142—Notwithstanding the provision of Article 31, such provisions of *Land* Constitutions as guarantee basic rights in conformity with Articles 1 to 18 of this Basic Law also remain in force.

Art. 142a—*added March 27, 1954*—The provisions of this Basic Law are not contrary to the conclusion and entry into force of the treaties signed in Bonn and Paris on May 26 and 27, 1952, (Treaty on Relations between the Federal Republic of Germany and the Three Powers and Treaty establishing a European Defense Community) with their related and additional conventions, especially the Protocol of July 26, 1952.

Art. 143—*as amended March 19, 1956*—The conditions under which it will be admissible to have recourse to the armed forces in case of a state of internal emergency, may be regulated only by a law which fulfills the requirements of Article 79.

Art. 144—(1) This Basic Law requires ratification by the representative assemblies in two-thirds of the German *Länder* in which it is for the time being to apply.

(2) In so far as the application of this Basic Law is subject to restrictions in any

Land listed in Article 23 or in any part of such *Land,* the *Land* or the part thereof has the right to send representatives to the *Bundestag* in accordance with Article 38 and to the *Bundesrat* in accordance with Article 50.

Art. 145—(1) The Parliamentary Council shall note in public session, with the participation of the representatives of Greater Berlin, the ratification of this Basic Law and shall sign and promulgate it.

(2) This Basic Law shall come into force at the end of the day of promulgation.

(3) It shall be published in the *Federal Gazette.*

Art. 146—This Basic Law shall cease to be in force on the day on which a constitution adopted by a free decision of the German people comes into force.

—Bonn/Rhine, May 23, 1949.

The Constitution of the U.S.S.R., 1936, as amended

Chapter I: THE SOCIAL STRUCTURE

Art. 1—The Union of Soviet Socialist Republics is a socialist state of workers and peasants.

Art. 2—The political foundation of the U.S.S.R. is the soviets of working people's deputies, which grew and became strong as a result of the overthrow of the power of the landlords and capitalists and the conquest of the dictatorship of the proletariat.

Art. 3—All power in the U.S.S.R. belongs to the working people of town and country as represented by the soviets of working people's deputies.

Art. 4—The economic foundation of the U.S.S.R. is the socialist system of economy and the socialist ownership of the instruments and means of production, firmly established as a result of the liquidation of the capitalist system of economy, the abolition of private ownership of the instruments and means of production, and the elimination of the exploitation of man by man.

Art. 5—Socialist property in the U.S.S.R. exists either in the form of state property (belonging to the whole people) or in the form of cooperative and collective farm property (property of collective farms, property of cooperative societies).

Art. 6—The land, its mineral wealth, waters,˙ forests, mills, factories, mines, rail, water and air transport, banks, communications, large state-organized and agricultural enterprises (state farms, machine and tractor stations and the like), as well as municipal enterprises and the bulk of the dwelling houses in the cities and industrial localities, are state property, that is, belong to the whole people.

Art. 7—The common enterprises of collective farms, and cooperative organizations, with their livestock and implements, the products of the collective farms and cooperative organizations, as well as their common buildings, constitute the common, socialist property of the collective farms and cooperative organizations.

Every household in a collective farm, in addition to its basic income from the common collective farm enterprise, has for its personal use a small plot of household land and, as its personal property, a subsidiary husbandry on the plot, a dwelling house, livestock, poultry and minor agricultural implements—in accordance with the rules of the agricultural artel.

Art. 8—The land occupied by collective farms is secured to them for their use free of charge and for an unlimited time, that is, in perpetuity.

Art. 9—Alongside the socialist system of economy, which is the predominant form of economy in the U.S.S.R., the law permits the small private economy of individual peasants and handicraftsmen based on their own labor and precluding the exploitation of the labor of others.

Art. 10—The personal property right of citizens in their incomes and savings from work, in their dwelling houses and subsidiary home enterprises, in articles of domestic economy and use and articles of personal use and convenience, as well as the right of citizens to inherit personal property, is protected by law.

Art. 11—The economic life of the U.S.S.R. is determined and directed by the state national economic plan, with the aim of increasing the public wealth, of steadily raising the material and cultural standards of the working people, of consolidating the independence of the U.S.S.R. and strengthening its defensive capacity.

Art. 12—Work in the U.S.S.R. is a duty and a matter of honor for every able-bodied citizen, in accordance with the principle: "He who does not work, neither shall he eat."

The principle applied in the U.S.S.R. is that of socialism: "From each according to his ability, to each according to his work."

Chapter II: THE STATE STRUCTURE

Art. 13—The Union of Soviet Socialist Republics is a federal state, formed on the basis of a voluntary union of equal Soviet Socialist Republics, namely:

The Russian Soviet Federative Socialist Republic
The Ukrainian Soviet Socialist Republic
The Byelorussian Soviet Socialist Republic
The Uzbek Soviet Socialist Republic
The Kazakh Soviet Socialist Republic
The Georgian Soviet Socialist Republic
The Azerbaijan Soviet Socialist Republic
The Lithuanian Soviet Socialist Republic
The Moldavian Soviet Socialist Republic

The Latvian Soviet Socialist Republic
The Kirghiz Soviet Socialist Republic
The Tajik Soviet Socialist Republic
The Armenian Soviet Socialist Republic
The Turkmen Soviet Socialist Republic
The Estonian Soviet Socialist Republic

Art. 14—The jurisdiction of the Union of Soviet Socialist Republics, as represented by its higher organs of state power and organs of state administration, embraces:

(*a*) Representation of the U.S.S.R. in international relations, conclusion, ratification and denunciation of treaties of the U.S.S.R. with other states, establishment of general procedure governing the relations of Union Republics with foreign states;

(*b*) Questions of war and peace;

(*c*) Admission of new republics into the U.S.S.R.;

(*d*) Control over the observance of the Constitution of the U.S.S.R., and ensuring conformity of the Constitutions of the Union Republics with the Constitution of the U.S.S.R.;

(*e*) Confirmation of alterations of boundaries between Union Republics;

(*f*) Confirmation of the formation of new Autonomous Republics and Autonomous Regions within Union Republics;

(*g*) Organization of the defense of the U.S.S.R., direction of all the armed forces of the U.S.S.R., determination of directing principles governing the organization of the military formation of the Union Republics;

(*h*) Foreign trade on the basis of state monopoly;

(*i*) Safeguarding the security of the state;

(*j*) Determination of the national economic plans of the U.S.S.R.;

(*k*) Approval of the consolidated state budget of the U.S.S.R. and of the report on its fulfillment; determination of the taxes and revenues which go to the Union, the Republican and the local budgets;

(*l*) Administration of the banks, industrial and agricultural institutions and enterprises and trading enterprises of all-Union importance; over-all direction of industry and construction under Union Republic jurisdiction;

(*m*) Administration of transport and communications of all-Union importance;

(*n*) Direction of the monetary and credit system;

(*o*) Organization of state insurance;

(*p*) Contracting and granting of loans;

(*q*) Determination of the basic principles of land tenure and of the use of mineral wealth, forests and waters;

(*r*) Determination of the basic principles in the spheres of education and public health;

(*s*) Organization of a uniform system of national economic statistics;

(*t*) Determination of the principles of labor organization;

(*u*) Establishment of the principles of legislation concerning the judicial system and judicial procedure, and of the principles of the criminal and civil codes;

(*v*) Legislation concerning Union citizenship; legislation concerning rights of foreigners;

(*w*) Determination of the principles of legislation concerning marriage and the family;

(*x*) Issuing of all-Union acts of amnesty.

Art. 15—The sovereignty of the Union Republics is limited only in the spheres defined in Article 14 of the Constitution of the U.S.S.R. Outside of these spheres each Union Republic exercises state authority independently. The U.S.S.R. protects the sovereign rights of the Union Republics.

Art. 16—Each Union Republic has its own constitution, which takes account of the specific features of the Republic and is drawn up in full conformity with the Constitution of the U.S.S.R.

Art. 17—The right freely to secede from the U.S.S.R. is reserved to every Union Republic.

Art. 18—The territory of a Union Republic may not be altered without its consent.

Art. 18a—Each Union Republic has the right to enter into direct relations with foreign states and to conclude agreements and exchange diplomatic and consular representatives with them.

Art. 18b—Each Union Republic has its own Republican military formations.

Art. 19—The laws of the U.S.S.R. have the same force within the territory of every Union Republic.

Art. 20—In the event of divergence between a law of a Union Republic and a law of the Union, the Union law prevails.

Art. 21—Uniform citizenship is established for citizens of the U.S.S.R. Every citizen of a Union Republic is a citizen of the U.S.S.R.

Art. 22—The Russian Soviet Federative Socialist Republic includes the Autonomous Soviet Socialist Republics: Bashkirian, Buryat, Daghestan, Kabardino-Balkarian, Kalmyk, Karelian, Komi, Mari, Mordovian, North Ossetian, Tartar, Udmurt, Chechen-Ingush, Chuvash, Yakut; Autonomous Regions: Adygei, Gorny, Altai, Jewish, Karachai-Cherkess, Tuva and Khakass.

[*Art. 23* repealed]

Art. 24—The Azerbaijan Soviet Socialist Republic includes the Nakhichevan Autonomous Soviet Socialist Republic and the Nagorno-Karabakh Autonomous Region.

Art. 25—The Georgian Soviet Socialist Republic includes the Abkhazian Autonomous Soviet Socialist Republic, the Adjar Autonomous Soviet Socialist Republic and the South Ossetian Autonomous Region.

Art. 26—The Uzbek Soviet Socialist Republic includes the Kara-Kalpak Autonomous Soviet Socialist Republic.

Art. 27—The Tajik Soviet Socialist Republic includes the Gorno-Badakhshan Autonomous Region.

Art. 28—The decision of questions relating to the Regional and Territorial Administrative structure of the Union Republics is left to the jurisdiction of the Union Republics.

[*Arts. 29, 29a,* and *29b* repealed]

Chapter III: THE HIGHER ORGANS OF STATE POWER IN THE UNION OF SOVIET SOCIALIST REPUBLICS

Art. 30—The highest organ of state power in the U.S.S.R. is the Supreme Soviet of the U.S.S.R.

Art. 31—The Supreme Soviet of the U.S.S.R. exercises all rights vested in the Union of Soviet Socialist Republics in accordance with Article 14 of the Constitution, in so far as they do not, by virtue of the Constitution, come within the jurisdiction of organs of the U.S.S.R. that are accountable to the Supreme Soviet of the U.S.S.R., that is, the Presidium of the Supreme Soviet of the U.S.S.R, the Council of Ministers of the U.S.S.R., and the Ministries of the U.S.S.R.

Art. 32—The legislative power of the U.S.S.R. is exercised exclusively by the Supreme Soviet of the U.S.S.R.

Art. 33—The Supreme Soviet of the U.S.S.R. consists of two chambers: the Soviet of the Union and the Soviet of Nationalities.

Art. 34—The Soviet of the Union is elected by the citizens of the U.S.S.R. voting by election districts on the basis of one deputy for every 300,000 of the population.

Art. 35—The Soviet of Nationalities is elected by the citizens of the U.S.S.R. voting by Union Republics, Autonomous Republics, Autonomous Regions, and national areas on the basis of twenty-five deputies from each Union Republic, eleven deputies from each Autonomous Republic, five deputies from each Autonomous Region, and one deputy from each national area.

Art. 36—The Supreme Soviet of the U.S.S.R. is elected for a term of four years.

Art. 37—The two chambers of the Supreme Soviet of the U.S.S.R., the Soviet of the Union and the Soviet of Nationalities, have equal rights.

Art. 38—The Soviet of the Union and the Soviet of Nationalities have equal powers to initiate legislation.

Art. 39—A law is considered adopted if passed by both chambers of the Supreme Soviet of the U.S.S.R. by a simple majority vote in each.

Art. 40—Laws passed by the Supreme Soviet of the U.S.S.R. are published in the languages of the Union Republics over the signatures of the President and Secretary of the Presidium of the Supreme Soviet of the U.S.S.R.

Art. 41—Sessions of the Soviet of the Union and of the Soviet of Nationalities begin and terminate simultaneously.

Art. 42—The Soviet of the Union elects a Chairman of the Soviet of the Union and two Vice-chairmen.

Art. 43—The Soviet of Nationalities elects a Chairman of the Soviet of Nationalities and two Vice-chairmen.

Art. 44—The Chairmen of the Soviet of the Union and the Soviet of Nationalities preside at the sittings of the respective chambers and have charge of the conduct of their business and proceedings.

Art. 45—Joint sittings of the two chambers of the Supreme Soviet of the U.S.S.R. are presided over alternately by the Chairman of the Soviet of the Union and the Chairman of the Soviet of Nationalities.

Art. 46—Sessions of the Supreme Soviet of the U.S.S.R. are convened by the Presidium of the Supreme Soviet of the U.S.S.R. twice a year.

Extraordinary sessions are convened by the Presidium of the Supreme Soviet of the U.S.S.R. at its discretion or on the demand of one of the Union Republics.

Art. 47—In the event of disagreement between the Soviet of the Union and the Soviet of Nationalities the question is referred for settlement to a conciliation commission formed on a parity basis. If the conciliation commission fails to arrive at an agreement, or if its decision fails to satisfy one of the chambers, the question is considered for a second time by the chambers. Failing agreement between the two chambers, the Presidium of the Supreme Soviet of the U.S.S.R. dissolves the Supreme Soviet of the U.S.S.R. and orders new elections.

Art. 48—The Supreme Soviet of the U.S.S.R. at a joint sitting of the two chambers elects the Presidium of the Supreme Soviet of the U.S.S.R., consisting of a President of the Presidium of the Supreme Soviet of the U.S.S.R., fifteen Vice-presidents—one from each Union Republic, a Secretary of the Presidium, and sixteen members of the Presidium of the Supreme Soviet of the U.S.S.R.

The Presidium of the Supreme Soviet of the U.S.S.R. is accountable to the Supreme Soviet of the U.S.S.R. for all its activities.

Art. 49—The Presidium of the Supreme Soviet of the U.S.S.R.:

(*a*) Convenes the sessions of the Supreme Soviet of the U.S.S.R.;

(*b*) Issues decrees;

(*c*) Gives interpretations of the laws of the U.S.S.R. in operation;

(*d*) Dissolves the Supreme Soviet of the U.S.S.R. in conformity with Article 47 of the Constitution of the U.S.S.R. and orders new elections;

(*e*) Conducts nation-wide polls (referendums) on its own initiative or on the demand of one of the Union Republics;

(*f*) Annuls decisions and orders of the Council of Ministers of the U.S.S.R. and of the Councils of Ministers of the Union Republics if they do not conform to law;

(*g*) In the intervals between sessions of the Supreme Soviet of the U.S.S.R., releases and appoints Ministers of the U.S.S.R. on the recommendation of the Chairman of the Council of Ministers of the U.S.S.R., subject to subsequent confirmation by the Supreme Soviet of the U.S.S.R.;

(*h*) Institutes decorations (orders and medals) and titles of honor of the U.S.S.R.;

(*i*) Awards orders and medals and confers titles of honor of the U.S.S.R.;

(*j*) Exercises the right of pardon;

(*k*) Institutes military titles, diplomatic ranks and other special titles;

(*l*) Appoints and removes the high command of the armed forces of the U.S.S.R.;

(*m*) In the intervals between sessions of the Supreme Soviet of the U.S.S.R., proclaims a state of war in the event of military attack on the U.S.S.R., or when necessary to fulfill international treaty obligations concerning mutual defense against aggression;

(*n*) Orders general or partial mobilization;

(*o*) Ratifies and denounces international treaties of the U.S.S.R.;

(*p*) Appoints and recalls plenipotentiary representatives of the U.S.S.R. to foreign states;

(*q*) Receives the letters of credence and recall of diplomatic representatives accredited to it by foreign states;

(*r*) Proclaims martial law in separate localities or throughout the U.S.S.R. in the interests of the defense of the U.S.S.R. or of the maintenance of public order and the security of the state.

Art. 50—The Soviet of the Union and the Soviet of Nationalities elect Credential Committees to verify the credentials of the members of the respective chambers.

On the report of the Credential Committees, the chambers decide whether to recognize the credentials of deputies or to annul their election.

Art. 51—The Supreme Soviet of the U.S.S.R., when it deems necessary, appoints commissions of investigation and audit on any matter.

It is the duty of all institutions and officials to comply with the demands of such commissions and to submit to them all necessary materials and documents.

Art. 52—A member of the Supreme Soviet of the U.S.S.R. may not be prosecuted or arrested without the consent of the Supreme Soviet of the U.S.S.R., or, when the Supreme Soviet of the U.S.S.R. is not in session, without the consent of the Presidium of the Supreme Soviet of the U.S.S.R.

Art. 53—On the expiration of the term of office of the Supreme Soviet of the U.S.S.R., or on its dissolution prior to the expiration of its term of office, the Presidium of the Supreme Soviet of the U.S.S.R. retains its powers until the newly-elected Supreme Soviet of the U.S.S.R shall have formed a new Presidium of the Supreme Soviet of the U.S.S.R.

Art. 54—On the expiration of the term of office of the Supreme Soviet of the U.S.S.R., or in event of its dissolution prior to the expiration of its term of office, the Presidium of the Supreme Soviet of the U.S.S.R. orders new elections to be held within a period not exceeding two months from the date of expiration of the term of office or dissolution of the Supreme Soviet of the U.S.S.R.

Art. 55—The newly-elected Supreme Soviet of the U.S.S.R. is convened by the outgoing Presidium of the Supreme Soviet of the U.S.S.R. not later than three months after the elections.

Art. 56—The Supreme Soviet of the U.S.S.R., at a joint sitting of the two Chambers, appoints the Government of the U.S.S.R., namely, the Council of Ministers of the U.S.S.R.

Chapter IV: THE HIGHER ORGANS OF STATE POWER IN THE UNION REPUBLICS

Art. 57—The highest organ of state power in a Union Republic is the Supreme Soviet of the Union Republic.

Art. 58—The Supreme Soviet of a Union Republic is elected by the citizens of the Republic for a term of four years.

The basis of representation is established by the Constitution of the Union Republic.

Art. 59—The Supreme Soviet of a Union Republic is the sole legislative organ of the Republic.

Art. 60—The Supreme Soviet of a Union Republic:

(*a*) Adopts the Constitution of the Republic and amends it in conformity with Article 16 of the Constitution of the U.S.S.R.;

(*b*) Confirms the Constitutions of the Autonomous Republics forming part of it and defines the boundaries of their territories;

(*c*) Approves the national economic plan and the budget of the Republic and forms the economic administrative Regions;

(*d*) Exercises the right of amnesty and pardon of citizens sentenced by the judicial organs of the Union Republic;

(*e*) Decides questions of representation of the Union Republic in its international relations;

(*f*) Determines the manner of organizing the Republic's military formations.

Art. 61—The Supreme Soviet of a Union Republic elects the Presidium of the Supreme Soviet of a Union Republic, consisting of a President of the Presidium of the Supreme Soviet of the Union Republic, Vice-presidents, a Secretary of the Presidium, and members of the Presidium of the Supreme Soviet of the Union Republic.

The powers of the Presidium of the Supreme Soviet of a Union Republic are defined by the Constitution of the Union Republic.

Art. 62—The Supreme Soviet of a Union Republic elects a Chairman and Vice-chairman to conduct its sittings.

Art. 63—The Supreme Soviet of a Union Republic appoints the Government of the Union Republic, namely, the Council of Ministers of the Union Republic.

Chapter V: THE ORGANS OF STATE ADMINISTRATION OF THE UNION OF SOVIET SOCIALIST REPUBLICS

Art. 64—The highest executive and administrative organ of the state power of the Union of Soviet Socialist Republics is the Council of Ministers of the U.S.S.R.

Art. 65—The Council of Ministers of the U.S.S.R. is responsible and accountable to the Supreme Soviet of the U.S.S.R., or, in the intervals between sessions of the Supreme Soviet, to the Presidium of the Supreme Soviet of the U.S.S.R.

Art. 66—The Council of Ministers of the U.S.S.R. issues decisions and orders on the basis and in pursuance of the laws in operation, and verifies their execution.

Art. 67—Decisions and orders of the Council of Ministers of the U.S.S.R. are binding throughout the territory of the U.S.S.R.

Art. 68—The Council of Ministers of the U.S.S.R.:

(*a*) Coordinates and directs the work of the all-Union and Union-Republican Ministries of the U.S.S.R. and of other institutions under its jurisdiction and exercises direction over the Economic Councils of the Economic Administrative Regions through the Union Republic Councils of Ministers;

(*b*) Adopts measures to carry out the national economic plan and the state budget, and to strengthen the credit and monetary system;

(*c*) Adopts measures for the maintenance of public order, for the protection of the interests of the state, and for the safeguarding of the rights of the citizens;

(*d*) Exercises general guidance in the sphere of relations with foreign states;

(*e*) Fixes the annual contingent of citizens to be called up for military service and directs the general organization of the armed forces of the country;

(*f*) Sets up, whenever necessary, special Committees and Central Administrations under the Council of Ministers of the U.S.S.R. for economic and cultural affairs and defense.

Art. 69—The Council of Ministers of the U.S.S.R. has the right, in respect to those branches of administration and economy which come within the jurisdiction of the U.S.S.R., to suspend decisions and orders of the Councils of Ministers of the Union Republics and the Economic Councils of the economic administrative Regions and to annul orders and instructions of Ministers of the U.S.S.R.

Art. 70—The Council of Ministers of the U.S.S.R. is appointed by the Supreme Soviet of the U.S.S.R. and consists of:

The Chairman of the Council of Ministers of the U.S.S.R.;

The First Vice-Chairmen of the Council of Ministers of the U.S.S.R.;

The Vice-Chairman of the Council of Ministers of the U.S.S.R.;

The Ministers of the U.S.S.R.;

The Chairman of the State Planning Commission of the Council of Ministers of the U.S.S.R.;

The Chairman of the Commission of Soviet Control of the Council of Ministers of the U.S.S.R.;

The Chairman of the State Committee on Questions of Labor and Wages of the Council of Ministers of the U.S.S.R.;

The Chairman of the State Scientific and Technical Committee of the Council of Ministers of the U.S.S.R.;

The Chairman of the State Committee on Aviation Technology of the Council of Ministers of the U.S.S.R.;

The Chairman of the State Committee on Defense Technology of the Council of Ministers of the U.S.S.R.;

The Chairman of the State Committee on Radio Electronics of the Council of Ministers of the U.S.S.R.;

The Chairman of the State Committee on Shipbuilding of the Council of Ministers of the U.S.S.R.;

The Chairman of the State Committee on Chemistry of the Council of Ministers of the U.S.S.R.;

The Chairman of the State Committee on Construction of the Council of Ministers of the U.S.S.R.;

The Chairman of the State Committee on Grain Products of the Council of Ministers of the U.S.S.R.;

The Chairman of the State Committee on Foreign Economic Relations of the Council of Ministers of the U.S.S.R.;

The Chairman of the Committee on State Security of the Council of Ministers of the U.S.S.R.;

The Chairman of the Board of the State Bank of the U.S.S.R.;

The Director of the Central Statistical Administration of the Council of Ministers of the U.S.S.R.

The U.S.S.R. Council of Ministers includes the chairman of the Union Republics' Councils of Ministers ex officio.

Art. 71—The government of the U.S.S.R. or a minister of the U.S.S.R. to whom a question of a member of the Supreme Soviet of the U.S.S.R. is addressed must give a verbal or written reply in the respective chamber within a period not exceeding three days.

Art. 72—The ministers of the U.S.S.R. direct the branches of state administration which come within the jurisdiction of the U.S.S.R.

Art. 73—The ministers of the U.S.S.R., within the limits of the jurisdiction of their respective ministries, issue orders and instructions on the basis and in pursuance of the laws in operation, and also of decisions and orders of the Council of Ministers of the U.S.S.R., and verify their execution.

Art. 74—The ministries of the U.S.S.R. are either All-Union or Union-Republican Ministries.

Art. 75—Each All-Union Ministry directs the branch of state administration entrusted to it throughout the territory of the U.S.S.R. either directly or through bodies appointed by it.

Art. 76—The Union-Republican Ministries, as a rule, direct the branches of state administration entrusted to them through corresponding ministries of the Union Republics; they administer directly only a definite and limited number of enterprises according to a list confirmed by the Presidium of the Supreme Soviet of the U.S.S.R.

Art. 77—The following ministries are All-Union Ministries:

The Ministry of Foreign Trade

The Ministry of Medium Machine Building

The Ministry of the Merchant Marine
The Ministry of Transportation
The Ministry of Transport Construction
The Ministry of Electric Power Plants
Art. 78—The following ministries are Union-Republican Ministries:
The Ministry of Internal Affairs
The Ministry of Higher Education
The Ministry of Geology and Conservation of Mineral Resources
The Ministry of Public Health
The Ministry of Foreign Affairs
The Ministry of Culture
The Ministry of Defense
The Ministry of Communications
The Ministry of Agriculture
The Ministry of Finance

Chapter VI: THE ORGANS OF STATE ADMINISTRATION OF THE UNION REPUBLICS

Art. 79—The highest executive and administrative organ of the state power of a Union Republic is the Council of Ministers of the Union Republic.

Art. 80—The Council of Ministers of a Union Republic is responsible and accountable to the Supreme Soviet of the Union Republic, or, in the intervals between sessions of the Supreme Soviet of the Union Republic, to the Presidium of the Supreme Soviet of the Union Republic.

Art. 81—The Council of Ministers of a Union Republic issues decisions and orders on the basis and in pursuance of the laws in operation of the U.S.S.R. and of the Union Republic, and of the decisions and orders of the Council of Ministers of the U.S.S.R. and verifies their execution.

Art. 82—The Council of Ministers of a Union Republic has the right to suspend decisions and orders of the Councils of Ministers of its Autonomous Republics, and to annul decisions and orders of the Executive Committees of the Soviets of Working People's Deputies of its Territories, Regions and Autonomous Regions and of the Economic Councils of the economic administrative Regions.

Art. 83—The Council of Ministers of a Union Republic is appointed by the Supreme Soviet of the Union Republic and consists of:
The Chairman of the Council of Ministers of the Union Republic;
The Vice-Chairmen of the Council of Ministers;
The Chairman of the State Planning Commission;
The Ministers;
The Chairmen of the State Committees, of the State Commissions and the directors of the other departments of the Council of Ministers created by the Supreme Soviet of the Union Republic in accordance with the Constitution of the Union Republic.

Art. 84—The ministers of a Union Republic direct the branches of state administration which come within the jurisdiction of the Union Republic.

Art. 85—The ministers of a Union Republic, within the limits of the jurisdiction of their respective ministries, issue orders and instructions on the basis and in pursuance of the laws of the U.S.S.R. and of the Union Republic, of the decisions and orders of the Council of Ministers of the U.S.S.R. and the Council of Ministers of the Union Republic, and of the orders and instructions of the Union-Republican Ministries of the U.S.S.R.

Art. 86—The ministries of a Union Republic are either Union-Republican or Republican Ministries.

Art. 87—Each Union-Republican Ministry directs the branch of state administration entrusted to it, and is subordinate both to the Council of Ministers of the Union Republic and to the corresponding Union-Republican Ministry of the U.S.S.R.

Art. 88—Each Republican Ministry directs the branch of state administration entrusted to it and is directly subordinate to the Council of Ministers of the Union Republic.

Art. 88a—The Economic Councils of the economic administrative Regions direct the branches of economic activity entrusted to them and are directly subordinate to the Union Republic Council of Ministers.

The Economic Councils of the economic administrative Regions, within the bounds of their competence, make decisions and issue directives on the basis and in execution of the laws of the U.S.S.R. and the Union Republic and of the decrees and directives of the U.S.S.R. Council of Ministers and the Union Republic Council of Ministers.

Chapter VII: THE HIGHER ORGANS OF STATE POWER IN THE AUTONOMOUS SOVIET SOCIALIST REPUBLICS

Art. 89—The highest organ of state power in an Autonomous Soviet Socialist Republic is the Supreme Soviet of the Autonomous Republic.

Art. 90—The Supreme Soviet of an Autonomous Republic is elected by the citizens of the Republic for a term of four years on a basis of representation established by the Constitution of the Autonomous Republic.

Art. 91—The Supreme Soviet of an Autonomous Republic is the sole legislative organ of the Autonomous Republic.

Art. 92—Each Autonomous Republic has its own Constitution, which takes account of the specific features of the Autonomous Republic and is drawn up in full conformity with the Constitution of the Union Republic.

Art. 93—The Supreme Soviet of an Autonomous Republic elects the Presidium of the Supreme Soviet of the Autonomous Republic and appoints the Council of Ministers of the Autonomous Republic, in accordance with its constitution.

Chapter VIII: THE LOCAL ORGANS OF STATE POWER

Art. 94—The organs of state power in territories, regions, autonomous regions, areas, districts, cities, and rural localities (stanitsas, villages, hamlets, kishlaks, auls) are the soviets of working people's deputies.

Art. 95—The soviets of working people's deputies of territories, regions, autonomous regions, areas, districts, cities, and rural localities (stanitsas, villages, hamlets, kishlaks, auls) are elected by the working people of the respective territories, regions, autonomous regions, areas, districts, cities, or rural locations for a term of two years.

Art. 96—The basis of representation for soviets of working people's deputies is determined by the constitutions of the Union Republics.

Art. 97—The soviets of working people's deputies direct the work of the organs of administration subordinate to them, ensure the maintenance of public order, the observance of the laws and the protection of the rights of citizens, direct local economic and cultural affairs and draw up the local budgets.

Art. 98—The soviets of working people's deputies adopt decisions and issue orders within the limits of the powers vested in them by the laws of the U.S.S.R. and of the Union Republic.

Art. 99—The executive and administrative organ of the soviet of working people's deputies of a territory, region, autonomous region, area, district, city, or rural locality is the executive committee elected by it, consisting of a chairman, vice-chairman, a secretary and members.

Art. 100—The executive and administrative organ of the soviet of working people's deputies in a small locality, in accordance with the constitution of the Union Republic, is the chairman, the vice-chairman and the secretary elected by it.

Art. 101—The executive organs of the soviets of working people's deputies are directly accountable both to the soviets of working people's deputies which elected them and to the executive organ of the superior soviet of working people's deputies.

Chapter IX: THE COURTS AND THE PROCURATOR'S OFFICE

Art. 102—In the U.S.S.R. justice is administered by the Supreme Court of the U.S.S.R., the Supreme Courts of the Union Republics, the Courts of the Territories, Regions, Autonomous Republics, Autonomous Regions and areas, the Special Courts of the U.S.S.R. established by decision of the Supreme Soviet of the U.S.S.R., and the People's Courts.

Art. 103—In all courts cases are tried with the participation of people's assessors, except in cases specially provided for by law.

Art. 104—The Supreme Court of the U.S.S.R. is the highest judicial organ. The Supreme Court of the U.S.S.R. is charged with the supervision of the judicial activities of all the judicial organs of the U.S.S.R. and of the Union Republics within the limits established by law.

Art. 105—The Supreme Court of the U.S.S.R. is elected by the Supreme Soviet of the U.S.S.R. for a term of five years. The Supreme Court of the U.S.S.R. includes the Chief Justices of the Supreme Courts of the Union Republics, ex officio.

Art. 106—The Supreme Courts of the Union Republics are elected by the Supreme Soviets of the Union Republics for a term of five years.

Art. 107—The Supreme Courts of the Autonomous Republics are elected by the Supreme Soviets of the Autonomous Republics for a term of five years.

Art. 108—The courts of Territories, Regions, Autonomous Regions and areas are elected by the Soviets of Working People's Deputies of the respective Territories, Regions, Autonomous Regions or areas for a term of five years.

Art. 109—The People's judges of district (city) People's Courts are elected by the citizens of the district (city) on the basis of universal, equal and direct suffrage by secret ballot for five-year terms.

The People's assessors of district (city) People's Courts are elected at general meetings of workers, employees and peasants at the place of occupation or residence of servicemen—in their military units, for two-year terms.

Art. 110—Judicial proceedings are conducted in the language of the Union Republic, Autonomous Republic or Autonomous Region, persons not knowing this language being guaranteed the opportunity of fully acquainting themselves with the material of the case through an interpreter and likewise the right to use their own language in court.

Art. 111—In all courts of the U.S.S.R. cases are heard in public, unless otherwise provided for by law, and the accused is guaranteed the right of defense.

Art. 112—Judges are independent and subject only to the law.

Art. 113—Supreme supervisory power to ensure the strict observance of the law by all ministries and institutions subordinated to them, as well as by officials and citizens of the U.S.S.R. generally, is vested in the Procurator-General of the U.S.S.R.

Art. 114—The Procurator-General of the U.S.S.R. is appointed by the Supreme Soviet of the U.S.S.R. for a term of seven years.

Art. 115—Procurators of Republics, Territories, Regions, Autonomous Republics and Autonomous Regions are appointed by the Procurator-General of the U.S.S.R. for a term of five years.

Art. 116—Area, district and city procurators are appointed by the Procurators of the Union Republics, subject to the approval of the Procurator-General of the U.S.S.R., for a term of five years.

Art. 117—The organs of the Procurator's Office perform their functions independently of any local organs whatsoever, being subordinate solely to the Procurator-General of the U.S.S.R.

Chapter X: FUNDAMENTAL RIGHTS AND DUTIES OF CITIZENS

Art. 118—Citizens of the U.S.S.R. have the right to work, that is, the right to guaranteed employment and payment for their work in accordance with its quantity and quality.

The right to work is ensured by the socialist organization of the national economy, the steady growth of the productive forces of Soviet society, the elimination of the possibility of economic crises, and the abolition of unemployment.

Art. 119—Citizens of the U.S.S.R. have the right to rest and leisure.

The right to rest and leisure is ensured by the establishment of an eight-hour day for industrial, office, and professional workers, the reduction of the working day to seven or six hours for arduous occupations and to four hours in shops where conditions of work are particularly arduous; by the institution of annual vacations with full pay for industrial, office and professional workers, and by the provision of a wide network of sanatoria, holiday homes and clubs for the accommodation of the working people.

Art. 120—Citizens of the U.S.S.R. have the right to maintenance in old age and also in case of sickness or disability.

This right is ensured by the extensive development of social insurance of factory and office workers at state expense, free medical service for the working people, and the provision of a wide network of health resorts for the use of the working people.

Art. 121—Citizens of the U.S.S.R. have the right to education.

This right is ensured by universal compulsory eight-year education, by extensive development of universal middle-school polytechnical education, of professional-technical education, of special middle-school and higher education on the basis of education's ties with life, with production, by all-out development of evening and correspondence instruction, by all forms of education being free of charge, by a system of state stipends, by teaching in schools in native languages, by the organization in factories, state farms and collective farms of free instruction of workers in vocational, technical and agronomic subjects.

Art. 122—Women in the U.S.S.R. are accorded equal rights with men in all spheres of economic, government, cultural, political and other public activity.

The possibility of exercising these rights is ensured by women being accorded an equal right with men to work, payment for work, rest and leisure, social insurance and education, and by state protection of the interests of mother and child, state aid to mothers of large families and unmarried mothers, maternity leave with full pay, and the provision of a wide network of maternity homes, nurseries and kindergartens.

Art. 123—Equality of rights of citizens of the U.S.S.R., irrespective of their nationality or race, in all spheres of economic, government, cultural, political and other public activity, is an indefeasible law.

Any direct or indirect restriction of the rights of, or conversely, the establishment of any direct or indirect privileges for, citizens on account of their race or nationality, as well as any advocacy of racial or national exclusiveness or hatred and contempt, is punishable by law.

Art. 124—In order to ensure to citizens freedom of conscience, the church in the U.S.S.R. is separated from the state, and the school from the church. Freedom of religious worship and freedom of antireligious propaganda is recognized for all citizens.

Art. 125—In conformity with the interests of the working people, and in order to strengthen the socialist system, the citizens of the U.S.S.R. are guaranteed by law:

    (*a*) Freedom of speech;

    (*b*) Freedom of the press;

    (*c*) Freedom of assembly, including the holding of mass meetings;

    (*d*) Freedom of street processions and demonstrations.

These civil rights are ensured by placing at the disposal of the working people and their organizations printing presses, stocks of paper, public buildings, the streets, communication facilities, and other material requisites for the exercise of these rights.

Art. 126—In conformity with the interests of the working people, and in order to develop the organizational initiative and political activity of the masses of the people, citizens of the U.S.S.R. are guaranteed the right to unite in public organizations; trade unions, cooperative societies, youth organizations, sport and defense organizations, cultural, technical and scientific societies; and the most active and political-conscious citizens in the ranks of the working class and other sections of the working people unite in the Communist party of the Soviet Union which is the vanguard of the working people in their struggle to strengthen and develop the socialist system and is the leading core of all organizations of the working people, both public and state.

Art. 127—Citizens of the U.S.S.R. are guaranteed inviolability of the person. No person may be placed under arrest except by decision of a court or with the sanction of a procurator.

Art. 128—The inviolability of the home of citizens and privacy of correspondence are protected by law.

Art. 129—The U.S.S.R. affords the right of asylum to foreign citizens persecuted for defending the interests of the working people, or for scientific activities, or for struggling for national liberation.

Art. 130—It is the duty of every citizen of the U.S.S.R. to abide by the Constitution of the Union of Soviet Socialist Republics, to observe the laws, to maintain labor discipline, honestly to perform public duties, and to respect the rules of socialist intercourse.

Art. 131—It is the duty of every citizen of the U.S.S.R. to safeguard and fortify public, socialist property as the sacred and inviolable foundation of the Soviet system, as the source of the wealth and might of the country, as the source of the prosperity and culture of all the working people.

Persons committing offenses against public, socialist property are enemies of the people.

Art. 132—Universal military service is law.

Military service in the armed forces of the U.S.S.R. is an honorable duty of the citizens of the U.S.S.R.

Art. 133—To defend the country is the sacred duty of every citizen of the U.S.S.R. Treason to the motherland—violation of the oath of allegiance, desertion to the enemy, impairing the military power of the state, espionage—is punishable with all the severity of the law as the most heinous of crimes.

Chapter XI: THE ELECTORAL SYSTEM

Art. 134—Members of all soviets of working people's deputies—of the Supreme Soviet of the U.S.S.R., the Supreme Soviets of the Union Republics, the Soviets of Working People's Deputies of the Territories and Regions, the Supreme Soviets of the Autonomous Republics, the Soviets of Working People's Deputies of the Autonomous Regions, and the area, district, city and rural (stanitsa, village, hamlet, kishlak, aul) soviets of working people's deputies—are chosen by the electors on the basis of universal, equal, and direct suffrage by secret ballot.

Art. 135—Elections of deputies are universal: all citizens of the U.S.S.R. who have reached the age of eighteen, irrespective of race or nationality, sex, religion, education, domicile, social origin, property status or past activities, have the right to vote in the election of deputies, with the exception of insane persons.

Every citizen of the U.S.S.R. who has reached the age of twenty-three is eligible for election to the Supreme Soviet of the U.S.S.R., irrespective of race or nationality, sex, religion, education, domicile, social origin, property status or past activities.

Art. 136—Elections of deputies are equal: each citizen has one vote; all citizens participate in elections on an equal footing.

Art. 137—Women have the right to elect and be elected on equal terms with men.

Art. 138—Citizens serving in the armed forces of the U.S.S.R. have the right to elect and be elected on equal terms with all other citizens.

Art. 139—Elections of deputies are direct: all soviets of working people's deputies, from rural and city soviets of working people's deputies to the Supreme Soviet of the U.S.S.R., are elected by the citizens by direct vote.

Art. 140—Voting at elections of deputies is secret.

Art. 141—Candidates are nominated by election district.

The right to nominate candidates is secured to public organizations and societies of the working people: Communist Party organizations, trade unions, cooperatives, youth organizations and cultural societies.

Art. 142—It is the duty of every deputy to report to his electors on his work and on the work of his soviet of working people's deputies, and he may be recalled at any time upon decision of a majority of the electors in the manner established by law.

Chapter XII: ARMS, FLAG, CAPITAL

Art. 143—The arms of the Union of Soviet Socialist Republics are sickle and hammer against a globe depicted in the rays of the sun and surrounded by ears of grain, with the inscription "Workers of All Countries, Unite!" in the languages of the Union Republics.

Art. 144—The state flag of the Union of Soviet Socialist Republics is of red cloth with the sickle and hammer depicted in gold in the upper corner near the staff and above them a five-pointed red star bordered in gold. The ratio of the width to the length is 1:2.

Art. 145—The capital of the Union of Soviet Socialist Republics is the City of Moscow.

Chapter XIII: PROCEDURE FOR AMENDING THE CONSTITUTION

Art. 146—The Constitution of the U.S.S.R. may be amended only by decision of the Supreme Soviet of the U.S.S.R. adopted by a majority of not less than two-thirds of the votes in each of its chambers.

Selected bibliography

GREAT BRITAIN

Historical works

Adams, G. B.: *Constitutional History of England,* rev. ed., New York, 1960.
————: *The Origin of the English Constitution,* 2d ed., New Haven, Conn., 1920.
Butler, David E.: *The Electoral System in Britain since 1918,* 2d ed., Oxford, 1963.
Hall-Albion-Pope: *A History of England and the Empire Commonwealth,* 4th ed., New York, 1961.
Keir, David Lindsay: *The Constitutional History of Modern Britain Since 1485,* 7th ed., London, 1964.
Macfarlane, L. J.: *British Politics 1918–1964,* New York, 1965.
McIlwain, Charles H.: *The High Court of Parliament and Its Supremacy,* Hamden, Conn., 1962.
McKechnie, W. S.: *Magna Carta: A Commentary on the Great Charter of King John,* Glasgow, 1914.
Maitland, Frederic W.: *The Constitutional History of England,* London, 1961.

Pasquet, D.: *An Essay on the Origins of the House of Commons* (trans. by R. D. G. Laffan), Cambridge, England, 1925.

Pollard, A. F.: *The Evolution of Parliament*, London, 1934.

Pollock, F., and F. W. Maitland: *History of English Law to the Times of Edward I*, Cambridge, England, 1952.

Porritt, E.: *The Unreformed House of Commons: Parliamentary Representation before 1832*, 2 vols., New York, 1963.

Stubbs, W.: *The Constitutional History of England*, 5th ed., Oxford, 1891.

Thompson, Faith: *The First Century of Magna Carta: Why It Persisted as a Document*, Minneapolis, 1925.

Thomson, David: *England in the 20th Century, 1920–1963*, London, 1964.

Trevelyan, G. M.: *The Two-party System in English Political History*, Oxford, 1926.

Articles:

Fellowes, E.: "Changes in Parliamentary Life, 1918–1961," *Political Quarterly*, Vol. 36, No. 3 (July–October, 1965), pp. 256–265.

General works

Amery, Leopold C. M. S.: *Thoughts on the Constitution*, 2d ed., Oxford, 1953.

Anson, Sir William R.: *Law and Custom of the Constitution*, 2 vols., New York, 1922–1935.

Bagehot, Walter: *The English Constitution*, Introduction by R. H. S. Crossman, London, 1963.

Bailey, Sidney D.: *British Parliamentary Democracy*, 3d ed., London, 1966.

Beer, Samuel H.: *The Government of Great Britain*, Chicago, 1958.

Brinton, Crane: *English Political Thought in the 19th Century*, New York, 1962.

Campion, Sir Gilbert, et al.: *British Government since 1918*, New York, 1950.

Dicey, A. V.: *Introduction to the Study of the Law of the Constitution*, 10th ed., London, 1959.

Greaves, H. R. G.: *The British Constitution*, 3d ed., London, 1955.

Jennings, Sir Ivor: *The British Constitution*, 3d ed., Cambridge, England, 1950.

————: *Cabinet Government*, 2d ed., Cambridge, England, 1951.

Keith, Sir Arthur B.: *The Constitution of England from Queen Victoria to George VI*, 2 vols., New York, 1940.

Kitzinger, U.: *Britain, Europe and Beyond*, Leyden, Netherlands, 1964.

Knaplund, Paul: *Britain, Commonwealth and Empire, 1901–1955*, New York, 1957.

Laski, Harold J.: *Parliamentary Government in England*, New York, 1938.

————: *Reflections on the Constitution*, New York, 1951.

Mathiot, A.: *The British Political System*, Stanford, Calif., 1958.

Moodie, Graeme C.: *The Government of Great Britain*, New York, 1961.

Morrison, Herbert: *Government and Parliament*, London, 1954.

Muir, Ramsey: *How Britain Is Governed*, 4th ed., London, 1940.

Ogg, Frederic A.: *English Government and Politics*, 2d ed., New York, 1936.

Robson, William A.: *The British System of Government*, 3d ed., New York, 1948.

Stout, Hiram M.: *British Government*, New York, 1953.

White, L. W., and W. D. Hussey: *Government in Great Britain, the Empire and the Commonwealth*, New York, 1958.

Wilson, F. M. G.: *The Organization of British Central Government, 1914–1956*, London, 1957.

Wilson, N.: *The British System of Government*, Oxford, 1963.

Articles:

Bromhead, P.: "The British Constitution in 1961," *Parliamentary Affairs*, Vol. 15, No. 2 (Spring, 1962), pp. 144–159.

————: "The British Constitution in 1963," *Parliamentary Affairs*, Vol. 17, No. 2 (Spring, 1964), pp. 142–159.

Christoph, J. B.: "Consensus and Cleavage in British Political Ideology," *American Political Science Review*, Vol. 59, No. 3 (September, 1965), pp. 629–642.

Harrison, W.: "The British Constitution in 1954," *Parliamentary Affairs*, Vol. 8 (Summer, 1955), pp. 303–317.

Political parties—general

Bailey, S. D.: *British Parliamentary Democracy*, 2d ed., New York, 1966.

———— (ed.): *The British Party System*, 2d ed., London, 1953.

Beer, S. H.: *British Politics in the Collectivist Age*, New York, 1965.

————: *Modern British Politics: A Study of Parties and Pressure Groups*, London, 1965.

Blondel, Jean: *Voters, Parties and Leaders: The Social Fabric of British Politics*, Baltimore, 1963.

Brand, Carl F.: *The British Labour Party: A Short History*, Stanford, Calif., 1964.

————: *The British Labour Party: From 1880 to the Present Day*, Stanford, Calif., 1965.

Bulmer-Thomas, Ivor: *The Growth of the British Party System*, London, 1965.

Butler, D. E.: *The Electoral System in Britain, 1918–1951*, London, 1953.

———— and Anthony King: *The British General Election of 1964*, Oxford, 1965.

Butler, R. A.: *Our New Frontier*, London, 1962.

Deakin, Nicholas: *Colour and the British Electorate 1964: 6 Case Studies*, London, 1965.

Finer, S. E.: *Anonymous Empire: A Study of the Lobby in Great Britain*, London, 1958.

————, et al.: *Backbench Opinion in the House of Commons, 1955–1959*, New York, 1961.

King, A. (ed.): *British Politics, People, Parties & Parliament*, Boston, 1966.

McCallum, R. B., and A. Readman: *The British General Election of 1945*, Oxford, 1947.

McKenzie, R. T.: *British Political Parties*, 2d ed., New York, 1963.

Shrimsley, Anthony: *The First Hundred Days of Harold Wilson*, New York, 1965.

Stewart, J. D.: *British Pressure Groups: Their Role in Relation to the House of Commons*, London, 1958.

Articles:

Abrams, M.: "Public Opinion Polls and Political Parties in Great Britain," *Public Opinion Quarterly,* Vol. 27, No. 1 (Spring, 1963), pp. 9–18.

Beer, S. H.: "Pressure Groups and Parties in Britain," *American Political Science Review,* Vol. 50 (March, 1956), pp. 1–23.

———: "Representation of Interests in British Government," *American Political Science Review,* Vol. 51 (September, 1957), pp. 613–650.

Brady, A.: "The British Two-party System," *Political Science,* Vol. 8 (March, 1956), pp. 3–18.

Butler, D. E.: "Some Notes on the Nature of British Political Parties," *Occidente,* Vol. 10 (March–April, 1954), pp. 137–153.

Clarke, David: "The Organization of Political Parties," *Political Quarterly,* Vol. 21 (1950), pp. 79–90.

Cross, J. A.: "Deputy Speakers and Party Politics," *Parliamentary Affairs,* Vol. 18, No. 4 (Autumn, 1965), pp. 361–367.

Epstein, L. D.: "Cohesion of British Parliamentary Parties," *American Political Science Review,* Vol. 50 (June, 1956), pp. 360–377.

Finer, S. E.: "The Anonymous Empire," *Political Studies,* Vol. 6 (February, 1958), pp. 16–32. (A study of lobbies in Britain.)

Fraser, L.: "On the Terms 'Left' and 'Right' in Contemporary British Politics," *Modern Age,* Vol. 7, No. 3 (Summer, 1963), pp. 291–300.

Jones, C. E.: "Inter-party Competition in Britain, 1950–1959," *Parliamentary Affairs,* Vol. 17, No. 1 (Winter, 1963–1964), pp. 50–56.

Lipson, Leslie: "Common Ground and Emerging Conflicts between the British Parties," *Political Quarterly,* Vol. 27 (April–June, 1956), pp. 182–193.

———: "The Two-party System in British Politics," *American Political Science Review,* Vol. 47 (1953), pp. 337–358.

McKenzie, R. T.: "Parties, Pressure Groups and the British Political Process," *Political Quarterly,* Vol. 29 (January–March, 1958), pp. 5–16.

———: "Power in British Political Parties," *British Journal of Sociology,* Vol. 6 (June, 1955), pp. 123–132.

Mackenzie, W. J. M.: "Pressure Groups in British Government," *British Journal of Sociology,* Vol. 6 (June, 1955), pp. 133–148.

Nicholas, H. G.: The Formation of Party Policy," *Parliamentary Affairs,* Vol. 5 (1951), pp. 142–153.

Potter, Allen: "British Party Organization," *Political Science Quarterly,* Vol. 43 (1949), pp. 65–83.

Rasmussen, J.: "The Implication of Safe Seats for British Democracy," *Western Political Quarterly,* September, 1966, pp. 516–529.

Rose, Richard: "Parties, Factions and Tendencies in Britain," *Political Studies,* Oxford, Vol. 12, No. 1 (February, 1964), pp. 33–46.

———: "The Political Ideas of English Party Activists," *American Political Science Review,* Vol. 56 (1962), No. 2, pp. 360–371.

The Conservatives

Birch, N.: *The Conservative Party,* London, 1949.

Block, G. D. M.: *A Source Book of Conservatism,* London, 1964.

Boyd-Carpenter, John: *The Conservative Case: Choice for Britain,* London, 1950.

Braine, Bernard: *Tory Democracy,* London, 1948.

Churchill, R. S.: *The Fight for the Tory Leadership: A Contemporary Chronicle,* London, 1964.

Conservative Party: The Right Road for Britain, London, 1949. Conservative Political Center, *Conservatism, 1945–1950,* London, 1950.

Hogg, Quintin (Viscount Hailsham): *The Conservative Case,* Baltimore, 1959.

————: *The Left Was Never Right,* London, 1954.

McKenzie, R. T.: *British Political Parties: The Distribution of Power within the Conservative and Labour Parties,* 2d ed., New York, 1965.

White, R. J.: *The Conservative Tradition,* 2d ed., London, 1964.

Articles:

Beer, Samuel H.: "The Conservative Party of Great Britain," *Journal of Politics,* Vol. 14 (1952), pp. 41–71.

Bulmer-Thomas, I.: "How Conservative Policy Is Formed," *Political Quarterly,* Vol. 24 (1953), pp. 190–203.

Butler, R. A.: "Conservative Policy," *Political Quaterly,* Vol. 20 (1949), pp. 317–325.

Potter, A. M.: "The English Conservative Constituency Association," *Western Political Quarterly,* Vol. 9 (June, 1956), pp. 363–375.

Salter, Sir Arthur: "British Conservatism To-day," *Yale Review,* Vol. 41 (1951), pp. 1–12.

Thomson, G.: "Parties in Parliament, 1959–1963: The Conservatives," *Political Quarterly,* Vol. 34 (July–September, 1963), pp. 249–255.

Urwin, D. W.: "Scottish Conservatism: A Party Organization in Transition," *Political Studies,* Oxford, Vol. 14, No. 2 (June, 1966), pp. 145–162.

Uthey, T. E.: "Implications of the Conservative Victory," *Fortnightly,* Vol. 177 (1952), pp. 15–19.

The Labor Party

Attlee, C. R.: *The Labour Party in Perspective; and 12 Years Later,* London, 1949.

Beer, M.: *A History of British Socialism,* London, 1948.

Brockway, Fenner: *Inside the Left,* London, 1947.

Clayton, J.: *The Rise and Decline of Socialism in Great Britain, 1889–1924,* London, 1926.

Cole, G. D. H.: *A History of the Labour Party from 1914,* London, 1948.

————: *A Short History of the British Working Class Movement, 1789–1947,* London, 1926.

Cripps, Sir Stafford: *Toward Christian Democracy,* London, 1946.

Crosland, C. A. R.: *The Future of Socialism,* London, 1956.

Hall, William G.: *The Labour Party,* London, 1949.

Jouvenel, Bertrand de: *Problems of Socialist England,* London, 1949.

Labour Party, National Executive Committee: *Labour Believes in Britain,* London, 1949.

Miiiband, R.: *Parliamentary Socialism: A Study in the Politics of Labor,* London, 1961.

Munro, Donald E. (ed.): *Socialism the British Way,* London, 1948.

Pritt, D. N.: *The Labour Government, 1945–1951,* London, 1963.

Rothstein, F. A.: *From Chartism to Labourism,* London, 1929.

Smith, Dudley: *Harold Wilson,* London, 1964.

Tracey, Herbert: *The British Labour Party,* 3 vols., London, 1948.

Webb, Sidney, and Beatrice Webb: *The History of Trade Unionism,* London, 1950.

Williams, Francis: *Socialist Britain,* New York, 1949.

Articles:

Burns, James MacGregor: "The Parliamentary Labor Party in Great Britain," *American Political Science Review,* Vol. 44 (1950), pp. 855–871.

Epstein, Leon D.: "Socialism and the British Labor Party," *Political Science Quarterly,* Vol. 45 (1951), pp. 507–531.

Hanham, H. J.: "The Local Organization of the British Labour Party," *Western Political Quarterly,* Vol. 9 (June, 1956), pp. 376–388.

Hornby, R.: "Parties in Parliament, 1959–1963: The Labour Party," *Political Quarterly,* Vol. 34, No. 3 (July–September, 1963), pp. 240–248.

Punnett, R. M.: "The Labour Shadow Cabinet, 1955–1964," *Parliamentary Affairs,* Vol. 18, No. 1 (Winter, 1964–1965), pp. 61–70.

Roche, John P.: "The Crisis in British Socialism," *Antioch Review,* Vol. 12 (1952–1953), pp. 387–398.

Schumacher, E. F.: "In Search of Socialism: Review of New Fabian Essays," *Twentieth Century,* Vol. 152 (1952), pp. 33–40.

Williams, Francis: "The Program of the British Labour Party: A Historical Survey," *Journal of Politics,* Vol. 12 (1950), pp. 189–210.

Liberals and minor parties

Cruikshank, R. J.: *The Liberal Party,* London, 1948.

Grimond, J.: *The Liberal Challenge,* London, 1963.

Laski, Harold J.: *The Secret Battalion: An Examination of the Communist Attitude to the Labor Party,* London, 1946.

McCallum, R. B.: *The Liberal Party from Earl Grey to Asquith,* London, 1963.

Pelling, Henry: *The British Communist Party,* New York, 1959.

Potter, A. M.: *Organized Groups in British National Politics,* London, 1961.

Rasmussen, J. S.: *Retrenchment and Revival: A Study of the Contemporary British Liberal Party,* Tucson, 1964.

Slesser, Sir Henry: *A History of the Liberal Party,* New York, 1944.

Thayer, G.: *The British Political Fringe,* London, 1965.

Articles:

Davis, Morris: "Some Neglected Aspects of British Pressure Groups," *Midwest Journal of Political Science,* Vol. 7, No. 1 (February, 1963), p. 42.

Fothergill, P.: "The Liberal Predicament," *Political Quarterly,* Vol. 24 (1953), pp. 243–249.

Grimond, J.: "The Principles of Liberalism," *Political Quarterly,* Vol. 24 (1953), pp. 236–242.

McKitterick, T. E. M.: "Radicalism after 1964," *Political Quarterly,* Vol. 36, No. 1 (January–March, 1964), pp. 52–58.

Rasmussen, J.: "The Implications of the Potential Strength of the Liberal Party for the Future of British Politics," *Parliamentary Affairs,* Vol. 14, No. 3 (Summer, 1961), pp. 378–390.

Willey, R. J.: "Pressure Group Politics: The Case of Sohyo," *Western Political Quarterly,* Vol. 17, No. 4 (December, 1964), pp. 703–723.

The Crown and the Executive

Baxter, Stephen B.: *The Development of the Treasury, 1660–1702,* Cambridge, England, 1957.

Beer, Samuel H.: *Treasury Control: The Co-ordination of Financial and Economic Policy in Great Britain,* 2d ed., Oxford, 1957.

Bridges, Sir Edward: *Treasury Control,* London, 1950.

Carter, Byrum E.: *The Office of Prime Minister,* London, 1956.

Chapman, Brian: *British Government Observed: Some European Reflections,* London, 1963.

Daalder, H.: *Cabinet Reform in Britain, 1914–1963,* Stanford, Calif., 1963.

Dimont, C.: *British Monarchy,* New York, 1955.

Harris, Joseph P.: *Parliamentary Control of the Executive in Great Britain,* Berkeley, Calif., 1962.

Heath, Sir Thomas: *The Treasury,* Whitehall Series, London, 1927.

Howard, A., and R. West: *The Making of the Prime Minister,* London, 1965.

Jennings, Sir Ivor: *Cabinet Government,* 3d ed., Cambridge, England, 1959.

Keith, Arthur B.: *The British Cabinet System,* 2d ed., London, 1952.

Mackenzie, W. J., and J. W. Grove: *Central Administration in Britain,* London, 1957.

Mackintosh, John P.: *The British Cabinet,* Toronto, 1962.

Martin, Kingsley: *The Crown and the Establishment,* London, 1962.

———: *The Magic of Monarchy,* New York, 1937.

Morrison, Herbert, et al.: *Vitality in Administration,* London, 1957.

Morrison, Herbert Stanley (Lord Morrison of Lambeth): *Government and Parliament: A Survey from the Inside,* 3d ed., London, 1964.

Richards, P. G.; *Patronage in British Government,* Toronto, 1963.

Schwartz, Bernard: *Law and the Executive in Britain: A Comparative Study,* New York, 1949.

White, L. W.: *Government in Great Britain, the Empire and the Commonwealth,* 3d ed., Cambridge, England, 1961.

Articles:

Bromhead, P.: "The Peerage Act and the New Prime Minister," *Parliamentary Affairs,* Vol. 17, No. 3 (Winter, 1963–1964), pp. 57–64.

Buck, P. W.: "The Early Start toward Cabinet Office, 1918–1955," *Western Political Quarterly,* Vol. 16, No. 3 (September, 1963), pp. 624–632.

Catlin, G.: "Considerations on the British Constitution," *Political Science Quarterly,* Vol. 70 (December, 1955), pp. 481–497.

Finer, S. E.: "The Individual Responsibility of Ministers," *Public Administration,* Vol. 34 (Winter, 1956), pp. 377–396.

Greaves, H. R. G.: "British Central Government, 1914–1956," *Political Quarterly*, Vol. 38 (October–December, 1957), pp. 383–389.

Hinton, R. W. K. "The Prime Minister as an Elected Monarch," *Parliamentary Affairs,* Vol. 13, No. 3 (Summer, 1960), pp. 297–303.

Jones, G. W.: "The Prime Minister's Power," *Parliamentary Affairs,* Vol. 18, No. 2 (Spring, 1965), pp. 167–185.

Moodie, G. C.: "The Crown and Parliament," *Parliamentary Affairs,* Vol. 10 (Summer, 1957), pp. 256–264.

Robson, W. A.: "The Reform of Government," *Political Quarterly,* Vol. 35, No. 2 (April–June, 1964), pp. 193–211.

Woods, J.: "Treasury Control," *Political Quarterly,* Vol. 25 (October–December, 1954), pp. 370–381.

Parliament

Bailey, Sidney D.: *The Future of the House of Lords,* New York, 1954.

Butt, Ronald: *The Power of Parliament,* Oxford, 1966.

Campion, Sir Gilbert: *An Introduction to the Procedure of the House of Commons,* 2d ed., London and New York, 1950.

———— (ed.): *Parliament: A Survey,* London, 1952.

Chester, D. N., and N. Bowring: *Questions in Parliament,* New York, 1962.

Gordon, Strathearn: *Our Parliament,* 2d ed., London, 1952.

Hemingford, Lord: *What Parliament Is and Does,* New York, 1948.

Herbert, Allen: *Independent Member,* New York, 1951.

Hogg, Quintin: *The Purpose of Parliament,* London, 1946.

Jennings, W. I.: *Parliament,* 2d ed., New York, 1957.

May, Sir Thomas Erskine: *A Treatise on the Law, Privileges, and Usage of Parliament,* 15th ed., rev. by Sir G. Campion, London, 1950.

Morrison, Henry: *Parliament: What It Is and How It Works,* London, 1935.

Morrison, Herbert Stanley: *British Parliamentary Democracy,* London, 1962.

Ranney, A.: *Pathway to Parliament: Candidate Selection in Britain,* Madison, Wis., 1965.

Richards, Peter G.: *Honourable Members: A Study of the British Backbencher,* New York, 1959.

Stewart, J. D.: *British Pressure Groups: Their Role in Relation to the House of Commons,* New York, 1958.

Young, Roland: *The British Parliament,* Evanston, Ill., 1962.

Articles:

Aikin, Charles: "The British Bureaucracy and the Origins of Parliamentary Policy," *American Political Science Review,* Vol. 33 (1939), pp. 26–46, 219–233.

Alderman, R. K., and J. A. Cross: "The Parliamentary Private Secretary: A Danger to the Free Functioning of Parliament," *Political Studies,* Oxford, Vol. 14, No. 2 (June, 1966), pp. 199–208.

Bromhead. Peter: "The General Election of 1966," *Parliamentary Affairs,* Vol. XIX, No. 3 (Summer, 1966), Hansard Society for Parliamentary Government, p. 332.

Buck, P. W.: "By-elections in Parliamentary Careers, 1918–1959," *Western Political Quarterly,* Vol. 14, No. 2 (June, 1961), pp. 432–435.

Chubb, Basil: "Parliamentary Control of the Public Accounts," *Parliamentary Affairs,* Vol. 5 (1950), pp. 344–351, 450–457.

Crick, B. R.: "What Should the Lords Be Doing," *Political Quarterly,* Vol. 34, No. 2 (April–June, 1963), pp. 174–184.

Davies, Ernest: "The Role of Private Members Bills," *Political Quarterly,* Vol. 28 (January–March, 1957), pp. 32–39.

Forsey, E.: "Parliament's Power to Advise," *Canadian Journal Econ. Polit. Science,* Vol. 29, No. 2 (May, 1963), pp. 203–210.

Greenleaf, W. H.: "Urgency Motions in the Commons," *Public Law,* London, Autumn, 1960, pp. 270–284.

Hanson, A. H.: "The Purpose of Parliament," *Parliamentary Affairs,* Vol 17, No. 3 (Summer, 1964), pp. 279–295.

Heasman, D. J.: "The Monarch, the Prime Minister and the Dissolution of Parliament," *Parliamentary Affairs,* Vol. 14, No. 1 (Winter, 1960–1961), pp. 94–107.

————: "Parliamentary Paths to High Office," *Parliamentary Affairs,* Vol. 16, No. 3 (Summer, 1964), pp. 315–330.

Hornby, R. "The Influence of the Back-bench: A Tory View," *Political Quarterly,* Vol. 36, No. 3 (July–October, 1965), pp. 286–294.

Johnson, N.: "Parliamentary Questions and the Conduct of Administration," *Public Administration,* London, Vol. 39, No. 2 (Summer, 1961), pp. 131–148.

Nicholas, H. G.: "The British Election," *Modern Age,* Vol. 8, No. 4 (Fall, 1964), pp. 368–376.

Pickles, W.: "Psychology Reconsidered: The 1964 Election Study," *Political Quarterly,* Vol. 36, No. 4 (October–December, 1965), pp. 460–470.

Ranney, A.: "Inter Constituency Movement of British Parliamentary Candidates," *American Political Science Review,* Vol. 58, No. 1 (March, 1964), pp. 36–45.

Ryle, M.: "Committees of the House of Commons," *Political Quarterly,* Vol. 36, No. 3 (July–October, 1965), pp. 295–308.

Shearer, J. G. S.: "Standing Committees in the House of Commons, 1945–1950," *Parliamentary Affairs,* Vol. 4 (1950), pp. 558–568.

Weare, V.: "The House of Lords: Prophecy and Fulfillment," *Parliamentary Affairs,* Vol. 18, No. 4 (Autumn, 1965), pp. 422–433.

Wolf-Phillips, L.: "Parliamentary Divisions and Proxy Voting," *Parliamentary Affairs,* Vol. 18, No. 4 (Autumn, 1965), pp. 416–421.

Wood, D.: "The Parliamentary Lobby," *Political Quarterly,* Vol. 36, No. 3 (July–October, 1965), pp. 309–322.

Yardley, D. C. M.: "The Work and Status of the Parliamentary Agent," *Parliamentary Affairs,* Vol. 18, No. 2 (Spring, 1965), pp. 162–166.

Law and justice

Amos, Sir Maurice Sheldon: *British Justice: An Outline of the Administration of Criminal Justice in England and Wales,* London, 1940.

Archer, P.: *The Queen's Courts,* Harmondsworth, England, 1956.

Ensor, Robert C. K.: *Courts and Judges in France, Germany and England,* New York, 1933.

Friedmann, W.: *Law and Social Change in Contemporary Britain,* London, 1951.

Hanbury, H. G.: *English Courts of Law,* 3d ed., London, 1960.

Hewart, Lord: *The New Despotism,* London, 1945.

Holdsworth, W. S.: *History of English Law,* 7th ed., London, 1956.

Holmes, O. W.: *The Common Law,* Boston, 1881.

Jackson, Richard Meredith: *The Machinery of Justice in England,* 4th ed., Cambridge, England, 1964.

Jenks, E.: *The Book of English Law as at the End of 1938,* 5th ed., London, 1956.

Jennings, Sir W. I.: *The Law and the Constitution,* 5th ed., London, 1959.

————: *Parliament,* 2d ed., Cambridge, England, 1957.

Patterson, C. P.: *The Machinery of Justice in Great Britain,* Austin, Tex, 1936.

Pollock, Sir F.: *The Expansion of the Common Law,* London, 1904.

————: *The Genius of the Common Law,* New York, 1912.

Potter, H.: *A Historical Introduction to English Law and its Institutions,* 4th ed., London, 1958.

Pound, Roscoe: *The Spirit of the Common Law,* Boston, 1921.

Radcliffe, C. R. Y., and G. Cross: *The English Legal System,* 4th ed., London, 1964.

Robson, W. A.: *Justice and Administrative Law,* 3d ed., London, 1951.

Sieghart, Marguerite A.: *Government by Decree: A Comparative Study of the Ordinance in English and French Law,* New York, 1950.

Slesser, Sir Henry: *The Administration of the Law,* New York, 1948.

Yardley, D. Ch. M.: *Introduction to British Constitutional Law,* London, 1960.

Articles:

Cooper, Lord: "Administrative Justice," *Public Administration,* Vol. 32 (Summer, 1954), pp. 165–171.

Gelinas, A.: "Judicial Control of Administrative Action in Great Britain and Canada," *Public Law,* London, Summer, 1963, pp. 140–171.

Harvey, H. J.: "Crown and the Common Law," *International Council,* Vol. 487 (1953), pp. 5–71.

Kilmuir, Viscount: "The Office of the Lord Chancellor," *Parliamentary Affairs,* Vol. 9 (Spring, 1956), pp. 132–139.

Marshall, G.: "The Recent Development of English Administrative Law," *Politico,* Vol. 24, No. 4 (December, 1959), pp. 637–645.

Mitchell, J. D. B.: "The Flexible Constitution," *Public Law,* London, Winter, 1960, pp. 332–350.

Richards, P. C.: "The Selection of Justices of the Peace," *Public Law,* London, Summer, 1961, pp. 134–149.

Local government

Attlee, C. R.: *Borough Councils,* 2d ed., London, 1946.

Block, G. D. M.: *Party Politics in Local Government,* published by Tonbridge Conservative Political Center, 1962.

Clarke, J. J.: *The Local Government of the United Kingdom,* 15th ed., London, 1955.

Cohen, E. W.: *Autonomy and Delegation in County Government,* London, 1953.

Cole, G. D. H.: *Local and Regional Government,* London, 1947.

Finer, Herman: *English Local Government,* 4th ed., London, 1950.

Finer, S. E.: *A Primer of Public Administration,* London, 1950.

Fogarty, M. P.: *Town and Country Planning,* London, 1948.

Haar, Charles M.: *Land Planning Law in a Free Society: A Study of the British Town and Country Planning,* Cambridge, England, 1951.

Harris, John S.: *British Government Inspection as a Dynamic Process: The Local Services and the Central Departments,* New York, 1962.

Jackson, Richard Meredith: *The Machinery of Local Government,* 2d ed., London, 1965.

Jennings, W. I.: *Principles of Local Government Law,* 4th ed., London, 1960.

Laski, H. J. W., and W. A. Robson: *A Century of Municipal Progress,* London, 1935.

Lipman, V. D.: *Local Government Areas, 1834–1945,* Oxford, 1949.

Local Government: Functions of County Councils and County District Councils in England and Wales, Cmd. 161, H. M. Stationery Office, London, 1957.

Robson, W. A.: *The Development of Local Government,* 2d ed., London, 1948.

————: *Local Government in Crisis,* London, 1966.

Smellie, K. B.: *A History of Local Government,* 3d ed., London, 1957.

Thomas, D.: *Local Government: An Introduction to the British System,* Oxford, 1964.

Warren, John H.: *The English Local Government System,* 8th rev. ed., London, 1965.

————: *Municipal Administration,* London, 1948.

Articles:

Banwell, H.: "The New Relations Between Central and Local Government," *Public Administration,* London, Vol. 37, No. 3 (Autumn, 1959), pp. 201–212.

Barratt, C.: "The Town Clerk in British Local Government," *Public Administration,* London, Vol. 41, No. 2 (Summer, 1963), pp. 157–171.

Black, Robert B.: "The British Central Land Board," *Public Administration Review,* Vol. 11 (1951), pp. 35–43.

Chipperfield, G. H.: "The City Manager and Chief Administrative Officer," *Public Administration,* London, Vol. 42, No. 2 (Summer, 1964), pp. 123–131.

Garner, J. F.: "Aldermen in English Local Government," *Journal Loc. Adm. Overseas,* Vol. 3, No. 1 (January, 1964), pp. 35–41.

Jones, Victor: "Recent Developments in the Government of Metropolitan London and Paris," *Western Political Quarterly Supplement,* Vol. 14, No. 3 (September, 1961), pp. 38–39.

Miller, J. V.: "The Organization of Internal Audit in Local Government in England and Wales," *Public Administration,* London, Vol. 38, No. 2 (Summer, 1960), pp. 137–156.

Sharp, E.: "The Future of Local Government," *Public Administration,* London, Vol. 40, No. 4 (Winter, 1962), pp. 375–386.

Usill, V.: "Democracy in British Local Government," *National Municipal Review,* Vol. 35 (1946), pp. 620–621.

Civil Service

Campbell, George Archibald: *The Civil Service in Britain,* 2d ed., London, 1965.

Critchley, T. A.: *The Civil Service To-day,* London, 1951.

Dale, Harold E.: *The Higher Civil Service,* New York, 1942.

Finer, Herman: *The British Civil Service,* 2d ed., London, 1947.

Great Britain, Treasury: *Political Activities of Civil Servants,* Cmd. 8783, London, 1953.

Greaves, Harold R. G.: *The Civil Service in the Changing State: A Survey of Civil Service Reform and the Implications of a Planned Economy on Public Administration in England,* London, 1947.

Griffith, L. W.: *The British Civil Service, 1854–1954,* H. M. Stationery Office, London, 1954.

Monk, Bosworth: *How the Civil Service Works,* London, 1952.

Robson, W. A. (ed.): *The Civil Service in Britain and France,* New York, 1956.

Stout, Hiram M.: *Public Service in Great Britain,* Chapel Hill, N.C., 1938.

Walker, Harvey: *Training Public Employees in Great Britain,* New York, 1935.

Wheare, K. C.: *The Civil Service in the Constitution,* London, 1954.

White, L. D.: *Whitley Councils in the British Civil Service,* Chicago, 1933.

Articles:

Attlee, C. R.: "Civil Servants, Ministers, Parliament, and the Public," *Political Quarterly,* Vol. 25 (October–December, 1954), pp. 308–315.

Brown, R. G. S.: "Organization, Theory and Civil Service Reform," *Public Administration,* London, Vol. 43, No. 3 (Autumn, 1965), pp. 313–330.

Campbell, G. A.: "Civil Service Recruitment," *Quarterly Review,* Vol. 608 (April, 1956), pp. 183–192.

Frankel, S. J.: "Arbitration in the British Civil Service," *Public Administration,* London, Vol. 38, No. 3 (Autumn, 1960), pp. 197–211.

Greaves, H. R. G.: "The Structure of the Civil Service," *Political Quarterly,* Vol. 25 (October–December, 1954), pp. 360–369.

Joelson, M. R.: "The Dismissal of Civil Servants in the Interest of National Security," *Public Law,* London, Spring, 1963, pp. 51–75.

Mallaby, G.: "The Civil Service Commission: Its Place in the Machinery of Government," *Public Administration,* London, Vol. 42, No. 1 (Spring, 1964), pp. 1–10.

Platt, A. J.: "Some Problems of Training in the British Civil Service," *Independent Journal of Public Administration,* Vol. 5, No. 2 (April–June, 1959), pp. 174–185.

National enterprise

Barry, E.: *Nationalization in British Politics: The Historical Background,* Stanford, Calif., 1965.

Brady, Robert A.: *Crisis in Britain: Plans and Achievements of the Labour Government,* Berkeley, Calif., 1950.

Chester, D. N.: *The Nationalized Industries: An Analysis of the Statutory Provisions,* 2d ed., London, 1951.

Cole, G. D. H.: *The National Coal Board: Its Tasks, Its Organization and Its Prospects,* London, 1948.

Haynes, William W.: *Nationalization in Practice: The British Coal Industry*, Boston, 1953.

Hutchison, Keith: *The Decline and Fall of British Capitalism*, New York, 1950.

Lewis, Ben W.: *British Planning and Nationalization*, New York, 1952.

Macdonald, D. F.: *The State and the Trade Unions*, New York, 1960.

Marsh, David C.: *An Introduction to the Study of Social Administration*, London, 1965.

Palmer, Cecil: *The British Socialist Welfare State: An Examination of its Political, Social, Moral and Economic Consequences*, Caldwell, Idaho, 1952.

Robson, W. A.: *Nationalized Industry and Public Ownership*, 2d ed., London, 1962.

———— (ed.): *Problems of Nationalized Industry*, London, 1952.

Rogow, A. A.: *The Labour Government and British Industry, 1945–1951*, Oxford, 1955.

Watkins, E.: *The Cautious Revolution*, London, 1951.

Weiner, Herbert E.: *British Labour and Public Ownership*, Washington, 1960.

Articles:

Abrams, M.: "Social Trends and Electoral Behaviour," *British Journal of Socialism*, Vol. 13, No. 3 (September, 1962), pp. 228–242.

Daniel, G. H.: "Public Accountability of the Nationalized Industries," *Public Administration*, London, Vol. 38, No. 1 (Spring, 1960), pp. 27–34.

"Denationalization of Iron and Steel," *Public Administration*, Vol. 31 (1953), pp. 277–284.

Dewey, D. J.: "Crisis in Britain: A Note on the Stagnation Thesis," *Journal of Political Economics*, Vol. 59 (1951), pp. 348–352.

Haynes, W. W.: "A Test Case from Britain: Does Nationalization Work?" *Harvard Business Review*, Vol. 31 (1953), No. 2, pp. 103–115.

Simmons, R. H.: "The Role of the Select Committee on Nationalized Industry in Parliament," *Western Political Quarterly*, Vol. 14, No. 3 (September, 1961), pp. 741–747.

Social services

Marsh, David C.: *The Future of the Welfare State*, Harmondsworth, Middlesex, England, 1964.

————: *National Insurance and Assistance in Great Britain*, London, 1951.

Robson, W. A. (ed.): *Social Security*, 3d ed., London, 1948.

Ross, Sir James: *The National Health Service in Great Britain*, Oxford, 1952.

Articles:

Smith, N. A.: "Theory and Practice of the Welfare State," *Political Quarterly*, Vol. 22 (1951), pp. 369–381.

Somers, H. M., and A. R. Somers: "The Health Service: Diagnosis and Prognosis," *Political Quarterly*, Vol. 27 (October–December, 1956), pp. 410–422.

Spenden, S.: "British Intellectuals in the Welfare State: How the New Climate Affects Science and Culture," *Commentary*, Vol. 12 (1951), pp. 325–430.

Wootton, Barbara: "Record of the Labor Government in Social Services," *Political Quarterly*, Vol. 29 (1949), p. 101.

Zink, Harold: "The New Role of the Government in Britain," *Western Political Quarterly*, Vol. 1 (1948), pp. 413–425.

The Commonwealth

Administration of the United Kingdom Dependencies, H. M. Stationery Office, London, 1957.

Attlee, C. R. A.: *Empire into Commonwealth,* London, 1961.

Bailey, Sidney D. (ed.): *Parliamentary Government in the Commonwealth,* New York, 1952.

Brady, A.: *Democracy in the Dominions,* 3d ed., Toronto, 1958.

Burns, A. C.: *In Defence of Colonies,* New York, 1957.

Burt, A. L.: *The Evolution of the British Empire and Commonwealth from the American Revolution,* Boston, 1956.

Carr-Gregg, John R. E.: *The Colombo Plan: A Commonwealth Program for Southeast Asia,* International Conciliation Pamphlet 467, New York, 1951.

Carter, Gwendolen M.: *The British Commonwealth and International Security: The Role of the Dominions,* Toronto, 1947.

Cowen, Z.: *The British Commonwealth of Nations in a Changing World: Law, Politics and Prospects,* Evanston, Ill., 1965.

Crocker, W. R.: *Self-government for the Colonies,* London, 1949.

De Smith, S.: *The New Commonwealth and Its Constitutions,* London, 1964.

Elton, Lord G. E.: *Imperial Commonwealth,* New York, 1946.

Hailey, W. M.: *Native Administration in British African Territories,* London, 1954.

Hodson, H. V.: *Twentieth Century Empire,* London, 1948.

Hussey, W. D.: *The British Empire and Commonwealth, 1500–1961,* Cambridge, England, 1963.

Jennings, Sir Ivor: *The British Commonwealth of Nations,* 4th rev. ed., London, 1961.

———: *Problems of the New Commonwealth,* London, 1958.

——— and C. M. Young: *Constitutional Laws of the Commonwealth,* 3d ed., Oxford, 1957.

Northedge, F. S.: *British Foreign Policy: The Process of Readjustment, 1945–1961,* Mystic, Conn., 1962.

Underhill, Frank H.: *The British Commonwealth: An Experiment in Cooperation among Nations,* Durham, N.C., 1956.

Wheare, K. C.: *The Constitutional Structure of the Commonwealth,* New York, 1960.

Wisemann, H. Victor: *Britain and the Commonwealth,* London, 1966.

Articles:

Hall, M. Duncan, et al.: "The British Commonwealth: A Symposium," *American Political Science Review,* Vol. 47 (1953), pp. 997–1040.

Millar, T. B.: "Commonwealth in Disarray," *International Relations,* Vol. 2, No. 7 (April, 1963), pp. 443–454.

Scott, T. R.: "The End of Dominion Status," *American Journal of International Law,* Vol. 38 (1944), pp. 34–39.

Wheare, K. C.: "Is the British Commonwealth Withering Away?" *American Political Science Review,* Vol. 44 (1950), pp. 545–555.

Wilson, R. R., and R. E. Clute: "Commonwealth Citizenship and Common Status," *American Journal of International Law,* Vol. 57, No. 3 (July, 1963), pp. 566–587.

FRANCE

History

Aron, Raymond: *France Steadfast and Changing: The Fourth to the Fifth Republic* (trans. by J. Irwin and L. Einaudi), Cambridge, Mass., 1960.
—————— (in collaboration with Georgette Elgey): *The Vichy Regime, 1940–1944*, New York, 1958.
Brogan, D. W.: *The Development of Modern France*, 2 vols., New York, 1965.
——————: *The French Nation: From Napoleon to Pétain, 1814–1940*, New York, 1958.
Duverger, Maurice: *The Government of France*, Chicago, 1958.
Earle, E. M.: *Modern France: Problems of the Third and Fourth Republics*, New York, 1964.
Martin, Kingsley: *French Liberal Thought in the 18th Century*, 3d ed., Oxford, 1962.
Meisel, James H.: *The Fall of the Republic: Military Revolt in France*, Ann Arbor, Mich., 1962.
Osgood, S. M.: *French Royalism under the 3rd and 4th Republics*, The Hague, 1960.
Pickles, D. M.: *France: The Fourth Republic*, London, 1955.
Roberts, J. M., and R. C. Cobb (eds.): *French Revolution Documents*, London, 1966.
Taine, H. A.: *The Origins of Contemporary France*, London, 1931.
Thomson, David: *Democracy in France since 1870*, 4th ed., Oxford University Press, 1964.
Viansson-Ponté, P.: *The King and His Court* (trans. by E. P. Halperin), Boston, 1964.
Werth, Alexander: *France, 1940–1955*, New York, 1956.
——————: *The Twilight of France*, New York, 1942.
Wright, Gordon: *France in Modern Times*, Chicago, 1960.
——————: *The Reshaping of French Democracy*, New York, 1948.
——————: *Rural Revolution in France: The Peasantry in the XXth Century*, Stanford, Calif., 1964.

Articles:

Anderson, M.: "The Myth of the Two Hundred Families," *Political Studies*, Oxford, Vol. 13, No. 2 (June, 1965), pp. 163–178.
Andrews, W. G.: "Swan Song of the Fourth Republic: The Committees of the Majority," *Parliamentary Affairs*, Vol. 15, No. 4 (Autumn, 1962), pp. 485–499.
Harrison, M.: "Government and Press in France during the Algerian War," *American Political Science Review*, Vol. 58, No. 2 (June, 1964), pp. 273–285.
King, J. B.: "Ministerial Cabinets of the Fourth Republic," *Western Political Quarterly*, Vol. 13, No. 2 (June, 1960), pp. 433–444.
Pinkney, D. H.: "A New Look at the French Revolution of 1830," *R. Polit.*, Vol. 23, No. 4 (October, 1961), pp. 490–506.

General works and discussion

Aron, Raymond: *An Explanation of De Gaulle*, New York, 1966.
——————: *France, the New Republic*, Introduction by D. W. Brogan, New York, 1960.

Barthélemy, Joseph: *The Government of France* (trans. by J. B. Morris), New York, 1924.

Duverger, Maurice: *The French Political System,* Chicago, 1958.

Furniss, E. S.: *De Gaulle and the French Army: A Crisis in Civil-Military Relations,* New York, 1964.

————: *France, Troubled Ally: De Gaulle, Heritage and Prospects,* New York, 1960.

Godfrey, E. D.: *The Government of France,* 2d ed., New York, 1963.

Goguel, François: *France under the Fourth Republic,* Ithaca, N.Y., 1952.

Hoffman, Stanley, et al.: *In Search of France: The Economy, Society and Political System,* Cambridge, Mass., 1963.

Luthy, Herbert: *France against Herself,* New York, 1955.

————: *The State of France: A Study of Contemporary France,* London, 1955.

Macridis, R. C.: *De Gaulle: Implacable Ally,* Introduction by Maurice Duverger, New York, 1966.

————: *The De Gaulle Republic, Quest for Unity,* Homewood, Ill., 1960.

Pickles, D. M.: *The Fifth French Republic,* New York, 1962.

Schoenbrun, David: *As France Goes,* New York, 1957.

————: *The Three Lives of Charles de Gaulle,* New York, 1966.

Siegfried, André: *France: A Study in Nationality,* New Haven, Conn., 1930.

Taylor, O. R.: *The Fourth Republic of France: Constitution and Political Parties,* New York, 1951.

Wahl, Nicholas: *The Fifth Republic,* New York, 1962.

————: *The Fifth Republic: France's New Political System,* New York, 1959.

Werth, Alexander: *The De Gaulle Revolution,* London, 1960.

White, Dorothy S.: *Seeds of Discord: De Gaulle, Free France and the Allies,* Syracuse, N.Y., 1964.

William, P. M.: *Politics in Postwar France,* London, 1961.

———— and M. Harrison: *De Gaulle's Republic,* London, 1961.

Articles:

Aron, R.: "The Political Methods of General de Gaulle," *International Affairs,* London, Vol. 37, No. 1 (January, 1961), pp. 19–28.

Ehrmann, H. W.: "Direct Democracy in France," *American Political Science Review,* Vol. 57, No. 4 (December, 1963), pp. 883–901.

Epstein, L.: "French Reformism," *Revue of Politics,* Vol. 25, No. 2 (April, 1963), pp. 225–240.

Goguel, F.: "L'Avenir des institutions françaises," *Bulletin SEDEIS,* (April 1, 1965), Futuribles, No. 89.

————: "Quelques aspects du problème politique français," *Revue française de science politique,* Vol. 13, No. 1 (March, 1963), pp. 5–24.

Gordey, M.: "The French People and De Gaulle," *Foreign Affairs,* Vol. 42, No. 4 (July, 1964), pp. 546–558.

Hoffman, S.: "De Gaulle's Republic," *Political Science Quarterly,* Vol. 75, No. 4 (December, 1960), pp. 554–559.

————: "Succession and Stability in France," *Journal of International Affairs,* Vol. 18 (1964), No. 1, pp. 86–103.

Johnson, D.: "The Political Principles of General de Gaulle," *International Affairs*, London, Vol. 41, No. 4 (October, 1965), pp. 650–662.

Macridis, R. C.: "De Gaulle: The Vision and the Record," *Yale Review*, Vol. 49, No. 2 (December, 1959), pp. 180–197.

Nordlinger, E. A.: "Democratic Stability and Instability: The French Case," *World Politics*, Vol. 18, No. 1 (October, 1965), pp. 127–157.

Ragoff, N.: "Social Stratification in France and in the United States," *American Journal of Sociology*, Vol. 58 (1953), pp. 347–357.

The Constitution

Chatelain, Jean: *La Nouvelle Constitution et le régime politique de la France*, Paris, 1959.

Colliard, Claude-Albert: *Précis de droit public: Les libertés publiques*, Paris, 1950.

The Constitution of the Fifth Republic (trans. by P. Campbell and B. Chapman, with commentary), Oxford, 1959.

Duverger, Maurice: *Manuel de droit constitutionnel et de science politique*, 5th ed., Paris, 1948.

Esmein, A.: *Eléments de droit constitutionnel, français et comparé*, 8th ed., Paris, 1927–1928.

Foundation for Foreign Affairs (Otto Kirchheimer): *A Constitution for the Fourth Republic*, Washington, 1947.

Freedeman, Charles E.: *The Conseil d'État in Modern France*, New York, 1961.

Pickles, W.: *The French Constitution of October 4th, 1958*, London, 1960.

Prélat, Marcel: *Pour comprendre la nouvelle constitution*, Paris, 1958.

————: *Précis de droit constitutionnel*, Paris, 1950.

Vedel, G.: *Manuel de droit constitutionnel*, Paris, 1949.

Articles:

Andrews, W. G.: "The By-election System of the Fifth French Republic," *Western Political Quarterly*, Vol. 17, No. 4 (December, 1964), pp. 690–702.

Blamont, E.: "La révision de la constitution," *Revue du droit public et de la science politique*, Vol. 69 (1953), pp. 415–422.

Campbell, P.: "The Cabinet and the Constitution in France, 1951–1956," *Parliamentary Affairs*, Vol. 9 (Summer, 1956), pp. 296–306.

Gooch, R. K.: "Reflections on the Constitution of the Fifth French Republic," *Journal of Politics*, Vol. 22, No. 2 (May, 1960), pp. 193–202.

Harrison, Martin: "The Constitution of the Fifth Republic: A Commentary," *Political Studies*, Vol. 8, No. 1 (February, 1959), pp. 296–306.

————: "The French Experience of Exceptional Powers: 1961," *Journal of Politics*, Vol. 25, No. 1 (February, 1963), pp. 139–158.

Hoffmann, Stanley H.: "The French Constitution of 1958: The Final Text and Its Prospects," *American Political Science Review*, Vol. 53 (1959), pp. 332–357.

Kirchheimer, Otto: "Decree Powers and Constitutional Law in France under the Third Republic," *American Political Review*, Vol. 34 (1940), pp. 1104–1123.

Meynaud, J.: "Constitution and Politics of the Fifth French Republic," *India Quarterly*, Vol. 15, No. 4 (October–December, 1959), pp. 327–347.

Pickles, W.: "The French Constitution of October 4, 1958," *Public Law,* London, Autumn, 1959, pp. 228–276.

————: "Special Powers in France: Article 16 in Practice," *Public Law,* London, Spring, 1963, pp. 23–50.

Pierce, Roy: "France Reopens the Constitutional Debate," *American Political Science Review,* Vol. 46 (1952), pp. 422–437.

Wahl, Nicholas: "The French Constitution of 1958: The Initial Draft and Its Origins," *American Political Science Review,* Vol. 53 (1959), pp. 358–382.

Parties and politics

Ambler, J. S.: *The French Army in Politics, 1945–1962,* Columbus, Ohio, 1965.

Blum, Léon: *For All Mankind,* New York, 1946.

Cantril, Hadley: *The Politics of Despair,* New York, 1958.

Capelle, Russell B.: *The MRP and French Foreign Policy,* New York, 1963.

Duverger, Maurice, et al. (eds.): *Les élections du 2 Janvier 1956,* Paris, 1957.

Ehrmann, Henry W.: *French Labor from Popular Front to Liberation,* New York, 1947.

————: *Organized Business in France,* Princeton, N.J., 1957.

Einaudi, M., et al.: *Communism in Western Europe,* Ithaca, N.Y., 1951.

Fauvet, Jacques: *Les Forces politiques en France,* Paris, 1951.

————: *Des Paysans et la politique dans la France contemporaine,* Paris, 1958.

Godfrey, E. Drexel, Jr.: *The Fate of the French Non-Communist Left,* Garden City, N.Y., 1955.

Goguel, François: *Géographie des élections françaises de 1870 à 1951,* Paris, 1951.

Goguel-Nyegaard, François, and Alfred Grosser: *La Politique en France,* Paris, 1964.

Hoffman, Stanley, et al.: *Le Mouvement Poujade,* Paris, 1956.

Laponce, J. A.: *The Government of the Fifth Republic: French Political Parties and the Constitution,* Berkeley, Calif., 1961.

Leites, N. C.: *On the Game of Politics in France,* Stanford, Calif., 1959.

Malraux, André, and J. Burnham: *The Case for De Gaulle,* New York, 1948.

Meynaud, Jean: *Les Groupes de pression en France,* Paris, 1958.

————: *Nouvelles études sur les groupes de pression en France,* Paris, 1962.

———— and Alain Lancelot: *La Participation des Français à la politique,* Paris, 1961.

Micaud, Charles A.: *Communism and the French Left,* New York, 1962.

Michelet, E.: *Le Gaullisme: Passionante aventure,* Paris, 1962.

Monnerot, Jules: *Sociology and Psychology of Communism* (trans. by Janes Degras and Richard Rees), Boston, 1953.

Pickles, Dorothy: *French Politics: The First Years of the Fourth Republic,* New York, 1953.

Pierce, R.: *Contemporary French Political Thought,* Oxford, 1966.

Tarr, Francis de: *The French Radical Party, from Herriot to Mendès-France,* London, 1961.

Thomson, David: *Two Frenchmen, Pierre Laval and Charles de Gaulle,* London, 1951.

Werth, Alexander: *Lost Statesman: The Strange Story of Pierre Mendès-France,* New York, 1958.

Articles:

Abel, Deryck: "The French Radical Party," *Contemporary Review,* June, 1961.

Almond, Gabriel A.: "The Christian Parties of Western Europe," *World Politics,* Vol. 1 (1948), pp. 30–58.

Alroy, G. C.: "The Secret Disappearance of French Radicalism," *International Review of the History of Political Science,* Vol. 2, No. 11 (June, 1965), pp. 41–52.

Aron, Raymond: "France, Still the Third Republic," *Foreign Affairs,* Vol. 30 (1951), pp. 145–151.

Bal, M.: "Les Indépendants," *Revue française de science politique,* Vol. 15, No. 3 (June, 1965), pp. 529–555.

Behr, E.: "The French Army as a Political and Social Factor," *International Affairs,* London, Vol. 35, No. 4 (October, 1959), pp. 438–446.

Belleville, P.: "Les Syndicats sous la Vème république," *Esprit,* Vol. 30, No. 3 (March, 1962), pp. 381–395.

Bouscaren, Anthony T.: "The European Christian Democrats," *Western Political Quarterly,* Vol. 2 (1949), pp. 59–73.

Brown, B. E.: "Pressure Politics in the Fifth Republic," *Journal of Politics,* Vol. 25, No. 3 (August, 1963), pp. 509–525.

Campbell, P.: "The Historical Element in Contemporary French Politics," *Political Science,* Vol. 6 (1954), pp. 52–67.

Colton, J.: "The French Socialist Party: A Case Study of the Non-Communist Left," *Yale Review,* Vol. 43 (1954), pp. 402–413.

Converse, P. E., and G. Dupeux: "Politization of the Electorate in France and the U.S.," *Public Opinion Quarterly,* Vol. 26, No. 1 (Spring, 1962), pp. 1–23.

Cook, G. C.: "Charles de Gaulle and the R.P.F.," *Political Science Quarterly,* Vol. 65 (1950), pp. 333–352.

Davis, M., and S. Verba: "Party Affiliation and International Opinions in Britain and France: 1947–1956," *Public Opinion Quarterly,* Vol. 24, No. 4 (Winter, 1960), pp. 590–604.

Duverger, Maurice: "Public Opinion and Political Parties in France," *American Political Science Review,* Vol. 46 (1952), pp. 1069–1078.

Ehrmann, Henry W.: "France Between East and West," *Western Political Quarterly,* Vol. 2 (1949), pp. 74–88.

———: "French Labour Goes West," *Foreign Affairs,* Vol. 26 (1947), pp. 465–476.

———: "French Views on Communism," *World Politics,* Vol. 3 (1950), pp. 141–151.

Einaudi, Mario: "The Crisis of Politics and Government in France," *World Politics,* Vol. 4 (1951), pp. 64–84.

———: "Western European Communism: A Profile," *American Political Science Review,* Vol. 45 (1951), pp. 185–208.

Godfrey, E. D.: "The Communist Presence in France," *American Political Science Review,* Vol. 50 (1956), pp. 321–338.

Graham, B. D.: "Theories of the French Party System under the Third Republic," *Political Studies,* Oxford, Vol. 12, No. 1 (February, 1964), pp. 21–32.

Hayward, J. E. S.: "Presidentialism and French Politics," *Parliamentary Affairs,* Vol. 18, No. 1 (Winter, 1964–1965), pp. 23–29.

Howell, R. F.: "The Philosopher Alain and French Classical Radicalism," *Western Political Quarterly,* Vol. 18, No. 3 (September, 1965), pp. 594–614.

Katzenbach, Edward L.: "Political Parties and the French Army since Liberation," *World Politics,* Vol. 3 (1950), pp. 533–548.

Kayser, J.: "The Radical Socialist Party as a Party of Government in the Third French Republic," *Parliamentary Affairs,* Vol. 13, No. 3 (Summer, 1960), pp. 318–328.

Kelly, G. A.: "The French Army Re-enters Politics, 1940–1955," *Political Science Quarterly,* Vol. 76, No. 3 (September, 1961), pp. 367–392.

Laponce, J. A.: "Mendès-France and the Radical Party," *Western Political Quarterly,* Vol. 11 (1958), pp. 340–356.

LeBras, Gabriel: "Géographie électorale et géographie religieuse," *Études de sociologie électorale,* Cahiers de la Fondation Nationale des Sciences Politiques, Paris, (1947), No. 1.

Macrae, D., Jr.: "Intraparty Divisions and Cabinet Coalitions in the Fourth French Republic," *Comparative Studies of Social History,* Vol. 5, No. 2 (January, 1963), pp. 164–211.

Macridis, C. R.: "The New French Politics," *Yale Review,* Vol. 52, No. 3 (March, 1963), pp. 352–365.

Meynard, J.: "Les Groupes de pression sous la Vème république," *Revue française de science politique,* Vol. 12, No. 3 (September, 1962), pp. 672–697.

Micaud, C. A.: "The Bases of Communist Strength in France," *Western Political Quarterly,* Vol. 8 (1955), pp. 354–366.

Neumann, Robert G.: "Formation and Transformation of Gaullism in France," *Western Political Quarterly,* Vol. 8 (1955), pp. 354–366.

———: "The Struggle for Electoral Reform in France," *American Political Science Review,* Vol. 45 (1951), pp. 741–755.

Noonan, L. G.: "Some Political Aspects of the French Fifth Republic," *Western Political Quarterly,* Vol. 13, No. 2 (June, 1960), pp. 464–478.

Pierce, Roy: "The French Election of January, 1956," *Journal of Politics,* Vol. 19 (1957), pp. 371–422.

Remond, R.: "Les Partis catholiques," *La vie intellectuelle,* Vol. 24 (1953), pp. 173–189.

Schlesinger, Joseph A.: "The French Radical Socialist Party and the Republican Front of 1956," *Western Political Quarterly,* Vol. 11 (1958), pp. 71–85.

Seigel, J. S.: "On the Sources of Political Divisions in France," *Social Research,* Vol. 22 (1955), pp. 325–346.

Siegfried, A.: "Stable Instability in France," *Foreign Affairs,* Vol. 34 (1956), pp. 394–404.

Velen, V. A.: "The New Left in France," *Foreign Affairs,* Vol. 40, No. 1 (October, 1961), pp. 71–85.

William, P.: "Compromise and Crisis in French Politics," *Political Science Quarterly,* Vol. 72 (1957), pp. 321–339.

Wright, Gordon: "French Farmers in Politics," *South Atlantic Quarterly,* Vol. 51 (1952), pp. 356–365.

Parliament

Goguel-Nyegaard, F.: *Le Référendum du 8 Janvier 1961,* Paris, 1962.

———: *Le Référendum du 8 Avril, 1962,* Paris, 1963.

Gooch, R. K.: *Parliamentary Government in France: Revolutionary Origins,* Ithaca, N.Y., 1960.
Lidderdale, D. W. S.: *The Parliament of France,* London, 1954.

Articles:

Bourne, H. E.: "American Constitutional Precedents in the French National Assembly," *American Historical Review,* Vol. 8 (1903), pp. 466–486.
Bromhead, P. A.: "Some Notes on the Standing Committees in the French National Assembly," *Political Studies,* Vol. 5 (1957), pp. 140–157.
Campbell, P.: "The French Parliament," *Public Administration,* Vol. 31 (1953), pp. 349–363.
Cobban, Alfred: "The Second Chamber in France," *Political Quarterly,* Vol. 19 (1948), pp. 223–235.
Debré, M.: "Trois caractéristiques du système parlementaire français," *Revue française de science politique,* Vol. 5 (1955), pp. 21–48.
Demichel, A.: "De l'incompatibilité entre les fonctions de ministre et le mandat parlementaire," *Revue de droit publique et science politique,* Vol. 76, No. 3 (May–June, 1960), pp. 616–647.
Goldey, D. B.: "The French Presidential Election of 5 and 19 December, 1965: Organization and Results," *Political Studies,* Oxford, Vol. 14, No. 2 (June, 1966), pp. 208–215.
———: "The French Referendum and Election of 1962: The National Campaigns," *Political Studies,* Oxford, Vol. 11, No. 3 (October, 1963), pp. 287–307.
Plaisant, Marcel: "Le Contrôle de la politique extérieure par le Conseil de la République," *Revue politique et parlementaire,* Vol. 52 (1950), pp. 113–122.
Stamps, Norman L.: "A Comparative Study of Legislative Investigations: England, France and Weimar Germany," *Journal of Politics,* Vol. 14 (1952), pp. 592–615.
Williams, P. M.: "The French Referendum, 1961," *Parliamentary Affairs,* Vol. 14, No. 3 (Summer, 1961), pp. 335–352.
———: "The French Referendum of April, 1962," *Parliamentary Affairs,* Vol. 15, No. 3 (Summer, 1962), pp. 294–306.
———: "The French Referendum and Election of October–November, 1962," *Parliamentary Affairs,* Vol. 16, No. 2 (Spring, 1963), pp. 165–173.
Wood, D. M.: "Issue Dimensions in a Multiparty System: The French National Assembly and European Unification," *Midwestern Journal of Political Science,* Vol. 8, No. 3 (August, 1964), pp. 255–276.

Local government

Chapman, Brian: *Introduction to French Local Government,* London, 1953.
———: *The Prefects and Provincial France,* London, 1955.

Articles:

Abbot, R. S., and R. Sicard: "A Postwar Development in French Regional Government: The 'Super Préfet'," *American Political Science Review,* Vol. 44 (1950), pp. 426–431.

Caumont, R. de: "Actualité et rajeunissement de l'administration départementale, I & II," *Revue administrative,* Vol. 10 (1957), pp. 221–231, 338–347.

Chapman, Brian: "A Development in French Regional Administration," *Public Administration,* Vol. 28 (1950), pp. 327–332.

Diamant, A.: "The Department, the Prefect and Dual Supervision in French Administration: A Comparative Study," *Journal of Politics,* Vol. 16 (1954), pp. 472–490.

Hermens, F. A.: "Local Autonomy in France and Italy," in *Constitutions and Constitutional Trends Since World War II,* ed. by A. J. Zurcher, New York, 1951, pp. 95–115.

Sharp, Walter R.: "France," in *Local Government in Europe,* ed. by William Anderson, New York, 1939, pp. 107–222.

Sweetman, L. T.: "Prefects and Planning: France's New Regionalism," *Public Administration,* London, Vol. 43, No. 1 (Spring, 1965), pp. 15–30.

The national administration

Bauchet, P.: *Economic Planning: The French Experience* (trans. by D. Woodward), New York, 1964.

Baum, Warren: *The French Economy and the State,* Princeton, N.J., 1958.

Blum, Léon: *La réforme gouvernementale,* Paris, 1936.

Colliard, Claude-Albert: *Le travail gouvernemental et ses méthodes,* Paris, 1948.

Crozier, M.: *The Bureaucratic Phenomenon: An Examination of Bureaucracy in Modern Organizations and Its Cultural Setting in France,* Chicago, 1964.

Einaudi, Mario: *Nationalization in France and Italy,* Ithaca, N.Y., 1955.

Fauvet, Jacques: *The Cockpit of France* (trans. by Nancy Pearson), London, 1960.

Grégoire, R.: *La fonction publique,* Paris, 1954.

Hamson, C. J.: *Executive Discretion and Judicial Control: An Aspect of the French Conseil d'État,* London, 1960.

Ridley, F., and J. Blondel, *Public Administration in France,* London, 1965.

Robson, W. A.: *The Civil Service in Britain and France,* New York, 1956.

Sharp, Walter R.: *The French Civil Service: Bureaucracy in Transition,* New York, 1931.

Articles:

Biswas, A. N.: "The Control of Public Expenditure in France," *Independent Journal of Public Administration,* Vol. 7, No. 4 (October–December, 1961), pp. 495–508.

Campbell, P.: "The Cabinet and the Constitution of France," *Parliamentary Affairs,* Vol. 5 (1951), pp. 341–361.

Cassin, René: "Recent Reforms in the Government and Administration of France," *Public Administration,* Vol. 28 (1950), pp. 179–187.

Chapman, Brian: "The Organization of the French Police," *Public Administration,* Vol. 29 (1951), pp. 67–75.

———: "Recent French Administrative Reforms," *Public Administration,* Vol. 32 (Summer, 1954), pp. 211–216.

Chatenet, P.: "The Civil Service in France," *Political Quarterly,* Vol. 25 (October–December, 1954), pp. 390–397.

Domenach, J. M.: "The French Army in Politics," *Foreign Affairs,* Vol. 39, No. 2 (January, 1961), pp. 185–195.

Ehrmann, H. W.: "French Bureaucracy and Organized Interests," *Administrative Science Quarterly,* Vol. 5, No. 4 (March, 1961), pp. 534–555.

Jumper, R.: "Recruitment Problems of the French Higher Civil Service: An American Appraisal," *Western Political Quarterly,* Vol. 10 (March, 1957), pp. 38–48.

Kingdom, T. D.: "The Public Service in France," *Public Administration,* Vol. 32 (Winter, 1954), pp. 450–453.

Langrod, G.: "Initial Administrative Tendencies of the Fifth French Republic," *Revue internationale de science administrative,* Vol. 25, No. 3 (1959), pp. 332–345.

Lewis, E. G.: "Parliamentary Control of Nationalized Industry in France," *American Political Science Review,* Vol. 51 (1957), No. 3, pp. 669–683.

Macridis, Roy C.: "Cabinet Instability in the Fourth Republic (1946–1951)," *Journal of Politics,* Vol. 14 (1952), pp. 643–658.

————: "The Cabinet Secretariat in France," *Journal of Politics,* Vol. 13 (1951), pp. 589–603.

Myers, Margaret G.: "Nationalization of the Industries and Credit in France after Liberation," *Political Science Quarterly,* Vol. 41 (1947), pp. 368–380.

Ridley, F.: "The French Educational System: Policy and Administrative Aspects," *Political Studies,* Oxford, Vol. 11, No. 2 (June, 1963), pp. 178–202.

————: "French Technocracy and Comparative Government," *Political Studies,* Vol. 14, No. 1 (1966), pp. 34–52.

Robson, William A.: "Nationalized Industries in Britain and France," *American Political Science Review,* Vol. 44 (1950), pp. 299–322.

Trouvé, Jean: "The French Civil Service Office," *Public Administration Review,* Vol. 40 (1951), pp. 180–186.

Law and justice

Brissaud, Jean: *A History of French Private Law* (trans. by R. Howell), Boston, 1912.

————: *A History of French Public Law* (trans. by J. W. Garner), Boston, 1915.

Ensor, Robert C. K.: *Courts and Judges in France, Germany and England,* Oxford, 1933.

Freedeman, Charles E.: *The Conseil d'État in Modern France,* New York, 1961.

Hamson, Charles J.: *Executive Discretion and Judicial Control: An Aspect of the French Conseil d'État,* London, 1954.

Rohkam, W., and O. C. Pratt: *Studies in French Administrative Law,* Urbana, Ill., 1947.

Articles:

Brown, L. N.: "The Reform of the French Administrative Courts," *Modern Law Review,* Vol. 22, No. 2 (July, 1959), pp. 357–380.

Deak, F., and M. Rheinstein: "The Development of French and German Law," *Georgetown Law Journal,* Vol. 24 (1936), pp. 551–583.

Diamant, Alfred: "The French Council of State: Comparative Observations on the Problem of Controlling the Bureaucracy of the Modern State," *Journal of Politics,* Vol. 13 (1951), pp. 562–588.

Garner, James W.: "French Administrative Law," *Yale Law Journal,* Vol. 33 (1924), pp. 597–627.

Hamson, C. J.: "Le Conseil d'État statuant aux contentieux," *Law Quarterly Review,* Vol. 68 (1952), pp. 60–87. (In English.)

Joelson, M. R.: "Legal Problems in the Dismissal of Civil Servants in the United States, Britain and France," *American Journal of Comparative Law,* Vol. 12, No. 2 (Spring, 1963), pp. 149–171.

King, J. B.: "Constitutionalism and the Judiciary in France," *Political Science Quarterly,* Vol. 80, No. 1 (March, 1965), pp. 62–87.

Langrod, Georges: "The French Council of State: Its Role in the Formulation and Implementation of Administrative Law," *American Political Science Review,* Vol. 49 (1955), pp. 673–692.

Lobinger, C. S.: "Administrative Law and Droit Administratif," *University of Pennsylvania Law Review,* Vol. 91 (1942), pp. 36–58.

Marx, F. M.: "Comparative Administrative Law," *University of Pennsylvania Law Review,* Vol. 91 (1942), pp. 118–136.

Riesenfeld, Stephan: "The French System of Administrative Justice: A Model for American Law?", *Boston University Law Review,* Vol. 18 (1938), pp. 48–82.

Wright, A. C.: "French Criminal Procedure," *Law Quarterly Review,* Vol. 44 (1928), pp. 324–341; and Vol. 45 (1929), pp. 92–107.

GERMANY

General history

Baraclough, G.: *The Origins of Modern Germany,* 3d ed., Oxford, 1957.

Craig, Gordon, A.: *From Bismarck to Adenauer,* Baltimore, 1958.

Dill, Marshall, Jr.: *Germany: A Modern History,* Ann Arbor, Mich., 1961.

Grosser, A.: *The Federal Republic of Germany: A Concise History* (trans. by N. Aldrich), New York, 1964.

Hartmann, F. H.: *Germany between East and West,* New York, 1965.

Hawgood, John A.: *The Evolution of Germany,* London, 1955.

Holborn, Hajo: *A History of Modern Germany,* London, 1959.

Lowenstein, Prince Hubertus zu: *A Basic History of Germany,* Bonn, 1964.

Mann, Hermann: *German History, 1933–45: An Assessment by German Historians* (trans. by A. Wilson and E. Wilson), New York, 1963.

Merkl, P. H.: *Germany: Yesterday and Tomorrow,* New York, 1965.

Pflanze, Otto: *Bismarck and the Development of Germany,* Princeton, N.J., 1963.

Pollock, J. K., et al.: *Germany in Power and Eclipse: The Background of German Development,* New York, 1952.

Rich, N.: *Friedrich Von Holstein: Politics and Diplomacy in the Era of Bismarck and Wilhelm II,* 2 vols., Cambridge, England, 1964.

Taylor, A. J. P.: *The Course of German History,* new ed., London, 1954.

Valentin, Veit: *The German People,* New York, 1946.

Articles:

Becker, Howard: "Changes in the Social Stratification of Contemporary Germany," *American Sociological Review,* Vol. 15 (1950), pp. 333–342.

Mann, G.: "Bismarck and Our Time," *International Affairs,* London, Vol. 38, No. 1 (January, 1962), pp. 3–14.

The Weimar Republic

Blachly, F. F. and M. E. Oatman: *The Government and Administration of Germany,* Baltimore, 1928.

Brecht, Arnold: *Federalism and Regionalism in Germany,* New York, 1945.

Brunet, Rene: *The New German Constitution* (trans. by J. Gollomb), New York, 1922.

Clark, Robert: *The Fall of the German Republic,* New York, 1964.

Dorpalen, A.: *Hindenburg and the Weimar Republic,* Princeton, N.J., 1964.

Edwards, M. L.: *Stresemann and the Greater Germany,* New York, 1963.

Eyck, E.: *A History of the Weimar Republic* (trans. by H. P. Hanson and R. G. L. Waite), Cambridge, Mass., 1962.

Gordon, Harold J.: *The Reichswehr and the German Republic, 1919–1926,* Princeton, N.J., 1957.

Halperin, S. W.: *Germany Tried Democracy,* Hamden, Conn., 1963.

Heneman, Harlow H.: *The Growth of Executive Power in Germany,* Minneapolis, 1934.

Hermens, F. A.: *Democracy or Anarchy,* Notre Dame, Ind., 1941.

Hertzmann, Lewis: *DNVP: Right-wing Opposition in the Weimar Republic 1918–1924,* Lincoln, Nebr., 1964.

Knight-Patterson, W. M. (pseud. W. W. Kolski): *Germany from Defeat to Conquest, 1919–1933,* London, 1945.

Rosenberg, Arthur: *A History of the German Republic,* London, 1936.

Scheele, Godfrey: *The Weimar Republic: Overture to the Third Reich,* London, 1946.

Sturmthal, A. F.: *The Tragedy of European Labor 1918–1939,* New York, 1951.

Waldman, Eric: *The Spartacist Uprising of 1919 and the Crisis of the German Socialist Movement,* Milwaukee, 1958.

Articles:

Helbich, W. J.: "Between Stresemann and Hitler: The Foreign Policy of the Brüning Government," *World Politics,* Vol. 12, No. 1 (October, 1959), pp. 24–44.

Kollmann, E. C.: "Reinterpreting Modern German History: The Weimar Republic," *Journal of Central European Affairs,* Vol. XXI (January, 1962).

The Nazi period

Bowen, Ralph: *German Theories of the Corporative State with Special Reference to the Period 1870–1919,* New York, 1947.

Buchheim, H.: *The Third Reich: Its Beginnings, Its Development, Its End,* London, 1961.

Bullock, Alan L. C.: *Hitler: A Study in Tyranny,* rev. ed., New York, 1958.

Butler, R. d'O.: *The Roots of National Socialism,* New York, 1942.

Dulles, Allen W.: *Germany's Underground,* New York, 1947.

Epstein, Klaus: *The German Opposition to Hitler,* Chicago, 1962.

Fraenkel, Ernst: *The Dual State: A Contribution to the Theory of Dictatorship,* New York, 1941.

Frank, Anne: *The Diary of a Young Girl* (trans. by M. Mooyaat), New York, 1952.

Gallin, Mary Alice: *German Resistance to Hitler: Ethical and Religious Factors,* Washington, D.C., 1962.

Gisevius, E. B.: *To the Bitter End,* Boston, 1947.

Heiden, Konrad: *Der Fuehrer,* London, 1944.

————: *A History of National Socialism,* New York, 1935.

Kogon, Eugen: *The Theory and Practice of Hell: The German Concentration Camps and the System behind Them* (trans. by H. Norden), New York, 1950.

Lowenstein, Prince Hubertus zu: *What Was the German Resistance Movement?,* Bad Godesberg, 1965.

Mosse, George L.: *The Crisis of German Ideology: Intellectual Origins of the Third Reich,* New York, 1964.

Neumann, Franz: *Behemoth: The Structure and Practice of National Socialism,* New York, 1942.

Pollock, James K.: *The Government of Greater Germany,* New York, 1940.

Rauschning, Hermann: *The Voice of Destruction,* New York, 1940.

Roberts, Stephen H.: *The House That Hitler Built,* New York, 1938.

Rothfels, Hans: *The German Opposition to Hitler,* rev. ed., Chicago, 1962.

Royce, H.: *Germans against Hitler, July 20, 1944,* 4th ed., Bonn, 1964.

Shirer, W. L.: *The Rise and Fall of the Third Reich: A History of Nazi Germany,* New York, 1960.

Trevor-Roper, H. R.: *The Last Days of Hitler,* 3d ed., New York, 1962.

Articles:

Epstein, K.: "A New Study of Fascism," *World Politics,* Vol. 16, No. 2 (January, 1964), pp. 302–321.

Herz, John: "German Administration under the Nazi Regime," *American Political Science Review,* Vol. 40 (1946), pp. 682–702.

Nyomarkay, J. L.: "Factionalism in the National Socialist German Workers Party, 1925–26: The Myth and Reality of the 'Northern Faction'," *Political Science Quarterly,* Vol. 80, No. 1 (March, 1965), pp. 22–47.

Samuel, R. H.: "The Origin and Development of the Ideology of National Socialism," *Australian Journal of Political History,* Vol. 9, No. 1 (May, 1963), pp. 59–77.

Szaz, Z. M.: "The Ideological Precursors of National Socialism," *Western Political Quarterly,* Vol. 16, No. 4 (December, 1963), pp. 924–945.

The reconstruction of Germany

Abosch, H.: *The Menace of the Miracle: Germany from Hitler to Adenauer* (trans. by D. Garman), London, 1962.

Adenauer, K.: *Memoirs, 1945–1953,* Chicago, 1966.

Almond, G. A.: *The Struggle for Democracy in Germany*, New York, 1965.

Balfour, Michael, and John Mair: *Four Power Control in Germany and Austria, 1945–1946*, Oxford, 1956.

Clay, Lucius: *Decision in Germany*, New York, 1950.

Ebsworth, Raymond: *Restoring Democracy in Germany: The British Contribution*, New York, 1962.

Freund, G.: *Germany between Two Worlds*, New York, 1961.

Friedman, W.: *The Allied Military Government of Germany*, London, 1947.

Friedrich, C. J., and Associates: *American Experiences in Military Government in World War II*, New York, 1948.

Golay, John F.: *The Founding of the Federal Republic of Germany*, Chicago, 1958.

Gottlieb, M.: *The German Peace Settlement and the Berlin Crisis*, New York, 1960.

Grosser, Alfred: *Colossus Again: Western Germany from Defeat to Rearmament*, New York, 1955.

————: *The Federal Republic of Germany: A Concise History* (trans. by N. Aldrich), New York, 1964.

Hiscocks, Richard: *Democracy in Western Germany*, London, 1957.

Holborn, Hajo: *American Military Government Organization and Politics*, New York, 1947.

Kehr, Helen: *After Hitler Germany, 1945–1963*, London, 1963.

Litchfield, E., and Associates: *Governing Postwar Germany*, Ithaca, N.Y., 1953.

McInnis, E.: *The Shaping of Postwar Germany*, London, 1960.

Meinecke, F.: *The German Catastrophe: Reflections and Recollections* (trans. by S. B. Fay), Boston, 1963.

Merkl, Peter: *The Origin of the West German Republic*, New York, 1963.

Middleton, Drew: *The Struggle for Germany*, Indianapolis, 1949.

Utley, Freda: *The High Cost of Vengeance*, Chicago, 1949.

Wallich, H. C.: *Mainsprings of the German Revival*, New Haven, Conn., 1955.

Warburg, James P.: *Germany: Bridge or Battleground*, New York, 1947.

Zink, Harold: *American Military Government in Germany*, New York, 1947.

————: *The United States in Germany, 1944–1955*, New York, 1957.

Articles:

Brecht, Arnold: "Re-establishing German Government," *Annals of the American Academy of Political and Social Science*, January, 1950, pp. 28–42.

Gimbel, J.: "American Denazification and German Local Politics, 1945–1949: A Case Study in Marburg," *American Political Science Review*, Vol. 54, No. 1 (March, 1960), pp. 83–105.

Griffith, William E.: "Denazification in the U.S. Zone of Germany," *Annals of the American Academy of Political and Social Science*, January, 1950, pp. 68–76.

Guradze, Heinz: "The Landerrat, Landmark of German Reconstruction," *Western Political Quarterly*, Vol. 3 (1950), pp. 190–213.

Herz, John: "The Fiasco of Denazification in Germany," *Political Science Quarterly*, Vol. 63 (1948), pp. 569–594.

Johnson, N.: "The Era of Adenauer and After," *Parliamentary Affairs*, Vol. 17, No. 1 (Winter, 1963–1964), pp. 31–49.

Kohn, H.: "Out of Catastrophe: Germany 1945–1960," *Revue of Politics,* Vol. 22, No. 2 (April, 1960), pp. 163–174.

Nettl, J. P.: "A Decade of Post-war Germany," *Political Quarterly,* Vol. 63 (1948), pp. 569–594.

Pollock, James K.: "Germany under Military Occupation," *Change and Crisis in European Government,* New York, 1947, pp. 15–61.

"Postwar Reconstruction in Western Germany," *Annals of the American Academy of Political and Social Science,* November, 1948, entire issue.

Political parties and politics

Bölling, Klaus: *Politics, Parties and Personalities in Postwar Germany,* New York, 1964.
———: *Republic in Suspense,* New York, 1964.

Braunthal, G.: *The Federation of German Industry in Politics,* Ithaca, N.Y., 1965.

Brentano, Heinrich von: *Reflections on German Foreign Policy,* New York, 1964.

Chalmers, Douglas: *The Social Democratic Party of Germany: From Working Class Movement to Modern Political Party,* New Haven, Conn., 1964.

Edinger, Lewis, J.: *Kurt Schumacher: A Study in Personality and Political Behavior,* Stanford, Calif., 1965.

Heidenheimer, Arnold J.: *Adenauer and the CDU: The Rise of the Leader and the Integration of the Party,* The Hague, 1960.

Kitzinger, U. W.: *German Electoral Politics: A Study of the 1957 Campaign,* Oxford, 1960.

Kohn, Hans: *Nationalism, Its Meaning and History,* Princeton, N.J., 1955.

Landauer, Karl: *European Socialism: A History of Ideas and Movements from the Industrial Revolution to Hitler's Seizure of Power,* 2 vols., Berkeley, Calif., 1959.

Lukomski, Jess M.: *Erhard and Germany,* New York, 1965.

Merkl, Peter H.: *Germany: Yesterday and Tomorrow,* New York, 1965.

Pinney, Edward: *Federalism, Bureaucracy, and Party Politics in West Germany,* Chapel Hill, N.C., 1963.

Speier, Hans, and W. P. Davison: *West German Leadership and Foreign Policy,* New York, 1957.

Stahl, Walter (ed.): *The Politics of Postwar Germany,* New York, 1963.

Articles:

Ascher, A.: "Radical Imperialists within German Social Democracy, 1912–1918," *Political Science Quarterly,* Vol. 76, No. 4 (December, 1961), pp. 555–575.

Barnes, S. H., et al.: "The German Party System and the 1961 Federal Election," *American Political Science Review,* Vol. 56 (1962), No. 4, pp. 899–914.

Braunthal, G.: "The Free Democratic Party in West German Politics," *Western Political Quarterly,* Vol. 13, No. 2 (June, 1960), pp. 332–348.

Duebber, U., and G. Braunthal: "Comparative Studies in Political Finance," *Journal of Politics,* Vol. 25, No. 4 (November, 1963), pp. 774–789.

Edinger, L. J.: "Continuity and Change in the Background of German Decision Makers," *Western Political Quarterly,* Vol. 14, No. 1 (March, 1961), pp. 17–36.

————: "Electoral Politics and Voting Behaviour in Western Germany," *World Politics,* Vol. 13, No. 3 (April, 1961)´, pp. 471–484.

————: "Post-totalitarian Leadership: Elites in the German Federal Republic," *American Political Science Review,* Vol. 54, No. 1 (March, 1960), pp. 58–82.

Epstein, K.: "Three American Studies of German Socialism," *World Politics,* Vol. 11, No. 4 (July, 1959), pp. 629–651.

Erler, F.: "The Alliance and the Future of Germany," *Foreign Affairs,* Vol. 43, No. 3 (April, 1965), pp. 436–446.

Freund, G.: "Adenauer and the Future of Germany," *International Journal,* Vol. 18, No. 4 (Autumn, 1963), pp. 458–467.

Freund, L.: "The De-Marxification of the Social-Democratic Party of Germany," *Modern Age,* Vol. 5, No. 3 (Summer, 1961), pp. 290–298.

Frye, C. E.: "Parties and Pressure Groups in Weimar and Bonn," *World Politics,* Vol. 17, No. 4 (July, 1965), pp. 635–655.

Hartenstein, W., and K. Liepelt: "Party Members and Party Voters in Western Germany," *Acta Sociologica,* Vol. 6 (1962), Nos. 1, 2, pp. 43–52.

Heberle, R.: "Parliamentary Government and Political Parties in West Germany," *Canadian Journal of Economic and Political Science,* Vol. 28 (1962), No. 3, pp. 43–52.

Heidenheimer, A. J.: "Federalism and the Party System: The Case of West Germany," *American Political Science Review,* Vol. 52 (1958), pp. 809–828.

————: "Foreign Policy and Party Discipline in the C.D.U.," *Parliamentary Affairs,* Vol. 13 (Winter, 1959–1960), pp. 70–87.

————: "German Party Finance: The C.D.U.," *American Political Science Review,* Vol. 51 (1957), pp. 369–385.

————: "Succession and Party Politics in West Germany," *Journal International Affairs,* Vol. 18 (1964), No. 1, pp. 32–42.

Heimar, B.: "Inner Struggle in the German Social Democracy," *International Politics,* Vol. 4 (1959), pp. 82–87.

Johnson, N.: "The Era of Adenauer and After," *Parliamentary Affairs,* Vol. 17 (1963–1964), No. 1, pp. 31–49.

————: "State Finance for Political Parties in Germany," *Parliamentary Affairs,* Vol. 18, No. 3 (Summer, 1965), pp. 279–292.

Kerr, Clark: "The Trade Union Movement and the Redistribution of Power in Post-war Germany," *Quarterly Journal of Economics,* Vol. 68 (1954), pp. 535–564.

Kitzinger, U. W.: "The West German Electoral Law," *Parliamentary Affairs,* Vol. 11 (1958), pp. 220–237.

Knappstein, K. H.: "The Projected European Union and the Question of German Unity," *American Academy of Political Science,* No. 348 (July, 1963), pp. 73–81.

Menzel, W.: "Parliamentary Politics in the German Federal Republic from 1957–1960," *Parliamentary Affairs,* Vol. 13, No. 4 (Autumn, 1960), pp. 509–519.

Neal, F. W.: "The Unsolved German Settlement," *American Academy of Political Science,* No. 351 (January, 1964), pp. 148–156.

Neumann, Robert G.: "The New Political Parties of Germany," *American Political Science Review,* Vol. 40 (1946), pp. 749–759.

Neumann, Sigmund: "Germany: Changing Patterns and Lasting Problems," in *Modern Political Parties* (ed. by S. Neumann), Chicago, 1956, pp. 354–392.

Oppen, B. R. von: "The End of the Adenauer Era," *World Today,* Vol. 19 (1963), No. 8, pp. 343–352.

Pulzer, P. G. J.: "Western Germany and the Three Party System," *Political Quarterly,* Vol. 33 (1962), No. 4, pp. 414–426.

Rueckert, G. L., and W. Crane: "C.D.U. Deviancy in the German Bundestag," *Journal of Politics,* Vol. 24 (1962), No. 3, pp. 477– 488.

Tauber, K. P.: "German Nationalists and European Union," *Political Science Quarterly,* Vol. 74, No. 4 (December, 1959), pp. 564–589.

————: "Nationalism and Social Restoration: Fraternities in Postwar Germany," *Political Science Quarterly,* Vol. 78, No. 1 (March, 1963), pp. 66–85.

Vardys, V. S.: "Germany's Postwar Socialism: Nationalism and K. Schumacher (1945–1952)," *Revue of Politics,* Vol. 27, No. 2 (April, 1965), pp. 220–244.

Williams, J. E.: "Federal Elections in West Germany," *World Today,* Vol. 17, No. 12 (December, 1961), pp. 512–518.

Constitutions and constitutional law

Friedrich, C. J.: "The Constitution of the German Federal Republic," in *Governing Postwar Germany,* ed. by E. Litchfield and Associates, Ithaca, N.Y., 1953, pp. 117–151.

Lewis, Harold O.: *New Constitutions in Occupied Germany,* Washington, 1948.

Pfitzer, Albert: *The Bundesrat* (trans. by Professor H. Arntz), Bonn, 1962.

Simons, Hans: *The Bonn Constitution and Its Government,* in *Germany and the Future of Europe,* ed. by Hans Morgenthau, Chicago, 1951.

U.S. Office of Military Government, Civil Administration Division: *Documents on the Creation of the German Federal Constitution,* September 1, 1949.

Articles:

Bachof, O.: "German Administrative Law," *International and Comparative Law Quarterly,* Vol. 2 (1953), No. 3, pp. 368–382.

Brecht, Arnold: "The New German Constitution," *Social Research,* Vol. 16 (1949), pp. 425–473.

Dietze, G.: "The Federal Republic of Germany: An Evaluation after 10 Years," *Journal of Politics,* Vol. 22, No. 1 (February, 1960), pp. 112–147.

Fliess, P. J.: "Freedom of the Press in the Bonn Republic," *Journal of Politics,* Vol. 16 (1954), pp. 664–684.

Foster, Charles R., and G. Stambuk: "Judicial Protection of Civil Liberties in Germany," *Political Studies,* Vol. 4 (1956), pp. 190–194.

Friedrich, C. J.: "Rebuilding the German Constitution," *American Political Science Review,* Vol. 43 (1949), pp. 461–482.

Johnson, N.: "Questions in the Bundestag," *Parliamentary Affairs,* Vol. 16, No. 1 (Winter, 1962), pp. 22–34.

Loewenberg, G.: "Parliamentarism in West Germany: The Functioning of the Bundestag," *American Political Science Review,* Vol. 55 (March, 1961), pp. 87–102.

Neumann, Robert G.: "New Constitutions in Germany," *American Political Science Review*, Vol. 42 (1948), pp. 448–468.
Rich, Bennett, M.: "Civil Liberties in Germany," *Political Science Quarterly*, Vol. 65 (1950), pp. 68–85.
Sawer, G.: "Federalism in West Germany," *Public Law*, London, Spring, 1961, pp. 26–44.
————: "Politics and the Constitution in West Germany," *Australian Outlook*, Vol. 14, No. 2 (August, 1960), pp. 136–146.

The operation of German government

Ellwein, Dr. Thomas: *Das Regierungssystem der Bundesrepublic Deutschland*, Stuttgart, 1963.
Erler, F.: *Democracy in Germany*, Cambridge, Mass., 1965.
Heidenheimer, A. J.: *The Governments of Germany*, New York, 1964.
Holbik, K.: *Postwar Trade in Divided Germany: The Internal and International Issues*, Baltimore, 1964.
Jacob, H.: *German Administration since Bismarck: Central Authority versus Local Autonomy*, New Haven, Conn., 1963.
Neumann, R. G.: *The Government of the German Federal Republic*, New York, 1966.
Plischke, E.: *Contemporary Government of Germany*, Boston, 1964.
Ullman, R. K., and S. King-Hall: *German Governments: A Study of the Development of Representative Institutions in Germany*, New York, 1955.

Articles:

Adenauer, Konrad: "The Development of Parliamentary Institutions in Germany since 1945," *Parliamentary Affairs*, Vol. 9 (1947), pp. 1–8.
Brandt, G.: "Socio-economic Aspects of German Rearmament," *Archives of European Sociology*, Vol. 6 (1965), No. 2, pp. 294–308.
Braunthal, G.: "Federalism in Germany: The Broadcasting Controversy," *Journal of Politics*, Vol. 24 (1962), No. 3, pp. 545–561.
Dietze, G.: "The Federal Republic of Germany: An Evaluation after Ten Years," *Journal of Politics*, Vol. 22 (1960), No. 1, pp. 112–147.
Kirchheimer, O.: "German Democracy in the 1950's," *World Politics*, Vol. 13 (1961), pp. 254–266.
Merkl, Peter M.: "Executive-Legislative Federalism in West Germany," *American Political Science Review*, Vol. 53 (1959), pp. 732–741.
Neunreither, K.: "Federalism and West German Bureaucracy," *Political Studies*, Vol. 7 (1959), No. 3, pp. 233–245.
————: "Politics and Bureaucracy in the West German Bundesrat," *American Political Science Review*, Vol. 53 (1959), pp. 713–731.
Oppen, B. R. von: "The End of the Adenauer Era," *World Today*, Vol. 19, No. 8 (August, 1963), pp. 343–352.
Pinney, E. L.: "Latent and Manifest Bureaucracy in the West German Parliament: The Case of the Bundesrat," *American Political Science Review*, Vol. 6 (1962), No. 2, pp. 149–164.

Poittie, T.: "The Federal German Parliament," *Parliamentary Affairs,* Vol. 10 (1956–1957), pp. 57–62.

Law and justice

Loewenstein, Karl: "Justice" in *Governing Postwar Germany,* ed. by Litchfield and Associates, Ithaca, N.Y., 1953, pp. 236–262.
Schmertzing, Wolfgang P.: *Outlawing the Communist Party: A Case History,* London, 1957.
Wunderlich, Frieda: *German Labor Courts,* Chapel Hill, N.C., 1946.

Articles:

Baade, Hans W.: "Social Science Evidence and the Federal Constitutional Court of West Germany," *Journal of Politics,* Vol. 23 (1961), No. 3, pp. 421–461.
Cole, T.: "The Role of Labor Courts in Western Germany," *Journal of Politics,* Vol. 18 (1956), pp. 479–498.
———: "Three Constitutional Courts: A Comparison," *American Political Science Review,* Vol. 53 (1959), No. 4, pp. 963–984.
———: "The West German Federal Constitutional Court: An Evaluation after Six Years," *Journal of Politics,* Vol. 20 (1958), pp. 278–307.
Leibholz, Gerhard: "The Federal Constitutional Court in Germany and the 'Southwest' Case," *American Political Science Review,* Vol. 46 (1955), pp. 805–839.
Loewenstein, Karl: "Reconstruction of the Administration of Justice in American-occupied Germany," *Harvard Law Review,* Vol. 60 (1948), pp. 419–467.
McWhinney, Edward: "The German Federal Constitutional Court and the Communist Party Decision," *Indiana Law Journal,* Vol. 36 (1959), pp. 546*ff.*
Nagel, H.: "Judicial Review in Germany," *American Journal of Comparative Law,* Vol. 3 (1954), pp. 233–241.
Rheinstein, Max: "Approach to German Law," *Indiana Law Journal,* Vol. 36 (1959), pp. 546–558.
Rupp, Hans G.: "Judicial Review in the Federal Republic of Germany," *American Journal of Comparative Law,* Vol. 9 (1960), pp. 29–47.
Trombetas, T. P.: "The U.S. Supreme Court and the Federal Constituional Court of Germany," *Revue hellenique de droit international,* Vol. 17, Nos. 3, 4 (June, 1964), pp. 281–298.

State and local government and Berlin

Plischke, E.: *Government and Politics of Contemporary Berlin,* The Hague, 1963.
Stanger, Roland J.: *West Berlin: The Legal Context,* Columbus, Ohio, 1965.
Strauss, Franz Josef: *The Grand Design: A European Solution to German Reunification* (ed. and trans. by Brian Connell), New York, 1966.
Well, Roger H.: *The States in West German Federalism: A Study of Federal-State Relations, 1949–1960,* New York, 1961.
———: *Local Government and State Government,* in *Governing Postwar Germany* (ed. by E. Litchfield and Associates), Ithaca, N.Y., 1953, pp. 57–83, 84–116.

Articles:

Fleming, D. F.: "The Future of West Berlin," *Western Political Quarterly,* Vol. 14, No. 1 (March, 1961), pp. 37–48.

Kirchheimer, Otto: "The Decline of Intra-state Federalism in Western Europe," *World Politics,* Vol. 3 (1950–1951), pp. 281–298.

McInnis, I.: "Berlin: Case Study in Coexistence," *International Journal,* Vol. 14, No. 4 (Autumn, 1959), pp. 244–249.

Plischke, E.: "Integrating Berlin and the Federal Republic of Germany," *Journal of Politics,* Vol. 27, No. 1 (February, 1965), pp. 35–65.

Pommerening, H. E.: "Local Self-government in West Germany," *Quarterly Journal of the Local Self-government Institute,* Vol. 25 (1954), pp. 299–306.

Shell, K. L.: "Berlin and the German Problem," *World Politics,* Vol. 16, No. 1 (October, 1963), pp. 137–146.

"The Siege of West Berlin: Fifteen Years of Divided Germany," *Round Table,* (March, 1961), pp. 160–165.

Wiskemann, E.: "Berlin between East and West," *World To-day,* Vol. 16, No. 11 (November, 1960), pp. 463–472.

The Eastern Zone

Bader, W.: *Civil War in the Making: The Combat Groups of the Working Class in East Germany* (trans. by E. Hinterhoff and P. Windsor), London, 1964.

Brant, Stefan: *The East German Rising,* London, 1955.

Glaser, Kurt: *Berlin and the Future of Eastern Europe* (ed. by D. S. Collier), Chicago, 1963.

————: "Governments of Soviet Germany," in *Governing Postwar Germany* (ed. by E. Litchfield and Associates), Ithaca, N.Y., pp. 152–183.

Hornstein, E. von: *Beyond the Berlin Wall by Refugees Who Have Fled to the West* (trans. by L. Wilson), London, 1962.

The Labour Code of the German Democratic Republic, Commentary by R. Schlegel, Berlin, 1962.

Nettl, J. P.: *The Eastern Zone and Soviet Policy in Germany, 1945–50,* London, 1951.

Solberg, R. W.: *God and Caesar in East Germany: The Conflicts of Church and State in East Germany since 1945,* New York, 1961.

Stern, C.: *Ulbricht: A Political Biography,* New York, 1965.

Wechsberg, J.: *Journey through the Land of Eloquent Silence: East Germany Revisited,* Boston, 1964.

Articles:

Cox, H. B.: "Establishment of the Soviet-sponsored East German Republics," *Department of State Bulletin,* Vol. 21 (1949), pp. 761–764.

Croan, Melvin, and Carl Friedrich: "The East German Regime and Soviet Policy in Germany," *Journal of Politics,* Vol. 20 (1958), pp. 44–63.

Dulles, E.: "The Soviet-occupied Zone of Germany: A Case Study in Communist Control," *Department of State Bulletin,* Vol. 36, No. 929 (Apr. 15, 1957), pp. 605–610.

Franklin, W. M.: "Zonal Boundaries and Access to Berlin," *World Politics,* Vol. 16, No. 1 (October, 1963), pp. 1–31.

Frei, O.: "The Barrier across Berlin and Its Consequences," *World To-day,* Vol. 17, No. 11 (November, 1961), pp. 459–470.

Herz, J. H.: "East Germany: Progress and Prospects," *Social Research,* Vol. 27 (1960), pp. 139–156.

Kuelz, H. R.: "The Soviet Zone of Germany," *International Affairs,* Vol. 27 (1951), pp. 156–166.

RUSSIA

General history

Dmytryshyn, Basil: *USSR: A Concise History,* New York, 1965.

Kerenskii, A.: *Russia and History's Turning Point,* New York, 1965.

Kliuchevsky, Vasily: *A History of Russia* (trans. by Hogarth), 5 vols., New York, 1960.

Labedz, L. (ed.): *Revisionism: Essays on the History of Marxist Ideas,* New York, 1962.

Maynard, Sir John: *Russia in Flux* (ed. by S. M. Guest), New York, 1959.

Mazour, Anatole G.: *Russia, Past and Present,* New York, 1951.

Meyer, Alfred G.: *Marxism since the Communist Manifesto,* Washington, 1961.

Pares, Sir Bernard: *A History of Russia,* definitive ed., New York, 1960.

Rauch, G. V.: *A History of Soviet Russia,* 4th rev. ed., New York, 1964.

Reshetar, J. S., Jr.: *A Concise History of the Communist Part of the Soviet Union,* rev. ed., New York, 1964.

Rothstein, Andrew: *A History of the U.S.S.R.,* Moscow, 1960. (In English.)

Schapiro, L.: *The Origin of the Communist Autocracy: Political Opposition in the Soviet State: First Phase, 1917–1922,* New York, 1965.

Schumann, Frederick K.: *Russia since 1917: Four Decades of Soviet Politics,* New York, 1957.

Seton-Watson, H.: *The Decline of Imperial Russia, 1855–1914,* New York, 1956.

————: *From Lenin to Khrushchev: The History of World Communism,* New York, 1960.

Sturley, D. M.: *A Short History of Russia,* New York, 1966.

Treadgold, Donald W.: *Twentieth Century Russia,* 2d ed., Chicago, 1964.

Vernadsky, George: *History of Russia,* 4th ed., New Haven, Conn., 1959.

————: *The Origins of Russia,* Oxford, 1959.

————: *Political and Diplomatic History of Russia,* Boston, 1936.

Werth, Alexander: *Russia at War, 1941–1945,* New York, 1964.

The Russian revolution

Berdyaev, N.: *The Russian Revolution,* Ann Arbor, Mich., 1961.

Carr, E. H.: *The Bolshevik Revolution, 1917–1923,* 3 vols., London, 1950–1953.

Chamberlin, W. H.: *The Russian Revolution, 1917–1921,* new ed., 2 vols., New York, 1965.

Kerenskii, Alexander: *The Catastrophe,* New York, 1927.

Treadgold, D. W.: *Twentieth Century Russia*, 2d ed., Chicago, 1962.
Trotsky, Leon: *History of the Russian Revolution*, 3 vols., New York, 1936.
————: *Lessons of October*, New York, 1937.
————: *My Life*, New York, 1930.
————: *The Revolution Betrayed*, New York, 1957.
Vernadsky, George: *The Russian Revolution 1917–1931*, New York, 1932.
Wolfe, Bertram D.: *Three Who Made a Revolution*, 4th ed., New York, 1964.

Lenin, Stalin, and Khrushchev

Brumberg, A. (ed.): *Russia under Krushchev*, New York, 1962.
Crankshaw, E.: *Krushchev: A Career*, New York, 1966.
Dallin, David Y.: *From Purge to Coexistence: Essays on Stalin's and Krushchev's Russia*, Chicago, 1964.
Fischer, Louis: *The Life of Lenin*, New York, 1965.
Krupskaya, N. K.: *Memories of Lenin* (trans. by E. Verney), New York, 1930.
Levine, I. D.: *Stalin*, New York, 1931.
Linden, Carl L.: *Krushchev and the Soviet Leadership, 1957–1964*, Baltimore, 1966.
McNeal, R. H.: *The Bolshevik Tradition: Lenin, Stalin, Krushchev*, Englewood Cliffs, N.J., 1963.
Mirsky, D. S.: *Lenin*, Boston, 1931.
Payne, P. S. R.: *The Life and Death of Lenin*, New York, 1964.
Possony, Stefan T.: *Lenin Reader*, Chicago, 1965.
Rondall, F. B.: *Stalin's Russia: A Historical Reconsideration*, New York, 1965.
Shub, David: *Lenin: A Biography*, New York, 1948.
Souvarine, B.: *Stalin*, New York, 1939.
Swearer, H. R.: *The Politics of Succession in the USSR: Materials on Krushchev's Rise to Leadership*, Boston, 1964.
Treadgold, D. W.: *Lenin and His Rivals: The Struggle for Russia's Future, 1898–1906*, New York, 1955.
Trotsky, Leon: *Lenin*, London, 1925.
————: *Stalin*, New York, 1941.
Tucker, Robert: *The Soviet Political Mind: Studies in Stalinism and Post-Stalin Change*, New York, 1963.
Von Lane, Theodore H.: *Why Lenin? Why Stalin?*, New York, 1964.
Werth, Alexander: *The Krushchev Phase: The Soviet Union Enters the Decisive Sixties*, London, 1961.
————: *Russia under Krushchev*, New York, 1962.

The theory of Communism

Berdyaev, Nikolai: *The Origins of Russian Communism*, Ann Arbor, Mich., 1960.
Burns, Emile (ed.): *A Handbook of Marxism*, New York, 1935.
Cole, G. D. H.: *What Marx Really Meant*, New York, 1937.
Dallin, A.: *Diversity in International Communism: A Documentary Record, 1961–1963*, New York, 1963.
Deutscher, Isaac: *The Prophet Outcast: Trotsky, 1929–1940*, London, 1963.

Djilas, Milovan: *The New Class: An Analysis of the Communist System*, New York, 1957.

Eastman, Max: *Marxism: Is It a Science?*, New York, 1940.

Engels, Friedrich: *Herr Eugen Dühring's Revolution in Science* (trans. by E. Burns), London, 1943.

Gregor, A. James: *A Survey of Marxism: Problems in Philosophy and the Theory of History*, New York, 1965.

Gurian, Waldemar: *Bolshevism: An Introduction to Soviet Communism*, Notre Dame, Ind., 1952.

Hook, Sydney: *From Hegel to Marx*, Ann Arbor, Mich., 1966.

————: *Towards an Understanding of Karl Marx*, New York, 1933.

Hunt, R. N. C.: *The Theory and Practice of Communism: An Introduction*, 5th ed., New York, 1960.

Laski, H. J.: *Karl Marx: An Essay*, New York, 1933.

Lenin, V. I.: *Imperialism: The Highest Stage of Capitalism*, Peking, 1965.

————: *State and Revolution*, Peking, 1965.

————: *What Is To Be Done?*, New York, 1929.

Lindsey, A. D.: *Karl Marx's Capital: An Introductory Essay*, New York, 1947.

Marx, Karl: *"Capital," "Class Struggle in France," "Critique of the Political Economy," "Manifesto of the Communist Party,"* New York, 1964.

Meyer, Alfred G.: *Leninism*, Cambridge, Mass., 1957.

————: *The Soviet Political System*, New York, 1965.

Morton, H. W. (ed.): *Soviet Policy Making: Studies of Communism in Transition*, New York, 1966.

Schwartz, H.: *The Many Faces of Communism*, New York, 1962.

Somerville, John: *Soviet Philosophy: A Study of Theory and Practice*, New York, 1946.

Stalin, V. J.: *Dialectical and Historical Materialism*, New York, 1940.

————: *Leninism*, 2 vols., New York, 1942.

————: *Marxism and the National and Colonial Question*, New York, 1935.

Sweezy, Paul M.: *Socialism*, New York, 1949.

Trotskii, L.: *Basic Writings*, New York, 1963.

Wetter, G. A.: *Dialectical Materialism*, New York, 1958.

Articles:

Historicus: "Stalin on Revolution," *Foreign Affairs*, Vol. 28 (1949), pp. 175–214.

General treatises, analyses, and observations

Andrews, William G. (ed.): *Soviet Institutions and Policies: Inside Views* (ed. by W. G. Andrews with the assistance of F. D. Scholz), Princeton, N.J., 1966.

Armstrong, J. A.: *Ideology, Politics and Government in the Soviet Union*, New York, 1962.

Barghoorn, F. C.: *Politics in the USSR*, Boston, 1966.

Barmine, Alexander: *One Who Survived: The Life and Story of a Russian under the Soviets*, New York, 1945.

Bauer, Raymond A.: *Some Views on Soviet Psychology*, Washington, 1962.

———— et al.: *How the Soviet System Works: Cultural Psychological and Social Themes*, New York, 1960.

Brown, J. F.: *The New Eastern Europe: The Krushchev Era and After*, New York, 1966.

Brzerzinski, Zbigniew K.: *Ideology and Power in Soviet Politics*, New York, 1962.

———— and Samuel P. Huntington: *Political Power: USA/USSR*, New York, 1962.

Chamberlin, W. H.: *The Russian Enigma*, New York, 1944.

Crankshaw, Edward: *Cracks in the Kremlin Wall*, New York, 1951.

————: *Russia and the Russians*, New York, 1948.

Dallin, A., and A. F. Westin: *Politics in the Soviet Union: 7 Cases*, New York, 1966.

Dallin, D. J.: *The Real Soviet Russia* (trans. by J. Shaplen), New Haven, Conn., 1947.

Deutscher, Isaac: *Russia: What Next?*, London, 1953.

————: *Russia in Transition*, New York, 1960.

Fainsod, Merle: *Smolensk under Soviet Rule*, Cambridge, Mass., 1958.

Fischer, G.: *Russian Liberalism from Gentry to Intelligentsia*, Cambridge, Mass., 1958.

————: *Soviet Opposition to Stalin*, Cambridge, Mass., 1952.

Florinsky, M. T. (ed.): *McGraw-Hill Encyclopedia of Russia and the Soviet Union*, New York, 1961.

Gurian, Waldemar (ed.): *The Soviet Union: Background, Ideology, Reality*, Notre Dame, Ind., 1951.

Hazard, J. N.: *The Soviet System of Government*, 3d rev. and enl. ed., Chicago, 1964.

Hendel, S.: *The Soviet Crucible: The Soviet System in Theory and Practice*, Princeton, N.J., 1963.

Librach, J.: *The Rise of the Soviet Empire*, rev. ed., New York, 1966.

Meyer, Alfred G.: *The Soviet Political System: An Interpretation*, New York, 1965.

Moore, Barrington, Jr.: *Soviet Politics: The Dilemma of Power*, Cambridge, Mass., 1950.

————: *Terror and Progress, USSR: Some Sources of Change and Stability in the Soviet Dictatorship*, Cambridge, Mass., 1954.

Moseley, Philip E.: *The Soviet Union since Krushchev*, New York, 1966.

Rosenberg, Arthur: *History of Bolshevism*, Oxford, 1939.

Rostow, W. W. (in collaboration with Alfred Levin): *The Dynamics of Soviet Society*, New York, 1953.

Schumann, Frederick L.: *Soviet Politics at Home and Abroad*, New York, 1946.

Scott, John: *Behind the Urals*, New York, 1942.

Smith, Walter Bedell: *My Three Years in Moscow*, Philadelphia, 1950.

Timasheff, Nicholas: *The Great Retreat: The Growth and Decline of Communism in Russia*, New York, 1946.

Treadgold, D. W.: *The Development of the U.S.S.R.: An Exchange of Views*, Seattle, 1964.

Trotsky, Leon: *The Real Situation in Russia*, New York, 1928.

Tucker, R. C.: *The Soviet Political Mind*, New York, 1963.

Ulam, A. B.: *The New Face of Soviet Totalitarianism*, New York, 1965.

Utley, Freda: *The Dream We Lost*, New York, 1940.

Webb, Sidney, and Beatrice Webb: *Soviet Communism: A New Civilization?*, 3d ed., 2 vols., New York, 1944.

Wetter, Gustav Andreas: *Soviet Ideology Today: Dialectical and Historical Materialism* (trans. by P. Heath), London, 1966.

Whiting, K. R.: *The Soviet Union Today: A Concise Handbook,* rev. ed., New York, 1966.

Articles:

Fainsod, Merle: "Controls and Tensions within the Soviet System," *American Political Science Review,* Vol. 44 (1950), pp. 266–282.

Moseley, Philip E. (ed.): "Russia since Stalin: Old Trends and New Problems," *Annals of the American Academy of Political and Social Science,* January, 1958, entire issue.

———— (ed.): "The Soviet Union since World War II," *Annals of the American Academy of Political and Social Science,* May, 1949, entire issue.

The Communist Party

Central Committee of the Communist Party of the Soviet Union: *History of the Communist Party of the Soviet Union* (Bolsheviks) *Short Course,* New York, 1939. (Credited to J. V. Stalin.)

Duranty, Walter: *Stalin & Co.: The Politburo—The Men Who Run Russia,* New York, 1949.

Grip, R. C.: *Patterns of Soviet Politics,* Homewood, Ill., 1964.

Kovalev, S.: *Ideological Conflicts in Soviet Russia,* Washington, 1948.

Leites, Nathan: *The Operational Code of the Politburo,* New York, 1951.

McClosky and J. E. Turner: *The Soviet Dictatorship,* New York, 1960.

Meissner, Boris: *The Communist Party of the Soviet Union* (ed. by John S. Reshetar, Jr.), New York, 1956.

Schneller, George K.: *The Politburo,* Palo Alto, Calif., 1951.

Articles:

Daniels, Robert G.: "The Soviet Succession: Lenin and Stalin," *Russian Review,* Vol. 12 (1953), pp. 153–172.

Fainsod, Merle: "The Komsomols: A Study of Youth under Dictatorship," *American Political Science Review,* Vol. 45 (1951), pp. 18–40.

Moore, Barrington, Jr.: "The Communist Party of the Soviet Union: 1928–1944," *American Sociological Review,* Vol. 9 (1944), pp. 267–278.

Nemzer, Louis: "The Kremlin Professional Staff: The 'Apparatus' of the Control Committee, Communist Party of the Soviet Union," *American Political Science Review,* Vol. 44 (1950), pp. 64–85.

Reshetar, John S., Jr.: "National Deviation in the Soviet Union," *American Slavic and East European Review,* Vol. 12 (1953), pp. 162–174.

Schlesinger, R.: "Notes on the Changing Functions of Party Congresses," *Soviet Studies,* Vol. 4 (1953), pp. 386–402.

Utis, O.: "Generalissimo Stalin and the Art of Government," *Foreign Affairs,* Vol. 31 (1952), pp. 197–214.

Constitution and institutions of government

Andrews, W. G. (ed.): *Soviet Institutions and Policies,* Princeton, N.J., 1966.

Braham, Randolph L.: *Soviet Politics and Government,* New York, 1965.

Fainsod, M.: *How Russia Is Ruled,* rev. ed., Cambridge, Mass., 1963.

Florinsky, Michael J.: *Towards an Understanding of the U.S.S.R.: A Study in Government, Politics, and Economic Planning,* rev. ed., New York, 1951.

Harper, S. N., and R. Thompson: *The Government of the Soviet Union,* 2d ed., New York, 1949.

Hazard, John: "Constitutional Problems in the U.S.S.R.," in *Change and Crisis in European Government* (ed. by James K. Pollock), New York, 1947, pp. 3–16.

————: *The Soviet System of Government,* 3d ed., Chicago, 1964.

Hendel, Samuel (ed.): *The Soviet Crucible: Soviet Government in Theory and Practice,* 2d ed., Princeton, N.J., 1963.

Krenskii, A.: *The Russian Provisional Government, 1917* (ed. by R. P. Browder), Stanford, Calif., 1961.

Maxwell, Bertram W.: "The Soviet Union," in *Local Government in Europe* (ed. by William Anderson), New York, 1939, pp. 383–447.

Meisel, J. H., and E. S. Kozera: *Materials for the Study of the Soviet System,* Ann Arbor, Mich., 1953.

Molotov, V.: *The New Soviet Constitution,* New York, 1937.

Moore, Barrington, Jr.: *Soviet Politics: The Dilemma of Power,* New York, 1965.

Mote, M. E.: *Soviet Local and Republic Elections,* Stanford, Calif., 1965.

Scott, Derek J. R.: *Russian Political Institutions,* 3d ed., New York, 1966.

Towster, J.: *Political Power in the U.S.S.R., 1917–1947,* New York, 1948.

Wesson, R. G.: *Soviet Communes,* New Brunswick, N.J., 1963.

White, Fedotoff D.: *The Growth of the Red Army,* Princeton, N.J., 1944.

Articles:

Alexeiev, N. M.: "The Evolution of Soviet Constitutional Law," *Review of Politics,* Vol. 2 (1940), pp. 463–476.

Aspaturian, V. V.: "The Theory and Practice of Soviet Federalism," *Journal of Politics,* Vol. 12 (1950), pp. 20–51.

Fainsod, Merle: "Recent Developments in Soviet Public Administration," *Journal of Politics,* Vol. 11 (1949), pp. 679–714.

Guins, George C.: "Soviet Centralism," *American Journal of Economics and Sociology,* Vol. 9 (1950), pp. 335–346.

Meissner, B.: "Die gesetzgeberische Tätigkeit des Obersten Sowjets der U.S.S.R. und die Entwicklung der Sowietexecutive von 1949–1953," *Europa-Archiv,* Vol. 8 (1953), pp. 5693–5706.

Nove, A.: "Some Aspects of Soviet Constitutional Theory," *Modern Law Review,* Vol. 12 (1949), pp. 12–36.

Forced labor, compulsion, and terror

American Federation of Labor: *Slave Labor in Russia,* New York, 1949.

Beck, F., and E. Goodin: *Russian Purge and the Extraction of Confession,* New York, 1951.

Dallin, O. J., and B. I. Nicolaevsky: *Forced Labor in Soviet Russia,* New Haven, Conn., 1947.

Lipper, Elinor: *11 Years in Soviet Prison Camps,* Chicago, 1951.

Mora, S.: *Kolyma,* Washington, 1949.

Pirogov, P.: *Why I Escaped,* New York, 1950.

Tchernavin, V. V.: *I Speak for the Silent,* Boston, 1935.

U.S. Department of State: *Forced Labor in the Soviet Union.* Washington, 1952.

Weissberg, Alexander: *The Accused,* New York, 1951.

Wolin, Simon, and Robert M. Slusser (eds.): *The Soviet Secret Police,* New York, 1957.

Articles:

Jasny, Naum: "Labor and Output in Soviet Concentration Camps," *Journal of Political Economy,* Vol. 59 (1951), pp. 405–419.

The Soviet economy

Arakelian, A.: *Industrial Management in the U.S.S.R.,* Washington, 1950.

Baykov, A.: *Development of the Soviet Economic System,* Cambridge, England, 1946.

Bergson, Abram: *The Economics of Soviet Planning,* New Haven, Conn., 1964.

———: *Economic Trends in the Soviet Union,* Cambridge. Mass., 1963.

———: *Structure of Soviet Wages,* Cambridge, Mass., 1944.

Bienstock, Gregory, et al.: *Management in Russian Industry and Agriculture,* New York, 1944.

Degras, Jane T.: *Soviet Planning: Essays in Honour of Naum Jasny,* Oxford, 1964.

Deutscher, Isaac: *Soviet Trade Unions: Their Place in Soviet Labor Policy,* New York, 1950.

Dobb, Maurice H.: *Soviet Economic Development since 1917,* London, 1960.

———: *Soviet Planning and Labor,* New York, 1943.

Hubbard, L. E.: *Soviet Labor and Industry,* London, 1942.

Jasny, Naum: *Essays on the Soviet Economy,* New York, 1962.

———: *The Soviet Economy during the Plan Era,* Palo Alto, Calif., 1951.

———: *Soviet Industrialization, 1928–1952,* Chicago, 1961.

Miller, Margaret: *Communist Economy under Change: Studies in Theory and Practice of Markets in Competition in Russia, Poland and Yugoslavia,* London, 1963.

———: *Labour in the U.S.S.R.,* London, 1942.

———: *Rise of the Russian Consumer,* London, 1965.

Nove, Alec: *The Soviet Economy: An Introduction,* New York, 1963.

Ploss, S. I.: *Conflict and Decision-making in Soviet Russia: A Case Study of Agricultural Policy, 1953–1963,* Princeton, N.J., 1965.

Schwartz, Harry: *Russia's Soviet Economy,* 2d ed., New York, 1958.

———: *The Soviet Economy since Stalin,* Philadelphia, 1965.

———: *The Soviet Union: Communist Economic Power,* Minneapolis, 1963.

Schwarz, Solomon M.: *Labor in the Soviet Union,* New York, 1952.

Shaffer, Harry G. (ed.): *The Soviet Economy: A Collection of Western and Soviet Views,* New York, 1963.

Voznesensky, N. A.: *Economy of the U.S.S.R. during World War II*, Washington, 1948.
Vucinich, Alexander: *Soviet Economic Institutions*, Stanford, Calif., 1952.

Articles:

Bennet, M. K.: "Food and Agriculture in the Soviet Union, 1947–1948," *Journal of Political Economy*, Vol. 57 (1949), pp. 185–198.
Berliner, Joseph S.: "The Informal Organization of the Soviet Firm," *Quarterly Journal of Economics*, Vol. 46 (1952), pp. 342–365.
Mosely, Philip E.: "Khrushchev's New Economic Gambit," *Foreign Affairs*, Vol. 36 (1958), pp. 557–568.
Volin, Lazar: "The Turn of the Screw in Soviet Agriculture," *Foreign Affairs*, Vol. 30 (1952), pp. 277–288.
Vucinich, Alexander: "The Kolkhoz: Its Social Structure and Development," *American Slavic and East European Review*, Vol. 8 (1949), pp. 10–24.

Law and justice

Aleksandrov, Nikolai G.: *Soviet Labor Law*, Delhi, 1961.
Berman, Harold J.: *Justice in Russia: An Interpretation of Soviet Law*, rev. enl. ed., New York, 1963.
Goliakov, I. T.: *The Role of the Soviet Court*, Washington, 1948.
Grzybowski, K.: *Soviet Legal Institutions: Doctrines and Social Functions*, Ann Arbor, Mich., 1962.
Gsovski, Vladimir: *Soviet Civil Law*, 2 vols., Ann Arbor, Mich., 1948–1949.
————: *Government, Law and Courts in the Soviet Union and Eastern Europe*, New York, 1959.
Hazard, John N.: *Law and Social Change in the U.S.S.R.*, London, 1953.
————: *Settling Disputes in Soviet Society: The Formative Years of Legal Institutions*, New York, 1960.
———— (ed.): *Soviet Legal Philosophy*, Cambridge, Mass., 1952.
———— and J. Shapiro: *The Soviet Legal System: Post-Stalin Documentation and Historical Commentary*, New York, 1962.
Schlesinger, Rudolf: *Soviet Legal Theory*, 2d ed., London, 1951.

Articles:

Berman, Harold J.: "The Challenge of Soviet Law," *Harvard Law Review*, Vol. 61 (1948), pp. 220–265; and Vol. 62 (1949), pp. 449–466.
Ginsburgs, George: "The Soviet Procuracy and Forty Years of Socialist Legality," *American Slavic and East European Review*, Vol. 18 (1958), pp. 34–62.
Gsovski, Vladimir: "Elements of Soviet Labor Law," *Monthly Labor Review*, Vol. 72 (1951), pp. 257–268.
————: "Marriage and Divorce in Soviet Law," *Georgetown Law Journal*, Vol. 35 (1947), pp. 209–223.
Guins, George C.: "Law Does Not Wither Away in the Soviet Union," *Russian Review*, Vol. 9 (1950), pp. 187–204.
————: "Soviet Law-Terror Incognito," *Russian Review*, Vol. 8 (1949), pp. 16–29.

Hazard, John N.: "Socialism, Abuse of Power and Soviet Law," *Columbia Law Review,*
Vol. 50 (1950), pp. 448–474.

———: "The Soviet Court as a Source of Law," *Washington Law Review,* Vol. 24
(1949), pp. 80–90.

———: "Soviet Socialism and Due Process of Law," *Michigan Law Review,* Vol. 48
(1950), pp. 1061–1078.

People, education, and religion

Anderson, Paul B.: *People, Church and State in Modern Russia,* New York, 1944.

Bauer, Raymond: *How the Soviet System Works: Cultural, Psychological and Social
Themes,* New York, 1960.

———: *The New Man in Soviet Psychology,* Cambridge, Mass., 1952.

Bowen, James: *Soviet Education,* Madison, Wis., 1962.

Counts, G. S., and N. P. Lodge: *The Country of the Blind: The Soviet System of Mind
Control,* Boston, 1950. (Excerpts from the book by Boris P. Esipov and N. K.
Goucharov.)

Grant, Nigel: *Soviet Education,* Baltimore, 1964.

Hecker, Julius F.: *Religion and Communism,* New York, 1934.

Inkeles, Alex: *Public Opinion in the Soviet Union,* Cambridge, Mass., 1958.

———: *The Soviet Citizen: Daily Life in a Totalitarian Society,* Cambridge, Mass.,
1959.

——— and Kent Geiger (eds.): *Soviet Society: A Book of Readings,* Boston, 1961.

Kondratovich, Aleksei: *The Soviet People Are Building a New Society,* Moscow, 1961.

Nicolaevsky, B. I.: *Power and the Soviet Elite* (ed. by J. Zagoria), New York, 1965.

Ritvo, Herbert: *The New Soviet Society,* New York, 1962.

Schlesinger, Rudolph (ed.): *Changing Attitudes in Soviet Russia: Documents and
Readings,* Vol. I, *The Family in the U.S.S.R.,* London, 1949.

Schwarz, Solomon M.: *The Jews in the Soviet Union,* Syracuse, N.Y., 1951.

Timasheff, Nicholas S.: *Religion in Soviet Russia, 1917–1942,* London, 1942.

Articles:

Anissimov, O.: "The Soviet System of Education," *Russian Review,* Vol. 9 (1950), pp.
87–97.

Brown, J. A.: "Public Opinion in the Soviet Union," *Russian Review,* Vol. 9 (1950),
pp. 37–44.

Timasheff, Nicholas S.: "Vertical Social Mobility in Communist Society," *American
Journal of Sociology,* Vol. 50 (1944), pp. 9–21.

The Soviet Union and the world

Barghoorn, Frederick C.: *The Soviet Cultural Offensive: The Role of Cultural Diplomacy,* Princeton, N.J., 1960.

———: *Soviet Foreign Propaganda,* Princeton, N.J., 1964.

———: *Soviet Image of the United States: A Study in Distortion,* New York, 1950.

Beloff, M.: *Foreign Policy of Soviet Russia, 1929–1941,* 2 vols., Oxford, 1956.

Berliner, Joseph S.: *Soviet Economic Aid: The New Aid and Trade Policy in Under-developed Countries*, New York, 1958.

Blueprint for World Conquest as Outlined by the Communist Internationale, Washington, 1946.

Borkenau, Franz: *European Communism*, New York, 1953.

————: *World Communism*, Ann Arbor, Mich., 1962.

Brzezinski, S. K.: *The Soviet Bloc: Unity and Conflict*, New York, 1963.

Carr, E. H.: *The Soviet Impact on the Western World*, New York, 1954.

Cultural Relations Between the United States and the Soviet Union, Department of State Publication 3480, Washington, 1949.

Dallin, David Y.: *The New Soviet Empire*, New Haven, Conn., 1951.

————: *Soviet Foreign Policy after Stalin*, Philadelphia, 1961.

————: *Soviet Russia's Foreign Policy, 1939–1942*, New Haven, Conn., 1942.

Ebon, Martin: *World Communism To-day*, New York, 1948.

Fischer, Louis: *Russia, America and the World*, New York, 1961.

————: *The Soviets in World Affairs*, 2 vols., New York, 1960.

————: *Trends in Russian Foreign Policy since World War I*, Senate Committee on Foreign Relations, 80th Cong., 1st Sess., Washington, 1947.

Fischer, Ruth: *Stalin and German Communism*, Cambridge, Mass., 1948.

Footman, David: *International Communism*, London, 1960.

Hammond, Thomas T.: *Soviet Foreign Relations and World Communism*, Princeton, N.J., 1965. (A selected annotated bibliography of 7,000 books in thirty languages.)

Hook, Sidney: *World Communism: Key Documentary Material*, Princeton, N.J., 1962.

Kennan, George F.: *Russia and the West under Lenin and Stalin*, New York, 1960.

————: *Soviet-American Relations, 1917–1920*, Princeton, N.J., 1956.

Laqueur, Walter, and Leopold Labedz: *Polycentrism*, New York, 1962.

Pentony, De Vere E. (ed.): *Soviet Behaviour in World Affairs: Communist Foreign Policies*, San Francisco, 1962.

Seton-Watson, Hugh: *From Lenin to Malenkov: The History of World Communism*, New York, 1953.

Taracouzio, T.: *The Soviet Union and International Law*, New York, 1935.

————: *War and Peace in Soviet Diplomacy*, New York, 1940.

Warth, Robert D.: *Soviet Russia in World Politics*, New York, 1963.

Articles:

Silone, Ignazio: "Farewell to Moscow," *Harper's Magazine*, November, 1949, pp. 93–99.

"Soviet Violations of Treaty Obligations: Documents Submitted by the Department of State to the Senate Committee on Foreign Relations," *Department of State Bulletin*, Vol. 18 (1948), pp. 738–744.

"X" (George Kennan): "The Sources of Soviet Conduct," *Foreign Affairs*, Vol. 25 (1947), pp. 566–582.

EUROPEAN INTEGRATION

Allen, James J.: *The European Common Market and the GATT*, Washington, 1960.

Andrews, W. G.: *European Political Institutions*, Princeton, N.J., 1962.

————: *European Politics,* Princeton, N.J., 1966.

Balassa, Bela A.: *The Theory of Economic Integration,* Urbana, Ill., 1961.

Ball, M. Margaret: *NATO and the European Union Movement,* New York, 1959.

Bebr, Gerhard: *Judicial Control of the European Communities,* New York, 1962.

Beever, Colin R.: *European Unity and the Trade Union Movements,* Leiden, Netherlands, 1960.

Beloff, Max: *The United States and the Unity of Europe,* Washington, 1963.

Beloff, Nora: *The General Says No: Britain's Exclusion from Europe,* Baltimore, 1963.

Benoit, Emile: *Europe at Sixes and Sevens: The Common Market, the Free Trade Association and the United States,* New York, 1961.

Bilgrami, Asaghar H.: *Britain, the Commonwealth and the European Union Issue,* Geneva, 1961.

Birrenbach, Kurt: *The Future of the Atlantic Community: Toward European American Partnership,* New York, 1963.

Bowie, Robert R., and Carl J. Friedrich: *Studies in Federalism,* Boston, 1954.

Brooks, John Nixon: *The European Common Market,* New York, 1963.

Calleo, David P.: *Europe's Future: The Grand Alternatives,* New York, 1965.

Campbell, Alan, and Dennis Thompson: *Common Market Law: Texts and Commentaries,* London, 1962.

Camps, Miriam: *Britain and the European Community, 1955–1963,* London, 1964.

Cerami, Charles A.: *Alliance Born of Danger: America, the Common Market, and the Atlantic Partnership,* New York, 1963.

Clark, Colin, et al.: *The Common Market and British Trade,* New York, 1962.

Committee for Economic Development: *The European Common Market and Its Meaning to the United States,* New York, 1959.

Coppock, John O.: *North Atlantic Policy: The Agricultural Gap,* New York, 1963.

Cottrell, Alvin J., and James E. Dougherty: *The Politics of the Atlantic Alliance,* New York, 1964.

Curtis, Michael: *Western European Integration,* New York, 1965.

Dell, Sidney Samuel: *Trade Blocs and Common Markets,* New York, 1963.

Deniau, Jean P.: *The Common Market: Its Structure and Purpose,* New York, 1960.

Deutsch, Karl W., et al.: *Political Community and the North Atlantic Area: International Organization in the Light of Historical Experience,* Princeton, N.J., 1957.

Diebold, William, Jr.: *The Schuman Plan,* New York, 1959.

Errera, J., et al.: *EURATOM: Analysis of and Comments on the Treaty* (trans. from the French by United States Joint Publication Service), Washington, 1958.

Frank, Isaiah: *The European Common Market: An Analysis of Commercial Policy,* New York, 1961.

Gladwyn, Lord: *The European Idea,* New York, 1966.

Glase, K., and D. S. Collier: *Western Integration and the Future of Eastern Europe,* Chicago, 1964.

Haas, Ernst B.: *Consensus Formation in the Council of Europe,* Berkeley, Calif., 1960.

————: *The Uniting of Europe: Political, Social, and Economic Forces, 1950–1957,* Stanford, Calif., 1958.

Haines, C. Grove (ed.): *European Integration,* Baltimore, 1957.

Hallstein, Walter: *United Europe: Challenge and Opportunity,* Cambridge, Mass., 1962.

Haviland, H. Field, Jr. (ed.): *The United States and the Western Community*, Haverford, Pa., 1957.

Kitzinger, U. W.: *The Politics and Economics of European Integration: Britain, Europe and the United States*, New York, 1963.

Kleiman, Robert: *Atlantic Crisis: American Diplomacy Confronts a Resurgent Europe*, New York, 1964.

Kraft, Joseph: *The Grand Design: From Common Market to Atlantic Partnership*, New York, 1962.

Lawen, R. (ed.): *International Regional Organizations: Constitutional Foundations*, New York, 1962.

Lichtheim, George: *The New Europe: Today and Tomorrow*, New York, 1963.

Lindberg, Leon N.: *The Political Dynamics of European Economic Integration*, Stanford, Calif., 1963.

Lindsay, Kenneth: *European Assemblies: The Experimental Period, 1949–1959*, London, 1960.

Liska, George: *Europe Ascendant*, Baltimore, 1965.

Marc, Alexandre: *L'Europe dans le Monde*, Paris, 1965.

Marjolin, Robert: *Europe and the United States in the World Economy*, Durham, N.C., 1953.

Mason, Henry L.: *The European Coal and Steel Community: Experiment in Supranationalism*, The Hague, 1955.

Middelton, D.: *The Atlantic Community: A Study in Unity and Disunity*, New York, 1965.

————: *The Supreme Choice: Britain and Europe*, New York, 1963.

Moore, Ben T.: *NATO and the Future of Europe*, New York, 1958.

Mulley, F. W.: *The Politics of Western Defense*, New York, 1962.

Munk, Frank: *Atlantic Dilemma: Partnership or Community*, New York, 1964.

Northrop, F. S. C.: *European Union and United States Foreign Policy*, New York, 1954.

Nutting, Anthony: *Europe Will Not Wait: A Warning and a Way Out*, New York, 1960.

Ouin, Marc: *The Establishment of the Customs Union*, Ann Arbor, Mich., 1960.

Pinder, John: *Europe against De Gaulle*, London, 1963.

Polach, Jaroslav G.: *EURATOM: Its Background, Issues and Economic Implications*, New York, 1964.

Robertson, A. H.: *The Council of Europe*, New York, 1956.

————: *Human Rights in Europe*, New York, 1963.

The Rules of Procedure of the Court of Justice of the European Communities, Leiden, Netherlands, 1962.

Scheingold, S. A.: "International Labor: The Regional Challenge," M.A. thesis, University of California, Berkeley, Calif., 1959.

————: *The Rule of Law in European Integration*, New Haven, Conn., 1965.

Schmitt, Hans A.: *The Past to European Union: From the Marshall Plan to the Common Market*, Baton Rouge, La., 1963.

Shanks, Michael, and John Lambert: *The Common Market Today and Tomorrow*, New York, 1962.

Stein, Eric, and Peter Hay (eds.): *Cases and Materials on the Law and Institutions of the Atlantic Area*, Ann Arbor, Mich., 1963.

Stein, Eric, and Thomas L. Nicholson (eds.): *American Enterprise in the European Common Market: A Legal Profile*, 2 vols., Ann Arbor, Mich., 1960.

Straus, Richard: *Coal, Steel, Atoms, and Trade: The Challenge of Uniting Europe*, New York, 1962.

Strauss, E.: *Common Sense about the Common Market: Germany and Britain in Postwar Europe*, London, 1958.

Strauss-Hupe, Robert, et al.: *Building the Atlantic World*, New York, 1963.

Uri, Pierre: *Partnership for Progress: A Program for Transatlantic Action*, New York, 1963.

Van der Beugel, E.: *From Marshall Aid to Atlantic Partnership: European Integration as a Concern of American Foreign Policy*, New York, 1966.

Van Oudenhove, Guy: *The Political Parties in the European Parliament*, Leiden, Netherlands, 1965.

Weil, Gordon Lee: *The European Convention on Human Rights: Background, Development and Prospects*, Leiden, Netherlands, 1963.

Articles and Pamphlets:

Acheson, Dean: "The Practice of Partnership," *Foreign Affairs,* Vol. 41 (January, 1963), No. 2, pp. 247–260.

"Action Program: Second Stage of the Common Market," *Common Market Reports,* (February, 1963), 63 pp.

Adler, G. M.: "EEC Court of Justice," *Canadian Bar Journal,* Vol. 7 (April, 1964), pp. 102–127.

Bebr, Gerhard: "The Balance of Power in the European Communities," *Annuaire européen,* The Hague, Vol. V (1959), pp. 53–79.

———: "European Coal and Steel Community: A Political and Legal Innovation," *Yale Law Journal,* Vol. 63 (November, 1953), pp. 1–43.

Becker, Loftus E.: "The 'Antitrust' Laws of the Common Market," *American Bar Association Section of Antitrust Law Proceedings,* Vol. 17 (1960), pp. 456–505.

Beloff, Max: "Federalism Is a Model for International Integration," *Yearbook of World Affairs,* New York, Vol. 13 (1959), pp. 188–204.

———: "National Government and International Government," *International Organization,* Vol. XIII (1959), pp. 538–549.

Benoit, Emile: "The External Relations of the Common Market," *The Record,* Association of the Bar of the City of New York, Vol. 15 (1960), pp. 276–285.

Birrenbach, Kurt: "Europe and the European Economic Community and the Outer Seven," *International Journal,* Vol. 15 (Winter, 1959–1960), pp. 59–65.

Bowie, Robert: "European Community and the United States," *India Quarterly,* Vol. 18, No. 3 (July–September, 1962), pp. 219–230.

———: "Prospects for Atlantic Community," *The Harvard Review,* Vol. 1, No. 1 (Fall, 1962), pp. 7–15.

———: "Studies in Aid of European Federation," *Harvard Law School Bulletin,* Vol. 3 (December, 1952), pp. 8–9.

"Budgetary Control in the European Economic Community: A Case Study in 'Supranational' Administration," *Occasional Paper No. 6,* London, March 28, 1960.

Camps, Miriam: "Britain, the Six and American Policy," *Foreign Affairs*, Vol. 39 (1960), pp. 112–122.

————: *Division in Europe*, Center of International Studies, Policy Memorandum 21, Princeton, N.J., 1960.

————: *The European Common Market and American Policy*, Center of International Studies, Memorandum 11, Princeton, N.J., 1956.

————: *The European Common Market and the Free Trade Area*, Center of International Studies, Memorandum 15, Princeton, N.J., 1957.

————: *The Free Trade Area Negotiations*, Center of International Studies, Policy Memorandum 18, Princeton, N.J., 1959.

Clayton, W. L., and Humphrey: "U.S. Trade and the Common Market," Foreign Policy Association, New York, 1962.

Coblentz, W. K.: "Schuman Plan: An Appraisal," *American Bar Association Journal*, Vol. 39 (March, 1953), pp. 201–205.

Comparative Tariffs and Trade: The United States and the European Common Market, Committee for Economic Development, Supplementary Paper 14, 2 vols., New York, March, 1963.

Deutsch, Harold C.: "America's Stake in Western Europe," Science Research Associates, Chicago, 1959.

Deutsch, Karl W.: "Political Community at the International Level," New York, 1954.

————: "Towards Western European Integration: An Interim Assessment," *Journal of International Affairs*, Vol. 16 (1962), No. 1, pp. 89–101.

Diebold, William, Jr.: "Britain, the Six and the World Economy," *Foreign Affairs*, Vol. 40 (1962), pp. 407–418.

————: "Theory and Practice of European Integration," *World Politics*, Vol. 11, No. 4 (July, 1959), pp. 621–628.

Donner, A. M.: "The Court of Justice of the European Communities," *The Record of the Association of the Bar of the City of New York*, Vol. 17, No. 5 (May, 1962), pp. 232–244.

Dougherty, James E.: "European Deterrence and Atlantic Unity," *Orbis*, Vol. 6, No. 3 (Fall, 1962), pp. 371–421.

Dwarkadas, R.: "The European Atomic Energy Community: Organization and Adminis-tration," *Indian Journal of Public Administration*, Vol. 5, No. 2 (April–June, 1959), pp. 186–198.

Efron, Reuben, and Allan S. Nanes: "The Common Market and Euratom Treaties: Supranationality and the Integration of Europe," *International and Comparative Law Quarterly*, Vol. 6, No. 4 (October, 1957), pp. 670–684.

Feld, W.: "Civil Service of the European Communities: Legal and Political Aspects," *Journal of Public Law*, Vol. 12 (1963), pp. 68–85.

————: "Court of Justice of the European Communities: Emerging Political Power," *Tulane Law Review*, Vol. 38 (December, 1963), pp. 53–80.

Franks, Lord: "Cooperation Is Not Enough," *Foreign Affairs*, Vol. 41, No. 1 (October, 1962), pp. 24–35.

Fulda, Carl H.: "Significance of the Anti-trust Laws of the European Economic Com-munity," *Oklahoma Law Review*, Vol. 16 (November, 1963), pp. 415–424.

Gaudet, Michel: "Euratom," edited by Herbert S. Marks, *Law and Administration*,

Vols. 1 and 2, *Progress in Nuclear Energy,* Series 10, New York (1959), pp. 140–179.

Goermahtigh, John: "European Coal and Steel Community," *International Conciliation,* No. 503 (May, 1955), pp. 343–408.

———: "European Integration," New York, *International Conciliation,* (1953), pp. 49–104.

Gordon, Lincoln: "Economic Regionalism Reconsidered," *World Politics,* Vol. 13, No. 2 (January, 1961), pp. 231–253.

———: "Myth and Reality in European Integration," *Yale Review,* Vol. 45, No. 1 (September, 1955), pp. 80–103.

———: "Nato and European Integration," *World Politics,* Vol. 10, No. 2 (January, 1958), pp. 219–231.

———: "The Organization for European Economic Cooperation," *International Organization,* Vol. 10, No. 1 (February, 1956), pp. 1–11.

Haas, Ernst B.: "The Challenge of Regionalism," *International Organization,* Vol. 12, No. 4 (Autumn, 1958), pp. 440–458.

———: *Consensus Formation in the Council of Europe,* Berkeley, Calif., 1960.

———: "International Integration: The European and Universal Process," *International Organization,* Vol. 15 (1961), pp. 366–392.

———: "Persistent Themes in Atlantic and European Unity," *World Politics,* Vol. 10, No. 4 (July, 1958), pp. 614–628.

———: "Regionalism, Functionalism and Universal Organization," *World Politics,* Vol. 8, No. 2 (January, 1956), pp. 238–263.

———: "The Uniting of Europe: Political, Social and Economic Forces, 1950–1957," Stanford, Calif., 1958.

——— and P. H. Merkl: "Parliamentarians against Ministers: The Case of Western European Union," *International Organization,* Vol. 14, No. 1 (Winter, 1960), pp. 37–59.

Hahn, Hugo J.: "Control under the EURATOM Compact," *American Journal of Comparative Law,* Vol. 7, No. 1 (Winter, 1958), pp. 23–46.

Hallstein, Walter: "NATO and the European Economic Community," *Orbis,* Vol. 6, No. 4 (Winter, 1963), pp. 564–574.

Hartley, Livingston: "On the Political Integration of the Atlantic Community," *Orbis,* Vol. 6, No. 4 (Winter, 1963), pp. 645–655.

Hasbrouck, Jan: "Common Market at the Grass Roots," *New York Herald Tribune,* Paris, June 7, 1960, and June 9, 1960.

Hay, Peter: "Federal Jurisdiction of the Common Market Court," *American Journal of Comparative Law,* Vol. 12 (Winter, 1963), pp. 21–40.

Hoffmann, Stanley H.: "Problems of Atlantic Partnership," *The Harvard Review,* Vol. 1 (Fall, 1962), pp. 16–25.

Hurtig, Serge: "The European Common Market," *International Conciliation,* No. 517 (March, 1958), pp. 321–381.

"Italy and the Common Market and the Free Trade Area," *The World Today,* Vol. 14 (April, 1958), pp. 152–162.

Kissinger, Henry A.: "Strains on the Alliance," *Foreign Affairs,* Vol. 41, No. 2 (January, 1963), pp. 261–285.

Kitzinger, U. W.: "Europe: The Six and the Seven," *International Organization,* Vol. 14, No. 1 (Winter, 1960), pp. 20–36.

Knorr, Klaus E.: "EURATOM and American Policy," A Conference Report, Center of International Studies, Princeton, N.J., 1956.

Kohnstamm, Max: "The European Community and Its Role in the World," John Findley Green Foundation Lectures, Westminster College, Fulton, Mo., 1963.

———: "Europe and Atoms for Power," in *Atoms for Power,* New York, 1957, pp. 140–149.

Kreinin, Mordechai E.: "European Integration and American Trade," *American Economic Review,* Vol. 49, No. 4 (September, 1959), pp. 615–627.

Lee, Linda K.: "European Integration and the Protection of Human Rights," *George Washington Law Review,* Vol. 31 (October, 1962), pp. 959–976.

Marjolin, Robert: "Prospects for the European Common Market," *Foreign Affairs,* Vol. 36, No. 1 (October, 1957), pp. 131–142.

McKesson, John A.: "The Schuman Plan," *Political Science Quarterly,* Vol. 67, No. 1 (March, 1962), pp. 18–35.

Miksche, F. O.: "The Case for Nuclear Sharing," *Orbis,* Vol. 5, No. 3 (Fall, 1961), pp. 292–305.

Monnet, Jean: "Peace Needs Quick Steps to Atlantic Union," *Freedom and Union,* Vol. 16, Nos. 7, 8 (July–August, 1961), pp. 12–16.

Moore, Ben T.: *EURATOM: The American Interest in the European Atomic Energy Community,* New York, 1958.

"A New Europe," *Daedalus,* Vol. 93, No. 1 (Winter, 1964), 576 pp., entire issue.

Nitze, Paul H.: "Collective Defense and the Atomic Community," *The Harvard Review,* Vol. 1, No. 1 (Fall, 1962), pp. 26–30.

North, Robert C., et al.: "The Integrative Functions of Conflict," *Journal of Conflict Resolution,* Vol. IV (1960), pp. 355–374.

Reuter, Paul: "Juridical and Institutional Aspects of the European Regional Communities," *Law and Contemporary Problems,* Vol. 26, No. 3 (Summer, 1961), pp. 381–399. (Part of a symposium on European regional communities.)

Riesenfeld, Stefan A.: "The Anti-trust Laws of the Common Market Countries," *Proceedings of the American Society of International Law,* Washington, 1962, pp. 27–39.

———: "The Decisions of the Court of Justice of the European Communities," *American Journal of International Law,* Vol. 56, No. 3 (July, 1962), pp. 724–728.

Schmitt, Hans A.: "The European Coal and Steel Community: Operations of the First European Antitrust Law, 1952–1958," *The Business History Review,* Vol. 38, No. 1 (Spring, 1964), pp. 102–122.

Schokking, Jan J., and Nels Anderson: "Observations on the European Integration Process," *Journal of Conflict Resolution,* Vol. IV (1960), pp. 385–410.

Stein, Eric: "Assimilation of National Laws as a Function of European Integration," *American Journal of International Law,* Vol. 58 (January, 1964), pp. 1–40.

———: "Common Market and the Free Trade Areas as Examples of Economic Regionalism," *American Society of International Law Proceedings,* Vol. 54 (1960), pp. 153–160.

———: "Developing European Regional Markets," in *Conference on Legal Problems in International Trade and Investment,* New York (1962), pp. 113–129.

————: "An Emergent Legal Community: The Common Market Countries' Plans for Harmonization of Law: A General View of Plans and Prospects," *American Journal of Comparative Law*, Vol. 9, No. 2 (Spring, 1960), pp. 351–358.

————: "European Coal and Steel Community: The Beginning of Its Judicial Process," *Columbia Law Review*, Vol. 55 (November, 1955), pp. 985–999.

————: "The European Parliamentary Assembly: Techniques of Emerging 'Political Control'," *International Organization*, Vol. XIII (1959), pp. 233–254.

———— (ed.): "The Court of Justice of the European Coal and Steel Community, 1954–1957," *American Journal of International Law*, Vol. 51, No. 4 (October, 1957), pp. 821–829.

Wilcox, Francis O., and H. Field Haviland, Jr. (eds.): "The Atlantic Community: Progress and Prospects," *International Organization*, Vol. 17, No. 3 (Summer, 1963), pp. 521–827.

Zellentin, Gerda: "The Economic and Social Committee," *Journal of Common Market Studies*, Vol. 1 (1962), pp. 22–28.

Index

Index

Abs, Herman J., 443

Abyssinia, 81

Academy of Science, U.S.S.R., 590

Acheson, Dean, 419, 666, 668

Act of Settlement, Great Britain, 14, 144

Act of Union with Scotland, Great Britain, 14

Action Française, 197

Action Group of Independent Germans, 441

Adams, Sherman, 456

Aden, 171

Adenauer, Konrad, 222, 366, 407, 411–412, 415–424, 429–431, 436–437, 439, 441, 444, 451, 453, 455–456, 465, 467, 474–475, 665–666, 682–683, 715

Adjubei, Alexei, 562

Afghanistan, 512

African Democratic Rally, 218

Agricultural production cooperatives, East Germany, 497

Agriculture of Soviet Union, 526–527, 539, 577–581

Albania, 646, 728

Albert, Prince, 70

Albert of Ansbach, 371

Alexander II, 512

Alexander III, 512, 515

Alexsandrov, G. F., 590–591

Algeria, 182–183, 203, 211–219, 225, 228, 237, 239, 245–246, 259–260, 267, 270, 273, 275, 289, 295, 300–301, 304, 312–313, 346–347, 356, 362, 683

All-German Bloc (GB/BHE) (Refugee party), 439–440

All-Union Central Council of Trade Unions (VTsSPS), 573

All-Union Leninist Communist League of Youth (*see* Comsomol)

Allied control of Germany, 366, 391, 402–405, 407, 484–485

American policy toward, 393, 395–397, 402–404

British policy toward, 393, 397, 402–404

French policy toward, 392–393, 397, 402–404

with local government, 486–489

Soviet policy toward, 392–393, 396–397, 402–403, 410

zones of occupation in, 392–395, 397–398, 402–403

Allied Control Council, 397, 400, 489

Allied occupation of Russia, 521

Alsace-Lorraine, 255

American colonies, 166–167

Amery, L. S., 170

Ancien régime, 185–186, 347

Andreyev, Andrei, 579

Anglo-Soviet treaty, 610

Anne, Queen, 14

Antier, Paul, 270

Antifascist Committees, 409

Anti-Semitism, 386, 389–390, 586–587

ANZAC forces, 167

Apparentement, 210, 224

Appropriation Act, Great Britain, 129

Aristotle, 545

Armand, Louis, 723

Army High Command, Germany, 377–379

Army Order No. 1, 519

Arnold, Karl, 415, 436

Arzhak, Nikolai (Yuli Daniel), 593

Asquith, Herbert, 18, 34, 72, 79–80, 135

Assemblée Nationale (*see* National Assembly, France)

Aswan Dam, 49

Atlantic partnership, 2, 657–658, 693

Atomic Energy Commission, United States, 725

Attlee, Clement, 39–44, 46–48, 50, 59, 64–65, 71, 74, 77, 80–82, 87, 93, 105, 675

Attorney General, Great Britain, 92, 149

Aube, l', 204, 255, 282–283

Auriol, Vincent, 217, 243, 247, 291

Aurore, l', 283

Australia, 132, 166–168, 170–172, 175

Austria, 93, 254, 389, 534

decline of, 370–371, 373

and European cooperation, 675, 677, 700

rivalry of, with Prussia, 373

Austrian-Hungarian Empire, 378

Austrian People's party, 415

Axelrod, Pavel, 515

Bacon, Paul, 257

Bagehot, Walter, 2, 4, 22, 70, 73–74, 108, 113, 119, 136

Bagirov, M., 537

Baldwin, Stanley, 16, 25, 37–40, 70, 81, 89, 168
Balkans, 403, 534
Ball, George, 666
Baltic states, 523, 531, 533
Bank of England, 102
Bank of France, 306
Bank of Rothschild, 232
Barangé Act of 1951, 245
Barbu, Marcel, 233
Barghoorn, Frederick C., 507
Barrès, Auguste Maurice, 264
Barzel, Fritz, 475
Barzel, Rainer, 422
Baudissin, Wolf von, 467
Baumel, Jacques, 276
Baumgartner, Josef, 414
Bavaria, 421, 424, 478, 484–485
Bavarian party (BP), 440
Bavarian People's party (BVP), 380, 414
Bayerische Volkspartei (*see* Bavarian People's party)
Bayernpartei (*see* Bavarian party)
Beaconsfield, Lord (*see* Disraeli)
Beerhall *Putsch*, 386
Belgian Christian Social party, 415
Belgium, 44, 337, 403, 429
   and European cooperation, 660, 662, 665–667, 675, 682–684, 687, 689, 697, 701, 704–706, 713, 724, 729–730, 738
   political parties of, 254, 260, 415
Belgrade Conference on Navigation on the River Danube, 642
Benjamin, Hilde, 498
Berg, Fritz, 443
Beria, Lavrenti, 530, 534, 536–539, 561, 566, 583, 620
Berlin, 540, 649–650
   blockade of, 416, 434, 489, 728, 730
   government of, 488–489
   wall of, 419, 491
Bernanos, Georges, 204
Besant, Annie, 35
Bevan, Aneurin, 40, 45, 48, 50, 62, 77, 115
Beveridge, Lord, 45
Bevin, Ernest, 74, 665, 675, 729
Bidault, Georges, 201, 204, 255, 259–260, 265–266, 668, 675
Bill of Rights, Great Britain, 14, 22
Birmingham Liberal Association, 33

Bismarck, Otto von, 192, 373–376, 384, 396, 410
Black Reichswehr, 381
Blackstone, Sir William, 140, 152
Blank, Theodor, 421, 467
Blanqui, August, 195
Blücher, Franz, 436
Blum, Léon, 194, 197–198, 202, 204, 211, 243, 306, 311
Board of the Budget, France, 310
Board of Trade, Great Britain, 48, 78, 92, 105
Bodin, Jean, 11
Boeckler, Hans, 441
Bolshevik Central Committee, 519
   (*See also* Communist party, in Soviet Union)
Bolsheviks, 516, 519–521, 524, 528–530, 532, 554, 570, 581, 586, 605
Bonaparte, Louis, 203
Bonapartists, 192, 221
Bonn Treaty (Petersberg Protocol of November 22, 1949), 405
Boulanger, General Georges, 203
Bourdet, Claude, 278
Bourgès-Maunoury, Maurice, 212, 247
Bracton, Henry, 140
Brandt, Willy, 425, 431–435, 438
Brauer, Max, 431
Brentano, Heinrich von, 416–417, 420
Brest-Litovsk, Peace of, 377–378, 521
Brezhnev, Leonid, 434, 543–544, 558, 565, 568, 580, 588–589, 593, 651, 655–656
Briand, Aristide, 662
Bright, John, 33
British Army of the Rhine, 176
British Broadcasting Corporation, 100–102, 201
British Chambers of Commerce, Association of, 66–67
British Commonwealth party, 34
British Electricity Authority, 101
British Employers' Confederation, 67
British European Airways, 102
British Medical Association, 67
British North American Act, 167, 172
British Overseas Airways Corporation, 102
British Socialist party, 34
British Supply Council, 666
British Union of Fascists, 121
Brodsky, Osip, 592

Bronstein, Leon (Leib) Davydovich (*see* Trotsky, Leon)

Brosio, Manlio, 731

Brougham, Lord, 153

Brown, Colonel Clifton, 115

Brown, George, 52, 76, 88

Bruce, David K., 668

Brüning, Heinrich, 382–383

Brussels Treaty of March 17, 1948, 675, 730

Brutelle, Georges, 248, 250

Bucharest peace treaty, 377–378

Budapest uprising, 540

Budënny, General, 522

Bukharin, Nikolai, 524–525, 530

Bulganin, Nikolai, 536, 538–539, 542–543, 566, 569, 583, 587, 618

Bulgaria, 645, 647, 728

Bund der Heimatvertriebenen und Entrechteten (BHE) (*see* Refugee party)

Bundesrat, German Federal Republic, 373, 376, 455, 468, 473, 480
    legislation by, 468–470
    membership of, 451, 460, 465, 467–468, 489
    organization of, 453, 467–468
    relation of, to *Länder* government, 449–451, 468
    role of, 467–468

Bundestag, German Federal Republic, 412, 422, 424, 441, 453, 463, 468, 471–472, 486, 715
    committees of, 464–466
    Council of Elders of, 463–464, 469
    and courts, 478, 480–482
    dissolution of, 453–455, 471–472
    election to, 460–462, 489
    Fraktionen in, 464–465
    legislation of, 468–471
    organization of, 422, 453, 462–464
    relation of, to executive (President and Chancellor), 453–454, 456, 468, 473–475
    in state of legislative emergency, 472
    and vote of confidence, 468, 471–472

Bundesverband der deutschen Industrie (Federation of German Industries), 443

Bundesverfassungsgericht (Federal Constitutional Court) (*see* Law and justice, in Germany)

Bureau of Administrative Affairs, Soviet Union, 616

Burke, Edmund, 32

Burma, 169

Butler, R. A., 46, 52, 87

Byelorussia, 598

Byng, Lord, 72

Cabinet, in France, 197, 218, 229, 232, 302, 304, 322
    Civil Service Office of, 299, 310
    Communists in, 303
    instability of, 211–212, 288, 299–300
    and Interministerial Council, 303
    and Minister of State, 247
    relation of, to legislature, 194, 210–213, 288, 297
  in Germany, 455, 474
    Chancellor leadership of, 453–456
    relation of, to legislature, 468, 473–475
  in Great Britain, 15–16, 22, 87–88, 93, 129
    advantages of, 80–81
    committees of, 86, 88
    composition of, 23, 86–88
    dissolution of, 80
    functions of, 83–85, 89–90
    "inner," 85–86
    ministers of, 24, 75–78, 81–82
    origin and development of, 74, 76–77, 85
    and Privy Council, 74, 85
    relation of, to legislature, 16–17, 22, 25, 76, 79, 83
    relation of, to monarch, 85–86, 88
    "sinecure" offices in, 77–78, 93
    War, 41–42, 45, 85, 167
  in Soviet Union (*see* Council of Ministers)

Cabinet secretariat, Great Britain, 74, 82

Cabinet system, Great Britain, 15–16, 80–85

Cagoulards, 197

Callahan, James, 52

Campbell-Bannerman, Sir Henry, 34

Canada, 16, 50, 166–172, 730, 732

Carbonnages de France (National Coal Authority), 307

Carew Hunt, R. N., 546

Castle, Barbara, 55

Catholicism, 13–14, 156, 187, 194, 245, 254–259, 264, 266, 279–282, 329, 371, 412, 414

Catroux, Georges, 246

Ce Soir, 283

Censure motion, France, 296

Center party, Germany (*Zentrum*), 380, 382–383, 412, 416
Central African Federation, 175
Central Electricity Board, 100–101
Central Gas Council, 101
Central Land Board, 157
Central Midwives Board, 155
Central Statistical Administration, 616
Centre Démocratique (*see* Democratic Center)
Centre national d'Études judiciares (National Center of Judicial Studies), 330–332
Ceylon, 169–171
Chaban-Delmas, Jacques, 273, 275–276, 318
Chadwick, Edwin, 154
Challe, Maurice, 231
Chamber of Deputies, France (*see* National Assembly, France)
Chamber of States (*Länderkammer*), East Germany, 495
Chamberlain, Joseph, 33, 151
Chamberlain, Neville, 40–41, 76, 79, 89, 151, 533
Chambord, Count, 192
Chancellor, of Duchy of Lancaster, 87, 93
   of Exchequer, 7, 18, 37, 54, 74, 87
   of Germany, 418–419, 425, 452–475
Charlemagne, 6, 140, 369
Charles, Prince (of Wales), 70
Charles I, 13, 69
Charles II, 13
Charles X, 190, 192
Chatenet, Pierre, 723
Cheka (*see* MVD–MGB)
China, 53, 66, 362, 512, 534, 541, 600, 646–651, 655, 740
Christian Democratic party, France, 202, 260
Christian Democratic Union (CDU), organization of, 414–416, 420
   policy of, 414–416, 422, 430
Christian Democratic Union–Christian Social Union (CDU/CSU), 407, 410–425, 431, 444, 455, 462, 465, 475–476, 486, 492
   electoral strength of, 413, 418, 423, 432–433, 436–437
Christian Federation of Labor (CFTC), 196, 259
Christian Labor Movement (*Christliche Gewerkschaftsbewegung*, CGB), 442
Christian People's party (*Christliche Volkspartei*, CVP), 441

Christliche Gewerkschaftsbewegung, CGB (Christian Labor Movement), 442
Christliche Volkspartei, CVP (Christian People's party), 441
Christlichdemokratische Union–Christlichsoziale Union, CDU/CSU (*see* Christian Democratic Union–Christian Social Union)
Church of England, 92, 128, 152
Churchill, Winston, 41–46, 48–49, 54, 58, 64, 69–71, 74, 76, 78, 85–88, 102, 115–117, 136–137, 200, 222, 265, 665, 670–671, 675. 731
Civil Service, in France, 299–301, 303–305, 342, 349, 351
   classes in, 310–311
   power of, 309
   rights of, 309–310
   training for, 311
   in Germany, 373, 460, 483
      character of, 458
      classes in, 459
      denazification of, 458
      history of, 372, 374
      under Nazis, 458
      of Weimar Republic, 458
   in Great Britain, 73, 93–100, 109–110
      in administration of nationalized industries, 100–104
      classes in, 97–100
      examinations in, 96–97
      by Treasury, control of, 95–96
      and Whitley Councils, 94, 98
Civil Service Act of 1946, France, 310
Civil Service Act of 1953, Germany, 459
Civil Service Commission, Great Britain, 89, 94, 96
Civil Service Office, France, 310
Clemenceau, Georges, 264, 377
Club Jean Moulin, 278
Clynes, John R., 39
Coal and Steel Community (Schuman Plan) (*see* European Coal and Steel Community)
Coalition government, Great Britain, 34, 41, 82, 118
Cobden, Richard, 33
Code Napoléon, 329–330
Coke, Lord (Sir Edward), 12, 140, 330
Colin, André, 255

Collectivization, Soviet Union, 526–527, 577–581

Colombey-les-deux-Églises, 216–217, 232, 247, 273

Columbo Plan, 175

COMECON (Council of Mutual Economic Assistance), 648

Cominform (Communist Information Bureau), 534, 643, 646–647, 729

Cominterm (Communist International), 524, 534, 643–646, 729

Commission for the Verification of Accounts in Public Enterprise, 308

Committee of Imperial Defence, Great Britain, 78, 85, 87

Committee of Ministers (*see* Council of Europe)

Committee on Ministers" Powers, Great Britain, 105

Committee of National Liberation, France, 205, 350

Committee on Nuclear Disarmament, Great Britain, 67

Committee for Party and State Control, U.S.S.R., 620

Committee of Public Safety, France, 189, 215–216

Committee for State Security, U.S.S.R., 538

Common Assembly (*see* European Economic Community)

Common law, 6–7, 10, 139–143, 332

Common Market (*see* European Economic Community)

Commonwealth, British, 13, 50, 87, 168, 172–173, 175

  acquisition of, 165–166, 168–171

  British colonial administration of, 165–166

  and British Empire, 166–168

  and "condominia," 174

  and Crown Colonies, 171, 174

  and desire for self-government, 166–167, 170–171, 175

  foreign relations of, 4, 166–167, 172–173

  nature of, 165, 168

  and "protectorates," 174

  relations of, with Britain, 166, 172–173

  and trust territories, 174–175

Commonwealth Conferences, 170, 173

Communal agriculture, Russia, 526–527, 539, 577–581

Communist Information Bureau (*see* Cominform)

Communist International (*see* Comintern)

Communist League, 643

Communist party, in East Germany, 492–495

  in Eastern Europe, 510, 542

  in France (PCF), 194, 196–198, 201–207, 219, 235–244, 248, 250, 254, 258, 261–262, 267, 283–284, 314–315, 318

  and Algerian crisis, 216, 219

  East-West orientation of, 224–225

  electoral strength of, 227, 229–230, 237–238, 240, 242, 249–250, 253, 267, 269–270, 272, 278, 316

  in Fourth Republic, 210–212, 216, 239

  historical development of, 196, 237–238

  and labor, 196, 238, 279–281

  organization of, 241

  post-liberation, 224–225

  program of, 224, 237, 242, 332

  and religious question, 224, 245

  in Resistance, 202, 205, 239

  view of, toward European cooperation, 224, 308, 672, 682

  in Germany (KPD), 336, 387, 410, 440–441, 449, 644

  dissolution of, 448, 482

  electoral strength of, 381–383

  in Great Britain, 30, 38, 40, 42, 47, 52, 95

  in Soviet Union, 493, 507, 509–510, 520, 524, 550, 575–577, 600, 602, 607–608, 613, 637

  and bureaucracy, 554–556, 587–590

  Central Auditing Commission of, 569

  Central Committee of, 219, 539–540, 542–543, 557, 562–564, 567–569, 582, 589, 591, 616, 618

  and collective farms and party leadership, 577–581

  Committee of Party Control of, 563–564, 569–570

  congresses of, 535, 539–540, 543, 551–552, 555, 561–565, 578–579, 588, 593, 624, 648, 650

  control of foreign Communist parties by, 534, 643–645, 647–648, 655

  and culture and science, 590–594

  "democratic centralism" in, 554–556

  and forced labor, 575–577

  General Secretary of, 517, 524, 537–539, 542–543, 565, 567–568, 587, 589, 591

Communist party, in Soviet Union, and labor unions, 573–575
  membership of, 553, 559–560
  organization of, 524–525, 555, 560–563
  and Orgburo, 535, 565, 567–568
  and Politburo, 506, 535–536, 540, 543–544, 555, 563, 568, 570, 579, 582–583, 588–589, 600–601, 612, 618, 621, 636
    (*See also* Presidium of Central Committee *below*)
  political control by, of Red Army, 534, 536, 567, 581–584
  Presidium of Central Committee of, 535–537, 539, 540, 543, 556–557, 564–570, 587–588, 593, 619, 622, 631
  propaganda of, 527, 534, 557–559, 649
  purges in, 528–533, 551, 572, 582
  and religion, 534, 584–587
  role of, 506, 510, 554
  Secretariat of, 525, 564–565, 567–568, 593, 605
  "self-criticism" in, 555–557
  theory of, 549–552, 558
  youth organizations of, 570–572
Communist Resistance Group (*Franc-Tireurs et Partisans*, FTP), 239
Comsomol, 526, 570–572, 577, 582–583, 585–586
Concentration camps, Germany, 387, 390, 398, 473, 529
Condorcet, 263
Confédération Française des Travailleurs Chrétiens (CFTC) (French Confederation of Christian Workers), 279–282
Confédération Générale de Travail (CGT) (*see* General Confederation of Labor)
Confédération Générale du Travail Unitaire (CGTU) (Unified General Confederation of Labor), 279–280
Congress of Vienna, 373
Connally, Tom, 730
Conrad of Masovia, Duke, 371
Conservative party, Great Britain, 30, 33–34, 37–41, 43, 51–52, 54, 56, 108, 134
  central office of, 61
  electoral strength of, 29, 42–43, 46–51, 57–58, 61
  organization of, 46, 59–61, 75–76, 110
  in Parliament, 58–59
  postwar growth of, 46–47

Conservative party, program and policy of, 42, 46, 50, 55, 57, 63–64
  return to power of, 47–52
  support of, from business, 28
  view of European cooperation of, 56
  view of nationalization of, 177
Conservative Workingmen's Clubs, Great Britain, 60
Consolidated Fund, Great Britain, 118, 129
Constant, Benjamin, 223
Constituent Assembly, of France, 322, 338, 348
  of Soviet Union, 519–520
Constitutional Council, France, 292, 294, 321, 324–325, 339–340
Constitutions, of East Germany, 495–496
  of France, 185–186, 189–192, 289
    amendment procedure of, 189, 198, 217, 293
    early development of, 185–188
    of Fifth Republic, 183, 191, 227–229, 272, 291–295, 301, 306, 348
    of Fourth Republic, 191–192, 206–208, 210, 290–293, 305, 325–326
    of 1791, 186, 188, 194
    of 1793, 188, 194
    of 1848, 190, 194
    of 1870, 191
    of 1946, 296, 319, 322–324, 331, 337, 339, 611
    of 1958, 274, 288, 290–291, 294–297, 299, 302, 305, 312, 316–317, 319, 322–324, 326–328, 331, 337, 339
    referenda, 218–219, 227–228
    of Second Republic, 190, 212
    of Third Republic, 191–194, 198, 208, 210, 290
    Vichy, 203
    of Year III, 188–189
    of Year VIII, 188–189, 191
  of Germany, 373, 375, 379, 418, 469
    amending procedure for, 470
    and civil rights 446–449, 479
    and dissolution of *Bundestag*, 471
    drafting of, 404–407
    and executive power, 452–460
    and federalism, 449–452
    interpretation of, 481–483
    and investigating committees, 465–466
    and judiciary, 475–476
    and *Länder* government, 485

Constitutions, of Great Britain, and customs
    and conventions, 2, 4, 21–26
  flexibility of, 20–26
  guiding principles of, 25–26
  and law and convention, 22
  monarch and, 71–72
  origins of, 3–26
  of the Irish Free State, 177
  of Soviet Union, 514–515, 552
    and civil rights, 633–639
    and Council of Ministers, 538, 565, 569,
      576–577, 587–589, 599–600, 609–610,
      614, 616, 618–619
    and court system, 627, 630
    and elections, 606–609, 631
    and federalism, 595–598
    of 1924, 612, 643
    of 1936, 528, 554, 596, 598–599, 601–
      602, 604–607, 609–611, 614, 616, 630,
      633–635, 637–639, 641
    and Presidium of the Supreme Soviet,
      539, 542–543, 600, 606, 609–612, 616,
      629–630
    and Soviets, 604–605, 612–613
    and Supreme Soviet of U.S.S.R., 606,
      609–611, 620, 653
Consultative Assembly (see Council of Eu-
    rope)
Control of Engagement Order, Great Britain,
    91
Convention Parliament, 13
Cooperative Union, Great Britain, 67
Corréze, 238
Corrupt and Illegal Practices Prevention Act
    of 1883, Great Britain, 111
Corsica, 216
Coste-Floret, Paul, 207, 312
Cot, Pierre, 339
Coty, René, 217, 267, 291
Coudenhove-Kalergi, Richard, 663
Council of Elders, Germany, 463–464,
    469
Council of Europe, 430, 673–680
  Committee of Ministers of, 675–677, 680
  Communist representation in, lack of, 676
  Consultative Assembly of, 675–680, 688,
    701
  on human rights, 679–680
  member nations of, 675–676
  origin and role of, 675–680

Council of Experts, Germany, 473
Council of German Prime Ministers, 399–400,
    403
Council of Ministers, of France, 292, 317, 349,
    354
  of Soviet Union, 538, 565, 587
    administrative pattern of, 619–620
    organization of, 610, 618–619
    power of, 569, 576, 609, 616, 618–620,
      622, 630
Council of Mutual Economic Assistance
    (COMECON), 648
Council of People's Commissars, of Soviet
    Union, 520, 605
  of Weimar Republic, 379
Council of the Republic, France, 207, 210,
    297, 312
Council of State, France, 299, 309–310, 321–
    322, 341–342, 350, 353, 479
Councils of Workers and Soldiers, Weimar
    Republic, 379
Cour des Comptes (see General Accounting
    Office)
Cousins, Frank, 55, 62, 77
Couve de Murville, Maurice, 218, 232, 311,
    358, 716
Crimea, 192, 512, 522
Cripps, Sir Stafford, 39–40, 47, 74, 117, 141
Croix de Feu, 197
Cromwell, Oliver, 13
Crossman, Richard H. S., 52, 55, 77
Crown of Great Britain and Commonwealth,
    and Civil List, 72
  control of, 8
  and monarch, and opposition, 73
    and Parliament, 122
    power and influence of, 15, 70–74
    and Prime Minister, 70–72
    reputation of, 70
    resignation of, and succession, 14, 70
    role of, 71–72
    as symbol, 68–70, 73
Cuban crisis, 229, 542, 650–651, 655, 737
Cuno, Wilhelm, 381
Curia Regis, 7, 9
Current Events Hour, Germany, 474
Curzon, Lord, 16, 58
Curzon line, 392
Cyprus, 166, 675, 677
Czechoslovakia, 281, 645, 647–649, 728–729

Daladier, Édouard, 197–198, 200, 533
Dalton, Hugh, 81
Daniel, Yuli, 593
Déat, Marcel, 198
Debré, Michel, 218, 270, 273–277, 298, 311, 326, 328, 682
Decembrists, The, 537
Declaration of the Rights of Man and of the Citizen of 1789, France, 186–187, 194
Defence of the Realm Regulation, Great Britain, 121
Defense Committee, Germany, 466–467
Defferre, Gaston, 233, 235, 240, 246, 248–250, 252–254, 261, 268
De Gaulle, General Charles, 4, 51, 54, 56–57, 66, 179–180, 183–184, 200–208, 213, 215–223, 225, 227–241, 243, 247–250, 253, 258, 260–262, 265, 267–277, 281, 283, 285–286, 288, 290, 293–294, 298, 302–304, 328, 340, 356–364, 416, 420–422, 425, 651, 666, 682, 691, 700, 702–703, 709, 715–719, 723, 727, 734, 738–739
Dehler, Thomas, 436–438
Delbecque, Léon, 215
Del Bo, Dino, 685
Demichev, P. N., 593
Democratic Alliance, France, 269
Democratic Center (Centre Démocratique), 235, 262–263, 268
Democratic League of Women (Demokratischer Frauenbund Deutschlands, DFD), 493
Democratic Peasant party, Germany, 493
Democratic Union of Labor (Union Démocratique du Travail), 229, 274
Demokratischer Frauenbund Deutschlands (DFD) (Democratic League of Women), 493
Denazification policy, American, 395, 398–402
    British, 401
    French, 401
    Soviet, 401–402
Denikin, General, 522
Denmark, 373, 675, 677, 730
Dépêche de Midi, 283
Dépêche de Toulouse, 283
Deschamps, Eugène, 282
Deutsch-nationale Volkspartei (German Nationalist People's party), 380

Deutsche Angestelltengewerkschaft (DAG), 442
Deutsche Beamtenbund (DBB), 442
Deutsche Demokratische Republik (DDR) (see specific institutions of East Germany)
Deutsche Friedensunion (DFU) (German Peace Union), 440–441
Deutsche Reichspartei (DRD) (German Reich party), 440
Deutsche Volkspartei (German People's party), 380
Deutscher Bauernverband (German Farmers' Federation), 443
Deutscher Gewerkschaftsbund (DGB) (German Trade Union Federation), 412, 441–442
Dien Bien Phu, 265
Dillon Round (see General Agreement on Tariffs and Trade)
Disraeli, Benjamin (Lord Beaconsfield), 1, 4, 16, 33, 41
Dissolution, of Bundestag, Germany, 453–455, 471–472
    of House of Commons, Great Britain, 80, 122, 293
    of National Assembly, France, 267, 293–294, 317, 328
Doenitz, Admiral Karl, 391–392
Döring, Wolfgang, 436
Dostoyevsky, Fyodor, 513
Douglas-Home, Sir Alec (Lord Home), 52–55, 58, 71–72, 75, 79, 112
Dru, Gilbert, 255–256
Duchet, Roger, 270
Dudintsev, 591
Dufhues, Herman, 414, 420
Dulles, John Foster, 419, 666
Duma, 514–515, 518–519, 605
Dunkirk Treaty of Mutual Assistance, 729
Durdenevski, V. N., 642
Dzhugashvili, Iosif Vissarionovich (see Stalin)

East Germany, 366, 647, 655
    government structure of, 493–498
    migration from, into West Germany, 419, 439, 490
    political developments in, 490–491
    political structure of, 492–493
    and West Germany, today and tomorrow, 499–503

East India Company, 166, 169

Eberlein, 644

Ebert, Friedrich, 379

Écho d'Alger, 215

Economic Council, Soviet Union, 621

Eden, Sir Anthony, 49–50, 58, 76, 79, 81, 93

Education Act of 1944, Great Britain, 45, 64, 156

Edward I, 9–10

Edward II, 140–141

Edward III, 10

Edward VII, 69, 71–72

Edward VIII (Duke of Windsor) 70, 123

Egypt, 49–50, 81, 721

Ehrenburg, Ilya, 591

Einsiedel, Otto von, 396

Eisenhower, Dwight D., 237, 419, 456, 665–666, 733, 738

El Alamein, 390

Elections, in France, of Council of the Republic, 299, 312

   and debates, 184

   and draft constitution, 207–208

   and electoral process, 312–316

   and electoral system, 316, 328

   and executive order of 1958, 313, 315

   law on, 247, 267, 270, 272, 301

   of National Assembly, 316, 717

   postwar, 206

   radio and television in, use of, 184, 233, 249, 279

   results of, 184, 192, 219, 225–227, 229–231, 234–236, 240, 244, 246–250, 252, 254–255, 261–262, 268–270, 272–275, 278–279, 281, 283–284, 302, 312–313, 328, 359, 717

   voter qualification in, 312–313

  in Germany, and electoral process, 460–462

   law on, 462

   results of, 411, 418–419, 422–423, 430, 432–433, 437, 489

   in Berlin, 427–435

   in 1933, 387

   of September 19, 1965, reproduction of ballot for, 461

   "sixty-forty" law on, 460

  in Great Britain, and campaigns, 109–110

   expenses for, 111–113

   candidates in, 109–112

   and constituencies, 108–109

   recent results of, 110

Elections, in Great Britain, voter qualifications in, 108–109

  in Soviet Union, 519–520, 606–609

Elizabeth II, 69–71, 73

Elysée Palace, 298, 328

Enabling Act of 1933, Germany, 387, 473

Engels, Friedrich, 515, 547–549, 551, 590, 595, 643

Equal Franchise Act of 1928, Great Britain, 18

Erhard, Ludwig, 366, 415–425, 432–433, 437–439, 454–457, 474–475, 715

Erler, Fritz, 430–435, 475

Estaing, Valéry Giscard de, 229, 231, 235–236, 262–263, 271

Estates General, France, 185–186, 188

Estonia, 522, 531, 533–534, 597

European Advisory Commission, Germany, 392, 403

European Assembly, 687

  (*See also* European Parliament)

European Atomic Energy Community (EURATOM), 275, 357–358, 502, 659, 673, 687

  Commission of (EURATOM Commission), 691, 700, 713, 719, 723, 725

  and Common Assembly, 687

  Consultative Committee for Nuclear Research of, 723

  Council of Ministers of, 722

  and Court of Justice, 687

  historical development of, 210, 231, 672, 720–722

  and Inter-Executive Energy Committee, 713

  organization of, 684, 696

  Scientific and Technical Committee of, 723

  and Treaty of Rome, 720

European Coal and Steel Community (Schuman Plan), 4, 184, 209, 259, 275, 357–358, 405–406, 429–430, 502, 659, 669, 673, 681–693, 716

  authority of, 688–691

  Common Assembly of, 684, 687–688, 701

  coordinating committees of, 687

  Council of Ministers, Special, 684, 687–689, 691, 696, 702, 722

  Court of Justice of, 684–686, 688–689, 700–701

  High Authority of, 674, 683–689, 693–694, 698, 700, 702–703, 713, 719

  institutions of, 684–688

European Coal and Steel Community (Schuman Plan), and Inter-Executive Energy Committee, 713
and International Ruhr Authority, 682
membership of, 682
organization of, 696
origin of, 668, 670–672, 678, 681, 684, 714
role of, 669, 685–688, 694
and Treaty of Paris, 684, 686–688, 690, 694, 703
European Commission of Human Rights, 679–680
European Convention for the Protection of Human Rights and Fundamental Freedoms, 679–680
European Court of Justice, 679–680, 696, 700–701
European Defense Community, 48, 184, 275, 362, 405, 416, 467, 670–672, 689, 692–693, 721, 730
European Economic Community (Common Market), 4, 51–53, 56–57, 66, 176, 182–184, 231, 233, 241–242, 261, 275, 357–359, 416, 420, 502, 651
Commissions of, 659–660, 674, 691, 696–707, 709, 711–714, 716–719, 722–723
Committee of Permanent Representation of, 697–698
and Common Assembly, 687–688, 698, 701–703, 716
concept of, 692
Council of Ministers of, 659–660, 696–703, 705, 707, 711–712, 714, 716–718, 722, 739
and Court of Justice, 683, 700–701, 703
and Economic and Social Committee, 703–704
and European Investment Bank, 704
and European Social Fund, 713
evaluation of, 704–719
institutions of, 696–704
and Inter-Executive Energy Committee, 713
member states of, 660
organization of, 684
origin of, 210, 672, 693–694
policies of, agricultural, 706–710, 716–719
commercial, 610–611, 711–712
political challenge to, 695, 714–719
relation of, to Communist states, 648, 712–713

European Economic Community (Common Market), and Treaty of Rome, 672–673, 689–690, 694–696, 699, 701, 703, 705, 707, 711, 718
European Free Trade Association, 704–705
European Investment Bank, 704
European Nuclear Energy Agency, 724
European Parliament, 660, 687–688, 696, 701–704, 714, 716, 726
(See also European Atomic Energy Community, and Common Assembly; European Coal and Steel Community; European Economic Community)
European Social Charter, 678
European unity, 660, 688–689, 727–728
concepts of, 661–673, 714
historical background of, 657–660, 692
and national sovereignty under unification, 658–659
view toward, of France, 665
of Germany, 665
of Great Britain, 665
of Italy, 665
European University, 725–726
Evian Conference, 228
Evtushenko, Evginy, 592–593
Exchequer, Great Britain, 7, 18, 37, 54, 74, 87
Express, l', 233, 249, 267
Extradition Act, Great Britain, 91
Extraordinary State Commission for the Investigation of German War Crimes, 584

Fabian Society, 34–36, 61–62
Fainsod, Merle, 588
Fanfani, Amintore, 693
Faure, Edgar, 246, 266–268, 293
Faure, Maurice, 248, 262, 268, 294
Faure, Paul, 205
Fauvet, Jacques, 235, 243–244
Fechner, Max, 492
Federal Constitutional Court (see Law and justice, in Germany)
Federalism, Soviet Union, 562, 595–598, 601–603, 606, 612–613
Federation of British Industries, 66–67
Fédération de l'Education Nationale (FEN) (National Teachers Federation), 285
Fédération des Gauches (see Federation of the Left)

Federation of German Industries (*Bundesverband der deutschen Industrie*), 443
Federation of the Left (*Fédération des Gauches*) 235, 240–241, 269
  origin of, 252–253, 268
  program of, 253–254
Fédération Nationale des Syndicats des Exploitants Agricoles (National Federation of Farm Syndicates), 285
Fellowship of the New Life (*see* Fabian Society)
Ferry, Jules, 191
Feudalism, 2, 6–7, 12, 139–140, 151, 185, 195, 329, 371
Fiery Cross (*Croix de Feu*), 197, 269
Fifth Republic, France, 207, 219, 227, 235, 248, 268, 272, 281, 285–288, 292–293, 297–298, 302, 305–306, 311, 314–315, 320–321, 326–328, 338–340, 348, 352
Figaro, le, 283
Finance Act, Great Britain, 129
Financial Secretary of the Treasury, Great Britain, 90
Finland, 40, 522–523, 533–534, 582, 729
First Lord of the Treasury, Great Britain, 74, 87, 89
Fitzherbert, Sir Anthony, 140
Five-Year Plans, Soviet Union, 524–525, 527, 529, 621–624
Flandin, Pierre-Etienne, 269
Fontanet, Joseph, 249, 260
For a Lasting Peace, for a People's Democracy, 646
Fortescue, 142
Fouchet, Christian, 714
Fourth Republic, France, 206–207, 209–221, 224–225, 227, 229, 231, 236, 239–240, 243, 247, 250, 259–260, 264, 267–268, 270–271, 274, 276, 281, 284–289, 291, 294–303, 305, 309, 312, 314–315, 317–320, 326–328, 338–340, 347–348
Fox, Charles James, 32
Frachon, Benoît, 203, 280
Franc-Tireurs et Partisans (FTP) (Communist Resistance group), 239
France, and European cooperation, 660, 665, 671–673, 675–676, 679–680, 682, 684, 687–688, 690–691, 693, 696–698, 700–705, 707–710, 714–719, 721–725, 729–730, 732–734, 739–740

France, map of, 181
  (*See also* specific government institutions)
Franco, Francisco, 635
Franco-Austrian War, 192
Franco-British Economic Coordination Commission, 666
Franco-German Friendship Treaty of January 22, 1963, 416, 420, 715
Franco-Prussian War, 192
Frederick II (the Great), 371–372
Frederick William (the Great Elector), 371
Frederick William I, 371
Free Democratic Party (FDP), 423–424, 444, 454–455, 475–476
  electoral strength of, 419–420, 435–438
"Free France," 204, 220, 265, 276
Free German Committee, 396
Free German Trade Union Federation (FDGB), 493, 497
Free German Youth (*Freie deutsche Jugend,* FDJ), 493
Free Social Union (*Freisoziale Union,* FSU), 441
Freie Demokratische Partei, FDP, (*see* Free Democratic party)
Freie deutsche Gewerkschaftsbund (FDGB) (Free German Trade Union Federation), 493, 497
Freie deutsche Jugend (FDJ) (Free German Youth), 493
Freisoziale Union (FSU) (Free Social Union), 441
French African Colonies, 346–347
French army, 214–216, 228, 231, 237, 239, 247–248, 260, 357
French Center for the Study of Foreign Affairs, 739
French Commission of National Liberation, 666
French Community, 346–347
  Court of Arbitration of, 347
  Executive Council of, 347
  Senate of, 347
French Confederation of Christian Workers (*Confédération Française des Travailleurs Chrétiens,* CFTC), 279–282
French Forces of the Interior, 201
French Institute of Public Opinion Research, 277
French Overseas Territories, 346–347

French Planning Commission, 666
French Revolution, 32, 180, 183, 185–189, 199, 250, 263, 329, 347, 372, 509, 611, 652
  of 1830, 190
French Social Party, 269
French Unified Movement of Reconstruction (*Mouvement Unifié de la Renaissance Française*, MURF), 205–206
Frey, Roger, 274–276, 302
Frick, Wilhelm, 387
Frunze, Mikhail Vasilyevich, 521
Fuel and Power Ministry, Great Britain, 87
Führer (*see* Hitler)

Gaillard, Félix, 213, 215, 247, 268
Gaitskell, Hugh, 59
Galbraith, Thomas, 51
Gallois, General, 359
Gamarnik, Jan, 530, 582
Gambetta, Léon, 191, 263
Gandhi, 170
Gapon, 514
Gasperi, Alcide de, 665–666, 683
GATT (*see* General Agreement on Tariffs and Trade)
Gaullists (*see* Rally of the French People)
Gay, Francisque, 255
General Accounting Office (*Cour des Comptes*) 308, 342, 350
General Agreement on Tariffs and Trade (GATT), 660, 700, 705–708, 718–719
General Board of Health, Great Britain, 154
General Confederation of Labor (CGT), 196, 203–204, 238, 244, 279
  and Workers Force (CGT-FO), 280–282
General Electric Company, 710
General Motors Corporation, 264
George I, 15
George II, 15
George III, 15
George IV, 15, 69
George V, 69, 71–72, 136
George VI, 69, 71, 73
German Confederation of 1815, 373, 460
German Defense Commissioner, 132
German Democratic Republic (DDR) (*see* East Germany)
German Economic Commission (DWK), 494

German Farmers' Federation (*Deutscher Bauernverband*), 443
German Federal Republic, and European cooperation, 660, 662, 665, 669, 675–676, 682, 687, 691, 693, 696–698, 701, 704–705, 708–709, 711–713, 715, 719, 721, 723–724, 730–731, 733, 737, 739–740
  evaluation of postwar developments in, 366, 490–492
  map of, 367
  (*See also* specific government institutions)
German High Command, 519
"German Labor Party," 385
German Municipal Act of 1935, 484
German Nationalist People's Party (*Deutschnationale Volkspartei*), 380
German party (DP), 439–440
German Peace Union (*Deutsche Friedensunion*, DFU), 440–441
German People's party (*Deutsche Volkspartei*), 380
German rearmament, 48, 197, 241, 360, 362–363, 730–731, 740
German Reich party (*Deutsche Reichspartei*, DRP), 440
German reunification, 416–417, 429, 434, 437–438, 445, 502–503
German Trade Union Federation (*Deutscher Gewerkschaftsbund*, DGB), 412, 441–442
Germany (West and East), today and tomorrow, 499–503
  (*See also* East Germany; German Federal Republic)
Gerstenmaier, Eugen, 422
Gesamtdeutscher Block, GB/BHE (*see* Refugee party)
Gestapo, 201, 256, 529
Ghana, 171
Gibraltar, 166, 171
Girondist party, 190
Gladstone, William, 4, 15, 28, 33, 71, 82, 95, 100
Glanville, 140
Globke, Hans, 456
Glorious Revolution, 13
Goebbels, Joseph, 388, 391
Goguel, François, 254–255
Goremykin, Ivan Longinovich, 515
Göring, Hermann, 387, 389, 391
Gosplan (*see* State Planning Commission)

Gouin, Félix, 243
Gouvernement Conventionnel, 187
Government of India Act of 1919, 169
Government of National Defense, France, 191
Governor-General, 168–169, 172
Grand Council (see Magnum Concilium)
Great Britain and Northern Ireland, and European cooperation, 665–675, 677, 680, 682, 709, 714–715, 721, 729–730, 733, 737–738, 742
    map of, 3
    (See also specific government institutions)
Great Corps of State (Les Grands Corps d'État), 311
Great Reform Bill of 1832 (see Reform Bill)
Greece, 646, 675, 700, 728–730
Greenwood, Arthur, 39, 59
Grévy, Jules, 326
Grotewohl, Otto, 427, 492–493, 495
Guadeloupe, 313, 316, 346
Guesde, Jules, 195, 242
Guiana, 313, 316, 318, 346
Guillaumat, Pierre, 218
Guingouin, Georges, 239
Guttenberg, Karl Theodor Freiherr zu, 422–423, 438

Habeas corpus, 399, 447
Habeas Corpus Act, Great Britain, 14
Haldane Committee of 1918, 83, 85, 88, 95, 155
Hallstein, Walter, 358, 717, 719
Hankey, Lord (Sir Maurice), 82
Hardie, Keir, 36
Hassel, Kai Uwe von, 467
Healey, Denis, 52, 55–56
Heath, Edward, 30, 53–59, 75–76, 715
Heine, Heinrich, 377
Henderson, Arthur, 36–37, 39, 76
Henry II (Plantagenet), 5, 7, 140
Henry III, 9
Henry VIII, 12, 140
Hermann of Salza, 371
Herriot, Édouard, 197, 205, 265–266, 318, 381
Herter, Christian, 666
Hertzog, General, 168
Hess, Rudolf, 509
Heusinger, Adolph, 467
Heuss, Theodor, 48, 418, 435, 453–454
Himmler, Heinrich, 388, 391

Hindenburg, Paul von, 378–379, 382–383, 387–388, 452
Hirsch, Etienne, 723, 725
Hitler, Adolf, 40, 183, 197–199, 222, 268, 371, 382–391, 397, 427, 444, 475, 496, 499, 527, 529–530, 532, 571
Hoare, Sir Samuel, 81
Hoare-Laval Agreement, 81, 83
Ho-Chi-Minh, 265
Hoffman, General, 521
Hohenzollern family, 371, 485
Holland, 254
Holmes, Oliver Wendell, 23, 143
Holy Roman Empire, historical development of, 369–370
Home, Lord (see Douglas-Home)
Home Secretary, 21, 148
Horner, Arthur, 52
Houphouet-Boigny, Félix, 218, 347
House of Commons, 56, 64, 78, 102
    bills in, 120, 127, 136
        private, 120, 126–128
        of private members, 124–127
    campaign expenses, 124–127
    chart of floor plan of, 114
    committees of, 11, 125–128
    composition of, 30, 108
    control of party in, 90, 120–121
    debate in, 115–116, 124
    dissolution of, 80, 122
    and elections, 18, 33–34, 42, 47–49, 108–112
    and grievances, 117–118, 130
    influence of, on public opinion, 113–115
    and legislation, 124–125
    membership of, 17–19, 108–113, 133
    and money bills, 11, 18, 125–126, 128–132, 136
    and opposition party, 115–118
    origin and development of, 9–15, 18
    power of, 10–16, 22
    privileges of, 121
    procedure in, 121–124
    relation of, to Cabinet, 79
        to House of Lords, 23, 135–138
    resignation from, 112
    and Royal Assent, 128–129, 136
    Speaker of, 70–71, 92, 109, 113, 115, 119–122, 124, 129, 319
    training for leadership in, 75, 116–117
    why it works, 53–54, 118–119

House of Lords, 12–13, 36, 92, 122
  composition of, 132–134, 136–137
  debate in, 134–135
  judicial function of, 145, 147, 149
  and legislation, 125–129, 136–137
  organization of, 135
  origin of, 10–11
  powers of, 11, 16, 18–19
    reduced, 136
  procedure in, 134–135
  reform of, 34, 135
  relation of, to Cabinet, 77
    to House of Commons, 23, 135, 137–138
Humanité, l', 196, 283, 593
Hundshammer, Alois, 414
Hungary, 239, 547, 572, 645
Hyderabad, 170
Hyndman, Henry M., 34

Iceland, 730
Ignatiev, N. G., 536
Imperial Conference, Great Britain, of 1917, 167
  of 1926, 168
Imperial League, Great Britain, 60
Independent Labor party, Great Britain, 34, 36, 38–40, 42, 61
Independent Liberal party, Great Britain, 42
Independent Republicans, France, 229, 235, 263, 271
Independents, of France, 224–226, 268
  historical development of, 270–271
  of Great Britain, 30, 32, 38, 42
India, Commonwealth status of, 166–171
  constitution of, 170, 172
  and Pakistan, 166, 170, 173
India Office, Great Britain, 87
Individualism, 180–183, 186
Indochina, 211, 214–215, 265, 304, 346, 646
Industrial Injuries Act, Great Britain, 45
Industrial Revolution, 133, 152, 546
"Inner" cabinet, Great Britain, 85, 88
Institute of Directors, Great Britain, 67
Insurance Commission, Great Britain, 155
International Atomic Energy Agency, 721
International Authority for the Ruhr, 405–406, 682
International Court of Justice, 568, 642, 679
International law, Soviet concept of, 642–643

International relations, Soviet concept of, 640–642
Ireland, Northern, 20, 28, 30, 33, 48, 91, 109–110, 133, 145–147, 150
Ireland, Republic of (Eire), 82, 167–169, 172, 675
Irish Nationalist party, 126
Iron and Steel Corporation, Great Britain, 101–102
Ismay, Lord, 731
Israel, 237, 421, 678
Italian Christian Democrats, 415
Italy, 254, 370, 386, 405, 408, 429, 665, 671
  and European cooperation, 660, 662, 675–676, 680, 682, 687, 697–698, 701, 704–705, 723–724, 726, 730–731, 733, 740
Ivory Coast, 218, 347
Izvestia, 239, 530, 538

Jacquet, Marc, 250
Jacquinot, Louis, 218
Jäger, Richard, 423
James I, 12
James II, 13, 69
Japan, 41–42, 600, 705
Jaurès, Jean, 195–196, 242
Jenkins, Roy, 55
Jennings, Sir Ivor, 15, 32
Jeune Republique, la (The Young Republic), 255
Jeunesses Patriotes (Patriotic Youth), 197
Jews, in Germany, 378, 389–390
  in Soviet Union, 587–588, 601
John, King, 8
Johnson, Lyndon B., 222, 360, 415
Jouhaux, Léon, 203, 280
Joxe, Louis, 232
Judicial Committee of the Privy Council, 25, 145, 147, 173, 175
Judicial review, in France, 188, 340, 388–389
  in Germany, 481
  in Soviet Union, lack of, 612, 630
Justice (*see* Law and justice)

Kaganovich, Lazar Moiseyevich, 538, 542–543, 583
Kahr, Gustav von, 388
Kaiser, Jakob, 415, 437
Kaiser, Wilhelm, 431
Kamenev, Lev Borisovich, 521, 524, 530

Kashmir, 170, 173

Katzer, Hans, 415

Kennedy, John F., 419, 650

Kennedy Round (*see* General Agreement on Tariffs and Trade)

Kenya, 166

Kerenski, Alexander, 518–519

KGB (*see* MVD–MGB)

Khachaturian, Aram, 591

Khruschev, Nikita, 434, 525, 536–544, 558, 563, 565–571, 578–581, 583, 587, 589, 591, 593, 599, 618, 620–622, 638, 646–647, 649–651, 655–656

Kielmansegg, Johann von, 467

Kiesinger, Kurt Georg, 366, 424–425, 433–435, 438, 455–456, 693, 719

Kipling, Rudyard, 165–166

Kir, Canon, 229

Kirilenko, 565

Kirov, S. M., 528, 530, 532

"Kitchen cabinet" of Hindenburg, 383

Kliuchevsky, Vasily, 511

Kohnstamm, Max, 694

Kolchak, Admiral, 521–522

Kolkhoz, 577, 580

Komandatura, 393, 397, 489

Kommunistische Partei Deutschlands (KPD) (*see* Communist party, in Germany)

Komsomolskaya Pravda, 571, 585–586

Koniev, Marshal Ivan, 538, 567

Konstantinov, F. B., 536

Korea, 237, 416, 649, 693

Kornilov, General, 519

Korovin, E. A., 642–643

Kostelnik, Dr., 586

Kosygin, Alexei, 434, 543–544, 558, 569, 580, 588–589, 618, 624, 651, 655–656

Kozhevnikov, F. I., 642–643

Kozlov, Frol, 544

Krokodil, 623

Krone, Heinrich, 418, 422, 457

Krylenko, N. V., 630

Krylov, S. B., 642

Krymov, General, 519

Kühlmann-Stumm, Knut von, 438, 475

Kurile Islands, 534

Kurland, 377

Labor courts, Germany, 479–480

Labor League of Youth, Great Britain, 61

Labor party, Great Britain, 19, 28, 30, 34, 40–41, 46, 48, 54, 62, 108, 110, 134, 162, 253, 282

conferences of, of 1958, 50

Scarborough, 53

ideology set by Fabian Society in, 35–36

leaders of, 30, 37, 50, 52–54, 75–76

leftist influence in, 40, 52, 54, 57, 62, 66

National Executive Committee of, 62–63, 138

in "national" government, 38–39

organization of, 36, 61–63

in Parliament, 58–59

origin of, 34–40, 61

postwar government reforms by, 42–45

program and policy of, 39–40, 42, 44, 46–47, 52–53, 55–57, 64–66, 100, 103–104

and results of elections, of 1945, 42–43, 110

of 1950, 29, 46–47

of 1951, 48

of 1955, 49

of 1959, 50–51

of 1964, 53, 110

of 1966, 56–57

shadow cabinet of, 48–50, 52

in War Cabinet, 41–42

Labor Representation Committee, Great Britain, 36

Labor unions, in France, 196–197, 246, 259, 279–282

Christian Federation of Labor, 196, 259

General Confederation of Labor, 196, 203–204, 238, 244, 279

in Germany, 441, 480

Christian Labor Movement, 442

Free German Trade Union Federation, 493, 497

German Trade Union Federation, 412, 441–442

in Great Britain, 34, 36, 40–41, 52, 61–63, 67, 94–95, 143

(*See also* Trades Union Congress)

in Soviet Union, 573–575

Laboulaye, Edouard René, 193

Lacordaire, 254

Lacoste, Robert, 214–215, 246, 259, 267, 271

Lamennais, 254

Länder government, Germany, 406–407, 439, 453, 487

under Allied Occupation, 484–485

Länder government, and courts, 449–451, 476, 478–479, 481, 483–486
  in education, 451–452
  and Federal Constitution, 446, 448
  and Federal government, 457
  and Federal legislature, 467–468
Länderkammer (Chamber of States), 495
Landwirtschaftliche Produktionsgenossenschaften (LPG) (Agricultural production co-operatives), 497
Laniel, Joseph, 265–266, 269–270
Lansbury, George, 39–40, 59
Latvia, 522, 531, 533–534, 597
Laue, Theodore H. von, 512
Laval, Pierre, 194, 197, 337
Lavigerie, Cardinal, 195
Law, Bonar, 16
Law on the Judiciary of 1938, Soviet Union, 630
Law and justice, in France, administrative courts, 340–346
  appointment of judges, 331–333
  chart of court system, 334
  Constitutional Council, 339–340
  Council of State, 180–189, 299, 341–345
  court system, 331–336
  criminal prosecution, 336–337
  High Court of Justice, 337–338
  influence of Roman law, 329–331
  judicial review, 188, 338–340, 345
  justice of the peace, 333–334
  Napoleonic Codes, 189, 329–330
  organization, 189, 333, 338
  State's Attorney's office, 333
 in Germany, administrative courts, 479
  chart of court system, 477
  Federal Constitutional Court, 440, 448, 450–451, 463–464, 470–471, 479–483, 486, 500
  judicial review, 481
  labor and specialized courts, 479–480
  Land courts, 370
  lay judges, 478
  under Nazis, 475, 479
  ordinary courts, 476–479
  Supreme Federal Court, 478–480
  in Weimar Republic, 479
 in Great Britain, administrative courts, 149
  chart of court system, 146
  common law, 6–7, 10, 12, 22, 139–141
  court system, 6–8, 143–149
Law and justice, in Great Britain, Courts of Chancery, 141–142, 145–148
  Curia Regis (King's Court), 7, 9
  equity, 140–143
  High Court of Justice, 145–148
  Inns of Court, 141–142
  judges, 6, 140, 142–147
  Judicature Act of 1873, 145
  jury, 6–7, 140, 144–145, 148
  legal profession, 141–142
  Magnum Concilium, 6–7, 133
  stare decisis, 332
  statute law, 22, 143
  "Supreme Court of Judicature," 145
 in Soviet Union, chart of court system, 628
  "comradely courts," 627–628
  court system, 626–630
  judges, 626–627, 630–631
  Judicial Committee, 599
  judicial review, lack of, 612, 630
  legal theory, 625–626
  Procurator-General, 600, 610, 629, 631–632
  Supreme Court, 612, 629–631
Law for the Liberation from National Socialism and Militarism, 400
Law on the Press Property, France, 282
League of Communist Youth (*see* Comsomol)
League of the Expellees and Disenfranchised, Germany (*see* Refugee party)
League of Nations, 93, 167, 174, 527, 666
Lecanuet, Jean, 233–235, 249, 260–263, 268
Ledru-Rollin, 263
Lefebvre, Theo, 693–694
Lemnitzer, Lyman L., 733
Lenin, Vladimir I. (Nikolai), 506, 510, 515–522, 524–525, 532, 536, 547, 549–551, 554, 563, 565, 573–574, 590, 595–596, 601–603, 605, 625–626, 641, 643–644, 647, 652
Lenin Academy of Agricultural Science, 591
Lenz, Otto, 456
Leo III, 369
Leo XIII, 195, 204, 255
Levant, 215
Liberal Democratic party, Germany, 410, 428, 492
Liberal party, Great Britain, 28–29, 39, 42–43, 47–48, 53, 57, 108, 110, 134–136
  future of, 177

Liberal party, Great Britain, with Labor party, 34, 36, 40
  policy of, 37–38
  voter support of, 30–32
  in War Cabinet, 41
Liberation of France, 203, 243, 277, 280, 306
Liebermann, Y., 541, 624
Lippe, Germany, 383
Lithuania, 377, 522, 531, 533–534, 597
Littleton, Lord Edward, 140
Lloyd, Selwyn, 54, 76
Lloyd George, David, 18, 34, 39, 72, 74, 82, 85, 135
Local government, in France, central control in, 189, 347
  evaluation of, 354–355
  Fourth Republic changes in, 347–348
  and General Councils, 348–349, 351–353
  historical development of, 189, 347, 350
  municipal, 349, 352–353
    in Paris, 272, 329, 350, 352–354
  prefects in, 189, 348–351, 353–354
  and taxation, 349
  territorial subdivisions in, 348–349
  in Germany, under Allied Occupation, 397, 402, 409–410, 486–487
    and Federal government, 457
    and German Municipal Act of 1935, 484
    during Nazi period, 388–389, 486
    in West Berlin, 488–489
  in Great Britain, and administrative county, 154–155, 163–164
    and boroughs, 152, 154, 157, 159–160
    and Boundary Commission, 162
    and central government control, 91, 153–155, 160–162, 164
    and counties, 151, 154–156
    and County Councils, 151, 154–158, 160, 163
    and education, 156–158
    historical development of, 150–155
    and justice of peace, 151–152, 154–155
    in London, 153, 161, 163–164
    politics and, 162–163
    services by, 150–151, 153–154, 156, 160–163
    and taxes, 152, 155–156, 160–161
    and town and country planning, 151, 156–158
    (See also Ministries, of Great Britain, Health, Housing and Local Government, Town and Country Planning)

Local Government Act, Great Britain
  of 1888, 154
  of 1894, 154
  of 1929, 158, 163
  of 1948, 161
Local Government Board, Great Britain, 154–155
Locke, John, 17
London, government of, 153, 161, 163–164
London Government Act of 1939, 163
London Passenger Transport Board, 100–101, 164
Lord Chancellor, 77, 122, 134–135, 145, 147–149
Lord Lieutenant, Great Britain, 152, 155
Lord Privy Seal, Great Britain, 93
Lords of Appeal in Ordinary, Great Britain, 133, 145
Louis XVI, 188, 190
Louis XVIII, 190
Louis Napoleon, Prince, 228
Louis Philippe, 190, 192
Lovett, Robert M., 730
Lübke, Heinrich, 418, 454–455
Luce, Sir David, 55
Ludendorff, Erich, 377–378, 519
Lutovinov, 557
Luxembourg, 403, 429
  and European cooperation, 660, 662, 667, 675, 682–684, 687, 697, 701, 704–705, 729–730
Luxembourg Conference of EEC, 231
Luxemburg, Rosa, 644
Lvov, Prince, 519
Lysenko, Trofim, 541, 590–591

Macauley, Lord, 51
MacDonald, Ramsay, 36–39, 59, 76
Machine Tractor Stations (MTS), 577
Mackenzie, W. J. M., 94
Macleod, Ian, 54, 61
MacMahon, Marshal, 192–193, 290
Macmillan, Harold, 50–52, 54, 56–58, 72, 74, 76, 78–79, 87, 115
McNamara, Robert S., 737
McNarney, General, 401
Magna Carta, 7, 9, 147
Magnum Concilium, 6–7, 133
Main Political Administration (MPA), 582
Maier, Reinhold, 437

Malagodi, Giovanni, 694
Malaya, 166, 171
Malenkov, Georgi, 534, 536–539, 543, 566, 568, 579, 583, 655
Malfa, Ugo La, 694
Malinovski, Rodion, 566, 583
Malraux, André, 277
Malvestiti, Piero, 685
Mansholt, Sicco, 258, 717, 719
Marie, André, 267–268, 308
Marin, Louis, 204, 269
Maritain, Jacques, 204
Marr, N. Ya., 591
Marshall, George C., 664–665, 729–730
Marshall, John, 330
Marshall Plan, 47, 237, 280, 308, 457, 663–664, 666–667, 728–729
Martinet, Giles, 278
Martinique, 313, 316, 346
Martov, L., 515
Marty, André, 239
Marx, Karl, 510, 515–516, 526, 536, 547–550, 580, 590, 595, 625, 643, 656
Marxism-Leninism, 34–35, 64, 195–196, 237, 242, 256, 376, 545–552, 557–558, 585, 625, 656
Massif Central, 239, 270
Massu, General Jacques, 215
Maude, Angus, 56
Maudling, Reginald, 54, 58–59, 76
Mau Mau, 166
Mauriac, François, 204
Max of Baden, 378
May, Sir George, 38
May, Sir Thomas Erskine, 122
"May 13 Movement," 216, 239
May Report, 38
Mayhew, Christopher, 55
Melville, Lord, 16
Mende, Erich, 423, 436–439
Mendès-France, Pierre, 214–216, 219, 225, 246, 249, 252, 254, 260, 265–269, 278–279, 671–672
Mensheviks, 516–517
Menthon, François de, 207, 255
Merkatz, Joachim von, 440
Meyer, René, 685
MGB (*see* MVD–MGB)
Michael, Grand Duke, 519
Middelhauve, Friedrich, 436
Middle East crisis of 1967, 236

Mikoyan, Anastas I., 543
Mill, John Stuart, 94
Millerand, Alexandre, 326
Ministers of the Crown Act, 1937, 24
Ministries, of France, 183–184, 299–304, 325, 458
    advisory agencies of, 305
    Agriculture, 304
    Armed Forces, 218, 302
    Defense, 302, 350
    Economic Council, 305–306, 323
    Finance, 299, 302, 304, 307–308, 310, 325
    Foreign Affairs, 211, 218, 299–300, 302
    Industry and Commerce, 304
    inner structure of, 304–305
    Interior, 216, 218, 299, 302, 304, 312, 348–351, 353–354
    Justice, 218, 331, 333, 342, 344
    ministers of state, 302
    Public Works, 304
    secretaries of state, 304
    War, 249, 299
  of Germany, Affairs of the Federal Council and the *Länder,* 457
    Agriculture, 457–458
    All-German Affairs, 457
    Economics, 457
    Family and Youth Affairs, 457–458
    Federal Border Police, 449
    Federal Defense, 457
    Finance, 457
    Foreign Affairs, 457
    Interior, 457–458
    Soviet Affairs, 457
  of Great Britain, 93, 160
    Agriculture and Fisheries, 78, 87, 91, 160
    Board of Trade, 78, 87, 92
    Colonial Office, 77, 87
    Commonwealth Relations Office, 77, 87
    Economic Affairs, 82, 87
    Education, 158
    Exchequer, 77, 88–90
    Food, 87, 91
    Foreign Office, 77, 87–88, 90–91, 93
    Health, 76, 78, 87, 91–92, 153–155
    Home Office, 21, 77, 87, 91, 93
    Housing and Local Government, 78, 87, 91, 157, 160–161
    Labor and National Services, 21, 78, 87, 91

Ministries, of Great Britain, Lord Chancellor, 77, 87, 92
   National Defence, 77, 87
   other, 83, 87–88, 90–92
   Prime Minister, 15–16, 24, 87–88
   Scottish Office, 77, 87
   "sinecure" offices, 77–78
   Supply, 87
   Town and Country Planning, 87, 91, 157–158
   Transport, Fuel and Power, 87–88
   Treasury, 77–78, 85, 87–90, 94, 129, 131, 160–161
  of Soviet Union, 538, 582, 589–590
   chart of central agencies for economic management, 617
   Defense, 582
   Finance, 543, 620
   Internal Affairs, 531, 538–539, 575–576
   State Control, 620
   State Security, 575–576
   (*See also* Council of Ministers)
Mitterand, François, 230, 233–235, 240, 249–250, 252–254, 261–262, 268
Moch, Jules, 216, 230, 243, 338
Moldavia, 533–534, 543
Mollet, Guy, 204, 212, 214, 217–218, 230, 233, 243, 246–254, 259, 267, 286, 302, 693
Molotov, Vyacheslav, 534, 537–539, 542–543, 583, 598, 620
Monarch (*see* Crown)
Monde, le, 283
Monnerville, Gaston, 268, 318
Monnet, Jean, 183, 210, 357, 665–669, 682–683, 685, 688, 693–694, 719
Montagne, Rémy, 268
Montalembert, Count of, 254
Montesquieu, Baron de (Charles de Secondat), 74
Montgomery, Field Marshal, 730
Moore, Barrington, 590
Morgenthau Plan, 395
Morocco, 246, 266
Morrison, Herbert, 48, 59, 93, 109, 121, 151
Moslem League, 170
Mosley, Sir Oswald, 38, 121
Mott, Bernard, 631
Motte, Bertrand, 262
Moulin, Jean, 201
Mountain (*La Montagne*), 263

Mouvement Républicain Populaire (MRP) (*see* Popular Republican Movement)
Mouvement Unifié de la Renaissance Française (MURF) (French Unified Movement of Reconstruction), 205–206
MPA (Main Political Administration), 582
MRP (*see* Popular Republican Movement)
Müller, Josef, 414
Mun, Count Albert de, 254
Munich Agreement of 1938, 533
Munich *Putsch,* 382, 386
Municipal Corporations Act of 1835, Great Britain, 153–154, 163
Municipal Corporations Consolidation Act of 1882, Great Britain, 153
Murphy-Beely Mission, 213
Mussolini, Benito, 40, 183
MVD–MGB, 377, 396, 525, 529–531, 537–539, 559, 575–576, 582–583, 588, 626, 629

Napoleon I, 189, 191, 329, 347, 350, 370, 372
Napoleon III, 190–192, 212, 263
Napoleonic wars, 512
Nasser, Gamal Abdel, 49–50, 721
Nation, la, 283
National, le, 338
National Assembly, France, 193, 207, 300, 331, 337–339, 349, 351, 357, 671, 716, 730, 739
   censure vote in, 228–229, 327–328
   committees of, 319–322, 324–326
   delegated legislation of, 322
   dissolution of, 267, 293–294, 317, 328
   elections to, 193–194, 205, 236, 314–315
   of Fifth Republic, 180, 182–184, 188, 193, 312, 318, 320
   finance bills in, 322–323, 325–326
   of Fourth Republic, 180, 184, 193, 210–213, 312, 317, 319–320, 327
   historical development of, 193–194
   legislation of, 299, 320–325
   "oral" and written questions in, 327
   organization of, 229, 276, 318–320
   powers in, 292–294, 305–306, 321–322, 326–327
   relations of, to cabinet, 320–321, 325–326
     to government, 296–297, 303, 321–322, 324–328

National Assembly, France, relations of, to President of the Republic, 192–193, 294–295, 317, 326
  of Third Republic, 180, 193, 197, 312, 317, 319–320
  vote of confidence in, 296–298, 326–328
National Center of Judicial Studies (*Centre national d'Études judiciaires*), 330–332
National Coal Authority (*Carbonnages de France*), 307
National Coal Board, Great Britain, 101–102
National Council of French Employers (*Conseil National du Patronnat Français*, CNPF), 285
National Council of Resistance, France, 201–202, 204, 243, 255, 269–270
National Credit Council, France, 307
National Defense Council, Germany, 457
National Democratic party, East Germany (*Nationaldemokratische Partei Deutschlands*, NPD), 440, 492–493
National Economic Councils, Soviet Union, 601
National Farmers' Union, Great Britain, 67
National Federation of Farm Syndicates (*Fédération Nationale des Syndicats des Exploitants Agricoles*), 285
National Front, East Germany, 493–496
National Health Act of 1946, Great Britain, 92
National Health Service Act, Great Britain, 45, 64
National Insurance Act, Great Britain, 45
National Insurance Council, France, 307–308
National Journal-Soldier's Journal (*Nationalzeitung-Soldatenzeitung*), 443
National Liberal party, Great Britain, 42
National Liberals, Germany, 380
National and Local Government Officers' Association, 67
National Republicans, France, 270
National School of Administration (*École Nationale d'Administration*), 311
National Service Act, Great Britain, 91
National Socialist German Workers' party (NSDAP), 386–387, 392
  "denazification" of, by Allies, 395, 397
  historical development of, 379, 381–383, 386–388
  organization of, 389
  and plot of July 20, 1944, 390–391

National Socialist German Workers' party (NSDAP), program of, 386, 388–389
  and purge of 1933, 388
National Teachers Federation (*Fédération de l'Education Nationale*, FEN), 285
National Union of British Manufacturers, 66–67
National Union of Conservative and Unionist Associations, Great Britain, 60
National Union of French Students (*Union Nationale des Etudiants de France*, UNEF), 285–286
National Union of Teachers, Great Britain, 67
Nationaldemokratische Partei Deutschlands, NPD (National Democratic party, East Germany), 440, 492–493
Nationalized industries, in France, 306–309, 687
  in Germany, 457
  in Great Britain, 100–104
Nationalsozialistische Deutsche Arbeiterpartei, NSDAP (*see* National Socialist German Workers' party)
Nationalzeitung-Soldatenzeitung (National Journal-Soldier's Journal), 443
NATO (*see* North Atlantic Treaty Organization)
Nazi party, Nazis (*see* National Socialist German Workers' party)
Nehru, Jawaharlal, 170
Neizevstny, Ernst, 593
Neo-Nazi, 366, 440, 443
NEP (*see* New Economic Policy)
Netherlands, 403, 429, 667
  and European cooperation, 660, 662, 675, 682, 684, 687, 691, 697, 701, 704–705, 724, 729–730, 738
New Caledonia, 346
New Economic Policy (NEP), Soviet Union, 524–526, 529, 573, 601
"New Party," Great Britain, 38
New Towns Act, Great Britain, 45, 157–158
New Zealand, 132, 168, 170–173
Newfoundland, 167–169
Newman, Cardinal, 119
Nicholas II, 512–513, 518–519
Nicolai, Metropolitan of Kiev and Galicia, 584
Nigeria, 171, 173
NKVD (*see* MVD-MGB)
Nord-Matin, 283
Norstad, Lauris, 733

North Atlantic Council (NAC) (*see* North Atlantic Treaty Organization)
North Atlantic Treaty Organization, and America, 737
  civilian aspects of, 731–733
  commands of, 733
  and crisis of 1966, 738–742
  and France, 210, 253, 359–362
  and Germany, 416, 467, 502
  and Great Britain, 176
  historical development of, 359, 727–731, 735
  national composition of forces in, 671, 731, 739
  and North Atlantic Council, 731–733
  and North Atlantic Treaty, 664, 670, 675, 730
  nuclear strategy of, 735–737
  and parliamentarians' Conference, 733–738
  perils and tribulations of, 734–738
  political consultation in, 737–738
  Secretary-General of, 731
  and Soviet Union and Eastern Europe, 651, 728–730, 740
  Standing Group of, 732–733
  structure of, 731–734
North German Federation, 373–374
Northcote-Trevelyan report of 1853, 94
Norway, 631
  and European unity, 675, 677, 730
Nouvel Observateur, le, 278
Nuclear weapons policy, of France, 357, 359–360
  of Germany, 416
  of Great Britain, 50–52, 55, 66–67
  of Soviet Union, 540
Nyasaland (Malawi), 171

OAS (Organization of American States), 658, 660
Occupation of Germany, 391–392, 394–401, 407
Occupation Statute of 1949, 404–406
Oceania, 346
Ochrana, 529
October Revolution (*see* Russian Revolutions of 1905 and 1917)
Oder-Neisse line, 392, 402, 429, 443, 490
OECD (*see* Organization for Economic Cooperation and Development)

OEEC (*see* Organization for European Economic Cooperation)
Official Secrets Act, Great Britain, 81, 144
Ogg, Frederic A., 9
OGPU (*see* MVD-MGB)
Ollenhauer, Erich, 429, 431, 693
Order in Council of 1870, Great Britain, 94
Order in Council of 1920, Great Britain, 94–95
Order of Teutonic Knights, 371
Organization of American States (OAS), 658, 660
Organization for Economic Cooperation and Development (OECD), 705, 724
Organization for European Economic Cooperation (OEEC), 664, 667
Orléanists, 192, 290
"Outer Seven" (*see* European Free Trade Association)

Pakistan, 166, 169–171, 173
Palais Burbon, France, 217, 289, 316, 327
Palewski, Gaston, 277
Palmerston, Lord, 4, 74
Pannell, Charles, 52
Papen, Franz von, 383, 471
Paris-Presse, 283
Parliament (*see Bundesrat; Bundestag;* Council of the Republic; House of Commons; House of Lords; National Assembly, France; Senate)
Parliament Act, Great Britain, of 1911, 18, 122, 129, 132, 136
  of 1949, 19, 132, 136, 138
Parliamentarians' Conference, 733–738
Parliamentary Commission, Great Britain, 132
Parti Communiste Français (PCF) (*see* Communist party, in France)
Parti Démocrate Populaire (PDP) (Popular Democratic party), 255
Parti des Fusillés (Party of Executed Men), 201
Parti Radical Socialiste (PRS) (*see* Radical and Radical Socialist party)
Parti Républicain de la Liberté (PRL) (Republican Party of Liberty), 269–270
Parti Socialiste, Section Française de l'Internationale Ouvrière (SFIO) (*see* Socialist party, France)

Parti Socialiste Unifié (PSU) (*see* Unified Socialist party)
Party of Executed Men (*Parti des Fusillés*), 201
Pasternak, Boris, 505, 591–592
Patriotic Youth (*Jeunesses Patriotes*), 197
Paulus, Friedrich von, 396
Peasant party, France, 270
Peasant's Revolt of 1381, Great Britain, 11
Peckenham, Lord, 93
Peel, Sir Robert, 16, 28, 75, 88
Pelletier, Émile, 218
People's Chamber (*Volkskammer*), East Germany, 495
People's Congress (*Volkskongress*), East Germany, 494–495
People's Council (*Volksrat*), East Germany, 494
People's Police (*Volkspolizei*, Vopo), East Germany, 496
Périer, Casimir, 193
Pétain, Marshal Philippe, 198, 201–202, 204–205, 243, 255
Peter III, 372
Peter the Great, 512, 520, 534
Petersberg Protocol of November 22, 1949 (Bonn Treaty), 405
Pethick-Lawrence, Lord, 170
Petrovna, Empress Elizabeth, of Prussia, 372
Petsamo, 534
Pflimlin, Pierre, 215–218, 247, 260, 262
Philby, Harold, 51
Philip, André, 243, 246, 675
Philip, Prince, Duke of Edinburgh, 70–71
Philippe, Louis, 290
Philippe-Égalité, 190
Pieck, Wilhelm, 396, 495
Pierrefitte, Alain, 249
Pinay, Antoine, 270, 272
Pitt, William (Earl of Chatham), 16, 32
Pitt, William, the Younger, 17
Pius X, 255
Plekhanov, Georgi, 515–516
Pleven, René, 416, 670, 694
Pleven Plan, 730
Poincaré, Raymond, 197, 361, 381
Poland, 281, 370–371, 392, 402–403, 491, 522–523, 533–534, 572, 645, 647, 729
Poliansky, N., 630

Politburo, 239, 388, 506, 535–536, 540, 543–544, 555, 563–568, 570, 579, 582–583, 588–589, 600–601, 612, 621, 636
(*See also* Communist party, in Soviet Union)
Political parties, in East Germany, 426, 492–493
in France, 183–184, 190, 195–196, 225, 227, 241, 248, 250, 264, 270
and election laws, 267, 270, 272
and electoral campaigns, 278–279
emergence of, during Third Republic, 194–195
and future of party system, 286–287
and party system, 223–224, 277–278, 300
and press, radio and television, 237, 243, 249, 255, 266–267, 278, 282–284, 292
and pressure groups, 284–286
and "religious question," 187, 195, 224, 241
shifts in, since Liberation, 224–226
and splinter parties, 277–278
and table of popular votes and seats in National Assembly, 226
in Germany, 388, 424, 433–435
in contemporary party system, 410–412
and election laws, 439–440
under Nazis, 408–409, 427
under occupation, 397, 402, 409–411
and pressure groups, 441–445
and two-party system, 439, 447
under Weimar Republic, 380, 408–410, 462
in Great Britain, 27–30, 32–34, 41, 43, 47–48, 50–51, 55–58, 79, 82, 177
and consequences of elections of 1950, 29, 46–47
and distribution of votes and seats in the House of Commons, 31
historical development of, 32–42
moderation in, 28–29
organization of, in Parliament, 57–58
postwar developments in, 42–46
and pressure groups, 66–67
prospects of, 177
and two-party system, 29–42, 74–75, 110, 118, 177
in Soviet Union, Bolsheviks, 516, 519–521, 524, 528–530, 532, 554, 570, 581

Political parties, in Soviet Union, Mensheviks, 516–517
  Social Democrats, 515–516, 518
  Socialist Revolutionary party, 518–520
Pollock, James K., 403
Pompidou, Georges, 232, 268, 270–271, 275–276, 296, 298, 303
Poor Law Act of 1834, Great Britain, 153
Poor Law Commission, Great Britain, 153
Populaire, le, 243, 282
Popular Democratic party, France (*Parti Démocrate Populaire* PDP), 255
Popular Front, France, 197–198, 230, 240, 243, 248, 255
Popular Republican Movement (MRP), 204–206, 215, 227, 229, 231, 233–235, 238, 241, 247, 249–250, 260, 266, 269–270, 282, 415
  and Algerian crisis, 259–260
  electoral strength of, 258–261, 263, 268
  and European cooperation, 259–260
  historical development of, 207, 212, 254–256, 263
  leaders of, 255, 260–261
  political philosophy of, 256–257
  program of, 224–225, 244–245, 258
Porritt, E., 17
Portugal, 730
Potemkin, rebellion of the, 514
Potsdam and Yalta agreements, 392–393, 403
Potter, Beatrice (*see* Webb)
Poujadists, 210–225, 267, 278
Powell, Enoch, 54, 56, 58–59
Pravda, 239, 538, 558
Premier, of France, 193, 292, 295, 298, 317
  of Soviet Union, 565, 568, 587
Presidency, of France, 291–293
  election to, 193, 228
  functions of, 180, 192, 290–295, 298, 302, 324
    judicial, 331, 337, 339
  historical development of, 190, 192
  relation of, to local government, 349
    to National Assembly, 192–193, 294–295, 319
  of German Federal Republic, 452–453, 470, 472
    and dissolution of *Bundestag,* 453–454, 471
  election to, 418, 453
  powers of, 418, 453–454

Presidium, Soviet Union (*see* Communist party, in Soviet Union; Constitutions, of Soviet Union)
Prime Minister, of France, 299, 303, 318, 326, 339
  role of, 290, 293–296, 298, 324
  vote of confidence in, 296–298
  of Great Britain, 15–16, 70–73, 78–79, 82
  choice of, 15, 58, 74–75, 78–79
  power of dissolution of, 109
  power and duties of, 24, 75–80, 85–89, 93
  relation of, with colleagues, 75–78, 80, 86, 88
  of Soviet Union, 538, 542, 588
Primrose League, Great Britain, 60, 154
Privy Council, Judicial Committee of, 25, 74, 92, 145, 147, 153–155, 160, 173
Profumo, John, 51–52
Proportional representation (PR), Germany, 460–462, 465
Protestantism, 180–181, 249, 371, 412, 414, 418
Proudhon, Pierre Joseph, 195
Provençal, le, 282
Provisional Government, Russia, 519–520
Prussia, 191–192, 379, 381, 383, 392, 402, 449, 467–468, 484–486, 534
  dissolution of, 389, 402
  dominance of, over Germany, 375–376
  rise of, 368, 370–374
Public Health Act of 1875, Great Britain, 154
Public Prosecution, Director of, Great Britain, 92, 147
Putna, General, 530
Pytakov, Y. L., 530

Queille, Henri, 267
Questions of History (Voprosy Istorii), 637

Radek, Karl, 524, 530
Radical and Radical Socialist party (*Parti Radical et Radical Socialiste*), 197, 202, 204–206, 235, 245, 250, 262, 269, 276, 283
  electoral strength of, 229, 259, 267–268
  historical development of, 263–266
  leaders of, 264–268
  organization of, 264, 267
  program of, 224, 263–265
  since the liberation, 224–225

Rally of the French People (RPF) (*Rassemblement du Peuple Français*), 210, 225, 238, 258, 276, 283, 314
electoral strength of, 272, 281
historical development of, 272–273
Rally of the Republican Left (RGR), 206, 276
Ramadier, Paul, 243, 303
Ramcke, Wilhelm, 442
Ramsay, Captain, 121
Rasputin, 518
Rassemblement des Gauches Républicains (RGR) (Rally of the Republican Left), 206, 276
Rassemblement du Peuple Français (RPF) (*see* Rally of the French People)
Red Army, 521–522, 530, 543, 581–584, 586
Redistribution of Seats Act, Great Britain, of 1885, 18
of 1944, 108
Reform Bill, Great Britain, of 1832, 17, 18, 32, 33
of 1867, 33
Refugee party (All-German Bloc, GB/BHE), 439–440
Rehmer, Ernst, 391, 440
Reich, First, 370
Second, 374
Third, 388–391, 409, 483
Reich President, Weimar Germany, 379
Reichstag, 387, 473, 500
in Imperial Germany, 376–377
in Weimar Republic, 379–382
Reith Commission, Great Britain, 158
"Religious question," France, 195, 224, 245, 257–258, 264
Renault Motor Works, 307–308
Representation of the People Act, Great Britain, of 1867, 18
of 1884, 18
of 1918, 18
of 1948, 108, 111–112
Republican Federation, France, 269
Republican Movement of Liberation, France, 256
Republican Party of Liberty (*Parti Républicain de la Liberté*, PRL), 269–270
Resistance movement, France, 199, 201, 203–205, 218, 237–239, 246, 252, 254–255, 260, 272, 274–276, 282, 306
Reunification of Germany, 428–429, 502–503

Réunion, 275, 313, 316, 346
Rey, Jean, 358, 719
Reynaud, Paul, 198, 269
RGR (Rally of the Republican Left), 206, 276
Rhodesia, Northern (Zambia), 171
Rhodesia, Southern, 55, 57, 64, 168, 171–173
Ribes, Champetier de, 255, 318
Ribière, Henri, 243
Richard II, 145
Ridgway, Matthew, 237, 733
Riom trials, 204, 243
Rivet law, France, 192
Romania, 361, 491, 645, 647, 728
Rommel, Field Marshal Erwin, 391, 442
Roosevelt, Franklin D., 222, 266, 339
Roosevelt, Theodore, 222
Rosebery, Lord, 33, 74, 137
Rossi, 238
Rousseau, Jean Jacques, 186, 188
Royal Absolutism, 12–13
Royal Assent, 18, 72, 128–129, 136
Royal Commission, Great Britain, 117, 126, 145
Royal Sanitary Commission, Great Britain, 154
RPF (*see* Rally of the French People)
Ruhr Valley, 381, 403–406, 484, 669, 687
Russian Empire, historical background of, 507, 511–513, 519
Russian Orthodox Church, 584, 587
Russian Revolutions of 1905 and 1917, 509, 514–522, 526, 529, 579–580, 596, 599, 643, 652
Russian Social Democratic Workers' party of 1898, 515, 518
Russo-Japanese War, 514
Rychkov, N. M., 630

Saar, 429, 436, 484, 669
SAC (*see* Strategic Air Command)
St. Laurent, Louis, 730
St. Pierre and Miquelon, 346
Sakhalin, 534
Sakhiet Sidi-Youssef, 213
Salan, General Raoul, 215–216, 231
Salisbury, Lord, 16, 23, 74, 76, 82, 93
Samuel, Lord (Sir Herbert), 39
Sangnier, Marc, 255
Scandinavia, 132, 181, 705

Scheel, Walter, 436, 439
Schiller, Karl, 435
Schleicher, Kurt von, 371, 383, 387
Schleswig-Holstein, 412
Schmid, Carlo, 418, 434
Schmidt, Helmut, 434
Schnadhorst, Francis, 33
Schneiter, Pierre, 318
Schröder, Gerhard, 416–417, 419, 421–426, 456
Schumacher, Kurt, 411, 427, 429–430, 475, 682, 693
Schuman, Robert, 183, 205, 209, 259–260, 301, 357, 657, 665, 667–670, 683, 688, 719
Schuman Plan (see European Coal and Steel Community)
Schumann, Maurice, 204, 261
Scotland, 14, 17, 60, 77, 91–92, 109, 125, 133, 145, 147, 150
SEATO (Southeast Asia Treaty Organization), 48
Second Republic, France, 263
Secret State Police (Gestapo), 377, 381, 390–391, 408
Sedan, Battle of, 191–192
Select Committee on Estimates, Great Britain, 131
Senat (see Senate, France)
Senate, France, 316–317, 357
    committees of, 324
    of Fifth Republic, 318
    finance bills in, 326
    of Fourth Republic, 318–319
    legislation in, 321–325
    organization of, 318–319
    powers of, 337–338
    president of, 319, 339
    relation of, to government, 326–328
    (See also Council of the Republic)
Senate of the Community, France, 323
Senegal, 247
Senghor, Léopold-Sedar, 347
Serigny, Alain de, 215
Servan, Marcel, 219
Servan-Schreiber, Jean Jacques, 267
Settlement Act of 1701, Great Britain, 14, 144
Seydlitz, Walter von, 396
SFIO (see Socialist party, France)
Sforza, Count Carlo, 675
Shadow cabinet, France, 253

SHAPE (Supreme Headquarters Allied Powers Europe), 733
Shaw, George Bernard, 35
Shawcross, Sir Hartley, 112
Shelepin, Alexander N., 565, 569–570, 620
Sheriff, Great Britain, 5, 151–152, 155
Shostakovich, Dmitri, 591
Siberia, 517, 519
Sieyès, Abbé, 611
Silkin, 158
Sillon, le, 255
Simon, Jules, 263
Simon, Lord (Sir John), 39
Simon of Montfort, 9
Simpson, Mrs., 70
Sinai Peninsula, 49–50
Singapore, 171
Sino-Soviet conflict, 510
Smith, Adam, 33
Smith, Ian, 171–172
Smuts, Field Marshal, 167
Smyrnov, 524
Snowden, Philip, 36–38
Soames, Christopher, 54
Social Democratic Federation, Great Britain, 34–36
Social Democratic party (SPD), German Federal Republic, 383, 387, 407, 410–411, 415, 442, 454–455, 460, 462, 465, 474–476, 492
    electoral strength of, 380–382, 426–430, 432–433, 435–436
    leaders of, 425, 431, 434–435
    organization of, 425–426, 428–429, 432
    program of, 421, 423, 426, 429–430
Socialist League, Great Britain, 40
Socialist party (SFIO), France, 197–198, 230, 235, 238, 240–241, 244, 247, 258–260, 264, 266, 269, 278–282, 302
    and Algerian crisis, 216–219, 245–246
    electoral strength of, 227, 229–230, 246–248, 267
    historical development of, 195–196, 242, 248
    inner contradictions in, 242–243
    leaders of, 243, 246, 249–251
    organization of, 251–252
    program of, 224, 249
Socialist Reich party (SRP), Germany, 440, 448, 482

Socialist Revolutionary party, Tsarist Russia, 518–520

Socialist Unity party (SED), East Germany, 402, 427–428, 489, 492–495, 497–498

Socialist Youth Movement, France, 251

Society of the Godless, 584

Society of Jacobites, 263

Society of Work and Savings, France, 257

Sokolnikov, Grigori, 530

Sokolovsky, Marshal, 402

Solicitor General, Great Britain, 92

Sostchenko, Michael, 591

Soustelle, Jacques, 214, 216, 273–274

South Africa, Republic of, 167–168, 170–171, 173–174, 214

South Arabian sheikdoms, 171

Southeast Asia Treaty Organization (SEATO), 48

Soviet-German Nonaggression Pact of 1939, 40, 201, 533, 610

Soviet Military Administration, 396, 410, 492–495

Soviet Union (*see* U.S.S.R.; specific government institutions)

Soviets in U.S.S.R., 604–606, 609, 612–613, 618–619, 622

Soviets of Workers' and Soldiers' Representatives, 605

Sovkhoz, 578, 580

Sozialdemokratische Partei Deutschlands (SPD) (*see* Social Democratic party, German Federal Republic)

Sozialistische Einheitspartei Deutschlands (SED) (Communist party, East Germany), 492–495

Sozialistische Reichspartei (SRP) (*see* Socialist Reich party)

Spaak, Paul-Henri, 665–666, 671–672, 675, 683, 692–693, 720, 731

Spain, 678

Spanish Civil War, 197

Speaker, Great Britain, 92, 109, 113, 115, 119–122, 124

Speaker's Conference on Electoral Reform, Great Britain, 18

Speaker's Conference on Electoral Reforms and Redistribution of Seats, Great Britain, 109

Special Accounting Offices, France, 308

Speidel, Hans, 467

Spiegel, Der, 417, 420, 444

Staatspartei (State party, Germany), 380

"Stab in the back" legend, 378–379, 386–387, 391–392

Stakhanovites, 527, 574, 636

Stalin, Joseph, 222, 238–239, 368, 388, 434, 506, 510, 517–518, 520, 524–540, 542–544, 550–551, 553, 557–558, 563–568, 570, 574–578, 580, 583, 586–587, 589–593, 595–596, 598–599, 601, 603, 608, 611, 616, 625, 633–634, 638, 641, 645, 647, 653, 655, 729

Stalingrad, Battle of, 390

State Committee of Defense, Soviet Union, 534, 616

State Council on Affairs of the Orthodox Church, Soviet Union, 584

State party, Germany, 380

State Planning Commission, Soviet Union, 535–536, 616, 621–624

Statute of Westminster, Great Britain, 25, 168

Stauffenberg, Claus Werner von, 390

Stewart, Michael, 54–55

Stikker, Dirk U., 731

Stockholm declaration, 649

Stolypin, 512, 515

Strasser, Gregor, 383

Strategic Air Command (SAC), 731

Strauss, Franz Joseph, 414, 419–422, 424–425, 433, 438, 467

Strauss, G. R., 40

Stresemann, Gustav, 380, 435, 662

Stuarts, 11–13, 32

Sudetenland, 389, 403

Suez campaign, 49–50, 81, 721

Suez Canal (*see* Universal Suez Canal Company)

Suffragettes, Great Britain, 67

Superannuation Act of 1859, Great Britain, 94

Superior Council of the Judiciary, France, 331–332

Supreme Headquarters Allied Powers Europe (SHAPE), 733

Sûreté Nationale, 350

Suslov, 565

Sweden, 512, 675, 677

Switzerland, 181, 675, 677, 679

Synyavsky, Andrei, 593

Tardieu, André, 194, 197

Tarsis, Valery, 593

"Technocrats," 182

Teitgen, Pierre-Henri, 255

Terre, la, 283

Tertz, Abram (Andrei Synyavsky), 593

Thiers, Adolphe, 191–192

Third (Communist) International (*see* Comintern)

Third Republic, France, 180, 191–194, 197–198, 201–205, 207, 211–212, 224–225, 242, 258, 264, 268–269, 285, 289, 291–293, 300, 302, 305, 312, 314–315, 317–322, 326, 331, 336, 347–348, 352

Thirty Years War, 370, 373

Thomas, J. H., 93

Thorez, Maurice, 201, 238–239, 647

Tikhon, Patriarch, 584

Tillon, Charles, 239

Timoshenko, Marshal, 567

Tito, Marshal Joseph Brosz, 534, 646–647

Tixier,Vignancour, Jean-Louis, 233–234, 261

Toleration Act of 1689, Great Britain, 14

Tomlin Commission, Great Britain, 96, 98

Tomski, M. P., 573

Tory Party, Great Britain, 28, 32–33, 39, 46, 152

Town and Country Planning Acts of 1944 and 1947, 45, 64, 156–157

Trade Disputes Act, 34, 37, 41, 94

Trade Expansion Act, United States, 706, 708

Trade-Union Council, 40

Trade Union of Electrical Workers, Great Britain, 52

Trade Unions, of France, 196–197, 246, 259, 279–282
  of Germany, 441, 480
  of Great Britain, 34, 36, 38, 41, 52, 61–63, 67, 94–95, 143, 177

Trades Union Congress, 34, 36–37, 52, 63, 103

Transport, Fuel-Power, Secretary of State for, Great Britain, 87

Transport Commission (Railroads), Great Britain, 101

Transport and General Workers Union, Great Britain, 62–63

Transport House, 63

Trans-Siberian railway, 521–522

Treasury, Great Britain, 77–78, 85, 87–90, 94, 129, 131, 160–161
  Permanent Secretary of, 94–95

Treasury bench, Great Britain, 124

Treaty of Brussels of 1948, 675

Treaty of Paris, 684, 686–689, 694, 701, 703

Treaty of Peace with Poland, of Riga, March 18, 1921, 523

Treaty of Rapallo of 1922, 524

Treaty of Rome, 358–359, 672–673, 689–690, 694–696, 699, 701, 703, 705, 707, 711, 718, 720

Treaty of Versailles, 403

Trevelyan, Sir Charles, 40

"Trew Law of Free Monarchies," 12

Trial for Treason Act, 1696, Great Britain, 14

Triennial Act of 1694, Great Britain, 14

Troquer, André le, 318

Trotsky, Leon, 517–521, 524–525, 530, 537, 564, 573, 604, 645

Trotskyites, France, 251

Truman, Harry S, 419, 665–666, 729

Truman Doctrine, 534, 729

Tudors, 11, 12, 152

Tukhachevski, Marshal, 521–522, 530, 582

Tunisia, 246, 266

Turkey, 675, 677, 700, 729–730, 733

Uborovich, General, 530

UDSR (*see* Union of Democratic and Socialist Resistance)

Ukraine, 522–523, 543, 598

Ulbricht, Walter, 493, 495, 647

Ulster Unionist Council, 60

Ulyanov, Vladimir Ilich (*see* Lenin)

Unified General Confederation of Labor (CGTU) (*Confédération Générale du Travail Unitaire*), 279–280

Unified Socialist party, France (PSU) (*Parti Socialiste Unifié*), 252, 254, 278

Union of Democratic and Socialist Resistance (UDSR) (*Union Démocratique et Socialiste de la Résistance*), 205–206, 252, 268

Union Démocratique et Socialiste de la Résistance (UDSR) (Union of Democratic and Socialistic Resistance), 205–206, 252, 268

Union Démocratique du Travail (Democratic Union of Labor), 229, 274

Union of German Officers, 396

Union of the Godless, 527

Union of Independents, France, 270

Union Nationale des Étudiants de France (*see* National Union of French Students)

Union for the New Republic, France (UNR), 220–222, 229, 270–271, 274–277, 281, 283, 286, 294, 298, 302, 327, 363
  electoral strength of, 229–230, 236, 238, 263, 274, 316
  historical development of, 225, 274, 276
  leaders of, 273–277
  program and policies of, 224, 277, 702
Union pour la Nouvelle République (UNR) (*see* Union for the New Republic)
U.S.S.R., foreign relations of, 640–651
  foreign understanding of, 506–507, 509–510
  map of, 508
  political regime of, evaluation of, 652–656
  (*See also* specific government institutions)
United Nations, 50, 53, 170–171, 173–174, 361–362, 598, 658–660, 677, 679, 741
United States, and European cooperation, 663–665, 668, 675, 705–708, 710–712, 715, 721–722, 724–725, 727–733, 735–736, 738–741
  constitution of, 187, 288, 290, 298, 319, 333, 338–339, 359–362, 364
United States-Euratom Agreement of 1963, 725
United States-Euratom Joint Research and Development Board, 724
"United States of Europe," 665, 693–694
Universal Declaration of Human Rights, 679
Universal Suez Canal Company, 49
Uri, Pierre, 253

Vandenberg, Arthur H., 730
Vandenberg Resolution, 730
Vanuxem, Paul, 231
Varga, Eugene, 641
Vassall, John, 51–52
Vatican, 255
Vavilov, S., 590
Vedel, Georges, 212, 289–290
Verdun, 198
Versailles Treaty, 500
Vichy Regime, France, 193, 198–199, 204–205
  constitution of, 203, 224–225, 238, 269, 279, 337, 347–348, 350, 353
Victoria, Queen, 23, 69–71, 169
Viet-Minh, 265
Vietnam, 54, 66, 361, 649–650, 738
Vladivostok, 650
Voice of America, 558

Volkov, Alexander, 539
Volkskammer (*see* People's Chamber)
Volkskongress (*see* People's Congress)
Volkspolizei (*see* People's Police)
Volksrat (*see* People's Council)
Voprosy Istorii (*Questions of History*), 637
Vorkuta, 576–577
Voroshilov, Klementi, 534, 566, 587, 611
Voznesensky, Andrey, 535
Voznesensky, Nikolai, 535–536
VTsSPS (All-Union Central Council of Trade Unions), 573
Vyshinsky, Andrei, 554, 602, 608, 625, 630, 632, 634, 642

Waldeck-Rochet, 241
Wales, 67, 77, 87, 91, 109, 126, 145–147
Walker, Patrick Gordon, 52, 54, 78
Wallas, Graham, 35, 94
Wallon, Henri Alexandre, 193
Walpole, Sir Robert, 15–16
Warsaw Pact, 361
Wavell, Lord, Viceroy of India, 170
Webb, Sidney and Beatrice, 35–36, 138, 530, 559
Wehner, Herbert, 430–435
Weimar Constitution, 294–295, 379, 446–450, 452, 464–465, 471–473, 475
  emergency powers of, 382–383
Weimar Republic, 290, 293, 379, 381–382, 387, 435, 445, 454, 458, 460, 463, 473, 475, 479, 483, 485, 500
  and elections of 1932, 382–383
  end of, 293–294, 383–384
  historical development of, 379–381
  political parties of, 380, 409–410, 412, 444, 462, 464
Weinert, Erich, 396
Wellington, Duke of, 136
Wells, H. G., 35
West European Union Treaty of 1954, 416
Western European Defense Organization, 730
Western European Union, 48, 362–363, 405, 416, 671, 693, 701, 730–731
Western Germany (*see* German Federal Republic)
Westminster, Statute of 1931, 25
Westphalia Treaty, 370–371
Westrick, Ludger, 456–457
Weygand, General Maxime, 522

Whig party, Great Britain, 32–33, 136, 152
White Army, Russia, 521–522
William I, 371, 374
William II, 378
William IV, 15, 72, 136
William the Conqueror, 6, 140
William of Orange, 13
Wilson, Harold, 30, 48, 52–57, 59, 64, 66–67, 71, 74–78, 84, 87–88, 115
Wilson, Sir Horace, 94, 98–99
Wilson, Woodrow, 26
Wilton, Lord Grey de, 142
Witte, Count, 512, 515
Woman Suffrage, 18, 194, 205
Women's Liberal Congress, Great Britain, 154
Woolton, Lord, 46, 61
World Federation of Trade Unions, 280
World War I, 15, 18, 34, 36, 67, 69, 82, 85, 167, 169, 174, 196, 205, 322, 377–378, 385, 387, 398, 466, 516, 518, 549
World War II, 15, 30, 40, 45, 49, 69, 83, 85, 91, 119, 121, 155 169, 177, 194, 196, 198, 204, 215, 274, 370, 390–393, 530, 532–534, 539, 543, 584, 590
Wrangel, General, 522

"X," Monsieur (Gaston Defferre), 249

Yakir, General, 530
Yalta and Potsdam Agreements, 392–393, 403
Yaroslavsky, 527
Young Communist League, 632
Young Republic (La Jeune République), 255
Yudenich, General, 521
Yugoslavia, 534, 645–647, 649, 655

Zaisser, General Wilhelm, 496
Zambia, 171
Zampolits, 582–583
Zasulitch, Vera, 515
Zentrum (see Center party)
Zhdanov, Andrei, 536–537, 561, 590–591
Zhebrak, A. R., 591
Zhukov, Marshal, 493, 538, 540, 566–567, 583–584
Zinoviev, Grigori, 524–525, 528, 530, 568, 644